AF732607

THE OXFORD HANDBOOK OF

ORGANIZATIONAL CHANGE AND INNOVATION

SECOND EDITION

THE OXFORD HANDBOOK OF

ORGANIZATIONAL CHANGE AND INNOVATION

SECOND EDITION

Edited by
MARSHALL SCOTT POOLE
and
ANDREW H. VAN DE VEN

OXFORD
UNIVERSITY PRESS

OXFORD
UNIVERSITY PRESS

Great Clarendon Street, Oxford, OX2 6DP,
United Kingdom

Oxford University Press is a department of the University of Oxford.
It furthers the University's objective of excellence in research, scholarship,
and education by publishing worldwide. Oxford is a registered trade mark of
Oxford University Press in the UK and in certain other countries

© Oxford University Press 2021

The moral rights of the authors have been asserted

First Edition published in 2004
Second Edition published in 2021

Impression: 2

All rights reserved. No part of this publication may be reproduced, stored in a retrieval system, or transmitted, in any form or by any means, without the prior permission in writing of Oxford University Press, or as expressly permitted by law, by licence or under terms agreed with the appropriate reprographics rights organization. Enquiries concerning reproduction outside the scope of the above should be sent to the Rights Department, Oxford University Press, at the address above

You must not circulate this work in any other form
and you must impose this same condition on any acquirer

Published in the United States of America by Oxford University Press
198 Madison Avenue, New York, NY 10016, United States of America

British Library Cataloguing in Publication Data
Data available

Library of Congress Control Number: 2020949091

ISBN 978-0-19-884597-3

Printed and bound by CPI Group (UK) Ltd, Croydon, CR0 4YY

Links to third party websites are provided by Oxford in good faith and
for information only. Oxford disclaims any responsibility for the materials
contained in any third party website referenced in this work.

PREFACE

Organizational change and innovation are central and enduring issues in management theory and practice. The need to understand processes of organization change and innovation has never been greater in order to response to dramatic changes in population demographics, technology, stakeholders' needs (customers, employees, investors, citizens), competitive survival, and social, economic, and environmental, health and sustainability concerns. Witness, for example, the Covid-19 virus pandemic that humanity is experiencing at the time of this writing, and of the necessity for public, private, and non-profit organizations throughout the world to respond to the pandemic. Unfortunately, with failure rates of organization change initiatives estimated at 50% to 70% (Zorn and Scott, Chapter 28), our track record for managing organization change and innovation has not been good. We critically need new and better ways to understand and manage change initiatives.

This Oxford handbook provides this understanding from a social science perspective by the world's leading scholars of cutting-edge theories and research on managing organizational change and innovation. It contains thirty-one chapters and five essays by sixty authors and co-authors from forty-seven universities located in twenty different countries. Of the sixty authors, 35% are female and 65% are male. We invited the lead chapter authors because of their distinguished and influential theories and research on organizational change and innovation. These leading scholars, in turn, invited a new generation of highly talented scholars to be their co-authors. Hence, this handbook represents the integrated work of a community of scholars from diverse perspectives, countries, genders, and generations. Figure 0.1 shows a picture of chapter authors attending a day-long workshop at Boston College in August 2019. The workshop provided a wonderful learning experience for chapter authors to present and get feedback from other chapter authors, and to gain insights on how their chapters contributed to the overall handbook.

Across the diverse chapters and essays of this handbook three basic questions consistently present themselves:

- ***What is the nature of change and process?*** New processes of organization change are emerging in many forms, including planned and unplanned, episodic and continuous, incremental and radical, alternative generating mechanisms or motors, and stability in changes.
- ***What are the key concepts in theories of change and innovation?*** They include human agency, time conceptions, causality and levels of analysis. In addition, we

FIGURE 0.1 Handbook Authors' Workshop August 14, 2019

add voices not heard in the first edition about affect and emotion, power and influence, paradox and conflict, critical and political perspectives on organization change, creativity, and innovation.

- ***How should we study change and innovation?*** Different questions beget different variance and process models and mathematical modeling based on alternative methods for archival, historical, and real-time collection of qualitative and quantitative data.

The handbook is organized into six major classes of models of organizational change and innovation, beginning with Van de Ven and Poole's (1995) core typology of teleology, life cycle, dialectics, and evolutionary process theories, followed by variations of more complex hybrid models of change. These variations represent important extensions to process theories that have emerged over the past twenty-five years since Van de Ven and Poole (1995).

The first edition of this handbook had its beginnings in the 1980s and 1990s, a time of emerging research on organizational change and innovation. For us, the need for a handbook was triggered by the Minnesota Innovation Research Program (MIRP), which began in 1983 with the objective of developing a process theory of innovation in organizations and society. Fourteen research teams, involving more than thirty faculty and doctoral students at the University of Minnesota, conducted longitudinal studies that tracked a variety of new technologies, products, services, and programs as they developed from concept to implementation in their natural field settings (see Van de Ven, Angle, and Poole, 1989; 2000; and Van de Ven, Polley, Garud, and Venkataraman, 1999; 2008).

The MIRP studies highlighted the need for theories of change processes and for methodologies specifically adapted to developing and testing process theories of organizational change and innovation. Workshops to address these needs led to our book (Poole, Van de Ven, Dooley, and Holmes, 2000) on methods for studying processes of change in terms of the sequence of events that unfold as things emerge, develop, grow, and terminate over time.

When designing the 1st edition in 2000 we found an emerging group of scholars who were breaking the mold of traditional stage theories, and introducing new theories of change and development that were based on processes of evolution, dialectics, social movements, structuration theory, and complexity theory, among others. Since the first edition in 2004, we have been struck by the growth and variety of theories and research on organizational change and innovation. The literature is vast and spread across a number of disciplines. A number of useful and powerful theories have evolved, but they often developed in relative isolation.

Fortunately, we found leading scholars who have been advancing this cutting-edge research. We asked them to develop broad, theoretically driven reviews that encompass the best of previous research and break new ground on their subject. Each chapter reviews, assesses, and advances the state of knowledge in its area. The chapters advance our thinking by developing integrative theories, by establishing connections among theories from different fields and research traditions, and by introducing new lines of inquiry. In our work with these authors we have been constantly impressed by their ability to combine careful scholarship with creativity. We thank them for undertaking the difficult task of bringing order to the extensive range of theory and research they synthesized.

The result is a second edition of this handbook that we hope will serve as a springboard for another two decades of research on organizational change and innovation. The great Elizabethan Francis Bacon wrote, "Some books are to be tasted, others to be swallowed, and some few to be chewed and digested." We think that this handbook offers something for those who just wish to taste and swallow. But we believe and hope that it proves to be a book that is chewed and digested by many students of organizational change and development.

We are grateful to Herbert Addison and David Musson of Oxford University Press who helped us envision the initial edition of this handbook and provided valuable guidance in the early years of this project. In their distinguished careers as Oxford's executive editors of business books, they made major contributions to management and organization science. Their able successor, Adam Swallow, was a source of encouragement and faith in the project, and his imprint on this book is lasting. Jenny King of Oxford University Press steered this project through its final stages, and we are grateful for her professional guidance. Christian and Morgan Durfee of the University of Minnesota contributed to the editing of several chapters, adding considerably to their readability.

Like the first edition, we continue to dedicate this second edition of the handbook in memory of parents, Edward and Helen Poole, and Arnold and Josephine Van de Ven.

References

Poole, M. S., Van de Ven, A. H., Dooley, K., and Holmes, M. E. (2000) *Organization Change and Innovation Processes: Theory and Methods for Research* (Oxford, UK: Oxford University Press).

Poole, M. S., and Van de Ven, A. H. (Eds.) (2004) *Handbook of Organizational Change and Innovation* (Oxford, UK: Oxford University Press).

Van de Ven, A. H., Angle, H., and Poole, M. S. (Eds.) (1989; and reissued 2000) *Research on the Management of Innovation: The Minnesota Studies* (Oxford, UK: Oxford University Press).

Van de Ven, A. H., Polley, D. E., Garud, R., and Venkataraman, S. (1999; reissued 2008) *The Innovation Journey* (Oxford, UK: Oxford University Press).

Van de Ven, A. H., and Poole, M. S. (1995). Explaining Development and Change in Organizations, *Academy of Management Review*, 20, 510–40.

Zorn, T. E. and Scott, J. (2020). must we change? The dark side of change and change resistance. In M. S. Poole and A. H. Van de Ven (Eds.), *The Oxford Handbook of Organization Change* (2nd ed.) (Oxford: Oxford University Press).

Contents

PART VII REFLECTIONS

List of Figures

List of Tables

List of Contributors

Daniel Albert is Assistant Professor of Management at the LeBow College of Business, Drexel University.

Jean M. Bartunek is Robert A. and Evelyn J. Ferris Chair and Professor of Management and Organization at Boston College.

Joel A. C. Baum is Professor of Strategic Management at the Rotman School of Management, University of Toronto.

W. Warner Burke holds the Edward Lee Thorndike Professorship of Psychology & Education at Teachers College, Columbia University.

W. E. Douglas Creed is Professor of Management at University of Rhode Island and Professorial Fellow, Department of Management and Marketing, The University of Melbourne

Mary Crossan is Professor of General Management and Strategy, Paul MacPherson Chair in Strategic Leadership at the Ivey School of Business, University of Western Ontario.

Gerald F. Davis is the Gilbert and Ruth Whitaker Professor of Business Administration at the Ross School of Business and Professor of Sociology, The University of Michigan.

James W. Dearing is the Brandt Endowed Professor in the Department of Communication, Michigan State University.

Stanley Deetz is President of Interaction Design for Innovation and Professor Emeritus at the University of Colorado, Boulder.

Kevin J. Dooley is a Distinguished Professor of Supply Chain Management in the W.P. Carey School of Business, Arizona State University, and a Senior Sustainability Scientist in the Julie Ann Wrigley Global Institute of Sustainability.

Moshe Farjoun is Professor of Strategy and Organization at the Schulich School of Business, York University, Toronto.

Martha S. Feldman is Professor of Urban Planning and Public Policy, Management, Political Science and Sociology and the Johnson Chair for Civic Governance and Public Management, University of California, Irvine.

Vibha Gaba is Professor of Entrepreneurship at INSEAD, and The INSEAD Fellow in Memory of Erin Anderson.

Martin Ganco is the Robert Pricer Chair in Enterprise Development, Academic Director of the Weinert Center for Entrepreneurship, and an Associate Professor in the Management and Human Resources department, University of Wisconsin-Madison.

Raghu Garud is Professor of Management and Organization and the Farrell Chair in Innovation and Entrepreneurship, Pennsylvania State University.

Zachary Gibson is a PhD student in the Technology and Social Behavior (TSB) program, Northwestern University.

Dennis A. Gioia is the Robert and Judith Auritt Klein Professor of Management at the Smeal College of Business, Pennsylvania State University.

Kenneth T. Goh is Assistant Professor of Strategic Management in the Lee Kong Chian School of Business and the Academic Director of the Business Families Institute at Singapore Management University.

David Grant is Pro Vice Chancellor (Business) at the Griffith Business School, Griffith University.

Royston Greenwood is Professor Emeritus, University of Alberta and Professorial Fellow University of Edinburgh Business School.

Timothy J. Hargrave is Associate Professor of Management at the College of Business, Central Washington University.

Tor Hernes is Professor of Organization Theory, Copenhagen Business School.

Anthony Hussenot is a Professor in Organization Studies, Université Côte d'Azur.

Quy Nguyen Huy is Professor of Strategy and the Solvay Chaired Professor of Technological Innovation, INSEAD.

Runtian Jing is a Professor of Organizational Behaviour in the Antai College of Economics and Management, Shanghai Jiao Tong University.

Eun Woo Kim is a Ph.D. candidate in the Management and Organizations department at the Stephen M. Ross School of Business, University of Michigan.

Laurie Lewis is Professor of Communication and Associate Vice Provost for Faculty Success, University of Texas at San Antonio.

Michael Lounsbury is Professor and Canada Research Chair in Entrepreneurship and Innovation and Academic Director of the Technology Commercialization Centre, University of Alberta.

Joel Malen is Associate Professor in the School of Commerce, Waseda University.

Saku Mantere is Associate Professor of Strategy and Organization and Director of the Marcel Desautels Institute for Integrated Management, McGill University.

Alfred Marcus is Professor and Edson Spencer Endowed Chair in Strategy and Technological Leadership, Carlson School of Management, University of Minnesota.

Cara C. Maurer is Assistant Professor in General Management and Strategy at the Ivey School of Business, Western University.

Alan D. Meyer is Professor Emeritus of Management at the Lunquist College of Business, University of Oregon.

Evelyn Micelotta is an Associate Professor in Management at the Telfer School of Management, University of Ottawa.

Anne S. Miner is an Emeritus Professor at the Wisconsin School of Business, University of Wisconsin- Madison.

Cliff Oswick is Professor of Organization Theory at Cass Business School, City, University of London.

Rosie Oswick is a Research Assistant at Cass Business School, City, University of London.

Brian T. Pentland is the Main Street Capital Partners Endowed Professor in the Department of Accounting and Information Systems, Michigan State University.

Marshall Scott Poole is the David L. Swanson Professor of Communication, Senior Research Scientist at the National Center for Supercomputing Applications, and Director of I-CHASS: The Institute for Computing in the Humanities, Arts, and Social Sciences, University of Illinois.

Craig Prichard is Programme Lead Specialist, Aquaculture, at Nelson Marlborough Institute of Technology.

Kätlin Pulk is Associate Professor and Vice Rector for Research, Estonian Business School.

Linda L. Putnam is a Distinguished Research Professor Emerita in the Department of Communication, University of California, Santa Barbara.

Hayagreva Rao is The Atholl McBean Professor of Organizational Behavior and Human Resources at the Stanford Graduate School of Business, Stanford University.

Davide Ravasi is Professor of Strategy and Entrepreneurship at the UCL School of Management, University College London.

Alexandra Rheinhardt is an Assistant Professor of Management at the University of Connecticut.

Saras D. Sarasvathy is Paul M. Hammaker Professor in Business Administration at the Darden School of Business, University of Virginia.

Majken Schultz is Professor of Management and Organization Studies, Copenhagen Business School and International Research Fellow, Centre for Corporate Reputation, Saïd Business School, Oxford University, UK.

Jennifer Scott is a Lecturer in the School of Management, Massey University.

Myeong-Gu Seo is an Associate Professor in the Department of Management and Organization at the Robert H. Smith School of Business, University of Maryland, College Park.

Michelle Shumate is a Professor in the School of Communication, Northwestern University.

Kathleen M. Sutcliffe is a Bloomberg Distinguished Professor in the Carey Business School, Johns Hopkins University.

Haridimos Tsoukas is the Columbia Ship Management Professor of Strategic Management, University of Cyprus and Distinguished Research Environment Professor of Organizational Behaviour, Warwick Business School.

Marja Turunen is a Postdoctoral Researcher in the Business School, University of Turku and in the School of Science, Aalto University.

Andrew H. Van de Ven is Professor Emeritus in the Carlson School of Management, University of Minnesota.

Sankaran Venkataraman is the MasterCard Professor of Business Administration and Senior Associate Dean for Faculty and Research at the Darden School of Business, University of Virginia.

Timo O. Vuori is Associate Professor of Strategic Management in the School of Science and the School of Business, Aalto University.

Rene Wiedner is Associate Professor at Warwick Business School, University of Warwick.

Jennifer L. Woolley is an Associate Professor of Management in the Leavey School of Business, Santa Clara University.

Theodore E. Zorn is Head of the Institute of Executive Education, Massey University.

CHAPTER 1

INTRODUCTION

Central issues in the study of organizational change and innovation

ANDREW H. VAN DE VEN AND
MARSHALL SCOTT POOLE

ORGANIZATIONAL change and innovation are central and enduring issues in management theory and practice. The need to understand processes of organization change and innovation has never been greater in order to respond to dramatic changes in population demographics, technology, stakeholders' needs (customers, employees, investors, citizens), competitive survival, and social, economic, environmental, health, and sustainability concerns. These concerns call for a better understanding and management of organization change and innovation. Organizational change is usually defined as an observed difference over time in organizational characteristics or activities (Van de Ven and Poole 1995). When this change is novel and unprecedented it is called innovation (such as creating a new product), and when the change has been repeated before it is often referred to as an organizational routine (such as reproducing an old product).

Why and what organizations change is generally well known, but the processes in which change unfolds remain obscure. Organizations may change for a number of different reasons, including environmental crisis, performance gap, new technology, identification of opportunities, reactions to internal or external pressures, mergers and acquisitions, imitating best practices, and abandoning investments in declining activities and reallocating them to innovation and new opportunities. In response to these "why" changes, what organizations change can include many areas and processes, such as changing organizational mission, vision, strategy and structure, technology, human resources training, hirings or layoffs, task-job design, culture, and relationships with stakeholders.

HOW organizations change is much less known than what and why they change. The how, or the process of change, is the central focus of this handbook. Many new concepts and findings on how organizations change have emerged since we edited the initial edition of this *Handbook of Organization Change and Innovation* (Poole and Van de Ven in 2004). Building upon and extending scholarly advances since then is the major purpose and contribution of this second edition of the handbook. Like the first edition, this handbook focuses on processes of change, or the sequence of events in which organizational characteristics and activities change and develop over time, and the factors that influence these processes. The organization is the central unit of analysis. Micro processes of change in individuals or groups, or more macro community or population changes are included insofar as they figure into organizational change. Chapters dealing with institutional and societal change perspectives keep the organizational implications at the center of the analysis.

This handbook is a rich tapestry of theories and findings about how organizational change and innovation processes unfold. As with many tapestries, what first strikes the eye is the amazing diversity of ideas and subject matter. But as we step back and look a little longer, patterns and central themes emerge. These patterns are the subject of this chapter.

Across the diverse and wide-ranging contributions to this handbook, three basic questions and themes have evolved in understanding processes of organization change and innovation:

A. *What is the nature of change and process?* Organization change comes in many forms, including planned and unplanned, episodic and continuous, incremental and radical, and with different generating mechanisms or motors.
B. *What are the key concepts and models for understanding organization change and innovation?* They include human agency, time conceptions, causality, and levels of analysis. In addition, we add voices not heard in the 1st edition about affect and emotion, power and influence, paradox and conflict, and political perspectives on organization change, creativity, and innovation.
C. *How should we study change and innovation?* Different questions beget different variance and process models and mathematical modeling based on alternative methods for archival, historical, and real-time collection of qualitative and quantitative data.

This chapter summarizes this evolving scholarship and explores its implications for future research and practice in organizational change and innovation.

What is the Nature of Change?

A variety of contrasting perspectives about the nature of organization change and innovation have emerged during the past fifteen to twenty years. They include contrasting views on whether an organization represents a thing as a noun, or process as a verb, and whether change is episodic or continuous, planned or unplanned, incremental or radical, triggered by different generating mechanisms or motors, unfolds over clock or kronos time, and maintains stability or change. Table 1.1 outlines these contrasting views that we will now discuss.

Episodic Versus Continuous Change

An important theme for understanding organization change is the distinction between episodic versus continuous change. Hernes, Hussenot, and Pulk in particular discuss this theme in Chapter 27. They expand on Weick and Quinn's (1999: 365) initial discussion of episodic change as "infrequent, discontinuous and intentional" (such as in Lewin's (1948) model of unfreeze-change-and refreeze), and continuous change as "ongoing, evolving and cumulative" (such as the bottom–up sensemaking process discussed by Rheinhardt and Gioia in Chapter 4). The two forms of change are associated with different metaphors of the organization, analytical frameworks, theories of intervention and roles attributed to change agents, as shown in Table 1.1. The distinction between episodic and continuous change is correlated with several others, including incremental versus radical change (e.g., Tushman and Romanelli 1985) continuous versus discontinuous change (Gaba and Meyer, Chapter 16), first-order versus second-order change (e.g., Meyer, Goes, and Brooks 1993) and competence-enhancing versus competence-destroying change (Abernathy and Clark 1985).

Most of the chapters in this handbook incorporate elements of both continuous and episodic change at different organizational levels or temporal periods. The various stage theories of development described throughout the book generally emphasize continuous change at the microlevel of system behavior, but stage changes are often conceptualized as episodic. Dooley's complex adaptive systems theory in Chapter 20 and Ganco and Albert's landscape modeling in Chapter 21 are built on both continuous and episodic elements. So also, Micelotta, Lounsbury, and Greenwood's Chapter 17 on institutional change incorporates continuous change at the level of concrete action that moves the process through episodic stages. While the theory focuses on episodic, stagewise changes, it presumes an underlying continuous process of activity as a means for constructing the stages.

Planned and Unplanned Change

Planned change is consciously conceived and implemented by knowledgeable actors. As Burke discusses in Chapter 2, practitioner models have historically emphasized planned change, including Beer et al. (1990), Burke and Litwin, 1992, Kotter (1996), Lewin (1948), Nadler and Tushman (1977), Tichy (1983), and Weisbord (1976). There is a prescriptive managerial orientation to these models of planned change: they attempt to improve an organizational situation with reference to a teleological desired end state. Burke (Chapter 2) discusses recent evidence-based management studies that substantiate

Table 1.1 Comparison of Different Views of Organization Change

Characteristic	Occasional Change in Organization	Ongoing Organizing Processes
Metaphor of Organization	Organization is a noun, the thing that is changed occasionally, but prone to inertia and stability.	Organizing is a verb, a never-ending process that emerges, evolves, and is partially cumulative over time.
Organization Change	Observed difference over time in an occasional interruption or divergence from equilibrium.	Perceived experiences and emotions of endless modifications in work processes and social practices.
Change continuity	Episodic, infrequent, discontinuous change.	Continuous, constantly ongoing, evolving change.
Time	Chronos, sequential clock-time before & after change.	Kairos, indivisible time experienced during change.
Change intentions, agency	Planned change, driven by human choice, goal-directed.	Unplanned change, purpose emerges in the process.
Change motors	Teleology, intentional, diagnostic change. Life cycle, regulated change.	Evolution, VSR competitive change. Dialectics, conflict, dialogical change, social movements.
Analytic Framework	Etic perspective: macro, distant, global, outsiders' view. Key concepts: inertia, interdependent parts, triggering, replacing, substituting, discontinuity, revolution, beginnings & endings.	Emic perspective: micro, close, local, insiders' view. Key concepts: recurrent interactions, response repertoires, emergent patterns, improvisation, transitions, sensemaking, affect & learning.
Intervention Theory	Intentional change: unfreeze, change, refreeze stages. Change is inertial, linear, progressive, and requires outside intervention.	Redirection of existing tendencies. Change is cyclical, processual, without an end state, equilibrium seeking, eternal.
Role of Change Agent	Prime mover who creates change by finding points of leverage in organization. Change agent changes meaning systems, schema, and punctuation.	Sense maker who redirects and shapes change. Change agent recognizes, makes salient, and reframes current patterns and momentum of change.

Adapted and modified from Table 1 in Weick and Quinn (1999)

many of the principles in these practitioner models. By contrast, unplanned change may or may not be driven by human choice, as in Chapters 13–17 on life-cycle models of change and in Chapters 18–21 on evolutionary models of change. In these models, change is not purposefully conceived ex ant, but emerges in the process, and may move the organization in either desirable or undesirable directions (as Sarasvarthy and Venkataraman discuss in Chapter 6). The contrast between planned and unplanned change focuses our attention on the degree to which change and innovation can be choreographed, scripted, or controlled.

While planned and unplanned change may be viewed as opposite ends of a continuum, it is also useful to consider them together, as is done in Chapters 22–26 on hybrid models of organization change. Because of the complexity and uncertainty of most organization change initiatives, plans go awry, and alternative goals and directions emerge during the process, as discussed by Sarasvathy and Venkataman in Chapter 6 and Garud and Turunen in Chapter 22. All planned change occurs in the context of the ambient change processes that occur naturally in organizations. For example, Chapter 16 by Gaba and Meyer reports on strategic planning processes in healthcare organizations that are going through their own life cycle and also adapting to hyperturbulent environmental jolts. The intersection of these three change processes, one planned and the other two unplanned, shapes the organization. Knowledge of the ambient change processes can enable the managers to conduct strategic planning more effectively. Conversely, unplanned change processes can be "domesticated" through interventions, and driven in useful directions. For example, in Chapter 19 Miner, Crossan, and Mauer discuss how a theory of unplanned population evolution can be transformed into a planned model of organizational evolution and innovation. In order to do this, the planner makes a virtue of necessity. Drawing on his or her knowledge of how natural change processes unfold, the planner uses the processes' momentum to push through needed measures. In Chapter 8, Jing advances this idea by discussing three strategies for seizing, entraining, and creating change momentum based on Eastern yin-yang philosophy.

Four Basic Motors of Change

Another way to define the process of change is in terms of the mechanisms that bring it about. Van de Ven and Poole (1995) defined four relatively simple theories that serve as ideal types for the explanation of change and innovation processes.[1] Figure 1.1 shows that each theory views the process of development as unfolding in a fundamentally different progression of change events, and is governed by a different generative mechanism or motor.

- A *life cycle* model depicts the process of change in an entity as progressing through a necessary sequence of stages or phases. The specific content of these stages or phases is prescribed and regulated by an institutional, natural, or logical program prefigured at the beginning of the cycle.
- A *teleological* model views development as a cycle of goal formulation, implementation, evaluation, and modification of actions or goals based on what was learned or intended by the entity. This sequence emerges through the purposeful enactment or social construction of goals or an envisioned end state among individuals within the entity.

[1] Related typologies of organizational change processes that complement these four basic motors of change are presented by Gaba and Meyer (Chapter 16) and Micelotta, Lounsbury, and Royston (Chapter 17).

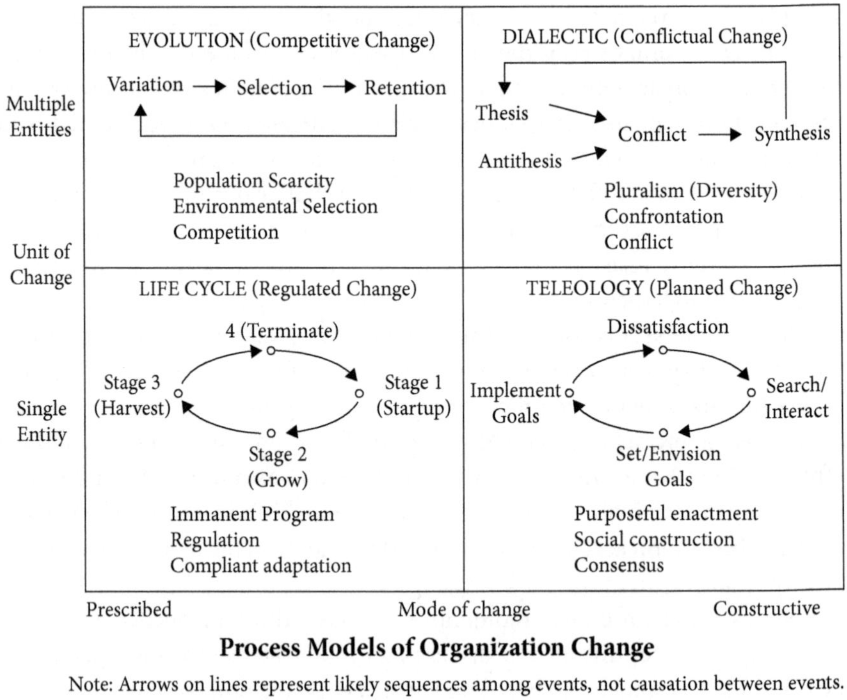

FIGURE 1.1 Handbook Organizing Framework of Process Theories of Organization Change
Source: Van de Ven and Poole, Explaining Development and Change in Organizations, AMR, 1995

- In *dialectical* models of development, conflicts emerge between entities espousing an opposing thesis and antithesis that collide to produce a synthesis, which in time becomes the thesis for the next cycle of a dialectical progression. Confrontation and conflict between opposing entities generate this dialectical cycle.
- An *evolutionary* model of development consists of a repetitive sequence of variation, selection, and retention events among entities in a designated population. This evolutionary cycle is generated by competition for scarce environmental resources between entities inhabiting a population.

The four theories are distinguished along two dimensions. The *unit of change* indexes whether the change in question is premised on the actions of a single entity or multiple entities. Evolutionary and dialectical theories operate on *multiple entities.* Evolutionary forces are defined in terms of their impacts on populations and have no meaning at the level of the individual entity. Dialectical theories require at least two entities to fill the conflicting roles of thesis and antithesis. On the other hand, life-cycle and teleological theories operate on a *single entity*. In the case of a life-cycle model, development is explained as a function of potentials immanent within the entity. While environment and other entities may shape how this immanence manifests itself, they are strictly secondary to the immanent potentials. The real push to development comes from within the single, whole, developing entity. Teleological theories, too, require only a single entity's goals, social construction, or envisioned end state to explain development. A teleological theory can operate among many members of an organization or a set of organizations when there is sufficient consensus among the members to permit them to act as a single organizational entity.

The generative mechanisms of the four process theories also differ in terms of whether the sequence of change events is prescribed *a priori* or whether the progression is constructed and emerges as the change process unfolds. A *prescribed* mode of change channels the development of entities in a pre-specified direction, typically of maintaining and incrementally adapting their forms in a definite, calculable way. A *constructive* mode of change generates unprecedented, novel forms that, in retrospect, are often discontinuous and unpredictable departures from the past. A prescribed motor evokes a sequence of change events in accord with a pre-established program or action routine. A constructive motor, on the other hand, produces new action routines that may (or may not) create an original (re)formulation of the entity. Life-cycle and evolutionary theories operate in a prescribed modality, while teleological and dialectical theories operate in the constructive modality.

The two dimensions of unit and mode of change define generative mechanisms in terms of their action and process. They differ from other dimensions such as incremental and radical change and competence-enhancing and competence-destroying change which classify organizational changes based on their consequences or outcomes, rather than by their starting or process conditions. One advantage of the typology is that it is possible to identify the motor(s) of a change process before it has concluded.

Major sections of this handbook are organized into chapters that reflect variations and extensions of process theories of teleology (Chapters 2–6), dialectics (Chapters 7–12), life cycle (Chapters 13–17), and evolution (Chapters 18–21). However, as these chapters discuss, theories of change are not always built around just one motor. This is clearly evident in Chapter 15 by Pentland and Goh who expand the traditional life-cycle model of organizational routines as regulating change to examine patterns in changing routines that can be driven by any of the four change motors (teleology, dialectic, life-cycle and evolution). So also, Bartunek, Putnam, and Seo in Chapter 3 trace the history of OD (organizational development) models of planned change that originated as teleological diagnostic approaches to OD and evolved to surface dialectical tensions and dialogical processes in the ongoing journey of OD.

There has been a major growth in hybrid models, which explain processes of change by combining two or more theories (or motors). As Poole and Van de Ven discuss in Chapter 13, Greiner's (1972) evolution and revolution model of organizational growth is a classic example of a hybrid model. It combined life-cycle stages of organizational growth that were propelled into the next stage by dialectical processes. Since then, there has been a growing number of nonlinear hybrid models of organization change. Six Handbook chapters (22–26) illustrate interesting variations of hybrid models.

In his Chapter 26, Farjoun traces the historical contributions of dialectics, Darwin, and Dewey on organization change. It provides a historical appreciation that traces the emergence and development of central concepts and philosophies of change in dialectics, evolution, and pragmatism. In doing so, Farjoun argues that to envisage new models, we need to consider how key ideas about change have historically evolved, and attend to their philosophical underpinnings.

Which model or combination of models to use to explain organization change depends on the questions asked. Process research studies tend to focus on four kinds of temporal questions that tend to be addressed with different process theories.

a. How did we get here? (looking into the past, life-cycle, and evolutionary models)
b. What is going on? (looking at the present, dialectical models)
c. How do we do something? (knowhow, process recipes for e.g., innovation, change something)
d. Where should we go? (looking at the future, teleological models)

Key Concepts in Theories of Change and Innovation

Whatever assumptions and approaches are taken, several fundamental issues face all students of organizational change and innovation. As discussed in the first edition of this handbook, *people, space* and *time* are fundamental to any human science: before all else, social life is comprised of people who exist through space and time. Since the first edition, a number of additional core concepts have emerged in the literature and are discussed in subsequent handbook chapters. They include *affect and emotion, power and influence, paradox and conflict, political perspectives, and beginnings and endings of organization change, creativity, and innovation.* This section will consider the roles these concepts play in understanding organization change and innovation.

People: Human Agency

What role should theories of organizational change and innovation grant to human agency? While there may well be an "invisible hand" that guides organizations, the role of human intention and human intervention is all too visible. Initially, the literature focused on change agents as individuals who take control, create, and remake organizations such as Steve Jobs with Apple. These "great individuals"—executives, entrepreneurs, organizational statespersons, transformational leaders, strategic decision-makers, planners, designers, change agents—represent a potent expression of the human will as maker of the organization. However, this "great leader" concept of agency is subject to several qualifications. For one thing, external conditions limit the agent's power and capacity to control events and manage organizational change. Second, agency is more complex when multiple interacting agents are involved. For example, it is possible that a less powerful agent may well take the crucial action that determines the success or failure of a change. Multiple agency is difficult to deal with, because it is difficult to know whose intention counts in such cases.

One way of dealing with this problem is to locate agency in the organization, group, work unit, or even industry. By rolling up the actions of multiple agents and the complexities of the organizational system into a single entity, this move makes agency manageable. Several research traditions take this approach to agency, and they differ mainly in the level of complexity attributed to the agent. One group of perspectives conceives of the organizational agent in fairly simple terms. The NK modeling framework discussed by Ganco and Albert in Chapter 21 relies on a simple learning system of stimulus and response model as found in psychological learning theory: the agent explores its environment, acting and learning in response to positive or negative outcomes. Evolutionary models of population ecology and community ecology research take organizations as members of populations or communities, and treat each member as operating according to a simple logic, such as survival or maximizing utility (See Chapter 18 by Baum and Rao).

Other perspectives treat organizational agents as more complex, to the extent that they cannot be fully described in terms of a learning cycle or rational behavior. The theories of groups as complex action systems discussed in Chapter 3 take this approach. While the nature of group processes can be described, how these processes unfold when a group acts are assumed to be indeterminate, and subject to the response of the group to its situation. Theories of organization culture and identity change in response to external events (Chapter 5 by Ravasi and Schultz) also adopt a complex view of how organizations adapt to events. The institutional theories discussed in Chapter 17 also adopt this approach. Institutions are taken to be complex entities whose histories shape their responses in complex ways. Though regularities in responses to institutional pressures and phases of institutionalization can be identified, these are assumed to be general patterns, and each organizational agent is assumed to craft its own response, much like a human agent would construct its own course of action.

For example, Chapter 14 by Marcus and Malen examines the hedging behavior of organizations in response to the many regulatory mandates of governments at local, regional, and national levels. The many changes governments require generally do not correspond to the changes organizations want to make, or those that they actually end up making. In response, a cat-and-mouse game often unfolds that leads to hedging behavior—that is a tendency by organizational agents to simultaneously take actions that align with some regulations while simultaneously taking actions to resist other regulations.

As these chapters indicate, the past decade has witnessed increasing sophistication of concepts of agency and the role it plays in organizational change and innovation. The multiple levels of agency in contemporary research on change and innovation suggest it is also important to consider the more general issue of levels of analysis, the "space" component of change and innovation.

Space: Levels of Analysis

There is general consensus that organizations are multilevel phenomena. A growing body of scholars hold that different concepts and dynamics are important to examine at micro, meso, and macro levels of organizations.

At the micro level, the characteristics, dispositions, and emotions of individuals are central to understanding organization change, as discussed by Burke in Chapter 2 on the Stouten, Rousseau, and De Cremer (2018) review of an extensive body of evidence-based knowledge, and by Nguyen and Vuori on emotionality and change in Chapter 28. Much of this knowledge can be traced to classical theories of individual adaptation level, affordance, and abduction.

Adaptation-level scholars have shown that the sensitivity of individuals to recognize a stimulus is based on their prior experiences and perceptions of familiar and stable stimuli (Helson 1964). This perception varies greatly from person to person and in different situations. Consequently, many people are insensitive to, and do not perceive, stimuli as being anomalous to which others may be attentive (Bowling, Beehr, Wagner, and Libkuman, 2005). Affordance theory (Gibson 1979) states that individuals perceive the world not in terms of objective stimuli, but also in terms of its action possibilities (affordances). Hence, an anomalous stimulus does not determine behavior; it's what you make of it (Norman 1988). Abduction, intuition and subconscious stimuli (Gandhok and Sammartino, 2018; Hodgkinson and Clarke, 2007) emphasize the importance of "cognitive versatility" for breakthrough ideation. This perspective argues for emergent intuition and a crucial role for "slow forms of intuition" in breakthrough ideation.

There is also a greater appreciation of meso-level workings of teams and groups in organization change processes. They include discussions of how power asymmetry and conflict influence social movements and activism (Chapters 9 by Davis and Kim and 10 by Prichard and Creed), and the festering effects of resistance to change (Zorn and Scott, Chapter 29).

When expanding context to macro-level inter-organizational networks (Chapter 25 by Shumate and Gibson) and ecosystems/infrastructures (Chapter 24 by Woolley) the organization becomes a participant in a much larger community that it does not control. At the macro-level there has been a significant growth of research on organizational ecosystems (or infrastructures), where the organization is no longer the central actor; instead it is a participant in a much larger network of inter-organizational actors. In her chapter on ecosystems, Woolley reviews the growing number of empirical studies that examine the macro emergence of ecosystems (or infrastructures) and the participant (not controlling) roles of organizations in them.

When examining change across levels it is important to distinguish *state changes* (when change occurs through units changing from one type to another) from *cross level influence* (when units at one level influence change in units at another level without a state change). State changes involve alterations in the entity undergoing change and have multiple level implications through bridging or moving through levels. Baum and

Rao's theory of co-evolution (Chapter 18) mingles cross level influence and state change: units at different levels of populations and communities influence each other across levels. In addition, communities may change state over time, as the populations that comprise them enter into relationships with different levels of complementarity and symbiosis. Communities with little symbiosis among populations are more akin to a group of independent units (and hence are weaker communities), whereas those with tighter linkages are more like heterogeneous or homogeneous groups (and hence stronger communities).

Garud and Turunen (Chapter 22) discuss Usher's model of partial cumulative syntheses, which represents a stochastic (or probabilistic) process of linking individual and collective acts of innovation. Based on his historical analysis of the history of mechanical inventions, Usher (1929; 1954) proposed a process model of four key activity stages to describe the emergence of novelty in thought and action for individuals and groups. Step 1. Observe anomaly or perception of an incomplete pattern. Step 2. Set the stage by confirming the anomaly. Step 3. Create hunches or acts of insight. Step 4. Evaluate hunches through critical revision and mastery. Micro and macro relationships unfold over time as individuals performing these four steps interact and combine with others performing different steps that produce a partial cumulative syntheses process of change and innovation.

Time: The "Ether" of Change

We judge that change has occurred against the background of time. We use metrics on this background for assessing when changes occur, the rate of change, and the consequences of change. For example, timing and rhythm of change affect organizational performance. In a study of sixty-seven European insurance companies, Klarner and Raisch (2013) found that regular and moderate changes had positive effects on long-term firm performance (3-year adjusted ROE), while focused, temporary, or punctuated change processes had negative effects on performance.

Different conceptions of time are often used in studies of organization change, including:

- *Newtonian time* is the time of classical physics.
- *Transaction time* is the time of significant events.
- *Dominant cultural time* is similar to the Newtonian conception of time, but the flow of time is regarded as unidirectional rather than bidirectional.
- *Organizational time* combines Newtonian and Transactional views.

These highlight several key issues: What is the nature of time? What is its role in theories of change and innovation? How do we best capture time as a metric and construct in our theories?

The time required to develop and implement organizational change often takes longer than participants expect. The implementation of a six-sigma program by a Dutch engineering company involved a seven-year punctuated equilibrium process (De Mast, Linderman, and Van de Ven, 2020). Moreover, consultants told the company that implementation of the six sigma program was expected to be a "turn-key" cut-and-paste process of following prescriptions, but the implementation process took seven years of nonroutine events. Of the events, 41 percent were observed to follow prescriptions, while 59% required adapting to exceptions. The timing of actions and decisions also affects outcomes. A study of new product development projects by Van Oorschot, Akkermans, and Sengupta (2013) found that delayed actions, deferred deadlines, and blurred perceptions of mixed signals created decision traps that mounted into failure over time.

As important as time is to the study of change and innovation, until recently it has remained as obscure as the ether of classical physics. Time is a profound and daunting subject, but it is important to engage it. As Hernes, Pulk, and Hassenot discuss in Chapter 27, the passing of time forces closure upon presents, which turns them into events. Events exhibit temporal agency which occur in "event formation" and may be seen as a structuring of events in time. Sarasvarthy and Venkataraman point out in Chapter 6 that in the flow of time, events are also viewed as chronos (clock) and kairos (peak) events.

Change and Stability, Beginnings and Endings

Another important theme emerging in this handbook is that seemingly enduring and objective organizational arrangements are underpinned by dynamic processes. Chapter 15 by Pentland and Goh examines how routines change in order to remain stable. They provide a vision of routines as generative systems by demonstrating how action taken to enact a routine also has the capacity to regulate conflicting organizational goals.

Stable organizational arrangements endure over time only through ongoing repair and reconstruction. Much more active *work* is required to maintain practices, organizations, and institutions than most management scholars would admit. Lok and de Rond (2013) show how the 175-year old institution of the Cambridge boat race has to be continually sustained and repaired as rules or principles are violated. Indeed each incident of rule violation brings these rules and principles to conscious awareness and provides opportunities to reaffirm them: in a very real sense, exceptions confirm the rule. These papers illustrate how dynamic processes underlie stability as well as change, much as a river is constituted by an ever-changing flow (Rescher 1996).

It is often thought that when a planned organization change is canceled, the organization returns to its former state. But as Mantere and Widner discuss in Chapter 30, research indicates that organizations do not return to their former states after changes are canceled (such as a canceled merger effort). This calls attention to the historical continuity of "sensemaking" and raises caution about the popular view that managers need to destroy organizational meaning to facilitate the realization of strategic changes.

Mantere and Widner in Chapter 30 also discuss endings, which are a crucial part of organizational change processes. For something new to emerge, something that has been needs to be concluded. Contemporary literature on organizational change seems to have lost at least some of its appreciation on conclusive aspects of change. Taking stock of contemporary literature, we seem to know much less overall on how to conclude things than how to start them.

Power and Influence

One cannot discuss organization change for long without addressing the asymmetric power and influence among organizational participants and units engaged in change. As is implicit in all the chapters, organizational changes do not simply reflect the social constructions of different affordant actors: they also reflect different power relations among actors and the models they have in their heads to guide change.

- Teleology views change as envisioned end states among agreeable cooperating actors
- Dialectics views change as confrontations and syntheses among conflicting parties
- Life-cycle views change as mandated prescriptions by more-powerful parties on less-powerful actors
- Evolution views change as variation, selection, and retention of scarce resources between competitors
- Garbage can views change as a probabilistic intersection of actors with problems, solutions, and resources
- Cumulative synthesis views change as an abductive process among numerous actors

The Prevalence of Conflict, Dialectics, and Paradox

A common theme throughout the handbook chapters is the recognition that conflict, tension, contradiction, paradox, and dialectics are prevalent in organization change and innovation. This is reflected in the six chapters in this handbook that examine important variations in dialectical processes of organization change. In Chapter 3, for example, Bartunek, Seo, and Putnam discuss the dualisms and dualities in organizational development in terms of diagnostic and dialogical approaches. The diagnostic approach is based on an assumption that an objective reality of conflict can be discovered using rational and analytic processes, and adopts an episodic goal-oriented view of organization change. The dialogical approach assumes there is no inherently real form of social organizing; "reality" is socially constructed and negotiated, and may involve power and political processes. It adopts a continuous and cyclical view of organization change.

In Chapter 9 Davis and Kim discuss how organizations are increasingly subject to political demands from outside actors and their own members. Information and communication technologies (ICTs) are enabling a flourishing of grassroots social innovations and demands for justice that challenge traditional top-down theories of change. Over the past twenty years, scholars have found that social movement theory provides a useful approach to understanding movements *within* organizations, movements that *target* organizations, and movements that *create* organizations and industries.

Hargrave compares paradox and dialectical perspectives on managing conflicts and contradictions in Chapter 7 The paradox perspective provides guidance to managers on how they can increase organizational effectiveness in the face of seemingly irreconcilable tensions. It presents contradictions as stable, separable, and controllable. The dialectical perspective, in contrast, depicts contradictions as difficult to disentangle from their contexts, and suggests that efforts to manage them will have unintended consequences and even undermine themselves. Further, whereas the paradox perspective depicts contradictions as persistent, dialectics treats them as continuously changing and transformed through oppositional processes in which a thesis is challenged by an antithesis, leading to the sublation of the two in a new element.

Critical perspectives of organization change are discussed by Oswick, Oswick, and Grant in Chapter 12. The critical enterprise consists, ideally, of three aspects: (1) explanation and critique of current systems and the historical currents that have given rise to them, (2) an alternative vision of organizations and society that resolves the problems and oppressions in the current systems, and (3) an account of how one moves from the current system to the envisioned one, either naturally or through planned change. Critical research on organizations has generally been weakest in terms of this third aspect. Living in a world dominated by current ideologies and disciplinary practices, many people experience difficulty understanding that there *are* alternatives, much less accepting them as plausible and attainable. Having devoted extensive labor to developing these two aspects, critical scholars have tended to pay less attention to explaining how one transforms the organization or the process by which transformation takes place. In some cases, there seems to be a presumption that raising subjects' awareness of control processes will be sufficient to effect change. In others, opening up the organization to increased participation is advocated. For the most part, critical and post-critical work has provided good portraits of what the end point of change should be, but much less insight on change or changing themselves.

Affect and Emotions of Change

In the past decade there has been an upsurge of interest in "non-cognitive" aspects of organizations, such as emotions and symbolism (Ashkanasy, Hartel, and Zerbe 2000;

Staw, Sutton, and Pelled 1994; Whetten and Godfrey 1998). This interest has also shaped scholarship on organizational innovation and change (e.g., Fiol and O'Connor 2002; Gioia and Thomas 1996; Huy 1999). Current thinking on organizational change and innovation is dominated by rational, instrumental viewpoints, which tend to neglect or downplay the nonrational side of human experience. This has not always been the case. As Nguyen and Vuori discuss in their Chapter 28, it now appears that these concerns are resurfacing in current thinking.

Change and innovation are passionate processes. Successful planned change requires a commitment grounded in an engaging vision and deep emotional involvement with the program. Visions have a cognitive component, but their appeal does not lie in reason. Rather it stems from their connection to participants' desires and identities, connections made through symbolic appeals that index fundamental values. When change occurs, it has an important emotional component because it involves giving up arrangements in which considerable energy and time has been invested. Fiol and O'Connor's (2002) study of community change offers an excellent illustration of the ways in which change affects and is affected by participants' identities and attendant emotional dynamics. They develop a model in which "hot emotional interpretations and relatively colder cognitive interpretations interact to initiate, mobilize, and sustain radical change" (Fiol and O'Connor 2002: 532).

Symbolic and emotional aspects of resistance to change are also in need of study. One example is the concept of nostalgia. Nostalgia, as discussed by post-modernists, is a common reaction to change. It involves an imaginary projection of good characteristics onto the past to recreate a past much better than the present situation. This past is constructed by inversion: undesirable characteristics of the present are mirrored with desirable characteristics of the past, which is then regarded as something to recapture and recreate in the present. Disregarding that "the good old days" were never as good as they are recalled, nostalgia can be a powerful emotional stimulus for resistance and reaction to change and innovation. Exploring the complex web of meaning and interpretation attached to concepts like nostalgia would illuminate aspects of resistance in ways that current rationality-based theories do not.

Greater attention to affect, identity, symbolism, aesthetics, and related subjects would provide a useful balance to change and innovation research. It is important to acknowledge the many sides of human beings and consider how they may figure in starting, sustaining, and resisting change.

Assemblages of Process Models

As mentioned in the handbook's first edition, appreciating the relational and heterogeneous nature of organization requires multiple divergent perspectives (or plots) because any one tends to come up short in relation to the complexity. It requires composite assemblages of worldviews, as Poole and Van de Ven discuss in Chapter 31.

Approaches to the Study of Change and Innovation

Mohr (1982) and Poole et al.(2000) first distinguished variance and process approaches to social scientific research, and the distinction has been quite influential in organizational studies. In general terms, a *variance theory* explains change in terms of relationships among independent variables and dependent variables, while a *process theory* explains how a sequence of events leads to some outcome. The two approaches yield quite different conceptualizations of change and imply different standards for judging research on change and innovation. Figure 1.2 provides a pictorial comparison of the two approaches.

A variance theory focuses on variables that represent the important aspects or attributes of the subject under study. Explanations take the form of causal statements or models that incorporate these variables (e.g., X causes Y which causes Z), and an implicit goal of variance research is to establish the conditions necessary and sufficient to bring about an outcome. Variance research employs experimental and survey research designs and is grounded in the general linear model that underlies most common statistical methods, including ANOVA, regression, factor analysis, and structural equation modeling. A key criterion for assessing variance theories is their generality, which refers to the range of cases, phenomena, or situations the causal explanation applies to.

The primary focus of a process theory is a series of events that unfold through time to bring about some outcome. Explanations in process theories tend to be more complex than variance explanations due to the complexity of events, the need to account for temporal connections among events, different time scales in the same process, and the

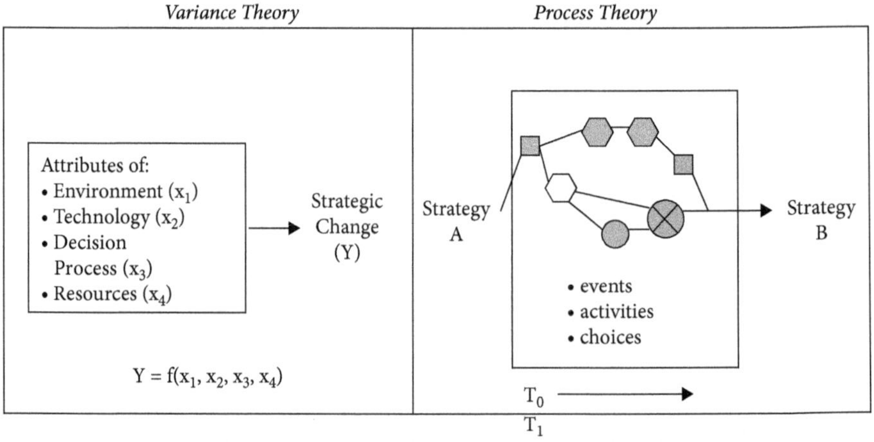

FIGURE 1.2 Two Approaches to Explaining Organization Change

Based on Mohr (1982) and Poole et al. (2000)

dynamic nature of processes. Process theories may incorporate several different types of effects into their explanations, including critical events and turning points, contextual influence, formative patterns that give overall direction to the change, and causal factors that influence the sequencing of events. Poole et al. (2000) argue that process explanations incorporate three of Aristotle's four causes, adding formal and final causation to the efficient causation that is the basis of causal explanation in variance research.

Process research employs longitudinal study designs that identify or reconstruct the process through direct observation, archival analysis, or multiple case studies. Analysis of process data requires methods (a) that can identify and test temporal linkages between events and also overall temporal patterns (Poole et al. 2000) and (b) that can cope with the multiple time scales that often occur in processes (where some events extend for years, other events embedded in them run for shorter periods, and others embedded within these even shorter periods) (Langley 1999). Whereas the great majority of variance research follows hypothetico-deductive procedures, process research employs a mixture of approaches. Most often, process studies derive theory from observation, but in some cases they test hypothesized models of the change process, and in others they use retroduction, whereby theories are used to guide observation that further specifies the theories (Poole et al. 2000: 115–17); indeed, in-depth studies of processes may employ two or even all three of these approaches (e.g., Van de Ven, Polley, Garud, and Venkatraman 1999). As a result, both qualitative and quantitative approaches are used in process research (see Langley 1999; Poole et al. 2000 for description of process methods).

The process approach is sometimes portrayed as opposed to the variance approach. However, it is more appropriate to view them as complementary. Variance studies can explore and test the mechanisms that drive process theories, while process studies can explore and test the narratives that ground variance theories. Rather than arguing that the two approaches are mutually exclusive, the relevant question is how to combine the two approaches.

Formal modeling using mathematical or simulation methodologies offers one way to bridge the gap between process and variance approaches. A discussion of several approaches to formal modeling is presented by Dooley in Chapter 20 and Albert and Ganco in Chapter 21. A model is a representation of a situated theory in some formal language, such as mathematics or a computer algorithm. The model draws on verbal theory and observation to derive a precise theory of a process in some specific context that can be used to project how the process would unfold, and compared to process data gathered in that context.

Concluding Thoughts

The assumptions that a theory of change and innovation make about agency, levels of analysis, and time are not always well articulated. Often they are part of the baggage that comes with adoption of certain perspectives and terms. However, there are benefits to explicitly considering these fundamental decision points in developing and testing theories. Deliberate consideration of the conception of levels, agency, and time in a theory encourages both theorists and readers to probe the theory for consistency and to ask what it has omitted. It invites readers to ask whether the theory may be oversimplifying things or, on the other hand, whether it is too complex. It also facilitates comparison and contrast of theoretical positions. It may be difficult to compare a theory of career development to a theory of individual decision-making in terms of their respective content, agency, levels, and time represent common denominators for all theories of change, development, and innovation. Comparative analysis of these aspects will show the degree to which the two theories are similar or incompatible in their basic workings. This, in turn, may facilitate the development of integrative positions or the delineation of basic differences among theories of change and innovation. The more conscious of our assumptions and the need to justify them we are, the stronger our theories will be.

Can the time and space elements of change and innovation theories be combined in a single manifold, as is the case in physics? Agents would then operate in a more homogeneous time–space continuum. While this is an appealing notion, it will not be straightforward to do so. Levels of analysis are not just dimensions of space, but social constructions with unique and sometimes complex structures of their own. For example, rather than just having a "group" level in an organization, there may be various types of groups—work units, informal cliques, cross functional teams—that are related in complex ways. As this example shows, level is far from a homogeneous construct. As the preceding discussion indicates, the same is true for time. While time and space are as fundamental to the human sciences as they are to the natural sciences, they are more variegated, lumpy, and idiosyncratic in the social world than in the physical world.

As mentioned in the handbook's first edition, appreciating the relational and heterogeneous nature of organization requires multiple divergent perspectives (or plots) because any one tends to come up short in relation to the complexity. It requires composite assemblages of worldviews.

References

Ashkanasy, N., Hartel, C., and Zerbe, W. (Eds.). (2000). *Emotions in organizational life*. New York: Quorum.

Beer, M., Eisenstat, R.A., and Spector, B. (1990). Why change programs do not produce change. *Harvard Business Review*, 68, 158–66.

Burke, W.W. and Litwin, G.H. (1992). A casual model of organizational performance and change. *Journal of Management*, 18, 532–45.

VanLear (Eds.), *Dynamic Patterns in Communication Processes* (pp. 215–30). Thousand Oaks, CA: Sage.

De Mast, J., Linderman, K., and Van de Ven, A. (2020). A process-learning view of system implementation: A case of six sigma. University of Minnesota, Carlson School of Management, Working paper.

Fiol, C. M., and O'Connor, E. J. (2002). When hot and cold collide in radical change processes: Lessons from community development. *Organization Science*, 13, 532–46.
Gandhok, T., and Sammartino, A., (2018). "'Managing intuition': Cognitive versatility and breakthrough ideation in strategy option generation.'" Paper presented at Strategic Management Society conference at Hyderabad, India, December.
Gersick, C. J. (1991). Revolutionary change theories: A multilevel exploration of the punctuated equilibrium paradigm. *Academy of Management Review*, 16(1), 10–36.
Gibson, J. J. (1979). The theory of affordances. In J. J. Gibson (Ed.), *The Ecological Approach to Visual Perception* (pp. 119–136). Hillsdale, New Jersey: Lawrence Erlbaum Associates, Inc..
Gioia, D. A., and Thomas, J. B. (1996). Identity, image and issue reinterpretation: Sensemaking during strategic change in academia. *Administrative Science Quarterly*, 41, 370–403.
Greiner, L. (1972). Evolution and revolution as organizations grow. *Harvard Business Review*, July–August, 165–74.
Guastello, S. J. (1995). *Chaos, Catastrophe, and Human affairs: Applications of Nonlinear Dynamics to Work, Organizations, and Social Evolution*. Mahwah, NJ: Erlbaum.
Helson, H. (1964). *Adaptation-Level Theory: An Experimental and Systematic Approach to Behavior*. Oxford, England: Harper & Row.
Hodgkinson, G.P., and Clarke, (2007). Conceptual note: Exploring the cognitive significance of organizational strategizing: A dual-process framework and research agenda. *Human Relations*, 60(1): 243–55.
Huy, Q. N. (1999). Emotional capability, emotional intelligence, and radical change. *Academy of Management Review*, 24, 325–45.
Klarner, P., and Raisch, S. (2013). Move to the beat—Rhythms of change and firm performance. *Academy of Management Journal*, 56, 1: 160–84.
Kotter, J.P. (1996). *Leading Change*. Boston: Harvard Business School Press.
Langley, A. (1999). Strategies for theorizing from process data. *Academy of Management Review*, 24, 691–710.
Lewin, K. (1948). *Resolving Social Conflicts*. New York: Harper.
Lok J. & de Rond, M.J. 2013. On the plasticity of institutions: Containing and restoring practice breakdowns at the Cambridge University boat club. *Academy of Management Journal*, 56(1), 185–207.
Meyer, A. G., Goes, J. B., and Brooks, G. G. (1993). Organizational reacting to hyperturbulence. In G. P. Huber and W. Glick (Eds.), *Organizational Change and Redesign* (pp. 66–111). New York: Oxford University Press.
Mohr, L. (1982). *Explaining Organizational Behavior*. San Francisco: Jossey-Bass.
Nadler, D.A. and Tushman, M.L. (1977). A diagnostic model for organization behavior. In J.R. Hackman, E.E. Lawler III, & L.W. Porter (eds.) *Perspectives on Behavior in Organizations* (pp. 85–100). New York: McGraw-Hill.
Poole, M.S. and Van de Ven, A.H. (Eds.) (2004). *Handbook of Organizational Change and Innovation*, Oxford, UK: Oxford University Press.
Poole, M. S., Van de Ven, A. H., Dooley, K., and Holmes, M. E. (2000). *Organizational Change and Innovation Processes: Theory and Methods for Research*. New York: Oxford University Press.
Rescher, N. 1996. *Process Metaphysics: An Introduction to Process Philosophy*. Albany, NY: State University of New York Press.
Staw, B., Sutton, R. I., and Pelled, L. H. (1994). Employee positive emotion and favorable outcomes at the workplace. *Organization Science*, 5, 51–71.

Stouten, J., Rousseau, D.M., and DeCremer, D. (2018). Successful organizational change: Integrating the management practice and scholarly literatures. *Academy of Management Annuals*, 12(2), 752–88.

Tichy, N.M. (1983). *Managing Strategic Change: Technical Political and Cultural Dynamics.* New York: Wiley.

Tushman, M., and Romanelli, E. (1985). Organizational evolution: A metamorphosis model of convergence and reorientation. In B. Staw and L. Cummings (Eds.), *Research in Organizational Behavior* (Vol. 7, pp. 171–222). Greenwich, CT: JAI Press.

Usher, A. P. (1929), (1954). *A History of Mechanical Inventions.* Cambridge, MA: Harvard University Press.

Van de Ven, A. H., Polley, D., Garud, R., and Venkatraman, S. (1999). *The Innovation Journey.* New York: Oxford University Press.

Van de Ven, A. H., and Poole, M. S. (1995). Explaining development and change in organizations. *Academy of Management Review,* 20, 510–40.

Van Oorschot, K., Akkermans, H., Sengupta K., and van Wassenhove, L.N. (2013). Anatomy of a decision trap in complex new product development projects. *Academy of Management Journal,* 56(1), 285–307.

Weick, K., and Quinn, R. E. (1999). Organizational change and development. *Annual Review of Psychology,* 50, 361–86.

Whetten, D., and Godfrey, P. C. (Eds.). (1998). *Identity in Organizations: Building Theory Through Conversations.* London: Sage.

Weisbord, M.R. (1976). Organizational diagnosis: six places to look for trouble with or without a theory. *Group and Organization Studies,* 1, 430–47.

PART I

TELEOLOGICAL MODELS OF CHANGE

CHAPTER 2

HISTORICAL CURRENTS IN SCHOLARSHIP OF ORGANIZATION CHANGE

W. WARNER BURKE

Historical Currents in Scholarship of Organization Change

It may be that many people, whether in the workplace or not, believe that organization change begins with the primary decision-makers, that is, what we currently call the C-suite, the chief executive officer, and those who report directly to him or her—the chief financial officer, the chief human resource officer, the chief of operations officer, etc. The belief goes that this group of executives sits around the boardroom table once a week or so, and decide among themselves whether certain changes in the organization need to be made, such as a revision of the organization's structure, a different version of the compensation system, or a change in hiring practices. In other words, an executive sees a need for some organizational change, perhaps has argued for it before, and continues to pound the table in the spirit of making the case for change. While this scenario may capture what happens some of the time in the boardroom, it does not account for how most change efforts today get underway. The scenario described concerns organizational change rather than organization change: "al" vs. "no al." Organizational means pertaining or relating to an organization not the organization itself. Moreover, the term "organizational" is an adjective, a modifier, and organization is a noun—changing some aspect of the organization compared with the organization as a whole. The point is that in today's fast-paced world change is a constant and expansive, with significant variation at the same time. Change is complex, affects the organization more as a whole than in pieces and parts, and comes from an organization's external environment more than from within. Rather than sitting around the boardroom table discussing the organization's structure, the more likely scenario is, or at least needs to be, one of perhaps pacing around the table in the boardroom and complaining in loud voices about how the competition is winning.

The argument being made is that the stimulus for change is predominantly an organization's external environment. And this stimulus today is multi-pronged, messy rather than orderly, touches most aspects of an organization, the business model as well as the bottom line, but not in the same way for all aspects, and is rarely predictable. The problem has become one of what Foster and Kaplan (2001) label as "cultural lock-in": the external environment changes more widely and rapidly than the organization's culture can change to respond quickly and effectively. They state that nothing breeds failure like success, that is, the more efficient organizations become in their day-to-day operations the more they become locked-in to their ways of doing things. This cultural lock-in prevents the change needed to respond to the external environment rapidly and with flexibility.

Even though the organization's culture is likely to be the most difficult component to change, it can be argued that it should not be the sole focus for change as Foster and Kaplan specify. Other important components that need to be environmentally responsive include the organization's strategy, technology, leadership, and diversity in the workforce, to name just a few other examples.

Complexities of the External Environment

Organization change therefore typically begins with what is happening in the organization's external environment: what is occurring in the arena of *capital* markets—at its most basic level acquiring sufficient funds to stay in business, in existence. A century ago this simply meant establishing a good relationship with one's local banker so that borrowing money to meet expenses, starting with the payroll, would become routine. Today there are myriad ways to finance a company. Other examples of the complexity in the external environment include new *technology* and the rapidly growing world of artificial intelligence, the different ways that businesses compete today and redefining markets, for example the advent of social media companies. Another form of competition at the present time is the battle for talent in the workforce. With this increased attention to the external environment, organizations currently, whether management realizes it or not, are operating more like an *open system* than ever before. If we had to identify a singular theory that drives organization change—and start-up businesses—it would be open system thinking which originated with biologists, in particular von Bertalanffy (1956). A living cell has an external environment and draws from it oxygen to sustain its life, but the cell does not need everything from these environmental inputs and thus eliminates ingredients that are not necessary for existence. These outputs return to the external environment and serve as feedback to the cell as to what may be needed and what is not required. This cycle of input—throughput—output followed by a feedback loop to the external environmental is the fundamental process of open system theory and depicted simply as

Input – Throughput – Output
Feedback

This conceptual framework has guided how we think about related theory, for example Lewin's Bf(P,E), organizational models, and change for quite a long time.

Open System Theory

Social psychologists Katz and Kahn (1978) were one of, if not the first, scholars in the world of organization change (the first edition of their book was published in 1968) to "translate" and expand on von Bertalanffy's work for the purpose of helping us to understand organizations in general and organizational behavior in particular. They define ten characteristics that distinguish open systems.

1. *Input*—the importation of energy; money in a business
2. *Throughput*—using the input to accomplish a goal
3. *Output*—goal accomplishment; delivery of a product and/or service
4. *Systems are cycles of events*—input-throughput-output with a feedback loop
5. *Negative entropy*—all forms of organization move toward disorganization or death
6. *Information input, negative feedback, and the coding process*—being selective about input
7. *Steady-state and dynamic homeostasis*—organizations may look steady and homeostatic but in reality are dynamic with driving forces pushing in one direction and restraining forces pushing in another
8. *Differentiation*—the natural process dividing labor into roles and functions
9. *Integration and coordination*—creating ultimately wholeness from the differentiations
10. *Equifinality*—an organization can reach a goal from different starting points and via a variety of paths and ways

In summary, open system theory begins with the life cycle of input-throughput-output with a feedback loop. In the life of an organization this cycle is fundamental, meaning that survival is dependent on the external environment and how well management deals with it in all of its complexities. The organization therefore is an open system and can be understood more specifically in terms of the ten characteristics that further define the organization accordingly. Therefore, organization change must be a systemic process—success depends on this mode of thinking. We now proceed to models, most of which are specific examples of applying open system theory ways of thinking.

Overview of Models for Understanding Organizations and Changing Them

With the overview section that follows of *what* to change and *how* to bring about the change, we begin an effort of tracing the earlier thinking about conceptual models of change and organizations, then we proceed more specifically toward an understanding of organizations and the processes of changing them.

What to Change

As noted already what to change organizationally is usually determined by what is happening in the organization's external environment, for example an economic downturn, the announcement of a merger between two competitors of the organization, new technology (from analog to digital), etc. A dramatic example from the 1980s was Prime Minister Margaret Thatcher's declaration that many if not most government-sponsored organizations would be changed to a private enterprise. British Airways (BA), formerly a government organization that had been hemorrhaging money year after year, became # 2 on PM Thatcher's long list of changing government organizations to privately held enterprises, primarily via stock ownership. The primary content focus for change at BA was its culture. One way to describe the change at BA was its response to a perturbation from the external environment, a "jolt" to the system from the Prime Minister, which in turn instigated a revolutionary or transformational change effort. This jolt created *what* needed to be changed. BA had been managed like other government agencies and that meant "meeting the annual budget," which as noted above, they rarely did. The content of the change might be characterized as moving from a budget model to a business model, from a government bureau to a business corporation. Thus, content became a focus of making a profit, not merely an attempt to hit budget targets. Moreover, BA changed its ownership from government to stockholders—individual investors and organizations, particularly foundations and investment firms.

The main interventions (the *how* to change) facilitating the change being conducted were over a five-year period. This process of change took many forms: training, pointed individual behavioral feedback for some 2,000 managers, and modifications of the system in terms of hierarchy and accountability structure, reward, and performance appraisals. These processes of change, the how, were also examples of content changes. For a more detailed account of this successful change effort at BA see Chapter 11 in Burke (2018).

The late Peter Drucker, management guru and perhaps *a* if not *the* philosopher of business, provided in his thirty-first article for the *Harvard Business Review* and no doubt one of his best among the thirty-one (Drucker 1994), a provocative claim. He argued that highly successful companies that do things right often end up doing them for naught or "fruitlessly" as he put it, and gradual decline occurs. This paradox, as Drucker called it, led to his "theory of the business."

Drucker's theory is a set of assumptions about how a business can succeed in a particular environment and marketplace. These assumptions "shape any organization's behavior, dictate its decisions about what to do and what not to do, and define what the organization considers meaningful results" (Drucker 1994: 96). Note that in this quote he uses the word "what" three times. In other words, *what* to change is Drucker's theory of the business. Companies get into trouble when "the assumptions on which the organization has been built and is being run no longer fit reality" (p. 95). Sound familiar? Foster and Kaplan (2001) called it "cultural lock-in." Drucker's (1994) theory of the business consists of three parts—Assumptions about the:

1. external environment of the organization, such as society and its structure, the market, the customer, and technology;
2. organization's mission, purpose, and *raison d être*;
3. organization's core competencies, that is, the skills and abilities required to accomplish the mission.

Drucker's criteria for a valid theory of the business:

1. The three assumptions must fit reality.
2. All three assumptions must fit or be congruent with one another.
3. The theory of the business must be known and understood by all organizational members.
4. The theory needs to be tested constantly.

Drucker's theory is not just an afterthought. His years of observation and study of the business world are distilled in these three assumptions and four criteria for validity. And this theory is not solely Drucker's. As noted, the Foster and Kaplan (2001) research fully support Drucker's thinking and conclusions. There is also support from empirical research. The study by Audia et al. (2000) provides strong evidence from both an archival, data-based study of the airline and trucking industries over a decade and the other was a laboratory experiment. Even the title of their article is supportive: "The paradox of success...." In summary their two studies showed that

> Greater past success led to greater strategic persistence after a radical environmental change, and such persistence induced performance declines. The laboratory study also demonstrated that dysfunctional persistence is due to greater satisfaction with past performance, more confidence in the correctness of current strategies, higher goals and self-efficacy, and less seeking of information from critics. (p. 837)

The content of organization change varies from one organization to another. It can be mission, strategy, culture, systems, or structure. The point is that whatever the content of change may be, for effective organization change to be achieved, that content *must* fit with and be a response to clearly identified factors from the external environment that influence or will have an impact on the business or overall performance of the organization now and/or in the future. Remember: the horse to bet on should probably not be the one that won the most recent race.

How to Change

While not always easy to identify what to change, it may be more difficult to be clear about how to bring about organization change. Over the years many different approaches have emerged. Van de Ven and Poole (1995) in fact conducted a study that lends support to this supposition. Using the key words of *change* and *development* they searched the extensive literature producing over 1 million articles. With considerable effort they boiled the search down to twenty theories of change and development and then clustered these twenty into four primary categories or schools of thought. They labeled these four: life cycle, teleological, dialectical, and evolutionary. The four are:

1. *Life cycle*: Organization change is a sequence of phases or steps which are cumulative and conjunctive.
2. *Teleological*: Organizations are about purpose—having goals and accomplishing a mission. Change concerns new goals.
3. *Dialectical*: Organizations compete for needed resources—thus, change involves conflict, negotiation, confrontation, and related skills.
4. *Evolutionary*: Organization change is a continuous cycle of selection and retention of talent and other resources. Change is continuous, transactional, and rarely if ever revolutionary.

For a more comprehensive explanation of these four categories and how they overlap to change organizations, see Chapter 1 by Van de Ven and Poole in this handbook.

To briefly summarize, we have in two parts reviewed models for understanding organizations in more depth and how to change them. The first part addressed what to change (as determined by the external environment) and used Drucker's theory of business to illustrate what we mean when covering the *what* to change. The second part concerned *how* to change and briefly defined the Van de Ven and Poole (1995) study which resulted in a consolidation of the many approaches to bringing about change into four primary categories or schools of thought—life cycle, teleological, dialectic, and evolutionary. These four definitions help us to understand what the larger landscape of how to change organizations looks like. We now consider what we refer to as "integrated" models, that is, frameworks that combine the what and the how. Initially it is important to define our terms—what is an organizational model? How and why do we use one? And what are some significant examples?

Integrated Organizational Models for Understanding and Changing Organizations

First, what is an organizational model? For our purposes it is a representation to demonstrate the construction or appearance of something, in this case, a representation of an organization. Staying with our open system theory, it is, at least metaphorically, an *organism*.

Second, why use a model? It can help us to categorize. We cannot expect to understand and keep track of everything about an organization, so "chunking" our information keeps us from being overwhelmed. An organizational model can also help us enhance our understanding, that is, it can guide us with how the components interact to areas that are in most need of change. A model can help us to interpret data about the organization. An organizational model can provide a common, shorthand language. And, finally, a model can help guide action for change.

There are at least two important cautions about using a model that helps to reduce complexity. It is not just the components of the model (mostly the what)—mission, culture, systems, etc.—that are important, but how these components fit together, with some carrying more "weight" than other areas. These interactions provide useful information for the *how* part of change. The second caution comes from Gareth Morgan (1997) when he stated: "Metaphor (an organism in this case) is inherently paradoxical. It can create powerful insights that also become distortions as the way of seeing created through a metaphor becomes a way of not seeing" (p. 5).

Integrated Models of Organizations and Organizations and Organization Change

There are many organizational models in the management literature. Mintzberg (1989) has described a number of them as has Morgan (1997) in his book about metaphors or "images" that depict organizational models. And the idea of organizational models has been around for at least fifty or more years. It may be that the first integrated model was created by Harold Leavitt (1965) of the Stanford University School of Business. His simple and straightforward framework had only four components depicted in the shape of a diamond with structure at the top, and then coming around clockwise occupying the remaining three corners were technology, people, and task. Perhaps Leavitt had a baseball diamond in mind. If so, structure is at second base, technology at first base, people at home base, and task at third base. Leavitt emphasized that change in any one of the four components would result in change for the other three. This statement implies system thinking but not *open* system theory. There is no accounting for the external environment (input) nor for output with a feedback loop. Leavitt's model covers only throughput, making it by definition a closed system.

The most popular organizational model in the world is no doubt McKinsey's 7-S framework. This consulting-firm model has been used since at least the early 1980s. The model was developed by Richard Pascale, Tom Peters, and others who were affiliated with McKinsey at the time. The model was apparently introduced to the general public via the Peters and Waterman (1982) best-selling book, *In Search of Excellence*. The model has seven components, all beginning with the letter "S" so that the seven can be more easily remembered. The irony here is that both Peters and Pascale were students of Leavitt at Stanford; thus, the widely used McKinsey model like Leavitt's original one of four components is based on the notion of a closed system. There is no accounting for the organization's external environment nor any reference to output or performance, much less a feedback loop. Therefore, we have a closed system consisting of seven components being connected with each other and arranged in a circle with structure at the top (like Leavitt), followed clockwise with systems, style, skills, strategy, and shared values, representing culture, in the middle, that is, surrounded by the other six. This well-known model, McKinsey 7-S, is systemic, with its seven components interacting, yet in the end it is not based on sound theory.

We will now summarize four models that are based on open system theory and illustrate the integrated idea of organization change models. These models have been chosen to summarize because they are popular with practitioners, especially those in the organization development arena. Displayed in Table 2.1, these summaries will bring us up to date regarding which models are in use today. We begin with Weisbord's Six-Box framework, then summarize the Nadler-Tushman Congruence model followed by Tichy's framework that emphasizes how to implement organization change, and end with a description of the Burke-Litwin Causal Model of Organizational Performance and Change.

Weisbord's Six-Box Organizational Model

Like McKinsey's 7-S model, Weisbord's (1976) six-box framework is arranged in a circle, but unlike the McKinsey model, Weisbord accounts for the external environment, although not prominently. He places "Environment" outside the circle with two arrows—one from the environment to the circle and one from the circle to the environment. At least this depiction helps to classify Weisbord's model as conforming to open system theory. The model nevertheless is primarily about throughput, that is, the six boxes. The six are placed in the circle with Purposes at the top followed clockwise with connecting arrows going in both directions by Structure, Rewards, Helpful Mechanisms, and Relationships, with Leadership in the center surrounded by the other five. The six boxes are defined by Weisbord as the labels imply, with Purposes meaning to define what business we are in, thus it is about mission, and Structure concerns how work is differentiated, Rewards focuses largely on incentives, Helpful Mechanisms emphasizes the technologies that support the work, Relationships is about the interactions among

Table 2.1 Open System Theory Models of Organization Change Models: What to Change, How to Change

Weisbord 6-Box Model	Six organizational components arrayed in a circle with purposes at the top then clockwise structure, Rewards, Helpful Mechanisms, Relationships and with Leadership in the center for purposes of coordination	Leaders coordinate and focus on the 5 other boxes with change projects for each one bearing in mind that all boxes are interconnected. Priorities based on data gathering for the 6.
Nadler-Tushman Congruence Model	Primary organizational components include Input (key resources; history) Throughput (strategy then the transformation process-task, informal organization, formal organizational arrangements and individual) followed by Output (organizational group and individual performance).	Focus on the identified organizational components especially *strategy* and their interactions with emphasis on incongruences among these components where innovation and conflict resolution may be realized as a result.
Tichy TPC Model	Primary organizational components are 3 subsystems—technical, political, and cultural. These 3 cut across 6 levers for change: Mission/strategy, tasks, prescribed network, people, processes, emergent networks forming a matrix of 18 alignments.	Data are gathered from the 18 categories of alignments, e.g., mission/strategy according to technical, political, and cultural—how well are these aligned? Misalignments become the targets for change, i.e., a combination of what and how to change.
Burke-Litwin Model of Performance and Change	Twelve boxes or dimensions that are interconnected within two broad categories: transformational and transactional. The primary contents for change are concerned more with the arrows than the boxes. How effectively the boxes interrelate become the primary content for change.	The process of change is top-down starting with how the external environment affects the organization as a whole. The data-gathering vehicle is a large-scale survey based on the 12 boxes, thus, the focus and process for change is based on feedback from the organization wide survey.

organizational members, with a special focus on how conflicts are managed, and Leadership has the responsibility of keeping the other five boxes in balance.

We can no doubt agree that Weisbord's model is straightforward, relatively simple to understand, and fairly easy to use. Moreover, its utility is to help relatively unsophisticated organizational members to think systemically, and to understand their organization as an open system and that plans for change should be crafted and implemented accordingly.

The Nadler-Tushman Congruence Model

This model by Nadler and Tushman (1977) was developed at about the same time as Weisbord's, and they made similar assumptions that an organization is an open system influenced by its external environment and that it in turn shapes this environment by way of its products and services. The Nadler-Tushman model is carefully designed to conform to open system theory using the direct language of input–output, etc. Rather than a circle we have a map of sorts traveling left to right with clear road signs of strategy, task, outputs with feedback loop, etc. The primary inputs are the environment, the organization's resources (capital, raw materials, technologies, etc.) and history (policy, types of people attracted to work for the organization, etc.). These inputs shape the organization's strategy, which in turn determines what the primary throughput of four components becomes, that is, the tasks (jobs), the informal organization (social structure, politics, etc.), the individual component (demographic data, diversity, etc.) and the formal organizational arrangements (structure, reward system, IT, etc.). All of these throughput variables in turn determine the outputs, that is, performance at three levels—organizational, group, and individual. The final point regarding this model is the notion of congruence. Nadler and Tushman viewed *fit* between pairs of inputs and throughputs, especially those pairs that constitute the "transformational process," their preferred term for throughputs, and the outputs. Their dominant diagnosis therefore was the degree of fit or congruence between and among all of these parts. The focus of change became the steps required for achieving congruence throughout the model. Getting all of this right, that is, the right fit for so many parts is obviously a complicated process. And it may have become too complicated or not quite the right change objective. In any case, Nadler and Tushman (1989) changed their minds about a dozen years after their original work on the model. They questioned their own position about the importance of congruence. Here was their conclusion from 1989 forward:

> While our model implies that congruence of organizational components is a desirable state, it is, in fact, a double-edged sword. In the short term, congruence seems to be related to effectiveness and performance. A system with high congruence, however, can be resistant to change. It develops ways of insulating itself from outside influences and may be unable to respond to new situations. (195)

Tichy's TPC Framework

The TPC stands for technical, political, cultural, and is similar to the previous two models, but Tichy's (1983) model focuses much more explicitly on organization change. It is therefore more about the how than the previous two models. Tichy's framework consists of nine components within familiar territory, but his "boxes" double as descriptors of organizational components and as *change levers*. Briefly the nine components or change levers are:

1. Organization's external environment and history—the input
2. Resources

3. Mission/Strategy (although placed in the same "box," Tichy nevertheless sees them as distinct levers)
4. Tasks
5. Prescribed networks—the formal organizational structure
6. Organizational processes—communicating, problem-solving, decision-making
7. People, which includes motivation and leadership
8. Emergent networks—the informal organization
9. Performance—impact on people; the output

The nine components are not unlike the previous two models. What makes Tichy's approach to organizations and change more unique is his framework of three primary systems—technical, political, and cultural—with which he then forms a matrix of the three with his previous levers. The technical system is based on science and represents a highly rational view of the organization. The political system is about power and who has it, who does not. The cultural systems consists of shared norms and values or "cognitive schemes" as Tichy calls them. Culture changes concerns creating new norms. Tichy's main argument is that these three systems must be aligned with the nine levers for effective change to occur. Data must be collected according to each of twenty-seven cells of the matrix. These twenty-seven then become the necessary levers for change.

The Burke-Litwin Causal Model of Organization Performance and Change

To be briefly covered, this final model actually emerged from practice. Both George Litwin and I were working together in the latter half of the 1980s as consultants to British Airways trying to make change happen and then to sustain it. The model was born out of our need to make sense out of what we were doing or not doing as the case might have been. Although not so clear then, it seems apparent today that we were following, at least implicitly, principles of open system theory and formulating ideas about what would work regarding organization change and why. It was a matter of reflection and bringing thoughts to the surface for challenge and discussion.

As can be seen from Figure 2.1 the model conforms to open system theory with input from the external environment, throughput according to ten components/boxes, and output in terms of performance from many levels, and a feedback loop represented by a bidirectional arrow meaning that organizations are shaped by their environment and at the same time have an impact on and shape to some extend future characteristics of that environment.

To depict the model more realistically there would need to be arrows or linkages between each component and all other components (boxes). To show all possible connections would look cluttered, to say the least, and probably indecipherable, so just

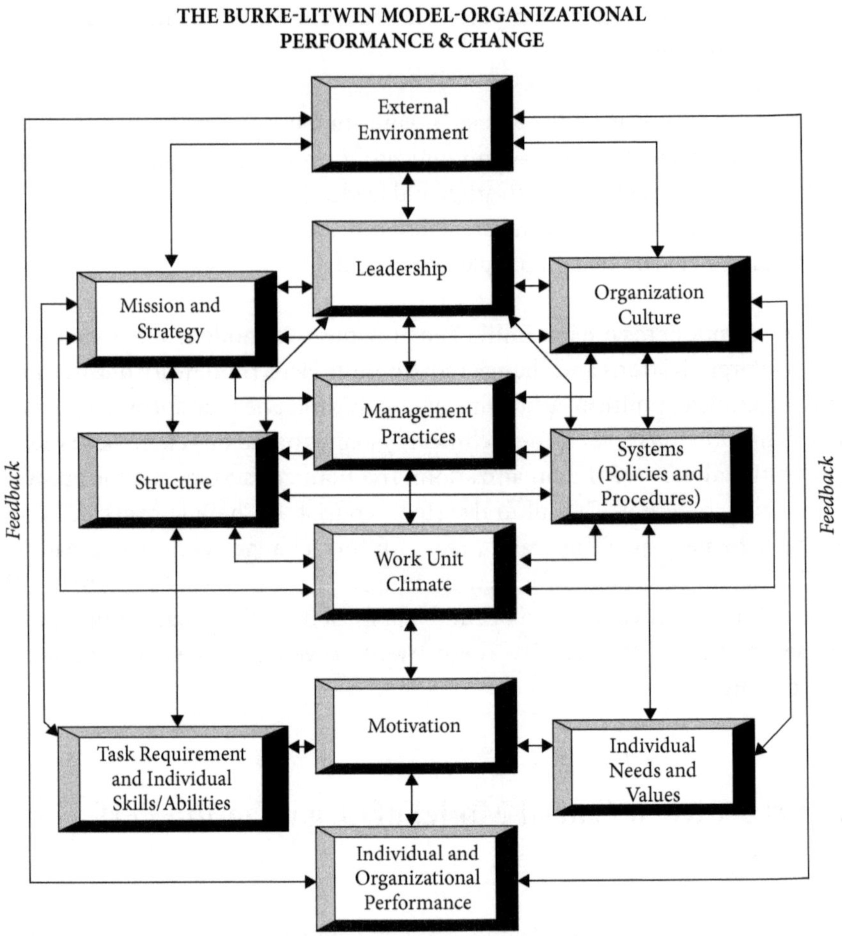

FIGURE 2.1 A Causal Model of Organizational Performance and Change

(W. W. Burke and G. H. Litwin)

some of the more important linkages are displayed. Also, we are limited to a page in a book which is two dimensional when circular arrows within a hologram would come closer to reality.

Our claim is that the model predicts causality, that the top boxes have more influence and "weight" than the lower boxes. When considering change, some directions in the model are more impactful than others. Consider a quick example between culture and systems. The arrow connecting the two components is bidirectional, but culture has a stronger effect on systems (e.g., rewards, information technology, budgetary processes, etc.) than the other way around. Evidence in partial support of this causal statement comes from a study by Kerr and Slocum (1987). Their research showed that an organization's reward system is a manifestation of its culture and that the reward system can be used to facilitate change in an organization's culture. In other words, the study at least clearly supports the idea of linkage. Culture carrying more weight was not demonstrated, but we are going further and hypothesizing that culture helps to *determine* the type of reward system that exists in the organization.

Our broader argument is that organization change occurs more from an environmental impact than from any other component. And as the model is displayed "weight" of the components is top-down. Mission, strategy, leadership, and culture have more influence on the total system than structure, management practices, and systems. Furthermore, the model is conceived as having two significant dimensions—*transformational*, which includes the external environment, mission/strategy, leadership, and culture, and *transactional*, which includes the remaining components. The point is that when the organization is attempting a change of mission and strategy as well as leadership and culture, transformational change is required. Change among the lower, transactional factors involves actions that can be characterized as continuous improvement.

Much more has been covered regarding this final, integrated organization change model; see particularly the original explanatory article (Burke and Litwin 1992) and Chapter 10 in Burke (2018).

Table 2.1 summarizes the four integrated models based on open system theory. They are presented in this particular order to reflect, at least roughly, the degree of complexity the model conveys, ranging from Weisbord, the least complex, to the Burke-Litwin Model, the most complex, in part due to the prediction of causality. All four reflect an open system theory way of thinking, starting with input and ending with output.

Finally the components of each model represent the content on *what* to change, for example, culture, strategy, etc. and the way these components are arranged and interact reflect the *how* of change, for example, the degree of "weight" or impact among the components, such as culture being more influential than systems, and the patterns of these interactions, such as the question of how one modifies structure when strategy is changed, or what the impact is on work unit climate when changes in management practices occur. Thinking about how to change an organization in this manner sets the stage for significant research among these components in terms of studying moderators and mediators in, say, a regression analysis.

Successful Organizational Change Based on an Integration of Management Practice and Scholarship

Up to this point in the chapter our focus has largely been historical. To bring the subject matter more to the present, we will now cover three recent reviews of organization change but from different perspectives. These reviews address both the content or *what* to change, and the process or *how* to change, but lean more toward the *how*, particularly in the initial review.

The first review article by Stouten et al. (2018) provides extensive coverage of what change practitioners recommend and follow in their work with client organizations. Then they compare these practice models with one another and research-based evidence that either supports or challenges the practitioners' approaches to organization change. Finally they synthesize best practices and research evidence to generate a list of ten principles and steps of change management.

The second review article by Suddaby and Foster (2017) concerns the importance of understanding and analyzing an organization's history when change is the goal. They consider four different perspectives or models of organization history that help to manage change more effectively than when the past is ignored. The four models are History-as-Fact, History-as-Power, History-as-Sensemaking, and History-as-Rhetoric.

And, finally, we have not overlooked the importance of leadership. The review paper by Oreg and Berson (2019) first call our attention to the gap, or chasm as they call it, between leadership and organization change. As we know leadership has an impact on organization change and, in turn, the consequences of organization change influence leaders, but this relationship has not been studied systematically. These reviewers then provide an overall framework for addressing the chasm followed by an extensive review of the literature to fill in the gaps suggested by their model.

What follows are summaries of these three reviews that address organization change and provide new perspectives.

Stouten et al. (2018) have made a significant contribution to the field of organization change by providing a summary and review of basic change management processes and principles in the form of popular change models. The change models they review begin with Lewin's three-phase process followed by six other models that span the 1980s, '90s, and up to 2006. Stouten et al. review the primary tenets of these models and the findings from research on organization change processes that provide evidence-based support or not as the case may be. Their coverage of the seven practitioner-oriented change models is followed by their own ten-steps framework in managing organization change that is evidence based.

Stouten et al. begin their article with the two primary challenges that they faced. First, they point out that the scientific literature is fragmented and lacks any consensus regarding basic change processes. They further contend that this fragmentation may be the main reason practitioners rely on popular writers of change management rather than evidence-based practice, which is difficult to pin down and be conclusive. A second challenge Stouten and his colleagues encountered is the difficulty of learning from experience. Organization change takes time and requires repeated measures from which to learn. Moreover, the nature of change can be very diverse from strategic change and restructuring to mergers and acquisitions, to facility relocations, to introductions of new technology, to name just a few examples. This diversity is difficult to learn from, to bring together in a coherent sense-making framework.

With these challenges in mind, the authors proceed with their review of seven popular models followed by their "synthesis of ten empirically supported steps in managing change based on scientific evidence, providing a foundation for an evidence-based approach to change management" (Stouten et al., 2018: 753).

Prescriptive Models of Planned Organizational Change

The *first* of these seven models is Kurt Lewin's (1948) three-phase process: unfreeze-change-refreeze which to some extent sets the stage for all subsequent models. The *second* practitioner model is Michael Beer's six-step developed with colleagues (Beer et al. 1990). The steps are diagnosis, change vision, establish a consensus of support, implementation, institutionalization, monitor, and make adjustments as needed. The *third* model is appreciative inquiry (Cooperrider and Srivastva 1987). The unique feature of this model is that it takes a positive perspective. Building on what organizational members feel are positive features of the organization they follow four stages in succession: discovery, dream, design, and destiny. The *fourth* model that Stouten et al. select is Judson's (1991) five steps: (1) analyzing and planning the change, (2) communicating, (3) gaining acceptance, (4) initial transition to the new situation, and (5) consolidation. The *fifth* model by Kanter et al. (1992) is more elaborate with ten steps: (1) analysis of need, (2) vision and direction, (3) separation from the past, (4) creating a sense that change is needed, (5) leadership, (6) political sponsorship, (7) implementation plan, (8) enabling structures, for example training program, (9) communication, and (10) reinforcement and institutionalized. Stouten and colleagues' *sixth* selection is Kotter's (1996) eight-step model which includes (1) establishing a sense of urgency, (2) forming a guiding coalition, (3) vision, (4) communication, (5) developing change plans, (6) short-term wins, (7) consolidation, (8) institutionalizing the change. And, finally, the *seventh* model is by Jeff Hiatt (2006). His change model is simplified to an acronym of ADKAR—awareness (need for change), desire (empowerment of employees), knowledge (to be developed), and reinforcement.

As can be seen from these seven change models there is considerable overlap. In a synthesis of these seven models, Stouten and his colleagues identified ten steps or success factors that were prescribed in the seven prescriptive models. These ten steps then provided the framework for testing their validity in the scientific research literature. The authors focused on peer-reviewed, empirical research studies from 1990.Their coverage included forty-two journals with these five leading the list: *Journal of Applied Psychology, Academy of Management Journal, Journal of Change Management, Journal of Applied Behavioral Science, and Journal of Organizational Behavior.*

In other words, how well does this literature support the elements (steps) of these prescriptive models?

See Table 2.2 for listing of the consolidated ten steps with the Stouten and colleagues' assessments for each step regarding the extent of agreement across the seven practitioner models and the degree of scientific support.

Stouten and colleagues (2018) summarize their consolidation process by pointing out that most of these practitioner models assume a top-down approach, essentially ignore the history of the organization, and emphasize the importance of empowerment and

Table 2.2 Integrated Summary of Seven Practitioner Models of Organization Change

Change Steps	Practitioner Agreement	Supportive Evidence
1. Data Gathering and Diagnosis	While important very little agreement as a first step.	No support for beginning with a sense of urgency.
2. Select and Support a Guiding Coalition	Considerable agreement but unclear about where top, middle, or lower levels of management.	As a rule, not addressed; not clear what the tasks of a coalition are.
3. Formulate a Clear, Compelling Vision for the Change	Considerable agreement	Support from research, e.g., Baum, Locke, and Kirkpatrick (1998).
4. Communicate the Vision	Very important how the vision is communicated like using multiple channels. Leaders must embody the vision.	Support for using multiple channels Oreg, Vakola, and Armenakis (2011); trust in management very important (Rousseau and Tijoriwala 1999) and clarity regarding possible downsides of change (Bies and Moag, 1986).
5. Mobilize Energy for Change	Mobilization is important but lack of agreement about the speed thereof.	Important but very little guidance except for Kim, Hornung, and Rousseau (2011).
6. Empower Others to Act	Agreement about the critical importance of empowerment and motivation.	Coch and French (1948) study regarding involvement leading to commitment and Knight Patterson and Dawson (2017); research also supports key role of procedural justice (Oreg et al. 2011), employees having a voice (Tyler and Blader 2003), and related bottom-up processes (Morrison and Phelps, 1999).
7. Develop and Promote Change–Related Knowledge and Ability	Most practitioners agree on importance of knowledge but at least one study showed that managers do not score very well on a test of knowledge about organization change (Burke, Clark, and Koopman 1984). Although practitioners rarely mention it, Stouten et al. (2018) emphasize the importance of developing a safe work environment where making mistakes and learning from them is supported.	Stouten el al. (2018) also cite the work of Edmondson (1999; 2002) regarding the importance and support of psychological safety, that is, developing a change environment that is safe.

Continued

Change Steps	Practitioner Agreement	Supportive Evidence
8. Identify Short-Term Wins and Use Them as Reinforcement of the Change Process	Considerable agreement regarding the importance of short-term wins and communication thereof.	There is research support for this step (Seijts and Latham 2005; Malina and Selto 2001).
9. Monitor and Strengthen the Change Process Over Time	In most practitioner models this step was included. Dealing with unintended consequences and using employee surveys are cited as actions that can support change over time.	Research supporting this step comes from the work of Buchanan, (2011) and Wiedner, Barrett, and Osborn (2017).
10. Institutionalize Change in Company Culture, Practices, and Management Succession	Most practitioner models include this step.	Overall research is limited. Establishing new routines into the larger organization is supported by Edmondson (2002) and Rerup and Feldman (2011).

Stouten, Rousseau, and DeCremer (2018).

learning plus the value of feedback. Research evidence largely supports these commonalities as well as the importance of alignment of structures and systems with the new practices that emerge as a result of the change. And, finally there is considerable agreement, with research support, that having a compelling vision for the change effort is an imperative. Scientific evidence supports the necessity of vision communication yet at the same time does not provides much clarity about the key attributes (degree of challenge, domain of focus) of the vision.

Although scientific evidence does not appear to exist for what needs to be the key attributes of an effective vision statement, the practice world does suggest what their attributes might be. Nanus (1992), in his book on *Visionary Leadership*, provides such a list. Using the term properties instead of attributes, he states that an effective vision has seven properties:

1. Appropriate for the organization at the present time and fits in terms of the organization's history, desired culture and values, and is attainable in the future
2. Sets standards of excellence and reflects high ideals
3. Clarifies purpose and direction
4. Inspires enthusiasm and encourages commitment
5. Is well articulated and easily understood
6. Reflects the uniqueness of the organization, its distinctive competence, what it stands for, and what it is able to achieve
7. Is ambitious, expands the organization's horizon, and may call for sacrifice and emotional investment by organizational members

Until a more definitive set of properties emerges this list by Nanus can be used to establish hypotheses for testing by researchers.

Stouten, Rousseau, and DeCremer conclude their extensive review of change models by (a) integrating the prescriptive and empirical literatures on change management and (b) addressing the research implications for the future.

Evidence-Based Principles of Change Management

Again, synthesizing the empirical literature Stouten and his colleagues conclude that there are ten principles and steps of effective change management. Some of these ten principles support the prescriptive models, for example communicating the vision, and some do not, such as the value of pilot testing and experimentation. Their ten are now summarized.

1. *Get Facts Regarding the Nature of the Problem(s)—Diagnosis Step 1*

Is change really needed? Gather two sets of facts to answer this question. The two are information regarding (1) the degree of need, and (2) historical conditions or constraints that might affect a change effort (Rafferty and Restubog, 2017).

2. *Assess and Address the Organization's Readiness for Change—Diagnosis Step # 2*

Determining an organization's readiness for change involves three primary diagnoses: (1) the organization's history regarding change successes and failures (Bordia et al. 2011), (2) the degree of stress currently experienced by organizational members (Oreg et al. 2011; Vakola and Nikolaou 2005), and (3) the degree of capability of senior leadership to guide and manage the change.

3. *Implement Evidence-Based Change Interventions*

Stouten et al. recommend that three sources of evidence need to be identified to support appropriate actions, that is, interventions: (1) Select a diverse group of people inside and outside the organization who have experience with the problem and can help with possible solutions, (2) identify key stakeholders to test ideas with, and (3) identify benefits and risks of specific kinds of change. The authors further remind us that change interventions differ with some being more appropriate for the organizations than others (Dutton et al. 2001; Neuman et al. 1989). Change interventions that develop learning for employees, provide rewards to motivate change and to practice change activities can be advantageous (Bos-Nehles et al. 2017; Marin-Garcia and Tomas 2016).

4. *Develop Effective Change Leadership Throughout the Organization*

Typically executives and managers in the organization who will be leading the change effort will require training in change-related skills (Bruch and Sattelberger 2001).

5. *Develop and Communicate a Compelling Change Vision*

There is strong agreement in the literature regarding the importance of this step. Stouten et al. state, however, that what is not clear from the literature is the nature of the content that makes a vision compelling. Although lacking support from research, useful criteria for an effective vision are provided by Nanus (1992). The authors state that there is greater clarity from the literature about the process of communication, that is, repetition and providing data that the change is working. They also remind us that research does not support urgency as a tactic (Staw et al. 1981).

6. *Work with Social Networks and Tap Their Influence*

Prescriptive models ignore this principle and step. Network relations augment individual skills, and attachment to one's professional group can be especially helpful (Battilana and Casciaro 2013).

7. *Use Enabling Practices to Support Implementation*

Enabling processes include goal setting, learning, employee participation, fairness and justice, and transitional structures such as task forces. These practices are clearly supported by the literature.

8. *Promote Micro-Processes and Experimentation*

These are processes that use multiple small interventions to support learning by doing and to create pilot tests for identifying new interventions.

9. *Assess Change Progress and Outcomes Over Time*

These processes provide important feedback to understand whether progress is being made and to make improvements (Wiedner et al. 2017).

10. *Institutionalize the Change to Sustain Its Effectiveness*

This step means integrating the change into larger systems of the organization such as HR practices, governance, etc. Stouten and colleagues argue that change in an organization's culture may not be necessary because not all change efforts require a shift in the organization's values and beliefs.

The breadth and depth of this extensive review by Stouten and colleagues has provided useful information regarding the phases or steps of planned organization change. Their final summary of ten principles is without doubt an important contribution to the field of planned organization change. At the same time their study shows where future research could focus to extend the accumulative knowledge so far. For example, they point to the need for a deeper understanding of the role of a *governing coalition* and suggest that change leadership at the middle management level, that is, not just at the top, may be particularly beneficial. The authors also repeat their earlier admonition of needing to know about factors that contribute to an effective vision statement to guide and provide inspiration for the change effort.

In the end, Stouten et al. argue for paying attention to the *nature* of planned organization change. First is the *temporal* nature of the change. Is it ongoing or a one-time only shift? Second, is the *scope* of the change effort. Are many aspects (strategy, structure, reward system) of the organization involved or only one? And, third, is the *scale* of the change. Is the entire organization affected or is the change more localized to a division or singular function such as HR or IT. The authors go on to conclude that

> The prescriptive literature largely ignores the kinds of change involved, but we suspect that there are opportunities for systematically reviewing studies according to their temporal, scope, or scale dimensions to identify patterns that can inform change practice and theory. (Stouten et al. 2018: 779).

Stouten et al. mention more than once the absence of an organization's history in the practitioners' models. They recognize its importance but do not delve into its meaning and role in managing organization change. Fortunately Suddaby and Foster (2017) have done that for us.

The Role of an Organization's History as Part of the Change Process

Suddaby and Foster (2017) have identified four implicit models of history that influence organization change: History-as-Fact, History-as-Power, History-as-Sensemaking, and History-as-Rhetoric. Their objective is to link views of history to organization change.

In summary:

- History-as-fact means that history is an inexorable accumulation of events that limit choice and cause inertia (Kelly and Amburgey 1991).
- History-as-power means that change is intended to consolidate the power of owners and managers, thus, the approach to implementation of organization change requires *punctuated equilibrium*.
- History-as-sensemaking means making interpretations of and how we experience events, not the events themselves, thus "change requires an interpretive shift in the cognitive frames that define the dominant reality of the organization" (Suddaby and Foster 2017: 30).
- History-as-rhetoric means that history is a narrative of the past and highly subjective, thus organization change must emphasize language and symbols that provide focus for the change.

Theory and history thereby strengthen our understanding of what is meant by the concept of change. These authors declare that their "central argument is that variations in how we conceptualize change are underpinned by different assumptions about

Table 2.3. Comparison of Integrated Organizational Models Based on Open System Theory with Recent Reviews of Organization Change Models and Concepts

Recent Reviews of Organization Change Models and Concepts	Integrated Models of Organizations and Organization Change Based on Open System Theory			
The 10 Evidenced-based Steps of Organization Change (Stouten et al. 2018)	Weisbord 6-Box (1976)	Nadler–Tushman Congruence (1977)	Tichy TPC Model (1983)	Burke–Litwin Causal Model (1992)
1. Data Gathering and Diagnosis	Yes: Formal vs. informal organization	Yes: Identify the overall system and strategy	Yes: Three sub-systems—technical, political, culture	Yes: 12 boxes—primary components of the model
2. Readiness for Change	Not assessed	Not assessed	Not assessed	Not assessed
3. Implement Interventions	Yes: Focus on 5 boxes guided by leaders	Yes: Transformative processes	Yes: The 9 levers	Yes: The 12 components
4. Develop Leadership	Yes: Central to the model	Implied via concepts, e.g., transformative	Implied in the political system	Yes: One of the 12 components
5. Vision	No	Not explicit	Implied perhaps	Not explicit
6. Social Networks	Recognizes importance of the informal organization	Informal organization perhaps	Yes: Prescribed and emergent networks	Not explicit
7. Enabling Practices	Leadership—keeping the boxes in balance	Transformative processes (throughput)	Fit between 3 systems (TPC) and 9 levers	Transactional factors
8. Micro Processes & Experimentation	Degree of fit between and among the 6 boxes	Congruence (goals structure, job design, etc.)	Fit between the 9 levers	Not explicit
9. Assess Progress	Not explicit	Not explicit	Not explicit	Yes: Time: 1 compared with Time 2 surveys
10. Institualization to Sustain Change	Leaders' responsibility	Not explicit	Not explicit	Yes: Implicit but not sufficiently emphasized
Consideration of History (Suddaby and Foster, 2017)	No	Yes: One of three major considerations from Input	Yes: Primarily the external environment not the organization per se	No: Only within the culture assessment
Emphasis on Leadership (Oreg and Berson, 2019)	Yes: Central to the model	Implicit	"Management occurs throughout the organization"	Yes: A transformational factor

history and its relationship to our capacity for change. We adopt a historical lens because, at their core, the study of change and history both involve the retrospective interpretation of past events. There are, however, important differences in how we theorize history... Our explicit theories of change and our ability to change, thus, vary by our implicit models" (Suddaby and Foster 2017: 20). These statements by the authors are summarized in the next to last row in Table 2.3.

A piece of my own history in the role of an organization change consultant has stuck with me. It involved a meeting that an experienced colleague and I were having with a client group from a larger corporation. At one point in the meeting due to some comment that a member of the group made, my colleague interrupted with a retort of "Spare me the history!" I thought that was a mistake at the time and I feel even more strongly about it today. Suddaby and Foster have provided an important contribution regarding the enormous role that history plays in any organization change effort.

Even though the leadership role in organization change has been mentioned from time to time in this chapter, it has been implied almost all of the time. It can also be assumed that leadership and organization change are intertwined. The change leader is a given. The bottom row of Table 2.3 addresses this interactive role of leadership more directly, and now in more detail we will summarize this timely review by Oreg and Benson (2019).

Leaders' Impact on Organization Change

To begin their extensive review of the relevant literature, the problem that Oreg and Berson (2019) address is what they refer to as the theoretical and methodological chasms between leadership and organization change. Leadership has an impact on organization change and organization change in turn affects leaders in terms of adjustments they may need to make regarding the overall change effort. Yet as Oreg and Berson claim: "[S]urprisingly the relationship between leadership and organization change have not been studied systematically" (2019: 272). Moreover, there is no conceptual foundation or road map to guide research and integrate findings. The authors' intent with their review is to rectify this problem.

Oreg and Berson begin with a very important distinction in terms of how leaders influence change. Accordingly they specify two key roles which will ultimately help to integrate distinct literatures. The two leader roles are (1) strategic choices that leaders make (Hambrick 2007), and (2) leaders' styles of leadership (Bass 2008; Graen and Uhl-Bien 1995). The outcomes of these two roles are traced in the literature via two paths of influence—the leader's impact on unit and organizational outcomes (Rubin et al. 2009) and the leader's influence on change recipients (Oreg and Berson 2011; Oreg et al. 2011). Using these two forms (strategy and style) as paths to outcome serves as the centerpiece of their overall integrative model of leadership and organizational change processes and outcomes.

Summary and Conclusion

As we come to the end of this chapter let us first be reminded briefly of what we have covered in the name of organization change and then how we might integrate our coverage. After defining open system theory we illustrated its usefulness by reviewing four relatively popular models of organizations with an emphasis on how the authors of these models—Weisbord, Nadler and Tushman, Tichy, and Burke-Litwin addressed organization change, bearing in mind that the four models cover both *what* to change and *how* to change. See Table 2.1 for a reminder of this coverage. We then went to literature to find, if it existed, recent reviews of organization change in one form or the other. We found three such reviews that were both relevant and timely—Stouten et al. (2018). On how to change, Suddaby and Foster (2017) on the relevance of an organization's history, and Oreg and Berson's (2019) review of related research on leadership. As a way of integrating our coverage we then drew a comparison of the four models with the three recent reviews. This comparison was an attempt to evaluate the four models of organizations and organization change—see Table 2.3.

In summary what does Table 2.3 tell us? It seems that overall in the decades since 1976 our four integrated models (Weisbord, Nadler-Tushman, Tichy, Burke-Litwin) remain reasonably useful. Yet they are "dated" in some significant domains. Are people in the organization prepared for change? You wouldn't know if relying on these models. While mission, strategy, and goals are emphasized, vision, is nowhere to be found. Only one model accounts for networks (Tichy) when it is clear that networks within organizations and simply networks per se are much more dominant today than a few decades ago. Two other omissions are serious—assessing progress over time and sustaining change once underway. And, finally, history and leadership need much more attention than they seem to be getting. More comparisons could be made, but the point appears to be made—our organization change models need updating and revisions.

Our lives today, at least in the working world are experienced by many of us as a blur. Time seems like a fly-by. Climate change is not some distant happening but on our doorstep. We have the luxury of storing tons of data including TV shows and movies we never seem to find the time to watch. We exercise to lose weight but exercising makes us hungry. So it is with organizations. Their external environments are highly cluttered and complex. Executives scramble to find the right talent (and search firms are making money), but hardly know anything about how to assess what the "right" talent is. The digital world looks like a godsend, making work more efficient with timely results, but we do not seem to be there yet. And what are these "new organizations" all about? Facebook is not GE. The latter makes products and makes money from selling them. Facebook makes money from social activities, but their business model or Drucker's theory of the business is difficult to determine. New forms of organizations continue to emerge but we do not quite understand them, much less how to relate to them from the standpoint of business deals and negotiation. And our organization change models may not be all that applicable to LinkedIn, Google, or Yahoo.

Besides attempting to describe present and perhaps some of future reality, what is the point of all this lather? In our complex and fast-paced world, especially the working world, it is comforting to have high-quality review articles like the three summarized here. It is comforting to learn that there is evidence to support a ten-stage model of how to establish and manage an organization change effort. It is comforting to learn that history is important. To ignore an organization's history particularly regarding its track record of dealing with a change is sheer folly. Doing so will ensure a repeat of history, some of it good and useful no doubt and will therefore serve as a source of what to do rather than what not to do. But some of the history if repeated will ensure failure, and if not addressed produce resistance to change. Many organizational members who have been with the organization for some period of time—years not months—have extensive memories and sort through the good, the bad, and the ugly. And, finally, it is comforting to learn that the chasm between leadership influence and organization change outcomes is no longer a chasm. The authors' review reveals many linkages. So, do leaders make a difference? Yes, indeed, and this final review article shows where and how.

And to come full circle, one final point: When I was a consultant at British Airways, I was fortunate to be able to make quite a few flights between New York and London via the Concorde. To make the trip in just over three hours and to see the curvature of our planet through a tiny window was one of those thrills that remain memorable. On one of my early trips the pilot invited me up to see the cockpit. Besides the relatively tight space I was stunned by the floor to ceiling flow of instruments, all of which were analogs, nothing digital. Although the Concorde was a spectacular airplane shuttling people 100 at a time across the Atlantic, it had a comparatively short lifespan. It was never profitable, experienced two crashes, and cost a small fortune for a ticket. It was not fuel efficient until reaching over 40,000 feet when the jet stream took over. In other words, the external environment was too relentless for the Concorde to overcome: primarily the cost of fuel, continuing with an analog system when the world was rapidly going digital, and serving a relatively small market of prime ministers, rock stars, and CEOs. It was a very complex external environment indeed.

So, the famous quote from former President Clinton, "It's the economy, stupid!" should be replaced with, "It's the entire external environment, stupid!"

References

Audia, P. G., Locke, E. A., and Smith, K. G. (2000), 'The Paradox of Success: An Archival and a Laboratory Study of Strategic Persistence Following Radical Environmental Change', *Academy of Management Journal*, 43, 837–53.

Bass, B. M. (2008), *The Bass Handbook of Leadership: Theory, Research and Managerial Applications* (4th edn) (New York: The Free Press).

Battilana, J., and Casciaro, T. (2013), 'Overcoming Resistance to Organizational Change: Strong Ties and Affective Cooptation', *Management Science*, 59, 819–36.

Baum, J. R., Locke, E. A., and Kirkpatrick, S. A. (1998), 'A Longitudinal Study of the Relation of Vision and Vision Communication to Venture Growth in Entrepreneurial Firms', *Journal of Applied Psychology*, 83, 43–54.

Beer, M., Eisenstat, R. A., and Spector, B. (1990), 'Why Change Programs Do Not Produce Change', *Harvard Business Review*, 68, 158–66.

Bies, R. J., and Moag, J. S. (1986), 'Interactional Justice: Communication Criteria of Fairness', in R. J. Lewicki, B. H. Sheppard, and M. H. Bazerman, eds., *Research on Negotiations in Organizations* (Greenwich, CT: JAI Press), 43–55.

Bordia, P., Restubog, S. L. D., Jimmieson, N. L., and Irmar, B. E. (2011), 'Haunted by the Past: Effects of Poor Change Management History on Employee Attitudes and Turnover', *Group & Organization Management*, 36, 191–22.

Bos-Nehles, A., Renkema, M., and Janssen, M. (2017), 'HRM and Innovative Work Behavior: A Systematic Literature Review', *Personnel Review*, 46, 1228–53.

Bruch, H., and Sattelberger, T. (2001), 'Lufthansa's Transformational Marathon: Process of Liberating and Focusing Change Energy', *Human Resource Management*, 40, 249–59.

Buchanan, D. A. (2011), 'Reflections: Good Practice, not Rocket Science—Understanding Failures to Change after Extreme Events', *Journal of Change Management*, 11, 273–88.

Burke, W. W. (2018), *Organization Change: Theory & Practice* (5th ed.) (Thousand Oaks, CA: Sage Publications).

Burke, W. W., Clark, L. P., and Koopman, C. (1984), Improve Your OD Project's Chances for Success', *Training and Development Journal*, 38/8, 62–8.

Burke, W. W. and Litwin, G. H. (1992), 'A Casual Model of Organizational Performance and Change', *Journal of Management*, 18, 532–45.

Coch, L. and French, J. R. P. (1948), 'Overcoming Resistance to Change', *Human Relations*, 1, 512–32.

Cooperrider, D. L., and Srivastva, S. (1987), 'Appreciative Inquiry in Organizational Life', in W. A. Pasmore and R. W. Woodman, eds., *Research in Organizational Change and Development* (Vol. 1) (Greenwich, CT: JAI Press).

Drucker, P. F. (1994), 'The Theory of the Business', *Harvard Business Review*, 72(5), 95–104.

Dutton, J. E., Ashford, S. J., O'Neill, R. M., and Lawrence, K. A. (2001), 'Moves that Matter: Issue Selling and Organizational Change', *Academy of Management Journal*, 44, 716–36.

Edmondson, A. (1999), 'Psychological Safety and Learning Behavior in Work Teams', *Administrative Science Quarterly*, 44, 350–83.

Edmondson, A. C. (2002). 'The Local and Variegated Nature of Learning in Organization: A Group-Level Perspective', *Organization Science*, 13, 128–46.

Foster, R. N., and Kaplan, S. (2001), *Creative Destruction: Why Companies That Are Built to Last Underperform the Market—and How to Successfully Transform Them* (New York: Currency).

Graen, G. B., and Uhl-Bien, M. (1995), 'Relationship-Based Approach to Leadership: Development of Leader-Member Exchange (LMX) Theory of Leadership over 25 years: Applying a Multi-Level, Multi-Domain Perspective', *The Leadership Quarterly*, 6/2, 219–47.

Hambrick, D. C. (2007), 'Upper Echelons Theory: An Update', *The Academy of Management Review Archive*, 32/2, 334–43.

Hiatt, J. M. (2006), *ADKAR: A Model for Change in Business Government and Our Community: How to Implement Successful Change in Our Personal Lives and Professional Careers* (Loveland, CO: Prosci Research).

Judson, A. (1991), *Changing Behavior in Organizations: Minimizing Resistance to Change* (Cambridge, MA: Basil Blackwell).

Kanter, R. M., Stein, B. A., and Jick, T. D. (1992), *The Challenge of Organizational Change* (New York: Free Press).

Katz, D., and Kahn, R. L. (1978), *The Social Psychology of Organizations* (2nd ed.) (New York: Wiley).

Kerr, J., and Slocum, J. W. (1987), 'Managing Corporate Culture through Reward Systems', *Academy of Management Executive*, 1, 99–08.

Kim, T. G., Hornung, S., and Rousseau, D. M. (2011), 'Change-Supportive Employee Behavior: Antecedents and the Moderating Role of Time', *Journal of Management*, 37, 1664–93.

Knight, C., Patterson, M., and Dawson, J. (2017), Building Work Engagement: A Systematic Review and Meta-Analysis Investigating the Effectiveness of Work Engagement Interventions', *Journal of Organizational Behavior*, 38, 792–12.

Kotter, J. P. (1996), *Leading Change* (Boston: Harvard Business School Press).

Leavitt, H. (1965), 'Applied Organizational Change in Industry', in J. March, ed., *Handbook of Organizations* (Chicago: Rand McNally), 1144–70.

Lewin, K. (1948), *Resolving Social Conflicts* (New York: Harper).

Malina, M. A., and Selto, F. H. (2001), 'Communicating and Controlling Strategy: An Empirical Study of the Effectiveness of the Balanced Scorecard', *Journal of Management Accounting Research*, 13, 47–90.

Marin-Garcia, J. A., and Tomas, J. M. (2016), 'Deconstructing AMO Framework: A Systematic Review', *Intangible Capital*, 12, 1040–87.

Mintzberg, H. (1989), *Mintzberg on Management: Inside Our Strange World of Organizations* (New York: Free Press).

Morgan, G. (1997), *Images of Organizations* (2nd ed.) (Thousand Oaks, CA: Sage Publications).

Morrison, E. W., and Phelps, G. C. (1999), 'Taking Charge at Work: Extrarole Efforts to Initiate Workplace Change', *Academy of Management Journal*, 42, 403–19.

Nadler, D. A. and Tushman, M. L. (1977), 'A Diagnostic Model for Organization Behavior', in J. R. Hackman, E. E. Lawler III, and L. W. Porter, eds., *Perspectives on Behavior in Organizations* (New York: McGraw-Hill), 85–100.

Nanus, B. (1992), *Visionary Leadership: Creating a Compelling Sense of Direction for Your Organization* (San Francisco: Jossey- Bass).

Neuman, G. A., Edwards, J. E., and Raju, N. S. (1989), 'Organizational Development Interventions: A Meta-Analysis of Their Effects on Satisfaction and Other Attitudes', *Personnel Psychology*, 42, 461–89.

Oreg, S., and Berson, Y. (2019), 'Leaders' Impact on Organizational Change: Bridging Theoretical and Methodological Chasms', *Academy of Management Annals*, 13, 272–07.

Oreg, S., Vakola, M., and Armenakis, A. (2011), 'Change Recipients' Reactions to Organizational Change', *Journal of Applied Behavioral Science*, 47, 461–24.

Peters, T. J. and Waterman, R. H. Jr. (1982), *In Search of Excellence: Lessons from America's Best-run Companies* (New York: Harper & Row).

Rafferty, A. E., and Restubog, S. L. D. (2017), 'Why Do Employees' Perceptions of Their Organization's Change History Matter? The Role of Change Appraisals', *Human Resource Management*, 56, 533–50.

Rerup, C., and Feldman, M. S. (2011), 'Routines as a Source of Change in Organizational Schemata: The Role of Trial-and-Error Learning', *Academy of Management Journal*, 54, 577–10.

Rousseau, D. M., and Tijoriwala, S. (1999), 'What's a Good Reason to Change? Motivated Reasoning and Social Accounts in Promoting Organizational Change', *Journal of Applied Psychology*, 84, 514–28.

Rubin, R. S., Dierdorff, E. C., Bommer, W. H., and Baldwin, T. T. (2009), 'Do Leaders Reap What They Sow? Leader and Employee Outcomes of Leader Organizational Cynicism about Change', *The Leadership Quarterly*, 20, 680–8.

Seijts, G. H., and Latham, G. P. (2005), 'Learning Versus Performance Goals: When Should Each Be Used?' *Academy of Management Executive*, 19, 124–31.

Staw, B. M., Sandelands, L. E., and Dutton, J. E. (1981), 'Threat Rigidity Effects in Organizational Behavior: A Multi-Level Analysis', *Administrative Science Quarterly*, 25, 501–24.

Stouten, J., Rousseau, D. M., and DeCremer, D. (2018), 'Successful Organizational Change: Integrating the Management Practice and Scholarly Literatures', *Academy of Management Annuals*, 12/2, 752–88.

Suddaby, R., and Foster, W. M. (2017), 'History and Organizational Change', *Journal of Management*, 43, 19–38.

Tichy, N. M. (1983), *Managing Strategic Change: Technical Political and Cultural Dynamics* (New York: Wiley).

Tyler, T. R., and Blader, S. L. (2003), 'The Group Engagement Model: Procedural Justice, Social Identity, and Cooperative Behavior', *Personality and Social Psychology Review*, 7, 349–61.

Vakola, M., and Nikolaou, I. (2005), 'Attitudes towards Organizational Change: What is the Role of Employees' Stress and Commitment?' *Employee Relations*, 27, 160–74.

Van deVen, A. H., and Poole, M. S. (1995), 'Explaining Development and Change in Organizations', *Academy of Management Review*, 20, 510–40.

Van de Ven, A. H., and Poole, M. S. (2021), 'Introduction: Central Issues in the Study of Organizational Change and Innovation', in M. S. Poole and A. H. Van de Ven, eds., *The Oxford Handbook of Organizational Change* (2nd edn) (Oxford: Oxford University Press),

Von Bertalanffy, L. (1956), 'General System Theory', in *General Systems, Yearbook of the Society for the Advancement of General System Theory* (Vol. 1) (London: Sage) 1–10.

Weisbord, M. R. (1976), 'Organizational Diagnosis: Six Places to Look for Trouble with or Without a Theory', *Group and Organization Studies*, 1, 430–47.

Wiedner, R., Barrett, M., and Oborn, E. (2017), 'The Emergence of Change in Unexpected Places: Resourcing across Organizational Practices in Strategic Change', *Academy of Management Journal*, 60, 823–54.

CHAPTER 3

DUALISMS AND DUALITIES IN THE ONGOING DEVELOPMENT OF ORGANIZATION DEVELOPMENT

JEAN M. BARTUNEK, LINDA L. PUTNAM, AND MYEONG-GU SEO

ORGANIZATION development (OD), an important approach to the theory and practice of organizational change, has itself been on a change journey for more than sixty years (Bartunek and Woodman 2015). This chapter addresses three major developments in OD, all of which involve tensions that some scholars label as dualisms and/or dualities, and all of which have been and are continuing to play integral roles in this journey. These are: 1) *intellectual distinctions* between "*diagnostic*" and "*dialogic*" approaches to OD, 2) the organizational *life* of OD that coexists with continued proclamations of its *death*, and 3) the progressive *separation* between the *scholarship* and the *practice* of OD. The first development depends on conceptual foundations within OD as described by Bushe and Marshak (2009); the second addresses conflicting opinions about the vitality of OD; and the third examines distinctions between how OD is carried out in practice and the scholarship pertinent to it. Table 3.1 presents a brief summary of these developments from the 1950s through the present day.

We discuss these developments in terms of contemporary approaches to dualisms and dualities. As Seo et al. (2004) and Putnam et al. (2016) show, scholars tend to cast opposites in the planned change literature as dualisms, mutually exclusive "*either-or*" relationships. Dualities, in contrast, focus on the interdependence of inseparable opposites, accepting both poles of a tension and treating them as complementary. Putnam et al. (2016: 60) suggest that such "*both-and*" responses can occur by means of paradoxical thinking. That is, both-and approaches may take the form of recognizing and accepting

Table 3.1 A Summary of the Evolution of OD over Time

Decade	Diagnostic/Dialogic OD		Death and Ongoing Life		Academic-Practitioner links
	Diagnostic OD	Dialogic OD	Death pronounced	New developments	Links and separations
1950s	OD as implicitly diagnostic begins	Some dialogic work, though not recognized as such			OD practitioners come largely from academia
1960s	Diagnostic OD continues	Publication of *Social Construction of Reality*		Action learning	OD practitioners come largely from academia
1970s	Diagnostic OD continues	Development of social constructionist thinking	"OD has run its course"	Quality of work life interventions	Many OD practitioners come from academia; some come from practice backgrounds and receive academic training
1980s	Diagnostic OD continues	Cooperrider uses a social constructivist approach		Organizational transformation; Introduction of appreciative inquiry	OD practitioners come largely from practice backgrounds
1990s	Diagnostic OD continues	Dialogic OD starts to emerge	OD has become irrelevant and should be replaced by change management	Recognition of large group interventions; Learning organizations	OD practitioners come from practice backgrounds; the development of scholar-practitioner doctorates
2000	Diagnostic OD continues	Dialogic OD is introduced	OD has diminished in importance	Expansion of large group interventions and action-learning	OD practitioners come from practice backgrounds; supple-mented by scholar-practitioner doctoral programs
2010	Diagnostic OD continues	Dialogic OD continues	There has been nothing new in OD since appreciative inquiry in the 1980s	Continued expansion of "collaborative" change and action-learning	OD practitioners come from practice backgrounds; supple-mented by scholar-practitioner doctoral programs

apparent opposites, moving back and forth between poles at different times, and reaching compromises between poles. These approaches can act positively to enable awareness of paradoxes and to address immediate needs. Over time, however, these strategies can sometimes disintegrate into dualisms (64).

Putnam et al. (2016: 64) also present "*more-than*" responses that accommodate "both poles through developing a novel, creative synergy." Some ways of accomplishing this include reframing and transcendence, connecting, third spaces, dialog, reflective practice, and serious play.

As we sketch out the developments in OD over its history, we focus on the major assumptions of each side of the tensions. We explore how these tensions have entered into OD activities and how scholars and practitioners are managing them in terms of the "either-or," "both-and," and "more than" approaches that Putnam et al. (2016) discuss. Thus, we present an updated and evolving approach to both our substantive topic and our theoretical foundation.

Tensions between Diagnostic and Dialogic OD

Gervase Bushe and Robert Marshak (2009, 2014, 2015) distinguished between *diagnostic* and *dialogic* approaches to OD. Based on their writings, we discuss several tensions, whether recognized or not, that play central roles in the intellectual differences between diagnostic and dialogic approaches and how scholars respond to them as dualisms or dualities. These tensions include positivist versus interpretivist epistemologies, treating data and organizations as objective realities versus socially constructed meaning systems, and changing behaviors versus changing mindsets. We also consider the relationship between dialogic OD and dialogic *communication*, since communication is an integral dimension of dialog. To begin this task, we summarize the history of OD and its implicit approaches to diagnosis or dialog.

The History and Emergence of OD Approaches

OD was developed in the 1950s (French 1969). It was based on an action research model developed initially by Lewin (1947) that involved groups of participants in a setting working with consultants or organizational researchers "to solve immediate, practical problems and also to make a scholarly contribution based on the outcome" (Rapoport 1970). Diagnosis of problems was thus an integral, taken for granted, dimension of action research. French (1969: 23) stated: "Although the specific interpersonal and task objectives of organization development programs . . . vary according to each diagnosis of organizational problems, a number of objectives typically emerge." Further, "organizational change efforts tend to fail if a prescription is applied unilaterally and without proper diagnosis" (p. 26).

Given this action research heritage, scholars and practitioners took for granted that diagnosis was integral to OD (French and Bell 1995; Weisbord 1976). This was explicit in all of the early intervention exercises developed as part of OD, including team building, survey feedback, Quality of Worklife interventions, and approaches to organizational transformation (Seo et al. 2004).

Beginning in the late 1960s and 1970s, and often drawing from Berger and Luckmann (1967), scholars began to develop a social constructivist epistemology to OD. As Gergen (1985: 266) argued, this approach "was principally concerned with explicating the processes by which people came to describe, explain, or otherwise account for the world (including themselves) in which they lived." It assumed that there was no "objective reality" that dispassionate social scientists could grasp independently from what they observed. Thus, it shifted the emphasis to how people were constructing and making meaning of situations, including through their shared discourse and interactions (Barrett 2015). Thus also, organizations were meaning-making systems in which what was real was continually created and re-created through social agreement (Marshak 2014).

This new epistemology began to influence the thinking of designers of OD interventions including learning organizations (Senge 1990), narrative approaches (Swart 2015), and the large group and/or whole systems interventions that began to be developed in the 1980s (Bunker and Alban 1992; Bushe and Marshak 2009; Marshak and Bushe 2013). The newer interventions (cf. Van de Ven 2007) focused on meaning-making rather than problem-solving.

One basic assumption that underlies many of these interventions is that (socially) constructing a positive future produced more energy for change than does focusing on problems (Bunker and Alban 2014). Another is that getting a whole system together enables many viewpoints to be heard, which in turn generates new understandings and fosters the development of shared meanings among participants (Bunker and Alban 1997). Appreciative inquiry (Cooperrider and Srivastva 1987: 137), in particular, has embraced these assumptions.

The continued application of a social constructivist approach within OD led Bushe and Marshak (2009) to claim that a new type of organization development, a *dialogic* form, had emerged. In actuality, these epistemological distinctions had been evolving since the 1960s, but were not considered dialogic until Bushe and Marshak labeled them as such (Bartunek and Woodman 2015). For example, Schein (2015) noted that the early T-groups included features that paralleled dialogic OD. Fisher and Torbert (1995) had previously shown that action research interventions actually included a good deal of meaning-making.

Comparing Diagnostic and Dialogic OD Approaches

When Bushe and Marshak (2009: 351) distinguished diagnostic from dialogic OD, they described diagnostic OD teleologically (Van de Ven and Poole 1995), as an "attempt to gather data to compare a given team or organization against a prescriptive model or a desired future state. Methodologies congruent with these assumptions... are then employed to help guide problem solving, decision making, and action planning." In contrast, they defined dialogic OD dialectically (Van de Ven and Poole 1995), as an attempt to engage a "system in dialog and synergistic relationships in such a way that: mental models are surfaced; new knowledge, structures, processes, practices, and stories are collaboratively created and shared; and diverse stakeholder voices and perspectives are heard" (p. 361). They claimed that dialogic OD was preferable, at least in complex situations (Snowden and Boone 2007) or for adaptive rather than technical problems (Heifetz et al. 2009).

Bushe and Marshak (2016) also argued that dialogic OD aimed to change the conversations that shaped everyday organizational processes through confronting difference and making change agents a part of the process rather than standing outside it. Specifically, participants, including change agents, engage in a type of reflexivity through questioning their own taken-for-granted assumptions and critically reflecting on the values and logics that influence their practices (Ripamonti et al. 2016). In this way, dialog triggers relational reflexivity through engaging difference as sources of knowledge and creativity from multiple voices (Oswick et al. 2000). Thus, proponents contended that it was an excellent approach for addressing dilemmas, traps, and wicked problems in which there was little agreement as to what was happening.

Table 3.2, adapted from Tables 1 and 2 in Bushe and Marshak (2009), highlights both the similarities and differences between the diagnostic and dialogic approaches to OD. Importantly, both approaches focus on OD as a process, not just as an intervention, although the idea of process functions differently in the two. For diagnostic OD, analytic processes aid in building capacity and using rational approaches to discover systemic problems to solve; organizational change is episodic and focuses on behavior. In contrast, dialogic OD centers on creating an organizational change process through using generative conversations and relational practice. It aims to help organizational members incorporate multiple voices and confront polar opposites in managing difference. In this way, diagnostic and dialogic approaches to OD differ in how they embrace dualities in organizational life.

Reflections on Dualisms and Dualities within Dialogic and Diagnostic OD

Bushe and Marshak (2015) emphasized differences (dualisms) between the two approaches, though it is evident from Table 3.2 that they do not exhibit a complete break. However, grey areas between the two often surface when implementing them (Duff and Dishman 2014; Gilpin-Jackson 2013). That is, consistent with Farjoun (2010), the two conceptually divergent poles (dialogic and diagnostic) operate as a duality and are often intertwined in the world of practice. Rather than making an either-or choice in which one pole drives out the other, practitioners often focus on the processes associated with each and how they emerge as complementary.

Table 3.2 Assumptions, Differences, and Similarities between Diagnostic and Dialogic OD

	Diagnostic OD	Dialogic OD
Assumptions	Valid data reflect an underlying objective reality that can be discovered using rational and analytic processes	There is no inherently real form of social organizing; "reality" is socially constructed and negotiated, and may involve power and political processes
Philosophical influences	Positivism and modernist philosophy	Social constructionism and critical philosophy
Values	– Humanism and democracy – Capacity building and System Development	– Humanistism and democracy – Capacity building and System Development
Change Constructs	– Collecting valid data using objective methods leads to change – Change is episodic and goal oriented	– Creating safe places and processes that produce generative ideas leads to change – Change is continuous and cyclical
Focus of change	Changing behavior	Changing how people think
Role of consultants	Focus on process issues in change	Focus on process issues in change

Adapted from Bushe and Marshak (2009)

Diagnostic and dialogic OD also share similarities as process-oriented interventions. In other words, the two offer the possibility of attaining "more than" as a way of responding to tensions. Dialog can both function as a container for new conversations and be a bottom-up process that disrupts ongoing social construction, generates new possibilities, and alters self-organizing (Barge and Andreas 2013). This activity can occur through communication designs that reflect a dialogic sensibility. Such designs can (potentially, at least) embrace both objective fact and social construction through incorporating reason and analytic processes with collective sensemaking and action. Tensions can serve as a means to sustain differences as participants share facts and stories, reflect on their own roles in creating situations, and generate new images linked to core narratives.

For example, Barge et al. (2008) drew on three tensions, inclusion–exclusion, preservation–change, and centrality–parity, to design a conversational structure for a dialog-based Circle of Prosperity aimed at advancing information technology that fostered economic development for several Native American tribal colleges and universities. In this way, diagnosis and dialog were not independent of each other; each provided foundations for the other to exist (Graetz and Smith 2008).

As this illustration suggests, although conceptually distinct, diagnostic and dialogical approaches are often intertwined and complementary in practice. Practitioners may conduct interventions by combining both dialogical and diagnostic dimensions. They are not necessarily seeking to apply particular conceptual understandings, but the processes that they use may connect apparently oppositional ideas (diagnosis and dialog), whether the practitioners are conscious of this or not. Academics sometimes create intellectual contrasts which may bear relatively little correspondence to what actually takes place in practice. Practice applications, in contrast with some academic understanding, may be more likely to embrace "more-than" approaches to managing tensions.

Tensions between the Death and Life of OD

This section might be summarized in Mirvis's (2014: 374) words as, "OD is dead, long-live OD". As the phrase suggests, a tension regarding the vitality and future of OD has been salient for decades and is often treated as a dualism. Multiple scholars contend that OD is dead, or least in decline. At the same time, other scholars and practitioners provide ongoing illustrations of its continuing vitality. Here we summarize pronouncements of OD as dead as well as illustrations of how it is alive. We then review the reasons and primary assumptions that underlie these arguments and the relationship of the two as a dualism.

OD as Dead

As Bartunek and Woodman (2012) showed, scholars and practitioners have claimed for more than forty years that OD (or at least the term "OD") is dead or at least close to death and in need of resuscitation. Initial concerns were largely about the term. In 1976, Burke expressed concern that the term *Organization Development* had "run its course" (p. 22–23). Perhaps it would be replaced by quality of work interventions or quality of working life". In 1977, Jones and Pfeiffer (p. 264) stated that "it is time to abandon the term *Organization Development*," because "the term OD has become such a catch-all that it has lost almost all of the specificity of its meaning."

By the late 1980s concern was more about the field itself. In 1989 (p. 11–12), Beer wrote that "the field of OD is dying" and "OD is in need of redefinition." In his distinguished presentation to the Organizational Development and Change Division of the Academy of Management, Quinn (1993) claimed that OD had become irrelevant (Worren et al. 1999) and should be replaced by *change management* that encompasses large-scale organizational changes that OD does not fully address.

Greiner and Cummings (2004: 374) argued that "the current diffuse nature of OD suggests that it is hardly recognizable in most organizations, portending its possible demise as a historical artifact." In a book edited by Bradford and Burke (2005) that largely bemoaned the state of OD, Argyris (2005: 112) said that "OD has appeared to diminish in importance and is usually relegated to the bottom of the organization" due to the "reasoning mind-sets" that OD professionals commonly rely on.

Concerns about the future of OD continue. Burke (2018: 186) argued that "little if any innovation has occurred in the field since 1987, when appreciative inquiry was introduced." Burke also argued that OD practitioners are not working with the clients who could most benefit from their work. Minahan (2019: 6) claimed that OD is on "the brink of our own demise." He added that it was time to retire organization development (p. 14) and to focus instead on strategic change (p. 15). Gilpin-Jackson (2018: 7) observed that "we appear to be stuck in a lens focused on the 'death of OD.'" It is useful to note that these concerns about the death of OD have been expressed by both academics (e.g., Argyris, Burke) and practitioners (e.g., Gilpin-Jackson, Minahan).

OD as Alive

Even though some declare it dead, the proliferation and active use of OD approaches attest to its livelihood for others. We discuss three examples: appreciative Inquiry, large group interventions, and action learning. Other newer approaches (e.g., Theory U, http://www.ottoscharmer.com/theoryu and learning organizations https://www.solonline.org/) could also be discussed. But we focus on a small number of illustrative approaches that are widely practiced and discussed in both scholarly and practitioner OD literature.

Appreciative inquiry (AI). Appreciative Inquiry is one of the most popular planned change methods in the world (e.g., Aldred 2009; Yaeger et al. 2005). As Bushe (2012) noted, AI began with David Cooperrider's (1986) doctoral research. Cooperrider was very excited about events taking place at the site he was studying (the Cleveland Clinic) for his dissertation and wondered if what he was observing could be seen in *positive* terms rather than problems that needed to be solved. Cooperrider's publication with Suresh Srivastva (1987) of the epistemology underlying AI provided an important and influential conceptual orientation to a positive approach.

Soon after this publication, an OD consultant, Jane Magruder Watkins, invited Cooperrider to work with her on developing the practice of appreciative inquiry. In the early 2000s, Cooperrider and several collaborators wrote books that explained the approach more completely (e.g., Cooperrider and Whitney 2005; Ludema et al. 2003), including as a *large group intervention*. These helped to spread AI to a large number of practitioners.

In practice, appreciative inquiry involves a "4D" process, often carried out in two to three-day sessions. Its phases include *Discovery*—mobilizing a whole system, multiple stakeholder inquiry into the positive core of the system; *Dream*—creating a results-oriented vision based on discovered potential and questioning higher purpose; *Design*—articulating a design capable of drawing on and magnifying the positive core to realize the newly expressed dream; and *Destiny*—strengthening the affirmative capability of a system by enabling it to build hope and sustain momentum for ongoing positive change and high performance (Cooperrider and Whitney 2007: 77–8).

The use of AI continues to grow, both in the US and internationally. As just a few examples, at the time of this writing Champlain College distributes educational materials, online resources, and stories through an Appreciative Inquiry Commons (https://appreciativeinquiry.champlain.edu/). A global Community of AI practitioners as well as multiple networks and groups exist around the world. There is a journal devoted entirely to appreciative inquiry, the *AI Practitioner* (https://aipractitioner.com). The Global Compact Leaders' Summit report (https://www.unglobalcompact.org/docs/news_events/8.1/summit_rep_fin.pdf) documented the successful impact of appreciative inquiry at a 2004 meeting involving UN Secretary-General Kofi Annan and nearly 500 business leaders.

Large group interventions. OD continues to emphasize large group or whole systems interventions (Holman and Devane 1999). These approaches began in the 1950s when Emery and Trist (1960), as consultants, engaged members of a whole organization in making major changes. Their foundational ideas were advanced by Harris and Beckhard (1987) and Weisbord (1987), who emphasized the importance of OD consultants working with an entire system. In practice this means engaging all decision-makers together, including stakeholders, for a particular decision.

Scholars did not recognize large group interventions as a coherent approach to change until Bunker and Alban (1992) included several of them in a special issue of the *Journal of Applied Behavioral Science*. Bunker and Alban (1997: xv) later defined large group interventions as "methods for involving the whole system, internal and external, in [a planned] change process." The methods they described included, among others, search conference (Emery and Purser 1996), future search (Weisbord and Janoff 1995), Real Time Strategic Change (Jacobs 1997), the conference model (Axelrod, 1992), and Open Space Technology (Owen 1994).

Since the 1990s, the number of whole system approaches has increased exponentially, and so have publications about them. Bunker and Alban (2006) published a second edition of their book, which included many more interventions than their 1997 volume. Holman and Devane published a *Change Handbook* in 1999 that included eighteen different methods, and then a second edition a few years later that covered sixty-one methods (Holman, Devane, and Cady 2007).

Despite the variety of methods, Bunker and Alban (1997: 155) note that they typically emphasize one or more of three goals: creating a desired future together rather than simply responding to what happens, redesigning work collectively as a whole system, and whole-scale participation that brings "the system together to do real work in real time on [immediate] problems, issues, and agendas that need to be addressed." We summarize the steps of one particularly highly regarded large group intervention, Future Search. It can be used for creating a desired future together as well as for working on immediate issues that need to be addressed.

The core principles of Future Search (Weisbord and Janoff, 1995; 2010) include convening decision-makers within an organization and external stakeholders; considering local actions within a global context; focusing on the future and common ground rather than on problems and conflicts; and self-management and responsibility for actions (Weisbord and Janoff 2010: 47). It usually takes place in three-day conferences preceded by several months of planning and succeeded by a lengthy period of implementing the plans developed during the conferences. Its average size is about sixty to eighty people, and this includes stakeholders as well as organization members. The conference includes six tasks: focusing on the past with regard to the Future Search topic; focusing on the present with regard to the topic; discussing key trends in groups; imagining and describing a preferred future; posting themes that reflect the preferred future; and then action planning over subsequent months. Weisbord and Janoff (2006) illustrated the successful use of this approach with US Federal Aviation Administration at a time it was trying to address a crisis regarding air-traffic patterns.

The number of whole system interventions has continued to expand since the Holman et al. (2007) compendium; there are at least 100 as of this writing. This increased number is reflected in *The Collaborative Change Library* (Cady and Gorelick, 2020, https://mylibraryworld.web.app/app/tabs/store/Collaborative%20Change%20 Library/toc). Cady and Gorelick use the term *collaborative* rather than *large group* or *whole systems* because they feel that term better captures new types of interventions that have come into existence. By collaborative, Cady (2019: 22) means "the achievement of mutually desired outcomes through the purposeful experience of sharing among two or more people."

Action learning. Action learning is an older intervention that has expanded in recent years. It differs from the interventions described above because it focuses explicitly on problems (i.e., takes a diagnostic approach), is generally conducted in small groups, and often takes several months to be accomplished.

Action learning originated in the UK in the 1940s based on activities that Reginald Revans (1907–2003) witnessed and participated in during and after World War II (cf., Yeo and Marquardt, 2015; Dillworth 2010; Pedler and Abbot 2013; Revans, 1983). It emerged formally in the late 1960s, through major projects in a consortium of London hospitals (Wieland and Leigh 1971; Clark 1972; Wieland 1981) and in the UK's General Electric Company (Casey and Pearce 1977). Its core principle is that managers can work together to solve significant problems and challenges without the help of experts.

An action learning website fleshes out its steps (see https://www.intrac.org/wpcms/wp-content/uploads/2016/09/Action-Learning-Sets-An-INTRAC-guide-1.pdf). First, action learning starts with the formation of sets (or groups) of three to seven people, whom Revans (1982: 720) referred to as *comrades in adversity*: "In structured half-day sessions, participants will talk in turns to present a significant challenge facing them in their day-to-day work. Set members help work on the problem through supportive, but probing questions. It is not about members giving advice or trying to provide answers. The focus is on learning from experience and putting it into action immediately."

Second, the sets meet for half days approximately every four to six weeks. When they meet for the first time, each person presents a challenge. Other group members ask questions of the presenter with the aim of helping him or her develop a deeper understanding of the problem. After this, not during it, presenters may respond. Then the meeting goes on to the next presenter.

Third, after the first meeting, the presenters work on the issues they originally described and reflect on what they are learning while doing this. At the next meeting, they discuss what they have done with regard to the issue and what they have learned from their experiences about the challenges they are facing. The set continues to meet until the issues have been resolved.

Given the successes that have occurred when action learning has been used properly, it is considered a very powerful organizational tool—powerful enough that "perceptive but faint-hearted souls... will not allow its use in their organizations because of the perceived risks to the organization and their careers" (Garratt 2011: 22). Action learning can be very challenging to participants. As Marsick and O'Neil (1999: 174) note, individuals "can find it difficult to learn from their experience through a messy struggle with real challenges. Participants in some programs are surprised when they are expected to take charge of their own learning, and often find it disturbing that they cannot easily 'name' or describe what that learning looks like."

To attest to its popularity, a *World Institute for Action Learning* (https://wial.org/) hosts annual conferences, offers consulting services, develops certification for action-learning coaches, and provides news and resources related to action learning practices. Since 2006, *Action Learning: Research and Practices*, a practitioner journal, has published articles biannually to "advance knowledge and assist the development of practice through the processes of action learning."

A number of organizations use this approach (e.g., Adler et al. 2004; Coghlan 2011; Coghlan et al. 2004; Dufresne and Offstein 2012; Leonard and Lang 2010; Raelin 2006; Trehan 2011). As one illustration, the Henley Forum (https://www.henley.ac.uk/research/research-centres/the-henley-forum-for-organisational-learning-and-knowledge-strategies) makes regular use of action learning as an integral part of management development. As another example, the Executive MBA program at the University of Maryland (https://www.rhsmith.umd.edu/programs/executive-mba/academics/action-learning-projects) incorporates action learning as a crucial dimension of training.

Assumptions about OD's Death and Life

Table 3.3 summarizes four underlying assumptions regarding the death and life of OD. One relatively straightforward assumption focuses on the appropriateness of the term. Throughout its history, OD, for many people, was associated with its earliest interventions (Seo et al. 2004), but these were superseded by other interventions that came along later. For scholars primarily of first generation OD, it is dying or dead.

Table 3.3 Summary of Assumptions Regarding the Death and Life of OD

Assumptions involving	Death	Life
Appropriateness	The term "OD" is outmoded; new change approaches have superseded it.	New types of change approaches, especially ones aligned with dialogic models, fit into the broad category of OD.
Specificity	"OD is a catch-all term."	OD is a container for multiple approaches.
Attention to present day concerns	OD isn't creating anything truly new and beneficial.	New approaches are being developed regularly (e.g., "collaborative change") to respond to contemporary concerns.
Energy	Low energy surrounding OD	High energy surrounding OD

A second assumption about whether OD is dead or alive focuses on specificity. For those who believe that OD is dying, the term "OD" itself is not helpful. For others, the term functions as a container for multiple contemporary approaches that are alive and well. A third assumption centers on attending to present-day concerns. Those who believe OD is dead believe that its interventions do not reflect present-day concerns or deal with the clients who could most benefit from it (Burke 2018). In contrast, those who believe OD is alive see new approaches that address contemporary concerns being introduced regularly. A fourth assumption centers on energy. Those who believe OD is dead do not see much novelty or energy linked to it; however, those who associate it with life see positive energy (such as AI interventions) emerging regularly. These differences affect how each side treats the other and how these dichotomous positions create divides in the field.

Reflections on Dualisms and Dualities within the Death and Life of OD

A tremendous amount of energy on the part of OD scholars and practitioners has gone into the debate as to whether OD is dead or alive. As suggested above, this debate has generally followed an either-or path. Proponents typically embrace one side and ignore the other, thus essentially casting them as mutually exclusive. Those who believe OD is dead rarely refer to newer change initiatives, such as large group interventions, while those who employ these new approaches typically do not acknowledge concern about OD's potential death.

It should be recognized that many of the signs of life have been initiated by practitioners and later codified by academics. This is particularly true of both large group interventions and action learning.

Moreover, especially with regard to the differing forums in which they are presented, it appears that both life and death are true, at least in part. For example, Burke's (2018) argument was that Harris and Beckhard (1987) had the basic idea for large group interventions in the 1980s. Even though designers of large group interventions partially agree with this, they also argue that the number and type of large group interventions keep increasing. Minahan (2019) is concerned that the number of people practicing OD, and the number of positions for such practitioners, is decreasing considerably, particularly within organizations. Nevertheless, new OD approaches are continually surfacing in the field. Marshak (2019: 17) responded to Minahan's (2019) paper, saying:

> I am increasingly of the mind that OD as it was originally practiced in the 1950s-1970s has largely atrophied or "died" except in the memories of old timers and gatekeepers like me. At the same time, newer ideas and practices have flourished including approaches that many of us might consider OD, but whose adherents know as something else and may never have even heard of OD. So, OD is dead. Long live OD.

This quotation, as does Mirvis's (2014), parallels a recommendation from Poole and Van de Ven (1989) about managing apparent contradictions. Marshak is essentially suggesting that the death and life of OD can be separated in terms of time period—the period when OD was getting started and recent years in which OD has evolved. For those who believe this is the case, then the two exist in a both-and rather than an either-or relationship.

The Dualism of OD Scholarship versus Practice

One of the major OD-related developments over the past fifty years has been a growing disconnection between the practice of OD and the academic scholarship on it. In its beginning, OD had explicit academic roots that were integrally linked to practice. Lewin's (1947) early theorizing and applied work that led to the development of OD took place primarily in academia. His work as well as that of early sociotechnical theorists was published in *Human Relations*, an academic journal. Due in large part to Lewin's work, the National Training Laboratories for Applied Behavioral Science (now NTL) was founded in 1947 and Leland Bradford (1990) was its first director. NTL offered its first experiential human relations conference that year and pioneered the technologies of group dynamics (https://www.ntl.org/about-us/ntl-legacy/). Lewin died just before he was to visit NTL for the first time. After his death, those who carried out the earliest OD work (cf. French 1969) included several academics, such as Douglas McGregor (MIT), Herbert Shephard (Case Western Reserve University), Robert Blake (University of Texas), and Ronald Lippitt (University of Michigan), many of whom contributed to the term "Organization Development" (Freedman 1999). Lippitt's (1983) work also laid a foundation for interventions that were future focused instead of attending to past problems.

As Bartunek (2014) noted, the broad understanding and practice of OD was developed originally in a number of major universities (such as MIT, Michigan, Columbia, and UCLA), and much of the early scholarship on OD was published in the *Journal of Applied Behavioral Science*, which began in 1965 under the sponsorship of NTL. The first editor of *JABS*, David Bradford (the son of Leland Bradford; 1965: 3) stated in its initial issue:

> Initiated through the cooperation of a number of major universities and with co-sponsorship of the Research Center for Group Dynamics (then at the Massachusetts Institute of Technology) and of the National Education Association, the National Training Laboratories has provided a meeting ground for research scientists, action leaders, and training methodologists. From this stream of merging interests and explorations have emerged a new direction and instrumentation for social progress and for basic research in the social sciences.

During the 1960s and 1970s, scholars produced considerable academic material on OD, including books such as *Social Intervention: A Behavioral Science Approach* (Hornstein et al. 1971), *Theory into Practice: Increasing Professional Effectiveness* (Argyris and Schön 1974), and monographs in the Addison-Wesley Organization Development series, edited by Warren Bennis, Richard Beckhard, and Edgar Schein. Authors included, among others, Beckhard (1969), Dyer (1977), and Schein (1969). All of them were academics, mostly in schools of business. Further, academics conducted OD studies of the early US-based quality of work life projects (e.g., Goodman 1979; Hanlon et al. 1985; Perkins et al. 1983).

However, over subsequent decades, as expectations for academic scholarship in management became far more rigorous, fewer scholars have shown interest in the application of OD (Beyer 1982). In addition, the study of organization change has moved away from the OD approaches discussed above. Prominent doctoral programs that once focused on OD were abolished and have been replaced by programs that focus on a range of organizational topics, but not OD.

Further, some of the academic research on organizational change has become more macro in orientation and addresses topics such as institutional pressures that are not amenable to OD consultation (e.g., Greenwood and Hinings 1996). Other studies are very micro in orientation, for example, conceptualizing the three components of employees' commitment to organizational change (affective, normative, and continuance) or examining their effects on different kinds of behavioral responses to organizational change (Herscovitch and Meyer 2002). These types of work address very different issues than does typical OD scholarship.

At the same time, OD practitioners express less and less interest in the organizational scholarship that appears in management and social science journals. This progressive separation is summarized in a series of YouTube videos that came from a Nexus4change conference that took place at Bowling Green State University in 2008. (https://www.youtube.com/ watch?v=_QAAUrRAnds, https://www.youtube.com/watch?v= R7qhaKWhBdg and https://www.youtube.com/watch?v=Vj8BIyDik1w).

As Bartunek (2014) noted, in those videos, participants who entered the field of OD at different times described what brought them to it. Those who joined in the 1960s and 1970s were mostly PhDs who were studying and applying OD. Those who entered the field in the 1980s "came in . . . through arts, through family therapy, working with criminals, carpentry, experiential work, [they]were all experimenting and found a home in the general field of OD." Those who entered the field in the 1990s "came from so many different directions." As the video notes, "[W]e connected with this work from very diverse backgrounds, and yet there was something about it that brought us all together." Those who entered the field in the 2000s noted that now there was "real democratization of the field" and raised the question of "Who are we in terms of quality?"

This progressive separation has had implications for OD-related research–practice relationships. *JABS* (as noted above) was designed to be a bridge journal between academics and practitioners. However, NTL, the sponsor of *JABS*, now also publishes an online journal, *Practising Social Change*, with a greater emphasis on practice-based information than on the scholarship that *JABS* publishes. NTL's website (https://www.ntl.org/about-us/publications/the-journal-of-applied-behavioral-science/) says about *JABS* that it "provides scholars with the best in research, theory and methodology, while also informing professionals and their clients of issues in group and organizational dynamics." The same NTL website says about *Practising Social Change* (http://www.ntl-psc.org/) that "[i]t is a collaborative and reflective meeting place for practitioners in Applied Behavioral Science who seek to work at their developmental edge: curious, conceptual thinkers charged with supporting change in work relationships, in teams, in communities or in the larger society, and who may be able to learn from the experience of others in different parts of the world." In other words, NTL itself, which over time has become much more a training organization, has noticeably split the academic side of change from its practice.

Further, additional organizations for OD practitioners have developed. The most prominent is the OD Network (https://www.odnetwork.org/) founded in 1968 out of NTL, which hosts its own conference and publishes its own journals (Burke, 2014). It defines itself on its website as "an international association of professionals who make organizations healthier and more efficient." The OD Network published a book, *Organization Development in Practice* (2016), edited by Rothwell, Stavros, Sullivan, and Vogelsang, in which most of the chapters were written by "experienced OD professionals" (p. v.); very few have primary university affiliations. In that book, the chapters by Alban and Bunker (2016) and Janoff (2016) discussed large group interventions in their reflections on the "life" of OD. The book also mentioned appreciative inquiry, but only in terms of when it was used and without discussion of its method. Action learning was not mentioned at all, nor was the term "dialogic." In other words, the "practice" of OD, according to the OD Network, includes only a few of the newer approaches to change developed under the broad umbrella of OD.

In addition to the OD Network, more specialized groups have formed, such as the *Organization Design Forum* (http://organizationdesignforum.org/), the *Taos Institute* (https://www.taosinstitute.net/), *Future Search Network* (https://futuresearch.net/), and the OD Education Association (ODEA) (https://www. odnetwork.org/general/custom. asp?page= ODEA) among others. These groups foster the development of particular approaches to the practice as well as the scholarship of OD.

Efforts to Treat OD Scholar-Practitioner Relationships as Dualities

Some writers have introduced both-and relationships that attempt to reconcile the academic and practitioner approaches to OD. In particular, the labels, *practitioner-scholar* and *scholar-practitioner*, developed some time ago and in common use, have embraced and connected the tensions between scholarship and practice. Tenkasi and Hay (2008: 49) defined scholar–practitioners as "actors who have one foot each in the worlds of academia and practice and are pointedly interested in advancing the causes of both theory and practice." Wasserman and Kram (2009) also focused on ways to develop complementarity between the two.

In addition, through the initiative of David Jamieson, who has played both consultant and academic roles, the Academy of Management now gives an annual scholar-practitioner award to individuals whose work has been informed by and contributes significantly to practice. The first winner of the award was Warner Burke, and early winners had OD backgrounds (e.g., Edgar Schein, David Nadler; David Jamieson). However, understanding what scholarship contributes to practice has expanded considerably over the years, and the 2018 award winner was Herminia Ibarra, whose work deals mostly with careers and professional identity, and not at all with OD. Further, it is not just those who identify with OD who consider themselves scholar-practitioners. Others, such as Gary Latham (2019), do as well.

The second effort is the development of several practitioner-based doctoral programs that focus on OD. Their explicit purpose is to train practitioner-scholars (e.g., Tenkasi 2011). These include, among others, programs at the Fielding Graduate University (https://www.fielding.edu/), Benedictine University (http://www.ben.edu/college-of-business/doctoral/organization-development/index.cfm), Case Western Reserve University (https://weatherhead.case.edu/degrees/doctorate/doctor-management/) and Bowling Green State University (https://www.bgsu.edu/dodc).

The training in these programs tends to emphasize the practitioner side of the duality more than it does the scholarly side. Moreover, these programs are often cohort-based and time-constrained and do not include extended training in research methods. This works well for informing organizations of scholarly findings (Banerjee and Morley 2013). It also creates potential problems, especially when students from OD-oriented professional doctoral programs think that their training prepares them to conduct, publish and review standard academic research.

A third effort is the growing tendency to publish online summaries of academic studies for practitioners. This activity is consistent with the original aim of OD to link scholarship with practice. As one of several examples, *Academy of Management Insights* (https://journals.aom.org/journal/ami) publishes short summaries of articles from the Academy of Management journals with the aim of making them accessible to practitioners. These summaries are often accompanied by short videos. In this way, *Insights* aims "to transform evidence-based research from the world's best sources into actionable insights to improve the workplace." A growing number of scholarly associations (e.g., the International Association of Chinese Management Research) and universities (e.g., *Rice Business Wisdom*, *Knowledge@Wharton*) are carrying out similar work. Even though these efforts do not put practitioners on equal ground with academics, they provide at least some academic recognition of the needs of practice.

As a reverse of this interplay, one recent "From the Editors" paper published in the *Academy of Management Review* (Ployhart and Bartunek 2019) indicates how much academics can learn from proficient practice. For the most part, however, there has been little effort in this direction.

Table 3.4 summarizes the increasing division between academics and practitioners who are involved in OD. For academics, the focus has been on the scholarly side, as indicated by the professional associations to which they belong, the research they do, the journals they read, and the material they publish. More recently, OD practitioners have entered the field without strong academic training or interest. They belong to different professional associations and publish in very different outlets. There have been attempts on both sides to create scholar-practitioner links, as in the scholar-practitioner award at the Academy of Management and the development of professional doctoral programs. A few academics and practitioners truly do influence both scholarship and practice in a continuing fashion, even though accomplishing this is very challenging. Professional doctoral programs designed primarily for practitioners have rarely accomplished complete bridges between theory and practice. Finally, the types of knowledge transfer in which academics are currently engaged (e.g., summaries of academic articles) are unlikely to create reciprocal links with practice.

Table 3.4 Assumptions Regarding the Separation between OD Scholarship and Practice

	Academia	Practice
Sources of new OD knowledge and practice	Academia	Primarily practice; some practitioner scholars
Membership organization	Academy of Management	OD Network
Illustrative journals	*Journal of Applied Behavioral Science*	OD practitioner; OD review; *Practising Social Change*
Attempts to create links across boundaries	Scholar Practitioner award; practitioner-scholar label	Professional doctoral programs; practitioner-scholar; practioner-academic gatherings
Knowledge transfer	Short magazine highlights of academic research findings	Possible learnings from practice

Reflections on Dualisms and Dualities within the Scholarship and Practice of OD

The scholar-practitioner interface represents multiple dimensions of dualities that have evolved over time within OD. Even though OD entered the field as a purposeful integration of scholarship and practice, this connection has frayed considerably over time. While efforts to link the two continue, tensions and differences expand, as many OD practitioners find much of academic writing impenetrable and valueless, and academics respond to the pulls to conduct rigorous research and publish in peer-reviewed journals (Bartunek and Rynes 2014).

One feature that characterizes this evolution over time is how much external pulls on one side of the binary affect its links to the other side. That is, tensions among academics about the scholar-practitioner relationship are often experienced as dualisms in light of the professional demands of scholars. Practitioners then remain largely outside and separate from the academy, even though they have sometimes contributed to the creation of interventions later studied by scholars.

Some attempts have been made to reduce this separation. In theory at least, scholar-practitioners represent a "more than" approach to these dualities, and when their full potential is accomplished, scholar-practitioners such as Ed Schein, Warner Burke, Kathy Kram, Laura Empson, Bob Marshak, and Phil Mirvis, are very influential in both the academic and the practice-based spheres. However, only a limited number of people have made such contributions. Further, even for luminaries, considerable tension exists in attempting to enact both roles. Empson (2013) has eloquently described the intense conflict she experienced in trying to do this (also see Kram et al., 2012). The presence of this conflict and the ways that a small number of people have handled it attest to what a "more than" approach to dualisms both accomplishes and costs.

Practitioner-scholar doctoral programs typically rely on "both-and" integration efforts to reach a middle ground or compromise between academic and practitioner poles. As we noted, integration as a "both-and" way of managing tensions may develop a kind of balance, but one that is less than optimal for either side. That seems to be the case here: the programs link well to work organizations, but often do not lead to academic credibility among scholars.

There are some ways to create more links. For example, the Case Western Reserve Doctor of Management program enables students to apply for the PhD in Management: Designing Sustainable Systems program (https://weatherhead.case.edu/degrees/doctorate/doctor-management/program-features/). Those who choose this option extend their coursework for an additional year, conduct independent doctoral research, and can earn a PhD.

Finally, knowledge sharing by means of summaries of scholarly articles is generally one sided, with academics passing on knowledge to practitioners, but doing so through translators (Ren and Bartunek 2020). It rarely invites contributions from practitioners. It does, however, represent an attempt to communicate in ways that can be understood by both groups.

To summarize this section, some academics and practitioners have made conscious and successful attempts to become scholar-practitioners, even with the challenges that this brings and the personal conflicts it entails. Further, university administrators have consciously established professional doctoral programs, and academics have developed means to summarize academic articles for practitioners. Thus, even amid considerable challenges, there have been attempts to speak to both sides of the divides.

Discussion and Implications for Organization Development

This chapter has focused on the tensions and contradictions linked to global OD practices as they have evolved over time and in different areas. We have examined the extent to which the tensions and contradictions have been handled in ways that reflect either-or, both-and more-than approaches (Putnam et al. 2016). Our work suggests that managing tensions associated with OD is often quite complex, and that how tensions are handled in practice sometimes differs from how they are handled in theory.

The first set of tensions we explored involves the dualism between diagnostic and dialogic OD. As Table 3.2 reveals, these conceptual distinctions started to appear after the 1980s, as dialogic approaches to OD surfaced in contrast to diagnostic methods. In identifying the distinctions between diagnostic and dialogic methods, Bushe and Marshak (2009) cast them primarily as a dualism with an either-or approach to managing the tension, although they also showed ways that the two could overlap. Yet, practitioners often intermingle these approaches in their work.

The second set of tensions centers on the future of the field itself, specifically, tensions between OD being dead or alive, with this tension typically treated as a dualism. As Table 3.3 shows, pronouncements of the death of OD began in the 1970s and have continued in each decade since that time. Yet, proclamations of death have occurred simultaneously with new practice developments that, for some, bring life. Approaches to the life and death debate have largely taken a form of either-or. Those who believe OD is dead rarely acknowledge the development of new initiatives or the ongoing success of old initiatives, such as action learning. Those who have developed new initiatives largely ignore those who claim that OD is dead, thus furthering the separation between the two. Mirvis (2014) and Marshak (2019) have articulated that OD is both dead and alive, a duality that has the potential to be generative.

A third tension is the dichotomy between scholars and practitioners. Initially, OD practitioners were also scholars who used practice to inform scholarship and used scholarship to inform practice. These dualities were initially ingrained in OD. In the 1980s, however, the two began to separate in terms of training, associations, and types of work, resulting in an increasing dualism between theory and practice. A few scholars have been able to create both-and or dualistic relationships between the two by becoming full scholar-practitioners, although considerable tensions accompany this move.

The major effort to decrease this dichotomy has been through creating doctoral programs aimed at training practitioner scholars. However, these efforts at integrating and finding middle ground between academia and practice have not produced sustained generative relationships between the two, and academic and practitioner communities typically remain separated.

Coming to the end of this discussion, we find ourselves in a contradictory situation. OD scholars, including those who have emphasized the importance of dialog as identified by Bushe and Marshak (2009), have not necessarily lived it out in generative ways. Multiple separations between factions and groups exist and attempts to resolve them have not succeeded. Death and life do not inform each other and, despite attempts at integration, academic and practitioner roles are often quite distinct. This is despite the fact that the practice of OD sometimes brings more (perhaps implicit) integration than does the scholarship of OD.

It is likely that most OD scholars and practitioners are conscious of these tensions on some level, although they do not explicitly describe them as ways of handling oppositions. What might they do if they were to recognize the opposites as tensions and if they could handle them from an overarching perspective of both-and dualities? What might they do to hold the poles of their differences together rather than separating them?

Putnam et al. (2016: 16) underscore the importance of both reflexive practice and serious playfulness as means of accomplishing both-and aspirations. To engage in reflexive practice (or praxis) and to "move forward amid complex circumstances," actors need to recognize tensions and understand their choices in responding to them. Through exploring these tensions, our chapter enables those experiencing the tensions to reflect on what is going on with them, what fosters treating them as dualisms, and what they might do to approach them as dualities. For example, Crosina and Bartunek (2017) described ways that some physical scientists and social activists joined forces to accomplish state regulation of a dangerous chemical. What might OD scholars and practitioners accomplish together?

Such reflection can be accompanied by serious play, in which individuals who experience the tensions play with them, perhaps using "irony and comic relief to surface tensions, expose contradictions, enact cynicism, and develop reflective practice" (Putnam et al. 2016: 66). For example, how can diagnosis be imagined taking place dialogically? How might OD scholars and practitioners imagine the death and life of OD while enjoying each other's company, perhaps by means of a Synectics excursion (https://synecticsworld.com/?s=excursion)? In other words, it is possible to bring tensions together through humor rather than treat them as either-or choices that require selecting one side as opposed to the other.

In theory, at least, these approaches to handling dualities enable thoughtful dialog between the poles in ways that welcome differences between opposites (Bartunek 2007). As we have shown, in practice there is not currently a great deal of dialog between proponents of dialogic OD and those of diagnostic OD; between those who proclaim the death of OD and those who declare it alive and well. There is some dialog, however, between scholars and practitioners of OD, and this is hopeful.

The opportunity and invitation exist for more frequent dialog and more-than responses; these are important for OD as a field. We hope that our chapter makes these options known and helps scholars and practitioners develop the capacity to enact them.

References

Adler, N., Shani, A. B., and Styhre, A. (2004), *Collaborative Research in Organizations* (Thousand Oaks, CA: Sage).

Alban, B. T., and Bunker, B. B. (2016), 'The ebb and flow of OD methods', in W. L. Rothwell, J. M. Stavros, R. L. Sullivan, and J. D. Vogelsang, eds., *Organization Development in Practice* (Washington DC Organization Development Network), 2–11.

Aldred, R. (2009), 'From Community Participation to Organizational Therapy? World Cafe and Appreciative Inquiry as Research Methods', *Community Development Journal*, 46/1, 57–71.

Argyris, C. (2005), 'On the Demise of Organization Development', in D. L. Bradford, and W. W. Burke, eds., *Reinventing Organization Development* (San Francisco: Pfeiffer), 113–29.

Argyris, C., and Schön, D. A. (1974), *Theory in Practice: Increasing Professional Effectiveness* (San Francisco: Jossey-Bass).

Axelrod, D. (1992), 'Getting Everyone Involved: How One Organization Involved Its Employees, Supervisors, and Managers in Redesigning the Organization', *The Journal of Applied Behavioral Science*, 28/4, 499–509.

Banerjee, S., and Morley, C. (2013), 'Professional Doctorates in Management: Toward a Practice-Based Approach to Doctoral Education', *Academy of Management Learning & Education*, 12/2, 173–93.

Barge, J. K., and Andreas, D. C. (2013), 'Communities, Conflict, and the Design of Dialogic Communication', in J. G. Oetzel and S. Ting-Toomey,eds., *The SAGE Handbook of Conflict Communication* (Los Angeles, CA: SAGE), 609–34.

Barge, J. K., Lee, M., Maddux, K., Nabring, R., and Townsend, B. (2008), 'Managing Dualities in Planned Change Initiatives', *Journal of Applied Communication Research*, 36/4, 364–90.

Barrett, F. J. (2015), 'Social Constructionist Challenge to Representational Knowledge: Implications for Understanding Organizational Change', in G. R. Bushe and R. J. Marshak, ed., *Dialogic Organization Development: The Theory and Practice of Transformational Change* (Oakland, CA: Berrett-Koehler), 67–83.

Bartunek, J. M. (2007), 'Academic-Practitioner Collaboration Need Not Require Joint or Relevant Research: Toward a Relational Scholarship of Integration', *Academy of Management Journal*, 50/6, 1323–33.

Bartunek, J. M. (2014), 'Academic-Practitioner Relationships: What NTL Started and What Management Scholarship Keeps Developing', *Journal of Applied Behavioral Science*, 50, 401–22.

Bartunek, J. M., and Rynes, S. L. (2014), 'Academics and Practitioners Are Alike and Unlike: The Paradoxes of Academic–Practitioner Relationship', *Journal of Management*, 40, 1181–201.

Bartunek, J. M., and Woodman, R. W. (2012), 'The Spirits of Organization Development, Or Why OD Lives Despite Its Pronounced Death', in K. Cameron and G. Spreitzer, eds, *Handbook of Positive Organizational Scholarship* (New York: Oxford University Press), 727–36.

Bartunek, J. M., and Woodman, R. W. (2015), 'Beyond Lewin: Towards a Temporal Approximation of Organization Development and Change', *Annual Review of Organizational Psychology and Organizational Behavior*, 2, 157–82.

Beckhard, R. (1969), *Organization Development: Strategies and Models* (Reading, MA. Addison-Wesley).

Beer, M. (1989), 'Towards a Redefinition of OD: A Critique of Research Focus and Method, *OD Practitioner*, 21/30, 11–12.

Berger, P. L., and Luckmann, T. (1967), *The Social Construction of Reality: A Treatise in the Sociology of Knowledge* (New York: Doubleday).

Beyer, J. M. (1982), 'Introduction to the Special Issue on the Utilization of Organizational Research', *Administrative Science Quarterly*, 27, 588–9.

Bradford, D. L., and Burke, W. W. (Eds.) (2005), *Reinventing Organization Development* (San Francisco: Pfeiffer).

Bradford, D. L. (1990), 'A Biography of Leland P. Bradford', *Journal of Applied Behavioral Science*, 26/1, vii–viii.

Bradford, L. P. (1965), 'Prologue', *Journal of Applied Behavioral Science*, 1, 3–5.

Bunker, B. B., and Alban, B. T. (1992), 'The Large Group Intervention—a New Social Innovation? '*Journal of Applied Behavioral Science*, 28, 473–9

Bunker, B. B., and Alban, B. T. (1997), *Large Group Interventions: Engaging the Whole System for Rapid Change* (San Francisco: Jossey-Bass).

Bunker, B. B., and Alban, B. T. (2006), *The Handbook of Large Group Methods: Creating Systemic Change in Organizations and Communities* (San Francisco: John Wiley & Sons).

Bunker, B. B., and Alban, B. T. (2014), 'Large Group Interventions', in B. B. Jones and M. Brazzel, eds., *The NTL Handbook of Organization Development and Change* (San Francisco: Wiley), 619–46.

Burke, W. W. (1976), 'Organization Development in Transition', *Journal of Applied Behavioral Science*, 12, 22–43.

Burke, W. W. (2014), 'Building a Loosely Coupled System: Origins of the Organization Development Network', *OD Practitioner*, 46/3, 4–6.

Burke, W. W. (2018), 'The Rise and Fall of the Growth of Organizational Development: What Now?' *Consulting Psychology Journal: Practice and Research*, 70/3, 186–206.

Bushe, G. (2012), 'Foundations of Appreciative Inquiry: History, Criticism and Potential', *AI Practitioner*, 14/1, 8–20.

Bushe, G. R., and Marshak, R. J. (2009). 'Revisioning Organization Development: Diagnostic and Dialogic Premises and Patterns of Practice', *Journal of Applied Behavioral Science*, 45, 348 68.

Bushe, G. R., and Marshak, R. J. (2014), 'The Dialogic Mind-Set in Organizational Development', *Research in Organizational Change and Development*, 22, 55–97.

Bushe, G. R., and Marshak, R. J. (2015), *Dialogic OD: The Theory and Practice of Transformational Change* (Oakland, CA: Berrett & Koehler).

Bushe, G. R., and Marshak, R. J. (2016), 'The Dialogic Organizational Development Approach to Transformation and Change', in W. Rothwell, J. Stavros, and R. Sullivan, eds., *Practicing Organizational Development* (San Francisco, CA: Wiley), 407–18.

Cady, S. H. (2019), 'Collaborative Change: Generative Approaches that Transform Organizations, Revitalize Communities, and Develop Human Potential', *Organization Development Review*, 51/2, 21–5.

Casey, D., and Pearce, D. (1977), *More than Management Development: Action Learning at GEC* (Aldershot: Gower).

Clark, P. A. (1972), *Action Research and Organizational Change* (London: Harper and Row).

Coghlan, D. (2011), 'Action learning research: The philosophy and methodology of practical knowing', in M. Pedler, ed., *Action Learning in Practice* (Farnham: Gower) 4, 357–367.

Coghlan, D., Dromgoole, T., Joynt, P., and Sorensen, P. (2004), *Managers Learning in Action: Management Education, Learning and Research*(London: Routledge).

Cooperrider, D. L. (1986), 'Appreciative Inquiry: Toward a Methodology for Understanding and Enhancing Organizational Innovation', Unpublished Ph.D. dissertation, Case Western Reserve University, Cleveland, OH.

Cooperrider, D. L., and Srivastava, S. (1987), 'Appreciative Inquiry in Organizational Life', In R.W. Woodman and W. Pasmore, eds., *Research in Organizational Change and Development* (Vol. 1) (Greenwich, CT: JAI Press), 129–69.

Cooperrider, D. L., and Whitney, D. D. (2005), *Appreciative Inquiry: A Positive Revolution in Change* (San Francisco: Berrett-Koehler).

Crosina, E., and Bartunek, J. M. (2017), 'The Paradoxical Mystery of the Missing Differences between Academics and Practitioners', In M. Lewis, W. K. Smith, P. Jarzabkowski, and A. Langley, eds., *The Oxford Handbook of Organizational Paradox* (New York: Oxford University Press), 472–89.

Cooperrider, D. L., and Whitney, D. (2007), 'Appreciative Inquiry: A Positive Revolution in Change', in P. Holman, T. Devane, and S. Cady, eds. *The Change Handbook* (2nd ed.) (San Francisco: Berrett-Koehler), 245–62.

Dillworth, R. L. (2010), 'Explaining Traditional Action Learning: Concepts and Beliefs', In Y. Boshyk, and R. L. Dilworth, eds, *Action Learning: History and Evolution* (New York: Palgrave-Macmillan), 3–28.

Duff, S., and Dishman, D. (2014), 'Transforming Joplin Leaders with Blended OD Design Post Tornado', *OD Practitioner*, 46/2, 19–24.

Dufresne, R. L., and Offstein, E. H. (2012), 'Holistic and Intentional Student Character Development Process: Learning from West Point', *Academy of Management Learning & Education*, 11/4, 570–90.

Dyer, W. G. (1977), *Team Building: Issues and Alternatives* (Reading, Mass: Addison-Wesley).

Emery, M., and Purser, R. E. (1996), *The Search Conference: A Powerful Method for Planning Organizational Change and Community Action* (San Francisco: Jossey-Bass).

Emery, F. E., and Trist, E. L. (1960), 'Socio-Technical Systems. Management Sciences, Models and Techniques', in C. W. Churchman, and M. Verhulst, eds., *Management Science, Models and Techniques* (Vol. II) (Oxford: Pergamon Press), 83–97.

Empson, L. (2013), 'My Affair with the "Other": Identity Journeys across the Research–Practice Divide, *Journal of Management Inquiry*, 22/2, 229–48.

Farjoun, M. (2010), 'Beyond Dualism: Stability and Change as a Duality', *Academy of Management Review*, 35/2, 202–25.

Fisher, D., and Torbert, W. R. (1995), *Personal and Organizational Transformations: The True Challenge of Continual Quality Improvement* (London: McGraw-Hill Book Company).

Freedman, A. M. (1999), 'The History of Organization Development and the NTL Institute: What We Have Learned, Forgotten, and Rewritten', *The Psychologist-Manager Journal*, 3/2, 125–41.

French, W. (1969), 'Organization Development Objectives, Assumptions and Strategies', *California Management Review*, 12/2, 23–34.

French, W. L., and Bell, C. H. (1995), *Organization Development* (5th ed.) (Englewood Cliffs, NJ: Prentice Hall).

Garratt.B. (2011). 'The power of action learning'. In M. Pedler (Ed.), *Action learning in practice* (Oxfordshire, UK: Routledge), 21–34

Gergen, K. J. (1985). 'The Social Constructionist Movement in Modern Psychology', *American Psychologist*, 40/3, 266–75.

Gilpin-Jackson, Y. (2013), 'Practicing in the Grey Area between Dialogic and Diagnostic Organization Development', *OD Practitioner*, 45/2, 60–5.

Gilpin-Jackson, Y. (2018), 'It's Time to Make Organization Development Our Client', *OD Practitioner*, 50/2, 7–15.

Goodman, P. (1979), *Assessing Organizational Change: The Rushton Quality of Work Experiment* (New York, NY: Wiley).

Graetz, F. and Smith, A. C. (2008), 'The Role of Dualities in Arbitrating Continuity and Change in Forms of Organizing', *International Journal of Management Reviews*, 10/3, 265–80.

Greenwood, R., and Hinings, C. R. (1996), 'Understanding Radical Organizational Change: Bringing Together the Old and the New Institutionalism', *Academy of Management Review*, 21/4, 1022–54.

Greiner, L. E., and Cummings, T. G. (2004), 'Wanted: OD More Alive Than Dead!', *Journal of Applied Behavioral Science*, 40, 374–91.

Hanlon, M. D., Nadler, D. A., and Gladstein, D. (1985), *Attempting Work Reform: The Case of 'Parkside' Hospital* (New York, NY: Wiley).

Harris, R. T., and Beckhard, R. (1987), *Organizational Transitions: Managing Complex Change* (Reading, Mass: Addison-Wesley Publishing Company).

Heifetz, R. A., Grashow, A., and Linsky, M. (2009), *The Practice of Adaptive Leadership: Tools and Tactics for Changing your Organization and the World* (Boston, Mass: Harvard Business Press).

Herscovitch, L., and Meyer, J. P. (2002), 'Commitment to Organizational Change: Extension of a Three-Component Model', *Journal of Applied Psychology*, 87, 474–87.

Holman, P., and Devane, T. (1999), *The Change Handbook: Group Methods for Shaping the Future* (San Francisco: Berrett-Koehler).

Holman, P., Devane, T., and Cady, S. (2007), *The Change Handbook: The Definitive Resource on Today's Best Methods for Engaging Whole Systems* (San Francisco: Berrett-Kohler).

Hornstein, H. A., Bunker, B. B., Burke, W.W., Gindes, M., and Lewicki, R. J. (1971), *Social Intervention: A Behavioral Science Approach* (New York: Free Press).

Jacobs, R. H. (1997), *Real Time Strategic Change: How to Involve an Entire Organization in Fast and Far-Reaching Change* (San Francisco: Berrett-Koehler).

Janoff, S. (2016), 'My Future Search Journey', in W. L. Rothwell, J. M. Stavros, R. L. Sullivan, and J. D. Vogelsang, eds., *Organization Development in Practice* (Washington DC: Organization Development Network), 22–33.

Jones, J. E., and Pfeiffer, J. W. (1977), 'On the Obsolescence of the Term Organization Development', *Group & Organization Studies*, 2, 263–4.

Kram, K. E., Wasserman, I. C., and Yip, J. (2012), 'Metaphors of Identity and Professional Practice: Learning from the Scholar–Practitioner', *Journal of Applied Behavioral Science*, 48/3, 304–41.

Latham, G. (2019), 'Perspectives of a Practitioner-Scientist on Organizational Psychology/Organizational Behavior', *Annual Review of Organizational Psychology and Organizational Behavior*, 6, 1–16.

Leonard, H. S., and Lang, F. (2010), 'Leadership Development via Action Learning', *Advances in Developing Human Resources*, 12: 225–40.

Lewin, K. (1947), 'Frontiers in Group Dynamics: I. Concept, Method and Reality in Social Science; Social Equilibria', *Human Relations*, 1, 5–40.

Lippitt, R. (1983), 'Future before you Plan', in R. A. Ritvo, and A. G. Sargent, eds., *The NTL Managers' Handbook* (Arlington, VA: NTL Institute), 36–45.

Ludema, J. D. Whitney, D., Mohr, B. J., and Griffen, T. J. (2003), *The Appreciative Inquiry Summit* (San Francisco: Berrett-Koehler).

Marshak, R. J. (2014), 'Organization Development as an Evolving Field of Practice', in B. B. Jones and M. Brazzel, eds., *The NTL Handbook of Organization Development and Change* (San Francisco: Wiley), 72–102.

Marshak, R. J. (2019), 'The Minahan Manifesto', *Organization Development Review*, 51/3, 17–18.

Marshak, R. J., and Bushe, G. R. (2013), 'An Introduction to Advances in Dialogic Organization Development,' *OD Practitioner*, 45/1, 1–4.

Marsick, V. J., and O'Neil, J. (1999), 'The Many Faces of Action Learning', *Management Learning*, 30/2, 159–76.

Minahan, M. (2019), 'Change Our Name, Change Our Game. It's Time for "Strategic Change"', *Organization Development Review*, 51/3, 6–16.

Mirvis, P. H. (2014), 'JABS at 50: Applied Behavioral Science and Something More?' *Journal of Applied Behavioral Science*, 50, 371–400.

Oswick, C., Anthony, P., Keenoy, T., Mangham, I. L., and Grant, D. (2000), 'A Dialogic Analysis of Organizational Learning,' *Journal of Management Studies*, 37, 887–901.

Owen, H. (1994), *Open Space Technology* (Potomac, MD: Abbott).

Pedler, M., and Abbott, C. (2013), *Facilitating Action Learning: A Practitioner's Guide.* (Berkshire, England: McGraw-Hill Education (UK).

Perkins, D. N., Nieva, V. F., and Lawler, E. E. (1983), *Managing Creation: The Challenge of Building a New Organization* (New York, NY: Wiley).

Ployhart, R. E., and Bartunek, J. M. (2019), 'Editors' Comments: There is Nothing so Theoretical as Good Practice—A Call for Phenomenal Theory', *Academy of Management Review*, 44, 493–7.

Poole, M. S., and Van de Ven, A. H. (1989), 'Using Paradox to Build Management and Organization Theories', *Academy of Management Review*, 14/4, 562–78.

Putnam, L. L., Fairhurst, G. T., and Banghart, S. (2016), 'Contradictions, Dialectics, and Paradoxes in Organizations: A Constitutive Approach', *The Academy of Management Annals*, 10/1, 65–171.

Quinn, R. E. (1993, August 8–11), 'The legitimate change agent: A vision for a new profession'. Organization Development and Change Division, Distinguished Speaker Address, 1993 Academy of Management meeting, Atlanta, Georgia.

Raelin, J. (2006), 'Does Action Learning Promote Collaborative Leadership?' *Academy of Management Learning & Education*, 5/2), 152–68.

Rapoport, R. N. (1970), 'Three Dilemmas in Action Research', *Human Relations*, 23, 488–513.

Ren, I. Y., and Bartunek, J. M. (2020), 'Creating Standards for Responsible Translation of Management Research for Practitioners,' in O. Laasch, D. Jamali, R. E. Freeman, and

R. Suddaby, *Research Handbook of Responsible Management* (Cheltenham, England: Edward Elgar), 726–41.

Revans, R. W. (1982). 'What is Action Learning?' *Journal of Management Development*, 1/3, 64–75.

Revans, R. W. (1983), *ABC of Action Learning* (Bromley, Kent: Chartwell-Bratt).

Ripamonti, S. Galuppo, L., Gorli, M., Scaratti, G., and Cunliffe, A. L. (2016), 'Pushing Action Research toward Reflexive Practice', *Journal of Management Inquiry*, 25/1, 55–68.

Rothwell, W. L., Stavros, J. M., Sullivan, R. L., and Vogelsang, J. D. (2016), *Organization Development in Practice* (Washington DC: Organization Development Network).

Schein, E. H. (2015), 'Foreword: Dialogic Organization Development, Past, Present and Future', in G. R. Bushe and R. J. Marshak, eds., *Dialogic Organization Development, the Theory and Practice of Transformational Change* (Oakland, CA: Berrett-Koehler), 6–13.

Schein, E. H. (1969), *Process Consultation: Its Role in Organization Development* (Reading, MA: Addison Wesley).

Senge, P. (1990), *The Fifth Discipline: The Art and Practice of the Learning Organization* (New York, NY: Currency Doubleday).

Snowden, D. J., and Boone, M. E. (2007), 'A Leader's Framework for Decision Making. *Harvard Business Review*, 85/11, 68.

Seo, M., Putnam, L., and Bartunek, J. (2004), 'Dualities and Tensions of Planned Organizational Change', in M. S. Poole and A. H. Van de Ven, eds., *Handbook of Organizational Change and Innovation* (New York, NY: Oxford University Press), 73–109.

Swart, C. (2015), 'Coaching from a Dialogic OD Paradigm', in G. R. Bushe and R. J. Marshak, eds., *Dialogic Organization Development: The Theory and Practice of Transformational Change* (Oakland, CA: Berrett-Koehler), 327–46.

Tenkasi, R. (2011). 'Integrating theory to inform practice: Insights from the practitioner-scholar'. In S. A. Mohrman and E. E. Lawler (Eds.), *Useful Research: Advancing Theory and Practice* (San Francisco, CA: Berrett-Koehler), 211–32

Tenkasi, R. V., and Hay, G. W. (2008), 'Following the Second Legacy of Aristotle: The Scholar–Practitioner as an Epistemic Technician', in A. B. Shani, S. A. Mohrman, W. A. Pasmore, B. N. Stymne, and N. Adler, eds., *Handbook of Collaborative Management Research* (Thousand Oaks, CA: Sage), 49–72.

Trehan, K. (2011), 'Critical Action Learning—From Theory to Practice', in M. Pedler, ed., *Action Learning in Practice* (4th ed.) (Surrey: Gower Publishing), 163–72.

Van de Ven, A. H. (2007), *Engaged Scholarship: A Guide for Organizational and Social Research* (New York, Oxford University Press).

Van de Ven, A. H., and Poole, M. S. (1995), 'Explaining Development and Change in Organizations', *Academy of Management Review*, 20, 510–40.

Wasserman, I. C., and Kram, K. E. (2009), 'Enacting the Scholar–Practitioner Role: An Exploration of Narratives', *Journal of Applied Behavioral Science*, 45, 12–38.

Weisbord, M. R. (1976), 'Organizational Diagnosis: Six Places to Look for Trouble with or without a Theory', *Group and Organization Studies*, 1, 430–47.

Weisbord, M. R. (1987), *Productive Workplaces: Organizing and Managing For Dignity, Meaning and Community* (San Francisco: Jossey-Bass).

Weisbord, M., and Janoff, S. (1995), *Future Search: Finding Common Ground for Action in Organizations* (San Francisco: Berrett-Koehler).

Weisbord, M., and Janoff, S. (2006), 'The FAA's historic growth without gridlock conference', in B. Bunker and B. Alban, eds., *The Handbook of Large Group Methods: Creating Systemic Change in Organizations and Communities* (San Francisco: Jossey-Bass), 176–89.

Weisbord, M., and Janoff, S. (2010), *Future Search: Getting the Whole System in the Room for Vision, Commitment and Action* (3rd ed.) (San Francisco: Berrett-Koehler).

Wieland, G. F. (1981), *Improving Health Care Management: Organization Development and Organization Change* (Ann Arbor: Health Administration Press).

Wieland, G. F., and Leigh, H. (1971), *Changing Hospitals: A Report on the Hospital Internal Communications Project* (London: Tavistock Publications).

Worren, N. A. M., Ruddle, K., and Moore, K. (1999), 'From Organizational Development to Change Management: The Emergence of a New Profession', *Journal of Applied Behavioral Science*; 35, 273–86.

Yaeger, T. F., Sorensen, P. F., and Bengtsson, U. (2005), 'Assessment of the State of Appreciative Inquiry: Past, Present, and Future', *Research in Organizational Change and Development*, 15, 297–319.

Yeo, R. K., & Marquardt, M. J. (2015), '(Re) Interpreting action, learning, and experience: integrating action learning and experiential learning for HRD'. *Human Resource Development Quarterly*, *26*(1), 81–107.

CHAPTER 4

UPSIDE-DOWN ORGANIZATIONAL CHANGE

Sensemaking, sensegiving, and the new generation

ALEXANDRA RHEINHARDT AND DENNIS A. GIOIA

SENSEMAKING is a process of meaning-making in which people attempt to comprehend ambiguous, unexpected, and/or confusing issues or events (see Maitlis and Christianson 2014 for a review). Sensemaking involves cycling between cognition (e.g., perceiving, interpreting) and action (Daft and Weick 1984; Thomas et al. 1993; Weick 1979; 1988), with the goal of creating a more ordered and comprehensible environment which, in turn, enables future cognition and action (Maitlis and Christianson 2014). The negotiation of "sense" can take place both intra- and interpersonally, with the latter being key to *organizational* sensemaking. For sensemaking at the organizational level to be successful, intersubjectively agreed upon (collective) meanings must emerge among multiple layers or hierarchies of individuals (e.g., Balogun and Johnson 2004; Meyer et al. 1998).

Planned organizational changes both trigger and are enacted through processes of sensemaking (e.g., Corley and Gioia 2004; Gioia and Chittipeddi 1991). The announcement of a change often initiates confusion and the subsequent need for organization members to make sense regarding new meanings, expectations, roles, practices, and/or ways of acting (Luscher and Lewis 2008). Change is ultimately enacted through successful sensemaking, such that the meaning of change is effectively negotiated and agreed upon by members (Corley and Gioia 2004; Denis et al. 1996). Conversely, planned organizational transformation suffers when sensemaking efforts fail, signaling a lack of agreement or buy-in regarding what is being changed and/or how best to accomplish change efforts (e.g., Mantere et al. 2012; Nag et al. 2007; Yu et al. 2005). Organizations and their members, therefore, implement actual changes through the process of making and giving sense about those changes.

We will be discussing the sensemaking processes involved in organizational change in more detail throughout this chapter. For now, however, we want to call attention to one aspect of these change efforts that set the stage for a different way of understanding organizational change. To date, the literature examining planned changes from a sensemaking perspective has largely taken a top-down approach, suggesting that it is primarily an organization's senior executives that both plan organizational changes and control the ensuing sensemaking process that aids the implementation of those changes (Gioia and Chittipeddi 1991; Howard-Grenville, Metzger, and Meyer 2013; Ravasi and Schultz 2006). These changes are usually formulated in response to environmental pressures (Barr, 1998; Nag et al. 2007), so it seems reasonable that most of the attention in the literature is devoted to these change initiatives, given that an organization's upper echelon is charged with the responsibility of monitoring notable environmental changes, as well as devising organizational strategies that are responsive to the changing environment (Ancona 2011; Smircich and Morgan 1982).

What is usually overlooked through this top-down approach, however, are the influences lower-level members contribute to organizational change. More specifically, characteristics of the new generation of employees (i.e., Millennials who now fill the ranks of the lower echelons of their organizations), combined with the current rapid rate of technological innovation, facilitate the increasing ability of lower-level employees to influence what will define their organization in the future. Millennials have a different sense of desirable organizational objectives and actions than their predecessors (Ferri-Reed 2014; Myers and Sadaghiani 2010)—a difference that will make a difference in trying to manage change. Furthermore, the advent of transformative forms of communication and technology (e.g., Internet, social media, smart phones) provide powerful vehicles for expression and influence (Kaplan and Haenlein 2010). Consequently, due to a combination of changing internalities and externalities, we argue that individuals in the lower echelons will play a much greater role in their organization's future change efforts than their counterparts in the past. We posit, in particular, that those in lower levels of organizational hierarchies may not only engage more extensively in their organization's sensemaking and sensegiving efforts—potentially resisting, obstructing, and/or reinterpreting change efforts—but they may also serve as the spark for radically different ideas and changes that may be further developed and enacted. As Maitlis (2005: 22) suggests, "[W]hile leaders are uniquely placed to influence how issues are interpreted and understood in organizations, their interpretations can be significantly shaped by the sensegiving efforts of others." Millennials are not bashful: they expect their preferences to be honored. We therefore suggest that we theorists and researchers need to place greater emphasis on the lower echelons of organizations in future work on organizational change if we are going to develop plausible models of future organizational change dynamics.

We first provide an overview of the literature integrating sensemaking and organizational change. We discuss both processes and outcomes of change, how change can be promoted and resisted via sensemaking efforts, as well as strengths and weaknesses of current sensemaking approaches to change. We additionally incorporate the related concepts of sensegiving and organizational identity change within our considerations. We then explore how current dynamics, including workplace composition and new technologies, influence modern organizational change and theories of change. We suggest that theories of change, including sensemaking perspectives on organizational change, need to more fully consider these recent workplace trends to better reflect coming organizational change efforts.

An Overview of Sensemaking and Organizational Change

Sensemaking as a Process of Teleological Change

Like other scholars subscribing to a "teleological" view of organizational change, those adopting a sensemaking approach tend to examine changes that are planned and deliberate, yet adaptive (Gioia and Chittipeddi 1991; Maitlis and Christianson 2014; Van de Ven and Poole 1995). This sensemaking perspective has guided many to focus on change efforts that are rooted in changing market and/or environmental demands (Dunford and Jones 2000; Nag et al. 2007). Some of these changes are more proactive; others are more reactive, depending on the timing, as well as the specific impetus for the change. Regardless of the orientation, however, these efforts tend to be purposefully-designed, planned, executed, and continuously monitored by the organization's top management (Gioia and Thomas 1996; Van de Ven and Poole 1995). Despite having an envisioned end-state in mind, however, the path to achieving the desired outcome is seldom fully laid out. The process of change therefore remains constructive, with changes often representing a notable break from the past (Van de Ven and Poole 1995). This constructive character enables non-executive organizational members and other stakeholders to enter into negotiations about the change, so they can help to modify or even resist the change (Gioia et al. 1994; Pratt, 2000; Sonenshein 2010). This social construction process often culminates in organizational members arriving at a consensus that serves as the basis for change implementation. The processes that take place within the teleological mode of organizational change are what scholars refer to as "sensemaking." More specifically, sensemaking is the process by which a shared sense of meaning and action is negotiated and produced (Gephart et al. 2010).

An Overview of Sensemaking and Sensegiving Processes in Planned Organizational Change

Scholars who employ a sensemaking approach to investigating organizational change often start by looking at the leader's sensemaking efforts that begin following the decision that a change is actually warranted. The starting point in these studies is therefore often the examination of the cognition and actions of the top leaders (e.g., Gioia and Thomas, 1996; Gioia et al. 1994). At this time, CEOs and/or their top management teams must make sense of how the intended change will fit within a revised meaning system (Bartunek 1984). Gioia and Chittipeddi (1991) described the beginnings of this process in their study of a strategic change initiative at a large university by noting that "the CEO must first develop a sense of the organization's internal and external environment and define a revised conception of the organization (via a process that is labeled as *sensemaking*). Following this interpretive work by the CEO (or top management team), some abstract 'vision' of the changed organization evolves..." This initial leader sensemaking, therefore, begins with an interpretation of proposed changes that is often influenced by the organization's current state of affairs, yet also accounts for what internal leaders want the organization to become (e.g., desired identity and future image) (Dutton and Dukerich 1991; Gioia and Thomas 1996; Ravasi and Schultz 2006).

Upon defining an organizational vision, leaders outline this desired outcome to organizational members and stakeholders (Corley and Gioia 2004; Dunford and Jones 2000; Gioia and Chittipeddi 1991). The necessity for such change is also established at this point so as to limit the confusion and/or resistance surrounding the change effort (Maitlis and Lawrence 2007). Research suggests that leaders employ tactics to encourage greater member buy-in at this time (Maitlis and Christianson 2014). This approach may include calling attention to flaws with the current (or previous) direction of the organization. For example, by focusing on the organization's poor performance or highlighting discrepancies between the identity of the organization and the image that external stakeholders have of the organization, leaders convey the necessity for change (e.g., Corley and Gioia 2004; Dutton and Dukerich 1991; Elsbach and Kramer 1996; Sonenshein 2010).

This process of providing sense for others is termed "sensegiving" (Gioia and Chittipeddi 1991) and is the spark that ignites subsequent sensemaking processes of organizational members lower in the hierarchy and/or those who were not involved in the initial planning efforts (Fiss and Zajac 2006; Gioia et al. 1994; Mantere et al. 2012). We note that regardless of how well planned or articulated proposed changes are, organization members must make sense of the elements of the change(s), both in broad organizational terms and also in terms of personal implications—for example, how the proposed change(s) will affect organizational routines and processes as well as the individual's tasks and roles (Balogun and Johnson 2004; 2005; Luscher and Lewis 2008). To be sure, actual change efforts begin only when members understand and agree with their leaders' proposals.

Although leaders might try to guide or control organizational sensemaking processes, members can "adopt, alter, resist, or reject the sense they have been given" through their own sensegiving efforts (Maitlis and Christianson 2014: 78; see also Gioia and Chittipeddi 1991; Sonenshein 2010). This two-way negotiation is deemed essential by some leaders who subsequently embrace the input of their members (e.g., Corley and Gioia 2004; Howard-Grenville et al. 2013; Ravasi and Schultz 2006). It is through this reciprocal sensemaking and sensegiving among and within various levels and layers of the organization that "organizational" sensemaking (as opposed to individual sensemaking) is achieved. A key point is that organization members must jointly or "collectively" create an understanding and embark upon action(s) for an organization-wide change to be implemented successfully (Berger and Luckmann 1967; Gioia et al. 1994). Without a collective "sense," individual changes in roles, tasks, and practices that together comprise the larger organizational change will not manifest and, therefore, broad-based change will not be achieved. Despite the recognition that multilevel input and feedback is paramount, the notion that leaders are the key drivers of organizational sensemaking during change efforts has tended to dominate the sensemaking literature. More recent work, however, has begun to recognize that lower-level employees might play a greater role in the sensemaking process than originally conceived (Balogun and Johnson, 2004, 2005; Maitlis 2005; Walsh and Bartunek 2011), bringing us one step closer to acknowledging that those in the lower echelons can actually drive sensemaking and organizational change processes.

Key Features of the Sensemaking Perspective on Organizational Change

Impetus for and Types of Change

As noted, scholars most often focus on changes that are planned and deliberate, which implies that organizations and, more specifically, organizational leaders, have desired outcomes in mind. How the plan comes into being and what the outcome will be, however, differ considerably across organizations and consequently across sensemaking studies. In this section we discuss some important drivers of internally- and externally-derived organizational change efforts. We also address two broad types of organizational change – "strategic change" and "organizational identity change" (which is often closely associated with major strategic change efforts).

Over several studies, Gioia and colleagues described a university's strategic change efforts to transition to a "top ten" public university (Gioia and Chittipeddi 1991; Gioia et al. 1994; Gioia and Thomas 1996). Although the authors alluded to the need to keep pace with changing market conditions to remain competitive within the higher education industry, it was really the arrival of a new university president that sparked the university's change efforts. Furthermore, while these efforts included projects that were designed with environmental and market factors in mind, it was also made clear that the president held a "personal interest" in strategic change. This reinforces the notion that "strategies often reflect the values of top managers" (Gioia and Chittipeddi 1991: 434) and thus may often be more internally driven, or as we suggest in this chapter, organizational strategies might sometimes reflect the strong values and desires of lower-level employees. The notion that the new leadership and new visions these leaders often provide can serve as the necessary impetus for change was further noted in a study by Denis et al. (1996). Although this study did not explicitly take a sensemaking perspective, it described the tactics leaders used to stimulate change—specifically leaders who were new to the organization. These new leaders also "brought with them different norms and more proactive modes of management" that differed from and conflicted with common industry practices (Denis et al. 1996: 679). These studies indicate that it can be a change in an organization's internal dynamics (e.g., leadership) that prompts or fosters larger-scale strategic changes.

Other sensemaking literature, however, more explicitly focuses on the external drivers of organizational change and leaders' perceived needs to respond to environmental changes (e.g., Balogun 2003; Corley and Gioia 2004; Nag et al. 2007; Ravasi and Schultz 2006). As one example, Dunford and Jones (2000) examined three New Zealand-based organizations and their response to deregulation efforts that affected their financial, labor, and goods markets. The authors studied the narratives used by the organizations' leaders in their attempt to make and provide sense surrounding the need to change following changes in environmental conditions. Similarly, in her study of six firms within the pharmaceutical industry, Barr (1998) analyzed interpretation efforts and planned changes by managers concerning amendments to the Food, Drug and Cosmetic Act which significantly altered the safety standards (and subsequently lengthened the time-to-market) for pharmaceutical products. Both these studies, as well as a host of others that either implicitly or explicitly utilize a sensemaking approach, make clear the notable influence environmental factors can have on organizations and subsequently provide the impetus for strategic organizational change. In each of the above-noted studies, what was being changed included organizational strategies, structures, routines, and/or processes. Other sensemaking studies have examined such changes as mergers and acquisitions (Yu et al. 2005), corporate spin-offs (Corley and Gioia 2004; Nag et al. 2007), and other forms of corporate restructuring, such as moving from a more hierarchically organized firm to one that is more decentralized (Balogun 2003; Balogun and Johnson 2004; 2005). Largely missing from this body of work, however, are the smaller-scale policy changes that are often initiated, not by external and/or top down conditions, but by members of the lower levels of their organizations—a point we turn to later in this chapter.

Organizational Identity Change

Recognizing that "any substantive change leads to the alteration of existing value and meaning systems" (Gioia and Chittipeddi 1991: 434; see also Gioia 1986), and that these values and meaning systems often comprise the essence of an organization (i.e., its identity), several scholars have focused explicitly on organizational identity change. At times, organizational identity change stems from changes that are labelled "strategic" and/or major changes that are planned (Corley and Gioia 2004; Nag et al. 2007; Tripsas 2009). At other times, organizational identity may evolve in response to identity threats (Dutton and Dukerich 1991; Elsbach and Kramer 1996; Ravasi and Schultz 2006). Given that there is another chapter in this handbook that is devoted to organizational identity change, we limit our discussion to the sensemaking efforts surrounding these identity changes.

We begin by discussing two studies that reflected organizational identity changes that directly stemmed from strategic change efforts. Both studies revealed that a planned strategic change initiative, which produced changed organizational structures and strategies, consequently spurred member ambiguity surrounding the new defining features of their organizations. Corley and Gioia (2004) noted this phenomenon in their study of a corporate spin-off, stating in the opening of their paper: "When we revise our familiar ways of describing our identity, or when our familiar ways of knowing who we are as an organization lose their meaning or have no meaning in new circumstances, the context for identity change arises." In essence, strategic changes (in this case a corporate spin-off) often call into question who or what an organization is or now stands for after a significant transformation. Members must make sense of who they are as an organization and, at times, may remain in an uncomfortable state of ambiguity while they attempt to piece together new meanings. Ultimately, organizational sensemaking efforts may suggest that rather than clinging to the labels of an old identity, new labels may be needed that more accurately reflect who the organization has become. And with new labels comes a new organizational identity.

Tripsas (2009) similarly examined an organization that had undergone a shift in strategy and consequently led to identity ambiguity, which spurred member sensemaking. In a lengthy process that extended over several years, members struggled in making sense of who their organization had become. A new organizational identity finally emerged when members collectively derived a sense of how the organization's revised strategy had reshaped their firm. Furthermore, there are times that an organization's environment spurs the need for change. These factors may constitute "identity threats" that call into question who an organization is or who it wants to be in the future. Dutton and Dukerich (1991) explored this phenomenon in their examination of the New York/New Jersey Port Authority, which suffered an image crisis resulting from the organization's response to the issue of homelessness. The public perception of the organization triggered member sensemaking whereby members collectively struggled to make sense of what they wanted their organization to be. Ultimately, NY/NJ PA's identity evolved via the process of member sensemaking and in conjunction with the organization's response to homelessness. Ravasi and Shultz (2006) similarly investigated an organization that was faced with a series of environmentally-induced identity threats, involving increased competition and an economic recession, that prompted organizational leaders to reevaluate their organization's core and distinct identity characteristics. The authors found that key to members' sensemaking efforts were facets of the organization's culture. Consequently, the organization's identity was revised, although it remained grounded in the organization's culture. As this body of work suggests, identity changes are often initiated by externally rooted identity threats which raise the issue of who/what an organization is or wants to be. At times, however, it is lower-level employees who raise these questions as they seek to make their organizations more closely aligned with their own identities—a point largely missing from the literature but one which we explore in more detail throughout this chapter.

Patterns and Outcomes of Organizational Change

> *Strategic change can be understood not only as a change in the position and fit of an organization in its environment, but perhaps more fundamentally as a change in the cognitive perspective represented by a new strategy. Strategy as cognitive perspective (cf. Ginsberg 1988, Mintzberg 1987) emphasizes the set of assumptions through which the problems and issues of the organization are identified and interpreted by top managers and key stakeholders (Hedberg and Jonsson 1978). The alteration of this "conceptual lens" represents a fundamental shift in the organization's belief structure, value system, and identity. (Bartunek 1984, Dutton and Dukerich 1991, Gioia and Chittipeddi 1991, Walsh 1988).*
>
> (*Gioia, Thomas, Clark, & Chittipeddi, 1994*)

This excerpt, taken from the study by Gioia et al. (1994) of a university's effort to undergo significant strategic change, identifies several factors relevant to appreciating the outcomes of change. First, many outcomes lay beyond formal, and perhaps more obvious, alterations in organizational forms, structures, and/or strategies, as well as the underlying individual behavioral and task changes that comprise larger-scale changes. Changes in member cognition bring about revisions to shared organizational meanings, values, beliefs, and identities (Bartunek 1984; Dutton and Dukerich 1991; Fiss and Zajac 2006; Labianca et al. 2000). These factors, although often less observable, are intertwined within the sensemaking process and thus are important to conceptions of change outcomes. Secondly, these same cognitive dynamics constitute the conceptual lenses through which organization members make sense of change (Gioia and Thomas 1996; Ravasi and Shultz 2006; Starbuck and Milliken 1988). Top managers and organizational stakeholders draw upon and then subsequently revise perceptions that are rooted in these lenses to bring about change. Old meanings and practices, at times, however, are too rigid and, therefore, undermine transformation efforts. Thus, we must first understand the underlying patterns of change to understand the outcomes of organizational change efforts (e.g., what is changed and/or whether change is successfully enacted).

As noted earlier, organizational sensemaking during change efforts tends to begin at the top of the organization, often in response to an environmental change or pressure that has implications for organizational strategy. Organizational leaders, in other words, first interpret and make sense of external dynamics. These leaders' interpretations may indeed be informed by the organization's identity (e.g., Gioia and Thomas 1996), construed external image (e.g., Dutton et al. 1994; Gioia et al. 2000), culture (Ravasi and Schultz 2006), knowledge and practices (Nag et al. 2007), and/or any other systems of meaning that may inform how an organization should respond to opportunities and threats. Upon constructing a new vision for the organization, leaders begin to provide sense to other organizational members and stakeholders. Sensegiving processes are often aided by use of symbols and symbolic action, metaphors, other discursive elements, and/or actions that help the leader convey the revised meanings they want others to adopt (Gioia et al. 1994; Hill and Levenhagen 1995; Maitlis and Lawrence 2007; Rouleau 2005; Sonenshein 2006). Organizational members and stakeholders are then prompted to engage in their own sensemaking and sensegiving efforts, wherein collective meanings emerge over time through this recursive cycle of leader, member, and/or stakeholder negotiation (Balogun and Johnson 2004; Gioia and Chittipeddi 1991; Isabella 1990).

The above depiction represents the predominant view of organizational change in the sensemaking literature. Scholars have begun to recognize, however, that variants in change patterns, such as major demographic shifts, can have unexpected effects on the process of change and/or the outcomes of change. Under such conditions, change efforts might not be quite so leader-centric. Some scholars believe that the roles other organizational members play in sensemaking processes often progress in the absence of overt guidance from top leaders. In a study spanning several papers, Balogun and Johnson (Balogun 2003; Balogun and Johnson 2004, 2005) noted the significant influence middle managers play in the combined sensemaking and implementation of organizational change. They studied the effortful role that these lower-level managers assumed, suggesting that not only do middle managers need to make sense of changes (often introduced by upper-level executives) for themselves, but they must also help others to understand the visions espoused by top leaders and implement changes as well (Balogun 2003). They also pointed to the multiple interpretations and subsequent unintended consequences that may arise in change initiatives that lack senior management control (Balogun and Johnson 2004).

Sonenshein's (2010) study of a Fortune 500 retailer undergoing strategic change revealed that greater examination of non-executive members is required to more fully understand change dynamics. Specifically, he found that lower-level employees tended to embellish management's change narratives, resulting in conflicting narratives that differed with regard to the attractiveness of the perceived change compared to the attractiveness of the status quo. Sonenshein suggests that better understanding is needed in terms of how employees make sense of and alter or embellish leaders' narratives to unpack why change is at times accepted and at other times resisted. He concluded that "strategic change is a series of multiple, sometimes conflicting narratives (Dawson and Buchanan 2005), in which understanding the differing narratives becomes vital to explaining how strategic change unfolds" (2010: 503).

Finally, Maitlis (2005) put forth a typology of sensemaking processes that differ in the degree to which leaders and other stakeholders engage in sensegiving (see Figure 4.1). Maitlis suggests that "guided" and "restricted" sensemaking are both characterized by a high degree of leader sensegiving. In the latter, the leader dominates sensemaking efforts while other stakeholders limit their involvement, whereas in the former other stakeholders take on a more animated sensegiving role as well. Conversely, in "fragmented" and "minimal" sensemaking processes, the leader assumes a lesser role and does not attempt to control the process. In fragmented sensemaking, stakeholders may engage in extensive sensegiving efforts whereas under conditions of minimal sensemaking, there

Leader Sensegiving	Stakeholder Sensegiving: High Sensegiving	Stakeholder Sensegiving: Low Sensegiving
High Sensegiving	***Guided Organizational Sensemaking*** Process Characteristics • High animation • High control Outcomes • Unitary, rich account • Emergent series of consistent actions	***Restricted Organizational Sensemaking*** Process Characteristics • Low animation • High control Outcomes • Unitary, narrow account • One-time action or planned set of consistent actions
Low Sensegiving	***Fragmented Organizational Sensemaking*** Process Characteristics • High animation • Low control Outcomes • Multiple, narrow accounts • Emergent series of inconsistent actions	***Minimal Organizational Sensemaking*** Process Characteristics • Low animation • Low control Outcomes • Nominal accounts • One-time, compromise action

FIGURE 4.1 "Four Forms of Organizational Sensemaking" by Maitlis

(From Maitlis, S. (2005). "The Social Processed of Organizational Sensemaking". *Academy of Management Journal*, 48, 21–49)

is little sensegiving done by any organizational stakeholders. Consequently, disparities exist in the number and consistency of accounts and actions generated. Overall, these findings suggest that sensemaking processes in general, and sensemaking processes associated with organizational change in particular, might not always follow the traditional patterns. Although leaders drive organizational sensemaking surrounding change efforts in many cases, at other times they do not take on such a significant role. There can be times when actual change is not even introduced by organizational leaders, but rather by lower-level employees, implying the significant influence these employees may have in their organizations' sensemaking and change efforts. This work thus brings us one step closer to an understanding of how bottom-up, or upside-down, organizational change works.

We next devote our attention to two broad change outcomes: successful and unsuccessful change efforts. We elaborate more on failed change efforts because: 1) most of the studies we have discussed so far have reflected successful organizational changes, and; 2) by understanding what leads to change failure we can arrive at a better understanding of what may lead to change success.

In their review of the organizational sensemaking literature, Maitlis and Christianson (2014) discuss conditions that may serve as deterrents to sensemaking and thus may impede change. Discussing the study by Nag et al. (2007) of an organization trying to reorient itself from an engineering focus to more of a business development focus, the authors concluded that it was the combination of a strong organizational identity, along with a desire to preserve collective knowledge-related practices, that ultimately prevented the change effort from being successfully accomplished. In their interpretation of this study, Maitlis and Christianson (2014: 76) suggested that the combined factors "buffered" organizational members "from leaders' efforts to trigger the construction of new meanings and purposes in the organization," which ultimately obstructed change efforts. Along similar lines, organizational members' sensemaking efforts were handicapped when a merger was cancelled in Mantere and colleagues' (2012) study. Rather than clinging to the organization's original identity as was the case in Nag et al.'s study, employees in this organization were not able to break away from the sensemaking they had done surrounding the merger. In essence, leaders' sensegiving efforts to facilitate the merger were so effective that when it was canceled members resisted the change reversal and the organization was left without a clear, consensual strategy.

These studies indicate that organizational change efforts do not always go as planned when guided by top managers. The process of change may essentially be derailed when organizational members disagree on a new direction for their organization—suggesting that regardless of hierarchical position, many members can influence organizational change. Furthermore, because change is usually largely implemented by lower-echelon members of an organization, leaders can lose their ability to influence change in the face of notable resistance from below, especially in the wake of a changing workforce that has greater voice and influence than previous generations of workers (due to a combination of internalities and externalities which we expound upon more later).

A Dynamic and Longitudinal Perspective on Organizational Change

Sensemaking scholars have largely recognized that sensemaking in general, and sensemaking with regard to organizational change in particular, is a dynamic and ongoing process (Hernes and Maitlis 2010; Louis 1980; Weick, 1995). In some cases, it may take many years for a change to be realized while in other cases change may be enacted over several months. Because organizational change is a dynamic process, rather than occurring at preconceived planned intervals or primarily at certain life stages, organizations are always evolving, and often in response to changing internal or external dynamics (Gioia et al. 2000; Van de Ven and Poole 1995). It is for these reasons that sensemaking scholars tend to engage in longitudinal studies of change efforts. Not only do they recognize that changes take time to emerge, but also that multiple pressures for change exist, and subsequent change initiatives may be introduced over a period of time. As one example, Ravasi and Shultz (2006) noted three separate threats to an organization's identity over a relatively short twenty-year period. Similarly, Mantere and colleagues (2012) reflected on an organization that had announced and then cancelled a planned merger, all within a two to three-year window. The implication is that organizations are always adapting and that to fully understand change efforts a longitudinal perspective is needed.

Strengths and Deficiencies of the Sensemaking Perspective on Organizational Change

Despite many strengths associated with a sensemaking perspective on organizational change, there are some deficiencies in this approach. In particular, we see a need for work on organizational change that more fully considers the role of new workforce dynamics and recent technological innovations. We touch on several strengths and weaknesses before turning to a discussion of future directions for change-related sensemaking research.

The four primary strengths of the sensemaking approach include its: 1) emphasis on both cognition and action; 2) accounting for multiple organizational members at differing organizational levels; 3) typically longitudinal perspective, and; 4) inclusion of multiple, interrelated concepts. Regarding cognition–action interrelationships, there is perhaps no approach that better captures how organizational members perceive and understand change initiatives and subsequently undergo cognitive shifts as a result of successful change efforts. And as sensemaking scholars make clear, this is of primary importance for understanding how planned changes get enacted (because it explicitly accounts for the reciprocal relationships between cognition and action). Secondly, this perspective considers varied member perspectives, addressing the responses of lower-level members to upper-level members' sensegiving efforts and vice versa. Change is most often viewed as a negotiated process that enables and takes into consideration multiple viewpoints. This perspective helps to explain when and why some changes are accepted and succeed, whereas others are rejected and fail. Third, change is viewed as dynamic and unfolding, often over extensive periods of time. Scholars studying organizational change from this perspective pay homage to this notion by engaging in fieldwork, often for several years, thereby capturing the ongoing dynamics of change. Finally, sensemaking studies often draw upon many concepts and perspectives, such as organizational identity and image, knowledge, and organizational practices and culture. This integrative approach better captures the complex dynamics of the change process.

On the other hand, there are several shortcomings in the current sensemaking approach to understanding organizational change. First, most of the change efforts that have been studied in the sensemaking literature are rooted mainly in external (environmental) dynamics. Economic recessions, market competition, and new legislation account for some of the environmental pressures driving organizational change. We see this (over)emphasis on external factors at the expense of internal influences as a deficiency and believe that more research is needed to better capture internal organizational change factors. Second, most of the work on organizational change that does address internal factors tends to emphasize formal organizational leaders (e.g., senior executives). This work recognizes that changes are typically initiated by upper echelon members, but tends to under-recognize the change-initiating potential, influence, and implementation role of lower-echelon members in organizational change—especially given the demographic shifts in the modern era. Future work needs to better account for bottom-up (i.e., upside-down, or more appropriately, *downside-up*) change, or change originating in the lower ranks of organizations. Lastly, most sensemaking studies tend to begin after a planned change has been announced (e.g., following the announcement of a merger or other corporate restructuring). This work has not adequately examined the processes leading up to the decision to instigate a planned change. Consequently, we know relatively little about how planned changes are actually formulated. In light of these shortcomings, we next discuss current workplace dynamics that have major implications for better understanding the organizational change process.

The New (Millennial) Workforce and The Shifting Workplace

The essence of how organizations and their members operate has been altered dramatically in this age of disruptive innovation, which is characterized by new and transformative forms of communication and technology (e.g., widespread access to the Internet, social media, smart phones, and the rise of artificial intelligence). These advances have led to bottom-up influences that are more important and more pervasive than ever before. Moreover, societal and/or generational changes have contributed to a workforce that harbors the potential for more—and more profound—change than in past generations. In this section we discuss these key workforce attributes and dynamics that are important to understanding coming organizational change processes. We orient our discussion around the changing *externalities* and *internalities* that have and will continue to contribute to making upside-down change more prevalent than in previous years. In doing so, we explain why and how today's lower-echelon employees are more likely to expand the scope of organizational sensemaking and sensegiving processes as they relate to strategic change initiation, formulation, and implementation (and, yes, our stated order of these processes is intentional—because the sensemaking perspective acknowledges that action often precedes cognition, so initiation frequently occurs before retrospective formulation processes occur).

Externalities Influencing Upside-Down Change

To appreciate the new context that actually encourages upside-down organizational change, we begin by noting that the amount of information to which everyone, including lower-level employees, has access has grown exponentially since the advent of the Internet. The creation of employer-based rankings like *Fortune*'s annual list of best places to work (created in 1998—see Levering and Moskowitz 1998), and the arrival of sites like Glassdoor and Indeed in the early 2000s (Polner 2020), have enabled employees to gather unprecedented amounts of data about their own organizations as well as their competitors, allowing for easy organizational comparisons (Widdicombe 2018). This includes, among other things, information on compensation, company policies, corporate social responsibility initiatives, etc. Front line employees may know more about how their company ranks among their competition than HR and strategic personnel did only a few years ago. This increased information consumption is augmented with even the lowest-level employees having the ability to contribute to the information pool. Organizational members now may provide information about the companies they work for on sites like Glassdoor, Indeed, Facebook, Instagram, Twitter, and many other social media platforms. The social media posting of relatively mundane information (e.g., someone having a disappointing workday) can reach thousands of people within a few hours—including those within the upper echelons of a given organization. Social media, a twenty-first-century innovation, provides a potentially influential public voice for *everyone* regardless of position in an organizational hierarchy. Studies suggest that 50% of employees post information about their employers on their social accounts like Facebook and Twitter, with 16% of this information being unflattering (Weber Shandwick, 2014). These figures reveal that employees frequently turn to social media as a means of venting their organization-based concerns. Regardless of intentions, these seemingly innocuous posts may serve to initiate the sensegiving and sensemaking processes underlying upside-down organizational change efforts, a point we discuss in more detail below.

The implication of this increased access to various communication channels is that employees, especially those in their organization's lower echelons, can use these media for their own personal sensemaking and, more importantly, as platforms for sensegiving. From sharing a Facebook post with a friend to actively organizing colleagues through Twitter, employees are afforded greater opportunities to engage in their organization's sensemaking and influence processes, albeit sometimes indirectly. As one recent example, Google employees organized and sent a mass email to their CEO demanding that Google terminate a contract with the Pentagon involving the use of artificial intelligence to analyze drone footage. They claimed they did not want Google being in the "business of war." The CEO responded by deciding *not* to extend the Pentagon contract for an additional year (Shane and Wakabayashi 2018).

Scholars have additionally begun noting a connection between the rise of social media and the increasing power of social movements, with the recognition that social media serves as a platform through which activists can connect, share information, and gain momentum for a cause (Lovejoy and Saxton 2012). The Occupy Wallstreet, Arab Spring, and Black Lives Matter movements all extensively relied on social media activism as a tool to organize diverse and geographically dispersed groups of people (Murthy 2018). Although these movements may have begun outside of any formal organization and consequently only indirectly influenced business, there is evidence that more recent socially-rooted movements have had greater influence. For example, both the NFL's "Take a Knee" movement (recognized as a part of the larger Black Lives Matter movement and which took place within the workplace setting), as well as the "Me Too" movement (which was aimed, in part, at addressing workplace sexual harassment policies) broadcasted a great deal of information and subsequently gained momentum through social media such as Twitter. Both movements, moreover, have direct implications for business. In the case of "Take a Knee," the NFL stepped up its corporate social responsibility efforts by agreeing to donate over $100 million to social justice causes (Dubin 2017). The "Me Too" movement, which was much more widespread and not confined to a single organization, led to many organizations, and even state legislatures, revising their sexual harassment policies (Gurchiek 2018).

We of course recognize that the public nature of the aforementioned cases and the subsequent inclusion of other organizational stakeholders (including consumers) undoubtedly influenced the resulting outcomes (a point we allude to later and which we see as being relevant to many similar cases of upside-down change). We suggest, however, that even in more contextually-bound cases, because of the rise of social media influence, organizations and their senior executives are now more likely to listen to their employees, engage with them in organizational sensemaking, and plan changes accordingly than in prior decades. A major reason is that today's workforce, increasingly composed of members of the Millennial generation (e.g., those born between 1981 and 1996), is less loyal to companies than previous generations. Today's employees rarely define career success in terms of workplace longevity. Younger people now change jobs, and often companies, in less than three years, thus prizing flexible career paths over long-term career stability (Carless and Wintle 2007; Smola and Sutton 2002). Surveys additionally indicate that Millennial-generation employees feel less connected and less committed to their organizations, despite feeling satisfied with their work (Stewart, Oliver, Cravens, and Oishi 2017). Together, these trends help to explain why turnover rates are much higher among Millennials than previous generations (Adkins 2016). These new workforce attitudes are a new fact of organizational life—and turnover has always been costly to organizations.

The implication is that companies that want to retain their employees, and therefore reduce turnover, benefit by being more attuned to their employees' needs and wants (Ferri-Reed 2014). In essence, a paradox exists whereby employers are working to retain employees who often do not wish to be retained. Nonetheless, organizations are indeed allocating time and resources to better understand what motivates this younger workforce, including how best to manage them, and ultimately how, if possible, to retain them (McGonagill and Pruyn 2010). This, in part, is why organizations are becoming more collaborative and changing to flatter organizational structures (Adler, Heckscher, and Prusak 2011), why companies are implementing more socially and environmentally responsible practices (Peretz 2017), and why many workplaces are adopting policies that are more work/life balance-friendly—all values which the Millennial generation holds and which we discuss more in our section on *internalities* (Hewlett et al. 2009). Citigroup, as one example, recently implemented new practices specifically designed to retain Millennials. These changes included providing employees the opportunity to take year-long leaves to pursue charitable work as well as working on micro-finance projects in developing countries (Rexrode 2016).

These externalities contribute to making upside-down organizational change more likely than in past decades. The increased information access that today's employees have in combination with the availability of technological influence platforms (i.e., social media) have resulted in lower-level employees both being more aware of and having greater ability to voice their organization-based concerns. The organizational trends of flatter hierarchies and increased rates of turnover have also contributed to making it more likely that higher-level executives will listen and respond to their employees' concerns. Flatter hierarchies put more decision-making power in the hands of more employees—making it more likely that issues will be heard. And, greater turnover has resulted in the paradoxical need to retain employees who wish not to be retained. Indeed, one way organizations are attempting to hold on to their Millennial-based workforce is by changing to become more aligned with employees' needs and wants.

Internalities Influencing Upside-Down Change

It is clear that the current workforce is advantaged with new technologies, communicative devices, and social media platforms that facilitate the expression of preferences, criticisms, suggestions, grievances, and even demands. Yet, this facilitation would be relatively meaningless if today's employees were not likely to initiate and advocate for change. Indeed, this new group of workers is increasingly likely to voice their opinions and advocate for or resist change than recent generations. For one, this younger cohort of workers tends to display more confidence in themselves than their senior counterparts did at a comparable age and organizational position (Myers and Sadaghiani 2010; Twenge 2009). Cole and colleagues suggest this heightened confidence is rooted in how Millennials were parented and taught at school (Cole et al. 2002). They were praised for every success (no matter how small) and were encouraged to talk to and befriend adults (e.g., the parents of friends). The combination of these experiences has resulted in a younger workforce that is not only more confident in themselves generally but also more comfortable in expressing their ideas to their seniors and demanding not only that they listen, but also take action. This has resulted in Millennials being more apt to question workplace norms, practices, policies, and expectations that upper-level organizational members have set in place (Curtis 2010).

Combined with this heightened confidence is a technological savviness that past generations lack. Being the first generation to grow up with the Internet, smartphones, social media, and other technologies, most Millennials are more knowledgeable about and comfortable using computer-based and/or digital technologies than their more senior counterparts (Gorman et al. 2004). This contributes to a tendency for Millennials to be early adopters of new technologies and also advocates for the adoption of new technological advancements within the workplace (Tapscott 1998). As one source suggested: "In effect, Millennials could become resident experts concerning CITs [communication and information technologies], offering their more senior coworkers opinions about what works, what can work, and how the organization can utilize CITs to improve operations and marketing" (Myers and Sadaghiani 2010: 232; see also Gorman et al. 2004).

This increasing desire to voice one's opinion is coupled with the notion that younger generations expect more from their workplaces than previous generations. Indeed, recent research suggests that younger employees are not merely concerned with the personal benefits they receive from their organizations, but increasingly want their organizations to act as responsible corporate citizens that are aligned with the needs of consumers and society at large (Hewlett et al. 2009). In fact, whereas workers from the "baby boomer" generation have/had a preference for higher pay and personal benefits, 75% of surveyed Millennials state they would rather take a pay cut in order to work for a company that prioritizes socially responsible practices (Cone Communications 2016). In addition to valuing companies that contribute to societal welfare, the Millennial generation also desires greater work–life balance which enables them to pursue their other interests and causes outside of work (Deloitte 2016). Deloitte represents one example of a company responding to their employees' changing preferences. In particular, the company changed their policies on flexible work schedules as well as the amount of time their travelling consultants spend away from home (Babcock and Laschever 2003).

This shift in values has led to what we label as "alignment inversion." More specifically, previous generations of workers, who sought workplace stability, tended to align themselves with their organizations and perceptions of their organizations' values (Kristof-Brown, Zimmerman, and Johnson 2005). The newer generation of workers, however, is changing the game and more often seeks their organizations to become more aligned with who they are as individuals (which often is entangled with societal interests). Should this alignment inversion not be achieved, Millennials are not afraid to leave their organizations and pursue opportunities that better align with their own identities and values. This desired alignment inversion directly influences the organizational change process—that is, organizations must respond if employee retention is important to them.

In sum, in part because of key externalities—such as increased information access, technological influence platforms, and organizational trends (i.e., flatter hierarchies and increased turnover)—as well as internalities—such as perceived increased voice, new values (i.e., for societal welfare), and alignment inversion by the Millennial workforce—this new generation is different—and different in a way that not only affects sensemaking processes but, more importantly, sensegiving and influence processes they can use to effect organizational change. Figure 4.2 depicts a model of how these new technologies and social dynamics can generate upside-down organizational change.

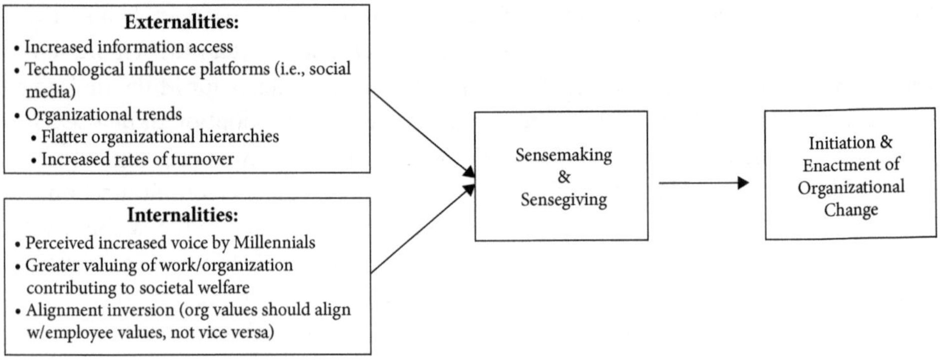

FIGURE 4.2 A Model of "Upside-Down" Organizational Change

To be sure, many of the changes that organizations have embraced in recent years and will continue to adopt in the future are rooted in the widespread usage of new technologies—a dynamic that has been with us for centuries. Yet, the recent shifts in demographics and the nature of widely available technologies could elide the deep-seated alteration in how organizational change will occur in the future. Business might be continuing to innovate by changing their product-base to one that is more electronic-focused, to engaging in online retail, and to increasingly rely on machine and digital technologies for production. But will business organizations change quickly enough to keep up with the consequences of the Millennial revolution? And what will be the implications for organizational change wrought by Millennials? The Millennial generation is the most advantaged in understanding and implementing these changes regardless of the organization-centered impetuses behind organizational changes (e.g., reducing costs, expanding markets). We now turn to a real-world example of upside-down organizational change to illustrate the dynamics and process of these change efforts from a sensemaking/sensegiving perspective.

The NFL's "Take a Knee" Movement: An Illustrative Case

> *Colin Kaepernick stood tall while sitting down. In fact, what he did in benching himself for the national anthem on Friday night was the hardest thing he could possibly do.... He made his statement loudly and clearly.* – Ian O'Connor, ESPN Columnist, August 27, 2016

Colin Kaepernick, a quarterback for the National Football League's (NFL) San Francisco 49ers, was troubled by racial inequality. He was troubled by police officers shooting, and getting away with shooting, Black youth. He was troubled by societal injustices. Kaepernick took a stand. He expressed his stance by sitting (and then later kneeling) during the playing of the National Anthem—a pregame tradition in the NFL since 2011—before a preseason game in late August of 2016. Kaepernick later explained his position, "I'm not going to stand up to show pride in a flag for a country that oppresses black people and people of color." Other like-minded players soon joined Kaepernick's cause. Kaepernick's grievance was not directed at the NFL (as he articulated in an interview) despite him expressing his position at his place of work. To be clear, there was no specific *organizational* complaint the quarterback was targeting. Furthermore, there was not a feature of the organization and/or its identity that Kaepernick wanted changed. Kaepernick and his small group of followers were targeting society itself with their individual, non-work identity(ies) informing their behavior. Yet, regardless of the intended audience, the implications for the organization (the NFL) were significant.

Many bottom-up organizational changes begin in this manner.[1] Unlike top-down changes which are led by organizational leaders who are primed to think and conceive of events, situations, and trends in terms of who or what their organization is (i.e., its identity) (Maitlis and Christianson 2014), upside-down changes are led by employees who are often primed to think in terms of who they are (i.e., individual identity). A scanning of Colin Kaepernick's press statements, interviews, and Twitter posts reflects that rather than the NFL (the focal organization) guiding Kaepernick's acts of activism, the quarterback was informed by a combination of his individual identities and characteristics including personal values and ethics (i.e., personal identity), the desire to represent those individuals lacking a voice (i.e., relational identity), membership in an underserved racial group (i.e., social identity), and membership in a society with perceived social ills (i.e., collective identity) (see Brickson 2000).

Upside-Down Sensemaking and Sensegiving in Action

People are complex and multifaceted beings who are and always have been continually informed by their various identities (Oyserman et al. 2012). What is new with the Millennial generation, who comprise mainly the lower echelons of the current workforce, is that they tend to bring more of their multifaced selves into the workplace (Gianniris 2018) and organizations are changing in response (e.g., Babcock and Laschever 2003; Hewlett et al. 2009). Rather than employees attempting to align more with their organizations, as in the past, organizations are beginning to align more with their employees. Now, and increasingly in the future, this realignment is (and will be) primarily and, sometimes intentionally, driven by (often lower-level) employees. As evidenced by the cases of organization-targeted employee activism, such as that which occurred within the employee-driven cross-company social movement that yielded

[1] As Margaret Mead so pithily put it: "Never doubt that a small group of thoughtful, committed citizens can change the world; indeed, it's the only thing that ever has."

greater same-sex benefits for employees and their partners (e.g., Bidwell et al. 2013), such social movements are giving impetus to many organizational change efforts. At other times, although the initial spark for change may be prompted by an employee, there are other stakeholders who might play a more active role in driving the sensemaking and sensegiving efforts underlying organizational change.

Kaepernick's act of sitting during the National Anthem went viral as it was publicly broadcast on August 26, 2016. Curiously, this was not the first time the 49ers quarterback had protested. He had actually sat the prior two weeks although it had gone unnoticed. Had it not gone viral, what would have happened? Would Kaepernick have continued his silent protest? Would the 49ers and/or the NFL have responded in any way? What occurred, however, was that the media drove a story about social activism within the NFL (giving sense to employee actions). Dozens more NFL players across various teams joined what became known as the "Take a Knee" movement throughout the next several NFL seasons (making sense of their role in the movement). Furthermore, the continued discussions between media representatives, fans, consumers, players, pundits, politicians, team owners, and anyone with a stake in the NFL or the larger Black Lives Matter movement transformed this event from a societally rooted personal issue to an organizational issue.

The NFL was confronted with two major questions, both of which had implications for the organization's identity as well as for its employees. First, should such social activism be tolerated in light of a fan-base and wider country being divided on the issue? Second, should the NFL address the root issues of their employees' cause and, if so, how? Perhaps two ESPN commentators best summarized the situation facing the NFL when they asked:

> What is the NFL's identity? Is it a strict entertainment company that Jones [owner of the Dallas Cowboys] and others envision, controlling the behavior of its players in service of its financial bottom line? Or should it attempt to transform itself into a more socially conscious league that would strive, through the forging of a rare and fragile owners-players partnership in this moment, to use its mammoth platform to try to change society for the good, even if the cost of that process, slow and complicated, would likely be measured in short-term declining popularity and lower revenues?
>
> Seth Wickersham and Don Van Natta Jr., ESPN, 10/27/17

It is perhaps too soon to tell whether the identity of the NFL has or will change. The NFL's actions, to date, provide mixed support. On the one hand, the NFL implemented a rule (which they later suspended) that directed NFL players not to protest during the anthem (yet allowed players who did not wish to stand during the anthem to remain in their locker room until the anthem was over—which was construed by many observers as an alternative mode of protest). Additionally, Colin Kaepernick continues to remain without an NFL job, which many attribute to his activism rather than his playing ability, and for which the ex-quarterback brought a conspiracy case against the NFL. On the other hand, the NFL has agreed to donate $100 million to social justice causes of the players' choosing over the next ten years. Many of these causes are additionally showcased on individual teams' websites, giving the impression that the NFL is taking social justice seriously. If this does not result in some form of league-wide identity change, it nonetheless would represent the adoption of an organizational CSR policy in response to employee desires.

The NFL case sheds light on some of the important underlying dynamics of upside-down organizational change. To begin, bottom-up changes are often influenced and initiated by lower-level employees' personal identities and values (i.e., internalities), though they may not always be planned—a point we return to later. Unlike top organizational leaders who think and respond on the basis of their organization's interests, lower-level employees (because of the advent of social media) have much more access to information—especially the kind of information that can fuel social movements, which grants them much more (sensegiving) influence on organizational thought and action (and is derived, in part, through key externalities). Consequently, they can now introduce issues that are removed from the organization's current strategy and/or identity and which are rooted in their own personal welfare and/or the welfare of other networks to which they belong. This explains why new employee practices, policies, and/or benefits, as well as new corporate social responsibility (CSR) practices and policies, are likely to be the most prevalent changes that are introduced by an organization's lower echelons.

The NFL case additionally highlights the influence of other stakeholders in bottom-up change processes. The sensemaking and sensegiving process involved in this kind of upside-down change is likely to be more extensive and recursive than the processes underlying top-down change because there are often other stakeholders involved. Why? For one thing, lower-level employees are more likely to use social media channels to promote their causes. With largely unfettered access to information, those in the media, consumers, and other stakeholders may become involved in an employee-initiated change effort, each party making and giving sense to each other. Additionally, the more complicated nature of upside-down changes (i.e., because of their reciprocality/recursiveness involving not only top-down/bottom-up, but also internal–external interactions) makes it more likely that a broader group of (loosely defined) organizational stakeholders will be interested in voicing their opinions. Whereas shareholders, for example, may find a proposed organizational merger to be significant, those in the broader public might find greater importance in issues of LGBTQ worker rights, proposed sexual harassment policies, etc.—even including cases where employees champion police brutality reform (like the Take a Knee protests). The involvement of a multitude of organizational stakeholders complicates the sensemaking/sensegiving processes involved in upside-down organizational change, thus increasing the likelihood that the process will be more involved than the related processes linked to top-down-only change efforts.

Furthermore, when lower-echelon issues do rise to the top of the organization, leaders must determine how these focal issues fit with the organization. This often is difficult given that issues initiated by lower organizational members are not always conceived of in organizational terms. Nevertheless, because of changing workplaces and the need to retain employees, combined with the increasing external stakeholder influences that are fueled by heightened information access, organizations are more likely to feel the pressure to respond to their employees today and in future years than they have in the past. This phenomenon therefore leads to the implementation of changes that are not necessarily aligned with the organization's identity but rather with employees' non-work identities. Consequently, organizations will increasingly need to adapt to align with the needs and wants of their employees. This signals a shift from the past wherein employees tended to try to align themselves, whether authentically or not, with their organizations (Kristof-Brown et al. 2005)—thus, representing an alignment inversion.

Future Directions (and Challenges) for Studying Upside-Down Organizational Change

The NFL case provides a glimpse of upside-down organizational change from a sensemaking perspective. To be sure, more work is needed in this area to derive a richer understanding of the dynamics that contribute to and/or influence these change efforts. We have already learned, however, that the types of change, the impetus for change, and the processes involved in change are likely to be distinct from more traditional top-down organizational change efforts. Moreover, the outcomes are also likely to be different. Change driven from the bottom-up involves organizations becoming aligned with who their employees are and/or what employees want their organizations to be, rather than change that is either aligned with the organization or with external pressures. The implications are likely to be far-reaching and thus of interest and consequence to future scholarship on organizational change.

In particular, future research may benefit from studying planned versus unplanned upside-down change efforts. For example, in the NFL case, players were not protesting as a means of advocating for organization-level change but rather for societal-level change. However, the NFL ultimately responded by agreeing to donate a significant sum to players' causes. From the perspective of the protesting employees, the *organizational*-level change was thus not planned, but was still brought about. In other cases, employees may bring their values and identities into the workplace without intending to change the organization, but over time the organization nonetheless changes and becomes more aligned with these same employees' values and identities. Sensemaking scholars would therefore benefit by examining the potentially distinct processes underlying planned and unplanned bottom-up change, and the consequences it may have for our model of upside-down organizational change.

Future scholarship should also consider the multiple, divergent, hybrid, and potentially opposing views involved in the bottom-up organizational change process. Or, in other words, sensemaking scholars might need to focus not only on generating more views, but also on evaluating and criticizing alternative views in collective settings. With the significant societal and generational trends influencing the key externalities and internalities underlying the process of upside-down organizational change (including greater access to information and communication channels, changing values, and voicing behaviors, etc.), there are likely to be far more stakeholders involved in upside-down change than in the past and in comparison to top-down change efforts. More voices involved ultimately complicates the sensemaking process. To disentangle these multiple and competing perspectives, scholars could benefit from research that is both inductive and longitudinal to better understand who is granted a voice, who is being listened to, how interactions unfold, as well as how potential power asymmetries come into play.

With regard to this latter point, we sense that the use of top-down power is somewhat mitigated by the communication channels employees now have access to. Relatively powerless employees can still initiate organizational changes if they are able to capture the (positive) attention of other stakeholders and/or the media—even if the organization's leadership is not supportive of the initiated change. There are likely important boundary conditions influencing the effectiveness or success of bottom-up change, however, including: 1) lower-level employees having higher societal status; 2) top managers being personally aligned with the underlying issues, and; 3) the issue itself being trendy or having significant societal ramifications such that the media and/or external agents and arbiters are more likely to get involved. These are all factors that may be examined through future research (in addition to others that may emerge through inductive work).

Finally, there appear to be important intersections between the sensemaking perspective of bottom-up organizational change and other change theories and processes. For example, as we allude to in this chapter, and as articulated in two other chapters in this handbook (see Chapters 9 and 10) social movements are becoming increasingly relevant to our understanding of bottom-up organizational change. For example, Davis and Kim explicitly analyze the connections between social movements and organizational change—topics they have aptly recognized as being treated separately until recent years (Chapter 9). In particular, they examine the role that activists (or social intrapreneurs) play in influencing four distinct types of organizational change and innovation (i.e., innovations related to products, practices, people, and the public). Following this theme of social movements, Prichard and Creed look at the emergence of activists in the organization and, consequently, how these activists initiate or engage in social movements that ultimately bring about organizational change (Chapter 10). Not only do we see sensemaking and sensegiving as being central to the influence processes these authors describe, but we believe these chapters also offer important insights for future work on the sensemaking perspective of bottom-up organizational change (change that may or may not be considered as stemming from social movements).

Furthermore, we think Hargrave's chapter and analysis on the dialectical and paradoxical processes of change (Chapter 7) as well as Ravasi and Shultz's work on organizational culture change (Chapter 5)—with their focus on the role of organizational identity, time, and history—offer important insights for the future study of upside-down change. In particular, both chapters may serve as useful tools for unpacking the potential tensions arising from the multiple stakeholders involved in the sensemaking processes underlying these change efforts. Employees at different levels of the organizational hierarchy as well as outside stakeholders may hold competing views of who or what their organization should be and/or the past histories they use to interpret current organizational realities—factors ultimately underlying the sensemaking processes leading to bottom-up organizational change. In conjunction, we believe further examination of these overlaps and/or collaboration among scholars in these distinct-but-related domains would be particularly fruitful for understanding future upside-down organizational changes.

Conclusion

Societal shifts are often rooted in younger generations. Younger generations are inclined to create a break from the past and adopt new ways of seeing and being. Past younger generations relied on physical forms of protest and street activism. Newer generations rely on social media and other channels of communication for self-expression, and these new technologies have changed the game in ways that differ from previous technological innovations. The new workforce is also changing the way business is conducted. They demand that organizations step up their social responsibility, incorporate progressive environmental and labor policies into their corporate strategies, and ultimately prompt big business to join them in producing and enacting societal change.

Past portrayals cast top-down organizational change as well planned and more transformative and revolutionary, whereas bottom-up change has been treated as more incremental and evolutionary. It is time to revise this portrayal and ask "more revolutionary for whom?" Implementing a merger or corporate restructuring undoubtedly has more direct and significant repercussions for the organization itself than adopting same-sex partner benefits that may directly benefit fewer employees. Yet, such corporate restructuring likely has minimal repercussions for society at large, whereas industry-wide adoption of same-sex partner benefits would have widespread collective impact. If Colvin (2007) is correct, that business is no longer in the business of solving customers' problems but is now in the business of solving the world's problems, then we scholars need to account for our portrayals of organizational changes that accompany this new orientation. Accounting for upside-down organizational change is aimed at doing just that.

We do not argue that externally rooted, top-down organizational changes are a phenomenon of the past and/or are less common than upside-down changes. Yet, we have entered an era in which lower-level employees are not only demanding that their voices be heard, but now have mastered the tools (social media) and thus the means of sensegiving and influence to make their voiced concerns come to pass. This new influence has significant implications for more traditional processes of organizational sensemaking, sensegiving, and change because lower-level employees are becoming notable agents of change. It is now necessary that sensemaking scholars take note of this Millennial-based trend, and do research that evolves with and responds to the changing workplace dynamics that are not only affecting the way business is conducted, but are contributing to changing the world in which we live.

References

Adkins, A. (2016), 'Millennials: The Job-Hopping Generation', Gallup, https://www.gallup.com/workplace/236474/millennials-job-hopping-generation.aspx/, accessed 8 August 2020.

Adler, P., Heckscher, C., and Prusak, L. (2011, July–August), 'Building a Collaborative Enterprise', *Harvard Business Review*, 95–101.

Ancona, D. (2011), 'Sensemaking: Framing and Acting in the Unknown', in S. Snook, N. Nohria, and R. Khurana, eds., *The Handbook for Teaching Leadership* (Thousand Oaks, CA: Sage Publications) 3–19.

Babcock, L., and Laschever, S. (2003). *Women Don't Ask: Negotiation and the Gender Divide.* Princeton, NJ: Princeton University Press.

Balogun, J. (2003), 'From Blaming the Middle to Harnessing its Potential: Creating Change Intermediaries', *British Journal of Management*, 14/1, 69–83.

Balogun, J., and Johnson, G. (2004), Organizational Restructuring and Middle Manager Sensemaking', *Academy of Management Journal*, 47/4, 523–49.

Balogun, J., and Johnson, G. (2005), 'From Intended Strategies to Unintended Outcomes: The Impact of Change Recipient Sensemaking', *Organization Studies*, 26/11, 1573–601.

Barr, P. S. (1998), Adapting to Unfamiliar Environmental Events: A Look at the Evolution of Interpretation and its Role in Strategic Change', *Organization Science*, 9/6, 644–69.

Bartunek, J. M. (1984), 'Changing Interpretive Schemes and Organizational Restructuring: The Example of a Religious Order', *Administrative Science Quarterly*, 29/3, 355–72.

Berger, P. L., and Luckmann, T. (1967). *The Social Construction of Reality: A Treatise in the Sociology of Knowledge.* Garden City, NY: Doubleday

Bidwell, M., Briscoe, F., Fernandez-Mateo, I., and Sterling, A. (2013), 'The Employment Relationship and Inequality: How and Why Changes in Employment Practices are Reshaping Rewards in Organizations', *Academy of Management Annals*, 7, 61–121.

Brickson, S. (2000), 'The Impact of Identity Orientation on Individual and Organizational Outcomes in Demographically Diverse Settings', *Academy of Management Review*, 25, 82–101.

Carless, S. A., and Wintle, J. (2007), Applicant Attraction: The Role of Recruiter Function, Work-Life Balance Policies and Career Salience', *International Journal of Selection and Assessment*, 15, 394–404.

Cole, G., Smith, R., and Lucas, L. (2002), 'The Debut of Generation Y in the American Workforce', *Journal of Business Administration Online*, 1/2,

Cone Communications. (2016), 'Three-Quarters of Millennials Would Take a Pay Cut to Work for a Socially Responsible Company, According to the Research from Cone Communications', http://www.conecomm.com/news-blog/2016-cone-communications-millennial-employee-engagement-study-press-release. Accessed 11 October 2020.

Colvin, G. (2007), 'The 500 Gets Religion: Why Big Companies are in the Business of Solving the World's Woes', Fortune, Cone Communications, Millennial Employee Engagement Study, https://static1.squarespace.com/static/56b4a7472b8dde3df5b7013f/t/5819e8b303596e3016ca0d9c/1478092981243/2016+Cone+Communications+Millennial+Employee+Engagement+Study_Press+Release+and+Fact+Sheet.pdf/, accessed 9 August 2020.

Corley, K. G., and Gioia, D. A. (2004), Identity Ambiguity and Change in the Wake of a Corporate Spin-Off', *Administrative Science Quarterly*, 49/2, 173–208.

Curtis, G. (2010, 3 September), 'Give your Workplace a Millennial Makeover: Learning to Think Like Your New Generation of Colleagues', CIO, www.cio.co.uk/article/3238071/give-your-workplacea-millennial-makeover/, accessed 9 August 2020.

Daft, R. L., and Weick, K. E. (1984), 'Toward a Model of Organizations as Interpretation Systems', *Academy of Management Review*, 9/2, 284–95.

Davis, G. F., and Kim, E. W. (2021), 'Social Movements and Organizational Change', in M. S. Poole and A. H. Van de Ven, eds., *The Oxford Handbook of Organizational Change and Innovation* (2nd edition) (Oxford: Oxford University Press),

Dawson P. and Buchanan, D. (2005), 'The Way It Really Happened: Competing Narratives in the Political Process of Technological Change. *Human Relations*, 58/7, 845–65.

Deloitte. (2016), 'The 2016 Deloitte Millennial Survey: Winning Over the Next Generation of Leaders', https://www2.deloitte.com/content/dam/Deloitte/global/Documents/About-Deloitte/gx-millenial-survey-2016-exec-summary.pdf/, accessed 9 August 2020).

Denis, J.-L., Langley, A., and Cazale, L. (1996), 'Leadership and Strategic Change under Ambiguity', *Organization Studies*, 17/4, 673–99.

Dubin, J. (2017), 'Report: Players Divided over NFL's $100 Million Social Justice Proposal: The Group of Players Negotiating with the League Has Been Fractured by Disagreements', CBS Sports, https://www.cbssports.com/nfl/news/report-players-divided-over-nfls-100-million-social-justice-proposal/, (accessed 9 August 2020).

Dunford, R., and Jones, D. (2000), 'Narrative in Strategic Change', *Human Relations*, 53/9, 1207–26.

Dutton, J. E., and Dukerich, J. M. (1991), 'Keeping an Eye on the Mirror: Image and Identity in Organizational Adaptation', *Academy of Management Journal*, 34/3, 517–54.

Elsbach, K. D., and Kramer, R. M. (1996), 'Members' Responses to Organizational Identity Threats: Encountering and Countering the Business Week Rankings', *Administrative Science Quarterly*, 41/3, 442–76.

Ferri-Reed, J. (2014), 'Are Millennial Employees Changing How Managers Manage? Leading a Multi-Generational Workforce: Learning to Leverage the Uniqueness of Every Age Group', *The Journal for Quality and Participation*, 37/2, 15–19.

Fiss, P. C., and Zajac, E. J. (2006), 'The Symbolic Management of Strategic Change: Sensegiving via Framing and Decoupling', *The Academy of Management Journal*, 49/6, 1173–93.

Gephart, R. P., Topal, C., and Zhang, Z. (2010), 'Future-Oriented Sensemaking: Temporalities and Institutional Legitimation', in T. Hernes and S. Maitlis, eds., *Process, Sensemaking, and Organizing* (Oxford: Oxford University Press), 275–312.

Gianniris, D. (2018), 'The Millennial Arrival and the Evolution of the Modern Workplace', Forbes, https://www.forbes.com/sites/forbestechcouncil/2018/01/25/the-millennial-arrival-and-the-evolution-of-the-modern-workplace/#67723d175a73/, accessed 9 August 9 2020.

Gioia, D. A. (1986), 'Symbols, Scripts, and Sensemaking: Creating Meaning in the Organizational Experience', in H. P. Sims, Jr., and D. A. Gioia, eds., *The Thinking Organization* (San Francisco: Jossey-Bass), 49–74.

Gioia, D. A., and Chittipeddi, K. (1991), 'Sensemaking and Sensegiving in Strategic Change Initiation, *Strategic Management Journal*, 12/6, 433–48.

Gioia, D. A., and Thomas, J. B. (1996), 'Institutional Identity, Image, and Issue Interpretation Sensemaking during Strategic Change in Academia', *Administrative Science Quarterly*, 41/3, 370–403.

Gioia, D. A., Thomas, J. B., Clark, S. M., and Chittipeddi, K. (1994), 'Symbolism and Strategic Change in Academia: The Dynamics of Sensemaking and Influence', *Organization Science*, 5/3, 363–83.

Gioia, D. A., Schultz, M., and Corley, K. G. (2000), 'Organizational Identity, Image, and Adaptive Instability', *Academy of Management Review*, 25/1, 63–81.

Gorman, P., Nelson, T., and Glassman, A. (2004), 'The Millennial Generation: A Strategic Opportunity', *Organizational Analysis*, 12, 255–0.

Gurchiek, K. (2018), 'One Year After #MeToo and "Weinstein Effect": What's Changed?' *Society for Human Resource Management*, shrm.org/resourcesandtools/hr-topics/employee-relations/pages/sexual-harassment-workplace-weinstein-effect.aspx.

Hargrave, T. J. (2021), 'The Paradox Perspective and the Dialectics of Contradictions Research', in M. S. Poole and A. H. Van de Ven, eds., *The Oxford Handbook of Organizational Change and Innovation* (2nd edn) (Oxford: Oxford University Press),

Hernes, T., and Maitlis, S. (Eds.). (2010). *Process, Sensemaking, and Organizing*. Oxford: Oxford University Press.

Hewlett, S., Sherbin, L., and Sumberg, K. (2009), How Gen Y and Boomers Will Reshape Your Agenda', *Harvard Business Review*, 87/7–8), 71–6.

Hill, R. C., and Levenhagen, M. (1995), 'Metaphors and Mental Models: Sensemaking and Sensegiving in Innovative and Entrepreneurial Activities', *Journal of Management*, 21/6, 1057–74

Howard-Grenville, J., Metzger, M. L., and Meyer, A. D. (2013), 'Rekindling the Flame: Processes of Identity Resurrection', *Academy of Management Journal*, 56/1, 113–36.

Isabella, L. A. (1990), 'Evolving Interpretations as a Change Unfolds: How Managers Construe Key Organizational Events', *Academy of Management Journal*, 33/1, 7–41.

Kaplan, A. M., and Haenlein, M. (2010), 'Users of the World, Unite! The Challenges and Opportunities of Social Media', *Business Horizons*, 53, 59–68.

Kristof-Brown, A. L., Zimmerman, R. D., and Johnson, E. C. (2005), 'Consequences of Individuals' Fit at Work: A Meta-Analysis of Person-Job, Person-Organization, Person-Group, and Person-Supervisor Fit', *Personnel Psychology*, 58/2, 281–342.

Labianca, G., Gray, B., and Brass, D. J. (2000), 'A Grounded Model of Organizational Schema Change during Empowerment', *Organization Science*, 11/2, 235–57.

Levering, R., and Moskowitz, M. (1998), 'The 100 Best Companies To Work For in America", Fortune, archive.fortune.com/magazines/fortune/fortune_archive/1998/01/12/236444/index.htm, accessed 9 August 2020.

Louis, M. R. (1980), Surprise and Sensemaking: What Newcomers Experience in Entering Unfamiliar Settings'. *Administrative Science Quarterly*, 25/2, 226–51.

Lovejoy, K., and Saxton, G. D. (2012), Information, Community, and Action: How Nonprofit Organizations use Social Media', *Journal of Computer-Mediated Communication*, 17, 337–53.

Luscher, L. S., and Lewis, M. W. (2008), 'Organizational Change and Managerial Sensemaking: Working through Paradox', *Academy of Management Journal*, 51/2, 221–40.

Maitlis, S. (2005), 'The Social Processes of Organizational Sensemaking', *Academy of Management Journal*, 48, 21–49.

Maitlis, S., and Christianson, M. (2014), 'Sensemaking in Organizations: Taking Stock and Moving Forward', *Academy of Management Annals*, 8/1, 57–125.
Maitlis, S., and Lawrence, T. B. (2007), 'Triggers and Enablers of Sensegiving in Organizations', *Academy of Management Journal*, 50/1, 57–84.
Mantere, S., Schildt, H. A., and Sillince, J. A. A. (2012), 'Reversal of Strategic Change', *Academy of Management Journal*, 55/1, 172–96.
McGonagill, G., and Pruyn, P. W. (2010). 'Leadership Development in the U.S: Principles and Patterns of Best Practice', *Bertelsmann Stiftung Leadership Series*, Berlin, Germany: S. Vopel.
Meyer, A., Frost, P. J., and Weick, K. E. (1998), 'The Organization Science Jazz Festival: Improvisation as a Metaphor for Organizing', *Organization Science*, 9/5. 540–2.
Murthy, D. (2018, Jan.–Mar.), 'Introduction to Social Media, Activism, and Organizations', *Social Media + Society*, 1–4.
Myers, K. M., and Sadaghiani, K. (2010), 'Millennials in the Workplace: A Communication Perspective on Millennials' Organizational Relationships and Performance', *Journal of Business Psychology*, 25, 225–38.
Nag, R., Corley, K. G., and Gioia, D. A. (2007), 'The Intersection of Organizational Identity, Knowledge, and Practice: Attempting Strategic Change via Knowledge Grafting', *Academy of Management Journal*, 50/4, 821–47.
Oyserman, D., Elmore, K., and Smith, G. (2012). 'Self, Self-Concept, and Identity', in M. Leary and J. Tangney, eds., *Handbook of Self and Identity* (New York, NY: Guilford), 69–104.
Peretz, M. (2017), 'Want to Engage Millennials? Try Corporate Social Responsibility', Forbes. https://www.forbes.com/sites/marissaperetz/2017/09/27/want-to-engage-millennials-try-corporate-social-responsibility/#7daf59696e4e/, accessed 9 August 2020.
Polner, E. (2020), 'The 10 Best Job Search Websites of 2020', The Balance Careers. http://www.thebalancecareers.com/top-best-job-websites-2064080, accessed 11 October 2020.
Pratt, M. G. (2000), 'The Good, the Bad, and the Ambivalent: Managing Identification among Amway Distributors', *Administrative Science Quarterly*, 45/3, 456–93.
Prichard, C. and Creed, D. (2021), 'Agency in Social Movements as Sources of Change', in M. S. Poole and A. H. Van de Ven, eds., *The Oxford Handbook of Organizational Change and Innovation* (2nd edn) (Oxford: Oxford University Press),
Ravasi, D., and Schultz, M. (2006), 'Responding to Organizational Identity Threats: Exploring the Role of Organizational Culture', *Academy of Management Journal*, 49/3, 433–58.
Ravasi, D. and Schultz, M. (2021), 'Organizational Identity and Culture Change', in M. S. Poole and A. H. Van de Ven eds., *The Oxford Handbook of Organizational Change and Innovation* (2nd edn) (Oxford: Oxford University Press),
Rexrode, C. (2016), 'Citigroup to Millennial Bankers: Take a Year off', *The Wall Street Journal*. wsj.com/articles/to-entice-millennial-bankers-citigroup-serves-up-new-perk-take-a-year-off-1458120603.
Rouleau, L. (2005), 'Micro-Practices of Strategic Sensemaking and Sensegiving: How Middle Managers Interpret and Sell Change Every Day', *Journal of Management Studies*, 42/7, 1413–41.
Shane, S., and Wakabayashi, D. (2018), '"The business of war": Google Employees Protest Work for the Pentagon', *The New York Times*. nytimes.com/ 2018/04/04/technology/google-letter-ceo-pentagon-project.html.
Smircich, L., and Morgan, G. (1982), Leadership: The Management of Meaning', *Journal of Applied Behavioral Science*, 18/3, 257–73.

Smola, K. W., and Sutton, C. D. (2002), Generational Differences: Revisiting Generational Work Values for the New Millennium', *Journal of Organizational Behavior*, 23, 363–82.

Sonenshein, S. (2006), Crafting Social Issues at Work', *Academy of Management Journal*, 49/6, 1158–72.

Sonenshein, S. (2010), 'We're Changing Or Are We? Untangling the Role of Progressive, Regressive, and Stability Narratives during Strategic Change Implementation', *Academy of Management Journal*, 53/3, 477–512.

Starbuck, W. H., and Milliken, F. J. (1988), Executives' Perceptual Filters: What They Notice and How They Make Sense', in D. C. Hambrick, ed., *The Executive Effect: Concepts and Methods for Studying Top Managers* (Greenwich, CT: JAI Press), 35–65.

Stewart, J. S., Oliver, E. G., Cravens, K. S., and Oishi, S. (2017), 'Managing Millennials: Embracing Generational Differences', *Business Horizons*, 60, 45–54.

Tapscott, D. (1998). *Growing up Digital: The Rise of the Net Generation*. New York: McGraw- Hill.

Thomas, J. B., Clark, S. M., and Gioia, D. A. (1993), Strategic Sensemaking and Organizational Performance: Linkages among Scanning, Interpretation, Action, and Outcomes', *Academy of Management Journal*, 36/2, 239–70.

Tripsas, M. (2009), 'Technology, Identity, and Inertia through the Lens of "The Digital Photography Company"', *Organization Science*, 20/2, 441–60.

Twenge, J. M. (2009), Change over Time in Obedience: The Jury's Still Out, but It Might Be Decreasing', *American Psychologist*, 64, 28–31.

Van de Ven, A. H., and Poole, M. S. (1995), 'Explaining Development and Change in Organizations', *Academy of Management Review*, 20/3, 510–40.

Walsh, I. J., and Bartunek, J. M. (2011), 'Cheating the Fates: Organizational Foundings in the Wake of Demise', *Academy of Management Journal*, 54/5, 1017–44.

Weber Shandwick (2014), 'Employee Activists Spark a New Social Movement in the Digital Age, According to Groundbreaking Global Study from Weber Shandwick', Weber Shandwick, https://www.webershandwick.com/news/employee-activists-spark-a-new-social-movement-in-the-digital-age/, accessed 9 August 2020.

Weick, K. E. (1979). *The Social Psychology of Organizing* (2nd ed.). New York: McGrawHill.

Weick, K. E. (1988), 'Enacted Sensemaking in Crisis Situations', *Journal of Management Studies*, 25/4, 305–17.

Weick, K. E. (1995). *Sensemaking in Organizations*. Thousand Oaks, CA: Sage Publications.

Widdicombe, L. (2018), 'Improving Workplace Culture, One Review at a Time: With its Emphasis on Transparency, the Jobs Site Glassdoor Aims To Upend Corporate Power Dynamics', The New Yorker (Annals of Human Resources, https://www.newyorker.com/magazine/2018/01/22/improving-workplace-culture-one-review-at-a-time/, accessed 9 August 2020.

Yu, J., Engleman, R. M., and Van de Ven, A. H. (2005), 'The Integration Journey: An Attention-Based View of the Merger and Acquisition Integration Process', *Organization Studies*, 26/10, 1501–28.

CHAPTER 5

ORGANIZATIONAL IDENTITY AND CULTURE CHANGE

DAVIDE RAVASI AND MAJKEN SCHULTZ

INTRODUCTION

IN the first edition of this handbook, Mary Jo Hatch's chapter examined what management scholars can learn from theories of culture change from anthropology and cultural sociology (Hatch 2004). She reviewed this literature to bring insights from these disciplines to bear on our understanding of whether and under what conditions organizational cultures change. She concluded by offering an expanded framework to understand the processes that underlie both cultural change and stability in terms of the ongoing interaction between the assumptions and values that shape members' behavior, and the symbols and artefacts that members use to account for this behavior (see also Hatch 1993).

After having briefly summarized the content of the original chapter, we explore one of the most interesting developments in research on culture change since that chapter was written: the acknowledgement of the interplay between organization culture and organizational identity—understood as members' relatively consensual answer to the existential question "Who are we as an organization?" (Albert and Whetten 1985; Gioia et al. 2013). We argue that a more nuanced understanding of the two constructs and how they interrelate, along with novel views on history, memory, temporality, and the importance of distant past and futures, enables a deeper conceptualization of how organizational identity influences members' commitment or resistance to culture change.

THEORIES OF CULTURE CHANGE

Sociological and Anthropological Theories of Culture Change

A longstanding assumption in anthropological and sociological research—Mary Jo Hatch reminded us in the original version of this handbook—is that change and stability tend to co-exist in cultures, because "at any given moment, culture is changing only in parts; other parts remain stable" (Hatch 2004: 192). "Change" – she observed, quoting anthropologist Melville Herskovits (1948) "is a constant in human culture. It is, however, always to be studied against a backdrop of cultural stability" (p. 635). At the time, organizational scholars overwhelmingly emphasized the inertial and conservative properties of culture, as opposed to its dynamism. Hatch's chapter drew on insights from other social sciences to encourage "a return to the seemingly lost project of explaining both stability and change" (Hatch, 2004: 191). To do so, she distinguished between three types of socio-anthropological theories of cultural change, and highlighted their relevance for our understanding of how cultures change in organization.

Mirroring theoretical developments in the natural sciences, early sociological theories of cultural change adopted an *evolutionary* perspective, positing that ongoing cultural changes are driven by technological change (White 1959) or adaptation to the environment (Sahlins and Service 1960). Some research in anthropology similarly adopted an evolutionary perspective, but focused instead on how variation within cultures gradually spread and came to be accepted. Herskovits (1964), for instance, pointed out that, even in the presence of widely accepted norms and conventions, "individual peculiarities" exist that induce people to act in novel and experimental ways. "Change"—Herskovits observed—"is brought about by a process whereby certain deviations from established norms are taken over by a number of people, thus initiating and continuing a tendency that becomes a trend (1964: 205; see also Kroeber 1944, for a similar view). A more recent explanation points to "repetition with a difference" (Roach 1995) whereby change may be the result of the accumulation of subtle variations and improvisations as a practice is repeated over time.

Theories of *change "from outside"* highlighted instead the mechanisms through which cultures change through external influences, as ideas and practices "diffuse" from one culture to another. Malinowski (1945), for instance, theorized how cultures change by coming in contact with one another, producing "new cultural realities" at the intersection of the two and as a reaction to one another. Other studies examined how the "transmission" (Kroeber 1944) of elements from one culture to another occurs through the selective borrowing of elements that seem advantageous and belong to "focal" areas in which members of a culture have immediate interests and concerns (Herskovits 1948, 1964). Borrowed elements, these theories observed, are likely to be merged with prior ones, and/or reinterpreted in ways that facilitate their assimilation within existing cultural patterns.

Finally, theories of *change "from within"* include mechanisms that explain cultural change based on internal dynamics. Weber's theory of charismatic leadership (Weber 1968/1978), for instance, highlighted the importance of the "systematization" of a charismatic leader idea into a coherent belief system that their "disciples" accomplish, and the "accommodation" of new beliefs and obligations in ways that enable these disciples to preserve their social position and economic interests. This "routinization" of the disruptive ideas introduced by charismatic leaders—according to Weber—enables them to promote cultural change, while at the same time maintaining some degree of stability.

Anthropologists also pointed out how the process of "enculturation" through which ideas, meanings, and practices are transferred from one generation to the next, occurs differently in early and late life. In maturity, Herskovits (1964) observed, individuals are able to engage more reflexively with new cultural content, and to examine consciously innovative modes of behavior that may eventually lead to culture change, allowing themselves to be "re-conditioned" to embrace innovation.

Organizational Culture

The notion of organizational culture generally refers to the largely tacit and taken-for-granted system of meanings and understandings that underpin organizational practices. Some scholars understand organizational culture as composed of both ideational and material elements (e.g. Smircich 1983; Martin 2002). The former are often associated with the assumptions that members use to interpret social reality, and the values that shape their attitudes and behavior (Schein 1985). The latter manifest more visibly in cultural forms (artifacts, stories, language, etc.), formal practices (policies, structures, and systems), and informal practices (unwritten norms and conventions) (Martin 2002) that reflect the underlying meaning system.

Early conceptualizations of organizational culture described it as a relatively stable set of norms and beliefs that provide the structural stability fundamental for the everyday functioning of an organization by shaping how members "act, think, and feel about their organization" in a coherent and predictable way, and (Schein 1985/2010: 18). Research in this tradition emphasizes how, due to their socialization into the organization's culture, members find it difficult to accept changes that clash with extant culture (Gagliardi 1986; Ogbonna and Wilkinson 2003).

Building on an increasingly influential perspective in cultural sociology (Swidler, 1986; DiMaggio 1997), more recent developments have questioned the view of organizational culture as a relatively unified system of beliefs constraining behavior, and proposed instead a notion of culture as a repertoire or "toolkit" (Weber 2005; Rindova et al. 2011; Harrison and Corley 2011; Giorgi et al. 2015). According to this view, culture is not to be understood as a strict and normative set of prescriptions, but more as a repertoire of cognitive and symbolic resources that members can flexibly draw upon to develop "strategies of action" (Swidler 1986, 2001).

Research in anthropology (D'Andrade 1981, 1995), cultural sociology (Vaisey 2009) and organization studies (Canato et al. 2013) suggests that these two perspectives—while often pitched as contraposed—are not really incompatible. In fact, both may be needed to fully understand cultural phenomena: the culture-as-norms perspective pointing to the deep, largely unconscious motivational structures that shape action; the culture-as-repertoire perspective pointing to the more conscious resources we use to understand and justify the actions we engage in.

Organizational Theories of Culture Change

In organizations, culture change is manifested in long-lasting changes in the way people act in various organizational situations (Rindova et al. 2011; Canato et al. 2013) and in the way they make and give sense of how they act (Rindova et al. 2011). In organization and management studies, several theories have been advanced over the years to explain how organizational cultures change. These theories have highlighted different mechanisms, reflecting different archetypal change theories (Van de Ven and Poole 2005).

Teleological theories of culture change. Early literature on organizational culture often reflected the perspective of practitioners, who viewed culture as a tool through which organizational leaders could control the organization (e.g., Deal and Kennedy 1982). This literature proposed teleological (Van de Ven and Poole 2005) models of change, often in the forms of prescriptive guidelines for organizational leaders to implement desired changes. Some of these models used well-known diagnostic frameworks for the analysis of culture—such as Quinn and Cameron's Competing Values Framework (Hooijberg and Petrock 1993)—to support a step-by-step process to raise awareness of cultural issues and direct cultural change.

Life cycle theories of culture change. Other theories of cultural change pointed to the likely modifications that organizational cultures go through as organizations age, grow, and diversify (Schein, 1985/2016; Greiner, 1998). These theories reflect a *life cycle* (Van de Ven and Poole 2005) view of change, and suggest that, as organizations mature, structural changes may require alterations in how people act and interact—often in the direction of increased formalization, routinization, and professionalization—that may be at odds with established cultural patterns, and become a source of stress and anxiety until they are accommodated within the culture.

Evolutionary theories of culture change. Other theories of cultural change, in organizations, reflect an evolutionary perspective on change (Van de Ven and Poole 2005), by pointing out how organizational cultures may undergo subtle and gradual changes as the composition and content of the workforce varies over time and generations of employees replace one another (see also Rheinhardt and Gioia, Chapter 4 of this volume), thereby gradually importing values and ideas that reflect more general trends in the external environment (Meyerson and Martin 1987). Van Maanen and Schein (1979), in particular, point out how newcomers may introduce cultural change by resisting, at least in part, the socialization process, and introducing alterations in the role assigned to them and/or the way in which they carry it out. Alvesson (2002) refers to this gradual, incremental, partly unintended change process as "culture drifting."

Dialectical theories of culture change. Dialectical theories of change (Van de Ven and Poole 2005) posit that change is the result of a synthesis between opposing efforts to impose or resist change, as discussed in Chapter 7 by Hargrave. As we mentioned earlier, the idea that cultural change is often the result of the integration between old and new ways (e.g., Malinowski 1945), or the mediation between established interests and emerging ones (e.g., Weber, 1968/1978) is well established in anthropology and sociology. Research on organizational culture, instead, traditionally emphasized either the transformational effects of leaders (Schein 1985; Trice and Beyer 1991), or their eventual failure to introduce significant change in the face of more or less overt resistance (Ogbonna and Wilkinson, 2003).

Building on a longitudinal study of culture change at 3M, one of us proposed a more nuanced, dialectical theory of culture change (Canato et al. 2013) that points out how, in the long term, some changes imposed from the top may affect habitual patterns of thought and action, while others will be rejected—depending on the relative compatibility of these changes with the organizational identity (we return on this point later). The resulting culture will combine both well-established and newly-introduced elements, without entirely embracing, nor entirely rejecting the changes introduced by a new leader.

Not all theories, however, fall neatly into one of the four types of change. Indeed, Schein's theory of cultural change (Schein 1985/2010) interestingly combines elements of different models. According to Schein, culture can be conceived as a set of taken-for-granted solutions to problems of external adaptation (how to survive in the environment) and internal integration (how to organize interactions among members) that every group faces. Cultures emerge, Schein points out, as groups experiment with different solutions and retain what seems to satisfactorily address their problems. This fundamentally evolutionary mechanism—whereby culture is conceived as the result of cumulative group learning—is combined with a teleological one, as Schein acknowledges the role of current and aspiring leaders in driving the formation and change of organizational cultures, and highlights the "mechanisms" available to them to "embed" new cultural assumptions and values. Schein recognizes that, as organizations age, and their size and complexity increase, they are likely to confront new problems, and these problems will likely induce cultural changes. By doing so, Schein also adds a life cycle perspective to his comprehensive theory. In addition, he argues, different stages in the life cycle of an organization may require different means of cultural change: whereas at an early stage, cultural change may by stimulated by organizational debate and self-insight, it may take a scandal or a crisis to induce culture change in a mature organization (Schein 2016).

Past theories of culture change, largely overlooked the role of identity in the process, with only one exception: Gagliardi's theory of how culture can be affected by strategic change. Gagliardi (1986) distinguishes between three different types of teleological cultural change—which he terms *apparent cultural change*, *cultural incre-*

mentalism, and *cultural revolution*—characterized by strategic change being congruent, compatible, or incompatible with current values and assumptions, respectively. To explain this difference, Gagliardi introduces an important distinction between culture, understood as values and tacit assumptions, and *cultural identity*, as a core set of elements that distinguishes the organization from others, which managers may therefore aspire to maintain, even amid changes. According to Gagliardi, apparent cultural change occurs in situations where organizations must engage in culture change in order to maintain their (cultural) identity—echoing the fundamental idea that "everything must change in order to stay the same" (as first espoused in *The Leopard* by Tomasi di Lampedusa 1958). Alternatively, organizations may encounter situations, where they feel pressed to change their (cultural) identity in order to survive; these changes—Gagliardi argues—can either be supported by a cultural revolution or resisted through cultural incrementalism.

Although, Gagliardi's theory remains firmly grounded within the concept of organizational culture, his conceptualization of "cultural identity", as an important and distinctive element of culture shaping its teleological dynamism, foreshadows more recent developments in our understanding of the interaction between organizational culture and identity in times of change. In the next section, we focus on this line of inquiry and begin to articulate the underlying socio-cognitive and temporal dynamics that characterize the interplay between these two phenomena.

Dynamics between Organizational Identity and Culture

Organization scholars have long debated whether and how organizational culture and identity differ (e.g. Fiol 1991; Schultz et al. 2000; Hatch and Schultz 1997, 2000, 2002; Alvesson and Roberson 2016; Ravasi 2016). Our own research, both jointly (Ravasi and Schultz 2006) and separately (Rindova et al. 2011; Canato et al. 2013; Hatch et al. 2015; Hernes and Schultz 2016) has contributed to sharpen our understanding of identity and culture by "operationalizing" these constructs and examining their interplay in times of change. In this section, we first introduce the concept of organizational identity and explain how it differs from culture, as a foundation to theorize the dynamic interplay between these two concepts over time. Next, we build on past research to elaborate the theory of identity dynamics (Hatch and Schultz 2002) by articulating more clearly opportunities for agentic intervention (vision and strategy) and the role of change agents.

Our (teleological) theory departs from a conceptualization of organizational identity dynamics as an ongoing (dialectical) accomplishment at the intersection between construed image and organizational culture (Hatch and Schultz 2002; Ravasi and Schultz 2006). Our elaboration adds a temporal dimension—with a particular view of identity as suspended between past and future. We acknowledge the possibility that, on occasions, identity dynamics can be leveraged by organizational leaders to promote cultural change, and begin to unpack how culture change can be inspired and directed by identity change or hampered and bounded by identity-related resistance. To do so, we partly reinterpret prior studies to emphasize temporal and agentic aspects that original analyses de-emphasized, to elaborate further the sensemaking and sensegiving processes that identity dynamics rest upon.

Organizational Identity

Research on organizational identity is concerned with collective self-definitions (Pratt et al., 2016) and how organizational actors "develop, express, and project their organizational sense of self" towards others (Hatch and Schultz 2002: 23), which entails continuous comparison and self-reflections (e.g., Corley et al. 2006). Drawing on the classic definition by Albert and Whetten (1985), organizational identity has been conceived as a set of claims and beliefs about an organization's "central, distinctive, and enduring attributes (...) as well as its rightful membership in a particular market category" (Navis and Glynn 2010: 440). This conception reflects the convergence between two different strands on research on organizational identity.

One, rooted in organizational behavior, conceived of organizational identity as "those features of an organization that in the eyes of its members are central to the organization's character (...), make the organization distinctive from other similar organizations, and are viewed as having continuity over time" (Gioia et al. 2013). This line of inquiry theorizes the construction of organizational identities as a process of claim-making (Ashforth and Mael 1996; Glynn 2000), whereby members advance representations of their organization that help address their needs to project a positive organizational image (Dutton and Dukerich 1991) and safeguard their self-esteem (Elsbach and Kramer 1996; Petriglieri 2015) and self-identity (Watson 2016), while preserving a sense of temporal continuity (Corley and Gioia 2004). This conceptualization entails that identity change may be initiated by changes in the process and substance of claim-making, which in turn may influence what organizational actors believe and understand about who they are as an organization—and eventually how they act.

A second stream of research, drawing on organizational sociology, has pointed to the "classification schemes" (Albert and Whetten 1985) that organizational members and stakeholders (investors, customers, critics, etc.) use to position organizations in a social space (Pontikes 2012; Rosa et al. 1999; Zuckerman 1999), and to the system of categories that constitute these classification systems (Khaire and Wadhwani 2010; Navis and Glynn, 2010). Research on this tradition conceives of organizational identity as a combination of claims to categorical memberships through which organizations establish similarity and difference from comparable organizations (Navis & Glynn, 2010). In this perspective, organizational identity change—at organizational level—may occur through self re-categorization, for instance, as an organization repositions itself into existing classification schemes (Cloutier and Ravasi, 2020), forges a new category and claims membership to it (Tripsas, 2009), or claims analogical membership to distant categories from other fields (Rindova et al. 2011). At field level, change my also occur as new categories emerge or established categories change, reflecting larger transformations in the underpinning industries and technologies.

Both these perspectives—identity-as-attributions and identity-as-categories—we argue, help us understand how members answer the fundamental question "Who are we as an organization" (see Cloutier and Ravasi, 2020). They do so by highlighting that members' answers will likely reflect a combination of cross-sectional ("What other organizations are we similar to, and what makes us different from them?") and inter-temporal ("What has remained the same over time and amid changes?") comparisons (see Clegg et al. 2007; Hernes and Schultz 2016).

Introducing Agency and Temporality in Identity Dynamics

In the original formulation of the theory of identity dynamics (see Figure 5.1), Hatch and Schultz (2002) applied Mead's theory of self to the organizational level to interpret identity construction as an ongoing process, shaped by the dialectical interplay between *culture*—as the historically received set of beliefs, values, and practices that inform our understanding of "who we are" as an organization—and *image*—as the external representation of the organization its members are exposed to. Organizational identity, the two authors argued, is interlinked to culture and image, to the extent that current claims and understandings results from a combination of "reflecting" on the former and "mirroring" the latter; at the same time, organizational identities "express" selected cultural content and are "projected" towards external constituents (Hatch and Schultz 2002).

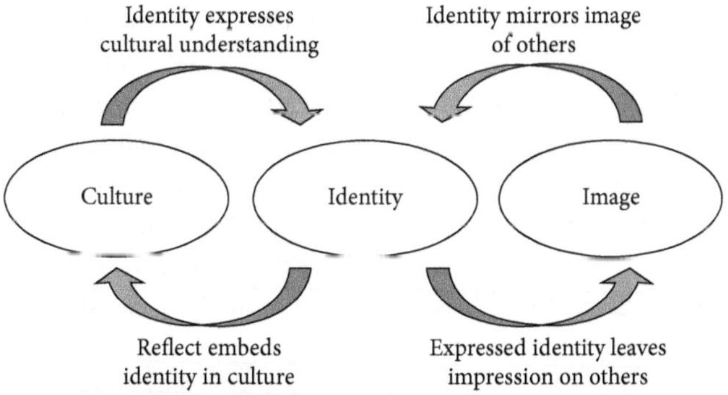

FIGURE 5.1 The Original Theory of Identity Dynamics

(Hatch and Schultz, 2002)

Research conducted in the last two decades enables us to extend these ideas to produce a more elaborate understanding of identity dynamics that accounts for the temporality of the process and highlights opportunities for agentic intervention.

Research on organizational identity has only begun recently to examine explicitly the temporality of identity-related processes (Schultz and Hernes 2013; Ravasi et al. 2019; Hernes and Schultz 2016, 2020). By this term, we refer to the extent to which organizational identity construction is shaped by attempts to link past, present, and/or future representations of "who we are" ("who we were", "will be," and/or "want to become"). Research suggests that identity construction is a process that unfolds over time, as persisting self-referred representations (Sasaki et al. 2020), commemoration of past accomplishments (Nissley and Casey 2002), and commitment to enduring practices (Ravasi and Canato 2010) induce members to accept some features as constitutive of "who we are" as an organization. A temporal perspective on identity, in particular, draws attention to the influence on this process of members' active attempts to trace meaningful intertemporal linkages among past events, accomplishments, and representations, to address present-day issues and shape future courses of action (Schultz and Hernes 2013; Ravasi et al. 2019). From this point of view, then, past and future become part of the ongoing reconstruction of identity.

These developments enable us to extend the theory of identity dynamics as originally developed by Hatch and Schultz (2002) by adding a temporal perspective on the process. Consistent with Mead's theory of self (Mead 1932) that originally inspired Hatch and Schultz, we can conceive of organizational identity as a process that occurs in an ongoing present—as members are periodically confronted with tasks that require them to make sense of "who we are" and "what makes us different" from other organizations (Schultz and Hernes 2013; Ravasi et al. 2019). In these circumstances, research shows, members' sensemaking tends to be influenced by their past, whether in the form of culture—as the legacy of a (distant) past (Ravasi and Schultz 2006) accessed through memory forms (Schultz and Hernes 2013)—or image—as (more recent) exposure to external representations (Dutton and Dukerich 1991).

In the following, based on these ideas, we elaborate each of the processes involved in identity dynamics. We first discuss how culture and image shape identity construction in organizations. Next we acknowledge how identity may in turn serve to consolidate culture and image, and discuss how it does so. Finally, we shift emphasis from how identity is shaped by the past to how it can influence the future. We do so by highlighting how organizational leaders can influence identity dynamics, by reshaping identity claims and beliefs to facilitate the implementation (in the near future) of a strategy aimed at realizing a vision cast further ahead in time. Our extensions of the identity dynamics are illustrated in Figure 5.2.

From Organizational History and Culture to Identity

Past studies have shown how organizational history—understood as an inevitably selective and partial account of the organizational past—is periodically re-written in light of managers' present-day aspirations and concerns about how the organization is officially represented and understood inside and outside (Rowlinson and Hassard 1993; Gioia et al. 2000; Suddaby et al. 2010).

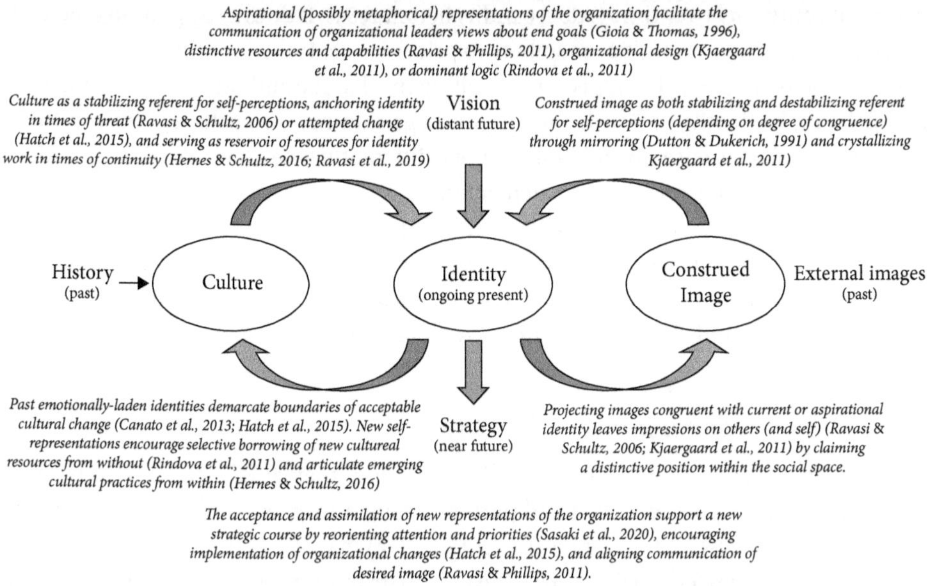

FIGURE 5.2 Identity Dynamics: An Extension

At the same time, research has shown that, when pressed to make sense of "who we are" as an organization, members often turn to their collective past. Our joint study of how managers at Bang and Olufsen responded to what they perceived as threats to the continued viability of their organizational identity (Ravasi and Schultz 2006), shows how, in these circumstances, they turned to a pool of cultural elements—stories, practices, and symbols—inherited from the past, in order to reformulate official definitions of "who we are" in ways that periodically reoriented the attention of the organization on a subset of these elements that managers considered relevant to current strategic concerns.

A study of organizational identity reconstruction in the LEGO Group (Schultz and Hernes 2013) further shows how organizational culture can support retrospective reflections on "who we used to be" to reconstruct a sense of "who we are." At the time, managers at LEGO struggled to develop a new set of identity claims in order to counter the increasing dilution of the original claim, which they defined as "the construction idea": offering timeless play combining creativity and logic. The dilution was caused by prior attempts to span multiple categories and become more like Disney (children's toys, computer-games, clothes, amusement parks, etc.). In these circumstances, recovering and re-using (as memory forms) textual, material, and oral cultural artifacts embedded in the past helped inspire and legitimate a new set of identity claims aiming to re-state the original idea by enhancing "systematic creativity".

Ravasi et al. (2019) extend the idea that members draw on the cultural heritage of the organization to make sense of "who we are", by highlighting variation in how they do so, reflecting different ways to relate past and present to inspire future-oriented action. This study questions the longstanding assumption that identity claims refer to features that, in the eyes of members, are central and distinctive to the organization, and possess some degree of continuity over time (Albert and Whetten 1985). It does so by pointing out that task characteristics may induce members to prioritize centrality, continuity, *or* distinctiveness (and disregard other aspects)—resulting in what the authors refer to as "identity evangelizing," "identity stewardship," or "heritage mining," respectively. This, in turn, will lead members to use history and memory differently when constructing an understanding of "who we are" to inform their actions.

Collectively, these studies suggest that culture acts as a stabilizing referent for self-perceptions, serving as a reservoir of resources for identity construction in times of continuity (Hernes and Schultz 2016; Ravasi et al. 2019), and anchoring identity in times of threat (Ravasi and Schultz 2006) or attempted change (Schultz and Hernes 2013; Hatch et al. 2015).

From Organizational Image to Identity

Members' beliefs and understandings of "who we are" may also be influenced by how the organization is portrayed by third parties. They do so, as members "mirror" themselves in these representations and use them to infer what others think about the organization (Dutton and Dukerich 1991). These "construed images" may operate both as stabilizing or destabilizing referents for collective self-perceptions, depending on their degree of congruence with members' own perceptions.

In the long run, cumulative exposure to consistent, widespread representations—what some scholars refer to as a "reputation" (Gioia et al. 2000)—may reinforce members' self-perceptions. Particularly positive representations may even "crystallize" a particular identity (Kjaergaard et al. 2011), thereby hampering its adaptation in the face of changing conditions. Danish producer of hearing aids Oticon, for instance, introduced a radical reorganization of its activities by dismantling both functional barriers and hierarchical layers. CEO Lars Kolind labeled the resulting structure a "spaghetti organization", and the term came to be widely used inside and outside the company to refer to its unconventional design. Eventually, however, the persisting representation of Oticon and its bold experiment in the national media made it difficult for members to envision a new identity for the organization (Kjaergaard et al. 2011).

From Organizational Identity to Culture

Just as organizational culture serves as an important referent for how members make sense of "who we are", as members' identity beliefs and understandings come to be deeply-felt, they will reinforce cultural practices by legitimizing and justifying their ongoing reproduction in light of a higher-order understanding of the organization (Fiol 1991). By doing so, organizational identity tends to shape the degree to which members will be willing to accept cultural changes.

Recent research suggests that cultural change may occur through prolonged exposure to ideas or practices borrowed from other cultures, which induces people to experiment with novel cultural forms and adapt them to their own reality (Canato et al. 2013; Howard-Grenville et al. 2011). Organizational identity influences this process as a deeply-felt understanding of "who we are," reflecting an inner layer of values that members perceive as central and distinctive, that demarcates changes that members are willing to accept from changes that they reject as identity-threatening.

A longitudinal study of the introduction of Six Sigma at 3M, for instance, revealed that members were willing—with some reluctance—to experiment with what they described as a new "data-driven culture," a "culture of accountability" that was quite different from how the company operated at the time (see Canato et al. 2013), and eventually modified habitual patterns of behavior accordingly. Resistance, however, picked up and intensified as they felt that changes—while beneficial for the efficiency and profitability of the company—began to threaten what they described as the "spirit," the "pillars" of the company. These foundational values—an entrepreneurial spirit, trust in people, tolerance for mistakes, constant push to innovate—were enshrined in the so-called "McKnight's principles" articulated by a legendary CEO of the past to explain the foundation of the managerial philosophy at the roots of 3M's success. The slowing down of growth rate, and the decreasing percentage of sales from new products on total revenues alerted the company that what Gagliardi would refer to as its "cultural identity" was at risk, eventually leading to the replacement of the CEO responsible for the introduction of Six Sigma with someone who would reverse identity-threatening changes. As an informant insightfully mused at the time: "Six Sigma changed our culture, but fortunately it did not change our values".

From Organizational Identity to Image

Just as consistent exposure to congruent external portrayals of the organization tends to reinforce the organizational identity, so these portrayals will likely be influenced—directly or indirectly—by the organizational identity. Organizational identity, according to Charles Fombrun (1996) lies at the foundation of corporate reputation, to the extent that the consistent stream of actions that cumulatively shape public perceptions expresses a clear and widely-shared sense of "who we are" (Schultz et al. 2000).

Often, the identity of the organization is expressed by explicit communication—in the form of corporate communication, corporate branding, advertising, etc. (Schultz et al. 2000)—aimed at drawing attention to corporate actions and helping external audiences interpret these actions in light of more general claims about what the organization stands for (Rindova and Fombrun 1999). By doing so, organizations attempt to claim a distinctive position in a social space by locating themselves in the system of categories that their audiences use to decide who to work for, who to buy from, or who to fund (Tripsas 2009) (i.e., "This is the type of organization we are"), and by highlighting what distinguishes them from other organizations in the same category (i.e., "this is what makes us different from other organizations of the same type").

While formally aimed at external audiences, these communications also serve the additional purpose of signaling to the rest of the organization what the identity aspirations of organizational leaders are (Gioia and Thomas 1996), and to promote consistent support to the expression of a unitary organizational identity (Ravasi and Phillips 2011).

Organizational Identity, Vision, and Strategy

While the original theory of identity dynamics explored in depth the relationships between organizational identity, culture, and image—and their mutually reinforcing interplay—it left the analysis of purposeful attempts to alter these dynamics relatively underdeveloped. Past research, however, has shown how formal claims about "who we are"—embodied in corporate mottos, slogans, or other identity statements—often help articulate the *vision* of organizational leaders' about an aspirational positioning for the organization (Gioia and Thomas 1996; Hatch and Schultz 2008), its distinctive resources and capabilities (Ravasi and Phillips 2011), organizational design (Kjaergaard et al. 2011), or dominant logic (Rindova et al. 2011).

The content of these identity statements, in turn, is expected to support the present course of action—or a future one—by orienting attention and priorities of members (Sasaki et al. 2020), aligning communication and action towards a desired image (Ravasi and Phillips 2011), and encouraging the implementation of cultural changes (Hatch et al. 2015). We elaborate on how leaders can actively attempt to shape identity claims and understandings to promote change in the following section.

Identity Dynamics and Pathways of Culture Change

In the previous section, we proposed an extended theory of identity dynamics that highlights room for agentic intervention in the interplay between identity, culture, and image. We now use this framework as a theoretical infrastructure to examine three ways in which purposeful reflections on who we are as an organization—triggered by internal or external events—may be used to initiate, facilitate, or consolidate cultural change. We refer to these three ways as pathways of culture change, and highlight the different roles that open reflections about "who we are" play in triggering, driving, or supporting changes in organizational culture.

Identity-Legitimated Cultural Change: Using New Claims to Consolidate Emerging Cultural Practices

A first way in which organizational leaders can stimulate reflections on "who we are" in order to support culture change is to use identity statements to draw attention to elements of the culture that they consider important to address current strategic issues and/or distinguish the organization from competitors (see for instance Ravasi and Schultz 2006; Ravasi and Phillips 2011). This statement can be taken to form a new (or revised) vision, mission, philosophy, or corporate motto (Sasaki et al. 2020). The purpose here is not so much to radically change the culture, but to consolidate incremental changes by raising awareness of the importance of these emerging elements of the culture for "who we are" (and, possibly, "who we want to be").

This change pathway acknowledges that, over time, culture changes incrementally as an organization—or one of its units—encounters problems that require new or modified solutions (Schein 2016). Deviant behaviour or demographic changes may also lead to the exploration or introduction of new solutions to old problems. Tentative new solutions, however, may not be incorporated immediately in the organizational culture—that is, widely accepted by its members as appropriate and desirable—because their adoption may be circumscribed to some groups, their effectiveness may not be widely recognized or possibly disputed, or their importance for the accomplishment of the organizational goals underestimated.

In these circumstances, organizational leaders may use identity statements to help emerging changes in "how we do things around here" to be assimilated, supported, and reproduced by all members by incorporating them in collective understandings of "who we are." New identity statements help them do so by encouraging people to make sense of emerging practices in terms of more general understandings of central and distinctive features—sometimes presented as "core values" or "competences" (Glynn 2000). By presenting emerging practices as central to "who we are," new identity statements justify the reallocation of resources among units and activities, and the rewarding of behavior consistent with desired changes. They may also prevent their inadvertent loss or deterioration (Ravasi and Phillips 2011).

It is important to recognize here that by "emerging" we do not necessarily refer to scattered and/or experimental practices introduced only recently in the organization. Practices we refer to as emerging may have been around for years, but awareness of their importance may still be limited, and their diffusion and/or reproduction over time still be in question. By purposefully intervening in the social processes that ensure the incremental modification of values and assumptions in light of these practices, this change model introduce a teleological element in an otherwise evolutionary path.

As Figure 5.3 illustrates, this change pathway directly connects identity, culture, and strategy, as the reflective efforts leading to the reformulation of identity statements tend

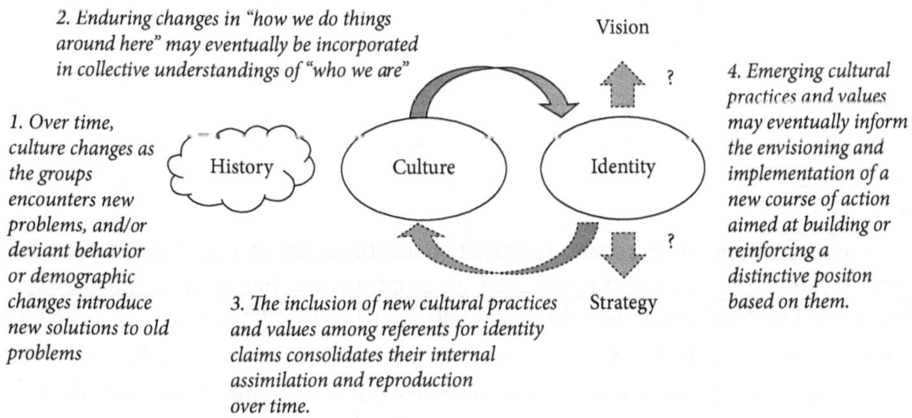

FIGURE 5.3 Identity-Legitimated Cultural Change

to be associated with the envisioning and implementation of a new course of action aimed at building or reinforcing a distinctive position based on these practices. The consolidation of cultural changes around new identity claims and beliefs is intended to support the implementation of the new course of action.

We observed similar dynamics in our longitudinal study of how managers at the Danish producer of high-end audiovisual equipment Bang and Olufsen addressed competitive threats between the early 1970s and the mid-1990s (Ravasi and Schultz 2006). In these circumstances, managers systematically turned to the past, by engaging in explicit reflections on cultural practices and artifacts to make (new) sense of the organizational identity in ways that enabled them to envision a new strategy to cope with competitive pressures, based on a renewed understanding of the elements that positively distinguished them from competitors. In the early 1970s, for instance, retrospective reflections on the philosophy that had guided product design in the past decade led to the codification of the Seven Corporate Identity Components: seven principles of design—such as Domesticity or Autovisuality—that managers believed characterized products and distinguished the company from fast-growing Japanese competitors. These principles—reflecting emerging practices in the design and development unit—were then extended to corporate communication, advertising and sales to ensure uniform support for a differentiation strategy built around them.

Image-Triggered Cultural Change: Using Identity as a Lens to Gauge the Desirability of Cultural Practices

According to Schein (2016), people generally tend to resist culture change. However, they may be induced to accept it by the shame they experience as events reveal aspects of their collective behavior that may be construed as socially undesirable, morally questionable, or otherwise inconsistent with the image that members want to have of themselves or their organization (Schein 2016)—in other words, with their "desired" organizational identity.

Organizational identity, here, serves as the lens through which members assess how they are portrayed by third parties such as news media, social movements, or social media. As members compare public portrayals of the organization with how they see themselves (or would like to see themselves) and review the decisions and actions in question, reflecting on the identity of the organization ("is this who we really are?"), it helps them articulate the source of their discomfort and envision a course of action to restore an alignment between external representations and internal aspirations (Dutton and Dukerich 1991).

These reflections may reveal inconsistencies between recent actions—possibly reflecting entrenched, if unacknowledged, assumptions and behaviors—and the aspirational self-image of members ("this is not who we want to be!"). These inconsistencies may be explained by the fact that the organizational culture is only partially reflected in identity claims and beliefs (Ravasi 2016). Some norms and assumptions—regarding, for instance, gender-based discrimination in managerial assignments or the acceptability of bribes when dealing with foreign officials—may be widely shared and strongly

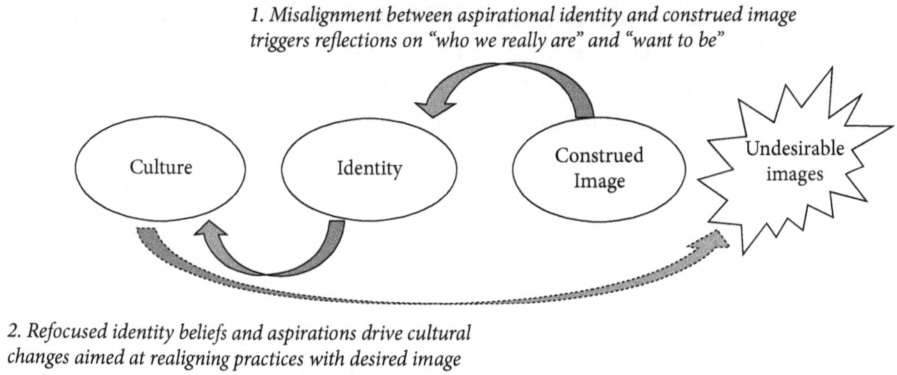

FIGURE 5.4 Image-Triggered Cultural Change

enforced, but not upheld as what the organization stands for or what positively distinguishes it from competitors. It is also possible that the events in question are the unexpected consequences of otherwise well-intended cultural norms and assumptions, or reflect deviant behavior revealing weaknesses in the enforcement of the organizational culture.

In these circumstances, members may simply engage in impression management aimed at repairing public perceptions, without really altering their behaviors (Gioia, Schultz, and Corley 2000). However, the severity of the misalignment and/or the intensity of external pressures may induce members to introduce more substantial changes in structures, policies, and incentive systems in order to bring action back in line with the aspirational identity and image. Shame at negative external portrayals may induce members to take these changes seriously and not limit themselves to ceremonial compliance, but alter their behaviors in a more lasting way to avoid similar experiences in the future. This change pathway is illustrated in Figure 5.4.

The case of the New York Port Authority described by Dutton and Dukerich (1991) exemplifies well how external representations of an organization that are incongruent with members' own perceptions and aspirations may induce them to re-examine their actions in light of the organizational identity and, possibly, to modify their behavior to realign internal and external perceptions. The New York Port Authority was induced to such reflections by a negative media coverage of the way they initially handled the problem of the homeless lingering in their facilities—representations that they felt collided with the "problem-solving" attitude that they believed characterized the organization (Dutton and Dukerich 1991). These reflections eventually led the NYPA to radically change their response to this problem.

Identity-Driven Cultural Change: Using New Claims to Encourage Culture Change

In an early attempt to disentangle the relations between identity and culture, Fiol (1991) suggested that organizational identity could be used to direct culture change by using novel identity claims to influence and stabilize new patterns of behavior. Later work built on this intuitive idea to illuminate a third change pathway, showing how new identity claims can help organizational leaders translate a vision of the future into a new conceptualization of the organization that helps members make sense of the new strategy and stimulate their identification with it (e.g., Kjaergaard et al. 2011; Rindova et al. 2011).

New claims may do so directly by expressing a desired end state in terms of an aspirational positioning (e.g. the idea of a "Top Ten University" driving changes at Penn State, as described by Gioia and Thomas 1996) and/or core drivers of competitive advantage (e.g., "Forward Forever" and "Honesty and Responsibility" at Tokyo Keizai University; see Sasaki et al. 2020). They may do so indirectly by presenting changes required to support the new strategic course as appropriate to the revised conceptualization of the organization (e.g., the idea of Alessi as an "artistic mediator" and "design factory" described below in more detail; see Rindova et al. 2011). Identity-driven cultural change is illustrated in Figure 5.5.

As Figure 5.5 shows, this third change pathway is grounded in a vision of a (distant) organizational future, which new aspirational (possibly metaphorical) representations of the organization help communicate. The acceptance and assimilation of these new representations support the new strategic course by reorienting attention and priorities, and encouraging the implementation of changes in the organizational culture (Hatch et al., 2015).

A longitudinal study by Hatch et al. (2015) of a post-merger integration process in the Carlsberg Group, for instance, revealed how organizational leaders challenged traditional notions of Carlsberg as a "brewing company" by offering an alternative view of Carlsberg as "fast-moving consumer goods company" to support the ambition to become the world's fastest-growing beer company. The ultimate goal of the top managers was to partly dismantle internal structures (e.g., the influence of local

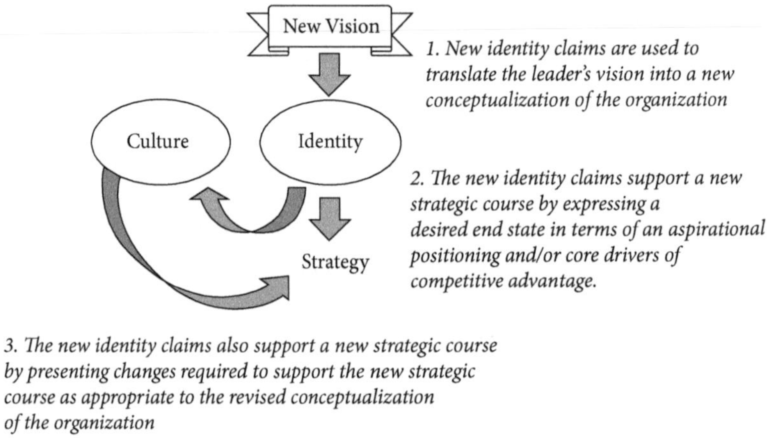

FIGURE 5.5 Identity-Driven Cultural Change

brewmasters on product-related decisions) and practices (e.g., emphasis on local brewing and specialty beers) that reflected the cultural heritage of the ultra-centenary organization, to transition to a marketing-led, consumer-driven model to simplify and homogenize a global portfolio. The new conceptualization, however, encountered the resistance of middle managers - who experienced it as clashing with deeply-held values and long-standing practices that were a source of personal or organizational pride, without offering an appealing alternative - and it was eventually set aside.

New categorical understandings of "who we are" may also encourage members to experiment with new practices that depart from current patterns of thought and action, by justifying them in light of new understandings of self, thereby facilitating acceptance and consolidation of cultural changes (Rindova et al. 2011). This interaction between identity and culture was revealed by a study of cultural changes at the Italian producer of designer kitchenware Alessi over the course of two decades (Rindova et al. 2011).

Between the early 1970s and the late 1980s, Alberto Alessi, grandson of the founder, endeavored to transform the way Alessi approached product design by importing ideas from the domains of arts (e.g., conceiving kitchenware as objects of art, designed by a recognized artist), craft (e.g., recovering ideas of virtuosity and variation in small-scale productions), anthropology (e,g., exploring archetypal forms of kitchenware, and their inclusion in consumption rituals), and psychoanalysis (e.g., exploring affect, fantasy, and playfulness in everyday objects). To persuade the rest of the organization to accept the incorporation of these new ideas in the cultural repertoire of the organization, and to inform their flexible use, Alessi gradually introduced new representations of the organization—such as a "publisher," a "workshop," an "artistic mediator," or a "design factory"—intended to justify the changes in the design, manufacturing, and commercialization of products inspired by the novel ideas imported from outside. By doing so, he effectively encouraged the organization to embrace new "ways of doing things around here"—that is, changes in its culture—in light of new claims and understandings of "who we are" as an organization.

The Dark Side of Identity and Culture Change

Our own work has largely focused on how the dynamics between identity and culture enable organizational change. Other studies, however, have shown how changes in organizational identity and culture can serve as means to reinforce social control and manipulation.

In an early contribution, Salancik (1977) theorizes how commitment may lead people to become collectively blindfolded, as they gradually embrace the fundamental goals and values of an organization and accept them as their own—that is, they identify with them. According to Salancik, commitment in itself is neither good nor bad, but it may develop in a direction, where individuals lose sight of what goals and values they are commiting themselves to, as occurs, for instance, in terrorist organizations or religious cults. Salancik describes commitment building as a nine-step process, beginning with selective recruitment and reinforced, among other things, by experiences of voluntary choice and individual accomplishments (Salancik 1977). Salanciks's theory reminds us about the powerful role that identity and identification may play in the socialization of new members into an organization culture, and the potential dangers of using identity and culture as a force of social control.

Others, such as O'Reilly (1989), examine the use of culture as a form of social control in organizations, suggesting how it may serve as a "normative order" creating motivation and direction for individual and organizational commitment (for a sharp critique of the practical and moral implications of encouraging the use of culture as a form of control, see Willmott 1993). Organizational identity, in this view, seems to reinforce this normative order by justifying it in terms of a higher-order conceptualization of a collective self—possibly inducing members, by doing so, to embrace norms and values that deviate from accepted society norms (see O'Reilly and Chatman 1996, for further discussion of the sociological and psychological forces behind organizational culture as systems as normative control).

Another example of the negative implications of strongly-held and mutually reinfrocing organizational culture and identity—and, in particular, of how strong socialization may lead to collective blindness—can be found in the concept of "groupthink" (Janis 1991). We interpret Janis's early study of the Bay of Pigs, and the later Challenger disaster as examples of how collectives may develop a shared collective identity through, among others, the "illusion of invulnerability, belief in inherent morality of the group, and out-group stereotypes" (Janis, 1991). This identity, Janis observes, may be enhanced by a culture of elitism, pressure for conformity, and fear of conflicts, with deleterious impact on the capacity of a group to respond to unexpected events.

Alvesson and Willmott (2002) similarly argue that identity regulation works as a means of social control by influencing identity work and self-identity. Although they do not address culture explicitly, they refer to how some means of social control derive from what we take to be changes in cultural elements, such as "influencing the hierarchical location" of employees by changing artifacts and rituals, "establishing and clarifying a distinct set of rules" leading to a push for new practices and behavioral patterns, or changing "categorization and affiliation," referring to the symbols and collective practices among workers. By doing so, these authors effectively suggest that cultural elements can be exploited as resources by managers, when seeking to obtain social control via identity regulation.

In fact, research shows that social control and manipulation may also occur in what appears to be more positive, apparently cheerful contexts. In his study of Disneyland as a "smile factory" (1991), for instance, Van Maanen shows how the employees are characterized by autonomously developed cultural elements—rituals, symbols, assumptions, and practices—that are misaligned with what is espoused by the organization, and by varying degrees of resistance to the organizational rules. These observations reveal an organizational culture—as practiced by employees—that differs considerably from the official claim for the park to be "The Happiest Place on Earth." By doing so, Van Maanen shows how cultural resources can also be used as a means of subtle resistance to dominant identity claims.

As this work collectively suggests, although the interplay between culture and identity can be harnessed to reinforce teleological changes reflecting the aspirations of organizational leaders, the dynamics may also reinforce social control in organizations in ways that may be dysfunctional and undesirable for society—by fueling hostility and isolation—or even for the organization itself—by leading to cognitive rigidity and inertia, if embraced too tightly, or to disengagement and more or less subtle resistance, if refused by members.

Conclusions

In this chapter, by highlighting elements of projective agency (Emirbayer and Mische 1999) in what was originally presented as an ongoing dialectical relationship (Hatch and Schultz, 2002), we have offered a teleological view of the dynamics between culture and identity. To do so, we have drawn upon recent developments within uses of history and temporality, which we argue are relevant, in particular, to understand the role of identity to teleological changes of culture.

The theory we have presented in this chapter is grounded in case-based research, carried out by the two authors, either jointly or independently, using a number of cases of organizational and cultural change (Bang and Olufsen, Carlsberg, Lego, Alessi, Oticon, 3M), as well as in findings from other studies of culture and/or identity change. Taken together these studies explored different facets of the process to gradually unpack the interplay between identity and culture, but left the role of organizational leaders undertheorized despite their central role to the observed dynamics. In this chapter, we addressed this limitation by reexamining these studies through the lens of a teleological model to produce a more agentic view of identity and culture change.

The three change pathways we have described show different ways in which organizational identity claims and beliefs may affect cultural change, and highlight the different temporalities inolved. The first pathway (Figure 5.3) shows how newly forged claims may be used to consolidate an emergent trajectory, rooted in a relatively recent past, to ensure its continuity in the future. The second pathway (Figure 5.4) shows instead how identity beliefs and understanding rooted in a distant past may shape how more recent events are interpreted, and induce members to adjust present behavior to realign past beliefs and future-oriented aspirations. The third pathway (Figure 5.5), finally, shows how visions of a distant future can be used to induce members to reconsider collective self-perceptions rooted in a distant past, thereby supporting changes in the present and near future.

More remains to be understood, however, about the conditions that affect the unfolding of the process. How organizational leaders select new categorical identities that successfully support cultural change, for instance, still remains a black box. Also, what induces members to accept new categorical identities and refuse others? How does the presence of multiple identities—possibly reflecting the prioritization of different temporalities, or temporally different experiences of the organization—affect the process? In this chapter, we have focused on culture change, and indirectly foreshadow teleological processes of identity change (e.g., borrowing categorical identities from other domains); can we also envision life cycle, evolutionary, or dialectical theories of identity change? The quest is far from over. Hopefully, when a new edition of this handbook is released, research will have helped us answer at least some of these questions.

References

Albert, S., and Whetten, D. A. (1985), 'Organizational Identity', *Research in Organizational Behaviour*, 7, 263–95.

Alvesson, M. (2002), *Understanding Organizational Culture* (London: Sage).

Alvesson, M. and Roberson, M. (2016), 'Organizational Identity: A Critique' in M. Pratt, M. Schultz, B. Ashforth, and D. Ravasi, eds., *Handbook of Organizational Identity* (Oxford: Oxford University Press), 160–80.

Alvesson, M., and Willmott, H. (2002), 'Identity Regulation as Organizational Control: Producing the Appropriate Individual', *Journal of Management Studies*, 39(5), 619–44.

Anteby M., and Molnár V. (2012), Collective Memory Meets Organizational Identity: Remembering to Forget in a Firm's Rhetorical History', *Academy of Management Journal*, 55, 515–40.

Ashforth, B. E., and Mael, F. (1996), Organizational Identity and Strategy as a Context for the Individual', *Advances in Strategic Management*, 13, 19–64.

Canato, A., Ravasi, D. and Phillips, N. (2013), 'Coerced Practice Implementation in Cases of Low Cultural Fit: Cultural Change and Practice Adaptation During the Implementation of Six Sigma at 3M', *Academy of Management Journal*, 1724–53.

Clegg, S. R., Rhodes, C., and Kornberger, M. (2007), 'Desperately Seeking Legitimacy: Organizational Identity and Emerging Industries', *Organization Studies*, 28/4, 495–513.

Cloutier, C., and Ravasi, D. (2020), 'Identity Trajectories: Explaining Long-Term Patterns of Continuity and Change in Organizational Identities', *Academy of Management Journal.*, 63/4, 1196–1235

Corley, K. G., and Gioia, D. A. (2004), 'Identity Ambiguity and Change in the Wake of a Corporate Spin-Off', *Administrative Science Quarterly*, 49, 173–208.

Corley, K. G., Harquail, C. V., Pratt, M. G., Glynn, M. A., Fiol, C. M., and Hatch, M. J. (2006), 'Guiding Organizational Identity through Aged Adolescence', *Journal of Management Inquiry*, 15/2, 85–99.

D'Andrade, R. G. (1981), The Cultural Part of Cognition', *Cognitive Science*, 5, 179–95.

D'Andrade, R. G. (1995), *The Development of Cognitive Anthropology* (Cambridge, UK: Cambridge University Press).

DiMaggio, P. J. (1997), 'Culture and Cognition', *Annual Review of Sociology*, 23/1, 263–87.

Deal T. E. and Kennedy, A. A. (1982), *Corporate Cultures: The Rites and Rituals of Corporate Life*, (Harmondsworth, Penguin Books).

Dutton J. E., and Dukerich J. M. (1991), 'Keeping an Eye on the Mirror: Image and Identity in Organizational Adaptation', *Academy of Management Journal* 34, 517–54.

Elsbach, K. D. and Kramer, R. M. (1996), 'Members' Responses to Organizational Identity Threats: Encountering and Countering the Business Week Rankings', *Administrative Science Quarterly*, 41, 442–76

Emirbayer, M., and Mische, A. (1998), 'What Is Agency?', *American Journal of Sociology*, 103(4), 962–1023.

Fiol, M. C. (1991), 'Managing Culture as a Competitive Resource: An Identity-Based View of Sustainable Competitive Advantage', *Journal of Management*, 17(1), 191–211.

Fombrun, C. J. (1996), *Reputation: Realizing Value from the Corporate Image*, (Boston, MA: Harvard Business School Press).

Gagliardi, P. (1986), 'The Creation and Change of Organizational Cultures: A Conceptual Framework', *Organization Studies*, 7/2, 117–34.

Gioia, D. A., Patvardhan, S. D., Hamilton, A. L., and Corley, K. G. (2013), 'Organizational Identity Formation and Change', *The Academy of Management Annals*, 7/1, 123–93.

Gioia, D. A., Schultz, M., and Corley, K. G. (2000), 'Organizational Identity, Image and Adaptive Instability', *Academy of Management Review*, 25/1, 63–81.

Gioia, D. A., and Thomas, J. B. (1996), 'Identity, Image and Issue Interpretation: Sensemaking during Strategic Change in Academia', *Administrative Science Quarterly*, 41, 370–403.

Giorgi, S., Lockwook, C., and Glynn, M. A. (2015), 'The Many Faces of Culture: Making Sense of 30 Years of Research on Culture in Organization Studies', *Academy of Management Annals*, 9/1, 1–54.

Glynn, M. A. (2000), 'When Cymbals Become Symbols: Conflict over Organizational Identity within a Symphony Orchestra', *Organization Science*, 11, 285–98.

Glynn, M. A. (2008), 'Beyond Constraint: How Institutions Enable Identities', in R. Greenwood, C. Oliver, R. Suddaby, and K. Sahlin-Andersson, eds., *The Sage Handbook of Organizational Institutionalism* (London, UK: Sage), 413–30.

Greiner, L. E. (1998), 'Evolution and Revolution as Organizations Grow', *Harvard Business Review*, 76(3), 55–64.

Hargrave, T. (2021), 'The Paradox Perspective and the Dialectics of Contradictions Research, in M. S. Poole and A. H. Van de Ven, eds., *The Oxford Handbook of Organizational Change and Innovation* (2nd edn) (Oxford: Oxford University Press),

Harrison, S. H., and Corley, K. G. (forthcoming), 'Clean Climbing, Carabineers and Cultural Cultivation: Developing an Open-Systems Perspective of Culture', *Organization Science*.

Hatch, M. J. (1993), 'The Dynamics of Organizational Culture', *Academy of Management Review*, 18(4), 657–93.

Hatch, M. J. (2004), 'Dynamics in Organizational Culture', in M. S. Poole and A. H. Van de Ven, eds., *The Oxford Handbook of Organizational Change and Innovation* (Oxford: Oxford University Press), 190–211

Hatch, M. J. and Schultz, M. (1997), 'Relations between Organizational Culture, Identity and Image', *European Journal of Marketing*, 31/5 356–65.

Hatch, M. J. and Schultz, M. (2000). 'Scaling the Tower of Babel: Relational Differences Between Identity, Image and Culture in Organizations', in Schultz, M., Hatch, M.J. and Larsen, M.H. (Eds.), *The Expressive Organization*, (Oxford: Oxford University Press), 11–36.

Hatch, M. J., and Schultz, M. (2002), 'The Dynamics of Organizational Identity', *Human Relations*, 55/8, 989–1018.

Hatch, M. J., and Schultz, M. (2008), *Taking Brand Initiative. How Companies Can Align Strategy, Culture and Identity through Corporate Branding* (San Francisco: Jossey-Bass).

Hatch M. J., Schultz, M., and Skov, A. M. (2015). 'Organizational Identity and Culture in the Context of Managed Change: Transformation in the Carlsberg Group, 2009–2013', *Academy of Management Discoveries* 1/1, 58–90.

Hernes, T., and Schultz, M. (2016), 'A Temporal Understanding of the Connections between Organizational Culture and Identity', in H. Tsoukas and A. Langley, eds, *Sage Handbook of Process Organizational Studies* (London: Sage Publications), Chapter 22.

Herskovits, M. J. (1948) *Man and His Works*, (New York: Knopf).

Herskovits, M. J. (1964) *Cultural Dynamics*, (New York: Knopf).

Hooijberg, R., and Petrock, F. (1993), 'On Cultural Change: Using the Competing Values Framework to Help Leaders Execute a Transformational Strategy', *Human Resource Management*, 32(1), 29–50.

Howard-Grenville, J., Golden-Biddle, K., Irwin, J., and Mao, J. (2011), 'Liminality as Cultural Process for Cultural Change', *Organization Science*, 22, 522–39.

Janis, I. (1991), 'Groupthink', in E. Griffin, ed., *A First Look at Communication Theory* (New York: McGrawHill), 235–46.

Khaire, M., and Wadhwani, R. D. (2010), 'Changing Landscapes: The Construction of Meaning and Value in a New Market Category—Modern Indian Art', *Academy of Management Journal*, 53(6), 1281–304.

Kjaergaard, A., Morsing, M., and Ravasi, D. (2011), 'Mediating Identity: A Study of Media Influence on Organizational Identity Construction in a Celebrity Firm', *Journal of Management Studies*, 48/3, 514–43.

Kroeber, A. L. (1944), *Configurations of Culture Growth*, (Berkeley, CA: University of California Press).

Lampedusa, G. T. (1958/1960), *The Leopard* (New York Pantheon).

Malinowski, B. (1945), *The Dynamics of Cultiure Change*, (New Haven, CT: Yale University Press).

Martin, J. (2002), *Organizational Culture: Mapping the Terrain* (Thousand Oaks, CA: Sage).

Mead, G. H. (1932), *The Philosophy of the Present*, (LaSalle, IL: Open Court Publishing)

Meyerson, D., and Martin, J. (1987), 'Culture Change: An Integration of Three Different Views', *Journal of Management Studies*, 24, 623–47.

Navis, C., and Glynn, M. A. (2010), 'How New Market Categories Emerge: Temporal Dynamics of Legitimacy, Identity, and Entrepreneurship in Satellite Radio, 1990–2005', *Administrative Science Quarterly*, 55/3, 439–71.

Nissley, N. and Casey, A. (2002), 'The Politics of the Exhibition: Viewing Corporate Museums through the Paradigmatic Lens of Organizational Memory', *British Journal of Management*, 13, 35–45.

O'Reilly, C. (1989), Corporations, Culture, and Commitment: Motivation and Social Control in Organizations', *California Management Review*, Summer, 31(4): 9–25.

O'Reilly, C., and Chatman, J. (1996), Culture as Social Control: Corporations, Cults, and Commitment', *Research in Organizational Behavior*, 18, 157–201.

Ogbonna, E., and Wilkinson, B. (2003), 'The False Promise of Organizational Culture Change: A Case Study of Middle Managers in Grocery Retailing', *Journal of Management Studies*, 40(5), 1151–78.

Petriglieri, J. L. (2011), 'Under Threat: Responses to and the Consequences of Threats to Individuals' Identities', *Academy of Management Review*, 36(4), 641–662.

Pontikes, E. G. (2012), 'Two Sides of the Same Coin: How Ambiguous Classification Affects Multiple Audiences' Evaluations', *Administrative Science Quarterly* 57, 81–118.

Pratt, M., Schultz, M., Ashforth, B., and Ravasi, D. (2016), 'Introduction', in M. Pratt, M. Schultz, B. Ashforth, and D. Ravasi, eds., *Handbook of Organizational Identity* (Oxford: Oxford University Press), 1–19.

Ravasi, D. (2016), 'Organizational Identity, Culture, and Image', in M. Pratt, M. Schultz, B. Ashforth, and D. Ravasi, eds., *Handbook of Organizational Identity* (Oxford: Oxford University Press), 65–78.

Ravasi, D., and Canato, A. (2010), 'We Are What We Do (and How We Do It): Organizational Technologies and the Construction of Organizational Identity. In N. Phillips, G. Sewell and D. Griffiths (eds.), *Technology and organization: Essays in honour of Joan Woodward*, (Emerald Publishing), 49–80.

Ravasi, D., and Phillips, N. (2011), 'Strategies of Alignment: Organizational Identity Management and Strategic Change at Bang and Olufsen', *Strategic Organization*, 9/2, 103–35.

Ravasi, D., Rindova, V., and Stigliani, I. (2019), The Stuff of Legend: History, Memory, and the Temporality of Organizational Identity Construction', *Academy of Management Journal*, 62/5, 1523–55.

Ravasi, D., and Schultz, M. (2006), 'Responding to Organizational Identity Threats: Exploring the Role of Organizational Culture', *Academy of Management Journal*, 49, 433–58.

Reinecke J., and Ansari, S. (2016), 'Time, Temporality, and Process Studies, in A. Langley, and H. Tsoukas, eds., *The SAGE Handbook of Process Organization Studies* (London, England: SAGE Publications), 402–16.

Rheinhardt, A. and Gioia, D. (2021), 'Upside-Down Organizational Change: Sensemaking, Sensegiving, and the New Generation', in M. S. Poole and A. H. Van de Ven, eds., *The Oxford Handbook of Organizational Change and Innovation* (2nd edn) (Oxford: Oxford University Press).

Rindova, V., Dalpiaz, E., and Ravasi, D. (2011), 'A Cultural Quest: A Study of Organizational Use of New Cultural Resources in Strategy Formation', *Organizational Science*, 22, 413–31.

Rindova, V. P., and Fombrun, C. J. (1999), 'Constructing Competitive Advantage: The Role of Firm-Constituent Interactions', *Strategic Management Journal*, 20, 691–710.

Roach, J. (1995) Culture and Performance in the Circum-Atlantic World. In A. Parker and E. K. Sedgwick (eds.), *Performativity and Performance*, (New York: Routledge), 45–63.

Rosa, J. A., Porac, J. F., Runser-Spanjol, J., and Saxon, M. S. (1999), 'Sociocognitive Dynamics in a Product Market', *Journal of Marketing*, 63, 64–77.

Rowlinson, M., and Hassard, J. (1993), 'The Invention of Corporate Culture: A History Of the Histories of Cadbury', *Human Relations*, 46, 299–326.

Sahlins, M. and Service, E. (eds.) (1960), *Evolution and Culture*, (Ann Arbor: University of Michigan Press).

Salancik, G. R. (1977), Commitment and the Control of Organizational Behaviour and Belief, in Staw and Salancik, eds., *New Directions in Organizational Behavior*. New York: Wiley, 54.

Sasaki, I., Kotlar, J., Ravasi, D., and Vaara, E. (2020), 'Dealing with Revered Past: Historical Identity Statements and Strategic Change in Japanese Family Firms', *Strategic Management Journal*, 41/3, 590–623.

Schein, E. H. (1985), *Organizational Culture and Leadership* (1st edn) (San Francisco, CA: Jossey-Bass).
Schein, E. H. (2016), *Organizational Culture and Leadership* (5th edn) (San Francisco, CA: Jossey-Bass).
Schultz, M., Hatch, M. J., and Larsen, M. H. (Eds.) (2000), *The Expressive Organization: Linking Identity, Reputation and The Corporate Brand* (Oxford: Oxford University).
Schultz, M., and Hernes, T. (2013), 'A Temporal Perspective on Organizational Identity', *Organization Science*, 24, 1–21.
Schultz, M., and Hernes, T. (2020). Temporal Interplay between Strategy and Identity: Punctuated, Subsumed, and Sustained Modes. *Strategic Organization*, 18(1), 106–35.
Schultz, M. (2016), 'Organizational Identity Change and Temporality', in M. Pratt, M. Schultz, B. E. Ashforth, and D. Ravasi, eds., *The Oxford Handbook of Organizational Identity* (Oxford: UK: Oxford University Press), 93–105.
Smircich, L. (1983), 'Concepts of Culture and Organizational Analysis', *Administrative Science Quarterly*, 28, 339–58.
Suddaby R., Foster W. M., and Trank C. Q. (2010), 'Rhetorical History as a Source of Competitive Headvantage', in J. A. C. Baum, and J. Lampel, eds., *The Globalization of Strategy Research*, Advances in Strategic Management (Vol. 27) (Bingley, UK: Emerald Group Publishing Limited), 147–772.
Swidler, A. (1986), 'Culture in Action: Symbols and Strategies', *American Sociological Review*, 51, 273–86.
Swidler, A. (2001), *Talk of Love: How Culture Matters* (Chicago: University of Chicago Press).
Trice, H. M., and Beyer, J. M. (1984), 'Studying Organizational Cultures through Rites and Ceremonials', *Academy of Management Review*, 9, 653–69.
Trice, H. M., and Beyer, J. M. (1991), 'Cultural Leadership in Organizations', *Organization Science*, 2, 149–69.
Tripsas, M. (2009), 'Technology, Identity, and Inertia through the Lens of "The Digital Photography Company,"' *Organization Science*, 20/2, 441–60.
Vaisey, S. (2009), Motivation and Justification: A Dual-Process Model of Culture in Action', *American Journal of Sociology*, 114: 1675–715.
Van de Ven, A. H., and Poole, M. S. (2005), 'Alternative Approaches for Studying Organizational Change' *Organization Studies*, 26(9), 1377–404.
Van Maanen, J., and Schein, E. H. (1979), 'Toward a Theory of Organizational Socialization, in B. M. Staw (ed.), *Research in Organizational Behavior* (Greenwich, CT: JAI), 209–64.
Van Maanen, J. (1991), 'The Smile Factory: Work at Disneyland', in B. Staw ed., *Psychological Dimensionsof Organizational Behavior* (2nd edn) (Upper Saddle River, NJ: Prentice-Hall).
Weber, K. (2005), 'A Toolkit for Analyzing Corporate Cultural Toolkits', *Poetics* 33, 227–52.
Weber, M. (1968/1978), *Economy and Society*, (Berkeley: University of California Press).
White, L. (1959), *The Evolution of Culture*, (New York: McGraw Hill).
Willmott, H. (1993), 'Strength is Ignorance; Slavery is Freedom: Managing Culture in Modern Organizations. *Journal of Management Studies*, 30/4, 515–52.
Zuckerman, E. W. (1999), 'The Categorical Imperative: Securities Analysts and the Illegitimacy Discount', *American Journal of Sociology*, 104/5, 1398–438.

CHAPTER 6

AN EFFECTUAL ENTREPRENURIAL MODEL OF ORGANIZATIONAL CHANGE

Acting on, reacting to, and interacting with markets as artifacts

SARAS D. SARASVATHY AND SANKARAN VENKATARAMAN

It is familiar to conceptualize organizations as existing in space—such as in markets or societies or other environments, and to see organizational change as a way to adapt to changes in the environment that are largely exogenous to the organization's own activities. However, we can also conceptualize organizations as moving through time, acting on environments in ways in which the environments themselves are shaped and even constructed through the activities of organizations in time. Effectuation offers a toolbox and a viewpoint to develop ideas around the latter conceptualization. In this chapter we attempt to outline the timescape of an effectual process of organizational change.

A time–space perspective of organizational change would at all times be cognizant of the temporal flows within which events and actions unfold. In other words, many actions, choices, events, actors, and outcomes in any change process will only take place in the future and cannot be fully determined, fully predicted, fully controlled, or fully anticipated in the present.

These temporal flows entail fundamental uncertainty in the change process, decoupling original or initial intentions from subsequent (especially final) states and outcomes in any change process. What can be said with any degree of certainty in the change process is that the *realized change* in the future will likely be very different from the initial *intended change*. Any model of the change process must first take into account this decoupling of intended change from the realized change and yet provide connective tissue between these two states. Derived from entrepreneurs' lived experiences in the face of such fundamental uncertainty, effectuation offers a useful process model applicable to organizational change.

The Effectuation Process

The effectuation process was derived from two studies: Sarasvathy (1998), which extracted a set of five heuristic principles from a think-aloud protocol study of expert entrepreneurs, and Dew (2003) that traced the history of the Radio Frequency Identification (RFID) industry. Note that RFID was a precursor to the Internet of Things (IOT) as we know the technology today.

Sarasvathy (1998) defined an expert entrepreneur as someone with ten or more years of full-time experience starting and running multiple ventures, including successes and failures, and at least one public company. In line with well-established precedents in studies of expertise in cognitive science (Ericsson and Smith 1991), this definition identified individuals who had been through every possible experience in entrepreneurship, along with evidence of proven performance. The study also used the protocol analysis method rigorously developed in cognitive science and widely used in over 200 studies of expertise in various domains (Ericsson and Simon 1984) ranging from chess playing (Gobet 2006) to scientific discovery (Klahr and Simon 1999; Schunn and Anderson 2001), the arts (Ericsson 2005) and athletics (Ericsson et al. 2018). Findings from this study revealed five heuristics that characterized entrepreneurial expertise:

1. *Bird-in-hand*: Continually distinguish means within and outside your control, and work only with things already within your control such as, who you are, what you know, and whom you know.
2. *Affordable loss*: Invest no more than what you can afford to lose, whether the investment is in terms of money, time, or other resources. In other words, keep the downside within your control.
3. *Crazy quilt*: Work with whoever wants to work with you. This sets in motion a process of stakeholder *self*-selection that we will elaborate below in terms of the effectual *process*. These stakeholders each provide commitments that underwrite the immediate next steps of the process. This brings the proximate future within the control of the venture.
4. *Lemonade*: When you encounter contingencies outside your control, work creatively to transform them into opportunities, for example by recombining them with bird-in-hand and crazy quilt or by reworking your affordable loss and what you can do with it. This converts the unpredictable itself into a resource.
5. *Pilot-in-the-plane*: Co-create the future of both your organization and its environment.

While it is not unusual in cognitive science to discover heuristics specific to the domain being studied, an unexpected bonus with this set of five heuristics was that they were internally logically consistent. This logic of *non-predictive control* became the basis for the theory of effectuation.

Note that each of the heuristics listed above enables effectuators to make decisions and take actions under uncertainty without relying on predictive information. In other words, the principles of effectuation allow actors to use control itself as strategy (Wiltbank et al. 2006). It is in this sense that effectuation is a logic of non-predictive control. Additionally, effectuation enables individuals and organizations to go beyond an adaptive to a co-creative stance toward their environments. In other words, organizational change need not only be in reaction to environmental changes, but can also be a proactive and interactive reshaping of environments. As Schumpeter pointed out, "It was not enough to produce satisfactory soap, it was also necessary to induce people to wash" (1939: 243).

In a historical study of the RFID industry, Dew (2003) examined interactions between a variety of stakeholders who came together effectually to build MIT's Auto-ID Center. Founded in 1999, this organization included Kevin Ashton, David Brock, Dr. Daniel Engels, Sanjay Sarma, and Sunny Siu, with funding from Procter and Gamble, Gillette, the Uniform Code Council, and a number of other global consumer products manufacturers. The organization developed the Electronic Product Code, a global RFID-based item identification system intended to replace the UPC bar code that led to ways of connecting physical devices and everyday objects to the Internet. Eventually this came to be called the Internet of Things (IOT). In-depth investigations of interactions between all these stakeholders showed that none of these stakeholders had been "induced" to come on board. Instead each had *self*-selected into the endeavor. This finding became embodied into a dynamic process of effectuation, first published in Sarasvathy and Dew (2005).

The above process not only spells out how new organizations emerge but also illustrates how new markets, institutions, and environments could result from these effectual interactions. What makes the interactions effectual is that each stakeholder (be they individuals or organizations) selects into the process for a variety of reasons and motivations, investing no more than each can afford to lose. And as these self-selected stakeholders iteratively transform both their ends and means while leveraging unexpected contingencies that come their way, the effectual network grows and co-creates bits and pieces of its own environment. And in cases like IOT, the resulting space (call it market or institutional or socio-political environment) is more like an artifact of human action than a product of natural evolution. More precisely, effectual entrepreneurship is an exemplar of a science of the artificial (Sarasvathy 2003; Simon 1996).

Figure 6.1 reproduces a graphical illustration of the effectual process from Sarasvathy and Dew (2005). Notice that the process is non-predictive, co-creative, and control-driven at every step. Every actor, at every step, divides the world into things within their control and things outside their control. Of course, it may not always be clear what may or may not be within one's control. Normatively speaking, when in doubt, it is better to

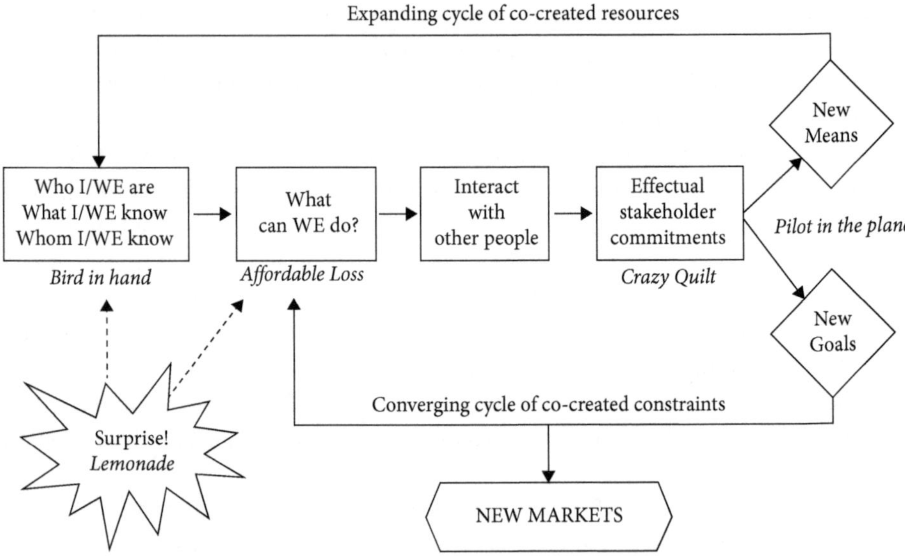

FIGURE 6.1 Effectual Process

(Modified from Sarasvathy and Dew (2005))

treat something as outside one's control than within it. For example, if we could figure out ways to co-create something for as close to zero resources as possible, we have less to worry about accuracy in determining what may or may not be within our control. An interesting practical observation coming from the classroom is that when students begin building ventures effectually, they learn that more things are within their control than they initially assumed. Another interesting observation is that one cannot lose what is not within one's control. We could thus infer that the process itself calibrates and reveals details of what is and is not within the control of effectuators.

Another aspect of the effectual process that has been highlighted in the literature is that it cannot proceed without creative and co-creative acts (Galkina and Lundgren-Henriksson 2017). By emphasizing the need to jump into action without pondering what actions should and should not be taken, the process focuses attention on possibilities, what can and cannot be done with resources already at hand (Sarasvathy and Venkataraman 2011). This shift in focus from "ought" to "can" drives attention away from resource constraints and brings to light slack in the system. In this the effectual process coheres well with approaches such as bricolage (Baker and Nelson 2005; Levi-Strauss 1966; Lévi-Strauss 1962) and affordance (Ansari et al. 2010; Hargrave and Van de Ven 2006; Mesgari and Azad 2013; Norman 1999). At the same time, effectuation explicitly de-emphasizes big goals and large opportunities as precursors to action, breeding sensitivity to mundane projects that are doable and worth doing, that may otherwise remain hidden and hence neglected. In effect, by unrelentingly focusing on both keeping the downside within one's control, while continually doing the doable, the effectual process takes away the most widespread reasons for *not* acting entrepreneurially (Read, et al. 2016a): namely:

- *I don't have a brilliant idea*: Effectuation suggests, just start with who you are, what you know, and who you know. Do the doable that is within your control and that you deem worth doing for any reason of your own. Most enduring ventures, including so-called "unicorns" begin as hobby ventures (e.g. eBay; Starbucks, Apple), or late-movers (e.g., Google was the sixty-fifth search engine; Sony began as a bamboo rice cooker manufacturer).
- *I don't have the resources*: Just think through what you are willing and able to lose for attempting something worth doing. For example, no need to resign from your job. Just commit a reasonable number of nights and weekends. Note that a third of successful ventures are started by hybrid entrepreneurs who concurrently work at full-time or part-time jobs (Folta et al. 2010).
- *I don't know what to do*: Effectuation provides detailed principles, techniques, and mechanisms on what to do starting Day One (Blekman 2011; Read et al. 2016a).
- *I'm afraid to fail*: Affordable loss shows you how to keep the downside within your control. Also, the process emphasizes keeping failures small and quick and the importance of not failing alone. When losses are distributed over a variety of stakeholders each of whom loses no more than they can afford, the process can both outlive failures and build on learnings from them. This diversification of losses over multiple stakeholders also offers psychological safety and the building blocks of solidarity for a longer stint at the process.

Temporally speaking, therefore, the effectual process could be argued to lengthen the viable duration for venturing while concurrently smoothing out turbulence during the venturing time frame. This implies that the overall performance implications of the effectual process have less to do with the probabilities of success and failure than with their temporal flow and magnitudes. Whatever one assumes to be the success/failure rates of any given venture, effectuation may offer the following conjectures about performance:

- When failures occur, they are likely to be smaller and happen earlier than if the venture were built using predictive approaches.
- When success occurs, it is more likely to lead to innovative products and markets, thereby increasing the magnitude of the upside, even if that upside may take longer to coalesce.
- Through a process of outliving failures and cumulating small successes through a co-creative stance, effectuators and their stakeholders are more likely to shape new futures and new markets, even when they themselves may not have predicted them.

An interesting question here is what happens to control as more stakeholders come on board. A pervasive preconception in entrepreneurship is that bringing other people on board entails loss of control over decisions, actions, and eventually over outcomes (Davidsson 1989). This confusion arises from the familiar, much-touted resource acquisition process (Martens et al. 2007) as a process of *necessity*: The necessity to obtain particular resources held by particular stakeholders who have to be appeased, incentivized, convinced, and "sold" to invest in the venture. That of course, entails loss of control through dilution of equity in one form or another. A deep dive into the effectual process entails challenging this preconception that resource requirements *necessarily* drive stakeholder acquisition. The effectual process can be conceptualized as one of *sufficiency*, not necessity. Whoever comes on board by making real commitments to the venture drives the goals of the venture (Sarasvathy and Dew 2005). Not vice versa. In other words, resources pledged by incoming stakeholders, who *self-select* and are *bought-in*, not necessarily "sold" into it, drive what the venture will turn out to be. This links well with concepts from human resources management such as personnel socialization, commitment, and motivation (Cable et al. 2013; Fang et al. 2011; Griffin et al. 2000). There is no necessity engendered by a preconceived vision or goal. This is perhaps the most non-trivial and non-intuitive hard-earned lesson of entrepreneurial expertise. In order to clarify this, it might be useful to turn to a real, worked out example of the effectual entrepreneurial process. Below is the Wikipedia description of the history of Chobani Yogurt.

> Chobani was founded in 2005 by Turkish-Kurdish businessman Hamdi Ulukaya. He chose the name Chobani as a variation of the modern Turkish word çoban,... meaning "shepherd." Chobani was inspired by Ulukaya's childhood raising sheep and goats and making cheese with his family. Not impressed by the yogurt options available in the United States, Ulukaya made strained yogurt at his home in Upstate NY. In 2005, after seeing an ad for a former Kraft Foods yogurt plant for sale in South Edmeston, New York, Ulukaya bought it with a Small Business Administration Loan. He launched the strained yogurt business with the help of a handful of the plant's former employees. His goal was to provide Americans with a more authentic, nutritious and accessible yogurt. In less than five years after launch, Chobani realized over $1 billion in annual sales and became the leading seller of Greek yogurt in America.

In many ways, this story is typical of many highly successful ventures. We can see traces of effectuation here in terms of an entrepreneur starting with who he was, what he knew, and who he knew, scraping together what he could for affordable loss and bringing on board anyone who wanted to work with him on it, including the handful of Kraft employees who were willing to stay on, supplemented by family and community members. But what makes the story starkly effectual is the fact that around the same time, $16 billion food-giant General Mills and owner of, at that time, leading yogurt brand Yoplait, had carried out intensive market research and testing of a "Greek" yogurt as part of their new product development division. Their rationally crafted best-practices-driven $2 million new product development process arrived at the conclusion that there was no market in the US for a Greek yogurt!

The above example raises intriguing issues about the temporal and ontological efficacy of simply doing that which is within one's control, working with whoever comes on board to co-create new futures and markets, *without having to predict "the" future and place a sizeable bet on it.* Before we turn to an exposition of these temporal and ontological aspects of the effectual process, we will briefly summarize the growing literature stream on effectuation.

A Non-Comprehensive Review of Effectuation Research

As mentioned above, effectuation was discovered and drawn from two empirical studies, both comprising doctoral dissertations. The first one (Sarasvathy 1998) consisted of think-aloud verbal protocol analyses of expert entrepreneurs and the second one (Dew 2003) investigated the forty-year history of the development of RFID. The basic theoretical framework consisting of the principles and the non-predictive logic undergirding them can be found in (Sarasvathy 2001). Sarasvathy and Dew (2005) then introduced the effectual process, spelling out a number of specific aspects of interactions between self-selected stakeholders. This was later combined with a two-by-two model of a space of prediction and control, yielding a typology of four strategies (Wiltbank et al. 2006).

Four publications based on empirical studies followed (Dew et al. 2009; Read et al. 2009; Read, Song, and Smit 2009; Wiltbank et al. 2009). These were co-authored by the core group of four researchers using protocol analyses, a scenario-based survey, and a novel form of meta-analysis respectively. As a recent review shows, since then the literature on effectuation has continued to grow through the efforts of others outside the original set of authors (Grégoire and Cherchem 2019). This review appeared in a special issue on effectuation in which the editors estimated that data using a variety of different methods have been collected from over fifty-one countries, multiple industries/domains, and historical periods (Alsos et al. 2019). In addition to standard quantitative analyses and qualitative case studies, methods used so far also include mathematical models (Kuechle et al. 2014; Mauer et al. 2018; Welter and Kim 2018) and historical analyses (Harmeling and Sarasvathy 2013; Olive-Tomas and Harmeling 2019).

Although publications began showing up in fields outside entrepreneurship and management, for example Coviello and Joseph (2012) in marketing, Yusuf and Sloan (2015) in public policy, and Pompe (2013) in ethics, many of the studies continued to investigate whether and when effectuation was used in various domains. For example, Brettel et al. (2012) examined R&D managers in large companies; Fischer and Reuber (2011) investigated social media; Berends et al. (2014) looked into product innovation processes; and several studies looked for effectuation in various aspects of internationalization (Galkina and Chetty 2015; Harms and Schiele 2012; Schweizer et al. 2010). Not all studies focused on merely showing that the effectuation phenomenon occurred. Some began examining its role within, or compared to, or in conjunction with other theories and processes. For example, Murnieks et al. (2011) considered effectuation in their study of the similarity effect in venture capitalists' evaluations of entrepreneurial firms; through an in-depth longitudinal case study of a social enterprise, Akemu et al. (2016) found that effectuation was co-constituted with distributive agency; and in an examination of a major natural disaster in Brazil, Nelson and Lima (2019) discovered new concepts such as diseffectuation and extended effectuation.

Along the way, studies began finding nuances and textures that opened new puzzles and unanswered questions. Garonne et al. (2010) asked whether strategy choices matter at all for nascent firms, and McKelvie et al. (2013) raised the issue of what would be an appropriate dependent variable for effectuation. Delving into uncertainty in new product decisions in software start-ups, McKelvie et al. (2011) interpreted their findings as follows:

> On one hand, the theoretical arguments developed in this article resonate well with Sarasvathy's logic. We suggest that state uncertainty may not meaningfully impede entrepreneurial action, because such uncertainty is assumed a priori in the decision policy of the entrepreneur—as Sarasvathy suggests. However, effectual reasoning also implies a process in which the decision-maker combines a set of available "means" to create some "end" that is only clear and definable post-action. This idea seems to be at odds with our suggestion that the inability to predict the consequences of one's own actions (response uncertainty)—represents a powerful impediment to entrepreneurial action. Such a finding would suggest limits to the utility of effectuation as a lens to inform entrepreneurial behaviors and outcomes comprehensively. (2011: 275)

These studies adjacent to effectuation were harbingers of the literature growing up beyond its infancy. In 2015, a critique of effectuation appeared in the *Academy of Management Review* (Arend, Sarooghi, and Burkemper, 2015) along with four dialog pieces responding to the critique (Garud and Gehman 2016; Gupta et al. 2016; Read et al. 2016b; Reuber et al. 2016). The crux of the critique had to do with difficulties of testing effectuation within a positivist agenda, and the responses offered opportunities to go beyond a positivist view while continuing to strive on the empirical front.

Most recently, scholars have begun diving more deeply into specific aspects of effectuation. Jiang and Rüling (2019), for example, identified two different types of effectuation processes, one externally motivated and the other internally motivated. These differed along five characteristics: perception of uncertainty, nature of aspirations, information processing, orientation of new goals, and attention to new goals. Kerr and Coviello (2019a) examined the literature on network development in depth to conceptualize why and how effectual networks develop and what networks result from the development process. Kerr and Coviello (2019b) elaborated on this by showing how the implementation of effectuation is influenced by the nodal, relational, and structural characteristics of pre-existing and emerging networks. Additionally, efforts to develop new theoretical frameworks to elaborate each principle of effectuation is also under way. For example, based on seven case studies of entrepreneurial teams from Curaçao, Martina (2018) developed an inductive model connecting prospect theory (Kahneman and Tversky 1979) with affordable loss. A theme that offers continuing challenges even as it attracts intrepid and intriguing efforts to overcome these, consists in measurement issues (McKelvie et al. 2019). In sum, exciting progress is under way. But much remains to be done as the pace of research picks up. It is in this spirit of an intellectual endeavor still very much in-the-making that we are undertaking the current task of connecting effectuation with theories of organizational change. We paint these connections in broad brushstrokes, hoping that young scholars better immersed in these two literatures will do the heavy lifting down the road.

An Effectual Process of Organizational Change

In a lovely little article titled "Footnotes to Organizational Change," March (1981) urged us to simultaneously study stability of processes as well as the changes they produce. He further emphasized interplays between rationality and foolishness in how these stable processes engender change. Evoking General Mills' decision not to introduce Greek yogurt, March pointed out, "The problem becomes one of introducing new ideas into organizations at a rate sufficient to sustain the larger system of organizations, when such action is not intelligent for any one organization" (1981: 578). Most importantly, he intuited, "Theories of change in organizations are primarily different ways of describing theories of action in organizations, not different theories." In March's spirit, we will now undertake the task of describing effectual action in organizations, not construct a different theory of effectuation for organizational actors and phenomena. As we do so, we will unmask temporal and ontological features of the effectual process.

A Timescape of the Effectual Process

The temporality of the effectual process is not a temporality driven by targeted consequences (March and Olsen 2010). In other words, in a teleological process, everything begins with prior intentions, goals, visions, and predetermined ends, etc., toward which decisions, actions, behaviors, and strategies move rationally and inexorably. Responses to exogenous events are actively adaptive, driven by desired outcomes that are predicted to be causally related to specific resources that need to be identified and particular stakeholders with those resources to be targeted. As we saw earlier in this chapter, effectuation is both non-predictive and non-adaptive. It is also non-teleological.[1] This implies that goals are endogenous to the effectual process, rather than exogenous antecedents to it. Temporality in an effectual process is driven by stakeholder commitments to particular possibilities that would not arise in the absence of those particular commitments.

While actors in the effectual process may act with several different ends-in-view, some of them clear, some ambiguous, some personal, others pecuniary or value-laden, they have to be open to multiple ways of embodying and even reshaping these through actual commitments forged through the stakeholder self-selection process. On the one hand, just as in a garbage can model (Cohen et al. 1972), various actors and problems and possibilities flow through the environments that effectual entrepreneurs live and build ventures in. On the other hand, through a series of intersubjective interactions leading to commitments from anyone and everyone who is accessible within this stream, a crazy quilt of viable and valuable artifacts is also co-created. In the latter, the process deviates from a stochastic design of the garbage can model into one of artificial desgn (Simon 1996) as the new organization and its environment concurrently come to be.

Artifacts in a Garbage Can?

In combining aspects of the garbage can model with an artifactual mode of action and interaction, one could argue that effectuation incorporates both Chronos and Kairos views of time. Each actor in the process experiences time chronologically as each day in their lives unfolds. Yet each is consciously sensitive to instances of Kairos, when purposeful action can stitch together new artifacts. Proximally speaking, this sensitivity is inherent in the process since the artifacts embody stakeholders' values and aspirations, even though the potential for distal positive consequences become visible only in the act of co-creation itself. In the Chobani case discussed earlier, Ulukaya could not and did not know that the venture would eventually become a massive success. From a proximal temporal perspective, his actions happened within the chronological flow of his life and embodied his values and tastes and childhood memories. Yet, seizing on the Kraft plant closing required a kairotic sensitivity that helped turn the chronological flow into an artifactual fork in yogurt history.

Such kairotic moments are rife in entrepreneurship history, just as they pervade mechanical invention (Usher 1954). Garud and Turunen (2020) in Chapter 22 of this book extend Usher's model to develop a process of organizational change and innovation. Within entrepreneurship, consider just three examples: Raskin arranging a visit by Steve Jobs (who also had just obtained funding from Xerox's venture capital arm) to Xerox PARC so he could understand the need for user friendly interfaces; Howard

[1] Later in this chapter we will see how this connects with the call from organization change scholars for the need to revise theories of planned change from predetermined ends to the emergence of in-process improvisation and learning of possibilities and opportunities as they arise.

Schultz visiting the Starbucks coffee-bean shop in Pike Place Market in Seattle, after noticing that the little shop was becoming a fast-growing client of Hammarplast, where he worked as general manager; more recently, the cofounders of Airbnb realizing the need to build a photography platform so good photographers would take compelling pictures of the rooms listed on Airbnb. In all of these stories, both the serendipitous flows of events and actors as well as the kairotic moments of active interactions and commitments are vividly illustrated. However, each of these kairotic moments can still be seen to be effectual in the sense that the actors did not and could not predict how big the positive consequences would eventually turn out to be. Even kairotic events consisted only in affordable loss commitments to co-create proximately viable and valuable artifacts that might or might not eventually result in major gains.

Control of Time Itself

It is important to emphasize that time itself is a resource, perhaps the most crucial and definitely the most inelastic of resources in human affairs. Yet time is often seen as "free" and therefore a major component of affordable loss investments. Familiar notions such as "sweat equity" in entrepreneurship capture this idea that time can substitute for money in the creation of new ventures. A more psychologically and emotionally salient interpretation of this principle concerns the way it structures choice in terms of what is worth doing. It is one thing to think of affordable loss as a risk minimization technique. Another, more radical consideration is the implicit value it imputes to the course of action at hand. Expert entrepreneurs are cognizant of the fact that committing to something *even if* it eventually fails is to deem that something as somehow intrinsically valuable.

While time is the most valuable resource for mortal actors, it is also a resource entirely within their control, after setting aside the portion of it necessary for basic survival and sustenance, of course. For example, as the literature on hybrid entrepreneurship (Folta et al. 2010; Raffiee and Feng 2014) shows, even people who need to work at a full-time job for a living have control over nights and weekends and other pockets of "free" time to invest in ventures they value. Additionally, as they invest this time in working with self-selected stakeholders, they can expand the quantity, quality, and flows of time invested in the venture. However, this accretion is subject to the particularities of "deals" negotiated with incoming stakeholders. If these deals entail unproductive temporal costs for coordination, monitoring, and conflict resolution, the crazy quilt process could devolve into black holes of unaffordable losses, especially in terms of time.

Larger organizations, those beyond an entrepreneurial stage of development, may have other ways of achieving control over time, for example, by simply hiring more people. However, as the organization changes over time, it may on the one hand experience tightness, or slack on the other, in terms of availability of time. We conjecture that putting in place effectual processes can then help "mop up" temporal slack, when available, and transform it into valuable new possibilities for the organization's future.

Connections of an Effectual Process with Themes from the Literature on Organizational Change

The preliminary exposition above of a timescape of the effectual process that includes kairotic stepping stones within a mundane chronological flow, combined with the exciting possibility of leveraging temporal slack, raises interesting issues in connection with themes from the literature on organizational change. We turn to exploring those next.

Effectual Artifacts Within the Continuous Flow of Time

In a comprehensive review of the literature on organizational change, Purser and Petranker (2005) hark back to Lewin's (Kurt Lewin 1951, 1958) seminal works on the unfreezing-moving-refreezing model, which incorporates iterative cycles of equilibrium followed by transition. Critiquing this stream of works (pardon the pun) as positing the possibility of standing outside the temporal stream to freeze and unfreeze things at will, Purser and Petranker offer a philosophical alternative to equilibrium-based framings of temporality that use "linear, detached and episodic" methods. The article points out the need for taking continuous change more seriously. In continuous models such as those advocated by Weick and Quinn (1999), organizational change is more emergent and improvisationally driven (Crossan et al. 2005) than planned. Echoing March (March 1976, 2006), the authors also call for eschewing pretensions to predictive rationality about the future and embracing a more improvisational temporal dynamic in line with Henri Bergson's (1911/1944) conceptualization of durée (the French word for duration), within which "[e]very attempt to reconstitute change out of states implies the absurd proposition, that movement is made of immobilities" (p. 308).

Such criticisms may also be brought to bear on entrepreneurship literature that is strongly influenced by notions of Schumpeterian disequilibration and Kirznerian re-equilibration (de Jong and Marsili 2015; Keyhani and Levesque 2016). Schumpeter postulated the entrepreneur as the agent of creative destruction in the economy, hence causing disruptions in equilibria (Schumpeter 1942). Energetic debates also continue on the notion of "alertness" attributed to entrepreneurs by Kirzner's works on market process (de Jong and Marsili 2015; Keyhani and Levesque 2016; Korsgaard et al. 2016). In Kirzner's exposition, the alert entrepreneur notices disequilibria and works diligently to bring the market back to equilibrium (Kirzner 1979).

Notwithstanding criticisms and debates about episodic conceptualizations, such as equilibria, it is important to note that while no one can entirely stand outside the flow of time, neither can anyone act without finding a few stepping stones in that flow. The existence of stepping stones is reinforced in Chapter 27 of this handbook where Hernes et al. (2021) refer to these as "bumps along the flow." The effectual process of stakeholder self-selection as explicated earlier offers a mechanism to cope with this temporal conundrum. By making affordable loss commitments to particular courses of action in the immediate future without looking to predict long-term outcomes, entrepreneurs and their stakeholders artifactually co-create stepping stones within the continual flow of time. This allows them to do more than aimlessly drift or merely adapt to their environments without having to act on knowledge of the future that neither they nor anyone else can or does have. Put differently, we propose that effectuators artificially construct episodicity with a continual flow of time.

Structural Inertia and the Co-creation of Identity

Parallel to discussions of episodic models of planned change in contrast to improvisational models of continuous change is another dominant literature stream in organizational change, kickstarted by Hannan and Freeman's (Hannan and Freeman 1984) article on structural inertia. This influential article that also appears within evolutionary views of entrepreneurship such as Aldrich and Martinez (2007) and Sarason et al. (2006), argues against the popular notion of evolution wherein selection processes mostly or even invariably favor adaptable organisms (organizations). In organizational ecologies, the authors show that environmental selection may favor organizations with structural inertia, "organizations whose structures are difficult to change" (1984: 149). This view stands in stark contrast to large literatures that seek to describe and prescribe planned ways to impel and facilitate organizational change. As Burke explains in Chapter 2 of this book, in their recent comprehensive review of seven different models of planned organization change, Stouten et al. (2018) encountered two major challenges having to do with (1) lack of cumulable results and (2) difficulties in learning from experience. The discussion in Burke coheres well with March and Olsen's (2010) exhortation to pay attention to stable as well as change processes within organizations in order to develop a deeper more temporally textured understanding of organizational change.

One important instantiation of the yin and yang of stability and change over time is captured in the notion of organizational identity. As Gioia et al. (2013) point out, there are "three putative 'pillars' of identity (i.e., that which is ostensibly central, enduring, and distinctive)" (2013: 124). An interesting puzzle here consists in the reconciliation of the very notion of "identity" in organizations that seek to navigate the continual flow of organizational change. An important example of this is provided by Ravasi and Schultz (2020) in Chapter 5 of this book in their examination of how organizational identity influences members' commitment or resistance to cultural change. Additionally, complexities inherent in multiple dimensions of organizational reality in which changes could be engendered also give rise to conflicts in institutional logics—that is, guidelines on appropriate interpretations and behaviors leading to successful functioning of organizations (Friedland et al. 1991; Thornton 2004). In this stream of work as in the one related to institutional theory, interesting problems related to change have led to an interest in understanding origins. For several decades, scholars studied problems of institutional change before they turned their attention to institutional entrepreneurship and the formation of new institutions. Similarly, Gioia et al. (2013) point out that organizational identity scholarship has only recently taken an interest in the formation of such identity. This interest, however, is yet to envelop entrepreneurship per se. Effectuation offers opportunities for gains from trade in this arena.

All entrepreneurs struggle with the problem of designing and fostering an identity for their ventures: everything from naming conventions and brand design, to shielding and nurturing sprouts of culture embedded in a soil made of the founders' personal values and preferences. While most entrepreneurs approach these either as purely subjective tasks or entirely objective market-driven prescriptions, effectual entrepreneurship highlights the role of intersubjective interactions with self-selected stakeholders. This is evocative of the need to overcome the dichotomy between inquiry from the inside and inquiry from the outside in organization science (Evered and Louis 1981). One way to do this comes from traditional models of branding in marketing that highlight the importance of market research and the use of professionals using design thinking or other systematic models to come up with brand design (Cooper et al. 2009). Another way can be found on the ground in entrepreneurial reality, where some of these decisions are simply a result of contingent encounters between two or more stakeholders coming together to cocreate the next step in venture creation.

A canonical story illustrates this and connects it up with the current discussion on stability and change in organizational identity formation. On September 7, 1998, Sun Microsystems co-founder, Andy Bechtolsheim, wrote a check to fund Stanford PhD students Larry Page and Sergiy Brin. The company was not yet incorporated. Since the check was made out to "Google, Inc.," the venture became Google, Inc. More interestingly, Page and Brin had to struggle to get funding in the early days when they raised amounts as small as $40 from their professors, until one of them introduced them to Bechtolsheim. By some accounts, Google was the sixty-fifth search engine. There were at least twenty other search engines before Google that had a shot at becoming market leaders. A particularly interesting one was Lycos, one of the earliest search engines, first developed in 1994 by Dr. Michael L. Mauldin and a team of researchers at the Carnegie Mellon University Center for Machine Translation. Lycos raised a lot of money and went public in 1995. By 1998, however, Dr. Mauldin had left Lycos, when the company developed as a portal network offering chat services, personal home pages, horoscopes, and other non-core features. Then in 1999, Lycos abandoned its own engine when it acquired FAST and now it uses Yahoo! to serve up search results. Lycos was purchased for $12.5 B by Terra Networks SA in 2000 and later sold to a Korean company named Daum that made around $250M in revenues with 450 employees in 2009. In 2010 it was sold for $35 M to an Indian company Ybrant and made $63 M in 2018. Google made $136 B in revenues in 2018 with over 100,000 employees worldwide.

Could this striking difference in stability in identity on the part of Google contrasted with incessant (impatient?) change in Lycos have something to do with who came on board and when in each venture and how they influenced both mission and values in the two? One could conjecture that whether stakeholders self-select into a venture for reasons that go beyond predictions of expected return or whether early stakeholders consist of investors with deep pockets placing large bets about expected return would make a substantive difference in the strength and stability of organizational identity as well as financial performance over time. A provocative corollary to this conjecture could be that too early a focus on financial performance as opposed to market co-creation may be detrimental to financial performance in the long run. Intriguingly, this corollary was emphasized by an overwhelming proportion of the expert entrepreneurs who participated in the study by Sarasvathy (1998) from which effectuation was originally derived.

The role of self-selected stakeholders in the formation of organizational identity and its navigation through subsequent cycles of stability and change as the organization grows over time suggests a shift in research focus in organizational studies, namely a shift from the boundary between organization and environment writ large to the boundary between organizations and their stakeholders, be they individuals or other organizational actors. This calls for building bridges between extant literatures on organizational change and identity and literatures on alliances between established organizations and new ventures (Bakker and Josefy 2018; Diestre and Rajagopalan 2012; Knoben and Bakker 2019; Kogut 1988; Mainela et al. 2018). An important attempt in this direction has been initiated by Rheinhardt and Gioia (2021) in Chapter 4 of this handbook, in which they point to remarkable changes in workplace dynamics due to generational factors such as the ethos of millennials as well as new communication technologies that enable them, leading to organizational changes initiated "bottom up" from rank and file employees rather than "top-down" through the C-suite.

Effectual Innovation in Causal Complexity

In addition to tensions between continuous versus episodic change, and the paradoxical advantages of structural inertia and stable identity, another issue of great interest to organizational change scholars consists in the need to innovate. Change is the quintessence of innovation. Yet innovation brings complexities of its own to the study of organizational change. In a special issue focused on the need to complicate and complexify organizational theories more generally, Tsoukas and Dooley (2011) offered an exciting array of possibilities for an effectual process to relate to and even overlap with organizational innovation. An extract from their introductory article describing just one specific contribution to the special issue speaks for itself:

> More specifically, Garud, Gehman and Kumaraswamy (2011) show how innovation at 3M is generated through the interweaving of actors, artifacts and practices over time, allowing for nonlinear innovation to occur. As they note, 3M designed its organization to allow for unexpected innovation; it recognized the critical role of luck and made space for it to (unexpectedly) occur. Taking time seriously, the authors show how constitutive temporality operates: how opportunities and favorable

> moments are endogenized in organizational life through the existence of several organizational arrangements that simultaneously activate different agentic orientations. The anti-dualist ontology is evident throughout the paper: chronos is connected with kairos, improvisation with design, serendipity with intentionality, and personal initiative with collective memory and business policy. (2011:733)

It is interesting to note how evocative the above passage is of the effectual process we described at the beginning of this chapter. Yet, Garud et al. (2011) are describing innovation within a large, albeit putatively "entrepreneurial" organization. In their in-depth study of 3M's processes and practices, Garud et al. paint vivid and detailed portraits of how exactly a variety of innovations came to be. The data included narratives from employees as well as management and spanned everything from organizational identity and coherence of visions of innovation to attitudes toward failure embodied in particular mechanisms within 3M's innovation processes. However, to construct an effectual view of 3M's innovation processes, it would be useful to know more about their employee recruitment practices and data from entry as well as exit interviews in order to highlight stakeholder self-selection. In other words, even the rich and textured data in this study highlights the fact that extant literature on organizational change, whether having to do with temporal flows or identity or innovation, mostly ignores the periphery between organizations and the people who move in and out of them.

Bringing an effectual lens to this literature would highlight these interactions and offer insights that could complement both the views from within and the views from the other boundary, between organizations and environments writ large, such as the one offered in Chapter 19 of this handbook (Maurer et al. 2021). In evolutionary terms, this would be akin to introducing more ecological, inter-species (organism to organism) concepts such as exaptation, wherein things which evolved for some other purpose in the past or even for no purpose at all get co-opted into use for a new purpose that enables an evolutionary advantage at that current time (Andriani and Cattani 2016; Gould and Vrba 1982); niche construction, the idea that niches can be constructed by organisms and are not pre-existing in the environment (Dew and Sarasvathy 2016); endosymbiosis, a process in which two interdependent species combine (including one engulfing the other) to form new organisms (Margulis 2004); epigenetics, namely, interactions with the environment including those with other species that can trigger heritable changes (Holliday 2006; Keller 2014); parasitism, the fact that most organisms are dependent on others and influence environments through others who are dependent on them (Combes 2001; Wilson 2000), etc. Each of these emerging concepts in evolutionary and ecological studies in a variety of sciences moves beyond the more familiar variation, selection, and retention processes that occur at the boundary between organism and environment.

One way to explore the above three new exciting spaces of overlaps is to view them within the temporal flow of a single exemplar organization. The turnaround of Ducati offers such an exemplar.

Turnaround of Ducati: An Example of Effectual Organizational Change

In the 1990s, American venture capitalist firm Texas Pacific Group (TPG) acquired Italian motorcycle manufacturer Ducati Motor SpA. At the time Ducati was moving from stagnation in the marketplace to negative territory in cash flows and earnings. In just one year, their market share had gone down from 4.5% to 3%. Other facts on hand were not encouraging. Even though Ducati's customers were appreciative of its racing achievements and open to repeat purchases, unfulfilled orders due to unpaid suppliers refusing to deliver parts led to soaring warranty costs resulting from deteriorating quality. The factory was in bad repair, production was "artisan" style, with a workforce consisting entirely of engineers and no managerial talent. Morale, not surprisingly, was low to say the least (Chung and Turpin 2004a).

The turnaround task fell to Frederico Minoli, the new CEO, who was given two clear goals: double-digit growth, and an EBITDA margin of about 20%, equal to the profit-level of Harley-Davidson, by far the highest in the industry (Gavetti 2001). While this double-goal was clear and precise, it was not at all clear what Minoli's immediate actions should be. For our purposes, the ensuing sequence of actions and events chronicled in a variety of cases and articles written by several different authors as well as in Minoli's own words in video and online interviews can be viewed in at least two different ways. First, as illustrated in the "standard" process flow in Figure 6.2 which is simply a redrawing of Figure 6.1 with the Ducati story mapped on to its boxes and arrows. Second, we can view the temporal flows within the story on their own. Such a holistic examination will highlight the three overlaps discussed above: the artifactual stones which sometimes interrupt the flows, thereby allowing us to frame them as episodes; the co-creation of identity inside the swirl of change; and, effectual innovation occurring within causal complexity.

In taking on the Ducati turnaround task in the first place, Minoli began with who he was, and what and whom he knew. He was born in Gallarate, Italy, home of the motorcycle racing icon Meccanica Verghera. In an interview with Gavetti on March 22, 2001, Minoli reflected on why and how he took on his task at Ducati:

> I was a University student between '68 and '72. It was a "hot" period in Italy. I remember spending full nights discussing the meaning of revolution, of Marxism... we were all little revolutionaries, we wanted to change the world, everything. Well, while these ideologies are well behind me, I can certainly say that this disposition towards change, the idea that everything should be continuously re-discussed is still the way I look at things. Any decision to change, even if well planned and analyzed, always leads to a new territory that needs to be discovered and charted. That's where I draw my professional satisfaction. I like the process of change, not success *per se*. I accepted [the chance] to run Ducati because I saw a

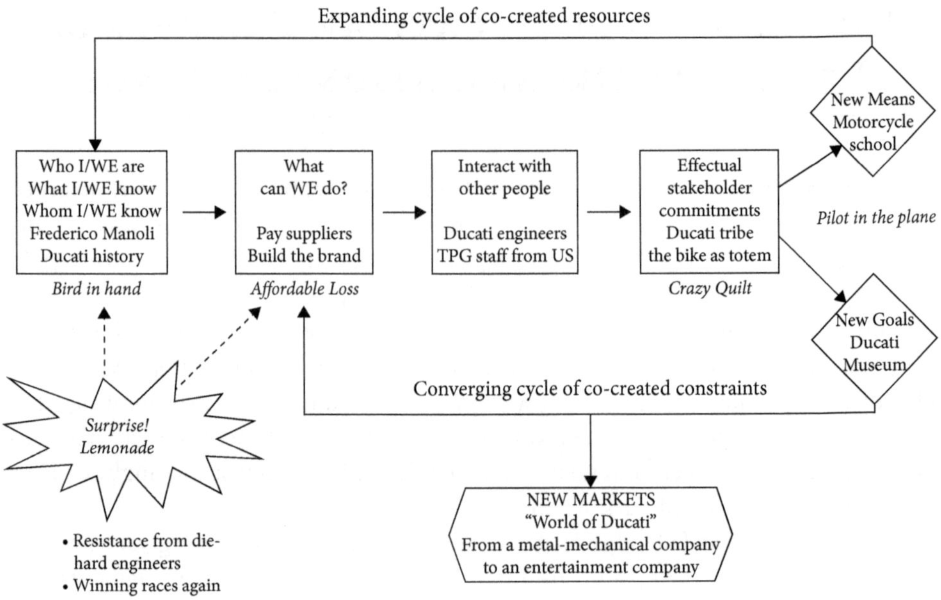

FIGURE 6.2 Ducati Turnaround Mapped Onto the Effectual Process

> company that, beyond its liquidity crisis, needed to be radically changed in order to fully exploit its enormous potential.

Even as a consultant at Bain in Boston, Minoli was not new to turnaround challenges. Earlier while working at McKinsey, he had successfully completed the turnaround of Benetton's US subsidiary.

> I liked to do the stuff that no one else wanted to do. I got involved in the "messy" industries like fashion and entertainment working with companies that had great products but crazy people in the organization.
>
> (Kuemmerle and Coughlin 2004)

With the new turnaround task at hand, Minoli moved to Bologna where the Ducati factory was located. He then dove headfirst into the history of the company, developing a visceral feel for the passion that drove the machine and its makers throughout its history to the current day. In his interview with Gavetti on March 22, 2001, he described it as follows:

> The company was driven by its excellent engineers and designers. These people were all purists, "knee down" riders, fanatics of the motorcycle: speed, performance and innovation were the attributes defining their world. They had an extreme notion of what a Ducati and therefore a Ducati rider, a "Duke," should be. When I came here for the first time, I left with the clear impression that it was almost by chance and not by strategic choice that Ducati had a product that the public loved. The market and

> market research were unknown to them…this place had an incredibly strong engineering culture with a real passion for races…and don't forget that we are in the middle of Emilia, the region of Ferrari, Lamborghini, Maserati and many others, a place where you can almost breathe the passion for races and mechanics.
>
> (Gavetti 2001)

His new-found visceral understanding of this passion led Minoli to a decision that flew in the face of standard management practice:

> Our workers were operating in an essentially obsolete plant. Conventional wisdom suggested investing in the floor and upgrading the manufacturing capability of Ducati. Much to the contrary, we decided to build the [Ducati] museum
>
> (Mitchell and Cassiman 2006).

Would it make sense to invest in a museum given problems in manufacturing, both in terms of factory floor and quality of products rolling off the line? What made the decision affordable loss was the ability to pay off unpaid suppliers to whom production could be outsourced once it became clear what to produce. In other words, the choice was between the conventional wisdom of building the product and then selling to customers versus building the passion brand and then cocreating products with those who were already bought into the passion. In his first week in Bologna, Minoli wrote 4,000 checks to local suppliers, in response to which one of the local priests thanked him since collection plates at the masses were fuller.

> Soon after my arrival I had 20 billion lire to invest. How to invest it? It was a difficult period. Our engineers were frustrated, and our workers were operating in difficult conditions. The roof of the factory was broken. It rained into the factory…and here we are in Bologna, the Italian communist stronghold…you can imagine the pressures from the unions. Well, in this situation, instead of fixing the roof, I decided to build the museum. It was a difficult decision, but it was an important one. It sent the right signal to the company. It symbolized the radicalness of the ideological change I was proposing: that Ducati is not only about beating Japanese bikes, that we have a powerful brand to preserve and develop, and ultimately that Ducati is not, or not only, a motorcycle company. We sell something more: a dream, passion, a piece of history, and the motorcycle is at its core.
>
> (Gavetti 2001)

In Minoli's own words, he realized the need for self-selected stakeholders who were committed to co-creating the brand:

> It was difficult to build the new culture at the beginning. I tried to find the common ground between my American and Italian staff, and then, I realized the passion for Ducati was the glue. The turnaround will be successful only if everyone wanted to be a part of it.
>
> (Mitchell and Cassiman 2006)

But how does one get people to do this? Again, in Minoli's own words:

> There was a tradition at Ducati, the managers of the company parked their cars in front of the main entrance of Ducati. Everybody else was parked half a mile away. We changed that. We said that anybody who had a Ducati could park in front of the entrance. Everyone else, even managers and myself would park far away, we couldn't care less. In the beginning it was strange, pulling some BMWs away from the front, but soon we had all the Ducatis there in the front. Then we all went to motorbike school so we could all ride. We organized buses to take us to watch races together. And we offered discounts to staff who wanted to buy Ducati bikes. (https://vimeo.com/39413912)

As Minoli and his staff began to live and breathe the Ducati experience, they learned to think not in terms of market segments, but in terms of a tribe that could grow into a world of its own:

> I also realized we don't actually have customers. All we have are passionate fans—Ducatisti! When I look at our fans, I cannot see any good ways of segmentation. Maybe the only thing they have in common is Ducati. I can think of them as a tribe in a village: it does not matter who they are, the link between them is the object they love and are passionate about. We used every opportunity to engage our fans in racing. In the Ducati tribe, what is important is not winning, but fighting together. (Chung and Turpin 2004b)

This was a kairotic commitment that not only triggered the transformation of Ducati from a metal-mechanical company into an entertainment company wrapped up in its passion brand, but also cocreated the market for Ducati, or perhaps more appropriately, what became the "world of Ducati" with a variety of events, stores, racing championships, the museum, apparel and accessories, desmodrome[2] clubs and of course, innovative new motorcycles. Every bit of the world of Ducati embodied and lived the "difference" that Livio Lodi, the curator of the Ducati Museum described as follows:

> People ask what's the difference between a Ducati and another racing bike. It's the same difference as eating homemade pasta in a small Italian village versus eating processed pasta in an Italian chain restaurant somewhere in New York. There's no comparison. (www.ducati.com/history/personalities/livio_lodi)

Interestingly, as Minoli acknowledged, this "difference" also mapped onto an important difference that his investors cared about, namely a valuation multiple of twelve to fourteen times earnings in the case of an entertainment company versus four to five times earnings in the case of a metal-mechanical company (https://

[2] The invention of the desmodromic engine by Ducati's legendary engineer Fabio Taglioni in 1955 was the origin of the distinctive sound or "voice" of Ducati bikes.

vimeo.com/39413912). Revenues of the company grew from €105.8 in 1996 to €388.2 in 2003, with a CAGR of 20.4%. EBITDA grew from €11.8 in 1996 to €45 in 2003, with a CAGR of 21.1%.

The Ducati turnaround not only offers instances of the use of effectuation principles in the sequence in Figures 6.1 and 6.2, it also highlights within its temporal flows the three areas of theoretical overlap discussed earlier:

1. Artifactual episodicity within a continual flow of time
2. Stakeholder self-selection in the co-creation of organizational identity
3. Effectual innovation within causal complexity

Discussion: Toward an Artifactual View of Effectual Timescapes of Organizational Change

In a perceptive article titled "Landscape Design" that was meant to complement the literature on "organizational design" Levinthal and Warglien (1999) showed how "actors' perceptions of landscapes are influenced by the manner in which they are framed by devices such as strategy frameworks…" Just as the crux of that article consisted in the manipulation of interdependencies between organizations and their environments with a view to enhancing organizational adaptation, our exposition here is a lens on temporal interdependencies between organizations and the actors who move in and out of them, with a view to enhancing organizational effectuation.

As we saw in the practical examples illustrating theoretical arguments above, flows of actors in and out of organizations reshape spaces both inside and outside organizations in terms of the products and services offered—that is, co-creating its markets—and the values and the organizational routines that embody them—that is, co-creating the identity of the organization both in terms of internal cultural and external reputational contours—as well as the ebbs and flows of its financial fortunes—that is, co-creating its revenues and profits. The way we frame these temporal flows, whether as actors inside the organizations actually engaged in co-creating these spaces or as researchers studying them and training those actors, will influence these flows in a real way.

An effectual frame offers an artifactual view of the spaces *within* which organizations were traditionally conceptualized as operating, thereby allowing us to see those spaces themselves as artifacts of a *process* that operates in a non-predictive, non-adaptive, and non-teleological manner. Put another way, an effectual process consists of individuals and organizations that work with things already within their control to proactively shape and cocreate their environments and futures. The effectual process illustrates the temporal flow of their actions and interactions. Einstein's theory of general relativity froze the universe into a four-dimensional solid in which time has come to be seen as an illusion. This unfortunately also contradicted the empirical observations in quantum mechanics where time appears to be very real indeed. Similarly, our theories of organizations and markets have made it difficult to deal with temporal flows, creating incompatible dichotomies such as episodic versus continual change, and stability versus flexibility in the face of innovations, etc. Returning to a more artifactual approach at the micro level of analysis in terms of an effectual process could allow us to see time as an intrinsic feature of organizational reality with internal and external spaces being engendered through the activity of *organizing*.

References

Akemu, O., Whiteman, G., and Kennedy, S. (2016), 'Social Enterprise Emergence from Social Movement Activism: The Fairphone Case', *Journal of Management Studies*, 53/5, 846–77.

Aldrich, H. E., and Martinez, M. A. (2007). 'Many are Called, but Few Are Chosen: An Evolutionary Perspective for the Study of Entrepreneurship', in *Entrepreneurship* (New York: Springer), 293–311.

Alsos, G. A., Clausen, T. H., Mauer, R., Read, S., and Sarasvathy, S. D. (2019), 'Effectual Exchange: From Entrepreneurship to the Disciplines and Beyond', *Small Business Economics*, 54/3, 1–15.

Andriani, P., and Cattani, G. (2016), 'Exaptation as Source of Creativity, Innovation, and Diversity: Introduction to the Special Section', *Industrial and Corporate Change*, 25/1, 115–31.

Ansari, S. M., Fiss, P. C., and Zajac, E. J. (2010), Made to Fit: How Practices Vary as They Diffuse, *Academy of Management Review*, 35/1, 67–92.

Arend, R. J., Sarooghi, H., and Burkemper, A. (2015), Effectuation as Ineffectual? Applying the 3E Theory-Assessment Framework to a Proposed New Theory of Entrepreneurship', *Academy of Management Review*, 40/4, 630–51.

Baker, T., and Nelson, R. E. (2005), 'Creating Something from Nothing: Resource Construction through Entrepreneurial Bricolage', *Administrative Science Quarterly*, 50/3, 329–66.

Bakker, R. M., and Josefy, M. (2018), 'More Than Just a Number? The Conceptualization and Measurement of Firm Age in an Era of Temporary Organizations', *Academy of Management Annals*, 12/2, 510–36.

Berends, H., Jelinek, M., Reymen, I., and Stultiëns, R. (2014), Product Innovation Processes in Small Firms: Combining Entrepreneurial Effectuation and Managerial Causation', *Journal of Product Innovation Management*, 31/3, 616–35.

Bergson, H. [1911] (1944). *Creative Evolution (A. Mitchell, Trans.)* (New York: Modern Library).

Blekman, T. (2011). *Corporate Effectuation: What Managers Should Learn from Entrepreneurs* (The Hague: Academic Service).

Brettel, M., Mauer, R., Engelen, A., and Küpper, D. (2012), 'Corporate Effectuation: Entrepreneurial Action and its Impact on RandD Project Performance', *Journal of Business Venturing*, 27/2, 167–84.

Burke, W. W. (2021), 'Historical Currents in Scholarship of Organization Change', in M. S. Poole and A. H. Van de Ven, eds., *The Oxford Handbook of Organizational Change and Innovation* (2nd edn) (Oxford: Oxford University Press),

Cable, D. M., Gino, F., and Staats, B. R. (2013), 'Breaking Them In or Eliciting Their Best? Reframing Socialization around Newcomers' Authentic Self-Expression', *Administrative Science Quarterly*, 58/1, 1–36.

Chung, R., and Turpin, D. (2004a). Rebuilding a Passion Brand: The Turnaround of Ducati (A), IMD-5-0666.

Chung, R., and Turpin, D. (2004b). Rebuilding a Passion Brand: The Turnaround of Ducati (B), IMD-5-0667.

Cohen, M. D., March, J. G., and Olsen, J. P. (1972), 'A Garbage Can Model of Organizational Choice', *Administrative Science Quarterly*, 17/1, 1–25.

Combes, C. (2001). *Parasitism: The Ecology and Evolution of Intimate Interactions* (Chicago, London: University of Chicago Press).

Cooper, R., Junginger, S., and Lockwood, T. (2009), 'Design Thinking and Design Management: A Research and Practice Perspective', *Design Management Review*, 20/2, 46–55.

Coviello, N. E., and Joseph, R. M. (2012), 'Creating Major Innovations with Customers: Insights from Small and Young Technology Firms', *Journal of Marketing*, 76/6, 87–104.

Crossan, M., Cunha, M. P. E., Vera, D., and Cunha, J. (2005), 'Time and Organizational Improvisation', *Academy of Management Review*, 30/1, 129–45.

Davidsson, P. (1989), 'Entrepreneurship—and After? A Study of Growth Willingness in Small Firms', *Journal of Business Venturing*, 4/3, 211–26.

de Jong, J. P., and Marsili, O. (2015), 'The Distribution of Schumpeterian and Kirznerian Opportunities', *Small Business Economics*, 44/1, 19–35.

Dew, N. (2003). *Lipsticks and Razorblades: How the Auto ID Center Used Pre-Commitments to Build the Internet of Things*. Available at SSRN 964507.

Dew, N., Read, S., Sarasvathy, S. D., and Wiltbank, R. (2009), 'Effectual versus Predictive Logics in Entrepreneurial Decision-Making: Differences between Experts and Novices', *Journal of Business Venturing*, 24/4, 287–309.

Dew, N., and Sarasvathy, S. D. (2016), 'Exaptation and Niche Construction: Behavioral Insights for an Evolutionary Theory', *Industrial and Corporate Change*, 25/1, 167–79.

Diestre, L., and Rajagopalan, N. (2012), 'Are all 'Sharks' Dangerous? New Biotechnology Ventures and Partner Selection in R&D Alliances. *Strategic Management Journal*, 33/10, 1115–34.

Ericsson, K. A. (2005), 'Recent Advances in Expertise Research: A Commentary on the Contributions to the Special Issue', *Applied Cognitive Psychology*, 19/2, 233–41.

Ericsson, K. A., Hoffman, R. R., Kozbelt, A., and Williams, A. M. (2018), *The Cambridge Handbook of Expertise and Expert Performance* (New York, NY: Cambridge University Press).

Ericsson, K. A., and Simon, H. A. (1984), *Protocol Analysis: Verbal Reports as Data*. (Cambridge, MA: The MIT Press).

Ericsson, K. A., and Smith, J. (1991), *Toward a General Theory of Expertise: Prospects and Limits*. (Cambridge: Cambridge University Press).

Evered, R., and Louis, M. R. (1981), 'Alternative Perspectives in the Organizational Sciences: "Inquiry from the Inside" and "Inquiry from the Outside"', *Academy of Management Review*, 6/3, 385–95.

Fang, R., Duffy, M. K., and Shaw, J. D. (2011), 'The Organizational Socialization Process: Review and Development of a Social Capital Model', *Journal of Management*, 37/1, 127–52.

Fischer, E., and Reuber, A. R. (2011), 'Social Interaction via New Social Media:(How) Can Interactions on Twitter Affect Effectual Thinking and Behavior?' *Journal of Business Venturing*, 26/1, 1–18.

Folta, T. B., Delmar, F., and Wennberg, K. (2010), 'Hybrid Entrepreneurship', *Management Science*, 56/2, 253–69.

Friedland, R., Alford, R. R., Powell, W. W., and DiMaggio, P. J. (1991), 'The New Institutionalism in Organizational Analysis', *The New Institutionalism in Organizational Analysis*, 232–63.

Galkina, T., and Chetty, S. (2015), 'Effectuation and Networking of Internationalizing SMEs', *Management International Review*, 55/5, 647–76.

Galkina, T., and Lundgren-Henriksson, E.-L. (2017), 'Coopetition as an Entrepreneurial Process: Interplay of Causation and Effectuation', *Industrial Marketing Management*, 67, 158–73.

Garonne, C., Davidsson, P., and Steffens, P. R. (2010), 'Do strategy choices matter for nascent firms? A study on effectuation and causation impacts on new ventures outcomes'. *Proceedings of the 7th AGSE International Entrepreneurship Research Exchange*.

Garud, R., and Gehman, J. (2016), 'Theory Evaluation, Entrepreneurial Processes, and Performativity', *Academy of Management Review*, 41/3, 544–9.

Garud, R., Gehman, J., and Kumaraswamy, A. (2011), 'Complexity Arrangements for Sustained Innovation: Lessons from 3M Corporation', *Organization Studies*, 32/6, 737–67.

Garud, R., and Turunen, M. (2021), 'Microfoundations of Innovation as Process: Usher's Cumulative Synthesis Model', in M. S. Poole and A. H. Van de Ven, eds., *Oxford Handbook of Organizational Change and Innovation* (2nd edn.). (Oxford, UK: Oxford University Press),

Gavetti, G. (2001). Ducati, *HBS No. 9-701-132*.

Gioia, D. A., Patvardhan, S. D., Hamilton, A. L., and Corley, K. G. (2013), 'Organizational Identity Formation and Change', *The Academy of Management Annals*, 7/1, 123–93.

Gobet, F. (2006), 'Expertise in Chess', in Cambridge University Press.

Gould, S. J., and Vrba, E. S. (1982), 'Exaptation—A Missing Term in the Science of Form', *Paleobiology*, 8/1, 4–15.

Grégoire, D. A., and Cherchem, N. (2019), 'A Structured Literature Review and Suggestions for Future Effectuation Research', *Small Business Economics*, 54/3, 1–19.

Griffin, A. E., Colella, A., and Goparaju, S. (2000), 'Newcomer and Organizational Socialization Tactics: An Interactionist Perspective', *Human Resource Management Review*, 10/4, 453–74.

Gupta, V. K., Chiles, T. H., and McMullen, J. S. (2016), 'A Process Perspective on Evaluating and Conducting Effectual Entrepreneurship Research', *Academy of Management Review*, 41/3, 540–4.

Hannan, M. T., and Freeman, J. (1984), 'Structural Inertia and Organizational Change', *American Sociological Review*, 149–64.

Hargrave, T. J., and Van de Ven, A. H. (2006), 'A Collective Action Model of Institutional Innovation', *Academy of Management Review*, 31/4, 864–88.

Harmeling, S. S., and Sarasvathy, S. D. (2013), 'When Contingency is a Resource: Educating Entrepreneurs in the Balkans, the Bronx, and Beyond', *Entrepreneurship Theory and Practice*, 37/4, 713–44.

Harms, R., and Schiele, H. (2012), 'Antecedents and consequences of effectuation and causation in the international new venture creation process', *Journal of International Entrepreneurship*, 10, 95–116.

Hernes, T., Hussenot, A., and Pulk, K. (2021), 'Time and Temporality of Change Processes, in M. S. Poole and A. H. Van de Ven eds., *Oxford Handbook of Organizational Change and Innovation* (2nd ed.) (Oxford, UK: Oxford University Press),

Holliday, R. (2006), 'Epigenetics: A Historical Overview', *Epigenetics*, 1/2, 76–80.

Jiang, Y., and Rüling, C.-C. (2019), 'Opening the Black Box of Effectuation Processes: Characteristics and Dominant Types', *Entrepreneurship Theory and Practice*, 43/1, 171–202.

Kahneman, D., and Tversky, A. (1979), 'Prospect Theory: An Analysis of Decision under Risk', *Econometrica*, 47/2, 363–91.

Keller, E. F. (2014), 'From Gene Action to Reactive Genomes', *The Journal of Physiology*, 592/11, 2423–9.

Kerr, J., and Coviello, N. (2019a), 'Formation and Constitution of Effectual Networks: A Systematic Review and Synthesis,' *International Journal of Management Reviews*, 21/3, 370–97.

Kerr, J., and Coviello, N. (2019b), 'Weaving Network Theory into Effectuation: A Multi-Level Reconceptualization of Effectual Dynamics', *Journal of Business Venturing*, 35/2, 105937.

Keyhani, M., and Levesque, M. (2016), 'The Equilibrating and Disequilibrating Effects of Entrepreneurship: Revisiting the Central Premises', *Strategic Entrepreneurship Journal*, 10/1, 65–88.

Kirzner, I. M. (1979). *Perception, Opportunity, and Profit: Studies in the Theory of Entrepreneurship* (Chicago: University of Chicago Press).

Klahr, D., and Simon, H. A. (1999), 'Studies of Scientific Discovery: Complementary Approaches and Convergent Findings', *Psychological Bulletin*, 125/5, 524.

Knoben, J., and Bakker, R. M. (2019), 'The Guppy and the Whale: Relational Pluralism and Start-Ups' Expropriation Dilemma in Partnership Formation', *Journal of Business Venturing*, 34/1, 103–21.

Kogut, B. (1988), 'Joint Ventures: Theoretical and Empirical Perspectives', *Strategic Management Journal*, 9/4, 319–32.

Korsgaard, S., Berglund, H., Thrane, C., and Blenker, P. (2016), 'A Tale of Two Kirzners: Time, Uncertainty, and the "Nature" of Opportunities', *Entrepreneurship Theory and Practice*, 40/4, 867–89.

Kuechle, G., Boulu Reshef, B., and Carr, S. (2014), *Antecedents of Entrepreneurial Decision-Making: Prediction and Control Oriented Strategies*.

Kuemmerle, W., and Coughlin, W. J. (2004), 'Ducati and Texas Pacific Group—A "Wild Ride" Leveraged Buyout', *HBS 9-801-359*.

Levi-Strauss, C. (1966). *The Savage Mind* (Chicago: University of Chicago Press).

Lévi Strauss, C. (1962). *La pensée sauvage* (Vol. 289) (Paris: Plon Paris).

Levinthal, D. A., and Warglien, M. (1999), 'Landscape Design: Designing for Local Action in Complex Worlds', *Organization Science*, 10/3, 342–57.

Lewin, K. (1951), 'Field Theory in Social Science' (D. Cartwright, Ed.) (New York: Harper & Brothers).

Lewin, K. (1958), 'Group Decisions and Social Change', in Maccoby, E. E., Newcomb, T. M. and Hartley, E. L., eds., *Readings in Social Psychology* (New York: Holt, Rhinehart and Winston),

Mainela, T., Puhakka, V., and Sipola, S. (2018), 'International Entrepreneurship beyond Individuals and Firms: On the Systemic Nature of International Opportunities', *Journal of Business Venturing*, 33/4, 534–50.

March, J. G. (1976). The technology of foolishness. In J. G. March, and J. P. Olsen, eds., *Ambiguity and Choice in Organizations* (Bergen, Norway: Universitetsforlaget), 69–81.

March, J. G. (1981), 'Footnotes to Organizational Change', *Administrative Science Quarterly*, 26/4, 563–77.
March, J. G. (2006), 'Rationality, Foolishness, and Adaptive Intelligence', *Strategic Management Journal*, 27/3, 201–14.
March, J. G., and Olsen, J. P. (2010), *Rediscovering Institutions* (New York, NY: Simon and Schuster).
Margulis, L. (2004), 'Serial Endosymbiotic Theory (SET) and Composite Individuality', *Microbiology Today*, 31/4, 172–5.
Martens, M. L., Jennings, J. E., and Jennings, P. D. (2007), 'Do the Stories They Tell Get Them the Money They Need? The Role of Entrepreneurial Narratives in Resource Acquisition', *Academy of Management Journal*, 50/5, 1107–32.
Martina, R. A. (2018), 'Toward a Theory of Affordable Loss', *Small Business Economics*, 54/3, 1–24.
Mauer, R., Wuebker, R., Schlüter, J., and Brettel, M. (2018), Prediction and Control: An Agent-Based Simulation of Search Processes in the Entrepreneurial Problem Space', *Strategic Entrepreneurship Journal*, 12/2, 237–60.
McKelvie, A., Chandler, G. N., DeTienne, D. R., and Johansson, A. (2019), 'The Measurement of Effectuation: Highlighting Research Tensions and Opportunities for the Future', *Small Business Economics*, 54/3, 1–32.
McKelvie, A., DeTienne, D. R., and Chandler, G. N. (2013), 'What is the Appropriate Dependent Variable in Effectuation Research?' *Frontiers of Entrepreneurship Research*, 33/4, 4.
McKelvie, A., Haynie, J. M., and Gustavsson, V. (2011), 'Unpacking the Uncertainty Construct: Implications for Entrepreneurial Action', *Journal of Business Venturing*, 26/3, 273–92.
Mesgari, M., and Azad, B. (2013), 'A selective review of affordance lens for organization-technology research'. Paper presented at the Academy of Management Proceedings.
Miner, A., Crossan, M., and Maurer, C. (2021). VSR Models of Change as Normative Practical Theory, in M. S. Poole, and A. H. Van de Ven, eds., *Oxford Handbook of Organizational Change and Innovation* (2nd edn.) (Oxford, UK: Oxford University Press).
Mitchell, J., and Cassiman, B. (2006). *Ducati: In Pursuit of Magic* (A), IES-168.
Murnieks, C. Y., Haynie, J. M., Wiltbank, R. E., and Harting, T. (2011), 'I Like How You Think': Similarity as an Interaction Bias in the Investor–Entrepreneur Dyad', *Journal of Management Studies*, 48/7, 1533–61.
Nelson, R., and Lima, E. (2019), 'Effectuations, Social Bricolage and Causation in the Response to a Natural Disaster', *Small Business Economics*, 54/3, 1–30.
Norman, D. A. (1999), 'Affordance, Conventions, and Design', *Interactions*, 6/3, 38–43.
Olive-Tomas, A., and Harmeling, S. S. (2019), 'The Rise of Art Movements: An Effectual Process Model of Picasso's and Braque's Give-and-Take during the Creation of Cubism (1908–1914)', *Small Business Economics*, 54/3, 1–24.
Pompe, V. (2013), 'Moral Entrepreneurship: Resource Based Ethics', *Journal of Agricultural and Environmental Ethics*, 26/2, 313–32.
Purser, R. E., and Petranker, J. (2005), 'Unfreezing the Future: Exploring the Dynamic of Time in Organizational Change', *The Journal of Applied Behavioral Science*, 41/2, 182–203.
Raffiee, J., and Feng, J. (2014), Should I Quit My Day Job? A Hybrid Path to Entrepreneurship', *Academy of Management Journal*, 57/4, 936–63.
Ravasi, D., and Schultz, M. (2021), 'Organizational Identity and Culture Change', in M. S. Poole, and A. H. Van de Ven, eds., *Oxford Handbook of Organizational Change and Innovation* (2nd edn.) (Oxford, UK: Oxford University Press).

Read, S., Dew, N., Sarasvathy, S. D., Song, M., and Wiltbank, R. (2009), 'Marketing under Uncertainty: The Logic of an Effectual Approach', *Journal of Marketing*, 73/3, 1–18.

Read, S., Sarasvathy, S. D., Dew, N., and Wiltbank, R. (2016a). *Effectual Entrepreneurship* (London: Routledge).

Read, S., Sarasvathy, S. D., Dew, N., and Wiltbank, R. (2016b), 'Response to Arend, Sarooghi, and Burkemper (2015): Cocreating Effectual Entrepreneurship Research', *Academy of Management Review*, 41/3, 528–36.

Read, S., Song, M., and Smit, W. (2009), 'A Meta-Analytic Review of Effectuation and Venture Performance', *Journal of Business Venturing*, 24/6, 573–87.

Rheinhardt, A. and Gioia, D. (2021), 'Upside-Down Organizational Change: Sensemaking, Sensegiving, and the New Generation', in M. S. Poole and A. H. Van de Ven, eds., *Oxford Handbook of Organizational Change and Innovation* (2nd edn.) (Oxford, UK: Oxford University Press),

Reuber, A. R., Fischer, E., and Coviello, N. (2016), 'Deepening the Dialogue: New Directions for the Evolution of Effectuation Theory', *Academy of Management Review*, 41/3, 536–40.

Sarason, Y., Dean, T., and Dillard, J. F. (2006), 'Entrepreneurship as the Nexus of Individual and Opportunity: A Structuration View', *Journal of Business Venturing*, 21/3, 286–305.

Sarasvathy, S. D. (1998). 'How Do Firms Come To Be: Toward a Theory of the Pre-Firm', Ph. D. dissertation. Carnegie Mellon University, Pittsburgh, PA.

Sarasvathy, S. D. (2001), 'Causation and Effectuation: Toward a Theoretical Shift from Economic Inevitability to Entrepreneurial Contingency', *Academy of management Review*, 26/2: 243–63.

Sarasvathy, S. D. (2003), 'Entrepreneurship as a Science of the Artificial', *Journal of Economic Psychology*, 24/2, 203–20.

Sarasvathy, S. D., and Dew, N. (2005), 'New Market Creation through Transformation', *Journal of Evolutionary Economics*, 15/5, 533–65.

Sarasvathy, S. D., and Venkataraman, S. (2011), 'Entrepreneurship as Method: Open Questions for an Entrepreneurial Future', *Entrepreneurship Theory and Practice*, 35/1, 113–35.

Schumpeter, J. A. (1942), 'Creative Destruction', *Capitalism, Socialism and Democracy*, 825, 82–5.

Schumpeter, J. A. (1939). *Business Cycles*,Vol. 1 (New York: McGraw-Hill).

Schunn, C. D., and Anderson, J. R. (2001). 'Acquiring Expertise in Science: Explorations of What, When, and How', in K. Crowley, C. D. Schunn, and T. Okada, eds., *Designing for Science: Implications from Everyday, Classroom, and Professional Settings* (Mahwah, NJ: Lawrence Erlbaum Associates), 83–114.

Schweizer, R., Vahlne, J.-E., and Johanson, J. (2010), 'Internationalization as an Entrepreneurial Process', *Journal of International Entrepreneurship*, 8/4, 343–70.

Simon, H. A. (1996). *The Sciences of the Artificial*. Cambridge, MA: MIT Press.

Stouten, J., Rousseau, D. M., and De Cremer, D. (2018), 'Successful Organizational Change: Integrating the Management Practice and Scholarly Literatures', *Academy of Management Annals*, 12/2, 752–88.

Thornton, P. H. (2004). *Markets from Culture: Institutional Logics and Organizational Decisions in Higher Education Publishing*. Stanford, CA: Stanford University Press.

Tsoukas, H., and Dooley, K. J. (2011), 'Introduction to the Special Issue: Towards the Ecological Style: Embracing Complexity in Organizational Research', Organizational Studies 32(6), 729–35.

Usher, A. P. (1954). *A History of Mechanical Inventions*. Courier Corporation.

Weick, K. E., and Quinn, R. E. (1999), 'Organizational Change and Development', *Annual Review of Psychology*, 50/1, 361–86.

Welter, C., and Kim, S. (2018), 'Effectuation under Risk and Uncertainty: A Simulation Model', *Journal of Business Venturing*, 33(1), 100–16.

Wilson, E. O. (2000). *Sociobiology*: Cambridge, MA: Harvard University Press.

Wiltbank, R., Dew, N., Read, S., and Sarasvathy, S. D. (2006), 'What To Do Next? The Case for Non-Predictive Strategy', *Strategic Management Journal*, 27/10, 981–98.

Wiltbank, R., Read, S., Dew, N., and Sarasvathy, S. D. (2009), 'Prediction and Control under Uncertainty: Outcomes in Angel Investing', *Journal of Business Venturing*, 24/2, 116–33.

Yusuf, J.-E., and Sloan, M. F. (2015), 'Effectual Processes in Nonprofit Start-Ups and Social Entrepreneurship: An Illustrated Discussion of a Novel Decision-Making Approach', *The American Review of Public Administration*, 45/4, 417–35.

PART II

DIALECTICAL MODELS OF CHANGE

CHAPTER 7

THE PARADOX PERSPECTIVE AND THE DIALECTICS OF CONTRADICTIONS RESEARCH

TIMOTHY J. HARGRAVE

INTRODUCTION

BEGINNING in the 1980s, and especially since a 1988 volume edited by Cameron and Quinn, the study of contradictions in organizations has coalesced into a "paradox perspective" on organizing. Scholars contributing to the paradox perspective have debated a number of core tensions as they have sought to establish a set of foundational concepts that define the perspective. One question that has long challenged paradox scholars is the relationship of dialectics to the paradox perspective. The purpose of this chapter is to compare and contrast stylized versions of the paradox and dialectical perspectives to identify the similarities and differences in their core assumptions. This is a timely task because scholars are currently debating what is included in the conceptual core of the paradox perspective, and whether there has been a premature convergence around a set of concepts that (as I will discuss) includes some elements of dialectical theory but excludes others. Following dialectics, I suggest that scholars move toward the development of a new perspective, which I refer to as the contradictions perspective. I broadly outline what this perspective might look like and examine recent works that have moved in its direction.

Since its emergence in the 1980s, the paradox perspective has had a managerial, prescriptive flavor. Its purpose has been to address the question of how organizational actors can increase organizational effectiveness by productively managing persistent contradictions in organizing. Major milestones in the development of paradox research, for example Lewis's 2000 article and Smith and Lewis's (2011) dynamic equilibrium model, are characterized by a focus on the intentional strategies that managers use to cope with persistent, irreconcilable tensions between mutually exclusive organizational elements. According to the dynamic equilibrium model, managers accept the persistent simultaneity of opposites and then search for synergies between them. Works building on these seminal contributions have adopted their managerial perspective.

Dialectical theory presents an alternative viewpoint to paradox theory. It is one of the "grand" theories of change (Farjoun 2017, 2020; Hegel 1807; Marx 1867; Van de Ven and Poole 1995) and provides a distinct way of interrogating reality that, in contrast to the paradox perspective, is concerned with the sweep of history rather than with management strategies. It posits that contradictions and the poles that constitute them are not static things but rather are incessantly changing, and can even be transformed into new, different entities; cannot be disentangled from other contradictions at multiple levels of analysis; and are not technical problems to be solved but rather must be addressed through political action. Further, from a dialectical perspective, the actions that actors take to manage contradictions invariably have unintended consequences and can even undermine themselves.

While paradox scholars have been interested in the dialectical perspective's assumption that contradictions can be transformed rather than persistently coped with, they have done so with an eye to understanding how managers can intentionally produce transformations (e.g., Cameron and Quinn 1988). Incorporating dialectics into the paradox perspective in this way is at odds with the fundamental nature and assumptions of dialectical theory, just discussed. Recently, in reaction to the sense that the dynamic equilibrium model and its underlying assumptions are prematurely coming to define the field (Cunha and Putnam, 2019), scholars have called for re-introducing dialectics into the paradox perspective in a way that captures its full flavor. This is a welcome move that could potentially open up new possibilities for contradictions research, because the dialectical perspective calls into question the notion that contradictions can be fully understood in their totality by boundedly rational managers, let alone effectively managed. The larger story that dialectics tells is that in the face of paradoxes, even the most willful and political astute managers can only grope their way toward a deeper understanding of reality, have little control of the process, and cannot predict or guide the process to its eventual "outcome"—which itself is just a single moment in a never-ending flow of activity. Dialectics suggests that the labeling of the relationship between two contradictory elements as a "paradox" is only convenient shorthand for something much more dynamic and multifaceted, and describes the relationship at just a moment in time in a perpetual process in which the relationship between the two elements continuously changes—and in which the elements themselves could change into something else.

After first defining key terms and describing the development of the paradox perspective, I then present dialectical theory, highlighting both the features that it shares with the received paradox perspective and those that distinguish it. I then consider the issue of integrating dialectics with the conceptual core of the paradox perspective, as suggested by Schad et al. (2016). I propose that scholars perhaps would be better served by thinking of their work in terms of the "dialectics of contradictions research" rather than in terms of the "paradoxes of the paradox perspective" (Smith et al. 2017). Doing so opens up the dialectical possibility of working to establish a new perspective that enfolds the paradox and dialectical perspectives. I outline the contours of such a "contradictions perspective" and review recent efforts to bring dialectical and paradox perspectives together. One of these is Hargrave and Van de Ven's 2017 article that depicts organizations as intentionally managing contradictions (in accordance with the paradox perspective) while also acknowledging that their efforts to do so will have unintended consequences and be influenced by political conditions within the organization (à la dialectical theory.) In addition, I discuss Raisch et al.'s (2018) "learning spiral" model. This model takes Hargrave and Van de Ven's model one step further, describing organizational learning spirals in which organizations cycle between convergence and divergence of contradictory elements, and between dynamic equilibrium between these elements and transformation of their relationship.

From a contradictions perspective that sublates dialectical and paradox perspectives, the paradoxes that managers address exist for a moment in time and are simplified representations of contradictions that are entangled with many other contradictions, only appear to be static, and can even come to take a new form. A contradictions perspective would accept the paradox perspective's assumption that managers try to establish order and increase organizational effectiveness in the face of seemingly impossible choices; however, it would also suggest these choices are even harder than they seem because they take place within a context that cannot be controlled. Ultimately, a contradictions perspective suggests managerial humility.

Overview of Literature: Contradictions, Paradoxes, and Dialectics

A contradiction is a dynamic tension between opposed, interdependent elements that presuppose each other for their existence and meanings and together form a unity (Werner and Baxter 1994). Some scholars have taken the view that contradictions are solely epistemological in nature, that is, that they are entirely a product of discourse (Putnam et al. 2016). More common among paradox and dialectics scholars, however, is the view that contradictions are both ontological and epistemological in nature, that is, that they are both inherent in reality apart from human experience (Bhaskar 1975; Schad and Bansal 2018) and at the same time subjectively experienced by actors based on their socially constructed knowledge of objective reality. A gap exists between the contradictions managers perceive (epistemological contradictions) and "real" objective (ontological) contradictions because of managers' perceptual and cognitive limitations (Schad and Bansal 2018). Addressing the gap between reality and our knowledge of it has been the work of philosophers and other scholars for thousands of years (e.g., Plato, *c.*380 BC; Hegel 1807, 1812), and understanding how managers address the gap is the work of management scholars today.

In the remainder of this section I present two leading perspectives on the management of contradictions, which I have already introduced briefly above. These are the paradox and dialectical perspectives. Table 7.1 provides a summary comparison of the two perspectives. It also refers to a third perspective, the contradictions perspective, which I outline near the end of the chapter.

Table 7.1 Paradox, Dialectical, and Contradictions Perspectives

	Paradox Perspective	Dialectical Perspective	Contradictions Perspective
Theoretical focus	Prescriptive, organizational. Focus on how organizations should manage contradictions.	Descriptive, historical. Focus on how contradictions are transformed over time.	Prescribes the management of contradictions that are recognized as continuously changing and situated within the social totality.
Ontology	Latent tensions inherent in reality become salient to actors under particular conditions. Nature of latent contradictions (material/ideal) typically not specified. Contradictions are stable and separable from each other.	Marxian: Contradictions in capitalism are inherent and dualistic. Hegelian: Socially constructed. Contradictions exist only in inadequate human understanding of existence. Contradictory elements continuously change quantitatively and qualitatively in relation to each other and can be transformed (sublated) into a single element. They are inseparable from each other and the totality.	Epistemological contradictions created through discourse are embedded in material reality (e.g., structure) and come to be experienced as objective reality. Contradictions can be discursive, material, or between discursive and material elements. Contradictions are continuously changing both quantitatively and qualitatively.
Epistemology	Actors construct salient contradictions at first as dualisms and then as dualities.	Marxian: Proletariat first unaware of contradictions (dualisms) of capitalism due to false consciousness, but then develop class consciousness through praxis. Hegelian: Humans uncover reality through oppositional learning processes.	Actors become aware of contradictions as they experience tensions between contradictory elements, and engage these contradictions humbly and practically in an effort to understand their complex and changing nature and therefore better manage them.

Process of Change	Emphasis on managerial control. Managers differentiate and coordinate contradictory elements in order to produce synergy—practices and arrangements that satisfy both poles.	Emphasis on mobilization, conflict, and actions with unintended consequences. Marxian: Proletariat engages in praxis and class conflict. Hegelian: Actors are unwitting instruments of Spirit.	Actors manage contradictions through social processes that involve learning, are constituted by power relations, and include elements of both conflict and cooperation. Even as actors learn, their efforts to produce order have unintended consequences.
Outcome of process of change	Persistence: Ongoing production of order through reproduction of dynamic tension between contradictory elements.	Transformation. Marxian: Overthrow of bourgeoisie, advent of communism. Hegelian: Progressively higher understandings of existence, with Spirit ultimately coming to recognize itself.	Relationship between contradictory elements can persist, change incrementally, or be transformed. These outcomes are contingent upon actors' ability to learn, their political skill, and the distribution of power. They are also unpredictable and temporary.

Adapted from Hargrave and Van de Ven, 2017

The Paradox Perspective

The dominant view in organization theory on how actors manage contradictions (both epistemological and ontological ones) has come to be known as the paradox perspective. According to this perspective, as the name suggests, organizational actors experience contradictions as paradoxes. A paradox is a tension between "contradictory yet interrelated elements—elements that seem logical in isolation but absurd and irrational when appearing simultaneously" (Lewis 2000: 760). Carson, Poole, Lambert, and Lammers refer to a paradox as a "no-win situation in which the alternatives are mutually exclusive and to fail to embrace either one will result in unacceptable consequences" (2017: 289). A key tenet of the paradox perspective is that managers cannot resolve paradoxes, so the management task is to accept them and productively use the tension between contradictory elements (Lewis 2000; Lewis and Smith 2014; Smith and Lewis 2011).

As discussed, the paradox perspective began to emerge in the 1980s. Although tensions between opposing forces have typically been grist for the mill of philosophers and other scholars interested in understanding and describing the course of human history (Hegel 1807, 1812; Marx 1867; Marx and Engels 1845–6; Van de Ven and Poole 1995), from its inception the paradox literature has had a narrower, more prescriptive, managerial flavor. In the opening chapter of their groundbreaking 1988 book *Organizational Paradox and Transformation*, Cameron and Quinn refer to paradox as "a problem to be solved" (298).

Lewis's seminal 2000 paper represented the first effort in organization studies to comprehensively and systematically consider the management of paradoxes. Lewis defined paradoxes as an epistemological problem, writing that "paradoxical tensions stem from polarized cognitive or social constructions" (761). In addition, she presented a taxonomy of common organizational paradoxes (the paradoxes of learning, organizing, and belonging) and identified three approaches to managing them. These were acceptance, confrontation, and transcendence. Notable for the purposes of this chapter was Lewis's definition of transcendence as "impl[ying] the capacity to think paradoxically" and as "critically examining entrenched assumptions to construct a more accommodating perception of opposites" (764). With this move, the paradox perspective came to define a paradox as a thing that persists indefinitely, as a tension that must be accepted and can be used productively, but cannot be resolved or transformed. For paradox researchers, this means that organizational learning about managing paradoxes involves developing a deeper understanding of the relationship between two stable contradictory poles and how to manage it. Lost was the idea of metamorphosis—the idea that the very nature of a focal contradiction can change from one thing into another.

The work on paradox that followed was characterized by a convergence on and refinement of the core concepts presented in Lewis's (2000) article. Researchers largely came to accept that managers experienced contradictions as paradoxes, that is, as tensions between stable opposing elements that had to be accepted and could not be transformed, and they sought to develop insights into where paradoxes come from and how they can be productively utilized. One noteworthy example came from Lüscher and Lewis (2008), whose empirical study of organizational change at Lego found that managers developed creative solutions to the frustrating paradoxes they faced by engaging in collective rounds of "sparring," which involved iterating between sensemaking and questioning. Lüscher and Lewis found that sparring enabled managers to move from viewing paradoxes as a "mess" to viewing them as a "more manageable mess" or "workable certainty" that provides a basis for action.

The definitive statement of the paradox perspective is provided by Smith and Lewis's (2011) dynamic equilibrium process model. An important contribution of this model is that in addition to identifying strategies for managing paradoxes, it prescribes a process—a sequential movement involving multiple strategies—for effectively managing paradoxes. The model first identifies the conditions—resources scarcity, plurality, and rapid change—under which managers begin to experience seemingly irreconcilable tensions between contradictory and functionally interdependent elements. It then posits that managers initially construct these tensions as dualisms—opposed and mutually exclusive (Farjoun 2010)—but can then effectively manage them by accepting their coexistence, constructing them as dualities—interdependent and complementary (Farjoun 2010), and iterating between them or finding synergies that accommodate both of them. Hence from the paradox perspective (as represented by the dynamic equilibrium model), paradoxes persist indefinitely, and managers can at best learn how to cope with them.

Dialectics

Dialectical theory provides a different perspective on contradictions. For the ancient Greeks, dialectics was an oppositional method of dialogue for progressively uncovering the truth (producing a greater correspondence between reality and knowledge of it). The dialectical method has found modern expression in places such as pragmatism and critical theory (Langley and Sloan 2011; Nielsen 1996), and was adopted as a lens on management in the 1970s and 1980s (Greiner 1972; Pettigrew 1979; Zeitz 1980.) In this same period, organizational theorists began to articulate dialectical management techniques such as devil's advocacy and dialectical inquiry (see discussions in Fairhurst 2019 and Langley and Sloan 2011). In addition, as noted, scholars such as Cameron and Quinn (1988) looked to dialectics for insights into how managers could stimulate breakthrough innovations.

This work notwithstanding, dialectics is typically thought of, not as a management tool or theory, but rather as a description of the constantly changing nature of reality and human understanding of it. Van de Ven and Poole (1995) identify dialectics as one of the four fundamental motors of change in social life, along with teleology (purposeful action), life cycle (organic growth), and evolution (competitive survival). Langley and Sloan (2011) argue that dialectics is not only a managerial method and mantra (orienting device for managerial thinking), but also a narrative for understanding history and a tool for critiquing oppressive social arrangements. Speaking to the grand scope of the dialectical perspective, Hegel referred to dialectics as "in general the principle of all motion, of all life, and of all activation in the actual world" (Hegel 1807: 128f).

The most prominent and influential dialectical theories come from Hegel (1807, 1812, 1817) and Marx (1867; Marx and Engels 1845–6, 1848). Both offer a triadic formulation of the dialectic often represented as thesis-antithesis-synthesis, although neither scholar used these terms and both actually rejected it. As the discussion proceeds, I will often distinguish Marxian and Hegelian dialectics because doing so allows me to tease out more specific recommendations for future research.

Hegel was interested in the trajectory of human history and the role of philosophy in it. He saw history as unfolding through a process in which the thesis, or current understanding of reality, is always found to be inherently incomplete as a description of reality and principle for action, and as implying its contradictory element. Mason (1996) writes that "Hegel claimed that all descriptions of things immediate, complete, or definitive turn out, on closer examination, to be inadequate" (295). In Hegelian dialectics, the interplay between the thesis and antithesis inevitably produces a new element, the synthesis or transformation (although Hegel most frequently referred to it as the "concrete"). The transformation is qualitatively different than the thesis and antithesis. Hegel referred to the process of transformation using the German word *aufheben*, which means to both preserve and destroy (Schneider 1971). The word is best translated into the English word "sublate," which means "to assimilate a smaller entity into a larger one" (Lexico, n.d.). According to Hegel (1812: 33), the transformation "is a new concept, but one higher and richer than the preceding—richer because it negates or opposes the preceding and therefore contains it, and it contains even more than that, for it is the unity of itself and its opposite." Once the transformation is produced it becomes the thesis and invariably suggests a new antithesis, as the dialectical process continues (Benson 1977; Hargrave and Van de Ven 2006; Nielsen 1996; Seo and Creed 2002; Van de Ven and Poole 1995). For Hegel, this process proceeds until the world ends or human knowledge of reality is complete. Thus Hegel presented a view of history in which humanity progressively moves toward truth through an oppositional learning process.

Marx's dialectical materialism also describes a process of change driven by contradictions. Yet whereas Hegel saw history as a process of employing human cognition to uncover hidden and even mystical truths, Marx started with material circumstances and social relations. Marx saw the contradictions in the capitalist mode of production as the generative force in human history. Most fundamentally, Marx observed that capitalism divides people into two groups, those who own the means of production (the bourgeoisie) and wage laborers (the proletariat), and at the same time establishes these groups as classes whose interests are in conflict (1845–6; Benson 1977). Building on Benson (1977), Seo and Creed (2002) write that according to the Marxian dialectical view, the deepening of structural contradictions in capitalism (which is the thesis) "sets the stage for the emergence of a transformational collective consciousness" (240) among actors whose interests are not served by existing arrangements, leading them to engage in political action (the antithesis) to build the power they need to challenge and ultimately transform existing arrangements and eliminate its contradictions (Prichard and Creed 2020). The force of change in this process is praxis, which Seo and Creed define as "political action embedded in a historical system of interconnected yet incompatible institutional arrangements" (223).

Although Hegelian and Marxian dialectics differ in obvious respects, they share important foundational features (Farjoun 2017, 2019, 2020; Schneider 1971). Most conspicuously, they both describe human world history as a process of change that is rooted in contradictions that are inherent in reality, and also as driven forward by actors seeking to resolve these contradictions. For Hegel, the dialectic is driven by a desire to know reality, while for Marx it is motivated by the desire to transform an inherently exploitative mode of production (capitalism). Marxian and Hegelian dialectical perspectives also share a number of other features, which I now discuss. These features challenge the conceptual foundation of the received paradox perspective.

Ontology of Becoming

Both Hegelian and Marxian dialectics insist that the very nature of contradictions is ceaseless immanent change. This "ontology of becoming" is also found in Chinese thought (Jing 2020; Jing and Van de Ven 2016; Peng and Nisbett 1999). From a dialectical perspective, the world and all the things in it are in a continuous state of becoming (Benson 1977; Jing 2020); in fact, the perspective challenges the idea that things (unchanging entities) even exist. Farjoun (2017) writes that "dialectics replaces the notion of 'thing' with notions of 'process' and 'relation'" (10). In one formulation of the dialectic, Hegel posited that "becoming" is the sublation of "being" (the thesis) and "nothing" (the antithesis.) By introducing the dimension of time, the concept of becoming incorporates and subsumes the more static categories of existence and non-existence. The concept of becoming captures that living things move from non-existence to existence and then return again, and that we are living and dying at the same time (Hegel 1812). When one looks at an organization through the lens of becoming, the ideas that stable contradictory elements exist and that their relationship can be managed are revealed to be analytical conveniences that managers and researchers use to simplify and make sense of a more complex, ever-changing organizational reality.

In dialectical theory, contradictory elements ebb and flow in relation to one another. As one element increases in quantity the other can decrease—even up to the point that the exertion of one leads to its own demise and the ascendancy of the other. For example, if we examine the contradiction between worker autonomy and control through the lens of becoming, we see that the exertion of more control by managers means less autonomy for workers—up until the point that the workers rebel or quit, at which point there is full autonomy and no control. At this point managers must establish new methods of control that allow for more autonomy, meaning that both control and autonomy come to have different constitutive definitions. In other words, the contradictory elements can change in both quality and quantity (Engels 1876; Farjoun 2017; Hegel 1812). And so the process continues. As already noted, though, sometimes the process of change is characterized not by quantitative and definitional changes in the contradictory elements but rather by their transformation into a new element that subsumes the earlier ones. I discuss such transformation further below.

The emphasis of dialectical theory on continuous becoming implies the inadequacy of the relatively static language and understandings that managers use to make sense of the world, and also the inadequacy of the paradox literature's tendency to depict contradictory elements as stable things that can be seen, named, studied, and managed. Benson (1977) saw dialectical theory as an antidote to the reification of categories. Dialectics suggests that while managers may sometimes experience tensions between contradictory elements as a stable state that must be accepted and coped with, the interplay between contradictory elements can be much more dynamic than this, involving shifts in power between the elements and ongoing re-definition of the elements themselves. Accepted categories are much more contingent than they appear, both to managers and paradox scholars.

Ontology: Inherent or Socially Constructed?

As Smith, Lewis, Jarzabkowski, and Langley (2017) state, the dialectical perspective raises another question about the ontology of contradictions, which is whether contradictions are inherent in reality or socially constructed. As noted, paradox scholars have tended to represent paradoxes as both. The inherent view depicts "paradoxes as living within systems, structures, processes, and routines...outside of individual agency" (Smith et al. 2017: 4). From this view, contradictions exist in sociomaterial reality whether or not they are enacted by organizational actors. They may for instance exist in an organization's production processes, human resource practices, or government relations, awaiting enactment by managers. In contrast, the constitutive, social constructionist view (Putnam et al. 2016; Schad et al. 2016; Fairhurst 2019) depicts contradictions as "arising from individual and collective sensemaking, discourse, and relationship dynamics" (Smith et al. 2017: 5). From this view, contradictions are created "bottom-up" through "discourses, social interaction processes, practices, and ongoing organizational activities" (Putnam et al. 2016: 67; also see Reinhardt and Gioia 2020). Contradictions do not exist "out there" waiting to be discovered but rather come into existence as actors interact with each other to reach agreement on meaning and action. The reason that the view is known as constitutive is that it depicts materiality as constituted by discourse, and structure as constituted by agency.

Paradox scholars have brought the inherent and constitutive views together by arguing that contradictions are latent, but then through processes of social construction come to be perceived as salient and managed by organizational actors (Smith and Lewis 2011). Schad and Bansal (2018) distinguish contradictions in "biophysical reality" from managers' experiences of them, while Hahn and Knight (forthcoming) distinguish latent contradictions from their enactment in sociomaterial reality.

The dialectical perspective also takes a both/and view of whether contradictions are inherent or socially constructed; however, the Marxian and Hegelian perspectives differ markedly. For Marx, as already noted, contradictions are inherent in the structure of capitalism, and in particular in the division of society into two classes with an antagonistic relationship based on their opposing relations to the means of production. While these contradictions are initially latent in the sense that they are not recognized by the proletariat, who are being exploited by the system, they come through praxis to be the basis of class consciousness and catalyze class struggle, leading to a new set of economic and social arrangements (socialism, communism). This perspective has a different emphasis than, but is not incompatible with the paradox perspective, because it depicts contradictions as inherent (in the structure of capitalism), initially latent, and then salient to actors, who then address them through praxis.

Hegel also saw contradictions as both the nature of reality and as produced through social processes. However, because he was an idealist, his dialectics had an entirely different starting point and purpose than Marx's (which it pre-dated). The Hegelian perspective on contradictions takes us into the realm of metaphysics. For Hegel, the nature of existence is not material; rather, it is Spirit (*Geist*; also translated as Mind) in the process of becoming. It does this ("becomes") through the dialectical process, which plays out through humans in the material realm, and more specifically through the triadic dialectical process. Through this process humans progressively move closer to "absolute knowledge," and Spirit achieves self-consciousness. Thus for Hegel (1807) humans are instruments for Spirit as it comes to know itself.

The Hegelian dialectical perspective poses a much greater challenge to the paradox perspective than does the Marxian perspective. It raises the difficult question of what it means to say that a contradiction is inherent in reality by suggesting not only that contradictions are processes not things, as described above, but also that they are inherent in an aspect of reality apart from the sociomaterial. The implications for paradox scholarship are profound. It is one thing to say that contradictions are socially constructed through discourse, another thing to say that they are inherent in socially constructed aspects of sociomaterial reality (such as class divisions), and an entirely different thing to say that they are inherent in an unseen aspect of reality which is the "real" reality. Hegelian dialectics suggests that the main task for managers is not to persistently cope with stable contradictory elements, as the paradox perspective suggests, but rather to continuously transform ever-changing contradictory elements. It is not to create a workable certainty (Lüscher and Lewis 2008) but to continue overcoming what we think is certain until there is nothing else to learn.

A forthcoming paper by Hahn and Knight (2019) significantly advances the ontology of contradictions. It does not explicitly address Hegel's metaphysics, but it comes very close by drawing on quantum theory in physics. (The relationship between quantum physics and metaphysics is of growing interest to philosophers of science; see for example Marmodoro 2015.) Hahn and Knight's quantum approach provides a novel account of the relationship between ontological and epistemological paradoxes. Drawing upon the quantum concept of superposition, it argues that paradoxes exist latently along with non-paradoxical possibilities prior to being observed by humans, but only as "potentialities." Paradoxes then become real when organizational actors creatively enact them in specific sociomaterial forms. At this point the unchosen potentialities collapse and are no longer possible. The implications for paradox scholars include the possibility that organizational paradoxes are real only to the extent that managers see them instead of other potentialities, and that they are more likely to persist to the extent that the organizational "apparatus," for example culture and incentives, influences managers to continue seeing them. In short, Hahn and Knight underscore an important implication of the ontology of Hegelian dialectics, which is that managers and paradox scholars must consider not just what is seen but also what is not seen.

Transformation

Another difference between the dialectical perspective and the paradox perspective is the former's insistence that while contradictory elements rise and recede with each other in dynamic tension, as just noted, they may also be transformed into something all-new that dissolves the tension. Clegg and Cunha refer to transcendence, that is, transformation, as "the defining characteristic of dialectics" (2017: 15).

For Marxists, transformation occurs through class conflict. The building of class consciousness in the proletariat and the efforts of the bourgeoisie to instill false consciousness (Gramsci 1926; Lukács 1923) oppose one another until praxis leads to the advent of socialism and eliminates the contradictions of capitalism. As already mentioned, transformation is also central to Hegel's idealistic dialectics, with history being a process of transforming human knowledge.

Both Hegel and Marx took deterministic views of the dialectic. For Hegel, the dialectical process proceeds until it produces human freedom through the realization of absolute knowledge, while for Marx it proceeds until there is freedom in communism. In *Capital*, Marx wrote that "capitalist production begets, with the inexorability of a natural process, its own negation. This is the negation of [the] negation. It does not re-establish private property [but rather communism], co-operation and possession in common of the land and the means of production" (1867: 929).

Other varieties of dialectical theory do not see transformation as inevitable, however. In their desk analysis of three case studies, Abdallah et al. (2011) conclude that while organizational leaders introduce transformational discourse into their organizations to resolve contradictions (e.g., the tension between the affordability and quality of healthcare), mechanisms that facilitate the acceptance of transformational ideas (e.g., strategic ambiguity) undermine the process of organizational transformation. Thus, transformation does not necessarily set the stage for further dialectical transformations but can instead be ephemeral. Werner and Baxter (1994) summarize that in some dialectical processes, "two opposing tensions may simply continue their ongoing struggle of negation in some cycling/spiraling and/or linear fashion" (352).

De Rond and Bouchikhi's 2004 study of a strategic alliance provides a strong challenge to teleological dialectical models. These scholars examine the playing out of tensions between planning and emergence, competition and cooperation, and control and autonomy. De Rond and Bouchikhi found that the strategic alliance was not able to transcend these tensions. They conclude that "dialectical tensions... are not there to serve an explicit or unconscious purpose. They just are. Thus, we are cautious in assuming that dialectical forces will collide and inevitably produce a new order, in a Hegelian or Marxist sense" (66).

Conclusions such as those of Abdallah et al. and De Rond and Bouchikhi suggest that transformation and persistent paradox, as described in the dialectics and paradox literatures respectively, are both possible outcomes of dialectical processes. There is no reason to assume that contradictions will definitively persist or be transformed. It should be noted, however, that these scholars' conclusions may not challenge the idea of transformation so much as provide insight into it by examining it from a closer distance over a shorter time period. One might see the dissipation of transformational ideas and the persistence of paradox when studying managers closely over a relatively small number of years, yet see the transformation of contradictions when taking a historical perspective.

Totality

Another important feature of dialectical perspectives is their insistence that the contradictions actors experience are entangled with other contradictions and embedded in a larger whole. This is perhaps clearest with the Hegelian perspective, which as noted posits that through the dialectical process we overcome our partial understandings and progressively move toward "absolute knowledge" of existence. Mason writes that through the Hegelian dialectical process, "all things show their necessary relation to something else and ultimately to the whole" (1996: 295). Marxian dialectics also view specific contradictions of capitalism as interconnected with many other contradictions across multiple levels of social organization (e.g., individual, group, department, organization, industry, society, the world). Particular contradictions cannot be understood without reference to other contradictions and "the totality" (Benson 1977; Werner and Baxter 1994).

Building upon Friedland and Alford (1991), Seo and Creed (2002) recognize that the contradictions in society's institutional orders produce contradictions within organizations. A manager addressing an organizational contradiction may not be able to transform or even cope with a focal contradiction without addressing the other contradictions to which it is linked, at multiple levels of analysis. For example, the approach a country takes to the tension between cultural unity and diversity (e.g., whether it embraces diversity or marginalizes and oppresses minority groups) could impact how its global trade policy negotiators address the tension between economic efficiency and respecting human rights, which could influence another country's national economic policies, which could in turn affect how a corporate manager experiences and addresses the tension between earning higher profits and creating benefits for many other stakeholders.

To date, paradox scholars have given little attention to the embeddedness of organizational contradictions within larger systems. Building off work by Cunha and Putnam (2017), Fairhurst writes that "best practices regarding paradox have had a tendency to decontextualize, abstract, and reify contradictions... Not so with dialectical research, in which contradictions are embedded in processes of struggle and confrontation in entwined social systems" (2019: 10). She continues: "It is not that scholars don't recognize that paradoxical tensions co-occur...; it is that they bypass how managers and other actors voice and perceive their co-occurrence" (13). In short, dialectics suggests that paradox researchers have not fully represented the contradictions that managers face.

Unintended Consequences

Another hallmark of the dialectical perspective, and one which is grounded in the perspective's process ontology and concern for totality, is the view that actions to address contradictions tend to have unintended consequences. Because contradictions are intertwined with many other contradictions, and because contradictory elements are continuously shifting in relationship to each other, qualitatively changing, and even being transformed, actors experience great uncertainty in trying to manage them. Unless managers operate in very loosely coupled environments so that their decisions are buffered and the impacts of these decisions are contained (Weick 1976), their actions are likely to have unpredictable impacts. Further, when the direct impacts of these actions are reinforced in positive feedback loops rather than dampened in negative feedback loops, they can reverberate across the totality in ways that no boundedly rational decision-maker could envision (Merton 1936).

As noted above, the unintended consequences of actions to address contradictions can be as dramatic as self-negation; efforts to promote one pole can undermine themselves by sowing the seeds for growth of the other pole. Thus the unintended outcome of exertion of control can be the loss of control; and the unintended outcome of focusing on long-term organizational viability is organizational death because short-term viability is undermined. (A similar point could be made about emphasizing short-term viability.) Max Weber took the view that every "idea, in the end, always and everywhere works against its original meaning and destroys itself" (Marianne Weber 1950: 385; cited in Schneider 1971: 674).

The role of unintended consequences in historical processes is evident in both Hegelian and Marxian dialectical perspectives. For Hegel, "world-historical" actors such as Napoleon Bonaparte drove history inexorably toward absolute knowledge, but these actors were not aware that their actions were contributing to realization of this end. Hegel spoke of Spirit's clever use of humans in this way as "the cunning of reason" (*c.*1822). This obviously is a very positive view of the role of unintended consequences in history. Marx, on the other hand, took a view that corresponds with that of Weber. As already discussed, he saw the efforts of the bourgeoisie to accumulate wealth through control of the means of production as unintentionally awakening praxis among the proletariat, and ultimately producing their (the bourgeoisie's) own demise.

Thus dialectical perspectives cast doubt on the paradox perspective's stance that contradictions can be effectively managed. They support that view that processes of change are "unowned" (Mackay and Chia 2013.) Efforts to divide and sequentially attend to contradictory elements, or to find synergies, among them are bound to go awry and will succeed only serendipitously. It should be noted, however, that dialectics' emphasis on unintended consequences does not undermine the assumption that paradoxes persist. In fact, they may be one of the reasons that they do persist.

Summary

Table 7.1 shows that the paradox and dialectical perspectives have different purposes and work from different assumptions about the nature of contradictions, how they change over time, and how actors engage them.

The purpose of the paradox perspective is to advance the practice of management. It seeks to provide guidance to managers on how they can preserve order and increase organizational effectiveness in the face of difficult, even paralyzing tensions. It presents contradictions as stable, separable, and, if accepted rather than resisted, controllable. The dialectical perspective asks challenging questions of paradox scholars by undercutting its key assumptions and even its raison d'être. It paints a picture of organizational contradictions as continuously changing in character as well as amount, and as difficult, if not impossible, to disentangle from the many other contradictions they are intertwined with at levels of analysis ranging from the individual to the global. Further, it depicts efforts to manage contradictions as "unowned" sequences of events in which the efforts of any particular actor are bound to have unintended consequences, even undermining themselves. In short, the dialectical perspective suggests that despite the best efforts of managers to produce order when managing contradictions, disorder will inevitably be a part of organizational life (Cunha and Putnam 2019).

Table 7.1 reveals another issue that must be addressed by paradox scholars as they move forward. This is the foundational issue of the nature of reality and contradictions in it. To date, paradox scholars have taken the view that paradoxes are both inherent in reality as well as socially constructed (e.g., Smith and Lewis 2011); however, it has not explained this position (Hahn and Knight, forthcoming.) Important questions that stem from this position must be addressed—but on these questions dialectical theory provides no clear critique or guidance. If contradictions are inherent in reality, where? In the very spiritual fabric of the universe, as Hegel thought? Or are they inherent in nature and then somehow come to also be present in the social world, as Schad and Bansal (2018) suggest? Or are they to be found in social structure, as Marx presented it—in which case, are they even inherent at all, since social structures are socially constructed?[1]

Paradox research could avoid these questions by taking a "constitutive approach" (Putnam et al. 2016) that sees contradictions as springing entirely from interactions, as artifacts of communication among people addressing shared problems. Adopting this stance is risky, however, for it suggests that managers should focus their attention only on what they can easily see. In contrast, the stance that contradictions are inherent in reality carries with it the massive suggestion that if managers are to understand and effectively manage contradictions, instead of practicing "management by exception" they should strive for deeper understanding of the totality.

Where are we Now? The Dialectics of Contradictions Research

As others have demonstrated, research into the management of paradoxes has grown considerably in recent years (Cunha and Putnam 2019; Schad et al. 2016; Putnam et al. 2016.) With this growth has come a convergence around a set of core assumptions and concepts, as elaborated in the dynamic equilibrium model (Smith and Lewis 2011).

[1] Those taking a constitutive view of contradictions would argue that the contradictions of capitalism are not actually inherent but rather are socially constructed. From this perspective, these contradictions are initially produced through discourse and then come through social construction processes to be taken-for-granted elements of objective reality. Berger and Luckmann (1967) describe this process as involving habitualization, institutionalization, objectivation, and legitimation. See also Giddens (1984).

While establishment of an accepted conceptual core is part of the development of any field of scholarship and a necessary precursor to the practice of normal science (Kuhn 1987), recently some scholars have suggested that the institutionalization of the paradox perspective as an established paradigm has been premature (Cunha and Putnam 2019). By coalescing around the viewpoint that paradoxes are technical problems that can be abstracted from their contexts and managed as part of the production of organizational order, paradox researchers have perhaps unintentionally marginalized perspectives such as the dialectical, which emphasize complexity, embeddedness, and disorder.

Of course, the paradox perspective is itself not an unchanging object, and we can view its changing nature through a dialectical lens. The thesis—the paradox perspective, which emphasizes simplicity, synergy, and order, has been found to be a cogent yet incomplete description of reality, inviting its own antithesis—dialectics, which emphasizes complexity, conflict, and disorder (Smith et al. 2019).

What is next in the development of the paradox perspective? How will the tension between these two contradictory elements play out? Will the development of the paradox perspective follow a paradox model or a dialectical model? Will the paradox perspective continue as the thesis, standing in contradiction to the antithesis of dialectics, with the two interdependent, and their boundaries shifting in relation to each other as they incorporate each other's ideas, or will there be a transformation that sublates the two perspectives? Or perhaps the two will develop together in parallel through a separation approach (Poole and Van de Ven 1989), with one being a management theory and the other an organizational and institutional theory.

Aware of the criticisms and limitations of the perspective, paradox researchers—including some of the key figures in the perspective's development—have sought to advance the field by incorporating elements of the antithesis into the intellectual core. In one prominent effort to define the contours of the paradox perspective, Schad et al. (2016) recognize the need for a more dynamic ontology of paradoxes; they suggest that paradox researchers treat "paradox as a verb, emphasizing the persistent interactions between opposing elements" (23). Further, they suggest that the concept of complex adaptive systems (Dooley 2020) be adopted as a meta-theoretical principle of the paradox perspective moving forward. They note that this principle, which resonates with the dialectical concept of totality, challenges the view that paradoxes can be managed and suggests instead possibilities such as self-organization and spontaneous order. These scholars even go so far as to advocate that dialectics also be adopted as one of the meta-theoretical principles guiding future paradox research. Smith and colleagues highlight some of these same points in their introductory chapter to the 2017 *Oxford Handbook of Organizational Paradox*. For example, they draw upon dialectics in discussing the need for a process ontology of paradox, referring to the "shifting and reforming" within contradictory elements as paradoxical changes, and the "ongoing fluid motion between ever-changing dualities" as dialectical changes (6).

While these efforts to expand the thesis (paradox theory) by incorporating the antithesis (dialectics) are useful and praiseworthy, they seek to assimilate the antithesis into the thesis rather than to sublate it (i.e., assimilate it into a higher understanding, the synthesis or transformation). According to Hargrave and Van de Ven (2017), assimilation impedes innovation because when it occurs, the elements of the antithesis that are incorporated into the thesis are justified "by appealing to the logic of the dominant element," and therefore "the logic of the subordinate element is not expressed, and the tension between the contradictory elements is not engaged" (331). This seems to be a good description of recent efforts to incorporate elements of dialectics into the paradox perspective, because they preserve the perspective's present conceptual core while deleting key aspects of the dialectical model. For example, Schad and colleagues recommend that dialectics provides a tool for understanding the dynamics of the "*persistence* of paradox" (43; italics added), thereby treating the transformation of paradox as an impossibility. Similarly, they suggest that "balance" be adopted as one of the metatheoretical principles for understanding the relationship between contradictory elements—thereby diminishing the role of politics and power imbalances in oppositional change processes. And while, as just noted, Schad et al. refer to the need to study the constant interplay between contradictory elements, they do not suggest the need to consider that the two elements themselves are changing from moment to moment in relation to each other.

The paradox literature is, in the language of Raisch et al.'s 2018 model (described further below), currently in a convergence mode, with paradox scholars seeking to incorporate major ideas from dialectics without fundamentally changing its character as a perspective that is concerned with how managers handle persistent paradoxes over a relatively short time horizon and few levels of analysis. Broadening the core of the paradox perspective to include dialectical theory—but only to the extent that it helps explain the persistence of paradox—is not really to incorporate dialectical theory at all, since it violates one of the theory's main principles. Incorporating dialectics in this way is not a step toward sublation.

Instead of discussing the paradoxes of paradox (Smith et al. 2019), perhaps scholars should begin to consider the dialectics of contradictions research. Doing so opens up the possibility of transforming the literature rather than preserving the thesis and assimilating the antithesis. It moves us toward a larger perspective that in addition to considering the short-term management of persistent contradictions to produce order and enhance effectiveness, also depicts a longer-term process of managers increasing and perhaps transforming their knowledge of reality.

A new perspective that sublated the paradox and dialectical perspectives might simply be called the contradictions perspective. I summarize this "proto-perspective" in column 3 of Table 7.1. While the precise conceptual foundation of this perspective is unknown at this point, it would both negate and preserve the foundations of the paradox and dialectical perspectives. With regard to its ontological foundation, it would probably negate the static ontology of the paradox perspective and incorporate dialectics' assumption of perpetual becoming, thereby capturing ongoing quantitative and qualitative changes in contradictory elements, with actors perceiving paradoxes at only particular moments in time. At the same time, it probably would eschew Hegel's metaphysics and adopt a realist philosophy such as critical realism (Archer, 1995; Bhaskar

1975; Mutch et al. 2006) that distinguishes but connects and preserves the tensions between ontology and epistemology, materiality and discourse, structure and agency (see Putnam 2015, for an excellent review of relevant theories). As such it would explain how socially constructed contradictions can "harden" into seemingly objective structures, which then influence but do not determine social construction processes (but see again the discussion of Hahn and Knight's forthcoming article.) It would also clarify the relationship between biophysical contradictions and sociomaterial ones. In addition, a transformational contradictions perspective would aim at managerial prescription yet also place actors' efforts to manage epistemological contradictions within the context of longer-term historical processes spanning multiple levels of analysis. It would negate the paradox perspective's assumption of the persistence of contradictions and incorporate the dialectical assumption that contradictions can be transformed, while also admitting of outcomes other than transformation (such as incremental change).

Towards a Contradictions Perspective

Some scholars have begun to undertake work that implicitly moves toward the development of a contradictions perspective by integrating dialectical and paradox perspectives. For example, Sheep et al. (2017) evoke the concept of totality by bringing the entanglement of contradictions into paradox research. Taking a constitutive approach, they study the contradictions produced when a parent company in the printing industry reacquired a subsidiary it had spun off. Sheep and colleagues find that the contradictions that organizational actors experienced could be understood as "Gordian knots," which they define as "discursive formulations in which members construct tensions, not only as co-occurring, but as... inseparable entanglements of interdependence" (463). They found, for example, that when they enacted contradictions, managers entangled the tension between parent and subsidiary interests with the tension between control and autonomy; and similarly, they constructed the tension between primary and secondary strategic goals as inseparable from the tension between cost and quality. A major finding of Sheep and colleagues is that one tension can either exacerbate or attenuate the tensions with which it is interwoven. While the interconnectedness of contradictions in some cases makes their management more feasible, in other cases it makes them unmanageable and justifies inaction.

As daunting as this implication of Sheep and colleagues' research is, it provides only a partial view of how difficult the management of intertwined contradictions could potentially be. This is because it addresses the management of only those organizational contradictions that managers "talk into being" (463), but not the contradictions at higher levels of analysis in which they are embedded but do not see. One can only imagine how much more difficult the task of managing contradictions would be if managers also tried to incorporate consideration of broader social, cultural, and institutional contradictions into their management practices.

A recent theoretical paper by Schad and Bansal (2018), mentioned above, speaks to this need to understand the totality. Taking an implicitly Hegelian view, Schad and Bansal (2018) argue that many of the paradoxes experienced by managers are epistemological rather than ontological, and that by engaging in systems thinking, managers will begin to consider ontological contradictions that had not previously caught their attention, develop a more complex understanding of the paradoxes they do enact, avoid partial solutions, minimize unintended consequences, and develop richer solutions. Schad and Bansal conclude that managers and researchers must both "zoom in" on the organizational level to understand the central tensions that managers experience, as paradox researchers generally have, and also "zoom out" to understand the higher-level contradictions that those tensions are nested in.

Other scholars have sought to more explicitly integrate paradoxical and dialectical perspectives. Hargrave and Van de Ven (2017) present a process model of managing organizational contradictions that accounts for both dialectical and paradox sequences of events, as well as sequences that include elements of both. Their model ties actors' approaches to managing contradictions to two factors: whether managers socially construct the relationship between contradictory elements as dualisms (per dialectics) or dualities (per the paradox perspective), and the distribution of power (a key feature of Marxian dialectical models.) The model provides a role for conflict and unintended consequences in processes of managing contradictions, and, unlike the deterministic dialectical perspectives of Marx and Hegel, allows for the possibility of both the persistence and transformation of paradox.

According to Hargrave and Van de Ven's model, the sequence of accepting paradox and managing it through synergy is but one possible sequence of events, one that plays out at a moment in time in which contradictory elements are seen as complementary, the balance of power between them is roughly equal (Carson et al. 2017), and (although Hargrave and Van de Ven do not say this), actors can identify contradictory elements that are constant in both quantity and quality, and are able to extract them from their embedding contexts and the contradictions with which they are intertwined. Hargrave and Van de Ven's integrated model provides a fuller range of sequences and outcomes than either the paradox model or the deterministic dialectical model. It suggests that managers can manage paradoxes and that paradoxes will persist—but only under particular conditions, and if managers undertake particular actions. A limitation of the integrated model is that it treats contradictions as isolated and manageable, disentangled from other contradictions.

Drawing upon both Marxian and Hegelian dialectical perspectives, Raisch et al. (2018) present a prescriptive learning spiral model that addresses this limitation. Raisch et al. agree with Schad and Bansal (2018) that managers and scholars should use systems thinking to uncover the social complexity of paradoxes; they note, however, that because of humans' cognitive limitations this learning process will unfold only gradually through a process in which actors successively improve upon their imperfect understandings. According to the learning spiral model, organizations move between stages of convergence, in which the contradictory elements exist in dynamic equilibrium, and managers cope with their persistence, and make incremental adjustments to their understandings as per the paradox perspective; and stages of divergence, in which dynamic equilibrium is disrupted by new discoveries and contradictory elements are transformed (consistent with dialectics). The switch from convergence to divergence occurs, Raisch and colleagues theorize, when organizational actors are motivated to engage in new rounds of sensemaking because they are learning little from their current representations of the contradiction, and existing arrangements do not serve their interests. Raisch, Hargrave, and Van de Ven explain that the learning spiral is never-ending because "convergence without divergence eventually leads to stasis and demise," and also that divergence must inevitably give way again to convergence, because "divergence without convergence eventually leads to chaos and vicious cycles." While Raisch et al. integrate dialectics and the paradox perspective, like Hargrave and Van de Ven they do not embrace the determinism of Marxian and Hegelian dialectics. They acknowledge the possibility that learning processes can be marked by "failures and disruptions," reproduce the status quo, or produce new understandings that combine but do not sublate contradictory elements (Marcus and Malen (2021) make a similar point in this volume).

One way of enriching the learning spiral model would be to clarify its ontological stance. The model explains how managers can engage in learning processes to progressively reduce the difference between ontological and epistemological contradictions, but it does not address the question of what the ontological contradictions actually are. What totality is it that managers should try to uncover? Raisch et al. allude to contradictions being material in nature and give the example of the tension between the short-term economic demands and long-term societal demands faced by the food company Nestle. This characterization is ambiguous, however. What is the objective reality of these demands? What is the set of intertwined contradictions that comprise them? These questions matter because their answers provide prescriptions for how managers should direct their attention. Managers who took the "real" contradiction to be the tension between short-term financial demands and long-term societal demands might curtail the learning process before considering encompassing contradictions at higher levels of analysis, such as tensions in the institutions governing global capitalism. Future research would benefit from an explicit conceptualization of what constitutes the reality that managers should try to uncover. The recent paper by Hahn and Knight discussed earlier provides an innovative take on this problem.

Conclusion

From its inception, paradox research has emphasized managerial prescription. Its purpose has largely been to understand what managers can do to maintain and promote organizational order and effectiveness in the face of seemingly irreconcilable, persistent tensions. As Table 7.1 demonstrates, for management researchers this has meant focusing on the contradictions that managers perceive, isolating those contradictions from other contradictions within the organization and their broader (e.g., industry, institutional, societal) contexts, and studying how managers address them over relatively short time frames. To the extent that dialectical theory has been considered, it largely has been used as a tool for understanding how managers can improve organizational effectiveness by influencing non-linear systems to produce surprising and beneficial outcomes (Cameron and Quinn 1988). This use of dialectical theory is based on the assumption that contradictory change processes can be controlled, which is at odds with the core of dialectical theory.

The paradox perspective provides an incomplete representation of reality and has invited its own antithesis. This antithesis comes in the form of dialectics. In contrast to the paradox perspective, dialectics sees contradictions as transitory and inseparable from other contradictions, and studies them over longer time horizons with reference to the totality. It depicts managers as awash in complexity, engaged in conflict, and taking actions that almost certainly will not have their intended effects because managers take them within a context that they do not understand. And finally, dialectical theory shows contradictions as inevitably being transformed, whereas the paradox perspective emphasizes that contradictions can only be coped with. It depicts managers as ultimately, through processes that none controls, transcending the inadequacy of their language, practices, logics, and structures.

I have proposed that instead of attempting to incorporate dialectics into the core of paradox theory, as paradox researchers have suggested, scholars should seek to create a new perspective that sublates dialectical and paradox perspectives. As discussed, a contradictions perspective would depict managerial perception of paradox as a moment of convergence within a never-ending dialectical process the course of which is not known, but which also could include moments of divergence and transformation. This perspective would both omit and enfold elements of both the dialectical and paradox perspectives. It would incorporate dialectics' assumption of perpetual becoming, adopt a realist perspective that explains how socially constructed understandings become taken-for-granted social structures, situate the management of contradictions within historical context and the totality, and allow for both the persistence and transformation of contradictions. As such, based on its recognition of the dynamic and complex nature of contradictions, a transformational contradictions perspective would counsel managers to proceed with humility, aware that they are participating in a never-ending process and that their actions will rarely have the desired effects.

At this point nobody knows what the conceptual core of a transformational perspective would look like, and nobody will control the process of creating it. Nobody even knows if it will be created. I certainly hope that a learning spiral process will play out and deliver this new perspective. In this chapter I have highlighted work that takes tentative steps toward sublation. Of course, a contradictions perspective that sublated paradox and dialectical perspectives itself might only exist for a moment in time on its way to becoming something else.

References

Abdallah, C., Denis, J-L., and Langley, A. (2011), 'Having Your Cake and Eating it Too: Discourses of Transcendence and Their Role in Organizational Change Dynamics', *Journal of Organizational Change Management*, 24, 333–48.

Archer, M. (1995), *Realist Social Theory: The Morphogenetic Approach* (Cambridge: Cambridge University Press).

Barnard, C. I. (1938), *The Functions of the Executive* (Cambridge, MA: Harvard University Press).

Benson, J. K. (1977), 'Organizations: A Dialectical View', *Administrative Science Quarterly*, 22, 1–21.

Berger, P.L., and Luckmann, T. (1967). *The Social Construction of Reality*. New York, NY: Anchor Books.

Bhaskar, R. A. [1975] (1997), *A Realist Theory of Science* (London: Verso).

Cameron, K. S., and Quinn, R. E. (1988), 'Organizational Paradox and Transformation', in R. E. Quinn and K. S. Cameron, eds., *Paradox and Transformation: Toward a Theory of Change in Organization and Management* (Cambridge, UK: Ballinger), 1–18.

Carson, E. J., Poole, M. S., Lambert, M. J., and Lammers, J. C. (2017), 'A Study of Organizational Responses to Dilemmas in Interorganizational Emergency Management', *Communication Research*, 44, 287–315.

Pina e Cunha, M., and Putnam, L. L. (2019), 'Paradox Theory and the Paradox of Success', *Strategic Organization*, 17, 95–106.

De Rond, M., and Bouchikhi, H. (2004), 'On the Dialectics of Strategic Alliances', *Organization Science*, 15, 56–69.

Dooley, K. (2021), 'Conceptualizing Organizational Change through the Lens of Complexity Science, in M. S. Poole and A. H. Van de Ven, eds., *Oxford Handbook of Organizational Change and Innovation* (2nd edn) (Oxford, UK: Oxford University Press),

Engels, F. [1876] (1964), *Dialectics of Nature* (Moscow: Progress Publishers).

Fairhurst, G. T. (2019), 'Reflections: Return Paradox to the Wild? Paradox Interventions and Their Implications', *Journal of Change Management*, 19, 6–22.

Fairhurst, G. T., Smith, W. K., Banghart, S. G., Lewis, M. W., Putnam, L. L., Raisch, S., and Schad, J. (2016), 'Diverging and Converging: Integrative Insights on a Paradox Meta-Perspective', *Academy of Management Annals*, 10, 173–82.

Farjoun, M. (2010), 'Beyond Dualism: Stability and Change as a Duality', *Academy of Management Review*, 35, 202–25.

Farjoun, M. (2017), 'Contradictions, Dialectics, and Paradoxes', in A. Langley and H. Tsoukas, eds., *The Sage Handbook of Process Organization Studies* (Thousand Oaks: Sage), 87–109.

Farjoun, M. (2019), 'Strategy and Dialectics: Rejuvenating a Long-Standing Relationship', *Strategic Organization*, 17, 133–44.

Farjoun, M. (2021), 'The Becoming of Change in 3D: Dialectics, Darwin and Dewey', in M. S. Poole and A. H. Van de Ven, eds., *Oxford Handbook of Organizational Change and Innovation* (2nd edn) (Oxford, UK: Oxford University Press),

Friedland, R. and Alford, R. R. (1991), 'Bringing Society Back In: Symbols, Practices and Institutional Contradictions', in W. W. Powell and P. J. Dimaggio, eds., *The New Institutionalism in Organizational Analysis* (Chicago, IL: University of Chicago Press), 232–63.

Giddens, A. (1984). *The Constitution of Society*. Berkeley and Los Angeles, CA: University of California Press.

Gramsci, A. [1926] (1971), *Selections from the Prison Notebooks* (New York: International Publishers).

Greiner, L. E. (1972), Evolution and Revolution as Organizations Grow', *Harvard Business Review*, 76, 55–60.

Hahn, T., and Knight, E. (forthcoming), 'The Ontology of Paradox: A Quantum Approach', *Academy of Management Review*. https://journals.aom.org/doi/10.5465/amr.2018.0408. Published online September 30, 2019, accessed August 16, 2020.

Hargrave, T. J., and Van de Ven, A. H. (2006), 'A Collective Action Model of Institutional Innovation', *Academy of Management Review*, 31, 864–88.

Hargrave, T. J., and Van de Ven, A. H. (2017), 'Integrating Dialectical and Paradox Perspectives on Managing Contradictions in Organizations', *Organization Studies*, 38, 319–39.

Hegel, G. W. F. [1807] (1977), *The Phenomenology of Spirit* (Oxford: Clarendon Press).

Hegel, G. W. F. [1812] (1969), *The Science of Logic* (London: Allen and Unwin).

Hegel, G. W. F. [1817] (1969), *Encyclopaedia of Philosophical Sciences* (Oxford: Oxford University Press).

Hegel, G. W. F. [*c*.1822] (1953), *Reason in History: A General Introduction to the Philosophy of History* (New York: Macmillan).

Jing, R. (2021), 'Eastern Yin-Yang Model of Change', in M. S. Poole and A. H. Van de Ven, eds., *Oxford Handbook of Organizational Change and Innovation* (2nd edn) (Oxford, UK: Oxford University Press),

Jing, R., and Van de Ven, A. H. (2016), 'Being versus Becoming Ontology of Paradox Management', *Cross Cultural and Strategic Management*, 23, 558–62.

Langley, A. and Sloan, P. (2011), 'Organizational Change and Dialectic Processes', in D. D. Boje, B. Burnes, and J. Hassard, eds., *The Routledge Companion to Organizational Change* (London: Routledge), 261–75.

Lewis, M. W. (2000), 'Exploring Paradox: Toward a More Comprehensive Guide', *Academy of Management Review*, 25, 760–76.

Lewis, M. W. and Smith, W. K. (2014), Paradox as a Metatheoretical Perspective: Sharpening the Focus and Widening the Scope', *Journal of Applied Behavioral Science*, 50, 127–49.

Lexico(n.d.). 'Sublate'. https://www.oxforddictionaries.com, accessed 16 August 2020.

Lukács, G. (1923), *History and Class Consciousness* (London: Merlin Press).

Lüscher, L. S. and Lewis, M. W. (2008), 'Organizational Change and Managerial Sensemaking: Working through Paradox', *Academy of Management Journal*, 51, 221–40.

Mackay, R. B., and Chia, R. (2013), Choice, Chance, and Unintended Consequences in Strategic Change: A Process Understanding of the Rise and Fall of Northco Automotive', *Academy of Management Journal*, 56, 208–30.

Marcus, A., and Malen, J. (2021), 'Organizational Routines and Organizational Change ', in M. S. Poole and A. H. Van de Ven, eds., *Oxford Handbook of Organizational Change and Innovation* (2nd edn) (Oxford, UK: Oxford University Press),

Marx, K. [1867] (1990), *Capital: A Critique of Political Economy* (Volume 1) (London, New York: Penguin Books).

Marx, K., and Engels, F. [1845–6] (2001), *The German Ideology*. Part 1: *Feuerbach* (New York: International Publishers).

Marx, K. and Engels, F. [1848] (1979), *The Communist Manifesto* (London: Penguin Books).

Marmodoro, A. (2015), 'Introduction: The Metaphysics of Quantum Mechanics', *Topoi*, 34, 309–11.

Mason, R. O. (1996), 'Commentary on Varieties of Dialectic Change Processes', *Journal of Management Inquiry*, 5, 293–9.

Merton, R. K. (1936), 'The Unanticipated Consequences of Purposive Social Action, *American Sociological Review*, 1, 894–904.

Mutch, A., Delbridge, R., and Ventresca, M. (2006), 'Situating Organizational Action: The Relational Sociology of Organizations', *Organization*, 13, 607–25.

Nielsen, R. P. (1996), 'Varieties of Dialectic Change Processes', *Journal of Management Inquiry*, 5, 276–92.

Peng, K., and Nisbett, R. E. (1999), 'Culture, Dialectics, and Reasoning about Contradiction. *American Psychologist*, 54, 741–54.

Pettigrew, A. M. (1979), 'On Studying Organizational Cultures', *Administrative Science Quarterly*, 24, 570–81.

Plato. [*c*.380 BC] (2019), *Republic*. Book VII. (B. Jowett, Trans.) (Ottawa: East India Publishing Co).

Poole, M. S. and Van de Ven, A. H. (1989), 'Using Paradox to Build Management and Organization Theories', *Academy of Management Review*, 14, 562–78.

Prichard, C., and Creed, D. (2021), 'Agency in Social Movements as Sources of Change', in M. S. Poole and A. H. Van de Ven, eds, *Oxford Handbook of Organizational Change and Innovation* (2nd edn) (Oxford, UK: Oxford University Press),

Putnam, L. L. (2015), 'Unpacking the Dialectic: Alternative Views on the Discourse–Materiality Relationship', *Journal of Management Studies*, 52, 706–16.

Putnam, L. L., Fairhurst, G. T., and Banghart, S. G. (2016), 'Contradictions, Dialectics, and Paradoxes in Organizations: A Constitutive Approach', *Academy of Management Annals*, 10, 65–171.

Raisch, S., Hargrave, T. J., and Van de Ven, A. H. (2018), 'The Learning Spiral: A Process Perspective on Paradox', *Journal of Management Studies*, 55, 1507–26.

Reinhardt, A., and Gioia, D. A. (2021), 'Upside-Down Organizational Change: Sensemaking, Sensegiving, and the New Generation', In M. S. Poole and A. H. Van de Ven, eds, *Oxford Handbook of Organizational Change and Innovation* (2nd edn) (Oxford, UK: Oxford University Press),

Schad, J. and Bansal, T. (2018), 'Seeing the Forest and the Trees: How a Systems Perspective Informs Paradox Research', *Journal of Management Studies*, 55, 1490–506.

Schad, J., Lewis, M. W., Raisch, S. and Smith, W. K. (2016), 'Paradox Research in Management Science: Looking Back to Move Forward', *Academy of Management Annals*, 10, 5–64.

Schneider, L. (1971), 'Dialectic in Sociology', *American Sociological Review*, 36, 667–78.

Seo, M-G. and Creed, W. D. (2002), 'Institutional Contradictions, Praxis, and Institutional Change: A Dialectical Perspective', *Academy of Management Review*, 27, 222–47.

Sheep, M. L., Fairhurst, G. T., and Khazanchi, S. (2017), 'Knots in the Discourse of Innovation: Investigating Multiple Tensions in a Reacquired Spin-Off', *Organization Studies*, 38, 463–88.

Smith, W. K. and Lewis, M. W. (2011), 'Toward a Theory of Paradox: A Dynamic Equilibrium Model of Organizing', *Academy of Management Review*, 36, 381–403.

Smith, W. K., Lewis, M. W., Jarzabkowski, P., and Langley, A. (2017), 'Introduction: The Paradoxes of Paradox', in W. K. Smith, M. W. Lewis, P. Jarzabkowski, and A. Langley, eds, *The Oxford Handbook of Organizational Paradox* (Oxford, UK: Oxford University Press), 1–24.

Van de Ven, A. H., and Poole, M. S. (1995), 'Explaining Development and Change in Organizations', *Academy of Management Review*, 20, 510–40.

Weber, M. (1950), *Max Weber: Ein Lebensbild* (Heidelberg: Lambert Schneider).

Weick, K. E. (1976), 'Educational Organizations as Loosely Coupled Systems', *Administrative Science Quarterly*, 21, 1–19.

Werner, C. M., and Baxter, L. A. (1994), 'Temporal Qualities of Relationships: Organismic, Transactional, and Dialectical Views', in M. Knapp and G. Miller, eds, *Handbook of Interpersonal Communication* (2nd edn) (Thousand Oaks, CA: SAGE), 323–79.

Zeitz, G. (1980). Interorganizational dialectics. *Administrative Science Quarterly*, 25: 72–88.

CHAPTER 8

EASTERN *YIN-YANG* MODEL OF CHANGE

RUNTIAN JING

HUMAN behaviors can be understood both socio-psychologically and historically (Rindova and Starbuck 1997). In this chapter, I intend to elaborate a theory of change behavior from an Eastern historical perspective.

Historically, the Western epistemologies of scientific inquiries were primarily rooted in Aristotelian formal logic, which emphasizes order and constancy in the world and decontextualizes facts and ideas as general laws and theories (Peng and Nisbett 1999). Based on this formal logic, Western philosophers and scientists developed an analytical and mathematical reasoning, which has been the foundation of the modern civilization and knowledge accumulation. From this perspective, people live their lives by their analytical practice of logic. By contrast, Easterners, especially the Chinese, have developed the *yin-yang* view of social existence by which they deny the true existence of contradiction and regard the opposite elements (such as *yin* and *yang*) as both contradictory and complementary in reality (See Chapter 7 by Hargrave, this volume; Jing and Van de Ven 2014; Li 2015). Such *yin-yang* view considers the opposites to be mutually embedded. This is called the *endogenous relatedness* of contradiction (Zhang and Han 2019: 1). With this cultural logic imbibed, people object to true contradictions and regard them as not being logically opposite (Peng et al. 2005). This is called *dialectical thinking*, referring to the "cognitive tendency toward acceptance of contradiction" (Peng and Nisbett 1999: 742), which encourages people to solve social problems, not by direct intervention but by unearthing and adjusting the higher-level factors governing the operation and cognition of existing conflicts. According to this *yin-yang* tradition, nothing is isolated or independent, the part cannot be understood except in relation to the whole, and people can recognize the fundamental orders of the world (called *Tao*, "道" in Chinese) only by their intuition through the context-specific perception. This *yin-yang* view can contribute fresh ideas to theorizing change and/or the process-related concepts in various organizational research areas, such as cultural beliefs in continuous change, dialectical change as mutual transformation, change agency as paradoxical leadership, and organizational momentum as driver of the change process.

Major Assumptions of the View

Change Process Driven by the Yin-Yang Duality

The Chinese cultures mostly assume the reality to be an "ever-changing flow" and not an event with clear beginning and ending points. Based on this process view, traditional cultural philosophies such as Confucianism, Buddhism, and particularly Taoism developed their assumptions and beliefs about change and its process, contradiction and paradox, time and momentum, change agents, and ideal roles. The Taoism or the Chinese *yin-yang* tradition is rooted in the ancient classic *The I-Ching* or *Book of Changes* (Wilhelm and Baynes, Trans. 1967), which is said to have originated with the legendary Chinese ruler Fu Hsi (*c.*3000 BC).[1] The change process by the *yin-yang* tradition was demonstrated most extensively in the symbolism of the archetypal poles *yin* and *yang*. Here, *yin* is a feminine aspect and corresponds to receptiveness, dimness, and softness, while *yang* is a masculine aspect and corresponds to activeness, lightness, and hardness (Javary 1997). As the black and white fish have shown in Figure 8.1, the *yin-yang* duality represents opposite and symbiotic relations, whereas the white dot in the black fish and the black dot in the white fish are the buds representing the seeds of their opposite. Thus, this view takes a dialectic mutualism approach toward the opposite aspects of organizations, such as competition vs. cooperation, exploration vs. exploitation, and change vs. stability (Smith and Lewis 2011). For instance, there is no absolute competition or cooperation since each aspect has its opposite embedded in its existence.

Moreover, the two opposites are assumed to be mutually transforming each other through a continuous change process, as the figure shows: what is black will become increasingly white until it is completely so; what is white will eventually become black (Jing and Van de Ven 2014). Such a cyclic change, in reality, is perceived as a constant paradoxical transformation between the duality of *yin* and *yang* in the human mind. Such a Taoist view of the contradiction is similar to the Hegelian expression that everything involves its own negation (Hargrave and Van de Ven 2017). As the Chinese proverb goes, when the development of anything brings it to one extreme, a reversal to the other extreme takes place (i.e., "物极必反" in Chinese). For example, the Chinese believe that success and failure take place mutually and transform each other. When people get successful, they become proud of their achievements, disregarding others, which turns out to be the seed of their possible failure. On the contrary, failure leads

[1] Here, we look to *yin-yang* duality in Taoism as the core logic in explaining various change activities and use Taoism to be synonymous with the *yin-yang* view.

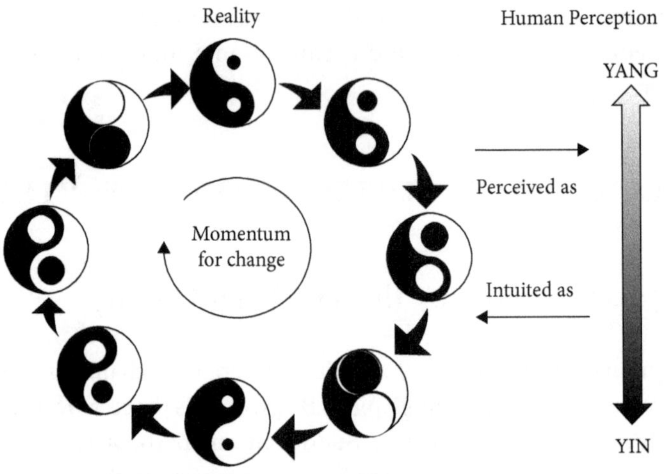

FIGURE 8.1 *Yin-Yang* View of Change

people to be humble, which brings gains to them in the next cycle of change. Underlying the various real cases of cyclical transformation, the saying *haughtiness invites losses, while modesty brings profits* is assumed to be a general governing order. Thus, dialectical thinking, a cognitive tendency toward the embracing of contradiction is salient in the Chinese culture (Cheng 2009). There are nearly four times as many dialectical proverbs that endorse contradiction and change in a Chinese proverb book (about 12%) than in an American proverb book (fewer than 3%) (Peng and Nisbett 1999). In essence, the mutual transformation between *yin* and *yang* duality is regarded as a principle of change in any social organization, which will be further demonstrated with the cases of organizational change in the next section.

In Chinese history, the *yin-yang* teaching is so powerful and pervasive that it has influenced many Chinese scholars; military strategists; and masters in medicine, literature, architecture, boxing (*taijiquan*, "太极拳" in Chinese), and other fields for thousands of years. As a reflection of this *yin-yang* dialectics, in 550 BC, Sun-Tzu observed in *The Art of War* (1971), "The thinking of the wisest individuals lies in considering both pluses and minuses. Think positively of yourself when in difficulty or crisis; consider your weaknesses when in a strong position" (p. 79). The Confucian book *The Doctrine of the Mean* also encourages people not to take extreme positions (Peng and Nisbett 1999).

The Favorable Chance to Change Determined by Momentum

Taoism highly values the dimension of time for people to achieve a successful change program, in the essence of doing *the right thing at the right time* (Jing and Van de Ven 2014: 34). From the *yin-yang* view, environments constantly and cyclically change, so the current situations eventually transform to their opposite, indicating either favorable or unfavorable momentum, called *shi* ("势") in Chinese.[2] Here, the momentum can be defined as power or energy that change agents perceive from interdependent transforming elements (such as *yin-yang* entities), which can afford a favorable timing opportunity for change (Jing and Van de Ven 2018). Notably, in the *yin-yang* tradition, the interaction between the actor and momentum can be indicated by a given hexagram ("卦" means judgment). A hexagram is a figure composed of six *yin* or *yang* lines. If a line gets either broken or solid, a change will happen, resulting in the transformation into a new hexagram. There are sixty-four hexagrams, and each is both a description of a condition of momentum and a strategy for handling it. The ancient Chinese invented a binary alphabet of solid and broken lines to represent the complicated transforming process of various structures (Capra 2010). A complicated method was developed to calculate and translate this interactive effect, which can help people to predict environmental variations. "By imaging yourself and your situation through the symbols of the oracle, you can redirect the manner in which you are thinking about things" (Karcher 2004: 72). After making sense of the situation, people realize the possible structures and developments of momentum and discover the most efficacious way to act. Thus, "all coincidence [is] meaningful" (Karcher 2004: 67). Because of the aim of this study, we focus only on theoretical and not methodological illustrations of these interactions.

As Orlikowski and Yates (2002) noted in their review on organizational time, most prior studies have taken an objective perspective toward time, assuming time to be objective and independent of human actions. What Taoism proposed is a subjective perspective of timing, which suggests that "time is experienced through the interpretive processes of people who create meaningful temporal notions such as events, cycles, routines, and rites of passage" (Orlikowski and Yates 2002: 689). By elaborating and applying this subjective perspective, Taoists emphasize how people perceive and adopt timing strategies to improve their change performance (Jing and Van de Ven 2018).

Deep Structure Formulating the Patterns of Change

As shown in Figure 8.1, to capture an appropriate time to change, people need to deepen their understanding about the underlying structure of momentum as a mechanism producing the empirical patterns of changes. Taking a similar epistemological view as critical realism (Bhaskar 1986; Mingers 2004), Taoism asserts that *the law that can be spoken of is not the eternal one*, implying that the momentum for change is not objectively "out there," but is intuited through implicit knowledge and reflexivity of the ongoing experi-

[2] The term *shi* has been translated into English as *situation* or *momentum*. We believe their meanings are slightly different and that *momentum* is a more accurate translation. The Merriam-Webster Dictionary defines *momentum* as "strength or force gained by motion or by a series of events," while *situation* means "position with respect to conditions and circumstances." For example, when situating a moving car on the road, we often refer statically to its current position or circumstance. But for its *shi* or *momentum*, we refer dynamically to show fast it is going to determine its direction and position in next few seconds. In this sense, *shi* has a more predictive capability about future than the *situation* during a changing process.

ences (called "悟道" in Chinese). To understand the observed sequences or patterns of events (e.g., pace, rhythm) in daily life, people need to constantly step back and reflect on the mechanism of momentum for change. Thus, the Chinese character for momentum *shi* is often used with the characters of patterns *xing* (i.e., *xing-shi*, called "形势" in Chinese), which implies the concrete forms of the reality provide the foundation on which social meanings of momentum are constructed.

From an evolutionary perspective, the change outcomes in one round become the inputs for the changes in the next round, implying a mutually constitutive relationship between the strategic action and momentum—as each change action shapes the action context for future choices (Michel 2014). Thus, creating incremental goals for change is a delicate art requiring actions and momentum to be subtly balanced in each stage.

"Becoming" Ontology of the Change Process

As shown in Figure 8.1, Taoism takes a "becoming" ontology to approach the change process, which insists that reality is continuously going on and coming about (Jing and Van de Ven 2016). Conversely, a common view in Western culture is the "being" ontology, which regards reality as an assembly of static individuals whose dynamic features are taken to be ontologically secondary and derivative.[3] Here, "being" refers to "a fixed, certain, and complete status or form of an existence before acquiring its relationships with other entities," while "becoming" refers to "an interdependent and interactive process with other entities before and after any entity acquires its status or form" (Li 2016: 50). According to Aristotelian formal logic, A is "A" (the law of identity), A is not "no-A" (the law of contradiction), and A cannot be "A and no-A," and "neither A nor no-A" (the law of the excluded middle). Based on formal logic, the Western dialecticism demonstrates how the opposing thesis and antithesis create a synthesis, and the thesis and antithesis can be totally different in their positioning and claims (Benson 1977). The *yin-yang* view contradicts these principles of "being" ontology in defining dialectics. As shown in Figure 8.1, the two entities (*yin* and *yang*) are contradictory, but each has the seed of its opposite by which it will transform. Thus, there is no pure *yin* or *yang* during the whole process. "The concept of polarity is critical to an understanding of *yin* and *yang*. It denotes an existential interdependence wherein each defines the other, unlike the concepts of dualism and dialectic wherein each exists independent of the other" (Marshak 1993: 298). Despite the huge economic and institutional change undergone in contemporary China, Faure and Fang (2008) found modern Chinese still remain anchored to the classical *yin-yang* way of thinking referring to business and society at large.

[3] It should be noted that many Western philosophers such as Heraclitus, Alfred Whitehead, Karl Marx, and Georg W. Hegel also advocated such a "becoming" ontology of change. For example, the ancient Greeks also had the cultural belief that the momentums in social and physical reality were infused by the movements of the heavens. Heraclitus's physical principles of Strife and Tension were applied to explain the social relations among people.

The Current State of Research Related to the View

Philosophy is a summary of the human wisdom based on daily life experience. In essence, *yin-yang* philosophy contributes an epistemological view about the continuous change process based on the "becoming" ontological assumption of reality. As Figure 8.2 shows, the current organizational research based on this *yin-yang* view mainly includes four areas: cultural belief in continuous change, momentum as driver of the change process, change agency as paradoxical leader, and dialectical change with mutual transformation.

Cultural Belief in the Continuous Change

Theoretically, the Western meaning of "change" tends to reflect the comparative statics of progressive events and stages of unfreezing, change, and refreezing (Lewin 1947). Consistent with the Aristotelian formal logic, this definition of change indicates stability, coherence, and resolution of contradiction through a synthesis of an entity or issue (Peng and Nisbett 1999). Because of their mutualism assumption about contradiction, the Chinese take a complex approach to understanding relationships among objectives and events, and their preconceived model of change is often non-linear, even cyclical (Nisbett 2003). For example, Professor Li-Jun Li and her colleagues have done many empirical studies in comparing the lay theories (or implicit theories held by the general public) of change in East Asia (particularly Chinese) and in North America. It was found that "North Americans tend to believe in inertia (i.e., things at rest tend to stay at rest; things in motion tend to stay in motion). In contrast, Chinese people tend to believe that things are changing constantly, and that sometimes the directions of development also changes" (Ji et al. 2004: 120).

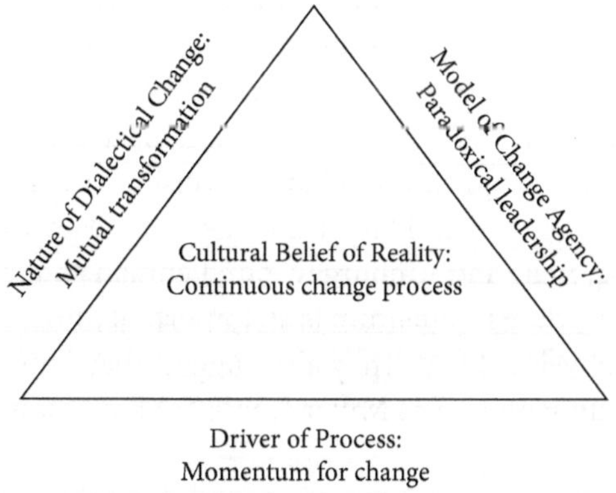

FIGURE 8.2 Organizational Research Based on *Yin-Yang* View

Driven by this cultural belief in continuous change, the Chinese have been shown to make more situational attributions than North Americans (e.g., Choi et al. 1999; Morris and Peng 1994); furthermore, they are more likely to see social problems from the relational perspective (Chen 2008), accommodate contradictory concepts, (Faure and Fang 2008), and adopt an inclusive attitude toward ambiguity (Li 2015). Similar to Kurt Lewin's (1947) force field theory, the *yin-yang* view highlights the importance of situational power in determining the impact of an action. For example, Alter and Kwan (2009) found that the Chinese usually anticipate more non-linear change (i.e., reversal and balance) than European Americans, but interestingly, when exposed to the *yin-yang* symbol, the European Americans demonstrated a greater increase in directional changes in the experimental contexts of stock-prediction and weather-prediction tasks.

Momentum as Driver of the Change Process

In business practice, momentum is often viewed as a key concept in increasing the success rate of change initiatives (e.g., Cross et al. 2003; Larreche 2008). In Chinese society, there are many famous sayings about "momentum," such as "momentum is like splitting the bamboo"("势如破竹"),[4] "implementing in favorable momentum" ("顺势而为"), "judging the timing and size up the momentum" ("审时度势"), and "saving up momentum to start out"("蓄势待发"). They provide a reflection of the effects of momentum on human life. Meanwhile, this view of momentum differs from its previous conceptualization in the Western literature in its assumptions about the roles of the human agency and the generating mechanism (Jing 2017).

The organizational literature has largely focused on resistance and inertia as the micro-foundation of an organizational change process and has explained how organizations would resist change even when environments threaten them with extinction (Hannan and Freeman 1977). Such an "inertia" view of organizational change was challenged by Miller and Friesen (1980). Based on a configuration view of organizations, they emphasized the integral interdependencies among the elements of organizational strategy, structure, and environment besides defining organizational momentum as "the tendency to keep evolving in the same direction" (Miller and Friesen 1980: 599). Since then, organization and strategy researchers have studied the organizational momentum in various research settings, such as organizational changes in the air carrier industry, mergers and acquisitions, change decisions by newspapers, creation of new ventures, cultural changes in military academies, and team sports games (e.g., Beck et al. 2008; Jansen 2004; Kelly and Amburgey 1991; Lehman and Hahn 2013). The previous studies indicate that while momentum is an important dimension of organizational change, it has not been well defined. They also suggest that continuing research in the field has proved to be difficult and as Miller (1990: 27) has commented, "[P]rogress in

[4] This idiom means that while splitting bamboo, as a knife cuts into the first section, the other sections yield to its advance.

the field has been halting." The momentum concept derived from a physical paradigm has been criticized for sticking to the assumption of mechanical momentum too doctrinally, and ignoring the role of human agency in a social context (Wiebe et al. 2012).

Taoism has developed a teleological approach to explaining how to manage momentum in a social context. According to the Taoist doctrine, the environment is enactive and constantly changing, bringing either favorable or unfavorable momentum for change. The concept of momentum has been further developed by Sun-Tzu in his book *Art of War*. In this book, he used a whole chapter to illustrate how skilled commanders can use momentum strategies to win a battle. Sun-Tzu is known as a Chinese military strategist and general in the sixth century BC, whose thinking about warfare was deeply affected by the Taoist philosophy. For example, the Taoist paradigm "reflects a horror of war and a deep-felt yearning for peace" (Koller 2007: 244) and Sun-Tzu's work reflects that the best way to achieve peace is by a swift victory or, better yet, by defeating an enemy before the war is even begun. As he writes, "[T]o fight and conquer in all your battles is not supreme excellence; supreme excellence consists in breaking the enemy's resistance without fighting" (Griffith 1971: 77). This so-called "indirect" approach to war is different from the "direct" approach in Western societies. For example, in his book, *On War*, Carl von Clausewitz (2007) emphasized that victory on the battlefield can be achieved only through a decisive battle of annihilation and destruction of the opposing force at any cost. Sun-Tzu's book has been considered a classic philosophical work on military strategy and has also been popularized by the business community in their pursuit of success in commerce. The *yin-yang* view and Sun-Tzu's thoughts can inspire us to conceptualize organizational momentum from the following aspects:

(1) Keeping harmony between human actions and momentum as a general law: According to Taoism, *xiangsheng* ("相生" means complementary) and *xiangke* ("相克" means conflicting) are the two sides of the relation between human action and momentum. When momentum is favorable, it can aid human change action, a positive relation called *xiangsheng*; when momentum is unfavorable, it dampens change, a negative relation called *xiangke*. Ultimately, when human action and momentum are no longer opposed, they have reached the pivot of *Tao* and can act in tandem.

(2) Teleological approach to managing organizational momentum: In Taoism, all the momentum analysis must unfold around people. As noted above, it has developed a dexterous methodology (i.e., sixty-four hexagrams) to help people comprehend the favorableness of momentum. To assist a social change process, people need to view the world of objects as "things-for-us" rather than "things-in-themselves" thereby making all the occurrences valuable to them (Yang 2008). With his theory of affordance, Gibson (1977) took a similar ecological view, arguing that people do not view the world as objective and inanimate; instead, they perceive external activities and events as inherently meaningful in relation to their purposes and attentions, which can afford various action possibilities.

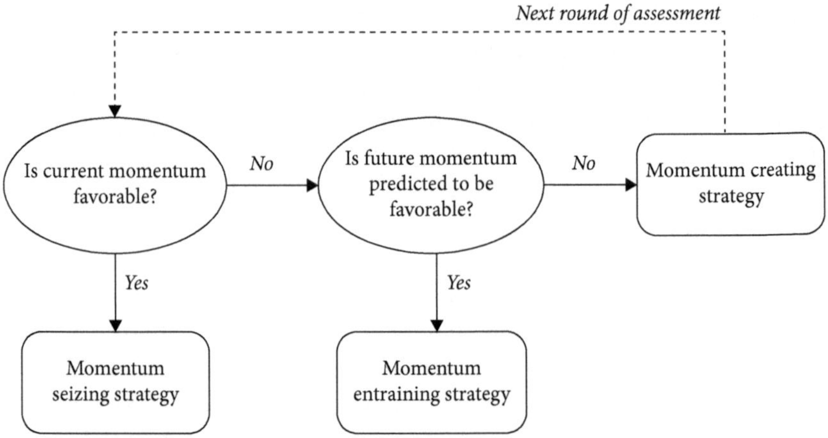

FIGURE 8.3 Linkages between Momentum Management Strategies

(3) Momentum created by the perception of interdependent systems inside and outside of organizations: To examine the internal momentum of organizations for a meaningful change, people need to consider the external momentum enabled by the environmental forces that may affect the internal movement. Thus, momentum is composed of two parts, which are internal momentum and external momentum. This distinction is consistent with our experiences in both the physical and organizational worlds that environmental conditions affect the internal momentum for change, which can afford accelerated, uniform, or decelerated processes of the organizational movement.

(4) Taoism has useful terms to describe temporal connections between past, current, and future momentum. As Figure 8.3 shows, momentum evolves over time and people can manage the momentum by three strategies:

(a) Momentum-seizing strategy (or *ying-shi* in Chinese). When the current momentum is perceived to be favorable, the change agents should promptly execute the change event that is being called for; otherwise, the opportunity may slip away.
(b) Momentum-entraining strategy (or *jie-shi* in Chinese). When the current momentum is unfavorable while future momentum is expected to be favorable, the agents can purposefully delay their change actions and be careful to entrain the change efforts into the rhythm of the momentum change.
(c) Momentum-creating strategy (or *zao-shi* in Chinese). When future momentums are assessed to be unfavorable or unclear, a better choice that the agents can make is to consciously affect the internal or external forces to redirect the momentum development for the next step.

The Chinese concept of "momentum" was introduced into Western societies by philosopher François Jullien's book *The Propensity of Things: Toward a History of Efficacy in China*. In this book, published in 1995, Jullien examined the historical evolution of this concept across different social areas (such as military strategy, political power, and aesthetic knowledge) in China, and termed it as a formal epistemology to explain and predict a particular configuration of the dynamism inherent in reality.

Change Agent as a Paradoxical Leader

Paradoxes are often defined as "contradictory yet interrelated elements...that seem logical in isolation but absurd and irrational when appearing simultaneously" (Lewis 2000: 760). Western views regard paradoxical opposites as mutually exclusive, presuming invisible but impermeable boundaries between them, which separate them as isolated elements (Smith and Lewis 2011). Compared with this "either/or" approach of contradiction, the *yin-yang* tradition assumes an "either/and" approach (Li 2015); it teaches that paradoxical components are both contradictory and complementary and each of the components contains a seed of its opposite (Zhang and Han 2019). In this sense, a paradox at a low level can be resolved by seeking the complementarities between the opposites at a high level (Jing 2017). Taking the *endogenous relatedness* of opposites as a cultural belief, leaders try to balance the interests between contradicting entities to maintain the harmony in an organization (Ma and Tsui 2015). This would make the visions and principles of change to be unclear, at least during the beginning stage. For example, leaders often consciously delay decisions or keep the information vague to gain more feedback about the underlying opposites or external entanglements. As indicated by the old proverb, "the master holds back secret tricks," Chinese society actually prizes the secrecy of leaders; they should learn to live with the high stress and anxiety caused by the ambiguity and uncertainty, to accomplish a mission of bringing about major change (Chen 2008).

This is called paradoxical leadership in the ongoing literature, defined as "leader behaviors that are seemingly competing, yet interrelated, to meet competing workplace demands simultaneously and over time" (Zhang et al. 2015: 539). The continuity of the passage of time is represented by the succession of situational momentum resulting from environmental variety. Through their perception and intuition of momentum, paradoxical leaders can seek or create a favorable chance to initiate a change in the present order through their knowledge and social skills. Both involvement and withdrawal are necessary means of an ultimate balance and completeness for a change agent. Such a flexible way to engage in social construction can be understood just as a mutual transformation between *yin* and *yang*: What goes up will eventually come down whereas what is decreasing will eventually increase.

In a recent study, Zhang and Han (2019) have highlighted the importance of paradoxical leadership in the context of long-term corporate development, which requires that CEOs of organizations can plant a solid present to grow a sustainable future (called the "present–future paradox"). This way they can develop organization–environment relationships that look toward future developmental possibilities (called the "organization–environment paradox"). Based on some field studies, they develop a scale to measure the paradoxical leader behavior in long-term corporate development, which demonstrates four factors: (a) combining short-term efficiency with long-term development, (b) conforming to while shaping collective forces in the environment, (c) focusing on both firm shareholders and the stakeholder community, and (d) maintaining both organizational stability and flexibility. Analyzing the empirical data on 340 small and medium-sized private firms in north China, the researchers found that paradoxical leadership in corporate development can well predict the long-term performance indicators of the firms, such as the percentage of the annual change in firm profit, R&D investment, and market share.

Dialectical Change as Mutual Transformation

Dialectics is a philosophical approach that involves a contradictory process between opposing sides. In the Western literature, the dialectical model of change was formally developed by applying Marxist or Hegelian dialectical thinking to the organizational context to address the internal dynamics of organizational change (Benson 1977; Seo and Creed 2002). As a key technical term in the dialectical model, "contradiction" is characterized by an opposing thesis and antithesis that combine to produce a synthesis (Van de Ven and Poole 1995). For example, the ideological and structural contradictions inside a free school, Innisfree, contributed to its final disintegration (Grimes and Cornwall 1987). A contradiction is the essence of social and political alienation in a dialectical process; it arises through the constant production of "inconsistent moves within the organization yielding contradictory structures, competing interest groups, and occasional periods of crisis" (Benson 1977: 15). Recently, Raisch, Hargrave, and Van de Ven (2018) combined dialectics and paradox theory to unpack the learning processes through which people build their capacity to understand and cope with complex tensions over time. They demonstrated how organizations experience a transformational cycle of divergence and convergence, which helps them to move ahead toward a deeper understanding of the low-level contradiction and then seek sustainable development.

Generally, the *yin-yang* view shares with dialectics the emphasis on wholeness, the whole being maintained by the balance of opposites such as *yin* and *yang*. Although balanced, *yin* and *yang* do not lose their identities in some puddled intermediate; thus, Taoist holism is a doctrine of harmony rather than development. In Taoism, since all opposites are interdependent, their conflict can never result in the complete victory of one side but will always be a manifestation of the dialectics between two opposites. By the very act of focusing the attention on any one concept, people create its opposite. As Lao Tzu says, "When all in the world understand beauty to be beautiful, then ugliness exists; when all understand goodness to be good, then evil exists." In current organizational practices, Chinese managers are found to be more ready to embrace contradiction in strategy episodes, and they tend to foster intra-episode plurality and emergent planning (Prashantham and Eranova 2019). Such dialectical thinking can even affect people's questionnaire response styles, and the respondents from East Asian culture exhibit more moderate and ambivalent responses compared to those from Western culture (Hamamura et al. 2008).

Meanwhile, we should also attend to the differences between the *yin-yang* view and the Western dialecticism. As mentioned above, the *yin-yang* view is based on a "becoming" ontology, while the Western dialecticism is based on a "being" ontology, which leads to the following two aspects of distinctions:

(1) Radical vs. incremental process—The Western dialectics reflects a radical change process, while what the *yin-yang* view contributes is an incremental process of change. Here, radical (or the so-called "second order," "transformational") change means a change altering the organization at its core (Newman 2000). Benson (1977: 4) phrases it: "radical breaks with the present order." Such a revolutionary tenet of dialectics originates from the "catastrophe" metaphor of Marxist theory in analyzing sharp contradictions between the capitalist and worker classes, entailed by Benson's model to describe the struggle for domination and power between oppositions. Burrell and Morgan (2017) classified the dialectical model as representing a "radical structuralist paradigm." By contrast, the *yin-yang* view approaches the change as incremental. Incremental (or the so-called "first order," "convergent") change may "involve adjustments in systems, processes, or structures, but it does not involve a fundamental change in strategy, core values, or corporate identity" (Newman 2000: 604). In a continuous change process, "small-win" and incrementalism is essential, and the change that the agent needs to do is "redirecting what is already under way" (Weick and Quinn 1999: 379).

(2) Exogenous vs. endogenous momentum—In the Western dialectical model, "momentum is an exogenous force emerging from the organizational discourse and from the broader institutional discourse," which can "reinforce internal movement by creating a 'burning platform' or a 'window of opportunity' for change" (Raisch et al. 2018: 1515). While for the Chinese *yin-yang* view, because of their conceptualization of the *endogenous relatedness* of opposites, the momentum can be created endogenously, as the above *zao-shi* strategy reveals.

Here, I disagree with Peng and Nisbett's (1999: 744) decision to term the *yin-yang* view a kind of *naïve dialecticism* because of its deviation from the Aristotelian ontology. As shown in Figure 8.2, rooted in a process ontology, the *yin-yang* view itself has constituted a coherent frame in explaining the entity ("what"), process ("how"), momentum ("when"), and leadership ("who") of the change. As shown in Figure 8.1, the dialectical *yin-yang* thinking is above all, metacognitive. It emerges when one realizes the manifold levels of the complexity involved in human cognition, including one's own. "Without such awareness, dialectical thinking remains an unrealized human potential" (Ho 2000: 1065). Dialectical thinking matters only when change agents systematically investigate the interrelations among constituent parts and part–whole relations within the "deep structure" of cognition.

A Case Vignette Illustrating the *Yin-Yang* Model of Change

The *yin-yang* model of change can be illustrated through a vignette of the Chengdu Bus Group (CBG) (Jing and Van de Ven 2014). The CBG is a large state-owned public transportation company, located in western China. For years, the company suffered from low employee morale and poor service quality. Although several CEOs attempted to address these chronic problems, their efforts were largely unsuccessful. Whereas most of the previous reform efforts were directed at changing a particular component of the system, She Chen—the newly appointed CEO—opted for a fundamentally different approach. He sought, in particular, to alter the systemic issues within the ecological system as a whole. For instance, CBG had a volume-based incentive system for frontline employees (i.e., bus drivers and conductors), where approximately 80% of their salaries were linked to passenger volume per month. As shown in Figure 8.4, this incentive system fueled intense competition among employees to increase the passenger volume and get assigned high-volume bus routes. Those assigned high-volume routes often made twice as much as their less fortunate peers, despite having the same overall workload. Although the inherent problems of the incentive system were well-recognized, previous attempts to alleviate the unhealthy competition among employees by equalizing wage levels were unsuccessful—and encountered strong employee resistance.

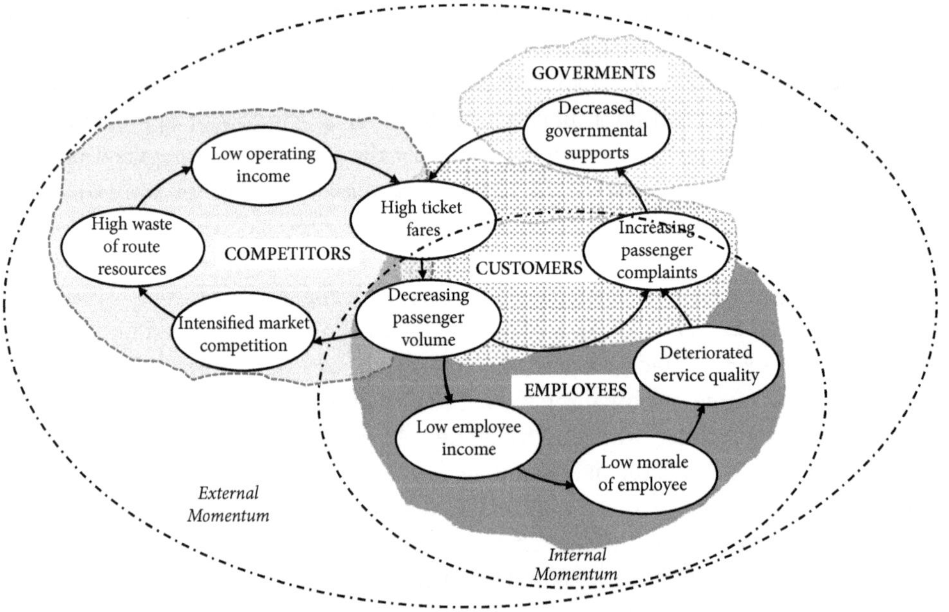

FIGURE 8.4 Illustration of the CBG Case

Instead of directly changing the incentive system, Mr. She Chen wanted to understand and eliminate the deep causes that had led to the introduction of this volume-based incentive system in the first place. He traced the cause to hyper-competition in the transportation sector, which pushed companies to maximize revenues by increasing passenger volume. At that time, there were five bus companies running public transportation services in the city (among them, two were wholly owned by CBG, while the other three were joint ventures where CBG was the minority partner). Less coordination among the companies and fierce competition between them, particularly on high-profit transportation routes, effectively cannibalized CBG's revenue. One way for CBG to resolve this issue would have been to buy out joint venture partners. However, the cost was prohibitively high and it would likely have triggered a protracted and challenging negotiation with joint venture partners.

In a highly unexpected move that has since been touted as the initial turning point of the whole reform, Mr. She Chen cut ticket prices in half. This move forced competitors to also cut their ticket prices to prevent customers from being siphoned away. Such a strategy seems to be irrational since it would intensify the competition. However, the competition in low prices was difficult to sustain because CBG's competitors relied on ticket revenues to maintain their operations. CBG, in contrast, was able to "afford" the significant drop in revenue because it had applied for a bank loan shortly before cutting ticket prices. Thus, the extreme condition of competition would inevitably lead to cooperation. Within three months, CBG had bought out joint venture partners at a highly discounted price. Because it no longer had to "fight" for passengers, CBG was able to abandon the volume-based incentive system and increase the income levels of frontline employees—thereby reducing workplace tension and unhealthy competition, whilst increasing morale and service quality. As a result of this continuous change process, three years later, the CBG had achieved remarkable outcomes. During 2006–09, the number of CBG's bus routes decreased from 202 to 175 due to optimization, while the passenger traffic volume increased from 67.5 to 85.9 million person per month. Despite the price-cutting impacts, the total income of the whole group increased from 75.0 to 79.7 million RMB per month; and the annual salary of employees increased from 22.6 to 34.4 thousand RMB. In 2010, CBG was recognized as an advanced management model in the public transportation industry by the Ministry of Transport of China, and its "reform miracle" became a popular case for many Chinese companies (Jing and Van de Ven 2014).

This case can help us understand the *yin-yang* view of change from the following aspects:

(1) Mapping out pace and sequence of complex changes: To implement an effective change, it does not simply mean to improve the employee change confidence by creating short-term wins (Kotter 1996) but to search for high-leverage ecological factors that can redirect the development of momentum from hostile to favorable and to work out change pace and sequence by mindfully experimenting with the momentum connections between major change problems for a continuous change

process (Amis et al. 2004). Chen started the reform process by solving external problems such as over-competition in bus routes. Comparatively, the previous CEOs had begun their reforms from internal problems such as the incentive system and service quality. Without optimized workloads and stable operating incomes, it would be difficult for those reforms to succeed since CBG could not afford to increase the salary of frontline employees; the low salary of employees led to unchangeably low work morale, hindering change efforts to increase service quality. Thus, the interdependencies among change problems made the sequence an important decision in reform. "There are sequential logics behind these reforms, and each should be examined by its possible impacts on others" (Jing and Van de Ven 2014: 46).

(2) Apprehending the deep structure of interdependent problems: In complex organizational contexts, it is sometimes hard to predict the resistance or readiness to change just by assessing the employees' change attitudes because of the complexity of interdependent change problems. In the CBG case, when Chen began his reform, almost everyone believed that it would inevitably fail. As the employees stated: "[A] t that time, we all thought CBG was hopeless, and no one could save it" (Jing and Van de Ven 2014: 39). Here, what change agents need to do is to step back and to understand employee resistance by apprehending the deep structure of interdependent problems and then affect employee attitudes by creating a favorable context. As Beer et al. (1990: 159) suggested: "This creates a situation that in a sense 'forces' new attitudes and behaviors on people." Here, interpreting what to change (change content) often takes precedence over the behavioral strategies of how to change (change behavior), and the impacts of each change decision need to be justified in the deep structure of change problems. Thus, the "deep structure" indeed works as a guide to sort change activities in a proper order for a desired outcome.

(3) Significant effects of momentum-based strategy as an indirect way of change: As a general principle, when facing a persistent unfavorable momentum, an immediate direct change in individual problems would be too costly since the momentum does not afford the change. On such occasions, the change agents may attempt to convert the unfavorable momentum into a favorable momentum by brokering ecological forces to increase the tensions of a divergent change in the environment. As Chen has commented during an interview: "To solve a tough problem, sometimes a leader needs to create another one first" (Jing and Van de Ven 2014: 48). In the CBG case, to resolve the external over-competition problem, one possible solution was buying back the external equities of joint ventures, but a direct purchase would result in high cost and resistance. To reverse the hostile momentum, CBG adopted a momentum-creating strategy. Specifically, what CBG did first was to affect customer choice by reducing ticket prices, which gradually weakened the competitors' bargaining power in transferring their equities. The possible impacts of this decision were examined by Chen through the interpretation of the "deep structure" of change problems (as shown in Figure 8.4). As a prerequisite, the buses of CBG and its competitors operated on very similar routes, and the customers were sensitive to

ticket prices. Thus, the CBG's price decision would force its competitors to respond similarly; otherwise, their customers would be quickly siphoned away. As a further step of the interaction, the CBG could afford a long-term, low-price competition, while its rivals could not do so since they relied on the ticket income to afford their operations and profits. Once they gave up the competition, their bargaining power in equities transferring to CBG was weakened, implying a favorable momentum for a change. Definitely, not all change issues have such high-leverage effects. The activities that are positioned at the intersection of internal and external systems of an organizational field (as shown in Figure 8.4) have a greater potential to be the ecological leverage to redirect the development of momentum.

Implications of the *Yin-Yang* View

The *yin-yang* change perspective has important implications for management. First, the perspective emphasizes that change agents synchronize their change actions with the rhythms of momentum favorableness. Emphasizing *doing the right thing at the right time* (Javary 1997: 9), Taoists view change momentum in an "indirect" way. In contrast to the common Western portrayals of organizational change processes as driven by strong leadership, the Taoist perspective advocates minimizing the actions and interventions of change agents. It highlights the agentic dimensions of momentum constructed by the affordant nature of momentum perception, the ecological leverage in momentum redirection, and the shift in temporal orientations of momentum responses. Correspondingly, it often involves spending a lot of time preparing and rehearsing for change and then spending a little time implementing the change. This is often termed "pacing" or "entraining" strategy in the prior literature on product development, acquisition, and alliance or new venture creation (e.g., Ancona and Chong 1996; Hernes 2014). Here, one important implication is that a faster pace of change is not always better in terms of final outcomes (Perez-Nordtvedt et al. 2008). To predict the trend of momentum development, change agents need to analyze the "deep structure" that holds organizational elements together and comprehend the links between the past and current momentum.

Second, change agents need to overcome the resistance to change by creating a favorable momentum rather than implementing strong interventions. Most literature on planned change emphasizes how leaders change the employees' resistance to the momentum for a change by their strong change visions and actions (See Chapter 3 by Bartunek et al., this volume; Kotter 1996; Piderit 2000). Meanwhile, there is evidence that 70% of these change initiatives fail just due to the unreliable assumption that leaders can change employee behavior by introducing new perspectives (Burnes 2011). "In fact, individual behavior is powerfully shaped by the organizational roles that people play. The most effective way to change behavior is, therefore, to put people into a new organizational context" (Beer et al. 1990: 159). This is exactly what the "indirect" concept of momentum implies. As such, employee resistance needs to be examined in the context of interdependent organizational elements. By creating a favorable momentum, the context has a potential to renew the very meaning of roles, responsibilities, and relationships in the workplace, which can help the employees change their attitudes and behaviors without exerting too much control.

Third, the perspective emphasizes that change agents should pay more attention to the "when to change" question. As Burke's review (Chapter 2, this volume) showed, organizational scholars are mostly interested in "what to change" or "how to change" questions; while in business practices, a proper chance often serves as the gate to organizational change (Jing and Van de Ven 2018), and such "when to change" question can be well addressed by the *yin-yang* model of change. Specifically, as Figure 8.3 shows, when current momentum is favorable, the change agents can use a momentum-seizing strategy to implement the change with less resistance. When the momentum is predicted to become favorable soon, the change agents may adopt a momentum-entraining strategy to explore the favorable opportunities of the future environment. When facing persistent unfavorable momentum, the change agents may adopt a momentum-creating strategy to enact ecological factors to redirect the situational momentum to create a better change opportunity.

Finally, the perspective has implications for understanding the diversified roles of leadership in the organizational change context. In the Taoist text, it is believed that the ultimate goal of leaders is to minimize their roles in a social change process. An ideal model is called "governing without interfering" ("无为而治" in Chinese), which implies that it is often better for leaders to think about the change in advance and plan to accomplish their change intentions by seizing, entraining, or creating favorable momentums rather than making a radical change. This same principle connects to the notion of "non-action" ("无为" in Chinese), which does not mean that people do nothing, but rather that they exercise forbearance and avoid doing pointless things (Lee et al. 2008). In the CBG case, during the three months following the price-cutting decision, CEO Chen just kept on waiting and seemingly doing nothing. In fact, the notion of "non-action" does not mean that change agents do nothing but rather that they wait and save their energy and credibility in a hostile momentum to take a better advantage of the next favorable one. Once the situational momentum turns favorable, they will take the opportunity to implement the change.

Strengths and Criticisms of the View

The *yin-yang* model of change has an advantage in explaining complicated organizational phenomena and activities from the "becoming" perspective. The embedded cultural wisdom has proved to be a useful frame to theorize the continuous change process or dynamic process of competition or paradox management (e.g., Chen 2008; Chen and Miller 2012; Smith and Lewis 2011; Weick and Quinn 1999).

Meanwhile, there are also some criticisms or drawbacks of this kind of theorizing. First, the *yin-yang* view and the other Chinese cultural philosophies may be over-interpreted by modern organizational scholars. Indigenous scholars adopting the frame from a historical legacy have constantly been reminded of an eisegesis problem, considering the differences between the original context of the indigenous knowledge (e.g., momentum strategies for warfare) and the organizational context (e.g., organizational change) in which it is now applied, as well as the strong impacts upon individual behaviors from other institutional and economic forces in history (e.g., Does *yin-yang* culture still matter to the modern Chinese?). Here, eisegesis refers to a technique where authors impose their own subjective judgment on a text. Thus, "great care is needed when using a work that is both from a different time and a different discipline for it can result in something of limited value" (Clydesdale 2017: 901). To overcome these problems, researchers need to follow an engaged scholarship model to adopt an insider's cultural view instead of running the risk of imposing their own presupposition on research subjects (Jing and Dong 2017). It is suggested that they conduct more empirical and field studies rather than just doing armchair theorizing works. Furthermore, they can cooperate with historians and cultural scholars to make sure that their understanding of *yin-yang* philosophy is correct.

Second, most Eastern change perspectives, including those of the Chinese, are "half-cooked" in the sense that they are often rich in philosophical thinking but lack in formal conceptualization and theorization (Kim 1978). For example, the Chinese concept of momentum for change was mostly developed by Sun-Tzu in his book *Art of War*. In this book, many vivid metaphors (such as rolling a stone from a high mountain, moving boulders on the surface of a torrential river, or shooting an arrow from a fully drawn crossbow) were employed to describe the meanings and effects of momentum, but throughout the book, no exact definition of this key concept was given. Thus, in the Chinese culture, "The logic [of momentum] was perceived so intuitively and shared so universally that it never became the subject of any theoretical discourse in Chinese civilization" (Jullien 1995: 69). To develop the indigenous insights into a formal theory, the researchers need to first provide a clear definition of the study concept and then make a good connection between the cultural and philosophical legacy and existing organizational literature.

Third, any theoretical view inevitably has trade-offs in terms of satisfying generality, accuracy, and simplicity, the criteria of a good theory (Thorngate 1976); the greater the complexity of a "becoming" ontological frame such as the *yin-yang* view, the more difficult it is to test or falsify it. The advantage of Chinese holistic thinking lies in its comprehensive consideration of problems and its preference for building complex theoretical frames by integrating various viewpoints. Meanwhile, the theoretical model based on holistic thinking is often criticized by readers as a result of retrospective sensemaking because it is always easy to find out a reason from a complex model to explain the occurrence of an event afterwards, making the model difficult to be falsified. Hence, "most Eastern philosophies are difficult to use a scientific approach to empirically verify and systematically operationalize" (Luo and Zheng 2016: 390). Here, I have two suggestions:

First, researchers should focus their attention on the cutting-edge questions that an indigenous concept can contribute. For instance, to advance further development of the paradoxical leadership theory, "[F]uture research might use qualitative methods to uncover paradox transformation processes in which the contradictory becomes complementary" (Zhang and Han 2019: 11). Second, they should carefully select methods that can help in resolving the above issues. In an empirical context, holistic epistemology is often associated with a research focus upon the organizational phenomena about configuration, complexity, or equifinality, which can be examined by some advanced methods such as dynamic modeling analysis, qualitative comparative analysis, and profile deviation analysis (e.g., Bartolucci and Nigro 2010; Fiss 2007; Vorhies and Morgan 2003). When its advantages, such as being more general or accurate in creating a complicated model or theory instead of a simple one, can be empirically justified, the contribution of this indigenous holism becomes indubitable.

The self-imposed cultural logic of Western philosophy has been the foundation that prosperous models of organizational change have been rooted in during the past eight decades, and these have greatly expanded our knowledge about business management practices (See Chapter 2 by Burke, this volume). Meanwhile, each category of knowledge is partial in the sense that "a way of seeing is a way of not seeing" (Poggi 1965: 284); we know that alongside the change questions that we can ask is also all the preconception that prompts us to ask those questions. Facing the challenges from the increasing complexity of organizational change problems, more fresh theoretical insights are called for to deepen our understanding of the ever-changing organizations. In this chapter, I summarized the coherent logic that underlies the Chinese *yin-yang* view of change even though it has never valued the conceptual formalization in history. I used the appreciation of this divergent and seemingly distant cultural view to decipher from outside the ongoing conversations in organizational change literature to reveal some priori assumptions underlying the existing theories and models and rediscover the joys of the scholarly inquiry in our organizational community.

References

Alter, A., and Kwan, V. S. Y. (2009), 'Cultural Sharing in a Global Village: Evidence for Extracultural Cognition in European Americans', *Journal of Personality and Social Psychology*, 96/4, 742–60.

Amis, J., Slack, T., and Hinings, C. R. (2004), 'The Pace, Sequence, and Linearity of Radical Change', *Academy of Management Journal*, 47/1, 15–39.

Ancona, D., and Chong, C. L. (1996), 'Entrainment: Pace, Cycle, and Rhythm in Organizational Behavior', *Research in Organizational Behavior*, 18/1, 251–84.

Bartolucci, F., and Nigro, V. (2010), 'A Dynamic Model for Binary Panel Data with Unobserved Heterogeneity Admitting a Root-n Consistent Conditional Estimator', *Econometrica*, 78/2, 719–33.

Bartunek, J. M., Putnam, L. L., and Seo, M-G. (2021), 'Dualities, Dualisms and Tensions in Organization Development', in M. S. Poole and A. H. Van de Ven, eds., *The Oxford Handbook of Organizational Change and Innovation* (2nd edn) (Oxford: Oxford University Press).

Beck, N., BrüDerl, J., and Woywode, M. (2008), 'Momentum or Deceleration? Theoretical and Methodological Reflections on the Analysis of Organizational Change', *Academy of Management Journal*, 51/3, 413–35.

Beer, M., Eisenstat, R. A., and Spector, B. (1990), 'Why Change Programs Do Not Produce Change', *Harvard Business Review*, 68/11, 158–66.

Benson, J. K. (1977), 'Organizations: A Dialectical View', *Administrative Science Quarterly*, 22/1, 1–21.

Bhaskar, R. (1986), *Scientific Realism and Human Emancipation* (London, UK: Verso).

Burke, W. W. (2021), 'Historical Currents in Scholarship of Organization Change', in M. S. Poole and A. H. Van de Ven, eds., *The Oxford Handbook of Organizational Change and Innovation* (2nd edn) (Oxford: Oxford University Press),

Burnes, B. (2011), 'Introduction: Why Does Change Fail and What Can We Do About It?' *Journal of Change Management*, 11/4, 445–50.

Burrell, G., and Morgan, G. (2017), *Sociological Paradigms and Organisational Analysis: Elements of the Sociology of Corporate Life* (London: Routledge Press).

Capra, F. (2010), *The Tao of Physics: An Exploration of the Parallels between Modern Physics and Eastern Mysticism* (5th edn) (Boston, MA: Shambhala).

Chen, M.-J. (2008), 'Re-Conceptualizing the Competition-Cooperation Relationship: A Trans-Paradox Perspective', *Journal of Management Inquiry*, 17/4, 288–304.

Chen, M.-J., and Miller, D. (2012), 'Competitive Dynamics: Themes, Trends, and a Prospective Platform', *Academy of Management Annals*, 6/1, 135–210.

Cheng, C. (2009), 'Dialectical Thinking and Coping Flexibility: A Multimethod Approach', *Journal of Personality*, 77/2, 471–93.

Choi, I., Nisbett, R. E., and Norenzayan, A. (1999), 'Causal Attribution across Cultures: Variation and Universality', *Psychological Bulletin*, 125/1, 47–63.

Clausewitz, C. (2007), *On War*. Trans. M. Howard and P. Paret (Oxford: Oxford University Press).

Clydesdale, G. (2017), 'Western Perceptions of Chinese Business: Sun Tzu and the Misuse of History', *Management and Organization Review*, 13/4, 895–903.

Cross, R., Baker, W., and Parker, A. (2003), 'What Creates Energy in Organizations?' *MIT Sloan Management Review*, 44/4, 51–6.

Faure, G. O., and Fang, T. (2008), 'Changing Chinese Values: Keeping Up with Paradoxes', *International Business Review*, 17/2, 194–207.

Fiss, P. C. (2007), 'A Set-Theoretic Approach to Organizational Configurations', *Academy of Management Review*, 32/4, 1180–98.

Gibson, J. J. (1977), 'The Theory of Affordances', in R. Shaw and J. Bransford, eds., *Perceiving, Acting, and Knowing: Toward an Ecological Psychology* (Hillsdale, NJ: Erlbaum), 67–82.

Grimes A. J., and Cornwall J. R. (1987), 'The Disintegration of an Organization: A Dialectical Analysis', *Journal of Management*, 13/1, 69–86.

Hamamura, T., Heine, S. J., and Paulhus, D. L. (2008), 'Cultural Differences in Response Styles: The Role of Dialectical Thinking', *Personality and Individual Differences*, 44/4, 932–42.

Hannan, M. T., and Freeman, J. H. (1977), 'The Population Ecology of Organizations', *American Journal of Sociology*, 82/5, 929–84.

Hargrave, T. (2021), 'The Paradox Perspective and the Dialectics of Contradictions Research', in M. S. Poole and A. H. Van de Ven, eds., *The Oxford Handbook of Organizational Change and Innovation* (2nd edn) (Oxford: Oxford University Press).

Hargrave, T. and Van de Ven, A. (2017), 'Integrating Dialectical and Paradox Perspectives on Managing Contradictions in Organizations', *Organization Studies*, 38/3–4, 319–39.

Hernes, T. (2014), *A Process Theory of Organization* (Oxford: Oxford University Press).
Ho, D. Y. F. (2000), 'Dialectical Thinking: Neither Eastern nor Western', *American Psychologist*, 55/9, 1064–5.
Jansen, K. J. (2004), 'From Persistence to Pursuit: A Longitudinal Examination of Momentum during the Early Stages of Strategic Change', *Organization Science*, 15/3, 276–94.
Javary, C. (1997), *Understanding the I Ching* (Boston and London: Shambhala).
Ji, L.J., Zhang, Z., and Nisbett R. (2004), 'Is it Culture or is it Language? Examination of Language Effects in Cross-Cultural Research on Categorization', *Journal of Personality and Social Psychology*, 87/1, 57–65.
Jing, R. (2017), 'Momentum for change: connecting Chinese and Western perspectives.' in Guclu Atinc, eds., Best Paper Proceedings of the Seventy-seventh Annual Meeting of the Academy of Management.
Jing, R., and Dong, M. (2017), 'Management Scholars' Learning from History: Direct vs. Indirect Approach', *Management and Organization Review*, 13/4, 905–11.
Jing, R., and Van de Ven, A. H. (2014), 'A "Yin-Yang" Model of Organizational Change: The Case of Chengdu Bus Group', *Management and Organization Review*, 10/1, 29–54.
Jing, R., and Van de Ven, A. H. (2016), 'Being versus Becoming Ontology of Paradox Management', *Cross Cultural and Strategic Management*, 23/4, 558–62.
Jing, R., and Van de Ven, A. H. (2018), 'Toward a Chance Management View of Organizational Change', *Management and Organization Review*, 14/1, 161–78.
Jullien, F. (1995), *The Propensity of Things: Toward A History of Efficacy in China* (New York, NY: Zone Books).
Karcher, S. (2004), *Total I Ching: Myths for Change* (Lancaster, UK: Time Warner Books).
Kelly, D., and Amburgey, T. L. (1991), 'Organizational Inertia and Momentum: A Dynamic Model of Strategic Change', *Academy of Management Journal*, 34/3, 591–612.
Kim, Y. K. (1978), 'Hegel's Criticism of Chinese Philosophy', *Philosophy East and West*, 28/2, 173–80.
Koller, J. M. (2007), *Asian Philosophies* (5th edn) (Upper Saddle River, NJ: Prentice Hall).
Kotter, J. P. (1996), *Leading Change* (Cambridge, MA: Harvard Business School Press).
Larreche, J. C. (2008), *The Momentum Effect: How to Ignite Exceptional Growth* (Upper Saddle River, NJ: Wharton School Publishing).
Lee, Y. T., Han, A. G., Byron, T. K., and Fan, H. X. (2008). 'Daoist Leadership: Theory and Application', in C. C. Chen and Y. T. Lee eds. *Leadership and Management in China: Philosophies, Theories, and Practices* (Cambridge: Cambridge University Press), 143–68.
Lehman, D. W., and Hahn, J. (2013), 'Momentum and Organizational Risk Taking: Evidence from the National Football League', *Management Science*, 59/4, 852–68.
Lewin, K. (1947), 'Frontiers in Group Dynamics', in D. Cartwright, eds, *Field Theory in Social Science* (London: Social Science Paperbacks), 188–237.
Lewis, M. W. (2000), 'Exploring Paradox: Toward a More Comprehensive Guide', *Academy of Management Review*, 25/4, 760–76.
Li, P. P. (2015), 'The Economic-Social Duality for Executive Rationale: The Interplay between Resource Pool and Game Rule for Sense-Giving and Sense-Making', *Management and Organization Review*, 11/2, 211–16.
Li, P. P. (2016), 'Global Implications of the Indigenous Epistemological System from the East: How to Apply Yin-Yang Balancing to Paradox Management', *Cross Cultural and Strategic Management*, 23/1, 42–77.

Luo, Y., and Zheng, Q. (2016), 'Competing in Complex Cross-Cultural World', *Cross Cultural and Strategic Management*, 23/2, 386–92.
Ma, L., and Tsui, A. S. (2015), 'Traditional Chinese Philosophies and Contemporary Leadership', *Leadership Quarterly*, 26/1, 13–24.
Marshak, R. J. (1993), 'Lewin Meets Confucius: A Review of the OD Model of Change', *Journal of Applied Behavioral Science*, 29/4, 393–415.
Michel, A. (2014), 'The Mutual Constitution of Persons and Organizations: An Ontological Perspective on Organizational Change', *Organization Science*, 25/4, 1082–110.
Miller, D., and Friesen, P. H. (1980), 'Momentum and Revolution in Organizational Adaptation', *Academy of Management Journal*, 23/4, 591–614.
Miller, D. (1990), 'Organizational Configurations: Cohesion, Change, and Prediction', *Human Relations*, 43/8, 771–89.
Mingers, J. (2004), 'Realizing Information Systems: Critical Realism as an Underpinning Philosophy for Information Systems', *Information and Organization*, 14/2, 87–103.
Morris, M. W., and Peng, K. (1994), 'Culture and Cause: American and Chinese Attributions for Social and Physical Events', *Journal of Personality and Social Psychology*, 67/6, 949–71.
Newman, K. (2000), 'Organizational Transformation During Institutional Upheaval', *Academy of Management Review*, 25/3, 602–19.
Nisbett, R. E. (2003), *The Geography of Thought: How Asians and Westerners Think Differently... and Why* (New York: Free Press).
Orlikowski, W. J., and Yates, J. A. (2002), 'It's About Time Temporal Structuring in Organizations', *Organization Science*, 13/6, 684–700.
Peng, K., and Nisbett, R. E. (1999), 'Culture, Dialectics, and Reasoning about Contradiction', *American Psychologist*, 54/9, 741–54.
Peng, K., Spencer-Rodgers, J., and Zhong, N. (2005), 'Naive Dialecticism and the Tao of Chinese Thought', in U. Kim, K. S. Yang, and G. Huang, eds., *Handbook of Indigenous and Cultural Psychology* (Malden, MA: Blackwell), 247–62.
Perez-Nordtvedt, L., Payne, G. T., Short, J. C., and Kedia, B. L. (2008), 'An Entrainment-Based Model of Temporal Organizational Fit, Misfit, and Performance', *Organization Science*, 19/5, 785–801.
Piderit, S. K. (2000), 'Rethinking Resistance and Recognizing Ambivalence: A Multidimensional View of Attitudes toward an Organizational Change', *Academy of Management Review*, 25/4, 783–94.
Poggi, G. (1965), 'A Main Theme of Contemporary Sociological Analysis: Its Achievements and Limitations', *British Journal of Sociology*, 16/4, 283–94.
Prashantham, S., and Eranova, M. (2019), 'Cultural Differences in Paradoxical Tensions in Strategy Episodes', Long Range Planning, in press.
Raisch, S., Hargrave, T. J., and Van de Ven, A. H. (2018), 'The Learning Spiral: A Process Perspective on Paradox', *Journal of Management Studies*, 55/8, 1507–26.
Rindova, V. P., and Starbuck, W. H. (1997), 'Ancient Chinese theories of control', *Journal of Management Inquiry*, 6/2, 144–59.
Seo, M-G. and Creed, W. E. D. (2002), 'Institutional Contradictions, Praxis, and Institutional Transformation: A Dialectical Perspective', *Academy of Management Review*, 27/2, 222–47.
Smith, W. K. and Lewis, M. W. (2011), 'Toward a Theory of Paradox: A Dynamic Equilibrium Model of Organizing', *Academy of Management Review*, 36/2, 381–403.
Sun-Tzu (1971). *The Art of War* (Trans. S. B. Griffith) (Oxford: Oxford University Press).

Thorngate, W. (1976), 'Possible Limits on a Science of Social Behavior', in J. H. Strickland, F. E. Aboud, and K. J. Gergen, eds., *Social Psychology in Transition* (New York, NY: Plenum), 121–39.

Van de Ven, A. H., and Poole, M. S. (1995), 'Explaining Development and Change in Organizations', *Academy of Management Review*, 20/3, 510–40.

Vorhies, D. W. and Morgan, N. A. (2003), 'A Configuration Theory Assessment of Marketing Organization Fit with Business Strategy and its Relationship with Market Performance', *Journal of Marketing*, 67/1, 100–15.

Weick, K. E. and Quinn, R. E. (1999), 'Organizational Change and Development', *Annual Review of Psychology*, 50/1, 361–86.

Wiebe, E., Suddaby, R., and Foster, W. M. (2012), 'The Momentum of Organizational Change', in S. Maguire and M. Schultz, eds., *Constructing Identity in and around Organizations* (Oxford: Oxford University Press), 235–60.

Wilhelm, R. and Baynes, C. F. trans. (1967), *I Ching or Book of Changes* (3rd edn) (Princeton, NJ: Princeton University Press).

Yang, G. R. (2008), 'Being and Value: From the Perspective of Chinese-Western Comparative Philosophy', *Philosophy: East and West*, 58/2, 267–82.

Zhang, Y., and Han, Y-L. (2019), 'Paradoxical Leader Behavior in Long-Term Corporate Development: Antecedents and Consequences', *Organizational Behavior and Human Decision Process*, 155/3, 42–54.

Zhang, Y., Waldman, D., Han, Y. L., and Li, X. B. (2015), 'Paradoxical Leader Behavior in People Management: Antecedents and Consequences', *Academy of Management Journal*, 58/2, 538–66.

CHAPTER 9

SOCIAL MOVEMENTS AND ORGANIZATIONAL CHANGE

GERALD F. DAVIS AND EUN WOO KIM

CORPORATIONS are increasingly experiencing change driven by activists inside and outside the organization. In November 2018, twenty thousand Google employees around the world walked out to protest the company's perceived history of protecting sexual harrassers. At Amazon, thousand of employee activists sought firm commitments from management to reduce the company's carbon footprint. Microsoft workers urged the company to annul an army contract for battlefield augmented reality headsets. And Salesforce workers pushed their company to cut ties to Customs and Border Protection over separating children from families on the US/Mexico border. Outside activists also used new tools to target corporations. After the Parkland school shooting in February 2018, a political website publicized a list of over thirty corporations offering discounted pricing to members of the National Rifle Association (NRA) and suggested a mass boycott of these firms. Within forty-eight hours, two dozen of these businesses had dropped their ties to the NRA, including well-known consumer brands such as Delta Airlines, Hertz, North American Van Lines, and MetLife.

In the world beyond corporations, social movements have become pervasive features of contemporary society, from the Arab Spring to the #MeToo movement against sexual harassment. These broad movements increasingly shape what happens within organizations, as internal activists take their cues from external efforts at social change.

Although social activism within organizations is not without precedent, what is new is its scale, pervasiveness, and success. Few organizations today are immune to politicized campaigns for change, from Applebee's restaurant to the Komen Foundation (Davis and White, 2015). But why now?

Advances in information and communication technologies (ICTs), coupled with generational shifts in values, have changed the landscape for social movements and organizations, and increasingly erase the boundaries between them. ICTs have created a situation in which nearly everyone in the industrialized world is accessible to everyone else, at least in principle, and information flows almost without cost. The result is that the transaction costs for collective action—say, the effort required to organize a large-scale protest—can now be trivially small. One Facebook post can be the spark that brings hundreds of thousands of people to a march on the capital the day after a presidential inauguration, something that would have taken large-scale formal organization just a generation ago. Anyone with a smartphone can be a change agent now.

The same shift in transaction costs has radically re-shaped organizations as well. It is increasingly feasible to "rent" rather than "buy" the inputs to an organization and coordinate them online, allowing tiny enterprises to scale up and down rapidly without the need to invest in fixed assets or permanent employees (Davis 2016). The global media brand Netflix had only seven thousand employees as of 2019 and rented server space from Amazon. Disruptive taxi firm Lyft had fewer than five thousand employees; Pinterest, Slack, and Zoom each had fewer than two thousand. And the maker of Instant Pot, the ubiquitous kitchen appliance that created a $300 million product category, had only fifty employees, relying entirely on outside contractors for production and distribution. Anyone with a credit card and a Web connection can be an entrepreur now.

These new forms of organizing create new challenges for theories of organizational change, new domains for activism, and new opportunities for research. This chapter reviews the nascent work on social movements and organizational change. The two scholarly domains, once strictly separate, are now increasingly joined by common interests. Moreover, social movement theory provides a robust and actionable account of organizational innovation and change that has gathered a large body of research evidence since the first edition of this handbook. Here, we review recent work and outline a framework for organizational change from a social movement perspective. We believe this framework can inform both research and practice.

We note at the outset that this domain is not entirely new. Donald Schon's (1971) classic book *Beyond the Stable State* lays out a life cycle analysis of social change that describes how ideas that emerge from the periphery can come to prominence in times of social change, and the model described here contains echos of Schon's work. But perhaps the pace of change today, enabled by ICTs, is new. And we believe that some of the most exciting work on change in the next decade will be research on grassroots social innovation and political action within organizations. As we write, major disruptions are washing over corporations and other organizations. If we are to take on the challenges that our species faces today, existing institutions will need to be substantially re-tooled, along the lines of the political revolutions of generations past. It is a fruitful time for research and theory on ICT-enabled change, and a critical time for research that can inform practice.

Organizations and Movements Converging

Research on organizations and social movements has traditionally been taken on by separate communities of researchers with very little overlap. Organizational scholars focused on formal, bounded organizations such as corporations, and examined questions of organization design, the boundaries of the firm, the sources of organizational diversity or homogeneity, and the factors associated with superior organizational performance (Scott and Davis 2007). Since the 1980s, organizational scholars have primarily been based in business schools. Social movement scholars, mostly in sociology, examined sources of social change, particularly those that took place outside the formal polity. Like organizations, movements entailed collective action among groups of people with more or less shared aims. But the action was more likely to take place on the streets than in the suites, and the changes they sought were more momentous than the addition of ranch flavoring to a snack food brand. And social movement scholars tended to be in departments of sociology and political science.

In an immensely perceptive 1978 article, Mayer Zald—who operated in both scholarly camps—recognized the commonalities between these two domains (Zald and Berger 1978). The article was entitled "Social movements in organizations: Coup d'etat, bureaucratic insurgency, and mass movement," and made the case that there was a strong analogy between states and organizations, and that this analogy extended to the forms of activism used by organizational members to create unsanctioned change. There were coups, in which CEOs are defenestrated by others high up in the hierarchy; insurgencies, in which middle managers conspired to change organizational products or processes outside the formal approval process; and mass insurrections among the rank and file workers. In each case there were strong parallels between processes at the national and the organizational level. Although the argument is widely hailed today, its reception at the time was quite muted: as Zald (2005: 162) put it, "It seemed to have sunk in the scholarly ocean of unread papers," and garnered few citations in its first twenty years. The two fields were like twins separated at birth, largely unaware of the other's existence.

In recent times, however, both domains have been unsettled by common underlying forces that make it clear that, in many ways, organizations and movements are more alike than different. Advances in ICTs have shifted the transaction cost profiles of coordinated action within and beyond organizations. This has dramatically shifted the landscape for both movements and organizations. Governments and organizations are increasingly transparent, subject to having their secrets going viral, from Edward Snowden's exposure of internal government surveillance programs to the Sony hack that made public the divergent salaries of male and female actors and the unflattering emails of executives. Social media enable nearly instantaneous marches and boycotts, as well as entirely new forms of coordination and activism. Informal movements can be crystallized into formal organizations; firms can be increasingly impromptu assemblies, like pop-up restaurants.

As a result, scholars over the past two decades have worked to build on commonalities and shared concerns across these two areas (Davis and McAdam 2000). Movements can target organizations and industries, or can create climates in which new kinds of organizations thrive (Rao et al. 2000). For instance, the alcohol prohibition movement was often fatal for breweries, but transformative for soft drink producers (Hiatt et al. 2009). Movements can also "infiltrate" organizations, changing their internal practices (Zald et al. 2005). For example, corporations with gay affinity groups were quickest to create programs offering benefits to the families of LGBT employees equivalent to those of straight employees (Briscoe and Safford 2008). And organizations can be components of movements themselves, taking on activist political stances. When Arkansas's legislature passed a bill enabling businesses to discriminate against LGBT customers on the basis of "religious freedom," Walmart successfully lobbied the state's governor to veto the bill, arguing for the benefits of diversity. Thus, the intersection of movements and organizations has become an increasingly fruitful scholarly domain, yielding dozens of articles and several collections (Davis, McAdam, Scott, and Zald 2005; Davis et al. 2008).

In this chapter, we review the recent outpouring of literature, but much of our focus is on a specific emerging domain: the rise of social movements within organizations as a significant new form of organizational change that connects societal concerns with dynamics within the organization itself.

Recent Research on Movements in and around Organizations

Since 2005 there has been a blossoming of research on movements *within* organizations, movements *targeting* organizations, and movements *creating or facilitating* organizations. We provide a brief review of research published over the past fifteen years, organized by theme, and provide some provisional conclusions. Our review provides a compact but fairly comprehensive update of what has been published in this domain since its foundational statements (Davis et al. 2005). After reviewing this work, we provide a synthetic account intended to spark further work on internal social movements.

Movements *within* Organizations

The literature on social movements within organizations highlights the fact that challengers face a high level of personal risk: their efforts often target incumbents in the same organization who hold higher power and can retaliate against them. In these circumstances, several factors enable activists to self-organize.

First, a physical "safe space" enables challengers to interact and discuss their ideas prior to going public. Kellogg (2009) defines *relational spaces* as areas of isolation, interaction, and inclusion where reformers can develop a unified collective for change. For healthcare professionals, afternoon rounds meetings in hospitals served as relational spaces: they were staffed with only reformers, and thus enabled reformers to build a new relational efficacy, identity, and frames without the fear of retaliation from defenders. Second, an *opportunity structure* inside an organization increases the chance of movement's success, thereby helping challengers take personal risks to mobilize themselves in the early phase of the movement. Briscoe et al. (2014) found that a CEO's political liberalism provided a cue that facilitated the formation of LGBT employee groups. Over time, however, as the movement developed and gained widespread acceptance, CEO ideology became less critical.

The existence of an *opportunity structure* also facilitates movement success. Kim et al. (2007) show that the weakened power of the government agents during the political democratization of the mid-1980s in South Korea enabled faculty in public universities to force their universities to abandon a conventional appointment system and adopt a direct voting system for the university presidential election. Kellogg (2011a) highlights the importance of political opportunities and the toolkits available to challengers. For activists seeking to reduce work hours for residents in their hospital, toolkits included facilitative staffing systems, openly supportive allies and non-repressive evaluation systems. It is important to note that organization-level political toolkits were partially available due to institution-level political opportunities. Institution-level political opportunities included the introduction of a new regulation supporting challengers' agenda, an increase in the size of the female workforce, and an undersupply of general surgery applicants. The level of challenger organization and cohesion also increased the odds of success.

Organized challengers have higher bargaining power than individuals, and they are under less threat of personal penalty that can be posed by incumbents. For example, Kim et al. (2007) find that universities with a faculty council were more likely to adopt new practices than those without. Thus, defenders may try to divide challenger coalitions. Kellogg (2012) finds that defenders rely on status distinctions as a tool to divide reformers, associating the proposed reforms with low-status markers and seeking to re-integrate higher-status reformers into the defender group.

Last, more recent work documents how organizations are not simply bounded entities that neatly contain movements, but are part of an overlapping field in which organizational and personal relationships provide conduits for tactics and ideas to spread (DeJordy et al. 2020). In the campaign to get equal rights for LGBT employees and their families in Minneapolis/St. Paul, activists were enmeshed in an "inhabited ecosystem" that cut across organizations. And as this article showed, progress is not inevitable.

Movements *Targeting* Organizations

How do social movements targeting organizations emerge and develop? There are several potential sparks for movement emergence. One category is cultural artifacts such as books, movies, and news stories. Vasi et al. (2015) report that activism against hydraulic fracturing (fracking)—an unconventional method of extracting natural gas—used the documentary "Gasland" as a mobilizing tool. Just as Rachel Carson's 1962 book *Silent Spring* raised public awareness of the danger of DDT, "Gasland" raised public consciousness about the dangers of fracking for drinking water and health. The documentary's nationwide release on HBO and nomination for an Oscar award increased online discussion about fracking on Twitter. Increased online discussion led to a higher number of organized events, and local screenings increased local mobilizations within the following two months, which in turn led to local bans on fracking.

News about other stakeholders' actions and reactions to target organizations affect the strength and nature of future reactions by focal stakeholders. This echoes the model of Schon (1971) described previously. Dorobantu et al. (2017) highlight the role of critical events for the emergence of a critical mass of social and political stakeholders targeting or defending an organization. Critical events are irregular, stakeholder-initiated actions and reactions targeting an organization such as court decisions that are unfavorable to the target organization. More specifically, the study highlights the roles of stakeholders' prior beliefs about a target organization, the nature of the reaction of peer stakeholders, and the status or visibility of reacting stakeholders on the development of social movement. Following a critical event, stakeholders who had positive prior beliefs about the organization mobilize to defend it, while stakeholders who had negative prior beliefs reinforce their opposition. Also, immediate positive reactions of peer stakeholders following a critical event lead to subsequent positive reactions, while immediate negative reactions of peer stakeholders lead to subsequent negative reactions. Finally, the study shows that the higher the status or visibility of the stakeholders that reacted after the critical event, the more pronounced the reaction by other stakeholders and shareholders.

We note that these critical events need not be construed as the *cause* of social movement activity. Grievances or innovations may be lying dormant, waiting for the right movement to gain tractions. This is one of the insights of the *political opportunity structure* view of social movements (esp. McAdam 1998). Key events, such as the Supreme Court's Brown v. Board of Education decision, did not conjure the civil rights movement out of thin air, but served as focalizing points for activism.

Several factors are associated with movement success in influencing target organizations. First, shareholders are typically more effective than other outsiders at bringing about change at the top management level. Vasi and King (2012) compare the effects of environmental activism by shareholders vs. non-shareholder outsiders in shaping perceived environmental risk, finding that shareholder resolutions are more influential than protests, demonstrations, boycotts, or lawsuits initiated by non-shareholder outsiders. Shareholder grievance are perhaps more legitimate in the eyes of risk managers than that of non-shareholder outsiders, as their economic interests are more closely aligned with those of the firms.

Second, directly influencing firms' political and regulatory environment is more effective than engaging in protests or boycotts. For example, Hiatt et al. (2015) compared the effectiveness of public political tactics (i.e., activists' testimony at congressional hearings) and private political tactics (i.e., protests) on firms' likelihood of adopting a new practice that addressed climate change, but at a cost to the firm. The public tactic increased practice adoption by increasing regulatory risk, while the private tactic led to more symbolic responses decoupled from actual change in practice. McDonnell and King (2013) similarly find that when firms are targeted by boycotts, they try to neutralize the reputational threats by making prosocial claims (e.g., issuing a press release associating themselves with pro-social activities) without directly addressing boycotters' concerns or changing their internal practices.

Boycotts or other campaigns by outsiders can still be effective when target firms are particularly vulnerable. King (2008) finds that companies were more likely to concede to boycotters' demands in the wake of declines in sales or reputations. Target firms were also more likely to concede to boycotts that receive high levels of media attention because they can disrupt organizational routine, impose costs, and shape negative public perception about the target firms. Zhang and Luo (2013) also highlight that a sense of organizational vulnerability spurs firms to respond to campaign demands more quickly. Firms were quicker to donate to disaster relief when they were targeted by online campains, when corporate donations were subject to greater online publicity, and when firms had higher reputations.

Fourth, social movements that affect firms' internal polity and perceived investment risk can lead to movement success. Weber et al. (2009) show that the anti-biotech movement in Germany influenced pharmaceutical firms' commercialization of biotechnology by threatening the status of internal elites inside organizations, undermining elite unity and increasing the perceived uncertainty of investment in biotechnology. Interestingly, movement activism was a source of imprinting. Firms that located their biotechnology operations abroad in response to the domestic opposition suffered from fragmented structure and increased coordination cost. These challenges continued to have an impact on firms by impeding development and commercialization of the new biotechnology. However, the movement's imprint was weak for new pharmaceutical firms that out-waited the peak of the social movements.

Fifth, social movements targeting firms in an industry can have a successful outcome when actors along the commodity chain in the industry share a low level of understanding about the nature and attributes of their products. Schurman and Munro (2009) explain that a critical factor that can create opportunities for activist challengers is incumbents' low cultural-economic cohesion—the degree to which actors along the chain share an understanding of their business worlds and of a product's attributes. The anti-biotech movement in Britain was largely successful because actors along the genetically modified food chain such as retailers, consumers, biotech companies, and farmers had low cultural–economic cohesion. In the US, in contrast, the movement had negligible impact because actors along the commodity chain had a high cultural–economic cohesion.

Practices that were initially adopted due to activism can also spread beyond targeted firms by standard diffusion processes. Briscoe and Safford (2008) find that the adoption of domestic partner benefits for LGBT employees was especially likely to influence later adopters when the earlier adopters were "activism resistant" firms, which they label the "Nixon in China" effect. In addition, different activist tactics have different effectiveness in inducing practice adoption among non-targeted organizations. Briscoe et al. (2015) find that the contagious effect of independent and evidence-based adoptions by targeted organization is greater than that of disruption-linked adoptions by targeted organization. The study examined a voluntary adoption of a practice by non-targeted universities and colleges during the Rein-in-Russell campaign organized by United Students Against Sweatshops (USAS). When USAS used disruption-linked tactics such as sit-ins against target organizations, non-targeted organizations make poor inferences about the merits of the new practice. On the other hand, when USAS used independent and evidence-based tactics such as organization of victim testimonial events against target organizations, non-targeted organizations have informed evidence about the merits of the new practice. During the victim testimonial events, university administrators at target organizations learned about the poor working conditions at their licensed suppliers, and this information was transmitted through their university networks, increasing voluntary adoptions of the practice among non-targeted organizations.

Who gets targeted? Bartley and Child (2014) find that the companies most likely to be targeted are larger companies, branded marketers (manufactures without factories), companies engaging in major advertising or brand activities, and firms with a positive reputation in the business communitiy. What are the effects of being targeted? McDonnell and Werner (2016) highlight a disruptive effect of activism on corporate political activity. The study finds that social activists' challenges decreased politicians' willingness to associate with the targeted firms. More specifically, boycotts led to a significant increase in the proportion of political contributions that were refunded to the donor, as well as a decrease in invited congressional appearances and awarded government contracts. Also, King and Soule (2007) found that a targeted firm's stock price was negatively affected when protests targeted issues dealing with critical stakeholder groups such as labor or consumers, and when protests generated greater media coverage.

Firms respond to being targeted by activists in diverse ways that vary in their effectiveness. McDonnell et al. (2015) find that when firms face more activist challenges such as boycotts, they are more likely to adopt social management devices such as instituting a formal CSR board committee and disseminating a CSR report. They also find that shareholder proposals, and not boycotts, lead firms to disseminate CSR reports because firms seek to counter the perceptions of risk among industry analysts and investors that are prompted by the proxy proposals. Once firms adopt social management devices, they become more receptive to future activist challenges. The study sheds light on the dynamic process through which corporate opportunity structures evolve over time in response to activist challenges. Other strategies that firms use to prevent future protests include participation in corporate-sponsored activisms (McDonnell 2015) and withdrawing a plan to open a new store if they face protests when released new store proposals in the region (Ingram et al. 2010).

Movements *Creating or Facilitating* Organizations and Industries

How do social movements enable the emergence of new industries? Weber et al. (2008) describe how social movements created a market for grass-fed beef and dairy products in the US. The study highlights that social activists used cultural codes to shape a new market and direct entrepreneurial activities. A coalition of activists employed cultural codes of authenticity, sustainability, and naturalness to motivate entrepreneurial production and shape the direction of innovation. Activists also utilized the cultural codes of manipulation, exploitation, and artificiality to establish external boundaries and foster internal cohesion, which helped create a positive collective identity for the new producer community. Furthermore, members of the coalition of activists helped create the nascent market by bridging the social distance between producers and consumers, creating an alternative infrastructure for distribution, and helping market participants agree on the quality dimension of the new product for valuation.

Similarly, Sine and Lee (2009) focused on the role of social movement organizations in promoting entrepreneurial activity to develop a wind energy sector. Environmental social movement organizations articulated problems associated with traditional technologies and inputs while promoting wind power as an environmentally benign alternative. In addition to constructing transformative framing that shifted values and norms surrounding electricity generation, environmental social movement organizations also staged lobbying campaigns directed towards regulators, which led to increased entrepreneurial activity in the wind power sector. Environmental social movement organizations also offered pre-existing social structures—a network of supporters of renewable energy—that are valuable to entrepreneurs. Greve et al. (2006) also highlight social movement's effort to attract entrepreneurs to create a new market. The study examines how microradio activists facilitated establishment of low-power FM (LPFM) radio stations in order to challenge the domination of radio by corporate chains. By putting diverse voices onto the airwaves, microradio activists sought to attract audiences for these new voices, and ultimately reduce the influence of corporate chain-owned stations. Microradio activists formed Micro-radio Empowerment Coalition, and elicited applications from entrepreneurs to found LPFM stations in local communities.

Second, groups of incumbent firms can initiate social movements to differentiate their products from those of peer firms. Bartley (2007) describes the process through which the market for certified wood was created through a political contestation among a wide array of actors that consist of firms, NGOs, SMOs, and governments. In response to tropical timber boycotts, environmentally conscious small specialty firms called for forest certification system that could differentiate their products from those produced by peer firms in the forest product industry. Discussions about the certification system continued and led to the formation of the Forest Stewardship Council (FSC) driven by environmental NGOs with support from governments and foundations. After the formation of the FSC, industry associations were able to develop forest certification programs, creating the market for certified wood.

Last, a new industry can be created as an unintended consequence of social movements that targeted other industry. Hiatt et al. (2009) describes how the Woman's Christian Temperance Union (WCTU) contributed to the decline of the brewery industry, which resulted in the unintended emergence and growth of the soft drink industry. The WCTU attacked the normative, regulative, and cognitive basis of the brewery industry by promoting temperance norms, supporting anti-alcohol laws, and campaigning for pro-temperance education. The movement not only resulted in the failure of the brewery industry, but also unintentionally created new entrepreneurial opportunities in the soft drink industry. The movement facilitated the founding of soft drink firms by inspiring entrepreneurs to produce alternative drinks, creating financial opportunities in the alternative market, and freeing up needed resources for the entrepreneurs to start their new businesses.

There are other ways that movements can enable the emergence of new types of organizations. Schneiberg et al. (2008) explain that the Grange—an anti-corporate movement in the US—fostered cooperatives and mutuals that were membership-based, mutual benefit associations which differed from for-profit corporations. In the face of blocked political access, the Grange shifted from politics to private strategies of economic self-organization, promoting alternative organizational forms. The authors describe the social movements as "organization-generating organizations." The authors argue that the Grange fueled cooperative forms as an alternative to politics or in response to blocked political access. This explanation is based on the finding that the positive effect of Grange membership on mutual self-organization was weaker in states where Grangers won political victories.

In addition, when challengers and incumbents can discover their convergent interests, they can collectively found a new type of organization that serves their collaborative goals. For example, O'Mahony and Bechky (2008) show that community projects in the open-source software movement and incumbent corporations in the proprietary software industry discovered convergent interests, and created nonprofit foundations to serve their mutual benefit. More specifically, members of the community projects were interested in enhancing the technical quality and expanding the user base of their code, which incumbent corporations could help. Incumbent corporations were interested in solving difficult technical problems and recruiting skilled programmers, and collaboration with the community projects allowed them access to talented programmers. The two parties created nonprofit foundations to serve as boundary organizations which help reinforce their convergent interests while allowing their divergent interests to coexist.

Social Movements within Organizations: A Model of Change and Innovation

Social movements have become increasingly pervasive in and around organizations. Social issues that used to be consigned to the environment outside organizations now penetrate everyday life within their walls. In this section, we provide a framework from the study of social movements to systematize the study of member-led movements within organizations as a form of organizational change and innovation, drawing on Davis and White (2015). We note at the outset that there has been relatively little research on the process of social movement activism within organizations, in part because the phenomenon has only recently emerged in force in the real world. Thus, we consider this framework to be a prospective guide to future work more than a well-validated theory.

The textbook synthesis model of social movements contains four core elements that give rise to movements aimed at social change and that shape their effectiveness (McAdam 1982; McCarthy and Zald 1977; Tilly 1978). These four elements in effect translate into four questions about movements: When? Why? Who? and How? Notably, social movement scholars in the "dynamics of contention" school see movements as inherently processual: movements should be examined, not in terms of covering laws (if X then Y), but in terms of the recurring mechanisms that underlie contentious politics (McAdam et al. 2001), and we take our cue from this turn. Thus, it is rarely the case that "whenever you see a grievance, you will see a successful movement mobilize." Instead, what we can hope for are regularities in *mechanisms*—that it often happens that A triggers B, and B may lead to C or D.

When: Opportunity Structure

The *political opportunity structure* describes the broad contours of the social context in which change occurs, and recent events that have made purposeful change more or less feasible (McAdam 1982). Why is now the right time for change? Why not last year, or next year? Consider the African-American civil rights movement. Why did it flourish and achieve its greatest successes in the late 1950s and 1960s and not earlier? If the timing of movements was driven entirely by the level of grievance experienced, then we might have expected the movement to crest after the end of Reconstruction led to a resurgence of white supremacist policies in the South, or after the Plessy v. Ferguson decision legalized segregation in public accommodations, or after President Wilson segregated the civil service, or after any number of large-scale injustices. Arguably, it was Truman's desegregation of the army and the Brown v. Board of Education decision that signaled that the political system was open to large-scale change that was impossible before—in short, that the opportunity structure had shifted (McAdam 1998).

Examining the political opportunity structure provides insights into the dynamics and timing of social movements and can be extended to explain the timing of successful innovations. It highlights the inherently processual nature of social movements: their emergence and success depend crucially on their timing.

In the context of organizations, the opportunity structure for employee activism includes an organization's strategy, structure, culture, and executive changes that make a change more or less timely. For instance, when William Clay Ford Jr. took over as chairman of Ford Motor Company in 1999, his environmental commitments signaled that employee-led green initiatives would face a more welcoming climate—as, indeed, they did (Davis and White 2015). Broader social trends, including external social movements, can also signal opportunity for internal activism. The #MeToo movement set the stage for the Google walkout in November 2018, and protests against the treatment of immigrants gave momentum to efforts by employees at tech firms to cut ties to the Customs and Border Protection agency.

This suggests two observations. First, member-led movements can be seen as a mechanism for connecting the social and political environment of the organization to change in its internal operations (cf. Zald et al. 2005). Organizational boundaries are permeable; politics flows in both directions. Second, researchers can use external movements as a cue to potential upcoming changes. One of the great extant research questions is what distinguishes those movements that make the transition from external social movement to internal practice (e.g., #MeToo) from those that do not.

Why: Framing

Framing describes how potential changes or innovations are conveyed to constituencies in ways that fit (or not) with broader cultural themes. It is the language and stories that are more or less compelling at persuading potential allies and decision-makers that a change is right. Frames suggest a diagnosis of a problem, a preferred set of solutions, and a motivation to pursue them (Snow and Benford 1988).

In the context of organizations, activists are more likely to be effective to the extent that the words, metaphors, and forms of evidence they use to make their case are aligned with the organization's culture (Weber 2005). Scholars have created increasingly sophisticated methods of analyzing corporate cultures to uncover the core underlying assumptions that shape what a compelling case is (Weber et al. 2013). What makes for a persuasive framing in a high-tech business may be very different than in a traditional manufacturer, or a family-owned business. The researchable implication is that the more closely a frame for change aligns with an organization's culture, the more effective it is at recruiting followers and the more likely it is to be successful. That is, rather than seeking the universal ingredients for a successful "pitch," it makes more sense to examine the fit between the organization's context and the character of the proposed frame.

We note here that there is a parallel stream of work on issue selling in organizations (Dutton and Ashford 1993; Dutton et al. 2001), which is reviewed elsewhere in this handbook.

Who: Social Networks

Change takes place through interactions among people and organizations, and understanding the *social networks* that connect potential allies and decision-makers can greatly speed the process of change by making ideas and innovations contagious. While "network" was once a relatively fuzzy metaphor for the social connections among people, it has evolved into an increasingly sophisticated toolkit for the social sciences and for activists. And with the advent of online social platforms such as Facebook, mapping and activating networks is now a nearly indispensable part of conscious efforts at social change. Moreover, the tools of network analysis are increasingly accessible to non-specialists, who throw around terms like "geodesic" (the shortest network path between two nodes) and "eigenvector centrality" (being well connected to the well-connected). With an Excel add-in and metadata from an organization's email server, almost anyone can draw a network map.

Network analysis suggests the conditions for success at efforts for change. Chuck Tilly (2004) argued that protests are more influential to the extent that participants convey that they are WUNC—worthy, unified, numerous, and committed. Similarly, the more numerous the supporters of a change initiative are perceived to be by decision-makers, the more likely their chances of success. Network analysis can be used to target new recruits, to find the shortest pathways to decision-makers, and to focus resources on the best-connected targets for influence. An accurate network map can be an extremely valuable tool for purposeful social change efforts. But not all movements go viral. For instance, in January 2001, the UN's Secretary General Kofi Annan spoke to a large group of members of the US Chamber of Commerce, imploring them to devote their resources—or at least their name—to the global effort to combat the HIV/AIDS pandemic. Joining the Global Business Coalition (GBC) cost only $25,000 ("Less than a benefit table at the opera," as its CEO Richard Holbrooke quipped), and the show of unity would be powerful. But while joining the GBC spread through networks—a handful of well-connected corporate directors evidently persuaded a number of the firms on whose boards they served to join—within a few years it had topped out at only 5% of the Fortune 500 (Davis and Anderson 2008). Not all efforts at change will succeed, even if the network processes are understood.

Here again, there is a clear agenda for future research on grassroots change initiatives to track the patterns of diffusion through networks. One might, for instance, track the spread of support for employee petitions in tech firms aiming to cut off disfavored clients by examining social networks and the sequencing of endorsements. As change efforts are increasingly organized online, they leave behind traces that can greatly aid research.

How: Mobilizing Structures

The fourth dimension describes the technological, social, and physical systems that can be used to *mobilize action*. Any social system contains vehicles that serve to channel social interactions and can translate latent support for change into active support. The civil rights movement, for instance, relied heavily on the network of Black churches in the South, as Aldon Morris (1984) has documented. Churches provided safe space for meetings, membership for recruiting, access to resources such as financial and legal support, and dense ties to local colleges and ministers in other locations. Moreover, they created a vehicle for the spread of particular movement tactics, such as lunch counter sit-ins.

ICTs have greatly changed the prospects for mobilizing by creating low-cost and pervasive channels of communication. Activists these days largely rely on social media such as Facebook and Twitter, and online infrastructure such as Slack or Loomio, to coordinate their actions most efficiently. Jennifer Earl and Katrina Kimport (2011) were pioneers in theorizing the effects of new online tools and platforms for organizing collective action. Both the speed and the content of movement organizing look different now. A Facebook post the day after an election can catalyze a march that brings a half-million people to Washington. Gender inequities in pay can be uncovered via a shared Google doc. And even websites can go on strike, as happened in response to the "Stop Online Piracy Act" that was opposed by Google, Wikipedia, and other online destinations.

Within organizations, the new online tools mean that management no longer has a lock on information. Both public forums such as Glassdoor, and internal vehicles such as Slack channels, allow members to share what goes on within the hidden domain of the workplace. Once again, as new tools spread, the prospects for member-driven change expand.

In its simplest form, this framework suggests that movements are effective to the extent that the political opportunity structure is receptive, the proposed change is framed in ways that fit the opportunity and motivate participants, the right allies are mobilized and the right decision-makers reached, using the appropriate tools for mobilizing and coordinating participation. But the *how* of movement mobilization and contestation is still somewhat under-specified. To date, the majority of published studies have sought to explain variation in observable indicators, as is encouraged by our academic journals and their love of regression tables. But not all changes fit this mold, and sampling only cases that yield observable success or failure (say, adoption of a policy or not) is methodologically suspect. Here, we must note the critical role of embedded ethnographic accounts, such as Kate Kellogg's exemplary work (Kellogg 2011b) and dense engagement across an entire interdependent field, such as DeJordy et al. (2020).

What exactly are member-activists trying to change? Interviews with social innovators in companies suggest that social activists pursue four kinds of innovation in organizations (Davis and White 2015). The first is influencing the kinds of *products and services* the organization offers to create value that extends beyond profit. This is sometimes called "intrapreneurship" or "corporate entrepreneurship," although we distinguish socially oriented intrapreneurship from more generic efforts at innovation. An example here might be Vodafone's M-Pesa, a mobile-phone-based payments system that piloted in Kenya and spread from there.

The second is *practices*, that is, making the operations of the organization more sustainable. Innovations in this domain can include efforts at lowering the firm's carbon footprint, greening supplier operations, and ensuring human rights and equitable labor practices in the supply chain. Here, Ford Motor Company's commitment to freshwater access as a human right, championed by one of its middle managers, ensured that its overseas factories would operate in a sustainable way.

The third is *people management* that is, making the workplace more just and rewarding. Thanks to the efforts of a committed human resource manager, Michigan's Cascade Engineering created an award-winning program to recruit employees from public assistance programs and provide support services for full-time employment, including an onsite social worker. The program has itself gone viral across the local labor market to other companies in Western Michigan.

The fourth is *engagement with the community* beyond the walls of the organization. IBM's Corporate Service Corps, which provides pro bono services by multidisciplinary teams to governments and nonprofits in low-income countries, was championed by a relatively junior MBA and former Peace Corps volunteer, and has become widely emulated in corporate America.

This rough typology highlights that member-led efforts at innovation and change can be aimed at a wide variety of organizational domains.

Principles of Change: A Movement-Based How-To

One of the virtues of the social movement framework on member-led change is that it creates a set of relatively straightforward guidelines for change that take the form of big questions (When? Why? Who? How?) as well as some more granular ones. Below we list some suggested queries to help guide the actions of member activists. These questions are primarily intended for changemakers, but can also spark questions for researchers seeking to explain choices and outcomes.

When?

- What has changed in terms of organizational priorities in the past few months? How does your initiative fit with current priorities?

- What has changed in terms of organizational leadership, which may open new opportunities to find a senior champion for this initiative?
- Would conditions become more or less favorable by waiting three months? Six months?

Why?

- What is the dominant culture of this organization like? What beliefs and values drive member behavior?
- What are the ingredients of a persuasive argument in this organization?
- What is a high-level pitch ("master frame") that speaks to this culture? How might this master frame be adapted to the interests and priorities of each of the key people in the decision-making system?

Who?

- Who are the most critical decision-makers for this initiative? What do they most care about? Who do they turn to for advice?
- When you think about the whole system that this initiative affects, who are the influencers? Who is especially well connected? Whom do others seek out for advice? Who is especially persuasive?

How?

- What are the existing mobilizing structures for getting this kind of initiative started, and supporting its ongoing viability? (Diversity councils, brown bags, corporate intranet, etc.)
- Where could you consider launching a pilot?
- What analogous initiatives have gone before and succeeded that you could use as favorable points of comparison? What unsuccessful initiatives should you differentiate from?
- How can you use technology to mobilize and organize people, especially in disparate geographies?

Strengths and Criticisms

Issues of social justice are increasingly central to organizations, from Walmart to Nike to Google. And although organizational leaders might prefer to avoid becoming entangled in politically contentious issues, for many of them this is no longer an option. In August 2013, Starbucks was the "beneficiary" of an unwanted nationwide demonstration by gun-toting fans of its laissez-faire policy on open carry in its stores, as well as counter-protests by opponents. Store managers found themselves to be unwilling front-line participants in the national debate on gun control, happening right in their stores. A few months later, Mozilla faced a storm of criticism inside and outside the organization, including employee walkouts, after appointing a new CEO who had previously supported a ban on same-sex marriage in California. And after Delta Airlines cut its NRA member discount program following the Parkland school shooting and a threatened boycott, the legislature in its home state of Georgia shelved a proposed tax break for the firm unless it reinstated the benefit. (Delta refused.)

Politics is no longer optional for many organizations. Employees, customers, and partners now scrutinize firms and their leaders for their political stances, and in a world where alternative products and services are just a click away, it is incumbent on firms to make informed choices. In this context, social movement theory offers an appealing toolkit for understanding and creating organizational change.

In the current synthesis, movement researchers are highly attuned to processes and mechanisms rather than simple mechanical rules for bringing about change. For movements (and change efforts) to succeed requires a series of phases of activity: choosing the right timing based on the opportunity structure, framing the case for change in a way that fits with the culture and setting, locating decision-makers and allies to create a network for change, and mobilizing via the appropriate platforms for action. Moreover, new tools for both research and activism create opportunities for fine-grained analysis, from mapping the social networks that support (or fail to support) change to computerized content analyses of corporate documents to diagnose the culture. And as movements are increasingly organized online, they leave behind archival data that should enable much more granular analyses of change efforts and what distinguishes those that succeed from those that do not.

To date, however, most research on movements and organizations has focused on external efforts at change rather than grassroots internal change initiatives. This is partly due to data availability: protests, boycotts, and shareholder proposals leave behind data that lend themselves to quantitative and comparative analysis. Internal change efforts are by definition less visible, and rarely leave systematic evidence available to the outside world. (Exceptions would include labor strikes and changes in policy, such as the adoption of domestic partner benefits—see Briscoe and Safford 2008). Moreover, while successful change efforts may become visible to the outside world, unsuccessful ones are likely to disappear from view. Thus, there is likely to be a built-in bias toward studying success and neglecting failure.

On the other hand, the fact that movements are increasingly mobilized via online platforms opens up the possibility of new and larger-scale comparative studies of change. Facebook and Twitter hosted much of the discourse around the Arab Spring, and Facebook played an infamous role in the 2016 US election. These data are, presumably, housed on servers somewhere. Similarly, the local chapters of the Indivisible movement that began in November 2016 overwhelmingly organized their activities on Loomio, a platform for dialogue, decision-making, and task allocation created by a worker-owned cooperative in New Zealand. For an intrepid doctoral student, this could be the raw material for an outstanding dissertation comparing the trajectories of more and less successful local chapters. And of course, Google hosts email servers for tens of thousands of organizations, many of them undergoing change efforts.

In short, we may be on the verge of an intriguing new era in research on organizational change, both in the "what" (member-led initiatives oriented toward social change) and the "how" (comparative large-sample studies using big data). In our estimation, social movement theory will be a critical component.

References

Bartley, T. (2007), 'Institutional Emergence in an Era of Globalization: The Rise of Transnational Private Regulation of Labor and Environmental Conditions', *American Journal of Sociology*, 113/2, 297–351.

Bartley, T., and Child, C. (2014), 'Shaming the Corporation: The Social Production of Targets and the Anti-Sweatshop Movement', *American Sociological Review*, 79/4, 653–79.

Briscoe, F., Chin, M., and Hambrick, D. C. (2014), 'CEO Ideology as an Element of the Corporate Opportunity Structure for Social Activists', *Academy of Management Journal*, 57/6, 1786–809.

Briscoe, F., Gupta, A., and Anner, M. S. (2015), 'Social Activism and Practice Diffusion: How Activist Tactics Affect Non-Targeted Organizations', *Administrative Science Quarterly*, 60/2, 300–32.

Briscoe, F., and Safford, S. (2008), 'The Nixon-in-China Effect: Activism, Imitation, and the Institutionalization of Contentious Practices', *Administrative Science Quarterly*, 53/3, 460–91.

Carson, R. (1962) *Silent Spring*. (New York: Houghton Mifflin.)

Davis, G. F. (2016) *The Vanishing American Corporation: Navigating the Hazards of a New Economy*. (Oakland: Berrett-Koehler.)

Davis, G. F., and Anderson, P. J. (2008), 'Social Movements and Failed Institutionalization: Corporate (Non) Response to the AIDS Epidemic', in R. Greenwood, C. Oliver, R. Suddaby, and K. Sahlin-Andersson (eds.), *The Sage Handbook of Organizational Institutionalism* (Thousand Oaks, CA: Sage), 371–88.

Davis, G. F., and McAdam, D. (2000), 'Corporations, Classes, and Social Movements after Managerialism', *Research in Organizational Behavior*, 22: 193–236.

Davis, G. F., McAdam, D., Scott, W. R., and Zald, M. N. (2005), *Social Movements and Organization Theory* (Cambridge: Cambridge University Press).

Davis, G. F., Morrill, C., Rao, H., and Soule, S. A. (2008), 'Introduction: Social Movements in Organizations and Markets', *Administrative Science Quarterly*, 53/3, 389–94.

Davis, G. F., and White, C. J. (2015), *Changing Your Company from the Inside Out: A Guide for Social Intrapreneurs* (Boston: Harvard Business Review Press).

DeJordy, R., Scully, M., Ventresca, M. J., and Creed, W. E. D. (2020), 'Inhabited Ecosystems: Propelling Transformative Social Change between and through Organizations', *Administrative Science Quarterly*, 65/4, 931–71.

Dorobantu, S., Henisz, W. J., and Nartey, L. (2017), 'Not All Sparks Light a Fire: Stakeholder and Shareholder Reactions to Critical Events in Contested Markets', *Administrative Science Quarterly*, 62/3, 561–97.

Dutton, J. E., and Ashford, S. J. (1993), 'Selling Issues to Top Management', *Academy of Management Review*, 18/3, 397–428.

Dutton, J. E., Ashford, S. J., O'Neill, R. M., and Lawrence, K. A. (2001), 'Moves that Matter: Issue Selling and Organizational Change', *Academy of Management Journal*, 44/4, 716–36.

Earl, J., and Kimport, K. (2011) *Digitally Enabled Social Change: Activism in the Internet Age* (Cambridge, MA: MIT Press).

Greve, H. R., Pozner, J.-E., and Rao, H. (2006), 'Vox Populi: Resource Partitioning, Organizational Proliferation, and the Cultural Impact of the Insurgent Microradio Movement', *American Journal of Sociology*, 112/3, 802–37.

Hiatt, S. R., Grandy, J. B., and Lee, B. H. (2015), 'Organizational Responses to Public and Private Politics: An Analysis of Climate Change Activists and US Oil and Gas Firms', *Organization Science*, 26/6, 1769–86.

Hiatt, S. R., Sine, W. D., and Tolbert, P. S. (2009), 'From Pabst to Pepsi: The Deinstitutionalization of Social Practices and the Creation of Entrepreneurial Opportunities', *Administrative Science Quarterly*, 54/4, 635–67.

Ingram, P., Yue, L. Q., and Rao, H. (2010), 'Trouble in Store: Probes, Protests, and Store Openings by Wal-Mart, 1998–2007', *American Journal of Sociology*, 116/1, 53–92.

Kellogg, K. C. (2009), 'Operating Room: Relational Spaces and Microinstitutional Change in Surgery', *American Journal of Sociology*, 115/3, 657–711.

Kellogg, K. C. (2011a), 'Hot Lights and Cold Steel: Cultural and Political Toolkits for Practice Change in Surgery', *Organization Science*, 22/2, 482–502.

Kellogg, K. C. (2011b), *Challenging Operations: Medical Reform and Resistance in Surgery* (Chicago: University of Chicago Press).

Kellogg, K. C. (2012), 'Making the Cut: Using Status-Based Countertactics to Block Social Movement Implementation and Microinstitutional Change in Surgery', *Organization Science*, 23/6, 1546–70.

Kim, T.-Y., Shin, D., Oh, H., and Jeong, Y.-C. (2007), 'Inside the Iron Cage: Organizational Political Dynamics and Institutional Changes in Presidential Selection Systems in Korean Universities, 1985-2002', *Administrative Science Quarterly*, 52/2, 286–323.

King, B. G. (2008), 'A Political Mediation Model of Corporate Response to Social Movement Activism', *Administrative Science Quarterly*, 53/3, 395–421.

King, B. G., and Soule, S. A. (2007), 'Social Movements as Extra-Institutional Entrepreneurs: The Effect of Protests on Stock Price Returns', *Administrative Science Quarterly*, 52/3, 413–42.

McAdam, D. (1982), *Political Process and the Development of Black Insurgency, 1930–1970* (Chicago: University of Chicago Press).

McAdam, D. (1998), 'On the International Origins of Domestic Political Opportunities in A. N. Costan and A. S. McFarland, eds., *Social Movements and American Political Institutions* (Lanham: Rowman & Littlefield), 251–67.

McAdam, D., Tarrow, S., and Tilly, C. (2001), *Dynamics of Contention* (New York: Cambridge University Press).

McCarthy, J. D., and Zald, M. N. (1977), 'Resource Mobilization and Social Movements: A Partial Theory', *American Journal of Sociology*, 82/6, 1212–41.

McDonnell, M.-H. (2015), 'Radical Repertoires: The Incidence and Impact of Corporate-Sponsored Social Activism', *Organization Science*, 27/1, 53–71.

McDonnell, M.-H., and King, B. (2013), 'Keeping up Appearances: Reputational Threat and Impression Management after Social Movement Boycotts', *Administrative Science Quarterly*, 58/3, 387–419.

McDonnell, M.-H., King, B. G., and Soule, S. A. (2015), 'A Dynamic Process Model of Private Politics: Activist Targeting and Corporate Receptivity to Social Challenges', *American Sociological Review*, 80/3, 54–678.

McDonnell, M.-H., and Werner, T. (2016), 'Blacklisted Businesses: Social Activists' Challenges and the Disruption of Corporate Political Activity', *Administrative Science Quarterly*, 61/4, 584–620.

Morris, A. D. (1984), *The Origins of the Civil Rights Movement: Black Communities Organizing for Change* (New York: Free Press).

O'Mahony, S., and Bechky, B. A. (2008), 'Boundary Organizations: Enabling Collaboration among Unexpected Allies', *Administrative Science Quarterly*, 53/3, 422–59.

Rao, H., Morrill, C., and Zald, M. N. (2000), 'Power Plays: How Social Movements and Collective Action Create New Organizational Forms', *Research in Organizational Behavior*, 22: 237–81.

Schon, Donald. (1971), *Beyond the Stable State* (New York: Random House).

Schneiberg, M., King, M., and Smith, T. (2008), 'Social Movements and Organizational Form: Cooperative Alternatives to Corporations in the American Insurance, Dairy, and Grain Industries', *American Sociological Review*, 73/4, 635–67.

Schurman, R., and Munro, W. (2009), 'Targeting Capital: A Cultural Economy Approach to Understanding the Efficacy of Two Anti–Genetic Engineering Movements', *American Journal of Sociology*, 115/1, 155–202.

Scott, R. W., and Davis, G. F. (2007), *Organizations and Organizing: Rational, Natural, and Open System Perspectives* (Upper Saddle River, NJ: Pearson Prentice Hall).

Sine, W. D., and Lee, B. H. (2009), 'Tilting at Windmills? The Environmental Movement and the Emergence of the US Wind Energy Sector', *Administrative Science Quarterly*, 54/1, 123–55.

Snow, D. A., and Benford, R. D. (1988), 'Ideology, Frame Resonance, and Participant Mobilization', in B. Klandermans, H. Kriesi, and S. Tarrow, eds., *From Structure to Action: Social Movement Participation Across Cultures* (Greenwich, CT: JAI Press), 197–217

Tilly, C. (1978), *From Mobilization to Revolution* (Reading, MA: Addison-Wesley).

Tilly, C. (2004), *Social Movements, 1768–2004* (Boulder, CO: Paradigm Publishers).

Vasi, I. B., and King, B. G. (2012), 'Social Movements, Risk Perceptions, and Economic Outcomes: The Effect of Primary and Secondary Stakeholder Activism on Firms' Perceived Environmental Risk and Financial Performance', *American Sociological Review*, 77/4, 573–96.

Vasi, I. B., Walker, E. T., Johnson, J. S., and Tan, H. F. (2015), '"No Fracking Way!" Documentary Film, Discursive Opportunity, and Local Opposition against Hydraulic Fracturing in the United States, 2010 to 2013', *American Sociological Review*, 80/5, 934–59.

Weber, K. (2005), 'A Toolkit for Analyzing Corporate Cultural Toolkits', *Poetics*, 33/3–4, 227–52.

Weber, K., Heinze, K. L., and DeSoucey, M. (2008), 'Forage for Thought: Mobilizing Codes in the Movement for Grass-Fed Meat and Dairy Products', *Administrative Science Quarterly*, 53/3, 529–67.

Weber, K., Patel, H., and Heinze, K. L. (2013), 'From Cultural Repertoires to Institutional Logics: A Content-Analytic Method', in M. Loundsbury and E. Boxenbaum, eds., *Institutional Logics in Action, Part B* (Vol. 39) (Bingley: Emerald Group Publishing Limited), 51–82.

Weber, K., Rao, H., and Thomas, L. (2009), 'From Streets to Suites: How the Anti-Biotech Movement Affected German Pharmaceutical Firms', *American Sociological Review*, 74/1, 106–27.

Zald, M. N. (2005), 'The Strange Career of an Idea and its Resurrection: Social Movements in Organizations', *Journal of Management Inquiry*, 14/2, 157–66.

Zald, M. N., and Berger, M. A. (1978), 'Social Movements in Organizations: Coup d'etat, Insurgency, and Mass Movements', *American Journal of Sociology*, 83/4, 823–61.

Zald, M. N., Morrill, C., and Rao, H. (2005), 'The Impact of Social Movements on Organizations', in G. F. Davis et al, eds., *Social Movements and Organization Theory*, 253–79. (Cambridge: Cambridge University Press.)

Zhang, J., and Luo, X. R. (2013), 'Dared to Care: Organizational Vulnerability, Institutional Logics, and MNCs' Social Responsiveness in Emerging Markets, *Organization Science*, 24/6, 1742–64.

CHAPTER 10

BECOMING AN AGENT OF CHANGE

CRAIG PRICHARD AND W. E. DOUGLAS CREED

INTRODUCTION

THE claim that social movements are the seedbeds of widescale organizational change in Western economies has become a well-traversed ground for recent management and organization scholarship (Davis et al. 2005; Davis and Kim, this volume; King and Soule 2007). In this vein, Rao and Dutta's recent paper (2018), which regards insurgent social movements as central to the development and management of successful corporate organizational strategy, is a welcome contribution. Using case material drawn from the development of Apple Computers, these authors show that the success of Apple founders, Steve Jobs and Steve Wozniak, was not necessarily a function of their brilliance as entrepreneurs and engineers, but rather their *embodiment of an insurgent social movement identity* emergent in the personal computing movement of the time. This movement sought to enhance the personal autonomy of end-users by democratizing access to computers controlled by a corporate "priesthood" of experts.

Consequently, Rao and Dutta argue, firms such as Apple owe their strategic success not to conventional managerialist prescriptions but to the fact that firms and their leaders *become activists in social movements*. Such movements turn market imperfections, for example, consumer "pains" over corporate computers in this case, into a sense of injustice or grievance that mobilizes people *not as consumers* but as loyal and devoted participants in social movements that challenge incumbent organizations, governments, and institutions. In contributing to this handbook, we pick up Rao and Dutta's discussion of activist identities as central to the process of strategic organizational change. However, drawing on relevant literatures, our focus is on the *process by which individuals and groups become change agents*.

For Rao and Dutta, successful organization change is not a function of planning, organizing, and communicating change to a rank and file, nor does it involve organizations playing for position in a market. Rather successful strategic change is played out in an "identity field" by activist change agents who seek to express, as Rao and Dutta argue, "subjugated identities." For Rao and Dutta, strategic organizational change is about change agents creating feelings of unity and worth through interaction among movement participants. Such feelings are, they say, communicated through cultural materials such as names, narratives, symbols, and rituals (2018: 316). But, if that's the case, then why and how do either people as actors –Jobs, Wozniak, or anyone, for that matter—or the groups and organizations that they build, take up these insurgent identities? This question exposes a broad gap in the organizational change literatures (Lok et al. 2020) that Rao and Dutta don't explore directly. But we can extract hints as to their possible answer from their text.

First, Rao and Dutta regard Jobs and Wozniak's embodiment of the personal computer movement's insurgent identity as a function of their efforts to "have some fun" as members of a counter-culture community. This "fun" involved uncovering and sharing exclusive or hidden knowledge in ways that challenged corporate control. In particular, it was their pursuit of "fun," which foreshadowed what became the broader hacker movements, that led Jobs and Wozniak to discover the tone system that organized the global telephone system of the time. Once they understood it, they then built a small machine that allowed them to hack that system and to make calls around the world for free. As Jobs later explained:

> We were at Stanford Linear Accelerator Centre one night and way in the bowels of their technical library way down at the last bookshelf in the corner bottom rack we found an AT&T technical journal that laid out the whole thing and that's another moment I'll never forget—we saw this journal, we thought, my God it's all real, and so we set out to build a device to make these tones. What we learned was that we could build something ourselves that could control billions of dollars worth of infrastructure in the world—that was what we learnt was that us two you know, we're not much, we could build a little thing that could control a giant thing and that was an incredible lesson. I don't think there would ever have been an Apple computer had there not been blue boxes. (Rao and Dutta 2017: 314)

While it might seem a rather strange question to ask, precisely what is it that produces this fun, this affective pleasure? Is it the recognition that Jobs and Wozniak garnered from other members of Home Brew Computer Club? Probably, yes, in part. But their account suggests that it may have been the epiphany itself. Their pleasure erupts when they find themselves, two young men who were "not much" in the world, able to "build a little thing" that controls a "giant thing." That revelation was *transformative*, seemingly producing a kind of conversion experience. Steve Jobs called it an "incredible lesson" without which there would not have been an Apple Computers. In other words, the epiphany was a pivotal moment in the process of Jobs' and Wozniak's becoming agents.

It propelled them personally, and later the movement they came to embody, to go further in challenging dominant interests in the computer industry at the time.

But what is at the core of this transformative moment? Rao and Dutta suggest that it involved a process of their claiming, and embodying through action, identities as protagonists; this process necessarily involves imputing *an antagonistic identity to another or others*, in this case, the telephone company owners and technicians. Steve Jobs himself, Rao and Dutta argue, understood this deeply.

> Even as he focused on the identity of the Apple product, he was always sensitive to the identity of the consumer and constantly sought to contrast Apple vis-à-vis an [corporate] opponent.

In what follows we explore how that combined process of claiming the identity of the protagonist and projecting the identity of antagonist onto another actor or subject, involves the co-mingling of two distinctive pre-conditions. On the one hand the process of claiming and projecting involves would-be change agents' ability to draw on their lived experiences of primal and necessarily conflictual relations with significant others (e.g., mothers and fathers). It is from these lived experiences that people develop the capacity for embracing and deploying oppositional identities. Drawing on these primal relationships is a purposeful if not fully conscious act. On the other hand, would-be change agents must also be able to draw on social movement resources and shared cultural narratives. We argue that to understand the first of these preconditions, we need to draw on psychoanalytic perspectives, while to understand the other we need to draw on sociological perspectives.

For example, biographies and movie accounts of Jobs' life (e.g. Isaacson 2011) suggest that Jobs' embrace of the identity of insurgent protagonist found in the Home Computing Movement and central to the Apple's insurgent organizational strategy as it battled IBM in the early years, alongside Jobs' insistent control over Apple's products, and his relentless focus on details, are all in part a consequence of his struggles with being an adopted child. Indeed, Jobs' official biographer, Walter Issacson, suggests that Jobs' controlling nature and episodic cruelty toward others was directly linked to his feelings about "being abandoned at birth." Based on interviews with key characters in Jobs' life, Issacson argues that: "The real underlying problem was the theme of abandonment in Steve's life' (Issacson 2011: 5). Of course, we are not arguing that successful organizational change agents must have problematic childhoods or relations with their parents. What we will argue is that insurgent organizational change agents, such as Jobs, derive their capacity to claim the identity of protagonist and project the identity of antagonist at least in part from a mix of *unconscious drives, traumatic experiences, and redemptive self-narratives* that many of us can draw upon but which is more pronounced and evident in some individuals.

To support our presentation, we draw on public sources that surround the emergence of two extraordinary organizational change agents' insurgent identities. Our first case focuses on the formative experience of the expatriate Jamaican, and prominent UK public intellectual, Stuart Hall. Our second case is that of anti-racism activist Christian Piccolini (2015; 2017) who, in his teenage and early adult years, led a white supremacist group in Chicago. Like the story of Jobs and Wozniak, the stories of both Hall and Picciolini brings to light the complex but identifiable process by which insurgent identities form as a consequence of encounters with what Piccolini terms *traumatic "potholes"*. From a psychoanalytic perspective, such traumatic "potholes" are interruptions or crises in relations between people (particularly the young) and their significant others (e.g. partners, parents, and care givers). Such "potholes" operate as obstructions or impediments to the formation of the maturing human being, waylaying the young person's emerging sense of self and redirecting in unwelcome ways the person's inchoate sense of purpose and aspirations. In Picciolini's case, a social movement, white supremacism, came to channel the expression of his underlying needs and unanswered desires by providing resources, for example collective practices, experiences, and social- and self-narratives, that organized his world and shaped his enactment of selfhood. As the home computing movement appears to have done for Jobs and Wozniak, the white supremacist movement provided the experiences, resources, and practices that enabled Picciolini to challenge and, in many instances, reject the conventions, rules, desires, values, and cultural treasures of significant others, such as his parents and grandparents. Doing so produces an exhilarating embodied sense of pleasure, purpose, and meaning, effectively achieving what psychologist William James describes as the core features of a conversion experience, the experience of new connectedness and the sense that one's life has a new centre and orientating principle.

Thus, we argue, that to greater or lesser degrees, insurgent change agents' identities are underpinned by the formative traumatic experiences and the related antagonistic relations with significant others; the change agents come to elaborate their insurgent identities through learning and deploying social movement framings and narratives that position them to claim the identity of protagonist and project on others the identity of antagonist.

We conclude our chapter by briefly discussing the implications of our argument for widescale organization changes. But before we can address this question and before we unravel the proposed pattern of insurgent identity formation, we need to firstly contextualize this work.

Contextualizing Social Movement Identities

When we began writing this chapter, the world was engulfed in protests against established institutions. Mass movements were seeking political freedom and fighting inequality and corruption in Bolivia, Chile, Ecuador, Gaza, Hong Kong, Iran, Lebanon, and elsewhere. Simultaneously, millions of people around the world, particularly youth, are marching in protest of the slow response by established institutions and politicians to the climate emergency. As we have concluded work on the chapter, protests at the brutal police killing of an unarmed black man in Minneapolis has flared up across the US. This has followed protests against the Covid-19 lockdown where conservative groups have protested stay-at-home orders. In one incident, Michigan State's legislature was closed as dozens of demonstrators, some heavily armed, gathered on the steps of the statehouse building to protest the stay-at-home order (Mena 2020).

Mass protest, civil disobedience, and resistance to perceived authoritative and oppressive conditions, figures, and institutions are ubiquitous and seemingly universal attributes of human organizing (Canetti 1962; Melucci 1989). The question of why, how, and in what form we become agents of such resistances, bent on challenging existing relations and conditions, is of course an enduring question for organization studies (McLaughlin 1969; Gusfield 1970; Davis et al. 2005).

Historically such work has tended to regard social, economic, and political conditions, and the perceived opportunities they afford for various repertoires of protest and resistance, as the seedbed of resistance (Gamson and Meyer 1999; Tilly 1986). More recent scholarship, meanwhile, has focused on how collectivities and movements *themselves* are agents of intentionality and change (Abdelnour et al. 2017). A key strand of this latter work asks how individuals and groups come to embrace and shape the activist identities that animate their participation in social movements (Meyer and Jepperson 2000, Seo and Creed 2002, Elidrissi and Courpasson 2019, Wright et al. 2012; Skoglund and Bohm 2019). Central to this work is the question of how individuals and groups *reflexively narrate activist identities and internalize social movement narratives* as their own (Polletta 1998; Creed et al. 2014; Lok et al. 2019). Before we turn to Christian Picciolini's self-penned account of his passage into (and out of) the white supremacist movement in the 1980s and 1990s to illustrate our discussion, we briefly draw out the concepts and frameworks from the organization change literature via our discussion of Stuart Hall's reflections on his own process of becoming a a change agent.

Psychoanalytic and Narrative Processes

Prominent UK sociologist, public intellectual, and political activist Stuart Hall (1932–2014) once wrote that "identity is formed at the *unstable point* where the 'unspeakable' stories of subjectivity meet the narratives of history" (Hall 1987: 44, *our emphasis*). Usefully, Hall, writes candidly of the "unspeakable stories" and narratives of history that formed his own identity. A Jamaican native who went to Oxford University on a Rhodes Scholarship in 1951, Hall wrote that he had migrated to escape his family and particularly his mother.

> The truth is, I'm [in Britain] because it's where my family is not. I really came here to get away from my mother. Isn't that the universal story of life? One is where one is to try and get away from somewhere else. That was the story which *I could never*

> *tell anybody about myself.* So, I had to find other stories, other fictions, which were more authentic or, at any rate, more acceptable, in place of the Big Story of the endless evasion of patriarchal family life. (ibid.: our emphasis)

Unlike Stuart Hall, most people are neither as honest nor as reflective of the underlying structure of their motivations. But the core process is clear. Identities form out of a breach in relations to significant others, producing a protagonist–antagonist structure. However, the origin of the original split is hidden in "more acceptable" historical narratives of, for example in this instance, enlightenment through education, and emancipation through metropolitan life.

Hall's notion of "unspeakable stories" draws from Freudian psychoanalytic tradition, where our unspeakable stories originate in the unremembered biographical history of our relations to significant others which are organized into a structure of largely unconscious demands, desires, and defenses. There is an extensive literature on psychodynamics of organizational change founded on the core Freudian assumption that the observable surface features of organizational life obscure a powerful set of unconscious forces (see, for example, original works by Levinson 1972; Zaleznik 1963; Gabriel, 1999). These forces, on the one hand, defend organizations, individuals, and groups against the threat of change. But on the other hand, they can also stimulate and mobilize organizational recruitment and change agency. The key psychoanalytic concept with respect to the latter is the notion of transference. As Gabriel and Carr (2003) explain, transference is the key process whereby an individual's feelings of admiration or love, which were at one point attached to parental figures, along with images of omnipotence, mystery and beauty, are transferred onto organizations and/or their leaders. Of course such instances of transference are inevitably unstable and illusionary. This means that change agents and innovative organizations struggle to live up to such billing. But once endowed with such idealized capabilities and gifts, such agents and organizations can have the effect of enhancing their followers' own ideal selves, which then leads to their having greater sense of worth, commitment, and capacity for self-sacrifice. But while idealization and transference explains the potential formation of would-be change agents' identities, commitments, and animating concerns (Creed, Hudson, Okhuysen, and Smith-Crowe, forthcoming), such potential requires some linkage to historic narratives, and particularly to their constituent redemptive narrative sequences—to which we now turn.

As readers will no doubt appreciate, Stuart Hall's forebears were brought from Africa to the West Indies by the English as enslaved people to work in sugar plantations after Jamaica was captured from the Spanish in the seventeenth century. Jamaica was a British colony until independence in 1962, a decade after Hall's emigration. In the 1950 and 1960s more than half a million Afro-Caribbean people immigrated to Britain, the so-call Windrush Generation, and found work in British factories desperate for labor following World War II. Consequently, a key historical narrative available to Hall, built upon British colonial relations of racial dominance, is that of upward mobility via elite British education.

> If you live, as I've lived, in Jamaica, in a lower-middle class family that was trying to be a middle-class Jamaican family trying to be an upper-middle class Jamaican family trying to be an English Victorian family…I mean the notion of displacement as a place of 'identity' is a concept you learn to live with, long before you are able to spell it.

At Oxford in the 1950s, Hall received a traditional education in the English literary canon of the times. However, and not surprisingly given his "unspeakable stories," he rebelled against this and, along with others, established the critical academic study of popular culture, for example, film, television, and rock music, that drew from the work of Marx, Freud, Gramsci, Foucault, and other French critical theorists. In later years he became famous as a left-wing public intellectual who railed against race, class, and gender inequalities, and particularly against the right-wing government of Margaret Thatcher.

What lessons can we draw from the Hall example? The drive of "unspeakable stories" of subjectivity, particularly the animating desire to escape authority figures (his mother and the patriarchal pressures of this family), necessarily has the effect of organizing Hall's trajectory from traditional Oxford English major to political activist engaged in social movements fighting racism and right-wing governments. In effect, Hall's identity as a change agent takes shape at the intersection of his "unspeakable stories" of patriarchal domination and the then available social movement narratives of resistance to colonial oppression (Cunha and Orlikowki 2008). These anti-colonialist narratives confirm his identity as protagonist in an emancipatory or redemptive struggle against an antagonist other. However, to understand Hall's process of becoming the change agent, we need to explain not simply the character of his personal "unspeakable stories" but also the structure of the available social movement narratives.

For this we turn to the work of social psychologist Dan McAdams (2006a, 2006b; McAdams and Bowman 2001) that draws on empirical analysis of the life stories of highly generative US citizens. This work shows that across the many domains of human experience, highly generative people account for the *emergence of their concern for others and action on behalf of future generations* through the use of *redemptive self-narratives*. Abstracting from the actual content and context, McAdam's identifies six particular redemptive self-narratives that his informants use to explain their experiences. These particular redemptive narratives pertain to atonement, emancipation, upward mobility, recovery, enlightenment, or development. Each of the six narratives bespeaks a movement or a "redemptive sequence," for example, from alienation to atonement, from ignorance to enlightenment, from rags to riches, or from addiction or disease to recovery and health.

Developing on this and drawing particularly on the work of William James from his *Varieties of Religious Experience* (2004), Creed et al. (2014) show in their analysis of the life stories of particular change agents how these redemptive narratives sequences not only shape protagonists' identities, but more importantly animate their capacity for organizational and social change. With our two key conceptual framings in place, we now further illustrate our discussion of the formation of a change agent with an analysis of the autobiography of former white supremacist leader, Christian Picciolini.

Piccolini Case (Identity Narrative and Desire)

In a little over 300 pages, Christian Picciolini's *White American Youth* (2017) offers an insightful, reflective biographical account of the author's recruitment into and eventual leadership of the US skinhead and white supremacist movement of the 1980s and 1990s. Picciolini attributes his entry into white supremacist activism to his search for identity and community following years of seeming parental neglect and after being bullied and ostracized in the school and community in which he lived:

> I believe, that many paths to radicalization emerge from an individual's fundamental search for identity and community, and a sense of individual purpose going wrong—and those paths are primed by a host of factors, including an individual's background, inclination toward violence and sometimes their mental health. (Picciolini 2017: xxiii)

As for his own background, on the face of it, Picciolini came from a loving, extended family that included nurturing grandparents. And yet, the early part of the book details how he resented his parents' absence due to their work commitments and particularly their decision to move from the Italian-American suburb of Blue Island, where he was born, to Oak Ridge, an English-speaking, upper-middle-class suburb with a better public school system. There, he was identified as different and bullied. He tells harrowing stories of his childhood years spent in a seemingly depressive state—alone, isolated, neglected by his parents and without friends. Much of the anger for this is directed, later in the book, at his father. He notes:

> I was relentless in my perseverance to piss off my Dad. For whatever reason I resented him for not being there when I was a kid more than my mother and it seemed like I never stopped acting out against him. (ibid: 130)

A key turning point came for the young Picciolini when he was forced, reluctantly, to fight the Oak Ridge school bully. To his surprise, he won, and within days he had become the most talked about and feared kid in the school. This had a dramatic impact on the young Picciolini as it signaled that violence was a means of securing recognition and approval. His description of his fists as the body part that signaled this transformation is instructive.

> During my first period math class, I flexed my fists, silently studying them, trying to take in the reality that these two bruised, balled up hands had become my ticket to respect and power. I took this lesson to heart, absorbed it in every fiber of every muscle in my body. It was to end up serving me in the years to come as I would help build one of America's most violent homegrown terror organizations. (ibid:12)

The family eventually moved back to the predominantly Italian-American suburb where his grandparents lived and the early teenage Picciolini joined the neighborhood boys' gang. However, not long after this, he encountered Clark Martell, a notorious and charismatic white supremacist in his late 20s, and from there he become increasingly engaged in skinhead punk and white supremacist music, literature, and groups. To the young Picciolini, Martell resembled a parental figure.

> So was I initially drawn to Martell's racist agenda? Not really. But he was magnetic. Charming. I wanted to be like him.... Why? Because Martell was the first adult—even though he was only twenty-six years old when I met him—who had ever disciplined me and provided me with a valid explanation for doing so. (2017: 48)

He recounts one particular night, when at 14, he was present at the formation of the Chicago chapter of the white supremacist Hammer Skins.

> That night was the most alien and intense thing that I've ever experienced. I was instantly hooked. I may not have come from a family that was down on its luck, and I hadn't been brought up to hate people different from me, *but something about what I was learning made it seem like a truth that had for years been hidden from me* and more than ever I wanted to be part of it.
>
> It was thrilling.
>
> Grown up.
>
> Real.
>
> And it was black and white, no middle ground. I couldn't sit on my hands any longer. I'd made my decision, and it was on this side of the fence where I landed with both feet.... I could keep Blue Island white, Italian. (ibid:72, italics added)

Many aspects of this passage make clear that it was an epiphany. The alien and intense experience revealed a hidden truth in unambiguous terms. He felt a sudden "grown-up" certainty about what he should do. This was a transformational experience in his becoming a white power activist.

Following this, the author was involved in street battles and vicious violence against Black, Mexican, and Irish teenagers. He distributed literature, organized events, recruited members and increasingly took on a recognized leadership role in the local chapter.

Music was central to the young Picciolini's engagement with the White Power movement as it provided a focal point for gatherings, as well as communicated the movement's central tropes and orienting narratives. Key to this was the music of Skrewdriver, the notorious UK National Front band.

> Skrewdriver wrote anthems with the relatable directives built in, unlike the whiny punk protest songs I'd become used to. The lyrics gave us truthful education our lying school teachers refused to deliver, for fear we'd see through their manipulated account of history. "*White Power.*" "*Blood and Honour.*""*Tomorrow Belongs to Me.*" "*Free my Land.*" Songs that filled me with pride and purpose instead of childish, nihilistic impulses like punk rock music did.
>
> Armed with my new cassette and a Walkman, I'd listen to Skrewdriver over and over and over until I heard the words in my head even when the batteries had run down. (ibid: 54)

Although Picciolini was expelled for violence from five schools during this period, he did develop a talent for recruiting the disenfranchised youth of his and surrounding neighborhoods.

> It took little skill to spot a teenager with a shitty home life. Somebody without many friends, looking confused or lonely, angry or broke. We would strike up a conversation, find out what they were feeling bad about, and move in with the pitch. 'Man, I know exactly how that is. If your dad hadn't lost his job then it wouldn't be like that. But the minorities get all the jobs, catch all of the breaks. They move into our neighborhoods and start getting handouts funded by us. Our parents work hard every day to put food on the table while the lazy blacks and Mexicans are cashing welfare cheques in their sleep.'
>
> Before I knew it, there were half a dozen newly shaved heads coming to our weekly meetings, *looking for something to belong to.* To be somebody. We gave their lonely, shitty lives purpose. They were just like me two years earlier...
>
> Soon there were dozens of kids falling all over themselves to help with recruitment tasks. (ibid: 109, italics added)

However, in his late teens Picciolini began to retreat from the movement. His passage out can be traced through his falling in love with a woman who abhorred violence and was not involved in the movement. She became his wife and they had two children together. This in turn led to a further retreat as the young dad was forced to work long hours in road construction and then in the record shop he started to support the young family. The record shop was significant in other ways. Its punk rock offerings attracted a wide range of customers, bringing him into direct contact with anti-racist, black skinheads who became his customers and friends. He initially started the shop to support his family and stay connected to the movement. But as he started to befriend anti-racists, he became ashamed of having white extremist music in stock. When he stopped carrying it, members of the movement came to regard him as a "sell out" and a "race traitor." Other events also contributed. His eventual divorce from his wife and estrangement from his young family, the death of his beloved younger brother in a gang-shooting, and the demise of the record store led not only to his retreat from the movement but to his rejection of white supremacism.

The next five years of his life were a kind of purgatory, entailing depression and self-examination. He attended college and entered a training program to become an IBM computer network administrator. By happenstance, his first posting found him back at a high school he had been expelled from. There, he had a pivotal experience:

> [a]nd who should I run into on my first week on the job but Mr. Johnny Holmes, the African American security guard at whom I had spewed all my racist bitterness on the day I was escorted out in handcuffs. [...] I tore after my former nemesis....
>
> He turned, his smile abruptly fading as he recognized me.
>
> "Excuse me. Do you remember me, Mr. Holmes?"
>
> "You're hard to forget," he said. [...]
>
> "I want to tell you...tell you I'm sorry."...All those terrible things I said. What I did. My hatred. I made your life miserable when I attended school here. I'd take it back if I could, though I understand that I can't—those memories are stuck with each of us and I just want to apologize. Thank you for helping to show me what it means to live a life of dignity even when I didn't deserve it."
>
> He studied me intently. After a short time, he held out his hand and gave a slight nod. "I'm glad to hear it, Mr. Picciolini. [...] It's your responsibility now to tell the world what healed you. Welcome home." [...]
>
> ...I looked down to see hands that were once squeezed into fists longing to lash out now locked together in forgiveness.
>
> The concept was pure. The only hope I had of trying to wash away the evil I'd paid tribute to was by exposing it to the light. (ibid: 248–50)

There is a wider political and economic context to the rise of neo-Naziism in the US at that time and in the particular location where Picciolini's story take place. But if we put this aside, how might we explain Picciolini's process of first becoming an agent in this particular social movement and his eventual renunciation of it?

One route is to locate this movement in the progressive engagement with and then retreat from McAdam's redemptive self-narratives (2016). As discussed above, McAdams' six redemptive self-narratives (of atonement, emancipation, upward mobility, recovery, enlightenment, and development) bespeak movement or "redemptive sequences," for example, from alienation to atonement. Working backwards, we would argue that the security officer, in one of the final moments in the collapse of Picciolini's white supremacist agentic identity, offered him *atonement* for his previous 'sins' via a sacred instruction, or charge, to repeat his story of healing which, in Picciolini's mind, became a condition for and product of forgiveness.

More generally, Picciolini's entire book can be read as two counterposed redemptive sequences both involving emancipation or liberation. The first is a narrative of liberation: the depressed child, with no friends and neglectful parents, trapped in an alien upper-middle-class school and suburb is transformed into a recognized skinhead who came to lead the local chapter of white power networks in his original Italian-American neighborhood. But there are many other redemptive sequences in his memoire. From the bullied to the most feared kid, from the deceived high schooler to the "enlightened" white supremacist, from the rudderless to the clearly directed, from benightedly certain to disabused, and from the marginalized to the newly welcomed. Embedded in Picciolini's story is also a narrative sequence of upward mobility where Picciolini moves from outsider and marginal character to leadership.

Meanwhile the last third of the book tells the emancipatory redemptive narrative of his exodus *from* the white supremacy movement. Inside this later sequence we can likewise identify the language of other redemptive self-narratives. His engagement with Black anti-racist skinheads in his record shop, for example, can be regarded as an expression of the enlightenment narrative. One dramatic scene exemplifies this narrative. Black anti-racist skinheads arrived in the shop in what Picciolini initially feared could become a robbery. However, the gang goes on to purchase his entire Skrewdriver collection which, at $300, becomes his single biggest sale. Through their recurring visits to the store, he realizes that those whom his movement had been targeting were themselves looking for belonging and recognition as a response to suffering and pain.

While there is precious little detail of what took place during the five years of depression that followed his divorce, the death of his brother and his unwinding from the movement, the turning point was clearly a friend's offer of a job in IT installations with IBM. This transition not only signals upward mobility, one of McAdams' redemptive self-narratives, but also two of his other generative self-narratives, healing and development. Both signal a return to conventional society, but more importantly show, that Picciolini was recovering and finding ways to re-engage and develop new identities beyond white supremacy.

McAdam's redemptive narrative sequences are helpful in identifying the key dynamics that organize Picciolini's delivery of his story. They carry his reflective account to a point at the end of the book where the author, and protagonist in the emancipatory sequence, reports that he has reconciled with his family, is deeply engaged with his own children, has fallen in love with and married another woman (an IBM employee he met at work), and through the writing of book has delivered on the promise made to the security officer to keep telling his story as a lesson for others. Such interpretative schemas help us identify the broad pattern of the particular modes of traffic between different identities over time and space and provide us with some of the key coordinates involved in becoming agents of change (see also Creed et al. 2010; Lok et al. 2020).

But McAdam's narrative framework has some weaknesses. His framework focuses on focal actor's internalization and response to contextual factors. It neglects the connection between the "unspeakable" stories of Picciolini's childhood, which he identifies as "potholes," that created conditions for the idealization of white supremacist leaders (Clark Martell and Skrewdriver) and his connection to the redemptive narrative sequences embedded in its movement's dogma. While useful, McAdams' framework, underplays the affective, somatic, and deeply emotional early experiences that support the formation and development of the particular agentic identities that change agents take up through such narratives. There is no question, as Creed et al. (2014) note, that narratives allow us to construct our pasts, imagine different futures, and maintain a degree of coherence and purpose (Creed et al. 2014: 115). However, narratives are not the only things that shapes our engagement with the world. They provide the coordinates and direct our attention, our activities, and practices in the world through our pursuit of particular characters, plots, and events. But the salience and resonance of such sequences draw on complex and hidden memories of original, primal, or formative experiences of relations with significant others. They may be built upon particular combinations of taste, sound, touch, and smell or our relations to various body parts, or particular places and settings. Such implicit memories, built on a fundamental need for love, care, and sustenance, and around the suppliers of such needs, create in us patterns of desire and longing, and if interrupted, feelings of rejection, exclusion, and subordination. In other words, available cultural narratives are taken up for a reason. There is always a back story dealing with unspoken forces that escape our attention when we rely solely on the joys of redemptive narrative. But we can go further.

In what follows we extend our discussion of why we become agents of change by drawing on more contemporary interpretive concepts from the psychoanalytic tradition. These concepts, which remain largely an anathema in North American managerial scholarship, allow us to dig more deeply into Christian Picciolini's story. Drawing from the Lacanian branches of the psychoanalytic tradition, the analysis offers a complementary, albeit at times, somewhat contrarian interpretation of Christian Picciolini's book. Our aim here is to explore more directly the repressed, less comfortable, "unspeakable stories," and how they connect with culturally available narrative sequences.

Inferiority and Desire

At the core of Lacan's understanding of subjectivity is the assumption that our engagement with the world is based on a ubiquitous struggle with a fundamental gap or a "lack" stemming from our earliest experiences of the world (Arnaud 2002; Driver 2009; Verhaeghe, 1995). As we develop our efforts to fill or suture this gap are magnified and filtered through language with its nexus of signfiers, key terms, symbols, images and remembered experiences.

Lacan's second assumption is that the structure of our desire or motivation to address this underlying lack is not simply of our own making, but reflects or is a reaction to the desires of significant others, particularly parents (e.g., the mother's desire for her child).

Christian Picciolini makes much in the early part of the book of the fact that his parents were young immigrants to the US and that his mother, in particular, was badly bullied and thwarted in her efforts to gain an education due to her poor English. The parents' sense of difference and marginality provoked both the family's move out of, and then back to the Italian-American neighborhood during the young Picciolini's childhood. The first move appears to have been an effort to take on the trappings of the dominant culture. It seems likely, then, that his parents unconsciously passed on to their first born their feelings of marginality, subordination, and inferiority, and that the young Picciolini's passage into white power is both a reflection of his early years of attempting to carry his parents' feelings of subordination and marginalization and a reaction against those feelings.

As Picciolini notes: "I thought I was 'white' but I was not, I was inferior." Consequently, despite his parents' explicit efforts to fit in, Picciolini both attributes his sense of inferiority and abandonment to the dominant external culture and transfers his ensuing resentment onto others in subordinate positions within that culture. In other words, a Lacanian psychanalytic explanation for his taking up the white power identity in his early teens would have it that he becomes an agent of his parents' underlying desires, fighting on their behalf, against their experience of inferiority and subordination. (This parallels Stuart Hall's embrace of his family's desire for upward mobility through an elite British education.) In addition, what makes the young Picciolini's "conversion" to a white power social movement identity so mobilizing and uplifting is that this process of becoming also involves rejecting his parents' acquiescence to subordination and thus breaking with their desires. In the first sense, his racist efforts are unconsciously aimed at winning "back" the parents' recognition and love. In the second, his "conversion" experience is based on the enlivening rejection of the values that animate their lives as immigrants and on the transference of his love and desire for recognition to his white power mentors and their organization. Central to this is his youthful success with violence which begins with a new found relationship with his fists—as discussed above.

In other words, the white power movement's sanction of violence against the supposed marginalization of white culture, which was neatly expressed in its explicit fourteen-word credo, "We must secure the existence of our people and a future for white children" (Picciolini 2017: 68), both aligns with the young Picciolini's desire to unconsciously fight on behalf of his parents (regardless of whether they wanted him to do so) and the rejection of his parent's seeming acceptance of marginality.

We further suggest that Picciolini's taking on of the language, practices, and relations of the white power movement is a function of his parents' immigrant positioning in relation to the dominant culture's subordination of other groups. The immigrant, unconsciously, comes to hate, violently, the dominant group's disdained subordinates as a means of recommending themselves to those in control. Despite their background, status, learning, and qualifications, new immigrants often find themselves flung into working-class jobs, with the associated intermittent poverty, as they struggle against an alien, dominant culture to recover some sense of recognition, standing, and regard. This suggests that part of the young Picciolini's estrangement from his father is a function of the contradictions between the family's sense of inferiority and his father's desire to own, at least, the trapping of upper-middle-class lifestyle (including a flashy house and a Corvette).

Yet this trajectory couldn't be maintained. The young Picciolini came to realize that others (Irish, Black skinheads, and Mexicans) also struggled. Others were in pain and felt inferior and this was not just a consequence of skin color or ethnicity. The loss of his wife's love (not to be desired by your wife is a big loss) and the loss of his son's innocent love of his father, could not be blamed on the white power movement's ideological targets. Rather, confrontation with real events in his life forced him to see that his own actions, not those of subordinated racial groups, had created some of the circumstances that he was struggling with. We argue that the security guard's compassion and charge to continue recounting his story of change finally unseats the nexus of signifiers that had justified resentment and hatred of others, signifiers that he had carried over unconsciously from his parents, in favor of a chain of signifiers that urge compassion, empathy, and love for the other. This is not to say that his parents explicitly adopted hatred of other groups, or were not appalled by the hatred Picciolini professed while in the white power movement. Rather, we argue that the young Picciolini unconsciously took on the parents' experience of marginalization and rejection, particularly the story of his mother's being bullied out of her education, which he alludes to repeatedly in the book. The importance of her story of being bullied, a formative part of his relations with his mother, is amplified by what he perceives as his parents' absence and neglect, a seeming rejection of him that he comes to blame on the others outside the family.

The key principle and pattern of the explanation we offer would have it that what underpins our taking on of social movement identities is a product of the unconscious desires of our significant others, much of which are known but not explicitly spelled out. In other words, when his parents told him that they never wanted him to have the same experiences they had as immigrants, he unconsciously came to hear this as the parent's wish that he fight on their behalf to release them from their pain and suffering. In a similar vein, in the context of his enlivening involvement with the skinhead movement's sympathetic older young men—with the heady experiences of punk music, alcohol, violence, and the repetition of the "fourteen word" credo—Picciolini's embrace of the movement's signifiers and practices appears as an unconscious rejection of his parents' accommodating, submissive, and obedient response to their positioning as immigrants. Such interpretations of the would-be change agent's unconscious experiences are themselves based on the assumption that there is an unconscious hope that either fighting on behalf of the desires of the significant others, against marginalization for example, or rejecting an accommodating and subordinating approach, will in some way return the child to completeness through communion with the significant other, in a place without pain or difference and alienation.

But this impetus to act on the unconscious wishes of significant others can become unseated when a person confronts the desires of *new others*. In Picciolini's case, the love of another woman, and the desire for a family of his own both provide some space for questioning and challenging his implicit and inherited desires. Of course, it is the case that the white power credo speaks of the need to secure the existence of one's people and children. This credo lends itself to being simply translated into claims of protecting one's family and community. But when his new wife asks him directly why he had so much hate inside him and he responds that is important for advancing his family's long-term interests, he recalls feeling even then that that the movement's standard answer had become less than convincing, salient, and compelling for him.

In his story, Christian Picciolini's love affair with Lisa, his first wife and mother of their two children, is central to his revaluation and eventual rejection of white supremacy. Lisa's distance from the movement and her abhorrence of violence, made it possible for him to begin to question the unconscious desires he carried over from his parents and which he articulated through the white power movement. These desires weaken and ultimately collapse under the pressure to take up the implicit desires and the signifying chain of new others, for example, the wife, one's children, the security guard, and the friend who secured Picciolini his IBM job. Of course, this perhaps predictable consequence raises the question of why Picciolini fell in love with a woman outside the movement. Was this an unconscious move to distance himself from violence, and to find an intimate relationship without violence, before he himself was in any way consciously willing to make this explicit? If we can accept that the young Picciolini's embrace of white power is firstly an unconscious move to take up the wishes of his parents, particularly of his mother, then it follows that we might accept the possibility that taking on the unconscious desires of a loving partner provides the initial basis of his ultimate rejection of white power movements' identity, practices, and violent relations to others. This suggests that from a psychoanalytic perspective, there is an agent within us who is already ahead of what we consciously understand to be our purpose. In this sense, such an unconscious agent is alertly awaiting signifiers/cultural meaning and practices that will create the imaginary or fantasy needed to change.

Conclusions

As a contribution to the study of organizational change, this chapter proposes a form of interpretative analysis for understanding the process of becoming a change agent. Our approach draws on McAdam's redemptive self-narrative sequences as culturally available framing devices, together with analysis using key concepts from the psychoanalytic traditions of the less obvious, largely unspoken (or even unspeakable) stories of subjectivity. Our aim in this regard has been quite specific. We have not, for example, attempted to explore how individuals and groups bring about organizational change (Moss-Kanter 1984; Katz 2003). We have neither attempted to contribute to the literature on the tools and tactics that organizations use to create activists (see for example Han 2014) nor attempted to contribute to the more general literature on organizational socialization, motivation, and commitment (Staw and Salancik 1979; Pearce and Larson 2006). We have also not attempted to contribute to the related literature on social movements and their contribution to organizational change. Classic studies in this regard (Davis et al. 2005) make movements themselves the agents of change and in particular explore the political processes involved as such movements attempt to reshape organizations (Zald and Berger 1978). Such work says little about the intimate process of developing change agents. Our focus has been on making a contribution to literature on how individuals and groups come to embrace activist identities that animate their participation in social movements (Meyer and Jepperson 2000, Seo and Creed 2002, Creed et al, 2010, Elidrissi and Courpasson 2019, Wright et al. 2012; Skoglund and Bohm 2019). As noted above, recent works around this question focus on how individuals and groups *reflexively narrate activist identities* and in the process internalize social movement narratives. Using two illustrative cases, our contribution to this has been to analyze in detail the complex interplay of unconscious dynamics and redemptive narrative sequences.

What our analysis brings to light is the familial, genealogical character of the process of becoming a change agent. In this regard, formative childhood experiences clearly play a role. Steve Jobs' struggle with feelings of abandonment stemming from his being adopted shaped his work as a computer industry change agent. Christian Picciolini's formative experience as the child of immigrants shaped his role as a leader of a US white supremacist movement. The key finding here, if we can put it that way, is that the process of becoming a change agent is a function of one's formative family history and particularly of the complex set of largely unspoken experiences that parents and grandparents and ancestors have had. We argue that Christian Picciolini's engagement in white supremacy arose from a largely unspoken desire to take up the fight on behalf of his immigrant parents in order, firstly, to recommend himself to them, and then to reject their position as compliant and submissive. While Picciolini says very little about his grandparents and their experience of immigration to the US, the fact that he spent much of his childhood in their care while his parents worked, would suggest that part of the unspoken desires that underpin his engagement with white supremacy likely flow also from his relations with his grandparents. In the same light, Stuart Hall's turn from the classical study of English literature to his study of popular culture, and his political activism, particularly in relation to racism, derived directly from his complex and somewhat contradictory efforts both to fulfill his family's desire for upward mobility, through an elite English education, and to escape his family's control through both his emigration to Britain and his turn to political activism.

So what then are the implications of our analysis for the understanding of movement-derived social and organizational change? It is of course obvious from the Picciolini case that the successful recruiting of member activists requires a core set of unique, mostly pleasurable activities that *exoticize opposition* to established authorities, conditions, and rules. Particular forms of dress, music, and physical engagement, including street violence in some instances, are clearly part of the wider repertoire of experiences that routinely contribute to the identity formation of social movement activists. But to be successful in forming the identities of insurgent change agents, social movement organizing must involve particular narrative sequences, as McAdams outlines. These offer the recipient some kind of *redemptive movement* away from what

William James referred to as the felt experience of falling short in some serious way. The redemptive narratives that social movements can offer, such as atonement or upward mobility or even emancipation (from police violence for example), can have the effect of creating what James described as a new "habitual center of... personal energy," that becomes an, if not the, animating force of the individual's agency (James 1902/2004: 147–8).

But such redemptive narrative sequences, in and of themselves, are not enough. To be successful and create a Steve Jobs, a Stuart Hall, or a Christian Picciolini, for example, such redemptive sequences must align with and express, in some form, unconscious desires buried in the often unspeakable stories derived from an individual's formative experience or, more likely the experiences of that individual's parents, grandparents, or even ancestors. In other words, it is then that the unspoken but nevertheless communicated patterns of traumatic experiences and unconscious desires intersect with the redemptive narratives on offer by social movements to produce change agents able to bring the energy, commitment, and desire required to reshape the status quo. In short, what this brings to light is an explanation for the formation of change agents that is not located within the individual or group, but rather spans generations, nations, and even archeological passages of time.

References

Abdelnour, S., Hasselbladh, H., and Kallinikos, J. (2017), 'Agency and Institutions in Organization Studies', *Organization Studies*, 38/12, 1775–92.

Arnaud, G. (2002), 'The Organization and the Symbolic: Organizational Dynamics Viewed from a Lacanian Perspective', *Human Relations* 55/6, 691–720.

Canetti, E. (1962), *Crowds and Power* (Harmondsworth, UK: Penguin).

Creed, W. E. D., DeJordy, R,, and Lok, J. (2010), 'Being the Change: Resolving Institutional Contradiction through Identity Work'. *Academy of Management Journal*, 53/6, 1336–64.

Creed, W. E. D., Hudson, B. A., Okhuysen, G., and Smith-Crowe. K. (Forthcoming). A Place in the World: Vulnerability, Wellbeing, and the Ubiquitous Evaluation that Animates Participation in Institutional Processes. *Academy of Management Review*.

Creed, W. D., DeJordy, R., and Lok, J. (2014), 'Myths to Work by: Redemptive Self-Narratives and Generative Agency for Organizational Change', in P. Tracey, N. Phillips, and M. Lounsbury, eds., *Religion and Organization Theory* (Bingley: Emerald Group Publishing Limited), 111–56

Da Cunha, J. V., and Orlikowski, W. J. (2008), 'Performing Catharsis: The Use of Online Discussion Forums in Organizational Change', *Information and Organization*, 18/2, 132–56.

Davis, G. F., and Kim, E. W. (2021), 'Social Movements and Organizational Change', in M. S. Poole and A. H. Van de Ven, eds., *The Oxford Handbook of Organizational Change and Innovation* (2nd edn) (Oxford: Oxford University Press),

Davis, G. F., McAdam, D., Scott, W. R., and Zald, M. N. (Eds.) (2005), *Social Movements and Organization Theory* (New York: Cambridge University Press).

Driver, M. (2009), 'From Loss to Lack: Stories of Organizational Change as Encounters with Failed Fantasies of Self, Work and Organization', *Organization*, 16/3, 353–69.

Elidrissi, Y. R., and Courpasson, D. (2019), 'Body Breakdowns as Politics: Identity Regulation in a High-Commitment Activist Organization', *Organization Studies*, 29, 423–44) (Online first).

Freud, S. (1989), *The Ego and the Id* (London: WW Norton & Company).

Freud, S., and Bonaparte, P. M. (1954), *The Origins Of Psychoanalysis* (Vol. 216) (London: Imago).

Gabriel, Y. (1999), *Organizations in Depth: The Psychoanalysis of Organizations.* London: Sage.

Gabriel, Y. and Carr, A. (2003), Organizations, Managementr and Psychoanalysis: An Overview, Journal of Managerial Psychology 17/5, 348–65

Gamson, W. A. and Meyers, D. S. (1996), 'Framing of Political Opportunity', in McAdam D. , McCarthy, J and Zald, M (eds), *Comparative Perspectives on Social Movements: Political Opportunities*, Cambridge: Cambridge University Press pgs. 275–90

Gusfield, J. R. (1970), *Protest, Reform, and Revolt: A Reader in Social Movements* (New York: Wiley).

Hall, S (1987). 'Minimal Selves', in L. Appignanesi, ed., *The Real Me: Post-Modernism and the Question of Identity* (London: Institute of Contemporary Arts), pgs 44–6

Han, H. (2014), *How Organizations Develop Activists: Civic Associations and Leadership in the 21st Century* (New York: Oxford University Press).

Isaacson, W. (2011), *Steve Jobs* (London: Little Brown)

James, W. (1902/2004), *The Varieties of Religious Experience* (New York: Simon & Schuster/ Touchstone).

Kanter, R. M. (1984), *Change masters.* Simon and Schuster.

Katz, R (2003), *The human side of managing technological innovation* 2nd Edition, Oxford: Oxford University Press.

King, B. G., and Soule, S. A. (2007), 'Social Movements as Extra-Institutional Entrepreneurs: The Effect of Protests on Stock Price Returns', *Administrative Science Quarterly*, 52/3, 413–42.

Lacan, J. (2006), *The Seminar of Jacques Lacan: The Other Side of Psychoanalysis* (Vol. Book XVII) (trans. Russell Grigg) (New York: W.W. Norton).

Levinson, H. (1972), *Organizational diagnosis* (Cambridge, MA: Harvard University Press).

Lok, J., Creed, W. E. D., and DeJordy, R. (2020), 'From "Church Cruise Director" to "Rabbi": Authoring the Agentic Self through Conventions of Narrative Necessity: Research in the Sociology of Organizations', in P. Haack, J. Sieweke, and L. Wessel, eds., *Micro Foundations of Institutions* (Bingley: Emerald Publishing), Chapter 4.

McAdams, D. (2006a), 'The Redemptive Self: Generativity and the Stories Americans Live By', *Research in Human Development*, 3/2&3, 81–100.

McAdams, D. (2006b), *The Redemptive Self: Stories Americans Live By* (New York, NY: Oxford University Press).

McAdams, D., and Bowman (2001), 'Narrating Life's Turning Points: Redemption and Contamination', in D. P. McAdams, R. Josselson, and A. Lieblich, eds., *Turns in the Road: Narrative Studies of Lives in Transition* (Washington, DC: American Psychological Association), Chapter 1: 3–34

McLaughlin, B. (Ed.). (1969), *Studies in Social Movements: A Social Psychological Perspective* (New York: Free Press).

Melucci, A. (1989), *Nomads of the Present: Social Movements and Individual Needs in Contemporary Society* (New York: Vintage),

Meyer, J. W., and Jepperson, R. L. (2000), 'The 'Actors' of Modern Society: The Cultural Construction of Social Agency', *Sociological Theory*, 18, 100–20.

Mena, Kelly (2020), "Michigan Governor Says Legislators 'Didn't Want To Be Around' for Anti-Lockdown Protests 'They Incited'", CNN, May 15, 1611 GMT, https://edition.cnn.com/2020/05/15/politics/whitmer-legislators-avoid-capitol-cnntv/index.html/, accessed 14 September 2020.

Pearce, N. J., and Larson, R. W. (2006), 'How Teens Become Engaged in Youth Development Programs: The Process of Motivational Change in a Civic Activism Organization', *Applied Developmental Science*, 10/3, 121–31.

Picciolini, Christian (2015), *Romantic Violence: Memoirs of an American Skinhead* (Chicago: Goldmill Group).

Picciolini, C. (2017), *White American Youth: My Descent into America's Most Violent Hate Movement—and How I Got Out* (New York: Hachette Books).

Polletta, F. (1998), 'Contending Stories: Narrative in Social Movements', *Qualitative Sociology*, 21, 419–46.

Rao, H., and Dutta, S. (2017), 'Why Great Strategies Spring from Identity Movements', *Strategy Science*, 3/1, 313–22.

Seo, M-G., and Creed, D. W. E. (2002), 'Institutional Contradictions, Praxis, and Institutional Change: A Dialectical Perspective', *Academy of Management Review*, 27, 222–48.

Skoglund, A., and Böhm, S. (2019), Prefigurative Partaking: Employees' Environmental Activism in an Energy Utility', *Organization Studies*, 9, 1257–83. (Online first).

Staw, B. M., and Salancik, G. R. (1977), *New Directions in Organizational Behavior* (Chicago: St Clair Press).

Tilly, C. (1986), *The Contentious Fench, Four Centuries of Popular Struggle* (Massachusetts, USA, Harvard University Press).

Verhaeghe, P. (1995), 'From Impossibility to Inability: Lacan's Theory on the Four Discourses, *The Letter: Lacanian Perspectives on Psychoanalysis*", 3, 1–14. Retrieved from http://www.psychoanalysis.ugent.be/pages/nl/artikels/artikels Paul Verhaeghe/From Impossibility to Inability.pdf/

Wright, C., Nyberg, D., and Grant, D. (2012), 'Hippies on the Third Floor': Climate Change, Narrative Identity and the Micro-Politics of Corporate Environmentalism. *Organization Studies*, 33/11, 1451–75.

Zald, M. N., and Berger, M. A. (1978). Social movements in organizations: Coup d'etat, insurgency, and mass movements. *American Journal of Sociology*, 83/4, 823–61.

CHAPTER 11

STAKEHOLDER MODEL OF CHANGE

LAURIE LEWIS

WHENEVER organizations move through change processes, individuals and groups may perceive threats and opportunities related to their stakes. A stake in an organization may take any number of forms, including finances, information access, goods/services, reputation, relationships, environmental conditions, and other resources. No matter the type, size, scope, or age of an organization, there will be sets of stakeholders who depend on the organization, or hope to derive benefit (or avoid harm) related to the organization's operation. When an organization changes in some significant way, stakes are invoked and often are cast into uncertainty. Organizational change can also result in the creation of new stakes, new stakeholders, alteration of stakeholder relationships, and shifting importance of stakes.

The notion of organizations as holders of stakes dates back to the earliest roots of Stakeholder Theory. According to DeBussy (2019) the word "stakeholder" first appeared in a Stanford Research Institute memo in 1963 and was first defined as "those groups without whose support the organization would cease to exist" (Freeman 1984: 31). From the earliest mentions of this lengthy line of theory development, scholars have debated the appropriate allocation of attention to various types of groups and individuals who hold stakes in organizations (excellent reviews of the history of stakeholder scholarship can be found in DeBussy 2019; Frandsen 2019; Freeman et al. 2010). Analysis of stakeholders of a variety of types and characteristics dominated much of the early scholarship in this area. Much of the debate surrounding stakeholders has focused on which of a variety of groups should be considered stakeholders by a focal organization, and on what basis organizations should allocate attention to various stakeholder groups. For example, Mitchell et al. (1997) suggest that the relative power, legitimacy, and urgency of various groups of stakeholders is used in determining among whom attention and resources should be divided. Their Theory of Stakeholder Identification and Salience (TSIS) views stakeholder salience as the extent to which managers prioritize competing stakeholder claims. The theory predicts that groups of stakeholders who possess more power, legitimacy, and urgency, will be more salient to the focal organization. According to TSIS, definitive stakeholders possess a high degree of all three attributes and are therefore very prominent in organizations.

The early work related to Stakeholder Theory drew attention to the very notion of "stakes" and those individuals and groups who perceived themselves to have a stake in an organization. Although typically, stakeholder scholars adopt the perspective of a focal organization, Mitchell et al. (1997) drew attention to the means by which stakeholder groups imposed their desires and demands on organizations. These authors detailed coercive, utilitarian, and normative power bases used to influence the decisions of organizations. It is important to notice that stakeholders are active agents in an organizational environment and are not mere passive actors who are granted more or less attention by active organizational managers.

The interplay between any given organization's recognition of, attention paid to, and relationships with stakeholder groups and individuals has dominated the literature. Much of the debate about stakeholders in the scholarly literature as well as within business practice has centered on the degree to which non-essential stakeholders need to be given attention. Essentially, should businesses only focus on those stakeholders on whom the business is dependent (e.g., core customers, shareholders, employees)? In the normative strand of Stakeholder Theory, scholars have debated the ethical requirements that dictate what organizations *should* do regarding their engagement with stakeholder groups (e.g., activists, community members, and advocacy groups) (Freeman et al. 2010). Debates continue about whether it is even possible to separate the business motivation for stakeholder engagement from consideration of ethical mandates to do so.

Shortcomings of Stakeholder Theory in the Context of Organizational Change

It is difficult to generalize across all of the Stakeholder Theory scholarship but there are some general tendencies of stakeholder perspectives and research that are sometimes problematic when considered in the context of organizational change. First, stakeholder theorists tend to describe stakeholders in terms of some rather generic buckets such as "customers," "employees," "vendors/suppliers," or "community." Even though some authors (including Freeman 1984) have described a process of stakeholder analysis that is more fine-grained, the sub-categories of the general types of stakeholders are typically also fairly non-descript buckets. For example, Frandsen (2019) uses the illustration of the Carlsberg Group where the most generic category of stakeholders is "customers," and more specific categories of customers might include "supermarkets," "bars," and "restaurants." What seems much less common in the stakeholder literature is a multi-dimensional methodology for describing/typing stakeholder groups. For example, in the above case, we could easily divide "customers" into high sales volume/low sales volume, or new/longstanding, or brand friendly/brand ambivalent among many other dimensions (See Table 11.1). In describing stakeholders not by categories or types but through characterizing dimensions of the relationships they have with an organization, we can add specificity and complexity. It could be that a bar and a supermarket could share identical scores along these dimensions while two restaurants have completely opposite ratings. It is also possible that some customers share more in common with some suppliers than with other customers.

This illustration leads to questions about assumptions in defining an organization's set of stakeholders. It also raises questions about a static approach to stakeholder mapping. If we think of Carlsberg's stakeholders as a static set of supermarkets, bars, and restaurants we would not likely expect them to change over time (even though we'd acknowledge new bars, restaurants, supermarkets would join the set, and some might leave it). However, if we see each stakeholder group in terms of dynamic dimensions which are indicated by our relationship with them (frequency/intensity/length/quality), we might describe the field of stakeholders in very different ways. Most importantly, we'd be highlighting that those stakeholder "buckets" (and the organizations/groups/individuals that fall into them) are likely to change over time in ways that are relevant to the stakeholder relationship with the focal organization.

In a dynamic model of stakeholder mapping, the dimensions or qualities of the relationship with the focal organization becomes most important. As managers decide to which groups to pay attention, they would consider not the choice between supermarkets, bars, restaurants, but between those with varying levels of sales volume, length of sales relationship, and degree of brand loyalty. It is likely that some combination of these (and other) qualities of the relationship will drive the attention paid to any given customer at any given point in time. And, of course, the important dimensions of stakeholder relationships may also evolve over time. For example, at the beginning of an organization's life, all stakeholders will have equal length of relationships (all new), and later in the organization's lifespan, there will be variation in the length of stakeholder relationships.

An overemphasis on the stakes stakeholders *have*, is a second problematic assumption in some applications of stakeholder theory. Again, this perspective implies a sort of static set of concerns, needs, demands, asks, and desires held by any given stakeholder group and the attendant assumption that such stakes are always in play. Aside from the obvious problematic assumption that stakeholders know what they want, need, and are

Table 11.1 Multi-Dimensional Description of a Set of Stakeholders

	High/low volume	New/longstanding	Friendly/Ambivalent
Stakeholder x	Low	New	Ambivalent
Stakeholder y	High	New	Friendly
Stakeholder z	High	Longstanding	Friendly

asking for, it is further problematic to assume that stakes are fixed and always situationally relevant. Stakeholder mapping often entails consideration of what the stakeholder group's stakes *are*. It is a more accurate approach to think about mapping stakeholders' assertion of stakes. In the example above, all of Carlsberg's customers have a stake in the pricing of the products. Presumably, they have a desire to have a low purchase price. However, not all of these stakeholders will be asserting a stake related to pricing at any given point in time. There could be a variety of reasons for not asserting a stake. There could be other stakes that are valued more. There could be a history of failure in asserting a stake that gives rise to hesitancy. There could be issues of incompetent or negligent stake-claiming on the part of representatives of a stakeholder group. Rather than attempt to map the "stakes" that each group has, it may be more useful to consider when and how stakes are asserted and with what effects.

A third critique of the stakeholder perspective concerns the tendency (especially in more classic stakeholder scholarship) to approach mapping of stakeholders merely from the standpoint of a focal organization. It is a limited perspective to adopt merely the perspective of a given organization rather than examine a network of groups, organizations, and subsets of collectives that seek to influence one another's actions and stakes. For example, in adopting a more networked approach, scholars may explore the dynamics related to a given community and the variety of businesses, agencies, nonprofits, and local governmental agencies as they interact around various topics and issues. Koschmann and Kopczynski (2017) ague that in some contexts, stakeholder relationships emerge around issues rather than the business deals of a given focal organization. Thus, in the above example, rather than focus on the stakeholders of Carlsberg, we might focus instead on relationships built surrounding public issues related to high alcohol consumption in the community (e.g., public drunkenness, drunk driving, violence in bars and other entertainment establishments, minors engaging in drinking, health issues related to alcohol abuse, and increases in crime). If a community group wished to see such negative outcomes associated with high alcohol consumption reduced, they might seek to assert their stakes with any number of target organizations (e.g., local government, local police, local bars, local alcohol distributers, health advocates, high schools, community groups, nonprofits). On the other hand, a vendor of alcohol might wish to maintain positive relationships with customers, government, police, and suppliers. It seems that a full engagement with Stakeholder Theory should include exploration of the means, methods, and choices of stakeholders in asserting stakes, and developing their stakeholder relationships with target organizations and with other groups of stakeholders of those organizations (e.g., voters, political action committees, school board members, media, police organizations). Some have argued for increasing focus on networks of stakeholders. Andriof and Waddock (2002) argues that this is a new trend in Stakeholder Theory:

> Generally, perspectives on stakeholder theory have moved away from an entirely corporate-centric focus in which stakeholders are viewed as subjects to be managed towards more of a network-based, relational and process-oriented view of

company-stakeholder engagement, where at least there is a consideration of mutuality, interdependence and power (as cited in Frandsen 2019: 19).

The argument for "joint stakes" is made clearly in Freeman et al. (2010) where they suggest that the problem of prioritization of stakes and stakeholders is a secondary problem. Rather than ask "which stakeholders are more important" these authors argue managers should consider all stakeholders as connected.

> No stakeholder stands alone in the process of value creation. The stakes of each stakeholder group are multifaceted, and inherently connected to each other. How could a bondholder recognize any returns without management paying attention to the stakes of customers or employees? How could customers get the products and services they need without employees and suppliers? How could employees have a decent place to live without communities?
>
> (Freeman et al. 2010: 27).

However, this approach maintains a focal–organizational perspective and eschews analysis of the network of stakeholder relationships from the perspectives of those groups. It seems more than a mere recognition of the ties among stakeholders is needed.

Understanding how stakeholders influence each other and form coalitions and rivalries is also a necessary component of an exploration of stakeholder networks. Mitchell et al. (1997) have noted that stakeholders who form alliances may increase the chances of the focal organization's compliance. Unions often seek community support or the endorsement by powerful political office-holders in order to put pressure on organizations during contract negotiations. Some scholars have started to explore the ways in which stakeholders not only recognize one another, but also assess the degree to which their stakes are competitive or complementary (Hendry 2005; Lewis 2019; Post et al. 2002).

As scholars adopt more of a network approach to fields of stakeholders and organizations, they must recognize that any given organization can be considered a stakeholder to any other organization/group. Essentially, they can be at once a "focal organization" and a stakeholder for multiple other "focal organizations." Further, stakeholder networks, like any other network based on interaction and exchange, shift and change over time and circumstances. They are dynamic and the interrelationships are fluid.

Stakeholder Theory and Organizational Change

Scholars often implicitly consider how stakes are asserted, claimed, and questioned during the process of organizational change. As stakeholders become aware that a change process is underway in an organization, they often assess for themselves how their stakes may be enhanced or threatened. Employees worry about job loss; managers worry about loss of resources; customers worry about affordability or availability of products; community members worry about impacts on environment, traffic, and quality of life. Other stakeholders may perceive the change will be helpful in their pursuit of some stake, such as raises, increased sales, updated infrastructure, or new external partners, etc. As stakeholders assess their own stakes as a change process unfolds, they also may reassess their relationships with other stakeholders and the relative balance of shared or opposing interests. Realignment of stakeholder relationships is common during organizational change. Throughout the change process, stakeholders inside and outside of an organization may influence one another's opinions and perceptions about the change, the process of changing, and the benefits and risks of the change itself.

The following section discusses a Stakeholder Model of Change (Lewis 2011; 2019) and highlights stakeholders' perceptions, and experiences of change over time, including the ways in which their stakeholder relationships evolve over the course of a change process.

A Stakeholder Model of Organizational Change

In 2011, I proposed a stakeholder model of organizational change (see Figure 11.1). The model presents the processes of change in the context of stakeholder communication (Lewis 2011). In the model and the discussion presented in the book (and subsequently updated in the 2019 revision), I explore stakeholders' assessments and perceptions of their own stakes and relationships with other stakeholders and the focal organization undergoing a planned change. The model also highlights the interaction among stakeholders and with the focal organization as they assess threats and opportunities viz their own and others' stakes throughout a change process.

The Lewis stakeholder change model brings a focus on process and interconnectedness among stakeholders, their communication and perceptions, and the outcomes for change in the organization and their environment. Here I will discuss implications of this model and other stakeholder approaches to organizational change in terms of (a) the alteration of stakes and stakeholders' perspectives of the change and (b) the changing nature of relationships among stakeholders throughout a change process.

Alteration of Stakes and Stakeholders' Perspectives Over a Change Process

Stakes change and shift over time. As noted earlier, individual stakeholders' awareness, interest, and actions in asserting various stakes will likely vary over time. During an

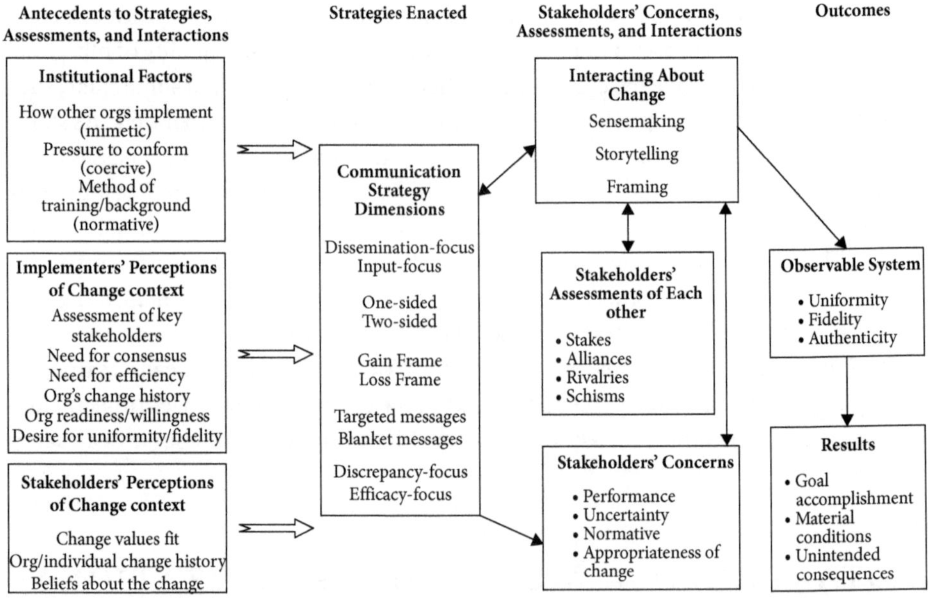

FIGURE 11.1 Lewis Change Process in Context of Stakeholder Communication

From Lewis, L. (2019). Organizational change: Creating change through strategic communication (2nd ed.)

organizational change, there is a more acute attention to the evaluation and assessment of one's own stakes and the stakes of adjacent stakeholders. Change often invokes real and perceived reallocation of resources. When individuals and groups perceive that their share of resources may be under threat and/or potentially increased through an organizational change, there is a heightened focus on evaluating stakes. Questions are raised concerning what is essential, what is optional, what can be discarded, and which future stakes should be claimed.

Organizational change involves a process of managing uncertainty. Bordia et al. (2004) argue that change involves three types of uncertainty: (a) strategic uncertainty, (b) structural uncertainty, and (c) job-related uncertainty. Stakeholders with strategic uncertainty will raise questions about the organization's future and environment. Structural uncertainty will give rise to operational and culture change that impacts how the stakeholder will be able to cope with the new processes, relationships, and values. Job-related uncertainty will typically impact an employee and be related to how that individual does his/her job, how rewards are allocated, and how status relationships are altered. In general, "[U]ncertainty concerns are related to the problems that occur for stakeholders when they do not know what to expect or what are likely outcomes of change" (Lewis 2019: 266). As stakeholders confront disruptions in procedures, administration of policies, shifting communication networks, unsteady resource-dependency relationships, altered role-relationships, and new standards and technology, among other changes, they will be confronted by uncertainty about outcomes, process, and values, and this will often trigger reconsideration of stakes that may be in play.

Scholars have explored the ways in which uncertainty is addressed and resolved through change processes. A key part of stakeholder communication during change is related to attempts to cope with or reduce uncertainty. Kramer et al. (2004) provide an example of this in their study of uncertainty in the context of an airline acquisition. Although much organizational research tends to assume that information seeking is the preferred method to reduce uncertainty during change, the success of those sorts of strategies has been called into doubt. For many stakeholders during change, increased acquisition of information can add to, rather than reduce, uncertainty. Kramer et al.'s (2004) study of an airline merger found that levels of uncertainty changed over time in some cases, and that the value of certain sources of information changed over time as well. The authors found that the pilots' value of official sources of information increased over time, while their value of information from union officials and media outlets decreased over time. Kramer et al., report, "Overall, pilots initially felt the media provided them with the most valuable information followed by peers. Over time, peers and then official sources became more valued. Union officials were consistently rated in the middle while outsiders were always rated lowest" (p. 87). This study also found that the ways in which stakeholders relied upon each other for information, peer support, and uncertainty reduction varied considerably. For example, these authors found that high information seekers (10 or 71% of respondents) actively sought more information in an attempt to manage their uncertainty. However, low information seekers (4 or 29% of respondents) tended to use internal techniques (passively allowing information to come to them; dismissing value of/reliability of any existing information) to manage uncertainty instead of seeking new information.

A part of this process is co-creating an understanding of which stakes are in play and in what ways an individual's stakes are advantaged or threatened. As stakes are reassessed and uncertainty is built and resolved, stakeholders' perceptions of their own stakes and stakes of other groups and individuals evolve. Changing perceptions and valuing of stakes is influenced through the sensemaking and strategic interactions among stakeholders. As information is shared, concerns are fomented, and stories are weaved, and stakeholders' understandings of the change and *what is at stake* are formed and altered. In the Kramer et al. (2004) study stakeholders sought out other employees for gossip and rumor communication. The pilots did not describe these encounters as providing "information" but rather as a means of connecting with and supporting each other;

> These peer-to-peer conversations seem to function differently than information seeking functions in URT. While the chats did not actually reduce uncertainty because they were not informative communication, the conversations provided supportive communication...and helped created an "in the same boat" consciousness of knowing that others were experiencing the same feelings. These conversations were valued because they provided a sense of comfort and created a sense of solidarity that consequently provided a way for employees to manage their uncertainty. (p. 93)

Although stakeholders' communication during change often is portrayed as reactionary or passive, these interactions are frequently strategic in nature (Lewis 2019). Stakeholders of all kinds (internal and external to an organization undergoing change) will be involved in the production of knowledge about a change—and participate in defining that change for themselves and for others. As Lewis (2019: 164) argues:

> They will be involved in clarification and sensemaking activity that involves asking questions and offering opinions to one another and to implementers. They may propose, especially to one another, alternative views of the change plan and purpose (reinterpreting it according to their best understandings or in terms of some version that suits political interests).

According to Achilles Armenakis and colleagues there are a set of five beliefs that influence whether they will support or resist a change effort. According to Armenakis et al. (1993), stakeholders must believe that (a) change is necessary for the organization, (b) the particular proposed change is the correct one to address an identified problem or gap, (c) the organization is capable of implementing the change, (d) opinion leaders are committed to the change, and (e) the change has positive implications for the stakeholder. Stakeholders may come to hold these or oppositional beliefs through their participation in analysis and diagnosis before any specific change is even selected or announced. In fact, according to the research evidence of Armenakis and colleagues' line of research on this topic, such first-hand early involvement is an ideal way to build these beliefs. Stakeholders may come to such beliefs through sharing with other stakeholders who already hold them (or their opposites) and/or through their own experience engaging with a change implementation process.

Story-sharing is a key means by which stakeholders, intentionally and unintentionally, influence each other's beliefs about a change. Through stories individuals might spread rumors, distort information upwards, highlight positives, launder negative information, and/or feign ignorance to further their individual goals. Further, "Both the process of storymaking as well as the resultant stories that are told afford opportunities for stakeholders to come together in shared stakes and/or to disassociate from others" (Lewis 2019: 254). Shelly Bird's (2007) investigation of a group of women coping with organizational change illustrates how alliances can be formed during change sensemaking and story-building. Bird found that elaborated and joint storytelling helped the women cope with uncertainty. She found that a terse telling (Boje 1991)—a truncated form of story-telling that involves reference to an elaborated story shared by the group—reflected bonding among the group members.

> Organizational storytelling is a social and collective activity. As Bird (2007) documents in her research, storytelling helps participants to order disparate facts, events, and experiences, create shared understanding of the past; and predict successful coping with future events and circumstance. Johansson and Heide (2008) argue: . . . whilst an ideal may be that people can make sense of strategic change

> through a coherent narrative that is credible for all parties, actors are making sense of situations differently, and are impacting on each other's sense-making processes. (p. 296)

Dewulf et al. (2009) argue that stakeholders use interactional frames to make collective sense of a situation. Together they categorize and arrange ambiguous events in meaningful ways. Framing and retrospective sensemaking help stakeholders communicate with one another and interpret a change. These are the conversations where people figure out "what is going on here," "what this means," and "why this is happening." This perspective views change as contextually enacted and created through communication among stakeholders. For instance, Leonardi (2009), in his study concerning technology implementation and sensemaking, argued that employees interpret technologies by assessing their functional value and through interactions with other users. Leonardi's research found that users of new technology developed one interpretation of the change that so informed these stakeholders' expectations and understanding of the change that it seriously shaped their material interactions with it. That shaping then led to a negative assessment of what the technology could do.

Storytelling and interactional framing clearly influence the perceptions that stakeholders have about their changing stakes in the organization and potential for threat or opportunity related to those stakes. The collective sensemaking may make individuals aware of competing and/or complementary stakes among stakeholder groups, and the cases made to support or resist the change.

Implementers' Attempts to Influence Stakeholders' Perspectives and Beliefs

Certainly, leaders, managers, and change implementers play active roles in influencing stakeholders' evolving beliefs, perspectives, and attitudes about change. Those who speak for the organization and who make decisions about the structural support for a change process will have a significant role in shaping both the interaction among stakeholders as well as directly impacting perceptions about the change, its consequences, and the stakes that are in play.

Those charged with implementing change often devote considerable communicative attention to disseminating information to stakeholders in order to clarify the goals, process, and desired outcomes of change. Typically, information is often portrayed as a possession of implementers and upper-level decision-makers (Larkin and Larkin 1994). Some studies have even suggested that employees prefer receiving their information from direct supervisors, and support the idea that information exchange must remain within the organizational hierarchy (Hargie and Tourish 2000). In such a conceptualization, employees and other stakeholders are perceived as mere receivers of information, lacking deeper understanding of the change. Employees (and other non-leader stakeholders) rarely are considered to possess the ability to assess change-related information or alternatives, therefore positioning implementers as the key holders and disseminators of information.

Change implementers typically focus on communication that they have designed to engage stakeholders in positive ways and to limit resistance. Often managers and implementers will attempt to sell change to stakeholder groups and to give rise to the key beliefs mentioned earlier (a point reflected in Burke's Chapter 2 in this volume, and challenged by Prichard and Creed's Chapter 10). Implementers want stakeholders to see the change in positive ways and to underscore how the change is necessary, likely to be successful, and as supported by opinion leaders. For example, in Applequist, et al.'s (2016) study of the implementation of a model for patient-centered care within twenty medical practices, examination of interviews with staff, administrators, and practitioners found evidence of the effectiveness of three over-arching themes: (1) open, consistent communication that encourages active listening and feedback; (2) appropriate reinforcement techniques; and (3) a clearly identifiable PCMH "champion" or change implementer.

Change scholars argue that change and change processes are interpreted through different frames used by various stakeholders (Lewis 2011). According to Fairhurst (2010), frames are structured ways of thinking where leaders can gain control of the situation. Framing is a means of bracketing important points of focus and eliminating other elements from view or consideration. Framing helps leaders connect with their audience by using, elaborating on, or eliminating meanings ascribed to circumstances or events. During change, framing helps highlight certain aspects of the process or goals while underscoring or obscuring others. Whittle et al. (2010) identified the "funnel of interests" phenomenon, where change agents create specific lens of interpreting and reinterpreting the change in order to realign the change to the recipient's interests.

Soliciting input is a general strategy employed to increase involvement and understanding, and garner approval for change. Lewis (2019) argues that participation itself may be of varied types, including direct or indirect/representative, voluntary or involuntary, and formal or informal. Specific designs issues for gathering input include timing, setting, anonymous access, choice of facilitator, and previous attempts at solicitation, to name a few. The specific design of input solicitation is highly consequential (Lewis, 2019). Sahay's (2017) study of a change process in a metropolitan hospital found that nurses often felt left out and skeptical about how individuals were selected to provide input. This chain of reactions certainly read to a resistance to the change (see for discussion, Zorn and Scott, Chapter 29 in this volume). Nurses were also reluctant to provide input after zealous announcements that celebrated the change initiative. Invitations to provide input in the context of a rally-like gathering about the change presents perceived risks, including stepping on the message and enthusiasm of implementers and organizational leaders. Barge et al. (2008) bring relevant observations to this discussion. Barge and colleagues collected data on a multistakeholder initiative and identified three dualities related to who should have voice: inclusion–exclusion, preservation–change, and centrality–parity. The duality of inclusion–exclusion surfaced as a design challenge and was specific to participation. This study elaborated the conflict faced by implementers when including different stakeholders in different phases of the change because who got invited to the table and at which phase was critical for the organization.

Earlier work (Lewis 2019; Lewis and Russ 2012) detailed the ways in which input solicitation can be more or less sincere (e.g., use of a resource or symbolic approach) and how that may influence the degree and nature of stakeholders' participation. Through the lens of a stakeholder perspective, we can view these design issues as predictors of stakeholders' willingness to name, claim, and assert stakes. Where stakes are highly relevant, but the circumstances of input solicitation are perceived as risky or insincere, stakeholders may be tentative about asserting their stakes. On the other hand, in contexts where many stakeholders are raising and asserting stakes, and there is an absence of negative repercussions, that may promote additional stakeholders to participate and assertively claim stakes.

Research concerning the likelihood of a stakeholder engaging in asserting stakes during change is very limited to date. In related work, scholars have assessed the processes of raising critique, concern, bad news, and dissent (cf. Garner 2009; Kassing 2009; Turnley and Feldman 1999). In general, when organizational change is perceived as sponsored by high-level decision-makers, lower-level stakeholders are often reluctant to participate in direct critique, especially when trust and authenticity are in question (Lewis 2019). In such circumstances, "input providers tend to hold back what they know, feign support, and conceal negative information" (Lewis 2019: 81). Self-censorship during input solicitation could easily give rise to management's misreading of the stakes in play and/or failure to recognize latent stakes not being vocalized by important stakeholders.

Outcomes Related to Stakeholder Interaction, and Stake Assertion

Resistance (see Zorn and Scott chapter) is perhaps the most consequential outcome discussed in change scholarship. Resistance in general is viewed negatively by organizations. The term itself is drawn from a metaphorical understanding of physical force that moves in the opposite direction and thus tries to maintain the status quo. The idea of overcoming resistance to change was first discussed in the 1940s and since then, resistors often have been stereotyped as dysfunctional, problematic, and sometimes irrational. Resistance can manifest in various ways and may be situated on a continuum with subtle forms (e.g., merely asking questions or seeking support) at one end and more forceful forms (e.g., protesting) at another (Lewis, 2019). Resistance is often perceived by management as a problem that needs to be quelled. The focus of the implementers is then placed on alleviating this dysfunctional state through communication. These communicative responses often include altering or discrediting their views, coercing them into silence, or negotiation of minimal levels of acceptable cooperation (Sahay 2017).

Expression of dissent and negativity towards a change may be a part of resistance to change. Such dissent typically is either peer-focused (i.e., voicing concerns to those close to us but lack the power to change the change) or upward-focused (i.e., targeted to those in the organization who have power). Peer-focused dissent may be more prevalent in places that label input providers as troublemakers or cynics and has negative consequences for them.

Resistance is often characterized in terms of emotional reactions to the idea of changing or as a manifestation of fear of the unknown. This notion of dispositional resistance has been the focus of Shaul Oreg's (2003, 2006) line of research. Oreg defines dispositional resistance as "an individual's tendency to resist or avoid making changes, to devalue change generally, and to find change aversive across diverse contexts and types of change" (Oreg 2003: 680). This conceptualization is rooted in a psychological profile of individuals who have a reluctance to lose control, tend towards rigidity, lack psychological resilience, and have intolerance to adjustment to change.

Although such types of personality characteristics likely account for a portion of change resistance in organizations, there is strong evidence that other concerns, causes, and assessments may be at the root of a larger portion of resistance behavior. Oreg's work has yet to assess the impact of the emotional and cognitive resistance profile to behavioral manifestations that would hinder a change from being fully implemented (such as expression of dissent, sabotage, protest). However, a more concerning outcome of the dispositional approach to resistance is failure to capture an understanding of the range of reasons that individuals and groups may resist change that are unrelated to their personalities. For many (I would argue, most) stakeholders, objections to and active resistance of change is likely rooted in their perspectives about a particular change as disadvantageous to themselves or the larger set of stakeholders with whom they are allied. Some *principled resistors* are highly analytic, evidence-based in their reasoning, and have high regard for principles and loyalties to the organization and/or to stakeholders impacted by change. Resistors acting out of an abundance of caution to avoid harming the stakes that they and others hold are of a different category than those with high dispositional resistance. This difference is quite significant if one's goal is to decrease resistance to a change effort. Appeals to calming fears, reassurance of a manageable period of uncertainty, and supportive communication intended to quell nervousness, would be ineffective to the principled resistor. The principled resistor is acting on his/her stakes in the organization and the perceived threat to those stakes. Appeals to the security or advancement of those stakes, or highlighting new stakes that might be viewed as more desirable, would be a more effective approach to reducing resistance.

Much of the organizational change literature focuses on the focal organization's goal to successfully implement a change with minimal resistance. Rates of "success" in change typically assesses the achievement of complete intended change and the costs associated with reducing or eliminating resistance. Other assessed outcomes concern whether the implemented change achieves the intended consequences of the initiative (e.g., increases in market share, improvement in productivity, or addition of customers/ clients). Often unintended consequences of the change effort are left unexamined. A key stakeholder-related consequence that often arises from change is the creation or destruction of alliances and the creation of rivalries among an organization's stakeholders.

> [A]s we work through stories and concerns that these stories invoke or resolve, we also may discover attractions to some and repulsions from others that ultimately shape our social network in the context of change. In short, we come to see shared fate with some stakeholders and see distance or even antagonistic goals with others. The sensemaking influences our world views of "what is going on" and those worlds sometimes collide, sometimes merge, and sometimes run parallel.
>
> (Lewis 2019: 273–4).

Change processes, especially ones that are highly consequential for resources, relationships, and the direction of organizations, are likely to give rise to disruptions of stakeholders' networks and perceptions of the alignment of stakes among groups. Change provides an opportunity for new stakes to be asserted, and new claims on stakes to be made. As this occurs, groups may discover that there are overlaps in needs, interests, and values. Change may also serve to raise tensions, conflicts, and competition over stakes.

Themes in Research of Stakeholder Approach to Organizational Change

Research that has explored stakeholders and their evolving perspectives and reactions to change has yielded important insights. In this section I will review a set of stakeholder perspective studies of organizational change. I will highlight research (see Table 11.2) that has embraced a focus on stakeholders' beliefs, perceptions, and behaviors as key explanations for important change outcomes and process.

The change scholarship adopting a stakeholder perspective has provided evidence that stakeholders' perspectives and concerns matter during change. As Widner et al. (2017) have demonstrated, understanding even how, why, or when strategic change may emerge requires an understanding of who is in a position to influence the design, selection, and implementation of change initiatives. These authors' study examines how through stakeholders' shifting and shaping sense of what is and is not valued, strategic change initiatives can allow some to gain control of, and alter, practices that the majority of individuals do not associate with highly valued resources. They suggest that those who do not control large amounts of valuable resources may not only lack sufficient influence to initiate and implement change, they may even hesitate to push for change

Table 11.2 Themes in Stakeholder-Related Research of Change

Stakeholder-related Focus	Authors	Date
Stakeholder Values	Widner, Barrett, & Oborn	2017
Framing of Change	Meyer, Cross, & Byrne	2016
	Cornelissen, Holt, & Zundel	2011
	Gallivan	2001
Storytelling and Perception of Change	Boje, Haley, & Saylors	2015
Relationships among Stakeholders	Hendy & Barlow	2012
Changing Networks & Support	Kim	2018
	Barrett & Stephens	2017
	Jacobs & Keegan	2018

by accepting their own subordinate position. They cite the example of Lockett et al. (2014: 1117) who found that a nurse who was tasked with introducing and implementing reforms in the NHS "scaled down her ambition" because she was not willing to challenge doctors who were in control of high-status medical knowledge.

We also see evidence in the research base related to stakeholder perspectives on change that supports the notion that framing of change among stakeholders has importance on outcomes. Meyer et al. (2016) sought to discover what processes occur within an organization to foster support for a new initiative among people with diverse values and perceptions on the initiative. Their study of a large public-school district found that when framing contests occur within an organization, the negotiation of frames requires specifically addressing various values held by stakeholders, and ensuring these values hold equal position in new change initiatives. Rather than focusing on the management/leadership's framing of the change (green-building), these authors turned their attention to the multi-framing attempts of numerous internal and external stakeholders. Meyer and colleagues illustrate through a detailed analysis of the assertion of stakes and framing of propositions how various stakeholders navigated discourse to alter the course of the change. Meyer et al. found:

> We set out to understand what processes within an organization affect the acceptance of and motivate action for a new initiative among stakeholders at different organizational levels and with diverse values. Using a case of green building adoption within a large school district, we found that framing processes were important to initial and continued support for organizational change such that stakeholders could agree that the new initiative was "the right thing to do." (p. 247)

Meyer et al. found that leadership was able to motivate pro-environmental behavior from people with a variety of values—even from staunch anti-environmentalists. The techniques of framing described in their research illustrates the importance of stakeholder interaction in shaping how a change is perceived and how stakes are invoked and created. They conclude, "frames are actively constructed and refined in group processes—in other words, framing is a shared interactive process" (p. 248). In a related vein, Cornelissen et al. (2011) explore the use of analogies and metaphors in the framing and legitimization of change. They make a propositional argument related to the differential utility of metaphors and analogies in the context of additive changes and substitutive changes; the relative use of relational metaphors and analogies as opposed to those that highlight common attributes; and the impact of cultural familiarity and motivational relevance to stakeholders.

Gallivan (2001) provides another example of empirical evidence of the importance of stakeholders' frames during organizational change. His study of a technology change illustrates how different stakeholder groups viewed a technology in different ways and that these differences were consequential in determining behavior towards and assessment of the change. In applying Orlikowski and Gash's (1994) "technology frames" as "the assumptions, expectations, and knowledge [that people] use to understand technology in organizations" (p. 178), he describes a company's efforts in reskilling computer programmers, systems analysts, and other IT professionals. He explores the ways in which stakeholders in different occupational groups, hierarchical levels, and specific job categories understood events, messages, and actions in different ways. Change managers described the vision for reskilling that relied on a partnership among themselves, IT managers, and IT employees. However, the IT managers and IT employees viewed the goals of the change as a narrow focus on updating technical skills and did not recognize the broader change to their level of business knowledge, job roles, and culture. Stakeholders who worked with IT viewed the change as radical and expected dramatic layoffs and new deskilled IT roles. There was a wide variation in perspectives and understandings of change-related messaging. Gallivan concludes:

> Stakeholders' behavior in response to a change initiative is shaped by the frames they hold about the initiative that are, in turn, based upon the context of their job roles and prior experiences. Furthermore, stakeholders' evaluation of the success of an initiative or their assessment of whether progress has been made toward its goals rests upon their distinctive understanding of the initiative's purpose and how they define progress. (p. 261)

Moving towards a fuller consideration of the ways in which stakeholders talk about change, Boje et al. (2015) explore storytelling in the context of stakeholder interaction about change. These authors describe antenarratives—not yet fully-formed narratives, that are pieces of organizational discourse that help to construct identities and interests. Embracing a processural view of storymaking, Boje et al. discuss how some stakeholders engage in retrospective sensemaking (Weick 1995), reviewing how past events will repeat to project future actions while others engage in prospective sensemaking (Boje 2016), betting through antenarrative processes on preferred futures which are not tied to clock time. Among their findings, they argue:

> We presented a plurality of contexts in which BKC [Burger King Corporation] operated that interconnected, embedded, and entangled with narrative ecologies. Grounding and embedding systems in multiple contexts allowed us to see struggles between and beneath grand narratives with living story webs, and the before and cyclical bets of antenarrative relationships. (p. 413)

The authors suggest that antenarratives linked living stories to grand narratives to construct identities and interests in time and space for unique discursive constructions of BKC's change.

Some research has examined stakeholder relationships. Hendy and Barlow (2012) examine "change champions" who are stakeholders who take on a special role of opinion leadership during change. These authors suggest that "[a] major aspect of the champions' role is to influence and facilitate change in others. Champions do this by demonstrating commitment, promoting innovation with passion and persistence, pulling together diverse groups of professionals, team-building, and developing informal networks to support them" (p. 349). Further, they play a role in networking among groups of stakeholders and between implementers and sets of stakeholders. The networking involves communicating messages, motivating others, and enacting typical boundary-spanning roles. Individuals who play this role are serving as "connectors" (Lewis 2019: 111) who (a) spread knowledge and counter-knowledge about change initiatives, (b) bring together diverse points of view on change from diverse stakeholder groups, and (c) broker alliances among stakeholders that may create aligned goals for the change. Oftentimes front-line and middle-level managers have been found to play connecting roles (cf. Coyle-Shapiro 1999; Gallivan 2001; Meyer 2006; Luscher and Lewis 2008).

Handy and Barlow's study found that organizational champions are highly effective in the first phase of adoption, when change is contained within distinct sub-sets of practice. However, moving beyond local contexts, the effectiveness of the champions varied. When champions were required to shift their work organization-wide, and share ideas outside their professional culture, some champions responded with resistance, resulting in a lack of innovation spread. "Some of the champions in our study perceived the involvement of other stakeholders as a threat to their status. This was expressed by a lack of engagement and by resisting input from others, regardless of whether this was beneficial for the wider organization" (p. 353).

In research related to coping with change, Kim (2018) notes that "organizational change—from strategic adaptation to market changes to a large-scale restructuring—may affect the characteristics of communication networks, and in turn, the changing nature of networks may reshape members' perceptions about their communication quality and knowledge-sharing practices" (p. 19). Kim's study of a restructuring in a multinational high-tech organization explores the implications of boundary-spanning and knowledge-sharing behaviors in disrupted networks during change. She argues that when new practices are implemented, a lack of prior history and common experience may impede learning from each other, and reorganization of work leads to lack of awareness about others' work and expertise, particularly in different teams. Kim argues:

> While experiencing organizational or environmental changes that impose potential coordination challenges, forming and maintaining connections across different job functions may heighten complexity and disagreement that subsequently preclude expertise awareness. (p. 21)

Kim concludes that employees who have strong ties will exchange knowledge more successfully than others who maintain far-reaching networks across functions and locations. She further concludes that greater emotional closeness with one's ties can help employees surmount knowledge-sharing obstacles stemming from organizational change. This study underscores the importance of shifting stakeholder relationships during change.

Other research has documented the influence of supportive communication among stakeholders during change. Barrett and Stephens (2017) investigated the role of socially supportive communication in the context of the implementation of electronic health records (EHR) technologies. They found negative relationships between social support and employees' attitudes about the change. They argue that some employees seeking social support may cause them to feel less competent (or be viewed so by co-workers). At times, receivers of support may have been impacted negatively through receipt of the wrong sort of support (e.g., emotional support instead of instrumental support). As stakeholders interact with one another either in ways that promote or critique change, or that seek to facilitate specific activity or behaviors regarding change, their relationships will influence the ways that the changes are perceived and the ultimate form the change takes in practice.

Scholars have often taken an assumption of paramount self-interest during organizational change (Jacobs and Keegan 2018). That is scholars (and practitioners) tend to assume that the primary question driving reactions to change is "what will happen to me?" Jacobs and Keegan argue that sensemaking about change is multidimensional and mostly ambivalent in nature and that in their assessment of organizational change, "recipients care not only about their own personal outcomes, but go beyond self-interested concerns to show a genuine interest in the impact of change on their colleagues and organization" (p. 73). Jacobs and Keegan cite the example of downsizings and the attendant concern that individual stakeholder has not just for themselves but for how colleagues are treated. They argue that "[i]n times of major restructuring, 'survivors' lower their organizational commitment... as a reaction to the perceived injustice towards the 'victims' of downsizing" (p. 74). They further argue that observations of the treatment of other stakeholders, as well as themselves, regarding perceptions of organizational justice, and violation of psychological contracts will impact their assessment of change and the organization as a whole. In their study of change recipients' reactions to twenty-six large-scale planned change projects in a policing context, data show that change recipients drew on observations with three foci (me, colleagues, and organization) to assess change. Most of the change recipients made sense of change based on ethical considerations, namely their observations and experiences of the impact of change—in positive as well as negative ways—on themselves, but to an even greater extent on "colleagues" and on general issues of work, organization, and policing. Their findings point to the importance of stakeholders' awareness of one another's stakes in less than strategic ways, but in ways that reflect morality and ethics.

Opportunities for Future Scholarship

It is ironic that most organizational change scholarship lacks a focus on stakeholders' evolving perspectives, attitudes, and behaviors through a process of change. Inherent in many of the single-point-in-time data collection strategies is an assumption that stakes and stakeholders are fixed, and that the continuous flow of interaction and influence among stakeholders is irrelevant to outcomes. Although some case studies of changes have adopted an over-time analysis of a process of change, they rarely highlight patterns and trends of changing stakes, stakeholder alliances/coalitions/relationship realignment, and shifting beliefs about a change. There is an implicit presumption that stakeholders are changing and that some start out unfavorable to the change and end up favorable (or the reverse), but the details of mapping their journey from one to the other point of view is most often absent.

The processes of change, or the sequence of events in which organizational characteristics change and develop over time and the factors that influence these processes are underdeveloped in the stakeholder approach to organizational change. Partly owing to the earlier mentioned tendencies in the stakeholder literature in general (assuming stakeholders and stakes are known and fixed; assuming a perspective of a focal organization in analysis of stakeholders/processes), the research has thus far provided scant insight to the ways in which stakeholders' stakes, relationships, and perceptions evolve throughout a change process. The contributions of the shaping of stakeholder networks, interaction flows, and rise and fall of the relevance of stakes is also left largely uncharted.

A process-oriented perspective on stakeholder change will need to adopt models of change that not only consider change to be a fluid process, but that also treat stakeholders' relationships, perspectives, and actions as dynamic. In order to move in this direction, it is important to frame our stakeholder-related change questions in more process terms such as:

- What rhetorical and relationship shifts within stakeholders' networks signal that change is becoming more or less contentious?

Change researchers ought to investigate early indicators that groups of stakeholders are forming antagonistic stances towards one another or when stakes in relation to the change are becoming staunchly oppositional. Examination of turning points in the evolution of key stakeholder groups' networks, transformation of groups' rhetoric from collaborative stances to contentious stances, and increases in oppositional language would provide insight into how groups of stakeholders move "sides" throughout a change. As we understand how coalitions form and dissolve and how that maps onto efforts to promote, resist, or accept change, we will be better positioned to explain how shifting loyalties forecast the path of a change.

- As a change moves from unknown to more fixed understandings, what patterns in statements of knowledge about the change will mark a convergence of perspectives and beliefs about the change?

Researchers interested in communication and change can provide analyses of ongoing sensemaking that reveals patterns of divergence and convergence. As meanings about what the change "is" and what it means are formed, shaken, reformed, and eventually solidified by various stakeholder groups, there may come a time when overall collective sense of the change becomes mostly fixed. Before that point, those who seek to reframe the change and influence understandings/perceptions of it have an opening. Once that window closes, it will be far more difficult to alter what stakeholders regard the change to "be." It is possible that changes are initially simply understood but are later questioned and shifted. So, patterns of initial closed understandings followed by divergent understandings and a return to a new closed and shared understanding may also occur. Depending on the approach of change implementers and organizational leaders it may be desirable for stakeholders to explore different applications and variations of a change (e.g., multiple uses of a new technology) and thus a flexible and open definition of the change at the outset of the implementation process may be useful. However, in other cases where a narrow and shared understanding of a change is the goal, ambiguity and debate surrounding the change may lead to misapplication, unnecessary cycles of negotiation, and even resistance.

- Do cycles of re-valuing stakes among key stakeholder groups indicate that a change is under threat or that the process is motivating real change among stakeholders?

As stakeholders react to the introduction of major change, they are often also estimating the degree to which the change will threaten or promote their closely held values. It is possible that some stakeholder groups will question the relative importance of their long-held values in these situations. For example, some employees might ask whether job security is more important than wages. Some customers might ask whether product prices are more important than level of service. Major change initiatives often force a collision of key values for stakeholders. It is possible that re-examination of key values is a sign that the organizational change is being fully realized as it motivates individual change. However, in some cases, re-examination of values during change may also serve as a clarifying exercise that leads to the rejection of a change that forces an unpleasant choice.

- Do patterns of emergence of new groups of stakeholders and/or amalgamation or dissolution of stakeholder groups indicate that strategies for implementing change will need revision?

The introduction of a major change initiative may create new stakeholder groups or the creation of perceptions that sets of stakeholders have new reasons to be in alliance. It is also possible that change programs essentially dissolve groups of stakeholders that existed prior to the change. Sets of customers or clients no longer served by an organization may simply lose interest in the organization and its activities. Stakeholders who had little relationship or awareness of each other may gradually discover common bonds through a change process. As these alterations in the stakeholder network surrounding an organization evolves, they will likely call upon implementers to rethink implementation strategies.

- What sort of stakeholder engagement strategies are best suited to different formations of stakeholder networks when a change is contentious and perspectives on the change are fluid and rapidly changing? Which are best suited to contexts of relative stability in networks and rigidity of perspectives on the change?

As we consider change as occurring in a fluid context of changing stakeholder relationships, interactions, influence, and intersecting values and stakes, it is clear that any given change may occur in hyper-active change contexts and others in relative calm and slow-changing contexts. Engaging stakeholders in these different types of contexts will, most likely, require different tactics and strategies. For example, it is likely that in highly fluid networks it will be important to actively monitor multiple sources and channels. However, in more stable networks, it may be most important to have quick responses to concerns that are raised so that they don't foment.

- What are patterns of stakeholder shifting beliefs about change that predict various outcomes (e.g., resistance, acceptance, cooperation)?

Scholars who are focused on patterns of shifting beliefs might uncover relationships between certain patterns and specific general change outcomes. For example, are patterns of initial resistance, followed by ambivalence, finishing with acceptance, a typical pattern associated with successful change outcomes? Are organizations that encounter initial resistance more likely to succeed in achieving intended goals of change than those who encounter initial acceptance (and thus, do not go through a period of testing the change idea)?

Such questions turn our attention to the ways in which a change process is altered by and alters the stakeholder network, and the changing context of stakeholders' views and experiences of change. A full dynamic model of stakeholder change would account for implications of:

- The order in which things happen and patterns of beliefs and perceptions as they evolve
- The patterns of stakeholder relationship creation and dissolution
- The speed with which stakeholders alter views, perceptions, and beliefs

- The number of cycles that stakeholders go through on the way to stable perspectives
- The dual influence of changing stakeholders and a changing organization

It is certainly beyond the scope of this chapter to provide such a dynamic model here. However, this review and the concluding recommendations for taking a process-oriented view highlight some key advantages of the approach. Such a reorientation will permit theorists and researchers to reject assumptions that stakes and stakeholders are fixed, and that the continuous flow of interaction and influence among stakeholders is irrelevant to outcomes. It will encourage a focus on highlighting patterns and trends of changing stakes, stakeholder relationship realignment, and shifting beliefs about a change. This, in turn, allows scholars to map the journey that stakeholders take from initial perspectives about a change to later ones. As scholars begin to track these shifts of relationships over time, and the influences regarding change perspectives and stakes, we will gain insight into stakeholder networks, interaction flows, and the rise and fall of the relevance of stakes. A process-oriented perspective on stakeholder change will afford understanding and explanation into the dynamics of change throughout a process of changing.

References

Andriof, J., and Waddock, S. (2002), 'Unfolding Stakeholder Engagement', in J. Andriof, S. Waddock, B. Husted, and Sutherland Rahmann, eds., *Unfolding Stakeholder Thinking: Theory Responsibility and Engagement* (Sheffield, UK: Greenleaf), 19–42.

Applequist, J., Miller-Day, M., Cronholm, P. F., Gabbay, R. A., and Bowen, D. S. (2016), 'In Principle We Have Agreement, but In Practice it is a bit More Difficult: Obtaining Organizational Buy-In to Patient-Centered Medical Home Transformation', *Qualitative Health Research*, 27/6, 909–22. doi: 10.1177/1049732316680601

Armenakis, A. A., Harris, S. G., and Mossholder, K. W. (1993), 'Creating Readiness for Organizational Change', *Human Relations*, 46/6, 681–703. doi: 10.1177/001872679304600601

Barge, J., Lee, M., Maddux, K., Nabring, R., and Townsend, B. (2008), Managing Dualities in Planned Change Initiatives', *Journal of Applied Communication Research*, 36, 364–90.

Barrett, A. K., and Stephens, K. K. (2017), The Pivotal Role of Change Appropriation in the Implementation of Health Care Technology', *Management Communication Quarterly*, 31/2, 163–93.

Bird, S. (2007), 'Sensemaking and Identity: The Interconnection of Storytelling and Networking in a Women's Group of a Large Corporation', *Journal of Business Communication*, 44/4, 311–39.

Boje, D. M. (1991), 'The Storytelling Organization: A Study of Story Performance in an Office-Supply Firm', *Administrative Science Quarterly*, 36/1, 106–26.

Boje, D. M., Haley, U., and Saylors, R. (2016), 'Antenarratives of Organizational Change: The Microstoria of Burger King's Storytelling in Space, Time, and Strategic Context. *Human Relations*, 69/2, 391–418.

Bordia, P., Hobman, E., Jones, E., Gallois, C., and Callan, V. (2004), 'Uncertainty during Organizational Change: Types, Consequences, and Management Strategies', *Journal of Business and Psychology*, 18/4, 507–32. doi: 10.1023/B:JOBU.000.

Burke, W. W. (2021), 'Historical Currents in Scholarship of Organization Change', in M. S. Poole and A. H. Van de Ven, eds., *The Oxford Handbook of Organizational Change and Innovation* (2nd ed.) (Oxford: Oxford University Press,

Cornelissen, J. P., Hold, R., and Zundel, M. (2011), 'The Role of Analogy and Metaphor in the Framing and Legitimization of Strategic Change', *Organization Studies* 32/120, 1701–16.

Coyle-Shapiro, J. A. M. (1999), 'Employee Participation and Assessment of an Organizational Change Intervention: A Three-Wave Study of Total Quality Management', *Journal of Applied Behavioral Science*, 35/4, 439–56.

DeBussy, N. M. (2019), 'Stakeholder'. Encyclopedia entry in W. Johanssen and B. Heath (Eds.), *International Encyclopedia of Strategic Communication* (Chichester, UK: Wiley-Blackwell), 1419–32.

Dewulf, A., Gray, B., Putnam, L. L., Lewicki, R., Aarts, N., Bouwen, R., and Van Woerkum, C. (2009), 'Disentangling Approaches to Framing in Conflict and Negotiation Research: A Meta-Paradigmatic Perspective', *Human Relations*, 62, 155–93.

Fairhurst, G. T. (2010), *The Power of Framing: Creating the Language of Leadership* (Vol. 290) (New York: John Wiley and Sons).

Frandsen, F. (2019), 'Stakeholder management', Encyclopedia entry in W. Johanssen and B. Heath (Eds.), *International Encyclopedia of Strategic Communication* (Chichester, UK: Wiley-Blackwell), 1432–44.

Freeman, R. E. (1984), *Strategic Management: A Stakeholder Approach* (Boston, MA: Pitman).

Freeman, R. E., Harrison, J. S., Wicks, A. C., Parmar, B. I., and DeColle, S. (2010), *Stakeholder Theory: The State of the Art* (Cambridge, UK: Cambridge University Press).

Gallivan, M. J. (2001), 'Meaning to Change: How Diverse Stakeholders Interpret Organizational Communication about Change Initiatives', *IEE Transactions on Professional Communications*, 44/4, 243–66.

Garner, J. T. (2009), 'Strategic Dissent: Expressions of Organizational Dissent Motivated by Influence Goals', *International Journal of Strategic Communication*, 3/1, 34–51.

Hargie, O., and Tourish, D. (2000), 'Charting Communication Performance in a Healthcare Organization', in O. Hargie, and D. Tourish, eds., *Handbook of Communication Audits for Organizations* (London: Routledge), 195–209.

Hendry, J. R. (2005), 'Stakeholder Influence Strategies: An Empirical Exploration', *Journal of Business Ethics*, 61, 79–99.

Hendy, J.,and Barlow, J. (2012). The role of the organizational champion in achieving health system change. *Social Science & Medicine*, 74, 348–55.

Jacobs, G., and Keegan, A. (2018), 'Ethical Considerations and Change Recipients' Reactions: It's Not All About Me', *Journal of Business Ethics*, 152, 73–90.

Johansson, K., and Heide, M. (2008), 'Speaking of Change: Three Communication Approaches in Studies of Organizational Change', *Corporate Communications: An International Journal*, 13/3, 288–305.

Kassing, J. W. (2009), '"In Case You Didn't Hear Me the First Time": An Examination of Repetitious Upward Dissent', *Management Communication Quarterly*, 22/3, 416–36.

Kim, H. (2018) 'Differential Impacts of Functional, Geographical, and Hierarchical Diversity on Knowledge Sharing in the Midst of Organizational Change', *Management Communication Quarterly*, 32/1, 5–30.

Koschmann, M. A., and Kopczynski, J. (2017), 'Stakeholder Communication', Encyclopedia entry in C. R. Scott and L. Lewis, eds., *International Encyclopedia of Organizational Communication* (Chichester, UK: Wiley-Blackwell), 2237–49.

Kramer, M., Dougherty, D. S., and Pierce, T. A. (2004), 'Managing Uncertainty during a Corporate Acquisition: A Longitudinal Study of Communication during an Airline Acquisition' *Human Communication Research*, 30/1, 71–101.

Larkin, T. J. and Larkin, S. (1994), *Communicating Change: How to Win Support for New Business Directions* (New York: McGraw-Hill).

Leonardi, P. M. (2009), 'Why Do People Reject New Technologies and Stymie Organizational Changes of Which They Are in Favor? Exploring Misalignments between Social Interactions and Materiality', *Human Communication Research*, 35, 407–41.

Lewis, L. (2011), *Organizational Change: Creating Change through Strategic Communication* (Chichester, UK, Wiley-Blackwell).

Lewis, L. (2019), *Organizational Change: Creating Change through Strategic Communication* (2nd ed.) (Chichester: Wiley-Blackwell).

Lewis, L. K., and Russ, T. L. (2012), 'Soliciting and Using Input during Organizational Change Initiatives: What are Practitioners Doing?' *Management Communication Quarterly*, 26, 267–94.

Luscher, L. S., and Lewis, M. W. (2008), 'Organizational Change and Managerial Sensemaking Working through Paradox', *Academy of Management Journal* 51, 221–40.

Meyer, C. (2006), 'Destructive Dynamics of Middle Management Intervention in Postmerger Processes', *Journal of Applied Behavioral Science*, 42/4, 397–419.

Meyer, M. A., Cross, J. E., and Byrne, Z. S. (2016), 'Frame Decoupling for Organizational Change: Building Support across Divergent Stakeholders', *Organization Environment*, 29/2, 231–51.

Mitchell, R., Agle, B., and Wood, D. (1997), 'Toward a Theory of Stakeholder Identification and Salience: Defining the Principle of Who and What Really Counts', *Academy of Management Review*, 22, 853–86.

Orlikowski, W. J., and D. C. Gash (1994), 'Technological Frames: Making Sense of Information Technology in Organizations', *ACM Trans. Inform. Syst.*, 12/2, 174–96.

Oreg, S. (2003), 'Resistance to Change: Developing an Individual Differences Measure. *Journal of Applied Psychology*, 88/4, 680–93.

Oreg, S. (2006), 'Personality, Context, and Resistance to Organizational Change', *European Journal of Work and Organizational Psychology*, 15, 73–101.

Post, J. E., Preston, L. E., and Sachs, S. (2002), 'Managing the Extended Enterprise: The New Stakeholder View', *California Management Review*, 45/1, 6–28.

Prichard, C. and Creed, D. (2021), 'Agency in *Social Movements as Sources of Change*, in M. S. Poole and A. H. Van de Ven, eds., *The Oxford Handbook of Organizational Change and Innovation* (2nd edn) (Oxford: Oxford University Press),

Sahay, S. (2017), 'Communicative Designs for Input Solicitation during Organizational Change: Implications for Providers' Communicative Perceptions and Decisions', Doctoral thesis, Rutgers University.

Turnley, W. H., and Feldman, D. C. (1999), 'The Impact of Psychological Contract Violations on Exit, Voice, Loyalty, and Neglect', *Human Relations*, 52/7, 895–922.

Weick KE (1995), *Sensemaking in Organizations* (Thousand Oaks, CA: SAGE).

Whittle, A., Suhomlinova, O., and Mueller, F. (2010), 'Funnel of Interests: The Discursive Translation of Organizational Change', *Journal of Applied Behavioral Science*, 46/1, 16–37. doi: 10.1177/0021886309357538.

Wiedner, R., Barrett, M., and Oborn, E. (2017), 'The Emergence of Change in Unexpected Places: Resourcing across Organizational Practices in Strategic Change', *Academy of Management Journal*, 60/3, 823–54.

Zorn, T. E., and Scott, J. (2021), 'Must We Change? The Dark Side of Change and Change Resistance', in M. S. Poole and A. H. Van de Ven, eds., *The Oxford Handbook of Organizational Change and Innovation* (2nd edn) (Oxford: Oxford University Press).

CHAPTER 12

CRITICAL APPROACHES AND PERSPECTIVES ON ORGANIZATIONAL CHANGE

ROSIE OSWICK, CLIFF OSWICK, AND DAVID GRANT

INTRODUCTION

IT has been long understood that organizations can be thought of as sites of conflict and contestation (Benson 1977; Edwards 1979; Steffy and Grimes 1986). The earliest perspectives on competing workplace interests and the pluralistic nature of organizations were developed within the field of industrial relations (Fox 1966, 1974). Here conflict and contestation played out in a largely antagonistic and material way (i.e., via trade union disputes and industrial action) (Hyman 1972). Within the field of organizational change, conflicting interests and contrasting perspectives typically manifest themselves in less overtly confrontational ways via discursive struggles and the subtle exercise of power and politics (Hardy 1995, 1996; Thomas and Hardy 2011; Thomas et al. 2011). For us, critical approaches to change are generally consistent with what has been described by Van de Ven and Poole (1995) as a "dialectical motor" of change where: "At least two entities exist (each with its own discrete identity) that oppose or contradict one other" (p. 525).

In this chapter, we explore the variety of ways in which the relationship between opposing and/or contradictory entities unfolds and plays out with regard to change in organizations. In doing so, we critically engage with organizational change and explore how it is constituted through "dialectic processes" (Langley and Sloan 2012). This is undertaken in two main ways. First, from a micro-phenomenological perspective we consider how insights derived from critical theory and other critical traditions have influenced the development of change strategies, interventions, and techniques. Second, at a more macro-level, we explore the extent to which particular schools of thought with regard to organizational change and organization development (OD) have embraced and/or resisted, the inevitable and unavoidable critical challenges and opportunities presented by opposing agents, competing interests, conflicting entities, and contrasting meanings in organizations.

There are three main parts to this chapter. In the next section we identify different critical traditions (i.e., critical theory, critical thinking, critical management studies, and critical realism), and discuss how they relate to how we see organizations and engage in processes of planned organizational change. We then consider how different schools of thought around change and OD have engaged with a critical approach and responded to dialectical conditions. Finally, we consider the scope for, and possible directions of, critical change scholarship and practice in the future.

Types of Critical Approach and Organizational Change

Arguably, the most prominent and well known of critical approaches is the notion of "critical theory" developed by the Frankfurt School (see, for example: Adorno 1973; Habermas 1971, 1984, 1987; Horkheimer 1937; Horkheimer and Adorno 1947a, Marcuse 1964). The popularity of critical theory is demonstrated by its inclusion as a chapter in a variety of edited collections and handbooks within the field of organization studies (see, for example: Alvesson and Deetz 1996; Mumby 2001, 2004; Scherer 2009).

Critical theory is primarily concerned with analyzing social conditions and social relations (Held 1980; Scherer 2009). It is dialectical in nature insofar as it considers the unequal distribution of power and resources between entities (Horkheimer and Adorno 1947a). This inequality is attributed to the positivist methods associated with the process of enlightenment (Kant 1784) where "the sciences have developed knowledge that serves the interests of powerful elites rather than helping people to emancipate themselves from the social conditions of dependency and suppression" (Scherer 2009: 35). Ideology and politics are central components in maintaining this imbalance of power. Citizens are socialized to see social inequality as normal, and as unreflexive, compliant members of society they are incapable of seeing alternatives (Marcuse 1964). The resultant hegemonic relationship (Gramsci 1971) between the privileged and the marginalized is perpetuated through the discourse and political processes that systematically distort communication and "create reality through ideological meaning systems" (Mumby 2001: 594).

Jurgen Habermas, as a central figure within the Frankfurt School, draws attention to the importance of communicative conditions and the need to discursively interrogate the assertions and claims made by institutions (Habermas 1984, 1987, 1990a, 1990b, 1990 c). In particular, Habermas argues that the "lifeworld" (i.e., an informed social world based on the skills and knowledge of its members) works on the basis of communicative reason while "social systems" are governed by "instrumental rationality" (i.e., on the logical calculation of means and ends). He asserts that the lifeworld becomes colonized as communicative reason is displaced by instrumental rationality (Habermas 1984, 1987). In order to address these problems, Habermas advocates a democratic process of open and free debate where the strength of the arguments made is the determinant of outcomes (Habermas 1996, 1998, 2001).

Although critical theory has been applied to the study of organizations (Steffy and Grimes 1986) and organizational change (Carr 2000a, 2000b; Grubbs 2000; Moss 2017), the work of the Frankfurt School has been primarily concerned with addressing problems at the societal level. The scope for utilizing critical theory in relation to organizational change will be explored later in this chapter. For now, we want to consider other forms of critical approach.

In terms of the dialectical motor (Van de Ven and Poole 1995), critical theory focuses on two distinctly separate opposing physical entities. More specifically, the entities are portrayed as two groups of different stakeholders: the powerful elite versus the oppressed. An alternative way of thinking about opposing or contradictory entities is as a tension between "perspectives" (e.g., ideas) rather than "entities" (e.g., people). When viewed in this way the resultant contrasting perspectives can be seen as an intrapersonal tension rather than an interpersonal one. This is the essence of "critical thinking" as an alternative form of critical approach. Critical thinking, which has emerged from the fields of psychology and education, requires actively thinking beyond the obvious or taken-for-granted way of conceptualizing a phenomenon or evaluating possible courses of action (Dewey 1910; Paul 1985; Paul and Elder 2001).

Whether or not the juxtaposing of two competing perceptions of a phenomena (i.e., a conventional obvious framing versus a radical or controversial alternative) is truly dialectical is perhaps contentious. We would assert, as we hope to demonstrate later in this chapter, that inner struggles between contrasting positions are highly pertinent in taking a critical approach to organizational change. Not least because struggles and tensions within individuals are often inextricably linked to how change resistance, change advocacy, and change ambivalence coalesce around discernible groups of stakeholders in organizational settings.

There are two discernibly different forms of critical thinking. First, there is "critical analysis" which is the active, real-time consideration of an alternative course of action (Facione 2011; Fisher 2001; Glaser 1941). The second variant is "critical reflection" which involves the retrospective consideration of an event or events (Dye 2011; Hullfish and Smith 1961). Probably the most widely used critical reflection model is Gibbs' (1988) six-stage reflexive cycle, involving: Step 1—description (what happened?); Step 2—feelings (what were you thinking or feeling?); Step 3—evaluation (what was good/bad about the situation?); Step 4—analysis (what sense can you make of the situation?)' Step 5—conclusion (what else could you have done?); Step 6—action plan (if it arose again, what would you do?); and then back to step 1. Within this model the two underlying oppositional entities are effectively "what you actually did" and "what you would do differently".

The implications of the processes of critical analysis and critical reflection in relation to organizational change will be discussed later in the chapter.

Beyond critical theory and critical thinking, a further critical approach which potentially has the most direct relevance to organizations and organizational change is the field of "critical management studies" (CMS) (Alvesson and Deetz 2000; Alvesson and Willmott 1996; Willmott 1997, 2008). CMS draws heavily on critical theory. However, unlike, critical theory which is concerned with issues at a societal level, CMS is typically concerned with issues at an organizational level. That said, as a field of inquiry, CMS does nevertheless consider the impact of society and social factors in terms of their specific effect upon management practices in the workplace. The overriding concern of CMS is interrogating the management practices and institutional arrangements that lead to the unequal distribution of power and resources in organizations. CMS challenges the attendant forms of domination and subordination that are driven by a set of wider social conditions, including patriarchy, neo-imperialism, and capitalism (Alvesson et al. 2009).

CMS advocates the de-naturalization of taken-for-granted social conditions within the workplace by questioning the extent to which they are inevitable and unavoidable (Grey and Willmott 2005). The performative nature of organizations is also challenged by CMS scholars who question the inherent instrumentality underpinning work arrangements and the overriding emphasis on profit maximization (Fournier and Grey 2000). In addition to being critical of the prevailing management practices, CMS also promotes ways of actually addressing what are seen as inherent problems in the workplace. More specifically, CMS calls for meaningful processes of reflexivity where conventional wisdom and dominant logics are outed and overturned (Thompson 2004). A case is also made within the CMS discourse for disruptive actions and subversive intervention against the dominant management practices and organizing processes (Spicer et al. 2009). Given the organizationally specific focus of CMS, this body of work has clear implications for organizational change activity, and these will be discussed later in the chapter.

The final area of critical engagement that warrants consideration is the "critical realist" perspective. This approach, developed by Bhaskar (1978, 1986) and extended by Sayer (2000), is critical of social constructivist explanations of reality; critical realism instead contends that what appear to be routine events are shaped by deep underlying structures and relations rather than simply discursive interactions (Reed 2009). Hence, the emphasis of the critical realism perspective is primarily on enduring structures and material conditions. In particular, there is a focus on how tangible outcomes can be attributed to the dynamic interplay between "conditions" (as generative mechanisms) and "contexts" (as structural and material inheritances) (Reed 2003; Sayer 2000). Although, not as popular or pervasive as the other three domains of critical inquiry, critical realism still has, as we will demonstrate later, implications for processes of organizational change.

The four critical approaches discussed above are summarized in Table 12.1. This provides a point of comparison across the different perspectives and outlines their key features. Having discussed the characteristics of the prevailing approaches, we now turn our attention to considering how they relate to organizational change.

Table 12.1 Characteristics of the Prevailing Critical Approaches

Critical Approach	Critical Emphasis	Definition(s)	Origins and Focus (Main Proponents)	Key Components of the Approach
Critical Theory	Ideological and communicative critique	"CT is a socio-philosophical school of thought which is part of the tradition of the Enlightenment. CT's basic concern is to analyse social conditions, to criticize the unjustified use of power, and to change established social traditions and institutions so that human beings are freed from dependency, subordination, and suppression" (Scherer, 2009).	**Frankfurt School**—*focus on "society"* (Adorno, 1973; Habermas, 1971, 1984, 1987; Horkheimer, 1937; Horkheimer and Adorno, 1947a, 1947b; Marcuse, 1964, 1970)	**Critiques of enlightenment**—positivist methods of the enlightenment mean that scientific knowledge has developed to serve the powerful elite through suppression and that the resultant inequality appears as natural and unavoidable. **One-dimensionality and consumerism**—through education and informal social control individuals in advanced capitalism are unable to envision their own emancipation and instead are unreflective and obedient consumers unable to imagine alternatives. **Critique of technocracy**—challenge to the scientific focus on efficiency and technical research because emancipation as an interest is largely ignored. **Communicative action**—propagates the notion that social rules and institutions are created and changed through communication. However, communicative reason tends to be displaced by instrumental rationality (via the colonization of the lifeworld). Hence, analysing language use is crucial to enabling emancipation and democracy.

Continued

Table 12.1 Continued

Critical Approach	Critical Emphasis	Definition(s)	Origins and Focus (Main Proponents)	Key Components of the Approach
Critical Thinking	Cognitive critique	"Critical thinking is the intellectually disciplined process of actively and skillfully conceptualizing, applying, analyzing, synthesizing, and/or evaluating information gathered from, or generated by, observation, experience, reflection, reasoning, or communication, as a guide to belief and action" (Scriven and Paul, 1987).	**Psychology/Education—***focus on the "individual"* (Dewey, 1910; Facione, 2011; Fisher, 2001; Glaser, 1941; Hullfish and Smith, 1961; Paul, 1985; Paul and Elder, 2001; Scriven and Paul, 1987).	**Critical analysis—**the real-time exploration of a variety of different approaches, options, and/or courses of actions. This involves actively and meaningfully considering the repertoire of available alternatives (including their respective merits and limitations). **Critical reflection—**the retrospective consideration of experiences/actions in terms of both the process and the outcomes. The focus is upon what can be gleaned from the event or issue by exploring: what happened; how and why it happened; what could have been done differently; what has been learned; and, what would you do differently in future circumstances.
Critical Management Studies	Institutional and organizational critique	CMS is concerned with "the study of, and sometimes against, management rather than with the development of techniques or legitimations for management. Critical of established social practices and institutional arrangements, CMS challenges prevailing relations of domination—patriarchal, neo-imperialist as well as capitalist—and anticipates the development of alternatives to them" (Alvesson, Bridgman and Willmott, 2009).	**Management scholarship—***focus on "organizations"* (Alvesson and Deetz, 2000; Alvesson and Willmott, 1992, 1996; Benson, 1977; Deetz, 1992, 1996; Fournier and Grey; 2000; Knights and Willmott, 1989)	**De-naturalization—**given that "naturalization" is the process which leads social conditions to appear inevitable and unchangeable, de-naturalization is the critical examination of these context-dependent and ideologically driven conditions. **Anti-performativity—**a specialized form of de-naturalization, concerning the taken-for-granted instrumentality of social relations. It challenges the adoption of a means-ends approach where the end is predetermined, "natural," and/or orientated towards status-quo maintenance.

Critical Approach	Critical Emphasis	Definition(s)	Origins and Focus (Main Proponents)	Key Components of the Approach
				Critical performativity—an extension of anti-performativity that advocates disruptive action and subversive intervention into management discourses and management practices. **Reflexivity—**recognizes that conventional knowledge is bound by the assumptions and routines of mainstream thinking. It problematizes the production of knowledge and questions how "facts" are produced.
Critical Realism	Critique of stratification and material conditions	CR is based "on a 'depth ontology' that presupposes the existence and causal powers or potentialities of underlying structures and relations that shape surface level events and outcomes" (Reed, 2009).	**Philosophy/Political Economy—** *focus on "structures and agency"'* (Bhaskar, 1975, 1986; Sayer, 2000)	**Retroductive methodology—**a form of analysis based on theoretical abstraction and modeling that seeks to explain tangible outcomes by considering how they emerge over time—via the interplay between "conditions" (generative mechanisms) and "contexts" (structural and material inheritances)—and, as such, how they become the entities that they are.

Critical Thinking and Change

The discussion of critical thinking within Table 12.1 draws a distinction between critical analysis and critical reflection. The difference between the two in relation to the actions of professionals, including change agents, is captured by Donald Schön (1983) in his seminal book, *The Reflective Practitioner*. Schön distinguishes between "reflection-in-action" (i.e., critical analysis *as* a real-time process) and "reflection-on-action" (i.e., critical reflection *as* a post-hoc process). At a surface level, it could be argued that a number of established OD techniques—such as "survey research and feedback" (Nadler 1977) and "action research" (Whyte and Hamilton 1964)—promote both real-time and post-hoc forms of reflection. However, we contend that the purpose of these techniques is to better apprehend and act upon a single reality (i.e., to get to "the truth" or "validate" a preferred pathway of change activity) rather than consider an alternative reality. In this regard, these change approaches are inherently positivistic rather than dialectic in nature.

For us, critical action and critical reflection, within the field of organizational change, requires the change practitioner to actively question himself or herself in terms of taken-for-granted assumptions and to develop alternative ways of seeing the problem and potential solutions. This is largely cognitive in nature, and involves deliberately reframing the issue and thinking outside-of-the-box. It requires a process akin to what has been described as "making the familiar strange" (Foucault 1977). We contend that this still constitutes a dialectical process, albeit an internal one. In effect, the change agent has personal responsibility for juxtaposing two opposing entities. In Van de Ven and Poole's (1995) terms, the individual engages in an active process of challenging the dominant or conventional view (i.e., thesis A) by developing an opposing antithesis (i.e., Not-A), with the internal conflict producing a synthesis (i.e., which is Not Not-A), or possibly following a process of due critical consideration a commitment to one of the two opposing views (i.e., still pursuing thesis A or switching to antithesis Not-A).

At present, much of the work within the field of organizational change is either geared to a positivistic drive to a single solution or relies on the assumption that opposing/contradictory perspectives are located "between stakeholders" rather than "within a stakeholder." This dominant logic is evident if one looks at the mainstream textbooks in the field (see, for example, mainstream textbooks: Brown 2010; Cheung-Judge and Holbeche 2011: Cummings and Worley 2005; French and Bell 1998).

Although there is a distinct absence of protocols and techniques for meaningfully embracing critical thinking within organizational change, there are some examples of good practice from the fields of education (Bolton 2010; Brookfield 2011) and professional practice (Cunliffe 2004). In particular, Cunliffe's (2004) work on becoming a "critically reflexive practitioner" offers grounded and very practical advice involving a process of journaling and mapping "to help situate reflective and reflexive practice" (p. 407).

We would posit that critical thinking is also inextricably linked to other forms of critical approach. For instance, Bolton (2010) draws attention to a connection between "critical thinking" and insights from "critical theory" and "critical realism" when she asserts that the individual engaging in critical reflection should think about "how to counteract seemingly *given* social, cultural and political structures" (2010: 4). This is, in effect, a call to engage in "critical action" rather than just "critical thinking." Hence, critical thinking can be seen as operating in a precursory or catalysing manner within change initiatives insofar as it provides a fruitful way into: (1) interrogating and addressing the systemic forms of domination identified within CT; (2) facilitating the emancipatory intent of CMS: and, (3) revealing the underlying structures and relations highlighted by CR. We will return to this theme when we consider different groupings of change intervention according to the degree of engagement with critical approaches.

Critical Theory And Change

As indicated in Table 12.1, critical theory is concerned with the challenges facing society rather than those facing organizations. The implications of this for organizations and organizational change can be seen as being either literal or metaphorical in nature. Taken metaphorically, critical theory can be used to explore how social relationships and social arrangements are analogous to work relationships and organizational arrangements (i.e., the organization *is like* a society). This enables the development of new and novel insights based on figurative similarities.

At a literal level, CT insights can be explored in terms of how societal inequalities play out within the workplace (i.e., the organization as a site of social activity and organizational change is treated as a particular example of social change). Many of the contributions in CMS have borrowed from critical theory in a figurative way (e.g., power elites in society as analogous to top management in organizations and subordinated groups in society as equivalent to workers in organizations). In this section we will mainly concentrate on the explicit and literal application of critical theory to organizational change, and the metaphorical process of borrowing from CT to inform CMS will be addressed in the subsequent section.

The extant literature which applies a critical theory perspective to organizational change is very limited. Some of the work that claims to be about "critical theory" is actually concerned with "theories that are critical" and, as such, are really examples of "critical thinking" rather than CT (Jansson 2013). For instance, Abel and Sementelli (2005) examine what they refer to as "evolutionary critical theory" in relation to organizations, without any reference to the work of any authors associated with the Frankfurt School.

Beyond this, there are several studies that meaningfully engage with actual critical theory and organizational change. One of the earliest contributions, by Carr (2000a), provides a call to action to start applying critical theory to the study of organizational change. In particular, he asserts that the dialectic logic championed by the Frankfurt School has strong contemporary relevance for change scholarship and offers a commentary on "how dialectics transcends binary oppositional thinking" (p. 208). In a further paper, Carr (2000b) makes a case for utilizing critical theory to engage with the psychodynamics of organizational change. He claims that by applying a dialectical orientation to their work change agents, through a process of individual and collective catharsis, we can discover and reflect upon the "social amnesia" (p.289) in the dominant institutional and social patterns within the organization.

In his work on cultural imperialism, Grubb (2000) posits that "theories of organization tend to discuss the management of change across networks in a grammar of instrumental reason, thereby offering legitimacy to the imperialism that emerges when groups come together in a shared-change experience" (p. 221). Having drawn attention to "instrumental reason," Grubb further enlists the work of Jurgen Habermas (1984, 1987) to identify the need to initiate change via dialogue to facilitate cultural emancipation. A further contribution to the application of critical theory to organizational change is provided by Moss (2017). She advocates a dialectic approach which involves "critical story sharing" to create conditions for "micro-emancipation" and to produce "tempered radicals" (Moss 2017: 295).

Beyond the limited body of work that directly connects critical theory and organizational change, there are a number of contributions that implicitly utilize the ideas developed by the Frankfurt School. This is most apparent in the work that critically engages with the exercise of power (Bradshaw 1998; Boonstra and Bennebrook Gravenhurst 1998; Hardy 1996), political behavior (Buchanan and Badham 1999; Feldman 1990; McClellan 2011), and forms of resistance (Thomas and Hardy 2011; Thomas et al. 2011). Much of this work is aimed at revealing the asymmetrical relations between stakeholders and the inherent dialectic problems associated with contemporary forms of organizing and organizational change.

Rather than focusing on how critical theory can reveal shortcomings and impediments to change (e.g., processes of domination and oppression), there is perhaps considerable scope to move beyond an emphasis on reactive critique and develop change approaches which integrate facets of critical theory in positive and constructive ways.

Critical Management Studies and Change

The foundations of CMS are built upon challenging management. A considerable amount of the work developed within the discipline questions the legitimacy of management and is highly critical of the dominant and taken-for-granted institutional arrangements that exist within organizations (Deetz 1992, 1996; Alvesson and Willmott 1992, 1996). Indeed, there has been a strong anti-management stream within CMS. This is exemplified in books like "Shut Down the Business School" (Parker 2018) and "Against Management" (Parker 2002). It is therefore unsurprising that the stance taken in relation to organizational change has tended to be largely skeptical and relatively hostile (Morgan and Spicer 2009; Voronov and Woodworth 2012; Mir and Mir 2012).

Much of the work of CMS is reactive insofar as it focuses on marshaling discursive critique via the deployment of "de-naturalization" (Grey and Willmott 2005) and "anti-performativity" (Fournier and Grey 2000) as responses to the prevailing forms of organization-based control and domination (see Table 12.1 for further descriptions of these responses). A proactive alternative to these responses is the notion of "critical performativity" (Spicer et al. 2009). This is a projective approach insofar as it promotes disruptive action and subversive intervention in management practices. It has been argued that "critical performativity" should be used to actively intervene in change processes and achieve emancipatory change ends (Spicer and Levay 2012). There is clearly potential value in actively intervening and challenging change processes within organizational settings. However, the action can still be seen as being in "opposition-to-change" rather than instigating and enacting critical forms of change.

One approach which adopts a critical stance as a means of enabling change has been developed by Cairns (2012). He proposes the "critical scenario method" which requires the development and consideration of a full range of scenarios that are "dependent upon consideration of all possible and plausible outcomes from human power plays and natural occurring events" (p. 207). He goes on to suggest that "decision making on the desirability of various change options and strategies should be guided by consideration of the Aristotelian concept of *phronesis*, or practical wisdom" (p. 207). The particular form of phronesis employed is based upon Flyvbergs's (2001) work which poses questions that require critical reflection on four issues: power, affect, desirability, and consideration of the extent to which it would be good for humanity. According to Cairns (2012), the "critical scenario method" provides a basis "to challenge predominant forms of 'business-as-usual' thinking in many organizations" (p. 207). The scope for constructive forms of CMS-inspired critical change activity will be explored later in the chapter.

Critical Realism and Change

A considerable amount of literature has been produced on the application of a critical realist ontology to the study of organizations (see, for example: Ackroyd and Fleetwood 2000, 2004; Fleetwood 2005; Reed 2003, 2009). However, there is a very limited amount that has been specifically focused on critical realism in relation to organizational change. The only area in which there has been some focused attention is IT-informed and technology-mediated processes of organizational change (e.g., Allen et al. 2013, Volkoff and Strong 2013; Volkoff et al. 2007). This area of inquiry has proved popular because of the evident material affordances and material embeddedness of technology. Hence, IT and technology-based forms of organizational change cannot easily ignore "structural and material inheritances" (see Table 12.1) in the way that other less materially anchored forms of change can.

Arguably, the two most significant contributions on critical realism and organizational change have been provided by Ackroyd (2012) and Fairclough (2005). Both argue for the consideration of material and structural factors across a variety of change initiatives. Fairclough (2005) is particularly critical of the dominance of social constructivist accounts of organizational change. He argues for meaningful integration of a critical realist perspective via the acknowledgement of two central principles concerning organizational change:

> (a) that while change in discourse is a part of organizational change, and organizational change can often be understood partly in terms of the constructive effects of discourse on organizations, organizational change is not simply change in discourse, and relations between change in discourse and change in other elements of organizations are matters for investigation, which entails a clear and consistent analytical distinction between discourse and other social elements; (b) that while ongoing change in social process, in social interaction, can contribute to organizational change, the relationship between change in social interaction and change in organizational structures is complex and subject to conditions of possibility which need to be investigated, which entails a clear and consistent distinction between social process (including texts), social practices (including orders of discourse), and social structures.
>
> (Fairclough 2005: 930–1)

Equally, Ackroyd (2012) contends that CR perspectives on organizational change have been systematically neglected. To counter this, he sets out an agenda for investigating processes of planned organizational change using critical realist research methods. He produces a continuum of research which ranges from "intensive designs" (focused case studies to establish the extant "mechanisms" based on an abductive logic) through to "extensive designs" (based on population studies using surveys and secondary data to establish the "context" based on a retroductive logic). The scope for meeting the challenge of meaningfully integrating a critical realist perspective and critical realist-informed methods, as part of the existing repertoire of change approaches, will be explored later in this chapter.

Towards Critically Informed Change Approaches

We posit that there are three discernible waves of interest in organizational change within the extant literature: *traditional diagnostic change*—where the change process is treated as a kind of forensic activity (i.e., a quasi-scientific endeavor); *contemporary dialogic change*—positions change as a dialogic process (i.e., as largely a discursive endeavor); *emerging critical OD*—views change as dialectical and inverts the dominant logic that change is a top-down process by presenting it as a more critically oriented bottom-up approach (i.e. a political endeavor).

Traditional approaches to change have tended to treat organizations in a largely unitarist way. This perceived absence of dialectic conditions means that critical approaches are typically neglected. More recently, there is a bundle of contemporary change techniques that can be captured under the umbrella term of "dialogic OD" (Bushe 2010, 2013; Bushe and Marshak 2008, 2009, 2016). Dialogic change approaches accept that organizations are essentially pluralistic and they attempt to address the resultant differences of opinion through processes of real-time face-to-face dialogue (Oswick 2009). However, rather than acknowledging dialectic conditions and embracing critical responses, this group of change interventions assumes that there is a rich variety of legitimate and contrasting, but not opposing, stakeholder interests and positions. The change emphasis is therefore on positively co-constructing consensus-based future outcomes rather than reconciling the conflict between opposing entities. Hence, critical perspectives do not play an active role in the enactment of dialogic interventions (Wolfram-Cox 2009).

Beyond diagnostic and dialogic forms of OD, a new bundle of change techniques has started to gain momentum. These change approaches see organizations as pluralistic sites of conflict and opposing interests which are hierarchically ordered and constituted through privileged and marginalized groups of stakeholders. The critically informed response to these circumstances is to engage with change in a radically different way which is more "bottom-up" than "top-down," and which hands over power to stakeholders who are traditionally marginalized.

The fundamental characteristics of these three change epochs and their respective connection to critical approaches are presented in Table 12.2. These perspectives, along with their critical/dialectical implications, are discussed more fully in the next three subsections.

Traditional Diagnostic Change Approaches and Their Critical Connotations

Table 12.2 points to the three different forms of OD having been particularly popular in different time periods. More specifically, if we focus on the "examples from the extant literature" contained in Table 12.2 we can see that "traditional OD" techniques and methods were prevalent from the early 1950s and up to the early 1980s. During this period an emphasis upon adopting a scientific approach was evident. The scientific foundations of traditional OD can be gleaned from the use of the term "science" in the title of French and Bell's (1973) leading textbook, "Organization Development: *Behavioural Science* Interventions for Organizational Improvement," and the fact that the main journal in the field is titled, *The Journal of Applied Behavioral Science*. Brown and Harvey state in their summary of key characteristics that: "OD is based upon *scientific approaches* to increase organisational effectiveness" (2006: 4). The enactment of traditional OD is epitomized in the prominence of a structured process involving phases typically referred to as "data gathering," "diagnosis," and "intervention" (Bennis 1969).

Traditional "diagnostic" OD is clearly systematic and structured in nature. This essence is captured in Beckhard's oft-cited seminal definition: "Organisation development is an

Table 12.2 A Comparison of Change Epochs, Critical Engagement, and Dialectic Conditions

	Traditional Approach to Change	Contemporary Approach to Change	Emerging Approach to Change
OD Epoch (and the general periodization)	**Diagnostic OD** (most popular between 1950s and 1980s)	**Dialogic OD** (most popular from the early 1980s to the present)	**Critical OD** (started in 2000s and gained more traction in 2010s)
General Approach to Change	Change as a *scientific process* achieved through *diagnosis* and *intervention*	Change as a *discursive process* achieved through *dialogue* and *co-construction*	Change as a *political process* achieved through *mobilization* and *emancipation*
Disciplinary Roots and Epistemology	*Socio-psychological*—positivism and functionalism	*Socio-linguistic*—social constructivism and interpretivism	*Socio-political*—critical theory and critical realism
"Ideal-Type" of Change (Van de Ven and Poole, 1995)	*Life cycle motor*—organic growth with pre-figured sequence and compliant adaptation	*Teleological motor*—purposeful cooperation with envisioned end state and consensus on means	*Dialectical motor*—oppositional with contradictory forces and conflict/confrontation
Perceived Need for Critical Engagement	*Critical approach unrequired*—due to a legitimate and dominant perspective with limited disparate and isolated alternative voices/entities (i.e., a quasi-unitarist context)	*Critical approach unrequired*—due to a conducive and cooperative environment, the absence of a dominant perspective, and many legitimate voices/entities (i.e., a multi-pluralist context)	*Critical approach required*—due to competing and opposing voices/entities that can be characterized as different, privileged, and marginalized groups or interests (i.e., a dialectic-pluralist context)
Response to Critical Circumstances	*Exercise hierarchical authority/power*—treat alternatives/resistance as negative and avoidable	*Participative exercise of power*—treat alternatives/resistance as positive and helpful	*Distributed and dispersed power*—treat alternatives/resistance as unavoidable and inevitable
Dialectic Assumptions	Maintain "thesis A" and overpower/suppress "not-A" antithesis	Provisional "thesis A" as a starting point for arriving at a "Not-A" consensus	React to "Not-A" thesis with "A" to arrive at a "Not not-A" synthesis

	Traditional Approach to Change	Contemporary Approach to Change	Emerging Approach to Change
Processual Characteristics	Reactive, punctuated and linear	Proactive, fluid, and recursive	Emergent, spontaneous, and rhizomatic
Temporal Orientation	Focus on the *past* to act in the *present*	Focus on the *future* to act in the *present*	Focus on the *present* to act in the *present*
Environmental Imperatives	Relatively stable and predictable world	Competitive and rapidly changing world	Turbulent and socially connected world
Hierarchical Ordering	*Top-down*—management conception and management execution (with some employee participation)	*Top-down (then peer-to-peer)*—tentative management conception and joint management/employee execution	*Bottom-up*—employee conception and management/employee execution
Change Logic	Change *of/for* employees	Change *with* employees	Change *by* employees
Examples from the Extant Literature	*Force-field analysis* (Lewin, 1951); *Action research* (Whyte and Hamilton, 1964); *Structural intervention* (Lawrence and Lorsch, 1969); *System 4 management* (Likert and Likert, 1976); *Survey feedback* (Nadler, 1977); *Job design* (Hackman and Oldham 1980);	*Appreciative inquiry* (Cooperrider and Srivastva, 1987); *Open space technology* (Owen, 1992); *Future search* (Weisbord and Janoff, 1995); *World cafe* (Brown and Isaacs, 1995); *Simu-real* (Klein and Broom, 1995); *Participative design* (Purser, 1998); *Dialogical scripting* (Oswick et al., 2000).	*Positive upward dissent* (Kassing, 2002); *Sociocracy* (Rau and Koch-Gonzalez, 2018); *Constructive deviance* (Warren, 2003; Robbins and Galperin, 2010); *Agonistic spaces* (Mouffe, 2000, 2007); *Employee activism* (Phillips, 2012); *Bottom-up change* (Moon, 2008).

effort: (1) planned, (2) organization-wide, (3) managed from the top, (4) to increase organization effectiveness and health, through (5) planned interventions in the organization's processes using behavioral science knowledge" (1969: 9). The use of terms like "planned" and "science" are especially telling. The scientific credentials of traditional OD are also apparent from the subtitles of a number of key texts published during the period, for example, *Developing Organizations: Diagnosis and Action* (Lawrence and Lorsch 1969) and *Feedback and Organization Development: Using Data-Based Methods* (Nadler 1977).

Embracing a scientific stance is consistent with a positivist epistemology. It also resonates with a core assertion of the Frankfurt School that the positivist methods associated with the process of enlightenment (Kant 1784) lead to the development of "knowledge that serves the interests of powerful elites rather than helping people to emancipate themselves from the social conditions of dependency and suppression" (Scherer 2009: 35). Hence, it could be argued that the appeal to scientific legitimacy of traditional approaches to change equally serve the interests of powerful organizational stakeholders.

The positivism of diagnostic OD techniques is aligned with a problem-centred way of thinking about organizations. Therefore, as an approach to change, it is consistent with the "life cycle motor" (Van de Ven and Poole 1995) with a linear "problem-to-solution" framing that promotes a view of organizational change as a discrete, punctuated, and knowable process (Bushe and Marshak 2009).

A further key facet of traditional OD is revealed if we revisit Beckhard's seminal definition of OD. Beyond being "planned" and "using behavioural science knowledge," it is also stated that the process should be "managed from the top" (Beckhard 1969:9). This "top-down" logic effectively means that OD is instigated and controlled by management, either directly or on behalf of management through the use of external consultants. Employees are relatively passive in the process insofar as change is positioned as something which is done "to employees" or "for employees," albeit that there is often some form of consultation and/or modest participation in the process.

Given the inherent positivism, and hierarchically organized emphasis, of "traditional diagnostic change approaches," there is no perceived need to meaningfully engage with dialectic ways of seeing organizations and organizational change processes because the assumption is that there is a "right" change approach which is implemented top-down through the exercise of the managerial prerogative. In such circumstances, it is presumed that there will be relatively little resistance and, where it does arise, it is seen as negative and futile.

Unfortunately, just because opposing entities and positions are not acknowledged in traditional diagnostic change approaches does not mean that they do not exist. Somewhat ironically, the largely top-down approach and the lack of critical engagement with opposing perspectives (i.e., an antithesis) is actually likely to lead to greater opposition. Indeed, the fact that directive forms of leadership and change are inclined to increase levels of both overt and covert forms of workforce resistance is well understood in the extant literature (Ford and Ford 2009; Piderit 2000; Thomas and Hardy 2011).

Contemporary Dialogic Change Approaches and their Critical Connotations

Following the domination of traditional "diagnostic" forms of organizational change, an alternative cluster of dialogic methods and approaches emerged in the mid-1980s and these remain popular. This collection of dialogic approaches positions organizational change as primarily a process of social construction (i.e., change is made possible through talk and interaction). There has been considerable academic work on organization development and change as a discursive process (Bushe and Marshak 2009; Ford 1999; Ford and Ford 1995; Grant et al. 2005; Marshak and Grant 2008; Shaw 2002). However, the genesis of contemporary OD can be traced back to the more practitioner-oriented work of Brown and Issacs (1995), Weisbord (1987), Owen (1992), Purser (1998), and Cooperrider and Srivastva (1987).

Unlike "traditional diagnostic OD" which is problem-centred, "contemporary dialogic OD" focuses more on improvement and, as such, the primary emphasis is less about the past (i.e., the retrospective scientific analysis of problems) and is far more future-oriented (the discursive construction of solutions and opportunities). Weisbord's articulation of "future search" (Weisbord 1987; Weisbord and Janoff 1995) as a form of large-scale intervention is explicitly "future-oriented". Moreover, it foregrounds dialogue insofar as it involves "getting the whole system in the room" (Weisbord 1987:19). And, the future is also prominent in other forms of dialogic OD. For example, if we take "World Cafe" interventions, Brown and Issacs' (1995) volume is titled, *The World Café Book: Shaping our Futures through Conversations that Matter*. The reference to "future conversations" simultaneously highlights both the projective and discursive nature of dialogic forms of OD. Equally, Cooperrider and Srivastva's (1987) development of "appreciative inquiry" (AI) has helped to shift the emphasis of OD from problems to solutions. The core elements of AI have been identified as: (i) appreciating and valuing the best of "what is"; (ii) envisioning "what might be"; (iii) dialoguing "what should be"; and, (iv) innovating "what will be" (Cooperrider and Whitney, 2001). The AI privileging of "improvement," "positive framing," "future orientation," and "dialogue" is clearly aligned with the characteristics associated with contemporary OD (see Table 12.2).

The contructivist and interpretivist credentials of "contemporary dialogic OD" means that it assumes that change is complex, emergent, and ambiguous and, as such, it cannot be structured and managed as an entirely predictable and scientific endeavor (Bushe and Marshak 2009; Oswick 2013). Hence, it is not possible to adhere to a strong "top-down" approach and in terms of the change process employees have more agency than is typically associated with traditional diagnostic OD. The emphasis on discursively co-constructing future realities means that change is done "with employees" through dialogue rather than "to employees" by managers. When viewed in that way, it could be argued that dialogic approaches to change embrace some of the core tenets of critical theory insofar as they are consistent with Jurgen Habermas' ideas on how to challenge the colonization of the lifeworld and promote democracy via open and free debate where outcomes are determined by the strength of the argument made, rather than governed by instrumental rationality (Habermas 1984, 1987, 1990c, 1996, 1998).

That said, although the outcomes and processes of dialogic change are not totally governed by management, these forms of intervention are nevertheless quite structured and controlled. The decision to use a form of dialogic intervention is typically organized, or the very least sanctioned, by management, the actual process is quite tightly structured (i.e., in terms of where, when, and how the dialogic intervention occurs), and the resultant outcomes are either supported or vetoed by management in terms of actual implementation. Hence, although employees are far from passive in the process, change is still instigated by management and governed, to a degree, through the existing hierarchy, albeit in a more relaxed manner than with traditional OD interventions. In this regard, they cannot be regarded as "power neutral" discursive sites of "open" and "free" debate in the manner advocated by Habermas (1984, 1987, 1990c).

Rather than being exemplary sites of discursive democracy, dialogic interventions perhaps unintentionally support a critical realist interpretation inasmuch as they demonstrate how these constructivist-informed events are shaped by deep underlying structures, power relations, and material inheritances (Reed 2003, 2009; Sayer 2000). One might even go as far as to conclude that dialogic interventions implicitly acknowledge dialectic tensions and critical conditions, and then provide overly optimistic, neo-liberal solutions. Put differently, they acknowledge dissensus (i.e., a variety of interests/positions), and address it by using dialogic processes to create a false and/or surface-level impression of consensus in which contrasting and opposing entities and interests are suppressed (i.e., marginal voices are overpowered and silenced by the majority).

Emerging Critical Change Approaches and their Critical Connotations

As can be seen from the examples from the literature offered in Table 12.2, a new family of OD methods and approaches has begun to develop over the past decade or so. We have chosen to refer to this body of change activity as "critical OD". It is a radical form of OD inasmuch as it is "bottom-up," and hands over the responsibility for change to employees (Heckscher and Adler 2006; Strand and Jung 2005). The role of management becomes one of accommodation and facilitation by creating the conditions for "employee activism" (Phillips 2012) and constructive forms of dissent (Mouffe 2007; Warren 2003). This alternative form of OD has emerged out of a need to consider the notion of "employee voice" (Klaas et al. 2012; Morrison 2011), but it is different from other forms of "bottom-up" initiatives—such as whistleblowing and staff suggestion schemes—which tend to be individualized, procedurally controlled by management, and not generally concerned with processes of planned organizational change.

There is also a substantive difference between the "constructive deviance" of emerging OD (Warren 2003) and the "destructive deviance" of some forms of collective action (i.e., industrial disputes and protests). While explicitly acknowledging dialectic conditions, critical forms of OD are primarily concerned with identifying and addressing areas of mutual interest and potential benefit within organizations (e.g., equality, inclusion, growth, sustainability, social responsibility, and mutual gain). In this regard, the emphasis is generative rather than distributive (i.e., how do we increase the size of the pie rather than how do we slice the existing pie?).

Critical OD has very obvious implications for hierarchy and governance. Formal hierarchical structures and control mechanisms are effectively set aside in favor of the utilization of informal networks, and the form of governance becomes more open and less formal as management control of the change process is relinquished. The role of the employee becomes one of a non-hierarchical change agent—a move from "change *for* employees" (diagnostic OD) and "change *with* employees" (dialogic OD) to a process of "change by employees" (critical OD).

The notion of manager-less, governance-free, non-hierarchically structured forms of organizing and organizational change may seem a little implausible and far-fetched. However, this is not what is being advocated. It is important to acknowledge that this new strand of OD is not about the "governance of organizations," it is about the "governance of OD and change activity." The typical infrastructure of an organization still exists (i.e., formal structures, rules, procedures, and roles), but these instruments of managing and governing are suppressed and/or set aside in relation to the scope and opportunities for OD-based change by encouraging and enabling bottom-up initiatives. It is entirely possible to use formal structures and governance arrangements to manage the day-to-day operations and the routine decision-making processes within an organization and have different, and more fluid arrangements for processes of significant organizational change. In short, "non-hierarchically organized" forms of OD can operate within "hierarchically organized-organizations."

As a relatively new phenomenon, "critical OD" has not yet become a fully established and commonplace form of change approach. It is however a significant development and it is gaining more traction.

A Critical Need for Critical Approaches to Change

We believe that critical-informed approaches are an important and necessary part of the organizational change landscape. In situations where the organizational context is relatively stable and the process of change is relatively straightforward and non-controversial, traditional diagnostic forms OD, based on a "life cycle motor" (Van de Ven and Poole 1995), can be highly effective. Equally, in a supportive organizational climate where there are generally agreed change goals and a conducive change environment, contemporary dialogic forms of OD, based on a "teleological motor" (Van de Ven and Poole 1995), can be highly effective. However, in organizations where there is a degree of inherent tension between groups of stakeholders (e.g., management and workers) and the change process is complex and contested, emerging forms of critical OD, based on a "dialectical motor" (Van de Ven and Poole 1995), are likely to have most purchase.

Change situations where there are dialectically based problems require dialectically based solutions. Unlike traditional diagnostic forms of OD, which largely ignore dialectical conditions, and contemporary dialogic forms of OD, which partially acknowledge dialectical conditions and provide unrealistic "dialectically insensitive" interventions, the emerging critical forms of OD acknowledge dialectic conditions and offer "dialectically sympathetic" interventions.

Sociocracy is a good example of a critical approach to both organizational governance and organizational change which is "dialectically-sympathetic." It advocates a process of democratic decision-making rather than hierarchically based forms of decision-making (Rau and Koch-Gonzalez 2018). However, rather than falling into the same trap as dialogic interventions, the aim is to reach a position of "consent" (i.e., a willingness to accommodate a position as a basis for action) rather than a position of "consensus" (i.e., unanimous agreement on a course for action). In this regard, sociocracy acknowledges the existence of opposition and it allows legitimate space for the consent offered by those with opposing views to be re-considered and re-visited at a later point in the process. By contrast, dialogic processes eschew dialectical-sensitivity because the drive for unanimity largely shuts off the space for dissent in real time, and subsequent dissent is typically discouraged (i.e., because you changed your mind or did not speak out at the time). We would go as far as to suggest that, in more extreme examples, the problems arising from a strong drive for consensus in dialogic interventions is remarkably similar to the problems associated with groupthink (Janis 1972). It is for this reason that the forms of "positive dissent" (Kassing 2002) and "constructive deviance" (Robbins and Galperin 2010; Warren 2003) associated with critical OD are crucial.

The emerging set of critical change approaches has significant implications for the leadership of change. In his bestselling book, *Leading Change*, Kotter (1996) contends that leadership involves creating vision and strategy; communicating and setting direction; motivating action and aligning people; and, transforming systems when needed. He places considerable emphasis on vision and persuasion in his approach to change leadership. The focus on strong leadership and vision resonates with aspects of "traditional OD" and "contemporary OD" (see Table 12.2) insofar as the centrality of vision (i.e., looking forwards) resonates with an emphasis on being future-oriented, and strong leadership (i.e., a directive, persuasive, and communicative leader) is congruent with a "top-down" perspective on OD.

Kotter's (1996) articulation of change leadership is at odds with the emerging forms of OD. In particular, it runs contrary to the core tenets of critical OD techniques, such as "positive upward dissent" (Kassing 2002) and "employee activism" (Phillips 2012), where initiatives are instigated by groups of workers rather than formal leaders. In this regard, the leadership of change in the future is far removed from that advocated in the mainstream leadership literature (Anderson and Ackerman Anderson 2001; Cran 2016).

An important imperative for rethinking the relevance and purchase of a new critical form of OD is the impact of generational shifts upon the workplace. The so called "Silent Generation" and the "Baby Boomers" have a very different attitude to change, hierarchy, governance, and leadership, than their "Millennial" and "Generation Z" counterparts. As Andrew Davidson (2014) observes:

> For traditional employers, Millennials pose new problems. Command-and-control is out. Having grown up with constant feedback from parents and teachers, they want dialogue, not orders, and a world of work that offers more opportunity and less hierarchy, and always new ways of doing things. (p. 19)

Millennials want to be engaged not managed. This has significant implications for change and change leadership which become acute as the baby boomers, that currently hold positions of power, become displaced by the increasing number of millennials in the workplace. We might expect that this will drive an inevitable shift in workplace attitudes and behavior with the established pillars of authority, hierarchy, and leadership being softened in favor of more democracy, networked activity, and self-organization.

The challenge going forwards for organizations is not so much about "leading change" as much as it is about creating the conditions in which employees can self-organize and instigate processes of meaningful positive change. The purchase of "change leadership," where visionary and charismatic leaders instigate processes of change, will become increasingly less effective in a world which is characterized by more distributed, emergent, fluid, and socially connected forms of organizing and decision-making, and which is more closely aligned to the tenets of "critical OD" (see Table 12.2). In this regard, organizations in the future may well look more like social movements than they do traditional organizations. That being the case, those involved in the study and practice of change will need to focus more on "change activists" and less on "change agents."

References

Abel, C. F., and Sementelli, A. J. (2005), 'Evolutionary critical theory, metaphor, and organizational change', *Journal of Management Development*, 24/5, 443–58.

Ackroyd, S. (2012), 'Contemporary Realism and Organizational Change', in D. M. Boje, B. Burnes, and J. Hassard, eds., *The Routledge Companion to Organizational Change* (Oxford: Routledge), 230–44.

Ackroyd, S., and Fleetwood, S. (2000), *Realist Perspectives on Management and Organisations* (London: Routledge).

Ackroyd, S., and Fleetwood, S. (2004). 'Developments in Critical Realism in Organisation and Management Studies', in S. Fleetwood and S. Ackroyd, S, eds., *Critical Realist Applications in Organisation and Management Studies* (London: Routledge), 1–13.

Adorno, T. W. (1973). *Negative Dialectics* (trans. E. B. Ashton) (New York, NY: The Continuum Publishing Company).

Allen, D. K., Brown, A., Karanasios, S. and Norman, A. (2013). 'How Should Technology-Mediated Organizational Change be Explained? A Comparison of the Contributions of Critical Realism and Activity Theory', *Management Information Systems Quarterly*, 37/3, 835–54.

Alvesson, M., Bridgman. T., and Willmott, H. (2009), 'Introduction', in M. Alvesson, T. Bridgman, and H. Willmott, eds, *The Oxford Handbook of Critical Management Studies* (Oxford: Oxford University Press), 1–26.

Alvesson, M., and Deetz, S. (1996). 'Critical Theory and Postmodernism Approaches to Organization Studies', in S. R. Clegg and C. Hardy, eds, *Handbook of Organization Studies.* (London: Sage Publications), 191–217.

Alvesson, M., and Deetz, S. (2000). *Doing Critical Management Research* (London: Sage Publications).

Alvesson, M., and Willmott, H. (Eds.) (1992), *Critical Management Studies* (London: Sage Publications).

Alvesson, M., and Willmott, H. (1996), *Making Sense of Management: A Critical Introduction* (London: Sage Publications).

Anderson, D., and Ackerman Anderson, L. A. (2001), *Beyond Change Management* (San Francisco, CA: Jossey-Bass).

Bhaskar, R. (1975). *A Realist Theory of Science* (London: Verso).

Bhaskar, R. (1986). *Scientific Realism and Human Emancipation* (London: Verso).

Beckhard, R. (1969). *Organization Development: Strategies and Models* (Reading, MA: Addison-Wesley).

Bennis, W. G. (1969). *Organization Development: Its Nature Origins and Prospects* (Reading, MA: Addison-Wesley).

Benson, J. K. (1977). 'Organizations: A Dialectical View', *Administrative Science Quarterly*, 22, 1–21.

Bhaskar, R. (1978) *A Realist Theory of Science* Hemel Hempstead, Harvester Wheatsheaf.

Bolton, G. (2010). *Reflective Practice: Writing and Professional Development* (Los Angeles, CA: Sage Publications).

Boonstra, J. J., and Bennebroek Gravenhorst, K. M. (1998). 'Power Dynamics and Organizational Change: A Comparison of Perspectives', *European Journal of Organizational Psychology*, 7/2, 97–120.

Bradshaw, P. (1998), 'Power as Dynamic Tension and its Implications for Radical Organizational Change', *European Journal of Organizational Psychology*, 7/2, 121–43.

Brookfield, S. D. (2011), *Teaching for Critical Thinking: Tools and Techniques to Help Students Question Their Assumptions* (San Francisco: Jossey Bass).

Brown, D. R. (2010). *An Experiential Approach to Organization Development* (8th edn) (London: Pearson).

Brown, D. R., and Harvey, D. (2006). *An Experiential Approach to Organization Development* (7th edn) (Upper Saddle River, NJ: Prentice-Hall).

Brown, J., and Isaacs, D. (1995), *The World Cafe Book: Shaping our Futures Through Conversations that Matter* (San Francisco, CA: Berrett-Koehler).

Buchanan, D., and Badham, R. (1999). 'Politics and Organizational Change: The Lived Experience', *Human Relations*, 52/5, 609–29.

Bushe, G. R. (2010), 'Being the Container in Dialogic OD', *Practicing Social Change*, ½, 10–15.

Bushe, G. R. (2013), 'Dialogic OD: A Theory of Practice', *Organization Development Practitioner*, 45/1, 11–17.

Bushe, G. R., and Marshak, R. J. (2008), 'The Postmodern Turn in OD: From Diagnosis to Meaning Making', *Organization Development Practitioner*, 40/4, 10–12.
Bushe, G. R., and Marshak, R. J. (2009), 'Revisioning Organization Development: Diagnostic and Dialogic Premises and Patterns of Practice', *Journal of Applied Behavioral Science*, 45/3, 348–68.
Bushe, G. R., and Marshak, R. J. (2016), 'The Dialogic Mindset: Leading Emergent Change in a Complex World', *Organization Development Journal*, 34/1, 37–65.
Cairns, G. (2012), 'Designing for Change with Critical Scenario Method', in D. M. Boje, B. Burnes, and J. Hassard, eds., *The Routledge Companion to Organizational Change* (Oxford: Routledge), 206–216.
Carr, A. (2000a), 'Critical Theory and the Management of Change in Organizations', *Journal of Organizational Change Management*, 13/3, 208–20.
Carr, A. (2000b), 'Critical Theory and the Psychodynamics of Change', *Journal of Organizational Change Management*, 13/3, 289–99.
Cheung-Judge, M. Y., and Holbeche, L. (2011), *Organization Development: A Practitioner's Guide for OD and HR* (London: Kogan Page).
Cooperrider, D. L., and Srivastva, S. (1987), 'Appreciative Inquiry in Organizational Life', in R. W. Woodman and W. A. Pasmore, eds, *Research in Organizational Change and Development* (Vol. 1) (Stamford, CT: JAI Press), 129–69.
Coopperrider, D. L., and Whitney, D. (2001), 'A positive Revolution in Change', in D. L. Cooperrider, P. Sorenson, D. Whitney, and T. Yeager, eds, *Appreciative Inquiry: An Emerging Direction for Organization Development* (Champaign, IL: Stipes), 9–29.
Cran, C. (2016), *The Art of Change Leadership: Driving Transformation in a Fast-Paced World* (Hoboken, NJ: John Wiley and Sons).
Cummings, T. G., and Worley, C. G. (2005). *Organization Development and Change* (8th edn) (Mason, OH: South-Western).
Cunliffe, A. L. (2004), 'On Becoming A Critically Reflexive Practitioner', *Journal of Management Education*, 28/4, 407–26.
Davidson, A. (2014, May), 'How Millennial Are You?' *Business Life*, 18–21.
Deetz, S. (1992), *Democracy in an Age of Corporate Colonization: Developments in Communication and the Politics of Everyday Life* (New York, NY: State University of New York Press).
Deetz, S. (1996), 'Crossroads—Describing Differences in Approaches to Organization Science: Rethinking Burrell and Morgan and their Legacy', *Organization Science*, 7/2, 191–207.
Dewey, J. (1910), *How We Think* (Lexington, MA: D.C. Heath and Co).
Dye, V. (2011). 'Reflection, Reflection, Reflection: I'm Thinking All The Time, Why Do I Need a Theory or Model of Reflection?' in D. McGregor and L. Cartwright, eds, *Developing Reflective Practice: A Guide for Beginning Teachers* (Maidenhead: McGraw-Hill Education), 217–34.
Edwards, R. (1979), *Contested Terrain: The Transformation of the Workplace in the Twentieth Century* (New York: Basic Books).
Facione, P. A. (2011). *Think Critically* (Englewood Cliffs, NJ: Pearson).
Fairclough, N. (2005), 'Peripheral Vision: Discourse Analysis in Organization Studies The Case for Critical Realism', *Organization Studies*, 26/6, 915–39.
Feldman, S. P. (1990), 'Stories as Cultural Creativity: On the Relationship between Symbolism and Politics in Organizational Change', *Human Relations*, 43/9, 809–28.

Fisher, A. (2001), *Critical Thinking: An Introduction* (Cambridge: Cambridge University Press).
Fleetwood, S. (2005), 'The Ontology Of Organisation And Management Studies: A Critical Realist Approach', *Organization*, 12/2, 197–222.
Flyvberg, B. (2001), *Making Social Science Matter: Why Social Inquiry Fails and How It Can Succeed Again* (Cambridge: Cambridge University Press).
Ford, J. D. (1999), 'Organizational Change as Shifting Conversation', *Journal of Organizational Change Management*, 12/6, 480–500.
Ford, J. D., and Ford, L. W. (1995), 'The Role of Conversations in Producing Intentional Change in Organizations', *Academy of Management Review*, 20, 541–70.
Ford, J. D., and Ford, L. W. (2009), 'Decoding Resistance to Change', *Harvard Business Review*, 87, 99–103.
Foucault, M. (1977), *The Archaeology of Knowledge* (London: Tavistock).
Fournier, V., and Grey, C. (2000), 'At the Critical Moment: Conditions and Prospects for Critical Management Studies', *Human Relations*, 53/1, 7–32.
Fox, A. (1966), 'Industrial Sociology and Industrial Relations', Research Paper 3, Royal Commission on Trade Unions and Employers' Associations (London: HMSO).
Fox, A. (1974), *Beyond Contract: Work, Power and Trust Relations* (London: Faber and Faber).
French, W., and Bell, C. H. (1973), *Organization Development: Behavioral Science Interventions for Organizational Improvement* (Englewood Cliffs, NJ: Prentice-Hall).
French, W., and Bell, C. H. (1998), *Organization Development: Behavioral Science Interventions for Organization Improvement* (6th edn) (Englewood Cliffs, NJ: Prentice-Hall).
Gibbs, G. (1988), *Learning by Doing: A Guide to Teaching and Learning Methods* (Oxford: Further Education Unit, Oxford Polytechnic).
Glaser, E. (1941), *An Experiment in the Development of Critical Thinking* (New York: Teachers College, Columbia University).
Gramsci, A. (1971), *Selections from the Prison Notebooks* (trans. Q. Hoare and G. Nowell Smith) (New York: International Publishers).
Grant, D., Michelson, G., Oswick, C. and Wailes, N. (2005), 'Discourse and Organizational Change', *Journal of Organizational Change Management*, 18/1, 6–15.
Grey, C., and Willmott, H. (2005), 'Introduction', in C. Grey and H. Willmott, eds., *Critical Management Studies: A Reader* (New York: Oxford University Press), 1–20.
Grubbs, J. W. (2000), 'Cultural Imperialism', *Journal of Organizational Change Management*, 13/3, 221–34.
Habermas, J. (1971), *Knowledge and Human Interests* (Boston, MA: Beacon Press).
Habermas, J. (1984), *The Theory of Communicative Action:* Volume 1 (MA: Beacon Press).
Habermas, J. (1987), *The Theory of Communicative Action:* Volume 2 (MA: Beacon Press).
Habermas, J. (1990a), 'Reconstruction and Interpretation in the Social Sciences,' in J. Habermas, ed., *Moral Consciousness and Communicative Action* (Cambridge, MA; MIT Press), 21–42.
Habermas, J. (1990b), 'Discourse Ethics: Notes on a Program of Philosophical Justification', in J. Habermas, ed., *Moral Consciousness and Communicative Action* (Cambridge, MA; MIT Press), 43–115.
Habermas, J. (1990c), *The Philosophical Discourse of Modernity* (Cambridge: Polity Press).
Habermas, J. (1996), *Between Facts and Norms* (Cambridge, MA: MIT Press).
Habermas, J. (1998), *The Inclusion of the Other* (Cambridge, MA: MIT Press).
Habermas, J. (2001), *The Postnational Constellation* (Cambridge, MA: MIT Press).

Hackman, J. R., and Oldham, G. R. (1980), *Work Redesign* (Reading, MA: Addison-Wesley).
Hardy, C. (1995), 'Managing Strategic Change: Power, Paralysis and Perspective', *Advances in Strategic Management*, 12(B), 3–31.
Hardy, C. (1996), Understanding Power: Bringing about Strategic Change', *British Journal of Management*, 7(special issue), S3-S16.
Heckscher, C. and Adler, P. A. (2006), *The Firm as a Collaborative Community: The Reconstruction of Trust in the Knowledge Economy* (Oxford: Oxford University Press).
Held, D. (1980), *Introduction to Critical Theory: Horkheimer to Habermas* (Berkeley, CA: University of California Press).
Horkheimer, M. (1937), *Critical Theory* (New York, NY: Herder and Herder).
Horkheimer, M., and Adorno, T. W. (1947a), *Dialectic of Enlightenment* (New York, NY: Herder and Herder).
Horkheimer, M., and Adorno, T. W. (1947b), *Eclipse of Reason* (New York, NY: Oxford University Press).
Hullfish, H. G., and Smith, P. G. (1961), *Reflective Thinking: The Method of Education* (New York: Dodd, Mead and Company).
Hyman, R. (1972), *Strikes* (London: Fontana Press).
Janis, I. L. (1972), *Victims of Groupthink: A Psychological Study of Foreign-Policy Decisions and Fiascos* (Boston, MA: Houghton Mifflin).
Jansson, N. (2013), 'Organizational Change as Practice: A Critical Analysis', *Journal of Organizational Change Management*, 26/6, 1003–1019.
Kant, I. [1784] (1974), 'An Answer to the Question: What is Enlightenment?' in I. Kant, ed., *Perpetual Peace and Other Essays* (ed. and trans. T. Humphrey) (Indianapolis: Hackett, 1983).
Kassing, J. W. (2002), 'Speaking Up: Identifying Employees' Upward Dissent Strategies', *Management Communication Quarterly*, 16/2, 187–209.
Klaas, B. S., Olson-Buchanan, J. B. and Ward, A. (2012), 'The Determinants of Alternative Forms of Workplace Voice', *Journal of Management*, 38/1, 314–45.
Klein, D. C., and Broom, M. F. (1995), *Power: The Infinite Game*, (Amherst, MA: HRD Press).
Knights, D., and Willmott, H. (1989), 'Power and Subjectivity at Work: From Degradation to Subjugation in Social Relations', *Sociology*, 23, 535–58.
Kotter, J. P. (1996), *Leading Change* (Boston, MA: Harvard Business School Press).
Langley, A., and Sloan, P. (2012), 'Organizational Change and Dialectic Processes', in D. M. Boje, B. Burnes, and J. Hassard, eds., *The Routledge Companion to Organizational Change* (Oxford: Routledge), 261–75.
Lawrence, P. R., and Lorsch, J. W. (1969), *Developing Organizations: Diagnosis and Action* (Reading, MA: Addison-Wesley).
Lewin, K. (1951). *Field Theory in Social Science* (New York: Harper).
Likert, R., and Likert, J. G. (1976), *New Ways of Managing Conflict* (New York: McGraw-Hill).
Marcuse, H. (1964), *One-Dimensional Man: Studies in the Ideology of Advanced Industrial Society* (Boston, MA: Beacon Press).
Marcuse, H. (1970), 'The End of Utopia', in H. Marcuse, ed., *Five Lectures: Psychoanalysis, Politics and Utopia* (Boston, MA: Beacon Press), 62–9.
Marshak, R. J., and Grant, D. (2008), 'Organizational Discourse and New Organization Development Practices', *British Journal of Management*, 19, S7-S19.

Mir, R and Mir, A. (2012) 'Organizational Change as Imperialism' in D. Boje, B. Burnes, and J. Hassard, eds., The Routledge Companion to Organizational Change. Oxon: Routledge, 425–39

McClellan, J. G. (2011), Reconsidering Communication and the Discursive Politics of Organizational Change', *Journal of Change Management*, 11/4, 465–80.

Moon, M. (2008), 'Bottom-Up Instigated Organisational Change through Constructionist Conversations', *Journal of Knowledge Management Practice*, 9/4, 1–14.

Morgan, G., and Spicer, A. (2009), 'Critical Approaches to Organisational Change', in M. Alvesson, T. Bridgeman, and H. Willmott, eds., *The Oxford Handbook of Critical Management Studies*. Oxford: Oxford University Press., 267–85

Morrison, E. W. (2011), 'Employee Voice Behaviour: Integration and Directions for Future Research', *Academy of Management Annals*, 5/1, 373–412.

Moss, M. A. (2017), 'Critical Story Sharing: A Dialectic Approach to Identity Regulation', in G. Jamissen, P. Hardy, Y. Nordkvelle, and H. Pleasants, eds., *Digital Storytelling in Higher Education: International Perspectives* (London: Palgrave Macmillan).

Mouffe, C. (2000), *Deliberative Democracy or Agonistic Pluralism*, Political Science Series (Wien Institute for Advanced Studies, Vienna).

Mouffe, C. (2007), 'Artistic Activism and Agonistic Spaces', *Arts and Research: A Journal of Ideas Contexts and Methods*, ½, 1–5.

Mumby, D. K. (2001), 'Power and Politics', in F. M. Jablin, and L. Putnam, eds, *The New Handbook of Organizational Communication* (Thousand Oaks, CA: Sage Publications), 585–623.

Mumby, D. K. (2004), 'Discourse, Power and Ideology: Unpacking the Critical Approach', in D. Grant, C. Hardy, C. Oswick, and L. Putnam, eds, *The Sage Handbook of Organizational Discourse* (London: Sage Publications), 237–58.

Nadler, D. (1977), *Feedback and Organization Development: Using Data-based Methods* (Reading, MA: Addison-Wesley).

Oswick, C. (2009), 'Revisioning or Re-versioning? A Commentary on Diagnostic and Dialogic Forms of Organization Development', *Journal of Applied Behavioral Science*, 45/3, 369–374.

Oswick, C. (2013), 'OD or Not OD that is the Question! A Constructivist's Thoughts on the Changing Nature of Change', *Journal of Change Management*, 13/4, 371–81.

Oswick, C., Anthony, P., Keenoy, T., Mangham, I. L., and Grant, D. (2000), A Dialogic Analysis of Organizational Learning', *Journal of Management Studies*, 37/6, 887–901.

Owen, H. (1992), *Open Space Technology* (Potomac, MD: Abbott).

Parker, M. (2002), *Against Management: Organization in the Age of Managerialism* (London: Polity Press).

Parker, M. (2018), *Shut Down the Business School! An Insider's Account of What's Wrong with Management Education* (London: Pluto Press).

Paul, R. W. (1985), 'Bloom's Taxonomy and Critical Thinking Instruction', *Educational Leadership*, 42/8, 36–9.

Paul, R. W., and Elder, L. (2001), *Critical Thinking: Tools for Taking Charge of Your Learning and Your Life* (Upper Saddle River, NJ: Prentice Hall).

Phillips, R. (2012), 'Employee Activists: Occupy Different Tents', Citizen renaissance, www.citizenrenaissance.com/2012/04/23/employee-activists-occupy-different-tents/, accessed 15 October 2019.

Piderit, S. K. (2000), 'Rethinking Resistance and Recognizing Ambivalence: A Multidimensional View of Attitudes toward an Organizational Change', *Academy of Management Review*, 25, 783–94.

Purser, R. (1998), *Participative Design* (Reading, MA: Addison-Wesley).
Rau, T. J., and Koch-Gonzalez, J. (2018), *Many Voices One Song: Shared Power with Sociocracy* (Amherst, MA: Sociocracy for All).
Reed, M. (2003), 'The Agency/Structure Dilemma in Organization Theory: Open Doors and Brick Walls', in H. Tsoukas and C. Knudsen, C., eds., *The Oxford Handbook of Organization Theory: Meta-Theoretical Perspectives* (Oxford: Oxford University Press), 289–309.
Reed, M. (2009), 'Critical Realism in Critical Management Studies', in M. Alvesson, T. Bridgman, and H. Willmott, eds, *The Oxford Handbook of Critical Management Studies* (Oxford: Oxford University Press), 52–75.
Robbins, D. L., and Galperin, B. L. (2010), 'Constructive Deviance: Striving toward Organisational Change in Health Care', *Journal of Management and Marketing*, 5, 1–11.
Sayer, A. (2000), *Realism and Social Science* (London: Sage Publications).
Scherer, A. G. (2009), 'Critical Theory and its Contribution to Critical Management', in M. Alvesson, T. Bridgman, and H. Willmott, H., eds, *The Oxford Handbook of Critical Management Studies* (Oxford: Oxford University Press), 29–51.
Schön, D. A. (1983), *The Reflective Practitioner: How Professionals Think in Action*. (New York: Basic Books).
Scriven, M., and Paul, R. W. (1987), 'Defining Critical Thinking', Retrieved from https://www.criticalthinking.org/pages/defining-critical-thinking/766 http://www.criticalthinking.org/University/univlibrary/library.nclk.
Shaw, P. (2002), *Changing Conversations in Organizations: A Complexity Approach to Change* (London: Routledge).
Spicer, A., Alvesson, M., and Kärreman, D. (2009), Critical Performativity: The Unfinished Business of Critical Management Studies', *Human Relations*, 62/4, 537–60.
Spicer, A., and Levay, C. (2012), 'Critical Theories of Organizational Change', in D. M. Boje, B. Burnes, and J. Hassard, J., eds., *The Routledge Companion to Organizational Change*. (Oxford: Routledge), 276–90.
Steffy, B. D., and Grimes, A. J. (1986), 'A Critical Theory of Organization Science', *Academy of Management Review*, 11/2, 322–36.
Strand, D., and Jung, D. I. (2005), 'Organisational Change as an Orchestrated Social Movement', in G. Davis, D. McAdam, W. R. Scott, and M. N. Zald, eds., *Social Movements in Organization Theory* (Cambridge: Cambridge University Press), 280–309
Thomas, R., and Hardy, C. (2011), 'Reframing Resistance to Organizational Change', *Scandinavian Journal of Management*, 27, 322–31.
Thomas, R., Sargent, L. D., and Hardy, C. (2011). 'Managing Organizational Change: Negotiating Meaning and Power-Resistance Relations', *Organization Science*, 22/1, 22–41.
Thompson, P. (2004), 'Brands, Boundaries and Bandwagons: A Critical Reflection on Critical Management Studies', in S. Fleetwood and S. Ackroyd, eds., *Critical Realism in Action and Organization Studies* (London: Routledge), 54–70.
Van de Ven, A. H., and Poole, M. S. (1995), 'Explaining Development and Change in Organizations', *Academy of Management Review*, 20/3, 510–40.
Volkoff, O., and Strong, D. M. (2013), Critical Realism and Affordances: Theorizing IT-Associated Organizational Change Processes', *Management Information Systems Quarterly*, 37/3, 819–34.
Volkoff, O., Strong, D. M., and Elmes, M. B. (2007), 'Technological Embeddedness and Organizational Change', *Organization Science*, 18/5, 749–883.
Voronov, M. and Woodworth, W. P. (2012). 'OD, Discourse and Domination' in D. Boje, B. Burnes, and J. Hassard, eds., The Routledge Companion to Organizational Change. (Oxon: Routledge), 440–56

Warren, D. E. (2003), 'Constructive and Destructive Deviance in Organizations', *Academy of Management Review*, 28/4, 622–32.
Weisbord, M. (1987), 'Toward Third-Wave Managing Consulting', *Organisational Dynamics*, 15, 19–20.
Weisbord, M., and Janoff, S. (1995), *Future Search: An Action Guide to Finding Common Ground in Organizations and Communities* (San Francisco, CA: Berrett-Koehler).
Whyte, W. F., and Hamilton, E. L. (1964), *Action Research for Management* (Homewood, IL: Irwin-Dorsey).
Willmott, H. (1997), Rethinking Management and Managerial Work: Capitalism, Control and Subjectivity, *Human Relations*, 50/11, 1329–60.
Willmott, H. (2008), 'Critical Management And Global justice', *Organization*, 15/6, 931–35.
Wolfram-Cox, J. (2009), 'Safe Talk: Revisioning, Repositioning, or Representing Organization Development', *Journal of Applied Behavioural Science*, 45/3, 375–77.

PART III

LIFE CYCLE MODELS OF CHANGE

CHAPTER 13

THE LIFE CYCLE PROCESS MODEL

MARSHALL SCOTT POOLE AND
ANDREW H. VAN DE VEN

One of the most common ways of thinking about change is to portray it as a sequence of steps or stages through which the change unfolds. A *life cycle* model depicts the process of change in an entity as progressing through a prescribed sequence of stages and activities over time. Activities in a life cycle model are prescribed and regulated by natural, logical, or institutional routines. In many organizational applications of a life cycle model, the rules prescribing the change process are based on routines learned in the past for managing recurrent changes in efficient and effective ways (Cohen and Sproull 1996; Feldman and Pentland, 2003). Alternatively, they may be externally induced (Rogers 2003) and regulated by sources outside of the organizational entity undergoing change. The life cycle is one of four basic motors of organizational change and development defined by Van de Ven and Poole (1995; Poole, Van de Ven, Dooley and Holmes 2000).

A life cycle theory does not have to be simply a model of passive compliance to mandated change by an entity. Life cycle theories may also consider how proactive individuals adapt to their environments and make use of rules to accomplish their purposes (Gibson 1977; Norman 1988).

The Basic Scheme of a Life Cycle Process Theory

Life cycle theories share three components. First, they posit a unitary sequence of stages that are invariant across cases. A stage is an internally coherent period of activity that serves a specific function for the developing entity. For example, organizational change might proceed through a four-stage sequence: problem recognition—deliberation—change—institutionalization. The sequence is presumed to be "universal" in that every change process will progress through these stages. The duration of stages may vary across cases, but the ordering of stages in the sequence is always the same. For example, for a three-stage sequence, ABC, for one organization A may be quite long, B short, and C midway between in length, while for another organization A might be short, B midway, and C very long. Notwithstanding differences in length and timing, the same sequence describes and explains the unfolding of the process for both organizations.

Second, a complete life cycle theory specifies the organizing principle behind the unitary sequence. There are three types of organizing principles. In some instances, the sequence derives from *logical necessity* in which each successive stage requires the previous ones to occur and there is a logical ordering of stages. Some normative models of decision-making or problem-solving specify a unitary sequence based on logical ordering, conceptual prescriptions of a series of stages that actors, groups, or organizations should go through in order to effectively achieve a goal, such as implementing an organizational change, making a decision, or running a communication campaign. Stouten et al. (2018) conducted an extensive review of one of the most common life cycle models, prescriptive models of planned organizational change. They integrated seven influential models of organizational change to derive a ten-stage model that encompasses the change processes described in the seven models:

1. Assess the opportunity or problem motiving the change
2. Select and support a guiding change coalition
3. Formulate a clear, compelling vision
4. Communicate the vision
5. Mobilize energy for change
6. Empower others to act
7. Develop and promote change-related knowledge and ability
8. Identify short-term wins and use as reinforcement of change progress
9. Monitor and strengthen the change process
10. Institutionalize change in company culture, practices, and management succession

This model is descriptive in that it attempts to show how change typically occurs. It is also purposely prescriptive, in that the steps show how we might organize an effective campaign to implement organizational change. This sequence is presumed to be the one that a rational change agent would follow in bringing about change systematically. Each successive stage depends on the previous stage and cannot be meaningfully undertaken without effective accomplishment of the previous stages. In this case, the argument is that change agents cannot mobilize the organization (step 5) unless they have previously built a coalition and communicated a clear and compelling vision for change. Successive steps empower others and give them the tools to bring about change, encourage change through short-term wins and monitor the change process before finally institutionalizing it.

Another class of organizing principles for life cycle models are *natural progressions* in which each successive stage builds on the accomplishments or growth of previous stages, which must be successfully navigated to move onto the next stage. Structural transitions as organizations grow (Stinchcombe 1965; Mintzberg 1979) represent an example of a unitary sequence based on natural progression. Mintzberg (1979) describes one such sequence: (1) organizations begin with *non-elaborated organic structures* in the entrepreneurial stage, then if they succeed and thrive (2) formalize their operations and management, moving into *bureaucratic structures*, and (3) with further growth, impose market or product groupings to move into *divisionalized structures*. This sequence of stages results from natural growth of the organization and later stages build on the structures of earlier stages, reconfiguring them to meet the demands of an ever larger organization.

A final class of organizing principles for unitary sequences are *legislated progressions* put into place by some regulatory body, such as a government or association. The sequence of activities that a new medicine must navigate in order to win Food and Drug Administration approval in the U.S.A is an example of a legislated progression. One description lists five phases: (1) discovery and development; (2) preclinical research; (3) clinical research (comprised of four sub-phases, each with increasing numbers of subjects involved); (4) FDA review; and (5) FDA post-market safety monitoring (http://diabetespac.org/fda-drug-approval-process/). This sequence is established by authority and mandates a series of activities that should be taken in the specified order. Legislated progressions, unlike logical and natural progressions, can be altered by changes in the law or regulations. The sequence set in place by a legislated progression is also more arbitrary than the logical or natural progressions.

The third component of a life cycle model is a generative mechanism that drives the progression through the stages. This generative mechanism is "where the action is" in the life cycle model and accounts (a) for how each of the stages is realized and "matures" and (b) for transitions from one stage to the next. In some cases, the same generative mechanism will account for both (a) and (b), while in others different generative mechanisms will be required. Stages are not simply "states" that the developing entity (person, organization, decision) is in: they involve particular activities that serve the goals of the stage, and as these activities are carried out the stage is realized. There are generally changes within each stage as its characteristic activities are carried out. For example, during problem analysis, the components of the problem are laid out, its causes explored, and its effects characterized, among other things. Each of these involve actions on the part of the decision-maker(s). As a stage is realized, it sets up the conditions for the next stage, through generating resources that can be used as a foundation for the next stage, and/or through creating problems that will be faced in the next stage, and/or through setting into motion transformations that will generate the next stage from the current one.

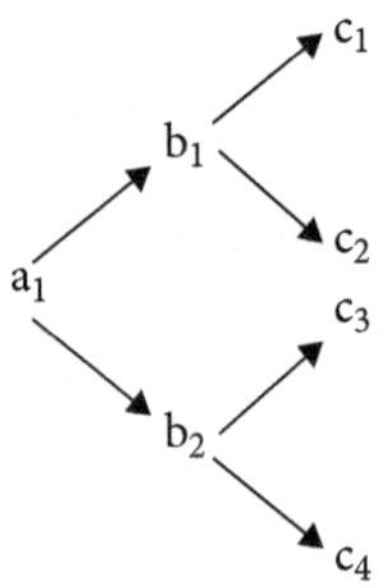

FIGURE 13.1 A Divergent Progression

Generative mechanisms may also describe what might lead to transitions from one stage to another and how the transition occurs. For instance, in Greiner's (1972) model of organizational growth, accumulating problems during each stage leads the organization to adopt new structures and processes to respond to the "crisis" it faces as the stage matures, which results in advancement to a new stage.

Typically, life cycles are depicted as a unitary sequence of stages, but they may be somewhat more complex. In a foundational analysis of life cycle models, van den Daele (1969) discussed several variations on life cycle models, including divergent progressions, in which a stage in the sequence divides into two or more alternatives, yielding a sequence similar to that in Figure 13.1.

For example, for a group following a life cycle the stage subsequent to stage a_1 might have two alternatives, such as conflict (b1) and no conflict (b2). This would yield a branching structure of alternative paths through the sequence. The model is still relatively simple, but there are some alternative paths that the individual, group, or organization may follow.

Qualifications for Life Cycle Process Models

Local adaptations are typically viewed as breakdowns by those who design and mandate a prescribed change routine such as a life cycle process. Prescriptions for change are perceived differently by "planners" who design a change program and "doers" who implement it but did not participate in its developments (Ford et al. 2008). As Pressman and Wildavsky's (1984) classic study of the Oakland rehabilitation complex found, breakdowns happen when "planners" are separated from "doers" because "learning fails when events are caused and consequences are felt by different people" (Pressman and Wildavsky 1984: 135). People are more likely to implement and comply with changes in which they have a part in planning and adapting to fit to their local situations (e.g., Katz and Allen 1982; Lichtenthaler and Ernst 2006). Adding to this, Cialdini (2009) describes a number of psychological experiments indicating that people are more likely to comply with requests of others when: a reason is provided for the request; reciprocity exists; an initial commitment is made; social proof exists that many similar others are complying; requests come from individuals they know and like; requests come from legitimate authority; or the opportunity is scarce, limited, or difficult to attain. All this is to say that a life cycle model, which posits a deterministic, unitary sequence of events, may be derailed by the role of active agents in implementing the sequence. While the sequence may be the optimal path from beginning to end, there are often "detours" on the way in order to gain adherence from agents participating in the life cycle that may complicate the sequence and cause it to diverge from a strict unitary sequence (Poole, 1983).

The chapter by Marcus and Malen in Chapter 14 of this volume, shows that relationships between the regulators and regulated of change can be highly interactive, co-evolving, and produce unintended outcomes. They show that the changes government regulators require generally do not correspond to the changes organizations want to make, or those that they actually end up making. Multiple and divergent regulations from local, regional, and national government regulators often lead organizations to engage in hedging behavior—that is a tendency to simultaneously take actions that align with the regulation while simultaneously taking actions to resist the regulation.

Rice and Rogers (1980) found that reinvention facilitates adopting and implementing change programs. Reinvention is a process of reverse engineering and adapting a change to fit a particular applied setting. It is fundamentally a learning process that is triggered by the inevitable setbacks and mistakes people encounter as they attempt to implement a change program. Reinvention requires some local autonomy to adapt mandated changes. Marcus and Weber (1989) showed that "autonomy," defined as customizing mandated safety guidelines, was necessary in order to implement new safety standards by twenty-eight American nuclear power plants. They found that prior poor implementation records yielded "rule-bounded" approaches, defined as "compliance with the standard technical specifications" (p. 545), and the "rule-bounded" approach produced a vicious cycle which perpetuated poor outcomes. Marcus and Weber (1989) concluded that managers or external regulators should be aware of the possible consequences of blind acceptance of prescribed changes, such as those mandated in the life cycle. Implementers who strictly obey the prescribed change may be complying in bad faith and may not achieve the results intended.

Finally, Piderit (2000), Ford et al. (2008), and Zorn and Scott (Chapter 29 of this volume) question the common assumptions of resistance to change. They note that change managers tend to dichotomize individuals' responses into those who support or resist the proposed change and to view the latter as being disobedient. Piderit (2000) and Ford et al. (2008) discuss a number of reasons why employees resist a prescribed change, including constructive intentions to correct errors that may prevent implementation. The ambivalence that employees feel toward an organizational change initiative does not necessarily represent opposition as disobedience; instead, it may reflect the complexity of most organizational changes as having both positive and negative characteristics.

Reflections and Critical Discussion of Life Cycle Theories

Life cycle process models have several strengths. They are clear and easy to describe. If the stages are defined clearly and cleanly differentiated, it is also generally easy to operationalize life cycle models. This in turn makes a clear test of the model possible, at least in principle.

There are also challenging elements in life cycle models. They are often framed in such a way that they are presented as necessary and deterministic. This implies agents have no freedom of choice, which runs counter to the typical account of the active, intentional nature of agents (Fay 1999). When we acknowledge that active agents are driving the life cycle forward, we need to add some type of "enforcement" mechanism to the life cycle that monitors the agents to ensure that they are moving through the life cycle in a systematic fashion.

The life cycle model is described as though there are clear demarcations between stages. However, stages may sometimes overlap. For example, in the Stouten et al. (2018) article, stages 3 and 4, which deal with vision, are likely to overlap. When this is the case stages "bleed" into each other and it may be difficult to determine when one ends and the next begins; indeed, sometimes this overlap is functional in that the second of the two stages facilitates completion of the first. Overlap definitely complicates testing a life cycle model, because the succession of stages may not be wholly clear.

Another issue is the typicality of the life cycle model. Attuned to human and biological development as we are, this sort of model tends to be the "default" mode of thinking about processes. As a result, it tends to preclude thinking in more complex terms about change, as we might if a dialectical or evolutionary process held. More complex models are harder to think through and test, and so there is a temptation to fall back to the life cycle, when in fact the "world" may be more complex.

Future developments advancing life cycle models should consider the role of agency and choice in these models, moving away from simple determinism. Certainly human agents can plan a sequence ahead and execute and enforce it, giving agency a clear role in life cycle models. In considering agency, it is also important to consider that there may be multiple forms of agency. Pickering (2010) has posited that there are material and cultural agencies, in addition to human agency. These different forms of agency interact in explaining social phenomena, and might be considered as we develop the role of agents in life cycles.

References

Cialdini, R. B. (2009), *Influence: Science and Practice* (London: Pearson Education).

Cohen, M. D., and Sproull, L. (1996), 'Introduction: Special Issue on Organizational Learning', *Organization Science*, 2, i–iii.

Fay, B. (1999), *Contemporary Philosophy of Social Science* (Malden, MA: Blackwell).

Feldman, B., and Pentland, A. (2003), 'Reconceptualizing Organizational Routines as a Source of Flexibility and Change', *Administrative Science Quarterly*, 48, 94–118.

Ford, J. D., Ford, L. W., and D'Amelio, A. (2008), 'Resistance to Change: The Rest of the Story', *Academy of Management Review*, 33, 362–77.

Gibson, J. J. (1977), 'The Theory of Affordances', in R. Shaw and J. Bransford, eds., *Perceiving, Acting, and Knowing* (Hillside, NJ: Lawrence Erlbaum), 67–82.

Greiner, L. (1972, July - August), *Evolution and Revolution as Organizations Grow, Harvard Business Review*, 165–74.

Katz, R. and Allen, T. J. (1982), 'Investigating the Not Invented Here (NIH) Syndrome: A Look at the Performance, Tenure, and Communication Patterns of 50 R & D Project Groups', *R&D Management*, 12, 7–20.

Lichtenthaler, U. and Ernst, H. (2006), 'Attitudes to Externally Organizing Knowledge Management Tasks. *R&D Management*, 36, 367–86.

Marcus, A. A., and Malen, J. (2021), 'Hedging: Organziational Responses to the Formulation, Implementation, and Enforcement of Government Mandated Changes', in M. S. Poole and A. H. Van de Ven, eds., *Oxford Handbook of Organizational Change and Innovation* (2nd edn) (Oxford, U.K. Oxford University Press),

Marcus, A. A. and Weber, B. (1989), 'The Deterrent to Dubious Corporate Behavior: Profitability, Probability and Safety Recalls', *Strategic Management Journal*, 10, 233–50.

Mintzberg, H. (1979), *The Structuring of Organizations* (Englewood Cliffs, NJ: Prentice-Hall).

Norman, D. (1988), *The Design of Everyday Things* (New York: Basic Books).

Pickering, A. (2010), '*The Mangle of Practice: Time, Agency, and Science* (Chicago: University of Chicago Press).

Piderit, S. K. (2000), 'Rethinking Resistance and Recognizing Ambivalence: A Multidimensional View of Attitudes toward Organizational Change', *Academy of Management Review*, 25, 783–94.

Poole, M. S. (l983), 'Decision Development in Small Groups III: A Multiple Sequence Theory of Decision Development', *Communication Monographs*, 50, 32l–4l.

Poole, M. S., Van de Ven, A. H., Dooley, K., and Holmes, M. (2000), *Organizational Innovation and Change Processes: Theory and Methods for Research* (New York: Oxford University Press).

Pressman, J. L., and Wildavsky, A. (1984), *Implementation: How Great Expectations in Washington Are Dashed in Oakland; Or, Why It's Amazing that Federal Programs Work at All, This Being a Saga of the Economic Development Administration As Told By Two Sympathetic Observers Who Seek to Build Morals on a Foundation* (Berkeley, CA: University of California Press).

Rice, R. E., and E. M. Rogers (1980), 'Re-Invention and Innovation: The Case of Dial-a-Ride', *Knowledge*, 1, 499–514.

Rogers, E. M. (2003), *Diffusion of Innovations* (5th ed.) (New York: Simon and Schuster).

Stinchcombe, A. L. (1965), 'Social Structure and Organizations', in J. P. March, ed., *Handbook of Organizations* (Chicago: Rand McNally), 142–93.

Stouten, J., Rousseau, D. M., and De Cremer, D. (2018), 'Successful Organizational Change: Integrating the Management Practice and Scholarly Literatures', *Academy of Management Annals*, 12, 753–88.

Van de Ven, A. H., and Poole, M. S. (1995), 'Explaining Development and Change in Organizations', *Academy of Management Review*, 20, 510–40.

Van den Daele, L. (1969), Qualitative Models in Developmental Analysis', *Developmental Psychology*, 1, 303–10.

Zorn, T. E. and Scott, J. (2021), 'Must we Change? The Dark Side of Change and Change Resistance', in M. S. Poole and A. H. Van de Ven, eds., *Oxford Handbook of Organizational Change and Innovation* (2nd edn) (Oxford, U.K. Oxford University Press).

CHAPTER 14

HEDGING: ORGANIZATIONAL RESPONSES TO THE FORMULATION, IMPLEMENTATION, AND ENFORCEMENT OF GOVERNMENT MANDATED CHANGES

ALFRED MARCUS AND JOEL MALEN

Introduction

To better align the behavior of organizations with the interests of society, governments make many demands on organizations to change their behavior. However, the changes governments require generally do not correspond to the changes organizations want to make, or those that they actually end up making. Organizations hedge in response to the numerous requirements that governments impose on them. This chapter develops a process model of the hedging behavior of organizations in response to government mandates.

Figure 14.1 illustrates the process model. Governments try to hold organizations accountable for their impacts on organizational stakeholders, including those who have ownership rights in organizations, those who work for organizations, those who consume the goods and services that organizations produce, and the effects that organizations have on the natural environment. Governments hold organization accountable by

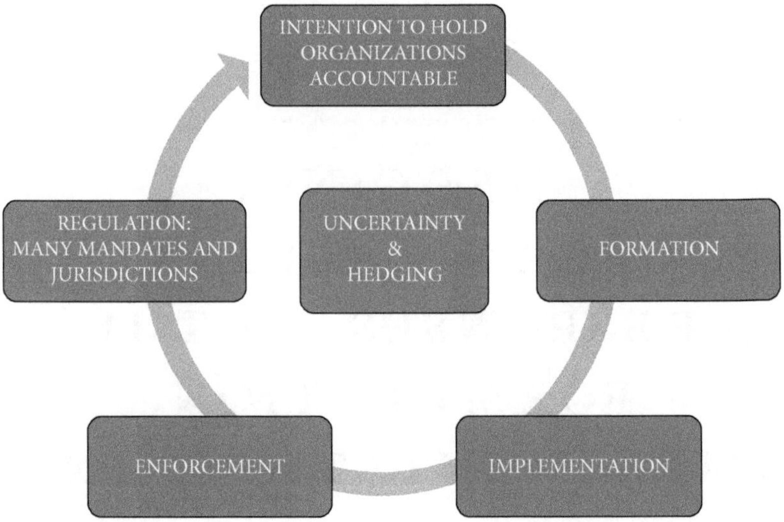

FIGURE 14.1 Organizational Change in Response to Mandatory Government Requirements

regulating their behavior. In order to regulate their behavior, governments at many levels—local, national, and international—must formulate, implement, and enforce laws, not a single law, but many laws that frequently have incompatible and inconsistent standards and means. Organizations are not passive at any stage of the regulatory process. Organizations and other parties mobilize, making the formulation, implementation, and enforcement of numerous regulatory mandates highly contested.

The outcomes of these many contests cannot be known beforehand. Further, the issues that stimulate the process rarely are resolved with a high degree of definiteness. They tend to linger, and any outcomes that do emerge are not stable over time. Regulatory issues leap into and fade from the attention of organizations and many other interest groups in society. They capture and lose media attention. They emerge, re-emerge, become salient, and lose salience again and again. As the arrows in the diagram suggest, the process, therefore, is recursive and takes place over long periods of time.

Thus, the precise changes in behavior across multiple salient domains necessitated by regulation are inherently uncertain. Because of this uncertainty to which organizations enmeshed in the regulatory process are subject, they rarely commit fully to a single strategy. Given the uncertain future conditions organizations subject to regulation face, they hedge their bets (Marcus 2019), that is, being unable to discern how government mandates for change will play out, organizations take steps to simultaneously engage in stonewalling and opportunism. In earlier work (Marcus 1984) labeled the responses that organizations make to regulation as stonewalling and opportunism. Stonewalling involves relying on public relations and employing legal and administrative processes to buffer organizations from regulatory change. Organizations may resort to stonewalling to avoid what they estimate to be costly and unnecessary changes that governments try to force them to undertake. Opportunism, on the other hand, involves embracing regulation. The reasons for embracing it vary. It can be the desire to improve an organization's image by appearing to be progressive. It can involve attempts to transform constraints into opportunities for gain. For instance, organizations benefit from regulations if they can exclude competitors, guarantee prices and profits, control complements and supplements, and/or obtain subsidies.

The term hedging is borrowed from finance where it means moving in more than one direction at once to offset the chance of adverse market movements. Technically, to hedge means to make investments that have a negative correlation, that is, it means to take the ambivalence felt about future directions and to make contradictory bets about what is to come next simultaneously. Hedging also draws on studies of organizational diversification (Sengul, et. al. 2019), which hold that when the future is unknown, organizations do not, and should not, place all their eggs in one basket (Ahuja and Novelli 2017). They should bet on more than one future states of world coming into being at the same time, in the hope that their positive choices more than offset the negative ones, or that these choices sustain them at different moments when different conditions prevail.

Highlighting a Process Model

This chapter highlights thE process model. It puts particular emphasis on three factors that appear in Figure 14.1.

- *The Formulation, Implementation, and Enforcement of Government Mandated Changes.* After legislatures pass laws, administrators carry them out, and courts clarify how they should be interpreted. The laws may be amended and bear little resemblance to their original formulation. Changes in a ruling party or regime can result in full-scale revision. Further, it needs to be recognized that lawmakers typically have a certain amount of cynicism when they formulate a law. They formulate laws for symbolic reasons to gain public approval, but understand that they cannot specify fully all the compliance and enforcement contingencies beforehand. They understand the limitations administrators have in carrying out the laws and the roles courts play in reinterpreting and changing them. Administrators and the courts change the substance of regulations over time in response to many factors including modifications in scientific and technical information and social movement activity. To the extent that organizations stonewall or are opportunistic, they play a role in how laws are implemented, enforced, and amended. They have some leeway in how they respond. Studies point out that regulations rarely are fully effective because organizations participate in the process (Stigler 1975; Peltzman 1976; Marcus 1980). Lapses in fully carrying out the intent of laws, as originally intended, therefore, are very common. To pass legislation in the US and in many other countries requires mobilizing support from a broad public, but once formulated, the legislation must be implemented and enforced. After a law is passed, regulated organizations continue to have power, interest, and the expertise to dictate outcomes. Organizations that wait long enough may be able to avoid full compliance with the laws meant to control their behavior. Their ability to avoid full compliance is a result of "cat and mouse" games that according to Funk and Hirschman (2014, 2017) they play with regulators and other interests in society over time.

- *Many Mandates and Jurisdictions*. In addition, organizations do not confront or engage with solitary government mandates in isolation. They deal with a host of requirements that cover many domains from corporate governance to how organizations treat employees and customers and impact the natural environment. National, local, and international governmental regulatory bodies have separate requirements in each of these domains and the requirements rarely are consistent. This lack of consistency provides organizations with more choices in how they respond—when and under what circumstances will they stonewall or be opportunistic; despite the power of law, organizations have autonomy to make these choices. They have room for maneuver. They can choose on which regulations to focus, which to give less attention to, which to give their endorsement, and which to resist. Though the scholarship on government regulated organizational change is vast, extant research studies overwhelmingly focus on the effects of single regulatory programs in isolation, overlooking the simultaneous impacts of the different regulatory mandates that have emerged in different jurisdictions. Pemer and Skjølsvik (2017), for instance, contend that regulatory change tends not to grapple with the combined effects of regulatory programs. This combined effect is of fundamental importance because of the autonomy it gives organizations and the uncertainty it introduces into the system (Marcus 1981).
- *Uncertainty and Hedging*. Temporal instability and multidimensional regulatory context augment uncertainty about whether the many laws governments formulate will be implemented fully, enforced, and achieve intended goals. Consider how Pressman and Wildavsky (1973) describe the process of how regulation unfolds. The instructions given by authorities of the many domains in which organizations are regulated are rarely clear. In each of the domains, there are numerous participants, perspectives, and decisions that have to be made across a series of steps. The conflict among competing interests and values does not go away after laws have been formulated. Ambiguity and resistance persist during implementation and enforcement, and therefore, neither implementation nor enforcement are likely to be simple and straightforward. The mix of mandates that organizations confront, moreover, is not stable over time, making the pathways for the unfolding of regulations even more complex, convoluted, and

uncertain, and the uncertainty provides organizations with considerable leeway in what they actually end up doing (Marcus and Van de Ven 2015; Hoffman and Ventresca 2002). The choices organizations make can be characterized along a continuum. At one end is a "fight all the way" approach whereby organizations do less or at most only what is required. At the other end is an actively progressive approach by which organizations take a leadership position and do more or even much more than is necessary. Typically, organizations will move in *both* of these directions simultaneously, depending on the mandate, the jurisdiction, their leadership at the time, social movement pressure, and other factors. Sometimes, they tilt more in the direction of stonewalling, while in other instances they tilt more in the direction of opportunism. In short, they hedge their bets. Their reactions to a multitude of different mandates is rarely consistent. The many responses to the changes governments try to compel them to make rarely can be classified collectively as entirely consisting of stonewalling or opportunism.

Taken together, the above three elements in the response of organizations to regulation combine to ensure the process of change that unfolds in response to government efforts to bring about change through regulation is neither smooth nor linear. Rather, it involves back and forth posturing by many governments and government entities that regulate organizational behavior and the organizations responsible for responding to these efforts at many stages across multiple jurisdictions. In this atmosphere of regulatory instability and organizational autonomy, each organization is likely to fashion a unique and distinct hedging strategy in the regulatory domains to which it is subject.

This chapter further explores this process by highlighting first, the reasons why governments attempt to regulate organizational behavior and what actually happens as regulations arise and governments attempt to control organizational behavior during regulatory formulation, implementation, and enforcement stages. Second, the chapter describes in more detail the types of regulations that organizations face in different arenas and jurisdictions. Specifically, it examines regulations that affect the ownership of organizations, their relations to employees and customers, and the impacts they have on the natural environment. Third, the chapter depicts how uncertainty takes hold and how organizations respond to this uncertainty with hedging strategies. In the face of a complex regulatory climate, mandating diverse and potentially inconsistent behaviors, organizations move back and forth between strategies that resist and that conform to the regulated changes governments attempt to promote.

In terms of bringing about desired organizational behaviors that are in the interests of the public, the cycles of regulation and organizational responses have been at times positive, at other times negative, and at other times neutral with not much progress achieved. Regardless of the outcome, the process nearly always unfolds in ways governments and regulated organizations rarely anticipated in advance.

The Formation, Implementation, and Enforcement of Regulatory Change

Extensive scholarship has analyzed how external mandates arise, what happens when they take effect, and to what degree governments implement and enforce them effectively (e.g., see Wilson 1980; Bernstein 1955). Though each instance is different, nearly every regulatory enactment results in unintended consequences that social movements and interest groups become aware of and try to fix by publicizing these problems. Marcus and Geffen (1998), for example, depict how the aim of the 1990 Clean Air Act amendments was to save East coast coal miners' jobs by having coal-fired power plants install scrubbers. Instead, to save money, the power plants lowered their emissions by importing low sulfur coal from strip mines in Wyoming, thus boosting the railroads' economic activity. While the increased demand helped the railroads to modernize, many coal miners in the East lost their jobs. In direct contrast to the intent of the regulation, the intended beneficiary—coal miners—was hurt, while a group that was not considered—the railroads—were restored to profitability at a point when many were close to bankruptcy. This example is just one of many where unintended consequences arise from the uncertainty of government-regulated change.

Government attempts to regulate organizational behavior are frequently preceded by a notable event, often a series of scandals, accidents or crises, that receives significant media coverage and stimulates governments to act. The process of developing legislation to the perceived problem is strongly contested by various stakeholders and interest groups, including the organizations whose behavior the government is attempting to change. Accordingly, any legislation that is passed often fails to go as far as lawmakers had originally intended when taking up the issue. Once put into legislation, there emerge notable gaps and weaknesses in the regulatory statutes lawmakers formulate. These gaps become apparent in implementation and enforcement stages.

Even under the best conditions, legislators cannot anticipate all the situations that administrators and enforcement officials will confront. There is an inherent ambiguity in all systems of rules (Mahoney and Thelen 2009). The typical regulation cannot, and does not, cover every case. During implementation, how best to induce organizations to change can become a technical issue lacking clear approaches that governments should follow.

Ambiguity of regulation can lead to what have been called "cat and mouse" games. Such games are especially pervasive when governments set far-reaching goals without providing sufficient clarity regarding how they expect organizations to achieve these goals (Funk and Hirschman 2017). For example, legislators in California tried to ban the sale of assault weapons in 1989, 1999, and again in 2006. However, gun makers consistently found ways to get around these restrictions by selling slightly altered semi-automatic weapons with the same rapid-fire lethal capabilities (Ellinson and McWhirter 2019). Regulatory games can last for long periods, from the time discussion first begins about the government formulating regulations to many years later when regulated changes have been in place for a long time and have been modified as they are implemented and subject to court challenges. While these "cat and mouse" games often distort and undermine regulatory intent (dos Santos 1996), they also can adjust regulatory goals to contexts regulators had not fully anticipated and better customize the rules to real-world conditions (Jarzabkowski et al. 2018; Marcus 1998a; Marcus 1998b; Marcus and Weber 1989).

Scholarship demonstrates that regulators have considerable latitude in how they choose to implement and enforce requirements (e.g., see Wilson 1980; Bernstein 1955). Funk and Hirschman (2014) show how this ambiguity, along with organizational participation in the rule-making process, allows organizations to undermine regulatory intent. Organizations can capture the agencies that are supposed to control their behavior. They attempt to put in place policies that will protect and exploit their capabilities and block policies that threaten these capabilities (e.g., see Lyon et al. 2018; Dal Bó 2006). This process often results in organizations being able to engage in activities analogous to those the government tried to restrict.

Courts frequently become the arbiter of post-enactment conflicts in how regulations are to be enforced. Eventually, regulators and enforcement officers, often under the influence of the organizations they are supposed to control, must offer their own interpretations of a legislative mandate. Interpretations of regulatory bodies can be, and often are, challenged repeatedly over time in the judicial system (Edelman 1992). However, important asymmetries exist with respect to the level of economic resources available to government to enforce regulations and organizations to resist those efforts—with organizations typically holding a major advantage. Organizations have the capacity to hire expensive, focused legal counsel who contend with overstretched government legal staff, and all too often the corporate attorneys overwhelm government attorneys in the courts. They bring about favorable rulings for regulated organizations that eviscerate the efforts to control their behavior.

Thus, regulated organizations typically have the power to stall, deflect, and fight regulation. They can, if they wish, push for fundamental regulatory reform and revision that is beneficial to their interests. They can attempt to stonewall the full force of regulatory mandates governments may try to impose. Of course they are free to choose whether or not to do so. Some organizations, rather than resisting, may be opportunistic and seize upon regulatory mandates to achieve some benefit. Within the same industry among organizations very similar in most respects, one finds both stonewalling and opportunism, thus demonstrating the degree to which organizations have discretion in how they respond to regulation. Such freedom of response compounds how the regulatory process unfolds. The interpretations and reinterpretations of regulatory statutes by judicial authorities brought about by the intervention of social movements as well as regulated organizations can lead to an enactment's revision, which restarts the regulatory process. Without the backing of the courts, enforcement officials have limited abilities to coerce organizations to comply. To some extent when legislators pass a law they must trust organizations to make good faith efforts to carry out the law.

They cannot impose compliance. The organizations generally are too powerful. There are information asymmetries between organizations and governments with respect to internal operations of organizations, and the number of regulated organizations enforcement officials must monitor is too vast.

Many Mandates and Jurisdictions

To understand the diversity of regulations a typical organization in the US faces, a brief review of some of the main regulatory enactments to which they are subject is worth carrying out (Marcus and Hargrave 2021). Here we describe only major regulatory areas covering an organization's primary stakeholders: shareholders, employees, customers, and the natural environment. The diverse laws depicted in this section are essential features of the regulatory programs in the US and, in their intent, of most countries of the world. Though the common aim of these programs is to compel organizations to alter how they would behave, how each of them has been formulated, implemented, and enforced varies greatly across jurisdictions as well as within jurisdictions over time.

Most countries in the world and most jurisdictions within countries have variations on these laws. Within countries, there also are differences by state, province, and/or municipality. Each state in the US, for instance, tends to have its own version of laws. US regulations are not uniform in that states typically modify national laws in addition to having their own existing statutes and histories of relevant judicial decisions. In other countries, a similar situation prevails. International bodies support or add to the laws with codes and standards of their own. The European Union (EU) has general regulatory authority for all countries that belong to it, but each country has the right to adapt these laws to its own circumstances. Within each European country, there are differences by province and metropolitan area. What pertains to Paris may not be relevant in Warsaw. China is the same. Its powerful centralized state might have to cede to provincial and local authorities with regard to the specifics of how a regulation is enforced. Beyond variation in content across jurisdictions, the means by which laws are enforced, and the actual degree of enforcement varies greatly. In sum, the US laws summarized next do not apply across the board or uniformly to each organization.

Organizations that are headquartered and operate in the US exist in a context in which there are many different global, national, and local regulatory enactments. There also are international frameworks, which also influence their behavior. All of the regulations both the mandatory ones and the voluntary international frameworks operate on their own timetable and they change at different rates. These variances provide organizations with choices in how to respond. They can move their operations from jurisdiction to jurisdiction, for instance; and these variances result in differences in how organization change their behavior. The following sections describe laws to protect shareholders, employees, consumers, and the environment that a typical organization would face in the US.

Laws to Protect Shareholders

Many US laws exist to protect shareholders. Congress enacted the main securities laws in the US in response to the stock market crash of 1929 and the subsequent Depression. These laws designed to protect shareholders require that companies provide full and accurate information about their financial position when they first offer stock and annually thereafter. In recent times, in response to a wave of financial scandals (dos Santos 1996), Congress has expanded upon these laws, in spite of vigorous business opposition. In 2002, Congress passed the Sarbanes-Oxley Corporate Fraud Accountability Act, the purpose of which was to further increase the protection afforded to investors. This law requires the board of directors of organizations to provide additional oversight of financial reports, and chief executive and financial officers to certify their accuracy. The main reason for these laws is to ensure that directors and managers work on behalf of shareholders as opposed to enriching themselves.

Regulatory frameworks for protecting shareholders vary within as well as across political jurisdictions. International bodies also have established cross-boundary standards to which they expect organizations to comply such as the OECD global framework.[1] In addition, in the US nearly every state has somewhat different incorporation laws. Delaware and Nevada, where most corporations are incorporated, call for shareholder primacy. Minnesota, where far fewer corporations are incorporated, obligates organizations to take into account the interests of all stakeholders. Globally, so-called Anglo-Saxon nations like the US, the UK, Canada, and Australia tend to follow the path of Delaware and Nevada, while nations in Europe like Germany are governed by co-determination rules which incorporate labor representation on boards of directors. In Asia, the laws of corporate governance often follow an approach similar to that employed in Japan, which has a balanced approach not quite like that of the Anglo-Saxon nations and not quite like that of Europe.

The point is that no single regulatory scheme exists globally in the realm of shareholder rights and that applies universally. Hence, US organizations have choices with respect to where they wish to incorporate and to what set of regulations they wish to subject themselves. This pattern of regulation that applies to shareholder rights is common to regulations in nearly every domain. The lack of uniformity within and across jurisdictions permits companies to craft their own regulatory strategies by cherry picking among the various jurisdictions that are trying to control their behavior.

[1] See for example Stilpon Nestor, International Efforts to Improve Corporate Governance: Why and How http://www.oecd.org/corporate/ca/corporategovernanceprinciples/1932028.pdf/, accessed 17 August, 2020.

Laws to Protect Employees

Another prominent domain covered by US regulation relates to the well-being of employees. During the Great Depression, the US Congress first enacted serious national laws in this domain. Under these laws, it set up the National Labor Relations Act (NLRA), which provides employees with the right to establish and operate unions and bargain collectively. The NLRA also prohibits employers from interfering with employees' ability to organize and bargain collectively. Labor laws also prevent unions from coercing employees to join a union. Hence, the actual rights of employees depend on how agencies like the National Labor Relations Board and the courts interpret them and how they are implemented in the different US states. Some states, for instance, have vigorously protected employees' rights to unionize. Other have not. Many corporations, including both Whole Foods and Walmart, have successfully fought unionization. In addition to laws permitting unionization, the federal Fair Labor Standards Act (FLSA) imposes a minimum hourly wage rate and mandates overtime pay. Yet each state and municipality is free to go its own way and many have adopted their own minimum wage laws which go beyond the federal mandate.

Another law applicable to labor is the Occupational Safety and Health Act which Congress passed in the 1960s. Under this law, Congress established the Occupational Safety and Health Administration (OSHA). Its goal is to protect workers' health and safety. These laws grant to employees rights and impose obligations on employers. Again, each state has its own occupational health and safety law and level of enforcement, which may differ in important ways.

Globally, the laws protecting labor are much stronger in Germany and much of the rest of Europe, where it is far harder to lay off an employee than in the US, where most employees can be fired for little or no cause. This difference played a role in Walmart's decision to withdraw from doing business in Germany and the European continent, despite the economic gains it could have achieved there. US automakers as well have seen their European operations consistently lose money, which they tend to blame on excessively stringent European labor requirements that do not allow them to fire workers easily and close down production facilities that are no longer profitable without bureaucratic delay.

Laws to Protect Consumers

In addition to protecting the rights of shareholders and employees, the US Congress also has enacted consumer protection laws. These laws are both broad in scope and hard to enforce since the US government typically can take up only one case at a time and the burden of proof on plaintiffs of winning such cases is very high. Nonetheless, the US does have extensive laws on the books designed to protect consumers. Among the most prominent are antitrust laws meant to prevent collusion, cartels, mergers, and acquisitions that would reduce competition and hurt consumers by increasing prices. Whether such changes in organizational scope actually hurt consumers is decided on a case-by-case basis. The counter argument to such change hurting consumers is that the economies of scale and scope and the efficiencies brought about by organizational restructuring and consolidation are in consumers' interest. In the merger between T-Mobile and Sprint, the Federal Communications Commission (FCC), tasked with deciding on the legality of that merger, split in its decision. While the two Democrats on the committee had concerns that prices would rise, their three Republican colleagues did not, and therefore the merger was allowed.

The interpretation of anti-trust laws is important and it changes over time. The change is a result not just of the political affiliations of appointed officials. The change comes from legal reinterpretation about what constitutes fairness in a capitalist economy. Until the Kennedy administration, an ultra-high market share indicated a company may have been violating anti-trust laws might. However, subsequent doctrine changed during the Nixon and Reagan administrations and the focus of violations shifted toward corporate misconduct; high market share had to be a result of wrongful corporate action. So long as the entry of new organizations was not blocked, a market share of 100 percent was not sufficient reason to start a case against a company.

Despite this alteration in the interpretation of anti-trust laws, significant rulings took place. These shook up whole industries and changed the global economy. The modern era of telecommunications was ushered in by dissolving AT&T's monopoly. The 1982 breakup of this company made possible a new era of telecommunications. On the other hand, the failure of anti-trust laws to bring about Microsoft's breakup in the late 1990s, arguably, slowed the pace of organizational and economic change. The government lost this case despite demonstrating some degree of wrongful conduct on Microsoft's part.

Anti-trust is not the only focus of US consumer protection laws. The Consumer Product Safety Commission (CPSC) has a broad mandate to assure the safety of a wide array of products people use. The National Highway Traffic Safety Administration (NHTSA) holds authority over motor vehicles. The Food and Drug Administration (FDA) focuses on food, pharmaceuticals, and medical devices. This agency often finds itself in the cross-hairs between the interests of large drug and medical device companies and individual safety. It has had several major failures in regulating these companies, for example with respect to Merck's Vioxx pain killer and Johnson and Johnson's DePuy hip replacement. In these instances, regulators had ample warning that consumers were seriously threatened, but they chose not to act until it was far too late (Marcus 2016); by that time, many people had died and suffered severe injuries. A reason for these lapses is the revolving door between positions of authority at the FDA and high level and lucrative positions in the companies that the FDA regulates.

The 1968 Truth in Lending Act is supposed to provide another form of consumer protection. This law requires financial institutions and credit card companies to offer easy-to-understand information about costs and terms, yet its inability to function effectively was a primary causes of the 2007-08 financial crisis, as consumers were duped into taking out automatic re-adjustable mortgages for which they were ill equipped to deal as interest rates rose and the economy tanked. After the financial crisis, Congress therefore, established the Consumer Financial Protection Bureau (CFPB) to better oversee banking, mortgage lending, and debt collection. As head of this agency under President Obama, Elizabeth Warren attempted to carry out the law, but the banking industry considered her efforts too energetic. With the change of administration under President Trump, this agency, like other regulatory agencies, was eviscerated, and there were calls for its elimination.

This pattern is not uncommon in the regulation of shareholder, employee, and consumer rights in the US. Legislation passed in the hope that it will correct a marketplace problem often weakens over time. Originally tough regulations meant to change organizational behavior may be pulled back or eliminated.

Globally, each nation has its own regulations to protect consumers. European Union (EU) anti-trust authorities have become stricter than US authorities and more willing to challenge major organizations, both on the grounds of wrongful practice and high market share. They have gone after tech giants like Microsoft, Facebook, and Intel in ways that US authorities have not. The EU also has demanded that product labels indicate whether a food contains GMOs (genetically modified organisms), a requirement that does not exists in the US and has not been seriously considered (Marcus 2016). Another example of where the EU has gone farther than regulatory authorities in US is in its regulation of Internet privacy where the EU has adopted laws to protect privacy, while no such laws exist in the US.

Laws to Protect the Environment

Starting in the 1970s, the US Congress made a concerted and comprehensive effort to address environmental issues (Marcus 1980). In that year it established the Environmental Protection Agency (EPA) in addition to enacting a suite of new national laws for the EPA to enforce. Prior to the EPA's establishment most US environmental protection laws were enforced on a state-by-state basis. Though the changes that took place in 1970 were vast, Congress explicitly chose not to pass a single comprehensive environmental bill. It did not pass such a bill despite the fact that it was well understood at the time that environmental problems intimately relate to each other; pollution that goes into earth or water, for instance, can be diverted to the air and so on. Laws applying to different environmental media may not be relevant to all of a factory's connected systems. The failure to pass comprehensive environmental regulation has sown confusion in the US and throughout the world as many nations have copied the US approach and also adopted separate regulation for different types of environmental impact. Organizations, as result, can often evade the need to eliminate pollution at its source; instead, moving the pollution from media to media, depending on what relevant laws are in place.

Each environmental law in the US has a different emphasis and is governed by different rules of administration and implementation. Table 14.1 is a list of some of the most significant environmental statutes the US Congress passed from 1970 to 1990. Water pollution laws are technology-based and designed to accomplish best available and achievable technology standards within specified time periods to assure that waterways are fishable and swimmable. Air pollution laws are goal-based and designed to achieve health standards. Further, air pollution laws are "grandfathered-in." They only apply technology standards to new facilities. This provision in the air pollution laws has created a perverse incentive for organizations *not* to build new facilities; instead, they rely on the technicality in the law to make a series of minor improvements rather than update their facilities out of a concern they will be designated new and therefore be subject to technology controls. The mishmash of environmental requirements in place provides firms with discretion in how they respond, which laws to prioritize, which changes to make, and how to make the changes.

The variance in corporate response, in turn, adds to the burden of enforcement officials, who must treat each facility on a case-by-case basis. Technical challenges also plague the process by which the laws are enforced. Understanding what constitutes "clean" as opposed to "unclean" air or what "best" available or achievable technology means is not simple. It has resulted in countless court cases. Idiosyncratic characteristics of individual facilities make it difficult to determine what enforcement officials should consider fair in comparison to other facilities. The appropriate solution to an environmental problem for a given facility never has been straightforward.

Controversy about feasibility and economic impacts also have affected the implementation of environmental protection laws in the US. From the beginning, such controversy has been intense.[2] Monitoring progress and compliance only adds to the challenge. The net result has been near continuous battles between regulated organizations, enforcement officials, communities, and national and local environmental organizations. Many of these battles have been conducted in the court of public opinion as well as the judicial system. Refinements of these laws through amendments have taken place, often stimulated by new ideas that economists or engineers introduce. At every turn, some organizations have resisted the implementation of environmental laws, fought against them in the courts, and lobbied to eliminate or change them.

[2] Stewart's analysis (1981) remains one of the best of this situation. He analyzes the tools used in environmental regulation and the standards, and the types of specifications on which authorities try to rely. His analysis takes up rulemaking, adjudication, and judicial review. It examines affordability criteria, moving targets, and overlapping requirements, and considers reliance on economic trade-offs, variances, and waivers. Stewart concludes that unpredictability and unintended consequences are the norm (also see Wilson 1967). He develops alternative decision processes that would make the system more predictable, but governments have implemented few of the modifications he recommended. The problems that Stewart has dissected persist.

Table 14.1 Major US Environmental Protection Laws: 1976–1990

Clean Air Act	• Sets national ambient air quality standards for various pollutants by determining their maximum concentrations. • Establishes emission standards for hazardous pollutants and individual source emissions limitations. • States make their own implementation plans though the EPA (environmental protection agency) administers the act.
Clean Water Act	• Aims to restore and maintain the chemical, physical, and biological integrity of US waterways. • Restricts effluent discharges into navigable waters through a permitting system known as the National Pollutant Discharge Elimination System (NPDES). • A separate statute, the Safe Drinking Water Act (SDWA), regulates drinking water.
Resource Conservation and Recovery Act	• Imposes cradle-to-grave liability on generators making them responsible for storage, transportation, and final treatment, or disposal of their waste.
Comprehensive Environmental Response, Compensation, and Liability Act	• Comprehensive national program for systematic control of hazardous waste. • Generators have *cradle-to-grave* liability for waste storage, transportation, and final treatment or disposal.
Toxic Substances Control Act	• Requires that chemicals be registered and screened for toxicity before use. • Covers toxic substances in everyday products and their by-products. • Puts the burden of proof of a chemical's safety on those proposing to use it.
Endangered Species Act	• Designed to protect endangered flora and fauna from extinction. • Species designated as either endangered, or threatened (likely to become endangered). • Requires protection of "critical habitat" of endangered species. • Administered by the US Fish and Wildlife Service and the National Marine Fisheries Service.
Clean Air Act Amendments	• Substantially strengthens penalties for noncompliant regions. • Addresses the problems of acid rain, urban smog, airborne toxins, and ozone-depleting chemicals. • EPA auctions a limited number of SO2 emissions allowances for each year. • Firms holding the allowances use them to emit SO2; firms also may bank them for later use or sell them.

At the same time, environmental organizations have sued the government and regulated organizations for not effectively carrying out the laws as required by statute. Rather than resist, some organizations voluntarily have gone beyond, even far beyond, what environmental laws require. They have done so either to gain commercial or reputational advantage, or both. However, such efforts often are selective. While 3M's manufacturing facilities have been notorious polluters of the waterways and land in and around the Saint Paul and Minneapolis area, the company also has been a pioneer in going beyond compliance with an innovative pollution prevention program that many other chemical companies copied for public benefit (Marcus et al. 2002).

Leakage in the enforcement of environmental laws comes about because organizations seek pollution havens outside the US. This exit from the US, in turn, has negatively affected the industrial base of the country in ways unanticipated when major environmental laws were passed. The natural environment in the US has improved, no doubt, partially as a result of the passage of and enforcement of environmental laws but also because of the exit of polluting facilities from the US. Too much of US pollution has been exported abroad, especially to China. Chinese officials, meanwhile, have had to stiffen their own environmental standards because of the rapid degradation of the health and welfare of the countries' citizens.

Laws to Prevent Climate Change

Regulations to mitigate climate further illustrate variations in regulatory enactments. Policies that regulate carbon exist at various supranational, national, and subnational levels, as well as across administrative bodies within jurisdictions. This variation simultaneously increases the degree to which organizations can craft their own strategies while making organizational change difficult. This phenomenon applicable to all climate mandates is especially pertinent to automobile companies (Marcus 2019; De Stefano et al. 2016; Aghion et al. 2016) that face different climate change policies at supranational, national, subnational, and global levels.[3]

Supranational Climate Change Regulation. Over the past decade, the EU, which signed the Kyoto Protocol—unlike the US—agreed to reduce its carbon dioxide emissions further than it originally promised. In 2014, it lowered its average carbon dioxide emissions target for light commercial vehicles to 147 grams per kilometer starting in 2020 and 95 grams per kilometer for passenger cars beginning in 2021. It also strengthened standards to limit emissions of diesel-powered vehicles and bring them down to a level equivalent to gasoline-powered vehicles.

National Climate Change Regulation. The US, not a signatory to the Kyoto agreement, only acted after a 2007 US Supreme Court ruling gave the EPA the authority to

[3] Temporal complexity further complicates this picture. Penna and Geels (2015) mapped the reorientation of US auto firms to environmental regulations from 1979 to 2012 as a series of stages consisting of: problem emergence and company neglect, rising public concerns and continued company defensiveness, political debates and controversies and company hedging, substantive policy formation and company diversification, and spillovers and strategic reorientation. The development of policies, however, were far more uneven in the subsequent 2012–2018 period (Marcus 2019). An amalgam of diverse laws and policies and their unpredictable unfolding stood in the way of rapid change.

regulate automotive greenhouse gases. Before that, it had been unclear if it had this authority under various versions of the Clean Air Act. The EPA then strengthened standards for a number of different pollutants in phases starting in 2017 through 2025 to bring them in line with California, which as a separate jurisdiction with special pollution problems, has the right to go further than the federal government to regulate pollution within its borders. Along with the National Highway Traffic Administration (NHTSA), the EPA set 2025 Corporate Average Fuel Economy (CAFE) standards at 163 grams of carbon dioxide per mile, equivalent to 54.5 miles per gallon, subject to re-evaluation in 2018.

The US standards were very different from those of the EU, which created a dilemma for automotive companies about what type of R&D to conduct, and to what extent they could harmonize global vehicle production. The Trump administration has tried to rescind the EPA and NHTSA standards, despite the objections of some of the auto companies, so that the standing of these controls in the US was in doubt.

Subnational Climate Change Regulation. The Trump administration also tried to eliminate California's special status. Lacking a national standard, the California Air Resources Board (CARB), which had the right to set its standards separate from the federal government, adopted a zero-emission requirement for model years 2005 and beyond. At the same time, the states of New York, Massachusetts, Connecticut, Maine, Maryland, New Jersey, New Mexico, Oregon, Pennsylvania, Rhode Island, Vermont, Washington, Delaware, and Colorado either adopted, or planned to adopt, regulations substantially similar to California's. Thus, global auto companies operating in the US faced a bevy of different requirements – some at the national and some at the state level, substantially complicating the challenge of how to respond. Without consistency among these laws, their concern was they might have to develop different models for different regions.

Climate Change Regulation outside the US. Outside the US, the EU and other countries, such as Korea, Mexico, Brazil, Taiwan, and India, introduced their own fuel-consumption regulations to reduce carbon emissions. These standards were customized to domestic requirements and adopted elements of approaches used in other countries based on local circumstances and needs. The result has been a patchwork of climate-related regulations throughout the world. On top of these diverse regulations, each country has additional policies relating to carbon emissions, including subsidies and other types of initiatives.

Among countries outside the EU and the US that regulated carbon emissions, Chinese regulations have been especially significant. They were influential because the Chinese auto market has been virtually the only market in the world experiencing meaningful growth in the sales of automobiles and other motor vehicles. In the rest of the world sales growth tended to be flat or under 2 percent per annum. China's climate change regulations called for the development of new technologies, such as high-performance batteries, and dictated limits on vehicle sales for manufacturers unable to develop such technologies within the timetable mandated by the government.

Uncertainty and Hedging

As shown, the burden the regulatory enactments place on organizations to comply differs from jurisdiction to jurisdiction. In every country in which an organization operates there also are likely to be laws, similar perhaps in intent but different in substance and content to those in place in their home country. Therefore, organizations have flexibility regarding which regulations they choose to comply with and how choose to comply. If an organization is not comfortable with a state's securities or tax laws, for instance, it can change jurisdictions. If it can save money by locating its production abroad where home country labor regulations do not apply or apply in a different way, it can make this change. If environmental regulations where it is located are onerous and stringently enforced, it can move its manufacturing facilities to another location where these regulation may not even exist, and if they do exist, their enforcement is at best nominal.

The aggregate result is that regulated organizations do not face a single, consistent set of regulations originating from a single government entity. Rather they face a host of different regulations emanating from different government bodies, some local, some national, and some international. Organizations face uncertainty not only because of different standards in different parts of the world but because they are uncertain if these standards will remain in place as governments change, the performance of the global economy fluctuates, and different types of technological advancement take place.

Uncertainty and Responding to Regulation

Uneven development of regulations creates substantial uncertainty for organizations (Marcus 1984; Rothenberg and Ettlie 2011; Marcus et al. 2011), which can deter or interfere with change. Because regulatory uncertainty shapes such factors as future prices, costs, demand and competitiveness, it makes forecasting and planning generally difficult. Without certainty, organizations cannot commit fully to a course of action. Neo-classical economic theory assumes that accurate predictions about price, demand, technology, and supply are possible. However, Rumelt and Lamb (1984) suggest that the type of regulatory uncertainty described can provoke results that depart significantly from rationality. After legislatures pass laws, agencies create regulations to implement and enforce these laws. At this point, no matter how detailed the laws and regulations, the laws are subject to modification. Complex negotiations among affected parties, regulators, social movements, and others shape regulations and the changes that take place in uncertain ways. Under these conditions, decision makers within organizations cannot readily assess the opportunities and risks and make the necessary trade-offs for the long-term investments they must make to yield the sizeable organizational changes that sometimes are needed. As decision-makers examine what is likely to happen next, they realize that contingencies are likely to increase and unexpected interactions likely to grow, and thus the orthodox approaches to decision-making that they might use are not likely to be reliable (Ghemawat 1991). With so much uncertainty, accurate predictions about the future are not possible. Decision makers must engage in simplified analysis; therefore, it is hard for them to make firm and lasting commitments (Ghemawat 1991). They must hedge their bets.

Regulatory uncertainty exacerbates the other types of uncertainty—state, effect, and response—that also exist (Milliken 1987). To make weighty changes, organizational decision-makers would have to commit scarce resources to future outcomes, but if they have little assurance these outcomes will come into being, their capacity to make these extensive changes decreases. The more organizational decision-makers must engage with uncertain conditions, in which they do not know the chances of payoffs/losses and their magnitude in advance, the less they can rely on rational/analytical decision-making and the more cognitive and collective errors they are likely to make. The less they rely on rational/analytical decision-making, the more other factors such as organizational politics and imitation of rivals are likely to influence what they do. The less they rely on rational/analytical decision-making, the more errors they can make and, because they are aware of this tendency, the more cautious they are likely to become.

One choice in how organizations respond is drift; that is to let the process of regulation take its course without an active response. Many organizations are not able to create a coherent response in a timely way. Although seemingly not a choice, the inability to forge a coherent response is in its own way a kind of choice. A related option is that organizations, while delaying a response, can observe what other organizations are doing and perhaps choose to join them or reject their approaches.

In the face of the multitude of regulatory programs that exist, organizations must make trade-offs, prioritizing some of the regulations that exist, while giving less attention to others. Decisions must be made based on many factors, including which markets they regard as most important and where social movement pressure, lobbying, and public attitudes operate in ways beneficial or not beneficial. Thus, each organization, if its responses to regulation are taken together, is likely to develop a unique set of strategies and to change differently in response to the regulatory challenges it faces.

Anticipating how the unique state of affairs in an organization influences its response depends on many factors internal and external to the organization. How organizations that face vast numbers of regulations prioritize each one is hard to foretell given differences in organizations' leadership, financial status, and operational capabilities, Even if organizations have reputations for a type of response—whether it be opposition and stonewalling or cooperation with the government and opportunism, their response may not be uniform across the different types of regulation they encounter. In some instances, they may willingly go along with government mandates, while in other instances they may try to circumvent regulations government imposes. Some regulations, they evade, others they support and embrace. They may or may not be able manage regulation for their benefit (Marcus 1984). Regulatory restrictions challenge managers' skills. They must identify the competitive impacts of regulations. Large and efficient organizations may gain because of economies of scale, while small and recent entrants may gain because they are technologically advanced and are ahead on the learning curve.[4] Who the winners and losers are is not obvious.

Organizations also appraise their political acumen and the extent to which they possess the capabilities to influence politicians, administrators, and the courts. The ability of organizations to influence regulatory direction arises not just from lobbying and contact with government officials and other organizational leaders. This ability also depends on the capacity to conduct sophisticated economic and technical analysis, to forge coalitions, and to make arguments that appear to be in the public interest and not just self-serving. Strictly classifying organizational responses as opportunism or stonewalling ignores the dynamic characteristics of actual responses which often involve simultaneous stonewalling and opportunism or movement from one type of response to another.

For instance, standard economic reasoning maintains that environmental regulation imposes costs on organizations (Jaffee et al. 1995; Majumdar and Marcus 2001). Since these costs tend to be rigid, inefficient, ineffective, and do harm to organizations, the response of organizations should be resistance. However, the strategic management literature emphasizes that organizations do not just resist. Rather, they respond in distinct and idiosyncratic ways. Environmental regulation can induce some to innovate, become more efficient, and perform better (Hart 1995; Aragón-Correa and Sharma 2003; Marcus and Fremeth 2009. Vogel (2007) contests the degree to which this outcome is common, but a growing body of work came to support the idea that under some circumstances it does "pay" to be "green" (Esty and Winston 2009). If it pays, then organizations respond in opportunistic ways. Some try to get ahead of the curve and embrace environmental regulation, whiles other continue to stonewall.

Hedging

In the face of uncertainty, organizations hedge their bets. That is, they may engage in both stonewalling and opportunism simultaneously or move in sequence from one type of response to another. Pursuing multiple responses is, however, difficult. If organizations

[4] When challenged by stringent pollution control requirements, 3M, for instance, relied on its superior technical and organizational capabilities in order to innovate and create more efficient processes and products (Marcus et al. 2002). When it conducted clean-ups at its own facilities and when it helped other companies do clean-ups at their facilities, yields grew and costs fell. Of course, this type of win-win scenario in which an organization benefitted at the same time the public benefitted is not always possible. The opportunity costs may be such that even if pollution prevention is profitable it does not allow organizations to pursue alternatives that are even more profitable.

invest too broadly in many options they experience the disadvantages of being a generalist, while if they invest too narrowly it becomes difficult for them to learn (Eggers 2012). Nonetheless, the purpose of hedging is to reduce downside risk and access upside opportunity. Thus, hedging draws on options theory (Kogut and Kulatilaka 1994, 2001; Tong and Reuer 2007), which examines how organizations defer, stage, and try to sequence investments in multiple interacting ways. They alter the scale of their investments, switch them around, abandon some, escalate commitment to others, deescalate commitments, and lump them together. They may grow and scrap their commitments. In uncertain regulatory environments, slack can facilitate their adaptability, as greater slack makes it easier for them to pursue multiple responses to the uncertainty (Kim and Bettis 2014).

The hedging behavior of organizations in this respect diverges from predictions of theories that maintain organizations' aim to optimize. Rather, their goal is to protect themselves from losses and preserve themselves in a way that is largely driven by the risk aversion behavior that Tversky and Kahneman (1991) describe at the individual level and accumulates throughout the organization. Such aversion to loss is driven by the recognition of an inability to predict whether any individual decision aimed at optimizing returns will actually pay off or turn out to be a miscalculation. Uncertainty about the future leads to ambivalence about the moves organizations should make (Ashforth et al. 2014). In the face of this regulatory uncertainty, organizations are apt to make contradictory moves simultaneously (Marcus, 1981). Assuming that different sets of events may happen leads to the well-known and investigated phenomenon of organizations, on the one hand, defending their current positions and exploiting current strengths, and, on the other hand, trying to be agile and innovative by exploring for new avenues of growth, while shielding themselves from losses (Benner and Tushman 2003; Lavie et al. 2010). In response to the uncertainties of regulation, they are prone to launching exploratory endeavors alongside their exploitative cores.

The literature has framed this problem as one of ambidexterity (Raisch and Birkinshaw 2008; Tushman and O'Reilly 1996). The issue ambidexterity presents to managers is how to accommodate the tensions. Poole and Van de Ven (1989) depict a number of coping methods for dealing with these contradictory tendencies: accepting and simply living with them; dividing them in space and time by allocating them to different organizational units, and emphasizing alternative tendencies at different moments (also see Carlson et al. 2017). Depending on their time perspectives, organizations are likely to manage the ambiguity of regulations differently (Kim et al. 2019; Marcus 2019; Zaheer and Zaheer 1999). Consider for instance that organizations in the oil and natural gas sector have time spans as long as thirty and forty years, since this is how long they need to exploit the resources they acquire. Organizations in the motor vehicle sector, on the other hand, tend to confine themselves to no more than a decade in the future, since this time is what they need to introduce new models and brands. These different time horizons influence how organizations in these sectors have responded to a diverse set of climate-change regulations.[5] Organizations in these sectors have hedged their bets by staking out paradoxical positions (Poole and Van de Ven 1989; Farjoun 2010; Schad and Bansal 2018). On the one hand, they have prepared for an uncertain regulatory future in which fossil fuels might be demoted from their role as the world's dominant energy source. On the other hand, they have focused on capturing as much gain as they could from dependence on fossil fuels, despite changing government mandates.

Recursive Cycles

Raisch et al. (2018) propose a spiral model of paradoxical learning in response to regulatory uncertainty. The learning is progressive over time and positive. This hopeful vision imagines a positive convergence, but perhaps there can be downward spirals of folly, as well as upward spirals, and rounds of imperfect sensemaking that lead to futile and endless cycles that achieve little progress (also see Hargrave and Van de Ven 2017). Hopefully, the positive cycles win out, but the outcomes of externally regulated change are hard to know because of the uncertainty, especially in advance, when it counts the most.

Pemer and Skjølsvik (2017) maintain that unexpected outcomes, conflicts, resistance, and significant gaps in achievement are common. The lasting and stable resolution of regulatory outcomes, which they illustrate in their study of procurement of the management consulting services in Sweden, is an exception. Jarzabkowski et al. (2018) also argue that unintended consequences can initiate action cycles that escalate and result in regulatory breakdowns. Heroic managers, who prevented breakdown in their study of a mandated change in a telecommunications company, are not that common.

[5] To summarize a complicated story that Marcus (2019) tells in his book *Strategies for Managing Uncertainty* in the oil and natural gas sector, companies responded in the following ways to the types of uncertainty that existed because of existing and possible future climate change regulation. ExxonMobil slightly changed its stance and widely publicized an effort to develop petro-algae. BP disgorged large amounts of fossil fuel assets to save itself from bankruptcy after the Deepwater Horizon oil spill. Shell restructured, letting go of oil assets and acquiring natural gas assets instead. As an owner of advanced battery and solar panel companies TOTAL started to secure European electric utilities. All of these companies at the same time remained committed to oil and natural gas. In the motor vehicle sector, where the time perspective differed, the decisions taken also diverged. GM introduced the all-electric Bold and exited from the unprofitable European market. Ford wavered in the face of weak financial results, unsure how much it should commit to its global bestselling F-150 series light truck versus moving to hybrids and to the opportunities of new transportation models. It made the F-150 series lighter by replacing some of the metal body with an aluminium one. VW, with its back against the wall because of its cheating on diesel emission standards, reversed its commitment to diesel as the world's "green" solution, and promised that it would make almost all its models available in some type of electric option no later than 2030. Toyota, while bringing on board more SUVs and small SUVs to the US market, pledged to make the most far-reaching transformation of any automaker with regard to offering hybrid and fully electric vehicles. These motor vehicle firms went farther than the oil and natural companies in making changes in the face of a future in which regulations might make dependence on fossil fuels far more difficult.

This case is inspiring, but it is not likely that it can be replicated in issues where the stakes are far higher. In highly contested regulatory contexts, such as that surrounding government efforts to mitigate climate change, respite from uncertain and unexpected outcomes (Giddens 1984) is less likely.

Two cycles may be possible (Marcus 1988a; Marcus 1988b; Marcus and Weber 1989). On the one hand, a vicious cycle can develop in which organizations that perform poorly are subject to increased government supervision and oversight. The increased supervision and oversight give them no choice but to respond with rule-bound changes. Since their flexibility is limited, it blunts their capacity for creative change and adaptation, which increases the chances that the poor performance persists. On the other hand, a beneficent cycle may materialize when an organization performs well. As a result, government grants autonomy from excessive supervision and oversight, and the release from close supervision provides these organizations with the freedom to make creative changes to government requirements, which reinforces their strong performance. Another result might be neutral, neither vicious nor beneficent.

Conclusion

Though numerous studies focus on regulatory formulation, implementation, and enforcement and reveal the unintended consequences that flow from the process, a limitation, as emphasized in this chapter, is that most consider a single regulatory program, rather than the combined effects of the diverse programs to which organizations are subject. Past research mostly examines the effects of regulatory programs separately. It does not consider their simultaneous impacts. This chapter has focused on the myriad impacts of multiple mandatory regulatory programs, the uncertainty created, the diverse responses of a host of different organizations to this mix of myriad uncertain regulatory mandates, the hedging in which these organizations engage to deal with the instability and uncertainty, and the contradictory results that follow. In the face of a full set of many different types of regulatory programs that change regularly over time, this chapter has argued that organizations hedge their bets. They make a series of trade-offs between resistance to change and acceptance of its inevitability.

This chapter has provided a model of an ongoing process that describes organizational responses to externally regulated change. Governments try to hold organizations accountable, they formulate, implement, and try to enforce many different regulations, and these regulatory programs proliferate at many levels and domains and are not stable. Uncertainty takes hold. Organizations respond by hedging their bets with stonewalling and opportunism depending on the circumstances and their characteristics. Their responses to regulation are distinct and varied. No two organizations are likely to respond in the exact same way. Their responses also are far from static. Responding to a fluid external and internal context leads decision-makers to branch out in many directions. As ultimate resolution of the attempts governments make to hold organizations accountable is indeterminate, the process begins afresh and repeats itself again and again as a series of "cat and mouse" games.

This chapter has shown that multiple government regulated mandates for organizational change exist. They cover organizations' major stakeholders and their relations to the natural environment, and they differ in their intensity and intent across many jurisdictions. Their source is in the many different government jurisdictions that regulate them—national, local, and international—and that regulate them in different ways. These laws are formulated, implemented, and enforced differently. They are inconsistent, contradict each other, and do not give organizations consistent and sufficient guidance about what to do. Administrators try to take over, the courts play an important role, and organizations have great leeway in what they choose to do. States, localities, and international bodies all impose requirements at national, international, and local levels and for organizations it is not at all clear what the organizations' responses should be. A jumble of mandates and jurisdictions regularly changing yields uncertainty about how organizations should respond. Given the uncertainty of how the mix of controls is likely to evolve into the future, organizations are reluctant to commit themselves too strongly to any particular course of action. They resist and try to preserve the current state of affairs through lobbying and court battles, sometimes going so far as to fund full-scale disinformation campaigns. They hedge their bets defensively by opposing regulations and act proactively by innovating in order to benefit from regulations. They try to maintain a balance between the status quo and the future, and they are not likely to go too far for too long in either direction. They also innovate, bringing into the world new processes and products in response to government regulations. The aggregate impact of diverse external regulatory pressures leads to a dynamic process. The process of government regulated change described in this chapter may be compared to a treadmill, or even to Sisyphus and his brave attempts to push the rock up the mountain even as it falls back again after each effort that is made.

References

Aghion, P., Dechezleprêtre, A., Hemous, D., Martin, R., and Van Reenen, J. (2016), 'Carbon Taxes, Path Dependency, and Directed Technical Change: Evidence from the Auto Industry', *Journal of Political Economy*, 124/1, 1–51.

Ahuja, G., and Novelli, E. (2017), 'Redirecting Research Efforts on the Diversification–Performance Linkage: The Search for Synergy', *Academy of Management Annals*, 11/1, 342–90.

Aragón-Correa, J. A., and Sharma, S. (2003), 'A Contingent Resource-Based View of Proactive Corporate Environmental Strategy', *Academy of Management Review*, 28/1, 71–88.

Ashforth, B. E., Rogers, K. M., Pratt, M. G., and Pradies, C. (2014), 'Ambivalence in Organizations: A Multilevel Approach', *Organization Science*, 25/5, 1453–78.

Benner, M. J., and Tushman, M. L. (2003), 'Exploitation, Exploration, and Process Management: The Productivity Dilemma Revisited', *Academy of Management Review*, 28/2, 238–56.

Bernstein, M. (1955), *Regulating Business by Independent Commission* (Princeton, NJ: Princeton University Press).

Carlson, E. J., Poole, M. S., Lambert, N. J., and Lammers, J. C. (2017), 'A Study of Organizational Responses to Dilemmas in Interorganizational Emergency Management', *Communication Research*, 44/2, 287–315.

Dal Bó, E. (2006), 'Regulatory Capture: A Review', *Oxford Review of Economic Policy*, 22/2, 203–25.

De Stefano, M. C., Montes-Sancho, M. J., and Busch, T. (2016), 'A Natural Resource-Based View of Climate Change: Innovation Challenges in the Automobile Industry', *Journal of Cleaner Production*, 139, 1436–48.

Dos Santos, J. C. (1996), 'Glass-Steagall and the Regulatory Dialectic', Economic Commentary, Federal Reserve Bank of Cleveland, February, 15.

Edelman, L. B. (1992), 'Legal Ambiguity and symbolic structures: Organizational mediation of civil rights law". *American Journal of Sociology*, 97/6, 1531–76.

Eggers, J. P. (2012), 'All Experience is Not Created Equal: Learning, Adapting, and Focusing in Product Portfolio Management', *Strategic Management Journal*, 33/3, 315–35.

Ellinson, Z., and McWhirter (2019), 'Gun Makers Adjust Rifles to Skirt Bans', *Wall Street Journal*, 6/22–3, A1.

Esty, D., and Winston, A. (2009), *Green to Gold: How Smart Companies Use Environmental Strategy to Innovate, Create Value, and Build Competitive Advantage* (Hoboken, NJ: John Wiley and Sons).

Farjoun, M. (2010), 'Beyond Dualism: Stability and Change as a Duality', *Academy of Management Review*, 35/2, 202–25.

Funk, R. J., and Hirschman, D. (2014), 'Derivatives and Deregulation: Financial Innovation and the Demise of Glass–Steagall', *Administrative Science Quarterly*, 59/4, 669–704.

Funk, R. J., and Hirschman, D. (2017), 'Beyond Nonmarket Strategy: Market Actions as Corporate Political Activity', *Academy of Management Review*, 42/1, 32–52.

Ghemawat, P. (1991), *Commitment* (New York, NY: Free Press).

Giddens A. (1984), *The Constitution of Society* (Cambridge, UK: Polity Press).

Hargrave, T. J., and Van de Ven, A. H. (2017), 'Integrating Dialectical and Paradox Perspectives on Managing Contradictions in Organizations,' *Organization Studies*, 38/3–4), 319–39.

Hart, S. L. (1995), 'A Natural-Resource-Based View of the Firm', *Academy of Management Review*, 20/4, 986–1014.

Hoffman, A. J., and Ventresca, M. J. (2002), *Organizations, Policy and the Natural Environment: Institutional and Strategic Perspectives* (Stanford, CA: Stanford University Press).

Jaffe, A. B., Peterson, S. R., Portney, P. R., and Stavins, R. N. (1995), 'Environmental Regulation and the Competitiveness of US Manufacturing: What Does the Evidence Tell Us?', *Journal of Economic Literature*, 33/1, 132–63.

Jarzabkowski, P., Lê, J. K., and Balogun, J. (2018), 'The Social Practice of Co-Evolving Strategy and Structure to Realize Mandated Radical Change', *Academy of Management Journal*, 62/3, 850–82.

Kim, A., Bansal, P., and Haugh, H. (2019), 'No Time Like the Present: How a Present Time Perspective can Foster Sustainable Development', *Academy of Management Journal*, 62/2, 607–34.

Kim, C., and Bettis, R. A. (2014), 'Cash is Surprisingly Valuable as a Strategic Asset', *Strategic Management Journal*, 35/13, 2053–63.

Kogut, B., and Kulatilaka, N. (1994), 'Options Thinking and Platform Investments: Investing in Opportunity', *California Management Review*, 36/2, 52–71.

Kogut, B., and Kulatilaka, N. (2001), 'Capabilities as Real Options', *Organization Science*, 12/6, 744–58.

Lavie, D., Stettner, U., and Tushman, M. L. (2010), 'Exploration and Exploitation within and across Organizations', *The Academy of Management Annals*, 4/1, 109–55.

Lyon, T. P., Delmas, M. A., Maxwell, J. W., Bansal, P., Chiroleu-Assouline, M., Crifo, P., Durand, R., Gond, J. P., King, A., Lenox, M., Toffel, M., Vogel, D., and Wijen, F. (2018), 'CSR Needs CPR: Corporate sustainability and Politics', *California Management Review*, 60/4, 5–24.

Mahoney, J., and Thelen, K. 2009, 'A Theory of Gradual Institutional Change', in J. Mahoney and K. Thelen, eds., *Explaining Institutional Change: Ambiguity, Agency, and* Power (Cambridge: Cambridge University Press), 1–37.

Majumdar, S. K., and Marcus, A. A. (2001), 'Rules versus Discretion: The Productivity Consequences of Flexible Regulation', *Academy of Management Journal*, 44/1, 170–9.

Marcus, A. A. (1980), *Promise and Performance: Choosing and Implementing an Environmental Policy* (Westport, CT: Greenwood Press).

Marcus, A. A. (1981), 'Policy Uncertainty and Technological Innovation', *Academy of Management Review*, 6/3, 443–8.

Marcus, A. A. (1984). *The Adversary Economy*. (Westport, Ct.: Quorum Books).

Marcus, A. A. (1988a), 'Responses to Externally Induced Innovation: Their Effects on Organizational Performance', *Strategic Management Journal*, 9/4, 387–402.

Marcus, A. A. (1988b), 'Implementing Externally Induced Innovations: A Comparison of Rule-Bound and Autonomous Approaches', *Academy of Management Journal*, 31/2, 235–56.

Marcus, A. A. (2016), *The Future of Technology Management and the Business Environment* (Old Tappen, NJ: Pearson).

Marcus, A. A. (2019). *Strategies for Managing Uncertainty: Booms and Busts in the Energy Industry*. Cambridge, UK: Cambridge University Press.

Marcus, A. A., Aragon-Correa, J. A., and Pinkse, J. (2011), 'Firms, Regulatory Uncertainty, and the Natural Environment', *California Management Review*, 54/1, 5–16.

Marcus, A. A., and Fremeth, A. F. (2009), 'Green Management Matters Regardless', *Academy of Management Perspectives*, 23/3, 17–26.

Marcus, A.A., and Geffen, D. (1998), 'The Dialectics of Competency Acquisition: Pollution Prevention in Electric Generation', *Strategic Management Journal*, 19/12, 1145–68.

Marcus, A. A., Geffen, D. A., and Sexton, K. (2002), *Reinventing Environmental Regulation: Lessons from Project XL* (Washington, DC: Resources for the Future).

Marcus, A.A. and Hargrave, T. (2021), *Managing Business Ethics: Making Ethical Decisions* (Thousand Oaks, CA.: Sage Press).

Marcus, A.A. and Van de Ven, A. (2015), 'Managing Shifting Goal Consensus and Task Ambiguity in Making the Transition to Sustainability', in R. Henderson, R. Gulati, and M. Tushman, M., eds., *Leading Sustainable Change: An Organizational Perspective* (Oxford, UK: Oxford University Press), 298–323.

Marcus, A. A., and Weber, M. J. (1989), 'Externally-Induced Innovation', in A. H. Van de Ven, H. L. Angle, and M. S. Poole, eds., *Research on the Management of Innovation: The Minnesota Studies* (New York: Harper & Row), 537–59.

Milliken, F. J. (1987), 'Three Types of Perceived Uncertainty about the Environment: State, Effect, and Response Uncertainty', *Academy of Management Review*, 12/1, 133–43.

Peltzman, S. (1976), 'Toward a More General Theory of Regulation', *The Journal of Law and Economics*, 19/2, 211–40.

Pemer, F., and Skjølsvik, T. (2017), 'Adopt or Adapt? Unpacking the Role of Institutional Work Processes in the Implementation of New Regulations', *Journal of Public Administration Research and Theory*, 28/1, 138–54.

Penna, C. C., and Geels, F. W. (2015), 'Climate Change and the Slow Reorientation of the American Car Industry (1979–2012): An Application and Extension of the Dialectic Issue Life Cycle (DILC) Model', *Research Policy*, 44/5, 1029–48.

Poole, M. S., and Van de Ven, A. H. (1989), 'Using Paradox to Build Management and Organization Theories', *Academy of Management Review*, 14/4, 562–78.

Pressman, J. L., and Wildavsky, A. (1973), *Implementation: How Great Expectations in Washington are Dashed in Oakland* (Berkeley: University of California Press).

Raisch, S., and Birkinshaw, J. (2008), 'Organizational Ambidexterity: Antecedents, Outcomes, and Moderators'. *Journal of Management*, 34/3, 375–409.

Raisch, S., Hargrave, T. J., and Van De Ven, A. H. (2018), 'The Learning Spiral: A Process Perspective on Paradox'. *Journal of Management Studies*, 55/8, 1507–26.

Rothenberg, S., and Ettlie, J. E. (2011), 'Strategies to Cope with Regulatory Uncertainty in the Auto Industry', *California Management Review*, 54/1, 126–44.

Rumelt, R. P., and Lamb, R. (1984), 'Competitive Strategic Management', *Toward a Strategic Theory of the Firm*, 26/1, 556–70.

Schad, J., and Bansal, P. (2018), 'Seeing the Forest and the Trees: How a Systems Perspective Informs Paradox Research', *Journal of Management Studies*, 55/8, 1490–506.

Sengul, M., Costa, A. A., and Gimeno, J. (2019), 'The Allocation of Capital within Firms', *Academy of Management Annals*, 13/1, 43–83.

Stewart, R. B. (1981), 'Regulation, Innovation, and Administrative Law: A Conceptual Framework', *California Law Review*, 69, 1256.

Stigler, G. J. (1975), *The Citizen and the State: Essays on Regulation* (Vol. 720) (Chicago: University of Chicago Press).

Tong, T. W., and Reuer, J. J. (2007), 'Real Options in Multinational Corporations: Organizational Challenges and Risk Implications'. *Journal of International Business Studies*, 38/2, 215–30.

Tushman, M. L., and O'Reilly, C. A. (1996), 'Ambidextrous Organizations: Managing Evolutionary and Revolutionary Change'. *California Management Review*, 38/4, 8–30.

Tversky, A., and Kahneman, D. (1991), 'Loss Aversion in Riskless Choice: A Reference-Dependent Model', *The Quarterly Journal of Economics*, 106/4, 1039–61.

Vogel, D. (2007), *The Market for Virtue: The Potential and Limits of Corporate Social Responsibility* (Washington, DC: Brookings Institution Press).

Wilson, J. Q. (1967), 'The Bureaucracy Problem', *The Public Interest*, 6, 3–9.

Wilson, J. Q. (1980), *The Politics of Regulation* (New York, NY: Basic Books).

Zaheer, S., Albert, S. and Zaheer, A. (1999), "'Time Scales and Organizational Theory', *Academy of Management Review*,' 24/4, 725–41.

CHAPTER 15

ORGANIZATIONAL ROUTINES AND ORGANIZATIONAL CHANGE

BRIAN T. PENTLAND AND KENNETH T. GOH

In theory and in practice, organizational routines have a problematic relationship with organizational change. On one hand, routines tend to stay the same when we want them to change. On the other hand, routines can change when we want them to stay the same. Routines are a source of inertia and path dependence (Schulz 2008; Sydow et al. 2009), but they can also drive innovation (Deken et al. 2016). One way or the other, routines are pervasive, paradoxical beasts that are central to organizing and organizational change (Becker et al. 2005; Cohen et al. 1996; Dönmez et al. 2016). It is not surprising that routines appear in other chapters in this handbook (e.g., Chapters 13, 22, and 28: Poole and Van de Ven; Garud and Turunen; Nguyen and Vuori).

In this chapter, we discuss current theory on how routines change and stay the same, and the implications of these dynamic processes for organizational change. We focus on the routine as the unit of analysis but consider the implications for change in organizations as well. Throughout this chapter, we use video game development as an example to make our concepts clear and concrete. Game development can be seen as a bundle of closely connected routines for generating novel products. Thus, it provides a good vehicle for exploring the paradoxical quality of routines as engines and anchors in a (n)ever changing world (Cohen 2007).

In our discussion, we consider each of Van de Ven and Poole's (1995) motors of change: life cycle, teleological, dialectic, and evolutionary. While each of these motors can be found in research on routines, fieldwork has identified change processes that do not fit well within these existing categories. By conceptualizing routines as networks of interdependent actions (Pentland and Feldman 2007), scholars in routine dynamics are beginning to create a novel perspective on change (and stability) referred to as *patterning*

(Feldman 2016; Danner-Schröder and Geiger 2016; Turner and Rindova 2018). Goh and Pentland (2019) suggest that patterning should be considered a new kind of change motor for processual phenomena. Patterning is the process through which action patterns accumulate and change over time, through repetition. Patterning can reinforce existing paths or generate new paths, so it provides an explanatory mechanism for the paradox of stability and change in routines.

Background

To understand the significance of current theory, it is helpful to locate it in the context of what has come before. The history of this topic reflects a move from a fairly static understanding of routines as things to a more processual understanding of routines as dynamic, generative systems. Here, we provide an extremely brief outline of this trajectory.

Routines versus Rationality

The concept of routinized behavior has always stood in contrast to idealized rational behavior. For example, Simon and March described performance programs and heuristics as a consequence of bounded rationality (Simon 1947; Simon and March 1958). Since rational decision-making is bounded in principle, routinized decision-making is necessary in practice. Empirically, routines like "mark-up" pricing in retail demonstrated that rationality was not a good model of managerial behavior. Routines provided a way to explain why managerial behavior does not always conform to rational models (Ashforth and Fried 1988).

Perhaps because of their relationship with cognitive efficiency, organizational routines are sometimes thought of as individual habits (Weiss and Ilgen 1985). In contemporary theory, organizational routines are a collective phenomenon, not an individual phenomenon (Feldman and Pentland 2003). Individual habits may contribute to organizational routines by shaping the interaction patterns of multiple individuals as they perform a routine (Cohen et al. 2014).

Evolutionary Theory of the Firm: Routines as Genes

At the organizational level, Nelson and Winter (1982) offered their evolutionary theory of economic change as an antidote to overly rational theories of the firm in micro-economics. Nelson and Winter (1982) theorized that firms change through an evolutionary process of selecting different routines and bundles of routines. In this theory, routines serve as the genetic material for organizations. Routines are conceptualized as genotypes that are expressed in firms, which are conceptualized as the phenotypes (Hodgson and Knudsen 2004; Knudsen 2008). The key point here is that this is an evolutionary theory of firms, not of routines. Routines serve as part of the *explanans* (the explanation), not the *explanandum* (the thing to be explained).

Dynamic Capabilities: Orchestrating of Bundles of Routines

Routines serve a similar role in theories of dynamic capabilities (Winter 2003; Teece et al. 1997; Eisenhardt and Martin 2000). Capabilities are built up from "bundles" of routines (Lewin and Massini 2004), and within a bundle, routines may be orchestrated differently to enhance capabilities. In some formulations (e.g., Winter 2003), there may be "meta-routines" for adapting to a changing environment by selecting or modifying operational routines, or the organizational capability may be attributed to superior executive expertise (Teece, 2012). Regardless of the specific formulation, dynamic capabilities are used as an explanation for organizational-level phenomena (e.g., competitive advantage). With some recent exceptions (Salvato and Vassolo 2018), research in this area does not rely on details about the internal aspects of routines.

Routine Dynamics: Beyond Routines as Things

In contrast, routine-level theories engage with empirical data about situated patterns of action within and between routines. The emerging field of routine dynamics (Feldman et al. 2016) seeks to understand how action patterns form and change (or do not change) over time. Over the last twenty years, research on routine dynamics has shifted from individual routines towards larger structures, such as clusters of routines (Kremser and Schreyogg 2016) and ecologies of routines (Sele and Grand 2016). Routine dynamics has been examined in a wide variety of settings, from aircraft manufacture (Swan et al. 2016) to ballet (Blanche and Cohendet 2019). Across these settings, the practice-based assumptions outlined below provide a robust framework for analyzing stability and change.

To summarize, firm-level theories address important questions about industry structure and competitive dynamics, but they tend to bracket off the internal dynamics of routines. Firms (phenotypes) may express particular routines (genotypes), but the ways that these routines are carried out and how they change over time is not part of the theory. Therefore, because we are interested in explaining how routines change and do not change, we focus on routine dynamics.

Basic Concepts and Assumptions of Routine Dynamics

Definition of Organizational Routines

We adopt Feldman and Pentland's (2003) definition of routines as repetitive, recognizable patterns of interdependent action carried out by multiple actors. This definition is very broad because routines are pervasive. Each element of the definition is important, as discussed by Feldman and Pentland (2003): repetition, recognizability, multiple actors, and interdependent actions. Others have suggested adding an explicit goal-seeking orientation to this definition (Salvato and Rerup 2018), but we prefer the more encompassing definition that includes patterns of action that emerge without an explicit goal to foreground actions over actors (or some other unit of analysis). In this chapter, we illustrate this idea of organizational routines with examples from videogame development.

Example. Videogame development involves a collection of routine tasks. For example, there is an established process for creating 3D animations. The routine to design and build an animated character for a game starts with developing concept artwork, using software graphical tools to model the art asset, adding textures to improve its visual quality, using a 3D animation software tool to build a skeleton rig for the animation, creating the animated movements, and then exporting the animation into the game engine.

Table 15.1 provides a simple visual definition of key concepts, inspired by Feldman's (2016) call for better visualization of action patterns in research on routines. Visualization is challenging because routines embody variation, and they can be represented in many ways, at different levels of abstraction. A clearly defined visual lexicon will help convey what we mean when we talk about change in action patterns.

This is an action-centric perspective, so the elemental units are actions/events (Feldman et al. 2016; Pentland et al. 2017). The first two rows of Table 15.1 show the basic elements: actions/events (□) and sequential relations (→). The width of the arrow is meant to indicate the frequency or weight of the sequential relation. Using this notation, the third row of Table 15.1 shows several performances of a routine as a set of sequentially related actions or events. For clarity, this is a simple, abstract example. However, as in most real routines, there are several different kinds of performances and each kind of performance can occur more than once.

We can aggregate the specific performances of the routine in row three into an overall pattern, as shown in row four (Pentland and Feldman 2007; Pentland et al. 2017). In doing so, we introduce an important distinction between performances and paths. Paths are possible ways of performing a routine inferred from multiple performances of the routine.[1] In contrast, a performance is a particular instance of a path. Research on

[1] The terminology comes from graph theory, where a path is a set of connected nodes (West, 2001).

Table 15.1 Visualizing Performances, Patterns, and Change in Organizational Routines

Term	Visualization	Definition
Actions or events	A B C D E	Single steps in a routine.
Sequential relation	→	Temporal relation between actions or events in a routine
Performances	A → B → C → D → E A → B → D → E A → B → C → B → C → D → E A → B → C → E → D → E A → B → D → C → B → D	Specific performances of a routine (e.g., specific attempts at creating 3D animation for different characters)
Routine	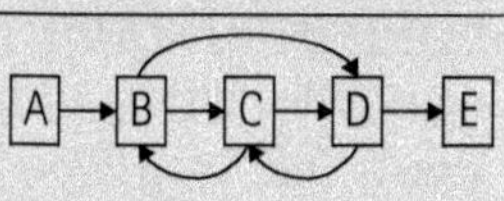	Overall set of possible paths that shows repetitive, recognizable pattern of interdependent actions
Patterning (change)	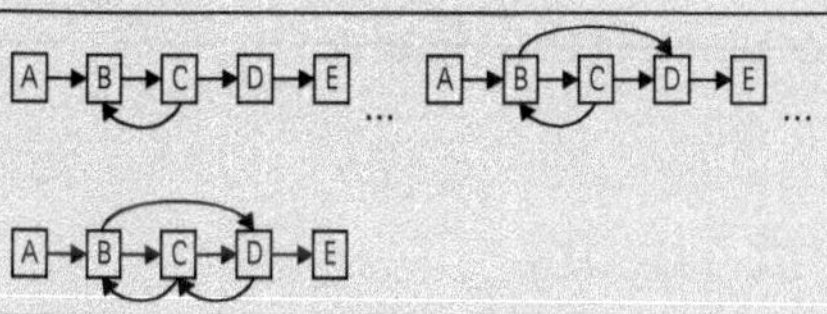	Diachronic progression of action patterns

process mining makes a similar distinction between a process variant and a process instance (Rosa et al. 2017). A variant is a typical way of performing a process. A process instance is one specific performance. Note that this is not the same as Abbott's (1990) distinction between incidents and events. For Abbott, incidents are *indicators* of events; incidents may be part of a larger event (e.g., an exchange of vows is an indicator of a wedding). However, a performance is not an indicator of a path. A performance is an *instance* of a path.

A physical path across a grassy field makes a clear, precise analogy: we tend to follow paths where the grass is worn. We could cut across in a new direction, but the existing paths show where people have gone in the past and where they are likely to go in the future. Through paths, past performances influence but do not determine future performances. Paths are the metaphorical "ruts in the road" that describe routines (Cohen 2007). The metaphors of *path* and *rut* make sense because the word "routine" derives from the French word *route*, which means *road.*

The conceptual leap here is that one routine can have multiple distinct paths. For example, there is more than one way to create a 3D character animation. Some might ask: why not treat each distinct path as a separate routine? There are three reasons. First, the paths are alternative ways of performing the same general task; they are equifinal.

Second, empirical research shows that even simple routines, such as invoice approval, can have hundreds of distinct paths (Pentland et al. 2010). Third, the paths are often closely related variants of each other, as suggested by the hypothetical example in Table 15.1. Therefore, we treat the overall set of possible paths as one routine and we represent it as a network (Pentland, Mahringer, Dittrich, Feldman and Ryan Wolf 2020).

Finally, we use the term *patterning* to talk about change in a routine, as shown in the last row of Table 15.1. Where prior literature has used the term *pattern* (e.g., Abbott 1990), it is used as a noun. For example, Abbott (1990) talks about patterns as consisting of typical sequences and families of sequences (TSFS) and asks about the antecedents and consequences of those typical sequences. The sequences unfold over time, but for the purpose of analysis, they are conceptualized as stationary (relatively fixed and unchanging, like things). In contrast, we use patterning as a verb that refers to pattern creation and re-creation.

In particular, patterning refers to the mechanisms of expanding or contracting the space of possible paths (Pentland et al. 2020) though adding, removing, or reinforcing possible paths. For example, an animator can try a new way to create a 3D character or stop using an old way. This will introduce a new path. Alternatively, the animator can follow an existing path. Empirically, patterning is reflected in a diachronic progression of changes in network structure (Pentland, Vaast, and Ryan Wolf In Press). This diachronic progression provides a way to conceptualize and measure change in a pattern of action, which is the focal phenomenon of this chapter.

Assumptions of Current Theory

Current theory on routine dynamics (Feldman et al. 2016) is based on a set of interrelated concepts and assumptions that reinforce the basic insight that routines are not fixed, mechanistic things. We will use videogame development to make these assumptions as clear as possible.

- *Temporality.* Routines are an inherently processual/temporal phenomenon. Routines unfold over time, step by step. We use the term *unfolding* to refer to the step-by-step performance of a routine along a particular path. For example, each character that is added to a videogame is created through a sequence of steps, as described above. However, in any particular instance, that sequence might unfold in a different way.
- *Situated and embodied.* As performances unfold over time, they unfold in particular places and they are performed by particular actors (Feldman and Pentland 2003). Routines are always situated in material contexts that include the actors performing the routine, which can be heterogeneous (human and non-human). For example, the animation routine in videogame development is performed by specific individuals, using specific tools, working on different parts of the routine at different times.

- *Performative.* As routines are performed, they create the world that they inhabit. In particular, through repetition, routines tend to create the conditions for subsequent performances. This recursive relation between past and future performances is referred to as *patterning* (Feldman 2016): adding and removing possible paths over time. For example, each performance of the animation routine sets conditions and expectations about each piece of work, and for the next performance of the routine itself.
- *Relationality.* Routines embody relationality in at least two ways. First, within a routine, the actions are interdependent and are related sequentially in time. Because actions within a routine are related, it makes sense to conceptualize them as a network (Pentland and Feldman 2007). Second, the function and significance of a routine depends on its relation to other routines. For example, the performance of the animation routine at a particular point in time is affected by the routine for integrating assets into the game engine because the software engineer may require the animated assets urgently, which limits the frequency of iterations in creating the animation. More broadly, the animation routine only exists (and makes sense) in relation to the rest of the game development routines.
- *Variability.* Routines (noun) are not necessarily very routine (adjective). The degree of variability is an empirical property of the pattern of action that makes up a routine (Feldman et al. 2016). For example, every performance of the animation routine is recognizable as such, but each one is performed differently.
- *Collective, not individual.* Organizational routines are distinguished from individual habits because, by definition, they are carried out by multiple actors. For example, the animation routine involves concept artists, technical artists, and animators working together with game designers and software engineers. Each of these actors perform or interact with different parts of the routine and have different understandings of the actions and timing of actions in performing the routine.
- *Heterogeneous actants.* The actors that perform routines need not be human. In keeping with the ontology of actor network theory (Latour 2005) and sociomateriality (Orlikowski and Scott 2008), we include computerized agents and other aspects of the material context that are essential to many routines in practice. Explanations of routines based on human psychology (e.g., motivation) tend to lose relevance as actors become more automated. For example, new technologies in computer animation that enable real-time rendering alters the animation routine such that animators no longer need to perform a separate step to generate a 3D image.
- *Effortful.* Contrary to the stereotype of routines as mindless habits, routines take work. Regardless of how a routine is formed, it takes effort to perform it consistently (Pentland and Reuter 1994). Effort is certainly evident in the case of 3D animation, as well as creativity. These routines are repetitive and recognizable, but certainly not automatic or mindless.

- *Emergent.* Contrary to the stereotype of routines as fixed entities, routines are capable of endogenous change (Feldman 2000). Through mere repetition, new patterns of action can emerge. For example, in each performance of the animation routine, new sequences could be formed, new actions could be taken, or old actions could be dropped.

Together, these assumptions add up to a practice-based perspective on routines (Parmigiani and Howard-Grenville 2011; Feldman and Orlikowski 2011; Feldman et al. 2016). Videogame development makes a good example because the routines involve collective, ongoing performance of the work by a heterogenous collection of actors (people and machines). The routines are effortful, emergent, embodied, and variable; at the same time, they are repetitive and recognizable. In making these assumptions, the practice-based concept has diverged from the psychological concept of routine (Ashforth and Fried 1988) that is more closely linked to the concept of habit (Cohen 2007). When there is confusion or disagreement about what counts as an organizational routine, it often arises from an outdated view that equates routines with individual human habits. It may also arise from confusing the noun *routine* (a recognizable pattern of actions) with the adjective *routine* (the degree to which that pattern is low skilled and follows explicit rules) (Autor et al. 2003).

Because of their roots in ethnographic fieldwork, these concepts are tuned to the situationally specific enactment of particular routines. They emphasize the processual aspect of routines. Ironically, while it is often referred to as a "practice-based" perspective, it is less oriented towards practical concerns such as cycle time, cost, and quality. Outcome metrics, like cost and cycle time, are more consistent with treating routines as static objects with variable properties.

Organizational Routines as Narrative Networks

Methodologically, empirical research on routine dynamics generally starts from situated action (performances) as the unit of observation and builds towards patterns of action (paths) as the unit of analysis (Feldman et al. 2016). Conceptually, the action pattern represents a generative system that can produce a variety of performances (Pentland et al. 2012). Cohen (2007) referred to this quality as "pattern-in-variety": within the action pattern of a routine, there are ongoing variations. The metaphor of paths across a field is helpful here: the history shapes but does not determine future performances.

Narrative networks (Pentland and Feldman 2007) provide a straightforward way to represent pattern-in-variety. First, we can think of each performance of a routine as a narrative: a sequence of specific events that unfolds over time. Then, we can summarize those performances by converting them into a network, where each kind of event appears as a node in the network (Pentland et al. 2017). Formally, a narrative network is a directed graph, where the nodes are events and the edges represent sequential relations between the events. The edges can also be interpreted as handoffs (Pentland et al. 2017) or organizing moves (Pentland 1992). The network is essentially a snapshot of an action pattern at one moment in time. Snapshot networks are an established approach to dynamics of social networks (Moody et al. 2005; Rosetti and Cazabet 2018).

The network representation has been used for comparing routines (Pentland et al. 2011). as well as measuring their complexity (Hærem et al. 2015). As we discuss below, it also provides a framework for describing routine dynamics as network dynamics, where change is operationalized by adding (or removing) nodes or edges in the narrative network (Goh and Pentland 2019). And of course, this provides a concrete way to operationalize patterning, which can be observed as diachronic change in the network over time.

Routine-Level Theories of Stability and Change

Before examining theories of change, it is worth examining theories that attempt to explain what routines are best known for: stability. In a sense, routine dynamics needs to overcome the tendency for patterning to result in a self-reinforcing, locked-in pattern. Narrative networks provide an explicit way to test for stability or change based on observable actions.

Inertia and Lock-In: The Classic View of Routines

The classic view of routines and routinization emphasizes the tendency of routines to follow fixed patterns. This is often referred to as inertia or lock-in (Sydow et al. 2009). To the extent that routines are truly locked into fixed patterns, it is easy to mis-recognize them as things.

Schulz (2008) provides an extensive survey of mechanisms that keep routines "on track," including habitualization, neuronal priming, reciprocal typification (mutual expectations), institutionalization, formalization, artifacts, competency traps, escalation of commitment, coercion, and leadership. In addition to shaping behavior directly, Schulz argues that these factors promote path dependence within routines (from one action to the next) as well as path dependence in the overall routine (from one performance to the next). Over time, as a routine is repeated, mere repetition tends to reinforce the existing pattern of action until it becomes locked in. Cohen's (2007) metaphor of ruts-in-the-road is a particularly apt way to describe this process.

In a similar vein, Cohen and Bacdayan (1994) suggest that we can understand routines as concatenated habits in which the actions of one actor trigger the response of other actors. As a routine is practiced, these stimulus–response relations become more predictable (Cohen et al. 2014). In their analysis, Cohen and Bacdayan use the speed and predictability of response as indicators that a routine has formed. It is worth noting that all of Schulz's (2008) mechanisms except one—artifacts—depend to some degree on humans as the primary actors. As digital technology becomes more advanced and more enmeshed in work processes, human-centric theories may become less relevant (Pentland and Hærem 2015).

Without question, some routines (noun) are extremely routine (adjective). The critical point is that lock-in does not just happen: it the result of a trajectory that leads to an action pattern with less and less variability. Nor does lock-in just persist; it is an "effortful accomplishment" (Pentland and Reuter 1994). Reducing variablity is an explicit goal of managerial practices such as Total Quality Management (TQM), Six Sigma, and business process management (Benner and Tushman 2003; van der Aalst 2011). However, as Lok and de Rond (2013) document in their fieldwork on boat racing in Cambridge, variations can produce stability by repairing transgressions to the rules. Routines can also function as shock absorbers (Berente et al. 2016) that allow a just-enough flexibility to keep a larger system stable.

The key point is that stability cannot be assumed: it is an effortful accomplishment (Pentland and Rueter 1994). Without a confluence of reinforcing factors and ongoing effort on the part of the people carrying out the routine, action patterns tend to change through mere repetition (Feldman 2000). Furthermore, routines are often not as consistent and fixed as the metaphor of lock-in suggests. Through fieldwork and archival research, close examination of actual performances of routines demonstrate that even simple routines (e.g., invoice processing) can have an enormous number of distinct performances (Pentland et al. 2011). Not only are routines more varied than one might expect, but they can also change.

Motors of Change in Routine Dynamics

Since Feldman (2000) identified routines as a source of change, the theoretical focus has shifted from stability to change. More precisely, the emphasis shifted to the balance between stability and change. As routines unfold, step-by-step, they may follow the same paths as prior performances, or they may deviate in some way. These differences may be temporary variations, or they may persist as changes that shape the trajectory of the action pattern (Pentland et al. 2012). This repetitive reinforcement and variation are the processes that Feldman (2016) refers to as patterning. In the following sections, we use Van de Ven and Poole's (1995) framework to review this literature (e.g., life cycle, teleological, dialectic, and evolutionary motors). Each of the four motors offers a distinct perspective on the practice-based view of routines as generative systems.

Motor #1: Life-cycle. A life cycle motor depicts change as an entity progressing through a prescribed sequence of stages regulated by an underlying logic, program, or code (Poole and Van de Ven 1995; Chapter 13, Poole and Van de Ven, this handbook). Routines are repetitive, so we can interpret each performance of a routine as following a brief life cycle, from start to finish. For example, the routine for developing an animated character consists of fixed steps of concepting, modeling, texturing, rigging, animating, and exporting. Even though each performance of the routine varies, these steps need to be performed in the prescribed sequence—the animation asset cannot be exported to the game engine before it is animated. In this sense, life cycles provide an excellent description of routine *repetition*, but they have not featured prominently as drivers of routine *dynamics*. Transitions from one step to the next in a life cycle are understood as changes within a stable pattern (e.g., from concepting to experimenting in the animation routine), not as changes in the pattern itself.

Of course, in many kinds of organizations, temporal and seasonal variation in routines are common (e.g., day versus night, weekday versus weekend, busy season versus low season). For example, Birnholtz et al. (2007) document seasonal variations in routines at Camp Poplar Grove, a summer camp that ceases operations in the winter. The point of the analysis, however, is that the routines spring back to life in clearly recognizable form year after year. They hibernate, so to speak, but they do not change very much. This example reinforces the distinction we made above between variation and change.

Motor #2: Teleology (goal seeking). The teleological motor explains change as a goal-directed process undertaken by an entity that involves a cycle of setting goals, performing the routine, evaluating outcomes, and modifying goals. As discussed by Burke in Chapter 2 of this volume on planned change models and by Gioia and Rheinhardt in Chapter 4 on bottom-up sensemaking, this is a socially constructed process because it depends on how the entity interprets and acts on performance feedback relative to a goal (Greve 2008). The teleological model has great face validity in that it attributes routine change to human agency. It aligns with Winter's (2003) view of dynamic capabilities: meta-routines that modify routines. In the animation routine for example, artists may skip certain steps if they are under pressure to meet a deadline. The teleological motor is widely used as an explanatory mechanism for change in the existing literature. For example, Rerup and Feldman (2011) discuss trial and error learning in a Danish research lab as a goal-seeking process.

While teleology is a powerful motor of change, its capacity to produce change in routines has limits. As Rice and Cooper (2010) point out, feedback is often unavailable or ineffective, in which case goal-seeking becomes meaningless. Furthermore, teleology may tend to exaggerate the role of human agency when routines are often performed by ensembles of actants that include artifacts such as tools, templates, and written procedures (Leonardi 2011; Orlikowski 2007). As an example, the step of rendering 3-D images in videogame development is performed entirely by software. New technologies for rendering 3-D images in real time substantially speed up the animation routine, which provides more opportunity for iteration and improvement.

Motor #3: Dialectic. Dialectic motors explain change as occurring through the synthesis of oppositional forces. The dialectic motor assumes multiple entities that are typically actors or stakeholders in the routine. Dialectical processes have featured in some theories of routine dynamics (e.g., Salvato and Rerup 2018; Turner and Rindova 2012).

For example, D'Adderio (2014) discusses the alternative, competing goals that are often at stake in transfer and replication.

Dialectic analysis provides an excellent fit with the concept of "routine as truce" (Nelson and Winter 1982; Zbaracki and Bergen 2010), where routine participants with competing interests may change the routine to one that is agreeable to all participants. The routine as truce is thus not a stable entity but a processual accomplishment (Salvato and Rerup 2018) driven by the dialectical motor of competing interests. Hargrave (Chapter 7) and Prichard, and Creed (Chapter 10) of this volume discuss how dialectical processes can produce a number of other types of routines. Like teleology, the dialectic motor has a great deal of face validity and provides a good description of certain situations. However, it faces similar conceptual problems as teleology, due to its emphasis on the agency of human actors and corresponding neglect of materiality in routines.

Motor #4: Evolution (variation, selection, retention). Feldman and Pentland (2003) suggested that routine dynamics could be explained by an evolutionary process of variation, selection, and retention (VSR), as Mauer, Miner, and Crossan discuss in Chapter 19 of this volume. While evolution makes a nice metaphor, it is difficult to operationalize in a rigorous way because this class of theory entails selection among a population of phenotypes (Hodgson and Knudsen 2004). When a variation of a routine (i.e., the genotype) has greater fitness, it may be expressed more often in the phenotypes (organizations) and therefore retained in the population.

While evolution works in biological systems, it can be difficult to apply to organizations because of problems in identifying the unit of analysis and the mechanisms. What entity is being varied, selected, and retained in the population? How, exactly, are phenotypes selected and genotypes retained? In a computer-based simulation, Pentland et al. (2012) used whole performances of the routine (whole paths) as the phenotypes being selected. The conceptual problem is that, in practice, routines are enacted one step at a time, not as whole performances. And in any case, as Rice and Cooper (2010) point out, the feedback mechanisms needed to support selection are often non-existent or unreliable. In the animation routine, the artists might modify particular steps, take more time to perform certain steps, or prioritize certain activities, but they cannot select (or de-select) whole performances, as in the simulation by Pentland et al. (2012). The idea of selective retention makes intuitive sense, but the formal genotype/phenotype model does not provide a clear connection between the situated actions that make up a routine, and changes in the overall pattern.

Patterning: A Motor of Change for Routine Dynamics

In the practice-based view of routine dynamics, the constitutive performances of a routine unfold one step at a time. This micro-production of meso-order has led scholars in routine dynamics to formulate other mechanisms to describe the processes through which routines change. In particular, the concept of *patterning* has gained popularity (Feldman 2016; Danner-Schröder and Geiger 2016; Dittrich and Seidl 2018).

Goh and Pentland (2019) suggest that patterning can be interpreted as a new motor of change for routines. Patterning refers to the effortful performance of the sequence of actions that forms a routine. When routines are represented as a narrative network, patterning can be operationalized in terms of the mechanisms that drive the addition (or removal) of nodes (actions) and edges (sequential relations) between actions (Pentland and Feldman 2007). These changes in the network can be tracked by comparing multiple "time-slices" (Rosetti and Cazabet 2018) of event sequences from particular time windows (e.g., Moody et al. 2005). But unlike social network dynamics that examine the formation/dissolution of ties between a fixed set of actors, capturing the dynamics of narrative networks involves tracing paths between a constantly changing set of actions (Goh and Pentland 2019).

Patterning is consistent with the practice-based assumptions about routines outlined above. First, it is based on the idea that routines unfold, step by step. This unfolding can be represented as paths in the network, which form recognizable patterns. Thus, patterning fits naturally with the representation of routines as narrative networks. Second, the network captures the sequential relations between steps and provides a way to express the multiplicity of a process – the space of possible paths encompassed by a process (Pentland et al. 2020) – as well. By emphasizing the mechanisms for adding (removing) nodes and edges in a network, patterning lays the foundation for developing explanations of routine dynamics that follows how the overall pattern of actions rather than specific actions within the pattern, stay the same or change.

Because each network summarizes an observed set of event sequences from a particular time window, it can be considered a time-slice or snapshot network (Rossetti and Cazabet 2018). This is an established methodology in network dynamics (e.g., Moody et al. 2005). To capture dynamics, we obviously need to collect and compare multiple slices. For example, Pentland et al. (in press) analyze process change in four dermatology clinics using two years of time stamped electronic health records (EHR). The EHR data provides a very fine-grained view of the record-keeping routines in each clinic. A separate network is computed for each day in each clinic, resulting in a history of 498 snapshots. Pentland et al. (in press) use this history to perform a diachronic analysis (Barley 1990) of the routines in the clinics. The analysis suggests that the routines are quite stable, except when there are exogenous shocks.

Patterning in Videogame Development

Goh and Pentland (2019) analyzed the patterning of actions in videogame development routines. In that study, they sliced the data into three-week time frames that corresponded to the blocks of time that the game developers referred to as "Sprints." During each Sprint, developers would act on specific tasks to accomplish project goals for that Sprint. The full study contained eleven sprints; we present three of them in Figure 15.1 for purposes of illustration. For each Sprint, the sequences of actions were mapped in a narrative network that presents a snapshot of the work. By comparing these time slices over time, they found that routines in videogame development changed from sprint to sprint.

The first thing to notice is that the real routines in Figures 15.1a,b,c are much messier than the idealized example in Table 15.1. Each node in the Figure 15.1 represents an action (building, testing, experimenting, etc.) taken by one of the roles (Art, Design, Sound, Tech, etc.) In other words, the nodes indicate activities: someone (role) doing something (action). Each edge in the network represents a handoff between those activities. For example, at the bottom of Figure 15.1a, we see loops between "Tech Testing" and "Tech Revision". This means that within that sprint, these activities were sequentially related in both directions (testing → revision and revision → testing).

Goh and Pentland analyzed these narrative networks to identify mechanisms that explained the addition/removal of activities (nodes) and handoffs (edges). One of the most striking findings concerned changes in the number of possible pathways in the network from sprint to sprint. The number of possible pathways is interesting because it is an indicator of task complexity (Hærem, Pentland and Miller 2015). A network with more paths is more complex than a network with fewer paths. For example, they found

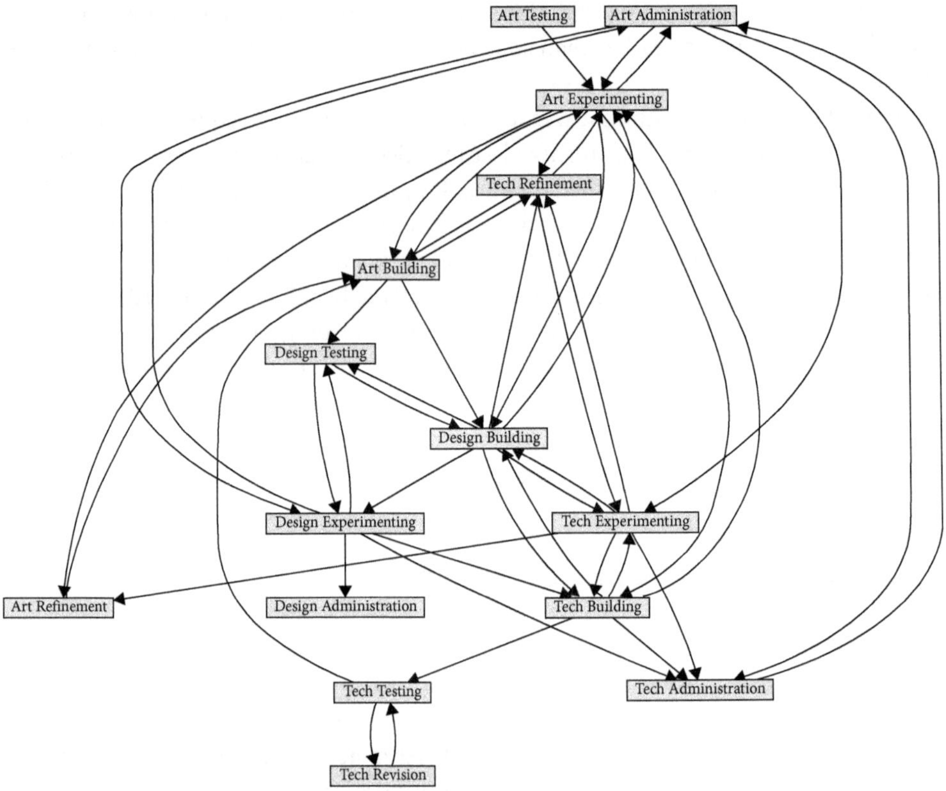

FIGURE 15.1A Narrative Network for Sprint 3

that the number of pathways increased from ~300 in Sprint 3 (Figure 15.1a) to over 43,000 in Sprint 4 (Figure 15.1b). The number of pathways decreased by almost the same amount in Sprint 5 (Figure 15.1c). These differences are impossible to "eyeball" from looking at the networks, but they can be estimated from the structure of the graph using a method presented by Goh and Pentland (2019). For our purposes, the key point is that the routines were changing from sprint to sprint.

The question is, what was causing the changes in the routines? Intuitively, one might hypothesize that the changes might be because of new activities entering the network (new roles, new actions, or some combination of the two). Further investigation revealed that the changes were driven primarily by differences in the number of unique

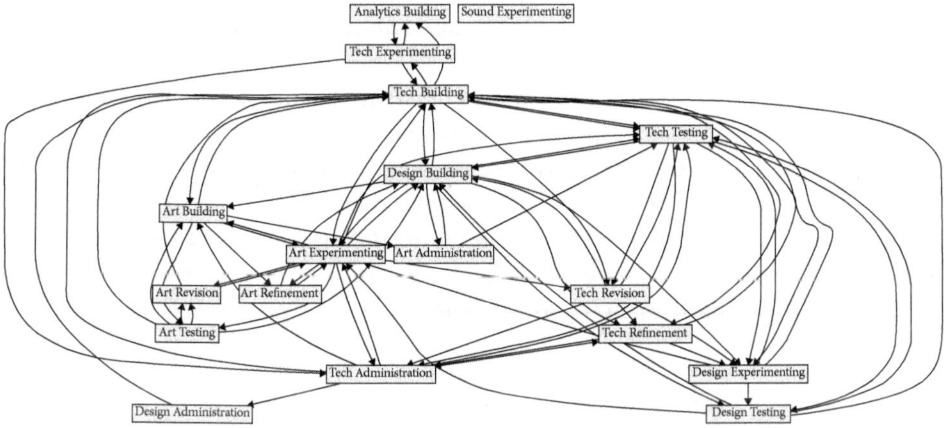

FIGURE 15.1B Narrative network for Sprint 4

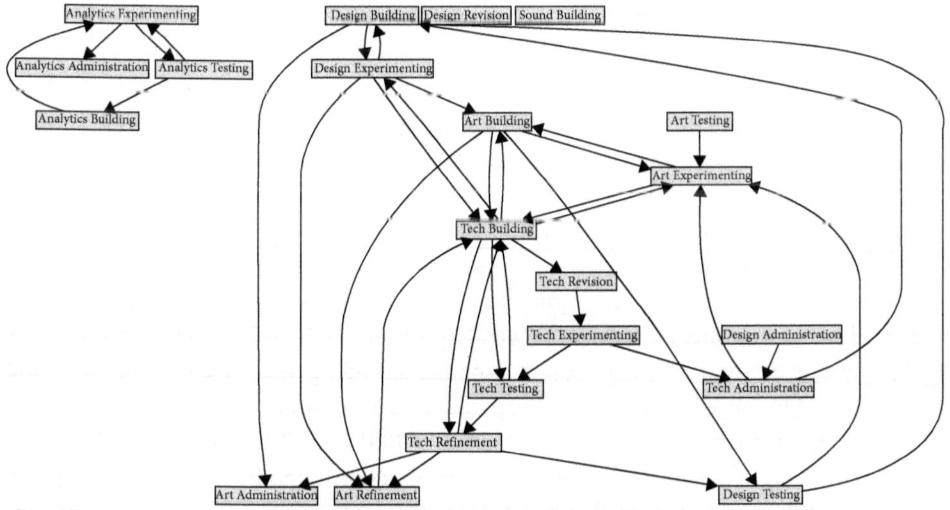

FIGURE 15.1C Narrative network for Sprint 5

handoffs in each sprint. Recall that handoffs between activities correspond to edges in the graph. They were doing roughly the same number of activities in each sprint, but the activities in Sprint 4 were more densely connected (with 87 edges, compared to 55 in Sprint 3 and 47 in Sprint 5).

Consistent with this finding, fieldwork revealed that the first prototype was scheduled to be delivered to the client at the end of Sprint 5. Developers' efforts to ramp up the testing of new ideas by iterating on early prototypes peaked in Sprint 4. These iterations involved a lot of back and forth work between different roles, which accounted for the higher number of handoffs in Sprint 4. By Sprint 5, the team had switched to a production focus to be able to meet the deadline for delivering the first prototype. This switch in focus was evident from the increase in frequency of Building tasks from eighty-one in Sprint 4, to 151 in Sprint 5. Furthermore, there was less iterating between roles and performances unfolded more "routinely" (adjective), which explained the reduction in the number of handoffs and paths.

This example shows how different motors of change blend together in practice. For example, the changes between sprints can be seen from a life cycle perspective (the first prototype is due soon). They can also be seen from a teleological perspective (we need to get this thing working). But in the moment, as the work unfolds, patterning results from specific activities (who does what?) and specific handoffs (what needs to be done next?). The overall pattern of the routine—and changes to that pattern—emerge from the situated practices of the participants (Feldman 2016).

Strengths and Weaknesses of Patterning as a Motor of Change

As of this writing, patterning is a new concept, so the strengths and weaknesses are somewhat theoretical, rather than practical. As compared to the other motors of change, patterning offers a processual model of change that does not invoke a substantialist account of routines as things. It assumes only patterns of action that unfold and accumulate over time, not a set of discrete entities. The idea of patterning as a motor of change more fully embraces the processual view by pointing to change as endogenously occurring through ongoing, repetitive performance. Simpson and Lorino (2016) offer a helpful critique of the original formulation of routine dynamics, which was based on a recursive relation between the ostensive and performative aspects of routines (Feldman and Pentland 2003). Among other things, Simpson and Lorino (2016) argue that this model lacks a sufficiently temporal account of how routines form and change. In contrast, performing and patterning (Feldman 2016) offers a more processual approach. Goh and Pentland (2019) argue that patterning exemplifies the process of dynamic unfolding described by Emirbayer and Mische (1998), because routines are performed one step at a time.

Patterning provides a mechanism that explains both stability and change. We would expect that many of the same theoretical factors that drive stability and change in other theories would apply here as well (e.g., teleology). To make sense from a patterning perspective, these motors would have to influence steps along the path as it unfolds. For example, in their study of videogame development, Goh and Pentland (2019) identify how revisions to the design led to more actions (nodes) and handoffs (edges) between different roles, which subsequently increased the complexity of the routines performed. In this way, patterning suggests a natural link from micro-level processes (where work is performed as a routine unfolds) and the more macro-level pattern of the routine.

Strengths and Weaknesses of the Narrative Network Model

The main advantage of the narrative network model is that it captures sequential relations between actions. As described above, it provides a way to move from the empirical observations of action, which can be highly fragmented, to overall patterns of actions (Pentland and Feldman 2007). At the same time, the narrative network approach has a number of important weaknesses and limitations. First, it does not necessarily capture the situated/embodied aspect of routines very well. By putting actions in the foreground, it tends to put actors and materiality in general in the background.

Second, it does not capture aspects of temporality other than sequence. It is based on event time, not clock time. Duration, simultaneity, co-occurrence, and subjectivity are not explicitly represented in the network. For example, if there are parallel (simultaneous) paths, or if two events need to happen at the same time, that is not explicitly represented. The narrative network captures only a basic model of sequential temporality, not the fully nuanced reality.

Third, the narrative network is essentially descriptive. It provides a detailed snapshot of a process, but it does not explicitly include feedback loops or other mechanisms that drive dynamics. These can be supplied as factors that shape the network. For example, Goh and Pentland (2019) identify several factors that shape the unfolding pattern of actions in videogame development such as time pressure and problems with quality, which lead to dramatic increases (and decreases) in the number of paths in the network.

Practical Applications

Process improvement has always been an important managerial goal. Generally speaking, the motivation for process improvement is teleological, since it involves some kind of gap analysis. Quality improvement programs such as Six Sigma (Conger 2015) are good examples of teleological process improvement initiatives. Process management can also be viewed as an exercise of managerial power subject to resistance (Erwin and Garman 2010), which would suggest the possibility of a dialectic change process, as well (Farjoun 2016).

The general area of "business process management" (BPM) (Benner and Tushman 2003) encompasses many specific techniques for managing process change. Within BPM, network models of organizational processes like those described here have become a practical tool for process monitoring and improvement (Leemans et al. 2019). It is important to note that these tools originate from research in computer science (van der Aalst 2013), not social science. For the most part, they have been developed independently of scholarly research on organizational routines (Breuker and Matzner 2014). The research on routines emphasizes a practice-based view where patterns of action are emergent, as described above. In contrast, the BPM literature tends to assume that processes are designed according to managerial goals. BPM has been most successful when applied to highly structured, transactional processes as opposed to less structured, knowledge-based, or creative processes (Dumas et al. 2018).

Business process management provides a number of related tools and techniques that are applicable to the problem of changing and controlling processes (Dumas et al. 2018; van der Aalst 2011). In particular, process mining uses digital event logs that provide a time-stamped record of how a process is executed. van der Aalst et al. (2011: 172) state that "the idea of process mining is to discover, monitor, and improve real processes (i.e., not assumed processes) by extracting knowledge from event logs readily available in today's (information) systems." They note that process mining "is an enabling technology for CPM, BPI, TQM, Six Sigma" and other process improvement programs. Because process mining provides objective evidence of how a process is currently working, it enables three key activities that are useful for organizational change management:

- Process discovery: How is a process working now? This is especially helpful for processes that are distributed over multiple locations or that occur on a time scale that makes them difficult to observe.
- Process improvement and redesign: How can a process be redesigned to avoid bottlenecks, errors, and delays?
- Conformance checking: How closely does the running process match the process as designed? Using computer generated event logs, process mining can provide up-to-the-minute diagnostic information about process conformance (including exceptions, errors, delays, etc.) Of course, the goal of conformance checking is to prevent change, not create it.

We are beginning to see interest in bridging between research on process mining and research on organizational routines (Grisold et al. 2020). Moving forward, it will be interesting to see whether concepts like patterning and emergence gain traction as practical tools for process management.

Future Research Directions

Routine Dynamics as Network Dynamics

Earlier, we suggested that narrative networks can be used to represent the patterns of action that constitute organizational routines (Pentland and Feldman 2007; Pentland et al. 2017). If so, then it suggests the possibility that changes in routines can be understood in terms of network dynamics. Goh and Pentland note that in social networks, we have a rich set of theories for explaining tie formation and dissolution, including reciprocity (Wasserman and Faust 1994: Chapter 13), preferential attachment (Barabási, and Albert 1999), homophily (McPherson et al. 2001), transitivity (Holland and Leinhardt 1977), and other features of the network. Furthermore, there are established models for predicting dynamics (Snijders 2001; Snijders et al. 2010) and for visualizing dynamics (Handcock et al. 2008).

However, in the realm of narrative networks, we are just beginning to explore the drivers of dynamics and change. Mathematical operations, such as paths and density, can be performed on any kind of network, but they will have different interpretations in different kinds of networks. We cannot simply borrow theories from social networks, because in a narrative network, "nodes are not individuals with cognition, motivation, and other personal characteristics. Consequently, the mechanisms that drive the dynamics of social networks do not apply" (Goh and Pentland 2019: 1904). Thus, we have a tremendous new opportunity to build theory about the dynamics of routines from a network perspective.

Multiplicity: Resistance and Change

The network perspective also provides insights about resistance and change via the concept of process multiplicity. Process multiplicity can be defined by the space of possible paths in a process or routine (Pentland et al. 2020). The routine dynamics literature suggests that multiplicity offers possibilities for change: the more variations that are present in a routine, the more ways endogenous changes can emerge. While multiplicity may facilitate *endogenous* change, Pentland et al (2020) argue that multiplicity may make efforts at managerial intervention and control more difficult. When there are multiple ways to get work done and multiple points of view about what to do and why to do it, there are also more opportunities for resistance. A more homogeneous routine, with a smaller space of possible paths, may be easier to control, replicate, or change. Understanding how process multiplicity influences organizational change and how actors resist or facilitate this change could be new avenues for research on routine dynamics.

Routine Dynamics and Morphogenesis

Morphogenesis is a concept that originated in developmental biology, but that been applied to social systems, as done by Gaba and Meyer in Chapter 16 of this volume, with their model of organizational morphogenesis. Morphogenesis (Archer, 2010) provides a theory of structural elaboration (i.e., change) that can be applied to routine dynamics using the network models. Archer (2010: 247) theorized that degrees of freedom and stringency of constraints are factors that drive morphogenesis: "the specification of degrees of freedom and stringency of constraints makes it possible to theorize about variations in voluntarism and determinism (and their consequences)...". Thus, routines with high degrees of freedom and low stringency of constraints are hypothesized to favor change.

The narrative network framework provides a way to operationalize morphogenesis in empirical research. By *degrees of freedom*, Archer (2010) means the set of choices available for actors to do something new or different in a given situation. In a narrative network, we can operationalize degrees of freedom as the out-degree of the current node (the number of outwardly directed edges). By *stringency of constraints*, Archer (2010) is referring to the fact that not all degrees of freedom are equally free to every actor at every time and place. Situational factors naturally make some options more expensive, difficult, or risky. With enough information, stringency of constraints could be modeled as a cost function assigned to each edge in the graph, depending on context.

Routine Dynamics and Organizational Change

Researchers in routine dynamics are just beginning to consider the move from change within routines, or clusters of routines (Kremser and Schreyogg 2016) to changes in larger structures. This limitation was articulated by Simpson and Lorino (2016) and it is still true today. There is a need to work across levels, from actions to paths, from paths to routines, and from routines to clusters and ecologies of routines. This kind of cross-level work has always proved a difficult challenge in organizational research. Frameworks like the one introduced by Salvato and Vassolo (2018) open the conversation across levels. Progress is being made, but detailed research on a large scale is difficult.

Conclusion

After nearly twenty years of research on routine dynamics, we are entering an exciting new phase. Network models are reshaping how we conceptualize routines and the processes through which routines form and change. By treating routines as dynamic systems, we can continue to explore their role in organizational change from a new point of view.

References

Abbott, A. (1990), 'A primer on sequence methods', *Organization science*, 1/4, 375–92.

Archer, M. S. (2010), 'Morphogenesis versus Structuration: On Combining Structure and Action." *British Journal of Sociology*, 61, 225–52.

Ashforth, B. and Fried, Y. (1988), 'The Mindlessness of Organizational Behaviors', *Human Relations*, 41, 305–29.

Autor, D. H., Levy, F., and Murnane, R. J. (2003), 'The Skill Content of Recent Technological Change: An Empirical Exploration', *The Quarterly Journal of Economics*, 118, 1279–333.

Barabási, A., and Albert, R. (1999), 'Emergence of Scaling in Random Networks', *Science*, 286, 509–12.

Barley, S. R. (1990), 'Images of imaging: Notes on doing longitudinal field work', *Organization Science*, 1/3, 220–47.

Becker, M. C., Lazaric, N., Nelson, R. R., and Winter, S. G. (2005), 'Applying Organizational Routines in Understanding Organizational Change', *Industrial and Corporate Change*, 14(5), 775–91.

Benner, M. J., and Tushman, M. L. (2003), 'Exploitation, Exploration, and Process Management: The Productivity Dilemma Revisited', *Academy of Management Review*, 28/2, 238–56.

Berente, N., Lyytinen, K., Yoo, Y., and King, J. L. (2016), 'Routines as shock absorbers during organizational transformation: Integration, control, and NASA's enterprise information system', *Organization Science*, 27/3, 551–72.

Birnholtz, J. P., Cohen, M. D., and Hoch, S. V. (2007), 'Organizational Character: On the Regeneration of Camp Poplar Grove', *Organization Science*, 18/2, 315–32.

Blanche, C., and Cohendet, P. (2019), 'Remounting a Ballet in a Different Context: A Complementary Understanding of Routines Transfer Theories,' in M. S. Feldman, L. D'Adderio, K. Dittrich, P. Jarzabkowski, eds., *Routine Dynamics in Action: Replication and Transformation* (Bingley: Emerald Publishing Limited), 11–30.

BreukerD. and Matzner M. (2014), 'Performances of Business Processes and Organizational Routines: Similar Research Problems, Different Research Methods—A Literature Review', Proceedings of the European Conference on Information Systems (ECIS), Tel Aviv, Israel.

Burke, W. W. (2021), 'Historical Currents in Scholarship of Organization Change' in M. S. Poole and A. H. Van de Ven, eds., *The Oxford Handbook of Organizational Change and Innovation* (2nd edn) (Oxford: Oxford University Press),

Cohen, M. D. (2007), 'Reading Dewey: Reflections on the Study of Routine', *Organization Studies*, 28, 773–86.

Cohen, M. D. and Bacdayan, P. (1994), 'Organizational Routines are Stored as Procedural Memory: Evidence from a Laboratory Study', *Organization Science*, 5, 554–68.

Cohen, M. D., Burkhart, R., Dosi, G., Egidi, M., Marengo, L., Warglien, M., and Winter, S. (1996), 'Routines and Other Recurring Action Patterns of Organizations: Contemporary Research Issues', *Industrial and Corporate Change*, 5, 653–98.

Cohen, M. D., Levinthal, D. A., and Warglien, M. (2014), 'Collective Performance: Modeling the Interaction of Habit-Based Actions.' *Industrial and Corporate Change*, 23/2, 329–60.

Conger, S. (2015), 'Six Sigma and Business Process Management', in J. vom Brocke, and M. Rosemann (eds.), *Handbook of Business Process Management* (Berlin, Heidelberg: Springer), 127–46.

D'Adderio, L. (2014), 'The Replication Dilemma Unravelled: How Organizations Enact Multiple Goals in Routine Transfer', *Organization Science*, 25/5, 1325–50.

Danner-Schröder, A., and Geiger, D. (2016), 'Unravelling the Motor of Patterning Work: Toward an Understanding of the Microlevel Dynamics of Standardization and Flexibility', *Organization Science*, 27/3, 633–58.

Deken, F., Carlile, P. R., Berends, H., and Lauche, K. (2016), 'Generating Novelty through Interdependent Routines: A Process Model of Routine Work', *Organization Science*, 27/3, 659–77.

Dittrich, K., and Seidl, D. (2018), 'Emerging Intentionality in Routine Dynamics: A Pragmatist View', *Academy of Management Journal*, 61/1, 111–38.

Dönmez, D., Grote, G., and Brusoni, S. (2016), 'Routine Interdependencies as a Source of Stability and Flexibility: A Study of Agile Software Development Teams', *Information and Organization*, 26/3, 63–83.

Dumas, M., La Rosa, M., Mendling, J., and Reijers, H. A. (2018), *Fundamentals of Business Process Management* (Heidelberg: Springer).

Eisenhardt, K. M., and Martin, J. A. (2000), 'Dynamic Capabilities: What Are They?' *Strategic Management Journal*, 21, 1105–21.

Emirbayer, M., and Mische, A. (1998), 'What is Agency?' *American Journal of Sociology*, 103/4, 962–1023.

Erwin, D. G., and Garman, A. N. (2010), 'Resistance to Organizational Change: Linking Research and Practice', *Leadership and Organization Development Journal*, 31/1, 39–56.

Farjoun, M. (2016), 'Contradictions, Dialectics and Paradoxes', in A. Langley and H. Tsoukas, eds., *The SAGE Handbook of Process Organization Studies* (Thousand Oaks, CA: Sage), 87–109.

Feldman, M. S. (2000), 'Organizational Routines as a Source of Continuous Change', *Organization Science*, 11/6, 611–29.

Feldman, M. S. (2016), 'Routines as Process: Past, Present, and Future', in J. Howard-Grenville, C. Rerup, A. Langley, and H. Tsoukas, eds., *Organizational Routines: A Process Perspective* (Oxford: Oxford University Press), 23–46.

Feldman, M. S., and Orlikowski, W. J. (2011), 'Theorizing Practice and Practicing Theory', *Organization Science*, 22/5, 1240–53.

Feldman, M. S., and Pentland, B. T. (2003), 'Reconceptualizing Organizational Routines as a Source of Flexibility and Change', *Administrative Science Quarterly*, 48/1, 94–118.

Feldman, M. S., Pentland, B. T., D'Adderio, L., and Lazaric, N. (2016), 'Beyond Routines as Things: Introduction to the Special Issue on Routine Dynamics', *Organization Science*, 27/3, 505–13.

Gaba, V. and Meyer, A. D. (2021), 'Discontinuous Change in Organizations and Fields', in M. S. Poole and A. H. Van de Ven, eds., *The Oxford Handbook of Organizational Change and Innovation* (2nd edn) (Oxford: Oxford University Press),

Garud, R. and Turunen, M. (2021), 'Microfoundations of Innovation as Process: Usher's Cumulative Synthesis Model', in M. S. Poole and A. H. Van de Ven, eds., *The Oxford Handbook of Organizational Change and Innovation* (2nd edn) (Oxford: Oxford University Press),

Goh, K. T., and Pentland, B. T. (2019), 'From Actions to Paths to Patterning: Toward a Dynamic Theory of Patterning in Routines', *Academy of Management Journal*, 62/6, 1901–29.

Greve, H. (2008), 'Organizational Routines and Performance Feedback', in M. C. Becker, ed., *Handbook of Organizational Routines* (Cheltenham: Edward Elgar), 187–205.

Grisold, T., Wurm, B., Mendling, J. and Vom Brocke, J. (2020), 'Using Process Mining to Support Theorizing About Change in Organizations', in Proceedings of the 53rd Hawaii International Conference on System Sciences.

Hærem, T., Pentland, B. T., and Miller, K. D. (2015), 'Task Complexity: Extending a Core Concept', *Academy of Management Review*, 40/3, 446–60.

Handcock, M. S., Hunter, D. R., Butts, C. T., Goodreau, S. M., and Morris, M. (2008), 'Statnet: Software Tools for the Representation, Visualization, Analysis and Simulation of Network Data', *Journal of Statistical Software*, 24/1, 1548–7660.

Hargrave, T. J. (2021), 'The Paradox Perspective and the Dialectics of Contradictions Research', in M. S. Poole and A. H. Van de Ven, eds., *The Oxford Handbook of Organizational Change and Innovation* (2nd edn) (Oxford: Oxford University Press).

Hodgson, G. M. and Knudsen, T. (2004), 'The Firm as an Interactor: Firms as Vehicles for Habits and Routines', *Journal of Evolutionary Economics*, 14, 281–307.

Holland, P. W., and Leinhardt, S. (1977), 'A Dynamic Model for Social Networks', *Journal of Mathematical Sociology*, 5/1, 5–20.

Knudsen, T. (2008), "Organizational Routines in Evolutionary Theory,' in M. C. Becker, ed., *Handbook of Organizational Routines* (Cheltenham: Edward Elgar), 125–51.

Kremser, W., and Schreyögg, G. (2016), 'The Dynamics of Interrelated Routines: Introducing the Cluster Level', *Organization Science*, 27/3, 698–721.

Latour, B. (2005), *Reassembling the Social: An Introduction to Actor-Network Theory* (Oxford: Oxford University Press).

Leemans, S. J., Poppe, E., and Wynn, M. T. (2019), 'Directly Follows-Based Process Mining: Exploration and a Case Study', in 2019 International Conference on Process Mining (ICPM), IEEE, 25–32.

Leonardi, P. M. (2011), 'When flexible routines meet flexible technologies: Affordance, constraint, and the imbrication of human and material agencies', *MIS Quarterly*, 35/1, 147–67.

Lewin, A. Y., and Massini, S. (2004), 'Knowledge Creation and Organizational Capabilities of Innovating and Imitating Firms', in H.Tsoukas and N. Mylonopoulos, eds., *Organizations as Knowledge Systems* (London: Palgrave Macmillan), 209–37.

Lok, J., and De Rond, M. (2013), 'On the plasticity of institutions: Containing and restoring practice breakdowns at the Cambridge University Boat Club', *Academy of Management Journal*, 56/1, 185–207.

McPherson, M., Smith-Lovin, L., and Cook, J. M. (2001), 'Birds of a Feather: Homophily in Social Networks', *Annual Review of Sociology*, 27/1, 415–44.

Miner, A., Crossan, M. and Maurer, C. (2021), 'VSR Models of Change as Normative Practical Theory', in M. S. Poole and A. H. Van de Ven, eds., *The Oxford Handbook of Organizational Change and Innovation* (2nd edn) (Oxford: Oxford University Press).

Moody, J., McFarland, D., and Bender-deMoll, S. (2005), 'Dynamic Network Visualization', *American Journal of Sociology*, 110/4, 1206–41.

Nelson, R. R., and Sidney, G. (1982), *An Evolutionary Theory of Economic Change* (Cambridge: Harvard University Press).

Nguyen, Q. H., and Vuori, T. (2021), 'Emotionality and Change', in M. S. Poole and A. H. Van de Ven, eds., *The Oxford Handbook of Organizational Change and Innovation* (2nd edn) (Oxford: Oxford University Press).

Orlikowski, W. J. (2007), 'Sociomaterial practices: Exploring technology at work', *Organization Studies*, 28/9, 1435–48.

Orlikowski, W. J., and Scott, S. V. (2008), 'Sociomateriality: Challenging the Separation of Technology, Work and Organization', *Academy of Management Annals*, 2/1, 433–74.

Parmigiani, A., and Howard-Grenville, J. (2011), "Routines Revisited: Exploring the Capabilities and Practice Perspectives', *Academy of Management Annals*, 5/1, 413–53.

Pentland, B. T. (1992), 'Organizing Moves in Software Support Hot Lines', *Administrative Science Quarterly*, 37/4, 527–48.

Pentland, B. T., and Rueter, H. H. (1994), 'Organizational routines as grammars of action', *Administrative Science Quarterly*, 39/3, 484–510.

Pentland, B. T., and Feldman, M. S. (2007), "Narrative Networks: Patterns of Technology and Organization', *Organization Science*, 18/5, 781–95.

Pentland, B. T., and Hærem, T. (2015), 'Organizational Routines as Patterns of Action: Implications for Organizational Behavior', *Annual Review of Organizational Psychology and Organizational Behavior*, 2/1, 465–87.

Pentland, B. T., and Rueter, H. H. (1994), 'Organizational Routines as Grammars of Action', *Administrative Science Quarterly*, 39/3, 484–510.

Pentland, B. T., Feldman, M. S., Becker, M. C., and Liu, P. (2012), 'Dynamics of Organizational Routines: A Generative Model', *Journal of Management Studies*, 49/8, 1484–508.

Pentland, B. T., Hærem, T., and Hillison, D. (2010), 'Comparing Organizational Routines as Recurrent Patterns of Action', *Organization Studies*, 31, 917–40.

Pentland, B. T., Hærem, T., and Hillison, D. (2011), 'The (N) Ever-Changing World: Stability and Change in Organizational Routines', *Organization Science*, 22/6, 1369–83.

Pentland, B. T., Recker, J., and Wyner, G. (2017), 'Rediscovering Handoffs', *Academy of Management Discoveries*, 3/3, 284–301.

Pentland, B.T., Mahringer, C., Dittrich, K., Feldman, M.S. and Ryan Wolf, J. (2020), 'Process Multiplicity and Process Dynamics: Weaving the Space of Possible Paths', *Organization Theory*, 1, 1–21.

Pentland, B.T., Vaast, E. and Ryan Wolf, J. *(in press), 'Theorizing process dynamics with directed graphs: A diachronic analysis of digital trace data', MIS Quarterly.*

Poole, M. S., and A. H. Van de Ven (2021), 'The Life Cycle Process Model', in M. S. Poole and A. H. Van de Ven, eds., *The Oxford Handbook of Organizational Change and Innovation* (2nd edn) (Oxford: Oxford University Press).

Prichard, C., and Creed, D. (2021), 'Agency in Social Movements as Sources of Change', in M. S. Poole and A. H. Van de Ven, eds., *The Oxford Handbook of Organizational Change and Innovation* (2nd edn) (Oxford: Oxford University Press).

Rerup, C., and Feldman, M. S. (2011), 'Routines as a Source of Change in Organizational Schemata: The Role of Trial-and-Error Learning', *Academy of Management Journal*, 54/3, 577–610.

Rheinhardt, A. and Gioia, D. (2021), 'Upside-Down Organizational Change: Sensemaking, Sensegiving, and the New Generation', in M. S. Poole and A. H. Van de Ven, eds., *The Oxford Handbook of Organizational Change and Innovation* (2nd edn) (Oxford: Oxford University Press).

Rice, R. E., and Cooper, S. D. (2010), Organizations and unusual routines: A systems analysis of dysfunctional feedback processes. (Cambridge: Cambridge University Press.)

Rosa, M. L., Van Der Aalst, W. M., Dumas, M. and Milani, F. P. (2017), 'Business Process Variability Modeling: A Survey', *ACM Computing Surveys (CSUR)*, 50/1, 1–45.

Rossetti, G. and Cazabet, R. (2018), 'Community Discovery in Dynamic Networks: A Survey', *ACM Computing Surveys (CSUR)* 51/2, 1–37.

Salvato, C., and Rerup, C. (2018), 'Routine Regulation: Balancing Conflicting Goals in Organizational Routines', *Administrative Science Quarterly*, 63/1, 170–209.

Salvato, C., and Vassolo, R. (2018), 'The Sources of Dynamism in Dynamic Capabilities', *Strategic Management Journal*, 39/6, 1728–52.

Schulz, M. (2008), 'Staying on Track: A Voyage to the Internal Mechanisms of Routine Reproduction', in M. Becker, ed, *Handbook of Organizational Routines* Cheltenham: Edward Elgar (228–55).

Sele, K., and Grand, S. (2016) 'Unpacking the Dynamics of Ecologies of Routines: Mediators and their Generative Effects in Routine Interactions', *Organization Science*, 27/3, 722–38.
Simon, H. S. (1947), *Administrative Behavior* (New York: The Free Press).
Simon, H., and March, J. G. (1958), *Organizations* (Oxford: Blackwell).
Simpson, B. and Lorino, P. (2016), 'Re-Viewing Routines through a Pragmatist Lens', in J. Howard-Grenville, C. Rerup, A. Langley, and H. Tsoukas eds., *Organizational Routines: A Process Perspective* (Oxford: Oxford University Press), 47–70.
Snijders, T. A. (2001), 'The Statistical Evaluation of Social Network Dynamics', *Sociological Methodology*, 31/1, 361–95.
Snijders, T. A. B., van de Bunt, G. G., and Steglich, C. E. G. (2010), 'Introduction to Stochastic Actor-Based Models for Network Dynamics', *Social Networks*, 32/1, 44–60.
Swan, J., Robertson, M., and Newell, S. (2016), 'The Paradox of Routines in the Ecology of Complex Innovation', in J. A. Howard-Grenville, C. Rerup, A. Langley, and H. Tsoukas, eds. *Organizational Routines: How They Are Created, Maintained, and Changed* (Vol. 5) (Oxford: Oxford University Press), 203–34.
Sydow, J., Schreyögg, G., and Koch, J. (2009), 'Organizational Path Dependence: Opening the Black Box', *Academy of Management Review*, 34/4, 689–709.
Teece, D. J. (2012), 'Dynamic Capabilities: Routines versus Entrepreneurial Action', *Journal of Management Studies*, 49/8, 1395–401.
Teece, D. J., Pisano, G., and Shuen, A. (1997), 'Dynamic Capabilities and Strategic Management', *Strategic Management Journal*, 18/7, 509–33.
Turner, S. F., and Rindova, V. (2012), 'A balancing act: How organizations pursue consistency in routine functioning in the face of ongoing change', *Organization Science*, 23/1, 24–46.
Turner, S. F., and Rindova, V. P. (2018), 'Watching the Clock: Action Timing, Patterning, and Routine Performance', *Academy of Management Journal*, 61/4, 1253–80.
Van de Ven, A. H., and Poole, M. S. (1995), 'Explaining Development and Change in Organizations', *Academy of Management Review*, 20/3, 510–40.
Wasserman, S., and Faust, K. (1994), *Social Network Analysis: Methods and Applications* (Cambridge: Cambridge University Press).
West, D. B. (2001), *Introduction to Graph Theory*, Prentice-Hall. *Englewood Cliffs, NJ.*
van der Aalst, W., (2011), *Process Mining: Discovery, Conformance and Enhancement of Business Processes* (Heidelberg: Springer).
van der Aalst, W., Adriansyah, A., De Medeiros, A. K., Arcieri, F., Baier, T., Blickle, T., Bose, J. C., et al. (2011), 'Process Mining Manifesto', in International Conference on Business Process Management, Berlin: Springer, 169–94.
van der Aalst, W. M. (2013), 'Business Process Management: A Comprehensive Survey', *ISRN Software Engineering*, 1–37.
Weiss, H. M., and Ilgen, D. R. (1985), 'Routinized Behavior in Organizations', *Journal of Behavioral Economics*, 14/1, 57–67.
Winter, S. G. (2003), 'Understanding Dynamic Capabilities', *Strategic Management Journal*, 24/10, 991–5.
Zbaracki, M. J., and Bergen, M. (2010), 'When Truces Collapse: A Longitudinal Study of Price-Adjustment Routines', *Organization Science*, 21/5, 955–72.

CHAPTER 16

DISCONTINUOUS CHANGE IN ORGANIZATIONS AND FIELDS

VIBHA GABA AND ALAN D. MEYER

INTRODUCTION

IN a 1987 symposium at the Academy of Management meetings in New Orleans, Alan Meyer presented a 2x2 framework for categorizing theories of change used by scholars in organization and management studies. This framework classified research reports by distinguishing modes of change (first-order vs. second-order change), and levels of analysis (organization-level vs. industry-level change). The framework identified mechanisms that were commonly adduced as drivers of change, and it cited exemplary research.

In two papers published in 1990 and 1993, Meyer and his colleagues refined this framework and used it in a historical analysis of medical–surgical hospitals in the San Francisco Bay Area. These papers noted the prevalence in the literature of research studies assuming organization-level adaptation, and remarked on the dearth of studies of discontinuous (second-order) change occurring at the field (or industry) level of analysis.

Our goal in this chapter is to review research addressing change that has been published since Meyer and his colleagues initially published their framework. Specifically, we will (1) summarize, evaluate, and extend the 1990 framework in light of subsequent work, (2) identify additional theoretical lenses and causal mechanisms that have been brought to bear on discontinuous change within organizations and organizational fields, and (3) propose fruitful constructs, methodologies, and directions for future research on change in and around organizations.

Classifying Theories of Organizational Change

Upon reviewing the literature on processes of organizational change, Meyer et al. (1990) reported finding diverse characterizations with contradictory implications.[1] They noted that some writers saw change as a continuous organizational process (March 1981); others saw it occurring during brief episodes interspersed between lengthy periods of stability (Miller and Friesen 1984). Some saw change flowing from volitional actions of effectual agents (Andrews 1971); others saw adaptations to and repercussions of unforeseen exogenous shocks (Meyer 1982). Meyer and his co-authors concluded that such inconsistencies arose from different assumptions, often left implicit, about the fundamental nature of change and the principal level at which change occurs.

Modes of Change

Continuous, or first-order change occurs within a stable system that remains unchanged (Watzlawick et al. 1974). Discontinuous, or second-order change transforms underlying properties or states of the system. This fundamental distinction has been drawn within virtually every unit of analysis examined by organizational scholars: single vs. double-loop learning by individuals (Argyris and Schön 1978), variations vs. reorientations in products (Normann 1971), adaptation vs. metamorphosis in organizations (Miller and Friesen 1984), competence-enhancing vs. competence-destroying advances in technology (Tushman and Anderson 1986), and evolution vs. revolution in industries (Schumpeter 1950).

Levels of Analysis

The level at which Management and Organizational Studies (MOS) authors assumed that changes occur provided the second dimension for classifying theories of change in Meyer and his co-authors' framework. They argued that most early twentieth-century theorists took the firm as the relevant unit of analysis and focused on actions designed to accomplish the goals of the dominant coalition (Cyert and March 1963; Thompson 1967) by aligning organizational attributes with environmental conditions (Ansoff,1965; Hofer and Schendel 1978). Beginning in the 1970s, however, concepts situated at the level of populations, industries, and fields attracted growing interest.

[1] This section summarizes and draws upon Alan D. Meyer, Geoffrey R. Brooks, and James B. Goes, 'Environmental Jolts and Industry Revolutions: Organizational Responses to Discontinuous Change,' *Strategic Management Journal*, 11 (Summer), 93–110. © 1990, John Wiley and Sons, Ltd.

Astley and Fombrun (1983) proposed the notion of collective strategy, and Bresser (1988) investigated the dilemmas that collective strategies pose regarding disclosure of proprietary information. Fennell and Alexander (1987) took an institutional theory perspective to examine interorganizational bridging strategies; others examined strategic implications of interlocking directorates (Zajac 1988) and interorganizational networks (Thorelli 1986; Jarillo 1988). Work grounded in the structure–conduct–performance paradigm (Scherer 1980) addressed the effects of industry structure, mobility barriers, and strategic groups (Caves and Porter 1977).

Based on the distinctions drawn above between mode of change (first vs. second-order), and level of change (organization vs. field), Meyer and his colleagues (1990) constructed Figure 16.1 to classify theories about how alignments between organizations and their environments are created and maintained.

Adaptation. The figure's northwest quadrant housed theories of first-order change constructed at the organization level of analysis. They termed these *adaptation* theories, which asserted that firms track their environments more or less continuously and adjust to them purposively. Two mechanisms of adjustment were identified. Theorists espousing the "strategic choice" perspective (e.g., Child 1972; Miles and Snow 1978; Mintzberg and McHugh 1985) maintained that subject to operational and technological constraints, power-holders within organizations had the latitude to decide upon structural arrangements and courses of strategic action. Successful actions were then encoded in firms' structures, processes, and product-market domains. An alternate mechanism of organizational adaptation was advanced in the resource dependence model (Pfeffer and Salancik 1978). Here, managers were relegated a lesser role because organizational changes were seen as responses dictated by external dependencies. Nevertheless, the organization remained the principal unit within which change was seen as occurring, and first-order change was the principal mode emphasized in resource dependence theory. Within both perspectives, the domain of theoretical explanation was limited to incremental changes within firms. Adaptation models posited firm-level changes that constructed idiosyncratic organizational structures and processes, and thus increased inter-organizational diversity over time.

Evolution. The figure's southwest quadrant included models considering how fields, industries, or populations of competing firms undergo first-order change. Meyer and his co-authors referred to these as *evolution* models, because they maintained that although individual organizations were relatively inert, various forces propelled populations of organizations toward alignment with prevailing external conditions. They differentiated two streams of theory by the dominant change mechanisms they posited. Population ecologists (e.g., Hannan and Freeman 1977, 1984; McKelvey 1982) emphasized blind variation, selection, and retention, arguing that differential rates in the entry and exit of firms cause populations to evolve gradually to fit the technical and economic constraints of environmental niches. Alternatively, institutional theorists (e.g., Meyer and Rowan 1977; Scott 1987; Zucker 1987) argued that organizations are pressured to conform to the normative expectations of their institutional environments. Achieving "isomorphism" with such expectations allowed organizations to gain legitimacy, garner resources, and enhance their survival chances. Whereas population ecology theory assumed that competition for resources shaped populations by affecting organizations' entry and exit rates, institutional theory focused on competition for legitimacy and entertained the possibility of change within intact organizations. But although they emphasized different causal mechanisms, ecological and institutional approaches both postulated population-level processes that increase homogeneity among organizations over time.

Metamorphosis. The northeast quadrant of Figure 16.1 contained firm-level theories focusing on second-order changes. Meyer and his colleagues dubbed these *metamorphosis* theories, because they maintained that organizations adopt stable configurations and possess inertia, but periodically realign by undergoing rapid, organization-wide transformations. Theorists had proposed various endogenous causal mechanisms that might drive metamorphic changes. These included progression through life cycle stages (Kimberly and Miles 1980), strategic reorientations (Tushman and Romanelli 1985), shifts between strategic types (Miles and Snow 1978), organizational archetypes (Hinings and Greenwood 1988), and structural gestalts (Miller and Friesen 1984). All of these metamorphosis theories focused on frame-breaking changes enclosed by the boundaries of single organizations.

	First-Order Change	Second-Order Change
	Adaptation	**Metamorphosis**
Organization Level	Focus: Incremental change within organizations Mechanisms: • Strategic choice • Resource dependence Authors: Child (1972), Lindblom (1959), Miles & Snow (1978), Pfeffer & Salancik (1978), Weick (1979)	Focus: Frame-breaking change within organizations Mechanisms: • Life cycles • Strategic reorientations Authors: Greenwood & Hinings (1988), Kimberly & Miles (1980), Miller & Friesen (1984), Tushman & Romanelli (1985), Greiner (1972)
	Evolution	**Revolution**
Field Level	Focus: Incremental change within established industries Mechanisms: • Natural selection • Institutional isomorphism Authors: Hannan & Freeman (1977), McKelvey & Aldrich (1983), Meyer & Rowan (1977), Scott (1987), Zucker (1987)	Focus: Emergence, transformation, and decline of industries Mechanisms: • Quantum speciation • Environmental partitioning Authors: Astley (1985), Barney (1986), Gould & Eldredge (1977), McCann & Selsky (1984), Schumpeter (1950)

FIGURE 16.1 Models of Change within Organizations and Fields

Source: Adapted from Meyer et al., 1990

Revolution. Finally, the figure's southeast quadrant housed theories focusing on second-order change in organizational fields. Following Schumpeter (1950), these were labelled *revolution* models, because they proposed that fields and industries are restructured and reconstituted during brief periods of discontinuous change which punctuate longer periods of stability. Quantum speciation, a biological notion, had been suggested as a mechanism whereby new organizational forms might emerge during such periods (Astley 1985), and environmental partitioning was proposed as a collective response to rapid field-wide change (McCann and Selsky 1984).

Based on their 1990 survey of the Management and Organizational Studies literature, Meyer and his co-authors asserted that MOS theorists had ventured into this fourth quadrant only occasionally. They claimed that first-order change had received far more attention than second-order change, and that more attention had been focused on change within organizations than within fields. Metamorphosis theorists had argued that progression between developmental stages (Kimberly and Miles 1980) or radical innovations in technology (Tushman and Anderson 1986) led to second-order changes within organizations—but they had not asked why or how second-order changes in the structure of an industry itself unfold. Van de Ven and Garud (1987) had addressed the emergence of new industries, but their framework did not consider second-order changes that restructure existing industries. Barney (1986) discussed industry-wide Schumpeterian shocks, but he did not delineate their dynamics. Population ecologists (Hannan and Freeman 1984) described how collections of competing firms evolve, but they had little to say about how exogenous second-order changes redefine viable environmental niches, or trigger the emergence of new organizational forms (Astley 1985; Carroll 1984). Institutional theorists argued that coercive, mimetic, and normative forces brought organizations into alignment with each other and with the institutions upon which they depend (DiMaggio and Powell 1983), but the processes whereby institutions themselves form and re-form had yet to be considered (Barley and Tolbert 1997).

Overall, Meyer, Goes, and Brooks concluded that most of the work published before 1990 attended to gradual, first-order environmental change and exhorted managers to respond by engaging in planning, forecasting, experimenting, and other first-order organizational responses.

Process Theories of Development and Change

Contemporaneously, Andrew Van de Ven and Marshall Scott Poole (1995) were constructing a typology of development and change processes that dovetailed with Meyer and his colleagues' framework. Van de Ven and Poole began by conducting an encyclopaedic multi-disciplinary literature review encompassing the social, biological, and physical sciences. They distilled out four "families of ideal-type theories of social change," which they termed 'Evolution', 'Life Cycle', 'Teleology', and 'Dialectic'. Each archetypical family was said to be endowed with a unique set of event sequences and developmental trajectories, which they called "motors." They proceeded to apply the typology to organization-focused theories of change processes by classifying theories in this area as hybridized combinations of the archetypes, and concluded that "most specific theories of organization change and development are actually composites of two or more ideal-type motors" (Van de Ven and Poole 1995: 527).

In contrast, Meyer and his colleagues had constructed their framework based upon a more narrowly circumscribed reading of the MOS literature addressing organizational change, with an emphasis on theories and mechanisms specifying how alignments between organizations and environments are developed and maintained. Given their departures from different bodies of literature, the parallels between Van de Ven and Poole's typology and Meyer, Goes, and Brooks' framework are striking, a convergence that lends support to the validity and utility of both approaches. The differences are also instructive. Van de Ven and Poole's typology includes a "family" of change models they label "dialectic," focusing on change arising from a Hegelian dialectic driven by confrontation and conflict—however, changes arising from power and political processes are absent from Meyer et al.'s framework. On the other hand, the "revolution" quadrant in Meyer et al.'s framework incorporates field-level change processes of emergence and discontinuity drawn from complexity theory—aspects of change that are not addressed by Van de Ven and Poole's typology.

Three Ensuing Decades of Change Research

The purpose of this chapter is to update the framework developed by Meyer and his colleagues by focusing on recent articles addressing discontinuous change.[2] Such work has proliferated in organization theory (Meyer et al. 1993), institutional theory (Greenwood et al. 2017), complexity theory (Anderson and Meyer 2017), strategy (Helfat and Peteraf 2015), and entrepreneurship (Sarasvathy 2001).

Literature Review Method

We conducted a literature review of the empirical work on change processes published after 1990 in Management and Organization Studies (MOS). We selected the papers for our corpus by conducting a Boolean search of the Social Science Citation Index[3] to

[2] Throughout the chapter we use the terms "discontinuous," "disruptive," and "second-order change" interchangeably.

[3] We searched for articles whose titles, abstracts, and keywords contained one or more terms from each of two sets. Set 1 contained the terms: organization*, firm*, field*, industr* and population*. Set 2 consisted of: change*, adapt*, disrupt*, discontinu*, emerge*, revolution*, reorient*, evol*, punctuat*, and metamorph*. To keep our review manageable, we limited the search to the following journals: *Academy of Management Journal, Administrative Science Quarterly, Management Science, Organization Science, Organization Studies, Journal of Management, Journal of Management Studies,* and *Strategic Management Journal.*

identify articles about change in organizations and/or fields. Our initial effort yielded 389 articles. After eliminating those papers that contained only brief usage of the terms and topics in question, we were left with a total of 189 articles. We sorted these articles into bins according to their year of publication, and within each bin, we ranked the articles according to the number of Google Scholar citations they had received. We examined the backward and forward citations of the most influential articles in the list. This led us to papers outside of the initial sample that had not used a variant of one of the original search terms, and papers in journals in adjacent fields. We continued with the exercise until we were confident we had identified the set of relevant and representative papers on discontinuous field and organization-level changes published in the last thirty years.

Social Mechanisms Causing discontinuous change

With relevant articles on discontinuous change in hand, we focused in at a more granular level to identify the social mechanism(s) that each paper's author(s) had theorized as driving change. We were inspired by recent calls for "mechanism-based theorizing" (Hedström and Swedberg 1998; Davis and Marquis 2005). "A mechanism is... about 'cogs and wheels'—the wheelwork or agency by which an effect is produced" (Hernes 1998: 74). A mechanism-based explanation "does not aim at an exhaustive account of all details but seeks to capture the crucial elements of the process by abstracting away the irrelevant details" (Hedström and Ylikoski 2010: 51). As Weber (2006: 121) puts it, social mechanisms "elaborate, sharpen, transpose and connect theories, but they do not substitute for them."

Following Hedström and Ylikoski (2010: 51), we define social mechanisms as causal accounts that describe a set of interacting parts producing an effect not inherent in any one of them. They are composed of "entities (with their properties) and the activities that these entities engage in, either by themselves or in concert with other entities [to] bring about change, and the type of change brought about depends on the properties of the entities and how the entities are organized spatially and temporally." Hedström and Ylikoski (2010: 51) write that a mechanism-based account of change provides a "how-possible explanation." It explains how the effect could in principle be produced by breaking "how" into smaller questions about the causal process: "What are the participating entities, and what are their relevant properties? How are the interactions of these entities organized (both spatially and temporally)?"

We studied the theoretical arguments made by the authors of the 189 change-focused articles in our corpus, seeking to identify the social mechanisms that they said or implied bring change about. We characterized papers' mechanisms in terms of three dimensions. (1) *Key components*: What entities does the theory specify or insinuate are central elements of the change process, and what are their essential properties? Key components can be cognitive, social, technical, or artifactual. (2) *Causal interactions*: What interactions between components are stated or implied as essential to bringing change into being? (3) *Triggers and catalysts*: What triggers, catalysts, or events are said or implied to initiate and drive the change process? In addition, we noted the level or levels of analysis at which authors viewed change as beginning and playing out. Table 16.1 explicates the primary social mechanisms we identified and cites representative empirical studies. ——————————————————-

Table 16.1 Social Mechanisms Invoked by Theories of Discontinuous Change

SOCIAL MECHANISM	BRIEF DESCRIPTION/DEFINITION	EXEMPLARY ARTICLES
Field-Level Mechanisms		
Shifts and hybridization of institutional logics	Change or amalgamation of dominant organizing principles that define the content and meaning of institutions. Networks of normative, cultural, and coercive influences supporting one or more logics or ideologies that justify and codify participants' action and behavior within the field.	Thornton and Ocasio, 1999; Greenwood, Suddaby, and Hinings, 2002; Battilana and Dorado, 2010
Institutional entrepreneurship	Socially skilled actors envision and strive to enact new institutions using varied influence tactics in order to advance interests they value that are being suppressed by extant field-level logics.	Fligstein, 1997; Sine and David, 2003; Battilana, Leca and Boxman, 2009
Shifting demand landscape	Evolving and uncertain consumer preferences or unrecognized dimensions along which consumers evaluate the offerings in the market shape technological evolution and perceptions of new opportunities in the market.	Adner and Levinthal, 2001; Adner and Snow, 2010; Benner and Tripsas, 2012; Danneels, 2003, 2008
Ecosystems nested in fields	Ecosystems emerge, organized around distinct yet interdependent organizations that jointly create value by purposively establishing cooperative linkage with each other through superior integrative capabilities.	Ansari et al., 2016; Cozzolino et al., 2018; McCann and Selsky, 1984; Meyer et al., 1993
Organization-Level Mechanisms		
Dynamic capabilities and managerial cognition	Strategic managerial and organizational cognitions influence the formation and execution of routines that achieve superior performance by realigning organizations with exogenous changes in their environments.	Teece, 2007; Tripsas and Gavetti, 2000; Gilbert, 2005; Eggers and Kaplan, 2009
Exaptation	Change occurs through emergence and/or recognition of an opportunity to re-purpose an existing capability, product, or innovation for a different, unanticipated purpose.	Andriani et al., 2017; Catani, 2005; Gould, 1991; Garud et al., 2016.

Continued

Table 16.1 (Continued)

SOCIAL MECHANISM	BRIEF DESCRIPTION/DEFINITION	EXEMPLARY ARTICLES
Organization-Level Mechanisms		
Effectuation/ Bricolage	Change agents take stock of resources and means at hand, asking "What can I do *now* that makes sense?" They invoke flexible decision logics that capitalize on environmental contingencies to experiment and sidestep constraints. Existing relationships are leveraged and choices are based on principle of affordable loss.	Sarasvathy, 2001; Baker and Nelson, 2005; Garud and Karnøe, 2003
Cross-Level Mechanisms		
Diffusion	New practices, structures, or technologies are adopted and/or abandoned through processes of contagion, social influence, and social learning.	Strang and Soule, 1998; Gaba and Meyer, 2008; Jonsson, Greve, and Fujiwara-Greve, 2009
Self-organization	Within a complex system, change emerges naturally from interactions among lower-level entities without intervention of a central controller.	Anderson, 1999; Chiles et al., 2001; Anderson and Meyer, 2017
Field-configuring events	Agents from diverse geographies, organizations, and/or professions assemble temporarily with the collective intent to construct specific organizational fields. This can create social microcosms that fore-shadow and simulate unrealized shared visions of a technology, market, or industry.	Meyer, Gaba, and Colwell, 2005; Anand and Watson, 2004; Lampel and Meyer, 2008; Garud, 2008; Hardy and Maguire, 2010

Social Mechanisms Driving Discontinuous Field-Level Changes

Shifts and Hybridization of Institutional Logics

Since the 1990s, the central focus of organizational institutionalism has shifted from explaining stability to explaining change (Greenwood et al. 2002). In the last three decades, institutional scholars have stepped up their efforts to explain field-level emergence and discontinuity. As part of that shift, they have examined how new logics take hold within a field (Friedland and Alford 1991; Thornton and Ocasio 1999; Lounsbury et al. 2003). Institutional logics are socially constructed justifications and templates for practices institutionalized in social systems (Thornton and Ocasio 2008). They encode cultural dimensions of institutions that enable and constrain social action. The recent proliferation of work in this domain reflects a growing interest in the origins and dynamics of field-level structures and processes, and has given rise to refined conceptions of fields themselves, the role of agency, and the processes through which change unfolds (see Schneiberg and Lounsbury 2008 for a review).

Many studies of change in institutional logics conceptualize field-level change as replacement, wherein a dominant logic engendering field-level practices is abandoned and another logic takes its place. For example, in publishing, a market logic replaced a craft logic (Thornton 2002), and in the culinary arts, nouvelle cuisine replaced haute cuisine (Rao, Monin, and Durand 2003). In finance, a regulatory logic replaced a thrift logic, until both were later replaced by a market logic (Haveman and Rao 1997; Lounsbury 2002). Historical contingency is a theoretical cornerstone of the mechanisms underlying shifts in institutional logics. That is, change is approached as a period effect, with a jolt or exogenous force ushering in a new dominant logic that separates one relatively stable era from another.

Other institutional change theorists assert that rather than definitive shifts from one logic to another, the more typical change mechanism involves ongoing interactions between two or more logics (Marquis and Lounsbury 2007; Dunn and Jones 2010; Greenwood et al. 2010). Several authors have noted that multiple competing logics can coexist within an organizational field, arguing that "an appreciation of heterogeneity and the relative incoherence of fields is crucial... for empirical explorations of institutional change." (Schneiberg and Clemens 2006: 210). This view asserts that institutional environments often are fragmented, with multiple logics advocating conflicting beliefs and prescribing different actions. Dunn and Jones (2010) reported that two logics—care and science—guided professionals teaching in medical schools between 1910 and 2005. They found that these logics were supported by distinct groups with different interests and fluctuated over time, imposing dynamic tensions on medical pedagogy and curricula.

Social movement dynamics can trigger logic replacements, destabilize fields, serve as sources of new logics, and generate resources mobilized by entrepreneurs (Lounsbury et al. 2003; Rao et al. 2003; Weber et al. 2009). Thus, conflict and pluralism within an organizational field may themselves be motivating forces for institutional change (Seo and Creed 2002; Lounsbury 2007). Multiple logics can trigger field-level contestation between factions formed around professional, ideological, religious, or political affiliations. Multiple logics can work from the macro level down to the micro. They can, for instance, be mapped into the structures and processes of "hybrid organizations" (Glynn and Lounsbury, 2005; Mars and Lounsbury 2009; Battilana and Dorado 2010), which "selectively couple intact elements prescribed by each logic" (Pache and Santos 2013), giving hybrid organizations legitimacy in the eyes of stakeholder groups whose logics are poles apart.

Institutional entrepreneurship

Disruptive changes in institutional logics can stem from the work of actors termed "institutional entrepreneurs." DiMaggio (1988) coined the term to explain how actors can cut through the stasis of embedded institutions to effect change. Fligstein (1997) argued that certain actors are "socially skilled" in enlisting other actors' assistance in undertaking novel actions, and noted that such institutional entrepreneurs are likely to be most effectual when fields are forming or in crisis. Battilana, Leca, and Boxenbaum

(2009) developed a model treating institutional entrepreneurship as a process distributed among a collective set of actors. The components of the social mechanisms that drive institutional entrepreneurship include an existing or nascent organizational field; exogenous shocks such as technological, regulatory, or political events; and socially skilled actors who are aware of new markets, technologies, business models, and/or ideologies. Other requisites for effective change include social networks through which entrepreneurs' visions and templates for novel institutional elements can be diffused, repositories where practices can be codified, and sufficient legitimacy to recruit new participants and solidify the support of stakeholders.

Sine and David (2003), for example, found that environmental jolts mobilized field actors—legislators, academics, technical innovators, and proponents of environmentally friendly technology—to reform the institutionalized industrial structure of regulated monopolies in the US power industry. Exogenous shocks (Haveman, Russo, and Meyer 2001; Hoffman 1999; Holm 1995), including social, technological, or regulatory changes (Greenwood et al., 2002), political crises (Fligstein and Mara-Drita 1996), or natural disasters (Phillips, Lawrence, and Hardy 2000) have all been identified as triggers that can disrupt a field sufficiently to enable institutional entrepreneurs to reinterpret their environment to support changes. Fligstein (1997) lists a number of tools and tactics plied by institutional entrepreneurs, including agenda setting, framing action, "wheeling" to ferment chaos, brokering, maintaining ambiguity, aggregating interests, and selectively networking with or isolating outliers.

Shifting Demand Landscape

In recent years, technology innovation, strategic management, and entrepreneurship scholars have suggested that heterogeneous and dynamic consumer markets are frequent sources of field-level disruptions. Inspired by Christensen's (1997) work on the innovator's dilemma, where incumbents focus on existing customers leads them to disregard disruptive technologies, the demand-side view "looks downstream from the focal firm, toward product markets and consumers, rather than upstream towards factor market and producers" (Priem et al. 2012: 347). Tripsas (2008) noted the impact of "customer preference discontinuities," rapid and significant changes in the attributes upon which customers base purchase decisions. Aggarwal and Wu (2015) examined the impact of the terrorist attacks of September 11, 2001 in the US defense industry. These attacks produced a significant industry-wide demand shock, shifting the industry's focus away from the Cold War mindset to a new security and counterterrorism orientation. Consequently, although the total demand for defense products increased significantly post 2001, the relative attractiveness of different product markets shifted suddenly. Similarly, Adner and Snow (2010) found that the introduction of a new disruptive technology in an industry can reveal latent heterogeneity in the old technology's broader demand environment by revealing customer segments that were previously unknown. Thus, demand-side mechanisms do not assume that customers' needs are constant; instead, they focus on market change and consumer heterogeneity.

Demand-side factors can shape the opportunities that firms pursue in the market (e.g., Danneels 2003, 2008), contribute to the emergence of dominant designs (Benner and Tripsas 2012), accelerate technological transitions (Adner and Levinthal 2001; Adner 2002; Tripsas 2008), reposition "old" technologies in the marketplace (Adner and Snow 2010), and highlight users' role in entrepreneurial innovation (Shah and Tripsas 2007). These studies show how unanticipated information from customers triggers demand uncertainty that sparks new understandings about product attributes induced by the new technology, and how those product attributes create value for the customers (Danneels 2004). Firms often are uncertain, ex-ante, about the combination of performance features that customers are likely to value in a disruptive product (Adner 2002). Studies have investigated the processes through which firms in an industry characterized by uncertain, shifting demand landscapes attempt to learn and adapt to changing consumer preferences. Benner and Tripsas (2012) found that prior industry affiliation of firms shaped their initial framing of the product market in the new digital camera market. Others studies show that when firms are uncertain about the combinations of performance features that customers are likely to demand, the stock of downstream complementary assets (assets that are used in "sales and distribution" of a product and in providing "training, support, and servicing" to customers) (Roy and Cohen 2017) or feedback from experientially diverse customers (customers who have previously interacted with diverse types of organizations in the market) (Hsu, Kovács, and Koçak 2019) can play a catalytic role in shaping the firms' adaptation during a disruptive technological change.

Ecosystems Nested in Fields

Quantum speciation (Grant 1963) is a biological process wherein a new species arises when a small segment of an ancestral population has been isolated near the periphery of its ecological domain. Harsh conditions and intense selection pressures exist there, because peripheries lie at the edge of the niche's tolerance for the species. Consequently, favorable mutations can spread quickly, particularly if unsaturated ecological space exists, allowing mutations to proliferate. Astley (1985) proposed a variant of quantum speciation as a social mechanism through which new organizational forms emerge in "speciation events." This field-level mechanism was invoked to explain the growth of the US semiconductor industry (Astley 1985), the rapid development of wireless communication technology (Levinthal 1998), and the rapid formation of regional networks brokered in California to create new competitive vehicles for financing and delivering healthcare (Meyer et al. 1993).

Recently, strategy scholars have appropriated the biological notion of an ecosystem to conceptualize networks of firms producing discrete but complementary products, while depending upon each other to jointly create value (Adner 2017; Kapoor 2018). Jacobides et al. (2018) drew a distinction between "business ecosystems" centered on a firm in a supply chain, "innovation ecosystems" centered on an innovation, and "platform ecosystems" assembled upon a novel platform technology. Ecosystems have been seen as both the result of discontinuous field-level change and as the cause of such change.

In the former, field-level disruptions have been viewed as triggering incumbent firms to restructure internally while forming unprecedented relationships with customers and suppliers. In some cases, upheavals in information technology have led incumbent firms to transform from product-divisional structures into multi-platform businesses. For instance, Cozzolino et al. (2018) described how an Italian news publisher, disrupted by Internet advances, switched from being a fully vertically integrated producer into a network organization coordinating multiple platforms, audiences, and advertisers linked thorough a mix of internal and external partnerships. In a case study of a disruptive new entrant, Ansari et al. (2016) described how TiVo pioneered the digital video recorder, and then assembled a ground-breaking new ecosystem by forming ties to AOL Time Warner, DirectTV, CBS, NBC, and Disney.

Thus, proactive management of alliances and networks with key firms in the ecosystem is crucial for both incumbents defending their positions in an existing market, and new entrants attempting to disrupt existing markets (Ansari and Krop 2012; Kapoor and Klueter 2015). Scholars have argued that such capabilities enable firms to reposition their products as a dominant design emerges (Furr and Kapoor 2018), develop successive technology generations (Helfat and Campo-Rembado 2016), orchestrate ecosystem and platform leadership (Helfat and Raubitschek 2018), and overcome bottlenecks (Hannah and Eisenhardt 2018).

Organization-Level Mechanisms

Dynamic Capabilities and Managerial Cognition

Dynamic capabilities have become a prominent social mechanism explaining why some firms respond better than others when their environments change discontinuously. Teece et al. (1997) define dynamic capabilities as those that enable a firm to adapt by changing its existing resource base. Teece (2007) disaggregated dynamic capabilities, for analytical purposes, into sensing, seizing, and reconfiguring components and suggested a role for managerial cognition in developing these capabilities. Because managerial cognition plays a crucial role in both interpreting firms' external environments and in shaping their internal responses, Adner and Helfat (2003) further posited that it is the interaction between a firm's existing resource base and its managers' cognitions that is crucial in shaping adaptive behavior when environments change discontinuously. They describe this interaction as capability to "build, integrate, and reconfigure organizational resources and competences" (Adner and Helfat 2003: 1012).

Several empirical studies link managerial cognition with organizational responses during periods of discontinuity. Because the scope, speed, and complexity of environmental change are unpredictable, the specific locus of impact and the appropriate response are not obvious *ex-ante*. Thus, managerial recognition and framing of discontinuities is needed to overcome organizational inertia rooted in established resources and routines (Gilbert 2005; Kaplan et al. 2003). Studies have shown how biases in managerial cognition inhibit firms' adaptive responses to environmental discontinuities. For example, Tripsas and Gavetti (2000) found that Polaroid's inability to transition from analogue to digital-imaging technologies can largely be explained by management belief structures that placed primacy on technical excellence and modeled economic success on a razor/blade business model that proved inappropriate in the digital world. Polaroid's actions were constrained not by a lack of organizational capabilities in digital technologies, but by managerial beliefs that were not aligned with the new market opportunity. Similarly, other studies have shown how CEO cognition (Kaplan 2008) and boards' unwillingness to engage in self-evaluation and self-reconfiguration can contribute to organizational inertia in the face of technical and/or regulatory changes in the environment (Hoppmann et al. 2019). Finally, Rosenbloom (2000) offered NCR as a counterfactual as it adapted its core products to radical changes in technology over four decades. He concluded that one reason NCR was able to survive was that changes in leadership provided the impetus to activate latent dynamic capabilities. That is, appointing leaders whose vision was not clouded by commitments to the old order supplied the impetus for a series of transformations.

Other studies have investigated the importance of aligning managerial cognitions and organizational capabilities. For example, Danneels (2010) examined resource alterations within Smith Corona, formerly one of the world's leading manufacturers of typewriters. He found that managerial cognition about firm resources was key to explaining the exercise of dynamic capabilities, because recognizing the path to renewal turned on understanding the fungibility of resources. Similarly, Eggers and Kaplan (2009) found that CEO attention was not only associated with the differences in communications technology firms' timing of entry into the new fiber optics product markets but that the CEO's attention to the emerging technology amplified the effects of industry orientation. Patala et al. (2019) further showed how incumbent firms can deploy blended rhetorical strategies to justify their investments in both renewable (legitimacy-gaining or novel) and non-renewable (legitimacy-losing or conventional) technologies.

Exaptation

Exaptation (Gould and Vrba 1982; Gould 1991) is a recently recognized mechanism propelling rapid evolution of technologies, organizations, ecosystems, and fields. Exaptation refers to the situation in which a useful structure or attribute—despite having arisen for entirely unrelated reasons—is appropriated or co-opted into a new role. Gould hypothesized, for example, that the feather originated as an adaptation that enabled the earth-bound ancestors of birds to regulate their body temperature—and was subsequently exapted for flight. Dew et al. (2004) discuss the exaptation of technologies, noting that Edison originally envisioned his phonograph as a business dictation machine, aspirin was used as an analgesic for over a century, and Viagra was developed to treat heart disease—before these inventions were subsequently exapted to become the jukebox, a blood thinner, and a libido booster. MOS researchers have invoked exaptation as a change mechanism to explain how Corning leveraged glass-making know-how to become a pioneer in the fiber-optics field (Cattani 2005, 2006), how factor markets generate pristine opportunities that are "poised for the taking" (Felin et al. 2016), and which attributes enabled selected commercial banks to cash in on regulatory changes (Marquis and Huang 2010). Andriani et al. (2017) measured the frequency of exaptation in the pharmaceutical industry and found that 42 percent of new uses derived from existing drugs were exaptations. They further showed that most radical innovations in drugs were exaptive (not innovative) and occurred in market areas very distant from the drug's original market. Garud et al. (2016: 156) describe the power of performative narratives to catalyze exaptive leaps by nudging people into "imagining the future, remembering the past, and seizing the moment".

Noting that "a concept without a name often lies hidden from identification and use," Gould (1991: 46) argued that failure to attach a name to exaptation has led to persistent errors in thought, and that this gap in syntax is consequential because the terms that researchers use "are not neutral or arbitrary hat-racks for a set of unvarying concepts; they reflect (or even create) different theories about the structure of the world" (Gould and Vrba 1982: 4). Because exaptation has been missing from our change mechanism menu, MOS researchers presume adaptive continuity, and "just cannot grasp the alternative of exaptive seizure of latent capacity that is present for other reasons" (Gould 1991:62).

Effectuation and Bricolage

Effectuation and bricolage are two related organizing concepts or theories of action that have recently been implicated in discontinuous change. Effectuation was proposed by Sarasvathy (2001: 245), who defined effectuation as "taking a set of means as given and focusing on selecting between possible effects that can be created with that set of means." The theory suggests that under conditions of uncertainty, entrepreneurs adopt a decision logic that is different from that explicated by a traditional rational model of entrepreneurship. She contrasted effectuation processes and causation processes, which "take a particular effect as given and focus on selecting between means to create that effect" (p. 245). Sarasvathy argued that when entrepreneurs employ effectuation in pursuing entrepreneurial opportunities, they start with a generalized aspiration and then attempt to satisfy that aspiration using the resources they have at their immediate disposal (i.e., who they are, what they know, and who they know). The overall objective is not envisioned clearly at the beginning, and those using effectuation processes remain flexible, take advantage of environmental contingencies as they arise, and learn as they go. The key components in applying effectuation as a mechanism in entrepreneurship entail (1) starting with means as opposed to establishing end goals, (2) evaluating options in terms of affordable loss instead of expected return, (3) leveraging relationships instead of competitive analysis when assessing relationships with other individuals and organizations; and (4) exploiting rather than avoiding contingencies (Sarasvathy 2008). Effectuation is viewed as most effective in settings characterized by extreme levels of uncertainty such as market creation (Sarasvathy and Dew 2005) and market transformation (Dew et al. 2011).

Like effectuation, bricolage provides a social mechanism in which actors recombine existing resources for a new purpose. Levi-Strauss (1966: 17) introduced the term to anthropology, defining bricolage as "making do with whatever is at hand" to solve problems and act on new opportunities. In a field study of twenty-nine resource-constrained firms, Baker and Nelson (2005) provided detailed accounts of entrepreneurial bricolage, showing how firms operating under conditions of tight resource constraint enacted idiosyncratic resource environments and persisted and grew by creating "something from nothing." Their conceptualization of bricolage includes three components: (1) a refusal to accept the resource limitations dictated by the environment (institutional or cultural), but focusing instead on 'trying out solutions, observing, and dealing with the results'; (2) recombining and reusing resources for new purposes; and (3) seeking resources that are inexpensive or are free, often available because others judge them to be useless or substandard. Bricolage has also been invoked as a mechanism by Garud and Karnøe (2003) to describe the innovative activities of engineers and entrepreneurs in the Danish wind turbine industry, by Baker, Miner, and Eesley (2003) in their study of improvisation in knowledge-intensive entrepreneurship, and by Perkmann and Spicer (2014) to understand the emergence of novel organizational forms. In all of these instances, bricolage is used as a theoretical concept to characterize activities in which actors repurpose resources creatively to shape their local contexts, resolve problems, or exploit opportunities.

Alternative theoretical perspectives such as effectuation (Sarasvathy 2001) and entrepreneurial bricolage (Baker and Nelson 2005) offer promise for understanding how human agents create and respond to discontinuous change. Both approaches provide an alternative to the causal model of rational choice and stipulate that under uncertain conditions, actors may follow a different route to identifying and exploiting opportunities. Further, as Sarasvathy argues, this may the best mode for adapting to dynamic and nonlinear environments where the future is unknowable or unmeasurable. These two theoretical mechanisms are reminiscent of the "technology of foolishness" which March (1983) advocated when making decisions and choosing actions in "environments that are complicated, endogenous, subjective and contested" (March 2006: 205). In such situations, actors act, and allow goals to emerge and change as they observe the outcomes of their actions. Overall, effectuation and bricolage provide alternatives to feedback-based adaptive processes, foregrounding experimentation to discover what may be worth doing in discontinuous environments.

Cross-Level Mechanisms

Upon categorizing 1990 theories according to the modes, levels, and mechanisms thought then to change organizations and fields over time, Meyer and his co-authors (1990: 97) noted that "adaptation, metamorphosis, evolution, and revolution are not independent and mutually exclusive forms of change." That is, change processes assigned to different cells in Figure 16.1 may occur simultaneously, and the occurrence or intensity of change in one cell can influence the occurrence or intensity of change in another.

To explore cross-level theorizing since 1990, we scrutinized the articles in our corpus, looking for social mechanisms that posited relationships crossing levels of analysis. We realized that several of the mechanisms we have classified as field-level are sometimes seen to operate across levels. Institutional entrepreneurship, for instance, can arise in the actions of an individual entrepreneur or organization, and catalyze discontinuous change field wide, as can exaptations unearthed by individual people or organizations. Three change mechanisms, however, struck us as fundamentally cross level in their causal trajectories. Driven by innovating individuals or early adopting organizations, diffusion processes radiate outward and upward, sometimes transforming fields as they spread. Similarly, self-organizing processes originate in the bottom-up actions of independent agents and reconfigure higher-level entities. Field configuring events assemble field-wide congregations of agents whose collective actions can reshape the landscape within which firms compete and individuals work.

Diffusion

Organizational scholars have proposed diffusion as a cross-level social mechanism to understand the processes through which field-level stability emerges and changes. In documenting the spread of various organizational practices, technologies, and innovations, studies have highlighted diffusion both as a mechanism for the emergence of "collective rationality" (DiMaggio and Powell 1983) at the field-level, and for the exercise of agency at the organizational level (Czarniawska-Joerges and Sevón 2005; Sahlin and Wedlin 2008). Diffusion as a mechanism for discontinuous change allows researchers to observe processes of social influence, learning, and mimicry and in doing so emphasizes both structural and cultural logics that integrate organizational action into models of field-level dynamics (see Strang and Soule 1998 for a review).

Several diffusion studies have highlighted field-level dynamics and connected them with organizational structure, culture, and practices. For example, Haveman et al. (2007) examined the replacement of community-based groups by bureaucracies in the early thrift industry in California. They found that many environmental changes such as the rise of social movements, regulatory and demographic trends, and shifts in cultural mores had altered the organizational forms within the field. Thrifts underwent dramatic change during and after the Progressive era, shifting from club-like associations that valued community and mutual aid to impersonal bureaucracies that celebrated the Progressive ideals of efficiency and individual rationality (Haveman and Rao 1997). Gaba and Meyer (2008) examined the incursion of venture capital practices into the population of information technology firms, and their subsequent diffusion in the form of corporate venture capital practices. They found both inter and intra-population effects in the spread of these practices and argued that the level of theorization of a practice affects the ease with which it can pass through population boundaries in an organizational field. Smets et al. (2012) provided a multi-level account of the interplay between institutional logics, organizations, and practices. They found that field-level institutional change in the legal profession emerged from the mundane activities of practitioners struggling to accomplish their work, became rationalized at the level of the organization, and then diffused within the field to solidify institutional change.

Other studies have looked at how adverse events or crises that strike one organization can spread to other organizations in the field. For example, Jonsson et al. (2009) found that an isolated act of organizational deviance can lead to the contagious loss of legitimacy among organizations categorized as similar. In addition, diffusion of information and distrust in organizations within a field can lead to financial panic triggering bank runs that whip up economic crisis (Greve and Kim 2014; Greve et al. 2016). Negative information about an organization can have a contagion effect because actors assess organizations they transact with based on multiple cues. These include the similarity of organization-level characteristics, the similarity of the communities in which organizations operate, and the presence of observable links between organizations (Greve et al. 2016). The diffusion of a tarnished reputation can penalize "innocent" organizations and undermine their viability, especially in sectors like banking and pharmaceuticals where reputation and legitimacy are paramount (Jonsson et al. 2009).

Self-Organization

Until recently, most social scientists scrupulously avoided emergence, electing to study established groups, organizations, or fields (Meyer et al. 2005). However, our review of the MOS literature indicates that accounts of discontinuous change that originate in self-organizing processes have increased substantially over the last three decades. Anderson (1999) introduced organization theorists to a menu of novel concepts and mechanisms linked with complex adaptive systems: agents with schemata, self-organizing networks sustained by importing energy, coevolution to the edge of chaos, system evolution based upon recombination, and sensitive dependence upon initial conditions. Authors have described how social systems self-organize as they pass through turning points (Abbott 2001), cross thresholds (Granovetter 1978), and undergo phase transitions (Prigogine and Stengers 1984). Chiles, Meyer, and Hench (2004) reported that a set of musical theatres clustered in Branson, Missouri passed through a series of "punctuated emergences."

Anderson and Meyer (2017: 3) presented eight distinctive features of changes that arise from complex system dynamics: (1) Self-organization is evident—complex systems evolve toward order with no central controller or authority generating the order. (2) Multiple interacting components are densely but not fully connected with each other—when there are few or no connections, a system produces additive and linear results, but when every element is interconnected with every other element, rippling effects produce random or chaotic outcomes. Self-organization occurs between these two extremes. (3) Novel collective structures emerge—unexpected structures appear at the collective level that are different in kind (not just in magnitude) from those found at a lower level. (4) Order emerges away from equilibrium—order does not demand or imply equilibrium, because self-organizing systems evolve naturally toward order without ever reaching a steady state. (5) Changes are distributed according to power laws—extreme outcomes are frequent and consequential, with power law relationships supplying a signature of self-organized systems. (6) Path dependencies are sensitive to initial conditions–two systems that start with only small differences can follow different paths, ending in states that are far apart. (7) Agents following simple rules construct complex structures–simple behaviors at one level produce emergent complexity one level higher. (8) System diversity increases–the system's structure, and outcomes grow more diverse over time.

When conditions such as these obtain, self-organizing processes serve as social mechanisms that can trigger non-linear causal relationships that catalyze discontinuous change. Self-organized changes may materialize at multiple levels of analysis, but they always arise from interactions between agents at a lower level of aggregation (Anderson, 1999).

Field Configuring Events

Field configuring events (FCEs) are social mechanisms that are said to catalyze discontinuous change in technologies, markets, industries, and organizational fields by enacting temporary organizations such as conferences, tradeshows, technology contests, and commercial ceremonies (Meyer, Gaba, and Colwell, 2005). These are "settings in which people from diverse organizations and with diverse purposes meet to announce new products, develop industry standards, construct social networks, recognize accomplishments, share and interpret information, and transact business" (Lampel and Meyer 2008: 1026). According to Lampel and Meyer, FCEs have six defining characteristics: (1) They assemble actors from diverse professional, organizational, and geographical origins. (2) Their duration is limited, running from several hours to several days. (3) They provide opportunities for unstructured social interaction. (4) They include ceremonial and dramaturgical elements. (5) They create occasions for information exchange and collective sensemaking. (6) They generate social and reputational resources that can be deployed subsequently.

In contrast to organizational economists who treat technologies, markets, industries, and organizational fields as preordained outcomes of the material conditions of economic competition, authors embracing FCEs as change mechanisms typically view these entities as collective products of social construction and intentional human agency. Anand and Watson (2004) studied how the Grammy Award ceremonies impacted the generation, allocation, and celebration of artists' prestige in the commercial music field over two decades. They reported that the Grammys surfaced conflicts over legitimacy and resolved them, and forged connections between central and peripheral actors in the field. In another FCE study, Hardy and Maguire (2010) observed the UN conference leading up to the Stockholm Convention on Persistent Organic Pollutants, an international treaty that established new global regulations for dangerous chemicals. They reported finding "narrative" social mechanisms at work generating "multiple discursive spaces that are governed by different rules and understandings regarding text production . . . distribution . . . and consumption." They remarked on how this FCE had enabled texts to "flow between discursive spaces," allowing actors to influence change despite holding positions of low power in the field. Other studies have shown how FCEs shaped fields by fostering shared cognitions in the legal field in pre-independence Israel (Oliver and Montgomery 2008); by setting technical standards in the emerging field of cochlear implants (Garud 2008); and by creating "conventionalizing" accounts of social life that triggered the emergence of "non-profit technology assistance" as an institutional field (McInerney 2008).

Adopting FCEs as a social mechanism offers researchers studying discontinuous change both theoretical and methodological advantages. Theoretically, taking the "event" as a fundamental platform allows researchers to observe cross-level effects–the impact of micro-level individual actions on macro-level field formation. At the same time, it nudges researchers into adopting a process perspective that recognizes temporal factors (Langley et al. 2013). Methodologically, FCEs bring together representative field participants and spark interactions that researchers can observe in real time. FCEs create microcosms that simulate the fields they represent and reshape. In addition, because FCEs are often scheduled to reoccur periodically, they allow researchers to track field evolution by collecting a series of cross-sectional snapshots of field structure (Lampel and Meyer 2008).

Why have MOS Theorists Ignored Discontinuous Change?

Our analysis of the post-1990 Management and Organization Studies literature turned up a diverse set of social mechanisms that authors have advanced as drivers of second-order change, as summarized above. Although attention devoted to second-order change has definitely increased, this shift has been gradual, and first-order organization-level models continue to dominate change theory. We believe that this results from five overlapping and mutually reinforcing factors: nebulous concepts, academic silos, adaptionist assumptions, equilibrium assumptions, and general linear reality.

Nebulous concepts and cross-level disorientation. Discontinuities in an organizational field can manifest as unexpected transitory shocks, sudden but permanent shifts in the landscape of a field, or oscillating cycles where expansion and contraction in field-level activities alternate (Meyer et al. 2005). Each of these dynamics presents idiosyncratic challenges for theorists, each demands theorization that spans at least two levels of analysis, and each requires collection of longitudinal or historical data.

Although considerable progress has occurred since 1990, we need to pay more attention to conceptualizing disruptions in organizational fields. One ongoing debate among scholars turns on the definition of disruption (e.g., Danneels 2004; Govindarajan and Kopalle 2006). In the wake of Christensen and Bower's (1996) seminal paper on the disk drive industry, the notion that disruptive innovation can disadvantage incumbents has piqued the interest of practitioners and scholars (e.g., Ansari et al. 2016; Danneels 2004; Markides 2006; McKinsey 2015). Christensen and his colleagues have expanded the locus of disruption to include technologies, products, and business models. Markides

(2006: 19) observes that "disruptive technologies" and "disruptive business models" create "different kinds of markets, pose radically different challenges for established firms, and have radically different implications for managers." Progress in studying organizational change over time at multiple levels may call for a discontinuous change in organizational theory and research methods themselves, which Pettigrew (1987) disparaged as ahistorical, aprocessual, and acontextual in character.

Academic solos and echo chambers. Management and organizational scholars know more about discontinuous changes in organizations and fields collectively than we recognize individually. Our review led us into unfamiliar scholarly terrain. There we discovered authors ensconced in adjacent fields positing similar causal mechanisms without acknowledging the connections, and following parallel lines of inquiry at different levels of analysis that should have informed each other. For example, strategy and innovation scholars have documented a variety of reasons for incumbents' inaction in the face of disruptive changes in their environments: resource dependence upon mainstream customers (Christensen and Bower 1996), rigidity of existing routines and competences (Gilbert, 2005), demand uncertainty (Adner 2002), and reliance on value networks within an ecosystem (Hill and Rothaermel 2003). These sources of organizational stasis provide important insights into the specific mechanisms and processes that prevent and allow organizations to adapt to discontinuities in their environments.

Adaptationist assumptions. Adaptation, a canonical cornerstone of Western thinking, originated largely from Charles Darwin's theory of evolution. According to paleontologist Stephen J. Gould, "the adaptationist paradigm...proceeds by breaking an organism into unitary 'traits' and proposes an adaptive story for each considered separately" (Gould and Lewontin 1979: 581). Gould says that "we tell adaptive stories as if trade-offs among competing, well-designed parts were the only constraint upon perfection for each trait." He contends that biologists' over-reliance on adaptationist explanations have kept them from "coming face to face with organisms as integrated wholes, not decomposable into independent and separately optimized parts."

Gould's indictment of biological thinking is equally applicable to mainstream MOS change theorizing. Most organizational change theorists have moved beyond the strict Darwinian view that change occurs solely through natural selection acting upon random variation, taking the Lamarckian position conceding the role of human agents in designing and deploying adaptations. Nevertheless, reductionism remains a dominant mode of inquiry, "whereby researchers seek to understand the behavior of a social entity by separately analyzing its constituent parts...implicitly [treating] organizations as loosely coupled aggregates whose separate components may be adjusted or fine-tuned individually" (Meyer et al. 1993: 1177). The adaptationist mindset has instilled habits of thought among organizational theorists that mask the possibility that organizations are bundles of interdependent attributes that often can only change simultaneously and discontinuously. Furthermore, organization theorists have used the term "adaptation" unreflectively to conflate fortuitous random mutations, Lamarckian innovations, and exaptations waiting to be co-opted for unintended uses.

Equilibrium assumptions. The notion of equilibrium originated in Newtonian physics and then diffused—first into neoclassical economics, and later into social science and organization theory. Meyer and his co-authors (1993: 71) note that "the assumption that social systems are in equilibrium—or at least gravitate toward quasi-stationary equilibria—permeates both theories of organizations and the methods used to test them." Virtually all organizational theories have implicitly presumed that equilibrium is sought and achieved (at least in due course) within firms, markets, industries, and organizational fields (Bromiley and Papenhausen 2003).

Economists disclose their equilibrium assumptions ritualistically and acknowledge the limitations they entail. Social scientists, on the other hand, seem blithely unaware of the profound influence that equilibrium assumptions have on their own theories and methods. Although social scientists roundly deride the economists' fiction that human beings are rational maximizers, rarely do they recognize or challenge their own equilibrium assumptions. All too often, we forget that like "rational man," equilibrium is a convenient fiction, and treat it instead as literal truth. This omission helps explain change theorists' tendency to ignore discontinuous change when building theory.

Organizational change unfolds over time as "a complicated mosaic of... interacting nested [social] units within an environment that is itself also evolving" (March 1994: 46). Adding equilibrium to this image of nested social units implies a hierarchical ordering of the pace at which change can happen, wherein lower-level units can change more swiftly than higher-level units. That is, equilibrium assumptions insinuate that organizations can adapt faster than their environments are being transformed. Change theories constructed by marrying adaptationist and equilibrium assumptions dissuade theorists from studying settings where the pace of institutional or field-level change outstrips organizational change. Theorists come to "expect individual human beings to change faster than human organizations; to expect organizations to change faster than the populations they constitute; to expect organizational populations to change faster than the ecological communities they inhabit" (Meyer, Gaba, and Colwell, 2005: 462).

Mired in "general linear reality." Andrew Abbott (2001) argues that the analytical hegemony of Newtonian mathematics' general linear model (GLM) has insidiously shaped social scientists' thinking about how society works. He observes that in order to use GLM methods "to actually represent social reality, one must map the processes of social life onto the algebra of linear transformations" (Abbott 2001: 39). Statistical assumptions morph into ontological assumptions about how the social world operates, inducing a mindset that Abbott terms "general linear reality" (GLR), which is 'infused with deeply held causal beliefs that treat linear models as representations of the actual social world' (Meyer et al. 2005: 451).

No wonder change theorists have steered clear of research settings undergoing the upheavals that accompany field-wide discontinuities. Not only does general linear reality render these discontinuities hard to frame theoretically, but the implicit assumption of equilibrium pervading social science research methods and designs makes them difficult to tackle methodologically.

As a result, industries and organizational fields in flux have been unappealing research settings. "Like earthquake victims, researchers... usually run for cover, wait for the dust to settle, and then return cautiously to search through the debris" (Meyer et al. 2005: 470). After all, when the ground is moving, it's hard to build grounded theory. Nevertheless, fields in flux are good places to study resilience, learning, and change. Harsh environments intensify selection pressures, increase readiness to change, and foster receptivity to new ideas. High velocity environmental changes accelerate organizational responses and make their effects easier to observe (Meyer 1982).

We can only get answers to questions that we are willing to ask. A host of research methods based on the general linear model have led organizational scholars to avoid asking questions about social systems away from equilibrium because they violate dogma about rigorous methodology (Meyer et al. 2005).

Prospects for Future Research

Based on our analysis, we offer the following recommendations for future studies of discontinuous organizational change processes:

Specify social mechanisms precisely. Our review has cataloged the toolkit of social mechanisms capable of triggering, propelling, and responding to discontinuous change. Change theorists should spell out which of these mechanisms they believe are at work and be alert for new ones, because "the quality of explanation is enhanced by an explicit focus on the cogs and wheels behind the regression coefficients" (Davis and Marquis 2005: 341).

Substitute process theorizing for variance theorizing. As a broad phenomenon, change is intrinsically temporal and processual. The specialized genre dubbed *discontinuous* change is explicitly delineated by a sudden loss of continuity. Thus, cross-sectional research designs seeking to account for variance cannot elucidate the causes, processes, or consequences of discontinuous change. Students of discontinuous change need to shift their orientation from explaining variance to apprehending process (Langley et al. 2013). "This will entail gathering more observational and qualitative data, switching to more longitudinal and temporally sensitive methods, and attending to unfolding events instead of verifying enduring relationships" Meyer et al. (2005: 460).

Build multilevel theories of discontinuous change. Even though multilevel thinking is becoming more evident in the MOS literature, we need more studies of discontinuous change that emphasize temporal and cross-level effects. This is especially important because discontinuous change cannot be understood as an exclusively organizational phenomenon. Discontinuities have fundamental transorganizational causes that unfold through complex technological, organizational, and social processes. For instance, we need more work linking micro-level individual actions to macro-level changes. Here, one approach is to classify changes using Hedström and Swedberg's (1998) typology that includes "situational mechanisms" (from macro to micro), "action-formation mechanisms" (from micro to micro), and "transformational mechanisms" (from micro to macro). In addition, more attention should be directed to hyperturbulence (McCann and Selsky 1984), which occurs when the pace of field-level change exceeds the collective adaptive capacity of the organizations inhabiting that field.

Incorporate non-linear concepts. Recent work highlights new causal mechanisms for change–field configuration, dynamic capabilities, exaptation, and demand heterogeneity–but we also need to more explicitly document the non-linear dynamics of discontinuous changes. This may allow us to understand the interaction of amplifying actions, contextual conditions, and initial small changes whose ultimate consequences may be unintended but can escalate and lead to discontinuous change (Plowman et al. 2007). The recent forays of machine learning (ML) methodologies into organization science seem more promising than traditional linear regression-based methods for illuminating the non-linear dynamics of discontinuous changes. ML methodologies rely on less stringent a priori assumptions about the functional form of the underlying data generation process, avoid overfitting the data, and are better at out-of-sample predictions. Accordingly, researchers can use these methods to explore novel and robust interactive and nonlinear effects between variables (Choudhury, Allen, and Endres, 2018). Such methods, can in turn, further aid in inductive theorizing of non-linear effects, while revealing robust, replicable associative patterns in data (Puranam et al. 2018).

Investigate exaptation. Researchers should explore the impact of exaptive change in organizations and fields. It is easier and faster to repurpose an existing attribute than to develop a new adaptation. Thus, exaptation within organizations is especially likely to be observed in settings where fields are undergoing discontinuous change. Exaptation leads to quirky and unpredictable functional shifts, and often produces a history of discontinuous transitions leading organizations and entire fields down unforeseen pathways. The concept suggests a middle ground between theoretical explanations based upon doctrinaire natural selection and those assuming unfettered human agency. It challenges the idea that adaptations are source of most or all organizational changes and suggests that the faster and more discontinuous the pace of change in an organization's environment, the larger the share of ostensibly "adaptive" responses may, upon closer examination, turn out to be exaptations.

Conclusion

Historically, organizational theory has addressed stability and incremental change far more extensively than process and radical change. Moreover, theories of change usually assume that larger social units (e.g., organizational fields, industries, and markets) change more slowly than the smaller social units that inhabit and constitute them (e.g., organizations, groups, and individuals). As a consequence, research has largely disregarded discontinuous field-wide change and ignored the possibility that profound changes in organizational structures, activities, and ideologies occur suddenly and may be caused by environmental discontinuities affecting all organizations in a field simultaneously.

But gradualism and equilibrium-seeking are assumptions of social theory, not facts of social life. This was demonstrated in 2020 when the global coronavirus pandemic crashed economies, filled hospitals, emptied public spaces, closed schools, grounded airplanes, and sent disruptions rippling through the lives of individuals, organizations, markets, fields, and global networks. Each of the social mechanisms that we had educed while studying change theories was switched on: ventilators were *exapted* from veterinary clinics, surgical masks were *effectuated* with 3D printers, *competing institutional logics* were hyped by public health experts and politicians, *demand landscapes shifted* as videoconference technology enacted social distancing, support networks *self-organized*, and *field configuring events* went online. It seems very likely that these social mechanisms will generate a global watershed—reshaping not just the world's future healthcare systems but our economies, politics, and cultures. Thus, the coronavirus pandemic underscores the urgency of our call to management researchers to shift their attention to the social mechanisms that drive discontinuous change.

References

Abbott, A. (2001). *Time Matters* . Chicago, IL: University of Chicago Press.

Adner, R. (2002). 'When Are Technologies Disruptive? A Demand-Based Perspective on the Evolution of Competition'. *Strategic Management Journal*, 23, 667–88.

Adner, R. (2017). 'Ecosystem as Structure'. *Journal of Management*, 43/1: 39–58.

Adner, R., and Helfat, C. E. (2003). 'Corporate Effects and Dynamic Managerial Capabilities'. *Strategic Management Journal*, 24/10: 1011–25.

Adner, R., and Levinthal, D. (2001). 'Demand Heterogeneity and Technology Evolution: Implications for Product and Process Innovation'. *Management Science*, 47, 611–28.

Adner, R., and Snow, D. (2010). 'Old Technology Responses to New Technology Threats: Demand Heterogeneity and Technology Retreats'. *Industrial and Corporate Change*, 19: 1655–75.

Aggarwal, V. A. and Wu, B. (2015). 'Organizational Constraints to Adaptation: Intrafirm Asymmetry in the Locus of Coordination'. *Organization Science*, 26/1: 1–309.

Anand, N., and Watson, M. R. (2004). 'Tournament Rituals in the Evolution of Fields: The Case of the Grammy Awards'. *The Academy of Management Journal*, 47/1: 59–80.

Anderson, P. (1999). 'Complexity Theory and Organization Science'. *Organization Science*, 10: 216–32.

Anderson, P., and Meyer, A. D. (2017). 'Complexity Theory and Process Organization Studies', in Ann Langley and Haridimos Tsoukas, eds., *Sage Handbook of Process Organizational Studies*. Beverley Hills, CA: Sage Publications, 127–43.

Andrews, K. R. (1971). *The Concept of Corporate Strategy*. Homewood, IL: Dow Jones-Irwin.

Andriani, P., Ali, A., and Mastrogiorgio, M. (2017). 'Measuring Exaptation and Its Impact on Innovation, Search, and Problem Solving'. *Organization Science*, 28/2: 320–38.

Ansari, H., Garud, R., and Kumaraswamy, A. (2016). 'The Disruptor's Dilemma: TiVo and the U.S. Television Ecosystem'. *Strategic Management Journal*, 37: 1829–53.

Ansari, S. M., and Krop, P. (2012). 'Incumbent Performance in the Face of a Radical Innovation: Towards a Framework for Incumbent Challenger Dynamics'. *Research Policy*, 41: 1357–74.

Ansoff, H. I. (1965). *Corporate Strategy*. New York, NY: McGraw-Hill.

Argyris, C., and Schön, D. (1978). *Organizational Learning: A Theory of Action Perspective.* Reading, MA: Addison-Wesley.

Astley, W.G. (1985). 'The Two Ecologies: Population and Community Perspectives on Organizational Evolution', *Administrative Science Quarterly*, 30: 224–41.

Astley, W., and Eesley, D. T. (2003). 'Improvising Firms: Bricolage, Account Giving and Improvisational Competencies in the Founding Process'. *Research Policy*, 32: 255–76.

Baker, T., and Nelson, R. E. (2005). 'Creating Something from Nothing: Resource Construction through Entrepreneurial Bricolage'. *Administrative Science Quarterly*, 50: 329–66.

Barley, S. R., and Tolbert, P. S. (1997). 'Institutionalization and Structuration: Studying the Links between Action and Institution'. *Organization Studies*, 18/1: 93–117.

Barney, J. B. (1986). 'Types of Competition and the Theory of Strategy: Toward an Integrative Framework'. *Academy of Management Review*, 11/4: 791–800.

Battilana, J., and Dorado, S. (2010). 'Building Sustainable Hybrid Organizations: The Case of Commercial Microfinance Organizations'. *Academy of Management Journal*, 53/6: 1419–40.

Battilana, J., Leca, B., and Boxenbaum, E. (2009). 'How Actors Change Institutions: Towards a Theory of Institutional Entrepreneurship'. *Academy of Management Annals*, 3: 65–107.

Benner, M. J., and Tripsas, M. (2012). 'The Influence of Prior Industry Affiliation on Framing in Nascent Industries: The Evolution of Digital Cameras'. *Strategic Management Journal*, 33/3: 277–02.

Bresser, R. K. F. (1988). 'Matching Collective and Competitive Strategies'. *Strategic Management Journal*, 9: 375–85.

Bromiley, P., and Papenhausen, C. (2003). 'Assumptions of Rationality and Equilibrium in Strategy Research: The Limits of Traditional Economic Analysis'. *Strategic Organization*, 1: 413–37.

Carroll, G. R. (1984). 'Organizational Ecology'. *American Review of Sociology*, 10: 71–93.

Cattani, G. (2005). 'Preadaptation, Firm Heterogeneity, and Technological Performance: A Study on the Evolution of Fiber Optics, 1970–1995'. *Organization Science*, 16/6: 563–80.

Cattani, G. (2006). 'Technological Pre-Adaptation, Speciation, and Emergence of New Technologies: How Corning Invented and Developed Fiber Optics'. *Industrial and Corporate Change*, 15/2: 285–318.

Caves, R. E., and Porter, M. E. (1977). 'From Entry Barriers to Mobility Barriers: Conjectural Decisions and Contrived Deterrence to New Competition'. *Quarterly Journal of Economics*, 91: 241–62.

Child, J. (1972). 'Organizational Structure, Environment and Performance: The Role of Strategic Choice'. *Sociology*, 6: 2–22.

Chiles, T., Meyer A.D., and Hench, T. (2004). 'Organizational Emergence: The Origin and Transformation of Branson, Missouri's Musical Theaters'. *Organization Science*, 15: 499–519.

Christensen, C. M. (1997). 'The Innovator's Dilemma: When New Technologies Cause Great Firms to Fail'. Cambridge, MA: Harvard Business School Press.

Christensen, C. M., and Bower, J. L. (1996). 'Customer Power, Strategic Investment, and the Failure of Leading Firms'. *Strategic Management Journal*, 17: 197–218.

Choudhury, P., Allen, R., and Endres, M.G. (2018). 'A machine learning methods framework for management research: Application to exploratory pattern detection'. Harvard Business *School* Working Paper, 19–32.

Cozzolino, A., Verona, G., and Rothaermel, F. T. (2018). 'Unpacking the Disruption Process: New Technology, Business Models, and Incumbent Adaptation'. *Journal of Management Studies*, 55: 7.

Cyert, R. M., and March, J. G. (1963). *A Behavioral Theory of the Firm*. Englewood Cliffs, NJ: Prentice-Hall.

Czarniawska-Joerges, B., and Sevón, G. (eds.) (2005). *Global Ideas: How Ideas, Objects and Practices Travel in a Global Economy*. Copenhagen: Copenhagen Business School Press, Vol. 13.

Danneels E. (2003). 'Tight-Loose Coupling with Customers: The Enactment of Customer Orientation'. *Strategic Management Journal*, 24/6: 559–76.

Danneels, E. (2004). 'Disruptive Technology Reconsidered: A Critique and Research Agenda'. *Journal of Product Innovation Management*, 21: 246–58.

Danneels, E. (2008). 'Organizational Antecedents of Second Order Competences'. *Strategic Management Journal*, 29/5: 519–43.

Danneels, E. (2010). 'Trying to Become a Different Type of Company: Dynamic Capability at Smith Corona'. *Strategic Management Journal*, 32: 1–31.

Davis, G. F., and Marquis, C. (2005). 'Prospects for Organization Theory in the Early Twenty-First Century: Institutional Fields and Mechanisms'. *Organization Science*, 16/4: 332–43.

Dew, N., Sarasvathy, S. D., and Venkataraman, S. (2004). 'The Economic Implications of Exaptation'. *Journal of Evolutionary Economics*, 14/1: 69–84.

Dew, N., Read, S., Sarasvathy, S. D., and Wiltbank, R. (2011). 'On the Entrepreneurial Genesis of New Markets: Effectual Transformations versus Causal Search and Selection'. *Journal of Evolutionary Economics*, 21/2: 231–53.

DiMaggio, P. J. (1988). 'Interest and Agency in Institutional Theory', in L. G. Zucker, ed., *Institutional Patterns and Organizations*. Cambridge, MA: Ballinger, 3–22.

DiMaggio, P. J., and Powell, W. W. (1983). 'The Iron Cage Revisited: Institutional Isomorphism and Collective Rationality in Organizational Fields'. *American Sociological Review*, 48: 147–60.

Dunn, M. B., and Jones, C. (2010). 'Institutional Logics and Institutional Pluralism: The Contestation of Care and Science Logics in Medical Education, 1967–2005'. *Administrative Science Quarterly*, 55: 114–49.

Eggers, J. P., and Kaplan, S. (2009). 'Cognition and Renewal: Comparing CEO and Organizational Effects on Incumbent Adaptation to Technical Change'. *Organization Science*, 20/2: 461–77.

Felin, T., Kauffman, S., Mastrogiorgio A., and Mastrogiorgio, M. (2016). 'Factor Markets, Actors, and Affordances'. *Industrial and Corporate Change*, 25/1: 133–47.

Fennell, M. L., and Alexander, J. A. (1987). 'Organizational Boundary Spanning in Institutionalized Environments'. *Academy of Management Journal*, 30: 456–76.

Fligstein, N. (1997). 'Social Skill and Institutional Theory'. *American Behavioral Scientist*, 40: 397–405.

Fligstein, N., and Mara-Drita, I. (1996). 'How to Make a Market: Reflections on the Attempt to Create a Single Market in the European Union'. *American Journal of Sociology*, 102/1: 1–33.

Friedland, R., and Alford, R. R. (1991). 'Bringing Society back in: Symbols, Practices, and Institutional Contradictions', in W. W. Powell and P. J. DiMaggio, eds., *The New Institutionalism in Organizational Analysis*. Chicago: University of Chicago Press, 232–63.

Furr, N., and Kapoor, R. (2018). 'Capabilities, technologies, and firm exit during industry shakeout: Evidence from the global solar photovoltaic industry'. *Strategic Management Journal*, 39/1: 33–61.

Gaba, V., and Meyer, A. D. (2008). 'Crossing the Organizational Species Barrier: How Venture Capital Practices Infiltrated the Information Technology Sector'. *Academy of Management Journal*, 51/5: 976–98.

Garud, R. (2008). 'Conferences as Venues for the Configuration of Emerging Organizational Fields: The Case of Cochlear Implants'. *Journal of Management Studies*, 45/6: 1061–88.

Garud, R., Gehman J., and Giuliani, A. P. (2016). 'Technological Exaptation: A Narrative Approach'. *Industrial and Corporate Change*, 25: 149–66.

Garud, R., and Karnøe, P. (2003). 'Bricolage versus Breakthrough: Distributed and Embedded Agency in Technology Entrepreneurship'. *Research Policy*, 32: 277–300.

Gilbert, C. G. (2005). 'Unbundling the Structure of Inertia: Resource versus Routine Rigidity'. *Academy of Management Journal*, 48: 741–63.

Glynn, M. A., and Lounsbury, M. (2005). 'From the Critics' Corner: Logic Blending, Discursive Change and Authenticity in a Cultural Production System'. *Journal of Management Studies*, 42/5: 1031–55.

Gould, S. J. (1991). 'Exaptation: A Crucial Tool for an Evolutionary Psychology'. *Journal of Social Issues*, 47/3: 43–65.

Gould, S. J., and Lewontin, R. C. (1979). 'The Spandrels of San Marco and The Panglossian Paradigm: A Critique of The Adaptationist Programme'. *Proceedings of The Royal Society of London*, 205/1161: 581–98.

Gould, S. J., and Vrba, E. S. (1982). 'Exaptation-A Missing Term in the Science of Form'. *Paleobiology*, 8/1: 4–15.

Govindarajan, V., and Kopalle, P. K. (2006). 'The Usefulness of Measuring Disruptiveness of Innovations ex post in Making ex ante Predictions'. *Journal of Product Innovation Management*, 23: 12–18.

Granovetter, M. S. (1978). 'Threshold Models of Collective Behavior'. *American Journal of Sociology*, 83: 1420–43.

Grant, V. (1963). *The Origin of Adaptations*. New York, NY, USA: Columbia University Press.

Greenwood, R., Díaz, A. M., Li, S. X., and Lorente, J. C. (2010). 'The Multiplicity of Institutional Logics and the Heterogeneity of Organizational Responses'. *Organization Science*, 21/2: 521–39.

Greenwood, R., and Hinings, C. R. (1988). 'Organizational Design Types, Tracks and the Dynamics of Strategic Change'. *Organization Studies*, 9: 293–316.

Greenwood, R., Oliver, C., Lawrence, T. B., Meyer, R. E. (2017). 'Introduction: Into the Fourth Decade *The SAGE Handbook of Organizational Institutionalism* (2nd edn). London: Sage Publications, 1–23.

Greenwood, R., Suddaby, R., and Hinings, C. R. (2002). 'Theorizing Change: The Role of Professional Associations in the Transformation of Institutionalized Fields'. *Academy of Management Journal*, 45/1: 58–80.

Greve, H. R. and Kim, J. Y. (2014). 'Running for the Exit: Community Cohesion and Bank Panics'. *Organization Science*, 25/1: 204–21.

Greve, H. R., Kim, J. Y., and Teh, D. (2016). 'Ripples of Fear: The Diffusion of a Bank Panic'. *American Sociological Review*, 81/2: 396–420.

Hannah, D. P., and Eisenhardt, K. M. (2018). 'How Firms Navigate Cooperation and Competition in Nascent Ecosystems'. *Strategic Management Journal*, 39/12: 3163–92.

Hannan, M. T., and Freeman, J. (1977). 'The Population Ecology of Organizations'. *American Journal of Sociology*, 83: 929–64.

Hannan M. T., and Freeman, J. (1984). 'Structural Inertia and Organizational Change'. *American Sociological Review*, 49: 149–64.

Hardy, C., and Maguire, S. (2010). 'Discourse, Field-Configuring Events, and Change in Organizations and Institutional Fields: Narratives of DDT and the Stockholm Convention'. *Academy of Management Journal*, 53/6: 1365–92.

Haveman, H., and Rao, H. (1997). 'Structuring a Theory of Moral Sentiments: Institutional-Organization Co-Evolution in the Early Thrift Industry'. *American Journal of Sociology*, 102: 1606–51.

Haveman, H., Rao, H., and Paruchuri, S. (2007). 'The Winds of Change: The Progressive Movement and the Bureaucratization of Thrift'. *American Sociological Review*, 72/1: 117–42.

Haveman, H., Russo M. V., and Meyer, A. D. (2001). 'Organizational Environments in Flux: The Impact of Regulatory Punctuations on Organizational Domains, CEO Succession, and Performance'. *Organization Science*, 12/3: 253–73.

Hedström, P. and Swedberg, R. (1998). *Social Mechanisms*. Cambridge: Cambridge University Press.

Hedström, P. and Ylikoski, P. (2010). 'Causal mechanisms in the social sciences'. *Annual Review of Sociology*, 36: 49–67.

Helfat, C. E. and Campo-Rembado, M. A. (2016). 'Integrative Capabilities, Vertical Integration, and Innovation Over Successive Technology Lifecycles'. *Organization Science*, 27/2: 249–64.

Helfat, C. E., and Peteraf, M. A. (2015). 'Managerial Cognitive Capabilities and the Microfoundations of Dynamic Capabilities'. *Strategic Management Journal*, 36/6: 831–50.

Helfat, C. E., and Raubitschek, R. S. (2018). 'Dynamic and Integrative Capabilities for Profiting from Innovation in Digital Platform-Based Ecosystems'. *Research Policy*, 47: 1391–99.

Hernes, G. (1998). 'Real Virtuality' in P. Hedström and R. Swedberg, eds., *Social Mechanisms: An Analytical Approach to Social Theory*. Cambridge, UK: Cambridge University Press, 74–101.

Hill, C. W. L., and Rothaermel, F. T. (2003). 'The Performance of Incumbent Firms in the Face of Radical Technological Innovation', *Academy of Management Review*, 28: 257–74.

Hinings, C. R., and Greenwood, R. (1988). *The Dynamics of Strategic Change*. Oxford: Basil Blackwell Ltd.

Hofer, C. W., and Schendel, D. (1978). *Strategy Formulation: Analytical Concepts*. St. Paul, MN: West Publishing.

Hoffman, A. J. (1999). 'Institutional Evolution and Change: Environmentalism and the U.S. Chemical Industry'. *Academy of Management Journal*, 42/4: 351–71.

Holm, P. (1995). 'The Dynamics of Institutionalization: Transformation Processes in Norwegian Fisheries'. *Administrative Science Quarterly*, 40/3: 398–422.

Hoppmann, J., Naegele, F., and Girod, B. (2019). 'Boards as a Source of Inertia: Examining the Internal Challenges and Dynamics of Boards of Directors in Times of Environmental Discontinuities'. *Academy of Management Journal*, 62/2: 437–68.

Hsu, G., Kovács, B., and Koçak, Ö. (2019). 'Experientially Diverse Customers and Organizational Adaptation in Changing Demand Landscapes: A Study of US Cannabis Markets, 2014–2016'. *Strategic Management Journal*, 40: 2214–41.

Jacobides, M. G., Cennamo, C., and Gawer, A. (2018). 'Towards a Theory of Ecosystems'. *Strategic Management Journal*, 39/8: 2255–76.
Jarillo, J. C. (1988). 'On Strategic Networks'. *Strategic Management Journal*, 9: 31–41.
Jonsson, S., Greve, H., and Fujiwara-Greve, T. (2009). 'Undeserved Loss: The Spread of Legitimacy Loss to Innocent Organizations in Response to Reported Corporate Deviance'. *Administrative Science Quarterly*, 54/2: 195–228.
Kaplan, S. (2008). 'Cognition, Capabilities, and Incentives: Assessing Firm Response to the Fiber-Optic Revolution'. *Academy of Management Journal*, 51: 672–95.
Kaplan, S., Murray, F., and Henderson, R. M. (2003). 'Discontinuities and Senior Management: Assessing the Role of Recognition in Pharmaceutical Firm Response to Biotechnology'. *Industrial and Corporate Change*, 12: 203–33.
Kapoor, R. (2018). 'Ecosystems: Broadening the Locus of Value Creation'. *Journal of Organization Design*, 7/1: 1–1.
Kapoor, R. and Klueter, T. (2015). 'Decoding the Adaptability-Rigidity Puzzle: Evidence from Pharmaceutical Incumbents' Pursuit of Gene Therapy and Monoclonal Antibodies'. *Academy of Management Journal*, 58/4: 1180–207.
Kimberly, J. R., and Miles, R. H. (1980). *The Organization Life Cycle: Issues in the Creation, Transformation and Decline of Organizations*. San Francisco, CA: Jossey-Bass.
Lampel, J., and Meyer, A. D. (2008). 'Field-Configuring Events as Structuring Mechanisms: How Conferences, Ceremonies, and Trade Shows Constitute New Technologies, Industries, and Markets'. *Journal of Management Studies*, 42: 1025–35.
Langley, A., Smallman, C., Tsoukas, H., and Van de Ven, A. H. (2013). 'Process Studies of Change in Organization and Management: Unveiling Temporality, Activity, and Flow'. *Academy of Management Journal*, 56: 1–13.
Levinthal, D. A. (1998). 'The Slow Pace of Rapid Technological Change: Gradualism and Punctuation in Technological Change'. *Industrial and Corporate Change*, 7/2: 217–47.
Levi-Strauss, C. (1966). *The Savage Mind*. London: Weidenfeld and Nicolson.
Lounsbury, M. (2002). 'Institutional Transformation and Status Mobility: The Professionalization of the Field of Finance'. *Academy of Management Journal*, 45/1: 255–66.
Lounsbury, M. (2007). 'A Tale of Two Cities: Competing Logics and Practice Variation in the Professionalizing of Mutual Funds'. *Academy of Management Journal*, 50/2: 289–307.
Lounsbury, M., Ventresca, M., and Hirsch, P. M. (2003). 'Social Movements, Field Frames and Industry Emergence: A Cultural-Political Perspective on US Recycling'. *Socio-Economic Review*, 1/1: 71–104.
March, J. G. (1981). 'Footnotes to Organizational Change'. *Administrative Science Quarterly*, 26: 563–77.
March, J. G. (1983). 'The Technology of Foolishness' in J. G. March and J. P. Olsen, eds., *Ambiguity, and Choice in Organizations*. Bergen: Universitetsforlaget.
March, J. G. (1994). 'The Evolution of Evolution' in J. A. C. Baum and J. V. Singh, eds., *Evolutionary Dynamics of Organizations*. New York: Oxford University Press, 39–49.
March, J. G. (2006). 'Rationality, Foolishness, and Adaptive Intelligence'. *Strategic Management Journal*, 27: 201–14.
Markides, C. (2006). 'Disruptive Innovation: In Need of Better Theory'. *Journal of Product Innovation Management*, 23: 19–25.

Marquis C., and Huang, Z. (2010). 'Acquisitions as Exaptation: The Legacy of Founding Institutions in the US Commercial Banking Industry'. *Academy of Management Journal*, 53: 1441–73.

Marquis, C., and Lounsbury, M. (2007). 'Vive la résistance: Competing Logics and the Consolidation of US Community Banking'. *Academy of Management Journal*, 50/4: 799–820.

Mars, M. M., and Lounsbury, M. (2009). 'Raging Against or With the Private Marketplace?'. *Journal of Management Inquiry*, 18/1: 4–13.

McCann, J. E., and Selsky, J. (1984). 'Hyperturbulence and the Emergence of Type 5 Environments'. *Academy of Management Review*, 9/3: 460–70.

McInerney, P-B. (2008). 'Showdown at Kykuit: Field-Configuring Events as Loci for Conventionalizing Accounts'. *Journal of Management Studies*, 45/6: 1089–116.

McKelvey, B. (1982). *Organizational Systematics: Taxonomy, Evolution and Classification*. Berkeley, CA: University of California Press.

McKinsey (2015, July). 'Disrupting beliefs: A new approach to business-model innovation'. *McKinsey Quarterly*.

Meyer, A. D. (1982). 'Adapting to Environmental Jolts'. *Administrative Science Quarterly*, 27: 515–37.

Meyer, A. D., Brooks, G. R., and Goes, J. B. (1990). 'Environmental Jolts and Industry Revolutions: Organizational Responses to Discontinuous Change'. *Strategic Management Journal*, 11: 93–110.

Meyer, A. D., Gaba, V., and Colwell, K. A. (2005). 'Organizing far from Equilibrium: Nonlinear Change in Organizational Fields'. *Organization Science*, 16: 456–73.

Meyer, A. D., Goes, J. B., and Brooks, G. R. (1993). 'Organizations Reacting to Hyperturbulence', in G. P. Huber, and W. H. Glick, eds., *Organizational Change and Redesign: Ideas and Insights for Improving Performance*. New York, NY: Oxford University Press, 66–111.

Meyer, J., and Rowan, B. (1977). 'Institutionalized Organizations: Formal Structure as Myth and Ceremony'. *American Journal of Sociology*, 83: 340–63.

Meyer, A. D., Tsui, A. S., Hinings, C. R. (1993). 'Configurational Approaches to Organizational Analysis'. *Academy of Management Journal*, 36: 1175–95.

Miles, R. E., and Snow, C. C. (1978). *Organizational Strategy, Structure, and Process*. New York, NY: McGraw-Hill.

Miller, D., and Friesen, P. (1984). *Organizations: A Quantum View*. Englewood Cliffs, NJ: Prentice-Hall.

Mintzberg, H., and McHugh, A. (1985). 'Strategy Formation in an Adhocracy'. *Administrative Science Quarterly*, 30/2: 160–97.

Normann, R. (1971). 'Organizational Innovativeness: Product Variation and Reorientation'. *Administrative Science Quarterly*, 16: 203–15.

Oliver, A. L., and Montgomery, K. (2008). 'Using Field-Configuring Events for Sense-Making: A Cognitive Network Approach'. *Journal of Management Studies*, 45/6: 1147–67.

Pache, A. C., and Santos, F. (2013). 'Inside the Hybrid Organization: Selective Coupling as a Response to Competing Institutional Logics'. *Academy of Management Journal*, 56/4: 972–1001.

Patala, S., Korpivaara, I., Jalkala, A., Kuitunen, A., and Soppe, B. (2019). 'Legitimacy under Institutional Change: How Incumbents Appropriate Clean Rhetoric for Dirty Technologies'. *Organization Studies*, 40/3: 395–419.

Perkmann, M., and Spicer, A. (2014). 'How Emerging Organizations Take Form: The Role of Imprinting and Values in Organizational Bricolage'. *Organization Science*, 25/6: 1785–806.

Pettigrew, A. M. (1987). 'Context and Action in Transformation of the Firm'. *Journal of Management Studies*, 24/6: 649–70.

Pfeffer J., and Salancik, G. (1978). *The External Control of Organizations*. New York, NY: Harper and Row.

Phillips, N., Lawrence, T. B., and Hardy, C. (2000). 'Inter-Organizational Collaboration and The Dynamics of Institutional Fields'. *Journal of Management Studies*, 37/1: 23–43.

Plowman, D. A., Baker, L. T., Beck, T. E., Kulkarni, M., Solansky, S. T., and Travis, D. V. (2007). 'Radical Change Accidentally: The Emergence and Amplification of Small Change'. *Academy of Management Journal*, 50: 515–43.

Priem, R. L., Li, S., and Carr, J. C. (2012). 'Insights and New Directions from Demand-Side Approaches to Technology Innovation, Entrepreneurship, and Strategic Management Research'. *Journal of Management*, 38/1: 346–74.

Prigogine, I. and Stengers, I. (1984). *Order Out of Chaos*. New York: Bantam Books.

Puranam, P., Shrestha, Y. R., He, V. F. and von Krogh, G. (2018). 'Algorithmic induction through machine learning: Opportunities for management and organization research'. Working Paper.

Rao, H., Monin, P., and Durand, R. (2003). 'Institutional Change in Toque Ville: Nouvelle Cuisine as an Identity Movement in French Gastronomy'. *American Journal of Sociology*, 108/4: 795–843.

Rosenbloom, R. S. (2000). 'Leadership, Capabilities, and Technological Change: The Transformation of NCR in the Electronic Era'. *Strategic Management Journal*, 21: 1083–103.

Roy, R., and Cohen, S. K. (2017). 'Stock of Downstream Complementary Assets as a Catalyst for Product Innovation during Technological Change in the U.S. Machine Tool Industry'. *Strategic Management Journal*, 38/6: 1253–67.

Sahlin, K., and Wedlin, L. (2008). 'Circulating Ideas: Imitation, Translation and Editing' in R. Greenwood et al., eds., *The Sage Handbook of Organizational Institutionalism*. Thousand Oaks, CA: Sage, 218–42.

Sarasvathy, S. D. (2001). 'Causation and Effectuation: Toward a Theoretical Shift from Economic Inevitability to Entrepreneurial Contingency'. *Academy of Management Review*, 26: 243–63.

Sarasvathy, S. D. (2008). *Effectuation: Elements of Entrepreneurial Expertise*'. Northampton, MA, US: Edward Elgar Publishing.

Sarasvathy, S. D., and Dew, N. (2005). 'New Market Creation through Transformation'. *Journal of Evolutionary Economics*, 15: 533–65.

Scherer, F. M. (1980). *Industrial Market Structure and Economic Performance*. New York, NY: Houghton Mifflin.

Schneiberg, M., and Clemens, E. S. (2006). 'The Typical Tools for the Job: Research Strategies in Institutional Research'. *Sociological Theory*, 24/3: 195–227.

Schneiberg, M., and Lounsbury, M. (2008). 'Social Movements and Institutional Analysis', in R. Greenwood, C. Oliver, R. Suddaby, and K. Sahlin (Eds.), *Handbook of Organizational Institutionalism*. Thousand Oaks, CA: Sage, 648–70.

Schumpeter, J. A. (1950). *Capitalism, Socialism and Democracy*. New York, NY: Harper &Row.

Scott, W. R. (1987). *Organizations: Rational, Natural and Open Systems* (2nd edn). Englewood Cliffs, NJ: Prentice-Hall.

Seo, M-G., and Creed, W. E. D. (2002). 'Institutional Contradictions, Praxis, and Institutional Change: A Dialectical Perspective'. *Academy of Management Review*, 27/2: 222–47.

Shah, S. K., and Tripsas, M. (2007). 'The Accidental Entrepreneur: The Emergent and Collective Process of User Entrepreneurship'. *Strategic Entrepreneurship Journal*, 1/1–2: 123–40.

Sine, W. D., and David, R. J. (2003). 'Environmental Jolts, Institutional Change, and the Creation of Entrepreneurial Opportunity in the US Electric Power Industry'. *Research Policy*, 32: 185–207.

Smets, M., Morris, T., and Greenwood, R. (2012). 'From Practice to Field: A Multilevel Model of Practice-Driven Institutional Change'. *Academy of Management Journal*, 55/4: 877–904.

Strang, D., and Soule, S. A. (1998). 'Diffusion in Organizations and Social Movements: From Hybrid Corn to Poison Pills'. *Annual Review of Sociology*, 24: 265–91.

Teece, D. J. (2007). 'Explicating Dynamic Capabilities: The Nature and Microfoundations of (Sustainable) Enterprise Performance'. *Strategic Management Journal*, 28/13: 1319–50.

Teece, D. J., Pisano, G., and Shuen, A. (1997). 'Dynamic Capabilities and Strategic Management'. *Strategic Management Journal*, 18: 509–33.

Thompson, J. D. (1967). *Organizations in Action*. Chicago, IL: McGraw-Hill.

Thorelli, H. B. (1986). 'Networks: Between Markets and Hierarchies'. *Strategic Management Journal*, 7: 37–51.

Thornton, P. H. (2002). 'The Rise of the Corporation in a Craft Industry: Conflict and Conformity in Institutional Logics'. *Academy of Management Journal*, 45: 81–101.

Thornton, P. H., and Ocasio, W. (1999). 'Institutional Logics and the Historical Contingency of Power in Organizations: Executive Succession in the Higher Education Publishing Industry, 1958–1990'. *American Journal of Sociology*: 105, 801–43.

Thornton, P. H. and Ocasio, W. (2008). 'Institutional logics', in R. Greenwood, et al., eds., *The Sage Handbook of Organizational Institutionalism*. Thousand Oaks: Sage Publications, 99–129.

Tripsas, M. (2008). 'Customer Preference Discontinuities: A Trigger for Radical Technological Change'. *Managerial and Decision Economics*, 29/2–3: 79–97.

Tripsas, M., and Gavetti, G. (2000). 'Capabilities, Cognition, and Inertia: Evidence from Digital Imaging'. *Strategic Management Journal*, 21: 1147–161.

Tushman, M. L., and Anderson, P. (1986). 'Technological Discontinuities and Organizational Environments'. *Administrative Science Quarterly*, 31: 1986.

Tushman, M. L., and Romanelli, E. (1985). 'Organizational Evolution: A Metamorphosis Model of Convergence and Reorientation, in L. L. Cummings and B. M. Staw, eds., *Research in Organizational Behavior*. Greenwich', CT: JAI Press, 7: 171–222.

Van de Ven, A. H., and Garud, R. (1987). 'A Framework for Understanding the Emergence of New Industries', in R. Rosenbloom and R. Burgelman, eds., *Research on Technological Innovation, Management and Policy*. Greenwich, CT: JAI Press, 4: 195–225.

Van de Ven, A. H., and Poole, M. S. (1995). 'Explaining Development and Change in Organizations'. *Academy of Management Review*, 20: 510–40.

Watzlawick, P., Weakland, J. H., and Fisch, R. (1974). *Change: Principles of Problem Formation and Problem Resolution*. New York, NY: Norton.

Weber, K. (2006). 'From Nuts and Bolts to Toolkits: Theorizing With Mechanisms'. *Journal of Management Inquiry*, 15/2: 119–23.

Weber, K., Davis, G. F., and Lounsbury, M. (2009). 'Policy as Myth and Ceremony? The Global Spread of Stock Exchanges, 1980–2005'. *Academy of Management Journal*, 52/6: 1319–47.

Zajac, E. J. (1988). 'Interlocking Directorates as an Interorganizational Strategy: A Test of Critical Assumptions'. *Academy of Management Journal*, 31: 428–38.

Zucker, L. G. (1987). 'Institutional Theories of Organizations'. *Annual Review of Sociology*, 13: 443–64.

CHAPTER 17

INSTITUTIONAL CHANGE

EVELYN MICELOTTA, MICHAEL LOUNSBURY, AND ROYSTON GREENWOOD

Introduction

Since the inception of this domain of research, scholars seeking to understand organizational change (i.e., changes in organizational characteristics over time) and innovation (i.e., changes that are novel for the organization) have been cognizant of the importance of the *broader environment* in which organizations operate. As part of interorganizational community, industry, population, and fields, organizations are impacted by their contexts and may be deeply affected by dynamics of change that alter the features and attributes of these environments. In a mutually shaping relationship, changes occurring within organizations may trigger bottom-up dynamic processes that significantly and permanently alter features and attributes at the macro-level.

The focus of this chapter is on institutional change—that is, "a difference in form, quality or state over time in an institution" (Van de Ven and Hargrave 2004: 261). In our view, institutions are relatively durable frameworks that provide stable sets of meanings, practices, rules, and norms on which organizations depend for their understanding of the world, engagement in social interactions, and evaluation of appropriate behaviors; as such, they are analytically distinct from individual organizations. This definition highlights the importance of devoting attention to unpacking the connection between macro-level institutional change processes and models of organizational change. Our goal is to shed light on novel facets of institutional change and highlight key issues pertaining to "organizational change" that we see as importantly connected to the institutional level. For example, institutional change may prevent organizational change, or drive it. Similarly, changes at the institutional level may prescribe and proscribe governance and management "archetypes," thus limiting the array of options of what legitimate organizational changes may look like. Examining the temporal dimension will also yield interesting insights, as the pace of accomplishment of institutional and organizational change are connected in meaningful ways.

While the change literature is vast and has a rich history, our discussion focuses on contemporary developments that have shifted analytical focus away from an emphasis on structure, stability, and isomorphism, and towards a foregrounding of agency, multiplicity, and variation. Recent scholarship has devoted deeper attention to empirically unpacking and theorizing the implications of understanding fields as plural, diverse, and heterogeneous, and in turn, how that alters previous theories that were developed through the empirical study of monolithic environments (Thornton et al. 2012). Critically, plural institutional environments may impose conflicting demands on organizations, and offer diverse opportunities for variegated organizational response (Greenwood et al. 2011).

The chapter is organized as follows. First, we offer a review of the current state of research on change processes from an institutional perspective. Based on our prior efforts to synthesize this vast body of work (Micelotta et al. 2017), we examine the longitudinal progression of research, illustrating the generative processes that drive change, the patterns of change over time, the mechanisms underpinning change, and its key outcomes. We also distinguish variance and process studies and zoom in on process-based research (i.e., temporal progression of event sequences), discussing implications for organizations, and similarities and differences between theoretical models of change.

Based on our typological analysis of the scope and pace of change, we discuss four *types* of institutional change processes—displacement, alignment, accretion, and accommodation—specifically highlighting their temporal patterns and underpinning mechanisms related to organizational change. We note that while we have a great deal of research on displacement and alignment, we have much less research on accretion and accommodation. To highlight the fruitfulness of directing more attention to these change processes, we provide an empirical illustration of pathways of institutional change based on the case of Open Access in higher education publishing. This case provides key insights into the dynamics of change, the mechanisms through which pathways are connected, and suggests implications for changes at various levels of analysis, including populations of organizations and organizational practices.

Current State of Research on Institutional Change: Triggers

As research on institutional change has intensified (Dacin et al., 2002; Scott 2010, 2014), so have efforts to summarize and clarify the large corpus of research that, somehow disconnectedly, has explored this topic. Even today, the term remains a sweeping categorization encompassing a broad spectrum of processes and outcomes. It includes the gamut of levels of analysis from populations and fields to single organizations and individual practices, with the primary focus on social structure, agency, or something in between. Scholarship has largely concentrated on institutional changes that are *triggered* either by exogenous disturbances (or "jolts," to use Meyer's 1982 term), to which organizations responded (e.g., Clemens and Cook 1999), or by the disruptive strategies of institutional entrepreneurs (e.g., Battilana et al. 2009), or most recently, by bottom-up changes that arise from the more mundane day-to-day practices within and between organizations (e.g., Smets et al. 2012).

Exogenous Change

The earliest studies theorized that changes in the institutional context (typically at the societal or field levels) would alter the environment of the organizations. Researchers postulated that change occurred in a top-down manner, from the environment to organizations. Thus, scholars studied a variety of macroenvironmental changes, such as shifts in political regimes in transitioning economies (Whitley and Czaban 1998), and sociopolitical upheavals (e.g., wars, revolutions) that affect the likelihood of survival of organizations and their strategic postures (Allmendinger and Hackman 1996). Others focused on competence-destroying technological changes and their effects (Romanelli and Tushman 1994), regulatory change (Lounsbury et al. 1998), to explain how competitive pressure and resource scarcity radically affect the rules of competition in established industries (Thornton and Ocasio 1999).

This line of research focused upon how macroenvironmental changes provide the impetus for processes of deinstitutionalization of incumbent organizational forms, not individual organizations, and for the transformation in the legitimacy-conferring criteria that dramatically alter the ability of organizational populations to survive (Davis et al. 1994). There was, however, a second line of research that conceptualized organizations as capable of adaptation and emphasized their successful responses to disruptive changes. For example, Ginsberg and Buchholtz (1990) observed the strategic conversion of health maintenance organizations to a for-profit model when the dramatic change in federal policies removed key advantages of nonprofit status. Research on organizational responses has also yielded insight on the factors that affect the responsiveness of organizations, as well as the organizational characteristics and strategies that increase the likelihood of successful conversion or that hinder strategic transitions, such as leadership style and strategic postures (Kriauciunas and Kale 2006). Typically, when a precipitating event makes action urgent and inevitable, change occurs in the form of strategic renovation guided by strong leadership. For example, Zajac and Kraatz (1993), Kraatz and Moore (2002) and Romanelli and Tushman (1994) emphasize the role of executives' leadership in enabling organizations to reconfigure after environmental changes.

A third line of research focused on shifts in field-level institutional logics (Thornton and Ocasio 1999). Institutional logics are "the socially constructed, historical patterns of cultural symbols and material practices, assumptions, values, and beliefs by which individuals produce and reproduce their material subsistence, organize time and space, and provide meaning to their daily activity" (Thornton and Ocasio 1999: 804). Thornton and Ocasio (1999) illustrate the shift from an editorial institutional logic to a market logic and its consequences for the collective understanding of the publishing industry. Similarly, Greenwood et al. (2010) revealed how the choice of firms to downsize in Spain (following the pressures of a market logic) were importantly counterbalanced by the family logic supported by the Catholic Church.

The institutional logics perspective is relatively recent, but it has become a highly influential theoretical orientation. Notably, it has introduced the conceptualization of change as a more complex and multifaceted process not reducible to selection or organizational adaptation processes (as implied in the above two research streams). Research drawing on the institutional logics perspective has tried to break down the theoretical boundaries between what is treated as exogenous versus endogenous, and more deeply puzzle about the role of organizations in both producing and reacting to aspects of institutional change.

Institutional Entrepreneurship

While a focus on triggers tended to emphasize how events external to organizations impact them, the institutional entrepreneurship literature highlighted endogenous processes that feature how particular actors, often organizations, are able to catalyze wider scale institutional change (see Battilana et al. 2009 for a review). This work stemmed from efforts to explicitly understand the role of actors and power in facilitating institutional dynamics (DiMaggio 1988). One key focal point in this literature has been to theorize how the structural position of organizational and individual actors—periphery (Leblebici et al. 1991) or core (Greenwood and Suddaby 2006)—enables institutional entrepreneurship. Much of this work grappled with the "paradox of embedded agency" (Seo and Creed 2002; see also Prichard and Creed 2021, this handbook), which refers to how actors embedded in highly constraining institutional arrangements can reflect and act in order to alter those institutions. One prominent development of this paradox has been to highlight that perhaps institutions are not as unitary and constraining as previously conceptualized; but in fact, institutional environments may be comprised on a plurality of logics that enable reflexivity and different forms of institution-altering behavior (Thornton et al. 2012).

Some scholars have also emphasized the importance of differences in the nature of fields—for example, emerging versus mature fields (Maguire et al., 2004), or the existence of 'institutional voids'—spaces that are institutionally less developed (Mair and Marti 2009). The characterization of fields and the study of their dynamics continues to provide a key focal point for the advancement of knowledge about the sources and consequences of institutional entrepreneurship, and more generally, institutional change (Zietsma et al. 2016; Furnari 2014).

Relatedly, other scholars have focused on institutional entrepreneurship associated with the introduction of innovations which are seen as nonthreatening to the institutional order, but can enable transformation, nonetheless. For example, various forms of cultural entrepreneurship (Lounsbury and Glynn 2001, 2019), including the use of bricolage (Rao et al. 2005), robust design (Hargadon and Douglas 2001), frames (Werner and Cornelissen 2014), and theorization (Greenwood et al. 2002) that provide key mechanisms associated with how institutional entrepreneurs have reshaped various fields. A similar perspective has been taken by the growing stream of research on "institutional work," where the focus is not primarily on the actors, but on the mechanisms through which institutions are disrupted, created, or maintained (see Hampel et al. 2017 for a review). Somewhat similarly, research at the interface of social movements and institutional change emphasizes more contextually situated approaches to agency rather than according substantial casual efficacy to individuals (Schneiberg and Lounsbury 2017; see also chapters in this handbook).

These developments have led to a diminution of attention to the "hero" narratives that infused early research on institutional entrepreneurship, instead directing attention to how change processes are often much more complicated, involving a wide variety of organizational actors, and unfold with varied pace and intention across space and time. Such focus, however, slightly shifted scholarly attention away from the analysis of change *within* organizations. For instance, within the vast literature on social movements, studies of collective action occurring inside organizations have been relatively scarcer than studies at the field level (Davis et al. 2008, see also Davis and Kim 2021, this handbook).

Emergent Practice-Driven Change

In contradistinction to the highly strategic characterization of prominent institutional entrepreneurs, scholars have strived to develop more grounded, actor and practice-centered approaches that seek to uncover and theorize the microfoundations of institutional change (Powell and Colyvas 2008; Barley 2008; Cardinale 2018). These recent developments build upon evolutionary approaches (e.g., Barley and Tolbert 1997; Berger and Luckmann 1967), that highlight the distributed—partaking—nature of agency and how change emerges from the bottom-up (Gray et al. 2015). Unlike prior foci, these more practice-centered approaches do not assume that change is precipitated by dramatic environmental shifts or by the purposeful efforts of powerful actors. Instead, change may be inadvertently triggered by the "mundane activities of practitioners struggling to accomplish their work" (Smets et al. 2012: 877; see also Smets et al. 2017).

In this line of inquiry, the analysis goes deeper into the organization to the micro-level. They show how local improvisations in practices concatenate to affect organizational characteristics and strategies that ultimately may become institutionalized through field-level dynamics. For example, Lounsbury and Crumley (2007) demonstrated how the performativity of mutual funds in investment firms led to problematic variations in mutual fund practices that were accommodated only through field-level restructurings in beliefs that would legitimate and accommodate new practices. Similarly, Smets et al. (2012) showed how gradually and unobtrusively new practices introduced within an organization moved up to the field level and stimulated a logic's shift of the legal professional field.

Practice-oriented studies have dovetailed with two critical trends: first, the growing interest in exploring opportunities for integration between institutional analysis and micro-level organizational perspectives (e.g., practice, identity, sensemaking, decision-making, framing); and second, the institutional logics perspective, which has explicitly focused attention on how broader configurations of meanings and practices affect organizational dynamics (Thornton et al. 2012: Chapters 4 and 6). As a result, new opportunities have been presented to combine theoretical lenses to theorize change processes as multilevel. The novel linkages and relationships between the macro-, meso-, and micro-levels of analysis have importantly enriched theories of organizational change.

Current state of research on institutional change: Pathways as integrative models

As Van de Ven and Poole note in the introduction to this handbook, since 2004 there has been much development in the literature about patterns and models of change. Scholars acknowledge the complexity characterizing change dynamics and processes and, as a result, we have seen a remarkable growth in nonlinear hybrid models of change. Compared to earlier conceptualizations, these models provide nuanced insights on both institutional and organizational change. Three elements are key: the temporal dimension; the centrality of paradoxes, contradictions, and dialectic; and the intertwined relationship between change and stability.

The concept of time and change are inherently related; thus, it is surprising that scholars have devoted thus far relatively limited attention to issues of temporality, velocity, and rhythm (but see Hernes, Chapter 27 this handbook; Lawrence et al. 2001). This gap is being rapidly filled, with more studies addressing theoretical and empirical questions about temporality of change, temporal institutional work, and the effect of timing decisions on key success and implementation outcomes (Klarner and Raisch 2013; Granqvist and Gustafsson 2016).

Along the same lines, the emphasis on change triggers has provided scholars with a theoretically convincing motivation for why stable institutional arrangements are altered; however, such focus has also bracketed the importance of other key mechanisms that contribute to keeping the momentum, steering the direction, and ultimately defining the outcomes of change. The emphasis on the triggers as the determinants of the form that change will take has also strengthened the tendency to overlook relational dynamics and feedback loops. Crucially, the role of balancing incompatibilities and/or contradictions, as well as settling conflicts, are increasingly seen as important mechanisms that drive and shape change in nonlinear ways. These key insights have been brought front and center by research on hybridity and hybrid organizations (Smets et al. 2015; Jay 2013) and institutional truces and settlements (Helms et al. 2012; Schildt and Perkmann 2017).

Finally, it is important to note the increasing focus on agency and work in both enabling change and/or preserving the status quo. The latest developments on institutional maintenance show that institutions are maintained by the active work of incumbent organizations, either through small "fixes" when breaches in institutional arrangements occur, or drastic repair work that restores the status quo after it has been dramatically disrupted (e.g., Dacin et al. 2010; Micelotta and Washington 2013). For example, Lok and de Rond (2013) showed how the 175-year old institution of the Cambridge boat race had to be continually sustained and repaired as rules or principles were violated. Each incident of rule violation reaffirmed institutions by bringing them to conscious awareness. An important insight of these studies is that dynamic processes underlie stability as well as change, and variations exist in the extent to which institutions and organizations can be successfully and permanently modified.

In sum, as scholarly attention has progressively moved away from the triggers of institutional change to dynamics related to time, contradictions and maintenance, the theoretical linkages between institutional and organizational change have become richer, and more opportunities have become evident. Inquiries now reveal the ways in which different triggers and forms of agency interplay with temporal variables such as pacing, sequencing, and duration in shaping the trajectory and outcome of institutional and organizational change processes. Institutional pluralism as a structural condition of fields is increasingly recognized, and the acknowledgement of multiplicity, paradoxes, and contradictions has offered scholars opportunities to better understand the complexity of modern change processes. At the organizational level, the idea of institutional complexity as the subjective experience of logic contradictions by organizations has provided new avenues to theorize complex and novel ways in which organizations appreciate and respond to change stimuli (Greenwood et al. 2011; Thornton et al. 2012).

An Integrative Framework

In our review (Micelotta et al. 2017), we analyzed 119 empirical articles to propose a novel integrative framework by which to understand the confusing array of studies on institutional change and help forge a more systematic way forward. We found that only thirty-nine papers utilized a variance approach to institutional and organizational change. These papers are mostly concentrated in the early years of theorizing (1990–2004) and become relatively rare afterwards. Thus, the majority of scholarship embraces a process-based lens. However, by examining the methods, main findings, and models of institutional change of these articles, the heterogeneity of processes of institutional and organizational change became evident.

Our suggested framework categorizes change processes according to two dimensions—the *scope* and *pace* of change. The y-axis categorizes change pathways based on pace—whether revolutionary or evolutionary. As noted earlier, "institutional change is inherently a longitudinal process, and many core questions revolve around temporal dynamics (Lawrence et al. 2001). We recognized that connections between agency and institutional processes and temporal variables (e.g., pace, sequence, linearity, readiness) in change processes have been minimally explored (Amis et al. 2004). The x-axis distinguishes change processes based on scope—whether they are transformational or developmental (see Thornton et al. 2012). We treated institutional change as transformational depending on whether a given empirical study detailed a "difference in form, quality or state over time in an institution" (Van de Ven and Hargrave 2004: 261).

Our typology joins a long-standing conversation about types of change at the organizational and institutional level. While there are a variety of typologies in the literature, existing typologies are a bit dated, and many have not yet been updated to account for recent developments. An interesting exception is the contribution of Gaba and Meyer (2021, Chapter 22, this handbook) that updates the typology originally elaborated by Meyer et al. (1993). The original typology categorized four kinds of changes in the literature of the 1990s: adaptation and metamorphosis at the organization level, and evolution and revolution at the industry level. The updated typology revisits these findings in light of recent studies and offers a more granular explanation of mechanisms underpinning discontinuous change. Our typology focuses on a different level of analysis, categorizing various approaches to institutional change at the field level based on published work mainly from the 1990s to the present. In addition, instead of conceptualizing evolution and revolution as forms of industry change, we believe those categories are better repurposed as differences in how institutional scholars theorize the pace of change.

Furthermore, older typologies reflected the literature at the time and anchored more exclusively on institutions as rule systems; thus, they focused mainly on the role of interests and politics as drivers of organizational and industry change. Our typology embraces more contemporary developments in institutional analysis that foreground the role of culture, cognition, and practice. In embracing culture, cognition and practice, the more contemporary institutional literature on institutional analysis has moved further away from the old institutionalist tradition of Commons, Selznick, and the like. This is most directly stated by DiMaggio and Powell (1991) in laying out the distinctions between the new and old institutionalisms, although they recognized the usefulness of older approaches to political processes (see also, Greenwood and Hinings 1996; Lounsbury and Hirsch 1997; Stinchcombe 1997). A key distinction of importance is the conceptualization of agency. Even though institutionalists like Commons emphasized that institutions enable, liberate, and constrain actors, institutions have been conceptualized primarily as regulations and norms that provide rule systems that *constrain* actors; within such systems change occurs mainly by interest-driven action, often in a pragmatic fashion (see e.g., Van de Ven and Lifschitz 2009). Alternatively, new institutionalist approaches draw on contemporary social theoretic developments (e.g., Giddens 1984) to conceptualize institutions as cultural systems that fundamentally constitute actors and their interests, providing a distinctly different ontological starting point (Emirbayer and Mische 1998; Lounsbury and Wang 2020; Meyer and Jepperson 2000; Sewell 1992). Nonetheless, we see opportunities for the pragmatic negotiations emphasized by Commons and other old institutionalists, in particular, the useful guidance for scholarship focused on practice-driven institutional change, which is most pronounced in studies of institutional accretion.

In the next section, we illustrate the four pathways of change—displacement, alignment, accretion, and accommodation—that emerged from our analysis. We discuss the typical process pattern and their underpinning mechanisms, with some examples as illustration (Figure 17.1).

SCOPE OF CHANGE

PACE OF CHANGE	**Developmental**	**Transformational**
	Q2 Institutional Alignment	**Q3. Institutional Accretion**
Evolutionary	***Form of change:*** A relatively low-paced process during which deviations are internalized into existing institutions ***Type of mechanisms:*** *propelling* (theorization, framing) *internalizing* (isomorphism, decoupling, intermediation) and *institutionalizing* (structuration, sedimentation) mechanisms ***Examples:*** Sherer & Lee, 2002; Wright & Zammuto, 2013; David et al., 2013	***Form of change:*** A relatively low-placed process during which deviations accumulate to replace institutions ***Type of mechanisms:*** escalating mechanisms: *technology-driven* (stickiness, similarity) and *practice-driven* (unobtrusive diffusion) ***Examples:*** Hargadon & Douglas, 2001; Ansari & Phillips, 2011; Smets et al., 2012
	Q4. Institutional Accommodation	**Q1. Institutional Displacement**
Revolutionary	***Form of change:*** A relatively high-paced process during which deviations are accommodated into existing institutions ***Type of mechanisms:*** de-escalating mechanisms: *conflict, partisan mutual adjustment, co-optation, and decoupling* ***Examples:*** Maguire & Hardy, 2009; Murray, 2010; Zietsma & Lawrence, 2010; van Wijk et al., 2012	***Form of change:*** A relatively high-paced process during which deviations swiftly replace institutions ***Type of mechanisms:*** displacing mechanisms: *selection* (disbandment and founding), *conversion* (Strategic renovation, strong leadership), and *socio-cultural reconfiguration* (identity reconstruction, change in meanings and values) ***Examples:*** Thornton & Ocasio, 1999; Kraatz & Moore, 2002; Hiatt et al., 2009

FIGURE 17.1 Pathways of Institutional Change

Institutional Displacement

Institutional displacement is a pathway of change with a revolutionary pace that results in transformational change in institutional arrangements and organizations. This pathway reveals how changes in the environment are reflected in the abandonment and replacement of forms of organizing, and associated structures and practices. This imagery of change is at the core of ecological theories of transformation and renewal through selection (Freeman et al. 1983), paradigms of quantum change and punctuated equilibrium in the technological innovation literature (Romanelli and Tushman 1994), economic theories of creative destruction (Schumpeter 1939), and institutional models of deinstitutionalization (Greenwood et al. 2002; see also Baum and Rao 2021, Chapter 16 in this handbook for a more extensive discussion of ecological and genealogical evolution).

Importantly, the mechanisms through which displacement occurs are diverse. For example, top-down regulatory and legislative reforms transform the field by forcing the disbanding of organizations; alternatively, dramatic political, market, and technological changes transform the field by pressuring organizations to change their structures and strategies in order to conform with the new environment; finally, socio-cultural changes in the form of change in institutional logics transform the field by orienting actors' attention and commitment towards alternative forms of organizing. More generally, three classes of mechanisms have been identified in the literature as underpinning institutional displacement: selection, conversion, and socio-cultural reconfiguration (see also Marcus and Malen 2021, Chapter 14 in this handbook for a discussion on the formation, implementation, and enforcement of different government regulations).

Selection. The first mechanism—selection—typifies the vantage point of scholars who consider organizations unable to change successfully to fit novel environmental conditions. Either because an environmental change is too extreme to bear or because change is pervasive and outside the control of organizations, institutional change takes the form of a displacement of unfitting organizational templates and their replacement with new forms. The selection process may be driven by actions that threaten and/or directly attack those organizations that lack adherence to changing environmental conditions. For example, Davis et al. (1994) describe the increased risk of acquisitions and takeovers faced by diversified firms whose structures and practices no longer embodied dominant systems of beliefs and values. Similarly, Hiatt et al. (2009) show the negative impact of collective action against alcoholic beverages and unfavorable regulations on the survival rates of breweries.

Selection may also occur because of the less menacing, yet equally impactful, resource scarcity that organizations experience as a result of environmental disruptions. For example, Tucker et al. (1990) document that when economic issues took precedence over social ones at the government level, social organizations lost precious resources and their legitimacy was questioned. Importantly, the resource most critical for organizations to lose is often legitimacy, because social acceptance is a prerequisite for the accrual of material support. In this regard, Holm's (1995) study of the rise and fall of the MSO organizational form in Norway is illustrative of how selection may be driven by the loss of integrity of the intricate web of both material *and* symbolic resources that undergird organizational forms.

Conversion. In contrast to selection, conversion reflects an adaptationist view of change. Rather than through the disbandment and founding of new organizational forms, displacement occurs as a result of substantial organizational changes. Notably, organizations change in the direction dictated by their environments, in order to maintain strategic and cultural "fit." This mechanism shows that not all adaptation is incremental or gradual, and some forms of change requires institutions to change at the core in order to adapt. For example, Ginsberg and Buchholtz (1990) observed the strategic conversion of health maintenance organizations to a for-profit model when the dramatic change in federal policies removed key advantages of nonprofit status. When a precipitating event makes action urgent and inevitable, change requires strategic renovation guided by strong leadership (e.g., Romanelli and Tushman 1994). For instance, White and Linden's (2002) comparison of the Polish and Chinese television manufacturing industries reveals that maintaining an adequate pace of adaptation, establishing managerial incentives to embrace change, and ensuring organizational capacity are critical responses that enable incumbent firms to survive in newly liberalized markets. Likewise, maintaining strengths and operational autonomy enabled orchestras in East Germany to successfully weather the sociopolitical transition following the collapse of socialism (Allmendinger and Hackman 1996). Conversely, the imprinting effect of firms' prior institutional and market environment (Kriauciunas and Kale 2006) and the entrenchment of values, motives, and actions of key managers (Clark and Soulsby 1995) are shown to negatively affect organizations' ability to adapt.

Socio-cultural reconfiguration. This third mechanism reflects the conceptualization of change as a complex process that is not reducible to organizational selection or adaptation to environmental changes. Unlike the first two mechanisms that explicate how changes in the institutional environment stimulate changes in organizations to ensure "fit," socio-cultural reconfiguration is based on the premise that organizations are embedded in complex fields where behaviors are entrenched in enduring institutional logics (Friedland and Alford 1991; Thornton et al. 2012). Thus, the process of displacement is not easy and entails discarding deeply held cultural elements (Greenwood et al. 2002). Beliefs, norms, values, rules, and meanings that guide behaviors, construct identities, and define legitimate practices have to be deinstitutionalized; then, new arrangements proposed by change agents need to be theorized and accepted before they can diffuse (Battilana et al. 2009). In this regard, Rao et al. (2003: 814) nicely showed the importance of identity as a motor of change; in their account of nouvelle cuisine, activists contributed to changing the logics dominating the gastronomic field by "delivering identity discrepant messages when they highlight institutional gaps, articulating problems with the existing logic and identity, and demanding redress." Several other studies highlight how the construction and reconstruction of meanings and values drove displacement of previously dominant organizational forms (Thornton and Ocasio 1999).

Summary. The conceptualization of institutional change as a displacement process was well understood and theoretically prominent in the early years of institutional analysis, when scholars had a somewhat "static" understanding of the relationship between the environment and organizations. Selection, conversion and sociocultural reconfiguration are three different ways of theorizing the one-way profound effect of environmental change on organizations. As more endogenous and processual views of change began to gain traction, this rigid separation between organizations and environments became less salient, as evident in the processual nature of the mechanisms underpinning the three other pathways—alignment, accommodation, and accretion.

Institutional Alignment

Institutional alignment is a change pathway that describes evolutionary processes leading to developmental change, thus providing a complementary perspective to institutional displacement. Alignment shows that institutions and organizations are relatively adaptable and may gradually co-evolve. The mechanisms that shape institutional arrangements are therefore endogenous, and the studies that exemplify this pathway focus attention on embedded human activity exploiting inconsistencies and contradictions. Accordingly, the theoretical foundations of this pathway of change are analytical models that connect macro and micro-institutional levels, such as institutionalization as structuration (Barley and Tolbert 1997), and dialectical perspectives that emphasize the role of collective human agency (or praxis) in creating change (Battilana et al. 2009). Examples include the introduction of novel organizational practices and rules that sustain central players' dominance (Greenwood and Suddaby 2006; Wright and Zammuto 2013), the emergence of new technologies, sectors, industries, and fields that do not substantially endanger existing arrangements (Munir and Phillips 2005), or the acknowledgement by "centrally" located actors of the practices and identities of marginalized groups (Maguire et al. 2004). Three intertwined mechanisms underpin institutional alignment: propelling, internalizing, and institutionalization mechanisms.

Propelling mechanisms. In the absence of disruptive triggers that command attention and urge actions, endogenous triggers propel the alteration of the status quo and catalyze change. Individuals and organizations seeking to exploit latent contradictions and bring about change need, firstly, to attract the attention of other field-level actors and, secondly, persuade them to embrace the change. At this stage, great emphasis is given to mechanisms such as theorization and framing, which explain how novel organizational forms, practices, and structural innovations are persuasively presented and justified to other field members so that they are not rejected or resisted (Greenwood et al. 2002). For example, in their study of the change in the professional business field, Greenwood and colleagues showed how the accounting profession introduced change by legitimating a new organizational form—the multidisciplinary practice—to *itself*. Specifically, professional regulatory agencies played a key role in framing the change as needed, progressive, and necessary; furthermore, the multidisciplinary practice was justified by aligning the idea with the values of the profession. Interestingly, the discussion around the functionality of the new form was implied, rather than explicitly emphasized.

While deviations from the status quo presented in a familiar way more easily attract attention and garner support, propelling mechanisms may not be sufficient to explain the form that change will take, when other actors are involved. In that scenario, institutional entrepreneurs' strategies need to address the potential resistance of "other actors" who are not part of the group that propelled the change. Despite the relative familiarity of the proposed revisions and the persuasiveness of entrepreneurs, consensus around changes might not be absolute, as the cooperation of other organizations is typically contingent upon individual interests. Internalizing mechanisms intervene at this point to orient actors and shape the direction of change, so that institutional arrangements maintain internal consistency and their taken-for-granted status.

Internalizing mechanisms. Internalizing mechanisms sequentially follow propelling mechanisms to enable the realignment of institutional arrangements around new relations, forms, and practices. For example, isomorphism and decoupling are two well-known mechanisms through which changes in the institutional environment are internalized into organizational actions and structures (Bromley and Powell 2012). Many studies in the institutional tradition point to (effective or ceremonial) institutional compliance as a primary way in which organizations regain alignment with their environments. For example, Glynn and Abzug (2002) demonstrate how institutional conformity led organizations to align their names – and identities – with institutionalized naming patterns. Along the same lines, studies of organizational forms of fashion companies (Djelic and Ainamo 1999), forms, and practices in professional services firms (Greenwood et al. 2002), and strategies of organizations seeking and/or granting academic accreditations (Durand and McGuire 2005) show that change arises from the need of organizations to preserve legitimacy and/or signal compliance. Intermediation between institutional actors may also be an effective internalizing mechanism. For instance, Wright and Zammuto (2013) elaborate the important mediating role of the group of organizational actors between center and periphery in the micro-processes that led top-down and bottom-up changes to be encoded, translated, and revised in the logics, scripts, and rules of professional cricket.

Institutionalizing mechanisms. The last stage of institutional alignment is typically seen as 'structuration' or 'restabilization.' This processual phase enables changed patterns of relations and actions to "acquire the moral and ontological status of taken-for-granted facts which, in turn, shape future interactions and negotiations" (Barley and Tolbert 1997: 94). For example, accepted deviations from institutionalized expectations can be formalized and reinforced through the codification of new institutional rules and the development of standards; novel organizational archetypes can be layered on previous ones in a process of sedimentation such as in the case of the multidisciplinary practices in professional service firms; also the reinforcement of boundaries and the localized encroachment of institutional logics provide examples of how newly established practices and forms can be legitimized and potentially diffuse (e.g., Wright and Zammuto 2013; Purdy and Gray 2009).

Summary. Institutional alignment is another well-understood process of institutional change through which scholars explain how flare-ups of contradictions and dialectical tensions, either occurring at the field or the organizational level, lead to developmental change. This pathway of change and its mechanisms theorize in a more precise and fruitful way the idea that institutions simultaneously enable and constrain human action. When the pace is evolutionary, change is gradual. Amendments to institutions and organizations can gradually internalize novel demands of actors and novel environmental conditions in a co-evolutionary process. It is important to note that many empirical examinations of institutional alignment focus on a single cycle, or even a single phase, of change. A fuller appreciation of this pathway of change may require extending this processual analysis to multiple cycles over a relatively long period of time.

Institutional Accretion

Institutional accretion is a pathway that describes evolutionary processes that lead to transformational change. Based on our review of the literature, accretion is a relatively less explored trajectory of change that requires further specification and theorizing. Thus far, only a handful of studies have examined instances of change in which seemingly localized and non-disruptive alterations cumulate to spawn institutional and organizational transformations. As a result, we have a more limited understanding of the mechanisms that underpin this pathway of change. For example, Lounsbury and Crumley (2007) theorized how initially ignored and dismissed "experimentations" with active investing strategies in the US finance industry led to the creation of new product categories that reconfigured the power structure of the industry. A similar dynamic is illustrated by Hargadon and Douglas (2001) and the ultimate displacement of the gas technology—and the industry built on it—enabled by Edison's 'robust design' strategy. The introduction of the innovation signaled continuity with dominant organizational practices but the accumulation of change provided the flexibility to create discontinuous change at the end.

Similar to institutional alignment, accretion is a pathway of change that originates from relatively non-disruptive events; it then unfolds through a concatenation of accretive mechanisms. Evolutionary triggers, such as shifting coordination problems within and between organizations, competitive pressures, entrance of new players in a field, or the availability of a new technology, are often the by-product of the ongoing activity of organizing. In the case of alignment, these events offer stimuli and opportunities for institutional actors to propel change, which is then internalized into existing organizational arrangements. As a result, the resulting change is developmental in scope. Accretion differs from alignment in that these seemingly ordinary and incremental variations are internalized into extant institutional arrangements, but are only partially institutionalized. Instead of acquiring a taken-for-granted quality—and therefore losing their catalytic potential—changes retain the generative capability to stimulate further changes. Small departures from the status quo may temporarily settle but, under appropriate conditions, they activate to prompt a sequence of magnifying cycles.

The mechanisms through which initial small deviations from the status quo are amplified to generate transformational change are still not well understood (see Garud and Turunen 2021, Chapter 10, this handbook for a discussion of partial cumulative syntheses theory and more). We know that these mechanisms need to have the ability to *escalate* change. Existing institutional and cognate literatures have yielded initial insights, in particular on what type of organizational feature has the ability to carry such an accretive, escalating power, but much more remains to be done. Extant studies suggest two types, namely *technology-driven* and *practice-driven* mechanisms. Both kinds of mechanisms require further study, and much more attention needs to be paid to identifying other mechanisms and the conditions under which they are catalytic.

Technology-driven escalating mechanisms. Despite the conventional imagery of technology as competence-destroying, research on innovation highlights that technology-driven change may unfold in an incremental way, driven by the co-evolution between institutions, organizations, and technology. Technology is a vital source of institutional variation and offers opportunities to peripheral players to introduce change. Notable examples include fringe radio broadcasters (Leblebici et al. 1991), inventors (Hargadon and Douglas 2001), and consumers (Ansari and Phillips 2011).

Importantly, these studies show that the effect of technology is often cumulative, and innovations typically gain initial acceptance from audiences when they are located "within the set of understandings and patterns of action that constitute the institutional environment." As discussed earlier, the "cloaking of innovations in the mantle of established institutions" (Hargadon and Douglas 2001: 478–9) and its institutionalization would be conducive to institutional alignment, if not for the essential condition that the evolutionary potential in a new technology is extremely hard to suppress. It is this intrinsic characteristic of technological development that drives the process of institutional accretion. For example, echoing the notion of robust design, Ansari and Phillips' (2011) investigation of mobile telephony in the UK confirms that compatibility between innovations and the interests of supporting organizations is essential for technological variations to be accepted. Technology, however, evolves over time beyond the initial limited understanding and use. As Hargadon and Douglas (2001: 499) elegantly put it: "[T]he early successes should arrive draped in familiar understandings and patterns of use. Over time, those systems that retain the flexibility to change with us will persist. Ultimately, these will be the innovations we look back on as radical and discontinuous." Importantly, the case of mobile texting reveals that novel technological practices may be more likely to catalyze change when they are "sticky," that is, easy to adopt but hard to give up. Such addictive property might be particularly important in circumstances where change revolves around practices that are seemingly trivial and uncoordinated (e.g., texting) as time is needed for a radically novel supporting institutional and organizational infrastructure to develop.

Practice-driven escalating mechanisms. Practice theory offers another useful theoretical lens to explore potentially powerful escalating mechanisms. According to this perspective, practices are not self-standing categories to be taken as given, but are the result of endless performances. It follows that "individual performances of a practice play a key role in altering a given practice through variation in its enactment" (Lounsbury and Crumley 2007: 996). For example, new practices and new actors can be initially ignored but may eventually precipitate transformational field-level change. In this scenario, the seemingly insignificant innovation contributed to altering the interrelations and mutual dependencies among field-level actors, as indicated by changes in field-level and organizational practices. Critically, escalation occurs when small innovations are theorized and then become part of the symbolic repertoire of the field. This is clearly illustrated by Smets et al. (2012) whose study offers a complementary view of practice-driven escalating mechanisms, where the escalation occurs through the material embodiment of small variations in more visible manifestations. These authors document that the shift in the institutional logics in the German legal sector originated from deviating practices within an organization that consolidated into a hybrid organization and "unobtrusively diffused" at the field level. In this case, an organizational change triggered a large-scale institutional change and, given the central position of the organization, we can assume that it significantly accelerated its pace; thus, an organizational change profoundly impacted the scale and pace of institutional change.

Summary. There is great research potential in understanding which organizational attributes and institutional features enable and/or constrain accretive changes. As empirical examinations accumulate, novel mechanisms are likely to emerge, hopefully leading to a redefinition and integration of the initial categorization of mechanisms that we offer. By integrating extant theories (e.g., Usher 1950) we will have a better understanding of institutional accretion as a process and its underlying escalating mechanisms.

Institutional Accommodation

The final change pathway—institutional accommodation—describes processes with revolutionary pace that lead to developmental change. Although the literature on institutional change is vast, this pathway is also understudied and seemingly the most elusive to capture in empirical examinations. Revolutionary pace is typically associated with institutional displacement and swift and dramatic change within organizations; hence, little is known about the circumstances that prevent transformational change from fully occurring and, instead, lead to developmental change. Along the same lines, extant accounts of developmental change typically rely on the evolutionary pace as an explanation for the relatively limited scope of change. This explanation does not hold when the process of change is revolutionary.

Similar to accretion, our theorizing of the processual mechanisms of accommodation is limited by the lack of extensive empirical research. We suggest that the key to understanding accommodation is to capture the *de-escalating* mechanisms that lead to a developmental rather than transformational outcome. De-escalating mechanisms allow institutions and organizations to recompose around altered arrangements, despite the revolutionary pace of change. Only four papers in the literature portray a process of change that is akin to institutional accommodation: Zietsma and Lawrence (2010), Maguire and Hardy (2009), Murray (2010), and van Wijk, Stam, Elfring, Zietsma, and den Hond (2013). We build on the insights of these investigations to provide illustrations of accommodation mechanisms. Our categorization of mechanisms is therefore tentative, and will require refinement and integration.

The paper by Zietsma and Lawrence (2010) explains accommodation as driven by *boundary* work and *practice* work performed by insider and outsider actors as theoretical anchors. Accommodation occurs through four institutional life cycles: stability, conflict, innovation, and restabilization. Institutional stability is abruptly interrupted by outsider actors who express grievances and manifest discontent. Breaching of organizational boundaries and disrupted practices lead to institutional conflict. In this cycle, the contestation reaches its climax, forcing incumbents to engage in interactions with challengers. In the following cycle of innovation, contestation defuses as new organizational boundaries are created to identify spaces of innovations where potential solutions can be elaborated. In the final cycle (institutional restabilization), these solutions are diffused from the initial organizations pushing it into the field (see also Lindblom 1965 and Lindblom 1977 for similar dynamics). The paper by van Wijk et al. (2013) illuminates similar interactional dynamics between challenger and incumbent organizations but proposes *mutual co-optation* as the primary de-escalating mechanism. The authors show that the more a movement is permeable, the more likely activists will engage in collaborative partnership with field-level incumbents. Importantly, cultural and relational structuration contributes to generating innovation—as shown in the vitality of Dutch sustainable tourism—but dilutes the originally transformational goals of collective action.

Three other papers document processes of accommodation and offer further insights. In Maguire and Hardy's (2009) examination of the abandonment of DDT, the authors emphasize the revolutionary pace of the change, once again triggered by collective and individual actions (i.e., outsider-driven change). While *Silent Spring* provided the initial opportunity, the growth in the intensity of the contestation led incumbent organizations to counteract with "defensive institutional work." Finally, the conflict between forces pushing for change and forces pushing for stability was settled by the recognition that the use of DDT was unnecessary, and the pesticide could be substituted with other chemicals. Critically, the authors describe a process of accommodation and show that a discursive mechanism—"*translation of problematizations*" in texts—enabled the conflict to be subdued and incumbents to experience relatively minor setbacks, despite the public outcry from the scientific community. Specifically, cumulative acts of translation reshaped the problematization of DDT in a way that selected out the most problematic issues (e.g., the necessity of chemicals). These dynamics heavily build on social movement dynamics, which are discussed more deeply in the handbook in Chapter 9 by Davis and Kim and in Chapter 10 by Prichard and Creed.

Finally, an equally insightful example is provided by Murray (2010) in her investigation of how academic geneticists skillfully transformed patenting from being seen as a threat to the logic of academic science, to a resource to protect and reinforce it. Once again, we can track a process of accommodation in Murray's account. At the outset, the possibility of patenting their discoveries came as a "shock" to mouse geneticists (2010: 351) in the midst of a "revolution" and "explosion of knowledge" in molecular biology (2010: 354). Confronted with the restrictions to exchange patented materials imposed by commercial entities, scientists strongly rejected the practice of patenting because its underpinning commercial logic was perceived as contradictory to the logic of science and its norms of open sharing. As the encroachment of the commercial logic within academia became more pressing, scientists acquiesced to commercial demands and eventually embraced patenting themselves. Murray shows that the process of change was not a simple story of scientists' relinquishment to the commercial logic. Scientists' adoption of patenting practices was driven by the crafting of sophisticated hybrid exchange strategies that transformed their meanings. Instead of encouraging industry encroachment, academics used patents to preserve the core institutional logic of science. In sum, the case shows that novel and potentially threatening practices were assimilated by *decoupling* the material act of the practices from its original meanings and then *infusing* them with meanings of the dominant logic (i.e., science). These studies have begun to reveal interesting mechanisms, although how these mechanisms are linked to delineate a process remains unclear. Nevertheless, they do offer promising directions for future explorations. Our hope is that future research will focus on this change pathway as a way to further enhance our knowledge about the mechanisms by which organizations participate as well as react to accommodative institutional change processes. In our next section, we present original research on the rise of Open Access in higher education publishing to further illuminate the relationship between these change pathways.

Pathways of Change: The case of Open Access Publishing

The case of Open Access publishing illuminates the connection between institutional change and organizational change in practice. We illustrate the ways in which the macro-level institutional change promulgated by the collective action around Open Access has altered practices and business models of various organizations within the field of publishing, including universities, professional societies and commercial publishers, libraries, and funding agencies. We begin with a historical overview of the field of scholarly publishing. We continue with an illustration of the Open Access movement and the attempt to instigate transformational institutional change in this field. Our discussion and conclusion offer insights from this case to explore temporal process relationships or patterns among the pathways of institutional change.

The Field of Scholarly Publishing

The field of scholarly publishing is a highly mature field governed by deeply institutionalized practices and norms of knowledge production and dissemination. In its most simplified structure, the field includes four primary organizational actors: *academics*, who are the primary producers (and consumers) of scientific publications; *funding agencies* who grant financial support, *publishers*, who support the dissemination of scientific results, and *university libraries*, who ensure access to publications in a timely fashion. Practices are assigned to different groups of organizations whose behaviors are informed by different institutional logics (Friedland and Alford 1991; Thornton et al. 2012). Specifically, the generation and validation of knowledge is a prerogative of academics, groups of experts that balance the logic of science (i.e., pursuit of truth and progress) with the logic of the profession (i.e., pursuit of career benefits, status, and prestige). The funding of research is a prerogative of the State, which provides resources through funding agencies on the basis that scientific progress is a national responsibility and duty (i.e., a public logic). Notably, dissemination of knowledge, which is the contentious target of the Open Access movement, is governed by the *commercial logic*. The commercial logic is dominant over the field-level practice of knowledge dissemination, as demonstrated by two elements: the dominance of the multinational for-profit corporation in this field and the widespread use of commercial exchange practices.

Open Access and Institutional Change in Scholarly Publishing

Until the Internet, there was no feasible (and cheaper) alternative to print publishing and the concentration of the market continued undisturbed. In the early 1990s, however, electronic publishing became available and its potential to dramatically lower the cost of knowledge dissemination did not go unnoticed. In 1997, a coalition of librarians and academics started a grassroots' mobilization that became later known as the Open Access (OA) movement. The movement pursued a radical goal: to use the Internet to revolutionize scholarly communication and design a more democratic system of knowledge dissemination. The movement started with a revolutionary pace, with a grassroots' mobilization of librarians and academics, calling for dramatic changes and boycotts. In 1997, the Association of US Research Libraries (ARL) took a stance against the dramatic increase in serials' subscription prices (the so called 'serials pricing crisis') and created a spin-off – the Scholarly Publishing Academic Resources Coalition (SPARC) – whose mission was to be a catalyst for change through the creation of a more competitive marketplace for research information.

The initially dispersed mobilization of activists became coordinated in 2002, when the Budapest Open Access Initiative (BOAI) was launched. At this meeting, Open Access was officially defined and strategies for implementation were elaborated. Notably, commercial publisher BioMed Central and the Public Library of Science pioneered the template of Open Access as a potential "business model." In order to recover the costs of dissemination, while ensuring free access to every reader, Open Access publishers charge authors with a fee (Article Processing Charges or APC) after the paper has been reviewed and accepted for publication. These fees are expected to be covered by scholars through the grants they receive by private and public funding agencies.

By 2005 the mobilization for Open Access had become a global movement, successfully capturing the attention of national governments, funding agencies, professional associations, and publishers. At this point in time, the possibility seemed real that the field of scholarly publishing could be turned upside down, moving away from a subscription-based model where the costs of accessing knowledge fall on the consumers of such knowledge. However, that was not the case. National policies in the United States, United Kingdom, and Continental Europe endorsed the principle of Public Access to research (National Institute of Health, 2005; Sherpa/Romeo, 2014), but not Open Access publishing as a "morally superior" business model that could (or should) displace the prevailing subscription-based model. Yet, some changes were implemented. Grant-giving organizations demanded that published research should be made freely available after a reasonable time after publication (embargo periods up to twelve months). Interestingly, the transformational change activists strived for was *not* realized. Despite a global collective mobilization and the intervention of national governments on the matter, the dissemination of knowledge still occurs in a closed system guided by the commercial logic. The subscription-based model, which entails the payment of a fee by readers in exchange for access, remains the dominant mechanism of dissemination of scholarly work.

The Case of Open Access as Failed Displacement Leading to Accommodation

By asking to make the scientific literature *immediately* available upon acceptance for publication on the Internet to *everybody* at *no cost* for the readers, the Open Access movement created a vision for a radical departure from the status quo. The proponents of Open Access strongly rejected the commercial logic that had come to dominate the exchange of knowledge and sought to restore and emphasize the key principle that scientific knowledge is a *public good* and a non-rival good; thus, it should be treated and distributed according to a public logic of unrestricted access (Willinsky 2006).

The mobilization for Open Access unfroze the field of scholarly publishing, questioning the principles of this community of organizations, where the relationships between networks of actors had been until that moment well understood, and institutionalized practices had been highly coordinated. While the movement has succeeded in making Open Access a component of the publishing field, change has been developmental. The intervention of the State (through funding agencies) has mandated that knowledge is a *semi-public* good, that if funded by the State, should be accessible after a reasonable time that protects the profits of publishers. Open Access has been accommodated, but dominant organizational forms and practices are still in place.

Discussion and Conclusions

How do we explain the failure of a potential institutional displacement and the fact that Open Access has become a permanent fixture of the field of publishing? The failure of transformational change can be explained with the failure of the deinstitutionalization process instigated by the proponents of change. Empirically, key actors in the field sought to maintain the jurisdictional boundaries of the dominant institutional logics. That required the need to assimilate Open Access within the organizational template of commercial publishers, rather than theorize Open Access publishing as a completely different template. As a result of the lack of endorsement of Open Access as an alternative template, deinstitutionalization of the dominant organizational form and associated field-level practices (*institutional displacement*) did not occur.

However, the revolutionary pace of institutional change prevents the field from going back to the status quo. This is not possible once the institutional field is in a state of relative entropy and a new template has been theorized by key field-level constituencies; further, the mediation of powerful actors (such as funding agencies) has introduced the possibility of change in the field, but change has not been implemented yet. Contradictions are still lingering as field-level actors wait for the 'dust to settle' and uncertainty to dissipate. The assimilation of Open Access into the field of publishing is explained by the possibility to temporally segment those practices and let the field reconfigure around a new arrangement. In the case of Open Access, arrangements were made so that a time limit is given to the dominant commercial logic and their representatives to control the practice. Segmentation establishes that the control of the dominant logic over the field-level practice will be *contracted* and some of the control is now taken over by a different logic (i.e., the public logic). The result of the negotiation is therefore a *settlement* (temporal segmentation) that ensures both logics have partial control over the same practice. Other examples of a similar arrangement can be found in the governance of artifacts that are considered as semi-public good. For instance, there is a time limit before a patent expires and the knowledge associated with the patent is released in the public domain; similarly, copyright laws on music expire after a certain number of years from the composition.

The case of Open Access shows how modern accounts of institutional change are likely to span across the quadrants in Figure 17.1. Thus, this empirical example sheds light on the theoretical complexity of institutional change and offers a great starting point to conceptualize temporal process relationships or patterns among the pathways of institutional change. It is theoretically interesting to think about other meta-mechanisms that may drive an episode of institutional change to begin as one pathway and end in a different pathway over time. For instance, change may start with a revolutionary pace and create the conditions for a transformational scope (*displacement*); however, over time, change may reduce its speed and become evolutionary. This may not alter the scope of change (transformational) but it may profoundly affect the length of time needed for the change to become part of the institutional field. For instance, the movement for Open Access may be following this trajectory. Started off as a revolutionary process with change proponents calling for a radical departure from the status quo, it has "cooled" off quite a bit in the last few years. Change agents are still working toward the goal of making the entire literature Open Access, but this may be the result of an accretive process of small changes, cumulating over time (*accretion*). Another interesting trajectory we can envision is the one where a change may start with a revolutionary pace and a transformational scope (*displacement*) and instead, reveal itself as being evolutionary and developmental (*alignment*). What mechanisms could underpin this trajectory? One possible mechanism could be the co-optation of key proponents of change. When co-optation occurs, change significantly slows down in pace—turning from revolutionary to evolutionary; similarly, the scope of institutional change almost inevitably is reconsidered, as tactics such as compromise and consensus makes it increasingly difficult to reform the status quo. These are theoretical speculations about possible temporal patters we could empirically observe in increasingly complex and pluralistic organizations and fields. We hope that scholars will take on the challenge of unpacking this complexity by examining institutional changes over time and across fields.

To conclude, in this chapter we have sought to delineate the state-of-the-art of the literature on institutional change to better understand the relationship between institutional change at various levels. As we discussed, once dominant assumptions about environmental fit and isomorphism dynamics between organizations and their broader contexts have been substantially loosened. This conceptual shift has enormously enriched our understanding of how change may unfold by opening up the exploration of multiplicity, variation, and increasing scholarly attention to the key role that contradictions, paradoxes, and conflict play in organizational life. Critically, the lesson from institutional theory that organizations seek legitimacy and optimal distinctiveness is still very much valid. Organizations do change to maintain coherence with their environments, while also protecting their distinctive competitive advantages, but they do so in much more complex ways than just selection of the 'fittest' or mere adaptation. In pluralistic environments, where demands exerted upon organizations are competing, responses may involve sophisticated mechanisms such as hybridity and selective decoupling. Notably, understanding how organizations change in heterogenous and complex environments requires appreciating the wider array of responses available to them.

Our typology of change pathways situates extant research to reveal important blind spots in the literature that require more systematic attention. By combining the dimensions of scope of change with pace of change, we are able to illuminate how different triggers of change lead to different kinds of institutional and organizational changes. The resulting four pathways—displacement, alignment, accretion, and accommodation—

provide insight into novel instantiations of institutional change, and explicate the heterogeneity of its manifestations at the level of the organization. Further, the recognition that institutional accretion and accommodation have gone largely undetected in the literature reveals that scholars still have plenty of room for investigating and explaining unexplored variation in paths of institutional change and their impact upon organizations. We encourage scholars to further unpack how theories of institutional and organizational change intertwine and, by doing so, continue to update and enhance our knowledge of modern organizations.

References

Allmendinger, J., and Hackman, J. R. (1996), 'Organizations in Changing Environments: The Case of East German Symphony Orchestras', *Administrative Science Quarterly*, 41/3, 337–69.

Amis, J., Slack, T., and Hinings, C. (2004), 'The Pace, Sequence, and Linearity of Radical Change', *Academy of Management Journal*, 47/1, 15–39.

Ansari, S. S., and Phillips, N. (2011), 'Text Me! New Consumer Practices and Change in Organizational Fields', *Organization Science*, 22/6, 1579–99.

Barley, S. R. (2008), 'Coalface Institutionalism', in R. Greenwood, C. Oliver, K. Sahlin-Andersson and R. Suddaby, eds., *The SAGE Handbook of Organizational Institutionalism*, (1st edn) (London: SAGE), 491–518.

Battilana, J., Leca, B., and Boxenbaum, E. (2009), "How Actors Change Institutions: Towards a Theory of Institutional Entrepreneurship", *Academy of Management Annals*, 3/1, 65–107.

Barley, S. R., and Tolbert, P. S. (1997), 'Institutionalization and Structuration: Studying the Links Between Action and Institution', *Organization Studies*, 18/1, 93–117.

Baum, J., and Rao, H. (2021), 'Multilevel Evolutionary Model', in A. H. Van de Ven and M. S. Poole, eds, *Oxford Handbook of Organizational Change and Innovation* (2nd edn) (Oxford: Oxford University Press),

Berger, P. L., and Luckmann, T. (1967), *The Social Construction of Reality: Everything That Passes for Knowledge in Society* (London: Allen Lane).

Bromley, P., and Powell, W. W. (2012), 'From Smoke and Mirrors to Walking The Talk: Decoupling in The Contemporary World', *Academy of Management Annals*, 6/1, 483–530.

Cardinale, I. (2018), 'Beyond Constraining and Enabling: Toward New Microfoundations or Institutional Theory'., *Academy of Management Review*, 43/1, 132–55.

Clark, E., and Soulsby, A. (1995), 'Transforming Former State Enterprises in the Czech Republic', *Organization Studies*, 16/2, 215–42.

Clemens, E. S., and Cook, J. M. (1999), 'Politics and Institutionalism: Explaining Durability and Change', *Annual Review of Sociology*, 25, 441–66.

Dacin, T., Goodstein, M. J., and Scott, W. R. (2002), 'Institutional Theory and Institutional Change: Introduction to the Special Research Forum', *Academy of Management Journal*, 45/1, 45–56.

Dacin, M. T., Munir, K., and Tracey, P. (2010), 'Formal dining at Cambridge Colleges: Linking Ritual Performance and Institutional Maintenance', *Academy of Management Journal*, 53/6, 1393–418.

Davis, G. F., Diekmann, K. A., and Tinsley, C. H. (1994), 'The Decline and Fall of The Conglomerate Firm in the 1980s: The Deinstitutionalization of an Organizational Form', *American Sociological Review*, 59, 547–7.

Davis, G. F., Morrill, C., Rao, H., and Soule, S. A. (2008), 'Introduction: Social Movements in Organizations and Markets'. *Administrative Science Quarterly*, 53/3, 389–94.

Davis, G. F., and Kim, E. W. (2021), 'Mobilizing Social Movements'. in A. H. Van de Ven and M. S. Poole, eds., *Oxford Handbook of Organizational Change and Innovation* (2nd edn) (Oxford: Oxford University Press).

DiMaggio, P. J. (1988), 'Interest and Agency in Institutional theory', in L. Zucker, ed., *Institutional Patterns and Organizations: Culture and Environment* (Cambridge: Ballinger), 3–21.

DiMaggio, P. J., and Powell, W. W. (1991), 'Introduction', in DiMaggio and Powell, eds., *The New Institutionalism in Organizational Analysis* (Chicago, ILL: University of Chicago Press), 1–38.

Djelic, M., and Ainamo, A. (1999), 'The Coevolution of New Organizational Forms in the Fashion Industry: A Historical and Comparative Study of France, Italy, and the USA', *Organization Science*, 10/5, 622–37.

Durand, R., and McGuire, J. (2005), 'Legitimating Agencies in the Face of Selection: The Case of AACSB', *Organization Studies*, 26/2, 165–96.

Emirbayer, M., and Mische, A. (1998), 'What Is Agency?' *American Journal of Sociology*, 103, 962–1023.

Freeman, J., Carroll, G. R., and Hannan, M. T. (1983), 'The Liability of Newness: Age Dependence in Organizational Death Rates', *American Sociological Review*, 48, 692–710.

Friedland, R., and Alford, R. R. (1991), 'Bringing Society Back In: Symbols, Practices and Institutional Contradictions', in W. W. Powell and P. J. DiMaggio, eds., *The New Institutionalism in Organizational Analysis* (Chicago: University of Chicago Press), 232–63.

Furnari, S. (2014), 'Interstitial Spaces: Microinteraction Settings and the Genesis of New Practices Between Institutional Fields', *Academy of Management Review*, 39/4, 439–62.

Gaba, V. and Meyer, A. (2021), 'Organizational Adaptation to Industry Revolution', in A. H. Van de Ven, and M. S. Poole, eds., *Oxford Handbook of Organizational Change and Innovation* (2nd edn) (Oxford: Oxford University Press).

Garud, R. and Turunen, M. (2021), 'Partial Cumulative Syntheses Model of Innovation', in A. H. Van de Ven and M. S. Poole, eds., *Oxford Handbook of Organizational Change and Innovation* (2nd edn) (Oxford: Oxford University Press).

Giddens, A. (1984), *The Constitution of Society: Outline of the Theory Of Structuration* (Berkeley and Los Angeles: University of California Press).

Ginsberg, A., and Buchholtz, A. (1990), 'Converting to For-Profit Status: Corporate Responsiveness to Radical Change', *Academy of Management Journal*, 33/3, 445–77.

Glynn, M. A., and Abzug, R. (2002), 'Institutionalizing Identity: Symbolic Isomorphism and Organizational Names', *Academy of Management Journal*, 45/1, 267–80.

Granqvist, N., and Gustafsson, R. (2016), 'Temporal Institutional Work', *Academy of Management Journal*, 59/3, 1009–35.

Gray, B., Purdy, J. M., and Ansari, S. S. (2015), 'From Interactions to Institutions: Microprocesses of Framing And Mechanisms for the Structuring of Institutional Fields', *Academy of Management Review*, 40/1, 115–43.

Greenwood, R., Díaz, A. M., Li, S. X., and Lorente, J. C. (2010), 'The Multiplicity of Institutional Logics and the Heterogeneity of Organizational Responses', *Organization Science*, 21/2, 521–39.

Greenwood, R., and Hinings, C. R. (1996), 'Understanding Radical Organizational Change: Bringing Together the Old and the New Institutionalism', *Academy of Management Review*, 21/4, 1022–54.

Greenwood, R., Raynard, M., Kodeih, F., Micelotta, E. R., and Lounsbury, M. (2011), 'Institutional Complexity and Organizational Responses', *Academy of Management Annals*, 5/1, 317–71.

Greenwood, R., and Suddaby, R. (2006), 'Institutional Entrepreneurship in Mature Fields: The Big Five Accounting Firms', *Academy of Management Journal*, 49/1, 27–48.

Greenwood, R., Suddaby, R., and Hinings, C. R. (2002), 'Theorizing Change: The Role of Professional Associations in the Transformation of Institutionalized Fields', *Academy of Management Journal*, 45/1, 58–80.

Hampel, C. E., Lawrence, T. B., Tracey, P., Greenwood, R., and Oliver, C. (2017), 'Institutional Work: Taking Stock and Making It Matter', in R. Greenwood, C. Oliver, T. B. Lawrence, and R. Meyer, eds., *The Sage Handbook of Organizational Institutionalism* (2nd edn) (London, Sage), 558–90.

Hargadon, A. B., and Douglas, Y. (2001), 'When Innovations Meet Institutions: Edison and the Design of the Electric Light', *Administrative Science Quarterly*, 46/3, 476–501.

Helms, W. S., Oliver, C., and Webb, K. (2012), 'Antecedents of Settlement on a New Institutional Practice: Negotiation of the ISO 26000 Standard on Social Responsibility', *Academy of Management Journal*, 55/5, 1120–45.

Hernes, T., Pulk, K., and Hussenot, A. (2021), 'Time and Temporality of Change', in A. H. Van de Ven, and M. S. Poole, eds., *Oxford Handbook of Organizational Change and Innovation* (2nd edn) (Oxford: Oxford University Press),

Hiatt, S. R., Sine, W. D., and Tolbert, P. S. (2009), 'From Pabst to Pepsi: The Deinstitutionalization of Social Practices and the Creation of Entrepreneurial Opportunities', *Administrative Science Quarterly*, 54/4, 635–67.

Hirsch, P. M., and Lounsbury, M. (1997), 'Ending the Family Quarrel: Toward a Reconciliation of "Old" and "New" Institutionalisms', *American Behavioral Scientist*, 40/4, 406–18.

Holm, P. (1995), 'The Dynamics of Institutionalization: Transformation Processes in Norwegian Fisheries', *Administrative Science Quarterly*, 40/3, 398–422.

Jay, J. (2013), 'Navigating Paradox as a Mechanism of Change and Innovation in Hybrid Organizations', *Academy of Management Journal*, 56/1, 137–59.

Klarner, P., and Raisch, S. (2013), 'Move to the Beat—Rhythms of Change and Firm Performance', *Academy of Management Journal*, 56/1, 160–84.

Kraatz, M. S., and Moore, J. H. (2002), 'Executive Migration and Institutional Change', *Academy of Management Journal*, 45/1, 120–43.

Kriauciunas, A., and Kale, P. (2006), 'The Impact of Socialist Imprinting and Search on Resource Change: A Study of Firms in Lithuania', *Strategic Management Journal*, 27/7, 659–79.

Lawrence, T. B., Winn, M. I., and Jennings, P. D. (2001), 'The Temporal Dynamics of Institutionalization', *Academy of Management Review*, 26/4, 624–44.

Leblebici, H., Salancik, G. R., Copay, A., and King, T. (1991), 'Institutional Change and the Transformation of Interorganizational Fields: An Organizational History of the US Radio Broadcasting Industry', *Administrative Science Quarterly*, 36/3, 333–63.

Lindblom, C. (1965), *The Intelligence of Democracy* (New York: Free Press).

Lindblom, C. (1977), *Politics and Markets* (New York: Basic Books).

Lok, J., and De Rond, M. (2013), 'On the Plasticity of Institutions: Containing and Restoring Practice Breakdowns at the Cambridge University Boat Club', *Academy of Management Journal*, 56/1, 185–207.

Lounsbury, M., and Glynn, M. A. (2001), 'Cultural Entrepreneurship: Stories, Legitimacy, and the Acquisition of Resources', *Strategic Management Journal*, 22/6–7, 545–64.

Lounsbury, M., and Crumley, E. T. (2007), 'New Practice Creation: An Institutional Perspective on Innovation', *Organization Studies*, 28/7, 993–1012.

Lounsbury, M., and Glynn, M. A. (2019), *Cultural Entrepreneurship: A New Agenda for the Study of Entrepreneurial Processes and Possibilities* (Cambridge: Cambridge University Press).

Lounsbury, M., Hirsch, P., and Klinkerman, S. (1998), 'Institutional Upheaval and Performance Variation: A Theoretical Agenda and Illustration from the Deregulation of Banking in the Field of Finance', *Advances in Strategic Management*, 15, 129–46.

Lounsbury, M., and Wang, M. (2020), 'Into the Clearing: Back to the Future of Constitutive Institutional Analysis', *Organization Theory*, 1, 1–27.

Maguire, S., and Hardy, C. (2009), 'Discourse and Deinstitutionalization: The Decline of DDT', *Academy of Management Journal*, 52/1, 148–78.

Maguire, S., Hardy, C., and Lawrence, T. B. (2004), 'Institutional Entrepreneurship in Emerging Fields: HIV/AIDS Treatment Advocacy in Canada', *Academy of Management Journal*, 47/5, 657–79.

Mair, J., and Marti, I. (2009), 'Entrepreneurship in and around Institutional Voids: A Case Study from Bangladesh', *Journal of Business Venturing*, 24/5, 419–35.

Marcus, A. and Malen, J. (2021), 'Externally-Regulated Change', in A. H. Van de Ven, and M. S. Poole, eds, *Oxford Handbook of Organizational Change and Innovation* (2nd edn) (Oxford: Oxford University Press).

Meyer, A. (1982), 'Adapting to Environmental Jolts', *Administrative Science Quarterly*, 27/4, 515–37.

Meyer, A. D., Goes, J. B. and Brooks, G. R. (1993), 'Organizations Reacting to Hyperturbulence', in Huber et al., eds., *Organization Change and Redesign* (New York, NY: Oxford University Press), 66–111.

Meyer, J. W., and Jepperson, R. L. (2000), 'The 'Actors' of Modern Society: The Cultural Construction of Social Agency', *Sociological Theory*, 18/1, 100–20.

Micelotta, E., Lounsbury, M., and Greenwood, R. (2017), 'Pathways of Institutional Change: An Integrative Review and Research Agenda', *Journal of Management*, 43/6, 1885–910.

Micelotta, E. R., and Washington, M. (2013), 'Institutions and Maintenance: The Repair Work of Italian Professions', *Organization Studies*, 34/8, 1137–70.

Munir, K. A., and Phillips, N. (2005), 'The Birth of the 'Kodak Moment': Institutional Entrepreneurship and the Adoption of New Technologies', *Organization Studies*, 26/11, 1665–87.

Murray, F. (2010), 'The Oncomouse that Roared: Hybrid Exchange Strategies as a Source of Distinction at the Boundary of Overlapping institutions', *American Journal of Sociology*, 116/2, 341–88.

Powell, W. W., and Colyvas, J. A. (2008), 'Microfoundations of Institutional Theory', in R. Greenwood, C. Oliver, K. Sahlin-Andersson, and R. Suddaby, eds., *The Sage Handbook of Organizational Institutionalism* (1st edn) (London: Sage), 276–98.

Prichard, C., and Creed, D. (2021), 'Agency in Social Movements', in A. H. Van de Ven, and M. S. Poole, eds, *Oxford Handbook of Organizational Change and Innovation* (2nd edn) (Oxford: Oxford University Press).

Purdy, J. M., and Gray, B. (2009), 'Conflicting Logics, Mechanisms of Diffusion, and Multilevel Dynamics in Emerging Institutional Fields', *Academy of Management Journal*, 52/2, 355–80.

Rao, H., Monin, P., and Durand, R. (2003), 'Institutional Change in Toque Ville: Nouvelle Cuisine as an Identity Movement in French Gastronomy', *American Journal of Sociology*, 108/4, 795–843.

Rao, H., Monin, P., and Durand, R. (2005), 'Border Crossing: Bricolage and the Erosion of Categorical Boundaries In French Gastronomy', *American Sociological Review*, 70/6, 968–91.

Romanelli, E., and Tushman, M. L. (1994), 'Organizational Transformation as Punctuated Equilibrium: An Empirical Test', *Academy of Management Journal*, 37/5, 1141–66.

Schildt, H., and Perkmann, M. (2017), 'Organizational Settlements: Theorizing How Organizations Respond to Institutional Complexity', *Journal of Management Inquiry*, 26/2, 139–45.

Schneiberg, M., and Lounsbury, M. (2017), 'Social Movements and the Dynamics of Institutions and Organizations', in R. Greenwood, C. Oliver, T. B. Lawrence, and R. Meyer, eds., *The SAGE Handbook of Organizational Institutionalism* (2nd edn) (London: Sage), 281–310.

Schumpeter, J. A. (1939), *Business Cycles: A Theoretical, Historical and Statistical Analysis of the Capitalist Process* (2 vols) New York: McGraw Hill.

Scott, W. R. (2010), 'Reflections: The Past and Future of Research on Institutions and Institutional Change', *Journal of Change Management*, 10/1, 5–21.

Scott, W. R. (2014), *Institutions and Organizations: Ideas, Interests and Identities* (Los Angeles, CA: SAGE).

Seo, M-G., and Creed, W. E. D. (2002), 'Institutional Contradictions, Praxis, and Institutional Change: A Dialectical Perspective', *Academy of Management Review*, 27/2, 222–47.

Sewell, W. H. Jr. (1992), 'A Theory of Structure: Duality, Agency, and Transformation', *American Journal of Sociology*, 98/1, 1–29.

Smets, M., Aristidou, A., and Whittington, R. (2017), 'Towards a Practice-Driven Institutionalism', in R. Greenwood, C. Oliver, T. B. Lawrence, and R. Meyer, eds., *The Sage Handbook of Organizational Institutionalism* (2nd edn) (London: Sage), 384–411.

Smets, M., Jarzabkowski, P., Burke, G. T., and Spee, P. (2015), 'Reinsurance Trading In Lloyd's of London: Balancing Conflicting-Yet-Complementary Logics in Practice', *Academy of Management Journal*, 58/3, 932–70.

Smets, M., Morris, T., and Greenwood, R. (2012), 'From Practice to Field: A Multilevel Model of Practice-Driven Institutional Change', *Academy of Management Journal*, 55/4, 877 904.

Stinchcombe, A. L. (1997), 'On the Virtues of the Old Institutionalism', *Annual Review of Sociology*, 23/1, 1–18.

Thornton, P. H., and Ocasio, W. (1999), 'Institutional Logics and the Historical Contingency of Power in Organizations: Executive Succession in the Higher Education Publishing Industry, 1958-1990', *American Journal of Sociology*, 105/3, 801–43.

Thornton, P. H., Ocasio, W., and Lounsbury, M. (2012), *The Institutional Logics Perspective: A New Approach to Culture, Structure, and Process* (Oxford: Oxford University Press).

Tucker, D. J., Singh, J. V. and Meinhard, A. G. (1990), 'Organizational Form, Population Dynamics, and Institutional Change: The Founding Patterns of Voluntary Organizations', *Academy of Management Journal*, 33/1, 151–78.

Usher, A. P. (1950), *A History of Mechanical Innovations* (Cambridge: Harvard University Press).

Van de Ven, A. H., and Hargrave, T. J. (2004), 'Social, Technical, and Institutional Change', in M. S. Poole, and A. H. Van de Ven, eds., *Handbook of Organizational Change and Innovation* (2nd edn) (Oxford: Oxford University Press), 259–303.

Van de Ven, A., and Lifschitz, A. (2009), 'John R. Commons: Back to The Future of Organization Studies', in Paul Adler, ed., *Classical Sociology and the Future of Organization Studies* (2nd edn) (Oxford, UK: Oxford University Press), 510–34.

van Wijk, J., Stam, W., Elfring, T., Zietsma, C., and den Hond, F. (2013), 'Activists and Incumbents Structuring Change: The Interplay of Agency, Culture and Networks in Field Evolution', *Academy of Management Journal*, 55/2, 358–86.

Werner, M. D., and Cornelissen, J. P. (2014), 'Framing The Change: Switching and Blending Frames and their Role in Instigating Institutional Change', *Organization Studies*, 35/10, 1449–72.

White, S., and Linden, G. (2002), 'Organizational and Industrial Response to Market Liberalization: The Interaction of Pace, Incentive and Capacity to Change', *Organization Studies*, 23/6, 917–48.

Whitley, R., and Czaban, L. (1998), 'Institutional Transformation and Enterprise Change in an Emergent Capitalist Economy: The Case of Hungary', *Organization Studies*, 19/2, 259–80.

Willinsky, J. (2006), *The Access Principle: The Case for Open Access to Research and Scholarship* (Cambridge, Mass: MIT Press).

Wright, A. L., and Zammuto, R. F. (2013), 'Wielding the willow: Processes of institutional change in English county cricket'. *Academy of Management Journal*, 56(1), 308–30.

Zajac, E. J., and Kraatz, M. S. (1993), 'A Diametric Forces Model of Strategic Change: Assessing the Antecedents and Consequences of Restructuring in the Higher Education Industry', *Strategic Management Journal*, 14/S1, 83–102.

Zietsma, C., Groenewegen, P., Logue, D., and Hinings, C. (2016), 'Field or Fields? Building the Scaffolding for Cumulation of Research on Institutional Fields', *Academy of Management Annals*, 11/1, 391–450.

Zietsma, C., and Lawrence, T. B. (2010), 'Institutional Work in the Transformation of an Organizational Field: The Interplay of Boundary Work and Practice Work', *Administrative Science Quarterly*, 55/2, 189–221.

PART IV

EVOLUTIONARY MODELS OF CHANGE

CHAPTER 18

EVOLUTIONARY DYNAMICS OF ORGANIZATIONAL POPULATIONS AND COMMUNITIES

JOEL A. C. BAUM AND HAYAGREVA RAO

THE ability of societies to respond to social problems may hinge crucially upon the diversity of organizational forms, and in the long run, in a dynamic environment, diversity can be maintained or increased by the rise of new forms.[1] Moreover, new forms are vital engines of organizational evolution. Indeed, an important component of organizational change, at the macro-level, consists of the selection and replacement of existing organizational forms by new organizational forms. Furthermore, since new organizational forms are structural incarnations of technologies, beliefs, values, and norms they emerge in tandem with social movements, new institutions, and new technologies and help to foster and reflect cultural and technical change in societies. For these reasons where new organizational forms come from is a central question for organization theorists.

New organizational forms are novel recombinations of goals, authority relations (including governance structures), technologies, and client markets. The evolution of a new organizational form involves a complex interplay between ecological and historical (i.e., genealogical) processes. A new form's emergence and character are shaped both by opportunities to create new resource spaces and the characteristics and creativity of, and competition among, existing organizations and entrepreneurs. It begins with the differential proliferation of variations within existing populations that lead, ultimately, to an organizational founding, the product of innovative thought, that jumps out of an

[1] An early version of this chapter was presented at the Macro-Level Perspectives on Organizational Change and Development symposium, Academy of Management, Chicago, August 1999. We are most grateful to Kim Bates, Scott Poole, and Andy Van de Ven for conversations, comments and ideas that helped us to improve this chapter.

established form to create a new one. New organizational forms congeal as the result of processes that isolate or segregate one set of organizations from another, including technological incompatibilities, institutional actions such as government regulations, and imprinting. The rise of new organizational forms is an essential source of organization variation, and plays a vital role in the creation of organizational diversity.

Organizational populations—local, coevolving groupings of organizations that embody the same organizational form—develop relationships with organizational populations engaged in other activities that bind them into organizational communities. Organizational communities constitute functionally integrated systems of interacting organizational populations (Hawley 1950). Organizational populations, not organizations, interact to shape communities. In an organizational community, the outcomes for organizations of any one population are fundamentally intertwined with those of organizations in other populations that belong to the same community system. At a still higher level, organizational communities interact to form organizational ecosystems, including national economies (Baum and Korn 1994).

Although Hannan and Freeman (1977) called for research at the population level as a first step toward the study of community-level phenomena, research in organizational ecology remains focused primarily on *Population Ecology* models of the growth and decline of local populations of established organizational forms. *Community Ecology* models emphasize processes of creation (i.e., speciation) and demise (i.e., extinction) of organizational populations and forms, and address the evolution of community structures that bind together a set of organizational populations and affect the persistence and stability of the community as a whole. The original question of organizational ecology—why there are so many kinds of organizations—has thus yet to be pursued fastidiously. Consequently, we still know too little about processes leading to the emergence of new organizational forms, or the structures of organizational inheritance that foster their persistence and transformation over time.

If, however, the current diversity of organizations is to be conceived as a reflection of the "cumulative effect of a long history of variation and selection" (Hannan and Freeman 1989: 20), then an explanation of how new organizational forms arise, become different, and remain different through time is required. In this chapter, we attempt to answer these questions by analyzing population and community-level dynamics through an evolutionary, Variation-Selection-Retention (VSR) lens (Aldrich 1979, 1999; Campbell 1965). We offer a view of organizational populations and communities as residing in a nested hierarchy where they coevolve and present a general framework—the "dual-hierarchy" model (Baum and Singh 1994a)—that identifies and interconnects the elements and processes we think are basic to organizational evolution. After presenting this framework, we turn to more detailed analyses of evolutionary dynamics at two levels of organization:

- *Micro-evolutionary* processes that shape persistence and change over time among organizations within a particular lineage, or organizational form
- *Macro-evolutionary* processes that shape persistence and change over time within a community of organizational forms, and through which new organizational forms arise

Our analysis of population and community-level evolution emphasizes the roles of institutional change (e.g., industry deregulation, globalization, market reforms), technological innovation cycles (e.g., technological discontinuities, dominant designs), entrepreneurs, and social movements as triggers of organizational variation. We explore how institutional and technological change transforms the dynamics of organizational communities by shifting the boundaries of organizational forms, destabilizing or reinforcing existing community structures, giving rise to consensus and/or conflict oriented social movements, and creating opportunities for entrepreneurs and venture capitalists to shape new organizational forms. Our analysis of population-level VSR aims to consolidate and refine earlier treatments of these processes; our analysis of community-level VSR, in contrast, represents one of the first comprehensive treatments of these processes (see also Aldrich 1999; Hunt and Aldrich 1998), and so will be, by necessity, more speculative in nature. We will conclude by highlighting some basic connections between evolutionary dynamics at population and community-levels that emerge from our analysis.

Evolutionary Dynamics of Organizations

Organizational evolution can be conceptualized as the interplay between two kinds of processes, *interaction* and *replication*, acting on two kinds of entities, *ecological* and *genealogical*, at a variety of levels of organization (Baum and Singh 1994a). Genealogical entities pass on their information largely intact in successive replications. Ecological entities, the structural and behavioral expressions of the genealogical entities, interact with the environment and this interaction causes replication to be differential. "Organizational evolution is the result of genealogical entities replicating, ecological entities interacting, the net effect of these interactions being the differential persistence of the genealogical entities that produced them" (Baum and Singh 1994a: 4).

A theory of organizational evolution, indeed any evolutionary system, minimally requires these two kinds of processes (i.e., interaction and replication) and two kinds of entities (i.e., ecological and genealogical). No theory of evolution can be complete without careful consideration of the structure and function of moment-by-moment ecological systems. Neither is a theory of evolution complete without consideration of the source of the information that supplies the entities to the ecological arena. In the evolutionary view, history and current function are intricately related. We need an understanding of the integration of interactive processes of resource exchange and transformation on the one hand, and historical processes of information conservation and transmission on the other.

Although research in organizational ecology has informed us about interaction processes within populations (for a review, see Baum 1996), it has yet to deal comprehensively with the community-level problem of the emergence and disappearance of organizational forms, and has only rarely attempted to link ecological processes of interaction and genealogical processes of replication. Consequently, we still know very little about the genealogical side of organizational evolution—the structures of organizational inheritance and speciation. Whereas biological inheritance is based primarily on propagation of genes, inheritance processes for social organizations appear very different, suggesting more equivocal organizational genealogies and evolutionary dynamics perhaps strikingly different from those expected with purely genetic transmission.

Fortunately, Darwin's idea of evolution—descent with modification—is not tied to particular features of biological inheritance. Natural selection is a very general mechanism likely to operate in any system of inheritance that meets two conditions: 1) there is heritable (blind) variation in form and 2) the variation in form is related to variation in survival and replication. Whenever these two conditions are met, the forms with the highest probability of being transmitted to the next generation will tend to increase in number (Campbell 1965).

The Dual Hierarchy of Organizational Evolution

Organizational evolution is frequently conceived to take place simultaneously at multiple hierarchical levels (e.g., face-to-face group, organization, population, community) (Aldrich 1979, 1999; Baum and Singh 1994a; Rosenkopf & Nerkar 1999). The hierarchies relevant to organizational evolution are *inclusive*, with levels nested one within the other. Wholes are composed of parts at lower levels of organization, and are themselves parts of more extensive wholes. Organizational communities, for example, are composed of populations of organizational forms, which themselves are composed of organizations, and so on. The nesting of entities into larger entities at a higher level of organization creates a system of levels. Each level constitutes a "node of selection" at which organizational entities are either retained or eliminated (Baum and Singh 1994a; Campbell 1974, 1994).

Ecological and Genealogical Entities

These entities form the various levels of two inclusive hierarchies, one *genealogical*, and the other *ecological* summarized in Table 18.1 (Baum and Singh 1994a). The *genealogical hierarchy* is formed by components of *institutional memory* engaged in the preservation and dissemination of production and organizing information. It is composed of *lineages*, entities that persist over time through replication in the same or a similar state. The *ecological* hierarchy reflects the economic structure and integration (i.e., resource exchange and transformation) of organizational systems. It is composed of *historical* entities, the result of the cumulative effect of variation and selection over time, and the structural and behavioral expressions of entities of the genealogical class.

Table 18.1 Genealogical and Ecological Entities

Genealogical Hierarchy	Ecological Hierarchy
	Ecosystem. A group of coevolving communities and its natural, social, technical, and economic environment, between which resources are regularly cycled.
Polythyletic Grouping. An aggregate of one or more organizational forms descended from two or more immediate common ancestors, though ultimately from a common ancestor.	**Community.** A group of coevolving organizational populations connected and integrated by a network of commensalistic and symbiotic interdependencies.
Organizational Form. A polythyletic group of competence sharing populations. A set of highly probably combinations of routines temporarily housed among all its included members at any given time.	**Population.** A group of coevolving organizations connected by commensalistic interdependencies that embody similar combinations of competences and routines.
Organization. A temporary repository of routines embodied in the organization's employees and technologies at any given time.	**Organization.** A group of coevolving workgroups and jobs. External expression of competences and routines embodied in the organization's employees and technologies at any given time.
Competence. An integrated set of interdependent routines.	**Workgroup.** A group of coevolving jobs. External expression of competences and routines embodied by group members at any given time.
Routine. An element of production and organizing knowledge and skill.	**Job.** A coevolving set of tasks or pattern of activity performed by a single individual. External expression of routines held by the employee at any given time.

Adapted from Baum and Singh (1994a: 10)

Organizations constitute a level in both hierarchies (Baum and Singh 1994a). As members of organizational forms (genealogical entities), organizations are packages of routinized competence, temporary repositories of production and organizing know-how (McKelvey 1982; Winter 1990). As members of populations (ecological entities), organizations are the external manifestation of the production and organizing competence they carry at any given time (McKelvey 1982). As such, organizations are transmitters of the routines that embody the knowledge, capabilities, beliefs, values, and memory of the organization and its decision-makers, bearers of adaptations, and expressors of variation in populations. And, organizations, varying among one another, are shuffled as units of selection. Organizations thus have both ecological and genealogical roles:

they are the nexus of environmental interaction and the conservation of lineages of production and organizing routines and competencies.

Interaction and Replication Processes

Two classes of processes, *interaction* and *replication*, distinguish the ecological and genealogical hierarchies, respectively (Baum and Singh 1994a). Processes in the ecological hierarchy are concerned with the mutual interactions between ecological entities at the same level of organization (e.g., between organizations within populations, and populations within communities) that are connected to the resource exchanges that propel ecological entities. Social, technical, and economic environmental conditions strongly implicated in patterns of organizational persistence and change, shape organizational evolution through their influence on ecological entities, and by forming part of the ecological hierarchy at the ecosystem level.

Dynamic interactions at each level hold together entities at the next-higher level of the nested ecological hierarchy. Interactions among jobs bind workgroups together, which in turn bind organizations together. Interactions among organizations of the same form constitute populations. Competition, mutualism, collective action, collective learning, and other ecological processes at this level are the characteristic phenomena responsible for producing the variables most frequently studied by organizational ecologists—organizational density, rates of founding, failure, and growth. When we become concerned with the interactions of populations of different organizational forms, we have moved up to the community level. Populations, not organizations, interact to shape communities. Ecological processes at this level include interpopulation competition, symbiotic interactions, institutional entrepreneurship and social movements related to new organizational forms, and changes in environmental carrying capacities. Finally, organizational communities interact to form ecosystems.

In the genealogical hierarchy, processes are those related to the production of new entities from old: the replication of lineages of routines, organizations, and organizational forms. Each level of the genealogical hierarchy is maintained by production of lower-level entities: routines must reproduce themselves for organizations to persist, organizations must produce more organizations for organizational forms to persist, and organizational forms must fragment for *polyphyletic groupings* to endure. Polyphyletic groupings are historical entities, comprised of one or more organizational forms, and formed by the production of new organizational forms from old, and constitute the highest level of organization in the genealogical hierarchy. Although reproduction occurs at all levels of the genealogical hierarchy, replication appears to be concentrated primarily at the lower levels of the genealogical hierarchy. That is, because they have short generation lengths compared to higher-level entities, most replication is replication of lower-level entities (e.g., routines, organizations) (see, e.g., Miner 1990, 1991). As a result, timescales are shorter, and the rate of evolution faster at lower levels of organization (Baum 1999; Campbell 1994).

VSR Processes

Evolution at all these levels of organization reflects the operation of three basic processes: *Variation, Selection,* and *Retention,* or *VSR* (Aldrich 1979, 1999; McKelvey 1982, 1997). This view of change, which is derived from Campbell's (1965) seminal article, is based upon an analogy between "natural selection in biological evolution and the selective propagation of cultural forms" (Campbell 1965: 26). The three key elements of Campbell's model are (1965: 27):

1. The occurrence of variations: heterogeneous, haphazard, "blind," "chance," "random," but in any event variable. (The mutation process in organic evolution, and exploratory responses in learning).
2. Consistent selection criteria: selective elimination, selective propagation, selective retention, of certain types of variations. (Differential survival of certain mutants in organic evolution, differential reinforcement of certain responses in learning).
3. A mechanism for the preservation, duplication, or propagation of the positively selected variants (the rigid duplication process of the chromosome gene system in plants and animals, memory in learning).

Campbell emphasized "blindness" to capture the accidental nature of variation and emergent nature of consequent behavior, processes, functions, and structure:

> 'Deliberate' or 'intelligent' variations would do as well as 'blind,' 'haphazard,' 'chance,' 'random,' or 'spontaneous' ones. They might be better insofar as they could be preselected. But they might be worse in that they could be restricted to the implications of already achieved wisdom and would not be likely to go beyond it. One of the services of terms like 'blind' and 'haphazard'... is that they emphasize that elaborate adaptive social systems... could have emerged, just as did termite societies, without any self-conscious planning or foresightful action. It provides a plausible model for social systems that are 'wiser' than the individuals who constitute the society, or than the rational social science of the ruling elite. It provides an anticipation of powerful 'inadvertent' social change processes in our own day, which may be adaptive in unforeseen or unwanted ways.
>
> (Campbell 1965: 28)

Campbell settled on the term *blind* variation to emphasize the danger of basing variations on *a priori* understanding or knowledge of their adaptive outcomes. Selection does not operate by comparing any one variation to some *hypothetical* best variation, it chooses among *presented* variations that which most improves an organization's fitness (Romanelli 1999). As Campbell (1988: 173) observed, "Being a purposeful problem solver... does not make one clairvoyant or prescient." Adaptation involves exploring the unknown, going beyond existing knowledge and recipes, and "fumbling in the dark" (Campbell 1974: 147).

In organizations, however, whether due to institutionalized understandings about right and appropriate forms of activity (Zucker 1977), or evolution of formal control systems (e.g., employment or accounting systems), members tend to develop preferences for certain responses or variations. Trial-and-error learning over the history of an organization's trials of variations may thus predispose its members to future trial or avoidance of certain kinds of variations. Such "vicarious selectors" act to shortcut purely blind variation by eliminating dangerous or inadequate actions before they are executed (Campbell 1965). As a result, variations may be differentially probable, limited to certain forms, and not independent of one another over successive trials. As long, however, as any regularity in exploration is independent of foreknowledge of the correct response, VSR processes will continue to operate effectively. Thus, new variations need not be blind with respect to outcomes of *prior* variations—but they must be blind with respect to their *own*outcomes. So, while vicarious selectors channel evolution in certain directions, evolution will occur as long as they are subject to selection themselves (Campbell 1965).

In the VSR model, simultaneous interaction of (blind) variation, (competitive) selection, and retention processes, termed a *Darwin machine* (Plotkin, 1993), unfold endlessly, moving systems toward greater fitness over time. Variation generates the raw material from which selection is made. Retention processes preserve the selected variation. Combined, (blind) variation and (competitive) selective retention generate "evolution in the direction of better fit to the selective system" (Campbell 1965: 27). If any of the three components is missing, however, no fit or order will occur.

Within and Cross-Level Processes

Darwin machines operate at each level of organization, setting the evolutionary process in motion by searching over time for more effective variations. This search can be envisioned as an ongoing exploration of possible configurations (variations) with differing values on some measure of goodness or fitness, where fitness is a function of the entity and its environment, and entities that have the highest fitness are selected and retained. At each level of organization, multiple Darwin machines operate simultaneously and interactively (e.g., multiple employees and workgroups search for more effective routines or combinations of routines). Their explorations can be visualized as movement through a fitness landscape, where configurations correspond to points in a two-dimensional (horizontal) space and fitness corresponds to the configuration's value on a third (vertical) dimension (Kauffman 1993). Local fitness maxima correspond to peaks in the landscape, local minima to valleys.

Processes within each level of each hierarchy (e.g., innovation, replication, competition), when taken alone, constitutes only one element of the overall evolutionary process, however. There are also interactive effects among levels within each hierarchy. Organizational evolution is above all a product of these coupled interactions. Although there is a degree of autonomy of event and process within each hierarchical level, and each level is taken to operate quasi-independently, a dynamic VSR system in its own right, there is also both upward and downward causation (Campbell, 1974, 1990). Interactions across levels limit the kinds of processes that can occur at a given level and regulate those that do. For example, people constitute, and are acted upon by, organizations and interactions among organizations. Their understanding of, beliefs about, and attitudes toward organizations help shape the decisions from which organizations are formed. These decisions (variations) are injected into the higher level of the populations, where selection, random drift, and entrepreneurship take over as dynamics. More generally, upward causation implies that, at each level, persistent features of the previous level constrain what emerges at the next level. Downward causation operates as follows:

Where natural selection operates through life and death at a higher level of organization, the laws of the higher level selective system determine in part the distribution of lower level events and substances. Description of an intermediate-level phenomenon is not complete by describing its possibility and implementation in lower level terms. Its presence, prevalence, or distribution... will often require reference to laws at a higher level of organization as well.... all processes at the lower levels of a hierarchy are restrained by, and act in conformity to, the laws of the higher levels (Campbell 1990: 4).

> Selection among higher-level entities thus shapes and constrains subsequent lower-level VSR processes. As a result, VSR processes at one level (e.g., organizational learning) can dramatically affect variability at lower levels (Tyre and Orlikowski 1994). Such cross-level interactions are likely to be strongest across contiguous levels with their significance declining as the levels involved become increasingly remote. Thus, what goes on at one level of the evolutionary hierarchy shapes processes and events at other levels, with dynamics connected most strongly at adjacent lower and upper levels. Systems of this type, hierarchical structures with feedback in which underlying components comprise and react to the overall organization, are termed *heterarchies*.
>
> (Hofstader 1979)

Importantly, higher-level adaptation does not arise automatically from lower level adaptation. It would be highly unusual in the evolution of nested hierarchical systems for a competence or routine that optimizes fitness for components of the system to optimize prospects for the higher levels of the system or the system as a whole (Baum 1999; Campbell 1994, March 1994). While selection among organizations can cause them to become well designed to survive, for example, adaptation at the level of individual organizations need not lead to adaptation at the level of populations. Selection within an organizational population acts on organizations' *relative* fitness and is insensitive to the fitness of the population per se. A competence or routine that decreases the fitness of the entire population will be favored if it yields individual organizations a bigger slice of the smaller pie. Similarly, one that benefits the entire population but involves a cost for individual organizations will be selected against. What is best for organizational entities at one level is not, however, generally best for those at other levels. As a result, while attempting to improve their own fitness, entities at different levels compete for resources across (as well as within) levels, complicating organizational evolution. Competitive saturation can serve to tighten relationships among levels, triggering positive and negative feedback, and influencing the mix of selection and adaptation events (Van de Ven and Grazman 1999).

A population of well-adapted individuals (in the sense of maximizing relative fitness) thus need not also be a well-adapted population. A well-adapted population might regulate its size to avoid overexploiting its resources, cooperate to defend itself against rival populations, or improve its common core technology, but none of these traits is likely to evolve when selection is insensitive to the welfare of the population per se. Functional organization at any level of the organizational hierarchy requires a corresponding process of selection *at that level*. Populations can become well designed only by a process of between-population selection, and communities can become well designed only by a process of between-community selection (Baum 1999; Campbell 1994; Sober and Wilson 1998). Relatedly, Van de Ven and Grazman (1999) suggest that the relationships among the various levels can be positive or negative, and that stability results from a balance between positive selection at one level (e.g., population) and negative selection at a higher level (e.g., community). Even if selection among entities at a given hierarchical level enhances their fitness, however, because the rate of evolution is faster at lower levels of organization, the fitness achieved at the higher level may be eroded constantly by lower level entities that "out-evolve" their higher-level counterparts.

Ecological and Genealogical Interactions

In the dual-hierarchy framework, however, it is interactions between ecological and genealogical hierarchies that integrate all the entities taking part in the process of organizational evolution. The elements of these two hierarchies interact, regulating change within one another, and, as byproducts, create the patterns and events of organizational evolution: the persistence and the modification of the entities comprising the ecological and genealogical hierarchies over time (Baum and Singh 1994a).

At any point in time, organizations, the members of populations, operate with other populations of organizations in more or less integrated communities. From a genealogical point of view, these ecological communities are integrated collections of populations drawn from various lineages of organizational forms. Polyphyletic groupings provide the organizational forms, which in turn provide the populations observed in each community, which are themselves integrated into the larger ecosystems of the ecological hierarchy. Thus, the genealogical hierarchy supplies the entities of the ecological hierarchy, their continued existence and characteristic features dependent on what is available in the genealogical hierarchy.

However, it is ecological entities, the visible structural and behavioral expressions of genealogical entities that are shuffled as units of selection. For example, within populations, the ongoing selection of organizations results in valuable configurations of routines (i.e., competencies) being retained and less valuable configurations being rejected.

And it is the unequal results of the interactions among ecological entities that determine what exists in the genealogical hierarchy in the next generation—which particular lineages of routines, organizations, and organizational forms survive over time, and in what form. In general, the ecological interactions that result in the differential perpetuation of genealogical entities occur at the same level or higher levels of the ecological hierarchy. Thus, most of the regulation of retention and modification of production and organizing competence over time results *not* from processes in the genealogical hierarchy, but from those in the ecological hierarchy responsible for the changing composition of ecological entities over time. Consequently, anything contributing to the differential birth, death, and persistence of ecological entities is material to an understanding of evolutionary processes. Of course, this does not mean that one hierarchy is causally prior to the other: both are necessary for a theory of organizational evolution.

Figure 18.1 overlays VSR processes on the dual hierarchy framework to depict one possible version of ecological–genealogical interactions. At each level of organization, Darwin machines connect ecological and genealogical hierarchies, continuously producing variations in genealogical entities, whose external expressions are shuffled as units of selection in the ecological hierarchy, with selected variations in turn retained as genealogical entities. Thus, "V" and "R" map onto replication processes and operate on genealogical entities, while "S" maps onto interaction processes and operates on ecological entities. In the scheme presented, Darwin machines operate at four levels of the dual hierarchy: job–routine, competence–workgroup, organization–organization, and population–organizational form. In other words, ongoing selection of jobs within

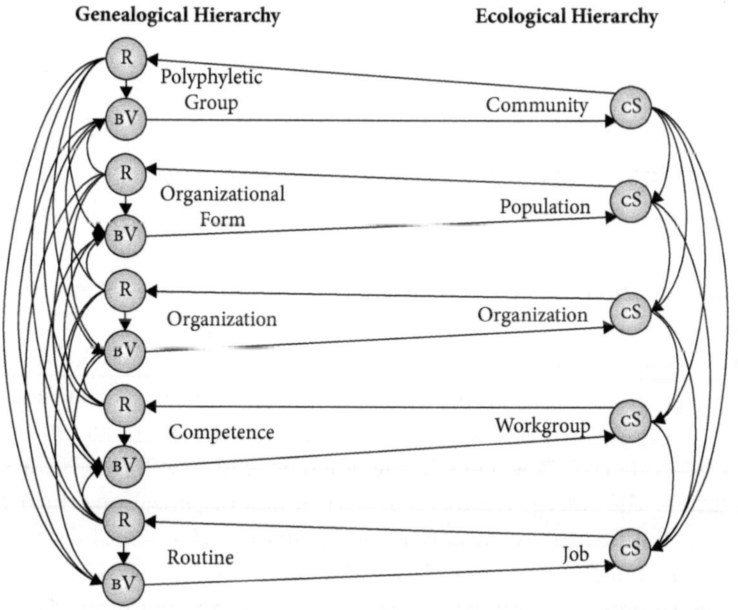

FIGURE 18.1 Multilevel VSR

BV = (Blind) Variation; CS = (Competitive) Selection; R = Retention workgroups, workgroups within organizations, organizations within populations, and populations within communities are conceived to directly affect replication of entities in the genealogical hierarchy, which in turn directly affect the variation among jobs, organizations, and populations.

Figure 18.1 also illustrates patterns of upward and downward interaction that constrain and regulate processes at adjacent levels within each hierarchy. Across levels of organization, Darwin machines interact through retention within the genealogical, and selection within the ecological hierarchy. In the genealogical hierarchy, retention at each level affects variation at other levels both *up* (e.g., the pool of available routines limits the range of organizational variation expressed within an organizational form) and *down* (e.g., integrating multiple interdependent routines into competencies rules out many lower-level combinatorial possibilities) the hierarchy. In the ecological hierarchy, the interactions that result in the differential selection of ecological entities cascade downward the selection of organizations, dependent on the selection of their populations, which in turn depend on the selection of the communities to which they belong. Thus, the ecological fates of organizations are tied inextricably to the fates of the populations and communities within which they are nested.

Although Figure 18.1 presents a detailed "snapshot" of the content, levels, and processes that constitute the dual-hierarchy model, it does not explicitly depict the implications of the model's dynamics over time. In the genealogical hierarchy, the result is a set of lineages tracing the temporal progression of changes in routines, competencies, organizations, and organizational forms (Van de Ven and Grazman 1999). In the ecological hierarchy, the result is a shifting distribution (e.g., changes in variability and average characteristics) of jobs, workgroups, organizations, and organizational populations.

Micro-Evolutionary Dynamics of Organizational Populations

Most new organizations constitute replications—with variation—of existing organizational forms (Aldrich and Kenworthy 1999). Such foundings are central to micro-evolutionary processes that produce persistence and change within lineages of established organizational forms. On occasion, however, an organizational founding, the product of innovative entrepreneurial initiative, jumps out of an established form to create a new one (i.e., "speciates"). The emergence of new forms is the domain of macroevolution. The emergence and character of new organizational forms is shaped both by opportunities to create new resource spaces (Hannan and Freeman 1989; Schumpeter 1934) and the characteristics and creativity of, and competition among existing organizations and entrepreneurs (Lumsden and Singh 1990). New organizational forms represent novel recombinations of core organizational features (Rao and Singh 1999), which include:

1. *Stated goals*—the basis on which legitimacy and other resources are mobilized (including not-for-profit, for-profit, cooperative, religious, and charitable orientations)
2. *Authority relations*—the basis of exchange within the organization and between the organization and its members (including governance structures—e.g., market, hierarchy, and clan)
3. *Core technology*—as encoded in capital investment, infrastructure, and the skills and knowledge of employees
4. *Market strategy*—the kinds of clients or customers to which the organization orients its production, and the ways in which it attracts resources from the environment

These core organizational features, which are difficult and hazardous to change (Hannan and Freeman 1984) and play central roles in the mobilization of resources and legitimacy, comprise a four-dimensional state space in which new organizational forms appear or disappear over time (Baum 1989; Rao and Singh 1999).[2] Hannan and Freeman (1984) distinguish these core features from more peripheral attributes of organizations, which are more amenable to change and serve to protect an organization's core from uncertainty by buffering it from, and broadening its connections to, the environment. Peripheral features include number and sizes of subunits, number of hierarchical levels, span of control, patterns of communication, and buffering mechanisms such as interlocking directorates and strategic alliances (Hannan and Freeman 1984:157). Although these and other organizational features (e.g., organizational culture) can be central to the character and identity of individual organizations, core features are intended to serve as a basis for characterizing the identities of organizational forms.

An advantage of using core features to identify and describe organizational forms is that they provide a compact list of relatively stable and adaptively significant attributes on which to base relatively stable and vital distinctions between organizational forms. These four features can also help assess how an organizational form is connected to ancestral forms and direct our attention to processes by which new discontinuities in configurations of goals, authority, technology, and market strategy arise. Organizational forms, then, are defined in terms of their core characteristics, and one form differs from another, primarily according to core characteristics of the form. Organizational forms constitute *polyphyletic groupings* (McKelvey 1982); that is, each member of a form shares common core characteristics, but may differ with respect to peripheral features.

There are considerable obstacles to the emergence of new organizational forms. Unless a new organizational form can rapidly acquire mechanisms that isolate it from its parent population(s) and external legitimacy that helps overcome a liability of newness (Stinchcombe 1965), its distinctive characteristics are unlikely to be maintained over

[2] There is considerable disagreement on how to define organizational forms and multiple definitions premised on different approaches to organizational classification have been discussed (see Baum 1989; McKelvey 1982: 35–65; Rao and Singh 1999; Rich 1992; Romanelli 1991).

time. Before we tackle the macro-evolutionary problem of the emergence of new forms, however, we must first characterize the ongoing, micro-evolutionary within-lineage dynamics of replication with variation within organizational forms.

Variation: Exploring Organizational Fitness Landscapes

Organizational variations are the result of human behavior. Any kind of change, intentional or blind, is variation. Individuals intentionally produce variations in, for example, technical and management competencies in their efforts to adjust their organization's relationship to the environment. Blind variations, in contrast, are accidental, the product of chance, luck, or unforeseen product of creative exploration. Most variations are small, serving mainly to perpetuate the existing order rather than displace it. Organizational variations provide the raw material from which selection can be made. Some variations prove more beneficial to organizations than others in acquiring resources in a competitive environment and are thus selected positively—not by some amorphous environment, but by managers inside organizations and investors, customers, and government regulators (McKelvey, 1994; Meyer 1994a; Miner 1994).

Selection criteria are set through operation of competitive and institutional processes, as well as the logic of technologies in use and organizational structures and incentives. Retention occurs when selected variations are routinized, reproduced, and carried forward into future actions and organizations. Internal criteria for selection (and retention) of variations are often more salient to people inside organizations than external, environmental criteria. Compared to the strong situations that characterize organizations' internal environments (Davis-Blake and Pfeffer 1989), their external environments are often inchoate, and rarely provide feedback with sufficient speed, frequency, or detail to yield clear cues about effective behavior. Most selection of variation within organizations, then, is driven by internal criteria defined by organizations including goals, subgoals, and organizationally based rewards for attaining these goals (Meyer 1994a).

When successful variations are known, or when environmental trends are identifiable, organizations can attempt to copy and implement these successful variations, or they can attempt to forecast, anticipate, plan, and implement policies in the context of the predictable trends (DiMaggio and Powell 1983; Nelson and Winter 1982). But when successful variations are unknown, because, for example, the behavior of consumers and competitors is unpredictable, the probability of choosing the correct variation and implementing it successfully is very low. Even when effective variations are identifiable, ambiguity in the causes of success may frustrate attempts at imitation. Under such conditions, variations can be viewed as experimental trials, some of which are consciously planned and some of which are accidental, some of which succeed and some of which fail (McKelvey, 1994; Miner 1994). Whether or not they are known, over time, selected variations are retained as surviving organizations come to be characterized by them.

If the survival odds are low for organizations with a particular variant, it does not mean that these organizations are destined to fail. Rather, it means the capacity of their members to change them successfully is of utmost importance to their performance and survival. However, individuals cannot always (or even often) determine in advance which organizational variations will succeed, and there are constraints on the capacity of individuals to change their organizations successfully, including established practices, norms, and incentives, competition for scarce resources, and limits to individual rationality. Consequently, in addition to variations introduced by members of ongoing organizations, evolutionary approaches also highlight the creation of new organizations as an important source of variation.

Intraorganizational Sources of Organizational Variation

The persistent centrality of issues of coordination and control in organization theory is a testament to the commonness of variation inside organizations (Aldrich 1999). New ideas—variations—emerge all the time and are tried out as a result of the inventiveness as well as the mistakes of an organization's fallible members. Organizational members forget standard routines and invent new ones while fulfilling their roles, or pursue their own creative (or destructive) insights when discouraged or bored. Random drift results as organizational members fulfill their roles independently of one another over time. Copying mistakes occur and information is imperfectly transmitted in attempts to transfer routines to new organizational members. Transferred personnel create hybrid routines, mixing ideas from their prior and current roles (Miner 1990, 1991). The problem is that not all this variation is beneficial: Although many variations turn out to be benign, some may prove harmful. While, required variations cannot be specified in advance, and outcomes of enacted variations are difficult to determine without a trial, organizations can still affect the types and level of variation they produce (Miner 1994).

Several organizational practices facilitate variation. One is *institutionalized experimentation* (Miner 1994). This includes formal research and development, introduction of "champion" and "intrapreneur" roles, adoption of total quality management and other continuous improvement practices, as well as use of parallel projects in which several teams work on solving the same general problem, generating intentional variation among potential solutions. A second is provision of *direct and indirect incentives* for producing variations. Many organizations use total quality, continuous improvement, and suggestion programs to establish innovation as a regular facet of work. Organizations also establish competitions between individuals or workgroups, and reward winners with resources and status. Others provide specific monetary incentives for discoveries, such as a percentage of licensing fees from patents produced by the new ideas. Sometimes, full-scale venture divisions or spin-off companies are established with participants sharing an equity interest in new products developed, or the venture itself (Burgelman 1983). A third is for organizations to officially tolerate unfocused variation or *playfulness* (March 1981). Research labs are purposely informal to encourage unplanned interactions and variations in ideas. A certain level of slack resources is tolerated to support informal work on unapproved projects.

Some organization theorists have come to view *complexity theory* as providing a general framework for understanding intraorganizational sources of variation (e.g., Baum 1999; Brown and Eisenhardt 1998; McKelvey 1998; Stacey 1995, 1996; Thietart and Forgues 1995; see Chapter 20 by Dooley). Complexity theory suggests that adaptive systems tend to steer themselves to "the edge of chaos" or "region of emergence" by regulating their level of autonomy/mutual dependence, both among components and between a system as a whole and other systems in the environment with which it interacts. Such regulation of interdependence is hypothesized to benefit an organizational system by admitting order and change, structure and surprise. Organizational complexity theorists conceive organizations as "complex adaptive systems" and emphasize how individuals, organizational subunits, and organizations "self-organize" into emergent aggregate structure.

Consider, for example, a large organization in need of a turnaround. If subunits comprising the organization are too tightly coupled, there may be excessive interdependence and rigidity—if every act of each subunit influences others throughout the organization, then the repercussions of any given action have the potential to destabilize the entire system. Coupling that is too tight leaves no room for desirable individual autonomy. If, in contrast, the organizational subunits are too loosely coupled, there is no coherence. Coordination is problematic, knowledge fails to diffuse and accumulate, and confusion sets in. In short, "too much structure creates gridlock... too little structure creates chaos" (Brown and Eisenhardt 1998: 14). The edge of chaos lies between these extremes, where partially connected organizational subunits never quite reach equilibrium, but never quite disintegrate either. It is a transitional realm in which emergent structures (e.g., new network formations, informal or formal group activities, departments, entrepreneurial ventures, technologies, and routines), resulting from responses to changing environmental conditions, form and produce new variations to resolve adaptive tensions, and then dissipate (McKelvey 1999). Such activity is very sensitive to small differences in initial conditions, leading to path-dependent behavior in which historical accidents "tip" outcomes strongly in a particular direction. As a result, complex behavior amplifies any initially random variation among organizational routines, which can follow radically divergent paths over time, providing a basis for a range of innovative behavior on which selection can act.

In the end, however, the source of variation does not matter as long as many blind variations are tried on a more or less regular basis.

Balancing Organizational Variation and Internal Selective Retention

There is an inherent tension in the VSR model: "variation and retention are at odds in most exemplifications of the model. Maximizing either one jeopardizes the other. Some compromise of each is required" (Campbell 1974: 27). Too much retention restricts the kinds of variations that can occur; too much variation prevents the system from systematically harvesting effective variations. Within organizations, although March (1981), Miner (1994), and others suggest that variation can be promoted through institutionalized experimentation and incentives that reward playfulness, over time a self-reinforcing bias toward preservation of current routines appears, inevitably, to tip the balance in favor of retention.

All organizations face the question of how to allocate energy between the exploration of new routines and the exploitation of old ones (March 1991). *Exploitation* refers to refinement and reproduction of existing routines. *Exploration* refers to search for new routines through concerted variation, planned experimentation and play. March (1991) advocates striking a balance between the two: too much emphasis on exploitation (retention) can lead to the adoption of suboptimal routines and stagnation; too much emphasis on exploration (variation) can lead to incurring the high costs of experimentation without harvesting any of the value of its benefits. In practice, however, sure short-run rewards of exploitation distract organizations from exploration, since each increase in competence at an activity increases the likelihood of obtaining rewards for engaging in that activity, while returns from exploration are systematically less certain.

Given initial success at applying a routine, organizations are likely to retain and reuse it because they know increasingly well how to, and because it is less risky and costly to apply an existing, proven routine than alternatives with which organizations have limited experience. Managers' attributions of success to their own abilities, and to the policies and practices (correct or not) they previously adopted limit the likelihood that they will initiate experimentation. This is especially true if there are few negative results, tempting managers to go just a little bit farther, and increasing the likelihood that any false or superstitious beliefs that managers hold will be reinforced (Levinthal and March 1993; Miller 1993). These managerial beliefs serve as powerful vicarious selectors within organizations, leading organizations to concentrate on what they believe they are good at, get worse at other things, attribute success to what they think they are good at, and attribute failure to not trying hard enough (Levitt and March 1988).

In the face of ambiguity and uncertainty, an emphasis on reproducing routines honed in the past can prevent organizations from adjusting their routines too quickly and detrimentally to idiosyncratic events and from engaging in costly explorations into highly uncertain domains. Exploitive learning may also enhance performance by reducing variability in the quality or efficiency of task execution (Argote and Epple 1990; Hannan and Freeman 1984). Exploitation can become harmful, however, if the criteria for organizational success and survival change *after* the organization has learned. Then the organization may perform poorly by doing well what it learned in the past; it may suffer the so-called *competency trap* (Levitt and March 1988). Organizations may thus often reduce exploratory activity prematurely and, in the case of a changing environment, may not renew exploratory search and learning activities despite the fact that new opportunities and threats are present (Starbuck 1983). This path dependency limits evolutionary possibilities, potentially overriding exploratory search and learning activities despite the fact that new opportunities and threats are present. Managers' internal selection criteria come to dominate external ones, leading organizations to employ routines of the past well beyond their point of usefulness to consumers and investors (Miller 1990, 1999; Starbuck 1983).

As noted above, there is nothing inherently problematic with limiting variations to certain forms, and nonindependence over successive trials. However, internal vicarious selectors that develop through a mutual positive feedback between experience and competence are often not subject to selection (Miller 1999), and also engender managerial confidence in their prescience about the outcomes of variation. Managers come to rely on inductive analysis to determine which variation will be best. Given an improvement, they conclude that the outcome was best based on comparison with presumed results of other variations that were never tried. Thus, rather than variations in routines and competencies that are subject to selection, internal vicarious selectors tend to produce singular changes that are *not*subject to selection. Ultimately, excessive attention to internal selection criteria that are not themselves subject to selection erodes an organization's competence as its goals become ends in themselves, and its members find easier (but not more effective) ways to achieve them (Meyer 1994b). This situation fundamentally and detrimentally reduces the ability of the organization to evolve: If multiple variations are not tried blindly, selection will not operate, or will operate through extreme failure, the result of organizational selection at a higher evolutionary level (Baum and Ingram 1998).

Although the threat exploitation and internal vicarious selectors pose for *individual* organizational survival is substantial, the resulting cycle of "specialization and replacement" may well be efficient for the organization's *population* (Levinthal and March 1993: 103). By combining advantages of learning at the organization level and advantages of selection at the population level, the "self-destructive" properties of organizational learning make the replacement of obsolescent organizations easier. Rigidities in one organization serve to exploit current knowledge and simultaneously make old markets vulnerable to new organizations with new capabilities.

Interorganizational Sources of Organizational Variation

Organizations' own experience is not the only source of variation, however. Organizations also learn vicariously or more directly from the experiences of other organizations, imitating or avoiding specific actions or practices based on their perceived impact (Cyert and March 1963; Miner and Haunschild 1995).

Interorganizational learning occurs when one organization learns by observing, exchanging knowledge, or generating knowledge through joint interaction with other organizations in its own or a different population. This learning may be either strictly vicarious when one organization observes but does not interact with another or interactive when the learning process arises from active contacts between two or more organizations (e.g., strategic alliances, research consortia). Vicarious interorganizational learning is a ubiquitous feature of contemporary organization theory (DiMaggio and Powell 1983) and in strategic management is the basis for the second-mover advantage (Lieberman and Montgomery 1988). Interactive interorganizational learning is widely held to be *the* primary incentive for (and benefit of) strategic alliances (Powell et al. 1996) and research consortia (Aldrich and Sasaki 1995; Mowery et al. 1996).

Interorganizational learning can also occur when members of one organizational population *collectively* observe members of other organizational populations or forms, and draw on their shared experience to enact or inform organizational routines (Miner and Anderson 1999). Members of one population might, for example, develop a formal collective entity after watching another population do so, as US semiconductor producers did after observing Japanese research consortia (e.g., SEMATECH; Mowery et al. 1996). An emerging industry's development of a trade association group in response to a common external threat also represents collective learning.

The experience of other organizations has some unique advantages over an organization's own experience. Of particular significance, while individual organizations tend to engage in too much exploitation, in the aggregate, they may explore the fitness landscape thoroughly. Unlike organizations, any one severely limited in how much it can explore, organizational populations and forms are nonhierarchical, faces limited demands for integration, and therefore can be more varied in their experience than individual organizations. The general lack of cohesion, the diversity of organizational goals, and the absence of any systematic harvesting or censoring of newly created routines all contribute to the proliferation of new ideas and routines as opposed to one that encourages incremental learning. Compared to individual organizations, then, organizational populations can explore a great deal of variation without violating internal or external standards for consistency and reliability (Baum and Ingram 1998).

Consequently, other organizations may offer a source of fresh variation for organizations that have fallen into competency traps. With such an approach, organizations mired in their own past can potentially learn the strategies, production and organizing competencies, and technologies employed by other successful organizations in their industry. A good strategy for any individual organization may thus often be to emphasize exploitation of the successful explorations of others (Levinthal and March 1993).[3] Although the politics of ingrained internal vicarious selectors can limit the potential of this strategy by channeling interorganizational search, widespread identification and imitation of "best practices" and the practice of "benchmarking" both typify this strategy (Imai, 1986). More generally, Haunschild and Miner (1997) identify three "modes" of interorganizational imitation: *frequency imitation* (copying the most common organizational routine), *trait imitation* (copying the routine of some organization based on a trait of that organization such as size, prestige, similarity to self, etc.), and *outcome imitation* (copying routines that appear to have good consequences for other organizations).

And what could be more efficient? The observing organization acquires the trial-and-error experience of another organization without ever investing resources in its

[3] Of course, if all organizations follow such a strategy, the population may produce no variations to imitate.

> own trial. What could be less risky? The chosen routine or practice, from among those observed, has demonstrated its ability to improve an organization's environmental fit."
>
> (Romanelli 1999: 87)

The problem is again prescience, which is typically the main objective of interorganizational learning. Organizations learning in this manner do not invest in learning without an expectation that they will discover new routines that will improve performance, and try to infer in advance which among possible variations will provide the greatest improvement. As long as no immediate decline in performance occurs that can be traced to the variation introduced, the action is likely to be interpreted as a success, but selection has had no chance to work (Romanelli 1999).

Selection: Defining Criteria and Organizational Fitness Landscapes

The contours of fitness landscapes that members of an organizational form must navigate, as well as the values of particular organizational variations they conjure are shaped by three main processes: *Competitive Isomorphism, Institutional Isomorphism*, and the *r-K Transition*. Competitive and institutional isomorphism focus on how exogenous environmental processes in the surrounding environment affect the "spatial" characteristics of selection criteria—how selection criteria affect the variability *within* organizational forms. The *r-K* transition captures processes endogenous to an organizational form's evolution that affect the "temporal" characteristics of selection criteria—how selection criteria change systematically as an organizational form ages and grows.

Competitive Isomorphism

Organizational ecologists contend that the degree of similarity or isomorphism among organizations is determined by *competition* among them (Hannan and Freeman 1977, 1989). Ecological models of competition focus on the importance of organizational niche similarity for intrapopulation competition. Niche overlap—the confrontation by organizations of a similar set of resources and constraints—is predicted to lead to competition, and the intensity of competition is expected to be a function of relative niche location. In particular, the more similar organizations' niche locations (i.e., the greater the degree of niche overlap), the more they require similar resources to thrive—raw materials, labor, financial support, institutional support, and customer demand—and the more intensely they compete (Hawley 1950; Hannan and Freeman 1977, 1989; McPherson 1983). At one extreme, if organizations' niches overlap completely, the potential for competition will be fierce. At the other extreme, if organizations' niches do not overlap at all, they will require entirely different resources and there will be no potential for competition.

In general, the niche is a location in multidimensional space defined by the resources in the environment. Although the niche is a concept well known in organizational ecology, the usual focus is on the niches of organizational forms (Hannan and Freeman 1977, 1989). In addition to the macro-niche of the form, however, individual organizations have micro- or organizational niches as well (Baum and Singh 1994b, 1994c; McKelvey 1982; McPherson 1983). Thus, organizational forms can encompass multiple organizational niches, and depending on the organizational niches they occupy, organizations face different competitive landscapes, and organizational niches provide a way to account for intra-form heterogeneity in capabilities and resource requirements (Baum and Singh 1994b, 1994c). Competition among organizations within and among organizational niches sets the evolution of organizational forms in motion. Variation in adaptive capacities at the organizational niche level is the raw material based on which organizations in competition are differentially selected for retention. Organizations with variations that are less proficient at adapting to and acquiring resources from the environment tend to be eliminated. Retention processes preserve the selected variation, setting the range of organizational variation that can be expressed within an organizational form—and its fitness relative to rival forms. Such competition can affect variability within organizational forms in several ways.

According to the principle of competitive isomorphism in organizational ecology (Hannan and Freeman 1977), selection processes link the variability of organizations to the variability of environments. Organizations are specialized, and these specializations, which follow from environmental selection pressures, create homogeneous organizational groupings that compete in different ways for different resources, and rely on different strategic and operational competencies. The more uniform the demands (e.g., consumer and investor) of an organizational environment, the greater the convergence of selection pressures on particular organizational variations and the greater the similarity of surviving organizations. This is because in homogeneous environments, few differentiated resources exist, and organizations prevail by virtue of their specialization to common environmentally imposed constraints. As a result, selection pressures reduce variation by eliminating organizations that deviate from those most proficient at acquiring the undifferentiated resources from the environment. Two different selection processes operate in homogeneous environments to lower organizational variability (Amburgey et al. 1994; Baum 2006; McPherson, Popielarz, and Drobnic 1992).

Stabilizing selection directs pressures against organizations whose features vary from the "optimum." Stabilizing selection leaves the features of the average organization unchanged and reduces organizational variation. Organizational forms undergoing stabilizing selection are in the process of *specializing*. Organizational size, for example, might be subject to stabilizing selection that favors organizations close to some "optimum" size while systematically selecting larger and smaller organizations out of the environment. *Directive selection* favors organizations at one tail of a distribution of organizational variation, while subjecting those at the other tail to negative selection pressures. For example, larger airlines (or, alternatively, labor unions, or life insurance companies) might be favored while smaller airlines are systematically eliminated, resulting in a larger mean size of airlines. Directive selection thus simultaneously reduces organizational variability and moves the features characterizing the average organization toward the favored tail of the distribution.

In contrast, heterogeneous environments contain many distinct resources and constraints, leading organizations to face varied circumstances, and requiring local adaptations. Under these conditions, differentiated organizations, adept at acquiring differentiated resources and carving out distinct niches, are favored by competitive selection, increasing organizational variation. *Diversifying* or *disruptive selection* increases variability by favoring organizations at the tails of the distribution, while discriminating against those in the middle, producing a bimodal or multi-modal distribution of variation (Hannan and Freeman 1977). For example, if large and small hotels (alternatively, banks, book publishers, or brewers) depend on different mixes of resources (e.g., conventions versus individual travelers), then patterns of resource use will be specialized to particular segments of the size distribution, hotels' niche location will vary with size, and similar-sized hotels will compete most intensely. As a result, large hotels pose a threat to medium-sized hotels but not small ones. Whatever strategy medium-sized hotels adopt to compete with large hotels makes them more vulnerable to competition from small hotels and vice versa. Therefore, the emergence of large hotels is accompanied by a decline in the number of medium-sized hotels, while small hotels flourish as their most intense competitors are removed from the environment (Baum and Mezias 1992).

Institutional Isomorphism

Neo-institutional theorists agree with organizational ecologists that organizational variability is a function of environmental heterogeneity. The central issue from the institutional perspective, however, is the level of fragmentation in the structure of the institutional environment (Scott 1995). Institutional theory emphasizes that environments are characterized by the elaboration of institutionalized beliefs, rules, and requirements to which organizations must conform if they are to receive support, acquire needed resources, and be perceived as legitimate. In contrast to ecologists' focus on *competitive isomorphism*, neo-institutionalists stress the degree of interdependence and connection among organizations. *Institutional isomorphism* is seen to result from powerful social forces—*coercive*, *normative*, and *mimetic*—in the interorganizational context that leads organizations to conform to institutionalized patterns (DiMaggio and Powell 1983).

Coercive isomorphism results from formal or informal pressures exerted by one organization on another. For example, organizations may conform to rules and regulations prescribed by superordinate environmental agents, such as the state, that are sufficiently powerful to impose particular structures or practices on them. Although conformity to such pressures may not increase a subordinate organization's ability to achieve its ends, it will at least enhance its legitimacy. Scott (1987) identifies two additional related mechanisms. *Authorization* involves legitimation of an organization's structural features or qualities by a superordinate institution (e.g., an accreditation agency). In this case, the subordinate organization is not compelled to conform, but voluntarily seeks out attention and approval of the authorizing agent. *Inducement* creates isomorphism by providing incentives to subordinate organizations willing to conform to the conditions of a superordinate agent, when the agent lacks the power or authority to impose its stipulations on subordinate organizations. Examples include venture capitalists and funding agencies that specify conditions for acquiring and remaining eligible for funding or being reimbursed for work performed.

Normative isomorphism is derived from professionalization and the belief systems promulgated by professional membership. Organizations may adhere to the norms and standards of business and professional circles that define routine or acceptable solutions to professional, managerial, and organizational problems. These solutions are institutionalized in the business, academic, or professional subcultures, and are transmitted through vehicles including educational institutions, conferences, training workshops, industry and professional journals, and the movement of the members of business or professional circles among organizations.

When influence in the institutional environment is centralized, coercive and normative institutional pressures are homogeneous and easily coordinated and imposed on subordinate organizations. In contrast, fragmented institutional structures suffer from ambiguity, coordinated action to influence organizations is difficult, and room for organizational discretion is created by the resulting uncertainty (Goodrick and Salancik 1996). In his study of the influence of government regulation on the evolution of the American life insurance industry Lehrman (1994: 631), for example, observes:

> The preferences of the institutional environment were initially neither stable nor uniform but over time shifted toward more technical, sober, and uniform standards. This resulted in decreased diversity of viable forms and increased conformity with a definition of life insurance as a financial service conceived and administered in a fairly specific manner.

Thus, consistent with the principle of competitive isomorphism in organizational ecology, the greater the number of distinct institutional resources and constraints in an organizational field (i.e., the greater the fragmentation of institutional structures), the greater the diversity of organizations that can be sustained in the field.

Mimetic isomorphism results from processes that induce the imitation of "normal" structures and practices. Faced with environmental uncertainty, organizations imitate or model themselves after other organizations in their field—especially similar organizations perceived to be more effective or successful, or with which they are in direct contact. Such imitation may be unrelated to goal attainment. Instead, becoming identified with the practices and characteristics of "successful" or "high-status" organizations is more critical. Like coercive and normative processes, effects mimetic processes also depend on the homogeneity of the institutional environment. When a widely accepted "normal" model exists, mimicry will tend to speed the predominance of the model and reduce organizational diversity. However, when such a "normal" model does not exist, mimicry tends to impede a "normal" model's rise (DiMaggio and Powell 1983: 155–6) and can increase organizational diversity if several qualitatively different alternatives, each with its own prestigious adopters and supporters, are the focus of imitation (Baum 2006).

The role of such institutional processes has figured with increasing prominence in recent ecological theory and research, and increasingly it is recognized that institutional processes are contextual to ecological processes (e.g., Aldrich and Fiol 1994; Barnett and Carroll 1993; Rao and Singh 1999; Tucker et al. 1992). In this view, institutional processes constitute the broader social context for ecological processes, prescribing the selection criteria on which ecological processes operate. Moreover, as an organizational form grows and its social impact becomes more widely recognized, community advocacy groups, government agencies, professional associations, and other social actors increasingly take an active role in monitoring its members' activities, distributing endorsements and rewards, and shaping the rules and standards for legitimate activities and outputs (Baum and Oliver 1992). Thus, the nature of selection criteria shaping organizational forms is influenced greatly by surrounding institutions, and these institutions may play an increasingly predominant role in defining selection criteria as an organizational form expands.

r-K Transition

The original application of the density dependence model in organization theory emphasized a dramatically different selection dynamic.[4] In it, Brittain and Freeman (1980) described how organizational forms undergo a transition over time from "*r*-selection" to "*K*-selection" as increasing the number of organizations relative to available resources alters the basis of competition from first-mover to efficiency advantages. The distinction between these two bases of competition is grounded in the logistic population growth functions in bioecology:

$$\frac{dN}{dt} = rN\left(\frac{K-N}{K}\right),$$

where K is the carrying capacity of the population's environment, r is the natural growth rate of the population, N is population density–the number of organizations in the population, and t is a time interval. According to this equation, when the number of organizations is initially low, the natural growth term r dominates and organizations enter at a slow but exponentially increasing rate. As population density increases, the carrying capacity term K becomes dominant, and the rate of growth slows. Growth stops when population density equals the carrying capacity.

In an emerging population, no organization or small group of organizations dominates, and entrants are typically similar in size to established organizations. Competition

[4] Here, we do not consider Hannan and Carroll's (1992) version of the density dependence model, which focuses on the dynamics of legitimation and competition to explain the growth trajectories of organizational populations, because it is cast at the population level. As a result, density-dependent legitimation captures relative fitness of populations, but does not address relative fitness of organizations *within* a population. Hannan and Carroll's formulation of density-dependent competition, which treats all organizations in a population as equal competitors, is similarly silent on relative fitness of organizations *within* a population. Therefore we present Brittain and Freeman's earlier formulation, which incorporates within-population variation among organizations.

is dominated by *r*-selection, which favors small organizations (*r*-specialists) capable of moving quickly to exploit new resource opportunities in the resource-rich but dispersed and uncertain environments that characterize low-density conditions. As the population continues to grow, its markets become connected, demand becomes more predictable, and some organizations begin making broad appeals to all customers to expand their market shares. Along with the increased potential for competition that accompanies increasing population size (relative to the abundance of resources), this begins to orient competition among the population's members toward cost and price reduction, favoring larger population members capable of achieving efficiency advantages.

When a population reaches its carrying capacity, the resources available to its members are fully exploited and competitive pressures shift to *K*-selection, which favors larger *K*-generalist organizations competing on the basis of efficiency for the mass market. The economic and competitive advantages of the population's large *K*-generalist members enable them to outcompete smaller *r*-specialist rivals, which are crowded out by asymmetric competition. This "shakeout" reduces the number of population members, raises the level of market concentration, and creates a log-normal or bimodal size distribution in which a few large organizations dominate many smaller ones (Hannan and Freeman 1977; Ijiri and Simon 1977).

Ultimately, however, increasing market concentration forces large organizations to compete increasingly with one another for central markets capable of sustaining their large-scale operations (Carroll 1985). This specializes resource use to particular segments of the size distribution and creates narrow pockets of demand that permits smaller, *K*-specialists to emerge and efficiently exploit without engaging in direct competition with the larger generalists. Thus, resource partitioning localizes the competitive effects of organizations—even large ones—to their particular segments of operations. Mature populations are thus comprised of *K*-generalists and *K*-specialists, with the mix depending on how heterogeneous the environment is, the ability of *K*-generalists to differentiate: the greater the differentiation of *K*-generalists (environments), the lower the consolidation and concentration of the market and the fewer potential resource pockets for *K*-specialists. Notably, because *K* strategists' organizational structures needed for generating competitive efficiency often preclude rapid adjustments needed to secure 1st-mover advantage, *r*-strategists may also re-emerge to compete for these new opportunities.

Competition at carrying capacity also initiates a more general process of niche elaboration based on functional and territorial differentiation within the population as competition pushes entrepreneurs to seek out distinct functions in which they hold a competitive advantage (Hawley, 1950). This creates organizational subgroupings that fulfill complementary roles in which they are dependent on, but noncompetitive with each other, and lowers the potential for competition by reducing the number of direct competitors each population member confronts. We will return to this process in detail in our discussion of organizational communities.

Often underlying *r*-to-*K* transitions are technology cycles that shape appropriate organizational forms and condition the basis of competition among organizations (Anderson and Tushman 1990; Dosi 1982, 1984; Schumpeter 1934). Technological evolution has long been characterized as a process of creative destruction in which technologies evolve over time through cycles of long periods of incremental change, punctuated by major technological innovations. Periods of incremental change enhance and extend an underlying technological regime and reinforce or institutionalize an existing technological order. Periods of incremental change end with technological discontinuities in which new, radically superior technologies displace old, inferior ones, making possible order-of-magnitude or more improvements in organizational performance.

The new technology can either be *competence-enhancing*, which builds on know-how embodied in the existing technology, or *competence destroying*, which renders the skills required to operate and manage the existing technology obsolete (Tushman and Anderson 1986). This distinction helps specify whether incumbents or newcomers are likely to become superior competitors as a result of technological change.[4] Competence-enhancing discontinuities reinforce stabilizing or directional selection favoring established *K*-strategists by making possible order-of-magnitude efficiency improvements. In contrast, introduction of multiple variants of a new technology during *eras of ferment* that follow competence-destroying changes produce disruptive selection conditions that create opportunities for *r*-strategists in emerging niche segments favoring their nimbleness. This technological variability and market uncertainty stimulates social, political, and market processes to reduce it (Tushman and Rosenkopf 1992). The ferment ends with the emergence of a *dominant design*, a single architecture that establishes dominance in a product class (Abernathy 1978; Anderson and Tushman 1990). Once a dominant design emerges, a stabilizing or directional selection regime re-emerges, and technological advance returns to incremental improvements to the dominant design. Emergence of dominant designs, which create economies of standardization and other complementary economies, also favors *K*-strategists competing on the basis of efficiency for the mass market. Thus, the dynamics of competitive selection shaping organizational forms is strongly influenced by the evolution of their underlying technologies.

Ruggedness of Fitness Landscapes

The number of distinct environmental resources and constraints, whether ecological, institutional, or technological, affects not only which variations are favored by selection, but also the *ruggedness* of the fitness landscapes for organizational forms. When there are only a few distinct environmental resources or constraints, fitness landscapes are highly correlated about a single, global peak. The fitness value for neighboring alternatives is similar, and any move toward increased fitness leads to the global optimum. As the number of distinct resources and constraints increases, landscapes becomes more rugged. The number of peaks (local optima) on the fitness landscape increase, peaks become increasingly steep, the level of fitness at any given optima declines, and the ability to predict a better than average fitness peak diminishes. The falling height of accessible fitness peaks makes it more likely that organizations will become trapped on suboptimal peaks. In precipitously rugged landscapes the increased likelihood of organizations becoming stranded on local (sub)optima can result in a "complexity catastrophe" that halts adaptive progression via VSR (Kauffman 1993). Then, even in the face of strong selection forces, the fittest organizations in the population exhibit characteristics that are little different from the entire population.

Retention: The Persistence of Organizational Forms

For biological species, persistence is based ultimately on inheritance processes involving the propagation of genes (and, for a few species, social learning along lines of descent). Inheritance processes for organizational forms appear more complex (Boyd and Richerson 1985; Hannan and Freeman 1989; McKelvey 1982; Singh and Lumsden 1990).[5] Transmission occurs *within* generations of organizations because the production and organizing routines being spread reproduce rapidly and have short generation lengths compared to their "host" organizations. As a result, information about organizing and production can potentially be inherited from diverse sources and the flow of information continues throughout the life of individual organizations as generations of its members come and go (McKelvey 1982; Miner and Haunschild 1995).

Organizational inheritance occurs through different processes at each level of the evolutionary hierarchy. At the organization level, an organization's current routines serve as templates for producing copies, making their replication through observation, formal training, and education, or, hiring proficient new employees, possible with some precision from day-to-day and over generations of organizational employees (Bandura 1977; McKelvey 1982; Nelson and Winter 1982).[6] Organizational routines not only record history, however, they shape its future course. Each time an organization uses a certain routine, it becomes more proficient at that routine and more likely to repeat it again in the future (Levitt and March 1988). Although this self-reinforcing process contributes to organizational stability, efficiency, and reliability, as described above, it can lead to competency traps that make the exploration of potentially adaptive alternatives difficult.

Other organizations' routines can also be inherited though selective copying or vicarious learning (e.g., reverse engineering, benchmarking); however, routines inherited in this manner may constitute substantial mutations because the "target" is often unavailable for direct observation and may be accompanied by unobservable subtle subroutines and tacit knowledge. More direct transmission of routines also occurs through personal and formal relationships between organizations and their members (e.g., personal ties, board of director interlocks, interorganizational relations), and still more directly when an organization hires employees from other organizations judged to possess knowledge of superior routines or absorbs a whole organization. Information can also be inherited in many different directions among generations of organizational members and organizations: *vertically forward* (i.e., young copy old); *horizontally* (i.e., young copy young, old copy old); and even *vertically backward* (i.e., old copy young)

[5] However, biological transmission is not so simple either. Hull (1988: 397–431) suggests that while familiar with the complexities of sociocultural transmission, social scientists may have an overly simple view of biological transmission.

[6] For a detailed account of organizational routines and their replication, see Nelson and Winter (1982: 96–136).

(Baum and Singh 1994a). Trial-and-error learning as well as more elaborate methods of adaptation (i.e., rational calculation based on collection of information, estimation of outcomes of various alternatives, and evaluations of the desirability of estimated outcomes according to some preference criteria) are forces that guide patterns of organizational inheritance. These features of organizational inheritance suggest evolutionary effects and levels of diversity and variation within organizational forms that are strikingly different from those expected with purely genetic transmission.

For one, the pace of organizational evolution is often likely to be very much faster than biotic evolution,[7] and quantum or punctuated evolutionary patterns may be more readily applicable to organizational than biotic evolution (McKelvey 1982; Miller and Friesen 1980; Tushman and Romanelli 1985).[8] In combination, transmission after birth and organizational learning may result in a preponderance of *Lamarckian* (versus *Mendelian*) inheritance in the sense that production and organizing competence acquired through learning can be *re*transmitted (Boyd and Richerson 1985; McKelvey 1982; but see Hull 1988: 452–7). Such social learning-driven inheritance mechanisms have the added advantage of easily admitting change in individual organizations and attending to the hierarchical nature of organizational evolution (Baum and Singh, 1994a). Consequently, the genealogies of organizational forms may often be equivocal and direct genetic analogies infeasible (Hannan and Freeman 1989; McKelvey 1982; but see Van de Ven and Grazman 1999).

Nevertheless, inheritance is certainly not completely unrestrained among organizational forms. The emergence and maintenance of distinctions among organizational forms requires barriers to the exchange of production and organizing competence. Without such barriers, organizational forms could not become or remain meaningfully different from each other over time. Instead, they would fall into a normal distribution of slightly varying forms with some average properties that are not heritable. In the world of organizations, although probably not rooted in a system of inheritance in the biological sense, it is obvious that differences can and do become deep enough that the gaps between them are rarely (if ever) bridged (Baum and Singh 1994a; McKelvey 1982).

Within organizational forms, organizations retaining similar bundles of production and organizing competence are reproduced over generations of employees and organizations as the result of barriers to inheritance from other organizational forms

[7] Of course, in terms of "generation time," organizational evolution occurs at the same rate as biological evolution. In "physical time," however, organizational evolution falls somewhere in the middle—between viruses on the one hand and sequoia trees on the other (see, e.g., Hull 1988).

[8] Use of these terms by some organizational scholars differs from their meanings in biology. In biology, the punctuation hypothesis is that rates of evolution are accelerated by rapidly divergent speciation. Species are conceived to change little during most of their history, but events of rapid speciation occasionally punctuate this stability, resulting in concentrated periods of change (Eldredge and Gould 1972). The punctuation model explains the rapid speciation as a result of the rapid appearance of new attributes in emergent populations (Stanley 1979). By comparison, organizational conceptions of the punctuation hypotheses typically entail the progression of single organizations (Miller and Friesen 1980; Tushman and Romanelli 1985) through a pattern of alternating periods of sustained inertial and discontinuous revolutionary change.

(Baum 1989; Boyd and Richerson 1985; Hannan and Freeman 1989; McKelvey 1982).[9] These "segregating" mechanisms include:

- *Technological interdependencies.* The dependence for successful performance of one element of organizational competence on the successful completion of others means the introduction of new kinds of production and organizing competence is potentially disruptive. As a result, gaps appear between organizational forms because certain combinations of goals, authority relations, market strategies, and modes of production are inconsistent technologically (Hannan and Freeman 1989; McKelvey 1982).
- *Transaction costs.* Transaction cost considerations (e.g., asset specificity, small numbers) lead to distinctive clusters of transactions within organizations engaged in different kinds of production (Williamson 1975, 1991). For example, integration into retailing occurs only for organizations whose products require considerable point-of-sale information and follow-up service, while integration into wholesaling occurs only for organizations whose products are perishable and branded.
- *Collective action.* Organizations working together (e.g., as lobbying association) creates distinctions between those engaged in collective action and those not so engaged (Hannan and Freeman 1989).
- *Institutional processes.* Coercive, normative, and mimetic processes (DiMaggio and Powell 1983) and the taken-for-grantedness of established organizational forms (Hannan and Freeman 1989) operate to accentuate and maintain the diversity of organizations. In either case, potentially arbitrary differences between organizations are transformed into differences with real social consequences, so that nominal classifications become substantive.
- *Social, professional, and personnel network closures.* Groups of organizations that repeatedly hire each other's employees or from the same educational or training institutions, (because they possess required skill and knowledge) develop a high degree of inbreeding with respect to production and organizing competence as well as language and culture and tend to become separate and different from other groups of organizations (Hannan and Freeman 1989; McKelvey 1982).
- *Complexity of learning.* The more difficult an organization's production and organizing competence is to learn and socially transmit (as a function of its complexity and distinctness), the less likely it is that organizations in different organizational forms will be able to acquire and comprehend enough of the competence to successfully implement it (McKelvey 1982).
- *Resistance to learning.* Organizations tend to prefer employing routines of the past (even beyond their point of usefulness) or to focus on refining current routines (e.g., updating and or managing more effectively the routines already held) rather than trying out new (potentially superior) ideas invented elsewhere (March 1991; McKelvey 1982; Nystrom and Starbuck 1984).

[9] For more detailed discussions of isolation mechanisms see Baum (1989, p. 25–33; 44–8), McKelvey (1982: 196–202), and Hannan and Freeman (1989, p. 53–7).

- *Conformist transmission.* Interorganizational imitation is biased toward adoption of majority or plurality practices when several competing beliefs are transmitted by different organizations (Boyd and Richerson 1985). Organizational inheritance is thus a strong homogenizing force that is *frequency-dependent*, varying with the commonness or rarity of organizational practices and structures, and *trait-* and *outcome-dependent*, with the most successful, similar organizations, the most attractive models for imitation (Miner and Haunschild 1995).
- *Imprinting.* The features acquired by organizations at the time of their founding, for example, by mimicking those features that are taken as the natural way to organize a particular form of collective activity, or as the result of environmental conditions, are retained into the future (Stinchcombe 1965).

These mechanisms foster stability of organizational forms, prevent breakdown of adaptive combinations of production and organizing knowledge, and keep worthless combinations from forming. However, they also decrease variability, limiting the ability of an organizational form and its members to explore new ways and means of adapting. Thus, organizational forms too can experience competency traps. As described earlier, however, compared to individual organizations, organizational forms can explore a great deal of variation without violating internal or external standards for consistency and reliability, and are therefore more likely to experience a proliferation of new ideas and competencies as opposed to incremental learning (Baum and Ingram 1998).

Inheritance is not nearly as effectively isolated socio-culturally as it is biotically, however. As a result, "speciation" of organizational forms is likely to be more frequent among organizational than biotic forms. Indeed, Campbell (1979) views the extent of "cross-lineage" borrowing that occurs in sociocultural evolution as the major *disanalogy* between it and biological evolution.

Macro-Evolutionary Dynamics of Organizational Communities

Now that we have explored micro-evolutionary VSR processes shaping the persistence and transformation over time within an existing organizational form, we are ready to begin our examination of the macro-evolutionary VSR processes through which new organizational forms arise, and the considerable challenges associated with their establishment. This requires us to shift from population-level thinking to community-level thinking. Community ecology examines the ways in which similar and dissimilar populations interact, attending in particular to the ways in which they develop collective modes of adaptation to the environment (Hawley 1950) and to the emergence of new kinds of organizational forms. It is only at this level that the creation of new populations and the erosion of boundaries of existing populations can be observed.

The idea of the community as a functionally organized unit has a troubled history in biology. The naturalists who preceded Darwin envisioned all of nature as part of a grand design. Darwin's theory, however, justified only limited functionalism: Natural selection can cause individuals to become well designed to survive and reproduce but, as we noted above, adaptation by individuals does not generally lead to the adaptation of populations, much less multi-population communities. Nevertheless, functionalism persisted, even flourishing after being recast in superficially Darwinian terms, and communities were compared to single individuals in their functional organization. These ideas were scrutinized and dismissed by evolutionary biologists in the 1960s (e.g., Williams 1966). As a result, most bioecologists with an evolutionary background regard the concept of community "superorganisms" dubiously.

Whether organizational communities have sufficient coherence as entities to be selected as entire units has also been argued (Baum and Singh 1994a; Hodgson 1993) and contested (Campbell 1994) in organization theory. Recently, Aldrich (1999) suggested that selection at the organizational community level depends upon the existence of a very tight coupling among populations, a condition most likely requiring strong centralized dominance by political authorities, as in authoritarian political regimes. Our hierarchical approach and analysis of organizational communities, which is informed by multilevel selection theory, does not require strong coupling for community-level selection. Below, we first describe the community concept in more detail and then elaborate the VSR engines shaping evolutionary dynamics within organizational communities.

Defining Organizational Communities

An organizational population built around an organizational form develops relationships with other populations engaged in other activities, but related to a common technical or institutional core, that binds them into organizational communities (Aldrich 1999; Astley 1985; Fombrun 1986; Hannan and Freeman 1989). A typical organizational form interacts with many different kinds of organizations. These include states and professions that regulate and monitor organizational activity, schools that train potential employees, suppliers of technical and material inputs, producers of similar and related (complementary and competitive) products and services, and consumers of the products and services (Baum and Korn 1994; Scott, Ruef, Mendel, and Caronna 2000). An organizational community is a set of populations linked by ecological ties of commensalism and symbiosis that coevolve with each other and their environment. The set of populations may inhabit a local geographic area (e.g., Silicon Valley, Route 128), or may encompass entire national, regional, or global economies, depending on its technical or institutional core (e.g., Wintel PCs). *Commensalism* refers to competition and cooperation between similar units, and *symbiosis* to mutual interdependence between dissimilar units (Hawley 1950). The resources that define these interdependencies vary across populations but generally include raw material, labor, technical knowledge, and market share (Baum and Korn 1994).

Community ecology attends explicitly to the structure and evolution of these ecological ties among organizational populations, and considers the community-level implications of these interactions for co-acting sets of populations. One consequence of adopting a community-level approach is that relationships among populations can begin to be understood as a dynamic system. Changes in interacting populations result not only from their *direct* interactions, but also *indirect* interactions and feedback processes. Consequently, a change in one population may produce a series of changes in other populations. As a result, the effects of change in one population may not follow the logic of direct cause-and-effect relations between populations (Baum and Korn 1994).

Community emergence and evolution depends on a steady stream of organizational foundings for the establishment of new populations and the reproduction (or revitalization) of established ones (Baum and Singh 1994a; Hunt and Aldrich 1998). Often, new organizational forms come into existence in organizational communities as a result of social movements led by institutional entrepreneurs—ideological activists who combine previously unconnected routines and competencies into an organizational solution to a problem—catalyzed by technological and institutional change that disrupts the status quo (DiMaggio, 1988; Rao 1998). Within a community, processes of commensalism and symbiosis sort populations into differentiated niches, and dominant populations drive others into subordinate positions and ancillary roles, resulting in community-level differentiation and integration, and a hierarchical ordering emerges (Astley 1985).[10] Hawley (1950, p. 221) felt that inequality was an inevitable result of functional differentiation because "certain functions are by their nature more influential than others; they are strategically placed in the division of labor and thus impinge directly upon a larger number of other functions." Populations occupying central locations are well positioned to play coordinating roles (Aldrich 1979). For example, the largest CPA firms in the United States molded the structure of the entire accounting community because they attracted the largest clients. Subsequently, their practices were imitated by middle-sized accounting firms and also in standards setting activity (Han 1994).

As community relationships stabilize, competition may shift from the population to the community level: What was once competition between populations becomes rivalry between communities. In Silicon Valley, symbiotic relationships developed among entrepreneurs, educators, venture capitalists, and other local residents that promoted

[10] Community dynamics have much in common with processes of organizational field (de)structuration (DiMaggio and Powell, 1993; Oliver, 1992). Organizational fields, "those organizations that, in aggregate, constitute a recognized area of institutional life: key suppliers, resource and product consumers, regulatory agencies, and other organizations that produce similar services or products" (DiMaggio and Powell 1983: 148). Indeed, as Scott (1994: 207–8, cf. Scott 1995) notes, "[T]he notion of a field connotes the existence of a community of organizations that partakes of a common meaning system and whose participants interact more frequently and fatefully with one another than with actors outside of the field." The primary difference appears to us to be one of levels, with organizational fields frequently constituted by multiple local organizational communities that vary in their degree and form of functional integration.

"collective learning and flexible adjustment among specialist producers of a complex of related technologies" (Saxenian 1994: 2). Law firms played a particularly important symbiotic role in the emergence of Silicon Valley's organizational community, brokering financing agreements between venture capital firms and start-ups (Suchman 1995). In contrast, firms in the Route 128 region around Boston perpetuated a competitive system in which large, independent firms looked to their own internal resources for much of what they needed, rather than developing links with other firms in the area. The region's culture encouraged stability and self-reliance, promoting competition based on secrecy and corporate loyalty (Saxenian 1994: 3). The major universities in the Boston area, MIT and Harvard, kept their distance from smaller companies, preferring ties to large firms that could fund the universities' own research priorities. DEC and other large firms experienced financial difficulties in the 1980s, as the bottom fell out of the minicomputer market. Route 128's lack of a network-based symbiotic community structure and culture dealt it a severe blow from which it had trouble recovering, in contrast to Silicon Valley's rapid recovery after its troubles in the 1980s.

Silicon Valley and Route 128 illustrate the concept of shared fate that is central to community ecology and multilevel selection theory (Sober and Wilson 1998; Wilson and Sober 1989, 1994). The activities of an organization can affect its performance relative to other organizations in the same and different populations in the local community, but they can also affect the abundance of all organizations in the local community as a unit. When multiple local communities exist that vary in their population composition, patterns of interaction, beliefs and customs, and social-organizational structures, those that function well as a unit contribute differentially to the next generation of local communities. Routines, beliefs, and norms can therefore spread, not by virtue of their advantage *within* local communities, but by virtue of the advantage that they bestow on their local community *relative* to other local communities. If the process of between-community selection is sufficiently strong, then, over time, local communities become functionally organized, increasing their contribution to future communities. Under such conditions, the often apparently functional form of organizational communities can be seen as adaptations that have evolved because communities expressing them outcompete other groups (Sober and Wilson 1998).

Of course, all of this requires an appropriate community structure. If there is only one local community, then the shared effect becomes irrelevant. If many groups are present but community-level selection is weak, then the activities that would turn the community into a functional unit will largely succumb to activities that succeed within the local community. Organizational communities frequently consist of a mosaic of semi-isolated patches, however. Some are geographically localized communities including Silicon Valley and Route 128, as well as North Carolina's Research Triangle, the US manufacturing belt, the tile cluster and textile district in northern Italy, and the German Machine-Tool District. The geographic localization of these (and other) organizational communities may derive from the nature of the community's technological core (Sorenson and Audia 2000). Others may not be geographically localized but instead linked by shared technologies or markets (Astley and Fombrun 1983). Ferguson (1998), for example, chronicles the gastronomic community in nineteenth-century France comprised of restaurants, critics, culinary magazines, and aristocratic consumers connected by the traditions of classical cuisine. von Burg and Kenney (2000) describe the local area networking (LAN) industry as an organizational community comprising mainframe, micro- and minicomputer manufacturers, which was initially driven into two groups championing Token ring and Ethernet systems until the latter triumphed. Ingram and Simons (2000) show how Israeli kibbutzim were located in a community of populations consisting of credit cooperatives, banks, and political parties, and Scott et al. (2000), offer a detailed account of the agencies, associations, hospitals, HMOs, and insurance companies constituting the San Francisco Bay area healthcare organization community. Regardless of the basis for their patchiness, local variations—either in physical or technological space—promote a process of natural selection at the community level.

Notably, the positive feedback inherent in conformist transmission of organizational practices, which biases imitation toward majority or plurality practices, implies that small differences in initial distributions of practices between communities will be reinforced, and variations within them erased (Boyd and Richerson 1985; DiMaggio and Powell 1983). This observation suggests a potentially important role for complexity theory, introduced earlier, in understanding community evolution. When community interactions are complex, sensitive dependence on initial conditions magnifies initially random variation among local communities, while simple interactions reduce it. Since selection at any level requires variation among entities, local communities characterized by complex interactions may be more prone to community-level selection than communities governed by simple interactions (Wilson 1997). Thus, in the same way that complex behavior produces variation *within* organizations, complex interactions among populations of organizations can produce variation among organizational communities.

Although the resulting homogeneities within groups and sharp differences between groups need not be interpreted as adaptive products of selection, they do, however, provide a basis for community selection. The community whose set of beliefs and social organization are most group-beneficial will have a higher global fitness and tend to replace communities with less adaptive beliefs and organization. In this context, "beneficial" implies beliefs that promote a synergetic pattern of interaction within the community. The more communities vary in fitness, the stronger such group selection becomes. Thus, the often-functional form of organizational communities can be seen as adaptations that have evolved because groups expressing them outcompete other groups (Sober and Wilson 1998). Consider, for example, returns to research activity within an organizational community. If other organizations in an organization's community invest in a high level of R&D activity, the pool of new knowledge into which the organization can tap will be quite rich. And, since research performs the dual role of both generating new knowledge as well as absorbing new knowledge generated by other firms (Cohen and Levinthal 1990), the organization will find it attractive to invest in R&D as well. Of course, low-level R&D equilibria in which the level of new knowledge is too limited to motivate individual organizations to invest are also possible. Thus, at the community level, there are increasing returns to R&D investment, and communities settling at high-level equilibria will tend to outcompete those settling at low-level equilibria.

Community Structure

Organizational communities thus emerge as sets of populations become interlinked by commensalism and symbiosis, and those linkages become increasingly important determinants of outcomes for members of the populations that comprise the community. Understanding the structure of these relationships, which define the community context, is a crucial step in understanding processes that govern the emergence and selection of new organizational forms: As organizational communities evolve, community structure changes, altering environmental opportunities and constraints facing potential entrepreneurs.

In our earlier discussion of competitive selection processes within organizational populations we introduced the following logistic population growth function to model competitive selection acting on the growth of a single population (recall that K is the carrying capacity of the population's environment, *r* is the natural growth rate of the population, *N* is population density–the number of organizations in the population, and *t* is a time interval):

$$\frac{dN}{dt} = rN\left(\frac{K-N}{K}\right),$$

Of course, when a population interacts with other populations as part of a community, it is difficult to understand the population's behavior and evolution without attending to the nature of its ecological relationships with those other populations. This single-population formulation is easily modified to account for a population's ecological interactions with other populations in the same community. Consider first the case of a two-population community:

$$\frac{dN_A}{dt} = r_A N_A\left(\frac{K_A - N_A - \alpha_{AB} N_B}{K_A}\right)$$

$$\frac{dN_B}{dt} = r_B N_B\left(\frac{K_B - N_B - \alpha_{BA} N_A}{K_B}\right)$$

The community represented by this pair of equations is composed of two populations, *A* and *B*, which affect each other's rates of growth and decline through their interdependence. The second equation is the mirror of the first. The coefficients $^{\alpha}$AB and $^{\alpha}$BA represent the interdependence of populations *A* and *B*. These coefficients represent the proportional effect each member in one population has on the carrying capacity of the other. Thus when α >0, the presence of a member of population *A* (*B*) reduces by the fraction $^{\alpha}$AB ($^{\alpha}B_A$) the resources available for population *B* (*A*), slowing *B*s (*A*s) growth or speeding its decline. When α <0, however, the presence of one population increases the resources available to the other, speeding its growth or slowing its decline. The two-population model can be generalized to a community of *J* populations as:

$$\frac{dN_i}{dt} = r_i N_i \left(\frac{K_i - N_i - \sum_{j \neq i}^{J} \alpha_{ij} N_j}{K_i} \right), \alpha_{ii} = 1.$$

Symbiotic relations (i.e., $\alpha_{AB}<0$, $\alpha_{BA}<0$) involve mutual "interdependence of unlike forms, that is, units of dissimilar functions" (Hawley 1950: 209), and imply that populations occupying different niches benefit from each other's presence, each enhancing the resource availability and growth prospects of the other. In the "information economy" interacting populations of "complementors" abound (Shapiro and Varian 1999). The populations of software vendors and original equipment manufacturers each producing and selling one component of the "Wintel" PC standard is perhaps the most visible example. Commensalism, in contrast, involves "co-action of like forms, i.e. units of similar functions" (Hawley 1950: 209) and implies potential competition between interacting populations. The degree of competition between populations depends on the degree of similarity or overlap of the niches they occupy. Aldrich (1999: 302) has identified six scenarios of commensalism (see also Baum 1996: 91–2; Brittain and Wholey 1988).

- *Full competition* (i.e., $\alpha_{AB} > 0$, $\alpha_{BA} > 0$), growth in each population leads to a decline in the other because their niches overlap. For example, an increase in the number of day care centers in Toronto stimulated the failure of nursery schools in Toronto, and an increase in the number of nursery schools stimulated failure of day care centers in return. (Baum and Oliver 1991).
- *Partial competition* (i.e., $\alpha_{AB} > 0$, $\alpha_{BA} = 0$), inter-population relations are asymmetric, with only one having a negative effect on the other. For example, an increase in the number of US craft labor unions both suppressed founding and increased failure of US industrial unions, but the number of industrial unions did not affect either the founding or failure of craft unions (Hannan and Freeman 1989).
- *Predatory competition* (i.e., $\alpha_{AB} > 0$, $\alpha_{BA} < 0$), one population expands at the expense of another. For example, in the United States, the population of television stations grew at the expense of the population of radio stations (Dimmick and Rothenbuhler 1984).
- *Partial mutualism* (i.e., $\alpha_{AB} < 0$, $\alpha_{BA} = 0$) obtains when inter-population relations are asymmetric, with only one population benefiting from the presence of the other. For example, an increase in the number of brewpubs in the US stimulated the founding of microbreweries, but the number of microbreweries did not affect brewpub founding (Carroll and Swaminathan 1992)

- *Full mutualism* (i.e., $\alpha_{AB} < 0$, $\alpha_{BA} < 0$) means that two populations are in overlapping niches and benefit from the presence of the other. For example, an increase in the number of single-exchange telephone companies lowered the failure rate of multi-exchange telephone companies, and an increase in the number of multi-exchange companies lowered the failure rate of single-exchange companies in return (Barnett 1990).
- *Neutrality* (i.e., $\alpha_{AB} = 0$, $\alpha_{BA} = 0$) means that two populations have no influence on each other, although they do affect other populations in the community. For example, the numbers of commercial and savings banks in Manhattan were unrelated to each other's founding rates (Ranger-Moore et al. 1991), and the numbers of Group and IPA HMOs were unrelated to each other's failure rates (Wholey et al. 1992).

Aldrich (1999) suggests that the apparent commonness of neutrality in organizational communities is a result of evolutionary selection favoring loosely coupled social systems whose various subparts can adapt autonomously. An alternative explanation is that when we attempt to detect competition in a community structure that contains the effects of competition we fail to detect it because we observe an evolved set of interactions reflecting the effects of past competition. Another is coevolution. Although coevolution has become an umbrella term for a variety of processes and outcomes, it is important to distinguish the *reciprocal evolution* of coevolution from the *mutual causation* of systems theory and ecology. This basic difference helps account for observing neutrality. Given similar resource requirements (ecological similarity), but *absent coevolution*, one population in a predator/prey interaction will outcompete the other—the inferior population either migrates niches or disappears. But *with coevolution*, organizations comprising two ecologically similar populations might evolve toward different niches such that both survive. Thus, "rapid-coevolution" can alter the nature of ecological interactions (McKelvey, 1999).

Caveats about Communities

Three cautions are in order here to avoid mistaken inferences about community-level structural organization and evolution. First, discussions of organizational communities often equate higher-level functional organization with evidence of strong ecological interactions and dynamic equilibria. However, these features are properties of many chemical, physical, biological, and social systems, and do not imply functional organization. An organizational population can have a carrying capacity, regardless of whether it manages or overexploits its resources. Even the most dysfunctional communities can be stable, responding in ways that resist perturbation—stability at the community level occurs when the overall system of interpopulation interactions is characterized by negative feedback (Puccia and Levins 1985). In general, the fact that organizational populations have strong effects on each other and on the environment should not be confused with higher-level functional organization.

Second, although mutualism certainly plays an important role in community-level functional organization, and may be more common in functional than dysfunctional organizational communities, the proportion of interactions in a community that are mutualistic says little about its functional organization. Functional community-level organization can involve competition and predation, in addition to mutualism. Indeed, mutualism is an inevitable byproduct of indirect effects and they will exist even in highly dysfunctional communities (Baum and Korn 1994).[11] Community-level functional organization must be studied by investigating the properties that contribute to functional design. Whether functional properties are created by mutualistic or competitive interactions among members of the community is a secondary issue.

Third, it is sometimes claimed that complex system dynamics can produce higher-level functional organization in the absence of natural selection (Kauffman 1993; McKelvey 1998, 1999). Although it is certainly true that complex systems dynamics can produce striking patterns in the absence of natural selection, similar to the often-striking "strange attractor" patterns that can be generated by complex systems of equations, *pattern* is not the same as *functional organization*. An object that is designed to do something well must be structured in a particular way. Complex system dynamics are no more likely than simple system dynamics to produce the right combination of properties in the absence of natural selection. As we noted earlier, however, the variability fostered by complex system dynamics may be highly relevant to community-level functional organization when combined with multilevel selection theory (Wilson 1997).

Variation: Entrepreneurs and New Organizational Forms

How do new organizational forms arise within communities? Although, as we noted above, segregating mechanisms isolate organizational forms from inheriting one another's production and organizing competence, they are not so strong and stable that they are never bridged, and organizational forms do "speciate" to produce new organizational forms. Social boundaries separating organizational forms are subject to blending processes that may weaken segregating mechanisms, causing boundaries among organizational forms to erode and become blurred as organizations once clearly distinguishable become more interpenetrated and alike (Hannan and Freeman 1989). Some social forces, for example, stable technologies and strong regulatory systems, work to maintain organizational forms as discrete, easily recognized entities. Such technological and

[11] For example, competition between two populations, A and B, which benefits a third population, C, because it also competes with B, would appear as mutualism between populations A and C even if A and C did not interact directly.

institutional barriers can be established and dismantled quickly, however, increasing the pace of divergence or convergence in the evolution of organizational forms.

Neo-institutional theorists emphasize entrepreneurs' recombination of existing templates as the primary source of variation in organizational forms. More generally, recombination involves working with routines and competencies. Pre-existing routines and competencies are thus seen as the building blocks with which entrepreneurs build new organizational forms. The creation of new forms through recombination implies that structure shapes action and in turn, action shapes structure (DiMaggio and Powell 1991; Friedland and Alford 1991). It also implies that entrepreneurs shortcut natural selection using vicarious selectors (Campbell 1965): Fit knowledge retained in the form of pre-existing templates accelerates organizational evolution by eliminating dangerous or inadequate actions before they are executed and increasing chances for survival of new forms.

Imitative and Innovative Entrepreneurship

Although the popular press portrays the typical entrepreneur as an innovator—a Michael Dell or a Jeff Bezos—in fact entrepreneurs mostly reproduce existing organizational structures (Aldrich and Kenworthy 1999). There is a crucial difference between the first instance of a new form, the act of speciation—innovative entrepreneurship—and the emulation of a new form—imitative entrepreneurship. Founding a new organization is always a risky business, but especially so when entrepreneurs have few precedents for the kinds of activities they want to found. Innovative entrepreneurs in the early years of a new organizational form face a greater set of challenges than imitative entrepreneurs who carry on a tradition pioneered by their many predecessors. The first instance of a new form represents an innovation that requires integration into the prevailing community social order to be viable. Building institutional context and institutional entrepreneurship including but not limited to acquiring legitimacy, are thus far more crucial challenges for innovative entrepreneurs.

Rao and Singh (1999) present a simple typology of recombinations that effectively captures the organizing processes involved in the construction of new forms through recombination. In their typology, new organizational forms represent novel incarnations of core features—goals, authority relations, technologies, and markets. Entrepreneurs can add or delete existing organizing elements from existing organizational forms, *both* add and delete elements, or they can neither add nor delete elements, the final case representing imitative entrepreneurship. Table 18.2 summarizes the four possibilities. Rao and Singh also distinguish between recombinations based on the number of changes. *Strong speciation* occurs when all four of the core features differ from existing forms. *Weak speciation* occurs when only one or two core attributes differ. Strategic groups within an industry, differing in markets served or technologies, illustrate weak speciation.

Table 18.2 A Typology of New Organizational Forms

	No addition of organizing elements	Addition of new organizing elements
No deletion of organizing elements	Cell I Imitative Entrepreneurship	Cell III Partial Enlargement
Deletion of organizing elements	Cell II Partial Contraction	Cell IV Radical Recombination

Adapted from Rao and Singh (1999: 72)

Cell I exemplifies imitative entrepreneurship. Such organizations, which reproduce an existing form, are likely to be accommodated easily into the current institutional order and legitimated on a nearly automatic basis because of existing precedents and tradition (Delacroix and Rao 1994). Many new organizations replicate existing forms because the entrepreneurs who found them use simple, conformist imitation rules that are *frequency-dependent*, varying with the commonness of organizational routines and capabilities, and *trait- and outcome-dependent*, with the most successful, similar organizations the most attractive models for imitation (Haunschild and Miner 1997). Faced with insufficient information and uncertainty, entrepreneurs turn to the actions of established organizations for clues about how to proceed. However, because it is not often possible to gauge the true value of other organizations' routines and competencies, more frequent use it taken as evidence that others find it valuable and appropriate, increasing its likelihood of entrepreneurial adoption. Entrepreneurs are also selective about which organizations to imitate, discriminating among organizations and imitating those that achieve the most desirable outcomes (e.g., high-status and superior performance). Organizational founders thus adopt institutionalized designs and attempt to model their new venture's structures and practices on patterns thought to be more modern, appropriate, and professional. As noted above, however, entrepreneurs who reflexively copy "industry recipes" (Spender 1989) not only reproduce existing organizational forms: they also fail to explore potentially superior alternatives (Romanelli 1999).

Coercive and normative processes at various levels of organizations also produce strong downward pressure to conform, reinforcing imitative behavior. At the organization level, parent companies pressure new branches and franchises to conform to their internal standards. At the population level, structuring of the immediate environment within which innovative entrepreneurs must operate, by standard designs and operating procedures, for example, can stand in the way of novelty. At the community-level, interpopulation relations affect the distribution of resources in the environment and the terms on which they are available to entrepreneurs. Resource providers, for example, reward entrepreneurs who signal their conformity to proven past predictors of success with easier (and cheaper) access to financial capital and social capital (Aldrich and Fiol 1994). At the institutional level, government regulations and policies, dominant professional models, and the skills and knowledge emphasized in educational curricula produce similar pressures for conformity (DiMaggio 1991; Sutton and Dobbin 1996). Cultural rules and norms also create powerful pressures toward conformity and cultural rigidity that can severely fetter innovative individual initiatives.

Although following conformist imitation rules can lead to a preponderance of imitative entrepreneurship that reproduces established populations, conformist imitation can, under certain conditions, produce eclectic recombinations of routines that bloom into innovative organizations (Miner and Raghavan 1999). For example, if entrepreneurs combine different modes of conformist imitation (frequency, trait, and outcome) in different mixes, they may bring about novel combinations of routines. Imperfect imitation can also introduce variety (Lippman and Rumelt 1982; Nelson and Winter 1982). For example, entrepreneurs can make copying errors, implementing imitated routines in different ways—for better or worse—or lacking complete information they may base their imitation on different samples of the outcomes for prior adopters, giving rise to novel combinations. Other important sources of variation in new organizations include the hiring and training of new employees from across several "training" populations. As a result of experiential learning processes, chance variations in the temporal sequences that entrepreneurs adopt or sample other organizations' actions or outcomes may also produce new mixes of routines.

Another path to nonconformity is ignorance of existing cultural norms and industry practices (Aldrich and Kenworthy 1999). Some individuals will simply be unaware of prevailing conformity-inducing forces. For entrepreneurs ignorant of the norms, rules, and practices that dictate organizational forms within a community or population, any conformity would be purely accidental. Perhaps only "outsiders," unencumbered by industry norms, practices, and recipes, are able to blindly (in Campbell's terms) assemble truly innovative organizations. This conjecture is at odds with the observation of highly visible habitual innovative entrepreneurs in many industries (Aldrich and Kenworthy 1999). What gives rise to habitually innovative entrepreneurs, and why is their success not contagious? Entrepreneurs' accumulation of tacit knowledge and social capital over a series of innovative successes provides one possible explanation for this phenomenon—innovative entrepreneurs with a track record become highly valued for their abilities, and may gain superior access to sources of capital and other forms of support. For them, "nonconformity" becomes a legitimate activity.

Regardless of how they "break the bonds" of conformity, innovative entrepreneurs can recombine core organizational features in three ways. *Partial contraction* (Cell II) results when organizational elements are deleted. Point-to-point airlines are the result of innovative entrepreneurs eliminating key elements of core technology from the value chain, including hub-and-spoke route networks, ticketing agents, transfer agreements with other airlines, and in-house maintenance. Cell II resembles imitative entrepreneurship to the extent that external endorsement may not be problematic because the new form entails eliminating some elements from pre-existing organizational forms, and so can readily draw on available institutional understandings. It may also be welcome by resource providers and consumers to whom it may represent a leaner, low-cost version of an existing form. Recombination through partial enlargement (Cell III), in contrast, creates new forms as entrepreneurs consciously add elements. Examples of such recombination are leading business schools getting actively involved in executive education or, more recently, US hospitals getting involved in the managed care business. Although in some instances legislative barriers may exist that prevent some types of enlargement, in other cases, regulators may, through deregulation, for example, encourage existing forms to add elements. Even when sanctioned by the state, however, new forms created by adding new elements may experience an external liability of newness because they are intelligible to resource providers and the general public. For example, diversified firms that combine unfamiliar elements may face poor market valuations, while non-profits that pursue multiple causes may find it difficult to gain philanthropists' support.

Radical recombination (Cell IV) involves both the addition and deletion of core organizing elements, resulting in new forms that embody new beliefs, values, goals, authority relations, technology, and new products or services to consumers. One illustration of such a recombination includes health maintenance organizations (HMO's). On the one hand, HMO's add elements that come with a profit orientation and greater cost consciousness, such as preventative care and careful review of referrals to specialists. On the other hand, routine access to sophisticated (and costly) diagnostic procedures, and the availability of significant discretion to physicians are typically curtailed. Such new forms cannot draw on existing institutional understandings and so must establish new understandings and new cognitive frames that establish a rationale for a new form (Meyer and Scott 1983). As a result, organizing challenges are likely to be greatest here, but may also offer the greatest potential rewards—if the challenges are successfully met (Rao and Singh 1999).

Imitation is thus the least disruptive form of entrepreneurship, but is also likely to secure the fewest rewards (Henderson 1999). New forms created through partial contraction of elements, and spawned by the addition of elements are more disruptive, and may gain substantial rewards. The relative advantages of leaner forms premised on the deletion of elements, and fatter forms composed of new elements hinge on consumer preferences, and institutional tolerances for costs and service. New forms produced through these processes also face more significant challenges and their proponents have to go the distance in erecting segregating mechanisms, gaining legitimacy, and buffering the new form from selection pressures.

Selection: Ecological Opportunity

The isolation of new organizational forms from their parent population(s) will succeed in establishing new populations only under certain ecological conditions. "Ecological opportunity" must be available for a novel form to establish itself successfully (Stanley, 1981: 96). Such opportunities exist where competitive saturation of the environment is low enough to weaken selection pressures. The environment must approximate an "unfilled ecospace," unoccupied by other populations (Gould and Eldredge 1977: 144). Otherwise, the novel form will be crowded out, as it would be in its parent population. Organizational communities are the contexts that govern the extent of ecological opportunity and the selection of new organizational forms (Astley 1985).

Within populations, the familiar *r*-to-*K* transition unfolds (see *r*-*K* Transition, above). While competition runs its course within populations, symbiotic interdependencies emerge between them. New populations branch out from established ones to fulfill ancillary roles in which they are dependent on but noncompetitive with their ancestors and each other (Hawley 1950: 203). Horizontal and vertical interdependencies among populations result from underlying technologies that define resource consumption patterns. As organizations struggle either to increase their autonomy (Burt 1980) or stabilize their interdependence (Pfeffer and Salancik 1978), they develop relationships with organizations in other neighboring populations, which, in part, serve to define the community's social structure (Fombrun 1986). This social structure itself unfolds nested within a set of institutionalized beliefs and understandings about competition and cooperation (DiMaggio and Powell 1983; Meyer and Rowan 1977).

In the early stages of community evolution, branching occurs frequently as competition at carrying capacity within populations initiates a process of functional and territorial differentiation that pushes entrepreneurs to seek distinct functions in which they hold a competitive advantage. Complementary functionalities and interpopulation dependencies can thus multiply rapidly as entrepreneurs create many novel organizational forms, some of which initiate new populations (Astley 1985; Hunt and Aldrich 1998; Romanelli 1989). Because communities contain multiple populations, each potentially at a different stage of the *r*-*K* transition, rates of entrepreneurship will differ across populations, as will—as a result—the favored organizational forms (Hunt and Aldrich 1998). The community evolves through a process of ecological succession in which change unfolds simultaneously in the structure of relationships *within* and *between* populations comprising the community along two axes–*commensalistic* and *symbiotic* (Hawley 1950: 201–3). As possible niches are progressively filled, the growth of internal complexity fosters community stability (Astley 1985; Hawley 1950).

Elaboration continues until the complexity of internal relationships can no longer increase without reducing the community's effectiveness as a functional unit (Hawley 1950: 203). At this stage, the community is "full," it is a closed, self-contained, self-maintaining, dynamic equilibrium system (Astley 1985). Tight integration of populations within the community makes it more likely that a new form will encounter a competitor that prevents it from being successful. New populations cannot be added without disturbing the system, and the size of each population is balanced against the needs of other populations in the community. Thus, community closure coincides with competitive saturation within its constituent populations, and its approach is a major factor regulating the extent of ecological opportunity. It also sets the stage for community collapse, however. If complex systems experience disturbances beyond a certain threshold, they may disintegrate as the result of a domino effect (Astley 1985; Pimm 1991). Thus, tightly coupled community systems can be fragile and prone to collapse and simplification when confronted with disturbances (e.g., technological and institutional change) that upset their equilibrium, and although they may be re-established though ecological succession—they also may not (Kauffman 1993; Pimm 1991).

Community Disruption

Stable technologies and strong regulatory systems, work to maintain organizational forms as discrete, easily recognized entities. At the same time, however, such technological and institutional barriers between forms can be erected and dismantled quickly, increasing the pace of divergence and convergence in the evolution of organizational forms. As a result, ecological opportunities and the potential for innovative entrepreneurship are closely tied to technological and institutional dynamics. Technological conditions shape the boundaries around organizational forms, determine the relative importance of resources and values of organizational routines and capabilities, and so the nature of interdependencies among organizational forms. Institutional conditions too define the boundaries around organizational forms, and the criteria for judging whether an organization or an organizational form is worthy of continued support and survival. Technological and institutional changes, which disrupt previously stable communities, are thus major catalysts for the creation of new organizational forms and the evolution of new community structures that bind new forms sharing a common orientation toward novel technological, normative, or regulatory conditions. Of course, communities experiencing major technological or institutional change present challenging contexts. Rules are disputed, technologies are contested, and social actors competing to create a new social order receive little guidance.

Technology Cycles

Technological disruptions spawn new forms by opening up spaces for new core technologies and possibilities for novel marketing strategies. Technological models of creative destruction through innovation (Schumpeter 1934; Tushman and Anderson 1986) hold that technological discontinuities create opportunities for entrepreneurs to establish new organizational forms as existing populations' sources of competitive advantage decay, freeing up resources for new organizations to take advantage of new opportunities for establishing competitive positions. Evolutionary models of technological change portray organizations as genealogical repositories of skills, routines, assets, and information (Nelson and Winter 1982; Winter 1988; Dosi 1988). Technological innovation produces new organizational forms through an ongoing recombinatory process of variation, selection, and retention (Abernathy and Utterback 1978; Basalla 1988; Bijker et al. 1987; Dosi 1982, 1984; Sahal 1985).

Anderson and Tushman (1990) integrate these diverse evolutionary analyses and outline how cycles of technological change affect entries and exits of organizations. They suggest that cycles of technological change are triggered by technological discontinuities, that is, radical product and process innovations that result in significant cost, performance, and quality improvements. *Competence-enhancing* discontinuities build on technologies of existing organizational forms, making possible order-of-magnitude improvements in their efficiency, and changes in the core technological characteristics of organizations. *Competence-destroying* discontinuities, in contrast, render existing organizational forms' know-how, skills, and resources obsolete, creating new possibilities for new actors (entrepreneurs and organizations from other domains) to enter, and novel organizational forms to emerge. By redefining the value and importance of organizational resources and capabilities, competence-destroying change alters the relational structure of an organizational community substantially, transforming exchange and power relationships, unraveling status orders, and fostering new types of linkages. Population boundaries give way as new actors enter, activities are reshuffled among organizations, and personnel blend and blur. Even the borders of the community may be realigned as the new technology in use redefines what types of activities and which types of actors are legitimate and which are more or less central or peripheral to those activities.

Competence-destroying technological discontinuities unleash an era of ferment characterized by variation and competition among multiple versions of the same technology and potential substitutes. Product diversity is high, and products tend to be made to customer specifications. The production process is nascent, labor intensive, and poorly codified. Performance criteria are ambiguous, the evaluation of technological alternatives is costly, and the trajectory of technological change is uncertain (Abernathy and Utterback 1978; Zuscovitch 1986). Eras of ferment culminate with the emergence of one design or technology as the dominant design, that is, a set of engineering ideas that constrain future technological progress. Dominant designs consist of the core product idea, the functions the product is to perform, and the processes by which it is to be manufactured, and they enable product standardization and generate stable linkages among firms, personnel, and capital markets (Clark 1985). A design becomes dominant as a result of its efficiency, legitimacy, or political support, and often entails intense political activity by entrepreneurs and organizations championing different ideas (Tushman and Rosenkopf 1992). The advent of a dominant design signals the start of an era of incremental technological change, which, as we noted earlier, can trigger an *r*-to-*K* transition within populations that create or use the technology. Innovations cumulate and refine the dominant design. Productivity and process improvements become more central, price competition becomes more important, and internal coordination in firms becomes formalized and routinized.

The era of incremental change lasts until it is broken by another product or process-based technological discontinuity that restarts the cycle. Product innovations are likely to be embodied in new organizational forms because the structure, decision-making, and learning processes of existing forms inhibits them from perceiving and effectively capitalizing on opportunities to modify subsystems and the linkages among subsystems (Baum et al. 1995; Henderson and Clark 1990). Thus, as we noted earlier, the "self-destructive" properties of organizational learning make the replacement of obsolescent organizations easier by making old markets vulnerable to new organizations with new capabilities. By contrast, process innovations are likely to inhibit new forms because they presuppose and capitalize on organizations' learning through doing, and create entry barriers (Abernathy and Utterback 1978; Kamien and Schwartz 1982).

Institutional Dynamics

Organizations exist not only in technical-resource environments, but also in worlds of beliefs, rules, and ideas that are referred to as *institutional environments*. The concept of the institutional environment refers to the cultural-cognitive belief systems and regulatory and normative structures that prevail in a given organizational community, constituting its organizing principles, and providing a basis for its coherence, meaning, and stability (Friedland and Alford 1991; Scott 1995). Although it is possible to separate material-resource and institutional environments analytically, what constitutes a "resource" and whether and how it can be used and combined are determined, in part, by institutional beliefs and rule systems (Scott 1995). In addition to such *indirect* influence, institutional environments influence organizations directly through the logics they legitimate, and the governance systems and rules of social action they support. Institutional environments specify what goals or values are to be pursued within a domain, indicate appropriate means for pursuing them, and organizational forms embody and enact the institutionally defined structures, practices, and identities.

Social actors—individuals as well as organizations—are capable of exercising their power to create and modify their institutional environments to have their interests reflected. Once institutional environments are in place, however, they operate as an external force, regulating and empowering social actors. Institutional arrangements, by their nature, are unlikely to change abruptly. Even when change appears sudden, it is usually possible to find evidence of earlier forces at work, undermining current arrangements, or precursors to new institutional logics and organizational forms (Scott, 1995). Thus, although there is often a "dominant" institutional logic that reflects the consensus of powerful institutional actors in a given community, secondary or repressed logics representing other, subordinated interests also exist that may, over time, become more influential, and even superordinate (Fombrun 1986). These secondary logics may serve as precursors to institutional change but, of course, not all vying will be successful.

Institutional models stress environmental imprinting, through which social conditions at the time of founding limit organizational inventions (Stinchcombe 1965), the importance of political upheavals, entrepreneurs' access to resources and power, and the role of the state in enabling (or constraining) competition and competence sharing between organizational forms (Aldrich 1979, 1999). The state and professions, for example, shape organizational communities and the potential for new organizational forms by providing cognitive and legal frameworks and spawning formal structures to create and defend jurisdictional claims (Abbott 1988; Rao 1998). When legal or other rules responsible for the emergence of or governing the maintenance of differences between groups of organizations are relaxed, or other forms of institutional pressures (e.g., normative rules, taken-for-granted assumptions) are removed, the existing distinctions among organizations may become blurred. Witness, for example, the empowerment of private military and security companies to perform critical national security and military tasks as institutional logics of state power, sovereignty, and the use of violence were transformed following the end of the Cold War (Baum & McGahan 2013).

For example, for a number of decades the US telecommunications industry experienced steady development, measured growth, and relative stability. But, suddenly, the onset of deregulation fostered an accelerating curve of new technologies and reshaping of industry structures (Astley and Fombrun 1983). This restructuring of telecommunications has now unfolded globally as countries around the world deregulated their telecommunications industries. Other industries (e.g., banking, airlines, and electric utilities) have experienced or are also now experiencing similar effects of deregulation. Beyond deregulation, perhaps most salient institutions to arise in the final decades of the twentieth century were the institutions of market reform in Latin American and European economies (e.g., Chile, Poland), and trade agreements giving rise to regionalization and globalization of economic organization (e.g., EEC and NAFTA).

More generally, Scott et al. (2000: 24–5) identify a range of outcomes of such institutional changes vital to community evolution:

- New logics. *The logics that direct, motivate and legitimate the behavior of actors in the community are changed. The types of ends pursued and/or means-ends chains that guide action undergo change, as do the types of justifications that are given for action.*
- New actors. *New types of social actors, both individual and collective, appear, sometimes representing new combinations or hybrids of existing organizational forms, sometimes representing new entrants from other [communities]. Existing actors may transform their identities. The cast of characters undergoes change.*
- New meanings. *The meanings associated with the attributes of behavior of actors in the community or the effects associated with them (that is, changes in the causal relations among variables) are modified. Old attributes are viewed in new ways or are observed to have different effects.*
- New relations among actors. *The nature and extent of relations among actors in the community, including, in particular, exchange and power relations, are transformed. New types of linkages are created and the relational structure of the community exhibits substantial alterations.*
- Modified population boundaries. *Boundaries once containing and separating organizational populations, organization, customary activities, and personnel blend and blur.*
- Modified [community] boundaries. *The borders of [the community] are expanded, reduced, or realigned. New definitions determine what types of activities and which types of actors are legitimate and which are more or less central or peripheral players.*

Changes in logics are likely to occur first, creating conditions for the construction of new roles and new types of organizations: "Logics lead the way because they are largely based on ideas. Ideas are often generated within a [community] by the 'creative odd ones' who formulate new concepts, models, and designs" (Scott et al. 2000: 174). The introduction of new actors can alter patterns of interaction, providing participants with new perspective on their situation that can precipitate changes in interpretation (i.e., logic). If new ideas and interpretations diffuse and gain acceptance—often they do not—they can become the basis for social movements. If successful, over time, logics become taken for granted as "how things are" and the "way things are done." Because they require a buildup of pressure and political will, changes in regulatory and normative structures (e.g., professional association policy) tend to lag the introduction of new logics and actors, but nevertheless, open up spaces for new core features—organizational goals, authority systems, client markets—and promote organizational diversity.

By dismantling segregating barriers, technological and institutional change create ecological opportunities for innovative entrepreneurs to construct new technical and institutional ideas, models, and designs, and found new organizations that represent new combinations of interests, personnel and technical capabilities. Technological and institutional change are thus essential, though not sufficient, preconditions for the birth of new organizational forms. New types of actors cannot come into existence in the absence of a supportive ideological based (Sinchcombe 1965; Aldrich and Fiol 1994). Social visionaries, intellectuals, inventors, and entrepreneurs create new possibilities—new designs for structures and new ways of acting. They propose new templates or archetypes for roles, groups, and organizations (Greenwood and Hinings 1993). But these ideas must find a receptive audience. More importantly, the new ideas must be instantiated in routines, roles, and social organizations if they are to persist over time.

Retention: The Institutionalization of New Organizational Forms

Although necessary, ecological opportunity is not sufficient for the creation of a new organizational form. Resources do not "pre-exist" as free-floating niches waiting to be filled with new forms, they have to be mobilized and niches carved out through individual and collective efforts (McKelvey 1982; Van de Ven and Garud 1989, 1992). Institutional entrepreneurship is needed to carve out a space for new organizational forms within a community of populations, either by creating a new niche for itself or by invading an already occupied niche. Entrepreneurs must mobilize resources, legitimate the goals, structures, and competencies embodied in their new forms, and integrate them within the organizational community. They must also rapidly acquire mechanisms that isolate their new form from its parent forms(s), or its distinctive characteristics are unlikely to be maintained over time. The balance of competition and symbiosis the new population achieves vis-à-vis other populations in the community ultimately determines its boundaries. Innovative entrepreneurs and their early imitators must learn and respond to constraints and opportunities as they construct their population's boundaries. Their struggle is very much a collective one, though not necessarily a collaborative one (Aldrich 1999). For new organizational forms, then, the burden of selection may stem more from the realm of *institutional selection* than *competitive selection* (Rao and Singh 1999). Central to the retention of any new organizational form, therefore, is the process by which the logic, technology, and values underpinning the new form are legitimated (Rao and Singh 1999; Stinchcombe 1968).

Organizational Legitimacy and the Liability of Newness

All new organizational forms face external and internal liabilities of newness (Stinchcombe 1965). Externally, new forms require the endorsement of the state and markets for capital and personnel. Internally, they must develop routines to perform and coordinate their work effectively. New organizational forms must also rapidly acquire mechanisms that isolate them from their parent forms(s), or their distinctive characteristics are unlikely to be maintained over time.

Among these challenges, a lack of legitimacy is especially critical: crucial stakeholders do not fully understand the nature of the new ventures, and their conformity to established institutional rules remains in doubt. These two entrepreneurial challenges reflect two forms of legitimacy: cognitive and sociopolitical (Aldrich and Fiol 1994; Hannan and Carroll 1992; Scott 1995). Cognitive legitimacy stresses conformity to institutionalized archetypes and schemas and emphasizes the legitimacy reflected in actors' taken-for-granted assumptions, conceiving an organizational form as legitimate when actors view it as the natural way to effect some kind of collective action. Sociopolitical legitimacy emphasizes how embeddedness in relational and normative contexts influences an organizational form's legitimacy by signaling its conformity to social and institutional expectations, rules, and practices. An organizational form achieves sociopolitical legitimacy when it becomes regarded as obligatory, buttressed by legal mandate or by widely shared cultural, professional, and political norms and values. Legitimacy is thus not merely a resource to be possessed or exchanged but a condition reflecting the alignment of an organization to normative, regulatory, and cultural-cognitive rules and beliefs prevailing in its organizational community and wider social environment (Scott, 1995). The extent to which an organization or organizational form is judged to be legitimate has critical implications for the level of support and sanction conferred on it by its environment and thus for its survival.

Aldrich and Fiol (1994) suggest that social contexts not only pattern established meaning to which imitative entrepreneurs conform, but also create opportunities for institutional entrepreneurs to initiate renegotiation of meanings. Aldrich and Fiol identify four nested levels of social context within which institutional entrepreneurs must progressively build trust, reliability, reputation, and, ultimately, cognitive and sociopolitical legitimacy for their novel forms. Table 18.3 shows the levels in their framework

Table 18.3 Strategies for Institutional Entrepreneurship

Level	Cognitive Legitimacy	Sociopolitical Legitimacy
Organization	Develop knowledge base via symbolic language and behavior	Develop trust by constructing internally consistent cognitive frames
Population	Develop knowledge base by encouraging convergence on a standard	Develop perceptions of reliability by mobilizing collective action
Community	Develop knowledge base by promoting activity through third-parties	Develop reputation by negotiating and compromising with other populations
Institutional	Develop knowledge base by creating linkages with educational institutions and professions	Develop legitimacy by organizing collective marketing and lobbying

Adapted from Aldrich and Fiol (1994: 649)

and strategies for institutional entrepreneurship at each level. The levels are tightly coupled. Gaining stakeholder trust at the organization level provides a basis on which to develop a codified knowledge base at the population level, which, in turn, makes it easier to organize collectively and establish a reputation facilitating interaction at the community level and cooptation of institutional actors. Legitimation of a new organizational form thus depends on individual efforts of institutional entrepreneurs to frame their new form and build trust in it, and collective efforts of early imitative entrepreneurs to establish standards, promote reliability, and advance the interests of the new form through institutional linkages (Friedland and Alford 1991).

Absent cognitive legitimacy, institutional entrepreneurs face the hurdle of winning approval of key stakeholders for their activities, who are unlikely to offer their unconditional support to the novel venture—and may actively oppose it (Baum & McGahan 2013). Institutional entrepreneurs must cognitively frame their new venture to foster others' trust in their competence and efforts. Cognitive frames are explanations that mobilize capital, personnel, and legitimacy by providing an institutional logic for the institutional entrepreneur's novel organizational solution (Rao 1998). Frames define the scope of the new organizational form, and justify it as indispensable, valid, and appropriate. They also define the interests of various constituencies, identify threats, and provide a vision (Snow and Benford 1992). Frames must be compatible with the established institutional order while at the same time concealing the new form's radical nature (Aldrich and Fiol 1994; Hunt and Aldrich 1998). Given the lack of externally validated frames, institutional entrepreneurs must construct a coherent case for their venture by recombining elements from existing cultural repertoires and organizational myths (Douglas 1986; Meyer and Rowan 1977). Institutional entrepreneurs are thus conduits though which new forms are infused with cultural and normative content.

Not only must institutional entrepreneurs convince various stakeholders of their novel venture's legitimacy, they must also fend off rival entrepreneurs offering alternate versions of their products and services, and competing with them for legitimacy by appealing to customers and investors to accept and endorse their version. When different institutional entrepreneurs champion incompatible frames, the choice between them hinges on power and social structure (Friedland and Alford 1991; DiMaggio 1991; Rao 1998). The fate of alternative frames depends on the relative sizes of the political coalitions that form around them, the attitudes of government actors, and levels of support from professionals. In such cases, stakeholder and institutional endorsements are critical if a new form is to take hold and proliferate.

Once institutional entrepreneurs have developed a basis of understanding and trust in their new form, they must develop strategies to enhance its performance reliability and establish stable relationships with early imitative entrepreneurs attempting to reproduce the new form. Intense competition among early entrants slows the growth of all ventures by reducing the chances that a champion will emerge and inspire efforts toward collective action, and by increasing confusion about what standards should be followed (Aldrich and Fiol 1994). Convergence is critical to establishing the new form's identity, boundaries, and role in the interorganizational community. Collective action and convergence toward a standard version are facilitated if entrepreneurs choose early on to imitate innovators, rather than seek further innovation.[12] Convergence is more likely if the original innovation is imitable, creating incentives for cooperating to stabilize competitive conditions (Aldrich and Fiol 1994). The likelihood of convergence also depends on the rate at which payoffs to new adopters accumulate; increasing returns to adoption stimulate imitative adoption (Arthur 1989). As we discuss further below, institutional entrepreneurs' efforts to convince others to accept and adopt their version of the new form often resemble social movements (Haveman and Rao 1997, Rao 1998). Social movements are collective attempts to construct the boundaries of new organizational forms and integrate them with the prevalent social order. Industry or trade associations, frequently founded by innovative entrepreneurs themselves, are often the centerpiece of such movements, taking leadership in formulating product and process standards, founding trade journals, running educational trade fairs, and representing the form to government agencies (Aldrich and Fiol 1994).

Although early imitative entrepreneurs will inevitably make frequent mistakes because so much of the knowledge about the new form is uncodified, repeated imitation and borrowing from earlier foundings fosters codification of knowledge about the form, fostering its spread and contributing to convergence on an organizational standard. Industry associations and other collective actors can facilitate codification and convergence by instituting accreditation procedures, or certification contests to evaluate organizations and their products or services according to performance on preset criteria (Rao 1994). Increasingly, accreditation has become a formalized process as professional associations establish criteria and assessment regimes to evaluate organizations'

[12] If, however, the organizational definition is settled before early entrepreneurs have had the chance to discover effective routines, the standard itself will be suboptimal, and this may prove disastrous for the form (Baum and Berta 1999).

conformity to their standards. Accreditation and certification offer standard social tests of an organizational form and its products and services. They also serve as knowledge diffusion mechanisms that help to establish the identity and cognitive legitimacy and accountability of the new form, and the reliability of its products or services and its producers. What is good for the organizational form is not necessarily good for the innovative entrepreneur, however (Aldrich and Fiol 1994). Codification and convergence facilitate replication, stimulating further imitative founding and lowering failure rates, but easy imitability also makes organizational survival more problematic as the market crowds with competitors whose survival depends on small differences. Under such circumstances, imitative entrepreneurs often survive at the expense of the original innovator (Delacroix and Rao 1994).

Converging on a common, well-codified definition helps create consumer awareness (e.g., through media attention) and provides financial institutions an opportunity to assess the credit-worthiness of the form. It also familiarizes government authorities with the form, and facilitates educational institutions' development of training programs. This familiarization in turn facilitates development of cognitive legitimacy—establishing the form as the taken-for-granted and natural way to organization a collective activity. Emergence of a consistent body of knowledge also provides entrepreneurs a basis on which to build a reputation for their new form as a taken-for-granted member of the larger inter-organizational community, facilitating stable relationships and economic transactions with other established populations, and raising the likelihood of sociopolitical approval. A new form becomes "established" when powerful actors endorse its claims by enacting rules and defining social and technical boundaries around the form, ensuring that its distinctive character—a novel incarnation of goals, authority relations, technology, and market strategy—will be preserved over time. The development of a regulatory framework of rules and guidelines (e.g., licensing) constitutes conditions conducive to the creation of organizations (Meyer and Rowan 1977).

Social Movements and Legitimation

Under certain conditions, social movements may also play a vital role in establishing new organizational forms. Social movements are collective endeavors to solve social problems. Social movement theory identifies process through which actors translate shared interests into collective action. In the same way that organizations working together (e.g., as lobbying association) can serve as a segregating mechanism, maintaining distinctions between those engaged in collective action and those not so engaged, collective action is also a vehicle through which such boundaries can be constructed in the first place. Contemporary social movement theory views the ability of institutional entrepreneurs to bring about change to depend on framing processes, mobilizing structures, and political opportunities (McAdam, McCarthy and Zald 1996).

Institutional entrepreneurs can mobilize legitimacy, finances, and personnel only when they are able to elaborate collective action frames that enable collective attribution processes to operate (Snow and Benford 1992). Opportunities to elaborate such frames are provided by major institutional and technological disruption and instability that undermines the status quo, increasing chances for a shared interpretation that a social system has lost legitimacy and is vulnerable to new demands from groups who seek to have their interests taken into account (McAdam 1994). Collective vehicles through which people mobilize and engage in collective action are also essential for social movements. Such structures include formal social movement organizations (McCarthy and Zald 1977), work and neighborhood organizations, and informal friendship networks (Tilly 1978) that shape the common identity and social ties linking individuals and organizations. The recognition of a shared identity, coupled with previously existing social ties, greatly increases the ability of a group to translate common interests into mobilization (Tilly 1978). Social connections are the conduits through which individuals join movements, and those most central in social networks are most likely to join social movements or otherwise become active and to do so early on. Homogeneous interests and dense social networks increase a group's capacity to mobilize its resources and the likelihood of the formation of a movement. Because organizations are the critical units in governmental policymaking, creating formal organizations to represent the movement is vital (Laumann and Knoke 1987).

Organized attempts to establish new structures also require political opportunity on which to thrive. Social movements thrive in times of social or political instability because the status quo is more vulnerable to successful challenge by outsiders. Disruptions change power relations and thus create opportunities for insurgency (McAdam 1994). While the social movements we focus on are aimed at institutionalization of new organizational forms, some are "counter-movements" aimed at unraveling some perceived regulatory or institutional injustice and so may themselves underlie institutional changes that create fertile conditions for new organizational forms to emerge. Political opportunity, mobilization structures, and framing processes are reciprocally intertwined such that skillful framing of an issue can create an opportunity and reduce mobilization costs, just as strong mobilization structures can broaden opportunity and reduce the need for an awe-inspiring frame. The background of conditions that create new possibilities for the rise of social movements often consist of a priori organizational and market failures (Rao et al. 2000). We consider three: influence costs, positive externalities, and negative externalities.

When a new organizational form involves a radical recombination (Table 18.2, Cell IV), it can jeopardize vested interests. It must acquire endorsements from powerful collective actors, such as the state, and must be transformed from a novel artifact into a social fact. A common presumption is that instances of a new organizational form can garner legitimacy by banding together through trade associations to secure governmental support and gain standing in consumer and financial markets. Trade associations can, however, be crippled by influence costs (Milgrom and Roberts, 1982). When decisions affect the distribution of wealth or benefits among constituents of trade assocations and elite coalitions, affected individuals can attempt to influence decisions to their benefit. As a result, agreements may be hard to negotiate, thus blocking sustained coordination among producers. When producers are unable to coordinate action because of influence costs, social movements can play vital roles in the legitimation of a new organizational form. For example, automobile clubs played an important role in legitimating the automobile in the United States due to the failure of collective action by trade associations for producers (Rao et al. 2000). As a novel product, the automobile was unfamiliar to prospective consumers who were confused because the source of power, the number of cylinders, systems of steering and control, and the mode of stopping were topics of considerable controversy. Sporadic opposition from vigilante anti-speed organizations constrained the use of the automobile by forcing municipal governments to impose speed ordinances. Firms within the new industry could not successfully band together to legitimate the automobile. The National Association of Automobile Manufacturers was established in 1900 in a bid to assure product quality, but was superseded by the Association of Licensed Automobile Manufacturers, formed in 1903, and then challenged by a rival, the American Motor Car Manufacturers' Association, established in 1905. Both associations had collapsed by 1911 following a legal battle. It was in this context that automobile fans banded together into automobile clubs and sought to legitimate the automobile as a reliable and safe means of transportation.

Positive externalities arise when those who incur the costs of an action are not the sole beneficiaries of the action and those who benefit have necessarily not shared in its costs. Standard economic theory holds that industry "pioneers" incur the costs of establishing a trade association, formulating technical standards and setting up supply and distribution networks, as well as playing key roles in familiarizing investors, personnel, consumers, and government agencies with the new organizational form. However, the benefits of these activities also extend to later entrants to the industry and not just to pioneers. In principle, pioneers should balk at incurring the costs of legitimating a new organizational form, but as standard economic theory points out they bear these costs because they have an opportunity to gain a large share of the market. Normal incentives can be inadequate, however, to motivate pioneers to incur these costs when collective goods such as technical standards are the result. In such cases, actors have incentives to free ride. New organizational forms may thus rely on social movement processes when "normal" incentives are insufficient to create public goods (Moe 1980; Olson 1965). For example, although technical standards benefit both producers and consumers, neither took the lead in creating standard setting organizations in the United States. Activists such as James Chase and Frederick Schlink (both employees of the National Bureau of Standards) wrote pamphlets that railed against the evils of wasteful variety, preached the virtues of standards, recruited members from the ranks of private corporations, and established standard-setting bodies. Their efforts peaked during World War I, when activists in the War Industries Board pushed producers to standardize products and conserve resources, leading to the formation of the American Standards Association in 1919.

Negative externalities obtain when some parties draw all the benefits of an action, while others face all of the costs. For example, steam locomotives, as Coase (1960) observed in a famous example, can emit sparks that set fire to fields, or deceptive advertising can harm the image of the advertising agencies and defraud consumers. In principle, one could claim that social costs can be reduced wholly through market mechanisms: For example, farmers can sell rights to emit sparks on their fields or purveyors of deceptive advertisements can be eliminated because they acquire a bad reputation. However, market mechanisms may not work when transactions span large distances, victims are uninformed, and lack recognized legal rights. Steel firms, for instance, can pollute air in another country. Consumers may not be able to discern honest from dishonest advertisers, and may even lack the right of legal redress. In such cases, social movements can arise to establish new firms to reduce social costs. New organizational forms may thus also rely on social movements for their legitimation when market mechanisms are inadequate to reduce negative externalities. For example, at the turn of the twentieth century in the United States, deceptive advertising may have benefited some firms, but harmed consumers and the image of advertising. Consumers were uninformed, free-rider problems prevented advertising agencies from engaging in collective action, and a social movement emerged to promote truth-in-advertising. Activists began forming advertising clubs in 1896, merging in 1904 to form the Associated Advertising Clubs of America. John Romer, publisher of *Printers Ink*, urged these clubs to establish vigilance committees to ascertain the truthfulness of advertisements issued by members, to discipline errant members, or even to take them to court. A National Vigilance Committee formed in 1912, and by 1914, twenty-four cities had founded vigilance committees in a bid to signal the advertising community's commitment to probity and professional conduct. In 1916, vigilance committees were renamed as Better Business Bureaus and by 1930 more than 10,000 businesses supported these bureaus in numerous cities (Samson, 1980: 343).

Micro–Macro Evolutionary Interactions

To this point, our examination of micro-evolutionary VSR processes within particular organizational forms and macro-evolutionary VSR processes that give rise to new organizational forms has emphasized primarily genealogical ("V" and "R") and ecological ("S") processes and their interactions *within* each level. What have remained implicit in our analyses are the interactions *between* VSR processes across micro and macro levels. Although process at population and community levels operate quasi-independently, each a dynamic VSR system in its own right, as we noted earlier there is also both upward and downward causation across hierarchical levels (Campbell 1974, 1990). These interactions constrain and enable the kinds of processes and events that can occur at a given level and regulate, in part, those that do occur. As a result, VSR processes at the population level (e.g., organizational learning, isomorphism) can dramatically affect VSR processes at the community level, while, at the same time, VSR processes at the community level (e.g., community disruption, coevolution, social movements) shape and constrain those at the population-level. To help us illustrate these cross-level interactions, Figure 18.2 overlays the main micro- and macro-evolutionary VSR processes that we identified at the population and community levels on the dual hierarchy model.

Across levels of organization, VSR processes interact through variation and retention within the genealogical hierarchy, and selection within the ecological hierarchy. In the genealogical hierarchy, retention processes at each level affect variation at other levels both up and down the hierarchy. For example, organizational learning and imitative entrepreneurship at the population level limit the range of organizational variation that is expressed within an organizational population, while institutional entrepreneurship and social movements within organizational communities foster new specializations that reshape competitive processes at the population level. Each of these upward and downward effects can, in turn, echo back and forth up and down the hierarchy as processes and events at each level react to each other (Hofstader 1979).

Within the ecological hierarchy, interactions that result in differential selection cascade downward, the fates of organizations dependent on the selection of their populations, which in turn depend on the selection of the communities to which they belong. Technological innovations at the community level, for example, may alter competitive selection and segregating mechanisms at the population level, reshaping the boundaries of populations. The convergence of telecommunications technologies, for instance, has created opportunities (and nightmares) for new kinds of organizations (e.g., cable companies) in the telecommunications community. More generally, the emergence of a

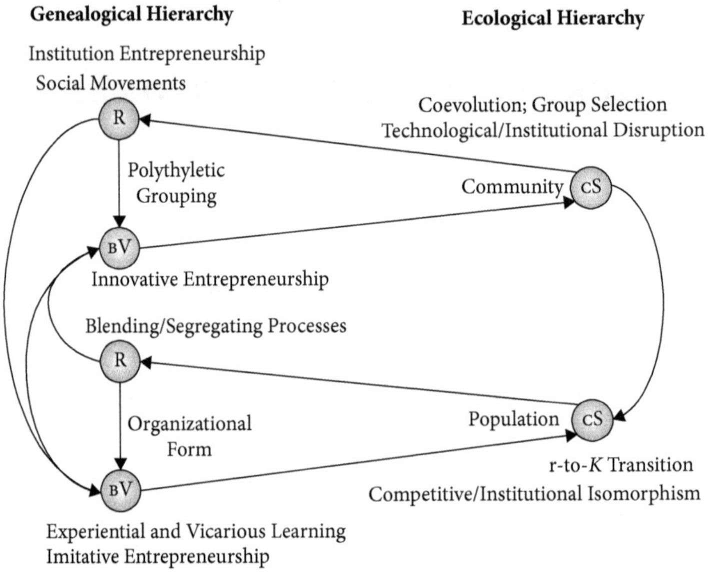

FIGURE 18.2 Micro-Macro Evolutionary Interactions

BV = (Blind) Variation; CS = (Competitive) Selection; R = Retention dominant design or technological discontinuity can alter the basis of competition at the population level by, for example, triggering an r-to-K transition or altering the relative importance of various competencies and resources.

Conversely, upward causation means that retained features of the lower level constrain what can emerge at the higher levels. Thus, organizations in one population can learn vicariously routines employed by organizations in another population belonging to the same organizational community, and the increasing homogeneity resulting from such imitation may, in turn, alter the structure of commensalisms within their community. Credit unions can, for example, imitate the practices and products of commercial banks, intensifying competition between them. Alternately, organizations in one population may establish cooperative relationships with organizations in another population, and in doing so alter the structure of symbiosis in their community. Hotels, car rental agencies, and airline companies, for example, are now bound together through a web of frequent-flyer programs. Community structures can also be reshaped as disruptive competitive selection or r-to-K transitions within populations promote new specializations and symbiotic relations as new populations emerge to fulfill ancillary roles (Hawley, 1950).

Complications of Hierarchical Evolution

These cross-level interactions of micro- and macro-evolutionary VSR processes complicate organizational evolution considerably. Units of organizational evolution are nested and overlapping so that some entities (organizations and populations) are integral parts of other adapting entities (communities). The structure of relations among them arises from interaction among various nested levels, each responding to its own and each other's VSR dynamics. As a result, selection pressures are often in conflict across levels, with adaptations that are beneficial for entities at one level harmful at others. Union power, for example, may enable some classes of jobs to be retained through industry-wide agreements, but may jeopardize the fates of individual organizations and the overall population. It is also possible for two entities to both compete and cooperate, depending on the level at which their interaction takes place. For example, a population of firms may band together into an effective trade association designed to ward off competition from other populations—but at the cost of more intense competition within the population. Analogously, what is good for an organizational form is not necessarily good for its innovative entrepreneur: While codification and convergence facilitate legitimation, easy imitability can results in imitative entrepreneurs surviving at the expense of the original innovator (Delacroix and Rao 1994).

Higher-level adaptation thus does not arise automatically from lower-level adaptation. Indeed, it would be very unusual in the evolution of a nested hierarchical system for an adaptation that optimizes fitness for components of the system to also optimize prospects for the higher levels of the system or the system as a whole (Baum,1999; Campbell 1994, March 1994). What is best for entities at one level is thus not generally best for those at other levels. As a result, while attempting to improve their own fitness, entities at different levels of organization compete for resources across (as well as within) levels, complicating organizational evolution. As we noted earlier, functional organization at any level of the organizational hierarchy requires a corresponding process of selection *at that level.* Populations can become well designed only by a process of between-population selection, and communities can become well designed only by a process of between-community selection (Baum 1999; Campbell 1994; Sober and Wilson 1998). Even if selection among entities at a given hierarchical level enhances their fitness, however, because the rate of evolution is faster at lower levels, the fitness achieved at the higher level may constantly be undermined by lower-level entities that "out-evolve" their higher-level counterparts.

Conclusion

Our goal in this chapter has been to provide a comprehensive framework and account of evolutionary dynamics in organizational populations and communities. We outlined the core premises of an evolutionary-ecological view of organizations drawing on core research findings amassed during twenty-five years of empirical research. After presenting our framework, we presented more detailed analyses of evolutionary dynamics at two levels of organization:

- *Micro-evolutionary* processes that shape persistence and change over time among organizations within a particular lineage, or organizational form
- *Macro-evolutionary* processes that shape persistence and change over time within a community of organizational forms, and through which new organizational forms arise

Our analysis of population and community-level evolution highlighted the roles of institutional change, technological innovation cycles, entrepreneurs, and social movements as triggers of organizational variation. We explored how institutional and technological change transforms the dynamics of organizational communities by shifting the boundaries of organizational forms, destabilizing or reinforcing existing community structures, giving rise to social movements, and creating opportunities for entrepreneurs to shape new organizational forms. Our analysis of population-level VSR serves to consolidate and refine earlier treatments of these processes; our analysis of community-level VSR, in contrast, represents one of the first comprehensive treatments of these processes (see also Aldrich 1999). We concluded by highlighting some basic connections between evolutionary processes at population and community-levels that emerge from our analysis.

Although we have attempted to be comprehensive in our treatment, in closing, we would like to point out two avenues for research into the evolutionary dynamics of populations and communities: spatial processes, and endogenous sources of change.

Our review finessed the issue of whether populations and communities change due to exogenous events or endogenous processes. Although our discussion depicted how organizations themselves are sources of variations and could learn from other organizations in populations, and hinted at the endogenous foundations of population-change, we need systematic research because seemingly exogenous shocks such as new laws, or economic crises could themselves well be the outcome of organizational action. For example, Edelman and Suchman (1999) describe- how new laws often are the outcomes of best practices in organizations, and therefore, have endogenous origins. Similarly, boom–bust phenomena in a given industry or a community may themselves be the outcomes of firms expanding capacity recklessly or exiting the market in droves (Fombrun 1986).

Our review also glossed over spatial aspects of population and community evolution. Spatial dimensions of population and community-level change are likely to become a rich avenue for work, not only because of the growing importance of industrial districts and multiunit chain organizations for which space is a vital strategic variable, but also because of the promise of joining hands with economic and social geographers to understand variation, selection, and retention at the level of regions. A growing line of research (Baum and Greve 2001; Baum and Haveman 1997; Baum et al. 2000; Baum and Sorenson 2003; Greve 1999a, b; Ingram and Baum 1997) bodes well for a deeper understanding of why many different kinds of organizations pockmark the landscape of our contemporary organizational society.

References

Abbott, A. (1988), *The System of Professions: An Essay on the Division of Expert Labor* (Chicago: University of Chicago Press).

Abernathy, W. J. (1978), *The Productivity Dilemma* (Baltimore, MD: Johns Hopkins University Press).

Abernathy, W. J., and Utterback, J. M. (1978), 'Patterns of Industrial Innovation', *Technology Review*, 80, 40–7.

Aldrich, H. E. (1979), *Organizations and Environments* (Englewood Cliffs, NJ: Prentice-Hall).

Aldrich, H. E. (1999), *Organizations Evolving* (London: Sage).

Aldrich, H. E., and Fiol, C. M. (1994), 'Fools Rush in? The Institutional Context of Industry Creation', *Academy of Management Review*, 19, 645–70.

Aldrich, H. E., and Kenworthy, A. L. (1999), The Accidental Entrepreneur: Campbellian Antinomies and Organizational Foundings, in J.A.C. Baum and B. McKelvey, eds., *Variations in Organization Science: In Honor of Donald T. Campbell* (Thousand Oaks, CA: Sage), 19–34.

Aldrich, H. E., and Sasaki, T. (1995), 'R&D Consortia in the United States and Japan', *Research Policy*, 24, 301–16.

Amburgey, T. L., Dacin, T., and Kelly, D. (1994), 'Disruptive Selection and Population Segmentation: Interpopulation Competition as a Segregating Process', in J. A. C. Baum and J. V. Singh, eds., *Evolutionary Dynamics of Organizations* (New York: Oxford University Press), 240–54.

Anderson, P., and Tushman, M. L. (1990), 'Technological Discontinuities and Dominant Designs: A Cyclical Model of Technological Change', *Administrative Science Quarterly*, 35, 604–33.

Argote, L., and Epple, D. (1990), 'Learning Curves in Manufacturing', *Science*, 247, 920–4.

Arthur, B. (1989), 'Competing Technologies, Increasing Returns, and Lock-in by Historically Small Events'. *Economic Journal*, 99, 116–31.

Astley, W. G. (1985), 'The Two Ecologies: Population and Community Perspectives on Organizational Evolution', *Administrative Science Quarterly*, 30, 224–41.

Astley, W. G., and Fombrun, C. J. (1983), 'Collective Strategy: Social Ecology of Organizational Environments', *Academy of Management Review*, 8, 576–87.

Bandura, A. (1977), *Social Learning Theory* (Englewood Cliffs, NJ: Prentice-Hall).

Barnett, W. P. (1990), The Organizational Ecology of a Technological System. *Administrative Science Quarterly*, 35, 31–60.

Barnett, W. P., and Carroll, G. R. (1993), 'How Institutional Constraints Affected the Organization of Early American Telephony', *Journal of Law, Economics, and Organization*, 9, 98–126.

Basalla, G. (1988), The Evolution of Technology (Cambridge: Cambridge University Press).

Baum, J. A. C. (1989), 'A Population Perspective on Organizations: A Study of Diversity and Transformation in Childcare Service Organizations'. Unpublished doctoral dissertation, University of Toronto, Canada.

Baum, J. A. C. (1996), 'Organizational Ecology', in S. Clegg, C. Hardy, and W. Nord, eds., *Handbook of Organization Studies* (London: Sage), 77–114.

Baum, J. A. C. (1999), 'Whole-Part Coevolutionary Competition in Organizations', in J. A. C. Baum and B. McKelvey, eds., *Variations in Organization Science: In Honor of Donald T. Campbell* (Thousand Oaks, CA: Sage), 113–35.

Baum, J. A. C. (2006), 'Competitive and Institutional Isomorphism in Organizational Populations, in W. W. Powell and D. L. Jones, eds., *Institutional Dynamics and Processes* Chicago: University of Chicago Press, 66–99.

Baum, J. A. C., and Berta, W. B. (1999), 'Sources, Dynamics and Speed: Population-Level Learning by Organizations in a Longitudinal Behavioral Simulation, in A. S. Miner and P. Anderson, eds., *Population-Level Learning and Industry Change Vol. 16: Advances in Strategic Management* (Stamford, CT: JAI Press), 155–84.

Baum, J. A. C., & Greve, H. R., eds. (2001), *Multiunit Organization and Multimarket Strategy – Advances in Strategic Management* Vol. 18. Oxford UK: Elsevier.

Baum, J. A. C., and Haveman, H. A. (1997), 'Love Thy Neighbor? Differentiation and Agglomeration in the Manhattan Hotel Industry', *Administrative Science Quarterly*, 42, 304–38.

Baum, J. A. C., and Ingram, P. (1998), Survival-Enhancing Learning in the Manhattan Hotel Industry, 1898–1980', *Management Science*, 44, 996–1016.

Baum, J. A. C., and Korn, H. J. (1994), 'The Community Ecology of Large Canadian Companies, 1984–1991', *Canadian Journal of Administrative Sciences*, 11, 277–94.

Baum, J. A. C., Korn, H. J., and Kotha, S. (1995), 'Dominant Designs and Population Dynamics in Telecommunications Services: Founding and Failure of Facsimile Service Organizations, 1969–1992', *Social Science Research*, 24, 97–135.

Baum, J. A. C., Li, S. X., and Usher, J. M. (2000), 'Making the Next Move: How Experiential and Vicarious Learning Shape the Locations of Chains' Acquisitions', *Administrative Science Quarterly*, 45, 766–801.

Baum, J. A. C., & McGahan, A. M. (2013), The Reorganization of Legitimate Violence: The Contested Terrain of the Private Military and Security Industry During the Post-Cold War Era, in B.M. Staw & A.P. Brief eds., *Research in Organizational Behavior* Vol. 33, 3–37.

Baum, J. A. C., and Mezias, S. J. (1992), 'Localized Competition and Organizational Failure in the Manhattan Hotel Industry, 1898–1990', *Administrative Science Quarterly*, 37, 580–604.

Baum, J. A. C., & Oliver, C. (1991), Institutional Linkages and Organizational Mortality. *Administrative Science Quarterly*, 36, 187–218.

Baum, J. A. C., & Oliver, C. (1992), Institutional Embeddedness and the Dynamics of Organizational Populations. *American Sociological Review*, 57, 540–59.

Baum, J. A. C., and Singh, J. V. (1994a), Organizational Hierarchies and Evolutionary Processes: Some Reflections on a Theory of Organizational Evolution', in J. A. C. Baum and J. V. Singh, eds., *Evolutionary Dynamics of Organizations* (New York: Oxford University Press), 3–20.

Baum, J. A. C., and Singh, J. V. (1994b), 'Organizational Niche Overlap and the Dynamics of Organizational Founding', *Organization Science*, 5, 483–501.

Baum, J. A. C., and Singh, J. V. (1994c), Organizational Niche Overlap and the Dynamics of Organizational Mortality', *American Journal of Sociology*, 100, 346–80.

Baum, J. A. C., & Sorenson, O., eds. (2003), *Geography and Strategy – Advances in Strategic Management* Vol. 20. Oxford UK: Elsevier.

Bijker, W., Hughes, T., and Pinch, T. (1987), *The Social Construction of Technological Systems* (Cambridge, MA: MIT Press).

Boyd R., and Richerson, P. J. (1985), *Culture and the Evolutionary Process* (Chicago: University of Chicago Press).

Brittain, J. W., and Freeman, J. H. (1980), Organizational Proliferation and Density Dependent Selection, in J. Kimberly and R. Miles, eds., *The Organizational Life Cycle* (San Francisco, CA: Jossey-Bass), 291–388.

Brittain, J. W., and Wholey, D. H. (1988), 'Competition and Coexistence in Organizational Communities: Population Dynamics in Electronics Components Manufacturing', in G. R. Carroll, ed., *Ecological Models of Organizations* (Cambridge, MA: Ballinger), 195–222.

Brown, S. L., and Eisenhardt, K. M. (1998), *Competing on the Edge* (Boston, MA: Harvard Business School Press).

Burgelman, R. A. (1983), 'A Process Model of Internal Corporate Venturing in the Diversified Major Firm', *Administrative Science Quarterly*, 28, 223–44.

Burt, R. S., Models of Network Structure, *Annual Review of Sociology*, 1980 6, 79–141.

Campbell, D. T. (1965), Variation and Selective Retention in Socio-Cultural Evolution, in H. R. Barringer, G. I. Blanksten, and R. W. Mack, eds., *Social Change in Developing Areas: A Reinterpretation of Evolutionary Theory* (Cambridge, MA: Schenkman, 19–48).

Campbell, D. T. (1974), 'Evolutionary Epistemology', in P. A. Schlipp, ed., *The Philosophy of Karl Popper* (Lasalle, IL: Open Court), 413–63.

Campbell, D. T. (1979), 'Comments on the Sociology and Ethics of Moralizing', *Behavioral Science*, 24, 37–45.

Campbell, D. T. (1988), 'A General "Selection Theory" as Implemented in Biological Evolution and in Social Belief-Transmission-with-Modification in Science, *Biology and Philosophy*, 3, 171–7.

Campbell, D. T. (1990), 'Levels of Organization, Downward Causation, and the Selection-Theory Approach to Evolutionary Epistemology', in G. Greenberg and E. Tobach, eds., *Theories of the Evolution of Knowing* (Hillsdale, NJ: Lawrence Erlbaum Associates), 1–17.

Campbell, D. T. (1994), How Individual and Face-To-Face-Group Selection Undermine Firm Selection in Organizational Evolution', in J. A. C. Baum and J. V. Singh, eds., *Evolutionary Dynamics of Organizations* (New York: Oxford University Press), 23–38.

Carroll, G. R. (1985), 'Concentration and Specialization: Dynamics of Niche Width in Populations of Organizations, *American Journal of Sociology*, 90, 1262–83.

Carroll, G. R., & Swaminathan, A. (1992), The Organizational Ecology of Strategic Groups in the Brewing Industry from 1975 to (1990), *Industrial and Corporate Change*, 1, 65–97.

Clark, K. B. (1985), 'The Interaction of Design Hierarchies and Market Concepts in Technological Evolution', *Research Policy*, 14, 235–51.

Coase, R. (1960), The Problem of Social Cost. *Journal of Law and Economics*, 3: 1–44.

Cohen, W. M., and Levinthal, D. A. (1990), 'Absorptive Capacity: A New Perspective on Organizational Learning and Innovation', *Administrative Science Quarterly*, 35, 128–52.

Cyert, R. M., and March, J. G. (1963), *A Behavioral Theory of the Firm* (Englewood Cliffs, NJ: Prentice-Hall).

Davis-Blake, A., and Pfeffer, J. (1989), 'Just a Mirage: The Search for Dispositional Effects in Organizational Research', *Academy of Management Review*, 14, 385–400.

Delacroix, J., and Rao, H. (1994), 'Externalities and Ecological Theory: Unbundling Density Dependence', in J. A. C. Baum and J. V. Singh, eds., *Evolutionary Dynamics of Organizations* (New York: Oxford University Press), 255–68.

DiMaggio, P. J. (1988), 'Interest and Agency in Institutional Theory', in L. G. Zucker, ed., *Institutional Patterns and Organizations: Culture and Environment* (Cambridge, MA: Ballinger), 3–21.

DiMaggio, P. J. (1991), 'Constructing an Organizational Field as A Professional Project: U.S. Art Museums, 1920–1940', In W. W. Powell and P. J. DiMaggio, eds., *The New Institutionalism in Organizational Analysis* (Chicago: University of Chicago Press), 276–92.

DiMaggio, P. J., and Powell, W. W. (1983), 'The Iron Cage Revisited: Institutional Isomorphism and Collective Rationality in Organizational Fields', *American Sociological Review*, 48, 147–60.

DiMaggio, P. J., & Powell, W. W. (1991), Introduction. In W.W. Powell & P. J. DiMaggio, eds., *The New Institutionalism in Organizational Analysis*. Chicago: Chicago University Press, 1–38.

Dimmick, J., and Rothenbuhler, E. (1984), 'Competitive Displacement in Communication Industries: New Media in Old Environments', in R. Rice and Associates, eds., *The New Media: Communication Research and Technology* (Beverly Hills, CA: Sage), 287–308.

Dooley, K. J. (2021), 'Conceptualizing Organizational Change through the Lens of Complexity Science', in M. S. Poole and A. H. Van de Ven, eds., *The Oxford Handbook of Organizational Change and Innovation* (2nd edn) (Oxford: Oxford University Press), Dosi, G. (1982), 'Technological Paradigms and Technological Trajectories', *Research Policy*, 11, 147–62.

Dosi, G. (1984), *Technical Change and Industrial Transformation* (New York: St. Martin's).

Dosi, G. (1988), Sources, Procedures, and Microeconomic Effects of Innovation, *Journal of Economic Literature*, 26, 1120–71.

Douglas, M. (1986), *How institutions think* (Syracuse, NY: Syracuse University Press).

Edelman, L. B., & Suchman, M. C. (1999), When the "Haves" Hold Court: Speculations on the Organizational Internalization of Law. *Law & Society Review*, 33, 941–91.

Eldredge, N., and Gould, S. J. (1972), 'Punctuated Equilibria: An Alternative to Phyletic Gradualism', in T. J. M. Schopf, ed., *Models in Paleobiology* (San Francisco: Freeman Cooper), 82–115.

Ferguson, P. (1998), 'A Cultural Field in the Making: Gastronomy in 19th Century France', *American Journal of Sociology*, 104, 597–641.

Fombrun, C. J. (1986), 'Structural Dynamics within and between Organizations', *Administrative Science Quarterly*, 31, 403–21.

Friedland, R., and Alford, R. R. (1991), 'Bringing Society Back In: Symbols, Practices, and Institutional Contradictions', in W. W. Powell and P. J. DiMaggio, eds., *The New Institutionalism in Organizational Analysis* (Chicago: University of Chicago Press), 232–63.

Goodrick, E., and Salancik, G. R. (1996), 'Organizational Discretion in Responding to Institutional Practices: Hospitals and Cesarean Births', *Administrative Science Quarterly*, 41, 1–28.

Gould, S.J., and Eldredge, N. (1977), 'Punctuated Equilibria: The Tempo and Mode of Evolution Reconsidered', *Paleobiology*, 3, 115–51.

Greenwood, R., and Hinnings, C. R. (1993), 'Understanding Strategic Change: The Contribution of Archetypes', *Academy of Management Journal*, 36, 1052–81.

Greve, H. R. (1999a), 'Branch Systems and Nonlocal Learning in Organizational Populations, in A. S. Miner and P. C. Anderson, eds., *Population Level Learning and Industry Change—Advances in Strategic Management* (Greenwich, CT: JAI Press), 57–80.

Greve, H. R. (1999b), 'Organizational Location Decisions: Competition, Learning, and Strategy in Tokyo Banking, 1894–1936', Institute of Policy and Planning Science. Unpublished manuscript, University of Tsukuba, Tsukuba, Japan.

Han, S-K. (1994), 'Mimetic Isomorphism and its Effect on the Auditor Services Market', *Social Forces*, 73, 637–64.

Hannan, M. T., and Carroll, G. R. (1992), *Dynamics of Organizational Populations: Density, Competition, and Legitimation* (New York: Oxford University Press).

Hannan, M. T., and Freeman, J. H. (1977), 'The Population Ecology of Organizations', *American Journal of Sociology*, 83, 929–84.

Hannan, M. T., and Freeman, J. H. (1984), 'Structural Inertia and Organizational Change', *American Sociological Review*, 49, 149–64.

Hannan, M. T., and Freeman, J. H. (1989), *Organizational Ecology* (Cambridge, MA: Harvard University Press).

Haunschild, P. R., and Miner, A. S. (1997), Modes of Interorganizational Imitation: The Effects of Outcome Salience and Uncertainty, *Administrative Science Quarterly*, 42, 472–500.

Haveman, H. A., and Rao, H. (1997), 'Structuring a Theory of Moral Sentiments: Institutional and Organizational Coevolution in the Early Thrift Industry', *American Journal of Sociology*, 102, 1606–51.

Hawley, A. H. (1950), *Human Ecology* (New York: Ronald).

Henderson, A. D. (1999), 'Firm Strategy and Age Dependence: A Contingent View of the Liabilities of Newness, Adolescence and Obsolescence', *Administrative Science Quarterly*, 44, 281–314.

Henderson, R. M., and Clark, K. B. (1990), Architectural Innovation: The Reconfiguration of Existing Product Technologies and the Failure of Established Firms', *Administrative Science Quarterly*, 35, 9–30.

Hodgson, G. (1993), *Economics and Evolution* (Cambridge: Polity Press).

Hofstader, D. R. (1979), *Gödel, Escher, Bach: An Eternal Golden Braid* (New York: Basic Books).

Hull, D. L. (1988), *Science as a Process* (New York: Oxford University Press).

Hunt, C. S., and Aldrich, H. E. (1998), 'The Second Ecology: Creation and Evolution or Organizational Communities', in B. Staw and L. L. Cummings, eds., *Research in Organizational Behavior* (Vol. 20) (Greenwich, CT: JAI Press), 267–302.

Ijiri, Y., and Simon, H. A. (1977), *Skew Distributions and the Sizes of Business Firms* (New York: North Holland).

Imai, K. (1986), *Kaizen: The Key to Japan's Competitive Success* (New York: Random House).

Ingram, P., and Baum, J. A. C. (1997), Opportunity and Constraint: Organizational Learning from Operating and Competitive Experience, *Strategic Management Journal*, 18 (Summer Special Issue), 75–98.

Ingram, P., and Simons, T. (2000), State Formation, Ideological Competition, and the Ecology of Israeli Worker Cooperatives, *Administrative Science Quarterly*, 45, 25–54.

Kamien, M. L., and Schwartz, N. L. (1982), *Market Structure and Innovation* (New York: Cambridge University Press).

Kauffman, S. A. (1993), *The Origins of Order: Self-Organization and Selection in Evolution* (New York: Oxford University Press).

Laumann, E. O., and Knoke, D. (1987), *The Organizational State: Social Choice in National Policy Domains* (Madison: University of Wisconsin Press).

Lehrman, W. G. (1994), 'Diversity in Decline: Institutional Environment and Organizational Failure in the American Life Insurance Industry', *Social Forces*, 73, 605–35.

Levinthal, D. A., and March, J. G. (1993), 'The Myopia of Learning', *Strategic Management Journal*, 14, 94–112.

Levitt, B., and March, J. G. (1988), Organizational Learning, *Annual Review of Sociology*, 14, 319–40.

Lieberman, M. B., and Montgomery, D. B. (1988), 'First-Mover Advantages', *Strategic Management Journal*, 9, 41–58.

Lippman, S. A., and Rumelt, R. P. (1982), 'Uncertain Imitability: An Analysis of Interfirm Differences in Efficiency under Competition', *Bell Journal of Economics*, 13, 418–38.

Lumsden, C. J., and Singh, J. V. (1990), 'The Dynamics of Organizational Speciation', in J. V. Singh, ed., *Organizational Evolution: New Directions* (Newbury Park, CA: Sage), 145–63.

March, J. G. (1981), 'Footnotes on Organizational Change', *Administrative Science Quarterly*, 26, 563–97.

March, J. G. (1991) 'Exploration and Exploitation in Organizational Learning', *Organization Science*, 2, 71–87.

March, J. G. (1994), 'The Evolution of Evolution', in J. A. C. Baum and J. V. Singh, eds., *Evolutionary Dynamics of Organizations* (New York: Oxford University Press), 39–49.

McAdam, D. (1994), 'Culture and Social Movements', in E. Larana, H. Johnston, and J. R. Gusfield, eds., *New Social Movements* (Philadelphia, PA: Temple University Press), 36–57.

McAdam, D., McCarthy, J. D., and Zald, M. N. (1996), 'Introduction: Opportunities, Mobilizing Structures, and Framing Processes—Toward a Synthetic, Comparative Perspective on Social Movements', in D. McAdam, J. D. McCarthy, and M. N. Zald, eds., *Comparative Perspectives on Social Movements: Political Opportunities, Mobilizing Structures, and Cultural Framings* (Cambridge, UK: Cambridge University Press), 1–20.

McCarthy, J. D., and Zald, M. N. (1977), Resource Mobilization and Social Movements: A Partial Theory', *American Journal of Sociology*, 82, 1212–41.

McKelvey, B. (1982), *Organizational Systematics* (Los Angeles, CA: University of California Press).

McKelvey, B. (1994), Evolution and organizational science. In J. A. C. Baum & J. V. Singh, eds., *Evolutionary Dynamics of Organizations* New York: Oxford University Press, 314–26.

McKelvey, B. (1997), 'Quasi-Natural Organization Science, *Organization Science*, 8, 351–80.

McKelvey, B. (1998), 'Complexity vs. Selection among Coevolutionary Firms: Factors Affecting Nash Equilibrium Fitness Levels', *Comportamento Organizacional E Gestto*, 4, 17–59.

McKelvey, B. (1999), 'Dynamics of New Science Leadership: An OB Theory of the Firm, Strategy, and Distributed Intelligence', Unpublished manuscript, Anderson School of Management, UCLA.

McPherson, J. M. (1983), 'An Ecology of Affiliation,' *American Sociological Review*, 48, 519–32.

McPherson, J. M., Popielarz, P. A., and Drobnic, S. (1992), 'Social Networks and Organizational Dynamics, *American Sociological Review*, 57, 153–70.

Meyer, M. W. (1994a), 'Turning Evolution inside Organizations', in J. A. C. Baum and J. V. Singh eds., *Evolutionary Dynamics of Organizations* (New York: Oxford University Press), 109–16.

Meyer, M. W. (1994b), 'Measuring Performance in Economic Organizations', in N. J. Smelser and R. Swedberg, eds., *The Handbook of Economic Sociology* (Princeton, NJ: Princeton University Press), 556–78.

Meyer, J. W., and Rowan, B. (1977), 'Institutionalized Organizations: Formal Structure as Myth and Ceremony', *American Journal of Sociology*, 83, 340–63.

Meyer, J. W., and Scott, W. R. (1983), 'Centralization and the Legitimacy Problems of Local Governments', in J. W. Meyer and W. R. Scott, eds., *Organizational Environments: Ritual and Rationality* (San Francisco, CA: Sage), 199–215.

Milgrom, P., and Roberts, J. (1982), 'Predation, Reputation and Entry Deterrence', *Journal of Economic Theory*, 27, 280–312.

Miller, D. (1990), *The Icarus Paradox: How Exceptional Companies Bring About their Own Downfall* (New York: HarperCollins).

Miller, D. (1993), 'The Architecture of Simplicity', *Academy of Management Review*, 18, 116–38.

Miller, D. (1999), 'Selection Processes inside Organizations: The Self-Reinforcing Consequences of Success', in J. A. C. Baum and B. McKelvey, eds., *Variations in Organization Science: In Honor of Donald T. Campbell* (Thousand Oaks, CA: Sage), 93–109.

Miller, D., and Friesen, P. H. (1980), 'Momentum and Revolution in Organizational Adaptation. *Academy of Management Journal*, 22, 591–614.

Miner, A. S. (1990), 'Structural Evolution through Idiosyncratic Jobs: The Potential for Unplanned Learning', *Organization Science*, 1, 195–210.

Miner, A. S. (1991), 'The Social Ecology of Jobs', *American Sociological Review*, 56, 772–85.

Miner, A. S. (1994), 'Seeking Adaptive Advantage: Evolutionary Theory and Managerial Action', in J. A. C. Baum and J. V. Singh, eds., *Evolutionary Dynamics of Organizations* (New York: Oxford University Press), 76–89.

Miner, A. S., and Anderson, P. (1999), 'Industry and Population Level Learning: Organizational, Interorganizational, and Collective Learning', in A. S. Miner and P. Anderson, eds., *Population Level Learning and Industry Change: Vol. 17. Advances in Strategic Management* (Stamford, CT: JAI Press), 1–30.

Miner, A. S., and Haunschild, P. R. (1995), 'Population Level Learning', in B. Staw and L. Cummings, eds., *Research in Organizational Behavior* (Vol. 17). (Greenwich, CT: JAI Press), 115–66.

Miner, A. S., and Raghavan, S. V. (1999), 'Interorganizational Imitation: A Hidden Engine of Selection', in J. A. C. Baum and B. McKelvey, eds., *Variations in Organization Science: In Honor of Donald T. Campbell* (Thousand Oaks, CA: Sage), 35–62.

Moe, T. M. (1980), *The Organization of Interests* (Chicago: University of Chicago).

Mowery, D. C., Oxley, J. E., and Silverman, B. S. (1996), 'Strategic Alliances and Interfirm Knowledge Transfer', *Strategic Management Journal*, 17, 77–92.

Nelson R. R., and Winter, S. G. (1982), *An Evolutionary Theory of Economic Change* (Cambridge, MA: Harvard University Press).

Nystrom, P. C., and Starbuck, W. H. (1984), 'To Avoid Organizational Crisis, Unlearn', *Organizational Dynamics*, 12, 53–65.

Olson, M. (1965), *The Logic of Collective Action* (Cambridge, MA: Harvard University Press).

Pfeffer, J., and Salancik, G. R. (1978), *The External Control of Organizations* (New York: Harper and Row).

Pimm, S. L. (1991), *Balance of Nature?* (Chicago: University of Chicago Press).

Plotkin, H. (1993), *Darwin Machines and the Nature of Knowledge* (Cambridge, MA: Harvard University Press).

Powell, W. W., Koput, K. W., and Smith-Doerr, L. (1996), 'Interorganizational Collaboration and the Locus of Innovation: Networks of Learning in Biotechnology', *Administrative Science Quarterly*, 41, 116–45.

Puccia, C. J., and Levins, R. (1985), *Qualitative Modeling of Complex Systems* (Cambridge, MA: Harvard University Press).

Ranger-Moore, J., Banaszak-Holl, J. J., and Hannan, M. T. (1991), 'Density-Dependent Dynamics in Regulated Industries: Founding Rates of Banks and Life Insurance Companies', *Administrative Science Quarterly*, 36, 36–65.

Rao, H. (1994), 'The Social Construction of Reputation: Certification Contests, Legitimation and the Survival of Organizations in the American Automobile Industry; 1895–1912', *Strategic Management Journal*, 15, 29–44.

Rao, H. (1998), 'Caveat Emptor: The Construction of Non-Profit Consumer Watchdog Organizations', *American Journal of Sociology*, 103, 912–61.

Rao, H., Morrill, C., and Zald, M. N. (2000), 'Power Plays: Social Movements, Collective Action and New Organizational Forms', in B. Staw and R. Sutton, eds., *Research in Organizational Behavior*, Vol. 22 (Greenwich, CT: JAI), 237–82.

Rao, H., and Singh, J. V. (1999), 'Types of Variation in Organizational Populations: The Speciation of New Organizational Forms', in J. A. C. Baum and B. McKelvey, eds., *Variations in Organization Science: In Honor of Donald T. Campbell* (Thousand Oaks, CA: Sage), 63–77.

Rich, P. (1992), 'Organizational Taxonomy: Definition and Design', *Academy of Management Review*, 14, 758–81.

Romanelli, E. (1989), 'Organizational Birth and Population Variety: A Community Perspective on Origins', in B. Staw and L. L. Cummings, eds., *Research in Organizational Behavior* (Vol. 11), (Greenwich, CT: JAI Press), 211–46.

Romanelli, E. (1991), 'The Evolution of New Organizational Forms', *Annual Review of Sociology*, 17, 79–103.

Romanelli, E. (1999), 'Blind (but Not Unconditioned) Variation: Problems of Copying in Sociocultural Evolution, in J. A. C. Baum and B. McKelvey, eds., *Variations in Organization Science: In Honor of Donald T. Campbell* (Thousand Oaks, CA: Sage), 79–91.

Rosenkopf, L., and Nerkar, A. (1999), 'On the Complexity of Organizational Evolution: Exploring Coevolution within and across Hierarchical Level in Optical Disc Technology, in J. A. C. Baum and B. McKelvey eds., *Variations in Organization Science: In Honor of Donald T. Campbell* (Thousand Oaks, CA: Sage), 169–83.

Sahal, D. (1985), 'Technological Guideposts and Innovation Avenues', *Research Policy*, 14, 61–82.

Samson, P. (1980), *The Emergence of a Consumer Interest in America*. University of Chicago Ph.D. thesis.

Saxenian, A. (1994), *Regional Advantage: Culture and Competition in Silicon Alley and Route 128* (Cambridge, MA: Harvard University Press).

Schumpeter, J. A. (1934), *The Theory of Economic Development* (Cambridge, MA: Harvard University Press).

Scott, W. R. (1987), 'The Adolescence of Institutional Theory', *Administrative Science Quarterly*, 32, 493–511.

Scott, W. R. (1994), 'Conceptualizing Organizational Fields: Linking Organizations and Societal Systems', in H-U. Derlien, U. Gerhardt, and F. W. Scharpf, eds., *Systemrationalität und partialinteresse* [*Systems Rationality and Partial Interests*] (Baden, Germany: Nomos Velagsgesellschaft), 203–21.

Scott, W. R. (1995), *Institutions and Organizations* (Thousand Oaks: Sage).

Scott, W. R., Ruef, M., Mendel, P. J., and Caronna, C. A. (2000), *Institutional Change and Organizations* (Chicago: University of Chicago Press).

Shapiro, C., and Varian, H. (1999), *Information Rules* (Boston, MA: Harvard Business School Press).

Singh, J. V., and Lumsden, C. J. (1990), 'Theory and Research in Organizational Ecology', *Annual Review of Sociology*, 16, 161–95.

Snow, D. A., and Benford, R. D. (1992), 'Master Frames and Cycles of Protest', in A. D. Morris and C. McClung Mueller, eds., *Frontiers in Social Movement Theory* (New Haven, CT: Yale University Press), 133–55.

Sober, E., and Wilson, D. S. (1998), *Unto Others: The Evolution and Psychology of Unselfish Behavior* (Cambridge, MA: Harvard University Press).

Sorenson, O., and Audia, P. G. (2000), 'The Social Structure of Entrepreneurial Activity: Concentration of Footwear Production in the United States, 1940–1989', *American Journal of Sociology*, 106, 424 62.

Spender, J-C. (1989), *Industry Recipes: The Nature and Sources of Managerial Judgment* (Oxford, UK: Blackwell).

Stacey, R. D. (1995), 'The Science of Complexity: An Alternative Perspective for Strategic Change Processes', *Strategic Management Journal*, 16, 477–95.

Stacey, R. D. (1996), *Complexity and Creativity in Organizations* (London: Berrett-Koehler).

Stanley, S. M. (1979), *Macroevolution: Pattern and Process* (San Francisco: W. H. Freeman).

Stanley, S. M. (1981), *The New Evolutionary Timetable* (New York: Basic Books).

Starbuck, W. H. (1983), 'Organizations as Action Generators', *American Sociological Review*, 48, 91–102.

Stinchcombe, A. L. (1965), 'Social Structure and Organizations', in J. G. March, ed, *Handbook of Organizations* (Chicago: Rand McNally), 153–93.

Stinchcombe, A. L. (1968), *Constructing Social Theories* (Chicago: University of Chicago Press).

Suchman, M. C. (1995), 'Localism and Globalism in Institutional Analysis: The Emergence of Contractual Norms in Venture Finance, in W. R. Scott and S. Christensen, eds., *The Institutional Construction of Organizations* (Thousand Oaks, CA: Sage), 39–63.

Sutton, J. R., and Dobbin, F. (1996), 'The Two Faces of Governance: Responses to Legal Uncertainty in US Firms, 1955 to 1986', *American Sociological Review*, 61, 794–811.

Thietart, R. A., and Forgues, B. (1995), 'Chaos Theory and Organization', *Organization Science*, 6, 19–31.

Tilly, C. (1978), *From Mobilization to Revolution* (Reading, MA: Addison-Wesley).

Tucker, D. J., Baum, J. A. C., and Singh, J. V. (1992), 'The Institutional Ecology of Human Service Organizations', in Y. Hasenfeld, ed., *Human Service organizations* (Newbury Park, CA: Sage), 47–72.

Tushman, M. L., and Anderson, P. (1986), 'Technological Discontinuities and Organizational Environments', *Administrative Science Quarterly*, 31, 439–65.

Tushman, M. L., and Romanelli, E. (1985), 'Organizational Evolution: A Metamorphosis Model of Convergence and Reorientation', in L.L. Cummings ed., *Research in Organizational Behavior* (Vol. 7) (Greenwich, CT: JAI Press), 171–222.

Tushman, M. L., and Rosenkopf, L. (1992), 'Organizational Determinants of Technological Change: Toward a Sociology of Technological Evolution', in B. M. Staw ed, *Research in Organizational Behavior* (Vol. 14) (Greenwich, CT: JAI Press), 311–47.

Tyre, M. J., and Orlikowski, W. J. (1994), 'Windows of Opportunity: Temporal Patterns of Technological Adaptation in Organizations', *Organization Science*, 5, 98–118.

Van de Ven, A. H., and Garud, R. (1989), 'A Framework for Understanding the Emergence of New Industries', in R. Rosenbloom, ed., *Research on Technological Innovation, Management, and Policy* (Greenwich, CT: JAI Press), 195–225.

Van de Ven, A. H., and Garud, R. (1993), 'Innovation and Industry Development: That Case of Cochlear Implants', in R. Burgelman and R. Rosenbloom, eds., *Research on Technological Innovation, Management and Policy*, Vol. 5 (Greenwich, CT: JAI Press), 1–46.

Van de Ven, A. H., and Grazman, D. N. (1999), 'Evolution in a Nested Hierarchy: A Genealogy of Twin Cities' Health Care Organizations, 1853–1995', in J. A. C. Baum and B. McKelvey, eds., *Variations in Organization Science: In Honor of Donald T. Campbell* (Thousand Oaks, CA: Sage), 185–209.

Von B., and Kenney, M. (2000), 'Venture Capital and the Birth of the Local Area Networking Industry', *Research Policy*, 29, 1135–55.

Wholey, D. R., Christianson, J. B., and Sanchez, S. M. (1992), 'Organizational Size and Failure among Health Maintenance Organizations', *American Sociological Review*, 57, 829–42.

Williams, G. C. (1966), *Adaptation and Natural Selection: A Critique of Some Current Evolutionary Thought* (Princeton, NJ: Princeton University Press).

Williamson, O. E. (1975), *Markets and Hierarchies* (New York: Free Press).

Williamson, O. E. (1991), 'Comparative Economic Organization: The Analysis of Discrete Structural Alternatives', *Administrative Science Quarterly*, 36, 269–96.

Wilson, D. S. (1997), Introduction: Multilevel Selection Theory Comes of Age. *The American Naturalist*, 150(S1), S1–S21.

Wilson, D. S., and Sober, E. (1989), 'Reviving the Superorganism', *Journal of Theoretical Biology* 136, 337–56.

Wilson, D. S., and Sober, E. (1994), 'Re-introducing Group Selection to the Human Behavioral Sciences', *Behavioral and Brain Sciences*, 17, 585–654.
Winter, S. G. (1990), 'Survival, Selection, and Inheritance in Evolutionary Theories of Organization', in Jitendra V. Singh, ed., *Organizational Evolution: New Directions* (Newbury Park, CA: Sage), 269–97.
Winter, S. G. (1988), On Coase, Competence and the Corporation', *Journal of Law, Economics and Organization*, 4, 163–80.
Zucker, L. G. (1977), 'The Role of Institutionalization in Cultural Persistence', *American Sociological Review*, 42, 726–43.
Zuscovitch, E. (1986), 'The Economic Dynamics of Technological Development', *Research Policy*, 15, 175–86.

CHAPTER 19

VSR MODELS OF CHANGE AS NORMATIVE PRACTICAL THEORY

CARA C. MAURER, ANNE S. MINER, AND MARY CROSSAN

Purpose of Chapter

In this chapter we suggest that wider use of a basic internal VSR (variation, selection, retention) model will offer a fruitful lens for organizational change agents and organization/strategy theorists. Evolutionary models are often seen as appealing to academics but less so to practitioners (March 1994). We explore the alternative possibility that a simple internal VSR model may have practical value for organizational change agents, separate from the development of increasingly complex computational models of more nuanced evolutionary change processes at higher levels of analysis.

The most basic VSR social science models arose initially as analogies from evolutionary biology in analyzing social systems. Some early applications resonated with cultural themes of "survival of the fittest" and were interpreted in popular culture to support class divisions or to justify eugenics and actual programs to weed out less fit human beings (Degler 1992; Leonard 2009). These misguided and ultimately rejected biological interpretations fortunately did not find a home in organizational and strategy theories in the past decades. Instead, Campbell (1960, 1975) and Weick (1979) actively introduced the basic VSR framework to organizational studies as a fertile model for understanding how social systems change (or not) and laid out the basic elements of a VSR approach.

Since the explicit introduction of these models in the 1960s and 1970s, academics have continued to develop VSR approaches to organization/strategy theory, for example, by trying to identify organizational analogues to genes in biological evolution (Aldrich et al. 2020; Burgelman 1991; Nelson and Winter 1982; Miner 1991). Over time, the

VSR-related literature developed three lines of work. One theoretical stream explicates specific links to material biosocial evolution with careful mapping to biological VSR processes and levels (see Chapter 18 by Baum and Rao, this volume). A second stream of work has moved to increasingly complex abstract models, including simulation models of evolutionary change (Bruderer and Singh 1996; Levinthal 1991). A third line of work includes a considerable body of theory-testing, data rich empirical research about industry, regional, population, technology, and community-level VSR processes and evolution (Dobrev et al. 2002; Murmann 2013). The trend towards more complex models and higher levels of analysis moves VSR models closer to accurate representations of evolving and nested organizational systems. More complex higher-level models have allowed scholars to sharpen understanding of external firm environments, but risk abandonment of internal VSR models as a useable tool for organizational change agents.

Hence, this chapter contributes a novel branch to the VSR tree: a simple normative model of *internal* VSR processes for change agents seeking to help a focal organization prosper and survive. The goal is to lay out an "umbrella" process model, based on three simple processes—variation, selection, and retention—that can shape change patterns and outcomes. Such processes have been theorized but have not generated an equivalent major body of theory-testing work or clearly linked normative theory.

We explore how organizational participants in general, and managers in particular, could use a simple yet credible VSR model to analyze and guide action in real time in any organization. We flag extant empirical work to offer evidence for the plausibility and usefulness of this model.

We also propose improvements to current VSR models that potentially increase their usefulness and applicability to day-to-day organizational processes. First, we suggest that the time is ripe to "bring the individual back" into VSR models as a way to frame normative theory for organizational participants seeking change, as well as for theorists who focus on change as a key organization process. Our attention on the role of individual organizational participants in VSR processes is perhaps a return to Campbell's psychological roots (Campbell 1960). Second, we draw attention to the potential impact of human emotions and imagination in VSR processes.

In the sections below, we consider how a change agent can attempt to: (1) directly influence each VSR process itself; (2) shape the balance of the three core processes; and (3) link internal with external VSR processes. Throughout these sections, we explicitly discuss how an individual change agent can actively utilize the VSR lens. We emphasize activities a VSR-guided manager might enact that are not obviously implied by standard normative top-down theories of consistent organizational action. These include deliberate use of micro-processes such as internal political processes and social influence. The internal/external linkage section highlights that the organization can attempt to create its own current and potential future contexts. This differs from a mechanical application of the traditional interpretations of the biological evolution analogy.

In the Discussion section, we briefly explain why it may be time to introduce emotions and imagination as vital additions to the VSR model approach. We discuss advantages and disadvantages of using the VSR model as a normative integrating lens.

We encourage academics to bring renewed enthusiasm to teaching practicing managers internal VSR models of change. The normative model can be used by change agents as a single framework of multiple micro-processes to understand and influence change—without falling into the trap of assuming all change is the result of simplified rational top-down processes. Initially, practitioners may find the model challenging, but can come to appreciate it for enacting change. The model offers an enriched role for managers who are willing to persist in efforts to create fruitful change and who embrace a role where they operate less as engineers who design and operate efficient machines, and more as gardeners of living and complex landscapes.

Background of VSR Models

VSR models have primarily developed within three generic streams: biosocial evolution, complex models of evolutionary change, and community-level VSR processes. The use of VSR models for practical normative theory is underdeveloped, but consistent with what March (1994) called the engineering of evolution. In this, actors accept the lack of total control, but look for possible, often non-obvious, intervention points in larger VSR systems. Our approach includes organizational members at large, which differs from the top-management focus in "guided evolution" (Lovas and Ghoshal 2000).

Prior work highlights three stylized engines of creating and sustaining VSR cycles: (1) deliberate and instrumental top-down actions/choices by top-management, (2) deliberate instrumental actions/choices at other organizational levels, including mid-level individuals who often drive enduring change, and (3) emergent patterns of action that are the result of deliberate instrumental action aimed at short-term or local goals, but that unintentionally spark long-term change.

Below, we first discuss each of the three VSR processes separately. We then consider possibilities for shaping VSR change by affecting the balance of the three core processes and their link to external change patterns. We draw on extant work on internal VSR (I-VSR) models.

Variation, Selection, and Retention as Distinct Processes

VSR models at the core envision three subprocesses which occur repeatedly and lead to systematic change in any system over time, without specific goals or deliberate pre-planning. For a VSR system to generate systematic organizational change, there must be (1) variability in some identifiable organizational unit (V-Variation), (2) processes that lead to differential survival of some types of units (S-Selection), and (3) processes that sustain the occurrence of these selected units (R-Retention). VSR-based theories envision nested systems in which VSR cycles repeatedly occur at multiple levels of analysis, even within one organization. Product-level variation in product platform technologies, for example, may be subject to organization-level selection when a top management team provide targeted resources to a focal product platform or technology standard (Lovas and Ghoshal 2000).

Variation

Variation in a unit is the first step in a cycle of VSR, followed by its differential selection, or not, and retention over time. Empirical studies of I-VSR models have focused on variation in organizational routines (Miner 1991; Nelson and Winter 1982) and organizational strategies (Burgelman 1994). However, the basic VSR model can apply much more broadly to any organizational context. We describe two major domains for deliberate organizational variation below: (1) Technology and (2) Routines and strategies.

Technology: Internal Variation

Formal R&D programs embody *top-down, deliberately* pursued variation. The organization may seek new product ideas but also new production processes or new materials with superior features in order to create possible future products—such as strength/lightness in metals for vehicles, or seed varieties that withstand climate extremes. Research-based technology management textbooks and practitioner guides encourage firms to develop deliberate engines to generate continuing variation (e.g., Schilling 2020).

In addition to top-down, deliberate variation, two other types of variation may occur. First, technical variation may still be deliberate and planned in advance but enacted without set goals or explicit awareness of top managers. Such *deliberate, bottom-up* variation occurs when lower-level employees champion products rejected by upper management, for example, or when organizations sponsors a small percent of time during which employees can pursue their own ideas of new technological materials or product features (Garud and Rappa 1994; Van de Ven et al. 1999). This type of technical variation is deliberate because some people in the organization have visions of possible technologies and pursue their development without top-down approval or possibly awareness (Van de Ven et al. 1999).

Emergent variation is a third type of technology variation process. Here, variation arises unintentionally through unplanned technological discoveries or cumulative impact of activities not deliberately aimed at creating variation. Classic accounts of technological innovation report serendipitous moments such as the observations at 3M that a failed glue could help attach notes in the famous case of 3M Post-it® notes (Garud et al. 2018). In some cases, variation arises from serendipitous recombination of existing technical knowledge or capabilities, and involves the act of noticing a new combination and pursuing it is a deliberate series of organizational actions unfolding over time. In that sense, emergent variation differs from a purely random occurrence of variation in an organization's output.

Tools to Shape Internal Technology Variation

The manager charged with R&D or product development goals has three levers suitable for promoting technological innovation. First, a manager can set specific top-down technological goals and direct coordinated efforts to achieve them. Second, a manager can promote incentive systems and processes to promote lower-level variation generation (Schilling 2020; Van de Ven et al. 2000). Historically, organizations have stimulated variation through prizes for technological inventions or incentives for individuals proposing new technologies (Galasso et al. 2018). Third, a manager can set in place scanning and alertness processes for early detection of unexpected variation. Scenario analysis, for example, is a management tool that explicitly encourages managers to visualize improbable or extraordinary situations outside current expectations (Hsia et al. 1994). Even when pursuing regularly established goals based on highest likelihood, organizational members are encouraged to stay vigilant to signs that unexpected scenarios might be unfolding, and then revise goals. Such actions improve chances that external variation is detected and acted upon.

This analysis implies that in practice, R&D or technical product development managers will be more effective if they approach their role with all three possible sources of variation in mind. A VSR-led manager would organize regular forms of top-down goal-driven research, but, in recognition of their limitations, also set up processes to harvest bottom-up variation, and recognize opportunities for serendipitous discoveries with unexpected value. Instead of being surprised by formal plans not working out as expected, managers would understand the whole organization as being involved in all three forms of variation, which would be their job to nurture and anticipate. In addition to tracking the existence of unplanned variation inside the organization, managers would attend to external variation sources, which we address in the later section on managing internal/external variation.

Organizational Routines and Strategies: Internal Variation

While the technological context offers an intuitive fit for using a VSR lens, other contexts are also applicable for understanding and nurturing change, as shown in extant research. Organizational routines are key units for VSR processes over time (Miner 1991; 1994; Nelson and Winter 1982). Formalized jobs, for example, are a type of organizational routine that play a role in organizational change, when viewed through a VSR lens (Rura-Polley and Miner 2002) In one research stream, most jobs in one organization were deliberately planned, vetted, and formally defined through written job descriptions, but a subset of jobs was not designed in advance by management (Miner 1987, 1991). In some of these jobs, incumbents began altering job implementation over time, and these variations in practice were sometimes institutionalized as new formal jobs. This example describes bottom-up variation, which was deliberate, but not initiated through top management and not necessarily enacted with the deliberate goal of long-term organizational-level change.

Around the same time period, Burgelman and colleagues developed a VSR approach with organizational strategies as the unit of analysis, and flagged two engines of variation (Burgelman 1994). One track came from top management teams engaged in formal planning efforts to consider possible variations in technology strategies (induced strategy). The second track (autonomous strategy) stemmed from lower organizational levels. In a key exemplar, manufacturing rules of thumb and routines that shaped actual production led to a de facto change in the product technology strategy being executed. Without using the VSR terminology, Mintzberg and Waters (1985) described similar patterns, in which some aspects of variation in strategy were deliberate, while others occurred through emergent processes, leading to variation in strategy being generated by accidental combinations of actions.

"Guided evolution" (Lovas and Ghoshal 2000) focused on strategic initiatives and human/social capital as two units on which VSR processes work to generate evolutionary change process. Here, the firm organized nearly all activities by projects. Members across the organizational hierarchy proposing new projects created new variation in key firm-level directions. In Burgelman's (1991) and Miner's (1991) visions, the sources of variation can be independent from, and possibly at odds with, the top-down strategy in place, while in "guided evolution," top management deliberately designs the system to allow for bottom-up strategies and selectively allocates resources to support them. Variation can arise at any organizational level and be selected, or not, through deliberate senior management choice. Our approach seeks to compensate for the over-emphasis on random and accidental adaptation and transformation embedded in many agent-based models. "Guided evolution" comes closest to the model presented here, but we suggest approaches that go beyond top management efforts to align enduring strategic intent with evolutionary processes that provide change agents with levers at all levels.

Role of Individuals: Variation

VSR processes require sufficient and appropriate variation as a starting point, so that selection can operate. The VSR model allows, but does not require, individual human beings as central actors in variation. Guided evolution (Lovas and Ghoshal 2000) argues that individuals have a distinct role to play in variation creation. Co-evolution between individual development of social capital (including both skills and social relationships) can occur over time and affect the nature of projects the organization undertakes. The organization picks projects in part based on available individuals to implement them. Over time, individuals make choices about what skills to acquire based on their guesses about likely important new projects, which in turn affects what future projects leaders can develop. Individual variation lies on the critical path to long-term organizational evolution at many levels, including strategies linked to project choices (Lovas and Ghoshal 2000).

To bring the individual back in certainly does not imply that individuals are unconditionally more effective at generating variation than groups or networks. Much practitioner-oriented work emphasizes the value of groups. A study of patents provides some support: some inventions by solo patent inventors had less value than those created in groups (Chan et al. 2020). Comparative solo versus group impact may depend upon problem modularity; solo inventors had less fruitful experience to draw on regarding variation creation. Also, the group-creation process may lead to wiser selection among inventions for patent, which improves quality.

Selection

We again consider internal processes that drive both technology and routines/strategy selection. In a later section, we discuss the crucial question of how actors affect the link between internal selection and external change.

Technology: Internal Selection

Many formal R&D management systems can be described as deliberate selection devices through which the organization picks among known technologies for future development. Formal assessment tools exist to characterize potential products and provide selection criteria and rules for selecting which ones to invest in. Firms may estimate ROI, time to break even, or total market size, rate each product and set up formal administrative systems to weigh factors and decide which technologies and/or products will survive the selection process. Such systems reflect a formal rational choice model. In some settings, firms draw on sophisticated finance assessment tools such as real options analysis to rate and select potential technology/product trajectories (McGrath and Nerker 2004).

Some firms set up process selection devices rather than outcome criteria-oriented tools. These include "shoot-out" systems, where competing teams are given resources to develop competing technologies or product designs, which in effect generates selection without an initial decision about direction (Miner 1994). Competing teams present results of their work and the dominant team wins. If competition alone drives product selection, such processes enact a political organizational system. In these, competition rather than a pre-set goal can represent a legitimate choice process, as seen in representative legislative bodies or embodied in courtroom processes, with competing advocates used to decide outcomes (March 1962).

Regardless of the formal system, many case studies reveal that informal political processes are hidden or tacit, but also drive selection of technologies/products. Subgroups and managers may work overtime to push for the use of criteria that they know will eventually favor the technologies/products they prefer, rather than promoting specific products. The underlying competition is subtle and tacit, consistent with an emphasis on the importance of setting decision criteria versus controlling individual decisions.

These tacit competitions over resources reflect a political form of an internal VSR selection process. In these cases, internal units' power and interpretive tools drive the selection process, rather than rational, consistently applied criteria.

Seasoned managers in such systems can become highly skilled at lobbying for internal resources to develop specific technologies, and at shaping perceptions about the relative potential of their preferred technology. Studies of the development of cochlear implants, for example, describe sophisticated and ongoing steps by which developers of cochlear implant technology repeatedly tried to influence perceptions about which technology platform would be most likely to meet customer values, or become a dominant design (Garud and Rappa 1994; Van de Ven et al. 1999). The VSR lens permits managers to participate in unstated or hidden political processes and understand them as another regular engine for selection, rather than as organizational flaws or departure from good practice.

Some internal technology selection processes, then, involve top-down rational choice (e.g., stage gate models of technology). Others involve mid-level deliberate efforts to shape which technologies survive and attract resources. Managers may observe shadow selection processes that are much less deliberate, similar to variation processes. Again, the VSR lens enables the alert manager to help shape organizational change by noticing non-obvious, serendipitous, or unexpectedly destructive mid-level selection processes, with a choice of promoting or undermining these undirected selection processes. For example, the VSR manager may deliberately scout firm and social events that are only loosely tied to technology in use by the firm, in order to become aware of hidden ways that employees are favoring or pushing away from particular technology variants that influence the organization's technical capabilities (Taylor 2010).

Organizational Routines and Strategies: Internal Selection

Turning to VSR selection processes for routines more generally, we again see three forms of deliberateness or intentionality in the focal process.

Top-down selection. Top-down funding, sanctioning projects, or approving formal strategies or policies, all manifest top-down rational actor models of selection. Organizations are urged to conduct formal reviews of organizational practices, such as popularization of Process Re-engineering overhauls (Hall et al. 1993), TQM, six sigma quality and lean production reviews (Cua et al. 2001; Zbaraki 1998). Many tools taught in finance, marketing, and operations compare potential new routines, practices, or policies. Organizations can use diverse metrics, such as ROI, net present value, operational efficiency, product market size, employee morale, or less formal tools to select which possible changes will be implemented. Here, traditional management theory can be seen as a special case of a VSR change process.

Mid-level deliberate selection. Actors at intermediate levels may engage in actions that lead to an overall selection process but are not derived from a top-down single organizational selection. For example, if competing units dominate the technology/product development through political processes over time, as described above, selection has occurred, but not as the result of top-down formal selection (Taylor 2010). These actions are deliberate but not planned by top management.

The manager, who uses the VSR lens will understand that lower-level political activities will shape overall selection. Anticipating or participating in such lower-level political activity is one way to affect higher-level selection. To impact these selection processes, the VSR manager will routinely map current power structures within the organization in anticipation. She would seek to shape the *criteria or contexts* for future selection of new routines, policies, or practices, gaining hidden influence over a broad set of choices (Krackhardt 1990). One well-known influencing tool is for a central office to nurture young professionals in a given functional area, and then to promote their careers so that over time they take influential positions across a large decentralized organization. The central office can count on a network of people willing to enact the values it instilled in them. If this is a deliberate strategy of the central office, it can be seen as a political modus of influencing selection. VSR managers, when setting up this long-term network, do not have a particular policy or practice in mind to be selected. Instead, they set in motion a set of resources and processes that will enable them to shape what will be selected, without the use of direct power or authority. Political processes still represent a deliberate set of actions and outcomes by the actors. Importantly, this kind of selection can easily lead to sets of selections that are not necessarily consistent over time (March 1962). However, because these mid-level selection processes are not formal, such inconsistencies are less likely to be noticed and adjusted.

Finally, the VSR approach implies that managers can benefit from seeking and utilizing emergent selection processes. This third type of selection process occurs when ongoing activities lead to de facto selection by the organization over time, but without the specific goal of influencing higher-level change. Emergent selection processes may also arise from repeated application of rules that have long-term unintended outcomes (Zhou 1993). Using a VSR lens, a manager may find it harder to detect or to influence these hidden processes, but not impossible. Close observation reveals that seasoned organizational actors already attempt to shape change in quiet ways using such approaches. Organizational actors who are skilled at symbolic activity can influence overall selection by actively shaping how potential new practices become interpreted within the organization (Van de Ven and Polley 1992;Van de Ven et al. 1999). They can set up influential de facto demonstration projects without top-down command or political power. Successful demonstration projects or punishment for a given rule violation can lead internal actors to voluntarily select new activities in a shadow selection process outside formal channels.

In scholarly work, Volberda and Lewin (2003) identified four different types of selection, including managed selection, in which managers intentionally aim to shape internal selection processes. Burgelman's (1994) study of the change in product market strategy in the chip industry illustrates emergent selection. The change of an internal production routine that drove production levels of memory chips enabled a de facto product market strategic change without a prior top-down decision or mid-level strategic intent. Miner (1990) flags lower-level unplanned jobs as another potential source of emergent selection.

Role of Individual: Selection

An individual organizational actor can directly enact selection processes that shape ongoing change. This routinely occurs when leaders or managers make choices between potential strategies, projects, technologies, or organizational values and culture. Here, standard models of top-down decision-making are simply a special case of VSR, where senior actors are aware of the variation in potential action and deliberately engage in selection. Formal strategic planning involves generating off-line action alternatives (V) and then picking which ones to enact (S) during ongoing implementation (R). The fact that individual-level top-management vision and change roles have been over-romanticized in prior theory and in the public imagination does not mean that it does not occur and play an important role in major organizational change and learning (Crossan et al. 2011).

A VSR lens encourages attention to individual-level impact across levels and types of selection in addition to top-down decision-making. An individual can drive organizational change at various levels, as shown in research on how product champions can influence product development in technology-based organizations (Howell and Shea 2006). More broadly, considerable research on internal policy advocacy and organizations as political systems underscore that individuals at all organizational levels can and do take actions that generate organization-level selection of key routines and even strategies (March 1962).

Illustrating nuanced ways individuals can affect internal selection, Lovas and Ghoshal (2000) describe how a firm pursued new projects, for example, by scouting which individuals were available to join the new project. Employees sometimes deliberately developed skills that they anticipated would be useful for promising new projects (Lovas and Ghoshal 2000). Individuals at all levels could shape change by affecting the criteria that drive choices for project members or to shape employees' choices of what capabilities to develop.

Retention

A system that creates good new things but then moves on to other new things cannot capture the full value of the new variants (March 1991). Evolutionary systems and learning scholars alike have long underscored that some form of replication is required for a system to adjust over time, including to adapt or learn (e.g., Crossan et al. 1999). The system may or may not be optimizing, but it is moving in some new direction in a sustained way (Aldrich et al. 2020). Retention refers, therefore, to the process through which selected variations are sustained in the system.

Technology: Internal Retention

Top-down retention activities. The core of retention lies in repetition of a given action. The impact of retention is to avoid selected changes eroding or fading away, which would make change temporary and non-systematic. Once an organization has selected a technical routine, project or technology, standard management theory emphasizes the importance of organizational focus and consistency. Admonishments to avoid specification-creep in product development, or to head off fragmentation in product platforms reflect this concern. Upper management affects technical retention when it designs or enforces new procedures to create more technical consistency, creates a quality control department to audit technology uses and consistency, promotes training programs that establish standards, or even promotes broader values that lead employees to enact consistency in their actions. The adoption of formal technological standards in product design also represents a retention process (Garud et al. 2002). Standardized product specifications, tolerances on designs, and procedural requirements for manufacturing all represent forms of organizational retention during the enactment of a new technology.

Mid-level retention. Lower-level and multi-level processes also drive organizational retention, above and beyond deliberate top-down efforts. Mid-level managers, who do not have the direct power to enforce adoption of a new technology or process across units, can nonetheless promote a new procedure, create a persuasive demonstration project, or lobby to have a design principle included in product/process reviews that will favor the practice they wish to see replicated. Change agents and product champions can attach their own technology preferences to large-scaled initiatives, which lead to broad replication in the organization, even without a formal top-down mandate (Taylor 2010). Hence, retention can be promoted by deliberate internal activity at lower levels of the organization in ways that are not designed in advance by upper management.

Mid-level actors can also slow down or weaken technical retention processes, for example by raising explicit technical doubts about the safety, reliability, or promise of a new technology the organization has adopted, or bringing in new information about a competing technology and sow doubt about which technology is a better focus. Studies of 3M's multiyear cochlear implant product development illustrate that internal actors can slow down the retention of a technology by offering evidence of the potential of a competing technology platform, a pattern seen often in product development efforts (Garud and Rappa 1994; Van de Ven and Polley 1992).

Organizational Routines and Strategies: Internal Retention

Top-down retention. Starting with the vision of scientific management at the turn of the last century, normative management theory emphasized the importance of consistent action to implement goals (Mintzberg and Waters 1985). Many management tools are designed to promote the consistent implementation of rational choices. These include incentives to align the interests of individuals with organizational goals, including through senior executives' stock holdings or individual pay incentives. Organizations also set up and enforce rules designed to promote consistent enactment of routines, or stipulate ethical standards deemed to be best for organizational prosperity and survival. They may create training tools and enforce norms through penalties or by expelling people as ways to sustain consistent behavior that has been previously selected as fitting the organization's interest.

Contrary to this century-old normative emphasis on retention and consistency, contemporary normative theory has highlighted innovation and organizational change as keys to ongoing prosperity and survival, at least in dynamic contexts. In some cases, however, the suggested approach to this apparent challenge is to maintain parts of the organization that emphasize retention and consistency through rules, milestones, and standardized practices, while also maintaining other units in which retention is deliberately downplayed, and variation emphasized instead. This strategy can be embodied in practices such as creating or tolerating "skunk works" projects, internal venture groups, or even "ambidextrous" units that combine retention and variation within the same group (Leybourne and Sainter 2012; Tushman and O'Reilly 1996). Contemporary efforts propose deeper integration of retention and variation processes to develop a paradox theory of action (Jay 2013).

Mid-level retention. An organizational change agent can affect administrative retention using many of the same tools noted above for affecting retention of technologies. Organizational members can speed up or strengthen known retention processes: they can lobby for the value of a particular project or process; encourage training in a given tool whether it be TQM, six sigma, or the use of emerging social media; they can nurture political and social processes to promote practices they favor. More subtly but perhaps with greater impact, they can work to embed particular priorities into the decision-making premises at work in various groups. In this tool for mid-level driven retention, the actors are not seen as advocating for particular outcomes. By embedding their preferred criteria within taken-for-granted decision premises, they not only affect selection processes, as noted above, but also promote retention of their preferred routines or strategies.

In non technical, administrative routines and strategies, mid-level managers and others can shape change by making retention slower or weaker. They can delay implementation, intentionally forget new proposed changes, place them low on priority lists, or create groups to make long studies that require large amounts of data. More nuanced tactics include introducing complicated arguments and re-interpretations of new practices, which reduces the chances they will be effectively retained in practice (March 1962; Alinsky 1969).

Qualitative research has shown that seasoned managers use these tools to shape change through weakening or strengthening retention of top-down newly initiated practices in large bureaucracies (Loavas and Goshal 2000; Taylor 2010). Normative management theory has often cast them as one-off moves, or "political" approaches to what should be rational organizations. In the VSR context, they are potentially useful tools, given the ongoing VSR engine of change that ought to be expected in a mature, viable organization.

Emergent retention. Prior research reveals many potential micro-processes that can create unplanned or non-deliberate retention. As noted, Cyert and March (1963) long ago argued that much activity unfolds through implementation of standard operating procedures, and Nelson and Winter (1982) generalized this idea into organizations enacting routines. Amburgey and Miner (1992) presented evidence that organizational inertia occurs when organizations not only continue to repeat prior actions, but take actions similar to, or related to prior strategies. Evidence from merger activity in US firms supported this theory. Miller and Friesen (1982) also found evidence of inertia and momentum in organizations. These theories postulate a baseline intrinsic tendency for organizational retention of any prior action.

Other descriptions of organizational stability and change emphasize more detailed micro-processes that can create emergent retention, such as the impact of taken-for-granted assumptions and organizational culture (Martin 2001). March (2010) argues that much action is guided by "the logic of appropriateness" in which actors choose to do something because it fits a sense of identity, or is consistent with norms about roles or values, independent of its potential instrumental impact. Institutional theorists also emphasize compliance with rules and norms. These processes are in effect retention processes that tend to sustain a given practice or trait once it is selected.

Considerable descriptive research supports ubiquitous retention processes in organizations. Many of these studies involve rich qualitative case studies and fine-grained descriptions of these processes. However, the conceptual development of internal VSR models has outstripped the publication of theory-testing of internal VSR models. As described above, Burgelman's (1994) detailed qualitative study describes how the selection of a new product market was in part shaped by the influence of standard procedures about how to allocate manufacturing output. The same rules supported the retention of these patterns over time. Miner's (1987, 1991) work on unplanned new jobs indicated that some, but not all, unanticipated novel bundles of job duties became formalized into official jobs that the organization continued to fill. This research also found that ongoing retention was shaped more by social factors in the presence of high local ambiguity and uncertainty (Rura-Polley and Miner 2002).

Role of Individual: Retention

We suggest it will be useful to refocus how individuals, along with groups and networks, play a role in how new organizational variations are retained and suppressed/amplified. Individuals can lead or participate in formal resistance or formal encouragement of retention of a given routine or strategy using mid-level and emergent process tools.

Such influence can go beyond visible lobbying and advocacy. In the Lovas and Ghoshal (2000) guided evolution example, employees' voluntary choice to be on a project influenced a project's existence, form, and its retention. In one case, a valued employee moved to a key new initiative, leaving behind another project, which was subsequently terminated. Individual action, here, affected retention of projects in a way that goes beyond top management choosing to continue to support projects. Individual persistence can support retention of organizational initiatives, as illustrated by descriptions of product champions or political advocates (Alinsky 1969; Howell and Shea 2006).

The sections above detail how change agents can influence each of the three separate VSR processes with special attention to mid-level action in hierarchies, or finding ways to magnify or decrease emergent processes. In addition to trying to influence separate processes, organizational actors can attempt to influence links between external change and internal VSR processes, and influence the balance between the three VSR processes. Individuals can affect such processes, which again highlights their potential importance in VSR models. Further, organizations and internal change agents can actively seek to shape their own contexts, rather than passively adapting to exogeneous change, as we emphasize below (Henderson and Stern 2004: Volberda and Lewin 2003).

Tracking and Shaping External Variation

Many firms devote resources to scan for changes in science/technology, as highlighted in contemporary textbooks on technological innovation (Schilling 2020). They maintain scientific advisory boards that detect long-term and immanent technological shifts; they engage in scenario planning exercises to envision potential shifts in what technologies can do; they create technology road maps, which estimate the timing of the arrival of new technologies, such as smaller, longer lasting batteries or sun-powered energy sources. Organizations also go beyond passively tracking technologies and seek to shape external technology evolution through research consortia, standard-setting bodies, and sponsored research in universities and research consortia (Miner 1994; Doz et al. 2000). Coalitions of technology organizations may create consortia to speed up processes of technological change.

Individuals play both visible and non-obvious roles in absorption and external creation of technical knowledge. Mid level actors accrue key insight through memberships in industry standard-setting groups, personal affiliation with scientific bodies, or open-source technology development projects. Such variation does not automatically permeate the working knowledge of the organization, making continuing efforts to improve internal knowledge-sharing critical but difficult to achieve. Individual change agents also sometimes advocate for specific technological platforms in external bodies, ultimately influencing variation available to their own firms. External technology change can also arise from ecologies of individuals within open-source settings. Scholarly research on the evolution of the LINUX kernel system (Lee and Cole 2003) illustrates the potentially complex role of community-based knowledge creation through dispersed volunteers rather than organizational formal cooperation.

Similarly, leaders often track political, legal, social, and international trends that may constrain action or offer opportunities. Official scouting occurs in professional associations, think-tanks, national foundations, and industry-level policy groups. Lower-level actors and emergent processes can influence such trends, however, and offer another window for change agents. The VSR-oriented change agent can independently track mid-level and emergent processes to detect and even influence societal trends, as seen when employees participate in social movements that affect organizations (Sine and Lee 2009). The lower-level agents can also track which external trends are already seen as crucial by leaders, and attach their specific issues to that trend (Alinsky 1969; Cohen et al. 1972). The complexity of potential salient exogenous societal trends far exceeds the information-tracking capacity of most organizations and individuals. This implies that change agents may need to prioritize external trends for attention. At the same time, truly unforeseeable external change sometimes creates danger and opportunity. This supports the potential value of individual use of scenario exercises to deliberately envision extreme unexpected changes, and the development of improvisational capabilities (Vera and Crossan 2004). Individuals can also participate in emergent variation creation involving external change. For example, Miner's (1990) research on idiosyncratic jobs describes cases where individuals accrued jobs duties in liaison roles with emerging community groups, which eventually led to long-term formal jobs reflecting those issues.

Matching Internal and External Selection/Retention

The link between external and internal selection processes represents one of the most crucial issues in any VSR model of evolutionary change. Nearly all important branches of evolutionary theories in the social sciences envision evolving systems in which VSR processes occur at multiple levels of analysis, ranging from individuals, groups routines, organizational units, whole organizations, populations, industries, regions, and communities of populations of organizations (March 1994; Aldrich et al. 2020). (See Chapter 24 by Woolley, this volume, for related work on organizational ecosystems).

In early VSR models, organizational external context provided the master selection framework for internal evolution, and the consequence of VSR change over time was to adapt the organization to exogenous forces and changes. This view was implied even by the title of Miner's 1994 essay "Seeking Adaptive Advantage: Evolutionary Theory and Managerial Action", the article that this chapter updates and amends. Contemporary models suggest instead that realistic models need to take into account organizations' agency relative to external contexts. This permits co-evolution across technologies, organizational forms, norms, and cultures (Henderson and Stern 2004; Murmann 2013). Our approach to internal VSR, envisions that organizations can and do actively "push back" against external factors. Thus, the balance of internal/external processes is another issue accessible to the change agent. We emphasize that organizations have the potential to create their context rather than only adapt to it, and that this remains an important frontier for additional attention. (See also Chapter 16 by Gaba and Meyer regarding external change.)

As the evolutionary perspective has increasingly emphasized, in many cases organizations do not adapt to, but rather co-create the very context in which they operate. Organizations lobby to protect legal systems that favor their survival and attempt to shape public attitudes about social norms or the legitimacy of new programs or products, whether through marketing, advertising, or contemporary social media processes

(Sine and Lee 2009) Organizations fund research related to topics they believe will shape their own futures. Research on new product markets such as wind power energy or grocery-van services reveal how early firms first collaborate to establish the legitimacy of the whole product class, and later spend energy differentiating themselves from competitors in that space (Navis and Glynn 2010). Organizations invest significant resources in standard-setting bodies, especially to shape systemic technologies that involve inter-organizational coordination, such as communication systems, wireless technologies, or energy transmission. Thus, the organizations are not engaged in adaptation to a fixed powerful exogenous environment, but instead actively seek to create the world in which they operate.

The VSR-oriented change agent can use external selection processes as a way to influence internal selection above and beyond formal actions by top management. Lower-level units may have preferences for a technology but be unable to convince their leaders of its superiority (Van de Ven et al. 1999). Members of these units may participate in professional associations that evaluate technologies, attend conferences with academia, interact with regulators and professionals, or individually seek to influence external standards or rules (Van de Ven et al. 1999). These lower-level activities can shape the external context even if the leaders are not aware of this impact.

Balancing Variation with Selection/Retention

Clearly, the nature and rate of organizational change driven by an internal VSR process depends not only on the content of each process separately, but on the relative speed or impact of each subprocess. There is not one variation, selection, and retention in an organization or industry, but a steady sequence of VSR phases, which over time lead to long-term change. In technology-driven product domains, balancing variation and selection/retention involves an organization's devotion of resources, including attention to research and product development versus investing in areas such as manufacturing efficiency or marketing activities. R&D investment represents an emphasis on variation, while product development stage-gate systems represent attention to selection, and post-product marketing efforts reinforce a given technical product choice, which involves some degree of retention of the original choice made.

The same logic applies to internal processes in administrative activities. Changing an organization's culture, for example, involves the same VSR phases, in which some new behavioral action is created or designed, and selected to be institutionalized in new slogans, rewards, physical environment, rules of thumb, or organizational stories (Martin 2001). Clearly, the impact of cultural VSR change will differ if the organization devotes most resources to retention, with a small degree of effort in creating new variations, versus if it devotes most attention to seeking variation in practices, values, and norms. The general challenge of finding a fruitful balance of variation versus selection/retention lies behind the popular contrast between exploration and exploitation (March 1991).

Contemporary practitioner-oriented management theory has increasingly emphasized variation and innovation (e.g., Schilling 2020). Senior managers can attempt to adjust the variation versus selection/retention balance through deliberate programs that enhance innovation, including promotion of organization-wide norms in which all employees are urged to actively look for new ways to execute activity in their areas, whether technology based or not. Contemporary ideals of ambidextrous organizations can be seen as efforts to find tools and practices that help regularize balances between variation and retention.

Work in this tradition confirms the difficulty of finding general principles that can be mastered and applied in organizations across the board, however. The prescriptive advice often must be so general as to leave change agents still without distinct guidance for practice. At the other extreme, sophisticated computational evolutionary models of change include very precise and nuanced details that are not overly general, but may contain so many contingencies that they are not useful or accessible to day-to-day organizational members and leaders.

It is certainly difficult, even for top managers, to deliberately shape the balance of variation versus selection/retention. The first issue is whether the balance of resources devoted to each is even in the conscious awareness of top leaders or change agents. In some settings, a particular balance may be taken for granted, leaving the issue dormant. In other cultural, geographical, or product areas, organizations may be spurred by failure or competitors and conclude that the organization's prosperity or survival depends on adjusting the relative resources of money, effort, and attention given to variation versus selection and retention. Using a VSR lens encourages deliberate, anticipatory attention to the relative balance of V versus S/R in both technical and non-technical areas. It can help managers avoid seeing the issues as only one of a particular innovation's potential value. It encourages a vision in which management does not assume there is a single fixed best ratio of variation to selection/retention, but is responsible for adjusting that mix to match context over time.

A VSR lens also draws attention to the importance of looking for nonobvious micro-processes that shape the balance of variation versus selection/retention. In the case of a changing technology, the top management team could scan lower-level processes that are shaping the actual product-market behavior, as seen in Burgelman's (1994) study, allowing more or less independence for local product design or manufacturing. Less obviously, top-level teams could change the balance of variation versus retention by making it easier or harder to create new rules new jobs, sets of job duties, or communication channels. The VSR lens also renews attention to the importance of considering the danger of too much innovation, if current management trends overemphasize its value. Lower-level participants can directly seek to increase either variation or selection/retention efforts in their own units if they perceive harmful imbalances. They can also alter the de facto presence of variation though participating in relevant hidden processes within the organization's workings (Batista et al. 2016). They can enhance retention, for example, through enforcing norms of working to rule, or boost variation through informal activities, such as skunkworks that operate outside management's formal approval (e.g., Schilling 2020; Van de Ven et al. 1999).

Model Improvement: Individuals, Imagination and Emotion

Throughout this chapter we have encouraged efforts to bring the individual back into VSR model development to improve model realism and increase its practical value for individual change agents. In this section, we propose another modification of contemporary VSR models, the addition of two concepts to the VSR framework: the roles of emotion and imagination in VSR processes.

These two elements apply at all levels of analysis, including individual and collective. Our goal here is not to develop fully articulated theory. Instead we highlight work that suggests the potential to improve VSR models by attending to emotion and imagination. Attention to the role of emotion and imagination in VSR processes makes these models more valuable as tools for change agents. In addition, careful incorporation of these two elements has the potential to change or even reverse standard findings in formal models of VSR outcomes.

Emotions and VSR Cycles

Research increasingly calls attention to the importance and feasibility of attending to shared emotion (Barsade and Knight 2015). Emotions have been shown to impact cognition and the social behavior of individuals and groups, especially under uncertain conditions (Elfenbein 2007), which highlights the applicability for strategic management (Levinthal 2011). There has been significant progress integrating emotion into strategy and organizational change theory (Huy 2011; Vuori and Huy 2016; see also Chapter 28 by Nguyen and Vuori). Emotions can be positive or negative and vary in valence (Elfenbein 2007). Thus, emotions will impact each of the three VSR processes uniquely, so that no unconditional single theory will capture their generic impact. Instead, careful attention to their role is necessary to understand and shape VSR change processes.

The nature of emotions plays a key role in *variation* processes. Emotions have been consistently linked to creativity (e.g., Baas et al. 2008; Isen 1999), which suggests higher variation. The "broaden-and-build perspective" (Fredrickson 2001) links positive emotions such as joy, happiness, and enthusiasm to broader thought-action repertoires, which are associated with higher creativity. However, others have shown that negative emotions, including frustration, distress, and anxiety can be useful because they signal that focused effort is required to improve a less than ideal situation (George and Zhou 2007). Emotional reactions to a triggering event supply individuals with the energy to engage in sensemaking (Maitlis et al. 2013). The link between emotion and creativity, thus, might be more complex, involving dynamic connections between positive and negative emotions (Bledow et al. 2013). Creativity increases in groups that experience high positive and high negative moods over time while also working in a supportive work context created by supervisors (George and Zhou 2007). Hence, both positive and negative emotions can increase variation and may also interact in complex ways, so there is no consistent simple linear impact.

Emotions also play a substantive role in *selection* processes. In rational actor and political models, individuals or subgroups have definable goals and their actions are intelligent in the sense of pursuit of those goals. This vision remains incomplete, however, because it omits the possibility that in some cases emotions rather than rational self-interest or perceived preferences will drive choices. Emotions can interrupt cognition and thereby send signals to shift attention, pause, and prioritize (Loewenstein and Lerner 2003). This can distort choices but can also provide opportunities for managers to carefully assess selection mechanisms in place. Entrepreneurship studies show that emotions influence evaluation of opportunities and their subsequent exploitation, which speaks to selection, indicating that subjectively felt experiences are as important as objective characteristics of opportunity recognition (Welpe et al. 2012).

Ingroup bias, presumably driven by emotions related to affiliation, impacted selection of innovation proposals in a major multinational consumer goods firm (Reitzeig and Sorenson 2013). Evaluators favored proposals submitted from their own unit, especially if the proposers belonged to high-status or small subgroups. In a qualitative study of Nokia's downfall between 2005 and 2010, Vuori and Huy (2016) concluded that managers' fear suppressed innovation processes and shaped long-term selection. Middle managers' internally oriented fear prevented them from sharing negative information with senior managers, who in turn left their unrealistically optimistic view of Nokia's capabilities unchallenged, and therefore failed to invest in long-term innovation processes. This case is an example of negative emotions restricting both variation and selection, by enforcing previously retained processes.

Change agents can use symbolic materials including narrative/stories to replace existing meaning systems with new ones in order to generate strategic change (Fiol 2002; Gioia and Chittipeddi 1991). Sonenshein 's (2010) study of managers' narratives and subsequent narratives by employees showed that employees embellish managers' narratives and thereby construct meaning about change, which leads to different and less controllable change outcomes.

Change makers skilled at symbolic management and active sensemaking can affect emotions during informal selection processes. Change leaders, who express positive emotions, including hope, empathy, sympathy, love, and fun, positively influence organizational change processes, such as receptivity to change and mobilization for change (Huy 2005). The importance of emotion in selection is consistent with the familiar pattern also in practice, in which objective data and forecasts fail to lead to change, while emotional appeals do affect selection (Kotter 2012).

We note that one prior theoretical approach to handle the role of emotions in rational choice processes has been to enfold emotions into a more general preference structure that drives any decisions (March 2010). Here, whatever the decision-maker does reveals their underlying preference structure, and the theory is agnostic on the origins of preferences. This definitional solution is not satisfying in probing VSR change processes and organizational observed behavior, however. Among other issues, emotional patterns will likely not follow even the most basic assumptions of rational choice models. In addition, the rational choice models remain instrumental and future oriented, and thus may not give adequate weight to actual selection criteria issues such as feelings of appropriateness or transcendence, regardless of outcomes (March 2010).

Emotions also play a role in the presence and nature of *retention* processes, but again cannot be viewed as uniform across different emotions or contexts. Early behavioral theories posited that organizations repeat current practices and only change when they fail to meet anticipated goals or levels of success, in part because of bounded rationality (Cyert and March 1963). Emotional attachment to projects or actions can however generate a separate vector that supports retention. Individuals' and groups' positive feelings can lead them to sustain old technologies or routines, even if it may hurt their own or organizational interest (Vuori and Huy 2016).

Positive emotions may encourage organizational members to persist long after objective data suggest they should switch routines or strategies, as is often discussed in practitioner-oriented work on product development and research and development (Schilling, 2020). Emotional attachment to outdated technologies at Intel, for example, may have enabled the inertia that negatively influenced the trajectory of Intel's attempt to adapt to new competitive demands (Burgelman 1994). Such persistence can represent a fatal danger but can also prevent the organization from abandoning a project prematurely, and thus overcome the dangers of overly rapid learning (March 1991). If a given new activity only has long-term value, persisting out of emotional commitment protects the organization from abandoning the path before it reveals value. In some contexts, positive emotions can produce persistence that leads to later discovery of valuable paths (Cardon and Kirk 2015). Similarly, Maurer et al. (2017) argue that actors may positively impact strategic renewal efforts by pursuing strategic insights which are fueled by emotion but face objection by others because of lack of objective evidence. Here, emotional persistence can lead to prosperity and survival that would otherwise not be possible.

Negative emotions can also enhance retention, for example through rigidity or inertia in organizational actors and units (Staw et al. 1981). Threats can trigger a tendency to avoid any change, which means stronger retention. Negative emotion can lead actors to exceed passive resistance and engage in active subversion of change sought in top-down change efforts (Elfenbein 2007). Emotion fueled resistance can exceed the retention one would expect from a rational calculation of risk or attention to expected outcomes. Political organizers have long understood the potential of deliberate efforts to ignite collective fear as a tool to drive resistance to change (Alinsky 1969).

Emotions can spread in groups and organizations through emotional contagion processes (Elfenbein 2007). Hence, a central role of VSR change agents is to shape collective emotions. Leaders have greater power in sparking social contagion of organizational emotional states because followers are more attentive to leaders (Sy et al. 2005).

Similarly, the passion of an entrepreneur impacts the emotional commitment of employees to the venture (Breugst et al. 2012). Instilling positive emotions such as optimism and enthusiasm nurtures strategic renewal efforts (Huy 2005).

Emotions can impact VSR processes even when actors try to avoid them. Leaders in a large technology firm, who had adopted an explicitly emotion-neutral approach to strategy implementation, inadvertently triggered middle managers' emotions via their social identities, (Huy 2011). This impacted how middle managers reacted to change initiatives even though their rational interests were not threatened. A change agent's ability to effectively influence patterns of collective emotion, which arise during strategic or organizational VSR change depends on a manager's "emotional aperture" or ability to recognize nuanced collective emotions in a collective, such as a group or business unit (Sanchez-Burks and Huy 2009).

Taken as a whole, these considerations imply that VSR change agents can take steps to influence emotional attachment or repulsion linked to each process. This lies within the repertoire of managers. However, its successful use requires the change agent to pick which emotion and which process deserves closest attention, requiring nuanced skills. From a theoretical viewpoint, it is important to identify settings where emotion can override, rather than simply, amplify, or mute rational and instrumental processes.

Imagination and VSR

Much VSR theorizing focuses on behavior that impacts social outcomes or material artifacts such as products (Miner 1994; Aldrich et al. 2020). This is consistent with a biological analogy where actions and reproduction drive genetic selection. Imagination opens the door to crucial issues that cannot be fully captured by a focus on action only. The concept of imagination has played a central role in the humanities and social sciences for many centuries (March 2010; Thompson 2018). A basic definition holds that imagination refers to "the act or power of forming a mental image of something not present to the senses or never before wholly perceived in reality" (Miriam Webster Dictionary, 2020). This implies that imagination is a creation of minds, and manifests creative activity. Thompson (2018) offers a theoretical integration of philosophy of imagination and philosophy of aesthetics. He envisions the process of imagining as a two-stage process that begins with primary sensory experience, involves individual and social elements and results in mental representations that are novel:

> Primary imagination encompasses the subconscious ability to blend and unify one's immediate sensory experiences with memories. This allows one to perceive of something—sensed only fragmentarily—as full of possibility and emotionally meaningful. The secondary imagination—as a continuation of the first—explains the conscious ability to perceive something not currently present.
>
> (Thompson 2018: 230)

We suggest that imagination can play a role in all three VSR processes. We envision that it can include not only individual imagining processes as described by Thompson, but group interactive processes that permit shared imagining.

Deliberate variation occurs when people imagine novel processes and outcomes, whether positive or negative. Organizations may design processes such as small group product development sessions, brainstorming, scenario planning, or science prize competitions, which all involve organizational efforts to increase the quality and volume of variation generated. These activities can involve variations in technology as well as in routines/strategies and templates. Underlying such processes is creative imagination.

Imagination is readily linked to individuals but also occurs at higher levels. Groups may even be able to create extraordinary ideas and breakthroughs more consistently than individuals (Harvey 2014). One study suggests that groups composed primarily of individuals who follow individualistic versus reciprocator motivations will generate less novel new action patterns than mixed groups (Bridoux et al. 2017). Garbuio et al. (2015) offer practitioner-oriented advice for design thinking, and specifically flag specific cognitive acts that facilitate creation in the generation of strategic options, such as imitation, induction, deduction, framing, analogical reasoning, and mental stimulation. The implicit outcome of these cognitive imaginative acts is to increase variation.

Human imagination can also profoundly impact selection processes. In standard planning processes, organizations compare "offline" (imagined) proposed new variations of action with current practice and then select one to enact. Managers can influence selection through imagining additional variations not yet proposed by others, which changes the selection landscape for the organization. Berg (2016) provides evidence for non-obvious ways that prior imagining may affect current selection. During "creative forecasting," subjects attempted to forecast the success of new creative projects. Prior creators were more accurate than managers in forecasting others' novel ideas, but not their own ideas. Berg (2016) theorized that the creators' role included both divergent and convergent thinking, while the managers' role emphasized convergent thinking. Individuals who had imagined projects were more accurate in selecting successful projects designed by others.

Group process matters here. Harvey (2014) proposes that instead of increasing divergence, or variance, in individuals' ideas, "creative synthesis"—through dialectic means—brings convergence of group members' perspectives. This facilitates consistent creation of breakthrough ideas. Synthesis, which characterizes selection, helps groups to evaluate novel ideas and thereby guides not only idea generation itself but also the process of idea generation and selection (Harvey, 2014).

Crucially, change agents can alter selection processes through the use of symbolic tools that change the meaning of events. Re-imagining meaning during selecting processes may alter their enactment and outcomes. Mirabeau and Maguire's (2014) study of a telecommunications firm described change processes that included discursive practices designed to impact sensemaking. Project champions invest energy in reframing the nature or future meaning of a product as a way to shape which products will or will not become part of the firm's realized strategy. This is consistent with conceptions of mid-level selection advocacy through active deployment of sensemaking. In one study, individuals absorbed rhetoric about TQM practices, implemented their own versions, and then filtered their own experience in order to create a perceived outcome of their own success (Zbaraki 1998). Over time, this repeated pattern led to a widespread, overly optimistic vision of TQM in the organization, which suggests that individual imagination and action interacted to create a hidden selection process favoring TQM ideology.

Incorporating imagination into retention processes further deepens the internal VSR model. Many shadow retention processes are not necessarily noticed by practicing managers, in part because of a failure to imagine that such hidden retention processes exist. An effective VSR manager can creatively unpack and see the shadow retention processes unfolding in the organization.

Imagination can also play a role in retention of action patterns when imaginative actors give new meaning to existing activities in ways that permit them to continue. Although retention is often seen as made up of passive processes, organizational actors may invest time in redefining actions as consistent. Organizations may retain the label of a technology standard but change its actual technical features through imaginative re-labelling of different parts of the standard (Garud et al. 2002). Retention occurs symbolically, but individual material elements of the technology standard actually change over time. Actors can actively redefine projects of interest to appear similar to better funded or legitimate projects in order to expand access to resources (Lovas and Ghoshal 2000).

Key VSR commentators have sometimes argued that individual imagination is too limited an engine of variation or selection for possible changes in technology or routines because individuals tend to imagine new states of the world that are close to current reality (March 1994 Weick 1979). We suggest, however, that imagination plays a vital role in the actual VSR change processes in organizations, worthy of attention from the change agent and theorist alike. Elon Musk, SpaceX, and NASA programs serve as practical examples of the possibilities and dangers. They have achieved major breakthroughs towards the goal of landing on Mars with the objective of settling humanity there, going beyond longstanding science-fiction visions of this possibility. Their progress towards this vision enacts an imagined radical new future well beyond a single organization.

Overall, these ideas imply that imagination offers an undertheorized factor in how VSR processes work and shape change. It appears that emotions and imagination may offer better predictors of VSR processes and outcomes than cognition alone, and that including them explicitly will enrich the manager's toolbox.

Discussion

This chapter has explored the idea that a basic internal VSR model may have value as an inclusive heuristic lens for use by practicing change agents. This contrasts with the dominant literature on evolutionary models of change, which tends to emphasize conceptual elaboration, rich case studies, and complex computational models of change. Much prior work that draws on evolutionary theory has focused on levels of analysis higher than the organization. This may have unfolded in part because key mechanisms in biological Darwinian evolution are assumed to operate at the level of species, but also because of the greater feasibility of developing consistent quantitative data on industry or regional levels, rather than on internal routines. Organization and strategy theory and practice, however, demands understanding at the organizational level as well. Important qualitative studies have provided nuanced insights into how VSR processes can, and do, unfold in organizations. Theory testing studies have presented a greater challenge: studying the birth and death of organizational routines within a given organization is exceptionally difficult and time consuming (Salvato and Rerup 2011). This has perhaps slowed down the building of a body of related internal VSR theory testing work. Computational modelling remains as a crucial domain for further work on evolutionary models, along with work grounded in field and experimental studies.

The VSR model as presented here promotes an intermediate view of agents' role in shaping change. It leaves the door open for individual leaders, who can detect core organizational dangers and can play active roles in strategic renewal inspired in part by emotion and making use of imagination (Maurer et al. 2017). However, it also highlights how organizational leaders in these co-evolutionary processes can attend to non-obvious mid-level interactions within their own organizations and to actors in the external environment. Agents then face choices about whether or not to attempt to influence such interactions.

Advantages of a Normative VSR Management Model

One of the crucial features of the VSR model is that it can illuminate patterned change without assuming deliberate prior design of the overall change (Aldrich et al. 2020). The fact that biological evolution represents such a powerful driver of change at world levels, and can be used as a vivid example of such emergent change, helps legitimize its use as an analogy, and illustrates its functioning. The organizational micro-processes that generate variation, selection, and retention can include rational instrumental action, political conflict, interpretive action, interactive dialectical interaction, and emergent processes. The VSR lens does not replace a rational actor model for the organization as a whole, but absorbs that model into a more credible framework.

The VSR lens can be used by change agents in all types of organizations, not just businesses. It does not require an ideological claim that VSR processes automatically lead to long-term efficiency, or social welfare. VSR models are agnostic about the benefits of outcomes. Instead, they force the user to address directly the ambiguity of how change affects long-term outcomes.

A VSR model still asks the manager to pursue standard activities, such as setting effective goals and implementing productive activities, but he or she also must deal with the hidden processes at different levels and different degrees of intentionality, in order to survive and prosper. The change agent executes these activities while also tracking external evolutionary change that may intersect with the organization's own pathway.

The VSR model pushes individuals to supplement the standard vision of management with awareness and conscious use of how to shape hidden VSR processes. This includes seeing political processes with internal tensions as a natural phenomenon that is not surprising and can even in some cases be used for positive organizational-level processes and outcomes. The VSR model also includes narratives of change that emerge through accidental discoveries, serendipitous impact of combinations of action, and luck. Using the VSR model allows the manager to start with a more realistic view of actual processes and to consciously develop indirect influence on specific diagnoses and actions. The manager can seek to effect change in the spirit of acting as a gardener or catalyst. In this VSR emergent world, managers may sketch a possible vision and leave large portions incomplete, or focus on harvesting the creativity of the other members.

For an organization's survival and prosperity, all three VSR processes have to work in effective cycles and fit the potential of the context. The change agent still plays a strategic role in assessing all three types of activities, shaping each, considering the balance between the VSR processes and also linking them to the context, including by actively shaping that context. Leaders using a VSR lens would expect deep internal and external surprises, given the nature of evolutionary processes, even though they could not predict a particular surprise. Leaders can prepare through maintaining organizational skills at interpreting surprises, at making pivots, and at rapid planning or improvising. Adding more explicit understanding of how imagination and emotion operate in VSR processes makes the model more realistic and gives the change agent a better chance of accurately anticipating possible outcomes of various actions. It will foster a deeper ability to work with the human beings of an organization and in surrounding societal groups.

In sum, a VSR lens protects against doomed efforts to rely fully on rational planning and control but offers a rich vision in which additional theories can co-exist. It draws attention to the existence of shadow change processes routinely at work, and encourages managers to carefully consider the possibility or desirability of influencing them. The VSR lens expects and enables managers to work with deliberate organizational goals and policies and to anticipate organizational emergent patterns. It includes the active interpretation of past and future actions as tools to shape all three VSR processes.

Disadvantages of a Normative VSR Management Model

One challenge to the widespread adoption of an internal VSR theory as a general framework for managers and change agents is that it does not match the taken-for-granted view of proper management in the modern world (Aldrich et al. 2020). Societies develop deep, often unstated norms about the proper way to organize human institutions and activity. This is a disadvantage to the extent that the VSR acceptance of less control is undesirable to organizational participants. It may also be seen as abdicating the responsibility for guiding organizations, which also may lead organizational participants to reject a VSR lens.

It seems likely that introducing the VSR theory in the context of a technology program may be most effective. The analogy between biological and technical evolution is intuitive for managers, and it is clear how leadership plays a role in balancing VSR processes or aligning them with external shocks and opportunities. Translation of VSR to organizational routines, strategies, and other units of actions for practicing managers could occur subsequently.

Managers may find it useful to work with case studies that give them opportunity to identify and shape VSR processes. Such engagement will help them to use the lens and encourage them to think automatically about how to influence hidden processes. At a minimum, managers will avoid maladapted actions because they failed to notice the hidden processes that actually drive organizational prosperity or survival.

The VSR model is a simple version of complex representations of organizational change processes. This has the benefit of practical use but the disadvantage of limitations as a scholarly theory of organizational change. Clearly, the schematic VSR lens does not remotely capture the actual complexity of change processes and micro-processes that lead to different prosperity or survival of organizations. Formal research on micro-reprocesses and specific causal loops remain crucial to ground abstract models in material reality. Computational and complexity models and broader systems theory offer much more accurate models of how change is progressing. Yet, such models have now developed to a point where practicing managers may need sophisticated modeling skills to make effective use of them.

We agree with the dangers of overconfident and misguided use of any management tool but propose that the benefits of a simple model outweigh the downsides. The main benefit of the basic VSR model—simplicity –makes it potentially valuable for daily use in short-term analyses and action, but also a tool to use with humility and patience. Adopting the stylized VSR lens as a practical tool requires a major but feasible shift that relies on attention to three elements, their interconnected nature, and their links to the external context.

Implications for Management Education

We suggest that including individuals in theories about internal VSR processes will encourage strengthening of individual reflection and action. We envision individual agents in organizations, who reflect more thoughtfully and can act more courageously, based on less privileging of formal strategic choice and analysis, and deliberate awareness of the distinct impact of imagination and emotion.

Contemporary management/leadership education already focuses on innovation in dynamic contexts. The VSR model that incorporates imagination and emotion can help expand the vision of what tools are useful. For example, if having sufficient variation is a problem, then deliberate efforts to train organizational members in imagining new meanings of existing processes or new organizational futures would have value. Imagining new meanings for existing practices or entities may represent a specialized skill similar to that of bricolage where participants imagine new uses of existing tools and materials (Baker and Nelson 2005). Hence, organizations may benefit from including training on re-imagination, in addition to training in standard design thinking or creativity training.

The strategy and management fields have perhaps seen evolutionary models of organizational change as more arcane models, of interest primarily to academics. Our chapter opens the door to an opposite idea: VSR models may instead have the greatest value as a simple heuristic lens that change agents at all organizational levels can use to analyze and influence organizational change over time. It may be one of the most, rather than the least, useful models when compared to the rich menu of change visions available today, including the many compelling models in this volume. VSR models offer an integrating lens for teaching not only about technology management/leadership but also about the general role of managers and change agents at all levels. A simple normative VSR model will be a useful and complementary addition to management education.

Conclusion

By sparking conversation about the simple, schematic VSR model as a tool for organizational actors, we clearly invite attention to the issue of guided evolution (March 1994; Lovas and Ghoshal 2000). The logic presented above does not assume that only top leadership can or should be the "guiding" force, which is in contrast to Lovas and Ghoshal's general approach. The spirit of this chapter falls more closely in line with March's (1994) essay on the engineering of evolutionary processes: it is a possible, but challenging, potential tool for the organizational change-seeker. March argues that limitations of human imagination and intention may mean that we are unlikely to be able to identify pathways for change that are helpful in the long run (March 1994). Our vision here is more hopeful. It implies that the change agent can in fact help nurture beneficial change that helps the organization prosper or at least survive.

Bringing the individual back into internal VSR models does not suggest a re-embrace of visions of the lone actor, who drives valued change heroically. Instead, we lay out pivot points where individuals can and do shape change through their deliberate as well as unintended impact on VSR processes and their interactions. We suggest that taking into account imagination and emotion will improve the accuracy and value of the VSR model. It reinforces the importance of research to deepen understanding about links between cognition, emotion, and imagination for strategy and organizational theory. At the same time, practicing change agents can use the core model of VSR processes for immediate value in designing and enabling fruitful actions and change through the processes. VSR models have historically been viewed as supporting passive adaptation to exogeneous contexts, along with being "cool" without integrating human imagination and emotions. We suggest a simple VSR model that embraces fully functioning individuals who draw on their cognition, emotion, and imagination to help their organizations' prosperity and survival.

Finally, explicit use of the schematic VSR model may give support and credibility to seasoned managers and change agents, who understand from experience that effective management is unlike the work of a master mechanic or engineer. Managers and change agents may be heroic, not because they can actually push levers to generate effective organizational change, but heroic in the mode of Greek tragedies or Don Quixote (March 2010), where leaders and change agents persist in pursuing valued dreams, even when fully understanding they cannot control them.

References

Aldrich, H. E., Ruef, J., and Egan, P. (2020), *Organizations Evolving* (3rd edn) (Thousand Oaks, CA: Sage).

Alinsky, S. D. (1969), *Rules for Radicals* (New York: Random House).

Amburgey, T. L., and Miner, A. S. (1992), 'Strategic Momentum: The Effects of Repetitive, Positional, and Contextual Momentum on Merger Activity,' *Strategic Management Journal*, 13/5, 335–48.

Baas, M., De Dreu, C. K. W., and Nijstad, B. A. (2008), 'A Meta-Analysis of 25 Years of Mood-Creativity Research: Hedonic Tone, Activation, or Regulatory Focus?', *Psychological Bulletin*, 134/6, 779–806.

Baker, T., and Nelson, R. E. (2005), 'Creating Something from Nothing: Resource Construction through Entrepreneurial Bricolage', *Administrative Science Quarterly*, 50, 329–66.

Barsade, S. G., and Knight, A. P. (2015), 'Group Affect', *Annual Review of Organizational Psychology and Organizational Behavior*, 2/1, 21–46.

Batista, M. D. G., Clegg, S., Cunha, M. P., Giustiniano, L., and Rego, A. (2016), 'Improvisation Prescription; Evidence from the Emergency Room', *British Journal of Management*, 27/2, 406–25.

Baum, J. A. C., and Rao, H. (2021), 'Evolutionary Dynamics of Organizational Populations and Communities' in M. S. Poole and A. H. Van de Ven, eds., *The Oxford Handbook of Organizational Change* (2nd edn) (Oxford: Oxford University Press).

Berg, J. M. (2016), "Balancing on the Creative Highwire: Forecasting the Success of Novel Ideas in Organizations', *Administrative Science Quarterly*, 61/3, 433–68.

Bledow, R., Rosing, K., and Frese, M. (2013), 'A Dynamic Perspective on Affect and Creativity', *Academy of Management Journal*, 56/2, 432–50.

Breugst, N., Domurath, A., Patzelt, H., and Klaukien, A. (2012), 'Perceptions of Entrepreneurial Passion and Employees' Commitment to Entrepreneurial Ventures', *Entrepreneurship Theory and Practice*, 36, 171–92.

Bridoux F., Coeurderoy R., and Durand R. (2017), 'Heterogeneous Social Motives and Interactions: The Three Predictable Paths of Capability Development', *Strategic Management Journal*, 38/9, 1755–73.

Bruderer, E., and Singh, J. V. (1996), 'Organizational Evolution, Learning, and Selection: A Genetic-Algorithm-Based Model', *Academy of Management Journal*, 39/5, 1322–49.

Burgelman, R. A. (1991), 'Intraorganizational Ecology of Strategy Making and Organizational Adaptation: Theory and Field Research', *Organization Science*, 2/3, 239–62.

Burgelman, R. A. (1994), 'Fading Memories: A Process Theory of Strategic Business Exit in Dynamic Environments', *Administrative Science Quarterly*, 39/1, 24–56.

Campbell, D. T. (1960), 'Blind Variation and Selective Retention in Creative Thought as in Other Knowledge Processes', *Psychological Review*, 67/6, 380–400.

Campbell, D. T. (1975), 'On the Conflicts between Biological and Social Evolution and between Psychology and Moral Tradition', *American Psychologist*, 30, 1103–26.

Cardon, M. S., and Kirk, C. P. (2015), 'Entrepreneurial Passion as Mediator of the Self-Efficacy to Persistence Relationship', *Entrepreneurship Theory and Practice*, 39/5, 1027–50.

Chan, T. H., Mihm, J., and Sosa, M. (2020), 'Revisiting the Role of Collaboration in Creating Breakthrough Inventions', Manufacturing and Service Operations Management, https://doi.org/10.1287/msom.2019.0858/, accessed 22 September 2020.

Cohen, M. D., March, J. G., and Olsen, J. P. (1972), 'A Garbage Can Model of Organizational Choice', *Administrative Science Quarterly*, 17/1, 1–25.

Crossan, M. M., Lane, H. W., and White, R. E. (1999), 'An Organizational Learning Framework: From Intuition to Institution', *Academy of Management Review*, 24/3, 522–37.

Crossan, M. M., Maurer, C. C., and White, R. E. (2011), "Reflections on the 2009 AMR Decade Award: Do We Have a Theory of Organizational Learning?', *Academy of Management Review*, 36/3, 446–60.

Cua, K. O., McKone, K. E., and Schroeder, R. G. (2001), 'Relationships between Implementation of TQM, JOT and TPM and Manufacturing Performance', *Journal of Operations Management*, 19/6, 675–94.

Cyert, R. M., and March, J. G. (1963), *A Behavioral Theory of the Firm* (Englewood Cliffs, NJ: Prentice-Hall).

Degler, C. N. (1992), *In Search of Human Nature: The Decline and Revival of Darwinism in American Social Thought* (Oxford University Press).

Dobrev, S. D., Kim, T., and Carroll, G. R. (2002), 'The Evolution of Organizational Niches: US Automobile Manufacturers, 1885–1981', *Administrative Science Quarterly*, 47, 233–64.

Doz, Y. L., Olk, P. M., and Ring, P. S. (2000), 'Formation Processes of RandD Consortia: Which Path to Take? Where Does it Lead?', *Strategic Management Journal*, 21/3, 239–66.

Elfenbein, H. A. (2007), 'Emotion in Organizations: A Review and Theoretical Integration', The *Academy of Management Annals*, 1/1, 315–86.

Fiol, C. M. (2002), 'Capitalizing on Paradox: The Role of Language in Transforming Organizational Identities', *Organization Science*, 13/6, 653–66.

Fredrickson, B. L. (2001), 'The Role of Positive Emotions in Positive Psychology: The Broaden-And-Build Theory of Positive Emotions', *American Psychologist*, 56/3, 218–26.

Gaba, V. and Meyer, A. D. (2021), 'Discontinuous Change in Organizations and Fields' in M. S. Poole and A. H. Van de Ven, eds., *The Oxford Handbook of Organizational Change* (2nd edn) (Oxford: Oxford University Press).

Galasso, A., Mitchell, M., and Virag, G. (2018), 'A Theory of Grand Innovation Prizes', *Research Policy*, 47/2, 343–62.

Garbuio, M., Lovallo, D., Porac, J., and Dong, A. (2015), 'A Design Cognition Perspective on Strategic Option Generation', *Advances in Strategic Management*, 32, 437–65.

Garud, R., Gehman, J., and Giuliani, A. P. (2018), 'Serendipity Arrangements for Exapting Science-Based Innovations', *Academy of Management Perspectives*, 32/1, 125–40.

Garud, R., Jain, S., and Kumaraswamy, A. (2002), 'Institutional Entrepreneurship in the Sponsorship of Common Technological Standards: The Case of Sun Microsystems and Java', *Academy of Management Journal*, 45/1, 196–214.

Garud, R., and Rappa, M. A. (1994), 'A Socio-Cognitive Model of Technology Evolution: The Case of Cochlear Implants', *Organization Science*, 5/3, 344–62.

George, J. M., and Zhou, J. (2007), 'Dual Tuning in a Supportive Context: Joint Contributions of Positive Mood, Negative Mood, and Supervisory Behaviors to Employee Creativity', *Academy of Management Journal*, 50/3, 605–22.

Gioia, D. A., and Chittipeddi, K. (1991), 'Sensemaking and Sensegiving in Strategic Change Initiation', *Strategic Management Journal*, 12/6, 433–48.

Hall, E. A., Rosenthal, J., and Wade, J. (1993), 'How to Make Reengineering Really Work', *Harvard Business Review*, 71, 119–31.

Harvey, S. (2014), 'Creative Synthesis: Exploring the Process of Extraordinary Group Creativity', *Academy of Management Review*, 39/3, 324–43.

Henderson, A. D., and Stern, I. (2004), 'Selection-Based Learning: The Coevolution of Internal and External Selection in High-Velocity Environments', *Administrative Science Quarterly*, 49/1, 39–75.

Howell, J. M., and Shea, C. M. (2006), 'Effects of Champion Behavior, Team Potency, and External Communication Activities on Predicting Team Performance', *Group and Organizational Management*, 3/2, 180–211.

Hsia, P., Samuel, J., Gao, J., Kung, D., Toyoshima, Y., and Chen, C. (1994), 'Formal Approach to Scenario Analysis', *IEEE Software*, 11/2, 33–41.

Huy, Q. N. (2005), 'Emotion Management to Facilitate Strategic Change and Innovation: How Emotional Balancing and Emotional Capability Work Together.' in C. E. Hä rtel, W. J. Zerbe, and N. M. Ashkanasy eds., *Emotions in Organizational Behavior*. (Mahwah, NJ: Lawrence Erlbaum Associates), 295–316.

Huy, Q. N. (2011), 'How Middle Managers' Group-Focus Emotions and Social Identities Influence Strategy Implementation', *Strategic Management Journal*, 32/13: 1387–410.

Isen, A. M. (1999), 'On the Relationship between Affect and Creative Problem Solving', in S. Russ, ed., *Affect, Creative Experience and Psychological Adjustment* (Philadelphia: Brunner/Mazel), 3–17.

Jay, J. (2013), 'Navigating Paradox as a Mechanism of Change and Innovation in Hybrid Organizations', *Academy of Management Journal*, 56/1, 137–59.

Kotter, J. P. (2012), *Leading Change* (Boston: Harvard Business Press).

Krackhardt, D. (1990), 'Assessing the Political Landscape: Structure, Cognition and Power in Organizations', *Administrative Science Quarterly*, 35/2, 342–69.

Lee, G. K., and Cole, R. E. (2003), 'From a Firm-Based to a Community-Based Model of Knowledge Creation: The Case of the Linux Kernel Development', *Organization Science*, 14/6, 633–49.

Leonard, T. C. (2009), 'Origins of the Myth of Social Darwinism: The Ambiguous Legacy of Hofsteder's Social Darwinism in American Thought', *Journal of Economic Behavior and Organization*, 71/1, 37–51.

Levinthal, D. A. (1991), 'Organizational Adaptation and Environmental Selection-Interrelated Processes of Change', *Organization Science*, 2/1, 140–45.

Levinthal, D. A. (2011), 'A Behavioral Approach to Strategy: What's the Alternative?', *Strategic Management Journal*, 32/13, 1517–23.

Leybourne, S. A., and Sainter, P. (2012), 'Advancing Project Management: Authenticating the Shift from Process to 'Nuanced' Process-Based Management in the Ambidextrous Organization', *Product Management Journal*, 43/6, 5–15.

Loewenstein, G., and Lerner, J. S. (2003), 'The Role of Affect in Decision Making', Handbook of Affective Science, 619(642), 3.

Lovas, B., and Ghoshal, S. (2000), 'Strategy as Guided Evolution', *Strategic Management Journal*, 21/9, 875–96.

Maitlis, S., Vogus, T. J., and Lawrence, T. B. (2013), 'Sensemaking and Emotion in Organizations', *Organizational Psychology Review*, 3/3, 222–47.

March, J. G. (1962), 'The Business Firm as a Political Coalition". *The Journal of Politics*, 24/4, 662–78.

March, J. G. (1991), 'Exploration and Exploitation in Organizational Learning', *Organization Science*, 2/1, 71–87.

March, J. G. (1994), 'The Evolution of Evolution', in J. A. C. Baum and J. V. Singh, eds., *Evolutionary Dynamics of Organizations* (New York: Oxford University Press), 3–20.

March, J. G. (2010), *The Ambiguities of Experience* (Ithaca, NY: Cornell University Press).

Martin, J. (2001), *Organizational Culture: Mapping the Terrain* (Thousand Oaks, CA: Sage Publications).

Maurer, C. C., Crossan, M. M., and Miner, A. S. (2017), 'Strategic insight for strategic renewal', *Strategic Management Society Conference*, Banff, Canada, June 4.

McGrath, R. G., and Nerkar, A. (2004), 'Real Options Reasoning and a New Look at the RandD Investment Strategies of Pharmaceutical Firms', *Strategic Management Journal*, 25/1, 1–21.

Merriam-Webster Dictionary, 2020.

Miller, D., and Friesen, P. H. (1982), 'Innovation in Conservative and Entrepreneurial Firms: Two Models of Strategic Momentum', *Strategic Management Journal*, 3/1, 1–25.

Miner, A. S. (1987), 'Idiosyncratic Jobs in Formalized Organizations', *Administrative Science Quarterly*, 32/3, 327–51.

Miner, A. S. (1990), 'Structural Evolution through Idiosyncratic Jobs: The Potential for Unplanned Learning', *Organizational Science*, ½, 195–210.

Miner, A. S. (1991), 'Organizational Evolution and the Social Ecology of Jobs', *American Sociological Review*, 56/6, 772–85.

Miner, A. S. (1994), 'Seeking Adaptive Advantage: Evolutionary Theory and Managerial Action', in J. A. C. Baum and J. V. Singh, eds., *Evolutionary Dynamics of Organizations* (New York: Oxford University Press), 76–89.

Mintzberg, H., and Waters, J. A. (1985), 'Of Strategies Deliberate and Emergent', *Strategic Management Journal*, 6/3, 257–72.

Mirabeau, L., and Maguire, S. (2014), 'From Autonomous Strategic Behavior to Emergent Strategy', *Strategic Management Journal*, 35/8, 1202–29.

Murmann, J. P. (2013), 'The Coevolution Of Industries and Important Features of Their Environments', *Organization Science*, 24/1, 58–78.

Navis, C., and Glynn, M. A. (2010), 'How New Market Categories Emerge: Temporal Dynamics of Legitimacy, Identity and Entrepreneurship in Satellite Radio, 1990–2005', *Administrative Science Quarterly*, 55/3, 439–71.

Nelson, R. R., and Winter, S. G. (1982), *An Evolutionary Theory of Economic Change* (Cambridge, MA: Belknap Press of Harvard University).

Reitzeig, M. and Sorenson, O. (2013), 'Biases in the Selection Stage of Bottom-Up Strategy Formulation', *Strategic Management Journal*, 34/7, 782–99.

Rura-Polley, T., and Miner, A. S. (2002), 'The Relative Standing of Routines: Some Jobs Are More Equal Than Others', in M. Augier and J. G. March, eds., *The Economics of Choice, Change and Organization: Essays in Memory of Richard M. Cyert* (Cheltenham: Edward Elgar), 272–303.

Salvato, C., and Rerup, C. (2011), 'Beyond Collective Entities: Multilevel Research on Organizational Routines and Capabilities', *Journal of Management*, 37/2, 468–90.

Sanchez-Burks, J., and Huy, Q. N. (2009), 'Emotional Aperture and Strategic Change: The Accurate Recognition of Collective Emotions', *Organization Science*, 20/1, 22–34.

Schilling, M. A. (2020), *The Strategic Management of Technological Innovation* (6th edn) (Irwin: McGraw-Hill).

Sine, W., and Lee, B. H. (2009), 'Tilting at Windmills? The Environmental Movement and the Emergence of the U.S. Wind Energy Sector', *Administrative Science Quarterly*, 54, 123–55.

Sonenshein, S. (2010), 'We're Changing—Or Are We? Untangling the Role of Progressive, Regressive, and Stability Narratives during Strategic Change Implementation', *Academy of Management Journal*, 53/3, 477–512.

Staw, B. M., Sandelands, L. E., and Dutton, J. E. (1981), 'Threat Rigidity Effects in Organizational Behavior: A Multilevel Analysis', *Administrative Science Quarterly*, 26/4, 501–24.

Sy, T., Côté, S., and Saavedra, R. (2005), 'The Contagious Leader: Impact of the Leader's Mood on the Mood of Group Members, Group Affective Tone, and Group Processes', *Journal of Applied Psychology*, 90/2, 295–305.

Taylor, A. (2010), 'The Next Generation: Technology Adoption and Integration through Internal Competition in New Product Development', *Organization Science*, 21/1, 23–41.

Thompson, N. A. (2018), 'Imagination and Creativity in Organizations', *Organization Studies*, 39, 229–50.

Tushman, M., and O'Reilly, C. A. (1996), 'Ambidextrous Organizations: Managing Evolutionary and Revolutionary Change', *California Management Review*, 38/4, 8–29.

Van de Ven, A. H., Angle, H. L., and Poole, M. S. (2000), *Research on the Management of Innovation: The Minnesota Studies* (New York: Oxford University Press).

Van de Ven, A. H. and Polley, D. (1992), 'Learning while Innovating', *Organization Science*, 3/1, 92–116.

Van de Ven, A. H., Polley, D. E., Garud, R., and Venkataraman, S. (1999), *The Innovation Journey* (New York: Oxford University Press).

Vera, D., and Crossan, M. M. (2004), 'Theatrical Improvisation: Lessons for Organizations', *Organization Studies*, 25/5, 727–49.

Volberda, H. W., and Lewin, A. Y. (2003), 'Co-Evolutionary Dynamics within and between Firms: From Evolution to Co-Evolution', *Journal of Management Studies*, 40/8, 2111–36.

Vuori, T. O., and Huy, Q. N. (2016), 'Distributed Attention and Shared Emotions in the Innovation Process: How Nokia Lost the Smartphone Battle', *Administrative Science Quarterly*, 61/1, 9–51.

Welpe, I. M., Spörrle, M., Grichnik, D., Michl, T., and Audretsch, D. B. (2012), 'Emotions and Opportunities: The Interplay of Opportunity Evaluation, Fear, Joy, and Anger as Antecedent of Entrepreneurial Exploitation". *Entrepreneurship Theory and Practice*, 36, 69–96.

Weick, K. E. (1979), *The Social Psychology of Organizing* (2nd edn) (Reading, MA: Addison-Wesley).

Woolley, J. (2021), 'Processes of Emergence and Change in Industry and Ecosystem Infrastructure', in M. S. Poole and A. H. Van de Ven, eds., *The Oxford Handbook of Organizational Change* (2nd edn) (Oxford: Oxford University Press),

Zbaraki, M. J. (1998), 'The Rhetoric and Reality of Total Quality Management', *Administrative Science Quarterly*, 43/3, 602–36.

Zhou, X. (1993), 'The Dynamics of Organizational Rules', *American Journal of Sociology*, 98/5, 1134–66.

CHAPTER 20

CONCEPTUALIZING ORGANIZATIONAL CHANGE THROUGH THE LENS OF COMPLEXITY SCIENCE

KEVIN J. DOOLEY

Introduction

Complexity science describes a broad and diverse group of concepts, theories, and models describing the systemic and dynamic properties of living systems (e.g., Gell-Mann 1994; Holland 1995; Jantsch 1980; Maturana and Varela 1992; Prigogine and Stengers 1984; Taleb 2007).[1] Complexity science evolved and differentiated itself from general systems theory by addressing phenomena that were particular to living systems, such as autopoiesis, negative entropy, self-organization, co-evolution between systems (Bateson 1972; Lewin 1992; Waldrop 1992; Anderson 1999; Guastello 2002). Complexity science has been used by organizational scientists to both develop and discover theory and has been accompanied by a wide range of methodological approaches, from qualitative case studies to quantitative models of nonlinear dynamical systems.

A common element of all complexity science models is that they explicitly incorporate the dimension of time—thus, they are particularly attractive to organizational theorists studying phenomena involving change, as change can only be defined and studied over time. In fact, it may be that part of the appeal of complexity science is due to the fact

[1] This chapter is derived from an original version: Dooley, K. (2004), 'Complexity science models of organizational change,' *Handbook of Organizational Change and Innovation*, S. Poole and A. Van De Ven, eds., Oxford: Oxford University Press, p. 354–73.

that few existing paradigms of organizational theory incorporate the dimension of time in any significant manner. Complexity science models tend to go beyond describing the mere progression of activities and events as is common, but instead detail the generative mechanisms responsible for change. Thus, complexity science models tend to have characteristics of both a variance theory, in that they conceptualize causal links between variables or constructs, as well as a process theory, in that they make explicit how change over time occurs. Complexity science models answer both the "how" and "why" of organizational change.

The explicit incorporation of a time dimension means that complexity science models assume that living systems are path dependent and historical (Turner and Baker, 2019). Additionally, complexity science models commonly assume that change is often unpredictable (and uncontrollable) due to nonlinear interactions in the system; structural and functional change can emerge, especially due to adaptive pressures; living systems usually operate between regimes of "order" and "chaos", that is. in a dynamic quasi-equilibrium; and organizing occurs from within (i.e., self-organization) in a manner irreducible to the systems' components (Turner and Baker 2019).

Complexity science-inspired models of organizational change can be categorized into four general areas. *Agent-based models* are simulation models or conceptual frameworks where agents within a system pursue teleological ends. Agents possess action rules (schema) that define how they interact with the environment, including resources and other agents. Agents are often modeled as being heterogenous in terms of their goals and capabilities and learn how to improve their fitness over time. Mechanisms within the models tend to be complicated. Complex adaptive system (CAS) models describe parts of the agent-based system (agents, objects, resources), and how they interact. The dominant disciplines underlying this approach are computer science and cognitive psychology. Researchers use agent-based models primarily in a deductive manner, as one must specify a model a priori and then simulate it in order to learn of the emergent properties and patterns in the system. Sometimes researchers qualitatively fit an agent-based model to an existing system to argue that it is better understood via a CAS lens than a more traditional conceptual lens. These studies can be insightful but lack verifiability in that the hypothesis of whether a particular system is a CAS or not cannot be empirically tested, because there is no standard definition of what a CAS is.

Computational models are simulation-based models where parts of a system co-evolve over time. These parts may be agents, or simply elements or attributes of the whole. Change is driven by non-teleological, local interactions between the parts. Mechanisms within the models tend to be simple. The dominant underlying disciplines are mathematics and computer science. Like agent-based models, computational models are primarily used in a deductive manner.

Dynamical models are mathematical models that formulate how, and often why, variables that we observe in complex systems change over time. Variables in such models may represent higher-level constructs that are not explicitly measurable or may represent measurable variables. Interactions between variables may be linear or nonlinear, discrete or continuous. The dominant underlying disciplines are mathematics and statistics. Researchers may use dynamical models inductively, by modeling empirical data and then theorizing how such observed patterns may have come about; or they may use them deductively, similar to how a computational model is used.

Far-from-equilibrium models are mathematical and conceptual models that formulate how order is created in the system from within. These models focus on the dialectic differences that exist within the system, and the role that energy (or other system inputs) plays in transforming structure. The models are based in thermodynamics and understanding how such systems create negative entropy, or order. Emphasis is placed on how significant structural changes occur, including how order is created from randomness. The dominant theoretical perspectives are biological and thermodynamic. Researchers use far-from-equilibrium models both inductively and deductively; first, emergent patterns are observed that hint at a self-organizing process, then the specific causal mechanisms behind such self-organization are hypothesized.

Thus, models within these four areas describe how parts of the system, and attributes of these parts, interrelate over time. The distinction of complexity science models into these four approaches is descriptive and not theoretical—in reality, there are features of models that overlap across these boundaries, and in general there is no consensus on a particular typology or taxonomy that categorizes complexity science models. A review of literature, however, suggests that far-from-equilibrium models have been far more popular amongst organizational scientists than models representing the other three approaches. This is most likely because agent-based, computational, and dynamical models all require empirical or computational effort, whereas far-from-equilibrium models, while conceptually complex, are typically applied in a qualitative manner.

Models within these four categories depict change consistent with the taxonomy posited by Poole and Van de Ven (1995). Agent-based models are teleological in nature, and portray constructive change brought about by individual agents pursuing improvement in their individual fitness level, although fitness can also have global, aggregate components. Evolutionary mechanisms, such as a genetic algorithm, may be embedded within the logic of an agent-based model, so that agents learn. Far-from-equilibrium models also formulate change as constructive, but from a dialectic versus teleological perspective. Whereas agent-based models depict agents as responsible for change, far-from-equilibrium models emphasize how the interconnections and interactions between parts of the system produce order and change. The teleology involved in a far-from-equilibrium model—why it wants to create order—is the system's desire to dissipate an influx of energy or information in more efficient ways. Dynamical models portray change as prescribed by the generative mechanisms within the system, and focus on single entities or variables, which may be attached to parts of the system or the system as a whole. Dynamical models are rarely teleological, but rather portray change as a life cycle process, inevitable and prescribed by the generative mechanism. Computational models also model change as an inherent property of the system, as it relates to the interaction of multiple entities. While computational models depict evolutionary processes, most do not have a component representing selection or adaptation. Thus, computational models have characteristics of both evolutionary and life cycle paradigms.

Complexity science models can be used to describe organizational change at various levels of conceptualization: an individual person, an object (e.g., entity, resource, technology), an organizational process, a team or subunit, the organization, or a market. In practice, many authors formulate models portraying the importance of the individual person, and their interrelationships with other individual people, but this is more a bias imposed by the research community rather than the models themselves. Complexity science models, like systems theory models, are generic enough to be employed at different levels of scale. Agent-based and self-organizing models can also address dynamic interactions that occur across scales of an organizational system.

The rest of the chapter is organized as follows. First, we shall contrast how complexity science conceptualizes change differently than its predecessor, systems theory. Next, each of the types of complexity science models as they relate to organizational change are described, and their application to organizational studies is discussed. An example is presented that demonstrates how each model might be applied in conceptualizing change within an organizational system. In the case of computational models the discussion is briefer, as the next chapter in this book by Ganco and Alvert goes into detail around the dominant computation model that organizational researchers employ, the NK (or rugged landscape) model (Kauffman 1995; Levinthal and Warglien (1999); Billinger et al. 2014). The chapter concludes by discussing some of the future challenges facing complexity science-based studies of organizational change, as it relates to both conceptual formulation and research methodology.

Organizational Change from Lens of Systems Theory

We start with a discussion of the manner in which general systems theory, the precursor to complexity science, conceptualizes phenomena of change. Systems theory has influenced the thoughts and models of social scientists since its inception midway through the twentieth century (Bateson 1972; Forester 1961; Haken 1984; Jantsch 1980; Simon 1957). The term "general systems theory" originates from Ludwig Von Bertalanffy, whose ideas were adopted by others, including Kenneth E. Boulding, William Ross Ashby and Anatol Rapoport working in mathematics, psychology, biology, game theory, and social network analysis. Systems theory models causal relationships between variables or constructs—but whereas traditional science posits a unidirectional relationship between cause and effect (i.e., motivated students tend to learn more), systems theory introduced the notion of bi-directional causality (i.e., motivated students tend to learn more, which in turn makes them more motivated). This bi-directional causality is not assumed to be instantaneous though, so variable A affects variable B, then B affects A, and so on. The effect of B on A is termed "feedback."

One type of feedback is a reinforcing loop, where variables A and B affect each other in a similar direction, and this leads to cascading processes and exponential growth in both A and B (theoretically). Thus, just as a microphone and audio speaker can positively interact to the point where feedback causes the system to "explode" to its physical limits, so too will (e.g.) motivation and learning interact with one another positively until the limits of performance are reached. A reinforcing loop also would imply that if motivation decreases, then learning will decrease, which will further decrease motivation, etc. Reinforcing loops are enacted in organizations in the form of incentives, social capital, economies of scale, some elements of performance evaluation, escalation of commitment, etc.

Feedback can also establish a balancing loop, and this is typically associated with a variable's level having a goal that it is attempting to achieve, or some type of limit. A balancing loop produces decreasing returns, and exponential decay in the associated variables. So, for example, as an automobile approaches a stop sign, the driver applies negative feedback (the brakes) to slow down the car, as it approaches its final destination. Natural limits can also act as sources of balancing loops, keeping the system within boundaries of feasibility. Balancing loops are enacted in organizations in the form of (constructive) criticism, management by exception, project management control systems, organizational policies and rules, etc.

Organizational researchers may theorize feedback within their models, but they rarely incorporate it within models that are subjected to empirical testing, because it requires the collection of longitudinal data. Strictly speaking, a model that posits that A causes B must demonstrate that A preceded B temporally. In order to demonstrate bi-directional causality between A and B, A must be observed at one particular time, B must be observed to occur at a later time, and then A again at yet a later time, thus requiring a minimum of three samples at different times. In practice, this has rarely been done, although the recent increased popularity of econometrics modeling via panel analyses suggests this will happen more in the future.

This temporal lag between cause and effect further complicates both the formulation of systems theory models, as well as the observation of these patterns, as the lag may be indeterminable, or may itself vary over time. For example, in models that link changes in levels of organizational investment in research to changes in the company's market share, the lag between investment and realization of successful new products must be taken into account, and this may vary across and even within particular industries, or may change due to technological and market forces.

Social scientists were quick to realize the conceptual value that systems theory offered, and its use quickly spread. In particular, interest in cybernetics was keen, as people attempted to understand how the brain worked, using the computer as a model of human thinking (Minsky 1986). Forrester (e.g., 1961) used computational models he named "system dynamics" to explore the relationship between key variables in large-scale social systems such as industries, communities, and ecologies. Relationships between variables were typically modeled using simple linear differential equations. While the behavior of a single relationship was relatively straightforward, it was the aggregate behavior that arose from complex coupling of the variables that led to surprising and revealing results (Sterman 2000).

While researchers continued to develop systems theory applications in the social sciences in the 1960s and 1970s, it was in the 1980s that systems theory enjoyed wider exposure within organizational studies and applications. This revived interest was in part because of the works of Deming (1986) and Senge (1990), who brought systems thinking concepts to business managers via the topics of total quality management and organizational learning.

While systems theory lays an important conceptual and intellectual foundation for studying complex systems, it did not adequately deal with the unique attributes associated with living systems, whether it is a cell, a biological entity, or a social system. While causal relationships may be modeled as being complicated, that is, many causes linked with many effects which may be bi-directional, models are still most often formulated in simple, linear ways. Systems theory does not describe how entities in a system interact but rather how variables interact, and these variables are traits or characteristics of entities within the system, or the system itself. Thus, systems theory models are top-down, in that they require the modeler to identify a priori the most significant variables and how they interrelate. Systems theory models portray life as something that is mechanically maintained through equilibrium-seeking processes.

It was during the 1980s that complexity science emerged from within systems theory. The Santa Fe Institute was started in 1984 as a major interdisciplinary think-tank to apply complexity science to the physical and social sciences. Three books fundamental to the complexity science paradigm were published in the 1980s: (1) Prigogine and Stengers (1984) model of self-organizing (thermodynamic) change in living systems; (2) Gleick's book "Chaos" (1987) which introduced the world to nonlinear dynamics and deterministic sensitivity to initial conditions; and (3) Holland's (1995) book that codified the components and principles of complex adaptive systems, enabling many other scholars to develop simulation models building from a common base of assumptions and architecture. In the 1990s, several popular books were published about the Santa Fe Institute and the topics it was studying (Waldrop 1992; Lewin 1994). The 1990s also saw the beginning of complexity science applications in the traditional organizational science academic literature (e.g., Brown and Eisenhardt 1998; Cheng and Van de Ven 1996; Dooley 1997; Eoyang 1997; Goldstein 1994; Guastello 1995; Kiel 1993; Stacey 1992; Wheatley 1992; Zimmerman and Hurst 1993). It was also during the 1990s that several institutions started which supported the application of complexity science in the study of organizations, such as the Chaos Network, the Society for Chaos Theory in Psychology and Life Sciences, the Plexus Institute, and the New England Complexity Systems Institute. Specialized business-complexity journals also started up in this period, such as *Nonlinear Dynamics in Psychology and Life Sciences* and *Emergence: Complexity and Organization*. It is from this point onwards where our review of scholarship begins.

Agent-Based Models of Organizational Change

Major Assumptions

Organizations can be thought of as examples of a general class of complex systems called *complex adaptive systems*, or CAS. Organizational theorists have traditionally associated the term "complexity" with a description of the inner workings of an organization (Dooley 2002), often related to size or variety. For example, a firm with many specialists is considered more complex than a firm with few specialists. In the case of CAS, complexity refers to the manner in which the system behaves relative to its internal structure. Its aggregate behavior is not predictable from, and cannot be reduced or understood from its component parts (Holland 1995). In a complex system, two plus two does not necessarily equal four. Many systems are complex—weather, ecologies, information networks, etc. A complex system is considered *adaptive* if it can change itself using evolutionary processes on timescales much shorter than bio-evolutionary time scales. Examples of a CAS include economies, automobile traffic, social organizations, and cultures (Gell-Mann 1994). It is worth noting that the most formal operational definition of CAS, by Holland (1995), is simultaneously a specification for a computer simulation language (*Swarm*). Thus, the connection between a CAS perspective and computer modeling is very strong.

The basic elements of an agent-based model (ABM) are agents. Agents are semi-autonomous units that seek to maximize their fitness by evolving over time. Agents scan their environment (both internal and external to the system) and interpret these scans via their schema. Agents can be representative of individual people, or can represent larger entities such as teams, divisions, or whole firms. Schemata are mental templates (within a computer model, computational templates) that define how reality is interpreted and what is an appropriate response for a given stimuli. These schemata are often evolved from smaller, more basic schema (Holland 1995). Agents are assumed to be rationally bounded, in that they have limited and perhaps biased access to information within the system, and schemata may differ across agents due to personal idiosyncrasies in how people make decisions (March 1994). Within an agent, multiple, contradictory schema may exist, competing via a selection-enactment-retention process (Weick 1979).

When an observation does not match what is expected, an agent can take action in order to adapt the observation to fit an existing schema. An agent can also purposefully alter schema in order to better fit the observation. A schema can change through random or purposeful mutation, or combination with other schemata. In most agent-based models, random mutations do not impact the agent's schema unless they correspond to an increase in the agent's fitness. When a schema changes it generally has the effect of making the agent more robust (it can perform in light of increasing variation or variety), more reliable (it can perform more predictably), or more capable in terms of its requisite variety (in can adapt to a wider range of conditions) (Arthur 1994).

Similar to a multi-attribute utility function, the fitness of the agent is often modeled as a complex aggregate of many factors, both local and global. Agents with low current fitness values are more likely to instigate change in their schema. Optimization of local fitness allows differentiation and novelty/diversity; global optimization of fitness enhances the CAS coherence as a system and induces long-term memory.

Schemata also determine how a given agent interacts with other agents both inside and outside of the system. Actions between agents involve the exchange of information and/or resources, occurring through lines of connectivity. These flows may be nonlinear. Information and resources can undergo multiplier effects based on the nature of connectivity in the system. Because an agent's schemata include information about other agents, an action by one agent can be considered information for other agents that are connected to it. Different types of connections exist. For example, Krackhardt and Carley (1998) define connectivity in an organizational system by a social network, a task network, and a resource network.

Agent tags help identify what other agents are capable of transacting with a given agent; tags also facilitate the formation of aggregates. For example, in an organizational AMB, tags may identify agents belonging to different functions or business units, or on particular project teams. Agent tags enable coordination and aggregation amongst like and unlike agents. At a basic level, agent tags help model the diversity and specialization within the CAS (Holland 1995). Agents also exist outside the boundaries of the ABM, and schemata also determine the rules of interaction concerning how information and resources flow externally.

A researcher using an ABM must specify what is inside versus outside of the system, or the system's boundary. In some cases, boundaries may be self-evident, such as the legal boundary of a firm. In other cases, boundaries are specified according to the research questions being addressed. Because systems are decomposable, boundaries may exist and be depicted at multiple scales, leading to nested behavior. Finally, the system's reason for being is defined by existence assumptions. These assumptions will tend to influence how the model incorporates contributions to agent fitness that are global in nature. For example, a simulation of a corporation may use economic criteria in the agents' fitness functions, whereas a simulation of a non-profit agency may use more altruistic criteria.

Current State of Research

Some papers (e.g., Colbert (2004); Garud et al. (2011); Wong and Chan (1999)) have used ABMs as a conceptual framework for developing or interpreting their theory. More rigorous applications develop a simulation model as an essential part of their theory building or testing (Fioretti 2012). These papers do not address organizational change writ large, but rather model topics or phenomena where an agent-based simulation is an effective methodological choice. For example, Wersching (2010) uses an ABM to study how industry characteristics and evolved structure impact knowledge-spillover effects. In similar vein, Carley and Morgan (2016) use ABM to examine information leakages within organizations, while Najed examines innovation diffusion (2016) in agent networks. Aros and Gibbons (2018) use ABM to study communication media options during a disaster response event. Gao et al. (2018) use ABM to study the impact of cognitive artifacts, such as operating rules, on organizational routines. Albino et al. (2006) examine the formation of industrial clusters using ABM. Meng et al. (2017) and Nguyen (2019) use ABM to study contract design and performance across multi-tier supply chains. This list is not meant to be exhaustive, but rather demonstrate the diversity of change-related applications for ABM.

Example

One model that demonstrates the application of an agent-based model is Axtell's (1999) computational model of the emergence of firms. Agents are individuals who self-organize into firms by considering their own fitness. First, each agent is assigned an "income-leisure" parameter that determines the amount of time it would prefer to spend working (making income) versus at leisure (any amount of time not allocated to work effort); these assignments are made randomly so agent heterogeneity is maintained. The agent's utility, or fitness, at any given time is a multiplicative function of the amount of effort they are expending, the return on that effort at the firm level, and the amount of leisure time available. At random intervals of time an agent will consider their current position and either (a) maintain their current effort level, (b) increase or decrease their current effort level, (c) start a new firm (solo), or (d) migrate to one of two friend's firms. The amount of return that a firm gets from the aggregated efforts of its members depends on the number of members, their individual efforts, and any synergistic effects that may be included (e.g., increasing returns). Returns to the individual are equally divided amongst all firm participants.

Despite the number of different parameters and starting conditions that can be varied, and the fact that the simulation itself is based on some rather simplistic assumptions about human nature, the results show a great deal of validity in mimicking actual firm formation behavior. For example:

- As firms become large, an individual agent's contribution becomes miniscule compared to the whole, which produces "free riders".
- As free riding becomes more commonplace, firm productivity decreases and those who most want "work" leave for other firms, bringing the large firm into decline.
- While "equilibrium" conditions theoretically exist that would lead to a static situation, there is sufficient dynamic instability such that these equilibrium conditions never arise.

- The history of any firm is emergent and path dependent.
- At the aggregate level, firm size, growth, and death rates mimic existing empirical evidence.

What is interesting here is not that there are free riders, or that firms die and emerge in a dynamic fashion, or even that real growth rates can be mimicked. Rather, the fundamental point is that all of these conclusions, found elsewhere in the organizational literature, emerge from a model with nothing more than semi-autonomous agents who seek to selfishly improve a simple fitness function. As more of these kinds of simulations are done, theories that emphasize local interactions leading to global, emergent patterns will become more prevalent.

Principles of Change

There are two types of change portrayed in agent-based models. First, because agents in the CAS are constantly interacting with other agents, and adapting to, or evolving with an environment, there is constant change in terms of flow of resources and information, learning by agents, and actions that agents take. CAS models portray change as something that is driven by the goals of individual agents, but the patterns that emerge are not necessarily deducible at the agent level because of the self-organizing nature of the system. Second, as a CAS model equates the organization to a particular set of elements (agents, schema, boundaries, interconnections), the deep structures of the system that portray the more quasi-permanent and stable elements of the organizational system will change as one or more of the elements of the CAS changes:

- Agents can be added or removed from the system, for example via expansion, downsizing, and mergers and acquisitions. This is also the basic manner in which the system's boundary can be altered.
- The fitness function of an agent can be thought of as containing both extrinsic and intrinsic components, and both individual and group components. It can be altered by changing reward and incentive systems, or by changing norms and values.
- The schema that agents have to interpret the world they see around them can evolve over time, being strengthened or weakened, can undergo mutation, can be combined with other schemata, or can be eliminated altogether. In an ABM, schema can be model basic rational processes (e.g., problematic search), but can also be modified to incorporate bounded rationality or even affective states. In most CAS formulations, schema change is linked to how actions and outcomes, as indicated by the fitness function, are associated. Thus, if an action rule consistently improves fitness, the strength of belief in that rule will tend to increase; this attribution process (Holland 1995) is the operational model of agent learning. Agents are assumed to be capable of single-loop, double-loop, or deutero-learning (Argyris and Schon 1978).

- Changing a flow's pace or timing can alter the flow of information or resources between two or more agents, increasing or decreasing exchanges. For example, information technology and the Internet increase the pace of information flow, while schedules and other forms of temporal coordination alter the timing of events.
- Connections between agents can be added or removed via restructuring and redesign of the system, including changing lines of command and increasing connectivity through information technology.
- Agent tags can be changed in either a specific or symbolic fashion. For example, salespeople in a growing firm may be separated into marketing and sales functions; people may be assigned titles indicating new levels of responsibility and communication.
- Changes in an organization's strategy (mission and vision) represent changes in its existence assumptions.

At a general level, a CAS model suggests means for and processes of organizational change that are not different from what already exists in the organizational literature. Many of the implications that authors draw by using CAS as a framework for how organizations work can also be found in literature within general systems theory, population ecology, organizational learning, and cognitive psychology (Dooley 1997). Novel insight comes not from the general conclusions as given above, but rather the specific conclusions based on the model at hand.

Strengths and Criticisms

An agent-based model of CAS has several advantages for theory building and testing in the study of organizational change. First, it can be used as an inductive tool capable of discovering surprising patterns of behavior unpredictable from the constituent components and rules. Second, the origin of the agent-based model is in part a software specification (Holland 1995). Thus, propositions or descriptions of the CAS, and the model's components and rules, are proximal to one another. Third, the community of scholars who have developed and used agent-based simulation models have developed common conceptual and software models, enabling shared resources that create increased research productivity. Finally, agent-based models have proven to be useful by real organizations for various sorts of design and operations problems.

The practical difficulty of using agent-based models for theory building or testing marginalizes their usefulness. Many scholars do not have or desire to obtain the skills needed to program software to create such computer simulations. It is also difficult to calibrate the numerous parameters than need to be determined and modeled; it is uncommon for such models to be calibrated to real data. Because an agent-based model is defined by such a large number of parameters, it can be unclear to a researcher how to constrain their theory and model to get meaningful comparisons. It is likely that as AI and machine learning are increasingly coupled with agent-based models for designing or managing real business systems, that resources will develop making it easier for organizational scholars to use agent-based models to study planned or emergent change.

Computational Models of Organizational Change

Computational models are similar to CAS agent-based models in that they depict parts of the system (agents or objects) that interact with one another through a set of rules. Insights from the models are gained from simulation. In contrast to agent-based models, most computational CAS models of organizational change are not teleological, and more often than not the rules that dictate local interactions are simple. Unlike agent-based models where there is a relatively agreed-upon framework and architecture for what models should have in terms of components, different computational models formulate the causal system differently. The most commonly used computational model by organizational change scholars is the NK model (Kauffman 1995). Since that model is covered extensively in the next chapter by Ganco and Albert, that model will not be discussed further here.

Other types of computational models of CAS are feasible (e.g., cellular automata, neural networks, genetic algorithms). For example, Morel and Ramanujam (1999) use a computational model self-organized criticality within their study of organizational evolution. Specifically, they posit the organization as a network and then use random graph theory to develop propositions about how organizations evolve without depending on a teleological premise. Similarly, Accard (2018) used the sandpile computational model to explain how small changes to organizational norms and routines diffuse unpredictably, sometimes leading to no change and sometimes leading to transformational change. However, these other computational models have gotten less attention from organizational change researchers.

Dynamical Models of Organizational Change

Major Assumptions

As Heraclitus said, you can never put your foot into the same river twice. At a microscopic level, the exact position of every water molecule is constantly changing, and their exact aggregate structure is never identical at different points in time. The structure of the river though, as defined by its three-dimensional boundaries, demonstrates resilience over time. The same is true of the human body. While millions of cells in our body die and are replaced daily, we are still recognizable because our structure remains roughly the same (Maturana and Varela 1992).

Systems and their elements change constantly; it is this constant dance that makes the system alive. If nothing changed and everything was at equilibrium, the system would be dead, quite literally (Dooley 1997). Life entails constant interplay between elements of the system. These life-giving processes, or generative mechanisms, drive the routine behavior of the system—and identifying and understanding these generative mechanisms is often the key to understanding the system at its most basic level. For example, many financial processes of the firm are driven by a temporal process of entrainment that requires the sequence and timing of actions to synchronize with state and federal taxation requirements. Likewise, the inventory levels of a firm may be driven by seasonal variations in the quality and quantity of raw material. At a micro-level, variations in the output of a process may be random, at any given time being affected by innumerable physical and operational factors.

Dynamical models portray this constant change and are used in three ways. Some organizational researchers collect empirical data and then use statistical methods to see what type of dynamics are present (e.g., Cheng and Van de Ven 1996; Poole et al. 2000; Thietart 2016). These dynamics then suggest something about the nature of the causal system. This is an inductive approach. Some researchers use the qualitative characteristics of dynamical patterns, especially chaos, to theorize about the nature of organizational change (e.g., Nonaka 1988; Wheatley 1992; Kiel 1993; Olson and Eoyang 2001).

There are four types of patterns that can be empirically observed through statistical modeling of an observed organizational variable: periodicity, chaos, white noise, and colored noise. These four patterns are indicative of four different, basic generative mechanisms. These mechanisms are defined by two variables: their dimensionality, and the nature of interdependence. Dimensionality refers to the number of variables driving behavior. For example, periodic (i.e., seasonal) processes may be low dimensional as they are driven by a few factors related to the environment (weather), while sales processes may be high dimensional as they are driven by the decisions of many independent agents (customers). These variables may behave independently, where the aggregate effect is the sum of the individual effects, or there may be significant interactions between them, representing contingencies.

Low-dimensional causal systems yield periodic and chaotic dynamics, while high-dimensional causal systems yield white and pink noise dynamics. Periodic and white noise dynamics stem from systems where causal factors act independently, or in a linear fashion, while chaotic and pink noise systems stem from systems where causal factors act interdependently, in a nonlinear fashion (Dooley and Van de Ven 1999).

White noise is what is typically referred to as pure randomness, and it is generated via a high-dimensional process (Peitgen et al. 1992). The law of errors (Ruhla 1992) also implies that the "many variables" affecting behavior are doing so in an independent fashion. If the observed behavior corresponds to collective social action, this implies that individuals are acting in a parallel manner, perhaps uncoordinated with one another. White noise processes progress with no memory of past behavior, so the system does not determine the future from the past—they are disconnected.

Pink noise is much the same as white noise, except that it is a sort of constrained randomness, whereby interactions between the factors/individuals constrain the system away from pure white noise (Schroeder 1991). These interactions between factors may stem from the presence of feedback loops and/or constraints within the system. These constraints and/or feedback loops are local rather than global, as the presence of global feedback and/or constraint would tend to greatly reduce the dimensionality of the system, and thus not be indicative of a pink noise process. Pink noise is commonly referred to as an inverse power law, as the frequency of an event is inversely related to its size. Inverse power laws have been found to be rather ubiquitous, showing up in social, economic, biologic, physiologic, geologic, and astronomical phenomena.

Chaotic processes are low dimensional, and nonlinear interactions exist between the factors/variables responsible for driving behavior. Low dimensionality may stem from the scope of the behavior in question, or it may imply that other mechanisms are reducing the dimensionality of the causal system via global feedback and/or constraints, because naturally a social system containing many agents will be (by definition) high dimensional, unless something is actively constraining the potential freedom and variety of possible behaviors. These mechanisms can be thought of as representing either control of individuals, and/or cooperation between the individuals. Control and cooperation may be managerial (Simon 1957), adaptive (March 1994), institutional (Scott 1995), or self-induced (Dooley 1997).

Periodic behavior is also low dimensional, where causal variables interact either not at all, or in a simple linear fashion. While such a system could arise naturally, it is also possible that interactions are linear (or absent) because the system was designed to be so. For example, the temporal regularity of required organizational action will entrain many processes to be periodic.

In summary, white noise processes consist of many significant factors acting in an independent fashion, and these processes demonstrate a lack of path dependency (i.e., the future is not predictable from the past). Pink noise processes consist of many independent factors being constrained in some fashion by local feedback loops. Chaotic processes consist of a few significant factors acting in an interdependent fashion, at a global level. Such processes demonstrate path dependency and are representative of control and/or cooperation. Periodic processes consist of a few significant factors acting in an independent, or simple linear fashion. These processes are also indicative of significant levels of control and/or cooperation.

These four different types of dynamical systems are empirically observed through statistical modeling. Linear and periodic patterns can be detected through regression, Fourier analysis, or other econometric methods. The residuals remaining after extracting any linear or periodic patterns from the data are noise; further analysis of the distribution of those residuals can distinguish white noise from pink noise. Finally, chaotic dynamics can only be detected with relatively sophisticated metrics that examine the difference between short and long-term autocorrelations in the time series of observations. See Poole et al. (2000) or Guastello (2002) for more details on these methods.

Current State of Research

There are only a few studies of organizational change that have used dynamical models. Cheng and Van de Ven (1996) used event history methods to study the dynamics of two different product innovations within 3M. They found that the actions taken, and associated outcomes, were chaotic at the beginning of the projects, and periodic (i.e., more orderly) at the end of the projects. Conversely exogenous events were random (white noise) throughout the projects. Analysis of the same data in Poole et al. (2000) came to slightly different conclusions, due to methodological differences. Thietart (2016) used event history methods to study an organization's evolution over several decades and found evidence of periodic and pink noise dynamics. Empirical applications of dynamical and other complexity science-related models are more common in the physical sciences, economics (e.g., De Fabritiis et al. 2003; Andriani and McKelvey 2007), and psychology (e.g., Guastello 2007).

Example

In Cheng and Van de Ven (1996) and Poole et al. (2000), event history methods were used to create longitudinal data describing the evolution of two different innovation projects within the same organization. Events were described as actions, outcomes, or other exogenous events. Events were identified via a variety of research tools, including direct engagement and observation of the projects as they were occurring. The identified events were also confirmed via feedback from managers. If an event was coded as an action, it was further coded as either constraining (-1) or expanding (+1); if an event was coded as an outcome, it was further coded as either positive (+1) or negative (-1) relative to impact on project objectives. The number of constraining and expanding actions, and positive and negative outcomes, were tallied into monthly counts, and time series were formed. That time series was subsequently analyzed for the four types of dynamical patterns described above. Differences in analyzing the same data between Cheng and Van de Ven (1996) and Poole et al. (2000) were mainly due to differences in the sequence of statistical modeling steps. In the former, chaotic dynamics were tested for on the raw event count data, while in the latter chaotic dynamics were tested on the residuals following extraction of periodic patterns via an ARIMA model.

Principles of Change

While empirical assessment of dynamics of potentially chaotic systems is not commonplace, many organizational researchers have taken the qualitative attributes of chaos and used this to theorize about organizational change (Thietart and Forgues 1995). One of the most common metaphors used is "the butterfly effect," which states that small changes in the system can have large impacts (Dooley 2009). This is a theme that is resonant and constant across all different complexity science models, but the ability to visualize this "sensitivity to initial conditions" brought an undue amount of attention to chaos in particular, above and beyond other complexity science phenomena. Most attention was paid to strategic planning—if chaos is present in real life, then sensitivity to initial conditions precludes prediction of the future, ever, regardless of how much information is at hand and how accurate the modeling effort is. The viability of strategic planning processes was particularly challenged (Stacey 1992).

Many organizational researchers have misunderstood the importance of sensitivity to initial conditions. As mentioned previously, the patterns that arise in dynamical systems are referred to as attractors (Guastello 1995). An attractor is a steady-state phenomenon; it represents the recurrent patterns of behavior or states of the system as it progresses into the future. This pattern however is not immediately realized. A period of time exists as the system moves from its "initial state" to its attractor. The behavior during this period of time is referred to as a transient. The amazing thing about transients is that they tend to end up at the same place—the attractor—for a wide variety of initial states. An attractor's "basin of attraction" is the set of initial states that converge towards it.

A chaotic system is sensitive to arbitrarily small changes in its initial conditions, with respect to its exact path into the future. This is significant in that we have believed until recently that deterministic systems were insensitive to such small perturbations. But note that this sensitivity is only with respect to the exact state (or level) of the variable in question, its exact *path* into the future. Typically, basins of attraction tend to be large relative to their corresponding attractor; that is, a large number of initial conditions lead to the same general pattern of behavior, or attractor. Thus, the system's attractor, or pattern, is not sensitive to changes in initial condition. Chaotic systems are sensitive in specific path, but not general overall pattern. So organizational processes that are predictive in nature may not be highly sensitive to chaos if they are qualitative in nature (i.e., strategic planning) but may be if they are quantitative in nature (i.e., demand forecasting).

Strengths and Criticisms

The empirical modeling of dynamical systems provides organizational change researchers a purely inductive way to generate theoretical explanations from observed systems. As large amounts of empirical data become more readily available, the opportunity for empirical modeling increases. There are challenges though. The empirical models and corresponding statistical methods are not simple to implement, even with the help of software. Data requirements can get in the way of successful modeling—data may be too brief in length, it may be too "noisy" to anything but noise, and systems may not fulfill assumptions of the statistical methods such as mean and variance stationarity. It is necessary to employ multiple analyses to time series data to determine if the underlying pattern is random, chaotic, or periodic.

Far-from-equilibrium Models of Organizational Change

Major Assumptions

A special type of systemic change in a complex system can occur when the level of energy within that living system is increased beyond a critical level. Far-from-equilibrium (FFE) models of change portray the system as self-organizing in the manner in which it renews its structure (Prigogine and Stengers 1984; Goldstein 1994). This re-organization occurs in an emergent fashion as internal and external forces push the system to a state of FFE. At an FFE state, the system's current organization is pushed to its maximum capacity for processing and dissipating energy. When it is pushed beyond this boundary, the system recognizes that its current structure is not capable of handling the excess energy, and its components re-organize to a different configuration that is more capable of dissipating the energy in an efficient manner. The transition of water from solid to liquid to gas portrays these state changes. At an FFE state, small fluctuations may be responsible for pushing the system to another attractive point of behavior, at which point convergent forces once again dominate and bind the system to its new attractor (Prigogine and Stengers 1984). In essence, change via FFE is a special case of the change process discussed in the previous section, whereby changing the initial state condition or a parameter within the system induces qualitatively new behavior.

Goldstein (1998) states that FFE self-organization is a

> radical reorganization of the structure of a system; the spontaneous emergence of novel patterns and configurations; the amplification and incorporation of random events; the discovery of creative alternatives for functioning; and the arising of new coherence and coordination amongst the parts of the system.

The environment does not change the system, and the system does not unilaterally change the environment; rather, the environment triggers internal mechanisms that are the source for transformation (Maturana and Varela 1992).

Current State of Research

Some authors have used an FFE model as a conceptual framework. For example, Macintosh and Maclean (1999) use an FFE model to propose a three-stage process model of conditioning, creating far-from-equilibrium conditions, and managing positive and negative feedback for strategic change. Madden et al. (2012) use it to explain the emergence of organizational capacity for compassion. Chiles et al. (2010) merge an FFE model with the concept of Austrian economics (Kirzner 2016) to discuss entrepreneurial dynamics. The FFE model specifically describes the timing of when a new venture can best take advantage of existing market dynamics to enter. Other papers (Schindehutte and Morris 2009; Selden and Fletcher 2015) have argued that entrepreneurship research needs to draw more from FFE models and complexity science in order to address some of the paradoxes within its studies.

Some authors have used an FFE model to interpret case studies, sometimes in the form of event history studies. For example, Chiles et al. (2004) study the emergence of the entertainment cluster in Branson, Missouri, illustrating a process of fluctuation, positive feedback, stabilization, and recombination. Plowman et al. (2007) use an FFE model to examine an organizational change event, stating, "radical change was unintended, emergent, and slow; destabilizing conditions helped small changes to emerge and become radical; subsequent actions amplified an initial small change and, though not intended to do so, promoted radical change; finally, the dynamic interaction of amplifying actions, contextual conditions, and small changes led to continuous radical change" (p. 515). Beck and Plowman (2014) analyze the Columbia space shuttle disaster to link collaboration between government agencies and departments to the emergence of relational trust and collective identity. Girod and Whittington (2015) use an FFE model and longitudinal data on the evolution of an auto company to demonstrate how small perturbations can sometimes lead to significant re-organizing. Lichtenstein et al.'s (2007) study draw nascent entrepreneurs and used an FFE model to describe the different pathways of successful new organization founding.

Example

Lichtenstein (2000, 2014) uses a model of FFE change to study entrepreneurism. He challenges the standard convention that in social systems information is akin to energy, and instead equates energy directly with the level of actual organizational activity. His life cycle model consists of three stages. First, increased resources generate increased organizing. In this phase small increases in resources will be readily adapted to, but the organization will resist major transformation. As the gap between required and actual performance begins to strain because the original configuration of the system becomes sub-optimal for handling a qualitatively different level of resources (i.e., energy), tension develops, and the system is pushed to the threshold of change. It is at this FFE state that a small change or perturbation to the organization, for example, the departure or arrival of an individual, a comment made by someone, a performance measure that slightly slips, can induce significant changes in organizing. The third stage of change brings about the emergence of a new configuration, which is path dependent and yet novel, has increased capacity to process the new level of resources, and often possesses greater complexity (via interconnectedness between elements of the system) than the original configuration.

Principles of Change

FFE models state the condition for qualitative change, rather than the exact nature of how change occurs. In general, these models state that change occurs when the system is far-from-equilibrium. Organizational researchers in turn have hypothesized about how a social system can be brought or find itself at an FFE state.

For example, crises are well known to be a trigger for individual or organization change. Nonaka (1988) advocates purposeful creation of crises as a means to keep the organization flexible and constantly renewed. Total quality management and other actions that open the boundaries between a firm and its customers may also be seen as a means to enable far-from-equilibrium conditions to arise. Goldstein (1994) suggests several different means by which to facilitate a system towards FFE:

- Increase the connectivity of the system to its environment, as the increase in information (energy) may push the system off equilibrium, if the information from outside the system does not conform to the norm of what is expected.
- Help people uncover latent assumptions they have about how the system works, and what the goal of the system is. Often these unquestioned assumptions form an unconscious barrier to recognizing that a system is in fact in an FFE state.
- Identify the "self-fulfilling prophecies" within the system that act as an attractor, and break the connections that maintain the recurrent pattern of behavior.

Olson and Eoyang (2001) present a general model of FFE self-organization in social systems: in order for self-organization to occur, there needs to be a container (a boundary that defines what is inside and what is outside the system, and that constrains interaction), differences that distinguish agents or elements within the system, and transforming exchanges. For example, in a project team, the norms of the group emerge in a self-organized fashion because of (a) boundaries that define the team as a real entity within the organizational system, creating "us and them", (b) differences that exist between team members, such as functional specialty or personality, and (c) exchanges (i.e., discourse) that moves the cognitive states of the agents from one position to another. Olson and Eoyang posit that organizational change can be induced by changing containers, focusing on different differences, or changing the nature of exchange.

Strengths and Criticisms

FFE models have shown great potential for insight into organizational change, having been used by numerous scholars already. The detailed nature of the FFE model's causal mechanisms makes it richer in explanation than previous, similar models such as punctuated equilibrium. It is also a qualitative model, which enables it to be used across a wide variety of organizational change phenomena, at different scales. Its qualitative nature also means that a researcher does not need to have statistical or computer coding skills to apply it. Because it is a qualitative model, however, the comparison of it to a real situation involves qualitative interpretation.

Conceptualizing Change

A single system will be used now to demonstrate how change may be conceptualized from these four different modeling perspectives. Consider the project management of a software development effort. The work of the project is accomplished by a team of software engineers, who report to a project manager. The team exists within the engineering function of an organization. We shall assume that the project has started and we are viewing this team (our system) in terms of what pattern of behavior is observed over time, and how it might change. The particular issue at hand is how the team collectively solves problems that arise in the coding of the software.

A researcher using an agent-based model would build a simulation of the team, with software engineers as agents. These agents would have a goal (i.e., to minimize problems with the product while expending the least energy), and schema to interpret the environment and other agents, and to produce action. The schema may be "if-then" rules in the form of a genetic algorithm that tell the agents which solutions to try, and agents may be able to see a corresponding representation of the problem at hand. So, within the computer, these agents are attempting to "recognize" the problem, and then apply a solution that fits the problem. Individual agents could be constrained in how much of the problem they see, or how accurately they recognize the problem, and thus interconnections between agents could be used to assimilate communication and coordination. Agents would probably also be programmed to learn, over time, how to respond to problems more effectively by giving parts of their schema "credit" according to the quality of their attempted solutions. Some typical research questions that could be investigated by the model would include:

- What level of connectivity provides enough collaboration and collective learning and yet does not swamp the agents with communication tasks?
- How do agents learn to generalize so they can solve problems they have not seen before?
- Is it better to have many agents having the same deep skills (ability to recognize and solve one type of problem), have agents with different deep skills, or have agents with broad skills?

A researcher using a computational model might focus on the cascading of errors that occur when one problem is solved, but the change incurs other errors. A network model of the software code could be built, where each node represents a variable within the software and the connections between the nodes represent connections within the algorithms embedded in the software. For example, if the code were a spreadsheet, the nodes could represent cells in the spreadsheet with connections indicating cross-referencing between the cells. The researcher could then induce different magnitudes of change in different nodes and examine how those changes cascaded across the entire system.

A researcher might also examine the problem-solving of the team from the perspective of Kauffman's NK model. By examining the nature of the software and modeling it as a genomic configuration, the researcher estimates the number of genes and their average connectivity, and uses Kauffman's simulation results to examine how long it would take to solve all of the code's problems, whether the software should be fixed in incremental or holistic steps, and how often the team would stop at a solution that was suboptimal.

A researcher using dynamical models could collect empirical time series data from the actual team and analyze it using a variety of statistical methods, in order to determine whether periodic, chaotic, random, or pink noise patterns were present. Variables that might be observed could include number of errors found, and/or fixed, per day; amount of time between error corrections, number of emails between team members per day, or the number of lines of code written by the team per day. Such diagnosis might reveal periodic patterns of entrainment between the team and other "clocks and calendars" defining the organization and its environments, or indicative of self-organized routines, chaotic patterns demonstrating adherence to general patterns with novelty moment-to-moment, or random or pink noise patterns indicating the open nature of their system and the multitude of causes impacting the observed variables.

A researcher using a far-from-equilibrium model to study change in the team would look for significant, qualitative changes in the way the team was organizing, and then look for the increased tension and the trigger that brought about that transformation. They would also examine the norms and routines of the team to see how they constrain the team from moving to a different pattern of behavior.

On the other hand, the project manager of the team, desiring to bring about changes in the team's behavior, might envision their leverage points differently depending on what model they had in their minds. Viewing the system in a traditional, non-complexity manner, the manager would likely ascertain the group's behavior due to individual motivation and/or skill, and/or the resources and processes the team is working with, and suggest changes in process and/or structure, or seek to give team members incentives and disincentives to push to the desired behavior. If the manager viewed the team as an agent-based system, they would focus on the mental models of the software engineers, and the simple rules that led their interaction. If the manager viewed the team as a dynamical system, they might focus on the interconnectedness of the engineers, and components of the problem. If the manager viewed the team specifically as chaotic, they might look for small changes they could make which would have a large effect. Finally, if the manager viewed the team as self-organizing, they might seek ways to bring the team far-from-equilibrium in order to induce self-change.

What then do complexity science models have in common, in terms of how they conceptualize change? First, all models are dynamic—time is the most significant variable in all the different models. Second, they are empirical. Data is either observed from a real system, or a system is simulated, and data from a real system or from a simulated system—and sometimes both—are analyzed. Patterns in these data become the fodder for theorizing. Third, they generate behavioral patterns that are emergent, inherently not deducible from the component parts. Fourth, they are only practically useful with the aid of a computer, to either simulate the system and/or detect patterns from observed data. Fifth, either explicitly within their component behaviors or implicitly through the coupling of components, the models depict behavior that is nonlinear, where changes in causes are not necessarily proportional to the corresponding changes in effects. Finally, these models depict change as having both divergent and convergent components (Dooley and Van de Ven 2016).

Conclusion

This chapter has organized complexity science-inspired models of organizational change into four categories. Agent-based models are simulation models or conceptual frameworks where agents within a system pursue teleological ends, and patterns of structure and behavior emerge via agent interactions with each other and the environment. Computational models like the NK model are simulation-based models where parts of a system are described as co-evolving over time. Dynamical models are mathematical models that formulate how, and often why, variables that we observe in complex systems change over time and are demonstrated through empirical modeling. Far-from-equilibrium models are conceptual models that formulate how order is created in the system from within, especially due to adaptive pressures. Far-from-equilibrium models have been the most popular amongst organizational scientists.

Complexity science models describe both the "how" and "why" of organizational change. They show how local change can lead to global change, and how the propensity for the system to undergo significant change differs depending on its current state. These models explain the duality that consistent small change is necessary for quasi-stability, and that a system can be hyper-sensitive in the specific path it takes but may share commonalities with many other systems in terms of its underlying pattern of behavior.

Application of complexity science models is uncommon, relative to its broader adoption in other areas of physical and social sciences. This is surprising given its perceived applicability to studying organizational change, and its ability to create novel theory and insight. Conversely, with the exception of far-from-equilibrium models, application requires computer coding or empirical analysis skills that many organizational scientists don't have. Thus, we might expect that in the future, organizational change phenomena are more likely to be investigated via a complexity science lens in applications where researchers do have those skills, or where they couple with other researchers who do within interdisciplinary teams. For example, the emerging discipline of data science combines operations research, statistical modeling, and artificial intelligence methods to explain and manage complex systems. These applications yield "big data" that is voluminous and longitudinal in nature. Complexity science models of change may help data science researchers explain the changes they are observing in the systems they are monitoring and managing.

References

Accard, P. (2018), 'Criticality: How Changes Preserve Stability in Self-Organizing Systems', *Organization Studies*, https://doi.org/10.1177/0170840618783342/, accessed 23 August 2020).

Albino, V., Carbonara, N., and Giannoccaro, I. (2006), 'Innovation in Industrial Districts: An Agent-Based Simulation Model', *International Journal of Production Economics*, 104, 30–45.

Anderson, P. (1999), 'Complexity Theory and Organization Science', *Organization Science*, 10, 216–32.

Andriani, P., and McKelvey, B. (2007), 'Beyond Gaussian Averages: Redirecting International Business and Management Research toward Extreme Events and Power Laws', *Journal of International Business Studies*, 38/7, 1212–30.

Argyris, C., and D. Schon (1978), *Organizational Learning: A Theory of Action Perspective* (Reading, MA: Addison-Wesley).

Aros, S., and Gibbons, D. (2018), 'Exploring Communication Media Options in an Inter-Organizational Disaster Response Coordination Network Using Agent-Based Simulation', *European Journal of Operational Research*, 269, 451–65.

Arthur, W. B. (1994), 'On the Evolution of Complexity, in G. A. Cowen, D. Pines, and D. Meltzer, eds., *Complexity: Metaphors, Models, and Reality* (New York: Addison-Wesley), 65–81.

Axtell, R. (1999), 'The emergence of firms in a population of agents'. Santa Fe Institute, paper no. 99-03-019.

Bateson, G. (1972), *Steps to an Ecology of Mind: Collected Essays in Anthropology, Psychiatry, Evolution, and Epistemology* (Chicago, Illinois: University of Chicago Press).

Beck, T., and Plowman, D. (2014), 'Temporary, Emergent Interorganizational Collaboration in Unexpected Circumstances: A Study of the Columbia Space Shuttle Response Effort', *Organization Science*, 25/4, 1234–52.

Billinger, S., Stieglitz, N., and Schumacher, T. (2014), 'Search on Rugged Landscapes: An Experimental Study', *Organization Science*, 25/1, 93–108.

Brown, S., and Eisenhardt, K. (1998), *Competing on the Edge* (Harvard Business, Boston, MA).

Carley, K., and Morgan, G. (2016), 'Inadvertent Leaks: Exploration via Agent-Based Dynamic Network Simulation,' *Computational and Mathematical Organization Theory*, 22, 288–317, doi: 10.1007/s10588-016-9215-3/, accessed 23 September 2020.

Cheng, Y. T., and Van de Ven, A. (1996), 'Learning the Innovation Journey: Order out of Chaos?' *Organization Science* 7, 593–614.

Chiles, T., Meyer, A., and Hench, T. (2004), 'Organizational Emergence: The Origin and Transformation of Branson, Missouri's Musical Theaters', *Organization Science*, 15, 499–519.

Chiles, T., Tuggle, C., McMullen, J., Bierman, L., and Greening, D. (2010), 'Dynamic Creation: Extending the Radical Austrian Approach to Entrepreneurship', *Organization Studies*, 31/1, 7–46.

Colbert, B. (2004), 'The Complex Resource-Based View: Implications for Theory and Practice in Strategic Human Resource Management', *Academy of Management Review*, 29/3, 341–58.

De Fabritiis, G., Pammolli, F., and Riccaboni, M. (2003), 'On Size and Growth of Business Firms', *Physica A: Statistical Mechanics and its Applications*, 324/1–2, 38–44.

Deming, W. E. (1986), *Out of the Crisis* (Cambridge, MA: MIT-CAES).

Dooley, K. (1997), 'A Complex Adaptive Systems Model of Organization Change', *Nonlinear Dynamics, Psychology, & Life Science*, 1, 69–97.

Dooley, K. (2002), 'Organizational Complexity', in M. Warner, ed., *International Encyclopedia of Business and Management* (London: Thompson Learning), 5013–22.

Dooley, K. (2004), 'Complexity Science Models of Organizational Change', in S. Poole and A. Van De Ven, eds., *Handbook of Organizational Change and Innovation*, (Oxford; New York: Oxford University Press), 354–73.

Dooley, K. (2009), 'The Butterfly Effect of the Butterfly Effect', *Nonlinear Dynamics, Psychology, and the Life Sciences*, 13/3, 279–88.

Dooley, K., and Van de Ven, A. (1999), 'Explaining Complex Organizational Dynamics', *Organization Science*, 10, 358–72.

Dooley, K., and Van de Ven, A. (2016), 'Cycles of Divergence and Convergence Underlying Processes of Organization Change and Innovation', in A. Langley and H. Tsoukas, eds., *Sage Handbook of Process Organization Studies* (London: Sage Publications), 574–92.

Eoyang, G. (1997), *Coping with Chaos: Seven Simple Tools* (Cheyenne, WY: Lagamo Corporation).

Fioretti, G. (2012), 'Agent-Based Simulation Models in Organizational Science', *Organizational Research Methods*, 16/2, 227–42.

Forrester, J. (1961), *Industrial Dynamics* (Cambridge, MA: Productivity Press).

Gao, D., Squazzoni, F., and Deng, X. (2018), 'The Role of Cognitive Artifacts in Organizational Routine Dynamics: An Agent-Based Model', *Computational and Mathematical Organization Theory*, 24, 473–99.

Garud, R., Gehman, J., and Kumaraswamy, A. (2011), 'Complexity Arrangements for Sustained Innovation: Lessons from 3M Corporation', *Organization Studies*, 32/6, 737–67.

Gell-Mann, M. (1994), *The Quark and the Jaguar* (New York: Freeman & Co).

Girod, S., and Whittington, R. (2015), 'Change Escalation Processes and Complex Adaptive System: From Incremental Reconfigurations to Discontinuous Restructuring', *Organizational Science*, 26, 1520–35.

Gleick, J. (1987), *Chaos: The Making of a New Science* (London: Heinemann).

Goldstein, J. (1994), *The Unshackled Organization* (Portland: Productivity Press).

Goldstein, J (1998), 'Glossary', in B. Zimmerman, C. Lindberg, and P. Plsek, eds., *Edgeware* (Irving, TX: VHA), 270.

Guastello, S. (1995), *Chaos, Catastrophe, and Human Affairs* (Mahwah, NJ: Erlbaum).

Guastello, S. (2002), *Managing Emergent Phenomena* (Mahwah, NJ: Erlbaum).

Guastello, S. (2007), 'Non-Linear Dynamics and Leadership Emergence', *The Leadership Quarterly*, 18, 357–69.

Haken, H. (1984), *The Science of Structure: Synergetics* (New York: Van Nostrand Reinhold).

Holland, J. H. (1995), *Hidden Order* (Reading, MA: Addison-Wesley).

Jantsch, E. (1980), *The Self-Organizing Universe* (Oxford: Pergaman Press).
Kauffman, S. (1995), *At Home in the Universe* (Oxford: Oxford University Press).
Kiel, D. (1993), 'Nonlinear Dynamical Analysis: Assessing Systems Concepts in a Government Agency', *Public Administration Review*, 53/2, 143–53.
Kirzner, I. (2016), 'The New Palgrave Dictionary of Economics', Austrian school of economics, Springer Link, https://link.springer.com/referenceworkentry/10.1057 percen t2F978-1-349-95,121-5_301-1/, accessed 23 September 2010.
Krackhardt, D., and Carley, K. (1998), 'A PCANS model of structure in organizations', *Proceedings of the 1998 international symposium on command and control research and technology*, June, Monterrey, CA.
Levinthal, D., and Warglien, M. (1999), 'Landscape Design: Designing for Local Action in Complex Worlds', *Organization Science*, 10/3, 342–57.
Lewin, R. (1992), *Complexity: Life at the Edge of Chaos* (New York: MacMillan).
Lichtenstein, B. (2000), 'Self-organized Transitions: A Pattern amid the Chaos of Transformative Change', *Academy of Management Executive*, 14, 128–42.
Lichtenstein, B. (2014), *Generative Emergence: A New Discipline of Organizational, Entrepreneurial, and Social Innovation* (Oxford: Oxford University Press).
Lichtenstein, B., Carter, N., Dooley, K., and Gartner, W. (2007), 'Complexity Dynamics of Nascent Entrepreneurship', *Journal of Business Venturing*, 22/2, 236–61.
MacIntosh, R., and MacLean, D. (1999), 'Conditioned Emergence: A Dissipative Structures Approach to Transformation', *Strategic Management Journal*, 20/4, 297–316.
Madden, L., Duchon, D., Madden, T., and Plowman, D. (2012), 'Emergent Organizational Capacity for Compassion', *Academy of Management Review*, 37, 689–708.
March, J. (2004), *Primer on Decision Making* (NY: Simon & Schuster).
Maturana, H. and Varela, F. (1992), *The Tree of Knowledge* (Boston: Shambhala).
Meng, Q., Li, A., Liu, H., and Chen, J. (2017), 'Agent-Based Simulation of Competitive Performance for Supply Chains Based on Combined Contracts', *International Journal of Production Economics*, 193, 663–76.
Minsky, M. (1986), *Society of Mind* (NY: Simon & Schuster).
Morel, B., and Ramanujam, R. (1999), 'Through the Looking Glass of Complexity: The Dynamics of Organizations as Adaptive and Evolving Systems', *Organization Science*, 10/3, 278–93.
Nejad, M. (2016), 'On the Contributions and the Validation of an Agent-Based Simulation Model of Innovation Diffusion', *European Journal of Marketing*, 50/3, 647–57.
Nguyen, H., Chiong, R., Chica, M., Middleton, R., Thi, D., and Pham, K. (2019), 'Contract Farming in the Mekong Delta's Rice Supply Chain: Insights from an Agent-Based Modeling Study', *Journal of Artificial Societies and Social Simulation*, 22/3, doi: 10.18564/jasss.4008/, accessed 23 September 2020.
Nonaka, I. (1988, Spring), 'Creating Organizational Order out of Chaos: Self-Renewal in Japanese Firms', *California Management Review*, 57–73.
Olson, E., and Eoyang, G. (2001), *Facilitating Organizational Change: Lessons from Complexity Science* (New York: John Wiley and Sons).
Peitgen, H-O., Jurgens, H., and Saupe, D. (1992), *Chaos and Fractals: New Frontiers of Science* (New York: Springer-Verlag).
Plowman, D., Solansky, S., Beck, T., Baker, L., Kulkarni, M., and Travis, D. (2007), 'The Role of Leadership in Emergent, Self-Organization', *The Leadership Quarterly*, doi: 10.1016/j.leaqua.2007.04.004/, accessed 23 September 2020.

Poole, M. S., and Van de Ven, A. H. (1995), 'Explaining Development and Change in Organizations', *Academy of Management Review*, 20, 510–40.
Poole, M., Van de Ven, A., Dooley, K., and Holmes, M. (2000), *Organizational Change and Innovation Processes: Theory and Methods for Research* (New York: Oxford University Press).
Prigogine, I., and Stengers, I. (1984), *Order out of Chaos* (New York: Bantam Books).
Ruhla, C. (1992), *The Physics of Chance* (Oxford: Oxford University Press).
Schindehutte, M., and Morris, M. (2009), 'Advancing Strategic Entrepreneurship Research: The Role of Complexity Science in Shifting the Paradigm', *Entrepreneurship Theory and Practice*, 33, 241–76.
Schroeder, M. (1991), *Fractals, Chaos, Power Laws* (New York: Freeman).
Scott, W. R. (1995), *Institutions and Organizations* (Thousand Oaks, CA: Sage).
Selden, P., and Fletcher, D. (2015), 'The Entrepreneurial Journey as an Emergent Hierarchical System of Artifact-Creating Processes', *Journal of Business Venturing*, 30/4, 603–15.
Senge, P. (1990), *The Fifth Discipline* (New York: Doubleday).
Simon, H. (1957), *Administrative Behavior* (New York: MacMillan).
Stacey, R. (1992), *Managing the Unknowable* (San Francisco: Jossey-Bass.
Sterman, J. (2000), *Business Dynamics: Systems Thinking and Modeling for a Complex World* (New York: Irwin).
Taleb, N. (2007), *The Black Swan: The Impact of the Highly Improbable* (New York: Random House).
Thietart, R-A. (2016), 'Strategy Dynamics: Agency, Path Dependency, and Self-Organized Emergence', *Strategic Management Journal*, 37, 774–92.
Thietart, R-A., and Forgues. B. (1995), 'Chaos Theory and Organization.' *Organization Science*, 6, 19–31.
Turner, J., and Baker, R. (2019), 'Complexity Theory: An Overview with Potential Applications for the Social Sciences', *Systems*, 7/4, 23. doi: 10.3390/systems7010004/, accessed 23 September 2020.
Waldrop, M. M. (1992), *Complexity: The Emerging Science at the Edge of Chaos* (New York: Simon and Schuster).
Wersching, K. (2010), 'Schumpeterian Competition, Technological Regimes and Learning through Knowledge Spillover', *Journal of Economic Behavior and Organization*, 75, 482–93.
Wheatley, M. (1992), *Leadership and the New Science: Learning about Organization from an Orderly Universe* (Oakland, CA: Berrett-Koehler Publishers).
Wong, Y. H., and Chan, R. (1999), 'Relationship Marketing in China: Guanxi, Favouritism and Adaptation', *Journal of Business Ethics*, 22, 107–18.
Zimmerman, B., and Hurst, D. (1993), 'Breaking the Boundaries: The Fractal Organization', *Journal of Management Inquiry*, 2/4, 334–55.

CHAPTER 21

LANDSCAPE MODELS OF COMPLEX CHANGE

DANIEL ALBERT AND MARTIN GANCO

INTRODUCTION

THE field of organization science has a long tradition in studying firms as complex systems (Thompson 1967; Weick 1976; Miller 1981), which has informed a variety of theoretical perspectives that built on the notion of organizational elements interacting in non-trivial ways. One of such influential perspectives focuses on organizational change and evolution as a process of search (Cyert and March 1963; Fleming and Sorenson 2001; Katila and Ahuja 2002). In the context of the search literature, organizations are viewed as boundedly rational agents performing iterative trial-and-error experimentation leading to gradual improvements of their performance (March 1991). Often the analogy of a complex landscape (or task environment) has been used to visualize the environment in which boundedly rational organizations search for viable solutions. In the stream of work viewing organizations as engaged in search over a complex landscape, scholars rely on the NK model as the main analytical tool to model and theorize about organizations (Kauffman 1993; Levinthal 1997). The NK modeling literature has emerged as an important part of research in strategic management and organizational theory.[1]

In this chapter, we contribute to the conversation about organizational change by reviewing the recent advances in the NK modeling literature conceptualizing organizational change and innovation as a search over a complex landscape. We discuss both strengths and limitations of this perspective as well as the potential for future research directions. Our key argument is that the NK model in its traditional form may be slowly reaching its limits in terms of the theoretical insights that it can provide to the field.

[1] Several review articles have been published recently explaining the NK model and providing an overview of the literature (Baumann et al. 2019; Csazsar 2018).

However, substantial modifications and extensions of the NK model or new classes of landscape models may still provide fresh insights. Specifically, we consider the modeling efforts that endogenize the landscape construction as the next frontier in this literature. We also discuss recent studies that incorporate various extensions of the NK model and allow for agent-driven changes to the landscape (Gavetti et al. 2017; Rahmandad 2019; Li and Csaszar 2019). Modeling deliberate landscape transformations allows examining important organizational research questions, such as the role of regulation and deregulation (Haveman et al. 2001; Li and Csaszar 2019) and firms' attempts to shape their industries (Gavetti et al. 2017). We close the chapter with describing new opportunities that such extensions provide and make a call for more modeling efforts that will help to advance the theoretical work on organizational change.

Organizational Change Through the Lens of a Complex Adaptive System

The organizational literature has a long tradition of conceptualizing and studying organizations as complex systems of interdependent elements (such as activity choices) (Thompson 1967; Weick 1976; Miller 1981). It is useful to distinguish between conceptual approaches that are configurational and those that embody a complex adaptive system lens (Van de Ven et al. 2013). The configurational approach of organizations was developed from the contingency theory. It focuses on studying holistic archetypes of organizations, that is, distinct organizational patterns along various design dimensions, such as the level of hierarchy, routinization, specialization, and decentralization (Miller 1981). Such system configurations are argued to be internally consistent while promoting different behaviors regarding adaptation to dynamically evolving environments (Miles et al. 1978; Mintzberg 1979). This stream of work also focuses on the interplay between internal consistency of a particular configuration (i.e., do the parts fit together) and external consistency (i.e., does the current configuration appropriately address external demands) (Miller 1992; Siggelkow 2001).

Importantly, the configurational literature has introduced the notion of "coupling" among otherwise independent parts as an important aspect of understanding how organizations evolve and change. Most notably, Weick (1976) discusses how loose coupling among organizational parts can lead to more desirable adaptive behaviors, such as localized adaptation, and more accurate understanding of the effects of changes in the immediate external environment. The potential benefits of local, or decentralized adaptation, together with the need for proper re-integration are reminiscent of Lawrence and Lorsch's (1967) work, and have further informed a growing literature stream that has become interested in the role of interactions among organizational parts.

Interactions have been studied at least in two different, yet related ways. First, interactions between organizational parts have been studied through the lens of governing rules, a perspective familiar to scholars in the tradition of complex adaptive systems.[2] Holland (1975, 1995) has viewed interdependencies as generative rules that underlie structure and behavior of the system. Using the example of a flock of birds, a system made up of individual birds, each bird follows a set of simple local rules, such as to keep a minimum and maximum distance from the birds around it and to fly around obstacles (e.g., a tree). By following such a rule, each bird adapts solely to the behavior of the birds around it without the need to know what is happening to the birds two or three degrees apart from its own position. Action is thus in response to locally distributed knowledge.[3] If the flock approaches a tree, the birds in the front will follow their rule to fly around such obstacle, while the following birds will adapt respectively to further enforce the rule of minimum and maximum distance. As a result, the obstacle has been avoided by all birds, even those who may never know that there was an obstacle because they are far in the back of the flock. The order of such system (i.e., the integrity of the flock) has been maintained and is robust to perturbations caused by the environment (i.e., encounter with the tree) thanks to the interdependent local rules. Interestingly, in this view of interdependency, the source of interaction resides with the agent/building-block (a rule the agent follows), rather than a physical law of interaction (e.g., gravity).

The second related view is one that focuses on interdependencies as a source of value. In a foundational paper, Milgrom and Roberts (1990) examine the value-creating aspects of organizational interdependencies and highlight their importance in the context of modern organizations. In the context of the organizational literature, they discuss interdependencies as a source of added value. In particular, Milgrom and Roberts (1990) develop a theoretical framework that defines the conditions under which interdependencies lead to elements being complementary—that is, when the whole is creating more value than the sum of its parts. Importantly, they draw on the concept of supermodularity to illustrate complementarity among two activities, A and B. Complementarity exists if the marginal benefit of doing more of activity A increases when doing more of B, and vice versa (see Ennen and Richter (2010) for a review of the complementarity literature and Jacobides et al. (2018) for a discussion of broader concepts related to complementarity). An important insight from the complementarity perspective explains why organizational change is difficult and often fails. When one activity reinforces the value of another activity, isolated changes may quickly render the value of the whole worse off than before. This implies that coordinated changes that consider interdependencies and reach internal consistency are critical for performance-enhancing organizational change (Whittington et al., 1999).

The complex systems view of organizations conceptualizes organizations as a set of interdependent activity choices (Levinthal 1997; Rivkin 2000).[4] It builds on and extends

[2] See also Chapter 20 of this volume by Kevin Dooley.

[3] Interestingly, this is like the notion of decentralized and distributed local knowledge in Austrian economics (Hayek 1945).

[4] Kevin Dooley in Chapter 20 of this volume discusses complex adaptive systems more broadly. The concept of interdependence is central to both NK models and many other complex adaptive systems models.

the value creation perspective of interdependencies (and remains rather silent on the role of interaction rules). The critical distinction between the complex systems view and the value creation/complementarity view is that interdependencies in the complex systems view can either create complementarity and value creation, or substitution and value destruction. In other words, the substitutional effects between activities implies that the marginal benefit of one activity decreases in the presence of an increase in another activity.[5] The canonical NK model in its general form has a landscape that is based on a random combination of value-creating and value-destroying interdependencies. Thus, the NK model has no pre-determined assumptions of what these interactions must look like and cannot be controlled in this sense (Porter and Siggelkow 2008). The extension of interdependencies beyond the notion of complementarities has important implications because it allows studying competition, collaboration, and coordination of organizations or units within organizations jointly.

The network of interdependencies between activities gives rise to a complex problem that is defined as NP-hard in the optimization theory (Rivkin 2000). The visualization of the complex problem is the rugged landscape. The more complex the problem, the more peaks and valleys the landscape has. Different configurations of activities correspond to different positions on this landscape while each position on this landscape has an assigned performance value, which is a function of the interplay between activity configurations and is represented by the height of the landscape. Central to the study of complex systems in the organizational literature is the question of how to navigate to higher performing solutions, that is, how to configure the system in the presence of interdependencies between the choices. Highly relevant here is the notion of bounded rationality and local information. If the searching organization had perfect foresight and full information about the landscape, the search process would be irrelevant as the organization can find the best configuration (i.e., the highest peak) immediately. Instead, organizations are argued to be limited in their knowledge of alternative solutions and temporal consequences of such (Simon 1947). Typical questions that existing studies have examined are focused on how to configure the search in the face of bounded rationality in terms of organizational units (Rivkin and Siggelkow 2003; Siggelkow and Levinthal 2003), the role of differences in managerial cognition of reality (Gavetti and Levinthal 2000), or how various forms of coordination across and within organizations affect outcomes (Aggarwal et al. 2011). Since the focus of complex systems organizational literature is inherently on the process of search, the organizations are conceptualized as dynamic and changing as they search the landscape. Further, the notion of organizational search has been explicitly linked to innovation, either in terms of organizations that are configured to produce innovative products and technologies (Ethiraj et al. 2008; Lenox et al. 2010), or organizations that innovate their organizational configurations and strategies (Rivkin 2000). Organizational change and innovation are thus at the core of the complex systems perspective of organizations.

[5] This type of "negative" complementarity is reminiscent of Porter's (1996) third-order fit, that is, optimization of efforts, and has been formally studied by Siggelkow (2002).

The theoretical development of the organizational complex systems literature has heavily relied on simulation modeling. The ability to use either verbal theorizing or formal modeling comes with limitations when developing theory about complex organizational phenomena. Verbal theorizing-based logic is limited to a small number of interacting variables to maintain clarity and internal consistency. However, several influential studies in the context of this literature have been produced using verbal theory. For instance, Gavetti and Rivkin (2007) focus on developing an understanding of strategy as emerging from the tension between boundedly rational search over a complex landscape and structures that facilitate such search but diminish the ability to change strategic decisions over time. Fleming and Sorenson (2001) rely on insights of the NK model to develop a set of propositions connecting technological complexity in the innovation process with performance. Similarly, formal analytical models providing closed-form solutions played a relatively limited role when developing this literature. While formal models provide a high level of internal consistency, when the focus of the theory is to understand patterns emerging from the interaction of more than few choices, the analytical closed-form models become intractable. Consequently, the work using formals models have focused on analyzing a small number or a single interdependence (Milgrom and Roberts 1990).

NK Models of Organizational Change and Innovation

The NK simulation model has emerged as a canonical approach to studying organizational change through a complex systems' lens. In fact, the NK framework is all about adaptation and evolution from the get go. It was developed by Stuart Kauffman (1993), an evolutionary biologist, to study how adaptation of genes affects organism's fitness and how organisms have evolved toward order because of epistatic interactions. The notion of fitness landscapes in evolutionary biology is fundamental and dates to the early twentieth century (Wright, 1931). The fitness landscape is analogous to a "performance function" that connects the genetic make-up of a species to its fitness with the external environment. The species are assumed to evolve over the landscape and climb its peaks through the processes of intergenerational mutation and recombination. Different positions on the fitness landscape represent different genetic configurations. The notion of a fitness landscape also introduces the concept of (local) peaks. A local peak is a stable configuration of genes that would decline in fitness if any single gene were to be changed. That is, local peaks represent various phenotypes. To "traverse" valleys toward a different phenotype (local peak), changes in multiple genes need to occur. The height of peaks is metaphorically used to describe the level of fitness (the higher the better the phenotype withstands selection forces). When selection forces are strong and change incremental in nature, the organisms may never find a path to deviate from the local peak, and the species will get "stuck" at the local peak. Also, higher fitness implies a greater likelihood of survival and small local peaks or valleys may imply a greater chance of being selected out. The models of fitness landscapes such as the NK model do not necessitate modeling selection, but selection may be built into such models (Levinthal 1997; Levinthal and Posen 2007). Consequently, the fitness of a position on the landscape can be explicitly linked to competitive dynamics.

Relying on the conceptualization of fitness landscapes, Kauffman (1993, 1995) developed a stochastic simulation model to study the relationship between several drivers that underscore fitness of species. These include the epistatic interactions between genes (the parameter *K*), the scope of the genetic make-up (i.e., the number of genes described in the parameter *N*), the performance of genetic operators such as mutation and recombination, and their effect on fitness. The notion of epistatic interactions in evolutionary biology is analogous to interdependencies and complementary or substitution effects. If two genes have an epistatic interaction, the relative fitness of one gene will be influenced by the other gene's state (whether it is switched on or off).

Because in evolutionary biology, the adaptation is unguided (i.e., mutation happens randomly) and becomes only visible through intergenerational selection forces, Kauffman was primarily interested in the landscape characteristics (i.e., the nature of the external environment) based on *N* and the underlying complexity among genes (*K*). He showed that, for a given set of genes, the number of stable phenotypes (that differed in more than one gene) (defined as local peaks), increases. This finding was termed the "ruggedness" of a landscape, implying many local peaks. Interestingly, he also showed that the average performance of local peaks decreases with increasing *K* (complexity). In other words, for a genetic organism, there are a plethora of viable make-ups (i.e., heterogeneity is large) that all are relatively similar in terms of their environmental fitness (i.e., fitness is relatively homogenous). In the context of evolutionary biology, this is related to the concept of neutral mutation and pre-adaptation (Kauffman 2007). Neutral mutations are changes in the genotype that have no or low impact on fitness. However, these changes may still be critical because they allow subsequent fitness-enhancing changes that would have not been possible from the original location.[6] In contrast, when there are no interactions between genes, there will be only one peak (i.e., the global and the local peak are the same), because genes' contribution to the overall fitness are additive (i.e., there is an optimal gene configuration for each gene independent of the state of all other genes) and non-epistatic, that is, independent from one another. Consequently, selection forces will drive all adapting organisms toward the global peak over time.

Kauffman's model has been introduced to the field of management by Levinthal (1997). Instead of genes, management scholars consider choices, which like genes, can

[6] Interestingly, these ideas have found only limited applications in the context of the organizational change literature. A notable exception is the study by Jain and Kogut (2014). Jain and Kogut (2014) developed an NK model to theorize how organizational memory and landscape neutrality are complements in improving the organizational adaptation and fitness.

be configured in multiple ways. The choices can represent many organizational decisions including decisions about technologies, products, employees, or strategies (Rivkin 2000). For example, a choice faced by a company may be to choose between two suppliers A and B. As in the original evolutionary biology context, choosing supplier A may contribute to the firm's performance differently than selecting B. If interdependencies are present, for example, this choice's value to the firm depends on other choices made previously, such as having adopted one product design over another one with which supplier A is more compatible than B. This logic is analogous in a more complex decision space, made up of a series of choices that together determine the value or usefulness of the solution mapped onto the "performance landscape."

An important reinterpretation of the Kauffman model for management purposes is that the agents adapt intra-generationally, that is a firm can explore different landscape positions and make value comparisons before it decides to make a move. Importantly, the search for alternative configurations is typically intelligent, that is, not random. Consequently, an agent is assumed to be capable of comparing the adapted performance to the original one before (also labeled "offline" search) or after the change has been implemented (i.e., "online" search). In the tradition of the behavioral theory literature, the search for alternative configurations of choices has typically been modeled as boundedly rational, that is, agents search incrementally within their local neighborhood (only few changes are considered at a time), and are therefore prone to getting stuck on local peaks. The focus of the research is then to model and theorize about various mechanisms and drivers that make firms less likely to get stuck at local optima and achieve higher positions on the landscape.

Since its introduction to the management field (Levinthal 1997), the NK model has motivated over seventy published studies in the broader field of management research (see Baumann et al. 2019, for a detailed review and list of these studies). See Csazsar (2018) and Ganco and Hoetker (2009) for a more technical discussion of the NK model in the context of management literature. Table 21.1 summarizes key terminology used in association with the NK framework. The fitness (or performance) landscape can be understood as a unique mapping of all possible configurations (all combinatorial alternatives of the N choices) to a performance value. Each choice is assigned $2^{(k+1)}$ unique values. This means that there are as many distinct values as the number of distinct combinations this configuration can take, given the design of k other choices that influence it. Each choice is then assigned a value called "performance contribution." Performance of a landscape position is the average of the N performance contributions of the individual choices. For example, let us assume that two choices (a_1 and a_2) are to be made (i.e., $N = 2$) and each choice can take the form of two distinct states 0 or 1. Further, we assume that a_1 influences the value of a_2 and vice versa. This implies four distinct positions on the landscape 00, 10, 01, and 11. In the next step, unique values from a uniform distribution between zero and one are drawn. For example, for $a1 = 02 = 0$, the random draw may have a performance contribution value for a_1 of 0.6 and for a_2 0.4. Consequently, the performance of the landscape position (00) is (0.6+0.4)/2 = 0.5. Note that while the values in the NK model are typically drawn from a uniform distribution,

Table 21.1 Basic Terminology in the NK Model

NK terminology	Explanation
Complex System	A system of interdependent elements
N	The number of elements considered. Each element may be configured in multiple ways but has mostly been applied in a simple binary form (e.g., 0 or 1, A or B, yes or no, etc.). Where elements have been described as company choices, policies, activities, resources, product components, and individuals.
K	The average number of elements that influence any given element within the system. This influence has been described as epistatic interdependence.
Composition	The distinct configuration of all N elements
Fitness/Performance landscape	The correspondent performance of all possible compositions
Local Peak	A composition on a given landscape, where all neighboring compositions' performance are lower than the focal compositions performance. Neighboring positions are typically defined as any composition that is different to the focal composition in exactly one element configuration.
Global Peak	The highest performing composition in a given landscape
Smooth vs. Rugged	This relates directly to the landscape's relative number of local peaks and is a result of its complexity (K). The greater the complexity, the more local peaks exist—termed rugged because of the analogy of a landscape with many hills and valleys. The opposite is true for low complexity landscapes, which have one global peak.

the qualitative properties of the model are invariant to the distributional assumptions. In fact, because the random draws for each choice are identical and independently distributed (i.e., "iid"), the landscape based on normally distributed choice values is numerically approaching the landscape with uniformly distributed choices as *N* increases due to the Central Limit Theorem. In other words, because of averaging of *N* choices' values, the landscape asymptotically approaches a normal distribution constrained between 0 and 1 with a mean of 0.5. The iid assumption about the contribution values has important benefits when using simulations. The assumption is conservative in nature because no skewness is being superimposed on the distribution of the performance landscape.

Using the NK Model to Study Organizational Change

Advantages of Using the NK Model to Study Organizational Change and Key Insights

The NK model has developed into one of the most prominent simulation techniques in the management literature to study change- and process-related research questions, particularly as they pertain to conceptualizing organizations as systems of interdependent choices. There are several reasons underscoring the relative appeal of the NK model in the study of these research questions. In the following we discuss two important areas in more detail: the model integrity, that is, framework-specific assumptions that render the NK model reliable and transparent, and the model applicability, that is, its relatively flexible nature of robust boundary conditions that allow for a broad application.

Model Integrity

The NK model is parsimonious and transparent in its assumptions and therefore tractable. While simulation models offer more flexibility and degrees of freedom than closed-form analytical models, the simulation models often become too complicated. When the model is too complicated, it becomes more difficult to discern the underlying mechanisms that are driving the results and the model becomes a "black box." The models are useful when they allow carefully pinning down theoretical mechanisms, and thus utilizing a complicated model with many moving parts defeats the purpose of using a model to develop new theory (Knudsen, Levinthal and Puranam 2019).

In their structure and assumptions, the NK models are relatively simple while still generating rich dynamics. As described above, a small set of parameters and assumptions defines the model. A relatively small number of "levers" allows for a deeper understanding of the model's dynamics and properties. Further, this allows easy replication of the model and relatively fast adoption of the model by other scholars. Over the last decade, scholars in the field have developed a firm grasp of the model. Researchers have a coherent understanding of the landscape properties and how they depend on the distinct choice states, the number of choices, and the degree to which choices influence one another. In other words, the modelers in the field have a strong shared understanding of the canonical NK framework which facilitates conversation about the model and helps publication of extensions and advancements related to it. Consequently, study results can be compared against the baseline NK model. Since the dynamics and properties of the baseline model are well understood, it is easier to show how and why various extensions change the baseline dynamics and it is easier to communicate new insights. This, in turn, facilitates progression of cumulative knowledge across the entire body of work. It is noteworthy that even mathematical analyses have been published that complement the simulation work. For instance, scholars have developed methods to analytically calculate landscape properties such as the expected number of local peaks (cf., Kaul and Jacobson 2006; Buzas and Dinitz 2013).

Another important aspect of model integrity is that the NK model is fully replicable. The replicability is facilitated by the small number of parameters and the transparent structure of the model, but it goes beyond that. As with many simulation models, scholars are not interested in specific realizations of the model but its average properties. Even though the landscapes and their characteristics are generated stochastically, the average characteristics and relationships between the landscape parameters (e.g., height of the global peak, number of local peaks) and the resulting agent behavior (e.g., performance accomplished, given a particular search rule) averaged over many landscapes are not random. This allows comparisons and replication across NK models to be generated using different software platforms and programming languages. In fact, the very nature of the NK model analysis is one of replication. A modeler specifies the simulation parameters and then runs the simulation multiple hundreds or thousands of times and then analyses statistical differences between the mean results based on the focal model as compared to mean results of a control model. Such an approach allows for identification of statistically significant differences and the detection of underlying causal mechanisms.

Model Applicability

Despite its parsimony, the NK model has non-trivial dynamics. The common issue with simulation modeling is that modelers unintentionally structure the model in a way that modeling predictions are immediately discernible from the modeling assumptions. In those cases, the model dynamics are trivial and not "emergent", and the model is unable to provide novel theoretical insights. This is the opposite extreme from the model being impenetrable, that is, "a black box." The insightful models thus strike the right balance by providing enough richness to be insightful but enough simplicity to be understandable. The NK model sits in this "Goldilocks" zone. It allows for rich emergent dynamics even with a small set of initial parameters. For example, merely manipulating the complexity parameter of *K* substantially alters the resulting performance landscape from a smooth, single peak landscape (*K* is zero) to a completely rugged, multipeak landscape. Further, changing *K* gives rise to qualitatively different patterns of performance that agents can achieve on the landscape. While in low complexity landscapes, it may be easy to find a global optimum, this may be very unlikely in complex landscapes using the same search strategy. In complex landscapes, agents are often stuck as sub-optimal local peaks. This property of NK landscapes is sometimes referred to as the "complexity catastrophe" because dislodging from a mediocre peak proves non-trivial (Kauffman 1993; McKelvey 1999).

A strength of the NK framework for studying organizational change are the degrees of freedom a modeler has available in specifying the external environment. By tweaking N and K, studies have tested how differences in the organization's external environment influence the efficacy of search strategies (Levinthal 1997). For example, Rivkin and

Siggelkow (2007) compared the topology and performance contribution as well as performance outcomes of various search strategies given a series of interdependence arrangements (such as hierarchical, centralized, and decomposable complexity patterns). While these studies compare distinct environmental characteristics, the NK framework has also been useful when modeling environmental change. Because of its parsimonious and tractable nature, one can model targeted changes in specific choices (by redrawing the contribution values of a decision) which can represent unpredictable changes (values are completely redrawn) (Levinthal 1997) or correlated changes (i.e., the changed environment is similar to the previous landscape) (Siggelkow and Rivkin 2009). Changes to the environment could also be the result of technological innovations in how components interact, that is, an architectural innovation (Albert and Siggelkow Forthcoming). Importantly, studies can introduce change to a particular aspect of the environment (e.g., new contribution values) while conserving other aspects of the environment (e.g., the order in which decisions influence one another) Consequently, the NK framework allows for a distinct and integrated study of organizational change as a means to find a better solution (usually within a stable environment) and organizational change as a means to adapt to a changing environment. Following this line of thought, it becomes clear why the NK model has become popular among scholars in the configurational, contingency tradition. The model allows one to observe the internal consistency (fit) together with external consistency. Internal fit is reflected in whether a configuration is a local peak (local optimum of configurations). External fit is reflected in the achieved performance in the landscape—that is, which peak the firm is occupying.

Model Relevance/Interpretability

The NK model and its findings have empirical relevance and provide testable results. While not trivial, the predictions of the model can be (and have been) tested using empirical datasets. While Fleming and Sorenson (2001), studying patent complexity in inventions, find only partial support for the NK model predictions, later studies found generally greater applicability and support (Lenox et al. 2010; Billinger et al. 2013; Ganco 2017). Even though the NK model is relatively abstract, it may be close enough to empirical phenomena that allows its examination. However, as we describe below when we discuss the NK model's limitations, the empirical relevance and the boundary conditions of the NK model for organizational phenomena is still relatively unknown and provide significant opportunities for future work. It is unclear whether some of the fundamental properties of the NK model are valid representations of real-life systems.

Relevance to the Field of Organization Science and Organizational Change

The NK model and its insights have been informative for central questions relevant for organizational scholars. The NK framework has been largely, albeit not exclusively, used to model the organizational search process inspired by the *behavioral theory of the firm* (March and Simon 1958; Cyert and March 1963). Organizational search can be conceptualized as problem-solving or adaptation due to changing environments

(March 1991). Such conceptualizations are naturally close to the imagery of the NK model, in which agents search for better solutions while facing a complicated problem embodied in the rugged landscape. Within the context of the behavioral theory of the firm, the NK modeling efforts have been focused on the tension between local and distant search which is analogous to the trade-off between exploitation and exploration (March 1991; Holland 1975). This tension highlights that organizations may "exploit" the comfort of a solution they have previously discovered, but at the expense of potentially forgoing a more suitable but distant solution. Similarly, an organization always chasing better novel solutions may end up never "cashing in" on the benefits of a specific opportunity. This conceptual tension spans multiple literature streams including core capability inertia (Leonard-Barton 1992) and path-dependency theories (Levinthal and March 1993). The tension is fundamentally grounded in the behavioral literature's key claim of decision-makers being boundedly rational (Simon 1987). While there are other prominent models, such as the bandit-model (Brand et al. 1956; Lave and March 1975; Puranam et al. 2015) that have helped to enhance our understanding of the exploitation and exploration trade-offs, the NK model introduced a novel perspective. The interdependence of choices is a central problem in organizational decision-making and the bandit-models in their canonical form assume independence of decisions (cf., Puranam et al. 2015 for an in-depth discussion of bounded rationality models). The NK model has thus significantly enhanced the ability to model managerial decision problems of high complexity, where decisions interact in non-trivial ways. In fact, the fitness landscape analogy has been illuminating in understanding why organizations may become inert and "stuck." This is because of their position on a local peak, which renders an incremental adjustment as not improving performance. Large coordinated changes may be necessary to "traverse a valley" and improve organizational performance. However, it may not be possible to discern how to implement such coordinated change. That is, inertia is not necessarily a sign of bad decision-making. Managers may end up on a local peak while acting quasi-optimally within the constraints of their bounded rationality. At the same time, the model and its results provide an understanding of why large-scale change will often require temporary decline in performance before climbing up a new local peak.

The NK modeling efforts have yielded many other valuable insights relevant for the organizational change literature. For instance, as the density of interdependencies increase, the landscape becomes more rugged with more local peaks and greater extremes in peak height. Consequently, as interdependencies increase, it may be more difficult to move away from a local peak and find a better solution. Coordinated exploration becomes more important in efforts to escape local peaks. At the same time, the average peak height is decreasing with interdependence which lowers returns from exploration and searching more broadly. This tension is explored in studies that highlight the role of managerial cognition in guiding search processes to make coordinated changes (Gavetti and Levinthal 2000; Sorenson et al. 2006). It is also useful to note that the NK model when focusing on the role of cognitive representations may be interpreted as formalizing the insights by Weick (1976). Weick sees strategy as a coordinating mechanism that allows an organization to achieve its objectives and find a profitable "solution" even when the immediate feedback from the environment is confusing or negative. Strategy can be thus recast as allowing the organization to traverse valleys in the NK landscape to achieve higher peaks. Another important insight is related to the distribution of extremely high peaks or a global peak on the landscape. As complexity increases, the height of the extreme peaks increases. Thus, even though each choice contribution is distributed uniformly (in the basic specification) and the landscape values are normally distributed, the skewness of the peak distribution and the thickness of the right tail of the peak height is increasing with interdependence. This insight is intuitively appealing because it suggests that, as complexity increases, there are significant rewards for "solving the problem" and such discoveries are rare and difficult. Consequently, the model and its imagery have been appealing as approximations of innvation processes (Fleming and Sorenson 2001; Sorenson et al. 2006).

The NK model and its dynamics also provide insights for organizational isomorphism, equifinality, and path dependence. A fundamental property of the NK landscapes is a positive correlation between the size of the basins of attraction and the peak height. Each peak is associated with a basin, which means that every agent that finds itself in the basin will gravitate toward the peak that gave rise to the focal basin of attraction. For a moment, let's imagine that the NK landscape is three-dimensional and defined over continuous dimensions, so it resembles an actual mountain range like the Himalayas (technically, the NK landscape is in an N-dimensional space defined over binary (0/1) dimensions). Then, it is useful to turn the landscape "upside-down" and think about the basins as "wells." Now, the deeper the well, the larger the area from which the objects will fall into the well. This property of the NK landscape implies isomorphism toward highly performing organizational forms. Even if organizations initiate their search with a variety of organizational configurations they will evolve toward a small number of dominant and high-performing organizations that have large basins of attraction (Levinthal, 1997). In the same vein, this provides a framework for our understanding of equifinality and path dependence. When the complexity is low, organizations will more likely end up on the same (global) peak independent of their initial starting configurations. In contrast, when the complexity is high and the performance landscape is rugged, firms will occupy local peaks close to their initial configurations. When the initial configurations (e.g., at founding) are heterogeneous, the organizational evolution will be path-dependent due to the ruggedness of the landscape, and the landscape may host a variety of distinct forms. If we impose a simple rule for selection such as the peak height will correspond to the likelihood of survival or that an agent is more likely to exit if it occupies a peak with other agents, we will obtain a result that more rugged landscapes will sustain more organizations that have different organizational configurations (Levinthal 1997).

The model also highlights limitations of simple search strategies. When the interdependencies are sparse, simple rules and local search perform very well. However, when the interdependencies are dense, local search is only suitable to fine-tune the position and find the local peak, but it is not powerful enough to escape the peak. In such settings, the "long jumps" (i.e., contemporaneous changes in multiple choices) become more important for performance. In the context of evolutionary biology, long jumps are accomplished by the genetic crossover operator. In the context of organizations, the long jumps could be conscious and planned such as when driven by managerial insights and cognition (Gavetti 2012), or by chance when the organization experiences a shock that forces it to change multiple choices at the same time. Similarly, the landscape may be reshaped, changing the local environment around the position that the organization occupies. Thus, in the context of the model, jumps, shocks, or environmental changes may be beneficial because they dislodge the firm from its suboptimal local peak and trigger new search. This provides some rationale for why success may follow from mistakes or shocks to the organization or its environment.

Another area where the NK modeling efforts yielded important insights is in the area of organizational design. The NK framework allows for structuring search by allocating decision-making responsibilities over certain choices to organizational subunits which can be thought of as reflecting organizational structure. This has typically been done by allowing for multiple agents searching independently, who make decisions for respective choice subsets. Using this approach, scholars have extended the NK models to shed light on the role of organizational structure in the change process. The processes that allow for dislodging from local peaks are highly relevant for these findings. For example, Siggelkow and Levinthal (2003) find that organizational forms that vacillate (temporarily) between decentralized and centralized forms are less likely to get stuck on a local peak early and find higher-performing solutions over time compared to permanently decentralized or centralized forms. Similarly, Ethiraj and Levinthal (2004b) find that reconfiguration of the organizational structure into new and recombined departments (via splitting and merging) leads to better long-term outcomes, especially when coupled with local search. More broadly, these findings suggest that structural reorganization improves organizational performance because departments locally optimize their performance, while temporally disregarded interdependencies between departments will dislodge the firm from the (mediocre) local peak. That is, such search is in the short run detrimental to the firm but triggers a new search that can help the firm to deviate from the local basin of attraction and gravitate toward more favorable peaks. However, some coordination is needed eventually, which can be accomplished via guided reorganization to improve department interdependency allocation or some form of centralization (Rivkin and Siggelkow 2003). It is useful to note that the results driven by the mechanism of "dislodging" from a local peak rely on the property of the NK model about the relationship between the peak height and its basin of attraction, for instance, if the organizational search is relatively weak (i.e., as it is in the case with any local search that only considers the immediate neighborhood of the current location). However, the mechanism holds even if the search is more powerful and encompasses a larger neighborhood, it will get stuck at the first local peak it encounters. Since higher peaks have larger basins of attraction, it is more difficult to dislodge sustainably from an already high peak. This makes it less likely that the agent will be dislodged from a high peak and will end up in a basin of a lower peak.

In a related stream of NK research, scholars have added new and qualifying insights to established problems of organizational design. For example, Rivkin and Siggelkow (2003) in their extension of the NK model show that top-level evaluation of change initiatives originating from lower levels of the organization may, in fact, lock-in the organization early, leading to mediocre performance and a local peak. This premature lock-in can be alleviated by introducing firm-wide incentives among lower-level decision-makers and incomplete task decomposition. Levinthal and Workiewicz (2018) explore the conditions under which a multiauthority (e.g., matrix) organization may outperform single authority structures. Their NK model suggests that multiauthority structures find better solutions when specialization is of importance while single authority structures fare better when subunits are interdependent and require integration efforts.

Underlying the research of organizational design and change in the NK framework is often the literature stream of near decomposability in complex systems. Often referred to as "modularity", near decomposability describes systems that can be organized into clusters (or modules) of elements that share many interdependencies within but only few across clusters. The clusters are weakly interdependent but sometimes hierarchical, that is, the modeler specifies an ordering of how clusters make decisions. Simon (1962) in his seminal work on the architecture of complexity illustrates these key attributes of complex systems (hierarchy and near decomposability) in biology and social systems, and in organizations. Because many task problems may exhibit a hierarchical and decomposable influence pattern among elements, researchers have devoted significant attention to understanding search and adaptation in such environments. For instance, research has explored the optimal degree of organizational modularity given a decomposable task environment (Brusoni 2005; Ethiraj et al. 2008), as well as how varying attributes of hierarchy affect performance in decomposable task environments (Ethiraj and Levinthal 2004a, 2004b). In addition, researchers have explored a variety of different interdependence patterns and how they influence organizational change efforts. Rivkin and Siggelkow (2007) investigated how the underlying design structure matrix (i.e., the interdependence pattern) of the task environment may favor or hinder exploration efforts. More recently, scholars have started exploring interdependence structures in the context of business ecosystems, that is, systems that go beyond firms or industries. For instance, Ganco, Kapoor, and Lee (2020) extend the NK model to include a "flow" architecture capturing how products are recombined in the context of ecosystems, and how different industries are connected. They show that ecosystem configurations give rise to differences in how firms perform combinatorial search depending on their position in the ecosystem.

Limitations of Using the NK Model to Study Organizational Change

While the NK model and its extensions have made significant contributions to our understanding of how organizations evolve and change, as is the case with any parsimonious approximation of real-life phenomena, the model imposes limitations. Further, there is a debate in the literature that the NK model must either be replaced or needs to evolve to be continually useful (Felin et al. 2014; Gavetti et al. 2017; Rahmandad 2019). We will first discuss the limitations and then a few recent advances that show promising future directions. The limitations of the model stem from both the assumptions of the model and some of its emergent properties.

The first limitation stems from the fixed landscape and the exogenous nature of the N and K parameters that are determining the shape and the statistical properties of the landscape. It is useful to reiterate that the exogenous landscape provides important benefits. It allows carefully teasing apart how the structural characteristics of the landscape and the nature of interdependencies interact with search processes to determine performance. Further, it allows for a controlled set of assumptions of how the organization should experience environmental change (e.g., redrawing of contribution values with or without a change to how decisions interact and so forth). The clean separation between the environment/landscape (i.e., the problem that is being solved) and the search facilitated the benefits of the model described above and ultimately helped the model flourish in the literature. However, the exogeneity of the landscape also imposes limitations. There is some debate on how serious this limitation is (Felin et al. 2014; Gavetti et al. 2017). On the one hand, scholars argue that an exogenous landscape imposes severe limitations on what can be modeled, and does not realistically depict endogenous landscape creation that is likely taking place in real-life systems (Felin et al. 2014; Gavetti et al. 2017). On the other hand, the exogeneity of a landscape may be just a matter of perspective. Even in the context of the NK model, it is possible to endogenize the focal landscape when it is modeled as a sub-landscape of a larger exogenous landscape through the NKC specification (Ganco, Kapoor, and Lee 2020; Ganco and Agarwal 2009; Gavetti et al. 2017). In the NKC specification, agents searching choices that are outside of the focal landscape but are interdependent with choices in the focal landscape, reshape the focal landscape (Gavetti et al. 2017). In an abstract sense, every endogenous landscape can thus be perceived as a subset of a larger exogenous landscape.[7] Aside from this debate, most scholars would likely agree that the exogeneity of the landscape makes the modeling of certain processes that are important for understanding organizations quite difficult. One may model endogeneity by using the NKC specification and specifying smaller, sub-landscapes as nested in a large, fixed landscape. However, the endogeneity would be no different from any epistatic interdependence of the standard Kauffman model. This is because the contribution values of the focal choices would be "redrawn" in response to changes stemming from "outside" of the focal sub-landscape. This limits the potential insights that researchers can obtain from such models and may not allow for a deeper understanding of how organizational structures evolve. Such modeling structure is not very viable when one wants to model an explicit process driving evolution of organizational structures. It is useful to note that

[7] This touches upon more abstract questions beyond the scope of this chapter of whether social systems can be approximated by (very large) but exogenous search spaces or whether an endogenous characterization is fundamentally needed.

existing work has generated insights about which organizational structures perform better and even made conclusions on which structures evolve due to selection (i.e., lower-performing structures are assumed to be selected out). However, these inferences have typically been made by generating performance outcomes across a variety of landscapes (e.g., by changing N and K parameters) and then comparing their performance. Again, such approach is imperfect because it does not allow modeling the processes that drive the evolution of organizational interdependencies and structures. Consequently, exogeneity of the NK landscapes represents a constraint of this approach and recent work has started exploring ways of relaxing it.

The second potential limitation stems from the emergent properties of the NK landscape and relatively unknown relevance of these properties for empirical phenomena. As we describe above, one of the fundamental properties of the NK landscapes is the positive relationship between the size of the basins of attraction and the peak height. This property underscores some of the findings emerging from the NK model. It is unclear whether this NK landscape property captures how interdependencies function in real-life systems. It is possible that sometimes very high peaks have small basins of attraction and low "pull" for searching agents. Agents need to begin their local search in proximity to such peak to discover it. It is worth mentioning landscape models' specification attempts, such as Harrison et al. (2017), that allow one to specify steepness and height of local peaks.

Perhaps a more relevant question is when do real-life systems resemble NK landscapes? What are the empirical boundary conditions of applicability of such systems? Consequently, we need much more empirical work examining the applicability of the NK models specifically as it relates to the NK landscape properties. Most of the existing empirical work testing the NK model has focused on examining whether the basic predictions of the model hold in real-life systems such as the "complexity catastrophe" (Fleming and Sorenson 2001; Lenox et al. 2006; Ganco 2017). The question of whether the assumption of the exogenous landscape is too constraining also affects empirical testing. We may need research allowing us to isolate exogenous and endogenous parts of the landscape. Because the interdependencies in the NK model are fixed, the model is agnostic about where they reside and who controls them. However, in real life, some interdependencies may reside in the environment and be fundamentally fixed (e.g., determined by technological limitations and "physics") and some may be more pliable and resulting from design choices. For instance, engine weight (lowering performance) and its horsepower (increasing performance) will likely always be positively related in automobiles even when innovation (i.e., design choices) will make this trade-off less pronounced (e.g., by adding a turbocharger).[8] Consequently, real-life interdependencies have both exogeneous and endogenous parts to them, but we have a very limited understanding of how and when such separation occurs.

[8] Porter and Siggelkow (2008) discuss that interdependencies between choices may not be a property of those choices but a function of other (contextual) choices made by a firm.

Another emergent property of the NK landscapes that has unclear empirical relevance is the relationship between the number of elements and the ruggedness of the space. The number of local peaks increases exponentially with the number of choices *N*, and thus the NK landscapes become very rugged quickly. This has important benefits because it allows producing rich dynamics with a relatively small space making modeling tractable and running large number of simulated runs computationally feasible. When the *N* is large, the computations even with fast parallel systems are relatively slow. Even though the fast increase of ruggedness in the NK model is computationally convenient, it is not clear whether or when the number of peaks and the number of choices have such property in real-life systems. It is unclear whether the low *N* in the NK model must be interpreted as a proxy for much larger systems, or if we can map N to (some) real-life systems directly. Rahmandad (2019) proposes a generalization of the NK model in which the number of peaks scale linearly with the number of choices. His landscapes are thus much smoother than the NK landscapes with the same number of choices. He argues that such structure may be a better representation of many real-life systems than the NK model.

Another limitation of the NK framework has been that the internal fit in the presence of environmental change can only be studied partially. Recall that internal fit exists when the set of choices are internally reinforcing (finding a local peak). External fit exists when the choices are particularly appropriate given its environment (a particularly high performance). Siggelkow (2001) elaborated on the landscape analogy and the role of internal and external fit in changing environments when studying the "rise and fall" of the fashion house Liz Claiborne. He observed an important type of environmental change that the NK model can theoretically accommodate but is difficult to deliberately study as a modeler, the so-called fit-conserving change. This type of change leaves internal fit intact, that is, the firm continues to occupy a local peak, but the environmental fitness (performance) has decreased, that is, the local peak has become a less favorable local peak in the environment. The stochastic nature and strength of the NK framework put limits on testing specific landscape topologies and changes, such as a decreasing and increasing local peak. However, this type of landscape evolution has been argued to have practical relevance. For example, Siggelkow (2001: 841) argues that Ford's production system enjoyed a high level of internal and external fitness in the early 1900s but this peak declined with the introduction of the Japanese production system, which has emerged as a new high-performing peak thanks to technological advances. Harrison and colleagues propose the attractor-based fitness landscape as framework, which allows to specify the number, height, and steepness of peaks (2017).

The questions surrounding the empirical relevance of the NK model is related to a broader discussion about testing formal and simulations models. Modelers always face trade-offs between the empirical relevance of their models and their conceptual parsimoniousness. When too many parameters are included in the model, the model may be closer to empirical phenomena, but it also becomes more complicated to uncover novel theoretical insights. That is, a model that predicts empirical phenomena well may not be very insightful for understanding theoretical mechanisms because it is much harder to tease apart the causal relationships in the model. NK models may be closer to the empirical phenomena than many formal closed-form models that are built around few basic axioms such as those based on full rationality in neoclassical economics. Prior literature related to organizational change applying the NK framework has informed our understanding of the mechanisms explaining why some change strategies may perform better than others. However, the existing literature also clearly shows an important limitation of (NK) computer simulations when studying organizational change. Simulation models are experiments where two or more alternatives are benchmarked. For example, one may compare two agents, one following an exploratory search and one agent following a local search rule. Fixing the problem space (i.e., the characteristics of the underlying performance landscape) allows one to attribute differences in search outcome precisely to the parameter of interest (here, the search scope). Such analytical models cannot inform us in the understanding why an organization may choose one search scope over the other. Therefore, it is crucial for simulation work that is interested in organizational change to draw on existing empirical patterns. For example, NK models can be specified to widen their search scope when performance falls below a desired aspiration level (e.g., relative performance to competitors), thereby formalizing empirically backed problemistic search (Cyert and March 1963).

To gauge the empirical relevance of the NK model, it is also important to reliably measure interdependencies in real-life systems. Prior work has relied on few empirical measures of interdependencies. One approach is based on surveys (Lenox et al. 2010) in which respondents are asked to rate the technological complexity in the focal industry. Specifically, survey respondents were asked for the degree to which a product/process innovation has been difficult for competitors to imitate due to sources of complexity such as secrecy, patents, complementary services, and product complexity. This measure has been used to study the implications of technological complexity for the industry-level questions such as the average level and distribution of profitability. The limitation of this approach is that it does not allow finer-grain analysis at the firm level. Further, it may be difficult to discern whether the survey responses proxy for interdependencies as conceptualized by the researcher. A multi-method triangulation may be needed to establish validity. The second common approach is to use patent data to construct a proxy of interdependencies (Fleming and Sorenson 2001; Sorenson et al. 2006; Ganco 2017). The benefits of using patent data to measure complexity stem from the vast number of observations that are available. The detailed information about patents allows constructing proxies for interdependencies. Specifically, scholars have used the patent classification systems to infer interdependencies. For instance, such inference may rely on assumptions including that subclasses represent components, that each component corresponds to a choice in the NK model, that subclasses that are frequently combined with different subclasses have low interdependence (Fleming and Sorenson 2001), or that pairs of subclasses that frequently appear on patents together are interdependent (Ganco 2017). A limitation of using patents to measure complexity is that the researcher needs to make a relatively large number of assumptions to map patent characteristics to interdependence. While some tests are possible, it is generally difficult to discern whether all assumptions are valid. Researchers may again need to triangulate patent-based measurement across multiple methods such as using qualitative validation (Ganco 2013). Further, patents represent selected outcomes of the technological search process. Only inventions that are in expectation above certain performance thresholds are observed. That is, only the higher peaks of the rugged landscape are observed, and the distribution of the observed peaks is truncated from the left. While scholars have acknowledged this issue and devised empirical methods to mitigate it in a focal context (Fleming and Sorenson 2001), not observing the entire landscape may have implications for the scope of empirical tests that can be performed using the patent-based measures. For instance, it is difficult to test whether the distributional properties of the NK landscapes resemble the distributional properties of the innovation process.

The limitations notwithstanding, measuring complexity using surveys and patents is important in the effort to advance the literature on complex change. The impact of the empirical work in this area is noticeable in the citation counts. For instance, the seminal study by Fleming and Sorenson (2001) using patent-based measures of interdependence has received more than 1,200 Google Scholar citations to date. We hope that this effort continues, and scholars will introduce new approaches to measuring interdependence as well as refine the existing ones.

Moving Forward: Toward Endogenous NK Landscapes

As we discuss above, one of the fundamental questions related to organizational change is how organizations and their structures evolve, adapt, and change, either in response to environmental changes or to their strategies and managerial decisions. Given that the landscape in the NK model is exogenous, the NK model in its canonical form can make only limited inroads into these important questions. Consequently, we see significant potential in the NK model extensions and new related models that endogenize the landscape creation. Such approaches allow modeling the explicit connection between the shape of the landscape and organizational or environmental processes, and help to dynamically simulate such processes. We discuss several recent examples of such models that may illustrate and foreshadow future research directions.

Gavetti et al. (2017) carefully develop the concept of landscape "shaping" as opposed to landscape searching and argue for the need to go beyond the basic NK model specification. Their refinement of the NKC model (Kauffman, 1995), defined as the NKES model, assumes that an endogenous landscape can be subsumed in a larger exogenous landscape where the additional choices (outside of the endogenous dimensions) are modeled as the "shaping" dimensions. This approach takes advantage of the NKC specification of the NK model in which multiple landscapes are connected through a set of interdependencies. Changing choices in a coupled landscape then changes performance contributions of choices in the focal landscape. In turn, this changes the shape of the focal landscape. Gavetti et al. (2017) assume that some agents searching in the endogenous landscape have access to and can search the coupled "shaping" choices. Consequently, some agents can change the shape of the landscape they are searching. While Gavetti et al. (2017) do not experiment with different specifications connecting the "shaping" dimensions to the focal landscape and the NKES specification does not allow studying the emergence of interdependencies, their model provides an interesting perspective recasting the NKC model and opening important questions relevant for endogenizing the NK landscapes.

Similarly, Li and Czaszar (2019) implement an extension of the NK model and examine how reshaping of the landscape by outside forces (i.e., industrial policy) affects firms' search behavior. In the model, they assume that regulators may change the peak height by providing incentives, imposing taxes or restricting the search scope (i.e., certain positions on the landscape are not accessible to the firms).[9] They study how the government's ability to impose interventions for configurations that represent peaks and the stability of government policies affect performance. In their model, government is thus an additional agent that can change the shape the landscape. While Li and Csazsar (2019) do not examine how the shape of the landscape depends on the behavior of organizations searching it, they design a clear and explicit mechanism capturing the effects of an external agent reshaping the landscape. Such research puts us closer to having a more general class of landscape models that will allow us to examine landscape dynamics as resulting from organizational processes.

Another step in that direction has been proposed by Rahmandad (2019). Rather than refining the NK model, Rahmandad introduces an alternative specification of a landscape that he defines as the PN landscape model. The PN model is grounded in the set of continuous interactions that resemble a linear regression where two-way, three-way, and so on, interactions are specified (while only linear direct effects are included—i.e., no polynomials). Generating a landscape as emerging from such an interacted linear model is in direct contrast to how the landscape is generated in the NK model. While changing any interdependent choice in the NK model leads to a new draw of the performance contribution of the focal choice, changes in the coupled choices in the PN model have potentially a much smaller effect. Further, higher-order interaction terms have increasingly smaller effects on the payoffs. This difference in the specification leads to different characteristics of the landscapes. For instance, the PN landscapes are much smoother and have a much smaller number of local peaks than the NK landscape with the same number of choices. In fact, the peaks scale linearly with choices in the PN model. Further, an interdependence between two choices in the PN model is given by more than one parameter because the lower and higher-order interactions contribute to the effect. This contrasts with the NK model where the interaction between two choices is given by one binary parameter (it is either present or not). Interestingly, Rahmandad

[9] See also the related Chapter 14 of this volume by Marcus and Malen.

(2019) shows that the NK model specification is a special case of the PN landscape—that is, he shows that for each NK landscape, there exists an interaction vector that generates an identical landscape (how the modeling parameters shape the landscape is very different in the two models). Rahmandad (2019) discusses that the applicability of the PN model vs. the NK model may depend on the characteristics of the system that is being modeled. While the PN specification is relatively new to discern how much follow-up research it will trigger and how insightful it will be, the specification has some important advantages.[10] For instance, modeling endogenous processes connecting interdependencies to organizational or environmental processes is very straightforward in the PN model. In fact, Rahmandad (2019) implements a simple example in which he allows the agents to search the space by changing choices, and "shape" the search space by changing the interdependencies (i.e., modifying the interaction "coefficients"). This results in agents creating a very smooth space and no substitution effects—that is, only complementary interactions are evolved.

Most recently, Albert and Siggelkow (Forthcoming) provide a variant of the NK model, where agents may not only search over an existing landscape but also across different landscape architectures. In their model, agents are at the discretion to add or remove interedependencies among elements and thereby manipulate the payoff-structure of the performance landscape. In that sense, the landscape becomes an endogenous consequence of an agent's search for alternative interdependencies.

Conclusion

The objective of our chapter was to provide in-depth discussion of the use of landscape models of organizational change. Specifically, we paid attention to the NK model as the most popular conceptualization of organizational search and change processes in the context of complex organizations and environments. We first grounded our conversation about the NK models in the literature while discussing their role in the broader context, discussing organizations as systems. Then, we proceeded to cover how researchers used the NK models to examine organizational change and innovation. We proceeded with discussing the key theoretical insights uncovered by the NK models and provided a discussion of the benefits of using the NK modeling approaches to study organizations. Further, we provide a brief overview of the empirical work aimed at testing the validity of the NK model and its empirical relevance.

As with any conceptual model, there are limitations. We addressed several shortcomings and assumptions underlying the model that may constrain its ability to address central questions in organizational research, such as those related to the emergence of organizational structures and processes. It is our belief that recent work is pushing the

[10] It is useful to note that the PN specification proposed by Rahmandad (2019) shows similarities with early continuous landscape models introduced by Chang and Harrington (2000, 2003, 2006).

boundaries by introducing refinements and new models that relax the limitations of the traditional NK model specifications. We discussed several examples that illustrate how alternative specifications of the landscape models may advance research in this area. In general, it is our hope to stimulate more research in this important and exciting research domain!

References

Albert, D. and Siggelkow, N. (Forthcoming), 'Architectural Search and Innovation', *Organization Science.*

Aggarwal, V. A., Siggelkow, N., and Singh, H. (2011), 'Governing Collaborative Activity: Interdependence and the Impact of Coordination and Exploration', *Strategic Management Journal*, 32, 705–30.

Baumann, O., Schmidt, J., and Stieglitz, N. (2019), 'Effective search in rugged performance landscapes: A review and outlook', *Journal of Management*, 45, 285–318.

Billinger, S., Stieglitz, N., and Schumacher, T. R. (2013), 'Search on Rugged Landscapes: An Experimental Study', *Organization Science*, 25, 93–108.

Brusoni, S. (2005), 'The Limits to Specialization: Problem-Solving and Coordination in "Modular Networks"', *Organization Studies*, 26, 1885–907.

Buzas, J., and Dinitz, J. (2013), 'An Analysis of Landscapes: Interaction Structure, Statistical Properties, and Expected Number of Local Optima', *IEEE Transactions on Evolutionary Computation*, 18, 807–18.

Chang, M. H., and Harrington, J. E. (2000), 'Centralization vs. Decentralization in a Multi-Unit Organization: A Computational Model of a Retail Chain as a Multi-Agent Adaptive System', *Management Science*, 46, 1427–40.

Chang, M. H., and Harrington, J. E. (2003), 'Multimarket Competition, Consumer Search, and the Organizational Structure of Multiunit Firms', *Management Science*, 49, 541–52.

Chang, M. H., and Harrington, J. E. (2006), 'Agent-Based Models of Organizations', in L. Tesfatsion and K. Judd, eds., *Handbook of Computational Economics* (Volume 2) (Amsterdam: North Holland), 1273–337.

Csaszar, F. A. (2018), 'A Note on How NK Landscapes Work', *Journal of Organization Design*, 7, 15.

Cyert, R. M., and March, J. G. (1963), *A Behavioral Theory of the Firm* (Oxford: Blackwell).

Dooley, K. J. (2021), 'Conceptualizing Organizational Change through the Lens of Complexity Science', in M. S. Poole and A. H. Van de Ven, eds., *The Oxford Handbook of Organizational Change* (2nd edn) (Oxford: Oxford University Press).

Ennen, E., and Richter, A. (2010), 'The Whole is More than the Sum of its Parts—or Is it? A Review of the Empirical Literature on Complementarities in Organizations', *Journal of Management*, 36, 207–33.

Ethiraj, S. K., and Levinthal, D. (2004a), 'Modularity and Innovation in Complex Systems', *Management Science*, 50, 159–73.

Ethiraj, S. K., and Levinthal, D. (2004b), 'Bounded Rationality and the Search for Organizational Architecture: An Evolutionary Perspective on the Design of Organizations and their Evolvability', *Administrative Science Quarterly*, 49, 404–37.

Ethiraj, S. K., Levinthal, D., and Roy, R. R. (2008), 'The Dual Role of Modularity: Innovation and Imitation', *Management Science*, 54, 939–55.

Felin, T., Kauffman, S., Koppl, R., and Longo, G. (2014), 'Economic Opportunity and Evolution: Beyond Landscapes and Bounded Rationality', *Strategic Entrepreneurship Journal*, 8, 269–82.

Fleming, L., Sorenson, O. (2001), 'Technology as a Complex Adaptive System: Evidence from Patent Data', *Research Policy*, 30, 1019–39.

Ganco, M. (2013), "Cutting the Gordian Knot: The Effect of Knowledge Complexity on Employee Mobility and Entrepreneurship', *Strategic Management Journal*, 34, 666–86.

Ganco, M. (2017), 'NK Model as a Representation of Innovative Search', *Research Policy*, 46, 1783–800.

Ganco, M., and Agarwal, R. (2009), 'Performance Differentials Between Diversifying Entrants and Entrepreneurial Start-Ups: A Complexity Approach', *Academy of Management Review*, 34, 228–52.

Ganco, M., and Hoetker, G. (2009), 'NK Modeling Methodology in the Strategy Literature: Bounded Search on a Rugged Landscape', *Research Methodology in Strategy and Management*, 5, 237–68.

Ganco, M., Kapoor, R., and Lee, G. (2020), 'From Rugged Landscapes to Rugged Ecosystems: Structure of Interdependencies and Firms' Innovative Search', *Academy of Management Review*, 45, 646–674.

Gavetti, G. (2012), 'Perspective—Toward a Behavioral Theory of Strategy', *Organization Science*, 23, 267–85.

Gavetti, G., Helfat, C. E., and Marengo, L. (2017), 'Searching, Shaping, and the Quest for Superior Performance', *Strategy Science*, 2, 194–209.

Gavetti, G., and Levinthal, D. (2000), 'Looking Forward and Looking Backward: Cognitive and Experiential Search', *Administrative Science Quarterly*, 45, 113–37.

Gavetti, G., and Rivkin, J. W. (2007), 'On the Origin of Strategy: Action and Cognition over Time', *Organization Science*, 18, 420–39.

Harrison, J. R., Kemp, A., and Saetre, A. S. (2017), 'Attractor-Based fitness landscapes for computational decision search'. 2017 Portland International Conference on Management of Engineering and Technology (PICMET): 1–8. IEEE.

Haveman, H. A., Russo, M. V., and Meyer, A. D. (2001), "Organizational Environments in Flux: The Impact of Regulatory Punctuations on Organizational Domains, CEO Succession, and Performance', *Organization Science*, 12, 253–73.

Hayek, F. A. (1945), 'The use of knowledge in society', *The American Economic Review*, 35, 519–30.

Holland, J. H. (1975), *Adaptation in Natural and Artificial Systems* (Ann Arbor, MI: University of Michigan Press).

Holland, J. H. (1995), *Hidden Order* (New York: Basic Books).

Jacobides, M. G., Cennamo, C., and Gawer, A. (2018), 'Towards a Theory of Ecosystems', *Strategic Management Journal*, 39: 2255–76.

Jain, A., and Kogut, B. (2014), 'Memory and Organizational Evolvability in a Neutral Landscape', *Organization Science*, 25, 479–93.

Katila, R., and Ahuja, G. (2002), 'Something Old, Something New: A Longitudinal Study of Search Behavior and New Product Introduction', *The Academy of Management Journal*, 45, 1183–94.

Kauffman, S. A. (1993), *The Origins of Order: Self-Organization and Selection in Evolution* (New York: Oxford University Press).

Kauffman, S. A. (1995), *At Home in The Universe* (New York: Oxford University Press).

Kauffman, S. A. (2007), 'Beyond Reductionism: Reinventing the Sacred', *Zygon*, 42, 903–14.
Kaul, H., and Jacobson, S. H. (2006), 'New Global Optima Results for the Kauffman NK Model: Handling Dependency', *Mathematical Programming*, 108, 475–94.
Knudsen, T., Levinthal, D. and Puranam, P. (2019), 'Editorial: A Model is Model,' Strategy Science, 4, 1–3.
Lave, C. A. and March, J. G. (1975), *An introduction to models in the social sciences* (New York, NY: Harper & Row).
Lawrence, P. R. and J. W. Lorsch (1967), *Organization and Environment: Managing Differentiation and Integration* (Boston: Harvard University Press).
Lenox, M. J., Rockart, S. F., and Lewin, A. Y. (2006), 'Interdependency, Competition, and The Distribution of Firm and Industry Profits', *Management Science*, 52, 757–72.
Lenox, M. J., Rockart, S. F., and Lewin, A. Y. (2010), 'Does Interdependency Affect Firm and Industry Profitability? An Empirical Test', *Strategic Management Journal*, 31, 121–39.
Leonard-Barton, D. (1992), 'Core Capabilities and Core Rigidities - a Paradox in Managing New Product Development', *Strategic Management Journal*, 13, 111–25.
Levinthal, D. A. (1997), "Adaptation on Rugged Landscapes', *Management Science*, 43, 934–50.
Levinthal, D. A., and March, J. G. (1993), 'The Myopia of Learning', *Strategic Management Journal*, 14, 95–112.
Levinthal, D. A., and Posen, H. (2007), 'Myopia of Selection: Does Organizational Adaptation Limit the Efficacy of Population Selection?', *Administrative Science Quarterly*, 52, 586–620.
Levinthal, D. A., and Workiewicz, M. (2018), 'When Two Bosses Are Better Than One: Nearly Decomposable Systems and Organizational Adaptation', *Organization Science*, 29, 207–24.
Li, C., and Csaszar, F. A. (2019), 'Government as Landscape Designer: A Behavioral View of Industrial Policy', *Strategy Science*, 4, 175–92.
March, J. G. (1991), 'Exploration and Exploitation in Organizational Learning', *Organization Science*, 2, 71–87.
March, J. G., and Simon, H. A. (1958), *Organizations* (New York: Wiley).
Marcus, A. and Malen, J. (2021), 'Hedging: Organziational Responses to the Formulation, Implementation, and Enforcement of Government Mandated Changes', in M. S. Poole and A. H. Van de Ven, eds., *The Oxford Handbook of Organizational Change* (2nd edn) (Oxford: Oxford University Press),
McKelvey, B. (1999), 'Self-Organization, Complexity Catastrophe, and Microstate Models at the Edge of Chaos', in J. A. C. Baum and B. McKelvey, eds., *Variations in Organization Science: In Honor of Donald T. Campbell* (Thousand Oaks: Sage), 279–307.
Miles, R. E., Snow, C. C., Meyer, A. D. and H. J. Coleman. (1978), 'Organizational Strategy, Structure, and Process', *Academy of Management Review*, 3, 546–62.
Milgrom, P., and Roberts, J. (1990), 'The Economics of Modern Manufacturing: Technology, Strategy, and Organization', *American Economic Review*, 80, 511–28.
Miller, D. (1981), 'Toward a New Contingency Approach: The Search for Organizational Gestalts', *Journal of Management Studies*, 18, 1–26.
Miller, D. (1992), 'Environmental Fit Versus Internal Fit', *Organization Science*, 3, 159–78.
Mintzberg, H. (1979), *The Structuring of Organizations: A Synthesis of Research* (Englewood Cliffs, NJ: Prentice-Hall).
Porter, M. E. (1996), 'What is Strategy?' *Harvard Business Review*, 74, 61–78.
Porter, M. E., and Siggelkow, N. (2008), 'Contextuality Within Activity Systems and Sustainability of Competitive Advantage', *Academy of Management Perspectives*, 22, 34–56.

Puranam, P., Stieglitz, N., Osman, M., and Pillutla, M. M. (2015), 'Modelling Bounded Rationality in Organizations: Progress and Prospects', *The Academy of Management Annals*, 9, 337–92.

Rahmandad, H. (2019), 'Interdependence, Complementarity, and Ruggedness of Performance Landscapes', *Strategy Science*, 4, 234–49.

Rivkin, J. W. (2000), "Imitation of Complex Strategies', *Management Science*, 46, 824–44.

Rivkin, J. W., and Siggelkow, N. (2003), 'Balancing Search and Stability: Interdependencies among Elements of Organizational Design', *Management Science*, 49, 290–311.

Rivkin, J. W., and Siggelkow, N. (2007), 'Patterned Interactions in Complex Systems: Implications for Exploration', *Management Science*, 53, 1068–85.

Siggelkow, N. (2001), 'Change in the Presence of Fit: The Rise, the Fall, and the Renaissance of Liz Claiborne', *Academy of Management Journal*, 44, 838–57.

Siggelkow, N. (2002), 'Evolution Toward Fit', *Administrative Science Quarterly*, 47, 125–59.

Siggelkow, N., and Levinthal, D. A. (2003), 'Temporarily Divide to Conquer: Centralized, Decentralized, and Reintegrated Organizational Approaches to Exploration and Adaptation', *Organization Science*, 14, 650–69.

Siggelkow, N., and Rivkin, J. W. (2009), 'Hiding the Evidence of Valid Theories: How Coupled Search Processes Obscure Performance Differences Among Organizations', *Administrative Science Quarterly*, 54, 602–34.

Simon, H. A. (1947), *Administrative Behavior: A Study of Decision-Making Processes in Administrative Organization* (New York: Macmillan).

Simon, H. A. (1962), 'The Architecture of Complexity', *Proceedings of the American Philosophical Society*, 106, 467–82.

Simon, H. A. (1987), 'Bounded Rationality', in J. Eatwell, M. Millgate, and P. Newman, eds., *The New Palgrave: Utility and Probability*(London: Palgrave), 15–18.

Sorenson, O., Rivkin, J. W., and Fleming, L. (2006), 'Complexity, Networks and Knowledge Flow', *Research Policy*, 35, 994–1017.

Thompson, J. D. (1967), *Organizations in Action* (New York: McGraw-Hill).

Van de Ven, A. H., Ganco, M., and Hinings, C. R. (2013), 'Returning to the Frontier of Contingency Theory of Organizational and Institutional Designs', *The Academy of Management Annals*, 7, 393–440.

Weick, K. E. (1976), "Educational Organizations as Loosely Coupled Systems', *Administrative Science Quarterly*, 21, 1–19.

Whittington, R., Pettigrew, A., Peck, S., Fenton, E., and Conyon, M. (1999), 'Change and Complementarities in the New Competitive Landscape: A European Panel Study, 1992–1996', *Organization Science*, 10, 583–600.

Wright, S. (1931), "Evolution in Mendelian Populations', *Genetics*, 16, 97–159.

PART V

HYBRID CHANGE PROCESS MODELS

CHAPTER 22

MICROFOUNDATIONS OF INNOVATION AS PROCESS

Usher's cumulative synthesis model

RAGHU GARUD AND MARJA TURUNEN

INNOVATION, always of importance to the growth and survival of firms, is even more important in today's environment characterized by the continual introduction of new products and services. Although innovation as an outcome is pleasing, navigating the processes that unfold is a difficult task (Coyne 1999; Van de Ven et al. 1999). As research has shown, innovation journeys are full of ups and downs, with success seldom guaranteed (Van de Ven et al. 1999). Yet, regardless of the specific outcomes, innovation serves as a generative force for change (Usher 1954).[1]

How might we understand innovation as process, and what are the implications of doing so? To address this question, we build on Usher's (1929, 1954, 1955) model of *cumulative synthesis*. Surprisingly, innovation scholars have not built on Usher's work as much as they have on the work of Usher's contemporary, Schumpeter (1934). We believe that Usher's work offers the microfoundations of innovation as process, one that lies in contrast to the macro perspective offered by Schumpeter. Besides introducing management scholars to Usher's model, another objective for writing this chapter is to extend his work with insights that have accumulated since he introduced his model. The payoff from this effort is the articulation of a perspective in which innovation can and should be *a part of* organizing rather than remain *apart* from it.

[1] We thank Marshall Scott Poole and Andy Van de Ven for giving us valuable feedback on earlier versions of this chapter. We thank the participants at a workshop organized in August 2019 for their useful comments on an earlier version of this chapter. In particular, we thank Jennifer Woolley and Marc Ventresca for their interest in our work, and for providing us with feedback. We are grateful to our colleagues, Hans Berends, Joel Gehman, Peter Karnøe, Arun Kumaraswamy, and Philipp Tuertscher, whose insights and friendship over the years have informed and sustained this work. Most importantly, we owe a debt of gratitude to our families.

The chapter is organized as follows: First, we provide an editorialized version of Usher's model of cumulative synthesis.[2] Second, we probe deeper into the assumptions underlying his model, after which we explore how his model has influenced contemporary scholars, and how it could be applied to enhance scholarship on, and the practice of innovation. Finally, we conclude the chapter with suggestions for future research.

Usher's Model of Cumulative Synthesis

Usher was intrigued by the question *How do new things happen?* To appreciate the significance of Usher's model in response to this question, it is first useful to revisit the theories on creativity, invention, and innovation that he confronted. There were two theories that Usher considered. The first, one that Usher labeled as "transcendentalism," attributed invention to the "inspiration of genius" and "as an array of independent items, each of them of massive proportions, each of them achieved by a process of revelation or intuitive perception that admits of no analysis." The second, advanced by sociologists, refuted the transcendentalists' position. Usher noted that these sociologists "establish[ed] the reality of the process as a whole, and demonstrate[d] vividly the length of the process in time." Abstracting from the work of these scholars, Usher concluded that "the emergence of novelty is presented as an accumulation of many individual items over a relatively long period of time. The magnitude of the individual item is small, but through cumulative synthesis the product becomes important."

While using the work of these sociologists to critique the transcendentalists' position (which Usher characterized as "naïve and ill grounded"), Usher in turn critiqued the sociologists' position, observing that they took "an essentially mechanistic position" because they considered the process of innovation "proceed[ing] under the stresses of necessity." Instead, and building on Gestalt psychology,[3] Usher explained that the process of invention "is intermediate between the mystic indeterminism of the transcendentalists and the mechanistic determinism of the sociological theories," and that "insight is not a rare, unusual phenomenon as presumed by the transcendentalist; nor is it a relatively simple response to need that can be assumed to occur without resistance and delay."

[2] To facilitate reading, we do not provide the specific source/page numbers after each quotation. They are to be found in Usher 1929, 1954, and 1955.

[3] Gestalt psychology emerged in Germany and Austria at the beginning of the twentieth century as a counterforce to a reductive science. Gestalt theorists such as Max Wertheimer, Wolfgang Köhler, and Kurt Koffka argued for holistic rather than analytic perception (i.e., considering phenomena as a whole rather than the summation of individual parts). Interestingly, Campbell (1960) offered a view on "blind variation in selection and retention in creative thought" based on trial-and-error learning, which he argued did not lie at odds with Gestalt thinking (except for the notion that geniuses had some direct way of knowing). It is beyond the scope of this chapter to align Campbell's ideas with Usher's, but we found many connections that we urge readers to explore on their own.

Usher then offered a generalized process model of cumulative synthesis based on his in-depth study of 100 years of mechanical innovations. The model was comprised of four "genetic steps"—the *perception of an unsatisfactory pattern*, the *setting of the stage*, the *primary act of insight*, and *critical revision and development* (Figure 22.1a). Distinguishing between the *primary act of insight* and the three other steps of his model, Usher argued that acumen is required for each of the remaining three steps as well. For instance, the *perception of an unsatisfactory pattern* (e.g., an unfulfilled want) requires acumen given that it is difficult to:

> perceive the inadequacy of a pattern of thought or action that has been sanctioned by tradition for so long a period that most members of the social group do not question the adequacy of a mechanism or a concept or a symbol that is in fact utterly inadequate.

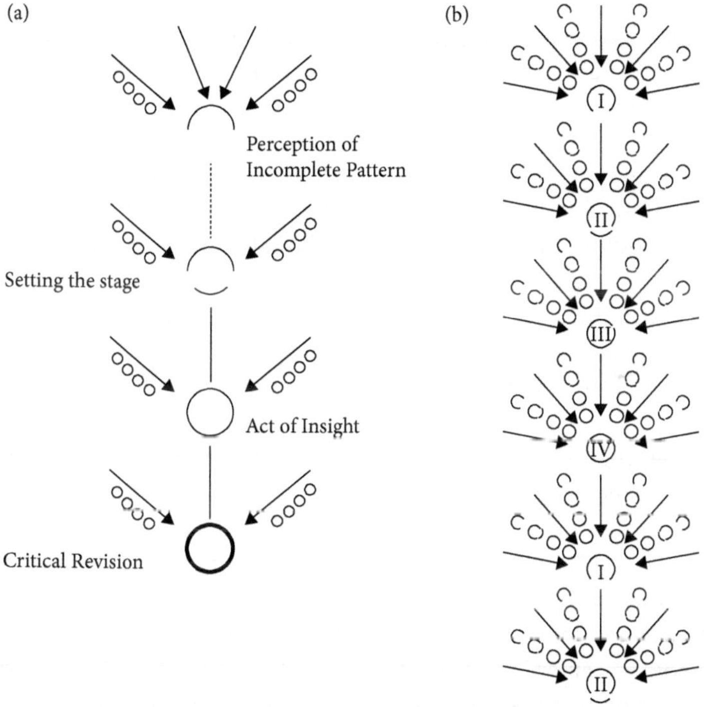

FIGURE 22.1A AND 22.1B Usher's Cumulative Synthesis Model. The emergence of novelty in the act of insight: synthesis of familiar items: (1) perception of an incomplete pattern; (2) the setting of the stage; (3) the act of insight; (4) critical revision and full mastery of the new pattern. b. The process of cumulative synthesis. A full cycle of strategic invention, and part of a second cycle. Large figures I-IV represents steps in the development of a strategic invention. Small figures represent individual elements of novelty. Arrows represent familiar elements included in the new synthesis.

From Usher [1929] (1954)

But, to the extent that one is attentive, an event could occur during the performance of an act of skill that triggers the recognition of an unsatisfactory pattern. Dealing with this unsatisfactory pattern through an *act of primary insight* is made possible by some fortuitous configuration of events and thought, which presents all the data essential to a solution. Considerable uncertainty surrounds these processes, which makes it impossible to predict the timing or the precise configuration of solutions in advance. As a result, for Usher, "the chance that appears in such events [i.e., acts of insight] exhibits the contingency of systems of events that disclose patterns and exhibit many interdependencies in a universe that is not wholly determinate...It is a chance occurrence in the sense of being unforeseen and unplanned." Here, it is useful to connect the notion of chance with other related terms including "blind variation," which Campbell (1960) defined as:

> variations produced without prior knowledge of which ones, if any, will furnish a select worthy encounter... [where] that specific correct trials are no more likely to occur at any one point in a series of trials than another, nor than specific incorrect trials... [and] a rejection of the notion that a variation subsequent to an incorrect trial is a "correction" of the previous trial or makes use of the direction of error of the previous one.

In our own investigation of creative acts, we have used the term "serendipity" rather than "blind" following Merton and Barber (2004). We agree with Campbell that foresight about the outcomes of creative thoughts and acts could get us into mysticism. At the same time, we have argued that actors can engage with phenomena in ways designed to enhance the likelihood of the discovery of novel ideas and the identification of uses for them through exaptation (Garud et al. 2018; see also Andriani and Cattani 2016; Nayak and Chia 2019). Our arguments are based on Usher's model, which highlights the possibility of increasing the likelihood of the occurrence of acts of insight by *setting the stage*. Again, acumen is required, as different stage-setting configurations generate different pathways for the emergence of novelty (Garud et al. 2018).

Usher went out of his way to note that the *act of primary insight* was not the end of the cumulative synthesis process. Although novel ideas are exciting, they must be "studied critically, understood in its fullness, and learned as a technique of thought or action." This is yet another step of Usher's model, which he labeled as *critical revision and full mastery*. In offering this label, Usher distanced himself from other perspectives that made a distinction between invention and imitation (Tarde's [1903] for instance), arguing that these interpretations failed to recognize the pervasiveness of novelty in everyday behavior.[4] Instead, Usher argued that the diffusion of a new technique

[4] It is interesting to explore the tension between invention and imitation by considering Elaine Sturtevant's practice of *copying inexactly*. We believe that Usher was reaching beyond a notion of agency implicated in copying inexactly to also include serendipitous variations that are bound to arise in the very act of copying.

throughout the economy presents a new set of problems, requiring new acts of insight. Indeed, the process of diffusion of an innovation, even after the act of primary insight, involves "a very intimate interweaving of minor acts of insight and acts of skill performed at high levels by persons of special training."[5]

Complicated as all of this might appear, Usher did not shy away from making further distinctions to offer a more complete perspective on cumulative synthesis. In particular, he distinguished between different types of inventions—*primary*, *secondary*, and *tertiary*. For Usher, inventions that generate a base of knowledge but are not directly carried forward to commercial use are primary inventions. Inventions that open up new practical uses (including ones that extend a known principle to a new field of use) are secondary inventions. Improvements in a given device that do not clearly extend the field of use are tertiary inventions.

After making these distinctions, Usher went on to elaborate his process model by detailing three examples—the development of the locomotive, the development of manufacturing processes using interchangeable parts, and the introduction of the Bessemer process in the iron and steel industry. He shared these examples to demonstrate the difficulties involved in the development and adoption of these innovations, and claimed that these difficulties were frequently ignored or underemphasized. Usher's careful re-examination of the historical events that led to the adoption of these innovations revealed a far more non-linear process than others had conceptualized, including the one articulated by Schumpeter. For instance, Usher found that: (a) the beginnings of commercial application preceded the full accomplishment of the secondary invention in some cases, and (b) the major invention remained to be achieved even during the process of critical revision. Contrasting this finding against Schumpeter's analysis, Usher noted, "Schumpeter's analysis suggests the opposite order of development: the completion of the secondary invention is represented as preceding the entrepreneurial work on application."

However, while departing from Schumpeter's theory, other observations that Usher offered resonated with Schumpeter's. For instance, Usher found that the activities of "scientist–inventors" that yielded primary innovations were more likely to be prominent during the early stages, whereas the activities of "inventor–entrepreneurs" yielding secondary inventions were more likely to be evident during later stages. While acknowledging that these dynamics were implicit in Schumpeter's work, Usher noted that "Schumpeter underestimated the degree of novelty involved in these acts of skill—of both the engineers and technicians and the administrative staff of the enterprise." Specifically, secondary inventions by engineers and technicians also require the

[5] We agree with Ingold (2014: 124) that the "wellsprings of creativity lie not inside people's heads, but in their attending upon a world in formation" and that "where it leads is not yet given." Yet, Usher's notion of *critical revision and full mastery* allows us to go beyond invention to also include all the events that occur during the process of innovation without any deterministic overtones (Garud, Tuertscher, and Van de Ven, 2013). Accordingly, in this chapter, we will use the term "innovation" to refer to an emergent (and non-deterministic) process that encompasses invention. Where appropriate, we will distinguish between the two terms (i.e., invention and innovation).

interweaving of acts of skill with acts of insight. Moreover, even more work is involved when firms engage in tertiary inventions.[6]

Assumptions Underlying Usher's Model

Now that we have introduced Usher's model and the intellectual context within which it was articulated, we delve deeper into the major assumptions underpinning it. Specifically, we examine: (a) how and why change occurs, (b) how relationality figures in his model, (c) how temporality figures in his model, (d) patterns of change, and (e) the ontological perspective on process.[7]

How and Why Change Occurs

We approach the question *How and why change occurs?* by drawing attention to three action modes theorized by Usher—*innate activities*, *acts of skill*, and *inventive acts of insight*. Innate activities are "unlearned modes of action that develop as responses to the structure of the organism or the biochemical processes that control its functions." Acts of skill, on the other hand, are "learned activities" regardless of whether such learning is induced by others, or is inherent in individuals. Acts of insight break away from acts of skill, and also are "unlearned activities." However, such activities are different from innate activities because acts of skill "result in new organizations of prior knowledge and experience."

Such reorganization necessarily involves a discontinuity. Because discontinuity implies a break from the past, actors encounter "resistance of undetermined magnitude." These actors then have to deal with such resistance through "the constructive assimilation of preexisting elements into new synthesis, new patterns, or new configurations of behavior . . . by establishing relationships that did not previously exist." These efforts can yield a synthesis, which is novel not only to the actors, but also to other social groups.

These observations are sufficient for understanding how and why change occurs. Change occurs through processes that involve not just the progressive improvements of innate skills mastered through doing, but also because of discontinuities that arise from probabilistic acts of insights that occur while carrying out acts of skills. Not only are the individuals transformed through this process, but, in addition, the organizations and the extant knowledge structures within which these individuals operate also are

[6] For other similarities and differences between Usher's and Schumpeter's views, please see Ruttan (1959).

[7] We thank Andy Van de Ven and Marshall Scott Poole for encouraging us to use these dimensions.

transformed. This process is ongoing, generating in its wake an accumulation of seemingly minor inventions and innovations (henceforth referred to as innovations), which in turn sets the stage for additional strategic innovations to emerge.

How Relationality Figures in Usher's Model

Usher realized that it is possible to increase the likelihood of novelty emerging through the recombination of resources, which led him to reformulate the question motivating his inquiry from "*How do new things happen?*" to "*How can the stage be set?*" In this regard, Usher observed that stage-setting could occur by influencing the field of perception for actors in order to increase the likelihood for an act of insight to occur. Here, he built on experiments conducted with chimpanzees by Köhler (1925) and his colleagues, wherein an experimenter would manipulate the visibility of a tool (a stick) with which the chimpanzees could access bananas, which otherwise were outside their reach.[8] In other words, the experimenters "set the stage" (in Usher's words) for chimpanzees to perceive the presence of a stick in their line of vision, and to probabilistically engage in acts of insight such as nudging the bananas towards them.

Koestler (1964), whose work influenced Usher, added further nuance to this process by noting: "Köhler and the Gestalt school... set their chimpanzees tasks for which they were ripe, or *almost ripe*, to prove that all learning was based on insight." Of particular importance here is the notion of ripeness (or readiness, in our words). Echoing Pasteur's maxim "chance favors only the prepared mind," a person has to be ready to recognize an opportunity for an act of insight to occur. In this sense, different individuals are more or less ripe for acts of insight leading to serendipitous discoveries. Relatedly, Campbell (1960) too explored individual differences in "creative intellect" arising from individual differences in (a) "the accuracy and detail of their representations of the external world", and (b) "the number and range of variations in thought trials produced."

It is easy to ignore the contexts within which individuals work, and to consider the capacity for generating insight to be solely located within particular individuals. However, Koestler departed from individualism by arguing that the environments within which individuals operate also play a key role (see also Burke in this volume). Noted Koestler (1964):

> Thus, one should not underestimate ripeness as a factor facilitating discoveries which, as the saying goes, are 'in the air'—meaning, that the various components which will go into the new synthesis are all lying around and only waiting for the trigger-action of chance, or the catalyzing action of the exceptional brain, to be assembled and welded together. If one opportunity is missed, another will occur.

[8] For more details, please visit http://www.pigeon.psy.tufts.edu/psych26/kohler.htm/, accessed 24 September 2020).

And, to bring the individuals and the settings within which they operate together, Koestler (1964) summarized:

> The 'ripeness' of a culture for a new synthesis is reflected in the recurrent phenomenon of multiple discoveries, and in the emergence of similar forms of art, handicrafts, and social innovations in diverse cultures. But when the situation is ripe for a given type of discovery, it still needs the intuitive power of an exceptional mind, and sometimes a favorable chance event, to bring it from potential into actual existence.[9]

How Temporality Figures in Usher's Model

At a surface level, it appears that Usher's model is based on a linear set of steps or stages—perception of an incomplete pattern and the setting of the stage, which, in a probabilistic way, leads to an act of insight to be followed by critical revision. But, it was just a matter of convenience for Usher to use this representation for a process that he discovered was not at all linear or progressive. To understand the more complex notions of time, timing, and temporality implicated in Usher's model, it is useful to probe alternative notions of time.

An interesting place to start is the act of insight. As is apparent in the many examples that Usher provides, the act of insight is a probabilistic event that occurs at an opportune moment. In Greek mythology, the notion of time that is implied here is *kairos* rather than *chronos*. Acts of insight occur not when the clock (*chronos*) is right, but instead at the opportune moment (*kairos*), that is, when the circumstances and the individuals are ripe with possibilities.

A failure to distinguish between *chronos* and *kairos* can lead to problems, especially when it comes to innovation. There is, in management studies, a push towards time management techniques, which advocate the efficient use of time. Time management techniques are predominantly chronos based initiatives where every chronological minute (including time to relax in order to be more efficient whilst at work) must be accounted for. However, by placing so much emphasis on *chronos*-based time management, *kairotic* moments can easily be lost. Cultivating *kairotic* moments requires a different way of thinking, a topic to which we will return when we further explore the implications of *kairos* for organizing.

Viewed purely from a *chronos*-based time management perspective, we can see that *chronos* and *kairos* could potentially be at odds with one another. However, the complementary relationship between the two become evident when we consider other facets of Usher's model. His theory makes it clear that besides strategic innovations

[9] The notion of ripeness of the environment is akin to the notion of "poisedness" that (Johnson and Powell 2017) offered. We thank Marc Ventresca for drawing this connection during a random coffee meeting at Peets' Coffee in Mountain View, California. Perhaps the situation was ripe, or we were ripe, or both, for this connection to be made.

(which are readily apparent to everyone), there are others that go unnoticed, or lie under the radar. But, these innovations, with perhaps little or no utility when they emerge, could, over chronological time serve as raw materials for cumulative synthesis to occur through acts of insight, thereby yielding discontinuous change.

If we examine the above proposition (i.e., the synthesis of minor innovations with others to generate discontinuities), we can see additional useful distinctions between other notions of time implicated in Usher's model. First, based on *chronos*, there is the notion of *asynchrony*, by which we mean that the various elements of a strategic innovation may develop at different rates and at different points in time. Relatedly is the notion of *diachrony*—by which we mean that the value of a discovery could fluctuate over time. For instance, what may be considered worthless and even a nuisance at one point in time could become valuable when combined with something else. But, to benefit from diachrony, actors must entertain long temporal horizons so as to take advantage of "the complexities of a cumulative process involving long sequences in time and many individual items of novelty."

It is useful here to introduce a third notion of time from Greek philosophy—*aion*. While *chronos* represents clock time and *kairos* opportune moment, *aion* represents a period of time that is cyclical. *Aion* is often depicted as a serpent with its tail in its mouth, an image that allows us to visualize how ideas from the past (in chronological terms) can become useful in the future through acts of insight when the moment is ripe (*kairos*). This point is best understood by considering an extended quote that Usher introduced from Ogden (whose work clearly influenced Usher) in the first edition of his book.

> A perception is any experienced circuit of events. In [chronological] time it has a beginning and an end, although in the mesh of continuous happening, in which different strands are consistently overlapping, it is often difficult, if not impossible, to determine either an absolute beginning or a finite end; which leads us to wonder if [chronological] time in its ever onflowing course, is really the safest guide in the analysis of experience. If it is not, then the conception of a circuit in which a want is satisfied is perhaps the truer description of adjustment. In turning full circle, the end coincides with the beginning; in satisfying a want, a gap is filled, and the want disappears.
>
> (Ogden 1926: 126)

Gestalt theory, which influenced Usher, is implicated here, which is also evident in Usher's observation: "It is truly difficult to impress on the individual that necessity of facing both past and future symbolized in the image of Janus." Understood in a different way, and building on Ricœur's (1984) notion of narrative time, cultivating a temporal orientation wherein both the past and the future is present in any moment implies that we are always in the midst of everything (i.e., *in midias res*). In such a view, every ending evokes several beginnings, and every beginning several endings. In addition, Ricœur offers the notion of *distentio*, which he uses to draw attention to the stretching of the soul (or agency) over time. From this perspective, some endings and beginnings are shaped by anticipations of pathways to be pursued, while others are shaped by a quest to find origins, given memories of pathways traversed. And, speaking to the plasticity of time implicated here, anticipations about the future and the memories of the past co-constitute attention in the present.

Patterns of Change

As already noted, the genetic sequence of four steps constitutes one pattern of change (Figure 22.1a). However, there is yet another pattern when we consider how this process repeats itself across time and space (Figure 22.1b). In order to explicate this pattern, we examine another approach to stage-setting (besides influencing the field of perception for actors)—namely, shaping the field of imagination. Shaping the field of imagination is challenging, as it involves "all the difficult problems of the analysis of memory and the phenomena of past perceptions not readily available to organized conscious interests." In this regard Usher noted:

> The accumulation of experience in the individual and the group becomes important as soon as organized communication has been achieved. The accomplishments of the social insects suggest the existence of organized systems of communication, but observation and inference present so many difficulties that we cannot deal with such problems with much confidence. Cumulative achievement becomes significant in human society at the dawn of culture in the Old Stone Age.

Recent work by Ingold (2019) on learning as an ecological process sheds light on these issues. By ecological learning (our abbreviation of his text), Ingold means that the environment within which living things operate plays a central role in the transmission of agency across generations. In developing his theory, Ingold was influenced by psychologist James Gibson who offered "the theory of affordances" (Gibson 1979). An affordance, for Gibson, is what an environment offers an animal, for good or ill, in its pursuit of the tasks of life. For instance, a stone offers shelter to the lizard, a tree is a place where birds can build a nest, and so on. One cannot think of these animals without thinking about the environments within which they flourish.

Thus, as new generations follow, the environments within which they emerge provide critical resources. Here is where Ingold offers a twist—the knowledge required to access these resources (especially for humans) is not automatically inherited, but instead must be reproduced and learned. To drive home this point, Ingold provides an example of the inheritance of a farm, arguing:

> What keeps the farm going as a habitable and productive environment is not the heritability of its assets but the continuity of the agricultural labour process. In its passage down the generations, this process is in the nature of a relay, wherein tasks once performed by older generations are gradually taken over by younger hands

> who have learned on the job. As the former slacken, the latter come up to speed. The life of the farm carries on. As this example shows, what is modelled as a mechanism of inheritance is not really that at all, but a process, namely the carrying on through time, and over generations, of an environment that is ever in the making.

In short, the transmission of skills across generations is a dynamic process wherein the environment itself is transformed as resources are reproduced in novel ways. To emphasize this point and to draw attention to the co-constitution of organisms and their environments, Ingold offered another example:

> An environment that exists and persists, by the same token, is *not* transmitted. It is no more transmitted than are the banks cut by the current of a flowing river transmitted from earlier waters to later ones. River and banks are co-constitutive, in a process that carries on through time. As with the river and its banks, so with organisms and environment.

Ingold captured the various strands of ecological learning by coining a new term—*perdurance*. As he explained:

> *perdurance, and not inheritance, is the sine qua non of evolution*. It lies not in the transmission, across generations, of an already constructed world but in the continual bringing forth, or production, of a world that—from generation to generation—is ever in formation.
>
> In short, knowledge does not 'descend' from one generation to the next but is regrown in each, through their practical overlap, as generations carry on their lives together. What each contributes to the next are the conditions of development for this regrowth to occur (Ingold 2000: 387). Practices, then, are not inherited through social learning. Nor are they subsequently implemented through individual learning. They are reproduced in the context of environmentally situated, collaborative work. To reproduce a practice is to produce it again; it is not to run off a replica from a model.
>
> In truth, nothing is transmitted (Ingold 2001). Learning occurs because lives overlap lengthwise, like fibres twisted in a rope. Although every fibre is only so long, the rope itself winds on indefinitely. Individual lives, then, are the strands of an inter-generational rope-work, and each extends the weave. That weave is evolution.

These observations are quite useful for understanding the patterns of change implicit in Usher's model of cumulative synthesis. In particular, environments provide valuable intellectual and cultural resources across generations to actors whose lives overlap "like fibers twisted in a rope." Again, evoking the notion of *aion*, one act of insight through synthesis (Figure 22.1a) is based on previous acts (Figure 22.1b), thereby opening up new assets from the past and new avenues into the future (the idea that *every ending evokes several beginnings, and every beginning several endings* that we introduced earlier).

Indeed, synthesis results in an expansion of the capacity of an environment that actors can conceivably use. As Usher observed:

> The environment is enlarged by new knowledge and skills. The distinctive feature of human evolution lies in this fact. Human societies not only select an environment, *they make their environment*. The processes by which "man makes himself" include those procedures by which men transform their environment. Human evolution is doubly dynamic; man and the geographic environment react upon each other, and both terms are transformed.

In this sense, Usher subscribed to what he labeled as "soft determinism" (following William James). As he explained, "The limitations of resources are relative to the position of our knowledge and of our technique. The limits of both actual resources and potential resources recede as we advance, at rates that are proportionate to the advances in our knowledge."

Ontological Perspective on Process

It is clear that Usher's model is not based on variance theorization wherein scholars establish efficient causation between a set of independent and dependent variables typical of variance studies. Instead, it is best conceptualized as falling within a range of process studies wherein a set of variables (or inputs) are necessary but not sufficient to generate certain outcomes (Mohr 1982). For instance, the sprouting of a plant may need sun, soil, seed, and water, but the presence of these inputs does not guarantee that the plant will spring forth. Similarly, the probability for the emergence of novelty may be enhanced by setting the stage, but stage-setting need not result in the emergence of novelty.

Mohr offered additional insights noting, "The predominant flavor of a process model is that of a series of occurrences of events rather than a set of relations among variables" (Mohr 1982: 54). The sequence of events matters, as evident in Mohr's observation: what comes out of a probabilistic process depends on what goes in, and what goes in almost always depends on what came out of a former one, so that their order must be faithfully rendered within the model (Mohr, 1982: 59–60).

The view of a process as a sequence of events representing changes in things is one way of understanding the emergence of phenomena over time. Things interact with one another to generate events that can be observed (Morgeson et al. 2015). These events, when placed in chronological order, can generate an explanation of how phenomena unfold. For instance, a person could be inflicted with malaria if a mosquito that has already acquired the parasite bites him or her. But, if a mosquito first bites a person and then acquires the parasite, malaria is not the outcome. In other words, the sequence of events matters.

The temporal sequence of events as changes in things based on substantive (or entative) metaphysics is one view of process (Van de Ven and Poole 1990; 2005). Process metaphysics (Rescher 1996) offers another. Process metaphysics views phenomena as unfolding journeys that materialize things along the way. Rescher (1996: 27) clarified that "process philosophy does not—or need not—deny substances (things), but sees them as subordinate in status and ultimately inhering in processes." In the management field, Langley et al. (2013: 4) highlighted the differences between process and substance views on phenomena by observing,

> Process and temporality...can be viewed from different ontologies of the social world: one a world made of things in which processes represent change in things (grounded in a substantive metaphysics) and the other a world of processes, in which things are reifications of processes (Tsoukas and Chia 2002) (grounded in process metaphysics).

So, where exactly does Usher's model fall within this spectrum? Our understanding is that it subscribes to both, that is, it not only subscribes to a process that is ever flowing and becoming, but, in addition, there are critical anchor points that emerge (Usher labeled them as "strategic"). In other words, innovation is both noun (an outcome) and a verb (a process) at the same time.

However, there are trade-offs in viewing innovation as both noun and verb, which is similar to the trade-off one makes in determining the precision with which the position of a particle or its momentum can be specified. According to the Heisenberg's uncertainty principle, the more precisely one specifies the position (momentum) of a particle, the less precisely one can specify its momentum (position). In a similar vein, the further we go in our understanding of innovation as process, the greater is the difficulty in specifying innovation as an outcome. And, conversely, precision in defining innovation as an outcome (and characterizing it with different labels such as incremental, radical, and discontinuous) comes at the expense of understanding innovation as process.

We believe Usher was aware of this dilemma. He understood that we tend to pay attention to strategic innovations because they are so visible, and not notice the minor innovations that play a key role in the overall process. As he noted, "The magnitude of the individual item is small, but through cumulative synthesis the product becomes important," and "Cultural achievement is a social accomplishment based upon the accumulation of many small acts of insight by individuals." Indeed, it is through the everyday acts of ordinary individuals, often imperceptible in their occurrences, that innovation unfolds, but not always in the same direction. Stated differently, differences in degrees can become differences in kind.

However, because scholars (especially transcendentalists) misunderstood this overall process and confused the "part for the whole," there emerged "an undue emphasis upon a relatively small number of acts which are presented without due regard to the conditions which made them possible, and to a concept of change at infrequent intervals in units of great magnitude." For Usher, cumulative synthesis involves all the steps found in the emergence of any individual innovation, which in turn sets the stage for other actors to "reproduce" (Ingold, 2019) (Figure 22.1b). Many tend to ignore or dismiss the intermediary steps and innovations, which in the grand scheme of the overall process play an important role in generating discontinuous innovations.

Overall, Usher's model is based on a distributed, decentered, and durational ontology. It is distributed in that many people are involved, and it is through the acts of insight of these individuals that strategic and minor innovations emerge. It is decentered in that these acts of insight are shaped by the arrangements in place (i.e., stage-setting). It is durational in that one has to go "back to the future", that is, maintain and reactivate smaller innovations to foster strategic innovations. Even failures can play an important role in this process:

> Failures are thus of explicit historical importance. They are not solutions, but they are not without relation to a solution. They reveal explicit consciousness of the potentialities of some new mode of action, or of some new contrivance. They are evidence of the emergence of tensions and strivings that are likely to result in a positive achievement, even if it be long postponed and realized only a generation or more after the earliest recognizable emergence of the new objective.

The Utility of Considering Usher's Model as the Microfoundations for Innovation as Process

So far, we have examined the assumptions underlying Usher's model after having introduced it briefly. In this section, we (a) critique the model, (b) examine the research-based principles of change, (c) summarize the current state of research related to the model, and (d) provide an example of the model in practice. In this way, we provide readers with justifications for considering Usher's model as the basis to develop further insights on innovation as process.

Critique of Usher's Model

Many years ago, Poggie (1965) observed that "a way of seeing is a way of not seeing." As applied to Usher's process model the question is—*What does his model help us see, and in doing so, what does it obscure?* We address this question in the spirit of appreciation, and to make a case as to why Usher's model can serve as the microfoundations for innovation as process.

As already explained, Usher's model widens the lens with which one can view phenomena. Relationally, it allows us to see that the emergence of novelty is based not on some mystical unexplainable force, but instead on a synthesis of resources that already exist along with new elements. Temporally, Usher's model takes us beyond chronological (clock based) and *kairotic* (event based) notions of time, to also appreciate *aionic* time (i.e., larger periods of time that are cyclical). Performatively, Usher's model recognizes that innovation is not an individual but a collective accomplishment, which unfolds within institutional settings. Within such settings, those who offer novel ideas will encounter resistance because institutional inhabitants become habituated to traditions (Hallet and Ventresca 2006). And, yet, novel ideas have an opportunity to emerge and grow, because they are based on a synthesis of existing ideas and because they offer a higher level of thought and action.

Given the possibility of such a wide inquiry frame, it is difficult to see what remains unexplained in Usher's model. Yet, despite its comprehensiveness, there is one facet of innovation that we believe deserves greater attention—projective agency (Emirbayer and Mische 1998). Although Usher's emphasis was on the "necessity of facing both past and future symbolized in the image of Janus," he nevertheless did not adequately explore the role of imagination and future expectations. After all, Usher was a historian who went out of his way to carefully reconstruct the events that had transpired before a moment of insight. One particular portion of his text is revealing:

> A particular system of historical events must show some clear presumption of positive genetic development. The techniques of action or the concepts must be based upon one or several related innovations preserved by tradition, and developed by further innovation. In so far as convergence occurs, we must think of the events prior to fusion in one system as a separate system of events. Practical problems of analysis center around the nature of the evidence that can be accepted as a basis for the presumption of common origins or independent development. The determination of the boundaries of major systems of events thus involves a careful analysis of cultural diffusion.

In this text, we can see how Usher carefully went about delineating the origins of events so as to determine whether or not they belonged to similar or different systems, a critical step in determining the genuine sequences that underlie his model. While commendable, these efforts may have led to an oversight on Usher's part in terms of gaining a deeper understanding and theorization of projective temporal agency on the part of actors during the emergence of novelty. Instead, his model draws attention to the past (iterational) and the present (practical–evaluative). To be fair, Usher did point to the importance of considering larger swaths of time, as noted earlier. But this is not the same as the role that imagination and future expectations play in driving the emergence of novelty.

Why is this important? We believe that no theory of innovation can be complete without the explicit consideration of the projections that individuals make in their attempts to initiate and carry out their projects. They may, as a result, stumble on novel ideas serendipitously, or drive processes teleologically, but without an understanding of projective agency, we have a theory of innovation which is at best about actors looking backward even while attempting to drive forward.

Research-Based Principles of Change

In the 1960s, the National Science Foundation (NSF) commissioned the Illinois Institute of Technology (IIT) to carry out a study of how non-mission related research contributes to the development of technological innovations. The report from the IIT team, completed in 1968, was entitled "Technology in Retrospect and Critical Events in Science" (TRACES). Similar to Usher's work, TRACES tracked critical events leading up to five major technological innovations—magnetic ferrites, the video tape recorder (VCR), the oral contraceptive pill, the electronic microscope, and matrix isolation. A visual representation of the events in the emergence of the VCR (adapted from Irvine and Martin 1984) is reproduced as Figure 22.2. As depicted in this figure, the scholars

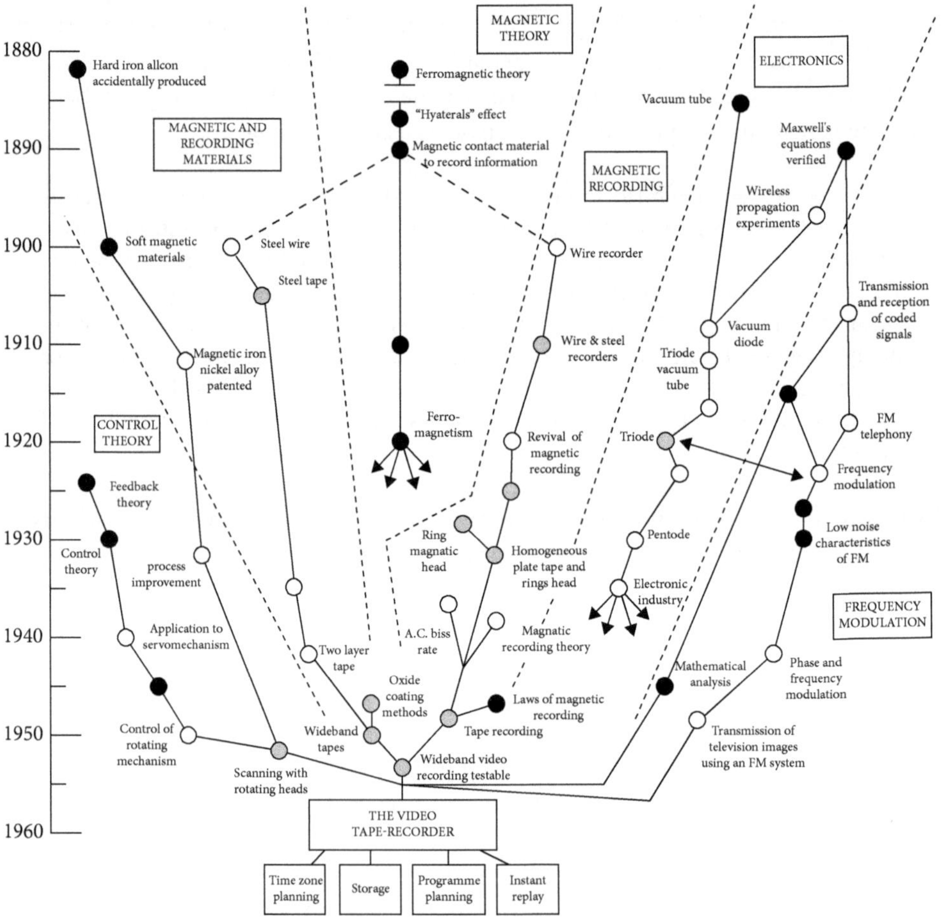

FIGURE 22.2 The Research Origins of the Video Tape Recorder Adapted from Irvine, J and Martin, B.R. Foresight in Science: Picking the Winners, 1984.

Note: BTL = Bell Telephone Laboratoriesl NRL = Naval Research Laboratory; AEG = Allgemeine Elektrizitats Gesellschaft

Source: •, Nonmission research; ○, mission-oriented research, ○, development and application.

found that the development of the VCR involved the merging of several streams of scientific and technological activities including control theory, magnetic and recording materials, magnetic theory, magnetic recording, electronics and frequency modulation.

Why do we share this with our readers? Because we see remarkable parallels between the findings from the TRACES study and the model of cumulative synthesis proposed by Usher based on his painstaking tracing of the events that led to multiple innovations. If we were to visually compare Figures 22.1 and 22.2, we see that the emergence of novelty involves convergence (in the TRACES case) or synthesis (in Usher's model). Moreover, behind the VCR as a strategic innovation are other strategic innovations in control theory, magnetic and recording materials, magnetic theory, magnetic recording, electronics, and frequency modulation. Each one of these strategic innovations is based on other not-so-strategic innovations. For instance, the research that led to the VCR falls into three categories (a) non-mission research leading to *primary inventions*, (b) mission-oriented research leading to *secondary innovations*, or (c) development and application work leading to *tertiary innovations*. Of these, the one that we want to draw attention to is the non-mission research—events that were purely driven by curiosity, leading to inventions whose role in the development of the VCR would have remained hidden if not for the IIT team.

The TRACES study, like Usher's, suggests that change may be promoted by paying attention to an ignored area of work—*mundane* innovations. By mundane we mean the many small discoveries (primary, secondary, and tertiary) that actors stumble upon during the course of their work. These mundane innovations do not immediately rise to the level of strategic innovations, but nevertheless can play an important part in the overall process of cumulative synthesis. Some mundane innovations may survive and eventually be used for strategic innovations. But many others may be ignored or forgotten. Moreover, when strategic innovations do emerge, the credit goes to those who claim the innovations as their own. Yet, these strategic innovations are based on other strategic and mundane innovations. A failure to recognize this process of change could, at the extreme, lead to impediments in our efforts to organize for innovations.

Current State of Research Related to the Model

As we noted before, scholars have not built on Usher's work as much as they have on Schumpeter's. Even those who have built on Usher's work (e.g., Rosenberg 1976; Ruttan 1959) draw on broader facets of innovation and technological change, probably because Usher, as a historian, was writing about changes over larger periods of time. But fewer scholars have explored how Usher's model can serve as the microfoundations for innovation as process, and how such a view informs organizing for innovation. It is one of the reasons why we decided to write this chapter.

We refer to our own work to illustrate the promise that Usher's model holds for innovation as process. For instance, building on the "ongoingness" of the process of cumulative synthesis, we have conceptualized innovation, not as a series of stages and phases from discovery to commercialization, but instead as an ongoing process wherein the functionality of materials and the identities of the people involved are materialized as the process unfolds (Garud et al., 2017). In this work, we go beyond innovation as a complex adaptive process occurring through the recombination of assets to also think of innovation as complex relational and temporal processes. The latter approaches (i.e., relational and temporal processes) progressively endogenize contexts and time to provide a flat ontology. No longer do we need to think of novel ideas having to somehow escape pre-existing selection environments (implicit in an evolutionary perspective), as the notion of relationality suggests the possibility of evaluation criteria emerging in and through the interactions between multiple sets of actors, including regulators and other institutional actors (see Garud and Karnøe 2003). From a temporal perspective, no longer do we need to make a distinction between the past, present, and the future, as innovation involves all three moments for the actors involved (Garud et al. 2017).

A second paper of ours illuminates other facets of Usher's work (Garud and Turunen 2017). In this paper (titled *The banality of organizational innovation*), we make a case for why it is important to think of innovation as an everyday mundane activity that draws upon organizational resources even while transforming them. These observations resonate with Usher's ideas such as: "Acts of insight thus occur in the normal course of the exercise of skills," and "Uncritical observation of behavior is likely to give too little stress to elements of novelty in acts of skill, and to present inventive acts of insight as completely unconditioned, isolated actions."

In addition, in our paper on the banality of innovation, we make the case that innovation as a process is distributed and decentered, an observation that resonates with Usher's comment:

> Social activity involves an interweaving of acts of skill with interspersed acts of insight. No particular field should be presumed to involve a single type of action. The term "innovator," as applied by Schumpeter to the entrepreneur, suggests a kind of differentiation from inventors in the technical fields that is likely to be misleading. Executives, like technicians, must be presumed to perform many acts of skill, and likewise to achieve many acts of insight and invention.

Finally, we also argue for *kariotic* time (i.e., eureka moments) and *aionic* time (i.e., taking a longer cyclical notion of time) besides *chronological* time. Taking such a durational view resonates with Usher's point:

> The research organizations of many corporations today provide a certain amount of free time for the personal projects and interests of the research worker. In some corporations, too, the general program of the staff includes many basic or primary problems not expected to yield immediate commercial results.

An Example of Usher's Model in Practice

Usher's model is based on insights that he derived from a careful analysis of the events that unfolded during the development and deployment of multiple mechanical innovations. These innovations include, among others, the water wheel and windmills, water clocks and mechanical clocks, printing, textiles, power, and machine tools. Because Usher described the events underlying these innovations in great detail, we encourage readers of Usher's work to appreciate how his model applies in practice.

As noted earlier, although Usher's descriptions are located at the technological level, his model holds great promise for how firms might organize for innovation. To illustrate the applicability of this model in practice, we provide details of the development and deployment of the Post-it® Notes at 3M Corporation. We begin by quoting Spence Silver, a person who played an important role in the development and deployment of Post-it Notes at 3M:

> In the course of the exploration I tried an experiment with one of the monomers in which I wanted to see what would happen if I put a lot of it into the reaction mixture. Before we had used amounts that would correspond to conventional wisdom. The key to the Post-it® adhesive was doing this experiment. If I had really seriously cracked the books and gone through the literature, I would have stopped. The literature was full of examples that said you can't do this.

In these reflections, we can see the makings of an act of primary insight described by the person who stumbled on a substance that eventually became Post-it Notes. Several points stand out in this quote. First, Silver was a skilled chemist, and a curious one at that. This curiosity is what drove him to experiment with the chemicals "to see what would happen if I put a lot of it into the reaction mixture." And, when something unexpected and strange happened, Silver did not throw away the substance, but instead kept it because he found it beautiful when he looked at it under the microscope. In other words, Silver was ripe (or poised) for the discovery, with the act of insight occurring not despite but because of his skills.

"When you realized that your adhesive was impermanent, did you consider the experiment a failure?" an interviewer asked Silver, to which he responded, "They want to call it 'a mistake that worked'. I like to think of it as a solution that was looking for a problem to solve." Based on this observation, we see a critical difference between what happened in the Post-it Notes case and the processes underlying Usher's model. To recapitulate, for Usher, the perception of an unsatisfactory pattern or an unfulfilled want is the trigger for an innovation. However, here we see that the innovation did not emerge because of a perception of an unsatisfactory pattern or an unfulfilled want, but instead because of a perception of a potential opportunity based on exapting uses for a discovery for which there was no immediate unfulfilled want (Garud et al. 2018). In other words, this innovation represents "solution-driven" and not "problem-driven" search.

Here, we connect with "abduction" as a key driver of solution-driven search. As we and others (e.g., Bartel and Garud 2003, Dougherty 2016, Garud et al. 2011, Sætre and Van de Ven 2019) have argued, actors other than those involved in a discovery often are key to finding functionality for such novelty. As these "others" view the novel items from their frames of reference (Pinch and Bijker 1987), (new) utility for a discovery emerges.

The exaptation that occurs through such interpretive flexibility is an abductive process, one that places novelty in the contexts of use.

One might wonder how the stage was set for this act of insight to occur. At any other company, the discovery of a substance that was counter to what was required (in this case a strong glue) would have been discarded. But not at 3M. In this company at the time of the discovery, many narratives of innovation celebrating the instincts of 3M's intrapreneurs on the commercial utility of their primary acts of insight were in circulation. Moreover, the environment at 3M itself was ripe with possibility as the company was founded on and continues operating on a way to organize for novel ideas including "mistakes" that can be combined with other resources to be developed for commercial purposes.

Silver had intimate knowledge of the field besides knowledge of the resources available at 3M, partly because of the repository of narratives of innovation that had accumulated over the years at the corporation. Inspired by these narratives, Silver decided to internally "crowdsource" his discovery. For instance, in answer to a question *Whom did you tell?* Silver responded: "Anyone who would listen."

Silver's discursive actions set off a sequence of events enabled by two facets of 3M's experimental culture. First was "bootlegging," a 3M meme encouraging intrapreneurs to use any of the company's idle resources to test out their pet projects. As Fry noted:

> At 3M we've got so many different types of technology operating and so many experts and so much equipment scattered here and there, that we can piece things together when we're starting off. We can go to this place and do 'Step A' on a product, and we can make the adhesive and some of the raw materials here, and do one part over here, and another part over there, and convert a space there and make a few things that aren't available.
>
> (Nayak and Ketteringham 1986: 66–7)

The second facet of the company that shaped the events that unfolded in the Post-it Notes case was 3M's 15% rule. Broadly translated, the 15% rule allows 3M employees (especially researchers) an opportunity to use some portion of their time to explore pet projects in the company's interest. It was this time (*kairotic* time, in our terms) that Silver used, and it was this time that he tapped into from the others that he approached through his narratives.

Bootlegging 3M resources, Silver and his colleagues began developing different kinds of prototypes (at one point, the adhesive was coated on the surface of a bulletin board). In other words, they engaged in experimentation. As Silver theorized about the practice of innovation at 3M, the process of emergence of the Post-it Notes was "more like a slow crescendo of things, which is typical of the discovery process. Things build up and you begin to see the options the discovery creates" (From Lindhal 1988: 14).

While these experiments were not successful, neither were they considered as failures by 3M employees. Instead, the experiments made it possible to keep the idea alive as various actors continued exploring a use for this strange glue during their 15% time (see

Garud and Nayyar [1994] for the value of keeping ideas alive as real options). Keeping the idea alive despite its non-success resonates with Usher's observation that we summarized earlier: "Failures are thus of explicit historical importance. They are not solutions, but they are not without relation to a solution. They reveal explicit consciousness of the potentialities of some new mode of action, or of some new contrivance."

The idea was kept alive for many years (by one estimate 12 years), which also speaks of the value of cultivating a diachronic temporal frame (i.e., cultivating an idea as an option over *aionic* time to make it possible to identify value for something that does not have immediate value). Indeed, it is because of the notion of time implicit in narratives (Ricœur 1984) where the future is constituted by looking at the past (as aptly captured by "Back to the Future", the title of an article on 3M) that an idea does not disappear. Instead, it lingers on as generative memory, interlaced across the circulating innovation stories (one 3Mer informed us that 90% of the innovation is accomplished by looking at the past). It is in this way that Art Fry, another scientist at 3M, remembered the strange glue when he encountered an *unsatisfactory pattern* (in Usher's terms)—the page markers of his hymn book would fall off during church choir practice. At that moment, Fry remembered Silver's glue that did not hold fast and, in a flash of insight, realized that it could be used on paper to serve as place markers.

Many tend to credit Art Fry with the discovery of Post-it Notes, but not Fry himself. Resonating with Usher's observation that any act of insight is based on other prior acts, both strategic and mundane, Fry noted:

> There are so many hoops that a product idea has to jump through. It really takes a bunch of individuals to carry it through the process. It's not just a Spence Silver or an Art Fry. It's a whole host of people. It's a classic 3M tale. I couldn't have done what I did without Silver. And without me, his adhesive might have come to nothing.
> (From Lindhal 1988: 17)

Similarly, when asked if Fry's insight was the culmination of the process, Silver responded, "Well, no. Then we started to deal with issues such as how to make large quantities of the adhesive, how to make a notepad, package it, market it, sell it. After the Post-it Note caught on in the marketplace, I guess then the rest was history." Indeed, the translation of Fry's idea into reality required multiple additional secondary and tertiary innovations such as the careful reformulation of the material so that it would have the specific level of stickiness to act as an "impermanently permanent" marker.

In addition, and very much consistent with Usher's observations on acts of insight required by engineers and technicians and the administrative staff of an enterprise (who Usher would consider as inventor–entrepreneurs as opposed to scientific-entrepreneurs such as Silver or Fry), critical revision and mastery required many secondary and tertiary innovations. These include the redesign of machine tools to allow for the mass scale manufacturing of paper with glue stuck on one side, and the reconceptualization of the practices followed in the corporate suites where it was felt that the product would be used most. What transpired with the Post-it Notes as explained by Nayak and Ketteringham (1986) is consistent with Usher's observations on the many additional innovations involved to deal with the social and technical difficulties before the widespread diffusion of an early act of insight.

Future Research and Methodological Implications

How might we investigate innovation as process to the extent that innovation journeys are decentered and distributed with many acts of insight occurring when actors are engaged in acts of skill? To offer some ideas, we draw upon Czarniawska's (2004) work on *Time, space and action-nets*. First, just like us, Czarniawska made a distinction between *chronos* and *kairos* noting that most actors provide chronological accounts of organizing but seldom reflect on the *kairotic* moments. Bringing *chronos* and *kairos* together, she noted "chronological accounts serve as raw materials for kairotically organized narratives" (Czarniawska 2004: 776). By this she meant rendering events relevant ("important or unimportant" in her words).

Complementing these observations on time, Czarniawska then turned her attention to space. Borrowing the concept of "centers of calculation" from the Science and Technology Studies (STS) literature (e.g., Latour 1987), she observed that multiple centers of calculation exist in an organization, and that the calculations that these centers engage in may be inconsistent with one another. Moreover, a calculation from one center can set in motion calculations across other centers. For instance, she observed that financial adjustments that were to be made because of calculations emerging from the budget meeting of the Department of Environment of a Swedish company filtered across other departments of the organization, triggering in their wake additional calculations. Eventually, from this experience and other studies, she concluded that calculation itself is dispersed and decentered.

Combining the two observations on time and space, Czarniawska offered the notion of "action nets." Action nets are interconnected sets of activities driven by people in specific places pursuing specific issues that become enmeshed to generate events. In order to grasp the practice of organizing, Czarniawska argued, it was not enough to study single events, as each event is related to others. Indeed, events take on meaning by connecting them with one another, a task that is accomplished through "story making."

These observations provide one way for exploring the methodological implications of Usher's model for a theory of innovation as an ongoing process. For instance, as with "story making," we have argued that the creation, use, and performation of innovation narratives offers one way to foster innovation as a decentered and distributed process (Bartel and Garud 2009). Not only does the accumulation of innovation narratives that emerge generate a collective consciousness of events (Turunen 2014), it also serves as an impetus for making sense of unusual events that can serve as triggers for acts of insights (Garud et al. 2011).

Resonating with these points, we return to 3M Corporation, a company that has survived and grown on innovation for more than a century. By institutionalizing narratives of innovation journeys, 3M has created a narrative infrastructure that not only memorializes past innovations, but also provides a springboard from which to generate new ways of navigating (and even encouraging) unusual experiences. This accomplishment is made possible by stories and narratives, as is evident in this observation offered by 3M employees:

> Stories are a habit of mind at 3M, and it's through them—through the way they make us see ourselves and our business operations in complex, multi-dimensional forms—that we're able to discover opportunities for strategic change.
>
> (Shaw et al. 1998)

Methodologically, then, to explore innovation as process, one approach is to follow the narratives, both made and in-the-making. Doing so affords several benefits. First, it allows us to understand innovation processes and organizational processes relationally in a part–whole fashion (Van de Ven 1986). Because of intertextuality, these stories are holons wherein the part (each story) contains the whole (the repository of stories that constitute organizational processes and its very culture), and the whole contains the parts.

Second, it allows us to see multiple notions of time implicated in innovation narratives. The chronological view is readily understandable given that many "plotted" stories have a beginning, a middle, and an ending. But, narratives have other notions of time embedded in them (Ricœur, 1984). For instance, it is in the narratives that people offer that we can also understand their temporal orientations—are they future oriented, past oriented, present oriented, or a combination thereof? Besides affording the ability to investigate these temporal orientations, narratives also allow us to explore *kairotic* and *aionic* notions of time. For instance, how are moments of eureka characterized? And, how are these moments informed by the time frames (i.e., durations that include the past, present, and the future) that actors take?

Third, by combining relationality and temporality (as noted above), these narratives allow us to explore the meanings that actors accord to their experiences. As Bruner (1991) noted, it is through narratives that individuals generate meaning. Correspondingly, Clandinin and Connelly (2000: 60, 189) provide what it means to analyze narratives narratively:

> Narrative inquiry is the study of experience, and experience as John Dewey taught, is a matter of people in relation contextually and temporally. Participants are in relation, and we as researchers are in relation to participants. Narrative inquiry is an experience of an experience. It is people in relation studying with people in relation.

In their view, narrative inquiry is a three-dimensional inquiry space wherein "…our terms are *personal* and *social* (interaction); *past*, *present*, and *future* (continuity); combined with the notion of *place* (situation)" (Clandinin and Connelly (2000: 50), emphasis in the original).

Van den Daele (1969) offers another way to analyze these narratives of innovations. Using set theory, Van den Daele (1969) developed a vocabulary to explore developmental patterns within and across individuals. To create this vocabulary, Van den Daele noted three dimensions of sequences based on *between-person differences*, *within-person differences*, and *relations of developmental elements*. Within each dimension, there are different kinds of progressions. Specifically, between-person differences are manifest as *unitary* or *multiple* progressions (with the latter further exhibiting convergent, divergent, or parallel patterns); within-person differences are manifest as being *simple* or *cumulative*; and the relations of developmental elements can be *conjunctive* or *disjunctive*.

This vocabulary, with some modifications, offers a more formal way to explore the non-linear process progressions within and between innovation trajectories and their developmental elements. For instance, one could follow the narratives of innovation to see if progressions are unitary or multiple, simple or cumulative, conjunctive or disjunctive over periods of time. A baseline hypothesis based on Usher's model is that over longer stretches of time (Figures 22.1b), one is likely to see innovation processes as (a) partially convergent/divergent, (b) partially cumulative, and (c) conjunctive. However, if we take smaller stretches of time, specific strands of innovation trajectories may exhibit other sequences. This becomes evident if we analyze narrower stretches of time during the development of the VCR (Figure 22.2).

To the extent they are valid, these hypotheses hold important organizational implications. Not only is there need to manage relational complexity, but also temporal complexity. By the latter we mean that organizations must be able to deal with multiple innovation trajectories and sequences simultaneously in order to remain innovative over the long run. The practices at 3M described here and elsewhere serve as one example of how such organizational arrangements can facilitate the simultaneous existence of multiple temporal patterns and sequences for productive purposes (Garud et al., 2011).

The End of a Beginning

Our objective in writing this chapter was to introduce Usher's model of cumulative synthesis to catalyze a new line of research on innovation processes. For instance, Usher's theorization of acts of insight emerging during the performance of acts of skill lies in contrast to the distinction that has emerged in the literature between exploration and exploitation (March, 1991). This distinction, that is, between exploration and exploitation, has led to considerable research on organizational ambidexterity, which advocates the spatial and temporal separation of the units that explore from the units that exploit (e.g., O'Reilly and Tushman 2013). There is a strand of inquiry in this discourse labeled "contextual ambidexterity" (Gibson and Birkinshaw 2004) that acknowledges the possibility of exploration occurring during exploitation. However, even this strand focuses more on the contexts for such possibilities and not on the micro-processes involved.

We suggest that Usher's model provides new insights on how exploration and exploitation can occur simultaneously. In particular, Usher's model highlights how innovation can be a natural by-product of daily work. But, the genesis of these ideas and their success depends on the extent to which any local effort connects with and builds upon other ongoing efforts distributed all across an organization. As local and global efforts become entangled to yield strategic outcomes, the whole organization is transformed.[10] These are the ingredients of innovation at work, wherein innovation grounded in daily activities and informed by other such activities across organizational boundaries leads to strategic outcomes that transform the organization. Usher's model provides us with some of the ingredients to theorize about how exploration and exploitation can occur simultaneously through such entangled ambidexterity.

[10] Our theorization, which is based on Usher's work, provides a complementary perspective to the one that Burke (Chapter 2, this volume) provides on organizational change. Burke argues for "organization" rather than "organizational" change in "today's fast-paced world [where] change is a constant and expansive with significant variation at the same time." In such a world, Burke argues that "Change is complex, affects the organization more as a whole than in pieces and parts, and comes from an organization's external environment more than from within." We agree with Burke that today's world is fast paced. In such a world, we cannot just rely on the external environment to act as a stimulus, but must set the stage for organizational elements to continually generate mundane innovation that can be synthesized to yield strategic innovations. And, during the process, the organizational elements and the connections between them are transformed, just as in the case of the Greek myth where Theseus' ship was transformed plank by plank even as it sailed.

References

Andriani, P., and Cattani G. (2016), 'Exaptation as Source of Creativity, Innovation, and Diversity: Introduction to the Special Section', *Industrial and Corporate Change* 25/1, 115–31.

Bartel, C. A., and Garud. R. (2003), 'Adaptive Abduction as a Mechanism for Generalizing from Narratives', in M. Easterby-Smith, and M. Lyles, eds, *Handbook of Organizational Learning and Knowledge* (Oxford: Blackwell), 324–42.

Bartel, C. A., and Garud, R. (2009), 'The Role of Narratives in Sustaining Organizational Innovation', *Organization Science*, 20, 107–17.

Bruner, J. S. (1991), 'The Narrative Construction of Reality', *Critical Inquiry*, 18/1, 1–21.

Burke, W. W. (2021), 'Historical Currents in Scholarship of Organization Change', in M. S. Poole and A. H. Van de Ven, eds., *The Oxford Handbook of Organizational Change and Innovation* (2nd edn) (Oxford: Oxford University Press),

Campbell, D. T. (1960), 'Blind Variation and Selective Retentions in Creative Thought as in other Knowledge Processes', *Psychological Review*, 67/6, 380–400.

Clandinin, D. J. and Connelly, F. M. (2000), *Narrative Inquiry: Experience and Story in Qualitative Research* (San Francisco, CA: Jossey-Bass).

Coyne, W. E. (1999), 'Foreword', in A. H. Van de Ven, D. E. Polley, R. Garud, and S. Venkataraman, eds., *The Innovation Journey* (New York: Oxford University Press), vii–viii.

Czarniawska, B. (2004), 'On Time, Space, and Action Nets', *Organization*, 11/6, 773–91.

Dougherty, D. (2016), *Taking Advantage of Emergence: Productively Innovating in Complex Innovation Systems* (Oxford: Oxford University Press).

Emirbayer, M, and Mische, A. (1998), 'What Is Agency?' *American Journal of Sociology* 103, 962–1023.

Garud, R., Dunbar, R. L., and Bartel, C. A. (2011), 'Dealing with Unusual Experiences: A Narrative Perspective on Organizational Learning', *Organization Science*, 22, 587–601.

Garud, R., Gehman, J., and Giuliani, A. P. (2018), 'Serendipity Arrangements for Exapting Science-Based Innovations', *Academy of Management Perspectives*, 32/1, 125–40.

Garud, R., Gehman, J., and Kumaraswamy. A. (2011), 'Complexity Arrangements for Sustaining Innovation: Lessons from 3M Corporation', *Organization Studies* 32/6, 737–67.

Garud, R., Gehman, J., Kumaraswamy, A., and Tuertscher, P. (2017), 'From the Process of Innovation to Innovation as Process', in A. Langley and H. Tsoukas, *The Sage Handbook of Process Organization Studies* (London: Sage), 451–65.

Garud, R., and Karnøe, P. (2003), 'Bricolage vs. Breakthrough: Distributed and Embedded Agency in Technology Entrepreneurship', *Research Policy*, 32/2, 277–300.

Garud, R., and Nayyar, P. (1994), 'Transformative Capacity: Continual Structuring by Inter-Temporal Technology Transfer', *Strategic Management Journal*, 15/5, 365–85.

Garud, R., Tuertscher, P., and Van de Ven, A. H. (2013), 'Perspectives on Innovation Processes', *Academy of Management Annals*, 7/1, 773–817.

Garud, R., and Turunen, M. (2017), 'The Banality of Organizational Innovations: Embracing the Substance-Process Duality', *Innovation: Organization & Management*, 19/1, 31–8.

Gibson, J. J. (1979), *The Ecological Approach to Visual Perception* (Boston: Houghton Mifflin).

Gibson, C. B., and Birkinshaw, J. (2004), 'The Antecedents, Consequences and Mediating Role of Organizational Ambidexterity', *Academy of Management Journal*, 47/2, 209–26.

Hallett, T., and Ventresca, M. J. (2006), 'Inhabited Institutions: Social Interactions and Organizational Forms in Gouldner's Patterns of Industrial Bureaucracy', *Theory and Society*, 35/2, 213–36.

Ingold, T. (2014), 'The Creativity of Undergoing', *Pragmatics & Cognition*, 22/1, 24–139.

Ingold, T. (2019), 'Evolution without inheritance: Steps to an ecology of learning'. University of Aberdeen Working paper.

Ingold, T. (2000), *The perception of the environment: essays on livelihood, dwelling and skill.* (London: Routledge).

Ingold, T. (2001), 'From the transmission of representations to the education of attention'. In *The debated mind: evolutionary psychology versus ethnography*, ed. H. Whitehouse. (Oxford: Berg), 113–53.

Irvine, J., and Martin, B. R. (1984), *Foresight in Science: Picking the Winners* (Dover, NH: Pinter).

Johnson, V., and Powell, W. W. (2017), 'Poisedness and Propagation: Organizational Emergence and the Transformation of Civic Order in 19th-Century New York City', in N. R. Lamoreaux and John Joseph Wallis, eds., *Organizations, Civil Society, and the Roots of Development*. National Bureau of Economic Research (Chicago: University of Chicago Press), 179–230.

Koestler, A. (1964), *The Act of Creation* (New York: The Macmillan Company).

Köhler, W. (1925), *The Mentality of Apes* (NY: Harcourt, Brace & Company Inc.).

Langley, A., Smallman, C., Tsoukas, H., and Van de Ven, A. H. (2013), 'Process Studies of Change in Organization and Management: Unveiling Temporality, Activity, and Flow', *Academy of Management Journal*, 56/1, 1–13.

Latour, B. (1987), *Science in Action: How to Follow Scientists and Engineers through Society* (Cambridge, MA: Harvard University Press).

Lindhal, L. (1988), 'Spence Silver: A Scholar and a Gentleman', *3M Today*, January 1988, 15/1, 12–17.

March, J. G. (1991), Exploration and Exploitation in Organizational Learning', *Organization Science*, 2/1, 71–87.

Merton, R. K., and Barber, E. (2004), *The Travels and Adventures of Serendipity* (Princeton, NJ: Princeton University Press).

Mohr, L. B. (1982), *Explaining Organizational Behavior: The Limits and Possibilities of Theory and Research* (San Francisco, CA: Jossey-Bass).

Morgeson, F. P., Mitchell, T. R., and Liu, D. (2015), 'Event System Theory: An Event-Oriented Approach to the Organizational Sciences', *Academy of Management Review*, 40/4, 515–37.

Nayak, A., Chia, R., and Canales, J. I. (2019), 'Non-Cognitive Microfoundations: Understanding Dynamic Capabilities as Idiosyncratically Refined Sensitivities and Predispositions', *Academy of Management Review*, 45/2, 280–303.

Nayak, P. R., and Ketteringham, J. M. (1986), *Breakthroughs!* (New York: Rawson Associates).

Ogden, R. M. (1926), *Psychology and Education* (London: Routledge).

O'Reilly, C., and Tushman, M. (2013), 'Organizational Ambidexterity: Past, Present and Future', *Academy of Management Perspectives*, 27/4, 324–38.

Pinch, T. J., and Bijker, W. E. (1987), 'The Social Construction of Facts and Artifacts: Or How the Sociology of Science and the Sociology of Technology Might Benefit Each Other', in W. E. Bijker, T. P. Hughes, and T. J. Pinch, eds., *Social Construction of Technological Systems* (Cambridge: MIT Press), 17–50

Poggie, G. (1965), 'A Main Theme of Contemporary Sociological Analysis: Its Achievements and Limitations', *British Journal of Sociology*, 16/4, 283–94.

Rescher, N. (1996), *Process Metaphysics: An Introduction to Process Philosophy* (New York: SUNY Press).

Ricœur, P. (1984), *Time and Narrative* (Chicago, IL: University of Chicago Press).

Rosenberg, N. (1976), *Perspectives on Technology* (Cambridge: Cambridge University Press).
Ruttan, V. W. (1959), 'Usher and Schumpeter on Invention, Innovation, and Technological Change', *The Quarterly Journal of Economics*, 73/4, 596–606.
Sætre, A. S., and Van de Ven A. H. (2019), 'Creating theory through abduction', University of Minnesota Working Paper',
Schumpeter, J. (1934), *The Theory of Economic Development* (Cambridge, MA: Harvard University Press).
Shaw, G., Brown, R., and Bromiley, P. (1998), 'Strategic Stories: How 3M is Rewriting Business Planning', *Harvard Business Review*, 76, 41–50.
Tarde, G. (1903), *The Laws of Imitation* (New York, NY: Henri Holt and Company).
Tsoukas, H., and Chia, R. (2002), 'On Organizational Becoming: Rethinking Organizational Change', *Organization Science*, 13/5, 567–82.
Turunen, M. (2014), 'Consciousness View of Organizations', in D. Boje and T. Wakefield, eds., *Being Quantum: Ontological Storytelling in the Age of Antenarrative* (Newcastle Upon Tyne, UK, Cambridge Scholars Publishing), 385–403.
Usher, A. P. [1929] (1954), *A History of Mechanical Inventions* (Cambridge, MA: Harvard University Press).
Usher, A. P. (1955), 'Technical Change and Capital Formation', in *Capital Formation and Economic Growth* (Princeton, NJ: Princeton University Press), 523–50.
Van de Ven, A. H. (1986), 'Central Problems in the Management of Innovation', *Management Science*, 32/5, 590–607.
Van de Ven, A. H., Polley, D., and Garud, R. (1999), *The Innovation Journey* (Oxford: Oxford University Press).
Van de Ven, A. H., and Poole, M. S. (1990), 'Methods for Studying Innovation Development in the Minnesota Innovation Research Program', *Organization Science*, 1/3, 313–35.
Van de Ven, A. H., and Poole, M. S. (1995), Explaining Development and Change in Organizations', *Academy of Management Review*, 20(3), 510–40.
Van de Ven, A. H., and Poole, M. S. (2005), 'Alternative Approaches for Studying Organizational Change', *Organization Studies*, 26/9, 1377–404.
Van den Daele, L. D. (1969), 'Qualitative Models in Developmental Analysis', *Developmental Psychology*, 1/4, 303–10.

CHAPTER 23

DIFFUSION OF INNOVATIONS

JAMES W. DEARING

INTRODUCTION

FEW social science paradigms have a history of conceptual and empirical study as long as does the diffusion of innovations. The robustness of the diffusion research and practice paradigm derives from the many disciplines and fields of study in which diffusion has been studied, from the international richness of many of these studies, and from the variety of new ideas, practices, programs, policies, and technologies that have been the objects of diffusion research. Early theorizing from the 1890s was gradually displaced by post hoc empirical research that described and explained diffusion processes. By the 1950s, diffusion researchers had begun to apply the collective knowledge learned about naturalistic diffusion in tests of process interventions to affect the rate of innovation adoption by individuals. The paradigm's strength in being able to reliably associate micro-level (individual-level) change with macro-level (community or societal) change has more recently been augmented with a dedicated focus on the mezzo-level of organizations and the professions that tie them together, especially in health services research (Dearing and Cox 2018).

WHY ARE WE STILL WRITING—AND READING—ABOUT THE DIFFUSION OF INNOVATIONS?

The diffusion research and practice paradigm has always brought together a number of ideas. There is *innovation* as a general desired state to which companies, governments, cities, and nations seem to strive. There is *an* innovation as that which is perceived to be new by a potential adopter and that, if adopted, achieves routine status before it is unceremoniously displaced. There is *innovativeness* as a categorical measure of time to adoption for individuals as innovators, early adopters, early majority, late majority, and laggards and, in organizations, of the organizational characteristics that correlate with *being innovative*.

There is the reality of uncertainty and cognitive dissonance and decision heuristics and bounded rationality and imitation, all of which contribute to the not infrequent adoption of ineffective innovations and the dismissal of worthy ones as decisions are made on the basis of who has already adopted, rather than waiting to learn whether an innovation works and is a good fit for an organization. There is time, and in studies of diffusion, usually a lot of it as most potential adopters enact psychological and sociological barriers to resist innovations (and sometimes for good reason). There are the many studies about receptivity to innovations and individual, organizational, and community readiness assessments. There is social system modeling to understand either mathematically or through simulation how variations and perturbations in the system affect measures of rate of adoption and reach of innovations, as well as demonstrations of how new media can give rise to convex rather than S-shaped curves. There are organizational fields, ecologic communities and—most promising for diffusion interventionists—societal sectors and the networks that tie them together (Scott and Meyer 1991), the former comprised of heterophilous organizations, the latter made up of homophilous organizations.

There is the common occurrence in organizations that innovative activity is very often at odds with diffusion; that is, that teams and units within organizations are encouraged to be creative and experiment and invent and are rewarded for such, all of which leads them to avoid, discount, and reject the evidence-based practices, programs, policies, and technologies from other teams and units, including those from within their own organization. There are the attributes of innovations and the long trail of studies about variance explained, knowledge-practice gaps and how channels of communication differentially function and figure at different points in the adoption–decision process. There are the burgeoning literatures about personal and impersonal influence, social norms, and opinion leadership. And then there are the rapidly growing literatures about innovation fidelity and adaptation, scale-up pathways and strategies, and organizational implementation and sustainability.

All in all, it's a lot. As D. Lawrence Kincaid summed up in 2004,

> The comprehensive nature of the model is one of its strengths and perhaps it[sic] primary weakness, leading to considerable confusion and criticism from those who use it as well as those who use alternative frameworks. Part of the problem is that the DOI is not a single theory but, rather, a model, framework, or paradigm large enough to drive a truckload of supporting theories through, including all existing theories of persuasion, knowledge acquisition, social learning, interpersonal communication and influence, social change, utilization of knowledge, and so forth (p. 37).

Theoretic and conceptual diversity within the paradigm has also meant methodological pluralism. Event history analysis sits alongside rhetorical analysis, archival analysis, simulation, case study research, survey research, social network analysis, and historical research, all in the service of the flowering of the paradigm's topical foci themselves: piracy and privateering as obstacles to the diffusion of sailing ship technology in the 1600s and 1700s (Walton 1970–1971); recommended practices for Rhode Island potato farmers (Spaulding 1955); radio broadcasting and the structuring of a diffusion system for popular music (Rossman 2012) and the global diffusion of jazz (Phillips 2013); diffusion of military weapons and warfare (Goldman and Eliason 2003); hysteria contagion within an organization (Kerckhoff et al. 1965); the diffusion of coal mine strikes in early twentieth-century France (Conell and Cohn 1995); and mosquito control in contemporary West Africa (Smith et al. 2018); creation of a diffusion extension system for primary care providers (Ono et al. 2018); and the diffusion of public management reforms (Wallis and Goldfinch 2013); the need for knowledge-sharing systems in organizations (O'Dell and Grayson 1998); and the diffusion of tobacco control across a continent (Studlar 1999); managerial fads and fashions (Abrahamson 1991; Abrahamson and Eisenman 2008); mechanized arm recycling trucks (Baer et al. 1977); golden parachutes (Fiss et al. 2012); kindergartens (Wollons 2000), and even democracy (Wejnert 2014).

In this chapter, I review the main concepts in this hybrid change paradigm that blends ideas that can be found in life cycle, evolutionary, and teleological theories of social change (Van de Ven and Poole 1995) and discuss why the paradigm developed in the ways that it did, including the shortcomings of this approach for studying the role of organizations in change processes. I attend to the rapid rise of studies of organizational implementation of innovations, which was long overlooked by diffusion scholars who were studying individuals rather than organizations as the units of adoption (Van de Ven and Rogers 1988), and studies of inter-organizational diffusion, and how a recognition of the activity of adopters and implementers is reshaping diffusion study, particularly as conducted by health services and public health researchers. Recognizing the agency of both those stakeholders who seek to spread innovations and of the eventual adopters and implementers in organizations is a way of seeing diffusion processes as translational processes (Latour 1986; Czarniawska and Sevon 2005). This applied, socially relevant use of diffusion concepts is a way for the diffusion paradigm, like the field of organizational studies, to amount to more than simply "a sprawling structure" (Davis 2015: 181). The paradigm has already proven useful conceptually and practically, for scholars and practitioners. Yet its potential still lies ahead as an organizing set of ideas and questions for structuring inquiry and guiding improvement in how organizational members go about their work. Twenty-five years ago, Everett Rogers was right when he wrote "[W]e do not need 'more of the same' diffusion research" (Rogers 1995).

The Classical Diffusion Paradigm

Diffusion is a social process that occurs among people in response to learning about an innovation such as a new belief, practice, program, policy, or technology. In its classical formulation, diffusion involves (1) an innovation that (2) is communicated through certain channels (3) over time (4) among the members of a social system (Rogers 2003). The typical dependent variable in diffusion research is time of adoption, though when complex organizations are the adopters, subsequent implementation is a more meaningful measure of change. Diffusion can be assessed among individuals and collectives including organizations, cities, states, and countries. When diffusion occurs and time of adoption data are graphed cumulatively, an S-shaped curve is common as the enthusiastic first to adopt are not closely followed by credible others with more to lose and who are more attentive to prior results as a basis for decision-making. If opinion leaders signal favorability, then this initial slow rate of adoption gives way to a cascade of adoptions, marked as a rapidly accelerating rate, which then slows as fewer and fewer skeptical non-adopters remain within the social system in question.

Figure 23.1 depicts this over-time process as a solid, dark S-shaped curve. Figure 23.1 also suggests the contextual realities not studied by most diffusion scholars, that (1) the vast majority of innovations fail to diffuse, (2) those innovations that do diffuse also decline in use, and (3) innovations exist in a dynamic competitive environment in which proponents of one innovation compete with the proponents of other innovations for the attention of potential adopters (proponents also effectively compete with themselves as subsequent products and services are marketed to displace prior adopted versions).

Not all instances of diffusion play out this way. Sometimes, the pressure to imitate by itself is sufficient to propel diffusion (Abrahamson 1991). Other times, the innovation in question is so inconsequential to how adopters work or live that they do not bother with social confirmation; they just adopt (this is how so-called social media often function, to alert individuals to new information so that "adoption" merely means knowing or sometimes believing). For other sorts of innovations such as government policies, time-to-adoption can be more rapid due to agenda-setting factors such as catastrophes, media

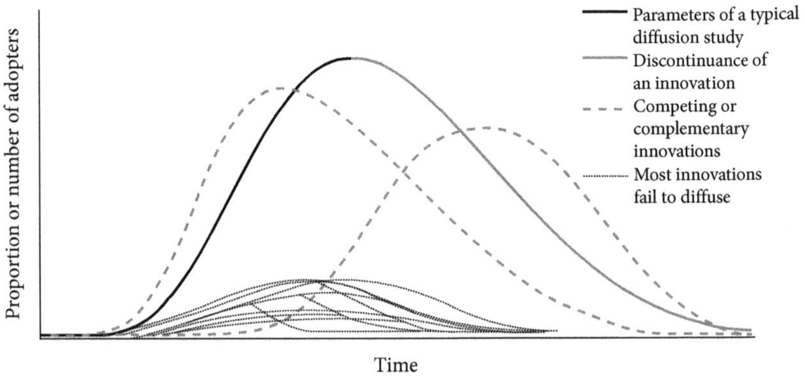

FIGURE 23.1 As shown in the solid dark line, diffusion typically begins with a slow rate of adoption that is followed by a rapid escalation, after which rate of adoption slows as saturation of the innovation in the social system is neared

coverage, political addresses, readiness for change among elected officials, motivated and active groups, and an innovative solution that is perceived positively (Boushey 2010). Often it is the focusing and framing by well-connected policy entrepreneurs that convinces decision-makers that the time has come to adopt a solution to a problem (Kingdon 1984; Mintrom and Norman 2009).

In the case of voluntary adoption decisions, acceleration in the rate of diffusion is usually the result of influential members of the social system making the decision to adopt, and their decision being communicated to others who then observe and follow their lead. Still, diffusion is an atypical outcome, since the vast majority of innovations fail to diffuse, never accelerating up an S-shaped curve (Lomas 1991; Berwick 2003). This can be a wholly warranted result since the definition of an *innovation* is simply that which is perceived to be new by potential adopters, not something that is necessarily better. Unworthy innovations sometimes diffuse, and effective innovations are sometimes stymied.

Over time through waves of innovations, diffusion changes societies. Sometimes these changes manifest as differences in knowledge, disproportionate access to government and commercial services, and worsening inequality because resource-rich organizations, communities, and states tend to adopt innovations early relative to poorer ones (Buchanan et al. 2011). A study of forty-four criminal justice policies and their diffusion from 1960 to 2008 shows that states are more likely to adopt policies that benefit privileged segments of the population and weaken marginalized segments (Boushey 2016). Fortunately, diffusion concepts can be operationalized to stimulate the spread of innovations specifically in low-resource settings (Green et al. 1991), a strategy known as *designing for diffusion* (Dearing et al. 2013).

Diffusion or the lack thereof is often well explained by three general sets of variables: (1) Each innovation's set of pros and cons, or *attributes*, (2) characteristics of adopters, especially potential adopter perceptions of earlier others' reactions, or *social influence*, and (3) the larger social and political *context* including issue salience, how proponents and opponents frame the meaning of an innovation, and the timing of its introduction. Perhaps unsurprisingly, given its many concepts and application by scholars in many fields, diffusion studies have helped to form the basis for a number of other areas of study (Estabrooks et al. 2008), such as dissemination and implementation science in health (Norton et al. 2017).

When an individual learns about an innovation that they think may have important consequences for them or for those they serve, uncertainty about how to respond typically leads to a search for further information so the potential adopter can better assess whether the innovation's attributes warrant further exploration. These pros and cons are rather well codified, especially:

- *Cost*, the perceived monetary, time, or other resource expense of adopting and implementing an innovation
- *Effectiveness*, the extent to which the innovation is perceived to work better than that which it will displace

- *Simplicity*, how easy the innovation is to understand and use
- *Compatibility*, the fit of the innovation to established ways of accomplishing the same goal
- *Observability*, the extent to which outcomes can be seen, and
- *Trialability*, the extent to which the adoption decision is reversible or can be staged

Whether individuals engage in such a cost/benefit assessment or not, if the innovation continues to seem promising and consequential to them, they may engage in a secondary search for the evaluative judgments of trusted, expert, and accessible others—*opinion leaders*—who are more discriminating and less susceptible to influence (Aral and Walker 2012). The seeking of advice or modeling one's own behavior on what others do is a heuristic, often reflecting an emotional desire for status, that allows the decision-maker to save time while reducing uncertainty.

Needs and motivations differ among people according to their degree of *innovativeness*: Based on a meta-review of empirical studies (Rogers 2003), the first to adopt (*innovators*) tend to do so because of excitement over novelty and feeling unconstrained by social norms; the next to adopt (*early adopters*, some of whom are opinion leaders) do so because of a measured appraisal that an innovation's advantages outweigh its disadvantages; and the subsequent *early and late majorities* adopt because they feel social pressure to adopt. *Laggards* are less susceptible to social pressure (like innovators) and feel free to take their time (Figure 23.2).

Campaigns to spread evidence-based innovations often target particular messages to the degree of innovativeness (or *readiness to change*) of potential adopters on the basis of formative evaluation data. Innovativeness reflects individual *thresholds* for change: Earlier adopters, being more certain of the worth of the innovation, need fewer in their *reference group* to have already adopted to make the decision themselves, whereas later adopters, being more skeptical, wait for more of their contacts to have adopted to in turn adopt (Valente 1995).

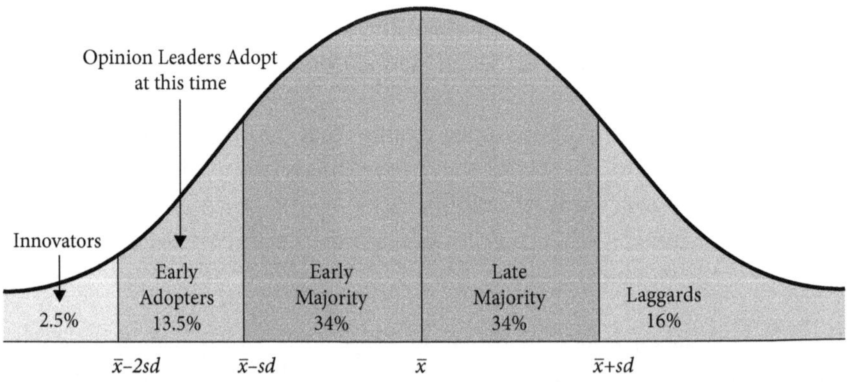

FIGURE 23.2 Units of adoption such as individuals can be grouped according to when relative to each other they adopted an innovation

Motivations and time of adoption can be predicted by each decision-unit's structural position in the network of advice-seeking and advice-giving relationships that tie a social system together, whether organization, community, or virtual network. When viewed sociometrically (who-to-whom) in two-dimensional space (Figure 23.3), the pattern of diffusion often begins on the periphery of a relational network as the first to try the innovation experiment with it; central members of the network—opinion leaders—observe and then adopt if they judge the innovation to have important advantages over current practice; and the many others then follow by paying attention to what highly connected opinion leaders do and advise. This form of social contagion, an outside-inside-outward progression of adoption, when graphed cumulatively, can reflect the S-shaped diffusion curve as in Kerckhoff et al.'s (1965) classic study of interpersonal communication and influence within a textile mill.

Potential adopters also perceive the relevance of innovations when others like themselves adopt—even if they are not relationally connected. This sort of imitative effect can result from having the same job title, same type of employer, common training, same hometown or shared beliefs or practices; all can lead them to reject or adopt innovations since homophilous others have done so. Modelers, forecasters, and experimentalists have spent considerable time testing the effects of both heterogeneous

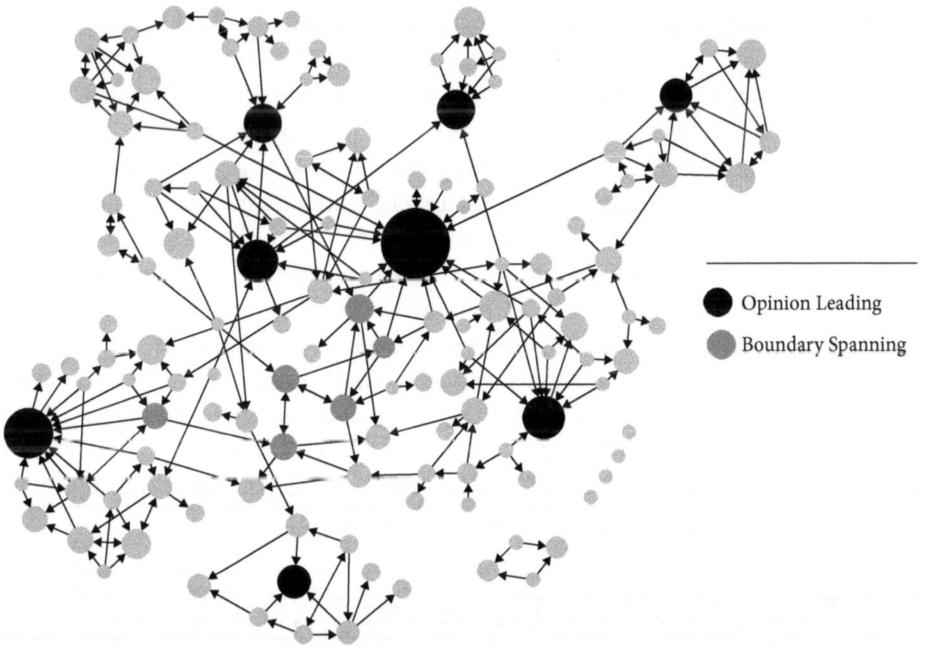

FIGURE 23.3 Sociometric mapping of advice seeking or social modeling in response to learning about an innovation can show how relational structure affects diffusion. This figure suggests the disproportionate nature of influence in which a few opinion-leading organizations affect the adoption decisions of many organizations, groups of which are tied together by boundary spanning organizations.

differences among units of adoption and homophilous characteristics of social system members on the decision to adopt (Meade and Islam, 2006; Centola 2011), showing, for example, that lagged introductions of innovations across countries can actually accelerate diffusion by allowing potential adopters in later-adopting countries to better assess the experiences of early adopters with an innovation (Kumar and Krishnan, 2002).

Dissemination is Not Diffusion

Dissemination activity and diffusion processes are related but distinct. *Dissemination* refers to activities by innovation proponents or intermediaries to inform others of an innovation, often via audience segmentation strategy. Information about an innovation is transmitted or advertised in what is usually a one-to-many process using social, mass, or specialty media channels, though simply making information available is probably more common. Thus, dissemination is an active process for what is usually a small number of individuals who are external to the system that they are attempting to influence. For the audience or potential adopters, the experience is typically a passive one except in those instances when the innovation catches on by eliciting the interest of the most innovative system members. That can be the start of a diffusion process among actual and potential adopters.

Diffusion is a social system response that disseminators hope to elicit. Without the triggering of interest or intrigue, dissemination efforts fail. Even when a lot is done to increase the reach of an innovation by establishing branch offices, licensing affiliate organizations as franchises, or partnering with distribution networks as a pathway to scale (Larson et al. 2017), demand from direct service providers such as clinicians and their patients or grocery stores and their customers is still essential for scale-up success and sustainability (Simmons & Shiffman 2007). So diffusion is a form of social activation that may or may not occur after the dissemination of information or scale up of services or products has occurred. Diffusion is a natural social phenomenon (Kincaid 2004); it can occur without any organized, intentional dissemination. Yet engaging in the dissemination of information and other strategies is not necessarily fruitless as Green et al. (1991) intimate: "Diffusion theory does not lead to the conclusion that one must wait for the diffusion of a new product or practice to reach the poorest people... In fact, one can accelerate the rate of adoption in any segment of the population through more intensive and more appropriate communication and outreach" (p. 114).

Forming the Paradigm and Early Application

The formulation of the social system in the classical model of diffusion, while informed by earlier macro-level perspectives of political philosophers and anthropologists, was set by the paradigmatic activity of rural sociologists who naturally conceived of the geographically defined farm community as the primary social system of interest. Mathematical modelers who studied diffusion sought to contrast external-to-the-community "broadcast" models of diffusion in which mass media and change agents from afar introduced ideas into communities, with internal-to-the-community "contagion" models of diffusion in which strong friendship ties, weak acquaintance ties, structural equivalence (similarity in network position as a basis for expecting similar adoption behaviors and timing), or proximity accounted for diffusion (Strang and Soule 1998).

Trained as a rural sociologist, Everett Rogers, too, conceptualized rural communities as the social systems of study (Rogers grew up on an Iowa farm watching his father *not* adopt innovations, so trying to explain this regressive behavior and in turn perhaps helping to improve farming conditions among poverty-stricken farmers came naturally to the son). Rural sociologists focused on community-level phenomena, on interpersonal networks, and on the boundedness of such social systems. They were open systems to be sure—how couldn't that be acknowledged in the era of television and satellites—but their strength, their resilience to keep out the many worthless innovations and to adapt the few good ones, rested in interpersonal relationships that functioned as very effective filters and gatekeepers—what the prominent sociologist and early diffusion scholar Elihu Katz labeled *interpersonal selectivity* (Katz 1980). If diffusion is about change and destruction and uncertainty, then interpersonal networks and opinion leaders were about stability, normative influence, and the measured appraisal of new ideas. Understanding the social dynamics of community-level systems was a main objective. The diffusion paradigm offered insight into strategies for community capacity building just as it also illustrated the divisive cumulative process by which the haves increasingly left the have-nots behind (Dearing and Meyer 2006), a product of repeated S-shaped "curves" of innovation diffusion among the haves, a social process akin to the great sociologist Robert K. Merton's individual-level concept of *cumulative advantage* (Merton 1968).

To spread agricultural, public health, and educational innovations—and many innovations were a combination of the three—diffusion systems had to be put into place to interact with rural communities. The 1950s, 1960s, and 1970s were decades of huge growth in US federal capacity and expansionism. Thus the diffusion systems were centralized in both administrative control and substantive expertise. Knowledge flowed from this core to the periphery with the objective of lessening the problems of farmers, public health officers, and teachers. The main model for these systems was the agricultural extension service that at the time was heralded for its international successes in crop production increases (the so-called Green Revolution). But the extension service model was expensive. There was not enough money to send change agents to regularly meet with all public health officers and teachers. The agricultural rural sociology lesson about finding and using opinion leaders to influence the decisions of their near-peers got lost at the same time that new information technologies promised so much. Accordingly, some of the dissemination systems that were created looked a lot like clearinghouses of published reports (Hutchinson and Huberman 1993).

So the classical diffusion paradigm found widespread application, both among academicians interested in different types of innovations and among practitioners who perceived the paradigm as a means for spreading solutions to real-world problems, yet it was also changed as it was adapted from agriculture to public health and education and as more efficient dissemination possibilities arose. Problems resulted, too. Criticism became particularly acute concerning international development, where the unintended and undesirable consequences of using the new "evidence-based" innovations were at times devastating to human health and the natural environment (McAnany 1984; Rogers 2003).

Diffusion concepts have been used in large-scale efforts to spread evidence-based practices, programs, and policies in the US off and on for several decades. The National Science Foundation created Teacher Institutes and used commercial publishers to disseminate curricular innovations beginning in the late 1950s and on through the 1980s. The US Department of Education instituted the Project Innovation Packages project, the Pilot State Dissemination Project, the Research and Development Utilization program, the National Diffusion Network (Raizen 1979), and the Educational Resources Information Center Clearinghouse, all in the 1970s, and all deriving part of their rationale from diffusion literature.

The diffusion-based strategy of using demonstrations of innovations as a stimulus for spreading complex and expensive and radical innovations has been widely applied by US agencies. The Atomic Energy Commission Power Reactor Demonstration Program in the 1950s is credited with having speeded commercial adoption of power reactor technology (Baer et al. 1977). The Energy Research and Development Administration demonstrated synthetic fuels. In the 1960s and 1970s, the Environmental Protection Agency demonstrated mechanized refuse collection, refuse firing, resource recovery, and poultry waste-processing technologies. The EPA continues to sponsor demonstrations of waste treatment, recycling, and hazardous waste clean-up technologies through its Superfund Technology Demonstration Division. The Urban Mass Transportation Administration sponsors demonstrations of intelligent highways, van pooling, dial-a-ride, and pedestrian malls. The largest use of demonstrations has been by the Department of Agriculture, through its Extension Service, state experimental stations, and state land-grant colleges. This integrated system made the demonstration of agricultural innovations a central part of a highly successful diffusion system.

In each of these cases of government use of diffusion concepts to spread evidence-based practices, application of diffusion concepts was pursued on a large scale but usually only concerned one or two concepts. A support network of change agents would be created, or innovation attributes would be used in the creation of message content, or peer-to-peer communication would be encouraged, or message content would be tailored to a type of individual's readiness to change, or implementation support would be provided. A notable exception has been the US Extension Service which has long applied multiple diffusion concepts in concert to affect change. Another exception is the Centers for Disease Control and Prevention's contemporary efforts in HIV prevention, the Diffusion of Effective Behavioral Interventions (DEBI) project, that has evolved into an online menu of dozens of evidence-based community-level HIV prevention programs with sufficient detail about each so that potential adopters from other cities can find and try a program that seems well suited to their own community and at-risk population (Collins et al. 2006).

The Active Adopter in the Process of Diffusion

The traditional approach to understanding diffusion processes emphasizes (1) the key generative role of centralized change agencies and those they fund as the sources of innovation, (2) the importance of perceptions by potential adopters of the attributes of an innovation to decrease uncertainty about what the innovation is and can do, and (3) the necessity of personal influence for signaling potential adopters that an innovation should be attended to, that it is consonant with prevailing local social norms, and that it is promising. But prevailing beliefs about how diffusion works are just that; related sets of concepts that have been the objects of study, in some cases considerable study. Researchers working in anthropology, agriculture, sociology, education, and other disciplines have over eight decades rarely studied all aspects of the process of diffusion; rather, they have emphasized those concepts most germane to their discipline (Katz et al. 1963). Yet there are still other ways of explaining the spread of new ideas, even if they are less supported yet through empirical research. Here I review several alternatives to traditional explanations of the diffusion process.

A Rhetorical Perspective on Diffusion. Green (2004) proposed a rhetorical explanation for the diffusion of managerial innovations. He argued that through their choices of language, managers increase or decrease the diffusion of new ideas and things within and across firms, such as Total Quality Management (TQM). The traditional approach to explaining diffusion includes the idea that when diffusion occurs, informational messages precede persuasive messages, since potential adopters first have questions about what an innovation is (knowledge-based questions), and then later have questions about the innovation's performance and, in particular, its negative aspects (evaluation-based questions) as they move nearer to making an adoption decision. The traditional explanation also includes the idea that what potential adopters say to each other—and especially what opinion leaders say to near-peers—affects the rate of adoption of an innovation.

In a set of propositions, Green (2004) posited that diffusion rates will vary depending on whether justifications for adopting the innovation are based in pathos (emotion), logos (effectiveness), or ethos (morality). Pathos appeals, he argued, would result in rapid diffusion and rapid discontinuance; logos appeals in moderately rapid diffusion and moderately rapid discontinuance; and ethos appeals in slow uptake and gradual discontinuance. Green reasoned that by combining the three types of justifications in this sequence (pathos arguments, then logos arguments, followed by ethos arguments), diffusion would be both accelerated and prolonged. This formula is different from that in Rogers (2003), where persuasive appeals rich in pathos are understood to be necessary just prior to the time of adopter decision, and after what rhetoricians would consider logical or logos appeals to explain to potential adopters what the innovation is and how it works.

In Green's theorizing about organizations, it is the managers as potential adopters who control the determination of such meaning and its communication. The agency for change within the corporation is placed with the managers as adopters, and less so with the outward-to-inward efforts of change agencies such as consulting firms. While to Green, external change agencies remain the sources of innovation, the meaning of those tools, techniques, and technologies is fomented and negotiated internally, by adopters. To him as well as to others (Strang and Meyer, 1994; Abrahamson and Fairchild 1999), discourse among adopters determines the fate of managerial innovations. This rhetorical perspective on diffusion is about framing the meaning of innovations. The theory reconceptualizes how we think about innovations; it is a means of explaining how characterizations of innovations influence our adoption of them.

A Trading Perspective on Diffusion. On the basis of a series of empirical studies, several management scholars have developed the theory that individual adopters employed by competing organizations frequently engage in the informal and asynchronous exchange of proprietary knowledge to solve work-related problems. First postulated by Eric von Hippel (1987) and subsequently further modeled and tested by Carter (1989) and Schrader (1991), "know-how trading" has been shown to well characterize how engineers and other technical and professional staff learn of process innovations. Though these researchers do not term it as such, know-how trading is an enactment of social capital: adopters access valuable information through extant relational contacts, on a need-to-know basis. Reciprocity is the guiding principle governing information exchanges through these relationships, just as it is with social capital of other types. What you help to solve this week for an acquaintance at a rival firm you will recoup at some unspecified later date. Schrader's (1991) study of 294 middle-level managers showed that the diffusion of knowledge through know-how trading benefitted both the individuals who were party to the exchanges and their employers.

Traditional theorizing about diffusion strongly suggests a directionality of diffusion, from sources to receivers (i.e., adopters). Diffusion research that incorporates the study of social networks has demonstrated the mediating role of interpersonal relations in speeding or slowing rate of adoption (Coleman et al. 1966). The theoretic importance of the trading perspective is its evidence of asynchronous reciprocity: that actors play the roles of sources and receivers at different times, according to the interpersonal request and supply for innovations. The implicit promise of engaging in exchange networks is the attendant obligation for reciprocal behavior, a strongly felt norm deriving from informal and tacit agreement. This sense of obligation, of brotherhood or sisterhood, facilitates bilateral diffusion, not just from A to B but from B to C to A. The informality, multiplexity, and strength of interpersonal work-based relationships means that the high value information usually required for successful technology transfer—so-called tacit knowledge—is precisely the type of knowledge that know-how trading facilitates. The trading perspective on diffusion is about the maintaining of important relationships. Whereas the rhetorical explanation for diffusion is about the meanings given to ideas and things, this trading perspective on diffusion of practices and innovative solutions is about relationships, not what you think but who you know. Know-how trading reconceptualizes how we think about adopters and the activities in which they engage. In know-how trading, adopters are mutually and maximally active. They do not merely reinvent innovations. They are the generative sources of innovative solutions to managerial and technical problems.

An Evolutionary Perspective on Diffusion. Douthwaite et al. (2002) studied what agricultural adopters did with six post-harvest technologies in the Philippines and Vietnam. They concluded in a cross-case analysis that learning and cycles of adaptation—analogous, they argue, to natural selection in the biological world—characterized how adopters interacted with technologies as a result of their social and work environments. In particular, Douthwaite, Keatinge, and Park identified instances of novelty generation (the creation of differences between adopters, their innovations, or the ways that they use innovations) and the subsequent selection by adopters of the most beneficial "novelties" to best fashion the technology in question. The authors observed that repeated instances of novelty generation and selection of the most well-suited novelties led to results (innovations) with "hybrid vigor," innovations that were most able to thrive in use by the adopters in question. The fittest innovations survived from plausible promise to successful adaptation in practice.

In this approach to understanding technological change, innovation and diffusion are inextricably intertwined processes. But unlike the rhetorical perspective that it is justifications that drive diffusion or the trading perspective that it is relational obligation that drives the spread of innovation, the key force in the evolutionary perspective that determines the adaptations that adopters make to innovations is the environment, which both enables and constrains the prosperity of any one "species" or innovative solution. Adopters change innovations to exploit a perceived niche in which they want to operate. So this perspective reconceptualizes how we think about environmental conditions in relation to diffusion, giving primacy to environmental conditions as a shaping force on innovation and propagation.

This theory suggests that while the environment determines what is possible, the agency necessary to take advantage of that opportunity is the adopters', whose activity is as much defined by a process of innovating as it is by a process of diffusion. The evolutionary perspective on diffusion is about adjusting the innovation-immediate context fit so that an opportunity made possible by the environment can be exploited. The result, according to these authors, is highly tailored innovation, often unique to each individual adopter–user.

Adopter Activity as a Common Thread

While the managerial and agricultural technology explanations for diffusion just reviewed are quite distinct from one another, they have in common a claim that adopters and implementers of innovations are by no means passive in the process of learning about and encountering innovations. Nor are they mere tinkerers or customizers, adapting at the margins of innovations from afar. These three disparate theories of diffusion suggest that adopters are not at all what we have been told they are. Rather, they are creators, inventors, and sources of change. They are, without overstating the case, extremely active in testing, manipulating, jerry-rigging, and doing what it takes to create both through language and through action an innovation that precisely addresses the requirements of an acutely felt local problem. If the purpose at hand is to create something radical or wonderful, then the type of adopter activity to which we refer will be of small import. On the other hand, if the purpose is to heighten the utility of a given innovation and hence transform it from something that one will not adopt or use into something that suits a felt need well enough to cause both adoption and implementation, then adopter activity is vital. It is perhaps what Maslow (1959) referred to as *secondary creativity*, individual activity that accounts for the majority of creative if modest output "which are essentially the consolidation and exploitation of other people's ideas" (p. 93.)

A distinction can be made between two types of adopter activity. Potential adopters can be active in relation to other adopters and potential adopters. They can also be active in relation to an innovation and their organizational context concerning implementation. First, I discuss activity in relation to individuals; then, I focus on the latter type of activity.

The traditional diffusion perspective is one in which potential adopters actively listen to, read about, and observe others' responses to innovations, and discuss those innovations with others. People are neither passive nor atomized individuals as much communication scholarship has characterized mass audiences. Except for the most venturesome and the most cautious, potential adopters think and act with reference to the social norms that characterize the networks or systems of which they are members. Thus for most people, their activity is of a social type that is normatively guided by prevailing attitudes and values. Their activity is with other adopters and potential adopters, defined more or less by their degree of innovativeness. The earliest adopters ("innovators" in Rogers' categorization) are highly active in scanning information environments, in seeking out new ideas from heterogenous sources, and in experimentation. Feeling few constraints on their behavior, they act nearly autonomously toward the group, though they often exhibit ties to others outside the immediate group. But innovators comprise only a small proportion (2.5 percent) of the adopters in any social system. The vast majorities of others (early adopters, early majority, late majority, laggards) are less active in how they behave, their activity being more a response to how they perceive that others within the group view the innovation in question. The last to adopt also exhibit a lesser degree of social integration, though they are more commonly passive rejecters rather than active in relation to others. The essential point is that activity is carried out through social relations. Conceptualizing one's activity as a property of interaction with others dominates both network and structural perspectives on innovation diffusion (see, for example, Burt 2003).

Adopter and implementer activity in relation to an innovation is much less prevalent in the diffusion literature. To be sure, there is support from studies that adopters actively change innovations during implementation (Rice and Rogers 1980; Dearing et al. 1998). But activity of this sort has usually been considered deviant or minor in relation to the original source-defined purpose of an innovation and how it was designed by that source. In the present chapter, I maintain along with Green (2004), von Hippel (1987), Douthwaite et al. (2002), and organizational management scholars (Czarniawska and Sevon 2005) that adopter activity in relation to innovations is far more important, common, and consequential than is reflected in the diffusion literature, and that such agency represents change processes that affect organizational context, too. Moreover, in studies of changes made to innovations, it is both innovation designers and proponents as well as those who adopt and implement who make changes to innovations. Designers reinvent for new market segments and opportunities (Dearing et al. 2019; Larson et al. 2017). Implementers adapt both organizational context and innovation to maximize fit, what Katz and others consider compatibility as a master attribute of innovations (Katz 1963; Dearing et al. 2019; Colyvas and Jonsson 2011).

Health services and public health researchers have long believed that adaptation is either good or bad. For decades in discussions of how to best diffuse or "scale up" effective educational programs, researchers have kept to this framing of the translational problem (Hutchinson and Huberman 1993): Adherents of program fidelity believe that working to ensure that adopters make as few modifications as possible is key to retaining the success of the original program. If the program is changed, how does one know if it is still effective? On the other hand, adherents of the program adaptation perspective counter that it is only through allowing adopters to change a program to suit their needs that the likelihood of sustainability is increased. If adopters do not feel ownership of the program, how can we ensure its persistence in practice? This debate has played out in disease prevention circles (Backer 1995; Elliott and Mihalic 2004). For many types of innovations, designing them to resist modification is futile; the baby may be tossed out with the bath water since adopters are free to look elsewhere for workable alternatives, or they will self-invent by borrowing from what their experience suggests will work and what impresses them from different sources. There is simply too much incentive at the individual or single organizational level to customize, to partly adopt, and to combine innovation components from elsewhere (Hippel 2005).

The simple adaptation perspective of encouraging sources to enable adopters and implementers to change innovations is incomplete. More than an innovation must change if a best fit between a program and one's work context is to be achieved. The context, too, should change. If one only changes an adopted program and not the work environment—or vice versa—technical, delivery system, and performance criteria misalignments are likely to characterize implementation. Over-time and incremental adjustments to both an innovation and a work environment characterize successful cases of technology transfer (Leonard-Barton 1988). "Mutual adaptation" of both an innovation and of its organizational context implies that an awful lot of the action of successful diffusion occurs not with the source nor with the end-beneficiary such as a student or customer or patient, but in direct service organizations such as schools, businesses, and clinics. How practitioners interpret the purpose and promise of an innovation will interact with how they choose to make accommodation for it in the workplace. The meanings we make of an innovation will contribute to what changes in the workplace we deem useful to best exploit it by deriving the most value from it. Second, adaptation is likely to intensify the meaning of an innovation for users since their actions in accommodation bring the innovation and its work environment more and more into harmony in achieving objectives that are important to each practitioner. Particularly if meaning is personalized and internalized, implementation could be greatly strengthened. Research has shown that people vest certain objects with sacred meaning. The attribution of sacred meaning to objects has been shown to occur across many types of people and across many types of objects. Marketing researchers Belk (1988) and Belk et al. (1989) argue on the basis of extensive data (Belk, 2005) that in attributing sacred meaning to objects, those objects become much more than possessions. They come to constitute an extended self of the individual.

The Need for Attending to the Issue of External Validity

To affect the diffusion of evidence-based innovations either within or across organizations, both internal and external validity are important concepts that must be understood and considered by both innovation developers and proponents, on the one hand, and adopters and implementers, on the other. Trying to broaden the reach or accelerate the rate of the adoption of an innovation makes no sense unless the innovation is worthy of being spread.

Internal validity is the extent to which a causal inference may be made between two or more variables (Campbell and Stanley 1966; Cook and Campbell 1979). In other words, internal validity is focused on whether or not innovation components cause specific and desired innovation outcomes. In practice, consideration of internal validity is often framed as, "Does the innovation work?" Internal validity is established through testing of the innovation under controlled conditions. The more highly controlled the environment within which an innovation is tested, the more confidence in the validity of the causal relationship(s) is established.

External validity refers to the extent to which the presumed causal inference may be generalized to other populations, settings, treatment variables, or measurement variables (Campbell and Stanley 1966). The more an intervention that was demonstrated and validated in one site can still achieve positive effects when translated in other places, other populations, other times, and other topics, the more externally valid the intervention. So *external validity* is the degree to which an innovation shown to be effective in an initial demonstration subsequently produces similar outcomes in other contexts. In Guala's (2003) words, "[I]t [the innovation] is *externally* valid if A causes B not only in E, but also in a set of other circumstances of interest F, G, H, etc." (p. 4, italics in the original). Consideration of external validity is often framed as, "Yes so the innovation works here, but will it work *there* (and *there*, and *there*)?"

The internal and external validity of innovations are both critical in efforts to trigger diffusion, given the premise that the most active users of innovations will be those who modify the innovation to best fit their circumstance as well as modify their circumstance to best fit the innovation (Leonard-Barton 1988). Consider first internal validity. Rather than posing the question, "Does the program work?", the question can be usefully reframed as, "Why does the program work?" and "What are the core components of the program that are thought to be integral to its effectiveness?" Rogers (2003) refers to this as principles knowledge or "information dealing with the functioning principles underlying how an innovation works" (p. 173).

A potential adopter who understands specifically why a program works will be better able to determine those aspects or core components of the program or environment that may be modified with minimal risk to program effectiveness. User activity will produce innovations of higher external validity to the extent that core components are known and understood. Developers may tailor communication efforts to explain why or how the program works. Precisely how to do this should not be assumed or guessed at, but rather derive from careful formative evaluation to assess potential adopter needs and wants, and their reactions to successive prototypes of an innovation.

In addition to communicating the conceptual basis for why a program works, developers may communicate in several alternative ways to bring about a desired outcome. Consider, for example, a performance improvement program that seeks to build team-efficacy as a core component. In other words, increased work group efficacy is determined to be causally related to improved team performance. In this case, developers may provide potential adopters a set of five different options for increasing team-efficacy (one innovation with five examples of how to replicate the desired effect). This gives the practitioner flexibility as well as guidance to adapt the intervention in a fashion most appropriate to the circumstance with little risk to fidelity. Such a strategy emphasizes what might be called *effect fidelity* (the achievement of the source's desired effects in subsequent external validity tests of the program) over *implementation fidelity* (replication of the program as originally demonstrated). Developers can enhance productive user activity by ensuring that users understand the underlying premise for desirable effects, and wherever possible, by providing users with alternative means to achieve the same effect.

Turning to external validity, the question, "Does the innovation work *there*?" may be reframed as, "How are aspects of the circumstance and environment here similar to and different from the circumstance and environment of demonstration at other sites?"

(Leviton and Trujillo, 2017). Answering questions of this sort is a complex task that is rarely achieved through the employ of just one research method (Leviton 2017).

Serious attention to issues of external validity was first given by the polymath Lee J. Cronbach in his large-scale studies of federal education programs (Shadish et al. 1991). Cronbach came to believe that internal validity was a poor measure of an innovation's ability to perform under diverse exogenous and organization conditions. The more an innovation that was demonstrated and validated in one site could still achieve positive effects when translated for other places, other populations, other times, even other topics, the more externally valid the innovation. Cronbach's (1982) focus was on theorizing about the process for translating a full-scale field test into altered or unaltered replications to achieve sector-wide social improvement through systematic investigation and comparison of the units (frequently individuals) studied and unstudied, the treatments they receive, how observations of effects are made, and differences between settings. This process he labeled *extrapolation*.

Cronbach's emphases were later incorporated by Cook (2000) and Shadish et al. (2002) as they continued fleshing out the concept of external validity so that it could be assessed. They focused on the extent to which prototypical characteristics of a model innovation are like those in second-order sites (what they term "surface similarity"), and on clarifying which differences between the original demonstration and the subsequent second-order sites are superfluous ("ruling out irrelevancies"). Stated differently, an important related means for communicating the core components that were causally responsible for the internal validity of the innovation is to also portray the peripheral components that were a part of the original demonstration of the innovation but determined to be not causally important, as well as the complementary assets of the organizations involved that implemented the innovation. Peripheral components of an innovation are those that adopters can be encouraged to change. And the listing of complementary assets or organizational capacities related to fielding an innovation can give subsequent adopters a strong sense of what it took to successfully implement the innovation in question. This is where the creation and expansion of knowledge-sharing systems among organizational implementers can function as a form of user-based guided adaptation (Dearing et al. 2011).

Literature about evidence-based medicine, in particular, is replete with the assumption of a research-to-practice progression or "pipeline" from efficacy tests to effectiveness trials to scale-up or dissemination. This assumption is often represented in different but synonymous language, as from basic to applied research, and from the establishment of internal validity to the establishment of external validity and on to societal-level practice implementation. The key to this assumption is the belief that there is a positive relationship between an innovation working well and its subsequent effectiveness in other settings, for other populations, at other times, under different contextual conditions. But is there a positive relationship between internal validity and external validity? Is it only the internally valid innovation that can prove externally valid? There is reason to doubt this assumed relationship. Moderating variables that differ from site to site can interact to differentially affect innovation performance across sites. An innovation implemented in precisely the same ways in multiple sites can, due to site moderating variation, show different results (Cronbach and Associates 1980). There is no logical reason why the factors that account for innovation success in one site will be similarly associated with innovation adoption, implementation, persistence, and success in subsequent sites unless sites are selected to be homogenous. And homogeneity of sites is not the point of external validity tests; indeed, Cronbach (1982) argued that the more diverse the sites, the more externally valid. Spread is easier when sites are similar to each other (Aarons et al. 2017).

Glasgow et al. (2003), referring to public health and healthcare interventions, posited that "it is highly unlikely that interventions that are successful in efficacy studies will do well in effectiveness studies, or in real-world applications" (p. 1262). The researcher's desire to design the most effective innovation frequently is the enemy of the good; that is, what can survive under realistic practice conditions of high staff turnover, few resources, and competing demands.

Reshaping Diffusion Study through Dissemination and Implementation Science

Driven by the interests of philanthropies and the needs of government agencies, and the persistent and growing applied problems that have been addressed but not solved by dominant scholarly paradigms in psychology, sociology, and political science, dissemination of innovations to and among organizations, as well as implementation and sustained use within those organizations, have become major topics of applied study, especially in health services and public health research (Brownson et al. 2018). Research about dissemination and implementation (D&I) is a response to a general acknowledgment that successful, effective practices, programs, and policies resulting from clinical and community trials, demonstration projects, and community-based research as conducted by academicians very often do not affect the services that clinical staff, community service providers, and other practitioners fashion and provide to residents, clients, patients, and populations at risk. In any one societal sector (populated, for example, by planners for healthcare delivery, or city-level transportation and parkway planners), the state of the science (what researchers collectively know) and the state of the art (what practitioners collectively do) co-exist more or less autonomously, each realm of activity having little effect on the other.

Dissemination science is the study of how evidence-based practices, programs, and policies can best be communicated to an inter-organizational societal sector of potential adopters and implementers to produce uptake and effective use, such as among clinics on behalf of patients or among elementary schools on behalf of children. This definition means that dissemination embeds the objectives of both external validity and *scale-up*, the replication of positive effects across settings and conditions (Moffitt 2007). Conceptualizing and operationalizing societal sectors of organizations as the locus of change fits well with the diffusion paradigm tendency to chart the over-time spread of an innovation throughout the units in a system. Since a societal sector is a collection of focal organizations of a common type that operate in the same domain but without respect to proximity, transformation from one state (non-adoption) to another (adoption) can be hypothesized and measured. Sector change is a learning process, one that is indicative of the active translation of research into practice and sometimes back again. When information about effective innovations is framed in ways meaningful to potential adopting organizations, packaged, and presented back to them as informational products, and then targeted first to influential organizations in the sector and met with a positive opinion leader response, knowledge is translated from science to art, research to practice. Networks of similarly trained specialists, professional societies, and trade associations are particularly useful partners in the conduct of dissemination research (Dearing et al. 2006; Dearing et al. 2017; LaJeunesse et al. 2019), which relies on formative evaluation to identify best-suited nodes in peer networks to influence adoption decisions (Donohue et al. 2018). Research about how to best disseminate or scale up innovations from management and marketing as well as health services includes identification and management of barriers to diffusion (Talke and Hultink 2010), seeding of innovations with policy entrepreneurs who bridge vertical boundaries sector to sector (Faling et al. 2019), diffusion path dependence (Greve and Seidel 2015), product launch timing (Calantone et al. 2012), and resistance to innovations by intermediaries (Ferlie et al. 2005; Jonsson 2009).

A call to action by the US Institute of Medicine (2001) led to a burst of attention that has focused on the implementation stage in organizations and the barriers to adoption and sustained use that innovations face (Fixsen et al. 2005; Damschroder et al. 2009; Stirman et al. 2015). *Implementation science* is the study of what happens prior to, and after, adoption occurs, especially in organizational settings. Many studies of implementation focus on field-based tests to understand the extent to which an evidence-based program or practice will still be effective when subjected to realistic practice conditions, and the extent to which knowledge of practice conditions in organizations should inform innovation design and, failing that, reinvention (Balas and Chapman 2018). A smaller proportion of implementation research concerns post-adoption behavior among practitioners under actual practice conditions, when implementation and sustainability traditionally have gone unobserved. The extent and quality of implementation and client or constituent responses to implemented innovations are often primary dependent variables in implementation studies (Yin et al. 1977).

The later-stage study of sustainability of innovations in organizations is an important aspect of implementation science and may be considered its most important focus (Scheirer and Dearing 2011). *Sustainability* is the continued use of program components and activities for the continued achievement of desirable program and population outcomes. Other terms that have been used by prior researchers in this domain include continuation, confirmation, maintenance, durability, continuance, and institutionalization (Damschroder et al. 2009; Century et al. 2010). There are some nuanced differences among these terms, but they all usually refer to the continued use of program components and activities beyond their initial funding period, and sometimes to desired intended outcomes, that are sustained in practice-based organizations (Stirman and Dearing 2019). Generally speaking, the likelihood of sustainability is heightened when there is an alignment, compatibility, or convergence of (1) problem recognition in the external organizational environment or community, with (2) the program in question, and (3) internal organizational objectives and capacities (Yin et al. 1977; Altman 1995; Gruen et al. 2008; Katz 1963). This orientation implies a multilevel system of health innovations being implemented by individuals, embedded in an organization, that operates within a community context or inter-organizational network over time (Schensul 2009). Therefore, research about sustainability can require several layers of data collection, in order to capture the multiple components of the systems involved in such continuation.

Taken together, dissemination and implementation science can be thought of as next generation applications of the diffusion paradigm. But there are differences, too:

1. Whereas diffusion is broadly construed to refer to any type of innovation, dissemination science only concerns efficacious (internally valid) *and* effective (externally valid) innovations;
2. Whereas diffusion studies often are designed to describe or explain diffusion, dissemination studies are designed as tests of which diffusion concepts most affect adoption and implementation, and why;
3. Whereas diffusion investigations are often conducted post hoc after adoption, dissemination science investigations are a priori interventions to affect adoption.
4. Whereas diffusion study has focused on adoption by end-users or beneficiaries of services or products, dissemination efforts target service or product providers; i.e., intermediaries between change agencies and end-users;
5. Whereas diffusion research has most often focused on individuals as the units of adoption, dissemination focuses on organizations as the units of adoption;
6. Whereas diffusion studies have often been conducted in geographically proximate communities, dissemination studies have the potential to focus on the societal sector, composed of organizations that offer similar services but often spanning many geographic areas; and
7. Whereas adoption has been the primary dependent variable of study in diffusion research, the study of implementation and maintenance becomes more critical in D&I science.

So there is a distinctiveness to dissemination and implementation science. Its normative orientation toward solving societal problems—long a basis for a minority of diffusion studies—means that dissemination science pairs strategies to achieve innovation adoption with strategies to achieve effective use. The dissemination and implementation scientist does not necessarily engage in the creation and efficacy testing nor even in the limited-site effectiveness testing of innovations themselves: for purposes of reducing bias in dissemination research projects a lack of involvement may be preferred. Rather, this scientist focuses on affecting the processes by which those innovations spread and are used. In doing so, a dissemination and implementation scientist applies certain concepts from diffusion of innovation theory as process intervention strategy. These concepts are the cumulative result of the classical diffusion research paradigm and of attendant work in organizational studies of implementation.

Conclusion

The diffusion of innovations research and practice paradigm has seen considerable evolution in theory and method over the decades, with the most consequential change being the formalization of dissemination and implementation science. For years, the diffusion literature was characterized by a dearth of studies about the spread of innovations across and within organizations. No longer. Dissemination science with its emphasis on intervention research, and implementation science with its emphasis on fidelity and adaptation, have added needed knowledge about how people and organizations respond to, and shape, innovations.

References

Aarons, G. A., Sklar, M., Mustanski, B., Benbow, N., and Hendricks Brown, C. (2017), '"Scaling Out' Evidence-Based Interventions to New Populations or New Health Care Delivery Systems.' *Implementation Science*, 12/111), 1–13.

Abrahamson, E. (1991), 'Managerial Fads and Fashions: The Diffusion and Rejection of Innovations', *Academy of Management Review*, 16, 586–612.

Abrahamson, E., and Eisenman, M. (2008), 'Employee-Management Techniques: Transient Fads or Trending Fashions?' *Administrative Science Quarterly*, 53, 719–44.

Abrahamson, E., and Fairchild, G. (1999), 'Management Fashion: Lifecycles, Triggers and Collective Learning Processes', *Administrative Science Quarterly*, 44, 708–40.

Altman, D. G. (1995), 'Sustaining Interventions in Community Systems: On the Relationship Between Researchers and Communities', *Health Psychology* 14/6, 526–36.

Aral, S., and Walker, D. (2012), 'Identifying Influential and Susceptible Members of Social Networks', *Science* 337/6092, 337–41.

Backer, T. (1995), 'Assessing and Enhancing Readiness for Change: Implications for Technology Transfer', in T. Backer, S. David, and G. Soucy, eds., *Reviewing the Behavioral Science Knowledge Base on Technology Transfer* (Rockville, MD: National Institute on Drug Abuse), 21–41.

Baer, W. S., Johnson, B., and Merrow, S. (1977), 'Government-Sponsored Demonstrations of New Technologies', *Science*, 196, 950–7.

Balas, E. A., and Chapmen, W. W. (2018), 'Road Map for Diffusion of Innovation in Health Care', *Health Affairs* 37/2, 198–204.

Belk, R. W. (1988), 'Possessions and the Extended Self', *Journal of Consumer Research*, 15, 139–68.

Belk, R. W. (2005), 'Possessions, Self, and the Sacred', in A. Griffin and C. C. Otnes, eds., *16th Paul D. Converse Symposium* (Chicago: American Marketing Association), 46–66.

Belk, R. W., Wallendorf, M., and Sherry, Jr., J. F. (1989), 'The Sacred and the Profane in Consumer Behavior: Theodicy on the Odyssey', *Journal of Consumer Research*, 16, 1–38.

Berwick, D. M. (2003), 'Disseminating Innovations in Health Care', *Journal of the American Medical Association* 289/15, 1969–75.

Boushey, G. (2010), *Policy Diffusion Dynamics in America* (Cambridge, UK: Cambridge University Press).

Boushey, G. (2016), 'Targeted for Diffusion? How the Use and Acceptance of Stereotypes Shape the Diffusion of Criminal Justice Policy Innovations in the American States', *American Political Science Review* 110/1, 198–214.

Brownson, R. C., Colditz, G. A., and Proctor, E. K. (eds.) (2018), *Dissemination and Implementation Research in Health: Translating Science to Practice* (Second edn) (New York, NY: Oxford University Press).

Buchanan, A., Cole, T., and Keohane, R. O. (2011), 'Justice in the Diffusion of Innovation', *Journal of Political Philosophy* 19/3, 306–32.

Burt, R. S. (2003), 'Social Origins of Good Ideas.' Unpublished manuscript, Chicago, Graduate School of Business, University of Chicago.

Calantone, R., Benedetto, A. D., and Rubera, G. (2012), 'Launch Timing and Launch Activities Proficiency as Antecedents to New Product Performance', *Journal of Global Scholars of Marketing Science* 22/4, 290–309.

Campbell, D. T., and Stanley, J. C. (1966), *Experimental and Quasi-Experimental Designs for Research* (Chicago: Rand McNally).

Carter, A. P. (1989), 'Knowhow Trading as Economic Exchange', *Research Policy*, 18, 155–63.

Centola, D. (2011), 'An Experimental Study of Homophily in the Adoption of Health Behavior', *Science* 334/6060, 1269–72.

Century, J., Rudnick, M., and Freeman, C. (2010), 'A Framework for Measauring Fidelity of Implementation: A Foundation for Shared Language and Accumuluation of Knowledge', *American Journal of Evaluation*, 31, 199–218.

Coleman, J. S., Katz, E., and Menzel, H. (1966), *Medical Innovation: A Diffusion Study* (New York: Bobbs Merrill).

Collins, C., Harshbarger, C., Sawyer, R., and Hamdallah, M. (2006), 'The Diffusion of Effective Behavioral Interventions Project: Development, Implementation, and Lessons Learned', *AIDS Education and Prevention* 18/Supplement A, 5–20.

Colyvas, J. A., and Jonsson, S. (2011), 'Ubiquity and Legitimacy: Disentangling Diffusion and Institutionalization', *Sociological Theory*, 29/1, 27–53.

Conell, C., and Cohn, S. (1995), 'Learning from Other People's Actions: Environmental Variation and Diffusion in French Coal Mining Strikes, 1890-1935', *American Journal of Sociology* 101/2, 366–403.

Cook, T. D. (2000), 'Toward a Practical Theory of External Validity', in L. Bickman, ed., *Validity & Social Experimentation* (Thousand Oaks, CA: Sage), 3–43.

Cook, T. D., and Campbell, D. T. (1979), *Quasi-Experimentation: Design & Analysis Issues for Field Settings* (Chicago: Rand McNally).

Cronbach, L. J. (1982), *Designing Evaluations of Educational and Social Programs* (San Francisco, CA: Jossey-Bass).

Cronbach, L. J., and Associates (1980), *Toward Reform of Program Evaluation* (San Francisco, CA: Jossey-Bass).

Czarniawska, B., and Sevon, G. (2005), 'Translation is a Vehicle, Imitation its Motor, and Fashion Sits at the Wheel', in Czarniawska and Sevon, eds., *Global Ideas: How Ideas, Objects and Practices Travel in the Global Economy* (Malmo, Sweden: Liber & Copenhagen Business School Press), 7–12.

Damschroder, L. J., Aron, D. C., Keith, R. E., Kirsh, S. R., Alexander, J. A., and Lowery, J. C. (2009), 'Fostering Implementation of Health Services Research Findings into Practice: A Consolidated Framework for Advancing Implementation Science', *Implementation Science* 4/50, 1–15.

Davis, G. F. (2015), 'Editorial Essay: What is Organizational Research For?' *Administrative Science Quarterly* 60/2, 179–88.

Dearing, J. W., Beacom, A. M., Chamberlain, S. A., Meng, J., Berta, W. B. et al. (2017), 'Pathways for Best Practice Diffusion: The Structure of Informal Relationships in Canada's Long-Term Care Sector', *Implementation Science* 12/11, 1–13.

Dearing, J. W., and Cox, J. G. (2018), 'Diffusion of Innovations Theory, Principles, and Practice', *Health Affairs* 37/2, 183–90.

Dearing, J. W., Greene, S. M., Stewart, W. F., and Williams, A. E. (2011), 'If We Only Knew What We Know: Principles for Knowledge Sharing Across People, Practices, and Platforms', *Translational Behavioral Medicine* 1/1, 1–11.

Dearing, J. W., Lapinski, M., Shin, S. Y., Hussain, S. A., Rumbold, Y., Osoro, R., and Shell, D. (2019), *A Model for Introducing Global Ideas to the U.S.* (East Lansing, MI: Health and Risk Communication Center, Michigan State University).

Dearing, J. W., Larson, R. S., Randall, L. M., and Pope, R. S. (1998), 'Local Reinvention of the CDC HIV Prevention Community Planning Initiative', *Journal of Community Health*, 23, 113–26.

Dearing, J. W., Maibach, E. W., and Buller, D. B. (2006), 'A Convergent Diffusion and Social Marketing Approach for Disseminating Proven Approaches to Physical Activity Promotion', *American Journal of Preventive Medicine* 31/4S, 11–23.

Dearing, J. W., Smith, D. K., Larson, R. S., and Estabrooks, C. A. (2013), 'Designing for Diffusion of a Biomedical Intervention', *American Journal of Preventive Medicine* 44/1S2, 70–6.

Donohue, J. M., Guclu, H., Gellad, W. F., Chang, C. H., Huskamp, H. A., et al. (2018), 'Influence of Peer Networks on Physician Adoption of New Drugs', *PLOS One* 13/10, 1–18.

Douthwaite, B., Keatinge, J. D. H., and Park, J. R. (2002), 'Learning Selection: An Evolutionary Model for Understanding, Implementing and Evaluating Participatory Technology Development', *Agricultural Systems*, 72, 109–31.

Elliott, D. S., and Mihalic, S. (2004), 'Issues in Disseminating and Replicating Effective Prevention Programs', *Prevention Science* 4/1, 47–53.

Estabrooks, C. A., Derksen, L., Winther, C., Lavis, J. N., Scott, S. D., and Wallin, L. et al. (2008), 'The Intellectual Structure and Substance of the Knowledge Utilization Field: A Longitudinal Author Co-Citation Analysis, 1945 to 2004', *Implementation Science*, 3, 49.

Faling, M., Biesbroek, R., Karlsson-Vinkhuyzen, S., and Termeer, K. (2019), 'Policy Entrepreneurship Across Boundaries: A Systematic Literature Review', *Journal of Public Policy* 39/2, 393–422.

Ferlie, E., Fitzgerald, L., Wood, M., and Hawkins, C. (2005), 'The Nonspread of Innovations: The Mediating Role of Professionals', *Academy of Management Review* 48/1, 117–34.

Fiss, P. C., Kennedy, M. T., and Davis, G. F. (2012), 'How Golden Parachutes Unfolded: Diffusion and Variation of a Controversial Practice', *Organization Science* 23/4, 1077–99.

Fixsen, D. L., Naoom, S. F., Blasé, K. A., Friedman, R. M., and Wallace, F. (2005), *Implementation Research: A Synthesis of the Literature* (Tampa, FL: Louis de la Parte Florida Mental Health Institute, University of South Florida).

Glasgow, R. E., Lichtenstein, E., and Marcus, A. C. (2003), 'Why Don't We See More Translation of Health Promotion Research to Practice? Rethinking the Efficacy-to-Effectiveness Transition', *American Journal of Public Health* 93/8, 1261–7.

Goldman, E. O., and Eliason, L. C. (eds.) (2003), *The Diffusion of Military Technology and Ideas* (Stanford, CA: Stanford University Press).

Green, L. W., Gottlieb, N. H., and Parcel, G. S. (1991), 'Diffusion Theory Extended and Applied', in W. B. Ward and F. M. Lewis, eds., *Advances in Health Education and Promotion* (Vol. 3) (London, UK: Jessica Kingsley), 91–117.

Green, S. E. (2004), 'A Rhetorical Theory of Diffusion', *Academy of Management Review* 29/4, 653–69.

Greve, H. R., and Seidel, M. L. (2015), 'The Thin Red Line Between Success and Failure: Path Dependence in the Diffusion of Innovative Production Technologies', *Strategic Management Journal*, 36, 475–96.

Gruen, R. L., Elliott, J. H., Nolan, M. L. Lawton, P. D., Parkhill, A., McLaren, C. J., and Lavis, J. N . (2008), 'Sustainability Science: An Integrated Approach for Health-Programme Planning.' *Lancet* 372/9649, 1579–89.

Guala, F. (2003), 'Experimental Localism and External Validity', Unpublished paper presented at the 2002 Philosophy of Science Association meeting.

Hippel, E. V. (1987), 'Cooperation Between Rivals: Informal Know-How Trading', *Research Policy*, 15, 291–302.

Hippel, E. V. (2005), *Democratizing Innovation* (Cambridge, MA: The MIT Press).

Hutchinson, J., and Huberman, M. (1993), *Knowledge Dissemination and Use in Science and Mathematics Education: A Literature Review*. NSF EHR/RED report 93–75 (Arlington, VA: National Science Foundation).

Institute of Medicine (2001), *Crossing the Quality Chasm: A New Health System for the 21st Century* (Washington, DC: Institute of Medicine).

Jonsson, S. (2009), 'Refraining from Imitation: Professional Resistance and Limited Diffusion in a Financial Market', *Organization Science* 20/1, 172–86.

Katz, E. (1963), 'The Characteristics of Innovations and the Concept of Compatibility', Unpublished manuscript. August 19.

Katz, E. (1980), 'On Conceptualizing Media Effects', *Studies in Communication*, 1, 119–41.

Katz, E., Levin, M. L., and Hamilton, H. (1963), 'Traditions of Research on the Diffusion of Innovation', *American Sociological Review* 28/2, 237–52.

Kerckhoff, A. C., Back, K. W., and Miller, N. (1965), 'Sociometric Patterns in Hysterical Contagion', *Sociometry*, 28/1, 2–15.

Kincaid, D. L. (2004), 'From Innovation to Social Norm: Bounded Normative Influence', *Journal of Health Communication*, 9, 37–57.

Kingdon, J. W. (1984), *Agendas, Alternatives and Public Policies* (Boston, MA: Little, Brown).

Kumar, V., and Krishnan, T. V. (2002), "Multinational Diffusion Models: An Alternative Framework', *Marketing Science*, 21: 318–30.

LaJeunesse, S., Heiny, S., Evenson, K. R., Fiedler, L. M., and Cooper, J. F. (2019), 'Diffusing Innovative Road Safety Practice: A Social Network Approach to Identifying Opinion Leading U.S. Cities', *Traffic Injury Prevention* 19/8, 832–7.

Larson, R. S., Dearing, J. W., and Backer, T. E. (2017), *Strategies to Scale Up Social Programs: Pathways, Partnerships and Fidelity* (East Lansing, MI: Diffusion Associates).

Latour, B. (1986), "The Powers of Association', in J. Law, ed., *Power, Action and Belief* (London, UK: Routledge), 261–77.

Leonard-Barton, D. (1988), 'Implementation as Mutual Adaptation of Technology and Organization', *Research Policy*, 17: 251–67.

Leviton, L. (2017), 'Generalizing about Public Health Interventions: A Mixed-Methods Approach to External Validity', *Annual Review of Public Health*, 38, 371–91.

Leviton, L., and Trujillo, M. (2017), 'Interaction of Theory and Practice to Assess External Validity', *Evaluation Review* 41/5, 436–71.

Lomas, J. (1991), 'Words Without Action? The Production, Dissemination, and Impact of Consensus Recommendations', *Annual Review of Public Health*, 12, 41–65.

Maslow, A. H. (1959), "Creativity in Self-Actualizing People', in H. H. Anderson, ed., *Creativity and Its Cultivation* (New York: Harper & Brothers), 83–95.

McAnany, E. G. (1984), 'The Diffusion of Innovation: Why Does It Endure?' *Critical Studies in Mass Communication*, 1, 439–42.

Meade, N., and Islam, T. (2006), "Modeling and Forecasting the Diffusion of Innovation—A 25-Year Review', *International Journal of Forecasting* 22/3, 519–45.

Merton, R. K. (1968), 'The Matthew Effect in Science', *Science*, 159/3810, 56–63.

Mintrom, M., and Norman, P. (2009), 'Policy Entrepreneurship and Policy Change', *Policy Studies Journal* 37/4, 649–67.

Moffitt, R. A. (2007), 'Forecasting the Effects of Scaling Up Social Programs: An Economics Perspective', in B. Schneider and S. McDonald, eds., *Scale-Up in Education* (Vol. 1) (Lanham, MD: Rowman & Littlefield), 173–86.

Norton, W. E., Lungeanu, A., Chambers, D. A., and Contractor, N. (2017), 'Mapping the Growing Discipline of Dissemination and Implementation Science in Health', *Scientometrics* 112/3, 1367–90.

O'Dell, C., and Grayson, C. J. (1998), 'If Only We Knew What We Know: Identification and Transfer of Internal Best Practices', *California Management Review* 40/3, 154–74.

Ono, S. S., Crabtree, B. F., Hemler, J. R., Balasubramanian, B. A., Edwards, S. T. et al. (2018), 'Taking Innovation to Scale in Primary Care Practices: The Functions of Health Care Extension', *Health Affairs* 37/2, 222–30.

Phillips, D. J. (2013), *Shaping Jazz: Cities, Labels, and the Global Emergence of an Art Form* (Princeton, NJ: Princeton University Press).

Raizen, S. A. (1979), 'Dissemination Programs at the National Institute of Education', *Knowledge* 1, 259–91.

Rice, R. E., and Rogers, E. M. (1980), 'Re-Invention in the Innovation Process', *Knowledge* 1, 499–514.

Rogers, E. M. (2003), *Diffusion of Innovations* (Fifth edn) (New York, NY: Free Press).

Rogers, E. M. (1995), *Diffusion of Innovations* (Fourth edn) (New York, NY: Free Press).

Rossman, G. (2012), *Climbing the Charts: What Radio Airplay Tells Us about the Diffusion of Innovation* (Princeton, NJ: Princeton University Press).

Scheirer, M. A., and Dearing, J. W. (2011), 'An Agenda for Research on the Sustainability of Public Health Programs', *American Journal of Public Health*, 101, 2059–67.

Schensul, J. J. (2009), 'Community, Culture and Sustainability in Multilevel Dynamic Systems Intervention Science', *American Journal of Community Psychology* 43/3–4, 241–56.

Schrader, S. (1991), 'Informal Technology Transfer Between Firms: Cooperation Through Information Trading', *Research Policy* 20, 153–70.

Scott, W. R., and Meyer, J. W. (1991), 'The Organization of Societal Sectors: Propositions and Early Evidence', in W. W. Powell and P. J. DiMaggio, eds., *The New Institutionalism in Organizational Analysis* (Chicago, IL: University of Chicago Press) 108–40).

Shadish, W. R., Cook, T., and Campbell, D. T. (2002), *Experimental and Quasi-Experimental Designs for Generalized Causal Inference* (Boston, MA: Houghton Mifflin, 341–73).

Shadish, W. R., Cook, T., and Leviton, L. C. (1991), *Foundations of Program Evaluation: Theories of Practice* (Thousand Oaks, CA: Sage).

Simmons, R., and Shiffman, J. (2007), 'Scaling Up Health Service Innovations: A Framework for Action', in Simmons, R., Fajans, P., and Ghiron, L., eds., *Scaling Up Health Service Delivery* (Geneva, Switzerland: World Health Organization.

Smith, R. A., Kim, Y., Zhu, X., Doudou, D. T., Sternberg, E. D., et al. (2018), 'Integrating Models of Diffusion and Behavior to Predict Innovation Adoption, Maintenance, and Social Diffusion', *Journal of Health Communication*, 23, 264–71.

Spaulding, I. A. (1955), 'Farm Operator Time-Space Orientations and the Adoption of Recommended Farming Practices', Bulletin 330. Agricultural Experiment Station (Kingston, RI: University of Rhode Island).

Strang, D., and Meyer, J. W. (1994), 'Institutional Conditions for Diffusion', in R. W. Scott and J. W. Meyer, eds., *Institutional Environments and Organizations: Structural Complexity and Individualism* (Thousand Oaks, CA: Sage), 100–11).

Strang, D., and Soule, S. A. (1998), 'Diffusion in Organizations and Social Movements: From Hybrid Corn to Poison Pills', *Annual Review of Sociology*, 24, 265–90.

Stirman, S. W., and Dearing, J. W. (2019), 'Sustainability of Cancer Practices and Programs', in D. A. Chambers, C. A. Vinson, and W. E. Norton, eds., *Optimizing the Cancer Control Continuum: Advancing Implementation Research* (New York: Oxford University Press), 312–29.

Stirman, S. W., Gutner, C. A., Crits-Christoph, P., Edmunds, J., Evans, A. C., and Beidas, R. S. (2015), 'Relationships Between Clinician-Level Attributes and Fidelity-Consistent and Fidelity-Inconsistent Modifications to an Evidence-Based Psychotherapy', *Implementation Science*, 10, 115.

Studlar, D. T. (1999), 'Diffusion of Tobacco Control in North America', *The Annals of the American Academy of Political and Social Science*, 566, 68–79.

Talke, K., and Hultink, E. J. (2010), 'Managing Diffusion Barriers When Launching New Products', *Journal of Product Innovation Management*, 27: 537–53.

Valente, T. W. (1995), *Network Models of the Diffusion of Innovations* (Cresskill, NJ: Hampton Press).

Van de Ven, A. H., and Poole, M. S. (1995), 'Explaining Development and Change in Organizations', *Academy of Management Review* 20/3, 510–40.

Van de Ven, A. H., and Rogers, E. M. (1988), 'Innovations and Organizations: Critical Perspectives', *Communication Research*, 15/5, 632–51.

Wallis, J., and Goldfinch, S. (2013), 'Explaining Patterns of Public Management Reform Diffusion', in S. P. Osborne and L. Brown, eds., *Handbook of Innovation in Public Services* (Cheltenham, UK: Edward Elgar), 15–28.

Walton, G. M. (1970–1971), 'Obstacles to Technical Diffusion in Ocean Shipping, 1675-1775', *Explorations in Economic History* 8/2, 123–40.

Wejnert, B. (2014), *Diffusion of Democracy: The Past and Future of Global Democracy* (New York, NY: Cambridge University Press).

Wollons, R. (eds.) (2000), *Kindergartens & Cultures: The Global Diffusion of an Idea* (New Haven, CT: Yale University Press).

Yin, R. K., Heald, K. A., and Vogel, M. E. (1977), *Tinkering With the System* (Lexington, MA: Lexington Books).

CHAPTER 24

PROCESSES OF EMERGENCE AND CHANGE IN INDUSTRY AND ECOSYSTEM INFRASTRUCTURE

JENNIFER L. WOOLLEY

Overview

INDUSTRIES and their ecosystem of related industries do not emerge suddenly fully formed, but rather require years, if not decades, of development by a wide range of stakeholders. As policymakers and politicians search for ways to accelerate the creation of new industries to promote economic growth, considerable attention has been paid to understanding how to support industrial development, particularly that related to technology and innovation. As such, the study of the context for industries and economic advancement has burgeoned. Embedded in larger social systems (Granovetter 1985; Granovetter and McGuire 1998), industries and ecosystems do not stand alone, but require infrastructure or the "physical, institutional, and organizational structures" that support innovative and economic activities such as entrepreneurship, technology commercialization, industry emergence, and ecosystem development (Woolley 2017a: 1).[1]

Infrastructure itself does not spontaneously appear. In some instances, infrastructure existing in other settings can be adapted to the challenge being addressed by a nascent industry or technology. In other situations, infrastructure components must be developed from scratch. This chapter examines the emergence and change of infrastruc-

[1] The focus of this chapter is on infrastructure that is particularly important for the development of industries and ecosystem. Some components of infrastructure, such as roads, utilities, and health systems are necessary for most economic activity and are not discussed here.

ture that supports industries and ecosystems. The next section reviews the ecological layers that make up the context of organizations and innovation and then summarizes the components of infrastructure particularly relevant to industry and ecosystem development. The second section reviews studies on the temporal dynamics of infrastructure across multiple perspectives, including community ecology, ecosystems, and economic geography. The third section incorporates the drivers and obstacles to industrial advancement and develops a model of infrastructure emergence and change.

Contextual Layers of Infrastructure

The environmental context for innovation, or the seeds of new industries, can be thought of in terms of layers as depicted in Figure 24.1. At the core of an industry is the foundational innovation on which it is based, including technological, social, and institutional innovations. This foundational innovation is developed in and across organizations in industries. While industries have been researched for some time, ecosystems have gained considerable attention as a useful level of analysis on which to build our understanding of innovation and entrepreneurship. The construct is not new but was borrowed from the study of biological systems and applied to groups of organizations (industries) with related production and consumption (Bahrami and Evans 1995; Garnsey and McGlade 2006; Moore 1993, 1997). Generally, ecosystems tend to center on a focal entity such as a firm or platform and the set of organizations that support that entity such as its supply chain and complementary actors. As work on ecosystems has expanded, research has focused on specific types, such as innovation ecosystems based on a technology or value proposition (e.g. Autio and Thomas 2013; Oh, Phillips et al. 2016), business ecosystems have focused on a firm and its environment (e.g. Kapoor and Agarwal 2017; Teece 2016), entrepreneurial ecosystems that support start-ups (e.g. Audretsch et al. 2019; Autio et al. 2018; Stam and Spigel 2017; Spigel and Harrison 2018), and platform ecosystems organized around market interaction facilitators (see Jacobides et al. 2018 for a review of work on ecosystems).

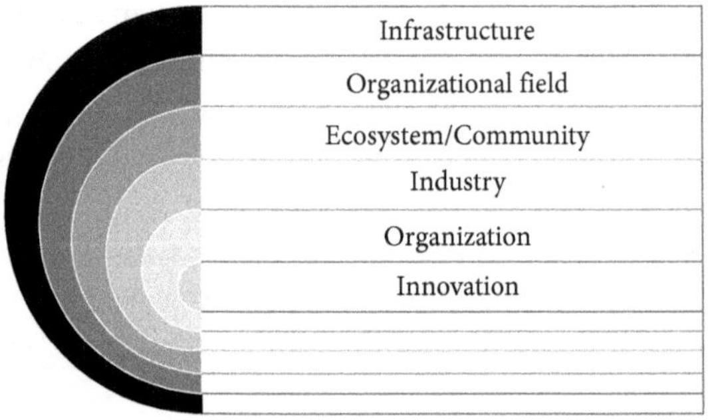

FIGURE 24.1 Contextual Layers of Infrastructure

A construct closely resembling ecosystems is an organizational community: a functionally integrated system of interrelated populations (Astley 1985). Organizational communities are not limited to industries with related production and markets (i.e., ecosystems), but also include symbiotic and commensalistic relationships of competing and non-competing industries. Although relatively neglected in organizational scholarship, this field of study predates that of ecosystems. Astley and Fombrun (1983) advocated for examining the interface between interrelated populations or communities in contrast to single populations as a useful level of analysis to improve our understanding of industrial and economic progress. Since then, organizational communities have been mainly defined in terms of geography (e.g. Baum and Korn 1994) or technological foundation (e.g. Brittain and Wholey 1988; Rao 2002; Ruef 2000; Wade 1995). Organizational communities do not include institutions, markets, governments, and other actors that also support industries and ecosystems.

An organizational field is the closest to the concept of infrastructure. An organizational field is an aggregation of organizations and communities that comprise a recognized area of institutional life such as suppliers, consumers, government agencies, and competitors (Dimaggio and Powell 1983). Interactions between individuals, organizations, and institutional structures are the cornerstone of organizational field configuration (Baum and Singh 1994; Garud 2008; Lampel and Meyer 2008; Oliver and Montgomery 2008). For example, the healthcare community is embedded in the medical field consisting of healthcare providers and facilities, regulatory bodies, insurance providers, and medical and nursing schools. Organizations and transorganizational structures that facilitate interactions between actors, such as medical associations and conferences, facilitate field convergence (Anand and Watson 2004; Garud 2008; Oliver and Montgomery 2008; Powell et al. 2005).

Infrastructure transcends levels of analysis as it includes the social, conomic and political factors that influence industrial activity (Van de Ven 1993). As such, it is a social system that includes tangible and intangible components (Venkataraman 2004) and their interactions beyond an organizational field. The components of social system infrastructure are outlined in Figure 24.2 that is adapted from Van de Ven et al. (2008). Initially, the social systems consisted of three main components: proprietary functions, resource endowments, and institutional arrangements (e.g. Van de Ven 1993; Van de Ven and Garud 1989). Later, market consumption was separated from resource endowments and the model was enlarged to consider infrastructure not only for an industry, but also for the development of technological innovations (Van de Ven et al. 2008; Van de Ven and Hargrave 2004).

Work on industrial infrastructure largely focuses on particular components or sets of interactions. Aldrich and Fiol (1994) emphasize the importance of gaining legitimacy for nascent ventures and innovations, particularly through interactions with collective action, third-party associations, other industries, and educational organizations. Gnyawali and Fogel (1994) consider five areas of infrastructure that support entrepreneurship: government policies and procedures, socioeconomic conditions, entrepreneurial and business skills, financial support to businesses, and non-financial support to businesses.

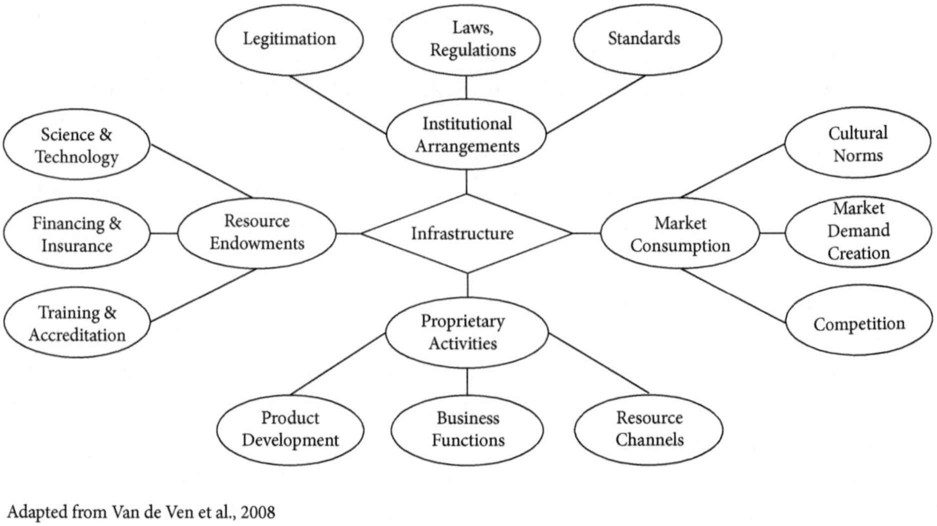

FIGURE 24.2 Industry Social System Infrastructure

Adapted from Van de Ven et al., 2008

Similarly, Bahrami and Evans (1995) identify six structures necessary for new ventures: universities and research institutes, venture capital, talent pool, lead users, entrepreneurial spirit, and services infrastructure. Leydesdorff and Etzkowitz (1998) break knowledge infrastructure into three components: economic dynamics (market competition), internal knowledge production (proprietary R&D), and governance of interactions (supply chain transactions). In their examination of the 3D printing industry in China, Xu and colleagues (2017) propose that innovation ecosystems are similar to infrastructure in that they are composed of three interacting sub-ecosystems: science, technology, and business. Similar to resource endowments, the science sub-ecosystem produces research and scientific knowledge. Proprietary functions and activities take place in the technology sub-ecosystem that produces applied R&D and industrial knowledge and the business sub-ecosystem comprised of organizations and firms involved in commercial activities. As evident in most work on ecosystems, this model does not include the institutional or many of the market-based components of infrastructure (Thomas and Autio 2018). As the framework built by Van de Ven and colleagues is the most comprehensive and incorporates those elements identified by other scholars, it guides the following review of relevant literature (see Woolley (2017a) for a review of literature on infrastructure related to technology entrepreneurship).

Resource Endowments

Infrastructure has three types of resource endowments that are critical for industries and ecosystems: 1) scientific or technological knowledge, 2) financing mechanisms, and

3) a pool of competent labor (Van de Ven and Garud 1989: 207). Basic scientific and technological knowledge provides the foundation for inventions that lead to the commercialization of innovation and industry creation (Audretsch and Feldman 1996). However, commercialization and diffusion of innovations requires knowledge beyond the source of invention to facilitate the advancement of commercial products. Knowledge resource endowments are often attributed to research and education in universities and applied research and development (R&D) activities in firms. Collaborations between university professors and firm researchers that are common in some industries such as biotechnology (Zucker and Darby 1997) aid knowledge resource development. Government laboratories and research centers also generate considerable commercializable technology and intellectual property (Mowery 1998; Smith and Ho 2006; Engardio 2008). The scientific research and innovation activities at universities, firms, and government research labs, in turn, educate and train potential employees and researchers needed to translate inventions into innovations (Bresnahan et al. 2001; Qian et al. 2013), use new technologies (Pennings 1982; Van de Ven 1993; Venkataraman 2004), and create new ventures (Forbes 2013). Similarly, universities and incumbent firms provide fodder for spin-off firms seeking to take nascent technologies to market (Agarwal et al. 2004). However, a skilled labor pool does not equate to an innovative one. To foster innovation commercialization, the workforce must also be entrepreneurial and supported by a risk-taking culture (Saxenian 2006).

The financing of scientific or technological knowledge development supports and shapes innovation and commercialization of discoveries (Etzkowitz et al. 2000; Clayton et al. 2018). Government science, technology, and innovation policies are some of the largest financial supporters of knowledge advancement (Roig-Tierno et al. 2015) through direct investments of universities, firms, national labs, and engineering centers (Etzkowitz 2002; Lerner 1999; Nelson 1994). Other sources of financial support such as angel investors and venture capital also support technology commercialization by sharing business knowledge and social capital (MacMillan et al. 1989; Sapienza 1992), which can increase market entry and deal flow (Pierrakis and Saridakis 2019). Jointly, universities, firms, and government agencies help build resource endowments for technology commercialization infrastructure.

Institutional Arrangements and Mechanisms

Institutional arrangements and mechanisms are organizations or structures that legitimate, regulate, and standardize a social system both internally and in relation to other industrial, social, and political systems (Van de Ven and Garud 1989; Scott 2008). In their function to establish norms, institutional arrangements help build legitimacy and reduce uncertainty that is inherent with nascent technologies and emerging industries (North 1990; Powell 1998).

Several actors engage in institutional arrangements and mechanisms including various associations, interest groups, finance and services providers, private regulators, and government agencies (Clayton et al., 2018). For example, industrial, scientific, and professional associations help shape standards, disseminate knowledge, and legitimate technologies (Aldrich and Ruef 2006; Greenwood et al. 2002; Sine et al. 2005). Governmental actors shape industrial commercialization of technology through regulations and standards implementation (Fligstein 1991; Spencer et al. 2005). Infrastructure that lacks intellectual property protection fails to support technology commercialization (Nakagawa 2001). Providers of resource endowments can also act as institutional arrangements and mechanisms since their support of scientific and technological knowledge development, training and education, and nascent ventures signals legitimacy to stakeholders.

Proprietary Functions and Activities

Proprietary functions are commercialization activities that transform technology into products and services for the market. Examples include product development, applied R&D, manufacturing, marketing, and supply chain mobilization (Van de Ven and Garud 1989; Venkataraman 2004). These activities enable the essential advancement of science and innovation that becomes new industries or transforms existing ones. Proprietary functions and activities occur mainly in firms and sponsoring organizations. Alliances between firms can help innovation through shared knowledge and increased legitimacy (Stuart 2000). Indeed, without proprietary functions, technological inventions would not become commercial innovations (Saxenian 1990).

Organizations that provide physical space and support services such as incubators and accelerators aid the proprietary functions of young, mainly high technology firms by providing business resources, networks, and services (Grimaldi and Grandi 2005; Mian 1996; Clayton et al. 2018; Schwartz 2009; Amezcua et al. 2013). Similarly, government and academic technology transfer agencies help firms appropriate inventions from universities and national labs (Cosh and Hughes 2010; Etzkowitz et al. 2000) and support the commercialization of faculty, staff, and student inventions (Clayton et al. 2018). Spinoffs from universities and national labs have proved to be successful examples of such proprietary activities that create the foundation for new industries (Smith and Ho 2006; Woolley 2017b).

Other organizations that support proprietary functions are often taken for granted (Bahrami and Evans 1995). However, infrastructure lacking mentoring and networking organizations, executive human resource placement firms, knowledgeable legal talent, communications technology, or informal forums, struggles to attract and keep firms seeking to advance innovation (Venkataraman 2004; Audretsch et al. 2015). For example, Silicon Valley's culture, informal networking structures (Saxenian 1994; 1990) and guidance from experienced law firms and venture capitalists (Suchman 2000; Saxenian, 1990) helped shape the configuration of semiconductor technology. These intangible resources are becoming better recognized for their role in industrial and regional transformation.

Market Consumption

Market consumption includes functions essential to a market economy such as customer demand, competition, market creation, and cultural norms (Van de Ven and Hargrave 2004). These mechanisms help build a market by informing and educating potential customers, steering institutional development, and guiding technology adoption (Cho and Mathiassen 2007). Technologies lacking market demand or entering areas already saturated with current alternative products are limited in their ability to appropriate rents for new innovations (Bresnahan et al. 2001; Nakagawa 2001). Market consumption mechanisms also determine how a technology is developed through entrepreneurial activity (Murmann and Tushman 2001).

Temporal Dynamics of Industry and Ecosystems Infrastructure Emergence and Change

Having outlined the major components of an industrial infrastructure, we now turn to the process questions of how infrastructure arises. And what are the temporal patterns or sequences of events in which the infrastructure components emerge and develop? There is a strong body of work that examines how industries are created (see Gustafsson et al. 2016 for a review of industry emergence literature) and how ecosystems emerge (see Jacobides et al. 2018 and Spigel and Harrison 2018). Similarly, there is a good amount of work on the individual components of infrastructure. However, this work is fragmented across multiple disciplines and perspectives. Work that does address infrastructure dynamics rarely attends to how it emerges or changes over time. As infrastructure is fundamental to the creation of industries and ecosystems, it merits considerable attention. The next section reviews work that provides insight into the temporal dynamics of infrastructure emergence and evolution, starting with research on community ecology, ecosystems and fields, and then geography more broadly. Table 24.1 summarizes the works representative of key themes from each perspective.

Community Ecology as a Forerunner

The community ecology perspective was developed in contrast to organizational ecology to highlight the role of organizational relationships and joint actions (Astley and Fombrun 1983). Several studies applying the community ecology perspective established the importance of understanding the interdependencies between organizations in different types of industries and sectors, as well as interactions between infrastructure

Table 24.1 Representative Studies on Infrastructure Components and Their Interactions

Perspective	Authors	Focus	Context	Findings
Community	Baum & Korn, 1994; Korn & Baum, 1994	Interaction	Largest public Canadian firms	Interdependence of populations includes operations, performance, and employment
	Wade, 1995	Interaction	Microprocessor	Competition between rival technology communities influences technology dominance
	Ruef, 2000	Interaction	Healthcare	Community and population density and mass and regulative legitimacy influence creation of new organizational forms
	Sorensen, 2004	Interaction	Denmark	Interaction of similar industry's firm failures employment with other industries' entrepreneurship
	Audia, Freeman & Reynolds, 2006	Interaction	Instrument manufacturers	Symbiotic and commensalistic relationships between populations influence entrepreneurship
Ecosystem	Ingram & Inman, 1996	Interaction	Hotel populations near Niagara Falls	Competitors work together to build institutions in reaction to common challenges
	Murtha, Lenway, & Hart, 2001	Interaction	Flat-panel industry	Academia, industry, and governments create knowledge for technology
	Lounsbury, Ventresca, & Hirsch, 2003	Components	Recycling	Government acts help build legitimacy for technology
	Giarratana, 2004	Firm actions	Software	Large incumbent firms develop technology breakthroughs
	Munir & Phillips, 2005	Interaction	Photography	Disparate stakeholders establish new institutions and competitive norms
	Powell et al., 2005	Interaction	Biotechnology & pharmaceuticals	Collaborations as key to knowledge creation
	Adner & Kapoor, 2010	Firm actions	Semiconductor	Incumbent firms' actions shape technology development and adoption
	Tuertscher, Garud, & Kumaraswamy, 2014	Interaction	ATLAS system	Experts across organizations coordinate technology creation across boundaries

Perspective	Authors	Focus	Context	Findings
	Khaire, 2014	Interaction	Fashion	How socio-cognitive legitimacy is built in a new industry
	Sanderson & Simons, 2014	Interaction	LED	Development of infrastructure relies on the interaction of stakeholders in all key infrastructure components
	Overholm, 2015	Interaction	Solar service	Firms shape opportunities for technology commercialization
Ecosystem	Ansari, Garud, & Kumaraswamy, 2016	Firm actions	Tivo & TV	Incumbent firms' actions influence how entrepreneurs enter a nascent market, and adjust its strategy and positioning
	Xu et al., 2017	Components	3D Printing in China	Ecosystems are composed of three sub-ecosystems: science, technology, and business
	Thompson, Purdy, & Ventresca, 2018	Interaction	Seattle	Disparate populations interact to garner ecosystems legitimacy
	Hannah & Eisenhardt, 2018	Firm actions	Solar ecosystem	The use of cooperation and competition to survive and shape new ecosystems
Geography	Nelson and Rosenberg, 1993	Component	Multiple technologies	Government is key to developing national innovation system
	Saxenian, 1994	Interaction	Silicon Valley	Institutional environment and social structures are necessary for the development of the technology across the cluster
	Saxenian, 1999	Interaction	Silicon Valley	Cultural and professional norms shape how innovation progressed and scaled
	Etzkowitz, 2002	Interaction	Multiple technologies	University-industry-government networks drive innovation
	Acs and Varga, 2005	Component	Europe	Entrepreneurship and human capital support technological development
	Pitelis, 2012	Component	Theoretical	Entrepreneurship drives ecosystems development
	Best, 2013	Component	Boston minicomputer	An ecosystem's ability to shift resources facilitates regional cluster growth
	Van de Wiele, 2017		12 Regions in Netherlands	A regions' resources and institutions influence its level of entrepreneurship
	Spigel & Harrison, 2018		Multiple ecosystems	Connectivity is essential for infrastructure

components. Baum and Rao (Chapter 18 of this volume) provide a detailed discussion of the levels within community ecology and temporal dynamics of genealogical evolution across these levels. Baum and Korn applied the community ecology perspective in two studies examining the performance of the largest public Canadian firms and found that populations of similar firms within a community are interdependent—influencing the operations, performance, and employment of other populations in the community over time (Baum and Korn 1994; Korn and Baum 1994). Wade (1995, 1996) finds that struggles for microprocessor market dominance can be conceptualized as competition between rival communities, each consisting of a set of interdependent populations using a different technology. Shifting to organizational forms, Ruef (2000) considers how, within an existing healthcare community, three factors influenced form creation: the number of other populations in the community, the density and mass of the focal population, and regulative legitimacy. Likewise, an increase in the entrepreneurial activity in one population in a community increased the legitimacy and opportunities for entrepreneurship in other populations in the emerging American film industry from 1895 to 1929 (Mezias and Kuperman 2000). Similarly, entrepreneurship is higher in an industry when similar industries are experiencing higher firm failures or have high employment (Sorensen 2004), or when the focal industry has symbiotic and commensalistic relationships with other populations in the field (Audia et al. 2006).

These studies focus on the influence of populations within the community on other populations, mainly considering their interdependence (Freeman and Audia 2006). Thus, this work highlights the development of proprietary functions and activities. However, as infrastructure extends beyond proprietary functions and industry interactions, we must turn to other work to gain additional insight into infrastructure emergence.

The Context of Ecosystems

Studies using an ecosystem approach that focus on the context of one industry as a complex system also provide insight into the temporal dynamics of infrastructure. For example, Murtha et al. (2001) find that multiple stakeholders including academia, industry, and governments created the resource endowment of knowledge needed to develop the flat-panel industry, and their involvement shifted over time as the technology was adopted. Likewise, large incumbent firms in the encryption niche of the early software industry developed the technological breakthroughs on which start-ups were founded (Giarratana 2004). Tuertscher and colleagues (2014) show how the complex technological system, ATLAS, was developed by over 3,000 experts across 175 separate institutions who relied on a common "boundary infrastructure" (Bowker and Star 1999) of language, tools, and models to coordinate activity, and additional technological knowledge resources that were developed over time through cycles of interactions. These experts would not have been able to utilize the boundary infrastructure had they not been educated in a common scientific language that transcended organizational and institutional boundaries (Tuertscher et al. 2014). Building on this study, Garud et al. (2019) find that these experts used deliberation, meshworking, and reflective judgment to diffuse tensions inherent in the large-scale community, which enabled them to make progress towards positive outcomes.

Populations not only influence each other's success, employment, and entrepreneurship, but also they can collaborate to build institutions in response to common issues (Ingram and Inman 1996; Khaire 2014) and shape opportunities for market consumption and commercialization (Overholm 2015). Indeed, individuals and groups that are initially fragmented and disparate can coalesce to build more coordinated patterns of social interactions that help garner legitimacy, build institutions, and develop competitive norms for an ecosystem such as United States recycling (Lounsbury et al. 2003), photography (Munir and Phillips 2005) and social impact initiatives (Thompson et al. 2018). Incumbent firms across industries in an ecosystem grapple with and influence technological development and commercialization in multiple ways. For example, the pace at which innovations are developed and adopted throughout an ecosystem is predicated on how incumbent firms manage the limitations of the new and old technologies (Adner and Kapoor 2010). Incumbent firms can shape how entrepreneurs enter and position themselves in a nascent market (Ansari et al. 2016). Both cooperation and competitive strategies are necessary for young firms while a technology is nascent and its trajectory is uncertain (Hannah and Eisenhardt 2018; Powell et al. 2005).

Studies using an ecosystem perspective tend to center on a focal industry or technology and examine the components and the interactions specific to aiding the focal industry (see Table 24.1). Research using a geographical lens takes a broader perspective across multiple technologies within a region or national context. It is to these studies we turn next.

Geography—Clusters and National Systems of Innovation

Research on geographically bound infrastructure mainly examines regional clusters (Feldman et al. 2005; Feldman and Francis 2004), national industrial clusters (Porter 1990), and systems of innovation (Etzkowitz and Leydesdorff 2000; Lundvall 1992; Lundvall et al. 2002; Nelson 1993). These works generally start with the premise that the co-location of organizations and institutions supports industrial progress (Krugman 1991; Nelson 1993; 1994), which helps to reduce uncertainty inherent for emerging technologies (Jansson 2011). Studies on cluster emergence and evolution tend to use one of four main models: industry life cycle, cluster lifecycle, complex adaptive systems, and micro-dynamics view of cluster life cycle (MacGregor and Madsen 2018). In one of the earliest studies of regional clusters, Saxenian (1994) highlights how the institutional environment and social structures of Silicon Valley supported continuous innovation and learning, findings which diverged from contemporary work that favored technology trajectories or path dependency. In fact, cultural and professional norms in the region needed to support challenging mainstream management practices that tended to stifle innovation and flexibility (Saxenian 1999).

Interactions between government agencies, universities, and industry are also critical as they can buoy the creation of innovation systems that enable economic growth (Etzkowitz 2002; Nelson and Rosenberg 1993). Such interactions were essential for the Boston area that had complementary turbine, chemical engineering, and optics industries, which were able to transition to other technologies by reorganizing human capital, technological capabilities, and funding (Best 2013). Sanderson and Simons (2014) found that similar interactions between researchers, firms, governance mechanisms, institutions, and markets were critical for the emergence of the solid-state lighting industry.

Scholars debate whether entrepreneurship catalyzes ecosystem development or if new ventures co-locate in locations with desirable infrastructure elements. Acs and Varga (2005) find that entrepreneurship and the labor market positively influence ecosystem innovation in Europe. Pitelis (2012) argues that entrepreneurs choosing a site or a pioneering firm expanding into a new location can spark ecosystem development. Van de Wiele (2017) focuses on two sets of resources—1) physical, financial, and human capital and 2) market consumption and services support—and institutions—including formal institutions, culture, and social networks—and finds that high levels of both support higher rates of entrepreneurship. However, Spigel and Harrison (2018) argue that in nascent ecosystems, the lack of interaction between organizations, creation or recycling of resources, worker mobility, and cultural support does little to support entrepreneurial activities. In this chicken and egg debate, the jury is still out.

Social Systems Approach and Emergence Across Industries and Technologies

Perhaps the most comprehensive treatment of infrastructure takes the social systems approach to address the larger context for industries and ecosystems. As the social systems approach crosses many levels of analysis, it is a uniquely useful perspective to shed light on infrastructure emergence and change, particularly the co-evolution of industry, science, technology, institutions and policy (see Nelson 1994; Van de Ven and Garud 1994; Rosenkopf and Tushman 1994; Geels 2004). Table 24.2 summarizes the core studies that speak to the process of infrastructure development, which are reviewed here. Please note that these studies start with a technology or innovation that can only be created through a long history of knowledge, skill, and insight (Usher 1954).

In their seminal work on technological discontinuities and change, Anderson and Tushman (1990; also Tushman and Anderson 1986) propose an evolutionary model of technological advancement that occurs over three main phases: breakthrough, ferment (competition), and convergence (dominant design and standardization). This model focuses on the technology itself, particularly the emergence of dominant designs and

Table 24.2 Summary of Process Models of Infrastructure Development

Authors	Foundation	Phase 1	Phase 2	Phase 3	Phase	Phase 5
Anderson & Tushman, 1990	Technology	Breakthrough	Ferment and competition	Convergence (dominant design and standardization)		
Leblebici, Salancik, Copay & King, 1991	Field change	Organize interdependence	Introduce new practices	New institutions create competition for resources	Dominant players adopt new practices	Field relation ships and structure institutionalized
Van de Ven & Garud, 1993	Technology (cochlear implants)	Endowment creation (scientific knowledge)	Appropriation (proprietary activities)	Expansion	Stabilization (dominant design)	
Saxenian, 1994; 1999	Geography (Silicon Valley)	Institutional environment	Social structure	Norms	Technology	
Hunt & Aldrich, 1998	Technology (WWW)	Innovation acts as catalyst	New firms, organizational forms and populations	Community growth	Legitimation	
Feldman, Francis, & Bercovitz, 2005	Geography (entrepreneurship)	Emergence	Commercialization	Maturation		
Aldrich & Ruef, 2006	Geography (Santa Barbara)	Shift in societal norms	Organizations created to support new norms	Creation of new regulatory regimes	Funding	Selection
Woolley, 2007	Technology (Nano)	Conceptualization	Foundational technology created	Funding support	Norms and values change and new regulatory regimes	Entrepreneurship
Woolley, 2010	Technology (Nano)	Conceptualization	Foundational technology created	Commercial application in upstream industries	Commercialization in downstream industries	
Oksanen & Hautamaki, 2014	Geography (Jyväskylä, Finland)	Groundwork	Deliberate interactions	Evaluation	Self-sustained growth	
Halse, 2017	Geography (Norway)	Exogenous event trigger	Governance changes	Cultural and normative changes, knowledge creation		
Davidian, 2018	Technology (Space tourism)	Initial research and knowledge sharing	Market entry through proprietary functions	Institutional legitimation		

standards by entrepreneurs and incumbent firms, but does not attend to the macro-level influences. Taking a field-level approach, Leblebici and colleagues (1991) argue that contextual changes such as that in infrastructure, take place over five stages: organization of the field's interdependence, introduction of new practices, creation of competition for resources by new institutions, adoption of new practices by dominant players, and institutionalization of field relationships and structures. However, in their studies of cochlear implant technology, Van de Ven and Garud (1993, 1994) highlight the uneven nature of infrastructure development over time. As shown in Figure 24.3, they found that the proprietary functions, resource endowments, and institutional arrangements emerged over a thirty-three-year period in the configuration of the infrastructure through four temporal patterns: (1) endowments creation when university researchers advance basic scientific knowledge, followed by (2) appropriation when firms collaborate with research institutes to gain proprietary rights to basic research knowledge and initiate commercial activities, (3) expansion of infrastructure development in both public and private sectors, and (4) stabilization when a dominant design emerges and the very infrastructure components that facilitated the earlier periods of industrial emergence began to constrain subsequent growth (see also Van de Ven et al. 2008). Garud and Rappa (1994) elaborate these findings by emphasizing the importance of reciprocal interactions between beliefs, artifacts, and evaluation by those involved in research, governance, and funding.

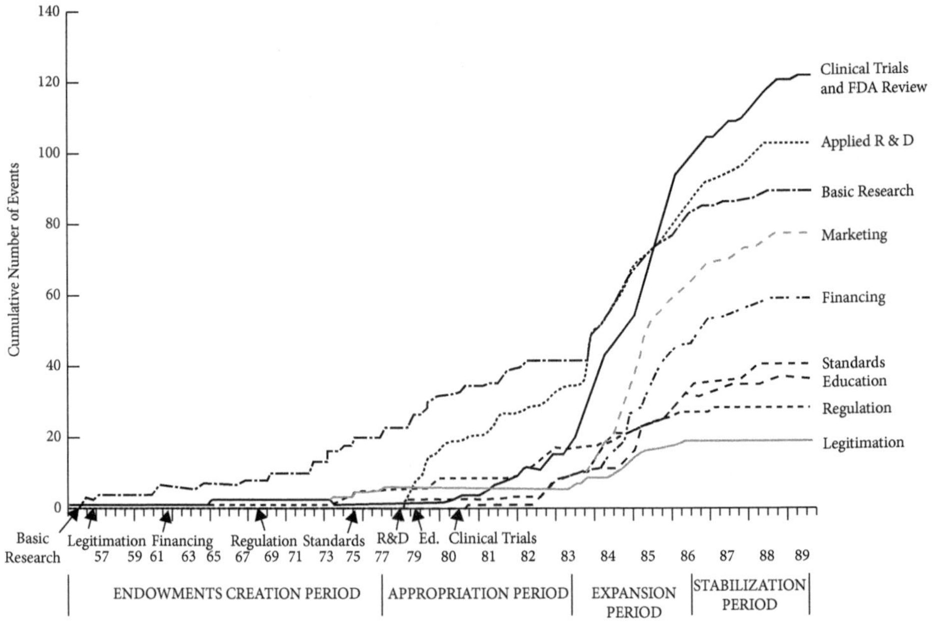

FIGURE 24.3 Cumulative Events in the Development of Functions for the Cochlear Implant Industry

From Van de Ven and Garud, 1993

As mentioned, Saxenian (1999) highlights how industrial development of technological innovations is a messy process that does not follow a predetermined paradigm. In her more holistic view of innovation commercialization, she argues that together the institutional environment, social structures, and culture enable innovation and further industrial growth (Saxenian 1994, 1999). Also focusing on innovation, entrepreneurship, and legitimacy, Hunt and Aldrich (1998) apply work on new organizational forms and populations to the evolution of organizational communities, and argue that technological innovation is a major catalyst for the creation of new firms, organizational forms and populations that promote and sustain the growth and evolution of a community. Furthermore, the development of an organizational community depends on social legitimacy at multiple levels of analysis, including organizations, populations, and communities (Hunt and Aldrich 1998: 267).

Other scholars find that innovative regions or clusters evolve in more regular, albeit still messy, stages. Focusing on the central role of the entrepreneur in the creation of innovative clusters, Feldman and colleagues (2005) find that these clusters evolve over three phases: 1) emergence when entrepreneurial innovation is sparked and relationships between firms and institutions begin to form; 2) commercialization of the nascent technology along with self-organized and deepening of self-reinforcing feedback among entrepreneurs, enterprises, institutions, and resources; and 3) industry maturation and convergence into an innovative and entrepreneurial system. This is a high-level treatment of context, and incumbent firms are not prominent. Looking at community-level emergence and evolution of the alternative-institutions movement in Santa Barbara in the late 1960s and early 1970s with the variation, selection, retention lens, Aldrich and Ruef (2006) find that as the societal norms concerning the role of organizations changed, other organizations were created to support these new norms, and a new community of symbiotically linked organizations emerged. They find that the creation of new regulatory regimes to organize and regulate rights, laws, responsibilities, and actions of existing populations provided opportunities for entrepreneurship that led to the creation of new populations and the revitalization of existing ones (Aldrich and Ruef 2006). Funding sources, such as venture capitalists and stock underwriting firms, supplied the much needed monetary and social capital for growing firms and organizations. Next, implicit selection forces, such as competition and conformity, that institutionalized norms, eliminated types of variation not well suited to the community (Aldrich and Ruef 2006).

In my own work on the emergence and evolution of nanotechnology, I have studied the infrastructure that influenced its configuration (Woolley 2007, 2010, 2014, 2017b; Woolley and Rottner 2008). Similar to other studies, I find that researchers in universities and incumbent firms were the first to advance nanotechnology towards industrial application (Woolley 2007). This was followed by interactions across academia and incumbent firms to legitimate the technology. Only then did funding from government agencies and subsequent private sources start to support industrial development. Later, the role of government changed from funding provider to coordinator and regulator. Simultaneously, norms and values coalesced and entrepreneurship strengthened.

Furthermore, when a technology is new and infrastructure lacks commercialization agents, entrepreneurship or intrapreneurship in upstream industries (e.g., basic materials and instrumentation for nanotechnology) is needed to develop the innovation and make it available for further development in downstream (consuming) industries (Woolley 2010). Thus, after a radical technological discontinuity, new firms tend to emerge first in upstream industries that build tools, inputs, and expertise necessary for supply chain mobilization.

Building on these studies, I next take a more holistic view to examine the configuration of infrastructure components as shown in Figure 24.4, which highlights the interdependence and interaction of the subcomponents (Woolley 2014). I find that the inherent risk and uncertainty associated with breakthrough inventions limits the availability of funding to support its development. For example, during the early years, most researchers could not find funding to support their work on nanotechnology since it was considered empirically impossible and, thereby, not worth funding. Additionally, most institutions lacked interdisciplinary activities and encouraged discipline-specific advancements. Thus, researchers funded their projects by framing them in light of their home disciplines and collaborated to create cross-discipline symposia, conferences and

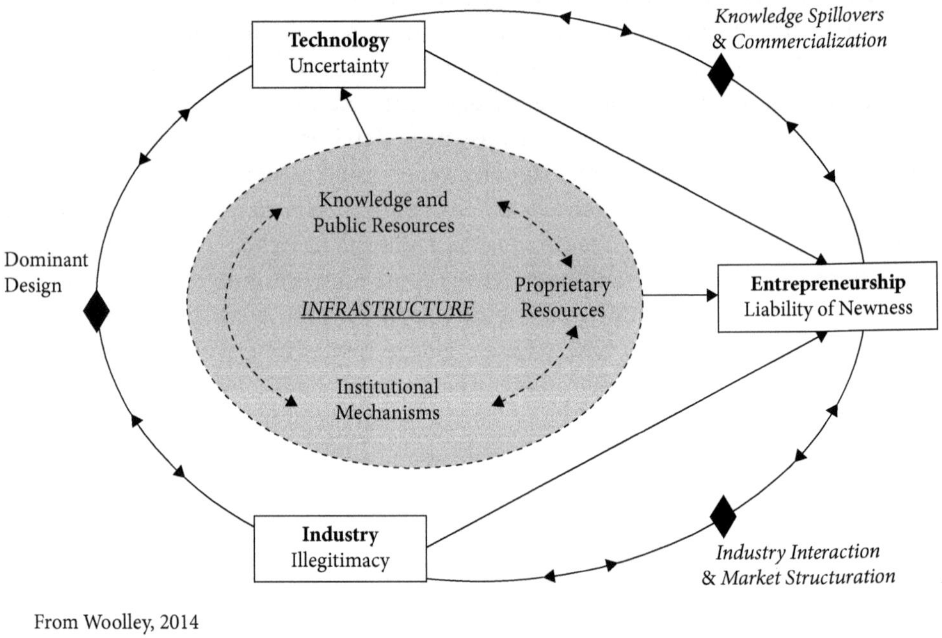

FIGURE 24.4 Infrastructure for Nascent Technology Entrepreneurship in Industries and the Trifecta of Burdens

From Woolley, 2014

labs to share knowledge, build legitimacy for the field, and shift norms of practice (Woolley 2014). Researchers in existing firms found that they did not have the tools needed to further their work and developed innovations out of necessity. These firms did not intend to commercialize these inventions though, and often the intellectual property was licensed to entrepreneurs for further development. Importantly, individual elements of infrastructure are necessary, but not sufficient to support industry creation and emergence. Indeed, through the process of systemic co-evolution, individual components interact and cross-develop to build the fabric of infrastructure (Woolley 2014). These findings support the argument that the process of infrastructure emergence requires actors to transcend organizational and disciplinary boundaries (Van de Ven et al. 2008).

Studies on innovation clusters find similar patterns. In their study of the Jyväskylä, Finland region, Oksanen and Hautamaki (2014) find that its transformation into an innovation cluster took place over four stages: 1) groundwork built through interactions between many different actors including universities, research labs, government, and firms; 2) deliberate network formation and instigation of educational and social interactions; 3) evaluation of the first two stages; 4) self-sustaining growth. This work suggests that the development of industrial infrastructure can be deliberately designed and coordinated. However, this is not always the case as often stakeholders act agentic in terms of their organization or the immediate future of the innovation (Cusumano et al. 1992). Furthermore, exogenous events influence the globalization of supply chains that shape the transformation of industrial clusters (Halse 2017). These changes are affected by, and themselves influence the cluster's culture, which subsequently alters how actors interact from relational to more formal transactions. These studies reinforce Garud and Rappa's (1994) findings that individual actors can influence infrastructure configuration when knowledge is built and applied to a new context.

Finally, Davidian (2018) applies the social systems infrastructure model to the emergence of space tourism. He finds that initially foundational resource endowments are accumulated through government-funded research, knowledge-sharing and education that builds cognitive legitimacy. Proprietary functions grew in new and incumbent firm through R&D, pre-production testing, and production activities. This finding supports the argument that intellectual property from universities, existing firms, and government research labs is important for commercializing nascent technologies (Woolley 2017b). Proprietary functions were supported by institutional arrangements such as endorsements, governance changes, and technology standards that created sociopolitical legitimacy. Although not identified specially, Davidian (2018) shows that market consumption was built through prize competitions, which also influenced legitimacy in other areas. At this point in space tourism, it is not clear that an adequate infrastructure has accumulated to support long-term viability of the industry.

Synthesis—A Process Model of Infrastructure Emergence and Change

The trajectory of a new industry is inherently unknown and unknowable. It is not a surprise that the models regarding processes related to infrastructure emergence vary greatly; however, patterns exist. Table 24.3 integrates these disparate perspectives by classifying the processes identified in these works as one of the infrastructure components proposed by Van de Ven and colleagues described earlier: resource endowments, proprietary functions and activities, institutional arrangements, and market consumption (Van de Ven 1993; Van de Ven and Garud 1989, 1993; Van de Ven and Hargrave 2004). Synthesizing findings from research, Figure 24.5 provides a model of infrastructure configuration. This model is not meant to be prescriptive or linear. It does, however, suggest a process model of infrastructure emergence that is based on five key propositions.

Emergence and change occurs in reaction to a spark—a stepping away from the status quo. Table 24.2 shows that researchers have called this by many different names—breakthrough, innovation catalyst, shift in societal norms, conceptualization, and exogenous trigger. Table 24.3 indicates this simply as *Spark*. It is important to note that a spark is not limited to a technological discovery (e.g., Anderson and Tushman 1990; Van de Ven and Garud 1993; Woolley 2007, 2010), but can be a shift in societal norms (Aldrich and Ruef 2006) that lead to a social movement (Sikavica and Pozner 2013; Weber et al. 2008), an institutional change (e.g., Leblebici et al. 1991) or regulatory shift (e.g., Aldrich and Ruef 2006; Lounsbury et al. 2003). This suggests that infrastructure emergence and change is triggered by a fundamental catalyst at the technological, social, institutional, or regulatory level.

> Proposition 1: The emergence of and changes in infrastructure are catalyzed by a fundamental spark that triggers component configuration and reconfiguration.

The components of infrastructure for industries and ecosystems are just that—structural components. Alone, they can do little to support industrial development. Yet, each one is necessary to support commercialization of innovation or the social, economic, and political landscape needed for long-term industrial advancement (Van de Ven 1993). Indeed, all studies regarding infrastructure and industrial development underscore the importance of each component and their interdependence (see Woolley 2014). And it was the lack of strong resource endowments, demand, and institutional arrangements that impeded the advancement of software technology in Asia (Nakagawa 2001). It is difficult, if not impossible, however, to determine how much of any individual component is enough as these will be context specific, or whether an abundance in one component can make up for a deficit in another. Nevertheless, the emergence of industries and ecosystems requires the systems-level interaction of all individual components, which suggests the following proposition:

Table 24.3 Integrated Process of Infrastructure Emergence and Change

Resource endowments	*Spark*	Invention and scientific knowledge building	Field defined	Continuous innovation, learning, and training					
				Exploratory funding support				Traditional funding mechanisms emerge	
Institutional arrangements		Knowledge-based institutional arrangements created	Institutional, social, and cultural support	Institutional definition of medium of exchange	Organizations created to support new norms	Governance changes and creation of new regulatory regimes		Convergence	Dominant design and institutionalization
Proprietary functions				Alliances between knowledge generators and commercialization firms	Appropriation (proprietary activities)	Commercial application in upstream industries	Support organizations emerge	Commercialization in downstream industries	Maturation support structures and culture)
Market consumption				Definition of and competition for critical tools and resources	Market pull	Ferment and competition	Industrial expansion	Evaluation and selection	Retention and self-sustained growth
Time		*Early*							*Late*

Proposition 2: Each component of the infrastructure social system is necessary, but not sufficient to support industrial emergence.

Industrial development also requires cross-component coordination, often by organizations that are not involved directly in the economic exchange of commercialization (Lynn et al. 1996). These actors must cross boundaries to induce the configuration of separate components into a cohesive infrastructure (Woolley 2014). For example, governments often fund foundational science and technology research through policies and initiatives, and universities support technology transfer of intellectual property created by professors and students, which leads to commercialization and entrepreneurship. Not only are the components necessary, but also their interaction and coevolution are paramount (Baum and Singh 1994). As far as entrepreneurship supporting or even driving industry creation and emergence goes, a trifecta of burdens must be considered, including technological uncertainty, lack of industry legitimacy, and the liability of newness, shown in Figure 24.4 (Woolley 2014). As such, interactions between economic, technological, and governance actors enable the development and commercialization of innovation (Garud 2008; Lampel and Meyer 2008; Leydesdorff and Etzkowit, 1998; Oliver and Montgomery 2008). Figure 24.5 shows how infrastructure components interact to combat these burdens by garnering support, reducing uncertainty, establishing knowledge spillovers and technology commercialization, aiding industry interaction and value chain creation, and enhancing commercial legitimacy and institutionalization. Thus, it is the interaction of the components that enables industrial development, leading to the proposition:

Proposition 3: To be effective, all of the components of infrastructure must interact to overcome the trifecta of burdens inherent in industry emergence.

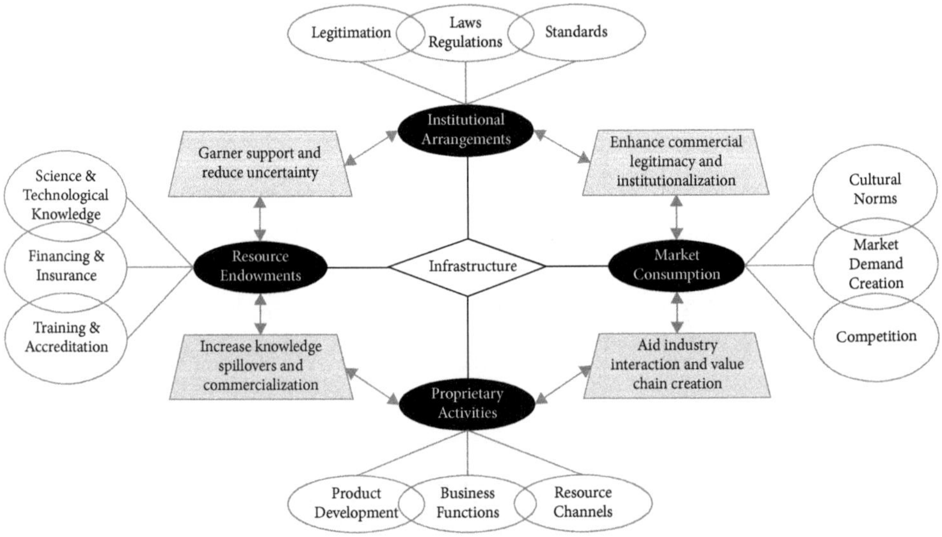

FIGURE 24.5 Model of Infrastructure Configuration

In terms of the temporal dynamics of infrastructure development, there is a certain degree of path dependence required as some activities and resources are needed before others can emerge. Not only do these components need to exist, but also infrastructure requires a cumulative synthesis of components such as knowledge and skills (Usher 1954; see also Chapter 22 by Garud and Turunen, this volume). This process takes place over a long period of time and is linear (Usher 1954). For example, advanced educational systems that support the knowledge creation necessary for the innovation on which new industries are formed are a foundational element of infrastructure and precede the configuration of other components. Certainly, after scientific discovery has accumulated a critical mass of researchers and scientists in universities, labs, and firms, these actors subsequently create industrial, scientific, professional, and trade associations to disseminate knowledge, build community norms, develop the market, and legitimate the technology (Aldrich and Ruef 2006; Sine et al. 2005). The further advancement of technologies requires skilled labor, which requires training by universities or incumbent firms familiar with the complexities of the technology. The training of skilled labor to commercialize and support the diffusion of an innovation is required before it can take hold. Thus, resource endowments develop through a cumulative synthesis of individual sub-components.

Similarly, financial resources for scientific discovery are needed before funding for commercialization of technology since invention itself must exist before knowledge spillovers between resource endowments and proprietary entities can occur. Furthermore, since it is more difficult to measure the value created by scientific discovery, support for basic knowledge and science is less risk averse than funding for industrial development is. These are different types of financial support with different motivations and objectives. For example, angel investment and venture capital support the commercialization of technologies that have been funded by government and academic organizations. Without the support of the innovations on which new industries are developed, there would be no entrepreneurial activities for more traditional funding mechanisms to support. Just as one infrastructure component alone is insufficient, a critical mass of a range of accumulated components is necessary to support industrial advancement. The process of accruing such a critical mass requires stakeholders across knowledge and technology development, market, and governance systems, which is time consuming and challenging. This suggests the following proposition:

> Proposition 4: The emergence of an infrastructure is a cumulative achievement involving the accretion of many interrelated institutional, resources, market, and proprietary events involving many actors in the public and private sectors over an extended period of time.

Infrastructure emergence is not completely without caution. In terms of the evolution of an innovation on which an industry or ecosystem develops, one would expect that a dominant design would not emerge until after a proof of concept, initial adoption, and commercial evaluation had occurred. However, at any point, the trajectory for an innovation can change. Indeed, innovation is heavily influenced by historical events (Feldman and Francis 2004; Kenney and von Burg 1999) and exogenous actions. For example, policy-makers at a US National Institute of Health and Food & Drug Administration sponsored conference decreed multiple channels the dominant design for cochlear implants before tests demonstrated the superiority of a particular channel designs (Van de Ven and Garud 1994). Thus, individual actors may alter the trajectory of a nascent technology or industry despite best efforts on the part of other stakeholders. Likewise, while policy-makers may create programs to support industrial emergence using extant knowledge, future conditions may make these programs obsolete.

Social systems such as industries are fluid and changing and the roles of infrastructure components shift over time. In some cases, the existing structures and actors in a field can hinder the advancement of a technology due to inertia and their own interests (Garud et al. 2002), which are difficult to overcome. Infrastructure that is inflexible or myopic may not be able to change should the foundational innovation be replaced or made redundant. For example, the supply chain and complementary industries that supported the diffusion of 2G telephony could not keep up with the pace of change needed to implement 3G successfully, thereby slowing its adoption (Ansari and Garud 2009). Inertia and inflexibility can take place at the geographic or institutional levels as well. For example, the creation of smaller innovation ecosystems or idiosyncratic regulations that conflict may preclude a wider development of an industrial system (Barnett and Carroll 1993). Should institutional arrangements fail to realign with changing norms and practices, they become irrelevant, leading to missed opportunities (Woolley and MacGregor 2019). Infrastructure must remain adaptable and responsive to stay relevant. Therefore, infrastructure components must be re-evaluated periodically or risk becoming inertial forces, bottlenecks, or hurdles that constrain subsequent industrial development.

> Proposition 5: The components necessary to facilitate the emergence of an infrastructure can become inertial forces, bottlenecks or hurdles that constrain subsequent industrial development.

Conclusion: Opportunities for Advancing Knowledge

The emergence and change of infrastructure that supports industries and ecosystems are important phenomena to understand. As this chapter has shown, researchers across multiple disciplines have examined various components of infrastructure. Unfortunately, several challenges have limited the progression of this body of work. Indeed, literature on infrastructure emergence and change seems disparate at first glance. The lack of coherent vocabulary and theory only add confusion. On the one hand, it could be argued that when research starts to explore a phenomenon, multiple perspectives will use their own lenses and language to improve understanding. On the other hand, researchers have been studying the context of industries for several decades and a common language has yet to materialize.

One reason for the limited progress in our understanding of infrastructure is the multitude of disciplines interested in the phenomenon. As many disciplines, unfortunately, do not converse with one another (or cross boundaries), several scholars have examined virtually the same research question using different language and coming to similar conclusions. For example, as reviewed above, several studies from different perspectives have identified components of infrastructure including evolutionary (e.g., Aldrich and Fiol 1994), entrepreneurship and social systems (e.g., Van de Ven 1993), innovation policy (e.g., Leydesdorff and Etzkowitz 1998), innovation ecosystems (Xu et al. 2017) and systems of innovation (e.g., Nelson 1993). Surprisingly, there is little cross citation between these perspectives. Instead of building on previous works, it is almost as though scholars in each perspective are starting fresh. This leads to fragmented views that, as time goes by and research accumulates within a discipline, is difficult to reconcile. As such, the overlapping of disciplines and parallel vocabularies leads to a lack of coherent theory (e.g., Forbes and Kirsch 2011).

The lack of common terminology within a discipline is even more problematic. For example, there is substantial overlap between the constructs of organizational field and ecosystem, yet studies on the topics rarely converse with one another. Yes, there are nuances within each area of research, but there is also much to be learned from each other as well. Certainly, our understanding of what supports industrial development would improve if similarities were acknowledged and studies built upon one another.

Progress on our understanding of infrastructure dynamics is also hindered by the difficulty of studying such a large, complex system. For one, studying the emergence of a social system requires an extensive amount of longitudinal data (Poole et al. 2000). In the case of infrastructure, comprehensive data must be collected on multiple populations and their interactions over time. Van de Ven and Garud (1993) found that twenty-two years of non-commercial activity transpired before the introduction of the cochlear implant. Studying the origins of nanotechnology required over three decades of data (Woolley 2007, 2014). Although individual industry histories are becoming more common, rarely do we have data on the histories of multiple, related industries and their contexts. Studying the creation of infrastructure requires data on the situation before the infrastructure emerged through its early years. This entails an overwhelming amount of archival data that can be difficult to obtain.

Nevertheless, understanding how to support industries and ecosystems with infrastructure is important for firms, policy-makers, and governments. The current state of our understanding includes a fairly robust set of infrastructure components and their interactions. As infrastructure shapes the ability how firms, technologies, and industries emerge and grow, the state of infrastructure holds important implications for entrepreneurs, firms, investors, and policy-makers. For example, entrepreneurs and entrepreneurial firms entering nascent markets should consider the state of infrastructure when determining their market entry strategy for two reasons: potential weaknesses and opportunities. Insufficient infrastructure can hinder a firm's launch. If this weakness is not addressed, a firm may struggle. At the same time, insufficient infrastructure can provide opportunities for enterprising actors who are willing to develop the deficient components. Similarly, investors should analyze the availability of infrastructure for their potential investees to determine fatal flaws in the business model. Potential investees entering markets that lack sufficient infrastructure may require considerably more time, energy, and resources to support their businesses than first considered.

Policy-makers and governments stand to benefit from understanding infrastructure as well. As locations (cities, regions, and nations) seek ways to promote innovation and economic development and growth, it follows that a solid understanding of the locations' infrastructure to support such activity is fundamental. Policy-makers and governments that identify and remedy weaknesses in their infrastructure can bolster the development of existing commerce and catalyze the creation of new industries.

Several opportunities for further research remain. Infrastructure work thus far tends to use high-technology settings. Few studies have looked at infrastructure for industries less driven by technological innovations (notable exceptions include Baum and Korn 1994 and Ingram and Inman 1996). It would be useful to compare and contrast the emergence of high and low technology industries to consider how the infrastructure needed to support each may differ. Furthermore, since the body of work is fragmented and lacks cohesion, it is not clear if the findings are generalizable. There may be technologies that emerge through the brute force of a few powerful actors, circumventing our current models of understanding.

Another opportunity for research is to expand our understanding of culture. Although work has mentioned the importance of culture (e.g. Saxenian 1994), little work has examined its role. The cultural component of infrastructure has been undertheorized and work has yet to identify the infrastructure mechanisms that lead to a supportive culture. Lundvall and colleagues (2002) argue that the time horizon of agents, trust, and predominant economic rationality are aspects of culture that are particularly important for innovation, but it is not clear how they influence industrial development.

The study of infrastructure has also relied on location-based contextualization of components. Technology is lowering barriers to entry and enabling access to resources, institutions, and markets from around the world. Resources are decreasingly geographically bound and proprietary functions occur across nations, generations, and culture. These trends may be influencing the foundations of industries and ecosystems. The very understanding of infrastructure may be shifting as industrial boundaries are blurred and markets become less geographically constrained.

Finally, just as the resources needed at the start-up of a firm are different from those needed for growth, little work has identified how infrastructure itself changes over time. As industries and ecosystems wax and wane, certainly the infrastructure and its components do as well. As industry creation and entrepreneurship are drivers of economic growth, infrastructure necessary for their continued growth and survival are also important. Our work to understand processes of emergence and change in industry and ecosystem infrastructure is far from complete.

References

Acs, Z. J., and Varga, A. (2005), 'Entrepreneurship, Agglomeration and Technological Change', *Small Business Economics*, 24/3, 323–34.

Adner, R., and Kapoor, R. (2010), 'Value Creation in Innovation Ecosystems: How the Structure of Technological Interdependence Affects Firm Performance in New Technology Generations', *Strategic Management Journal*, 31/3, 306–33.

Agarwal, R., Echambadi, R., Franco, A. M., and Sarkar, M. B. (2004), 'Knowledge Transfer Through Inheritance: Spin-Out Generation, Development, and Survival', *Academy of Management Journal*, 47/4, 501–22.

Aldrich, H. E., and Fiol, C. M. (1994), 'Fools Rush In? The Institutional Context of Industry Creation', *Academy of Management Review*, 19/4, 645–70.

Aldrich, H. E., and Ruef, M. (2006), *Organizations Evolving* (Thousand Oaks, CA: Sage).

Amezcua, A. S., Grimes, M. G., Bradley, S. W., and Wiklund, J. (2013), 'Organizational Sponsorship and Founding Environments: A Contingency View on the Survival of Business Incubated Firms, 1994–2007', *Academy of Management Journal*, 56/6, 1628–54.

Anand, N., and Watson, M. R. (2004), 'Tournament Rituals in The Evolution of Fields: The Case of The Grammy Awards', *Academy of Management Journal*, 47/1, 59–80.

Anderson, P., and Tushman, M. L. (1990), 'Technological Discontinuities and Dominant Designs—A Cyclical Model of Technological-Change', *Administrative Science Quarterly*, 35/4, 604–33.

Ansari, S. M., and Garud, R. (2009), 'Intergenerational Transitions in Socio-Technical Systems: The Case of Mobile Telephony', *Research Policy*, 38/2, 382–92.

Ansari, S. M., Garud, R., and Kumaraswamy, A. (2016), 'The Disruptor's Dilemma: TiVo and the US Television Ecosystem', *Strategic Management Journal* 37/9, 1829–53.

Astley, W. G. (1985), 'The Two Ecologies: Population and Community Perspectives on Organizational Evolution', *Administrative Science Quarterly*, 30/2, 224–41.

Astley, W. G., and Fombrun, C. J. (1983). 'Collective Strategy: Social Ecology of Organizational Environments', *Academy of Management Review*, 8/4, 576–87.

Audia, P. G., Freeman, J. H., and Reynolds, P. D. (2006), 'Organizational Foundings in Community Context: Instruments Manufacturers and Their Interrelationship with Other Organizations', *Administrative Science Quarterly*, 51/3, 381–419.

Audretsch, D. B., Cunningham, J. A., Kuratko, D. F., Lehmann, E. E., and Menter, M. (2019), 'Entrepreneurial Ecosystems: Economic, Technological, and Societal Impacts', *Journal of Technology Transfer*, 44/2, 313–25.

Audretsch, D. B., and Feldman, M.P. (1996), 'Innovative Clusters and the Industry Life Cycle', *Review of Industrial Organization*, 11/2, 253–73.

Audretsch, D. B., Heger, D., and Veith, T. (2015), 'Infrastructure and Entrepreneurship', *Small Business Economics*, 44/2, 219–30.

Autio, E., Nambisan, S., Thomas, L. D. W., and Wright, M. (2018), 'Digital Affordances, Spatial Affordances, and the Genesis of Entrepreneurial Ecosystems', *Strategic Entrepreneurship Journal*, 12/1, 72–95.

Autio, E., and Thomas, L. D. W. (2013), 'Innovation Ecosystems: Implications for Innovation Management', in M. Dodgson, D. M. Gann, and N. Phillips, eds., *The Oxford Handbook of Innovation Management* (Oxford UK: Oxford University Press), 204–88.

Bahrami, H., and Evans, S. (1995), 'Flexible Re-Cycling and High-Technology Entrepreneurship', *California Management Review*, 37/3, 62–89.

Barnett, W. P., and Carroll, G. R. (1993), 'How Institutional Constraints Affected the Organization of Early United-States Telephony', *Journal of Law Economics and Organization*, 9/1, 98–126.

Baum, J. A. C., and Korn, H. J. (1994), 'The Community Ecology of Large Canadian Companies, 1984–1991', *Canadian Journal of Administrative Sciences*, 11/4, 277–94.

Baum, J. A. C., and Rao, H. (2021), 'Evolutionary Dynamics of Organizational Populations and Communities', in M. S. Poole and A. H. Van de Ven, eds., *Oxford Handbook of Organizational Change and Innovation* (2nd edn) (Oxford UK: Oxford University Press).

Baum, J. A. C., and Singh, J. V. (1994), 'Organization-Environment Coevolution', in J. A. C. Baum and J. V. Singh, eds., *Evolutionary Dynamics of Organizations* (New York: Oxford University Press), 279–401.

Best, M. (2013), 'Greater Boston's Industrial Ecosystem: A Manufactory of Sectors', *Technovation*, 39–40/1, 4–13.

Bowker G. C., and Star S. L. (1999), *Sorting Things Out: Classification and Its Consequences* (Cambridge, MA: MIT Press).

Bresnahan, T., Gambardella, A., and Saxenian, A. (2001), '"Old Economy' Inputs For 'New Economy' Outcomes: Cluster Formation in The New Silicon Valleys', *Industrial and Corporate Change*, 10/4, 835–60.

Brittain, J., and Wholey, D. R. (1988), 'Competition and Coexistence in Organizational Communities: Population Dynamics in Electronics Components Manufacturing', in G. Carroll, ed., *Ecological Models of Organizations* (Cambridge, MA: Ballinger), 195–222.

Cho, S., and Mathiassen, L. (2007), 'The Role of Industry Infrastructure in Telehealth Innovations: A Multi-Level Analysis of a Telestroke Program', *European Journal of Information Systems*, 16/6, 738–50.

Clayton, P., Feldman, M., and Lowe, N. (2018), 'Behind the Scenes: Intermediary Organizations That Facilitate Science Commercialization Through Entrepreneurship', *Academy of Management Perspectives*, 32/1, 104–24.

Cosh, A., and Hughes, A. (2010), 'Never Mind the Quality Feel the Width: University-Industry Links and Government Financial Support for Innovation in Small High-Technology Businesses in the U.K. And the USA', *Journal of Technology Transfer*, 35/1, 66–91.

Cusumano, M. A., Mylonadis, Y., and Rosenbloom, R. S. (1992), 'Strategic Maneuvering and Mass-Market Dynamics: The Triumph of VHS Over Beta', *Business History Review*, 66/1, 51–94.

Davidian, K. J. (2018), 'Accumulation Model Processes of Human Suborbital Space Transportation Industry Emergence', PhD. Dissertation. University of Cape Town, SA.

DiMaggio, P. J., and Powell, W. W. (1983), 'The Iron Cage Revisited: Institutional Isomorphism and Collectivity Rationality in Organizational Fields', *American Sociological Review*, 48, 147–60.

Engardio, P. (2008), 'Los Alamos and Sandia: R&D treasures', *BusinessWeek*. www.businessweek.com/stories/2008-09-10/los-alamos-and-sandia-r-and-d-treasures/, accessed 26 August, 2020.

Etzkowitz, H. (2002), 'Incubation of Incubators: Innovation as A Triple Helix of University-Industry-Government Networks', *Science and Public Policy*, 29/2, 115–28.

Etzkowitz, H., and Leydesdorff, L. (2000), 'The Dynamics of Innovation: From National Systems And "Mode 2" To A Triple Helix of University-Industry-Government Relations', *Research Policy*, 29/2, 109–23.

Etzkowitz, H., Webster, A., Gebhardt, C., Cantisano, T., and Branca, R. (2000), 'The Future of The University and The University of The Future: Evolution of Ivory Tower to Entrepreneurial Paradigm', *Research Policy*, 29/2, 313–30.

Feldman, M. P., and Francis, J. L. (2004), 'Homegrown Solutions: Fostering Cluster Formation', *Economic Development Quarterly*, 18/2, 127–137.

Feldman, M. P., Francis, J. L., and Bercovitz, J. (2005), 'Creating a Cluster While Building a Firm: Entrepreneurs and the Formation of Industrial Clusters', *Regional Studies*, 39/1, 129–41.

Fligstein, N. (1991), 'The Structural Transformation of American Industry: An Institutional Account of the Causes of Diversification in the Largest Firms, 1919-1979', in W. W. Powell and P. J. DiMaggio, eds., *The New Institutionalism in Organizational Analysis*, (Chicago: University of Chicago Press), 311–36.

Forbes, D. P. (2013). 'The Infrastructure of Entrepreneurial Learning', in R. Mitchell and B. Randolph-Seng, eds., *Handbook of Entrepreneurial Cognition* (Cheltenham, UK: Edward Elgar), 364–82.

Forbes, D. P., and Kirsch, D. A. (2011), 'The Study of Emerging Industries: Recognizing and Responding to Some Central Problems', *Journal of Business Venturing*, 26/5, 589–602.

Freeman, J. H., and Audia, P. G. (2006), 'Community Ecology and the Sociology of Organizations', *Annual Review of Sociology*, 32, 145–69.

Garnsey, E., and McGlade, J. (2006), *Complexity and Co-Evolution: Continuity and Change in Socio-Economic Systems* (Cheltenham, UK: Edward Elgar).

Garud, R. (2008), 'Conferences as Venues for the Configuration of Emerging Organizational Fields: The Case of Cochlear Implants', *Journal of Management Studies*, 45/6, 1061–88.

Garud, R., Gray, B., and Tuertscher, P. (2019), 'Dialectical engagement at Atlas, CERN: A model for the functioning of large-scale scientific communities', Pennsylvania State University, Working paper.

Garud, R., Jain, S., and Kumaraswamy, A. (2002), 'Institutional Entrepreneurship in The Sponsorship of Common Technological Standards: The Case of Sun Microsystems and Java', *Academy of Management Journal*, 45/1, 196–214.

Garud, R., and Rappa, M. A. (1994), 'A Socio-Cognitive Model of Technology Evolution: The Case of Cochlear Implants.' *Organization Science*, 5, 344–362.

Garud R., and Turunen, M. (2021), 'Microfoundations of Innovation as Process: Usher's Cumulative Synthesis Model', in M. S. Poole and A. H. Van de Ven, eds., *Oxford Handbook of Organizational Change and Innovation* (2nd edn) Oxford UK: Oxford University Press),

Geels, F. W. (2004), 'From Sectoral Systems of Innovation to Socio-Technical Systems: Insights about Dynamics and Change from Sociology and Institutional Theory', *Research Policy*, 33/6–7, 897–920.

Giarratana, M. S. (2004), 'The Birth of a New Industry: Entry by Start-Ups and The Drivers of Firm Growth—The Case of Encryption Software', *Research Policy*, 33/5, 787–806.

Gnyawali, D. R., and Fogel, D. S. (1994), 'Environments for Entrepreneurship Development: Key Dimensions and Research Implications', *Entrepreneurship Theory and Practice*, 18/4, 43–63.

Granovetter, M. (1985), 'Economic Action and Social Structure: The Problem of Embeddedness', *American Journal of Sociology*, 91/3, 481–510.

Granovetter, M., and McGuire, P. (1998), 'The Making of an Industry: Electricity in the United States', *Sociological Review*, 46/1, 147–73.

Greenwood, R., Suddaby, R., and Hinings, C. R. (2002), 'Theorizing Change: The Role of Professional Associations in the Transformation of Institutionalized Fields', *Academy of Management Journal*, 45/1, 58–80.

Grimaldi, R., and Grandi, A. (2005), 'Business Incubators and New Venture Creation: An Assessment of Incubating Models', *Technovation*, 25/2, 111–21.

Gustafsson, R., Jääskeläinen, M., Maula, M., and Uotila, J. (2016), 'Emergence of Industries: A Review and Future Directions', *International Journal of Management Reviews*, 18/1, 28–50.

Halse, L. L. (2017), 'The Evolution and Transformation of Industrial Clusters: A Conceptual Model', *International Journal of Manufacturing Technology and Management*, 31/1–3, 176–91.

Hannah, D. P., and Eisenhardt, K. M. (2018), 'How Firms Navigate Cooperation and Competition in Nascent Ecosystems', *Strategic Management Journal*, 39/12, 3163–92.

Hunt, C. S., and Aldrich, H. E. (1998), 'The Second Ecology: Creation and Evolution of Organizational Communities', *Research in Organizational Behavior*, 20, 267–301.

Ingram, P., and Inman, C. (1996), 'Institutions, Intergroup Competition, and the Evolution of Hotel Populations around Niagara Falls', *Administrative Science Quarterly*, 41/4, 629–58.

Jacobides, M. G., Cennamo, C., and Gawer, A. (2018), 'Towards a Theory of Ecosystems', *Strategic Management Journal*, 39/8, 2255–76.

Jansson, J. (2011), 'Emerging (Internet) Industry and Agglomeration: Internet Entrepreneurs Coping with Uncertainty', *Entrepreneurship and Regional Development*, 23/7–8, 499–521.

Kapoor, R., and Agarwal, S. (2017), 'Sustaining Superior Performance in Business Ecosystems: Evidence from Application Software Developers in The IOS and Android Smartphone Ecosystems', *Organization Science*, 28/3, 531–51.

Kenney, M., and Von Burg, U. (1999), 'Technology, Entrepreneurship and Path Dependence: Industrial Clustering in Silicon Valley and Route 128', *Industrial and Corporate Change*, 8/1, 67–103.

Khaire, M. (2014), 'Fashioning an Industry: Socio-Cognitive Processes in The Construction of Worth of a New Industry', *Organization Studies*, 35/1, 41–74.

Korn, H. J., and Baum, J. A. C. (1994), 'Community Ecology and Employment Dynamics: A Study of Large Canadian Organizations, 1985–1992', *Social Forces*, 73/1, 1–31.

Krugman, P. (1991), *Geography and Trade* (London: MIT Press).

Lampel, J. and Meyer, A. D. (2008), 'Field-Configuring Events as Structuring Mechanisms: How Conferences, Ceremonies, And Trade Shows Constitute New Technologies, Industries, and Markets—Introduction', *Journal of Management Studies*, 45/6, 1025–35.

Leblebici, H., Salancik, G. R., Copay, A., and King, T. (1991), 'Institutional Change and the Transformation of Interorganizational Fields: An Organizational History of the U.S. Radio Broadcasting Industry', *Administrative Science Quarterly*, 36/3, 333–63.

Lerner, J. (1999), 'The Government as Venture Capitalist: The Long-Run Impact of the SBIR Program', *Journal of Business*, 72/3, 285–318.

Leydesdorff, L., and Etzkowitz, H. (1998), 'The Triple Helix as a Model for Innovation Studies', *Science and Public Policy*, 25/3, 195–203.

Lounsbury, M., Ventresca, M., and Hirsch, P. M. (2003), 'Social Movements, Field Frames and Industry Emergence: A Cultural–Political Perspective on US Recycling', *Socio-Economic Review*, 1/1, 71–104.

Lundvall, B. Å. (1992), *National Systems of Innovation. Towards a Theory of Innovation and Interactive Learning* (London: Pinter).

Lundvall, B. Å., Johnson, B., Andersen, E. S., and Dalum, B. (2002), 'National Systems of Production, Innovation and Competence Building', *Research Policy*, 31/2, 213–31.

Lynn, L. H., Reddy, N. M., and Aram, J. D. (1996), 'Linking Technology and Institutions: The Innovation Community Framework', *Research Policy*, 25/1, 91–106.

MacGregor, N., and Madsen, T. L. (2018), 'Cluster Evolution', in *Oxford Research Encyclopedia of Business and Management*. doi: 10.1093/acrefore/9780190224851.013.141/, accessed 26 September 2020.

MacMillan, I. C., Kulow, D. M., and Khoylian, R. (1989), 'Venture Capitalists' Involvement in Their Investments: Extent and Performance', *Journal of Business Venturing*, 4/1, 27–47.

Mezias, S. J., and Kuperman, J. C. (2000), 'The Community Dynamics of Entrepreneurship: The Birth of the American Film Industry, 1895–1929', *Journal of Business Venturing*, 16/3, 209–33.

Mian, S. A. (1996), 'Assessing Value-Added Contributions of University Technology Business Incubators to Tenant Firms', *Research Policy*, 25, 325–35.

Moore, J. F. (1993), 'Predators and Prey: A New Ecology of Competition', *Harvard Business Review*, 71/3, 75–86.

Moore, J. F. (1997), *The Death of Competition: Leadership and Strategy in the Age of Business Ecosystems* (New York: Harper Collins).

Mowery, D. C. (1998), 'The Changing Structure of The US National Innovation System: Implications for International Conflict and Cooperation in R&D Policy', *Research Policy*, 27/6, 639–54.

Munir, K. A., and Phillips, N. (2005), 'The Social Construction of Events: A Study of Institutional Change in the Photographic Field', *Organization Studies*, 26/1, 93–112.

Murmann, J. P., and Tushman, M. L. (2001), 'From the Technology Cycle to the Entrepreneurship Dynamic', in C. B. Schoonhoven and E. Romanelli, eds., *The Entrepreneurship Dynamic: Origins of Entrepreneurship and The Evolution of Industries*, (Palo Alto: Stanford University Press), 178–203.

Murtha, T. P., Lenway, S. A., and Hart, J. A. (2001), *Managing New Industry Creation: Global Knowledge Formation and Entrepreneurship in High Technology* (Palo Alto, CA: Stanford University Press).

Nakagawa, T. H. (2001), 'SAP – A Globally Enterprising Company: European Lessons from the Enterprise Software Industry', *Business and Politics*, 3/2, 109–34.

Nelson, R. R. (1993), *National Innovation Systems: A Comparative Analysis* (Cambridge, UK: Oxford University Press).

Nelson, R. R. (1994), 'The Co-Evolution of Technology, Industrial Structure, and Supporting Institutions', *Industrial and Corporate Change*, 3/1, 47–63.

Nelson, R. R., and Rosenberg, N. (1993), 'Technical Innovation and National Systems', in *National Innovation Systems: A Comparative Analysis* (Cambridge, UK: Oxford University Press).

North, D. C. (1990), *Institutions, Institutional Change and Economic Performance*. (Cambridge, UK: Oxford University Press).

Oh, D. S., Phillips, F., Park, S., and Lee, E. (2016), 'Innovation Ecosystems: A Critical Examination', *Technovation*, 54/1, 1–6.

Oksanen, K., and Hautamaki, A. (2014), 'Transforming Regions into Innovation Ecosystems: A Model for Renewing Local Industrial Structures', *Public Sector Innovation Journal*, 19/2, 1–16.

Oliver, A. L., and Montgomery, K. (2008), 'Using Field-Configuring Events for Sense-Making: A Cognitive Network Approach', *Journal of Management Studies*, 45/6, 1147–67.

Overholm, H. (2015), 'Collectively Created Opportunities in Emerging Ecosystems: The Case of Solar Service Ventures', *Technovation*, 39–40, 14–25.

Pennings, J. M. (1982), 'Organizational Birth Frequencies: An Empirical Investigation', *Administrative Science Quarterly*, 27/1, 120–44.

Pierrakis, Y., and Saridakis, G. (2019), 'The Role of Venture Capitalists in the Regional Innovation Ecosystem: A Comparison of Networking Patterns Between Private and Publicly Backed Venture Capital Funds', *Journal of Technology Transfer*, 44/3, 850–73.

Pitelis, C. (2012), 'Clusters, Entrepreneurial Ecosystem Co-Creation, and Appropriability: A Conceptual Framework', *Industrial and Corporate Change*, 21/6, 1359–88.

Poole, M. S., Van de Ven, A. H., Dooley, K., and Holmes, M. E. (2000), *Organizational Change and Innovation Processes: Theory and Methods for Research* (Cambridge, UK: Oxford University Press).

Porter, M. E. (1990), *The Competitive Advantage of Nations* (New York, NY: Free Press).

Powell, W. W. (1998), 'Learning from Collaboration: Knowledge and Networks in the Biotechnology and Pharmaceutical Industries', *California Management Review*, 40/3, 228–40.

Powell, W. W., White, D. R., Koput, K. W., and Owen-Smith, J. (2005), 'Network Dynamics and Field Evolution: The Growth of Interorganizational Collaboration in the Life Sciences', *American Journal of Sociology*, 110/4, 1132–205.

Qian, H., Acs, Z. J., and Stough, R. R. (2013), 'Regional Systems of Entrepreneurship: The Nexus of Human Capital, Knowledge and New Firm Formation', *Journal of Economic Geography*, 13/4, 559–87.

Rao, H. (2002), "Interorganizational Ecology', in J. A. C. Baum, ed., *Blackwell Companion to Organizations* (Malden, MA: Blackwell Publishers), 541–56.

Roig-Tierno, N., Alcazar, J., and Ribeiro-Navarrete, S. (2015). 'Use of Infrastructures to Support Innovative Entrepreneurship and Business Growth', *Journal of Business Research*, 68/11, 2290–4.

Rosenkopf, L., and Tushman, M. L. (1994), 'The Coevolution of Technology and Organization', in J. A. C. Baum and J. V. Singh, eds., *Evolutionary Dynamics of Organizations* (New York: Oxford University Press), 403–24.

Ruef, M. (2000), 'The Emergence of Organizational Forms: A Community Ecology Approach', *American Journal of Sociology*, 106/3, 658–714.

Sanderson, S. W., and Simons, K. L. (2014), 'Light Emitting Diodes and The Lighting Revolution: The Emergence of a Solid-State Lighting Industry', *Research Policy*, 43/10, 1730–46.

Sapienza, H. J. (1992), 'When Do Venture Capitalists Add Value?', *Journal of Business Venturing*, 7/1, 9–27.

Saxenian, A. (1990), 'Regional Networks and the Resurgence of Silicon Valley', *California Management Review*, 33/1, 89–112.

Saxenian, A. (1994), *Regional Advantage: Culture and Competition in Silicon Valley and Route 128* (Cambridge, MA: Harvard University Press).

Saxenian, A. (1999), 'Comment on Kenney and von Burg, "Technology, Entrepreneurship and Path Dependence: Industrial Clustering in Silicon Valley and Route 128"', *Industrial and Corporate Change*, 8/1, 105–10.

Saxenian, A. (2006), *The New Argonauts. Regional Advantage in a Global Economy* (Cambridge, MA: Harvard University Press).

Schwartz, M. (2009), 'Beyond Incubation: An Analysis of Firm Survival and Exit Dynamics in The Post-Graduation Period', *Journal of Technology Transfer*, 34/4, 403–21.

Scott, W. R. (2008), *Institutions and Organizations* (2nd ed.) (Thousand Oaks, CA: Sage).

Sikavica, K., and Pozner, J-E. (2013), 'Paradise Sold: Standards, Social Movement Identification and Competition in Identity-Partitioned Markets', *Organization Studies*, 34/5–6, 623–51.

Sine, W. D., Haveman, H. A., and Tolbert, P. S. (2005), 'Risky Business? Entrepreneurship in the New Independent-Power Sector', *Administrative Science Quarterly*, 50/2, 200–32.

Smith, H. L., and Ho, K. (2006), 'Measuring the Performance of Oxford University, Oxford Brookes University and the Government Laboratories' Spinoff Companies', *Research Policy*, 35/10, 1554–68.

Sorensen, J. B. (2004), 'Recruitment-Based Competition Between Industries: A Community Ecology', *Industrial and Corporate Change*, 13/1, 149–70.

Spencer, J. W., Murtha, T. P., and Lenway, S. A. (2005), 'How Governments Matter to New Industry Creation', *Academy of Management Review*, 30/2, 321–37.

Spigel, B., and Harrison, R. (2018), 'Toward a Process Theory of Entrepreneurial Ecosystems', *Strategic Entrepreneurship Journal*, 12/1, 151–68.

Stam, E., and Spigel, B. (2017), 'Entrepreneurial Ecosystems', in R. Blackburn, D. De Clercq, and J. Heinonen, eds., *Handbook for Entrepreneurship and Small Business* (London: SAGE), 407–22.

Stuart, T. E. (2000), 'Interorganizational Alliances and the Performance of Firms: A Study of Growth and Innovation Rates in a High-Technology Industry', *Strategic Management Journal* 21, 791–811.

Suchman, M. C. (2000), 'Dealmakers and Counselors: Law Firms as Intermediaries in The Development of Silicon Valley', in M. Kenney, ed., *Understanding Silicon Valley: The Anatomy of an Entrepreneurial Region* (Palo Alto: Stanford University Press), 71–97.

Teece, D. J. (2016), 'Business Ecosystems', in M. Augier and D. J. Teece, eds., *Palgrave Encyclopedia of Management* (London: Palgrave Macmillan), 1–4.

Thomas, L. D. W., and Autio, E. (2018), 'Ecosystem Value Potential: An Organizational Field Perspective'. Academy of Management Proceedings.

Thompson, T. A., Purdy, J. M., and Ventresca, M. J. (2018), 'How Entrepreneurial Ecosystems Take Form: Evidence from Social Impact Initiatives in Seattle', *Strategic Entrepreneurship Journal*, 12/1, 96–116.

Tuertscher, P., Garud, R., and Kumaraswamy, A. (2014), 'Justification and Interlaced Knowledge at ATLAS, CERN', *Organization Science*, 25/6, 1579–608.

Tushman, M. L., and Anderson, P. C. (1986), 'Technological Discontinuities and Organizational Environments', *Administrative Science Quarterly*, 31/3, 439–65.

Usher, A. P. (1954), *A History of Mechanical Inventions* (Cambridge: Harvard University Press).

Van de Ven, A. H. (1993), 'The Development of an Infrastructure for Entrepreneurship', *Journal of Business Venturing*, 8/3, 211–30.

Van de Ven, A. H., and Garud, R. (1989), 'A Framework for Understanding the Emergence of New Industries', in R. S. Rosenbloom and R. A. Burgelman, eds., *Research on Technology Innovation, Management, and Policy* (Vol. 4) (New York: Elsevier), 195–225.

Van de Ven, A.H., and Garud, R. (1993), 'Innovation and Industry Development: The Case of Cochlear Implants', *Research on Technological Innovation, Management and Policy*, 5, 1–46.

Van de Ven, A.H., and Garud, R. (1994), 'The Co-Evolution of Technical and Institutional Events in The Development of an Innovation', in J. A. C. Baum and J. V. Singh, eds., *Evolutionary Dynamics of Organizations* (New York: Oxford University Press), 425–32.

Van de Ven, A. H., and Hargrave, T. J. (2004), 'Social, Technical, and Institutional Change', in A. Van de Ven and M. S. Poole, eds., *Handbook of Organizational Change and Innovation* (New York: Oxford University Press), 259–303.

Van de Ven, A. H., Polley, D. E., Garud, R., and Venkataraman, S. (2008), *The Innovation Journey* (New York: Oxford University Press).

Van de Wiele, Z. (2017), 'Entrepreneurial Ecosystems: A Literature Review', Master's Dissertation, University of Gent.

Venkataraman, S. (2004). 'Regional Transformation through Technological Entrepreneurship', *Journal of Business Venturing*, 19/1, 153–67.

Wade, J. B. (1995), 'Dynamics of Organizational Communities and Technological Bandwagons—An Empirical Investigation of Community Evolution in the Microprocessor Market', *Strategic Management Journal* 16 (Summer), 111–33.

Wade, J. B. (1996), 'A Community-Level Analysis of Sources and Rates of Technological Variation in the Microprocessor Market', *Academy of Management Journal*, 39/5, 1218–44.

Weber, K., Heinze, K., DeSoucey, M. (2008), 'Forage for Thought: Mobilizing Codes in the Movement for Grass-Fed Meat and Dairy Products', *Administrative Science Quarterly*, 53/3, 529–67.

Woolley, J. L. (2007), 'Understanding Organizational Community Creation: The Nanotechnology Community', PhD Dissertation, University of California, Irvine.

Woolley, J. L. (2010), 'Technology Emergence Through Entrepreneurship Across Multiple Industries', *Strategic Entrepreneurship Journal* 4/1, 1–21.

Woolley, J. L. (2014), 'The Creation and Configuration of Infrastructure for Entrepreneurship in Emerging Domains of Activity', *Entrepreneurship Theory and Practice* 38/4, 721–47.

Woolley, J. L. (2017a), 'Infrastructure for Entrepreneurship', *Oxford Research Encyclopedia of Business and Management* doi: 10.1093/acrefore/9780190224851.013.33/, accessed 26 September 2020).

Woolley, J. L. (2017b), 'Origins and Outcomes: The Roles of Spin-Off Founders and Intellectual Property in High-Technology Venture Outcomes', *Academy of Management Discoveries* 3/1, 64–90.

Woolley, J. L., and MacGregor, N. (2019), 'The relationship between science, technology, and innovation policy timing and entrepreneurship', Santa Clara University, Leavey School of Management, Working paper.

Woolley, J. L., and Rottner, R. M. (2008), 'Innovation Policy and Nanotechnology Entrepreneurship', *Entrepreneurship Theory and Practice* 32/5, 791–811.

Xu, G., Wu, Y., Minshall, T. and Zho, Y. (2018), 'Exploring Innovation Ecosystems across Science, Technology, and Business: A Case of 3D Printing in China', *Technological Forecasting and Social Change* 136/1, 208–21.

Zucker, L. G., and Darby, M. R. (1997), 'Present at the Biotechnological Revolution: Transformation of Technological Identity for a Large Incumbent Pharmaceutical Firm', *Research Policy* 26/4–5, 429–46.

CHAPTER 25

INTERORGANIZATIONAL NETWORK CHANGE

MICHELLE SHUMATE AND ZACHARY GIBSON

Interorganizational networks describe a transorganizational system of connections among organizations. Such networks stand apart from *interpersonal* connections between members of different organizations (e.g., friendship, advice). At the *interorganizational* level, a variety of relations are possible, including interlocking directorates (e.g., Beckman et al. 2004), supply chains (e.g., Andersson and Mölleryd 1999; Akkermans 2001), strategic alliances (e.g., Gulati and Gargiulo, 1999), scientific collaboration (e.g., Cassi et al. 2012), co-membership (e.g., Fortune 2003), and multiplex ties, including client referrals, exchanges, and information flow (e.g., Morrissey et al. 1997). Scholars who study networks, by and large, come from two perspectives: those who utilize social network analysis to understand the underlying structure of interdependence between organizations (e.g., Gulati 1995) and those who consider networks an organizational form (e.g., Powell 1990; Uzzi 1997). In this chapter, we review both lines of scholarship because we believe they could benefit from cross-fertilization.

Interorganizational networks can change in a variety of ways, including the addition or subtraction of organizations (e.g., Rosenkopf and Padula 2008), the shifting of network boundaries (e.g., Woo 2019), mergers of nodes within the network (e.g., Rogan 2014), changes to the ties between organizations (e.g., Powell et al. 2005), and changes to organizations that are embedded within the network (e.g., Pennings and Harianto 1992).

This chapter examines interorganizational network change, including its antecedents, processes, outcomes, and management. We concur with Cummings (1984: 367), who argued that interorganizational networks "constitute a distinct logical type higher than that of single organizations, [and that] they require a theory and practice of planned change commensurate with that higher level." Based on our scan of the literature, we could identify no systematic treatment of the topic writ broad. Therefore, we conducted a systematic literature review of research, dating back to the early 1970s, across management, organizational studies, public administration, organizational communication, and technology studies sub-disciplines. In this review, we describe what we do and do not know about interorganizational network change.

We orient the chapter around two key distinctions in the literature. The first is Kilduff and Tsai's (2003) discrimination between the trajectories of networks that are primarily goal-directed and those that are serendipitous. We come to this distinction by way of Provan and Kenis (2007) who use it to separate organizational scholars who examine named networks with a clear identity and goals from research that primarily uses social network analysis to detect networks. We argue that interorganizational change antecedents, processes, and outcomes are heavily influenced by the presence of a shared identity and goal. Moreover, scholars from these two traditions rarely cite one another. Considering the distinct nature of these two networks types, we argue that different models of change best explain their movement and transformation. In this chapter, we connect these two literatures and demonstrate both how they align and differ.

We also utilize the framework of change provided by Mohr (1982) and expanded by Van de Ven and Poole (1995). Following their lead, we distinguish between variance and process approaches to studying interorganizational network change. Process models describe how and why the entire network changes over time. In contrast, the variance models describe how organizations make changes in their portfolio of ties or are differentially impacted by these changes.

Moreover, we draw on Van de Ven and Poole's four process models of change—evolutionary, teleological, life cycle, and dialectical—to classify the ways that scholars have understood the nature and dynamics of change. Although this framework was quite helpful to us, it was not initially applied to interorganizational networks. In our application, life cycle models describe the stages of whole interorganizational network evolution that occur in a linear fashion. Evolutionary models describe changes that occur in the network which affect the fitness of either organizations in a network or the network as a whole. In contrast, when leaders make goal-directed changes to the whole network, or organizations make goal-directed changes to their portfolio of ties, we consider these to be teleological models of change. Finally, when scholars describe managing tension between multiple sets of demands or two phases of change, we describe the research as dialectical. Echoing our earlier expectation of distinct change processes, we structure the chapter so that we explore how each model of change appears with respect to the two network types. In doing so, we hope to capture how goal-directed and serendipitous networks develop over time.

Using these two distinctions as touchpoints, we report the results of an expansive systematic literature review. Through this review, we answer four interrelated questions. First, how does the literature define change? Second, what theories are used to understand change in goal-directed networks, serendipitous networks, and organizations embedded in networks? Relatedly, how does time figure into these theories? Third, what are the mechanisms by which change might be promoted? Fourth, what are the commonly studied outcomes of network change? We structure the chapter around these questions with the intent of displaying how the two literatures have treated the networks under their study. Through this, our aim is to identify gaps both within and between the literatures.

Method

This chapter draws on a systematic review of interorganizational network change studies. The search covered *ABI/INFORM*, *Business Source Premier*, and *Communication Source*, searching for terms related to interorganizational networks (i.e., "interorganizational network," "inter-organizational network," "alliance network," "contract network," "social movement network.") together with terms related to change (i.e., "change," "development," "evolution"). We note here our decision to exclude the interorganizational *relationships* (IOR) literature. The basis for this exclusion is that the IOR literature has traditionally taken a dyadic focus, often emphasizing a pair of organizations or a single relationship. In contrast, the interorganizational *network* literature has traditionally taken a more whole-network focus, examining a large number of organizations and the many relationships among them.

The original search, performed July 5, 2018, returned 830 unique articles. From there, we performed two rounds of screening to narrow the size and focus of the review. The first round, examining only the titles and abstracts, eliminated 538 studies because they: (1) did not include an interorganizational network, (2) did not include some form of change, or (3) focused on adoption and implementation of an interorganizational information or technology system. The second round, now examining the full text of the articles, eliminated an additional 137 articles based on the same criteria above. Lastly, after reading through these papers, we identified six commonly recurring citations that did not appear in the original database search. Adding these papers, we examined 161 articles in total.

With the review database compiled, we split the database and coded each article on five features: publication, methodology, the studied network(s), how change is formulated, and the outcomes studied. For publication, we marked the year and discipline of each article to examine temporal and disciplinary trends in this area of research. For methodology, we tracked the data collection and analysis approach of each paper. We identified whether each paper was theoretical, empirical, a simulation, or a meta-analysis, and whether the study involved an intervention. For the networks, we captured the specific type of relationship (e.g., collaboration, exchange, alliance) and the kinds of organizations involved (e.g., businesses, governments, community-based organizations). For change, we identified how each article defined change, whether it treated change as either variance or a process (Mohr 1982), and which theory of change it exhibited (van de Ven and Poole 1995). Finally, we coded the outcomes the studies examined (e.g., firm performance, network structure, learning), and at which levels these outcomes occurred.

Using this information, we can provide a brief characterization of the studies in our database before we dive more deeply into interorganizational network change. To start, we find a predominance of case studies and quantitative analyses of archival data, with these two kinds of studies characterizing over two-thirds of the empirical papers in our database. In addition, the few theory pieces we collected tended to serve more as advancements on existing theories (e.g., Ainsworth and Feyerherm 2016; Jenssen and Nybakk 2013; Yang and Taylor 2015). We also find that the disciplines of management, organization studies, and strategy together account for nearly half of the work done in this area. Although a variety of other fields participate (e.g., communication, economics, futures studies, public management), their voices have been substantially smaller to date. That said, to our pleasure, we note that research into interorganizational network change has steadily grown in popularity, with the earliest study identified in 1973 (i.e., Pfeffer and Leblebici 1973), a scattering of studies between the mid-1990s to mid-2000s ($n = 35$ between 1995 and 2005), and finally a starker increase in the last decade ($n = 100$ between 2009 and 2018). We see this as an area burgeoning with research and interest, and so take this as necessitation for a survey of what has been done to date and the future directions we should move.

How to Define Change

Following Mohr (1982) and Van de Ven and Poole (1995), we distinguish between research and theory that takes a variance approach and a process approach to differences in interorganizational networks over time. A little more than half of the articles we examine ($n = 84$) took a variance approach, where scholars sought to determine the relationship between independent variables and dependent variables in a longitudinal analysis. Soda's (2011) study of organizational innovativeness is a good example of this approach. He examined the number of patents that organizations received as a function of their position in the interorganizational network two years prior (i.e., cohesion, brokerage) and includes a number of controls. Using negative binomial regression to estimate the model, he shows that lower cohesion (i.e., the extent to which partner organizations are connected) and higher brokerage (i.e., the extent to which partner organizations are *not* connected) increase the number of patents organizations attain.

Variance approaches, like this one, provide more generalizable estimates of the relationships between variables. However, they do little to explain *how* and *why* interorganizational networks, and the organizations within them, change. Process theories and the research derived from them, take a different shape entirely. Huxham and Vangen's (2000) theory of interorganizational network membership dynamics provides a helpful example. They note, "[T]he structure of collaborations is continually changing, partly because of external pressures and changes within the member organization have a direct influence on who can and should be a member, and partly because the inevitable changes to the collaborative purpose imply different membership needs" (789–90).

They go on to detail how each of these factors explains both how and why organizations join and leave the interorganizational network.

In this review, following the focus of this handbook, we are primarily interested in process approaches to interorganizational network change. As such, our discussion hereafter will refer to theory and research that takes a process approach ($n = 74$). From this review, we've identified several ways that interorganizational networks change, using the distinction between goal-directed and serendipitous networks.

Kilduff and Tsai's (2003) work is foundational to our choice to categorize interorganizational network change research into studies focusing on goal-directed or serendipitous networks. They argue that the operational and structural dynamics of network change differ depending on whether the network has a defined goal and identity. They summarize their argument thus: "[T]he serendipitous network trajectory evolves through a predictable process of clustering and bridging as individual actors make choices based on dyadic attraction. The goal-directed network trajectory, in contrast, is driven forward through phases of development in the pursuit of a goal" (2003: 94).

Exploring this first distinction, we find that research on goal-directed networks generally describes changes to network ties (e.g., Koza and Lewin 1999), network governance (e.g., van Raak and Paulus 2001), network activities (e.g., Swan and Scarbrough 2005), network orchestrator activities (e.g., Gardet and Mothe 2011; Paquin and Howard-Grenville 2013), and membership (e.g., Sydow 2004). Most research in this model uses qualitative methods or case study analysis to examine the factors that influence how and why a network changes over time. Management, organization studies, organizational development, and public management disciplines dominate the set of articles that we examined in this category.

In contrast, serendipitous network research most commonly examines changes in network structure (e.g., Gulati 1995; Madhavan et al. 1998; Powell et al. 2005; Liu et al. 2015). Less commonly, research examines changes in market incentives (Zikos 2010; Lin et al. 2012), the economic risks and rewards of network embeddedness (Uzzi 1996), changes in how individuals representing organizations acted (Chetty and Agndal 2008; Son and Rojas 2011), or changes in organizational activities (Estivalete et al. 2008) or resources (Dittrich et al. 2007; De Reuver and Bouwman 2012). The majority of articles investigating these networks come from the management, project management, and economics disciplines. A wide variety of analytic methods were used in research on serendipitous networks, including social network analysis, case studies, regression-approaches, and grounded theory approaches.

Comparing the types of change studied when networks are goal-directed or serendipitous reinforces Kilduff and Tsai's (2003) argument about trajectories for network change. Most changes in goal-directed networks originate from network leadership or changes at the whole network level. In contrast, change in serendipitous networks tends to originate from each organization. These changes include individual agent behavior when they represent the networks, organizational changes, and strategic changes in organizations' portfolio of network relationships. Thus, most change in goal-directed networks is described as top-down and planned, whereas, in contrast, most change in serendipitous networks is bottom-up and emergent, or a result of macro-level incentive changes in the market. Further discussions of this theme related to sensemaking, conflict, and opposing interests can be found in Chapters 3, 4, 7, 9, and 12 of this handbook.

Change in Goal-Directed Networks

Research in goal-directed networks is easy to identify. Authors can name the network that they are studying, not just the industry or a set of bounded organizations. Often the set of organizations meets together on a regular basis, and membership may be fluid or tightly regulated. Scholars have created a variety of theoretical models to describe these networks, including the bona fide group collaboration theory (Stohl and Walker 2002), the diagnostic model of transorganizational systems (Ainsworth and Feyerherm 2016), and theories of network governance (a.k.a. network orchestrator activities) and interorganizational change (Dagnino et al. 2016).

Bona fide group collaboration model. Bona fide group collaboration theory focuses on goal-directed networks as a special type of group (Stohl and Walker 2002). It conceptualizes interorganizational collaboration as a temporary system that spans organizational boundaries. In this context, the negotiated temporary system is "enacted by the representative of the collaboration partners specifically for the completion of a collaborative project and is the collaborating group" (243). It focuses on communication as central in the generative and processual nature of the group dynamics. The model notes that membership, group boundaries, and identity each evolve over time as the group interacts with each other and with their larger environment. They highlight that this larger environment, and in particular individuals' alignment with or roles in organizations, create varying levels of commitment and involvement with the network. These environmental exigencies, then, have implications for decision-making processes, commitment, trust, power, and knowledge management. In research, scholars have taken up the model to explain the emergence of less goal-directed groups (Cooper and Shumate 2012) and the ways participants try to negotiate their presence in the next interorganizational collaboration after a network disbands (Woo 2019).

Beyond consideration of the particulars of the model, the bona fide group collaboration model directs researchers' attention to at least three elements of goal-directed interorganizational networks that are poorly described in other models. First, membership in the bona fide group collaboration model is dynamic, and the model seeks to both account for and explain this dynamism in terms of tasks, group dynamics, and environmental exigencies. Second, the model explicitly recognizes that groups are the mechanism by which most work gets done in goal-directed networks. It is the only theory that brings group dynamics to bear in the explanation of interorganizational network change. Finally, the theory operates with the assumption that the network is temporary, and its structure is negotiated through communication. Indeed, many goal-directed interorganizational networks are temporary structures that only exist until a project is completed, as project management research has long held. In such temporary arrangements, communication processes play an outsized role in the emergence and change that occur in the network.

Diagnostic model of transorganizational systems. Ainsworth and Feyerherm (2016) offer an open systems model to address interorganizational change. Extending Cummings and Worley's (2014) systems model, the essential argument is that interorganizational networks transform inputs into a set of outcomes through their design. The model operates as a tool that allows both researchers and practitioners to examine the causes of network inertia (i.e., lack of change or growth in network ties) and/or various levels of performance. Inputs include the problem or opportunity that leads the interorganizational network to form. Design components include mission and vision, constituency, governance structure, measurement systems, negotiated order, information systems, and trust. Outputs include organizational effectiveness, network effectiveness, the degree to which the problem is partially or fully solved, and the creation of new knowledge. The model is iterative so that outputs result in changes to both design and inputs.

The diagnostic model is helpful in directing research to a broad set of design features that may influence the unfolding of interorganizational network change. In addition, as a teleological model, it helpfully directs researchers to pay attention to the ways that changes are a result of both past actions and the evaluation of the results of those actions. Moreover, the model usefully directs researchers to three levels of outcomes that result from the network: organizational, network, and societal (see Popp et al. 2014 for more on these levels). By developing trust and negotiated order through iteration on factors such as governance structure, shared mission and vision, and membership, the model suggests that interorganizational networks can improve their capacity to tackle societal problems while also supporting organizational performance and productivity.

Theories of network governance/orchestration and network change. Finally, a line of research has emerged around the topic of network orchestration and network governance. Network orchestration refers to the work of the "triggering organization" that "recruits organizational members and shapes their actions" (Paquin and Howard-Grenville 2013: 1624). Relatedly, network governance is the process that ensures "participants engage in collective and mutually supported action, that conflict is addressed, and that network resources are acquired and utilized efficiently and effectively" (Provan and Kenis 2007: 231). Network orchestration turns our attention to the activities of a single organization that is purposively shaping the interorganizational network, whereas network governance is a larger concept that encompasses both those activities and other types of coordination where a single catalyzing organization is not in charge (see Chapter 24 of this handbook for a discussion of this process in the technology industry). Analogous to some conceptions of change management (Hayes 2018), the network orchestrator is often the purposive change maker who elicits the support of other organizations in moving the network toward some goal.

Theories of network governance and orchestration are often interested in the ways that network management changes over time as networks mature, situating them between the teleological and life cycle model of network change. Provan and Kenis (2007) argued that if a network survives, it will naturally move from a pattern of more shared governance to a more brokered form of governance. Further, they argue that if a network begins with brokered governance, it is unlikely to move to a more shared governance model. Similarly, Paquin and Howard-Greenville (2013) describe orchestrator activities changing as the network evolves. In the first phase, called "assembly," they primarily focus on managing the dilemma of internal versus external legitimacy. The assembly phase is marked by engagement with external and potentially internal stakeholders. During the capturing value phase, phase two, they balance encouraging formal ties and allowing ties to emerge organically from the network. Key activities include strategically introducing potential partners and getting more involved in the project activities of the network. In the third and final phase, strategic growth, network orchestrators turn to replication, focusing their efforts on exploiting existing relationships that have produced value for the network. Both Provan and Kenis and Paquin and Howard-Greenville assume that the network aims to continue long into the future and will become a permanent but evolving organizational entity.

Goal-directed network research. These three theories represent different ways of understanding interorganizational network change. However, most research on change in goal-directed networks uses either more generic theories of societal change, such as structuration theory (e.g., Sydow et al. 2003; Sydow 2004; Berends et al. 2011) and theories of organizational learning (e.g., Hartley and Allison 2002; Coughlan and Coghlan 2004; Morris et al. 2006), or uses theories that do not explicitly address change, like exchange theory (e.g., Stern 1979) and institutional theory (e.g., Honig and Lampel 2000).

Almost all research on goal-directed networks uses a variant of a case study approach (e.g., longitudinal case study, comparative case study) or a type of qualitative analysis (e.g., grounded theory, discourse). A little less than a third of these articles explicitly examine the impact of an intervention on interorganizational network change (see the section on Practical Management).

Research on goal-directed networks primarily focuses on the purposive change of interorganizational networks, or natural changes that occur after the accumulation of a set of purposive activities have occurred. As such, goal-directed network research to date has not taken an evolutionary perspective. Instead, the majority takes a teleological ($n = 19$) or lifecycle ($n = 15$) view of interorganizational change. A minority of articles take a dialectical approach ($n = 7$).

Teleological research can be categorized into two camps. The first camp is concerned with organizational learning (e.g., Hartley and Allison 2002; Coughlan and Coghlan 2004; Sotiriadou et al. 2017). In this set of research, network interactions are a new source of information for the organization. Organizations take advantage of this information, depending on their level of absorptive capacity. Absorptive capacity is "a firm's ability to utilize externally held knowledge through three sequential processes: (1) recognizing and understanding potentially valuable new knowledge outside the firm through exploratory learning, (2) assimilating valuable new knowledge through transformative learning, and (3) using the assimilated knowledge to create new knowledge and commercial outputs through exploitative learning" (Lane et al. 2006: 856). Change in these models is a result of participation in a network, which in many cases, includes organizational learning as one of its explicit goals.

The second camp focuses on changes to network structure as a result of an intervention or planned change; these changes include a search conference (e.g., Clarke 2005), network activities (e.g., Morris et al. 2006; Matinheikki et al 2016), and implementation of a new set of tools designed to integrate the network (Alin et al. 2013). Many times, the structure of the network is tied to another level of outcome, such as organizational learning (Johnson and Wechsler 1990) or network goals (Clarke 2005).

Life cycle research, in contrast, is concerned with the particular stages that networks progress through. Our review includes both theoretical models that pertain to particular types of interorganizational networks (Wegner et al. 2016; Albareda and Waddock 2018) and empirical research. These papers commonly identify stages that networks progress through as they develop over time, but the names and numbers of those stages vary widely. Huybrechts and Haugh (2018) identify three stages: building field-level receptivity to institutional pluralism, collectively codifying the new hybrid organizational form, and consolidating legitimation toward plural audiences. Wegner and colleagues (2016) review several models of network development and then propose their own six-stage model: conception, birth and formalization, development, consolidation and maturity, decline, and dissolution. While the number of stages and end state of these models differ, all suggest a relatively linear model of network change.

Most research using a life cycle approach is interested in one of two outcomes. Some research is interested in the formation of the network itself (e.g., Schermerhorn, Jr. et al. 1985; Albareda and Waddock 2018). However, most life cycle research is interested in network performance, either in terms of market share (van den Ende et al. 2012) or establishing the legitimacy of a new standard (Gerst and Bunduchi 2005) or organizational form (Huybrechts and Haugh 2018).

In contrast to research from the teleological and life cycle perspectives, research from the dialectical perspective views change as reactive, not progressive (e.g., Koza and Lewin 1999; Beech and Huxham 2003; Provan et al. 2004). These changes can come from the external environment (e.g., Stern, 1979; Provan et al. 2004) or as the result of interactions within the collaboration (Beech and Huxham 2003). The results of these changes are varied.

Provan and colleagues (2004) provide an emblematic example of changes from the environment. They examined the ways that the Community Partnership of Arizona responded to a significant change in the states' funding mechanism for mental health providers. This environmental change shifted the way that the agencies providing mental health services would be compensated. They argue in their longitudinal case study that the structure of the network, in particular the presence of a form of network governance where a network administrative organization acted as a coordinating body, helped the network remain resilient and find creative ways to work around the new policy. In these models, the dialectic is between the network's norms and environmental demands.

In contrast, Beech and Huxham's (2003) research is suggestive of how dialectics might play a role in the internal dynamics of the network. They develop the cycle of identity formation through their discourse analysis of a learning network. The cycle demonstrates the way that an individual's actions and others' perception of their identity interact until members of a network crystallize their perception of each other's' identity, if only temporarily. In this model, the dialectic is between (a) an individual's self-identity and subsequent action connected to that identity and (b) others' perception of their identity.

Open questions in the study of goal-directed networks. In many ways, the literature on goal-directed networks is more coherent than the research on serendipitous networks. However, the review of both theory and research on goal-directed interorganizational network change reveals a significant opportunity for consolidation and theorizing. Such a project faces three challenges that must be addressed.

First, researchers and theorists are not clear about what role shared identity and goal orientation might play in interorganizational network formation, change, and dissolution. We suggest the difference between these two forms might be captured by entitativity, a concept introduced by Campbell (1958) and housed in the groups literature. Though we do not have the space to unpack this rich construct, we encourage scholars to explore how entitativity (i.e., perceiving an aggregate as a unitary entity) could contribute to the differences in the structure, dynamics, and theorizing around these networks (see Yzerbyt et al. 2000; Brewer et al. 2003 for a review of prominent research).

Second, there is a clear divide in the research between scholars who are studying temporary, project-based networks and enduring goal-directed networks. Those who study temporary networks often rely on extensions of group processes or life cycle approaches. In contrast, those who study enduring networks tend to eschew any type of group dynamics, instead focusing on the network's interaction with the environment. Research in both veins could benefit by reading and invoking concepts from each other's work.

Third, scholarship should take into account changes that may be attributed to network maturation and planned changes. In doing so, theory and research should account for expected temporal variation and events that create disruptions in the expected progression of the network. In doing so, they will better account for the way that time influences the pace and degree of network change.

Change in Serendipitous Networks

In contrast to goal-directed networks, work on serendipitous networks appears less cohesive and more varied in terms of the networks studied, the perspectives taken, and the theories and contexts explored. Broadly, research on serendipitous networks exhibits two methodological tendencies. One, it examines either industry- or market-based networks (e.g., Larson 1992; Lazerson 1995; Uzzi 1997). Two, it takes a cumulative view of some sets of organizations' alliance portfolios and constructs an interorganizational network by connecting those portfolios (e.g., Gulati 1995). These trends likely emerge due to the defining characteristic of serendipitous networks—the absence of a shared identity or boundary. Theories around serendipitous networks seek to explain the basis of their emergence (Gulati and Gargiulo 1999), their development over time (Hite and Hesterly 2001; Schurr et al. 2008), how change occurs at multiple levels (Håkansson and Snehota 1995; Halinen et al. 1999), and the tensions these networks straddle (Oliver 2004; Zikos 2010).

The origin of serendipitous networks. In their seminal work, Gulati and Gargiulo (1999) describe five factors driving the formation of strategic alliances between organizations: three types of embeddedness, strategic interdependence, and structural differentiation. Each form of embeddedness—relational, structural, and positional—detail different ways in which organizations are connected to one another. Relationally embedded organizations share many direct relationships; structurally embedded organizations share many indirect relationships; and positionally embedded organizations share similarly central positions in the network. Together, these network positions suggest the importance of status in the network and access to unique information. Organizations want to connect with other organizations whom they perceive as reliable, reputable, and resourceful. In a similar fashion, strategic interdependence acknowledges how organizations facing the same environmental challenges, resource scarcity, and market uncertainty, will come together in order to stabilize their positions.

Structural differentiation, by contrast, explains how occupying *different* roles within the network increases the likelihood of alliance formation. More specifically, a network with a higher level of structural differentiation provides more relational information to its member organizations. That is, organizations are better able to discern the value of potential partners when structural differentiation is higher. The differences in relational profiles characterize what roles an organization fulfills in a network and what resources it may have to offer. Altogether, embeddedness, interdependence, and differentiation provide foundational mechanisms through which serendipitous relationships can develop between any pair of organizations. As these relationships proliferate, a serendipitous network emerges.

Developmental theories of serendipitous networks. Hite and Hesterly (2001) provide the theoretical first steps for how serendipitous networks transition from emergence to "early growth." In their framework, emerging networks tend to emphasize identity and to *whom* organizations connect. At this initial stage, organizations seek to connect to other organizations who are of higher status or legitimacy, with the intent of legitimating their own identity. This effectively provides an opportunity for the organization to enter whichever space it is targeting. From there, organizations shift their attitude to more "calculative" partnering (i.e., transactional ties). Whereas the initial ties emphasize identity, these latter ties emphasize resources and *what* other organizations can offer. At this early growth stage, networks transition from being identity-based to resource-based, establishing an exchange network.

Schurr and colleagues' (2008) definition of "interaction episodes" offers further ground from which this development can continue. As they characterize it, interaction episodes comprise a set of "interacts" (e.g., brainstorming, discussing, recommending) within some common context (e.g., problem-solving). Over time, organizations engage in many different interaction episodes with others in the same space, be it market, industry, or otherwise, and these episodes color their relationships with each other. Positive interaction episodes may serve as the basis for forming a new alliance or deepening an already existing collaboration between some pair of organizations. Additionally, they may serve to foster new resource exchanges or information-sharing. Negative interaction episodes, however, may weaken or even fracture those relationships, depending on the criticality and frequency of such episodes. Combined, these two pieces offer a neat sequence and mechanism through which serendipitous networks develop. Uzzi and Spiro (2005) in their study of Broadway networks suggest such a trajectory as well, noting that infant networks tend to be very exploratory but eventually must come to a balance between exploration and exploitation in order to maintain success.

Multilevel theories of network change. Notably, the changes described by Schurr and colleagues (2008) occur at the lowest level of the relationship (i.e., interaction). Håkansson and Snehota (1995), in their book, argue that network change may occur within a focal relation, but it may also occur elsewhere, including organizations, other relations in the network, and the environment in which the network is situated. As they put it, "[C]hange in a [network] is to a large extent endogenous in relation to the network but exogenous of the single actor" (271). Due to the interdependent and inherently multi-level nature of networks (i.e., actors, dyads, triads, subgroups, whole networks), change may come from many different directions.

Halinen and colleagues (1999) further echo this complexity and expand on it by describing two forms of change that networks may experience. Using a punctuated-equilibrium model, they suggest that networks undergo both incremental and radical change. During periods of stability, networks undergo relatively *incremental* changes, where shifts in relationships or the activities of a single actor do not spill over into the broader network. Yet, during a period of turbulence following some critical event (e.g., executive turnover, mergers, economic recession, technological discontinuities), changes in network structure and activity may be much more rapid and expansive. Once-dominant organizations may find themselves slipping out toward the market periphery (Dittrich et al. 2007) as previously smaller organizations rise to prosperity (Koza and Lewin 1999). Crucially, these theories highlight the complex, even chaotic, nature of change in serendipitous networks.

Duality theories of serendipitous networks. The existence of such complexity is not unexpected, however. Several authors have wrestled with the tensions that serendipitous networks face. Oliver (2004) attempts to explain how member organizations simultaneously try to both compete and collaborate with network partners. Meanwhile, Zikos (2010) suggests that organizations will oscillate between periods of collaboration and periods of competition, contingent on other environmental factors. Other empirical articles then examine how networks cope with exploitation versus exploration, or both occurring at the same time (Elg and Johansson 1996; Chiaroni et al. 2010). In summary, serendipitous networks exist in rather tenuous states. Yet, despite their seemingly chaotic nature, scholars have propagated this area of research with a variety of perspectives and approaches to sift out order.

Serendipitous network research. The study of serendipitous networks offers a fairly balanced representation among the four models of change. Specifically, we find explanations frequently drawing on evolutionary ($n = 8$), teleological ($n = 6$), life cycle ($n = 5$), and dialectical models ($n = 4$). Considering the relatively shared coverage using these different models, we explore what authors have had to say when using each. As illustrated below, each model offers insight into some aspects of network change, though none explain it completely.

Starting with evolutionary approaches, studies commonly acknowledge the reactionary behavior of focal organizations to other organizations in the same environment. For instance, two papers by Andersson and Mölleryd (1997, 1999) address how some organizations taking strategic action with their supply chains led to similar actions by other organizations. As a result, the individual, uncoordinated actions of these organizations shaped the structure of the telecommunication supply chain network over the course of twenty-five years. In a similar vein, other studies have highlighted how these kinds of self-focused actions lead to changes in R&D networks (Margolin et al. 2015), exchange networks (Chetty and Agndal 2008), NGO collaboration networks (Shumate et al. 2005), project networks (Shumate, Ibrahim, and Levitt 2010), and networks more generally (Schurr et al. 2008). Yet, in an interesting contrast to this egocentric approach, a variety of other studies taking an evolutionary perspective have pointed to the importance of external events. Policy changes (Knight and Pye 2004; Song and Vannetelbosch 2007; Margolin et al. 2015), subsidization (Zikos 2010), and technological discontinuities (Rosenkopf and Padula 2008) all affect the behavior of the network as a whole and of member organizations. This divide suggests that network change may emerge as either a culmination of organizational actions or as an adaptive reaction to broader environmental shifts.

Such a concept contrasts neatly with the substantially more agentic focus of the teleological perspective. Whereas the evolutionary perspective portrays network emergence as more of a byproduct of individual actions, the teleological perspective suggests that networks can intentionally be forged, or at the very least be guided in certain directions. Broadly, work has emphasized the former. A number of papers capture the strategic actions of organizations to broaden or diversify their alliance portfolios across a variety of industries, including: biotechnology (Powell et al. 2005; Chen and Lin 2017), computing (Dittrich et al. 2007), healthcare (Stadtfeld et al. 2016), construction (Son and Rojas 2011), and nonprofit (Ihm and Castillo 2017). Together, these papers describe different conditions under which organizations shape their egocentric networks (i.e., alliance portfolios) to improve their performance (e.g., innovation, efficiency, revenue) and gain an advantage in their respective markets. On the other hand, much less attention has been given to how serendipitous networks might seek to manage themselves.

Our review found only one paper that examines how a serendipitous network, as a whole, shifts its activities for the benefit of its member organizations. De Reuver and

Bouwman (2012) explore how mobile service organizations collectively shift the governance of their collaborations as they iterate through three different phases of new service development. They show that as these collaborative networks shift back and forth through these phases, they engage in distinct styles of governance to promote different outcomes. For instance, networks tend to rely on power- or authority-based governance when in the R&D phase, both to gain access to market leaders and to maintain accountability among competitors. Later, in the roll-out and market phases, networks tend to rely on contract-based and trust-based governance systems to protect market share. Notably, this model hints at circumstances where industry networks might become more goal-directed and less serendipitous.

Unlike the other approaches, we find that life cycle approaches attempt to characterize the changes of the network as a whole, rather than as a result of organizational actions. Several papers, for instance, describe how networks develop in response to changing learning goals of the networks (Estivalete, Pedrozo, and Cruz 2008; Dantas and Bell 2011; Filieri et al. 2014). These papers describe not only differences in the kinds of ties being formed, such as bridging versus bonding (Filieri et al. 2014), but the depth of trust and activity at different stages of development (Estivalete et al. 2008; Dantas and Bell 2011). In a similar vein, several other papers examine how collaboration networks evolve in tandem with traditional industry (Lin et al. 2012; Nikulainen 2012) and innovation life cycles (Chiaroni et al. 2010). Chiaroni and colleagues (2010) and Lin and colleagues (2012) suggest that as industries mature, networks expand and become increasingly dense and decentralized. In contrast, some networks evolve alongside stages of an external event. For instance, Doerfel and colleagues (2013) describe how a disaster response network, an interorganizational network responsible for restoring infrastructure and operations to a disaster-struck region, developed in New Orleans in the aftermath of Hurricane Katrina. Notably, despite their serendipitous nature, all of these networks develop around some kind of focal activity (e.g., learning, innovation, recovery) yet exhibit varying life cycles.

The few papers we find incorporating dialectical perspectives seem to echo this idea as well. Unlike the other approaches, they focus on some kind of central contradiction or conflict that serves as the impetus for change. Capaldo (2007) and Elg and Johansson (1996) both describe networks straddling the challenge of exploration (i.e., expanding their network) versus exploitation (i.e., reinforcing their networks) in innovation settings. Capaldo suggests networks will oscillate back and forth between these two network activities in reaction to market changes. Elg and Johansson add a dimension to this oscillation, noting, for example, that organizations may switch between exploiting in their vertical supply chain relationships or exploiting in their horizontal supply chain relationships. Araujo and Brito (1997) identify a similar clash in the port wine industry between increasing profit for individual organizations through free production versus maintaining the stability of the market through market-wide production quotas.

Looking across all these studies, serendipitous network change occurs through emergent (i.e., bottom-up) processes. The culmination of each member organization's relational changes (i.e., tie formation, dissolution, reinforcement, membership churn) creates an emergent network structure. In contrast to goal-directed networks, no collective agreement or shared cognition exists in structuring the network's relations or its activities.

Open questions in the study of serendipitous networks. In some ways, the diversity of models of serendipitous interorganizational network change is encouraging. It suggests an active and interested engagement with the issues serendipitous networks face. However, it also suggests that we lack a unified understanding of how change occurs in these networks. We lack a consensus of whether a change in serendipitous networks follow some natural lifecycle, results from something evolutionary, dialectical, or teleological, or some combination thereof. It thus seems that one clear line of research is creating such a unified understanding that incorporates these different forms of change.

Kilduff and Tsai (2003) contend that network conflict is inevitable in both goal-directed and serendipitous networks and that cohesive subgroups are likely to result from this conflict. However, we find very few studies of serendipitous networks that integrate conflict into their model. We see this as fertile ground for understanding: a) the factors that instigate goal conflict in serendipitous networks; b) how these networks manage that conflict; and c) how the networks transform through those conflicts.

Change in Organizations through Network Membership

Despite our emphasis on interorganizational *network* change, we would be remiss if we ignored that such networks indeed are comprised of organizations. Without member organizations working together in some form, interorganizational networks would not exist. Surprisingly, we find little theory that provides a processual account of organizational change resulting from network membership. We do, however, find several pieces that draw on variance theories to explain how organizations might change through network membership. Specifically, they offer explanations of how organizations might improve their innovation (Jenssen and Nybakk 2013), adapt their interlocking strategies (Heracleous and Murray 2001), restructure their relationships (Kim et al. 2006), and undergo more generic organizational change (Ferreira and Armagan 2011), all through interactions with their interorganizational networks.

Member organization research. Eleven papers provide process accounts of how *organizations* change resulting from their participation in an interorganizational network. From an organizational lens, this change may occur in a variety of ways, such as: joining or leaving a network, forming or dissolving relationships with other member organizations, reinforcing existing relationships, increasing or decreasing engagement with the network as a whole, or changing the nature of their activities in the network. The majority of processual accounts take a teleological perspective ($n = 6$), followed by life cycle ($n = 2$), dialectical ($n = 2$), and evolutionary ($n = 1$) perspectives.

Beginning with teleological research, we find that half of the papers draw on some form of organizational learning theory (i.e., exploration vs. exploitation; tacit vs. explicit knowledge), whereas other studies are more varied. Some focus on the ways that organizations gain new competencies or knowledge as part of their participation in networks. For example, Coughlan and Coghlan (2004) and Hartley and Allison (2002) both describe action learning approaches to improve organizations' abilities from learning networks and to gain better technical and process knowledge of a network-wide strategic plan. Other outcomes in teleological studies include the decision whether to join, leave, or re-join a network, formation or dissolution of ties, and changes in work goal (i.e., what research discipline to emphasize). For example, Dittrich et al. (2007) show how IBM managed to reposition themselves from the deteriorating industry of mainframe computers to the growing industry of information and communication technology by shifting from an exploitation to an exploration strategy. Specifically, over the course of eleven years, IBM rapidly expanded its alliance network and joint ventures with other organizations in the industry to move into a position to keep up with the changing nature of computing.

Life cycle models describe how organizations leverage their networks in order to develop their own capacities across phases. Chiaroni and colleagues (2010) develop a model of how organizations make the change from closed innovation to open innovation through three phases. In "unfreezing," the organization recognizes its own innovative production is slowing down or is already stagnant, and begins to activate extant collaboration ties in response. The organization then "moves," expanding its collaboration ties, often through executive relationships, shifting its position in the network, and improving its innovation output. Then, through "institutionalization," the organization formalizes its new collaborations into longer-term R&D relationships. Estivalete et al. (2008) develop a similar model but in the context of organizational learning. In their model, organizations go through a process of identifying areas in which they lack competency or skill, begin forging new relationships with organizations who do possess those skills, then commit to those relationships through formalizing actions such as mutual investment. In both cycles, the last stage, whether institutionalizing or formalizing, serves as the precedent for the next cycle. Organizations must break away from the new norm or identify their next weakness and then perform the cycle again.

Dialectical models describe how organizations within the network balance competing demands, including cooperation versus competition (Koza and Lewin 1999) and intentionality versus serendipity in forming their network ties (Benson-Rea and Wilson 2003). In both papers, organizations choose to manage the dialectical tension one way and then, upon entering a new phase, are pulled to the other side of the tension (see also Chapters 7 and 8 of this handbook for more on dialectical models). For instance, Benson-Rea and Wilson suggest that organizations straddle a tension between serendipitous relations and intentional ones. Often, organizations tend toward one strategy (e.g., serendipity), a behavior that eventually results in them leaning the other way (e.g., intentionality). This oscillation, however, tends to be a greater struggle for younger firms than older ones, suggesting that there may be a degree of learning necessary to navigate the dialectics.

Song and Vannetelbosch's (2007) simulation-based research describe yet another tension organizations may face, from an evolutionary perspective. Their model describes how firms straddle a tension between international R&D collaboration and personal profit, which is in turn colored by whether national governments can subsidize R&D. Through several mathematical proofs, they suggest that triads (i.e., groups of three organizations) will often cycle between four structural configurations: (1) a network with no relations (i.e., the empty network), (2) a single relation between A and B (i.e., the partial network), (3) a pair of relations between A and B, and B and C (i.e., the star network), and (4) all relations among A, B, and C (i.e., the complete network). Moreover, the sequence of the cycle and the time spent in each stage of the cycle can change as a result of the degree of government subsidies and public spillover (i.e., effect of research on social welfare). They describe this in terms of pairwise stability and strong stability. Pairwise stability refers to a circumstance when no organizations benefit from breaking their ties and no two agents benefit from adding ties. In contrast, strong stability refers to a circumstance in which the network is resistant to a reconfiguration of links among a group of organizations. When there are no subsidies or public spillovers, the complete network (4) is pairwise stable and the partial network (2) is strongly stable. Once public spillovers are introduced, the partial network becomes only pairwise stable. In this absence of strong stability, they suggest organizations will rely on competitive policies that result in cycles from one network structure to the next. Specifically, the complete network (4) gives rise to the star network (3); the star network (3) gives rise to the partial network (2); and the partial network (2) gives rise to the complete network (4). This points to the potential instability of interorganizational relationships and their vulnerability to environmental conditions. Extrapolating further, this would suggest that organizations would view networks opportunistically, thereby creating more unstable networks and more rapid changes in organizational network position and performance.

Open questions in the study of member organizations. Research on organizational change as the result of network participation emphasizes the benefits organizations can gain (Coughlan and Coghlan 2004; Dittrich et al. 2007; Estivalete et al. 2008; Chiaroni et al. 2010). What remains unclear, however, is what costs organizations incur as a result of joining these networks. What kinds of resources must an organization allot or dedicate to network activities in order to maintain membership? How do benefits compare with the opportunity costs lost by deploying resources in a different way?

Moreover, beyond the learning approaches described above, we lack a processual theory that examines how organizations change as a result of their interorganizational relationships. Such a theory might fruitfully examine how interorganizational networks and organizations co-evolve. Moreover, a dialectical theory might highlight how organizations and networks oscillate between self-interested goals and joint goals.

Practical Management

Relatively few articles address interventions designed to spur interorganizational network changes ($n = 12$). These articles generally described four categories of intervention: events and hosting, training and/or technical assistance, network management, and government intervention.

Research that examines events and hosting suggests that, through greater interaction, stronger and more diverse interorganizational ties will form. For example, Munoz and Lu (2011) examine the impact of the Creapolis Innovation Centre on the formation of ties among Spanish businesses. Ihm and Castillo (2017) examine how a regular nonprofit capacity-building event created new ties and strengthened old ties among participants. These types of interventions are among the least prescriptive and costly. They induce network change by reducing the exploration costs of interorganizational relationships.

Many action research studies describe training or technical assistance programs that they implemented to improve the composition, design, and/or functioning of the network (Schermerhorn, Jr. et al. 1985; Akkermans 2001; Coughlan and Coghlan 2004; Clarke 2005). For example, the National Action Learning Programme and CO-IMPROVE approaches are highly structured models of action learning that aim to promote collaborative continuous quality improvement across extended manufacturing enterprises (Coughlan and Coghlan 2004). Akkermans (2001) describes the Renga approach, a group workshop where participants engage in model-building, multi-level process mapping, and a system dynamics and modeling simulation. In a case study, Akkermans demonstrates how Renga can promote trust, communication, and productivity among organizations involved in the same supply chain.

Finally, some research notes that government intervention can transform networks. For example, Lin and colleagues (2012) describe how China's policies transformed the network of relationships among organizations in China's 3G industry. Similarly, Song and Vannetelbosch (2007), in a simulation study, demonstrate how government investment can influence interorganizational network stability and efficiency.

The dearth of research on interorganizational network interventions suggests difficulty in identifying the causes of positive interorganizational network change or, alternatively, that such changes cannot yet be catalyzed effectively. This represents a significant opportunity for solution-based social science to test some of the prescriptions about the efficacy of particular levers for mobilizing interorganizational network change.

Critique and Future Directions

Following Kilduff and Tsai (2003), we argue that interorganizational network change in goal-directed and serendipitous networks follows different trajectories. This foundational argument should serve as the basis for future theorizing and research. Goal-directed interorganizational change is more likely to be teleological and/or operate through a life cycle model. In contrast, serendipitous interorganizational networks are more likely to follow evolutionary models of change in the context of different life stages. However, one of the areas that is ripe for future research examination is how serendipitous networks can become goal-directed and how goal-directed networks become serendipitous. Kilduff and Tsai hint at this potential when they acknowledge that goal-directed networks sometimes rely on individuals' personal networks (i.e., serendipitous networks) to recruit potential members. Relatedly, Koza and Lewin (1999) describe how an informal, interpersonal relationship developed into a sprawling, goal-directed interorganizational network. Conversely, when goal-directed networks fall apart, the remnants are often a serendipitous network of latent ties that may be reactivated in the presence of another opportunity (Mariotti and Delbridge 2012; Woo 2019). Moreover, some network orchestrators encourage greater serendipity in the formation of interorganizational ties than others (Paquin and Howard-Grenville 2013). All of these arguments suggest that a future direction might lie in the degree of interdependence required for various tasks, the degree to which ties are arranged, or intriguingly, a hybrid goal-directed/serendipitous approach. Goal-directed network change may spur serendipitous network change, undermine it, or interact with it in heretofore unexplored ways. Similarly, the structure and evolution of serendipitous networks may serve as the initial conditions for goal-directed networks. As we conclude this chapter, we offer four prescriptions for future research.

First, we encourage researchers interested in interorganizational network change to draw from the theories of interorganizational change processes instead of trying to adapt old models of interorganizational networks to the topic of change, as we saw frequently done in this systematic review. Although resource dependence (Pfeffer and Salancik 1978), exchange theory (Das and Teng 2000), and classical institutional theory (DiMaggio and Powell 1983) have been foundational to the study of interorganizational networks, they do not provide a model of processual network change. As such, scholars researching processual network change need to situate their research within theoretical frameworks that better describe the sequence of events or processes that they hope to elucidate. Failure to heed these differences has left the field with very little synthesis or lines of research that build on a common understanding of the processes. In order to move the field forward, key touchstone models need to be used by many scholars, across many types of interorganizational networks, to determine the generalizability of our knowledge. Moreover, processual theories should further consider how the four broad models highlighted by Van de Ven and Poole (1995) might connect or blend to explain the dynamics of change in interorganizational networks.

A second issue that emerges from this review is positivity bias. The bias is evident in that we have very few studies that examine the costs of participating in interorganizational networks and how those costs might negatively influence the organizations within the network. Huxham and Vangen (2009), in their work on interorganizational relationships, argue that unless organizations cannot achieve their desired outcomes in any other way, they should avoid working with other organizations: the costs of networking are too high and the likelihood of payoff too remote. However, we see no similar caution in the study of either goal-directed or serendipitous networks. The studies of interorganizational network change seem to suggest that almost all networking is good.

Relatedly, we have very few studies on network inertia. This is a particularly striking gap in the study of goal-directed networks, where network orchestrators might find a network resistant to change. Given the attention that is given to this topic in organizational change management (e.g., Hayes 2018), the omission is striking.

A third key issue in the study of interorganizational network change is the lack of quantitative research. When networks are examined longitudinally using a variance approach, almost all the work is quantitative (96%). Researchers mostly examine archival data (65%) and use forms of regression or general linear modeling. However, once we turn to the study of process, very few articles (11%) use quantitative research methods. While the case study research that dominates the study of the process of interorganizational change is useful, it cannot produce a generalizable model of how and why networks change, and how network managers and leaders might influence that change. One possible reason for this empirical divide may be that scholars are unfamiliar with statistical methods that are appropriate to the study of process, including simulation models, longitudinal models from social network analysis research (e.g., temporal exponential random graph models, relational event models, SIENA), time series, and event history models.

But opportunities abound for researchers who do not have the background in these methods. One of the most important opportunities is to test the effectiveness of various network interventions, where a pre-post test or a control/treatment test might be used to understand the efficacy of various strategies. A model of this type of work comes from prevention science; van Horn et al. (2014) conducted a randomized control model to test the efficacy of Communities that Care, an intervention designed to help organizational coalitions reduce the rate of risky adolescent behaviors in their communities. In their study, twelve intervention community coalitions were trained in the Communities that Care model, which includes technical assistance, and twelve control community coalitions received resources but no training. We call for similar types of research that proposes and examines network interventions. In doing so, scholars can bridge the gap between academic knowledge and managerial practice. Moreover, solution-science calls the academy to greater, not less rigor; interventions require disentangling the levers of change from contributing factors and non-essential correlates.

Fourth, there are relatively few theories that focus on the process of interorganizational network change. Among the theories that we identified and reviewed in this chapter, only theories of network governance (Provan and Kenis 2007) and learning theories (e.g., Lane et al. 2006) have catalyzed a cumulative body of empirical research. If research is going to generate knowledge that extends beyond the results of one or two studies, a comprehensive model that addresses the elements of interorganizational network change must be developed.

One tactic would be to extend theories of interorganizational relationship dynamics (Ring and van de Ven 1994; Doz 1996), organizational change (Weick and Quinn 1999; Pettigrew et al. 2001; Cummings and Worley 2014), or group change (Forsyth 2018) to the study of interorganizational networks. For example, Ring and Van de Ven's (1994) theory of the processual development of interorganizational relationships is ripe for extension into understanding serendipitous networks. In that serendipitous networks may be the collection of these interorganizational relationships among a field of actors, the theory may be fruitfully scaled up to address the interdependencies and dynamics of these networks. Similarly, the developmental cycle described in the serendipitous network theory section of this chapter may easily be expanded to describe goal-directed networks.

An alternative tactic is to begin with a foundational understanding of the different models of change (van de Ven and Poole 1995). Although we found many models of life cycle change (e.g., Sydow 2004; Chiaroni et al. 2010; Lin et al. 2012; Wegner et al. 2016) and the IMP group (Håkansson and Snehota 1995; Halinen et al. 1999) provides a robust model of evolutionary change, very little theoretical work has been done to develop teleological and dialectical models of change. This leaves significant opportunities for scholars who hope to focus on the role that network leaders and managers play in the trajectory of both goal-directed and serendipitous networks.

Finally, one intriguing possibility is to construct a multi-level model of interorganizational network change in which different theories of change operate at different levels. For example, dialectical models might be fruitfully applied to how individuals interact as a part of their roles representing organizations in these networks. At the organizational level, evolutionary models might operate, describing how the dyadic relationships are selected and retained. At the interorganizational level, life cycle models might best describe how the network change occurs. Such theorizing would then also necessitate explanation of how the models operating at these different levels affect each other. In closing, the study of interorganizational network change is in its early formation, where no clear theoretical model has emerged; such states are ripe with opportunities for scholarship.

References

Ainsworth, D., and Feyerherm, A. E. (2016), 'Higher Order Change: A Transorganizational System Diagnostic Model, *Journal of Organizational Change Management*, 29/5, 769–81, https://doi.org/10.1108/JOCM-11-2015-0209/, accessed 26 September 2020.

Akkermans, H. (2001), 'Renga: A Systems Approach to Facilitating Inter-Organizational Network Development, *System Dynamics Review*, 17(3), 179–93, https://doi.org/10.1002/sdr.215/, accessed 26 September 2020.

Albareda, L., and Waddock, S. (2018), 'Networked CSR Governance: A Whole Network Approach to Meta-Governance, *Business & Society*, 57/4, 636–75, https://doi.org/10.1177/0007650315624205/, accessed 26 September 2020.

Alin, P., Maunula, A. O., Taylor, J. E., and Smeds, R. (2013), 'Aligning Misaligned Systemic Innovations: Probing Inter-Firm Effects Development in Project Networks', *Project Management Journal*, 44(1), 77–93, https://doi.org/10.1002/pmj.21316/, accessed 26 September 2020.

Andersson, P., and Mölleryd, B. G. (1997), 'Telecommunication Services in Context: Distribution Consequences of Technological Change and Convergence', *International Journal of Service Industry Management*, 8/5, 453–73, https://doi.org/10.1108/09564239710189853/, accessed 26 September 2020.

Andersson, P., and Mölleryd, B. G. (1999), Channel Network Change and Behavioral Consequences of Relationship Connectedness', *Journal of Business Research*, 46/3, 291–301.

Araujo, L., and Brito, C. (1997), 'Agency and Constitutional Ordering in Networks: A Case Study of the Port Wine Industry', *International Studies of Management & Organization*, 27/4, 22–46, https://doi.org/10.1080/00208825.1997.11656717/, accessed 26 September 2020.

Bartunek, J., Putnam, L., and Seo, M-G. (2021), 'Dualism and Dualities in the Ongoing Development of Organization Development,' in M. S. Poole and A. H. Van de Ven, eds., *The Oxford Handbook of Organizational Change and Innovation* (2nd edn) (Oxford: Oxford University Press).

Beckman, C. M., Haunschild, P. R., and Phillips, D. J. (2004), 'Friends or Strangers? Firm-Specific Uncertainty, Market Uncertainty, and Network Partner Selection', *Organization Science*, 15/3, 259–75, https://doi.org/10.1287/orsc.1040.0065/, accessed 26 September 2020.

Beech, N., and Huxham, C. (2003), 'Cycles of Identity Formation in Interorganizational Collaborations', *International Studies of Management and Organization*, 33/3, 28–52, https://doi.org/10.1080/00208825.2003.11043686/, accessed 26 September 2020.

Benson-Rea, M., and Wilson, H. (2003), 'Networks, Learning and the Lifecycle', *European Management Journal*, 21/5, 588–97. https://doi.org/10.1016/S0263-2373(03)00108-7

Berends, H., van Burg, E., and van Raaij, E. M. (2011), 'Contacts and Contracts: Cross-Level Network Dynamics in the Development of an Aircraft Material', *Organization Science*, 22/4, 940–60, https://doi.org/10.1287/orsc.1100.0578/, accessed 26 September 2020.

Brewer, M. B., Hong, Y.-Y., and Li, Q. (2003), 'Dynamic Entitativity', in V. Yzerbyt, C. M. Judd, and O. Corneille, eds., *The Psychology of Group Perception* (1st ed.) (New York, NY: Psychology Press), 19–30.

Campbell, D. T. (1958), 'Common Fate, Similarity, and Other Indices of the Status of Aggregates of Persons as Social Entities', *Behavioral Science*, 3/1, 14–25, https://doi.org/10.1002/bs.3830030103/, accessed 26 September 2020.

Capaldo, A. (2007), 'Network Structure and Innovation: The Leveraging of a Dual Network as a Distinctive Relational Capability', *Strategic Management Journal*, 28/6, 585–608, https://doi.org/10.1002/smj.621/, accessed 26 September 2020.

Cassi, L., Morrison, A., and Ter Wal, A. L. J. (2012), 'The Evolution of Trade and Scientific Collaboration Networks in the Global Wine Sector: A Longitudinal Study Using Network Analysis', *Economic Geography*, 88/3, 311–34. https://doi.org/10.1111/j.1944-8287.2012.01154.x

Chen, S.-H., and Lin, W.-T. (2017), 'The Dynamic Role of Universities in Developing an Emerging Sector: A Case Study of the Biotechnology Sector', *Technological Forecasting and Social Change*, 123, 283–97, https://doi.org/10.1016/j.techfore.2016.06.006/, accessed 26 September 2020.

Chetty, S., and Agndal, H. (2008), 'Role of Inter-Organizational Networks and Interpersonal Networks in an Industrial District', *Regional Studies*, 42/2, 175–87, https://doi.org/10.1080/00343400601142696/, accessed 26 September 2020.

Chiaroni, D., Chiesa, V., and Frattini, F. (2010), 'Unravelling the Process from Closed to Open Innovation: Evidence from Mature, Asset-Intensive Industries', *R&D Management*, 40/3, 222–45. https://doi.org/10.1111/j.1467-9310.2010.00589.x

Clarke, N. (2005), 'Transorganization Development for Network Building', *Journal of Applied Behavioral Science*, 41/1, 30–46. https://doi.org/10.1177/0021886304272655/, accessed 26 September 2020.

Cooper, K. R., and Shumate, M. (2012), 'Interorganizational Collaboration Explored Through the Bona Fide Network Perspective', *Management Communication Quarterly*, 26/4, 623–54, https://doi.org/10.1177/0893318912462014/, accessed 26 September 2020.

Coughlan, P., and Coghlan, D. (2004), 'Action Learning: Towards a Framework in Inter-Organisational Settings', *Action Learning: Research and Practice*, 1/1, 43–61, https://doi.org/10.1080/1476733042000187619/, accessed 26 September 2020.

Cummings, T. G. (1984), 'Transorganizational Development', *Research in Organizational Behavior*, 6, 367–422.

Cummings, T. G., and Worley, C. G. (2014), *Organization Development and Change*. Stamford, CT: Cengage learning.

Dagnino, G. B., Levanti, G., and Mocciaro Li Destri, A. (2016), Structural Dynamics and Intentional Governance in Strategic Interorganizational Network Evolution: A Multilevel Approach. *Organization Studies*, 37/3, 349–73, https://doi.org/10.1177/0170840615625706/, accessed 26 September 2020.

Dantas, E., and Bell, M. (2011), 'The Co-Evolution of Firm-Centered Knowledge Networks and Capabilities in Late Industrializing Countries: The Case of Petrobras in the Offshore Oil Innovation System in Brazil', *World Development*, 39/9, 1570–91, https://doi.org/10.1016/j.worlddev.2011.02.002/, accessed 26 September 2020.

Das, T. K., and Teng, B.-S. (2000), 'A Resource-Based Theory of Strategic Alliances', *Journal of Management*, 26/1, 31–61.

Davis, G. F. and Kim, E. W. (2021), 'Social Movements and Organizational Change', in M. S. Poole and A. H. Van de Ven, eds., *The Oxford Handbook of Organizational Change and Innovation* (Oxford: Oxford University Press),

De Reuver, M., and Bouwman, H. (2012), 'Governance Mechanisms for Mobile Service Innovation in Value Networks', *Journal of Business Research*, 65/3, 347–54, https://doi.org/10.1016/j.jbusres.2011.04.016/, accessed 26 September 2020.

DiMaggio, P., and Powell, W. W. (1983), 'The Iron Cage Revisited: Collective Rationality and Institutional Isomorphism in Organizational Fields', *American Sociological Review*, 48/2, 147–60.

Dittrich, K., Duysters, G., and de Man, A.-P. (2007), 'Strategic Repositioning by Means of Alliance Networks: The Case of IBM', *Research Policy*, 36/10, 1496–511, https://doi.org/10.1016/j.respol.2007.07.002/, accessed 26 September 2020.

Doerfel, M. L., Chewning, L. V., and Lai, C.-H. (2013), 'The Evolution of Networks and the Resilience of Interorganizational Relationships after Disaster', *Communication Monographs*, 80/4, 533–59, https://doi.org/10.1080/03637751.2013.828157/, accessed 26 September 2020.

Doz, Y. L. (1996), 'The Evolution of Cooperation in Strategic Alliances: Initial Conditions or Learning Processes?' *Strategic Management Journal*, 17, 55–83. Retrieved from JSTOR.

Elg, U., and Johansson, U. (1996), 'Networking when National Boundaries Dissolve', *European Journal of Marketing*, 30/2, 61–74, https://doi.org/10.1108/03090569610106653/, accessed 26 September 2020.

Estivalete, V. de F. B., Pedrozo, E. A., and Cruz, L. B. (2008), 'The Learning Process in Interorganizational Relationships', *Brazilian Administration Review*, 5/4, 319–31, https://doi.org/10.1590/S1807-76922008000400006/, accessed 26 September 2020.

Ferreira, M. P., and Armagan, S. (2011), 'Using Social Networks Theory as a Complementary Perspective to the Study of Organizational Change', *Brazilian Administration Review*, 8/2, 168–84, https://doi.org/10.1590/S1807-76922011000200004/, accessed 26 September 2020.

Filieri, R., McNally, R. C., O'Dwyer, M., and O'Malley, L. (2014), 'Structural Social Capital Evolution and Knowledge Transfer: Evidence from an Irish Pharmaceutical Network', *Industrial Marketing Management*, 43/3, 429–40, https://doi.org/10.1016/j.indmarman.2013.12.011/, accessed 26 September 2020.

Forsyth, D. R. (2018), *Group Dynamics*. Samford, CT: Cengage Learning.

Fortune, A. (2003), 'The Other Side of the Network Coin: Cost Considerations of Network Structure', *Computational and Mathematical Organization Theory*, 9/2, 109–25, https://doi.org/10.1023/B:CMOT.0000022751.56620.99/, accessed 26 September 2020.

Gardet, E., and Mothe, C. (2011), 'The Dynamics of Coordination in Innovation Networks', *European Management Review*, 8/4, 213–29. https://doi.org/10.1111/j.1740-4762.2011.01020.x

Gerst, M., and Bunduchi, R. (2005), 'Shaping IT Standardization in the Automotive Industry—The Role of Power in Driving Portal Standardization', *Electronic Markets*, 15/4, 335–43, https://doi.org/10.1080/10196780500302872

Gulati, R. (1995), 'Social Structure and Alliance Formation Patterns: A Longitudinal Analysis', *Administrative Science Quarterly*, 40/4, 619–52.

Gulati, R., and Gargiulo, M. (1999), 'Where Do Interorganizational Networks Come From?' *American Journal of Sociology*, 104/5, 1439–93,https://doi.org/10.1086/210179/, accessed 26 September 2020.

Håkansson, H., and Snehota, I. (1995), *Developing Relationships in Business Networks* (London: Routledge.

Halinen, A., Salmi, A., and Havila, V. (1999), 'From Dyadic Change to Changing Business Networks: An Analytical Framework', *Journal of Management Studies*, 36/6, 779–94. https://doi.org/10.1111/1467-6486.00158

Hargrave, T. (2021), 'The Paradox Perspective and the Dialectics of Contradictions Research'. in M. S. Poole and A. H. Van de Ven, eds., *The Oxford Handbook of Organizational Change and Innovation* (Oxford: Oxford University Press),

Hartley, J., and Allison, M. (2002), 'Good, Better, Best? Inter-Organizational Learning in a Network of Local Authorities', *Public Management Review*, 4/1, 101–18, https://doi.org/10.1080/14616670110117332/, accessed 26 September 2020.

Hayes, J. (2018), *The Theory and Practice of Change Management* (Basingstoke: Palgrave).

Heracleous, L., and Murray, J. (2001), 'Networks, Interlocking Directors and Strategy: Toward a Theoretical Framework', *Asia Pacific Journal of Management*, 18, 137–60, https://doi.org/10.1023/A:1010655621305/, accessed 26 September 2020.

Hite, J. M., and Hesterly, W. S. (2001), 'The Evolution of Firm Networks: From Emergence to Early Growth of the Firm', *Strategic Management Journal*, 22/3, 275–86, https://doi.org/10.1002/smj.156/, accessed 26 September 2020.

Honig, B., and Lampel, J. (2000), 'Interorganizational Entrepreneurship in the Global Arena', *International Journal of Organizational Analysis*, 8/4, 343–63, https://doi.org/10.1108/eb028922/, accessed 26 September 2020.

Huxham, C., and Vangen, S. (2000), 'Ambiguity, Complexity and Dynamics in the Membership of Collaboration', *Human Relations*, 53/6, 771–806, https://doi.org/10.1177/0018726700536002/, accessed 26 September 2020.

Huxham, C., and Vangen, S. (2009), 'Doing Things Collaboratively: Realising the Advantage or Succumbing to Inertia?', in J. O'Flynn, J. Wanna, J. O'Flynn, and J. Wanna, eds., *Collaborative Governance—A New Era of Public Policy in Australia?* (Canberra: ANU E Press), 29–44, http://epress.anu.edu.au/anzsog/collab_gov/pdf/ch04.pdf/, accessed 26 September 2020.

Huybrechts, B., and Haugh, H. (2018), 'The Role of Networks in Institutionalizing New Hybrid Organizational Forms: Insights from the European Renewable Energy Cooperative Network. *Organization Studies*, 39/8, 1085–108, https://doi.org/10.1177/0170840617717097/, accessed 26 September 2020.

Ihm, J., and Castillo, E. A. (2017), 'Development and Transformation of Collaborative Networks in Events', *Journal of Convention &Event Tourism*, 18/3, 205–24. https://doi.org/10.1080/15470148.2017.1322021/, accessed 26 September 2020.

Jenssen, J. I., and Nybakk, E. (2013), 'Inter-Organizational Networks and Innovation in Small, Knowledge-Intensive Firms: A Literature Review', *International Journal of Innovation Management*, 17/02, 1,350,008. https://doi.org/10.1142/S1363919613500084/, accessed 26 September 2020.

Johnson, J. A., and Wechsler, B. (1990), 'The Development of an Interorganizational Network in State Government: Improved Performance through Action Research', *International Journal of Public Administration*, 13/5, 689–706, https://doi.org/10.1080/01900699008524690/, accessed 26 September 2020.

Kilduff, M., and Tsai, W. (2003), *Social Networks and Organizations* (Thousand Oaks, CA: SAGE).

Kim, T.-Y., Oh, H., and Swaminathan, A. (2006), 'Framing Interorganizational Network Change: A Network Inertia Perspective', *Academy of Management Review*, 31/3, 704–20, https://doi.org/10.5465/amr.2006.21318926/, accessed 26 September 2020.

Knight, L., and Pye, A. (2004), 'Exploring the Relationships between Network Change and Network Learning', *Management Learning*, 35/4, 473–90, https://doi.org/10.1177/1350507604048274/, accessed 26 September 2020.

Koza, M. P., and Lewin, A. Y. (1999), 'The Coevolution of Network Alliances: A Longitudinal Analysis of an International Professional Service Network', *Organization Science*, 10/5, 638–53, https://doi.org/10.1287/orsc.10.5.638/, accessed 26 September 2020.

Lane, P. J., Koka, B. R., and Pathak, S. (2006), 'The Reification of Absorptive Capacity: A Critical Review and Rejuvenation of the Construct', *The Academy of Management Review*, 31/4, 833–63. https://doi.org/10.5465/amr.2006.22527456

Larson, A. (1992), 'Network Dyads in Entrepreneurial Settings: A Study of the Governance of Exchange Relationships', *Administrative Science Quarterly*, 37/1, 76–104, https://doi.org/10.2307/2393534/, accessed 26 September 2020.

Lazerson, M. (1995), 'A New Phoenix? Modern Putting-Out in the Modena Knitwear Industry', *Administrative Science Quarterly*, 40/1, 34–59. https://doi.org/10.2307/2393699/, accessed 26 September 2020.

Lin, R., Zhang, H., Fan, J., and Hou, R. (2012), 'Alliance Network and Innovation: Evidence from China's Third Generation Mobile Communications Industry', *Journal of Asia Business Studies*, 6/2, 197–222, https://doi.org/10.1108/15587891211254407/, accessed 26 September 2020.

Liu, L., Han, C., and Xu, W. (2015), 'Evolutionary Analysis of the Collaboration Networks within National Quality Award Projects of China', *International Journal of Project Management*, 33/3, 599–609, https://doi.org/10.1016/j.ijproman.2014.11.003/, accessed 26 September 2020.

Madhavan, R., Koka, B. R., and Prescott, J. E. (1998), 'Networks in Transition: How Industry Events (Re)Shape Interfirm Relationships', *Strategic Management Journal*, 19/5, 439–59. https://doi.org/10.1002/(SICI)1097-0266(199805)19:5<439::AID-DIA952>3.0.CO;2-2

Margolin, D. B., Shen, C., Lee, S., Weber, M. S., Fulk, J., and Monge, P. (2015), 'Normative Influences on Network Structure in the Evolution of the Children's Rights NGO Network, 1977–2004', *Communication Research*, 42/1, 30–59, https://doi.org/10.1177/0093650212463731/, accessed 26 September 2020.

Mariotti, F., and Delbridge, R. (2012), 'Overcoming Network Overload and Redundancy in Interorganizational Networks: The Roles of Potential and Latent Ties', *Organization Science*, 23/2, 511–28, https://doi.org/10.1287/orsc.1100.0634/, accessed 26 September 2020.

Matinheikki, J., Artto, K., Peltokorpi, A., and Rajala, R. (2016), 'Managing Inter-Organizational Networks for Value Creation in the Front-End of Projects', *International Journal of Project Management*, 34/7, 1226–41. https://doi.org/10.1016/j.ijproman.2016.06.003/, accessed 26 September 2020.

Mohr, L. B. (1982), *Explaining Organizational Behavior* (1st ed.), San Francisco: Jossey-Bass.

Morris, M., Bessant, J., and Barnes, J. (2006), 'Using Learning Networks to Enable Industrial Development: Case Studies from South Africa', *International Journal of Operations and Production Management*, 26/5, 532–57, https://doi.org/10.1108/01443570610659892/, accessed 26 September 2020.

Morrissey, J. P., Johnsen, M. C., and Calloway, M. O. (1997), 'Evaluating Performance and Change in Mental Health Systems Serving Children and Youth: An Interorganizational Network Approach', *Journal of Mental Health Administration*, 24, 4–22. https://link.springer.com/article/10.1007/BF02790476

Munoz, P., and Lu, L. (2011), 'Interorganizational Networks and Open Innovation Environments: Addressing Emerging Paradoxes', *International Journal of Entrepreneurship and Innovation*, 12/4, 227–37, https://doi.org/10.5367/ijei.2011.0051/, accessed 26 September 2020.

Nikulainen, T. (2012), R&D Collaboration and Nanotechnology—An Opportunity for Traditional Industries', *International Journal of Innovation and Technology Management*, 09/03, 1,250,023, https://doi.org/10.1142/S021987701250023X/, accessed 26 September 2020.

Oliver, A. L. (2004), 'On the Duality of Competition and Collaboration: Network-Based Knowledge Relations in the Biotechnology Industry', *Scandinavian Journal of Management*, 20/1–2, 151–71, https://doi.org/10.1016/j.scaman.2004.06.002/, accessed 26 September 2020.

Oswick, R., Oswick, C. and Grant, D. (2021), 'Critical Approaches and Perspectives on Organizational Change', in M. S. Poole and A. H. Van de Ven, eds., *The Oxford Handbook of Organizational Change and Innovation* (Oxford: Oxford University Press),

Paquin, R. L., and Howard-Grenville, J. (2013), Blind Dates and Arranged Marriages: Longitudinal Processes of Network Orchestration', *Organization Studies*, 34/11, 1623–53, https://doi.org/10.1177/0170840612470230/, accessed 26 September 2020.

Pennings, J. M., and Harianto, F. (1992), 'Technological Networking and Innovation Implementation', *Organization Science*, 3/3, 356–82, https://doi.org/10.1287/orsc.3.3.356/, accessed 26 September 2020.

Pettigrew, A. M., Woodman, R. W., and Cameron, K. S. (2001), 'Studying Organizational Change and Development: Challenges for Future Research', *Academy of Management Journal*, 44/4, 697–713.

Pfeffer, J., and Leblebici, H. (1973), 'Executive Recruitment and the Development of Interfirm Organizations', *Administrative Science Quarterly*, 18/4, 449, https://doi.org/10.2307/2392198/, accessed 26 September 2020.

Pfeffer, J., and Salancik, R. (1978), *The External Control of Organizations: A Resource Dependence Perspective* (New York: Harper Row).

Popp, J. K., Milward, H. B., Gail MacKean, M., Ann Casebeer, M., and Lindstrom, A. (2014), *Inter-Organizational Networks*. IBM Center for the Business of Government website: https://www.researchgate.net/profile/H_Milward/publication/266142659_Collaborating_Across_Boundaries_Series_Inter-Organizational_Networks_A_Review_of_the_Literature_to_Inform_Practice/links/542739210cf26120b7b34992.pdf/, accessed 26 September 2020.

Powell, W. W. (1990), 'Neither Market nor Hierarchy: Network Forms of Organization', *Research in Organizational Behavior*, 12, 295–336.

Powell, W. W., White, D. R., Koput, K. W., and Owen-Smith, J. (2005), 'Network Dynamics and Field Evolution: The Growth of Interorganizational Collaboration in the Life Sciences', *American Journal of Sociology*, 110/4, 1132–205, https://doi.org/10.1086/421508/, accessed 26 September 2020.

Provan, K. G., Isett, K. R., and Milward, H. B. (2004), 'Cooperation and Compromise: A Network Response to Conflicting Institutional Pressures in Community Mental Health', *Nonprofit and Voluntary Sector Quarterly*, 33/3, 489–514. https://doi.org/10.1177/0899764004265718/, accessed 26 September 2020.

Provan, K. G., and Kenis, P. (2007), 'Modes of Network Governance: Structure, Management, and Effectiveness', *Journal of Public Administration Research and Theory*, 18/2, 229–52, https://doi.org/10.1093/jopart/mum015/, accessed 26 September 2020.

Rheinhardt, A., and Gioia, D. (2021), 'Upside-Down Organizational Change: Sensemaking, Sensegiving, and the New Generation', in M. S. Poole and A. H. Van de Ven, eds., *The Oxford Handbook of Organizational Change and Innovation* (Oxford: Oxford University Press),

Ring, P. S., and van de Ven, A. H. (1994), 'Developmental Processes of Cooperative Interorganizational Relationships', *The Academy of Management Review*, 19/1, 90–118, https://doi.org/10.2307/258836/, accessed 26 September 2020.

Rogan, M. (2014), 'Too Close for Comfort? The Effect of Embeddedness and Competitive Overlap on Client Relationship Retention Following an Acquisition', *Organization Science*, 25/1, 185–203. https://doi.org/10.1287/orsc.2013.0833/, accessed 26 September 2020.

Rosenkopf, L., and Padula, G. (2008), Investigating the microstructure of network evolution: Alliance formation in the mobile communications industry. *Organization Science*, *19*(5), 669–87. https://doi.org/10.1287/orsc.1070.0339/, accessed 26 September 2020.

Runtian, J. (2021), 'Eastern *Yin-Yang* Model of Change', in M. S. Poole and A. H. Van de Ven, eds., *The Oxford Handbook of Organizational Change and Innovation* (Oxford: Oxford University Press),

Schermerhorn, Jr., J. R., Bussom, R. S., Elsaid, H., and Wilson, H. K. (1985), 'Managing the Inter-Organisational Context of Management Development in a Developing Country: A Case Study', *Leadership & Organization Development Journal*, 6/1, 27–32. https://doi.org/10.1108/eb053569/, accessed 26 September 2020.

Schurr, P. H., Hedaa, L., and Geersbro, J. (2008), 'Interaction Episodes as Engines of Relationship Change', *Journal of Business Research*, 61/8, 877–84, https://doi.org/10.1016/j.jbusres.2007.09.006/, accessed 26 September 2020.

Shumate, M., Fulk, J., and Monge, P. (2005), 'Predictors of the International HIV–AIDS INGO Network Over Time', *Human Communication Research*, 31/4, 482–510. https://doi.org/10.1111/j.1468-2958.2005.tb00880.x

Shumate, M., Ibrahim, R., and Levitt, R. (2010), 'Dynamic Information Retrieval and Allocation Flows in Project Teams with Discontinuous Membership', *European Journal of International Management*, 4/6, 556–75, https://doi.org/10.1504/EJIM.2010.035589/, accessed 26 September 2020.

Soda, G. (2011), 'The Management of Firms' Alliance Network Positioning: Implications for Innovation', *European Management Journal*, 29/5, 377–88. https://doi.org/10.1016/j.emj.2011.03.004/, accessed 26 September 2020.

Son, J., and Rojas, E. M. (2011), 'Evolution of Collaboration in Temporary Project Teams: An Agent-Based Modeling and Simulation Approach', *Journal of Construction Engineering and Management*, 137/8, 619–28. https://doi.org/10.1061/(asce)co.1943-7862.0000331

Song, H., and Vannetelbosch, V. (2007), 'International R&D Collaboration Networks', *The Manchester School*, 75/6, 742–66. https://doi.org/10.1111/j.1467-9957.2007.01044.x

Sotiriadou, P., Brouwers, J., De Bosscher, V., and Cuskelly, G. (2017), 'The Role of Interorganizational Relationships on Elite Athlete Development Processes', *Journal of Sport Management*, 31, 61–79.

Stadtfeld, C., Mascia, D., Pallotti, F., and Lomi, A. (2016), 'Assimilation and Differentiation: A Multilevel Perspective on Organizational and Network Change', *Social Networks*, 44, 363–74, https://doi.org/10.1016/j.socnet.2015.04.010/, accessed 26 September 2020.

Stern, R. N. (1979), 'The Development of an Interorganizational Control Network: The Case of Intercollegiate Athletics', *Administrative Science Quarterly*, 24/2, 242, https://doi.org/10.2307/2392496/, accessed 26 September 2020.

Stohl, C., and Walker, K. (2002), 'A Bona Fide Perspective for the Future of Groups: Understanding Collaborating Groups', in L. R. Frey, ed., *Communication Yearbook*, 28 (Mahwah, NJ: Lawerence Erlbaum), 189–231.

Swan, J., and Scarbrough, H. (2005), 'The Politics of Networked Innovation', *Human Relations*, 58/7, 913–43, https://doi.org/10.1177/0018726705057811/, accessed 26 September 2020.

Sydow, J. (2004), 'Network Development by Means of Network Evaluation? Explorative Insights from a Case in the Financial Services Industry', *Human Relations*, 57/2, 201–20, https://doi.org/10.1177/0018726704042927/, accessed 26 September 2020.

Sydow, J., and Windeler, A. (2003), 'Knowledge, Trust, and Control: Managing Tensions and Contradictions in a Regional Network of Service Firms', *International Studies of Management & Organization*, 33/2, 69–100, https://doi.org/10.1080/00208825.2003.11043679/, accessed 26 September 2020.

Uzzi, B. (1996), 'The Sources and Consequences of Embeddedness for the Economic Performance of Organizations: The Network Effect', *American Sociological Review*, 61, 674–98.

Uzzi, B. (1997), 'Social Structure and Competition in Interfirm Networks: The Paradox of Embeddedness', *Administrative Science Quarterly*, 42, 35–67.

Uzzi, B., and Spiro, J. (2005), 'Collaboration and Creativity: The Small World Problem', *American Journal of Sociology*, 111/2, 447–504,https://doi.org/10.1086/432782/, accessed 26 September 2020.

van de Ven, A. H., and Poole, M. S. (1995), 'Explaining Development and Change in Organizations', *Academy of Management Review*, 20/3, 510–40, https://doi.org/10.2307/258786/, accessed 26 September 2020.

van den Ende, J., van de Kaa, G., den Uijl, S., and de Vries, H. J. (2012), 'The Paradox of Standard Flexibility: The Effect of Co-Evolution between Standard and Interorganizational Network', *Organization Studies*, 33/5–6, 705–36, https://doi.org/10.1177/0170840612443625/, accessed 26 September 2020.

Van Horn, M. L., Fagan, A. A., Hawkins, J. D., and Oesterle, S. (2014), 'Effects of the Communities That Care System on Cross-Sectional Profiles of Adolescent Substance Use and Delinquency', *American Journal of Preventive Medicine*, 47/2, 188–97, https://doi.org/10.1016/j.amepre.2014.04.004/, accessed 26 September 2020.

van Raak, A., and Paulus, A. (2001), 'A Sociological Systems Theory of Interorganizational Network Development in Health and Social Care', *Systems Research and Behavioral Science*, 18/3, 207–24, https://doi.org/10.1002/sres.389/, accessed 26 September 2020.

Wegner, D., Begnis, H. S. M., Alievi, R. M., and Maehler, A. E. (2016), 'The Dynamics of Cooperation: Proposal of a Life-Cycle Model of Small-Firm Networks', *Gestão and Regionalidade*, 32/94, https://doi.org/10.13037/gr.vol32n94.2805/, accessed 26 September 2020.

Weick, K. E., and Quinn, R. E. (1999), 'Organizational Change and Development', *Annual Review of Psychology*, 50/1, 361–86.

Woo, D. (2019), 'Exit Strategies in Interorganizational Collaboration: Setting the Stage for Re-Entry', *Communication Research*, 0093650219851418, https://doi.org/10.1177/0093650219851418/, accessed 26 September 2020.

Woolley, J. (2021), 'Processes of Emergence and Change in Industry and Ecosystem Infrastructure', in M. S. Poole and A. H. Van de Ven, eds., *The Oxford Handbook of Organizational Change and Innovation* (2nd edn) (Oxford: Oxford University Press).

Yang, A., and Taylor, M. (2015), 'Looking over, looking out, and Moving Forward: Positioning Public Relations in Theorizing Organizational Network Ecologies. *Communication Theory*, 25/1, 91–115. https://doi.org/10.1111/comt.12049/, accessed 26 September 2020.

Yzerbyt, V., Castano, E., Leyens, J.-P., and Paladino, M.-P. (2000), 'The Primacy of the Ingroup: The Interplay of Entitativity and Identification', *European Review of Social Psychology*, 11/1, 257–95, https://doi.org/10.1080/14792772043000059/, accessed 26 September 2020.

Zikos, V. (2010), 'R&D Collaboration Networks in Mixed Oliopoly', *Southern Economic Journal*, 77/1, 189–212, https://doi.org/10.4284/sej.2010.77.1.189/, accessed 26 September 2020.

CHAPTER 26

THE BECOMING OF CHANGE IN 3D: DIALECTICS, DARWIN, AND DEWEY

MOSHE FARJOUN

Introduction

WHERE can new theories of organizational change come from? In answering this question, Van de Ven and Poole (1995) advised us to look at how the different ideal-type change models in their typology interconnect.[1] As they explained: "the interplay among the theories produces a wide variety of more complex theories of change and development in organizational life." Their framework therefore "promotes new theories by identifying possible explanations of organizational change and development that do not yet exist in the literature" (1995: 510–11).

In this chapter, I seek to extend this vision. I propose that we can better understand the interplay among theories by delving into their historical interconnections and their philosophical underpinnings. Learning from prior intersections and roads less travelled, and grasping conceptions of change at their roots, may yield novel, significant departures from the status quo, or at least generate interesting alternatives (Weick 1989; Abbott 2004).

To develop this idea, I use dialectics as my main anchor. Within organization studies, dialectics is often regarded as a close cousin to organizational contradictions, paradoxes,

[1] I'd like to thank the editors for providing valuable feedback on earlier drafts of this chapter, and for encouraging me to write it in the first place. I am also indebted to Markus Becker, Kenneth Benson, Chris Ansell, and William Jackson for their instructive comments and suggestions and for Gerda Kessler for her skilled copyediting. All remaining errors or omissions are mine.

and dualities (Putnam et al. 2016; Farjoun et al. 2018; See Chapter 7 by Hargrave, this volume). It has also been viewed as synonymous with a Hegelian development through a conflict change process, which consists of an affirmation, negation, and synthesis triad (Hernes, 1976; Van de Ven and Poole 1995). As I have argued elsewhere (e.g., Farjoun, 2019), while valuable, these views are incomplete, and fail to do justice to the richness of dialectics and the breadth of its contributions, actual and potential.

For the purpose of this chapter, I will consider dialectics to be a general view of social relations and processes, which is abstracted from the ideas of Hegel, Marx, and their key followers, but is not limited to the specific arguments of these scholars (Benson 1977). Thus undesrtood, dialectics is broader than common views admit in several respects.

First, while it highlights contradictions and tensions, dialectics does not regard them merely as external, decontextualized problems for individuals to address. Rather, it regards them as grounded in specific social arrangements and historical interactions, as endogenous mechanisms for explaining how social orders develop, change, and transform, and as means for individuals and social collectives to mobilize action and reconstruct existing orders (Benson 1977; Ollman 2015; Farjoun 2017).

Second, although as an *ideal type*, the Hegelian triadic model best represents the notion of development through conflict; dialectics accommodates other variants. For instance, it recognizes the possibility of no synthesis or of several syntheses. Furthermore, through their extensive writings, Hegel and Marx uncovered other change patterns as well. For these reasons, dialectics may better be viewed as comprising a *family* of conceptual or social (and sometimes even natural) change models, variously stressing interconnection, tension, contradiction, opposition, and conflict as their key motor (e.g., Schneider 1971; Hernes 1976; Bhaskar 1993).

Third, within dialectics, the notions of contradiction and change are not standalone principles but belong to a wider *relational process ontology*, which informs a set of loosely interrelated principles, such as totality, the unity and interplay of opposites, and praxis (e.g., Benson 1977; Seo and Creed 2002; Farjoun 2019). Dialectics views the world as a ceaseless interplay of opposing tendencies (Baxter and Montgomery 1996) and a manifold of nested and interrelated processes (e.g., Nicholson and Dupre 2018), rather than a configuration of "dead things" (Ollman 2003). In contrast to social atomism, the commitment of dialectics to relationality highlights how "one thing cannot exist without the other, that one acquires its properties from its relation to the other, and that the properties of both evolve because of their interpenetration" (Levins and Lewontin 1985). Dialectics also views the world as in a continuous state of *becoming*, a work in progress rather than a final product (Tsoukas and Chia 2002); social arrangements that seem fixed and permanent are temporary, arbitrary patterns, and any observed social pattern is regarded as one of several possibilities (Benson 1977). Illustrating this unconventional processual worldview, Marx conceptualized capital not merely as economic input ('a thing'), but as a social relation which can change its form over time (Ollman 2015). Echoing Marx's view of capital, the recently developed blockchain technology—used as a basis for cryptocurrencies such as bitcoin—can too be viewed not as a '*thing*" but as a historical, cumulative process of transactions.

This more nuanced appreciation of dialectics—which recognizes its specific view of contradiction, the broader menu of change models it includes, and its relational process perspective—enlarges its capacity to stimulate new models of change. Importantly and most immediately, dialectics offers both an ideal type model of *organizational* change, and a template for synthetic, meta-theoretic, *conceptual* change, premised on the confrontation of existing change models.

Here, I'd like to highlight two other generative capacities of dialectics: as a process philosophy, and as an evolutionary theory. In the first instance, dialectics wears its philosophical hat, and its relational process principles serve as heuristics, or "means to find things out" (Abbott 2004), like discovering or inventing new ideas about change. Consider Giddens' (1984) notion of structuration, Weick's (1979) theory of "organizing," and Feldman and Pentland's (2003) reconceptualization of routines as sources of change—all regarded as key conceptual innovations within our field. Each of these advances required profound, ontological departures. At the same time, each intellectual move offered a different interpretation of a broader—"process within structure" dialectical heuristic (e.g., Abbott 2004; Bakken and Hernes 2006; Langley 2007; Ansell 2011).[2] Therefore, along with the deep, and at times radical insights it can yield, a relational process perspective's interpretive flexibility can also inspire a playful approach—indispensable to the theorizing process.

Dialectics can also stimulate new ideas about change by wearing its theoretical, evolutionary hat. In this capacity, dialectics offers specific theoretical ideas regarding mechanisms and patterns of change, comparable to those included in other equivalent dynamic approaches, whether founded on a similar philosophy or not. The dialectical view particularly underscores how past and present developments affect, but do not determine, future ones (Levins and Lewontin 1985); for instance, it highlights how any system contains the seeds of its own destruction or transformation. In this, historical sense, dialectics is considered an *evolutionary* perspective.

Thus viewed, dialectics invites a systematic contrast with another, better known, evolutionary theory: Darwin's theory of natural selection. Within organization studies, these two influential, living approaches have largely developed along separate paths and, in their ideal-type formulations are commonly viewed as offering contrasting perspectives on organizational change and development (e.g., Van de Ven and Poole 1995; See Sections 2 and 4 in this handbook). These differences remain important, and in the interest of stimulating debate and imagination, ought to be preserved. At the same time, extracting key and often overlooked historical and conceptual complementarities between dialectics and evolutionary theory may yield new, creative directions too.[3]

I illustrate these dual engines for new theory development by showing how they coalesced in pragmatist philosophy, and in Dewey in particular. Dialectics and Darwin's

[2] I prefer to use the term "dialectical" to convey attributes such as non-linear, synthetic, recursive, and oppositional. Others have grouped these heuristics in alternative terms, such as flux (Morgan, 2006) and irony (Sztompka 1986).

[3] Increasingly recognized, for instance, is the influence exerted by Darwin's and Hegel's ideas on process philosophy (Langley and Tsoukas 2017), as well as the joint contribution of Darwin and Marx to the development of historical, institutional and evolutionary perspectives in economics (Hodgson 2014).

evolutionary theories have intersected in other intellectual approaches, notably institutional economics, Schumpeter's analysis of capitalism and technological change, and systems and complexity theories; however, pragmatism exemplifies their convergence at a key, and relatively less familiar chapter in the history of ideas. Furthermore, like dialectics, pragmatist philosophy is premised on a relational process worldview and shares many of the heuristics of dialectics (Ansell 2011; Farjoun et al. 2015; Farjoun 2019). I draw on Dewey to discuss the challenges in bringing together different philosophical and evolutionary traditions, and to extract lessons from his innovative solutions. Dewey's work is also significant, since, as Cohen (2007) observed, it collates the seeds for much of subsequently developed organizational theories.[4]

Inspired by Dewey, but also abstracting from his synthesis, I will also propose two additional pathways for future change theorizing. To illustrate dialectics' first hat, I will show how combining specific ideas drawn from evolutionary and dialectic theories—particularly about knowledge and power—can help form richer models of change, relevant to present-day developments. In addition, I will illustrate how new change models can draw on one of the key principles of dialectics—the interplay between the implicit and explicit orders variously associated with notions such as potentialities and actualities, generativity and affordances.

My key aspirations in this chapter are twofold. My first aim is to encourage organizational scholars to consider philosophy, the history of ideas, and tradition, as important and relatively underutilized sources for modeling change. My second, indirect objective is to make novel connections across a wide range of literatures that are not often brought together. While this chapter highlights the contrast between dialectics and evolutionary theory, it also helps uncover less apparent linkages between other models of change, such as institutional change [See Chapter 23 by Dearing, this volume], effectuation [See Chapter 6 by Sarasvathy and Venkataraman, this volume], discontinuous change [See Chapter 16 by Gaba and Meyer, this volume], and complex adaptive systems [See Chapter 20 by Dooley and Chapter 21 by Albert and Garco, this volume].

My additional hope is to spark curiosity in what dialectics brings to organizational theory's drawing table. Working with, and against, other approaches, such as evolutionary theory and pragmatism, is not only inherent to the dialectical view, but can help reassert it in its proper place within organization studies. In this vision, dialectics appears not as a footnote to newer research streams but as a rich, playful, and highly relevant social science and processual perspective, a precursor to central ideas in the field of organization studies, and a companion to other influential traditions in its class.

The rest of the chapter is organized into two main sections, respectively dealing with the history of ideas and with resources for theorizing change. The first section provides a broad-brush historical overview of key intellectual traditions that deal with change, transformation, and flux. Stretching from Greek philosophy to dialectics, to Darwin, to

[4] Among other things, one can find in it fragments of institutional, evolutionary, sensemaking, learning, and transaction costs theories of organization.

pragmatism, this section interweaves historical continuities with conceptual ones. The second section illustrates the philosophical and evolutionary new idea generators at work: by reading Dewey's pragmatism anew, and by proposing additional directions pertinent to contemporary phenomena. I conclude with a discussion of the chapter's main themes.

Models of Change: Selected Chapters and Developments in the History of Ideas

Throughout history, philosophers, social and natural scientists, and many others, have continuously mused about the nature of change and transformation and the mechanisms that best explain them. From ancient Greek philosophy and onwards, conceptions have shifted from change as a *teleology*, leading to a final cause or a state of completion, to change as a *progress*, a movement away from ignorance, to change as *development* driven by scientific and technological knowledge, and to change as *continuous in time* (Patterson, 2018). More recently, observers have started regarding *crises* and revolutions as recurrent too (Harari, 2015). A key notion that has been rejected is the belief that change always entails improvement or the working out of a grand scheme (Patterson 2018). Along with these conceptual shifts, some ideas about change have persisted. For instance, as underscored by Trompf's (1979) historical analysis, theories of change that involve notions of recurrence and renewal gain currency in times of flux.

This section retrieves selected milestones in the history of ideas about change. It particularly highlights three processual, "becoming" perspectives relevant to organizational change—dialectics, evolutionary theory, and pragmatism—and places them in a historical context. As Figure 26.1 indicates, these perspectives combine ideas from natural sciences, humanities and social sciences. Furthermore, all three are active traditions, coevolving with each other and with broader contextual developments. Although none of them was originally developed as a theory of organization, the ideas contained in these perspectives are highly present in organization studies and inform dominant conceptions of change in the field.

Dialectics and process philosophy in ancient Greece: Heraclitus. Heraclitus of Ephesus (544–483 BC) is considered the father of dialectics and the founder of "process" philosophy (e.g., Rescher 1996). His key departure from the philosophy preceding him lies in his emphasis on human affairs (Graham 2019), but it was his perspective on process and change that subsequently captivated the imagination of others. Well remembered is his reflection that no one could step twice in the same river as it is no longer the same river.

Less familiar are some of his other insights. In his writings, Hercalitus maintained that: (1) the cosmos was a "unity of opposites"'simultaneously change and non-change (continuity); (2) the cosmos is in a continual state of flux because of the continually shifting interrelations of change and permanence; (3) the world is changed through transformations ordered in and by time; (4) time is responsible for the existence of a stable world; (5) the cosmos exists through the transformation of substances into one another; (6) the substances are not permanent; and (7) fire is simultaneously the most unstable (changeable) and the most enduring of its predecessors' generating substances, and it is also the one into which everything else turns (Patterson, 2018).

A lasting insight that Heraclitus provided is that one cannot explain change merely as separate from, and in opposition to, stability. For Heraclitus, both change and permanence are constant and continually interacting features of the cosmos, and the two may occur simultaneously at different levels of the totality. Constancy requires ongoing change and ongoing change produces stability (Patterson 2018: 15). Another, subtle and profound message of his river metaphor is that some things (i.e., the river) stay the same only by changing (i.e., the flow and turnover of water), an insight that has clear resonance with contemporary models of change (e.g., Ansell et al. 2015). Similar ideas permeate dialectics—an evolutionary tradition Heraclitus and other Greek philosophers have stimulated.

Dialectics: Hegel and Marx. In the nineteenth century, particularly, scholars increasingly emphasized that progress was inevitable and that it occurred through successive stages of intellectual and social development. They called it "evolution" in order to convey the idea of continuous change in time (Patterson 2018). Evolutionary concepts entered people's minds at the time by two different routes and in two different forms. On the European continent they were first introduced through Hegel, and later in the materialist teachings of Marxism. In the English-speaking world they were popularized through the teachings of Herbert Spencer, Darwin, and T. H. Huxley, who conformed to the native empirical traditions (Novack 1975).

Key dialectic scholars, mainly Hegel (1770–1831) and Marx (1818–1883), have absorbed many influences—from political economy, to the humanities, to the natural sciences. They have been particularly influenced by Greek philosophy (Heraclitus, but also Aristotle, Socrates, Plato, and others), and by its key carriers, notably Kant. While it retained and refined its philosophical core, dialectics gradually assumed other roles—becoming more theoretical, empirical, and activist as a result.

Hegel saw history as the gradual unfolding of reason and freedom and as the evolution of the human spirit, which he viewed as a set of potentials waiting to be actualized and developed. Marx's broader version of dialectics built on, but also significantly reconceptualized, Hegel's idealistic version (Kaufmann 1965). Whereas Hegel saw dialectics as operating in the realm of ideas and ideals, Marx stressed that the contradictions that produce a dialectical pattern of historical change have their roots in the material conditions of social existence, which can be scientifically studied. Moreover, conflicts between abstract social forces, such as technological and economic ones (productive forces and relations of production), are manifest in conflicts between groups in the society, specifically classes, and help explain human history (Blau, 1972; Adler 2009). For Marx, history is not about the struggle of ideas but of men and women attempting to achieve their own aims, working with and against nature and each other.

The differences between Hegel and Marx notwithstanding, these dialectics scholars have significantly developed and applied its relational process philosophy. Table 26.1 lists several key principles associated with a relational process ontology, and provides illustrations from dialectics, pragmatism, and evolutionary theory. As we will subsequently discuss, as two philosophical and social traditions, dialectics and pragmatism have greater overlap with one another.[5] However, evolutionary theory too shares several underlying principles, albeit implicitly.[6]

Enter Darwin (1809-1882). The nineteenth century, a bedrock for several social and political revolutions, was also the time for an important crossover between dialectics and another evolutionary perspective: Darwin's theory of natural selection. Within biology, and prior to the second half of the nineteenth century, the term "evolution" was used primarily, if not exclusively, to designate the development of the individual embryo. Therefore, in 1859, when Darwin introduced his theory of natural selection, the concept of evolution was already in the air. Since Darwin's work, the designator "evolution" has been typically, if not exclusively, linked with the theory of natural selection as the primary cause by which such species change has occurred over historical time (Sloan 2019a).

In the initial public presentation of his revolutionary theory, Darwin relied on the novel claim that small individual variations—the kind of differences considered by an earlier tradition as merely "accidental'"formed the raw material upon which, by unlimited addition through the action of natural selection, major changes could be produced sufficient to explain the origin and subsequent differences in all the various forms of life over time (Sloan 2019a). Darwin realized that in nature individual organisms compete for limited resources and those fortuitously better adapted to changes in the local environment, through advantages in coloration, speed, or vision, for example, are more likely to survive and reproduce and pass on these advantages to their offspring, thereby bringing about changes in the population. Darwin called this natural selection because the forces of nature select which organism will survive. This principle was not of *progress* but of local *adaptation*: the survivors are not better in any cosmic way; they are just better fit in a local sense.

The primary distinguishing feature of Darwin's theory that separates it from previous explanations of species change centers on the causal explanation he offered for how this process occurred (Sloan 2019b). According to Lewontin (1974: 10), Darwin's stunning insight was that the differences between organisms within a species are converted into

[5] The philosophical principles underlying pragmatism and dialectics are compatible mainly from a theoretical standpoint. Taking a more fine-grained approach, philosophers are likely to regard differences between the two traditions, such as about the role of ontology, as more significant than our discussion suggests.

[6] While they are not explicitly linked with dialectics, relational process principles also appear in several other organizational theories, such as in Weick's theory of organizing. As Morgan (2006) recognized in his flux metaphor, relational process principles have equivalents in modern natural sciences; other than in complexity theory, these principles appear in chemistry (Stein 2004), biology (Levins and Lewontin 1985; Jablonka and Lamb 2005; Nicholson and Dupre 2018), and physics (Barad 2007).

Table 26.1 A Relational Process Philosophy—Illustrative Parallels in Dialectics, Pragmatism, and Evolutionary Theory*

Tradition: Key inter-related principles, or dialectical heuristics:	*Philosophy and Social Theory:* *Dialectics*	*Pragmatism (Dewey)*	*Natural Sciences:* *Evolutionary Theory (Implicit)*
Recursive relations *Mutual causality; reflexivity, circularity, interplay.*	Interplay between organizations and environments (niche construction), and between process and structure.	Illustrated in the relation between stimulus and response, in the notion of experimentation, and in institutional change model.	Coevolution—how two or more species reciprocally affect each other's evolution; enactment; highlights information feedback and endogenous selection.
Contradiction/ Unity and interplay of opposites *Conflict, struggle, tensions; disequilibrium*	Struggle (such as between ideas or classes). Evolution as a self-negating process. Uneven development (leading to crisis and revolution). Synthesis	Conflict as part of thinking and inquiry. Democracy as a means for settling conflicts through dialogue.	Struggle or competition (e.g., between species). Contradiction as a sub case of variation. Uneven development (a form of inertia). Hybridization and recombination
Totality *Systems; holism, interdependence, interpenetration.*	An inter-related and nested whole with partially autonomous parts (e.g., capitalism). Contradictions as interconnected.	Human nature as an integrated system. Character as the interpenetration of habits. Culture as integrating science, religion, and other spheres.	Ecology (entangled bank metaphor; ecosystem). Complex interactions (competition and cooperation) between species.
Implicit and explicit order *Generative systems; affordances.*	Interplay between potentialities and actualities, or essence and appearance. Stratified ontology.	Individuals' creative potentials as best actualized in specific environments. Habits as dispositions	Genotype (heredity information) and Phenotype (observed properties). Habits and routines as dispositions
Transcending dualisms *Distrust of dualism and rigid categories. Union of processes; Mediation.*	Highlighting interplay and overlap. Allowing for middle ground. Stability and change as nested and intertwined (a continual transformation also serves to preserve existing social structures).	Duality A transactional view Creating new concepts by unifying opposites in a single processual term. Alienation as the converse of continuity and transaction. Mediating science, practice and philosophy	Processual orientation diffuses boundaries, categories, and levels. Stability and change as nested and intertwined (stable structures enable the creation of transformed structures)

* Each of the above traditions includes a variety of principles and concepts not summarized here.

the differences between species in space and time. Thus, the differences between species are already latent within them, and all that is required is a motive force for the conversion of variation. That force is natural selection (Patterson 2009).This theory was both radical, and unsettling to many at the time: it went not only against the science of the time but also against religion, and other aspects of the established social order. It suggested that new species, and human beings specifically, have evolved rather than being created through some grand design.

Around the time Darwin published his radical ideas in *The Origin of Species* (1859), Marx and Engels were working on their Manifesto, a radical text against the then established order. Like many others in years to come, Marx recognized Darwin's newly published book as highly original and significant. While he later criticized some of Darwin's ideas as closely mirroring the political and social order prevailing in England at his time, Marx saw parallels between Darwin's account of natural selection and his own ideas, partly developed with Engels, on how human societies developed historically.

The key parallel centered around Marx' ideas about class *struggle*, somewhat analogous to the competition between species for key resources highlighted in Darwin's theory. Both scholars were influenced by the ideas of key classical, political economists (Figure 26.1). Whereas Marx mainly drew on Ricardo, it is commonly believed that

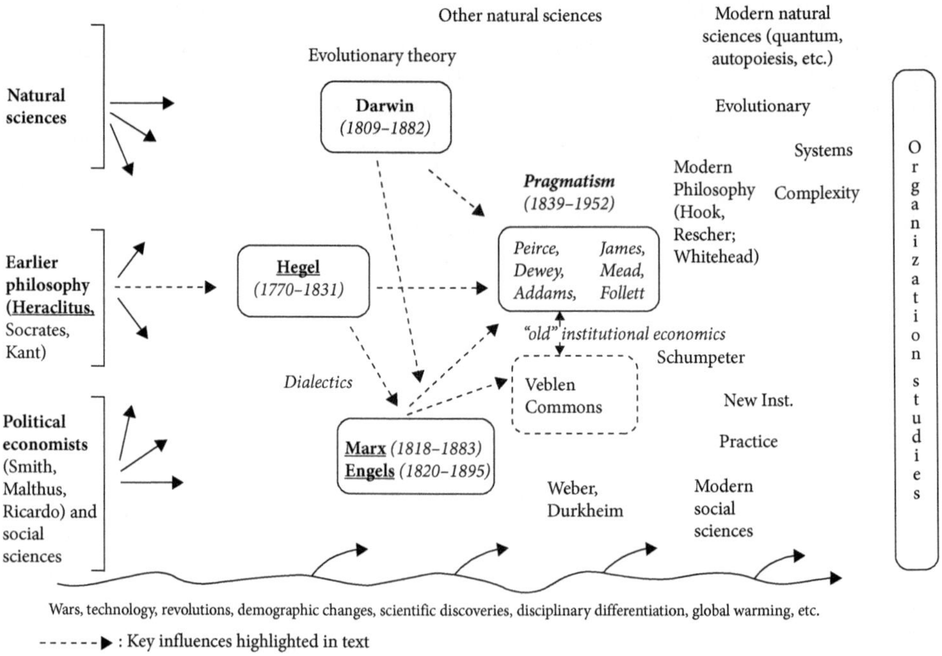

FIGURE 26.1 Dialectics, evolutionary theory and pragmatism—situating three "becoming" perspectives in the history of ideas (see also table titles in introduction chapter).

Darwin was heavily influenced by Malthus' theory that the geometrical increase of population coupled with the only arithmetical increase of food supply would lead to a crisis. The idea of struggle proved useful to Darwin when he developed the notions of selection and "struggle for existence", central to his theory. According to Sloan (2019b), Darwin reinterpreted Malthus's principle, which was formulated only with reference to the human population in relation to food supply, as a general principle governing all organic life.

In a remarkable twist in the history of ideas, whereas Darwin initially generalized Malthus's notion of struggle from human economy to natural world, subsequent work proceeded in the opposite direction: from natural to social science. Starting with Spencer (1898), scholars have been interested in applying evolutionary analysis to the social and organizational world, a development that has been intensified in recent years (e.g., Nelson and Winter, 1982; Hannan and Freeman 1984; Hodgson and Knudsen 2010).[7] Contemporary organizational scholarship views evolution as a generic approach, applicable at multiple levels, that directs attention to the processes of variation, selection, retention, and struggle (or competition) over scarce resources that jointly produce patterned change in evolving systems (Aldrich and Ruef 2006: 4).[8]

While both are considered as grand processual, "becoming" perspectives, the potential for an exchange between dialectics and evolutionary theory has always been a matter of debate: whereas some highlighted their differences, others stressed their complementarities. For reasons known only to himself, Darwin, was more reserved about connecting with Marx and his economic and social analysis of history.[9] Years later, key contemporary evolutionary theorists, Nelson and Winter (1982: 43–5), also qualified such connections. As they made clear, political power was not central to their theory as it was for Marx, nor did they find much use in their theory for his ideas about contradictions and class conflict. Nevertheless, like other contemporary economists—notably, institutional economist Douglas North and technology historian Nathan Rosenberg—Nelson and Winter were quite receptive to the general scheme of Marx's dialectical materialism. Resonating with their own approach, they characterized much of Marx's economic theory as evolutionary, and as consistent with their own stress on endogenous change. They also viewed some of

[7] Evolutionary theorizing found its way to organization studies mainly through two dominant theories. Hannan and Freeman's (1984) ecological framework applied evolutionary theory at the level of populations of organizations. In their theory, change occurs through the changing demographics (i.e., entry and exit) of relatively inert organizations. A wholly different model of change was offered by Nelson and Winter (1982) who applied the natural selection metaphor and evolutionary principles at the level of organizational routines. In their evolutionary theory of the firm, change and innovation mainly occur through the mutation and recombination of relatively stable organizational routines. The conceptual shift in unit of selection leads to viewing organizations as more flexible than depicted in a population ecology perspective.

[8] Organizational theorists have not used the term "evolution" uniformly. For simplicity and unless otherwise stated, I will not mention the different variations, refinements, and organizational applications of Darwin's ideas and will mainly use the broad term "evolutionary theory" instead.

[9] For additional details on this exchange, see Ball (1979) and Rejon (2018).

their own ideas as quite compatible with those of Marx, in that he highlighted how the capitalist organization of production defines a dynamic evolutionary system.

Two evolutionary theories compared. Ostensibly, the view of dialectics and evolutionary theory as separate, and perhaps antithetical theories, is hardly surprising. Darwin's evolutionary theory has not been formulated as a philosophy. It concerns adaptation to the natural world, views blind variation and chance as central explanatory mechanisms, involves the development, retention, and selection of *information* concerning adaptive solutions to survival problems faced by entities in their environment (Hodgson and Knudsen, 2010), and in its ideal-type formulation, it stresses gradual, adaptive change.

By contrast, while it has been applied to the natural world too, dialectics originated in philosophy and developed mainly to theorize about the social world and human history—recent in origins compared to the natural world. Unlike Darwin, who sought to explain the origins of observed diversity, complexity, and novelty in nature, Hegel and Marx were more interested in the structure, varieties, and evolution of social orders and societies, and in the role of individuals within these contexts. This led them to focus on human agency and intentionality, both at the individual and collective level, and to highlight how self-aware agents not only adapt but actively construct and shape their social and natural environments. In line with this focus, dialectics highlights interests, power, ideologies, and institutions, more than feedback and information. Finally, Hegel, Marx, and Engels assigned a greater role to non-gradual, revolutionary changes.[10]

The broad differences between dialectics and evolutionary theory notwithstanding, the two perspectives exhibit several, non-obvious affinities, particularly around key principles and heuristics: recursive relations, contradiction/unity, and the interplay of opposites, totality, implicit and explicit orders, and transcending dualisms (e.g., stability and change) (Table 26.1).

Perhaps the most intuitive affinity lies in their stress on recursive, coevolutionary relations, manifest in terms such as mutual causality, reflexivity, and interplay. The biological concept of coevolution highlights feedback and endogenous selection and is used to describe how two or more species reciprocally affect each other's evolution. In evolutionary models of organizations, coevolution refers to the systematic way that organizations (and populations) influence their environments and how organizational environments comprised of other organizations and populations in turn influence those organizations (Baum and Singh 1994; McKelvey 1997; Nelson 2005; See Chapter 18 by Baum and Rao, this volume). Closest to the biological concept of coevolution is the dialectics-inspired niche construction theory (Levins and Lewontin 1985). However, recursive relations are pervasive in dialectics—manifested in its Hegelian change model, the interplay between agency and structure and more. The recursive relations of dialectics are linked with other of its relational process principles and do not stress information

[10] Dialectics and evolutionary theory differ in their broad scientific orientations. Darwin's natural selection theory enlisted vast and cumulative empirical evidence in its support. By contrast, while it too has drawn on broad empirical, comparative historical data, and has generated many theoretical propositions, dialectics is more cumulative in its deep insights and the applications of its principles than in its specific empirical findings.

exchanges as much; further, in the dialectical view, the two sides of a relation do not simply interact or oscillate but rather interpenetrate and develop over time.[11]

As we have seen, the notion of struggle was key to the historical intersections between the two theories. The concept of *contradiction* connects the two theories in other, subtle ways. Within evolutionary theory, contradiction is viewed as a form of variation (Aldrich and Ruef 2006). From the alternative, dialectical viewpoint, the Darwinian evolution by selection among variants constitutes a contradictory, *self-negating* process, which consumes the variation that fuels it and so destroys the condition for its further development (Levins and Lewontin 1985). A related idea that appears in both theories stresses development as stimulated by imperfections and incompleteness. Similarly, the idea of synthesis as retaining the useful aspects of two or more terms or entities has a parallel in Darwin's discussion of breeding and artificial selection.

Dialectics and evolutionary theories also parallel each other in highlighting how uneven developments, disequilibria, and similar temporal forms of contradictions stimulate change. Having each engaged in a comparative history of sorts, Hegel, Marx, and Darwin, became sensitized to the uneven nature of development: for Darwin, it occurred across species and geographies; for Hegel and Marx, across different societies or realms of society, such as institutions and technology. These similarities notwithstanding, the two theories differ in how they draw on uneven development as a theoretical mechanism. For instance, in organizational evolutionary theory, this mechanism mainly appears in discussions of organizational inertia, whereas in dialectics, it features as a disequilibrium phenomenon, a potential source of revolutions and crises.

Another concept connecting the two evolutionary perspectives is the notion of *totality*. Both adopt a non-reductive, holistic style of argumentation (Patterson 2009). Dialectics' stress on ecology, systems, and complexity, and its recognition of their nested nature, is well reflected in its notion of totality (e.g., Harvey 2018). However, Darwin's theory is deeply ecological too: it highlights complex interactions between species (Sloan 2019b), where entities face immediately scarce resources and struggle to survive, whether through conflict or cooperation (Hodgson and Knudsen 2010).[12]

Furthermore, and as will be subsequently illustrated in greater detail, dialectics highlights the interplay between the potential and the actual, or essence and appearance. A parallel in evolutionary theory is the contrast between genotype, which designates the organism's full heredity information, and phenotype, which refers to the organism's actual observed properties. In similar vein, contemporary evolutionary views highlight habits and routines as latent dispositions which may or may not be realized in specific interactions.

Finally, evolutionary theory does not explicitly discuss the *transcendence of dualisms*; nevertheless, its processual view makes it consistent with this dialectical principle. This affinity of the two theories is manifest in their joint emphasis on the unity, interplay, and

[11] Some may view the dialectics notion of interpenetration, often associated with less dualistic views, as incompatible with evolutionary reasoning, particularly with the idea that selection operates on a population of cohesive individual units.

[12] This holistic view is reflected in Darwin's entangled bank metaphor, which is said to summarize his natural selection theory.

nested nature of stability and change (Seo and Creed 2002; Farjoun 2010). This interplay, or duality, is expressed differently in each theory, however. For instance, within the evolutionary tradition, selection and transformation are viewed as fundamentally related: stable structures which are selected because they best fit their contexts and enable the creation of transformed structures (Levinthal, 1991). The dialectical materialism of Marx highlights too how social transformation is enabled (or constrained) by the existing social arrangements. However, it also highlights the inverse relation whereby transformation and change function to preserve existing social structures. In Marx's view, chronic mutation, innovation, and technological change are integral to capitalism and help reproduce it.

Other than in underlying principles, dialectics and evolutionary theory have several parallels in the patterns of change they highlight:

First, while not confined to them, both evolutionary and dialectical models accentuate endogenous sources of change. Darwinian theory is viewed as a powerful scientific theory of endogenous change, where variation provides differences, but selection determines which differences survive (Kelm 1997). This stress on internal, bottom-up, motors of change characterizes dialectical models as well. In the dialectical view, rather than only originating in external shocks, change has structural sources and often arises endogenously, from within the existing system or order. Related to endogenous change, dialectics also calls attention to how the world of appearances often conceals and actively suppresses latent potentialities for transformation, such as those stemming from individuals' creativity and desire for freedom. The mechanisms underlying endogenous change differ. In Darwin's theory biological evolution is self-generating; by contrast, in the Marxian scheme, specifically, evolution is directed by willful, conscious, active people and molded by historical forces (Basalla 1988).

A second affinity concerns the tempo and scope of change considered in each theory. Once one relaxes their ideal-type formulations, the two theories recognize a broader and fuzzier spectrum of change patterns, the specific form of which may be best revealed empirically, in specific contexts. In evolutionary formulations the pace of change is set by the intersection of external selection and external forces (Aldrich and Ruef 2006). In zooming in and out through different spatial and temporal scales, dialectics too accommodates both gradual and revolutionary patterns of change. Hegel, for instance, viewed history as the gradual unfolding of reason and freedom. Yet, he also discussed how the gradual accumulation of minor changes leads to qualitative change and sudden reversals.

A relational, ecological sensitivity is also manifest in both theories' appreciation of recursive coevolutionary and cumulative changes, which can occur at both the dyadic and the ecological level. In his writings on nature, Engels, highlighted how organisms and social actors select and shape their environments (Levins and Lewontin 1985). Similarly, central to Marx's view of history is the recursive notion that a group (or a class) can change itself by modifying its environment (Hernes 1976).

Finally, evolutionary theory is non-deterministic and non-teleological. Contemporary views of dialectics have also distanced themselves from a teleological conception of change, highlighting instead change as more open ended and possibilistic (e.g., Benson 1977). In this view of change as *contingent development*, the effect of a force cannot be specified in general but only in a context (Levins and Lewontin 1985; Patterson 2018).

The pragmatist fusion.[13] The historical and conceptual linkages between dialectics and evolutionary theory—evident in their underlying relational process principles and views on change—set the stage for examining their synthesis in pragmatist philosophy and in Dewey. Pragmatist thinking, as mainly represented by Charles Peirce, John Dewey, William James, and Herbert Mead, as well as associated intellectual figures such as Jane Addams, Mary Parker Follett, John Commons, and Thorstein Veblen, developed into a distinctive, problem-solving philosophy towards the end of the nineteenth century (Elkjaer and Simpson 2011; Farjoun et al. 2015; Lorino 2018). Pragmatists particularly stressed that ideas are more than mere accretions of experience out there to be discovered, their importance lying in their projected influence on future experiences, as tools to cope with problems and to promote social change (Menand 2001). Pragmatism's problem-solving orientation brings together its distinctive ideas about experience, habit, action, and reflexivity, and highlights human activities such as interpretation, inquiry, deliberation, creativity, and learning.

In developing their ideas, pragmatists built on the diverse sources of philosophers, historians, natural scientists, social scientists, and political theorists. Like other key philosophers before them, pragmatists developed their own views of the natural and material world. Particularly influenced by Darwin's ideas about natural selection, they sought to apply these ideas to the social world and thereby "evolutionize" philosophy.

Dewey was born in 1859, the year Darwin published *The Origin of Species*, and he came to maturity when the evolutionary theory was conquering the scientific world. Deeply influenced by Darwinism, Dewey (1910) contains an essay on the influence of Darwin on philosophy (of nature and knowledge). Dewey's reflections provide a window into how Darwin, mostly regarded as a highly influential theorist, immensely contributed to philosophy, and to its processual, "becoming" strand.[14]

In his 1910 essay, Dewey proposed that Darwin's contributions can be best assessed against the conceptions that reigned before him, mainly the assumption of the superiority of the *fixed* and the *final*. He credited Darwin's *The Origins of Species* for introducing a new mode of thinking that in the end was bound to transform the logic of knowledge, and hence the treatment of morals, politics, and religion. Darwin's theory saw change in living things as orderly and cumulative. For Dewey, a key implication of the view that the transient aspect of nature also implies a different, provisional

[13] An earlier version of the ideas contained in this section were presented at the 2019 'Celebrating the Pragmatist Turn' workshop, Glasgow, Scotland, and appear in Farjoun et al. (2015). The references to Dewey are mainly drawn from The Essential Dewey (Hickman and Alexander 1998), which provides a survey of Dewey's rich ideas, and incorporates influences from Peirce, James, and Veblen, and, to a lesser degree, Mead.

[14] See Lennox (2019) for a further discussion of Darwin and philosophy.

view of knowledge and knowing was that things are subject to experimental test. Consequently, philosophy and truth cannot remain in the realm of ideas but need to be evaluated in practice.[15]

Whereas the impact Darwin had on pragmatism is well recognized, the distinctive influence exerted by dialectics is often overlooked (Figure 26.1). For instance, building on the heritage of Hegel, pragmatism also broke down the traditional subject–object dichotomy and regarded thought as a natural process bound up with the rest of the natural world. Peirce, James, Dewey, and Mead were greatly influenced by Hegel, but they rejected his idealist bias.[16] Still significant, the direct influence exerted by Marx on pragmatism is more implicit. Although they disagreed on the means for effecting social change, pragmatists' quest to make philosophy practical, actionable, even activist, clearly echoes Marx's similar agenda.[17]

Dewey's (1859–1952) long career overlapped with those of many important characters in our historical overview, from Darwin to Marx to organization theorists, such as March and Simon. His ideas "drifted" (in Dewey's own terms) from what he called absolutism to experimentalism. In the main this shift indicates a reduced influence of Hegel's idealist metaphysics and a growing influence of Darwin's ideas. Nevertheless, Hegel's influence remained evident in much of Dewey's work. In his autobiographical essay, Dewey (1930) observed that except for Plato, there was greater richness and greater variety of insight in Hegel than in any other single systematic philosopher.

Dewey and Marx both gradually moved from Hegel's idealism (Phelps 2005), and both sought to synthesize it with other sources: Marx with materialist scholarship; Dewey with Darwin's theory. Often opposed to Marx's ideas, Dewey was significantly influenced by them, nevertheless. Particularly, while he drew on Hegel's political theory in developing his own conceptions of community and democracy, Dewey had to relate to Marx's influential political theory too. Furthermore, Dewey seems to have drawn on Marx's keen, and at times cynical, insights—on class struggle, power, hypocrisy, exploitation, and manipulation—as a check on his own, perhaps more romantic view of reality.

Ultimately, the pragmatist project, in which Dewey and others engaged, aimed at developing a social and processual philosophy, one that was practical and scientific at the same time. Addressing this challenge often required using one of the poles—philo-

[15] Dewey's profound appreciation of Darwin's evolutionary ideas was not unconditional. For instance, he observed how Darwin's revolutionary theory became possible only by some conceptual advances made before him. Similarly, he identified the evolution of the environments as an unwritten chapter in Darwin's natural selection theory.

[16] In addition to being present in Dewey's work, Hegel's influence is highly visible in the work of Mead and Follett and is present in Peirce and James. Thorstein Veblen, usually considered an institutional economist rather than a founding figure of pragmatism, had Peirce as his mentor and Dewey as a colleague. Greatly inspired by Marx, Veblen also served as an indirect conduit of dialectical ideas to pragmatism. John Commons also drew on Dewey and was highly influenced by Veblen. Commons' stress on relationality (e.g., "transactions") contrasts with Veblen's relative emphasis on history, evolution, and process.

[17] As Marx wrote in the eleventh thesis on Feuerbach: "The philosophers have only interpreted the world in various ways; the point, however, is to change it."

sophical principles, social practice, and science—to mediate the tensions between the other two. Thus, as much as they evolutionized philosophy, pragmatists went in the other directions too: using philosophical ideas and principles about uncertainty and freedom, for instance, to flesh out Darwin's evolutionary ideas, or developing concepts such as experimentation and design, to bring Darwin's ideas closer to the social and to the world of practice.

Resources for Theory Construction: Dewey and Beyond

> I envy, up to a certain point, those who can write their intellectual biography in a unified pattern, woven out of a few distinctly discernible strands of interest and influence. By contrast, I seem to be unstable, chameleon-like, yielding one after another to many diverse and even incompatible influences; struggling to assimilate something from each and yet striving to carry it forward in a way that is logically consistent with what has been learned from its predecessors.
>
> Dewey (1930)

Dewey's career was in large measure devoted to mediating and harmonizing contrasting views of the world (Hildebrand 2018). While he wrote extensively about the role of synthesis in human thinking, Dewey did not provide a clear account of his own complex synthesizing process. Absent such record, a reverse engineering of this process remains somewhat speculative. Nevertheless, reviewing several ideas and concepts developed by Dewey may still indicate to change theorists how he might have wrestled with diverse and often incompatible approaches. His work particularly illustrates how dialectics' two hats—as an evolutionary theory and as a relational process philosophy—can stimulate new conceptions of change.

In the following I will discuss each of these generators of new ideas, as reflected in Dewey's work and as can be abstracted from it.

A) Drawing on Two Evolutionary Theories

Dewey's synthetic approach. Bringing together two seemingly incompatible perspectives on change, such as dialectics and evolutionary theory, presents an intellectual challenge. For instance, Dewey pondered how the notions of fit and survival should be viewed in relation to the social order. Similarly, in thinking about social and organizational change, Dewey weighed the respective roles of chance and intentionality.

To mediate such contrasts, Dewey exercised ingenuity, playfulness, and maneuvering, and combined several tactics. *First*, he rejected any ideas that he did not deem fitting, and often translated, reinterpreted, and reframed existing concepts in a new way.

A case in point of this selective approach is Dewey's conceptualization of conflict. He recognized conflict and disharmony as ubiquitous—in nature, as well as in human affairs and society. Like Hegel, Marx, and Darwin, he stressed the generative role of conflict as a mechanism for transformation and change. Yet, Dewey was careful to avoid the destructive ways in which many interpreted the ideas of Marx and Darwin about conflict as a means for social change. As indicated by his phrase "conflict is the gadfly of thought", Dewey's main solution was to give conflict a central place as a stimulus for creativity, and imagination. This conceptual move—from conflict as explaining history and society, to conflict as central to thinking—departed from Marx's more radical dialectical materialism, and brought Dewey closer to Hegel's theorizing on cognition, sensemaking, and problem-solving. Conflict was also central to Dewey's political theory. Here, he readjusted Hegelian ideas about the self and community and developed his views of democracy. He saw the institution of democracy as encouraging the settling of conflicts through dialogue and as a means for surfacing and evaluating competing claims by subjecting them to test.

Dewey also seems to have drawn on a second tactic: using both dialectics and evolutionary theory to theorize about a common concept. For instance, core to Dewey's work is the mechanism of experimentation. Dewey's idea of experimentation implies that thinking and acting are inseparable elements in the same adaptive and recursive sensemaking process. While experimentation can be derived directly from Darwin's stress on the becoming, provisional, and cumulative aspects of the evolutionary process, it can be equally derived from dialectics. In Marx's view, for instance, human thought is founded in human activity and in the social relations (or "world") brought about by this activity (Berger and Luckmann 1967). Echoing Hegel, Dewey maintained that "every experience modifies the experiencer, which means every experience counts" (Novack 1975).

The key notion of habit can also be derived from both traditions. For Dewey, habit, or what may more broadly be called "learned behavior", mediates between impulse (also affect, creativity) and intelligence (also deliberation or cognition). When interlocked with other learned behaviors, the notion of habit serves pragmatists to conceptualize larger ensembles or totalities such as character and customs. Remarkably, the concept of habit has important roots in the dialectics' tradition too. Weber, Veblen, Dewey, and Bourdieu all drew, directly or indirectly, on Hegel's discussion of habits and its collective form "habitus." Building on Hegel and earlier ideas, Dewey and Weber stressed habits' plasticity and viewed individuals as creatures of habit (Malabou 2005).

A third tactic Dewey used was to pit evolutionary and dialectics ideas against one another. This clash led Dewey to favor one theory or to transcend both views to create new concepts. In this blending process, the pretensions of each side to constitute the whole of a relation were denied.[18]

[18] This process also involved confronting Hegel's dialectical idealism with Marx's materialist writings, for instance through their respective stress on cognition and meaning, and on action.

Both solutions are illustrated in Dewey's theory of institutional change. In theorizing about the tempo and scope of change, Dewey recognized that qualitative change can arise from the gradual accumulation of smaller pressures. To avoid the harsh consequences of crises and catastrophes—such as those highlighted in Marx's thought, Dewey prescribed a more moderate, renewal approach of continuous reconstruction and improvement. Consistent with the dialectical distinction between essence and appearance, Dewey doubted the wisdom of sweeping changes and the sustaining power of revolutions. In his opinion, habits of thought and beliefs are more durable, and persist despite any surface revolution in practices.

Dewey's model of institutional change also blended the two traditions. Consistent with dialectics, Dewey saw institutional change as an endogenous process arising from the recursive interaction of agents' creative potential and contradictions or breaches in the existing order. Drawing on Darwin's ideas, Dewey saw chance and accident as important mechanisms, potentially more significant to social and historical change than human intelligent design.

As Dewey's work illustrates, fusing elements drawn from dialectics and evolutionary theory can stimulate new ideas about change and related notions, such as habit and experimentation. To encourage future synthetic work, it may be useful to offer a different case, not directly derived from Dewey's writings. In the following brief example, I will combine ideas about power as stressed in dialectics with ideas about knowledge highlighted in evolutionary theory. I will show how this fusion can lead to a rich, more complete model, relevant to contemporary phenomena such as fake news and the influence digital monopolies exert over their users.

Change at the interplay of knowledge and power. Knowledge and power are analytically distinct but interrelated in practice. Evolutionary and dialectical change models can accommodate both notions, but their traditional focus privileges one idea over the other. In evolutionary theory the emphasis is on information and its correlates such as experimentation, knowledge, habits, and learning, whereas dialectics is more concerned with interests such as those associated with power, conflict, and influence. Consistent with this distinction, evolutionary theory's notion of stability highlights memory and the retention of knowledge, whereas dialectics highlights the conservative role of vested interests, ideologies, institutions, and traditions. This division is also manifest in organizations' theories. For instance, in Weick (1979) and Nelson and Winter (1982), power and conflict appear to be secondary, whereas change models associated with power theories, such as resource dependence, tend to downplay learning and experimentation.

The respective stress on power and knowledge of dialectics and evolutionary theory impinges upon their views of social development and change. The evolutionary view is more epistemological and developmental—it stresses knowing as a way for agents to learn, grow, and adapt. Adding to this position, dialectics would regard knowledge as central to social conflict—a means for agents to attain power and advantage over others.

In the social world, agents do not simply learn and accumulate knowledge: occasionally, they are in a position to shape what others, often with different and opposing interests, learn and know. This influence is particularly heightened under conditions of power asymmetry. As developments such as fake news and digital monopolies' control of user data illustrate, political parties and business organizations may deliberately affect other agents, such as voters and consumers, with the result that these other constituents will not know enough, or know or believe in the wrong things.

A particular form of shaping others' knowledge occurs when companies encourage their customers (or other resource providers) to routinize their transactions. In industries, such as tobacco, gambling, pharmaceuticals, and online games, firms sometimes promote behaviors which can become addictive in their users and customers. Similar consumer habits can appear in a wider range of settings in milder or less visible forms. In its ultimate form, habituation would have consumers not think about spending at all. As a credit card company official recently explained, the aim of the company is for the customer to be unaware of their payments.

An integrated evolutionary–dialectic model can shed light on such contemporary phenomena. Along with the evolutionary view (e.g., Nelson and Winter 1982), agents experiment or probe the environment, their ideas are validated through a selective process and then retained in the form of habits, routines, and knowledge, to be subsequently tested and refined in an ongoing fashion. Consistent with the dialectic view, however, this learning process is also conflictual and contested. In this complementary view, as they intervene in the world, powerful agents do not simply seek to enhance their own knowledge, but also to preserve or improve their position by actively making others unaware and less knowledgeable. Conversely, and for the less powerful, greater awareness, knowledge, and the adoption of a critical stance, become a prerequisite for social change and transformation.

This integrated and more complete model of change highlights several points: first, thinking and acting, habit and conflict, and power and knowledge are inseparable elements in the same adaptive and recursive process; second, when power imbalances exist, as they often do, agents' learning is mutual but not necessarily symmetric; finally, knowledge may act both to reproduce existing social and political arrangements and to challenge them.

B) Drawing on Relational Process Philosophy

Dialectical heuristics in Dewey. In its second hat, dialectics supplies generative principles for thinking about change, complexity and flux. Hegel not only provided Dewey with specific and deep ideas, on topics such as freedom, thinking, and education, he also helped him cultivate specific, playful modes of thinking, or what we call "dialectical heuristics" (see Table 26.1). Dewey credited Hegel for supplying "a demand for unification" and remarked how

> Hegel's synthesis of subject and object, matter and spirit, the divine and the human, was, however, no mere intellectual formula; it operated as an immense release, a

> liberation. Hegel's treatment of human culture, of institutions and the arts, involved the same dissolution of hard-and-fast dividing walls, and had a special attraction for me. (Dewey 1930)

Consistent with the dialectical perspective, Dewey saw the world in oppositional terms—a combination of stability and change, movement and culmination, certainty and unpredictability. At the same time, he clearly recognized the potential of a processual approach to dissolve and transcend categories, dualisms, and levels of analysis, and unite them in a single, processual notion which includes both elements and their connection. For instance, Dewey's concept of action synthesizes body (thesis) and mind (antithesis); similarly, the notion of coordination helped Dewey transcend the separation of stimulus and response.

Like dialectics, the pragmatist relational view, which following Dewey is referred to as the "transactional view", reacts against a view of individuals as atomistic entities; it emphasizes instead that their essential characteristics and "traits" are outcomes of relations with others (Hodgson 1994: 61ff; Simpson 2009). An important application of Dewey's innovative transactional view is provided in his view of adaptation. Rather than considering this evolutionary concept simply to mean an adjustment to a given environment, Dewey viewed adaptation as including both accommodation to conditions and the modification (or construction) of the environment to accommodate it to our wants, habits, and purposes. Extending his transactional view to the system level, Dewey conceptualized culture as an ecology—a state of interaction of many factors, such as law, politics, industry, the arts, and people's social philosophy. Also of interest to Dewey was the reverse image of continuity and transaction, which he framed, like Marx, as a form of alienation (Medearis 2015). For instance, he wrote about the risks of separating thinking and acting, turning habit and routine into "dead." mindless activities.

Furthermore, pragmatists viewed habit as a disposition to act—habits may or may not become manifest in observable behavior, and constitute dormant powers, waiting to be invoked under certain conditions. This dispositional view of habit joins Darwin's style of reasoning, which highlights tendencies and probabilities, with the dialectics' principle of the interplay between the potential and the actual. Consistent with his transactional approach, Dewey saw habit as an interaction between agents and their social and natural environment, within which habit might incorporate aspects of the environment. Furthermore, for Dewey, environmental objects—social, cultural, natural—"avail and counter avail" and thus help individuals learn and refine their habits and skills.

Dewey's work illustrates two complementary ways in which researchers can use dialectical heuristics for new concept and theory development. First, the same principle can be reinterpreted in varied applications. For instance, Dewey's ecological view is evident in how he conceptualized both human nature and culture (Table 26.1). Second, being parts of a configuration, dialectical heuristics can also be applied in tandem with other principles. For instance, Dewey's model of institutional change (e.g., Farjoun et al. 2015) is buttressed by several dialectical principles such as contradiction, the transcendence of dualisms, and the interplay of potentialities and actualities.

In the following, final example, I will focus on how one key dialectical principle can stimulate new theorizing on change.[19]

Beyond Dewey: Change as the interplay between the implicit and the explicit orders. Building on the heritage of Dewey's and others' innovative use of dialectical heuristics, organizational change scholars can leverage similar heuristics, or "ideas behind ideas," to further develop new change models and categories. One illustrative pathway for theorizing change lies in the interplay between the implicit and explicit. Specifically, dialectics highlights how potentialities and dispositions, such as latent contradictions, habits, structural arrangements, capacities, and processes, serve as endogenous, generative, and developmental forces that may get realized in specific interactions (Dewey 1922; Bhaskar 2009). For organizational scholars, the distinction between potentialities and actualities, offers a prism for considering such notions as "deep structure," mechanisms, tacit and explicit knowledge, for examining how the seeds of the future are concealed in the present, and for discussing how unanticipated and even unconscious consequences can be in tension with stated, intended, and observed consequences.[20]

This distinction holds several opportunities for new theorizing about change. A first opportunity lies in better conceptualizing the range of potentialities that stimulate change "from within." The different traditions we have discussed highlight several endogenous mechanisms such as conflicts and contradictions, the creative potentials of individuals or groups, and uneven developments. Unused or "invisible" resources, and transportable schema offer other illustrations. Discussion of potentialities also calls attention to how latent capacities and developments such as anomalies, surprises, and innovations, incubate and develop, and at what point they overcome the forces and arrangements that hold them so that they become manifest changes.

A second opportunity in conceptualizing the potential–actual interplay lies in differentiating between apparent change and actual change. Organizations' display of stability and order may hide accumulating hidden, disruptive developments waiting to erupt. Alternatively, organizations often build up facades of transformation and reforms while in fact not much changes. Portrayed as a big transformation, Facebook's recent announcement of its own blockchain cryptocurrency is a case in point. The original intent of the blockchain technology founders was to transfer power, centralized in the state and in large financial institutions, to the hands of individual users. Facebook's initiative leaves the balance of power between users and big organizations largely intact. In this case, claims about drastic changes mask the reproduction of the current order.

A third opportunity involves theorizing the interaction of potentials in the organization with those residing in its environment, such as in other organizations and institutions. Within organizational theory, one arrow highlights how institutions and actors

[19] Other than in Dewey, the use of a broader range of dialectics principles appears in the work of social scientists such as Selznick, Merton, Simmel, Bourdieu, and Giddens.

[20] Reality, for Marx, is structured by processes, relations, and "inner mechanisms" that are not always apparent on the surface (Patterson 2009). The distinction between potentialities and actualities is considered by some to be the "entire secret of Hegel's dialectics."

affect individuals' unconscious, hidden layers. A different arrow operates in the reverse direction: it views individuals' unconscious, creative capacities as the roots of larger-scale innovations in organizations and environments. Future modelling efforts can therefore be devoted to the entire circuit. In Dewey, for instance, both structure and agent have a built-in capacity for change. Future research can model interactions where each agent serves as an environment for the other. These relational meeting points can occasion habitual, reproductive processes or lead to transformations instead.

Finally, potentialities and actualities are moments in the broader dynamics of development and transformation. There is a continuous accumulation of effects of earlier actualizations which turn to potentialities for later actualizations. Furthermore, the process of actualizing potentialities may diminish or enlarge their capacities. Exemplifying such dynamics, several of today's large, visible organizations were unknown start-ups years ago, and may themselves be displaced by similar rivals whose operations and ideas are still hidden from view. Much of what is real today was unimagined not long ago.

Discussion

In this discourse on the interplay of three processual, "becoming" perspectives—dialectics, evolutionary theory, and pragmatism—I build on the history of ideas to put forward a case for dialectics as a rich and stimulating philosophical and evolutionary tradition. Against this backdrop I call attention to relatively underutilized sources for modeling change, and highlight linkages between several literatures and change models that are not commonly connected. I reflect on these themes below and discuss how others can extend them in the future.

Untapped Sources for Modeling Change

Dialectics' philosophical and evolutionary hats. This chapter highlights two of dialectics' generative hats: as a source of abstract and relatively enduring principles, as well as a fount of more specific ideas and observations about the mechanisms and patterns of change and evolution. As indicated by Darwin's theory and in many other examples, the generation of new and radical ideas about change, either through conceptual work or empirical observations, does not depend on the explicit use of philosophical principles. Still, incorporating philosophical principles in theorizing about change provides several advantages.

First, as we have seen, conceptual innovations are often accompanied by revised ontological assumptions. The relational process ontology has historically been pivotal to such innovations because it offers a clear antidote to other worldviews based on atomistic, linear, dualistic, and equilibrium assumptions. Dialectical heuristics offer a second advantage: they involve irony, paradox, and circularity—attributes often associated with playful, creative problem-solving. Third, a philosophical kernel shared by several "becoming" traditions (Table 26.1) allows change scholars to approach real-world phenomena more eclectically, that is, without being committed to a single perspective such as dialectics or complexity theory.

When it comes to considering new models of change, scholars can draw on other complementarities between dialectics, evolutionary theory and pragmatism, particularly since as these traditions coevolved, they also retained their signature: dialectics with its contrarian as well as synthetic approach, evolutionary theory with its stress on spontaneity and chance, and pragmatism with its focus on experimentation and experience.

The kinship between the three processual "becoming" traditions can also sharpen their differences vis-à-vis other, less compatible perspectives. For instance, while significant in other respects, reductionist approaches that locate the mechanisms of social and historical change solely in biology or human nature (e.g., neuroscience, behavioral strategy), may not be as consistent with the key tenets of the relational process philosophy.

History and tradition as sources of new ideas. Several ideas in this chapter may elicit a déjà vu reaction from readers. This is particularly expected from adherents of contemporary theories such as institutional logics, practice, and complexity. To be sure, these literatures introduced new ideas of their own, and have assimilated ideas from other sources. Still, many of their key ideas were inspired by dialectics, if not descended from it, and reflect its relational process worldview.

For evolutionary theorists such as Darwin, dialectic scholars such as Hegel and Marx, and pragmatists such as Dewey, innovation and tradition were not necessarily contradictory. While they all broke the mold of prevailing ideas at their time, they neither abided by tradition nor abandoned it, but rather respected it and worked with what tradition could offer. In line with the views of sociologist of knowledge Robert Merton, just as these intellectual giants entered a critical dialogue with their masters, so should we interpret their ideas in the light of new perspectives and approaches, later discoveries, experiences, and newly gathered data. The masters are honored, not by zealous repetition of their earlier findings, but by extensions, modifications, and often enough, by rejection of some of their ideas and findings (Sztompka, 1986).

In the dialectical view, an observed social pattern is regarded as one of several possibilities. Consistent with this processual view, the history of ideas contains many "roads less travelled" and potential gems available for reuse. For one, the same source can stimulate more than one synthesis. Thus, for example, Marx synthesized Hegel with materialist ideas, and Dewey combined Hegel and Darwin. Moreover, since theorists usually assimilate what fits their interests and tastes, they often reject significant ideas that others can recruit. Thus, for instance, Marx rejected Hegel's idealism in favor of his materialist approach; however, Weber reasserted ideas as a key motor in human history. Similarly, while Nelson and Winter's (1982) evolutionary theory of the firm highlighted the role of routines, they left much room for considering how a firm's routines interact with those of other constituents in the firm's ecology.

Connecting the (Often) Unconnected

Consistent with Van de Ven and Poole's (1995) proposal to explore the interplay between different change models, this chapter brings together several literatures that are not commonly linked, promoting a new view of each literature in the process. Such linkages are not limited to modeling change, and extend to other realms of organizational and social life. I highlight the challenges, as well as the benefits, of viewing the Darwinian tradition and dialectics as distinct members of a broader "evolutionary theories" umbrella. Future research can explore other historical intersections. For instance, both institutional economics and Schumpeter's work on technological change have built on Marx's dialectical materialism as well as on evolutionary theory.

Similarly, I show how relational process principles bind together several literatures and change models mostly considered as separate. These and other historical and conceptual continuities highlighted in this chapter reinforce Van de Ven and Poole's typology of ideal-type change models; at the same time these linkages re-segment the original typology along alternative dimensions, such as conflict, recursive relations, and power and information.

As my comparison of dialectics and evolutionary theory reveals, the commonalities between these two perspectives on change may be greater, and more fundamental, than usually recognized. What lies behind this puzzling affinity? While this question requires much more scrutiny, my analysis may offer some tentative clues.

One explanation that can be ruled out is that dialectics scholars and Darwin have simply borrowed each other's ideas. Although it is possible that Marx incorporated some of Darwin's evolutionary ideas in his own work, several of Marx's important texts came prior to Darwin's publication of *On the Origins of Species*. Furthermore, most of Hegel's career preceded Darwin. Equally unlikely is that Darwin drew on Hegel's philosophy.

Other possibilities merit more consideration. For instance, although not in the terms developed in the theory of natural selection, ideas about evolution long preceded Darwin and Hegel. Furthermore, as Rescher (1996) discussed, the idea of system has ever been prominent among process theorists with organic, biological systems as a paradigm. Therefore, it may well be that Darwin, Hegel, and Marx, and subsequently Dewey, were all inspired by nature to develop some of their own views. Noteworthy, and highly inspiring, is the fact that in the nineteenth century, the humanities, natural sciences, and social sciences were not as demarcated as they are today. The stew of ideas and observations from nature, philosophy, political economics, history, and other spheres, with which the great thinkers played (Figure 26.1), provided many opportunities for knowledge transfer through analogical reasoning and other means.

Conclusion

In seeking to innovate, scholars of organizations and change are often hesitant to turn to philosophy, history, and tradition. As this chapter shows, processual traditions—

evolutionary theory, but dialectics and pragmatism no less—have been instrumental to the historical development of organization studies. The potential of these "becoming" perspectives is far from being exhausted: for those interested in understanding organizations and change in dynamic, holistic, and at times unorthodox terms, they are likely to remain relevant, productive, and highly inspiring.

References

Abbott, A. (2004), *Methods of Discovery: Heuristics for the Social Sciences*, Contemporary Societies Series (New York, NY: W.W. Norton & Company).

Adler, P. S. (2009), 'Marx and Organization Studies Today', In P. S. Adler, ed., *Oxford Handbook of Sociology and Organization Studies: Classical Foundations* (Oxford: Oxford University Press), 62–91.

Albert, A. and Garco, M. (2021), 'Landscape Models of Complex Change', in M. S. Poole and A. H. Van de Ven, eds., *The Oxford Handbook of Organizational Change and Innovation* (Oxford: Oxford University Press).

Aldrich, H., and Ruef, M. (2006), *Organizations Evolving* (London, UK: Sage Publications Ltd).

Ansell, C. K. (2011), *Pragmatist Democracy: Evolutionary Learning as Public Philosophy* (New York, NY: Oxford University Press).

Ansell, C. K., Boin, A., and Farjoun, M. (2015), 'Dynamic Conservatism: How Institutions Change to Remain the Same', in M. Kraatz, ed., *Institutions and Ideals*, Research in the Sociology of Organizations (Vol. 44) (Bingley, UK: Emerald Group Publishing), 89–119.

Bakken, T., and T. Hernes (2006), 'Organizing is Both a Verb and a Noun: Weick Meets Whitehead', *Organization Studies*, 27/11, 1599–616.

Ball, T. (1979), 'Marx and Darwin: A Reconsideration', *Political Theory*, 7/4, 469–83.

Baxter, L. A., and Montgomery, B. M. (1996), *Relating: Dialogues and Dialectics* (New York, NY: Guilford Press).

Barad, K. (2007), *Meeting the Universe Halfway: Quantum Physics and the Entanglement of Matter and Meaning* (Durham, London: Duke University Press).

Basalla, G. (1988), *The Evolution of Technology* (Cambridge: Cambridge University Press).

Baum. J. A. C., and Rao, H. (2021), 'Evolutionary Dynamics of Organizational Populations and Communities', in M. S. Poole and A. H. Van de Ven, eds., *The Oxford Handbook of Organizational Change and Innovation* (Oxford: Oxford University Press).

Baum, J. A. C., and Singh, J. V. (1994), 'Organization-Environment Coevolution', in J. A. C. Baum and J. V. Singh, eds., *Evolutionary Dynamics of Organizations* (New York, NY: Oxford University Press), 379–402.

Benson, J.K. (1977), 'Organizations: A Dialectical View', *Administrative Science Quarterly*, 22/1, 1–21.

Berger, P. L., and Luckmann, T. (1967), *The Social Construction of Reality* (New York, NY: Doubleday Anchor).

Bhaskar, R. (1993), *Dialectic: The Pulse of Freedom* (London: Routledge).

Bhaskar, R. (2009), *Scientific Realism and Human Emancipation* (London: Routledge).

Blau, P. M. (1972), 'Dialectical Sociology: Comments', *Sociological Inquiry*, 42/2, 182–8.

Cohen, M. D. (2007), 'Reading Dewey: Reflections on the Study of Routine', *Organization Studies*, 28/5, 773–86.

Darwin, C. (1859), *On the Origin of Species by Means of Natural Selection*, or preservation of favored races in the struggle for life (London: John Murray).

Dearing, J. (2021), 'Diffusion of Innovations', in M. S. Poole and A. H. Van de Ven, eds., *The Oxford Handbook of Organizational Change and Innovation* (Oxford: Oxford University Press).

Dewey, J. (1910), 'The Influence of Darwin on Philosophy,' in Dewey, ed., *The Influence of Darwin on Philosophy and Other Essays* (New York, NY: Henry Holt and Company), 1–19.

Dewey, J. (1922), *Human Nature and Human Conduct* (New York, NY: Henry Holt and Co).

Dewey, J. (1930), 'From Absolutism to Experimentalism', in L.A. Hickman and T.M. Alexander, eds, (1998), *The Essential Dewey* (Vol. 1: Pragmatism, Education, Democracy) (Bloomington: Indiana University Press), 14–21.

Dewey (1931), From 'Science and Society', in L. A. Hickman and T. M. Alexander, eds., (1998), *The Essential Dewey* (Bloomington: Indiana University Press).

Dooley, K. (2021), 'Conceptualizing Organizational Change through the Lens of Complexity Science', in M. S. Poole and A. H. Van de Ven, eds., *The Oxford Handbook of Organizational Change and Innovation* (Oxford: Oxford University Press).

Elkjaer, B. and Simpson, B. (2011), 'Pragmatism: A Lived and Living Philosophy. What Can It Offer to Contemporary Organization Theory?' in H. Tsoukas and R. Chia, eds., *Philosophy and Organization Theory* (Vol. 32, Research in the Sociology of Organizations (Bingley, UK: Emerald Group Publishing), 55–84.

Farjoun, M. (2010), 'Beyond Dualism: Stability and Change as a Duality', *Academy of Management Review*, 35/2, 202–25.

Farjoun, M. (2017), 'Contradictions, Dialectics and Paradox', in A. Langley and H. Tsoukas, eds., The *SAGE Handbook of Process Organization Studies* (London: SAGE), 87–109.

Farjoun, M. (2019), 'Strategy and Dialectics: Rejuvenating a Long-Standing Relationship', *Strategic Organization*, 17/1, 133–44.

Farjoun, M., Ansell, C. K., and Boin, A. (2015), 'Pragmatism in Organization Studies: Meeting the Challenges of a Dynamic and Complex World', *Organization Science*, 26/6, 1787–804.

Farjoun, M., Smith, W., Langley, A., and Tsoukas, H., eds., (2018), *Dualities, Dialectics, and Paradoxes in Organizational Life* (Oxford: Oxford University Press).

Feldman, M. S. and Pentland, B. T. (2003), 'Re-Conceptualizing Routines as a Source of Flexibility and Change', *Administrative Science Quarterly*, 48, 94–118.

Gaba, V. and Meyer, A. (2021), 'Discontinuous Change in Organizations and Fields', in M. S. Poole and A. H. Van de Ven, eds., *The Oxford Handbook of Organizational Change and Innovation* (Oxford: Oxford University Press).

Giddens, A. (1984), *The Constitution of Society: Outline of the Theory of Structuration* (Berkeley and Los Angeles: University of California Press).

Graham, D. A. (2019), 'Heraclitus', in *Stanford Encyclopedia of Philosophy*, https://plato.stanford.edu/entries/heraclitus/, accessed 27 September, 2020.

Hannan, M.T., and J. Freeman (1984), 'Structural Inertia and Organizational Change', *American Sociological Review*, 49/2, 149–64.

Harari, Y. N. (2015), *Sapiens: A Brief History of Mankind* (New York: Harper).

Harvey, D. (2018), *The Limits to Capital* (London: Verso Books).

Hernes, G. (1976), 'Structural Change in Social Processes, *American Journal of Sociology*, 82/3, 513–47.

Hickman, L. A. and Alexander, T. M. (eds.) (1998), *The Essential Dewey* (Vol. 1: Pragmatism, Education, Democracy). (Bloomington, IN: Indiana University Press).

Hildebrand, D. (2018), 'John Dewey', in *Stanford Encyclopedia of Philosophy*, https://plato.stanford.edu/entries/dewey/, accessed 27 September, 2020.
Hodgson, G. M. (1994), 'The Return of Institutional Economics', in N. J. Smelser and R. Swedberg, eds., *The Handbook of Economic Sociology* (Princeton, NJ: Princeton University Press), 58–76.
Hodgson, G. M. (2014), *Economics in the Shadows of Marx and Darwin* (Cheltenham and Northampton: Edward Elgar Publishing).
Hodgson, G. M., and Knudsen, T. (2010), *Darwin's Conjecture: The Search for General Principles of Social and Economic Evolution* (Chicago, IL: University of Chicago Press).
Jablonka, E., and Lamb, M. J. (2005), *Evolution in Four Dimensions: Genetic, Epigenetic, Behavioral, and Symbolic Variation in the History of Life* (Cambridge, MA: MIT Press).
Kaufmann, W. A. (1965), *Hegel: Reinterpretation, Texts, and Commentary* (Garden City, NY: Doubleday).
Kelm, M. (1997), 'Schumpeter's Theory of Economic Evolution: A Darwinian Interpretation', *Journal of Evolutionary Economics*, 7/2, 97–130.
Langley, A. (2007), 'Process Thinking in Strategic Organization', *Strategic Organization*, 5/3, 271–82.
Langley, A., and Tsoukas, H. (eds.), (2017), *The SAGE Handbook of Process Organization Studies* (London: SAGE).
Lennox, J. (2019), 'Darwinism', in *Stanford Encyclopedia of Philosophy*, https://plato.stanford.edu/entries/darwinism/notes.html/, accessed 28 September, 2020.
Levins, R., and Lewontin, R. (1985), *The Dialectical Biologist* (Cambridge, MA: Harvard University Press).
Levinthal, D. A. (1991), 'Organizational Adaptation and Environmental Selection: Interrelated Processes of Change', *Organization Science*, 2/1, 140–45.
Lewontin, R. C. (1974), *The Genetic Basis of Evolutionary Change* (New York, NY: Columbia University Press).
Lorino, P. (2018), *Pragmatism and Organization Studies* (Oxford: Oxford University Press).
Malabou, C. (2005), *The Future of Hegel: Plasticity, Temporality, and Dialectic* (London: Routledge).
McKelvey, B. (1997), 'Quasi-natural Organization Science', *Organization Science*, 8/4, 352–80.
Medearis, J. (2015), *Why Democracy is Oppositional* (Cambridge, MA: Harvard University Press).
Menand, L. (2001), *The Metaphysical Club* (New York, NY: Farrar, Straus and Giroux).
Morgan, G. (2006), *Images of Organization* (Thousand Oaks, CA: SAGE).
Nelson, R. R., (2005), *Technology, Institutions, and Economic Growth* (Cambridge, MA: Harvard University Press).
Nelson, R. R., and Winter, S. G. (1982), *An Evolutionary Theory of Economic Change* (Cambridge, MA: Belknap Press).
Nicholson, D. J., and Dupré, J. (eds.) (2018), *Everything Flows: Towards a Processual Philosophy of Biology* (Oxford, UK: Oxford University Press).
Novack, G. (1975), *Pragmatism vs. Marxism: An Analysis of John Dewey's Philosophy* (New York, NY: Pathfinder Press, Inc).
Ollman, B. (2003), *Dance of the Dialectic: Steps in Marx's Method* (Urbana and Chicago: University of Illinois Press).
Ollman, B. (2015), 'Marxism and the Philosophy of Internal Relations; or, How to Replace the Mysterious "Paradox" with "Contradictions" That Can Be Studied and Resolved', *Capital & Class*, 39/1), 7–23.

Patterson, T. C. (2009), *Karl Marx, Anthropologist* (Oxford: Berg Publishers).

Patterson, T. C. (2018), *Social Change Theories in Motion* (New York, NY: Routledge).

Phelps, C. (2005), *Young Sidney Hook: Marxist & Pragmatist* (Ann Arbor, MI: University of Michigan Press).

Putnam, L. L., Fairhurst, G. T., and Banghart, S. (2016), 'Contradictions, Dialectics, and Paradoxes in Organizations: A Constitutive Approach', *The Academy of Management Annals*, 10/1, 65–171.

Rejon, M. R. (2018), 'Two Clashing Giants: Marxism and Darwinism', in OpenMind: BBV's knowledge community. https://www.bbvaopenmind.com/en/science/leading-figures/two-clashing-giants-marxism-and-darwinism/, accessed 28 September 2020.

Rescher, N. (1996). *Process Metaphysics: An Introduction to Process Philosophy* (New York: SUNY Press).

Sarasvathy, S. and Venkataraman, S. (2021), 'An Effectual Entrepreneurial Model of Organizational Change: Acting on, Reacting to, and Interacting with Markets as Artifacts', in M. S. Poole and A. H. Van de Ven, eds., *The Oxford Handbook of Organizational Change and Innovation* (Oxford: Oxford University Press).

Schneider, L. (1971), 'Dialectics in Sociology', *American Sociological Review*, 36/4, 667–78.

Seo, M-G., and Creed, W. D. (2002), 'Institutional Contradictions, Praxis, and Institutional Change: A Dialectical Perspective', *Academy of Management Review*, 27/2, 222–47.

Simpson, B. (2009), 'Pragmatism, Mead and the Practice Turn', *Organization Studies*, 30/12, 1329–47.

Sloan, P. (2019a), 'Evolutionary Thought Before Darwin', in *Stanford Encyclopedia of Philosophy*, https://plato.stanford.edu/entries/evolution-before-darwin/, accessed 28 September 2020.

Sloan, P. (2019b), 'Darwin: From Origin of Species to Descent of Man', in *Stanford Encyclopedia of Philosophy*, https://plato.stanford.edu/entries/origin-descent/, accessed 28 September 2020.

Spencer, H. (1898), The Principles of Sociology (Vol. 3) (New York, NY: D. Appleton & Company).

Stein, R. L. (2004), 'Towards a Process Philosophy of Chemistry', *Hyle: International Journal for Philosophy of Chemistry*, 10/4, 5–22.

Sztompka, P. (1986), *Robert K-Merton: An Intellectual Profile* (London: Macmillan International Higher Education).

Trompf, G. W. (1979), *The Idea of Historical Recurrence in Western Thought* (Berkeley, CA: University of California Press).

Tsoukas, H., and Chia, R. (2002), 'On Organizational Becoming: Rethinking Organizational Change', *Organization Science*, 13/5, 567–82.

Van de Ven, A. H., and Poole,M. S. (1995), 'Explaining Development and Change in Organizations', *Academy of Management Review*, 20/3, 510–40.

Weick, K. E. (1979), *The Social Psychology of Organizing* (2nd edn) (Reading, MA: Addison Wesley).

Weick, K. E. (1989), 'Theory Construction as Disciplined Imagination', *Academy of Management Review*, 14/4, 516–31.

PART VI

CORE ASPECTS IN ALL CHANGE MODELS

CHAPTER 27

TIME AND TEMPORALITY OF CHANGE PROCESSES

Applying an event-based view to integrate episodic and continuous change

TOR HERNES, ANTHONY HUSSENOT, AND KÄTLIN PULK

"Is it a revolt?" asked Louis XVI. The duke replied: "No, sire, it's not a revolt; it's a revolution."

Chaussinand-Nogaret (1988, p. 102)

INTRODUCTION

AN incisive observation made by Gersick (1994: 11) is that change research sometimes fails to grasp the complexity of change because research methods are aimed at detecting whether a change has or has not happened. This, she argues, prevents researchers from understanding the obstacles faced by actors in making decisions about change. Works on organizational change have tended to assume that change takes place as isolated happenings at certain points in time. For example, new technology is introduced at a certain point in time, and the change associated with that technology is ascribed to that point in time. Underlying such a view of change is a sequential view of time, which subscribes to what time philosopher McTaggart (1908) called a "before and after" logic of time. A sequential view of time invites an understanding of change as a difference in states at different points in time. Importantly, such a view presupposes that change happens at a certain point in time and will forever have taken place as "that change" at that point in time. In a sequential view of time, the primary ordering mechanism of events is that of chronological ordering (e.g., Langley et al. 2013; Van de Ven and Poole 1995). In such a logic, an event (such as a change) that took place before another event will forever have taken place before that event (McTaggart, 1908). An often-cited theory of change, which reflects a pattern of change underpinned by a sequential view of time, is Lewin's (1947) model of change as "unfreeze, move and freeze." Although Lewin' contribution is sometimes mistakenly referred to the "unfreeze, change and refreeze" model (Cummings et al. 2016), its underlying idea of change happening at distinct times is still upheld and has been conducive to the search for patterns in and around change events (Weick and Quinn 1999). Lewin's model also lends itself to explaining a change in terms of antecedents and consequences, which helps explain why studies of organizational change tend to take a sequential view (e.g., Weick and Quinn 1999).

Conversely, works based on a continuous (process) view of change, posed as antitheses to the Lewinian view, have argued against sequential views (Tsoukas and Chia 2002) argue that change needs to be understood "from within" (Shotter, 2006), as an ongoing process of becoming. Langley and Tsoukas (2010), for example, criticize episodic views of change for not being able to explain the processes by which change unfolds. In a continuous change view, change is never really settled as an event that stands before and after; therefore, there is no given state "before" that can be compared to the state "after" (Weick and Quinn 1999). Tsoukas and Chia argue for a view of change as experienced in time: "experienced by practitioners as an unfolding process, a flow of possibilities, and conjunction of events and open-ended interactions occurring in time" (Tsoukas and Chia 2002: 572). The underlying idea of the continuous change view is that a sequential view of change cannot transcribe the subtle and ongoing change occurring on a daily basis. In this, Tsoukas and Chia's (2002) view of continuous change resonates with a Bergsonian view of time as indivisible "durée," in which ultimate positions in time are avoided. In taking a Bergsonian view of time, they also reject the spatialized notion of time that Bergson associated with clocks and calendars, which is considered imposed exogenously on the human experience.

However, although Tsoukas and Chia, as well as other scholars of continuous change (Chia 1999; Feldman 2000; Orlikowski 1996), consider actors to be in a state of experiencing change, they do not take into consideration the effect of events that lie in the actors' past or future. According to the philosophers of time, such as Whitehead (1929), Mead (1932), and Schütz (1967), distant events are immanent parts of actors' experience of time. This point is important because events that take place in actors' trajectory are sometimes expressive of episodic change along the actors' own temporal trajectory. In an event-based view inspired by process philosophy (Hernes 2014; Hussenot and Missonier 2016), however, events are not seen as fixed "bumps in the road" waiting to happen, but as reconstructed breaks in an immanent trajectory that signify past or future episodic change in the actors' own time. An event-based view as defined here is different from the use of events by other scholars (Clark 1985; Reinecke and Ansari 2016). In the view taken here, events constitute the very making of time (Hernes 2014) and are always in a state of becoming as "those events that mattered". When we in the following use the term "event-based" view we really imply an "event-process" view. In this view, events are not finalized sequential accomplishments but becoming phenomena. In the words of Whitehead (1929), events do not change, they *become*.

Nevertheless, such events are associated with change, not as episodic changes as dramatic changes observed from the outside (Weick and Quinn 1999), but as "breaks" in actors' experience that are associated with change. They are, in other words, a part of actors' own trajectories of episodic changes. As breaks in actors' experience, they constitute potentialities that actors may evoke from the past or project upon the future as they move through time. Past and future changes are important to actors as potential changes in the current experience as they imagine their trajectory into the past and future (Hernes 2017). Changes recalled from the past or changes imagined for the future are episodic, although not as Weick and Quinn (1999) viewed episodic change, but as breaks marked by events that are ongoing accomplishments (Feldman 2000) rather than accomplished changes. Also, in this view, events are not considered closed occasions with fixed features, but more in terms of their affordances (Gibson 1986), as potentialities for redefinition and change.

Drawing upon an event-based view (Hernes, 2014; Hussenot et al. 2020; Hussenot and Missonier 2016; Pulk 2016) rooted in a process ontology (Rescher, 1996), we will discuss how episodic changes in the past or future are immanently connected to ongoing efforts at continuous change. In this view, episodic change is associated with past or future events that mark "breaks" in the temporal trajectory envisaged by actors while they perform the continuous change in an indivisible (Tsoukas and Chia 2002) and ongoing (Schultz and Hernes 2013) present. Actors address events marking episodic changes, typically through problem solving activity in the present, associated with continuous change (Tsoukas and Chia 2002). Such activity enables them to be selective of which changes to address. Following this view, episodic and continuous change belong to the same movement. On the one hand, this movement consists of making tangible past and future change events through ongoing continuous change. On the other hand, continuous change lived by actors is what defines episodic events of change as being in a state of becoming rather than as accomplished states. Central to this argument is that events associated with certain changes are not accomplished events (i.e., van Oorschot et al. 2013) but events in the making that are continually subject to redefinition.

The main contribution of the chapter is to suggest an integrative way to define and study episodic and continuous change. Rather than see change as either episodic or continuous, we suggest understanding change as an "immanent temporal trajectory." By drawing upon the concept of immanent temporal trajectory, change is here defined as the interplay between ongoing continuous change in the moment, and past and future episodic events of change. Such a contribution enables implications for organization studies by questioning the common assumption that ruptures, radical changes, disruptions, novelties (etc.) would be imposed or planned intentionally by actors.

The chapter is organized as follows: the first section deals with the relation between time and change and shows how the way we conceptualize change depends on the definition we apply to time. The second section introduces the classic ontological divide between episodic and continuous views of change. The third section suggests a different definition of episodic change to make it ontologically compatible with the continuous view of change. The fourth section introduces an event-based view of change as a way to integrate the episodic and continuous view of change into the concept of immanent temporal trajectory. The last section discusses the contributions and implications of such an integrative view on our understanding of organizational phenomena.

Time and Change

Change and time are mutually intertwined. Aristotle suggested famously in Chapter IV in his *Physics* that without change, there would be no experience of time. In their analysis of episodic and continuous change, Weick and Quinn (1999: 362) emphasize, that "change is a phenomenon of time." Scholars of social or organizational change have used time extensively to study change. In the introduction to the first edition of this volume, for example, Poole and Van de Ven define change as "a difference in form, quality or state over time in an organizational entity" (2004: xi), a definition that goes back to Van de Ven (1987) and Van de Ven and Poole (1995). An inference to be drawn from this definition is that the observed, measured, or experienced change (difference) depends on the timespan chosen. Hypothetically, if the timespan is extremely short, say a day after a major organizational change has been announced, the actual "change" will be minimal, as people will wonder what will happen, and how. If the timespan is a year from the same announcement, and new technologies have been introduced, functions have been eliminated or established, and new markets have been defined, most people in that organization will most likely agree that the resulting change is substantial. Such examples suggest that time is inherent to the very definition of change (Reinecke and Ansari 2016) and that sequential time imposes a particular understanding of change as defined by accomplished events.

If we pursue the line of argument, of time being inherent to the definition of change; we are obliged to explore the definitions we apply to time and how those definitions influence the definition of change. Put crudely, what form of change is consistent with what view of time? The most common notion of time in the organizational analysis is sequential, "Newtonian" definition, characterized by equal units that provide an objective, universal measure of time. As pointed out above, it also represents what McTaggart (1908) called a "before and after" logic of time, whereby an event that took place before another event will forever have taken place before that event. This may also be seen as the type of timeless and unchanging reality that Parmenides advocated in saying, "whatever is *is*, and what is not cannot be." This means that we can move through time with a standard ordering of events in terms of their succession. In this view, change can be understood as the difference in the state of affairs from one point in time to the next. Change that has taken place between two points in time will always be that change because the events that were used to describe that change will not change even as those events recede into the past. What makes the sequential time a powerful concept for studying change is that it enables change to be put down to a specific time, defined once and for all. Thus, an event associated with a certain change is given by the time at which it took place, which is important because it took place before some events and after some others.

The significance of clock-time for understanding the change is that it provides a backdrop that helps us order the sequence of changes. Thus (returning to events related to the quote at the beginning of the chapter), the beheading of Louis XVI (a change both from being head of state *and* having a head to no longer being the head of state and no longer *having* a head) is a consequence of the storming of the Bastille in the sense that we can say that it led to his execution. Although we may question the implicit causality when we use the expression "led to," we accept that there is a forward causal pattern given by sequence in time. It is possible that he might not have been beheaded if the storming of the Bastille had not taken place, just as he might have been beheaded even if the Bastille had not been stormed. Still, the causal analysis assumes that once they take place, events are "accomplished" (Tsoukas and Chia 2002), and hence their causal powers are settled once and for all. By "accomplished," we imply that the meaning given to events remains unchanged over time in the sense of what those events led to.

But what happens if we do not define events as accomplished states? What if events are phenomena in the making and become redefined as actors move through time, as assumed by process theories of time (Hernes 2017)? What came before and what came after will then be less significant, and so will the chronological distance between events. We are still grappling with the fact that there is change, but we no longer have the understanding of afforded to us by the sequential view of time. On the contrary, in an event-based view, change takes place not as a result of the accomplished event, but as events in the making, continually redefined in terms of its meaning as actors move through time. An event may remain unchanged as having taken place, such as the storming of the Bastille, but the meaning of that event will be open to continual redefinition, such as what caused it and what it led to in turn.

The distinction between clock-time and event time is important because it enables different understandings of change. In a sequential view, events can be plotted against a fixed timeline, such as a calendar, and they can be grouped in terms of that same timeline (Bluedorn, 2002). In an event-based view, on the other hand, the various changes leading up to the storming of the Bastille (Sewell 1996) would be linked less by chronological order and more by how they would be interlinked and redefined on an ongoing basis, from acting within the events, to building up over time into more complex sets of events that would be defined and redefined by actors as they move through time. As people were storming the Bastille, they were probably conscious of events that preceded the storming and events that might follow, both of which would signal some form of change. However, the events associated with past and future change were in the making; they were not defined sequentially but relationally, and therefore their meaning would change with time. For example, the storming of the Bastille would be in response to the King's sacking of his minister of finance some days earlier and the subsequent gathering of crowds earlier on 14 July, which would in the minds of people signify a different path forward than if other sets of events had been taken into consideration. These events (and others), together with the lynching of the guards, laid the foundations for a trajectory of future changes, which eventually led to the beheading of Louis XVI on 21 January 1793, which marked the end of the absolute monarchy in France. Whereas in chronological time the beheading of the king took place after the storming of the Bastille and could be seen as caused by the storming, in an events-based view of time his beheading could be seen as a possible future event in the minds of those who did the storming, for then to be seen as a meaningful (however appalling) part of the overall trajectory of the French Revolution.

Underlying an event-based view of time (Hernes 2014) is the idea that events that mark change are perpetually in the making and hence subject to redefinition as actors move through time. In this view, as mentioned above, events are seen as offering changing affordances (Gibson 1986) of re-interpretation as actors move through time. Being in the making means that events are open to redefinition as actors relate them to other events. For example, Hernes and Pulk's (2019) study of an episode in a shipbuilding company shows how a seemingly mundane meeting may turn into immediate, yet minor change, but eventually trigger strategic change, and hence become defined retrospectively as something much more important than how the actors present felt at the time. When Hernes and Pulk entered the organization several years after that event, several people kept bringing it up as an event that had marked a new era for the company. However, although those present at the actual event had an inkling at the time that it might turn into something important, they were highly uncertain as to what the implications, if any, might be from their activities at the event.

The Ontological Divide between Episodic and Continuous Change

Episodic and continuous change (Tsoukas and Chia 2002; Weick and Quinn 1999) represent salient categories of change in organizations, although deemed ontologically incompatible by some scholars (Colville and Hennestad 2004). Despite their ontological difference, they are also complementary forms of change that may help explain how organizations can maintain a sense of continuity while at the same time pursuing radical change. As Pettigrew (1985: 1) has pointed out, "The more we look at present-day events, the easier it is to identify change; the longer we stay with an emergent process and the further back we go to disentangle its origins, the more likely we are to identify continuities." Moreover, as Pillemer notes, identified and experienced continuities are "punctuated by distinctive" and "influential episodes" (2001: 123). However, although scholars have developed convincing modes of integration between the two forms of change (e.g., Orlikowski and Hofman 1997), their ontological differences still hamper integration.

Episodic change (Weick and Quinn 1999; see also Feldman and Pentland 2003; Howard-Grenville et al. 2011; Pettigrew et al. 2001; Wiebe et al. 2012) represents an ontological assumption of organizations as inert systems that require the imposition of force, principally by management, in order to change (Feldman and Pentland 2003; Weick and Quinn 1999). The very term "episodic" refers to its temporally discontinuous and intermittent nature (Pettigrew et al. 2001), which is different from the Bergsonian view proposed by Chia (1999). Episodic change is to a varying extent synonymous with other concepts of change, such as revolutionary, radical structural, or planned change (Maes and Van Hootegem 2011; Orlikowski 1996). Hence implementing episodic change is mostly assumed to be led by decision-makers in response to perceived organizational inertia in relation to "jolts" in the external environment (see Gaba and Meyer, Chapter 16 in this volume) that set off collective processes of adaptation (Howard-Grenville et al. 2011).

Continuous change, referred to also as an emergent change (Livne-Tarandach and Bartunek 2009; Maes and Van Hootegem 2011), is rooted in an ontology of fluidity and immanence (Chia, 2005) expressed through ongoing processes in problem-solving, improvisation, practices, and routine work (Feldman and Pentland 2003; Orlikowski 1996; Tsoukas and Chia 2002; Weick and Quinn 1999; see also Pentland and Goh, Chapter 15 in this volume). It expresses a view of organizations as self-organizing, emergent, evolving, and cumulative systems (Weick and Quinn 1999). Being rooted in a view considering organizations as situated practices (Orlikowski 1996), continuous change is pervasive and ongoing (Brown and Eisenhardt, 1997; Feldman 2000; Orlikowski 1996; Tsoukas and Chia 2002) rather than momentary or periodic. It is an "everyday" type of change expressive of a view of organizations as emergent, gradual, and evolving. Arguing for change being inherently continuous, Tsoukas and Chia (2002) propose that change is never settled and shared between people as a "frozen" account of differences between before and after certain events. This, Tsoukas and Chia (2002) argue, is how change is perceived "from within," as opposed "from without," which is consistent with a clock-time view. In this view, continuous change takes place at the practice level, involving, for example, micro-level improvisation (Moorman and Miner 1998), accommodations to and experiments with everyday contingencies (Orlikowski 1996), or executing routines (Feldman 2000). Change is here a much more situated account of differences that always opens to a reinterpretation. Rather than being seen as accomplished (i.e., van Oorschot et al. 2013), events are forever emerging either as they are left behind in the flow of time or projected upon the future for then to becoming towards actors.

Whereas episodic change involves, according to Weick and Quinn, so-called "triggers," which we may translate as "trigger events," Tsoukas and Chia (2002) would argue that such "triggers" never really take place. They argue against the episodic view of change on the basis of its underlying view of time (see Dawson 2014 for a fuller discussion). Relatedly, Isabella (1990) uses the term "trigger events" with reference to Lewin's (1947) model of change as freeze, unfreeze, and re-freeze, consistent with Gersick (1991), who states that periods of relative stability are punctuated by more compact periods of metamorphic change. In contrast, Tsoukas and Chia argue that change takes place, not as isolated events in or across time, but rather as a continuous experience *through* time.

The interplay between episodic and continuous change remains currently undertheorized (Livne-Tarandach and Bartunek 2009), and attempts at bridging the divide between the views are hampered by works that see them as ontologically inconsistent through the lens of time. Chia (1999, 2005) argues in particular that the underlying assumption of movement in continuous change is what makes it ontologically inconsistent with "frozen snapshot" (Chia, 1999) logic of episodic change. Chia contrasts the episodic view with a Bergsonian view of time as a movement of "single unity" (1999: 216). Tsoukas and Chia (2002) consider the two ontologies to be inconsistent with one another, since one assumes fixity of accomplished events over time, whereas the other assumes time as indivisible movement, that is, events as emergent. They criticize episodic change as associated with accomplished events, a view largely consistent with Weick and Quinn's (1999) definition of episodic change as "occasional interruption from equilibrium" and tending "to be dramatic."

We would argue, however, that the ontological inconsistency between episodic and continuous change proposed by Tsoukas and Chia (2002) boils down to a one-sided view of events. When they define events as being episodic, punctual, and as accomplished states, Tsoukas and Chia overlook the process view of events, which sees events as emergent and open to actors' redefinition as they move through time. In this view, episodic change is experienced by the actors themselves, in their own flow of time and not as substantial change as observed from the outside. As pointed out in the introduction, events may be associated with episodic change without being attributed fixity as accomplished states. If events are in the making and not considered accomplished states, then nor will change associated with events be attributed to fixity.

Our argument here is that the above-mentioned becoming versus being gap may be "de-ontologized" to allow for the continuous and episodic change to be intertwined and mutually constitutive, both being experienced "from within" (Shotter 2006). This is necessary because the gap hampers a deeper understanding of the dynamics of change. It is, therefore, not just important, but also possible, to conceive of continuous as well as episodic change from the same ontological view. The continuous change view, as championed in the past, denies the attempt of actors to temporarily consider past or future changes as tangible series of events, while an episodic view of change denies the subtle and constant change that ongoingly occurs in organizational phenomena. It is important not to forget that people in organizations talk about events in the past that they associate with the change, but that they use that talk in the present, which means that they translate episodic change that they see as significant into their ongoing processes of continuous change.

Bridging the Ontological Divide between Episodic and Continuous Change

In this part, we will suggest a different definition of episodic change to make it ontologically compatible with the situated (Orlikowski 1996) and processual nature of the continuous change proposed by Tsoukas and Chia (2002). We will argue that the continuous change view as proposed by Tsoukas and Chia (2002) and supported by Feldman (2000) and Orlikowski (1996) can be extended to include episodic changes from the actors' temporal trajectory, defined as "breaks" in experience. A "break" is a point on the temporal trajectory that signals a difference between before and after. Although little changes go on all the time, there are, at times, what we may call a distinctive break that marks the difference between before and after that come to be seen as significant by organizational members. As Hernes and Pulk (2019) registered when they began their study of change at a shipbuilding company, numerous changes had taken place a few years earlier, but defined in terms of a particular event that was expressive of the process of change during that period. Such a redefinition of episodic change is made possible if one considers past, present, and expected changes not as defined and displayed once and for all along a timeline by actors but instead constantly redefined and reconfigured as a way to define the contingencies of the present. Research shows that this happens in organizations. For example, Hatch and Schultz (2017) relate the story of how the people at Carlsberg Group were inspired to use a century-old motto inscribed in granite to relaunch a novel brand of beer. Schultz and Hernes (2013) describe how LEGO managers evoked the past transition to LEGO bricks in order to reorient their current strategy to bring about change towards a "brick-based" future.

This implies approaching episodic change from "within," as pointed out by Shotter (2006), much the way that continuous change is theorized. In this view, episodic change is not a transition from one state to another that is achieved once and for all. Instead, it is seen as an "immanent" (Chia 2005; Tsoukas 2018) experience of a difference in time, which is evoked and projected on the future by actors as they move through time. Instead of being seen as an unchanging "decisive break," episodic change becomes, consistently with continuous change, episodic change "in the making." Thus, one way to make episodic change analytically consistent with continuous change is to define episodic change as significant "breaks" that are experienced, evoked, or anticipated by actors as they move through time. Referring to various scholars, Weick (2005) offers different labels for such changes, such as interruptions, breakdowns, or shifts. Similarly, Wiebe (2010) refers to "discontinuities" that mark a difference between periods, which may lie in the actors' past or future. Such discontinuities, he argues, are changes that are defined by the actors themselves. We would add, though, that from a temporal perspective, for an interruption, breakdown, shift, or discontinuity to qualify as episodic change, it would need to leave some traces through time that the actors themselves perceive as significant. Moreover, actors may (or may not) recall such breaks differently as they encounter new situations at other points in time as well as anticipate future ones.

How Episodic Change Emerges in the Present

Conceptualizing past, or future anticipated breaks as emerging, this view invites us to study how episodic change may emerge in the present, how it may be evoked from the past, or how it may be projected for the future. To liken episodic changes to breaks in actors' experience is a means to arrive at a definition of episodic change that is ontologically closer to continuous change, but it leaves open the interplay between continuous and episodic change. The overall question may be posed as, how episodic events emerge and are maintained and redefined by actors while they practice continuous change? Conversely, how does continuous change enable the emergence of episodic change? How does it enable past and present episodic change to be brought forward to the current moment, and how does it enable the projection of future episodic change?

A question is how episodic change emerges from an ongoing continuous change in the present. In the present actors experience the continual process of transforming the future into the past while drawing upon the past to confront a novel future. The present, however, is not a fixed temporal entity, and a challenge is, therefore, to work with a notion of the present that follows actors as they move through time. A definition that follows the actors through time is particularly important if we wish to study how, for instance, an episodic change emerging at one point in time becomes evoked by actors at later stages in time. With its primary focus on imminent problem-solving, micro-level improvisation (Moorman and Miner 1998), accommodations to and experiments with everyday contingencies (Orlikowski 1996), or executing routines (Feldman 2000), continuous change exhibits a present-orientation, which suggests that the very acts of performing continuous change may be used as a proxy for the actors' present. Mead (1932) provides a fitting definition of the present for our purpose, which is as the locus of experience; the present is the "going on", and that which is going on is never-ending continuous change.

Continuous change in the present sometimes emerges as events that become associated with episodic change. For example, in their study of change at a mission church, Plowman, Baker, Beck, Kulkarni, and Travis (2007) show how a handful of young people at Mission Church initiated the idea to start offering Mission Church Sunday morning breakfast to the homeless, and how this idea transformed both the Mission Church and its immediate neighborhood. Within a short period after serving the first breakfast, church volunteers were offering more than 200 Sunday morning meals to homeless people. In a few months, a physician volunteer started to offer medical examination, which in turn grew to a full-scale Sunday morning medical program. The initial idea of serving hot breakfast to people in need led to a tax-exempt organization financed partly by city grants "providing a 'day center' for several thousand homeless people and serving over 20,000 meals a year" (Plowman et al. 2007: 516). Soon, in relation to these developments, the mission of the church began to shift. Although the initial group of young people did not intend any transformation either in church or its environment, they "planted the small seed of the idea that led to radical change" (Plowman et al. 2007: 539). That is to say, that although transforming the church's mission, opening a day center, or medical clinic, each of which could be viewed as an episodic change, were not intended or planned, the possibility of their emergence was established with starting to offer breakfast, which eventually became associated with episodic change events.

The Present as the Vantage Point for Past and Future Episodic Change

Whereas the present is the locus of the emergence of episodic change, it is also the vantage point from which actors have access to more distant past and future events across varying temporal spans (Bluedorn 2002; Hernes 2014). As we define such events as an episodic change in the form of breaks, those changes are addressed by actors as they practice continuous change in the present.

For example, in the study of the shipbuilding company by Hernes and Pulk (2019) described above, the ship designers could recall from previous events the discussions about the rationale of the new bow design. As mentioned above, the so-called "NewBow event" was a regular meeting at which staff, together with a visiting CEO, decided to put a radically new bow design on a ship that was already under construction. The meeting was essentially an ordinary business meeting, but a number of occurrences during the meeting made them decide to experiment with a new bow-design on the new ship, which turned out to lead to consequential change for the company. During the meeting, the client CEO caught a glimpse of a mock drawing of a ship fitted with a NewBow. The NewBow was a novel design with a backward sloping bow, which was first conceived by one of InnoShip's designers in 1997 while he was working for another naval design company. That company did not want to pursue the idea; he then brought it up during one of the product development sessions at InnoShip in 2001–2003, in other words, approximately three years before the meeting.

Although the ongoing project had been conceived for a conventional bow, and preparations for construction were already underway, the client CEO asked the InnoShip representatives about the ideas behind the concept. The InnoShip designers replied cautiously that it was something they "had been playing around with" during their internal product development sessions. The NewBow had been selected from a number of other ideas that they had been working on during the product development sessions months and years earlier. At that time, the entry of the NewBow concept into their product development sessions represented a break in the experience, which for the designers was a change event at the time that made a difference to how they went about their sessions.

Moreover, they were able to envisage how the new bow could be designed and fitted. By projecting themselves into the future, they were able to work out solutions through continuous change during the meeting. The *future* episodic change foreseen at the NewBow event was the realization of the NewBow on the vessel under construction. The designers saw an opportunity to realize a revolutionary design that had simmered for several years, but the materialization of the concept was still a change event in the making as experienced in the present during the meeting. What that change eventually might become was not at all clear to them. Nevertheless, they saw the materialization of the concept as the first step of a potential process of change, and the materialization would in itself be a change event, although on a relatively small scale. The change event they saw for themselves at the time of the meeting was the event of the first vessel complete with the new bow mounted. Still, given that they realized an idea that had been years in the making meant that this projected change event would signify a break with ongoing practices.

Whereas past changes were brought forward at the NewBow event, that event also turned into a change event in turn, not at the time that it took place, but retrospectively when people at the company realized that more substantial organizational change had taken place, including a change in strategy based on the NewBow and other related concepts. While at the time of the NewBow event, employees did not see it as a moment of change but perceived it primarily as an opportunity to solve an imminent challenge using an old idea, the NewBow event became later seen as representative of a discernible shift in the strategic trajectory of InnoShip. Materials, such as website postings and annual reports, show how the design defined during the "NewBow event" helped set the company in a new strategic direction. Although it was a change in the making at the time, it came to symbolize what Tsoukas and Chia (2002) and MacKay and Chia (2013) call synoptic accounts of change. However, our analysis suggests that when associated with key events in the organization's own past, synoptic change may no longer be incompatible with continuous change when it becomes an immanent part of the actors' temporal trajectory.

Integrating the Episodic and Continuous Views of Change into an Event-Based View

In an event-based view of change (Hernes 2104; Hussenot et al. 2020; Hussenot and Missonier 2016; Pulk 2016), episodic change events should not be considered ontologically different from the continuous change. Events in actors' past or future experiences that are expressive of change are not inconsistent with Bergson's view of time as indivisible experience, which informs Tsoukas and Chia's time view. For Bergson (1907), life is an indivisible experience, but through its materialization (events or any other "things"), we can define a tangible and actionable reality from it (Hussenot, forthcoming). For example, decisions are made based on our ability to enact these past, present, and/or projected events in our current moments. These events forming a situated temporality enable us to make this current moment tangible in order for decisions to be made about how to move into the future. This view not only brings a theoretical explanation but invites empirical studies about how actors constantly (re)define and configure episodic events of change as well.

For example, organizational scholars working from a temporal view have shown how actors may draw upon distant past events (Basque and Langley 2018; Hatch and Schultz 2017; Schultz and Hernes 2013) and how they may imagine a more distant future in the present (Slawinksi and Bansal 2012). While it is common in temporality studies to study how past, present, and future events are brought into the current moment, it is important to recognize that past, present, and future events are enacted differently by actors over time as well. The past, having been experienced, may be reached through evocation (Schultz and Hernes 2013) or invocation (Basque and Langley 2018), whereas the future is enacted through anticipation (Kaplan and Orlikowski 2013; Slawinski and Bansal 2012), projection (Emirbayer and Mische 1998), or imagination (Schnaars 1987). In such a view, past, present, and future episodic events of change are never really the same, as they are constantly re-enacted by actors. What remains relatively stable is the events associated with change, but they typically start as a future projection of a desired state of affairs. As execution unfolds through many smaller events and activities, the projected event of change becomes past, which is evidently not the same as the projected change. Although there are to our knowledge no studies dedicated to understanding how projected change becomes past, there is every reason to assume that the process of transforming from a future possibility to a past memory is a temporally challenging yet potentially very interesting study. It would be a temporally informed study of episodic change in the making, sustained by ongoing continuous change.

Immanent Temporal Trajectory, Change, and Continuity

In an event-based view, events that mark change are seen as continuously in a state of becoming; that is, they do not change, they become. In this view, events are related less by their relative positions in time than by their connecting on the basis of forming mutually meaningful interplay. Importantly, it means that past, present, as well as future (projected) events may also be events in the making, including the change associated with those events. The main difference from a sequential view of change is that here events are continuously in the making; they are temporal resources available for actors' meaning-making.

We have relied on an event-based view to integrating the episodic and the continuous views into the same ontological framework. More precisely, we have suggested understanding episodic change as past, present, or future tangible breaks of experience that are enacted through continuous change. This view, viewing episodic and continuous changes "in tandem" not as two different views of change, either ontologically different or occurring at different moments in time, but instead, as two dimensions of the same movement through time, allows to "overcome the natural deficiencies of each" (Evered and Louis 1981: 393). In this last section, we discuss the contributions and implications of such a view in our understanding of organizational phenomena. The main contribution of such a view is that change can be defined as an immanent temporal trajectory in which past, present, and future episodic events of change are brought continuously, redefined and reconfigured through continuous change. Such a contribution also leads to interesting implications as by defining change through the lens of immanent temporal trajectory, it questions numerous analyses based on the assumption that ruptures, radical change, disruptions, novelties (etc.) are considered accomplished changes once and for all.

A trajectory is an expression of continuity in the sense that it connects events through time. It enables actors to establish a sense of continuity between different events (changes) over time, although, to an outsider, those events seem very different from one another. Every event may be seen as an occasion of episodic change because it stands out by being a break in experience, being what Bateson (1972: 459) called the "difference that makes a difference." However, although such events are changes in their own right, they also form a sense of continuity over time. This means that events are connected relationally, giving meaning to one another by defining one another. Following this, totally different events may make perfect sense to actors as continuity as well as change. Such a view is different from, for instance, Brown and Eisenhardt (1997) for whom continuous change is a succession of changes. On the contrary, in the view offered here, changes as events serve to define one another into a meaningful temporal trajectory that embodies both continuity and change.

The concept of immanent temporal trajectory, thus means firstly that episodic changes are forms of enactment of past, present, or anticipated events bringing a sense of continuity to the lived moment. Secondly, this constant enactment of past, present, and future events takes part in the experience of a continuous change, as the meaning or definition of episodic changes constantly evolves. Whitehead's (1929) take on events and immanence become helpful here; he used the term "immanence" to describe how events connect *internally* to one another (Hernes 2014). Consequently, the continuous change is both the result of the constant re-enactment of episodic changes and the experience of unexpected events in the current moment. The concept of immanent temporal trajectory is thus a way to express the idea that actors define a sense of direction and continuity to their activity. It is this sense of direction and continuity that also brings a sense of stability, which paradoxically also contains a sense of disorder and novelty. What this means for our framework, is that while actors perform the continuous change, such as solving unexpected day-to-day problems, they remember or imagine events of change at other times and draw inspiration from those events (Hernes and Schultz 2020). By inspiration, we mean that actors connect their current moment (e.g., solving an unexpected problem) with these remembered and imagined events.

Defining change as breaks that are experienced, evoked, or projected by actors, enables the very interplay between the continuous and episodic change to be analyzed. In a way, this view reconnects and extends the idea of the life cycle motor of change suggested by Van de Ven and Poole (1995: 531): "The immediate process of organizing is driven through a life-cycle motor and influenced by a teleological motor of participants' choices of adaptations and retentions. However, over the longer run, these short-term actions contribute to an evolutionary process through which different practices, structures, and ideas are selected and retained." The life cycle motor is similar to the idea of an immanent temporal trajectory. Although trajectories seem at first linear, they are arguable made up of multiple interconnected recursive cycles (Hernes and Bakken 2003).

The event-based view also connects with Van de Ven and Poole's idea of "choices and retentions." As actors move through time, they retain certain epochal breaks represented by events in their trajectory from their past, present, or future (as projected or expected) while adapting or ignoring others. Which ones they retain and how they connect the ones they retain, come to form temporary causal maps that are brought into the present and extended to the future through a continuous change in the present.

The idea of immanent temporal trajectory means that change and continuity are not two different states occurring at two different moments in time, but rather are two dimensions of the same movement (Pettigrew 1985). The implication of this view of change is that organizational change should be studied as attempts to define a sense of continuity in their activity by chopping up the continuous change in episodic events considered as either novelties or stabilities. More precisely, the sense of continuity constantly reconstructed by actors means that neither change nor continuity is given but rather are always in need of enactment. What actors consider as states of change and continuity are primarily the temporary result of their representation of their continuous experience of change. This materialization is supported by actors' narratives, or through management tools and artifacts at large.

Studying organizational change as an immanent temporal trajectory that actors constantly redefine as a way to define the continuity of their activity means that researchers have to focus over time on the way actors redefine this continuity; that is, how they constantly redefine and reconfigure past, present, and future events as similar, different, radically different, etc. As such, the nature of change (or not change) lived by actors is not given to researchers as exogeneous categories, but rather it is defined by actors. Considering episodic events of change as representations made by actors means that the researcher cannot impose predefined categories of change but rather let the actors express the way they (re)define and (re)qualify episodic events of change. The event-based view of change claims that the nature of change lived by actors is always situated, analytical, and immanent.

Conclusion

Theories of organizational change have been strongly influenced by assumptions about time. The Bergson-inspired view of time as "natural duration," or as "permeated whole" (Abbott 2001: 216) is a view that does not let actors escape from the continuous flow of time. By locking actors into the flow of time, Tsoukas and Chia (2002) did not invite episodic change to avoid the spatializing of time that Bergson's "natural duration" was meant to avoid. We have introduced an event-based view as an alternative to allow for the fact that actors actually do take past and future events into consideration *through* their continuous change activities. Our view extends from a Bergsonian view of time as a "permeated whole" to include how they address events that are distanced from the present (Mead 1932). By defining episodic changes as past or future "breaks" that actors address from present, we have been able to bridge the ontological divide between episodic and continuous change. In doing so, we also invite conceptual as well as empirical challenges.

A conceptual challenge is to identify what counts as a change. By introducing the notion of "breaks," we have taken an endogenous view and departed from Weick and Quinn's (1999) formulated definitions of episodic change, which include terms, such as radical, intentional, macro, and discontinuous. In our definition, we have left it to actors' own subjective views of what counts as an episodic change along their own temporal trajectory. In the absence of external criteria for episodic change, what counts as episodic change becomes more of an empirical question. It also means that any change is idiosyncratic and cannot be generalized to other organizations. The NewBow event, from Hernes and Pulk's rendering, was considered unique to the members of InnoShip. This does not mean that it cannot be translated into other studies. For other studies to be related to that change, the translation would be done by the use of the concept of immanent temporal trajectory. All organizational actors have an immanent temporal trajectory that is continually in the process of enactment, and some breaks may be shared by different actors across trajectories. Zerubavel (2003), for example, provides numerous examples of breaks along historical trajectories. Our concept of immanent temporal trajectory departs from Zerubavel's by including future imagined breaks. However, what we share with Zerubavel's work is that although actors attach dates and locations to events, the meanings of those dates are constructed in the present and are therefore likely to change as actors move through time. What changes is not their date but how the events are related to one another. We recall his perspicuous observation, that "In Irish time, 1651 and 1981 were only moments apart" (Zerubavel 2003: 38).

References

Abbott, A. D. (2001), *Time Matters: on Theory and Method* (Chicago: University of Chicago Press).

Aristotle (2008), *Physics* (Oxford: Oxford University Press).

Basque, J., and Langley, A. (2018), "Invoking Alphonse: The Founder Figure as a Historical Resource for Organizational Identity Work', *Organization Studies*, 39/12: 1685–708.

Bateson, G. (1972), *Steps to an Ecology of Mind* (Northwhale, NJ: Jason Aronson Inc).

Bergson, H. (1907 [2009]), *L'évolution créative* (Paris: Presses Universitaires de France).

Bluedorn, A. C. (2002), *The Human Organization of Time: Temporal Realities and Experience* (Stanford, CA: Stanford University Press).

Brown, S. L., and Eisenhardt, K. M. (1997), 'The Art of Continuous Change: Linking Complexity Theory and Timepaced Evolution in Relentlessly Shifting Organizations', *Administrative Science Quarterly*, 42, 1–34.

Chaussinand-Nogaret, G. (1988), *La Bastille est Prise* (Paris : Éditions Complexe.

Chia, R. (2005), 'Organization Theory as a Postmodern Science', in H. Tsoukas and C. Knudsen, eds., *The Oxford Handbook of Organization Theory* (Oxford: Oxford University Press), 113–40.

Chia, R. (1999), 'A "Rhizomic" Model of Organizational Change and Transformation: Perspective from a Metaphysics of Change', *British Journal of Management*, 10, 209–27.

Clark, P. (1985), 'A Review of the Theories of Time and Structure for Organizational Sociology', *Organizational Sociology: Research and Perspectives IV*, 33–79.

Colville, I., and Hennestad, B. (2014), 'Organizing, Changing and Learning: A Sensemaking Perspective on an Ongoing "Soap Story"', *Management Learning*, 45/2, 216–34.

Cummings, S., Bridgman, T., and Brown, K. G. (2016), 'Unfreezing Change as Three Steps: Rethinking Kurt Lewin's Legacy for Change Management', *Human Relations*, 69/1, 33–60.

Dawson, P. (2014), 'Reflections: on Time, Temporality and Change in Organizations', *The Journal of Change Management*, 14/3, 285–308.

Emirbayer, M., and Mische, A. (1998), 'What is Agency?' *American Journal of Sociology*, 103/4, 962–1023.

Evered, R., and Louis, M. R. (1981), 'Alternative Perspectives in the Organizational Sciences: "Inquiry from the Inside" and "Inquiry from the Outside"', *Academy of Management Review*, 6/3, 385–95.

Feldman, M. (2000), "Organizational Routines as a Source of Continuous Change', *Organization Science*, 11/6, 611–29.

Feldman, M. S., and Pentland, B. (2003), 'Reconceptualizing Organizational Routines as a Source of Flexibility and Change', *Administrative Science Quarterly*, 48/1, 94–118.

Gaba, V. and Meyer, A. (2021), 'Discontinuous Change in Organizational Fields', in M. S. Poole and A. H. Van de Ven, eds., *Oxford Handbook of Organizational Change and Innovation* (2nd edn) (Oxford: Oxford University Press).

Gersick, C. (1991), 'Revolutionary Change Theories: A Multilevel Exploration of the Punctuated Equilibrium Paradigm', *Academy of Management Review*, 16/1, 10–36.

Gersick, C. J. (1994), 'Pacing Strategic Change: The Case of a New Venture', *Academy of Management Journal*, 37/1, 9–45.

Gibson, J. J. (1986), *The Ecological Approach to Visual Perception* (New York and Hove: Psychology Press).

Hatch, M. J., and Schultz, M. (2017), 'Toward a Theory of Using History Authentically: Historicizing in the Carlsberg Group', *Administrative Science Quarterly*, 62/4, 657–97.

Hernes, T. (2014), *A Process Theory of Organization* (Oxford: Oxford University Press).

Hernes, T. (2017), 'Process as the Becoming of Temporal Trajectory', in H. Tsoukas, H. and A. Langley, eds, *Sage Handbook of Process Organizational Studies* (London: Sage Publications), 601–7.

Hernes, T., and Bakken, T. (2003), "Implications of Self-Reference: Niklas Luhmann's Autopoiesis and Organization Studies', *Organization Studies*, 24/9, 1511–36.

Hernes, T., and Pulk, K. (2019), *A Temporal View of the Interplay between Continuous and Episodic Change* (Boston: Academy of Management Conference).

Hernes, T., and Schultz, M. (2020), 'Translating the Distant into the Present: How Actors Address Distant Past and Future Events through Situated Activity', *Organization Theory*, 1, 1–20.

Hernes, T., and Schultz, M. (forthcoming), 'A Situated View of Organizational Temporality', *Organization Theory*. https://doi.org/10.1177/2631787719900999

Howard-Grenville, J., Golden-Biddle, K., Irwin, J., and Mao, J. (2011), 'Liminality as Cultural Process for Cultural Change', *Organization Science*, 22, 522–39.

Hussenot, A. (forthcoming), 'A Modus Vivendi between Movement and Materiality: Henri Bergson and the Matter of Organization', *Unplugged M@n@gement*.

Hussenot, A., Hernes, T., and Bouty, I. (2020), 'Studying Organization from the Perspective of the Ontology of Temporality: Introducing the Event-Based Approach', in J. Reinecke, R. Suddaby, A. Langley, and H. Tsoukas, eds., *About Time: Temporality and History in Organization Studies* (Oxford: Oxford University Press).

Hussenot, A., and Missonier, S. (2016), 'Encompassing Novelty and Stability: A Process Event-Based Approach', *Organization Studies*, 37/4, 523–46.

Isabella, L. A. (1990), 'Evolving Interpretations as Change Unfolds: How Managers Construe Key Organizational Events', *Academy of Management Journal*, 33, 7–41.

Kaplan, S., and Orlikowski, W. J. (2013), 'Temporal Work in Strategy Making', *Organization Science*, 24/4, 965–95.

Langley, A., Smallman, C., Tsoukas, H., and Van de Ven, A. (2013), 'Process Studies of Change in Organization and Management: Unveiling Temporality, Activity and Flow', *Academy of Management Journal*, 56/1, 1–13.

Langley, A., and Tsoukas, H. (2010), 'Introducing : Perspectives on Process Organization Studies', in T. Hernes and S. Maitlis, eds, *Process, Sensemaking and Organizing* (Oxford University Press), 1–26.

Lewin, K. (1947), 'Frontiers in Group Dynamics: Concept, Method and Reality in Social Science; Social Equilibria and Social Change', *Human Relations*, 1, 5–41.

Livne-Tarandach, R., and Bartunek, J. M. (2009), 'A New Horizon for Organizational Change and Development Scholarship: Connecting Planned and Emergent Change', in A. B. Shani, R. W. Woodman, and W. A Pasmore, eds, *Research in Organizational Change and Development*, Vol. 17, 1–35. (Bingley, UK: Emerald)

MacKay, R. B., and Chia, R. (2013), 'Choice, Chance, and Unintended Consequences in Strategic Change: A Process Understanding of the Rise and Fall of Northco Automotive', *Academy of Management Journal*, 56, 208–30.

Maes, G., and Van Hootegem, G. (2011), 'Toward a Dynamic Description of the Attributes of Organizational Change', in A. B. Shani, R. W. Woodman, and W. A. Pasmore, eds, *Research in Organizational Change and Development*, Vol. 19, 191–231. (Bingley, UK: Emerald)

McTaggart, J. (1908), 'The Unreality of Time', *Mind*, 17, 457–74.

Mead, G. H. (1932), *The philosophy of the present*. Prometheus.

Moorman, C., and Miner, A. S. (1998), 'Organizational Improvisation and Organizational Memory', *Academy of Management Review*, 23/4, 698–723.

Orlikowski, W. J. (1996), "Improvising Organizational Transformation over Time: A Situated Change Perspective', *Information Systems Research*, 7/1, 63–92.

Orlikowski, W. J. and Hofman, D. J. (1997), 'An Improvisational Model for Change Management: The Case of Groupware Technologies', *Sloan Management Review*, 38, 11–21.

Pentland, B. T., and Goh, K. T. (2021), 'Organizational Routines and Organizational Change', in M. S. Poole and A. H. Van de Ven, eds., *Oxford Handbook of Organizational Change and Innovation* (2nd edn) (Oxford: Oxford University Press).

Pettigrew, A. M. (1985), *The Awakening Giant: Continuity and Change in Imperial Chemical Industries* (Oxford: Basil Blackwell).

Pettigrew, A. M., Woodman, R. W., and Cameron, K. S. (2001), 'Studying Organizational Change and Development: Challenges for Future Research', *Academy of Management Journal*, 44/4, 697–713.

Pillemer, D. B. (2001), 'Momentous Events and the Life Story', *Review of General Psychology*, 5, 123–34.

Plowman, D. A., Baker, L. T., Beck, T. E., Kulkarni, M., Solansky, S. T., and Travis, D.V. (2007), 'Radical Change Accidentally: The Emergence and Amplification of Small Change', *Academy of Management Journal*, 50/3, 515–43.

Poole, M. S., and Van de Ven, A. H. (2004), *Handbook of Organizational Change and Innovation* (New York: Oxford University Press).

Pulk, K. (2016), 'Making Time While Being in Time: A Study of the Temporality of Organizational Processes', Frederiksberg: Copenhagen Business School [Phd]. PhD series No. 43.2016.

Reinecke, J., and Ansari, S. (2016), 'Time, Temporality, and Process Studies', in A. Langley and H. Tsoukas, eds, *The SAGE Handbook of Process Organization Studies* (London: SAGE), 402–16.

Rescher, N. (1996), *Process Metaphysics: An Introduction to Process Philosophy* (Albany (NY), State University of New York Press).

Schnaars, S. P. (1987), 'How to Develop and Use Scenarios', *Long Range Planning*, 20/1, 101–14.

Schultz, M., and Hernes, T. (2013), 'A Temporal Perspective on Organizational Identity', *Organization Science*, 24/1, 1–21.

Schütz, A. (1967), *The Phenomenology of the Social World* (London: Heinemann Educational Books).

Sewell, W. H. (1996), 'Historical Events as Transformations of Structures: Inventing Revolution at the Bastille', *Theory and Society*, 25, 841–81.

Shotter, J. (2006), 'Understanding Process from within: An Argument for 'Withness'-Thinking', *Organization Studies*, 27/4, 585–604.

Slawinski, N., and Bansal, P. (2012), 'A Matter of Time: The Temporal Perspectives of Organizational Responses to Climate Change', *Organization Studies*, 33, 1537–63.

Tsoukas, H. (2018), *Philosophical Organization Theory* (Oxford: Oxford University Press).

Tsoukas, H., and Chia, R. (2002), 'On Organizational Becoming: Rethinking Organizational Change', *Organization Science*, 13/5, 67–582.

Van de Ven, A. H. (1987), 'Review Essay: Four Requirements for Processual Analysis', in A. M. Pettigrew, ed., *The Management of Strategic Change* (Oxford: Blackwell), 330–41.

Van de Ven, A. H., and Poole, M. S. (1995), 'Explaining Development and Change in Organizations', *Academy of Management Review*, 20, 510–40.

van Oorschot, K. E., Akkermans, H., Sengupta, K., and Van Wassenhove, L. N. (2013), 'Anatomy of a Decision Trap in Complex New Product Development Projects', *Academy of Management Journal*, 56/1, 285–307.

Weick, K. E. (2005), 'Theory and Practice in the Real World', in H. Tsoukas and C. Knudsen, eds., *The Oxford Handbook of Organization Theory* (Oxford: Oxford University Press), 453–75.

Weick, K. E., and Quinn, R. (1999), 'Organizational Change and Development', *Annual Review of Psychology*, 50, 361–86.

Whitehead, A. N. (1929), *Process and Reality* (New York: The Free Press).

Wiebe, E. (2010), 'Temporal Sensemaking: Managers'' Use of Time to Frame Organizational Change', in T. Hernes and S. Maitlis, eds., *Process, Sensemaking, and Organizing* (Oxford: Oxford University Press), 213–41.

Wiebe, E., Suddaby, R., and Foster, W. M. (2012), 'The Momentum of Organizational Change', in S. Maguire and M. Schultz, eds., *Constructing Identity in and around Organizations.* Series: Perspectives in Process Organization Studies (Vol. 2) (Oxford: Oxford University Press), 235–60.

Zerubavel, E. (2003), *Time Maps: Collective Memory and the Social Shape of the Past* (Chicago: University of Chicago Press).

CHAPTER 28

EMOTIONALITY AND CHANGE

QUY NGUYEN HUY AND TIMO O. VUORI

Introduction

MAJOR organizational change often triggers strong emotions. These emotions could help or hinder the realization of change. Change leaders could increase the odds of change success by making their followers feel inspired about the proposed new direction. And change leaders often struggle to deal with employees' negative emotions that drive resistance to their proposed changes.

Research on emotionality and change has sought to describe and explain how and why people in organizations experience emotions in relation to change, and how leaders and organizations could better take those emotions into account in managing the change process.

Even though there has been a growing literature on emotions and change, the relevance of emotions for effective workplace behaviors remains under-recognized. Business cultures in various national settings include the belief that emotions do not belong in the workplace and, for example, the Protestant work ethic is particularly antithetical to emotions. Some people even believe that emotions reflect weakness and might be experienced only by some inferior groups. Yet, anecdotal evidence since the time of Odysseys and more recent, rigorous case studies and experiments have shown that all people—including business leaders—experience emotions and that emotions influence their choices and behaviors (Damasio 1994).

There is even neurological evidence that emotions are necessary for decision-making under uncertainty (Damasio 1994). The evaluation of choice options happens through emotions: the option that activates the most positive emotion is considered the best option (Lerner et al. 2015; Phelps et al. 2014). In many cases, the emotional reaction is consistent with what might be called rational choice, such as when an option that maximizes financial results generates the most positive emotional reaction in a leader. Even rule-based decision-making (March and Simon 1958) can be viewed from an emotional perspective: a person who identifies with a set of rules feels good when he or she makes a decision according to the rules and would feel bad about a decision that violates the rules.

Furthermore, there is evidence that when an emotional reaction is eliminated, decision-making under uncertainty is paralyzed: "Elliot" had a good job at a business firm before he lost his ability to feel emotions due to a brain tumor (Damasio 1994).[1] He was able to list the pros and cons of different alternatives, but unable to make decisions. For example, he could spend hours choosing between two restaurants and discussing their location, menu, and other factors, without arriving at a final conclusion. Often, decision-making under uncertainty involves comparing options that cannot be fully quantified on similar dimensions (the incommensurability problem).

Incorporating emotions into our theorizing on change is important because emotional perspectives explain dynamics that cannot be easily explained with purely cognitive or structural theories. At the individual level, people take various actions, such as eating unhealthy food or shouting at their spouse, due to an emotional impulse, even though they are cognitively aware of their harmful consequences. At the organizational level, communication patterns between different organizational groups can be influenced by how the groups feel toward one another rather than by rational considerations of what is best for the organization as a whole or even in the best interests of a particular group (Vuori and Huy 2016a). The goal of the research on emotionality and change is to increase understanding of how change triggers emotions and how those emotions influence change-related behaviors and change outcomes. The practical benefit of such a theory is that it helps leaders to manage change in ways that generate change-enabling rather than change-resisting emotions.

Emotions—Adaptive Responses to Changing Circumstances

Emotions refer to a process which "begins with a focal individual who is exposed to an eliciting stimulus, registers the stimulus for its meaning, and experiences a feeling state and physiological changes, with downstream consequences for attitudes, behaviors, and cognitions, as well as facial expressions and other emotionally expressive cues" (Elfenbein 2007: 315).

According to the circumplex model of emotions, emotions can vary in terms of their valence (positive vs. negative) and arousal (high vs. low arousal) (Russell and Barrett 1999; Russell 2003). Anger is a high-arousal negative emotion, whereas sadness

[1] See also https://www.thecut.com/2016/06/how-only-using-logic-destroyed-a-man.html/, accessed 29 September 2020.

is a low-arousal negative emotion; excitement is a positive, high-arousal emotion, whereas satisfaction is a positive, low-arousal emotion.

Emotions are associated with action tendencies that help individuals cope in particular situations. For example, anger activates the action tendency for fighting and prepares the body physically for fight (e.g., blood flows to arms and heart-rate goes up), which benefits survival in conflict situations. In this sense, all emotions that people experience are adaptive. The implication for the research on emotionality and change is that one should not construe some emotions as always harmful or beneficial, but consider the context in which the emotion is experienced and how the emotion influences (adaptive) behaviors in that context. For example, a middle manager's anger can make him or her assertively challenge a change plan and, in this way, help the organization's leaders identify some unrealistic assumptions in the plan, helping them take corrective actions before costly errors in implementation.

Even though emotions are also associated with physiological antecedents (e.g., small dose of alcohol typically improves a person's mood), the way emotions are generated by people's appraisals of the changes in their situation relative to their environment is central for organizational theorizing. People evaluate their relationship with the environment and when there is a change that is perceived to threaten their survival or goal achievement, a negative emotion results, whereas when there is a change that is perceived to benefit their survival or goal achievement, a positive emotion results (Lazarus 1991). The more immediate and impactful the change, the higher the emotional arousal. Furthermore, the specifics of the situation, such as whether the change was caused by someone intentionally or not, influence which discrete emotion people feel. For example, if there is someone to blame, anger is more likely than sadness (Lazarus 1991). The appraisal process provides a fundamental framework for change scholars to predict which specific emotions will likely be experienced by organization members (Huy 2011). In addition, as appraisals have a subjective component, the appraisal theories explain why sensegiving and sensemaking may influence which emotions organization members end up experiencing during change.

Due to their evolutionary roots (e.g., immediate dangers by predators), emotions tend to emphasize short-term outcomes more than long-term ones (Bechara and Damasio 2005). Traditional change management has emphasized the need for generating early wins (Kotter 1995) and people's emotional reactions might be part of the reason why such a practice could be beneficial. Emotional reactions to short-term outcomes could lead employees to react negatively to change initiatives that are intended to improve the company's and their own situation in the long term but generate discomfort in the short term. Employees may engage in various change-resisting behaviors, even if by doing so they could harm their own well-being in the long term. These resisting actions might generate irreversible harmful effects on the success of change.

On the other hand, even short periods of enthusiasm might trigger decisions and actions that move the change process on an energizing path (Vuori and Huy 2016b). To illustrate, an intense feeling of fear may cause an individual to get a vaccination that saves his life five years later. Similarly, a fleeting fear reaction might cause members of an organization to double-check potential threats and take preemptive actions to counter the threats; or a brief moment of enthusiasm might motivate members of an organization to publicly support a change initiative, which in turn might help convince other skeptical members to support the initiative and help it reach a critical mass.

Even though people often experience similar emotions in similar situations—in part due to social selection and shared identities (Huy 2011), there are individual-level factors that shape each individual's emotional experience and generate interpersonal differences in emotions (Sanchez-Burks and Huy 2009). Starting from trait-like and biological factors, individuals vary in terms of their affectivity such that some individuals' emotional reactions are more intense than others in similar situations (Hamann and Canli 2004). Traits also influence people's tendency to experience positive versus negative emotions (Watson and Clark 1984), the duration of their emotions (Verduyn et al. 2015), and various other qualities of the emotional experience. In addition to traits, personal experiences and learning shape people's emotional reactions.

Variance in individuals and sub-groups' emotions in an organization is a key reason why managers' emotional aperture—the ability to recognize the distribution of different emotions in a group—is an essential emotional skill to deal with change situations (Sanchez-Burks and Huy 2009). The same change proposal could lead a sub-group of people (e.g., production) to feel fearful or depressed whereas another subgroup (e.g., sales) to feel enthusiastic and hopeful. In some situations, managers need to acknowledge the emotions of a minority instead of assuming that the whole group or organization is feeling the same emotion. Once they recognize and acknowledge the different clusters of emotions in the focal group, managers can customize their communication and actions to different sub-groups to increase the likelihood that each sub-group will react favorably to the proposed change.

Yet, there are mechanisms that operate in organizations that contribute to the convergence of individuals' and sub-groups' emotions (Menges and Kilduff 2015). These mechanisms make collective emotions particularly relevant for organizational change.

Collective Emotions in Organizations

The core assumption of the theory on emotionality and change is that *collective emotions matter more than personal emotions in organizational change*. This is because collective emotions systematically influence patterns of behaviors of many individuals. Such behaviors are likely to influence organizational outcomes due to their critical mass: if many people start doing specific things in new ways due to their emotional reactions, the organization as a whole is energized to change. In contrast, individual-level emotions typically only influence the focal individual and the people around him or her, but do not lead to patterns of behaviors displayed by a large number of individuals.

Collective emotions refer to emotions that are shared by many individuals in a group or an organization. The emotions experienced by each individual need not be exactly similar in terms of valence and intensity, but rather reflect common tendencies and themes, such that there is congruence between the emotions experienced by the members of a particular collective. For example, shared fear does not mean that all members of an organization experience fear at a similar intensity at the same time; rather, shared fear means that many members of an organization tend to feel various degrees of fear toward similar targets—such as their superiors (Vuori and Huy 2016a).

Researchers have identified three core mechanisms that generate collective emotions in organizations (see Menges and Kilduff, 2015 for a review). First, exposure to the same situation facilitates shared appraisals between people working in the same context, increasing the likelihood of them experiencing similar emotions. For example, during a heavy storm, all passengers in an airplane are exposed to noises and shaking, which can make them all feel fear. In a similar manner, members of an organization may face an emotion-triggering situation together and therefore feel similar emotions. For example, an aggressive leader can activate fear among many members of a collective (see also, Vuori and Huy 2016a). Second, social identification with the collective entity makes various individuals appraise situations on behalf of the collective entity and thus experience emotions that relate to the goals and well-being of the collective entity. For example, various individuals may identify with a football team and feel positive emotions when the team wins and negative emotions when the team loses. In a similar way, members of an organization may feel positive emotions when something good happens to their organization and negative when something bad happens (see also, Huy 2011).

Third, emotional contagion makes people's emotions converge via non-verbal elicitation that unconsciously spreads to others (Barsade 2002). For example, in an airplane, during a storm, people may see other passengers' terrified facial expressions and hear their screams, which in turn can amplify their own fear and make the fear ever more shared and collective. In a similar way, an employee may see another employee express enthusiasm about a goal and start feeling similar enthusiasm as a result.

These three mechanisms together explain how organization-level factors such as structure and processes can generate various collective emotions inside the organization (Vuori and Huy 2016a). Structures and processes place different groups into different situations. Hence, these groups are exposed to different information and cues; and interact more frequently with members of the same group than with members of the other groups, leading to higher social identification within the group, which makes emotional contagion more likely within the group than between groups.

Ebb and Flow of Emotions during Organizational Change

In terms of process ontology (e.g., Hernes 2014), the theory on emotionality and change does not espouse a hard or extreme view of process, but considers how emotional dynamics emerge within the structural context of the organization and influence change formulation and execution activities. The theory assumes that collective emotions influence collective action tendencies and cognitive interpretations, which shape the evolution of organizational change. During an organizational change process, specific events trigger emotions in various organizational groups, emotions which in turn influence group members' interpretations and actions. As change only progresses when people take actions that promote the change and, as emotions influence their actions, emotions become a fundamental socio-psychological component of change.

How events and actions trigger emotions, which in turn influence perceptions and actions that either promote or undermine organizational change is well illustrated by Huy and colleagues' (2014) longitudinal study of change, legitimacy judgments, and emotions. They found that middle managers initially perceived their new CEO's rhetoric and actions as legitimate and felt positive emotions as a consequence. They therefore supported the CEO and took actions to promote his change agenda. However, the CEO then took actions that the middle managers perceived as illegitimate and experienced negative emotions as a consequence. Middle managers reduced their engagement in supporting the change progress; this led the CEO to react with decisions and actions that the middle managers perceived as even less legitimate, and their emotions became even more negative, which led to change-undermining actions and mutiny and ultimately led to the failure of the change process.

Three emotional phases in change processes can be identified: (1) change leader emotions that contribute to the initiation of a change, (2) change recipient emotions about a communicated change, and (3) change leader and recipient accumulative emotions about actual change actions and progress.

Change Leader Emotions and Change Initiation

Even though changes can be emergent, organizational leaders often consider initiating a change program before communicating such a plan. Research on emotionality and change has recognized that leaders' emotions influence which kinds of change needs they perceive for their organization. For example, when leaders perceive a new external threat, they may feel high-arousal negative emotions (e.g., fear), which may contribute to change initiatives that reinforce the organization's existing core activities (Staw et al. 1981). Organizational leaders may also feel highly unpleasant emotions related to threats and avoid attending to them fully, which also reduces the likelihood of them initiating a radical change (Hodgkinson and Healey 2011).

On the other hand, leaders may also experience pleasant emotions, such as excitement and hope. Some studies indicate that positive emotions enable leaders to think more creatively and therefore generate better change plans (Fredrickson and Losada 2005). In the extreme, leaders may end up in the state of hubris, which makes them envision and initiate radical organizational changes that are by nature more risky (Hiller and Hambrick 2005).

A small number of studies have also focused more on how leaders regulate their emotions during change planning. In particular, Healey and Hodgkinson (2017) theorize and Vuori and Huy (2021) show empirically how emotions can influence top managers' strategic decision-making and that emotion regulation activities can help them transcend their initial emotional impulses and preferences and select strategic goals and plans that diverge from these initial preferences. They show that a general sense of psychological safety reduces the intensity of defensive emotional reactions in difficult situations and therefore enables broader thinking (see also, Edmondson 1999). Furthermore, Vuori and Huy (2018) indicate that a board-induced formal process for information processing can nudge top managers to internalize more new information that alters their appraisals of strategic options and therefore influences which kind of change they end up proposing for the organization.

Organization Members' Initial Emotions and Actions

Once leaders have created a change plan, they communicate it to their organization. Organization members make sense of their organization's situation and their leaders' communication. This sensemaking triggers emotions among the members and influences their actions. Sometimes leaders' communication can activate emotions that benefit change implementation: For example, Carton (2018) studied NASA during the moon project in the 1960s and found how President Kennedy communicated in ways that generated perceptions of meaningfulness among the employees and, according to our interpretation, also generated positive emotions such as excitement, pride, and hope among them. These perceptions of meaningfulness and associated positive emotions made the employees commit to their work strongly, which contributed to substantive progress of the project.

Often the emotional dynamics in interpreting a change involve a combination of negative and positive emotions. As emotions are not reactions to absolute states of the world, but rather reactions to perceived changes in the world and perceived implications for the focal individual, the order in which specific things happen and how they are framed (and interpreted) influence which emotions people experience as a result. A classic example is the practice of generating dissatisfaction with the prevailing situation through "unfreezing" (Lewin 1951/1997), establishing a "sense of urgency" (Kotter 1995), dissatisfaction or "sensebreaking" (Pratt 2000), or "ambiguity-by-design" (Gioia and Chittipeddi 1991), before proposing a new strategic direction. As individuals are first made to feel negative about the prevailing situation, they are more likely to react with positive emotions to the proposed change because the proposed change might improve their situation. (Note that in the moon project example described above, the Cold War provided the threat-related motivation for the project).

The jury is still out in regard to whether the initiation with a negative emotion and prevention motivation, such as a threat, is the more effective way to motivate change, or whether a more positive approach could be equally or even more effective. The Positive

Organizational Scholarship perspective challenges the dominant, overly negative way of thinking about emotions and change (Cameron et al. 2003). For example, Dutton et al. (2010: 282) suggest that a more positive change could be initiated: "Appreciative jolts arise when the experience of affirmation changes an individual's sense of who he or she can be or desires to be. In this case the prompt to alter one's self-definition comes from movement toward the positive or desired state instead of movement away from the negative or undesired state."

Accumulating Emotions during Change

As the above examples illustrate, in the early stages of a change process emotions that elicit new actions tend to be instrumental: change leaders seek to motivate people to take actions to build a better organization and/or address a threat. However, as change actions are initiated and continue over time, additional emotional complexity emerges: in addition to experiencing emotions related to the desired target state and associated future actions, members of the organization may start feeling emotions that are associated with the organizational change actions that have been enacted. To illustrate at the individual level: in the early stages of a new exercise program, it is easy to envision how one will become physically fit by running every morning and following a strict diet, but as weeks go by, one might get increasingly annoyed by the time-consuming exercises and frustrated by the constant hunger resulting from the diet. These emotions might start acting against the change program, despite the excitement generated by the initial envisioned goal. Hence, recognizing and managing the emotions that are generated during the process of implementing change can become equally as important as the emotions generated by the goal of the change.

At the organizational level, our recent study with Natalia Vuori (N. Vuori et al. 2018) generates theory on how organizational dynamics can convert short-term emotions into longer-lasting affective sentiments that influence change dynamics. We studied a post-acquisition integration process for over three years. Members of the acquiring and acquired firm were initially positively excited about the integration of the two companies. However, the target firm's members experienced various negative emotions due to the changes imposed on them by the acquiring firm. These emotions were initially fleeting and did not directly cause dysfunctional behaviors. However, the members of the target firm did not reveal their negative emotions to the acquiring firm, and this positive emotional façade misled members of the acquiring firm. They did not show sympathy or initiate corrective actions to address the causes of acquired members' negative emotions. Rather, the acquiring firm continued imposing requirements that caused frustration among the target firm's members. Over time, as the target firm's members experienced negative emotions for various reasons that they associated with the acquiring firm, they started developing more stable affective sentiments toward the acquiring firm. That is, they started believing and feeling that the acquiring firm's members were incompetent and disrespectful. So, it was not any strong emotional reaction that persisted, but many emotional reactions accumulated and formed a more stable, affectively-charged negative sentiment. These sentiments, in turn, influenced acquired members' behaviors and contributed to the failure of the integration process.

Fiol and O'Connor (2002) provide another illustration of how accumulating emotions can contribute to organizational change. They acknowledge that radical changes challenge organization members' identities which may elicit negative emotional reactions and change resistance. This explains why change approaches that start from a dominantly "rational" external perspective often fail. Yet, they also recognize that "inside-out" approaches that start from the existing identity are unlikely to lead to sufficient radical changes because if people start from an internal perspective, they are unlikely to challenge what they are doing. Hence, Fiol and O'Connor suggest—based on a field study—that initial small projects where both insiders and outsiders participate to create something novel can trigger positive emotions. One small project is unlikely to be enough to foster radical change, but when it's complemented by other small projects, support to people, and explicit communication about their success, the internalization and institutionalization of new identity beliefs become more likely. This can generate a virtuous cycle where people get repeatedly excited about the change process.

More generally, emotions may appear rapidly and fade quickly or keep recurring. Understanding this temporal dynamic is important because the longer change-promoting emotions last, the smoother the implementation of the change; and the longer the change-resisting emotions last, the more difficult the implementation. However, existing theory is underdeveloped in regard to explaining and predicting the duration of collective emotions. To illustrate, we described how change-hindering shared fear lasted for several years at Nokia during the early years of the smartphone industry (Vuori and Huy 2016a). We did not argue that all managers were afraid all the time but rather that they experienced fear repeatedly toward the same targets during those years because the problematic situation was not resolved. Middle managers were under the threat of top managers' aggression when they interacted with top managers and therefore felt fear toward them. On the other hand, Vaara and Monin (2010) described a case in which the enthusiasm for a change generated by an inspiring vision waned in a few months because the situation of the company did not progress as smoothly as the vision promised.

These examples suggest that there are some characteristics of the change process that influence whether the emotions associated with the change persist, intensify, or decline. By drawing on research on habituation (Rankin et al. 2009), one could infer that change-related emotions remain intense if members of the organization are neither under- nor over-exposed to the stimuli that generates the emotions. That is, facing an angry top manager once in every two months is likely to remain scary because of the relative infrequency of the situation, whereas hearing the same top manager shout every day might become less scary because one gets used to the aggression. Likewise, change-promoting emotions might last longer if the stimuli that activates the emotions occurs sparingly rather than all the time. A visionary CEO may sound inspiring when employees listen to her every now and then, but not if they listen to her every day. These speculative hypotheses have yet to be tested in organizational settings, however.

Huy's (2002) study on emotional balancing is consistent with the notion that repeated, but varying stimuli likely create favorable emotional dynamics during a change program. Huy found that change progressed more smoothly in units where different middle managers took very different roles in relation to emotion management during change. In these units, some of the middle managers took a nurturing, empathic role, enabling the employees to express and process their concerns related to change, while other middle managers took a more assertive and change-promoting role, pushing the employees to commit to the change and take actions accordingly. The combination of these two types of behaviors—called emotional balancing—ensured that the employees did not get overwhelmed by the change-promotion actions nor did they become apathic or complacent due to too much empathy.

Current State of Research and Next Steps

Theory on emotionality and change at the organizational level builds on a relatively well-developed foundation of psychological studies at the individual and group-levels. A very large number of experimental studies have specified the mechanisms through which individuals experience emotions, how their emotions might diffuse to others, and how emotions influence their behaviors (Elfenbein 2014). At the organizational level, however, theory on emotionality and change has mainly been developed through conceptual works and inductive field studies (e.g., Huy et al. 2014). From these studies and conceptual works (Ashkanasy et al. 2017), we start developing a clearer understanding of how organizational change is influenced by various emotion-related mechanisms. An important foundation for an overall theory of emotionality and change is Huy's (1999) work on emotional capability and change. His model suggests how emotion-attending behaviors in organizations influence change receptivity, mobilization, and learning during changing.

Important next steps in the development of the theory could include more inductive fieldwork to unpack a richer set of core mechanisms, further conceptual work, and large-sample testing of the key propositions of the theory. We have identified five streams that would benefit from further research.

First, more work is needed to increase understanding of how organizational structures, practices, and processes relate to emotionality in the organizations. We currently have some general understanding that structural factors influence which information middle managers attend to, which further shapes their collective emotions, which influence their behaviors and change implementation (Vuori and Huy 2016a). However, more work integrating collective emotions into organization theory is needed: Collective emotions occur in organizational settings and hence we need to investigate how other various tangible organizational factors influence which collective emotions people experience and how those collective emotions shape their behaviors.

Second, the temporal dimensions of emotions in organizational change should be further investigated: It is currently understood that emotions and events co-evolve over time, but topics such as the duration of different collective emotions, sequences of change-enabling vs change-disabling emotions, and other temporal factors such as social time, pacing, sequencing, rhythm, and change polychronicity have remained understudied (Kunisch et al. 2017).

Third, studies on emotionality and change need to identify more explicit assumptions about the psychological qualities of change leaders. Change studies tend to assume that top managers are dominantly rational and should be able to control their emotions so that emotions do not influence substantively their decision-making, communication, and conflict resolution activities, whereas lower-level middle managers and employees tend to be portrayed as more "irrational" and influenced by their emotions. Furthermore, some studies seem to assume that middle managers are unable to regulate their own emotions, but top managers should design processes to nudge middle managers and employees to experience organizationally desirable emotions. Current research could make asymmetrical assumptions about how emotions influence top managers versus middle and low-level managers. Future studies should investigate more systematically this assumption and explore to what extent it is realistic to posit that top managers could influence and manage others' emotions.

Fourth, the theory on emotionality and change should further incorporate recent developments in positive organizational scholarship (Cameron et al. 2003). Currently, much of what we know about emotions and change comes from case studies that have documented a failure case (e.g., Huy et al. 2014; Huy 2011; Vuori and Huy 2016a; Vuori et al. 2018). We therefore seem to have more direct evidence about what change leaders should not do, rather than what they should do to implement change successfully. Research and theory would benefit from documenting emotion-related practices and explaining their beneficial effects for organizational change more systematically.

Fifth, theory on emotionality and change could be extended to inter-organizational settings. Most research has so far focused on intra-organizational dynamics. Yet, as ecosystems are becoming more common, inter-organizational dynamics and collective emotions may become increasingly important (Huy and Zott 2019; Vuori and Huy 2016b).

Research-Based Principles of Change

A core principle for managing change based on the theory of emotionality and change is that leaders should actively attend to various groups' diverse emotional reactions during change planning and implementation such that arising emotional reactions would support rather than hinder the intended change. This includes attending to both stimulating change-supporting emotions and reducing the likelihood of change-resisting emotions.

There are various practices that change leaders can use to stimulate change-supporting emotions among their followers (see also, chapters by Hargrave 2021; Davis and Eun, 2021, in this volume). Rhetoric and sensegiving seem the most used approaches, as leaders may express ideas in ways that make others feel inspired, scared, angry, or otherwise activated for specific types of action readiness. In addition, how to nudge people to act to change their emotions seems like a promising, albeit under-investigated topic in organizational change. For example, in some situations it might be more effective to make people test-drive an electric car to make them excited about the potential of a new technology than to seek to persuade them through verbal sensegiving (Vuori and Huy 2016b).

In regard to reducing the effects of change-resisting emotions, leaders need to first consider how to communicate the proposed change and orchestrate change actions such that they are perceived as minimally harmful to the recipients' well-being. In addition, they should acknowledge that negative emotions are almost inevitable during the process of change and enact practices that reduce their harmful effects. For example, some changes might generate destructive conflicts among organizational groups and activate anger and other hostile emotions among various groups. In such situations, it seems advisable to let the initial intense emotional reactions cool down for some time, before trying to reactivate a more constructive dialogue among groups.

In addition to investigating specific beneficial emotion management actions in organization settings, it is useful to explore how various emotion management tasks are distributed among various actors (Vuori and Huy 2021). For example, diverse managers could handle different aspects of emotion management (Huy 2002). Change processes often activate a variety of emotions and their management. The complexity is often beyond what an individual manager can address; hence, multiple organizational roles seem necessary to enable members of the organization to experience an adaptive set of collective emotions.

A third core principle involves ensuring sufficient transparency and richness in communication such that top and middle managers remain aware of each other's context and concerns, as well as the changing external situation of the organization (Vuori and Huy 2016a; Vuori et al. 2018). Dialogical approaches provide one means for achieving transparency (Raelin 2012). It is important for change leaders to remain attuned to how various groups in the organization are feeling about the ongoing change so that leaders could adjust the change process in a timely manner and reduce the risk of mounting resistance and increase positive momentum.

Conclusion

Change is driven in part by emotions and generates diverse emotional reactions among various organizational groups that have different identities, preferences, and interests. In this chapter, we have described an active approach to anticipating, managing, and responding to various organizational groups' emotions. Organizational change does not automatically trigger a predetermined grief-cycle (Kübler-Ross 1973) or "the change curve." Various groups' emotional reactions to change can evolve in different directions depending on how each group construes various aspects of the content and process of change, including how they react differentially to leaders' rhetoric and actions. By taking a more proactive and socially textured approach toward groups' diverse collective emotions, leaders could shape a more emotionally enabling organizational change context.

References

Ashkanasy, Neal M., Humphrey, Ronald H., and Huy, Quy Nguyen (2017), 'Integrating Emotions and Affect in Theories of Management', *Academy of Management Review*, 42/2, 175–89.

Barsade, S. G. (2002), 'The Ripple Effect: Emotional Contagion and its Influence on Group Behavior', *Administrative Science Quarterly*, 47/4, 644–75.

Bechara, Antoine, and Damasio, Antonio R. (2005), 'The Somatic Marker Hypothesis: A Neural Theory of Economic Decision', *Games and Economic Behavior*, 52/2, 336–72.

Cameron, K. S., Dutton, J. E., and Quinn, R. E. (2003), *Positive Organizational Scholarship* (San Francisco: Berrett-Koehler).

Carton, Andrew, M. (2018), '"I'm not Mopping the Floors, I'm Putting a Man on the Moon": How NASA Leaders Enhanced the Meaningfulness of Work by Changing the Meaning of Work', *Administrative Science Quarterly*, 63/2, 323–69.

Damasio, A. R. (1994), *Descartes' Error: Emotion, Rationality and the Human Brain* (New York: Putnam).

Davis, G. F. and Kim, E. W. (2021). 'Social Movements and Organizational Change', in M. S. Poole and A. H. Van de Ven, eds., *The Oxford Handbook of Organizational Change and Innovation* (Oxford: Oxford University Press),

Dutton, Jane E., Roberts, Laura Morgan, and Bednar, Jeffrey (2010), 'Pathways for Positive Identity Construction at Work: Four Types of Positive Identity and the Building of Social Resources', *Academy of Management Review*, 35/2, 265–93.

Dutton, J. E., Roberts, L. M., & Bednar, J. (2010). Pathways for positive identity construction at work: Four types of positive identity and the building of social resources. *The Academy of Management Review*, 35(2), 265–293. https://doi.org/10.5465/AMR.2010.48463334

Edmondson, A. (1999), 'Psychological Safety and Learning Behavior in Work Teams', *Administrative Science Quarterly*, 44/2, 350–83.

Elfenbein, Hillary Anger (2007), '7 Emotion in Organizations', *The Academy of Management Annals*, 1, 315–86.

Elfenbein, Hillary Anger (2014), 'The Many Faces of Emotional Contagion An Affective Process Theory of Affective Linkage', *Organizational Psychology Review*, 4/4, 326–62.

Fiol, C. M. and O'Connor, E. J. (2002), 'When Hot and Cold Collide in Radical Change Processes: Lessons from Community Development," *Organization Science*, 13/5, 532–46.

Fredrickson, B. L., and Losada, M. F. (2005), 'Positive Affect and the Complex Dynamics of Human Flourishing', *American Psychologist*, 60/7, 678.

Gioia, Dennis A., and Chittipeddi, Kumar (1991), 'Sensemaking and Sensegiving in Strategic Change Initiation', *Strategic Management Journal*, 12/6, 433–48.

Hamann, Stephan and Canli, Turhan (2004), 'Individual Differences in Emotion Processing," *Current Opinion in Neurobiology*, 14/2, 233–38.

Hargrave, T. J. (2021), 'The Paradox Perspective and the Dialectics of Contradictions Research', in M. S. Poole and A. H. Van de Ven, eds., *The Oxford Handbook of Organizational Change and Innovation* (Oxford: Oxford University Press),

Healey, Mark P., and Hodgkinson, Gerard P. (2017), 'Making Strategy Hot', *California Management Review*, 59/3, 109–34.

Hernes, Tor (2014), *A Process Theory of Organization* (Oxford: Oxford University Press).

Hiller, Nathan, J. and Hambrick, Donald, C. (2005), 'Conceptualizing Executive Hubris: The Role of (Hyper-) Core Self-Evaluations in Strategic Decision-Making', *Strategic Management Journal*, 26/4, 297–319.

Hodgkinson, G. P., and Healey, M. P. (2011), 'Psychological Foundations of Dynamic Capabilities: Reflexion and Reflection in Strategic Management', *Strategic Management Journal*, 32/13, 1500–16,

Huy, Q. N. (1999), 'Emotional Capability, Emotional Intelligence, and Radical Change', *Academy of Management Review*, 24/2, 325–45.

Huy, Q. N. (2002), 'Emotional Balancing of Organizational Continuity and Radical Change: The Contribution of Middle Managers,' *Administrative Science Quarterly*, 47/1, 31–69.

Huy, Q. N. (2011), 'How Middle Managers' Group-Focus Emotions and Social Identities Influence Strategy Implementation', *Strategic Management Journal*, 32/13, 1387–410.

Huy, Quy, and Zott, Christoph (2019), 'Exploring the Affective Underpinnings of Dynamic Managerial Capabilities: How Managers' Emotion Regulation Behaviors Mobilize Resources for their Firms', *Strategic Management Journal*, 40/1, 28–54.

Huy, Quy, Corley, Kevin, and Kraatz, Matthew (2014), 'From Support to Mutiny: Shifting Legitimacy Judgments and Emotional Reactions Impacting the Implementation of Radical Change', *Academy of Management Journal*, 57/6, 1650–80.

Kotter, John P (1995, March-April), 'Leading Change: Why Transformation Efforts Fail', *Harvard Business Review*, 59–67.

Kübler-Ross, Elisabeth (1973), *On Death and Dying* (London: Routledge).

Kunisch, Sven, et al. (2017), 'Time in Strategic Change Research', *Academy of Management Annals*, 11/2, 1005–64.

Lazarus, R. S. (1991), *Emotion and Adaptation* (New York: Oxford University Press).

Lerner, Jennifer S. et al. (2015), 'Emotion and Decision Making', *Annual Review of Psychology*, 66/1, 799–823.

Lewin, Kurt (1951/1997), *Resolving Social Conflicts & Field Theory in Social Science* (Washington, DC: American Psychological Association).

March, James G., and Simon, Herbert A. (1958), *Organizations* (New York: Wiley).

Menges, Jochen I and Kilduff, Martin (2015), 'Group Emotions: Cutting the Gordian Knots Concerning Terms, Levels-of-Analysis, and Processes', *The Academy of Management Annals*, 9, 845–928.

Phelps, Elizabeth A., Lempert, Karolina M., and Sokol-Hessner, Peter (2014), 'Emotion and Decision Making: Multiple Modulatory Neural Circuits', *Annual Review of Neuroscience*, 37, 263–87.

Pratt, M. G. (2000), 'The Good, the Bad, and the Ambivalent: Managing Identification among Amway Distributors', *Administrative Science Quarterly*, 45/3, 456–93.

Raelin, Joseph A. (2012), 'Dialogue and Deliberation as Expressions of Democratic Leadership in Participatory Organizational Change', *Journal of Organizational Change Management*, 25/1, 7–23.

Rankin, Catharine H. et al. (2009), 'Habituation Revisited: an Updated and Revised Description of the Behavioral Characteristics of Habituation,' *Neurobiology of Learning and Memory*, 92/2, 135–38.

Russell, J. A. (2003), 'Core Affect and the Psychological Construction of Emotion,' *Psychological Review*, 110/1, 145.

Russell, J. A. and Barrett, L. F. (1999), 'Core Affect, Prototypical Emotional Episodes, and Other Things Called Emotion: Dissecting the Elephant,' *Journal of Personality and Social Psychology*, 76/5, 805–19.

Sanchez-Burks, J. and Huy, Q. N. (2009), 'Emotional Aperture and Strategic Change: The Accurate Recognition of Collective Emotions,' *Organization Science*, 20/1, 22–34.

Staw, B. M., Sandelands, L. E., and Dutton, J. E. (1981), 'Threat Rigidity Effects in Organizational Behavior: A Multilevel Analysis," *Administrative Science Quarterly*, 26/4, 501–24.

Vaara, Eero and Monin, Philippe (2010), 'A Recursive Perspective on Discursive Legitimation and Organizational Action in Mergers and Acquisitions,' *Organization Science*, 21/1, 3–22.

Verduyn, Philippe et al. (2015), 'Determinants of Emotion Duration and Underlying Psychological and Neural Mechanisms,' *Emotion Review*, 7/4, 330–35.

Vuori, Natalia, Vuori, Timo O., and Huy, Quy N. (2018), 'Emotional Practices: How Masking Negative Emotions Impacts the Post-Acquisition Integration Process,' *Strategic Management Journal*, 39/3, 859–93.

Vuori, Timo O., and Huy, Quy N. (2016a), 'Distributed Attention and Shared Emotions in the Innovation Process How Nokia Lost the Smartphone Battle,' *Administrative Science Quarterly*, 61/1, 9–52.

Vuori, Timo Olavi and Huy, Quy N. (2021), 'Regulating Top Managers' Emotions during Strategy Making: Nokia's Socially Distributed Approach Enabling Radical Change from Mobile Phones to Networks in 2007–2013,' Academy of Management Journal, in press.

Vuori, TO and Huy, Q. (2016b), 'Mental Models and Affective Influence in Collaboration for New Technology', Proceedings of the Academy of Management Annual Meeting.

Watson, David and Clark, Lee A (1984), 'Negative Affectivity: The Disposition to Experience Aversive Emotional States," *Psychological Bulletin*, 96/3, 465.

CHAPTER 29

MUST WE CHANGE? THE DARK SIDE OF CHANGE AND CHANGE RESISTANCE

THEODORE E. ZORN AND JENNIFER SCOTT

Introduction

THIS chapter addresses two interrelated dimensions of organizational change: its dark side and its resistance by stakeholders. Much of the research on organizational change over the years has largely adopted and reproduced an ideology of change as an unquestioned good. Yet, as commonly noted by scholars, a large percentage of change initiatives are unsuccessful (Hughes 2011) and people are often negatively affected in and by many change initiatives. Thus, our focus is on a more recently emergent critical approach highlighting the dark side of change (Dawson 2003; Helms-Mills 2003; Morgan and Spicer 2009). By the "dark side of change," we refer to change initiatives undertaken for ethically questionable reasons, using ethically questionable means, or resulting in harmful or negative outcomes.

In addition, we explore the closely related issue of resistance to change initiatives. We focus particularly on perspectives on resistance that treat it not simply as an obstacle to be overcome, but as a multifaceted phenomenon and one of a range of possible responses to change initiatives. Change is often resisted precisely *because* stakeholders perceive a dark side to initiatives that are presented as innocuous, necessary, or beneficial. Essentially, what we are calling the "dark side" of change is a perception or judgment about the change initiative, and resistance as an aversive cognitive, emotional, and/or behavioral response to change.

Our intention is not to disparage all change initiatives nor to discredit continued research focused on improving organization change. Instead, we highlight the value of multiple perspectives on a phenomenon such as change (e.g., Zorn et al. 2000), and believe that bringing substantive consideration to a darker side of organizational change can ultimately make change initiatives better understood and more acceptable to stakeholders.

We begin our discussion by further articulating our use of "dark side of" and "resistance to" organizational change, as issues that arise when change initiatives are undertaken. We then apply a framework of three dimensions—substance, processes, and outcomes—to both the perception of the dark sides and the response of resistance.

Preliminary Considerations

A consideration of the dark side of organizational change looks through a critical lens at potentially negative aspects of change. This then raises at least three important preliminary considerations: perspective, multi-dimensionality, and dynamism (or the time-bound nature of change). First is the question of perspective, or who decides whether change is positive/bright or negative/dark? To answer the question directly, and perhaps obviously, no single perspective should, prima facie, be accepted as conclusive. Exploring multiple perspectives on organizational phenomena such as change initiatives is important since the phenomenon is elucidated through such exploration (see also Jacobs et al. 2013). Thus, examining the dark side of change is bound to lead to contestation among perspectives over which changes are laudable, which are contemptible, and which are somewhere in between. A multiple-perspectives approach legitimizes the opportunity for critique of change initiatives, even when most or all stakeholders embrace the change. For example, an external observer may usefully identify problematic elements within an otherwise widely accepted change initiative.

Similarly, one issue that clouds judgments of change as "good" or "bad" is the multi-dimensionality of change (Cooper 1998; Piderit 2000). That is, any change initiative has multiple elements, some of which may be judged positively and some negatively by the same stakeholder, and some of which may be given greater weight than others in judging the change. For example, a change focused on adopting a new technology may offer the promise of greater efficiencies, opportunities, and reputation while at the same time threaten job losses and decreased demand for certain skills. Dent and Powley's (2002) typology of changes is useful here. They argue that the degree to which perspectives will differ is influenced by the nature of the change proposed. Specifically, they discuss three very different categories of changes. First, there are changes that almost no one will see as *positive*, but may see them as *necessary*, such as downsizing or budget cuts. They refer to these as "take-your-medicine" changes; they might also be referred to as "change as a necessary evil." Other changes may be seen as positive overall, with likely benefits for the organization as a whole and most of its stakeholders, but with a clear understanding that some individuals or groups will be hurt or inconvenienced. These might include reorganizing for efficiency or for customer service improvement or introducing new technology to replace technology widely acknowledged to be outdated. These can be referred to as "be-a-team-player" changes. Finally, "improvements" are those changes that are widely expected to be welcomed—although they are not always.

Beyond differences in the changes themselves, one useful way to begin to unpack the multiple dimensions is by separating the *substance* (content or rationale) of change programs from the *processes* (methods) used to implement change and the *outcomes* (consequences) of change. These three dimensions offer a way to deconstruct those aspects that contribute to judgments about the dark side of change.

A final preliminary consideration is the dynamic and time-bound nature of perspectives on change and of the process of resistance (Jones and Van de Ven 2016). Consistent with the process focus of this handbook, we see the labeling of a particular change as "positive" or "negative" as a situated judgment that can, and usually does, evolve over time, and which then impacts the evolving responses to change, including resistance. Perceptions of change are subject to multiple influences over time, not the least of which is social interaction with others who have different information and perspectives regarding the change. For example, one may start by seeing a change initiative as primarily negative and as a result resist the change, but with additional information and interaction with others, come to see the initiative as acceptable or even positive. Similarly, a negative or positive view can also become more extreme. The authors have seen this dynamic process play out in our own university, whereby university leaders announced that a substantial amount of funding would be taken from the general budget each year to be set aside for specific strategic initiatives. Some colleagues, who initially supported the change, soured on it as certain projects failed to produce outcomes of which they approved. Others became more positive about the change as they garnered benefits they had not anticipated.

All three of the above considerations—perspective, multidimensionality, and dynamism—suggest the necessity to avoid a simplistic view of the issues on which we are focusing in this chapter. While the chapter focuses on dark sides and resistance, implicitly suggesting bifurcated views of dark versus bright and resistance versus acceptance, we will strive toward a more nuanced view of these phenomena that acknowledges their fluidity and ambiguity.

These issues bring to the fore the question of how organizational change is conceptualized. Van de Ven and Poole (1995) articulated four models underlying conceptualizations of change. Their dialectical model that highlights oppositional forces in tension with each other is particularly useful in considering the dark side of change, while avoiding simplistic views of change as either good or bad, bright or dark. Dialectical models of change highlight the tensions that inevitably accompany change and highlight the notion that tensions emerge when opposing forces both have appeal but simultaneously negate each other.

An obvious example is the tension between change and stability. Zorn et al. (2014) adopted a dialectical framework to explain organizations participating in a "Best Places to Work" competition as a means of improving and promoting their human resources management practices. A dialectical perspective in that study highlighted how organizations experienced a constant tension between *substance* and *image*, for example making substantive changes to practices that actually improved working conditions versus symbolic actions that had the effect of promoting the organization as a good place to work. This tension was at the heart of many stakeholders' skepticism about the process; they often saw the dark side as being what they perceived as disingenuous public relations maneuvers that had little substantive impact on working conditions.

The considerations above also highlight the relationship between the two major foci of our chapter—the dark side of change and resistance to change—as integrally linked. People resist change initiatives based on their perceptions and judgments, conscious or not, that there is a dark side to the change proposed. That is, they resist change because they hold a view that something about the change itself, the means of change, or the likely outcomes, are problematic.

With these preliminary issues having been addressed, we turn to the first of our two major foci: the dark side of change.

The Dark Side of Change

In this section, we address the dark side, or negative aspects, of organizational change, with a focus on change initiatives that are—or are perceived to be—undertaken for ethically questionable reasons, using ethically questionable means, or having negative or harmful consequences.

By focusing on the substance (content or rationale), processes (methods), and outcomes (consequences) of change initiatives, we explore the issues raised in research and practice that are associated with the dark side. This framework provides a basis for critiquing prominent change practices and research findings for their dark side dimensions, to contribute to enhanced understanding of change initiatives by stakeholders.

Substance: Change Logics and Management Ideas

We return to the question in our title: Why change? What a change is about, what it entails, why it is being undertaken, and how it is labeled are all part of what we are calling the *substance* of organizational change. The essence of the substance of change is the rationale for, the content of, or the *logic* of the change. Change is initiated for many reasons, and an important part of an evaluation of change as negative or dark is the substance, rationale, or logic behind the initiative. That is, beliefs about *why* a change is being initiated are integrally involved in judgments about its appropriateness or "goodness." When a change is undertaken motivated by (or *perceived* to be motivated by) the initiator's self-interest or for other unethical, frivolous, or irresponsible reasons, dark side concerns come to the fore.

By "change logic" we mean a more or less coherent rationale for adopting or initiating an organizational change. This is similar to the idea of social accounts that has been used in some organizational change literature (Tucker et al. 2012), but broader in scope. Whereas social accounts refer more narrowly to explicit explanations for one's decisions or actions, change logics may be implicit and more diffused.

The idea of "organizational logic" is well established in the change management literature. For example, Drazin et al. (2004: 163) define organizational logics as "cognitions, or organizing principles, encoded in the minds of those who create organizations.... The mental conception of how an organization should be structured and then how that conception is mapped onto practice." Similarly, the notion of "institutional logics" is used to describe the "practices and beliefs inherent in the institutions of modern western societies" (Thornton and Ocasio 2008: 101).

What is not addressed in the change literature is that change initiatives themselves have distinguishable logics that may be separated from organizational or institutional logics. Changing from one organizational logic to another—such as a move from a single to triple bottom line logic (e.g., Norman and MacDonald 2004)—may be undertaken for different reasons. For example, the move may reflect (a) a sincere embrace of social conscience by the top management team, (b) an effort to garner positive public relations for the organization, or (c) a new CEO's effort to enhance his or her reputation as a hero or celebrity leader (Morris et al. 2005). Each of these reflects a different change logic—a different rationale for initiating the change.

Change logics may be multi-layered, in that a single change initiative may embody more than one logic. In light of our focus on the dark side of change and resistance, it is important to recognize that change logics may be ambiguous and contested. To illustrate this, consider that change logics may be usefully viewed along two dimensions: explicit versus implicit and public versus private, which suggests four broad categories of change logics:

- *Publicly expressed logics (explicit and public).* Publicly expressed logics are the officially sanctioned rationales expressed in press releases or other official texts explaining or justifying a change, typically emphasizing instrumental reasoning. Examples might include the opportunity to improve customer service, increase efficiencies, or improve competitive advantage, and often focus on the material aspects of the change, such as new technologies or methods that will deliver tangible payoffs to stakeholders. They are also typically articulated by senior members of an organization or their representatives (e.g., head of public relations) to a wide audience, including key stakeholders (e.g., customers, employees, shareholders, government regulators) and the wider public.
- *Privately expressed logics (explicit and private).* These are logics embedded in change agents' conversations with selective audiences, usually management

insiders, or people with whom they have close personal relationships. As with publicly expressed logics, these may emphasize instrumental reasoning; however, they are more likely to also include symbolic elements of the change, such as the "symbolic capital" or public relations benefits to be garnered from a change or political elements, for example using a restructuring to dismiss individuals or organizational units deemed problematic.

- *Private, unexpressed logics (implicit and private).* These are logics that pro-change managers and other change agents (e.g., key professionals—such as IT experts and consultants) hold individually or implicitly share. The logics may be discerned in their discourse, but are not overtly expressed, although they may "leak" from change agents' communication, for example, in jokes, in moments of anger, or in patterns of behavior, such as questions asked (see for example, Schein's (2017) list of behaviors that convey culture and values) and become obvious to perceptive observers. These logics are often of a political nature, involving personal gain to the change agents or disadvantage to the change agents' enemies or rivals that may be envisioned as resulting from the change.
- *Underlying discourses or pressures (implicit and public).* These are logics embedded in broader discourses that influence managers to initiate change. They may vary from those shared at a societal or cultural level (e.g., shared beliefs in many Western countries about the superior efficiency of the private sector compared to the public sector for delivering services) to those shared within an organizational culture (e.g., shared beliefs about continuous innovation being the key to organizational survival).

With every change being *about* something, where at its core an idea, practice, structure, or vision captures how the organization can be improved, the alignment or misalignment of these four logics is fundamentally linked to dark side concerns and resistance. For example, when publicly expressed logics align with privately expressed and unexpressed logics and are buttressed by underlying discourses, a change initiative is likely to be seen as warranted, or at least sincere, lacking a hidden agenda, and based on widely shared assumptions. But when public logics conflict (or stakeholders *suspect* they conflict) with privately expressed or privately unexpressed logics, questions of ethics and transparency arise. As a result, stakeholders' suspicions emerge and resistance may ensue.

With this understanding of change logics and their contribution to dark side perceptions (potentially leading to resistance), we extend our focus to the study of management ideas. Scholars of management fads and fashions (e.g., Abrahamson and Piazza 2019; Zorn 2018) have documented how some management ideas become highly popular and then fade over time. While a change initiative's status as fashionable or not does not determine whether it comes to be seen as "dark" or "bright," nor whether it is resisted or accepted, our change logics framework can help to demonstrate important connections between the content and logic of a change initiative. Specifically, implementation of a highly fashionable change program, such as agile management or advanced analytics (Rigby and Bilodeau 2018), will be supported by underlying discourses bolstering its status as timely and at the leading edge of management thinking. Such a perception may help the change initiative gain acceptance but can also engender cynicism as *merely* a fad. As an example of the latter, a manager in a company adopting a knowledge management program wryly explained their company's rationale for the change to one of us as, "a bandwagon drove by and we jumped on it."

Because of the currency of a fashionable management idea, the language and symbols associated with the underlying discourse of the idea is also likely to find its way into the publicly expressed logic for a particular change. Such language and symbols are likely to resonate with others who will have exposure to public discourse such as seen in the promotion of the idea from the "management fashion industry." For example, the business press, consultants' advertising, and public seminars (Jackson 2001) might provide a ready-made set of arguments for organizations to use in supporting their implementation. Additionally, the underlying discourse may find its way indirectly into privately expressed and privately unexpressed change logics as well. Privately expressed logics may emerge in managerial discussions about the reputational advantages to be gained by the organization for adopting fashionable management ideas, and an individual manager may imagine the kudos to be personally gained for being a champion in adopting an idea currently in vogue.

Ideally, stakeholders will trust that publicly expressed logics are not dissimilar from privately expressed and privately unexpressed logics—that is, that the rationales provided to them can be trusted as authentic and that there are no hidden agendas. Dark side concerns can emerge; however, if stakeholders suspect that the various logics are not in alignment, for example if publicly expressed logics seem inconsistent with privately expressed or privately unexpressed logics or are not bolstered by their understandings of underlying discourses.

Process: Means of Change

The next element of our consideration of the dark side is the *process* of change, that is, the method or emergence, evolution, and means of enacting organizational change. Even when stakeholders may agree on the substance, rationale, or change logics of an initiative, choices made in implementing a change can raise concerns. Specifically, stakeholder suspicions are raised when they perceive unethical behaviors in change processes, which they interpret as incompetence, deception, hidden agendas, or inappropriate use of power.

Power, variously defined as the ability of actors to exert their will (Finkelstein 1992) or "asymmetric control over valued resources" (Magee and Frasier 2014: 307) is essential in implementing change. As change is enacted by deploying power to move an organization from one state or condition to another, the act of utilizing power in and of itself is neither positive nor negative, but a necessity. However, the application of power, or *how* power is used in the process of change, and stakeholders' perceptions of the ethical or unethical conduct of power as a means to implement change, is critical to understanding the dark side of change. Magee and Frasier's highlighting of the asymmetric control over resources is central here. In enacting change, when power is perceived to be employed unethically, the change process will likely be viewed negatively.

One of the ways that power is used in change processes to avoid such negative perceptions is to employ it in such a way that its use is not obvious or obtrusive. Thus, Foucault's (1982) claim that power works most effectively when it masks its own mechanisms is relevant here. Scholars have identified a continuum of mechanisms by which control may be exercised over employees (e.g., Gossett 2009), which can be seen in the context of change as more or less obtrusive ways of exercising power to enact change. Research based on Tompkins and Cheney's (1985) distinction between obtrusive and unobtrusive control has distinguished among forms of influence that vary from the direct, obtrusive, and visible (e.g., a manager issuing a directive to demand a change) to the indirect, unobtrusive, and invisible (e.g., developing a strong organizational culture in which workers propose changes that management supports).

The most unobtrusive forms of influence rely on encouraging workers to embrace the organization's or work team's values as their own and thus use self-imposed or work team pressure as primary forms of influence. Team surveillance effectively replaces management surveillance (Barker 1993). Embracing organizational values such as being innovative or "cutting edge" can be particularly useful, especially when they are supported by underlying discourses (i.e., implicit and public change logics). Here again, we see the value of a dialectical and multiple perspectives approach to considering change. From a bright side perspective, the use of unobtrusive forms of influence may be seen as more humane and empowering, as workers choose to participate and to be guided by organizational values rather than by heavy-handed management tactics. Simultaneously, though, they may be seen from the dark side to be manipulative and underhanded.

Another means by which power mechanisms can be masked is through "discursive closure" (Deetz 1992), a process by which alternatives to a favored position are kept hidden or closed from consideration. This can include establishing meeting agendas that allow some topics for discussion but not others or that allow lists of options for consideration but enable only a subset of possible alternatives to be considered. In a change process, it would be common practice to consider alternative scenarios for the change; through discursive closure, discussion might be limited to scenarios that favor one set of interests over others.

Adding to the complexity is the dynamic nature of change initiatives. Stakeholders' perceptions and interpretations of forms of influence and exertion of power may change over the duration of the implementation of change. That is, depending on both the perspective and the point in time over the course of a change implementation, a stakeholder might reasonably consider the process ethical, unethical, or a combination, which contributes to a fluid or ambiguous perception of the change process.

A number of studies of organizational change processes highlight the emergence of distrust and suspicion as a result of change implementers' choices. A few examples are illustrative. Lewis et al. (2013) found in an experimental study that using two-sided messages (those that acknowledged both the risks and the benefits of the change) decreased workers' assessments of trust and honesty of the change initiators and favorability of the change itself. Although they had hypothesized that being transparent about the potential risk would be advantageous in change situations in which the potential for negative outcomes was high, they found that one-sided messages (those that focused solely on the benefits of the change) were consistently superior in terms of generating favorable responses from stakeholders.

Similarly, Tucker et al. (2012) found the particular ways that individuals who were responsible for implementing change accounted for the initiative influenced the way workers understood the change as well as workers' trust in management. They investigated three types of social accounts that change implementers used to frame the decision to implement a change. *Referential accounts* pointed to comparable organizations or situations as a rationale for the change, whereas *causal accounts* identified the forces, both internal and external, that created a need for the organization to change, and *ideological accounts* focused on the underlying values or reasons for the change and its likely benefits. Although causal and ideological accounts both predicted the workers' understanding of the change, only the use of ideological accounts predicted higher levels of trust in management.

In line with our consideration of how the *process* of change, and stakeholders' understanding and perception of the process, impact dark side judgments and resultant resistance behaviors, the two examples above are particularly relevant. They each demonstrate how choices made in the change implementation process may generate trust or distrust in the change initiative and in the individuals leading the change. In neither case is the *substance* of the change the factor that raises concerns. Rather, the process, or *how* the change was introduced and justified, was the key factor.

Finally, research by Higgins et al. (2012) focused on the use of implementation teams in the change process, whereby the teams are formed to develop and implement a strategic vision for the change. Higgins et al.'s research focused on the use of implementation teams in a school district in which the teams were tasked with designing and implementing an instructional improvement strategy. While their research was primarily focused on factors affecting team member learning rather than the efficacy of teams for change implementation, we highlight this study because of its relevance to our discussion above on unobtrusive control. The use of change implementation teams may well be an effective means of garnering buy-in to a change process, given that such a process will make change implementation decisions more democratic and broadens responsibility for the change success beyond management. For those same reasons, however, the use of power may be masked when co-workers rather than management apply pressure to accept the change.

Change processes, thus, have the potential to raise dark side concerns even when the substance of the change is noncontroversial. As shown in the discussion, concerns about abuses of power, ethically questionable methods, or methods that decrease trust may lead stakeholders to object to a change initiative. Even when the use of power and control is unobtrusive, it can raise concerns if people perceive they are being manipulated.

Outcomes: Negative Consequences of Change

Observed and expected negative outcomes of change initiatives are at the heart of negative evaluations of change and are thus fundamental to discussions of the dark side. Many scholarly discussions of dark side phenomena focus primarily on outcomes. For example, according to Griffin and O'Leary-Kelly (2004: 4), dark side behavior is "motivated behaviour by an employee or group of employees that has negative consequences for an individual within the organization, or the organization itself." Similarly, Linstead et al. (2014: 167–8) suggest that "dark side behaviours [fall] into two broad categories, those that harm others and those that harm the organization." Linstead et al. also highlight the importance of considering both intended and unintended consequences.

The purported high rate of failure of change initiatives must be considered a primary cause of suspicion regarding change initiatives. With failure rates estimated at 50% to 70% (Barrett and Stephens 2017; Hughes 2011), it is not surprising that stakeholders are skeptical of change initiatives. Many people have both personal experience as well as familiarity with high-profile cases of problematic change initiatives. Large and catastrophic IT implementations seem especially prominent. In the authors' personal experience, our university recently went through a two-year process of implementing a multimillion-dollar student management system that created havoc with many critical university functions and generated negative press for the university. In addition, there have been high profile cases of large IT system implementations in New Zealand—as well as in many other countries—that have made repeated headlines (e.g., Asgarkhani et al. 2017). Given the tendency of the media to focus on negative examples, success stories are rarely reported. Thus, large change initiatives are, not surprisingly, met with suspicion by many.

Beyond the overall failure rate of change are other negative outcomes of change that have been documented in research, including change fatigue, cynicism, and work intensification. For multiple reasons, including the widespread embrace of continuous change as a norm and the valuing of cultures of innovation (Zorn et al. 1999), change has been a constant in many organizations. As a result, change fatigue (e.g., Bernerth et al. 2011) has been documented as a consequence of change. Bernerth and colleagues found that change fatigue was positively associated with exhaustion, and that exhaustion was in turn negatively related to organizational commitment and positively related to turnover intentions.

Change cynicism represents feelings that "often combine pessimism about the likelihood of successful change with the blame of those responsible for change as incompetent, lazy, or both" (Reichers et al. 1997: 48). A recent meta-analysis (Thundiyil et al. 2015) examined a range of antecedents and consequences of this phenomenon. Among the more interesting findings, change cynicism was less likely if there were high levels of organizational and supervisory support, a perception of trustworthiness, and good communication. Additionally, cynicism was found to have an adverse influence on employees' organizational commitment, motivation, and involvement, and increased their intention to quit.

Work intensification involves an increase in the amount of work performed for a unit of time (Green 2004). A number of scholars have pointed to an increasing rate of change in organizations as part of an overall process of social acceleration (Rosa 2010). Felstead and Green's (2017) work in the United Kingdom has shown an increasing level of work intensification both in the long term, that is, since at least the late nineteenth-century (even though actual working hours have declined), as well as in the last several decades. Work intensification is a direct result of both a higher occurrence of organizational change and particular change programs.

The introduction of technology as part of change initiatives is particularly impactful on intensity. Even change programs intended to improve the quality of working life, such as flexible work practices, can increase intensification (e.g., Kelliher and Anderson 2010). Changes associated with computerization and teamwork have also been found to increase work intensification (Felstead et al. 2019). Importantly, work intensification has been found to be associated with increases in emotional exhaustion (Korunka et al. 2015) and health problems (Felstead and Green 2017) as well as decreases in job satisfaction (Korunka et al. 2015).

While there are documented examples of positive outcomes of change noted throughout this volume (e.g., Lewis in Chapter 11 illustrates examples of various stakeholders benefitting from change initiatives), the negative outcomes noted in this section not surprisingly lead to suspicions about change initiatives and dark side accusations. Such suspicions and accusations sometimes result in subsequent actions (or inactions) that are seen as resistance to change—which we consider in the next section.

Resistance to Change

When the dark side of change emerges—that is, the substance, process, and/or outcomes of organizational change are perceived as harmful or ethically questionable—stakeholders likely resist the change. In this section, we consider how and why resistance arises, is manifested in action, and results in consequences that ultimately support, undermine, or modify change initiatives.

In the same way that organizational change research has evolved from a position of seeing change as an unquestioned good that should be supported under all circumstances to a recognition of a dark side, so too has resistance research evolved from a traditional position of seeing resistance in stark terms as undesirable behavior to a more contemporary view that sees it in more nuanced terms with positive as well as negative qualities (Bareil 2013; Schweiger et al. 2018). At the risk of oversimplifying, we will refer to these as the "traditional" and "contemporary" approaches. Rather than a comprehensive literature review, our intention is to contrast these perspectives and highlight the contemporary—a view that sees resistance not simply as an obstacle to be overcome, but as a multifaceted phenomenon and one of a range of possible responses to change initiatives.

We return to the parallel structure from the previous section, wherein we consider *substance, processes*, and *outcomes*, in this case focused on resistance to change.

Substance: The Nature of Resistance

By the *substance* of resistance, we mean the nature of the construct—the content or rationale of what it entails and the dynamics underlying it or causing it to emerge. Resistance has been given substantial attention by scholars of organizational change, and yet defining and conceptualizing it remain contentious. Despite a long history of scholarship, scholars have come to quite different conclusions about just what resistance is (e.g., Dent and Powley 2002). As Deline (2019: 4) stated, "A key contention between scholars concerns the definition of resistance itself, ranging from an objective fact... to a co-constructed social reality." Kurt Lewin is typically credited with introducing the concept, borrowing it from physics and defining it as a restraining force that pushes back against change to maintain the status quo (Piderit 2000; Dent and Goldberg 1999). According to Dent and Goldberg, Lewin saw resistance as a system phenomenon, but subsequent treatments tended to personalize it as a characteristic or response of individuals or groups. As the concept evolved, authors often treated resistance as one of two bifurcated responses to change, with support or acceptance as the other option available.

A number of assumptions have been made about resistance in the traditional approach that have been challenged by contemporary approaches. First, for much of the history of change research in organization studies, resistance has been assumed to be the primary and nearly involuntary response to organizational change (Dent and Powley 2002). As an example, consider Craine's (2007: 44) statement:

> Resisting change is as congenital as being frightened of the dark, having a crush at age 16, or laughing at the Three Stooges. Little can be done to avoid these reactions. They are natural, emotional, and inevitable. This innate resistance to change occurs because most people like things to be comfortable and familiar.

However, Dent and Powley, among others, questioned this assumption, finding in their qualitative research that interviewees were nearly twice as likely to make positive responses about change than negative.

Second, resistance in the context of organizational change has traditionally been viewed as a negatively valanced construct, especially an act of problematic employee behavior. Lewis (2011: 190) suggested that it has traditionally been viewed as "an act of disobedience, defiance, and/or... a reactive process by which employees (or others) oppose initiatives by change agents." Such approaches privilege managers' and change agents' perspectives and tend to see resistors as problematic and resistance as an obstacle to inherently positive and valued change initiatives. Resistance is thus seen as undesirable—something to be avoided or overcome. Davidson (1994: 94) took an even more extreme view, arguing that resistance has come to include "anything and everything that workers do which managers do not want them to do, and that workers do not do that managers wish them to do." And finally, Krantz (1999: 42) suggested that resistance "has been transformed over the years into a not-so-disguised way of blaming the less powerful for unsatisfactory results of change efforts."

Third, resistance has also traditionally been considered as something only done by the less powerful in response to change initiated by those in power; typically, this means the assumption is that management initiates change and employees resist it. However, as Agócs (1997) pointed out, many changes are initiated by the less powerful or those acting on their behalf, such as unions or professional bodies. In such cases, management may be the ones engaging in resistance. Agócs argues that the powerful have institutionalized structures and practices to resist changes in various forms, including denying the need for change, refusing to act on a proposed change, and repressing or undermining efforts to implement the change.

Ford et al. (2008: 363) concluded that, as a result of assumptions such as these, "[W]e have a one-sided view of resistance that is treated as received truth, even though this view is both theoretically and practically limited, overly simplistic, and perhaps even misguided." A number of contemporary efforts have critiqued these assumptions as biased, simplistic, and overly narrow and have attempted to offer a less pejorative and more nuanced view of resistance. In keeping with the multiple perspectives approach we articulated in the introduction, consider several alternative perspectives on resistance. One perspective is to see resistance as a natural and necessary response to change initiatives. For example, Thomas and Hardy (2011: 326) argue that "resistance is an adaptive response to power, it operates in tandem with power, and it forms at the points where relations of power are exercised." From this perspective, resistance is to be expected and even accepted. Ford et al. (2008) added that resistance is often a rational response brought on by change agents' actions or inactions.

Another perspective is to see resistance and support not as bifurcated options, but part of a wider array of possible responses that can include cynicism, withdrawal, compliance, support, and commitment (Oreg et al. 2018). Oreg and colleagues conceptualized this range of possibilities as not only differing on a positive–negative dimension but also on an activation dimension. That is, responses to change vary not only in how positively or negatively they view the change, but also in how active or passive they are. They argue (2018: 79) that the activity dimension is at least as important as positivity in terms of constructively enabling good results, noting that "passive responses, even if positive, may retard change, whereas active responses, even if negative, may sometimes facilitate it in the long run by clarifying problems with the change."

The quote above hints at a final and particularly consequential perspective, which is that resistance, rather than a negative response to be avoided, can in fact be constructive. First, the emergence of resistance can be a reminder that there is value in stability in that stability allows the organization some level of predictability necessary for effective functioning, as well as a reminder that it may be naïve to assume that change is always inherently good (Waddell and Sohal 1998; Zorn et al.1999). Second, resistance injects energy

(Waddell and Sohal 1998) and stimulates conversations about the change that can ultimately be constructive. As Ford et al. (2008: 368) argue:

> Although talking in a negative way—for example, complaining and criticizing—has been labelled as resistance... it can nevertheless be functional because it keeps the topic 'in play'—that is, in existence—giving others an opportunity to participate in the conversation.

By stimulating conversation, people engage more fully in the change process. In doing so, they may also gain new information, encounter other perspectives, and perhaps identify ways to improve the proposed change. On the latter point, Waddell and Sohal (1998: 545) further suggested that "resistance plays a crucial role in drawing attention to aspects of change that may be inappropriate, not well thought through, or perhaps plain wrong."

The substance of resistance, then, has been contentious, but in recent years is recognized as an important and complex part of the change process, not simply an obstacle to overcome in the process of change.

Process: The Unfolding of Resistance

The discussion above makes clear that responses to change initiatives are far more complex than the positive/support versus negative/resist bifurcation often depicted. Given that responses are likely to be complex, dynamic, and fluid, it is important to consider how resistance and related responses to change emerge and evolve as a process. In this section, we discuss the emergence and progression of resistance (e.g., Dent and Goldberg 1999) and patterns discernible in resistance efforts (e.g., Ford et al. 2008). This reflects the importance of a longitudinal perspective, considering the sequences of activities or processes that transpire over time and may result, for example, in the evolution of resistance into support or the relabeling of behaviors from resistance to constructive questioning—or vice versa.

To consider resistance as a *process*, it is important to acknowledge first that any organizational change and responses to it do not emerge in a vacuum but in the context of existing relationships that have a history. So, the process in that sense starts well before a change is formally announced or even suspected. There are pre-existing relationships between change initiators and stakeholders that may be characterized by, for example, trust or perceived credibility—or their opposites. Individual stakeholders as well as stakeholder groups differ in terms of their predispositions toward and histories with the organization and its leaders, as well as toward the type of change introduced. Jacobs et al. (2013: 779) suggested that:

> Ambiguous procedures and regulations are interpreted in numerous different ways and different parties develop different responses in relation to procedural ambigu-

> ities. In this sense, idiosyncrasies develop in each specific work relationship and (organizational, national) culture provides a general setting by providing a lens for sensemaking.

Thus, the pre-change situation with its network of relationships and meanings will likely have a strong influence on the responses to a change (see also Andersén and Andersén 2014).

Additionally, changes may be anticipated, leaked, and/or hinted at before any formal announcement, and each of these events evokes responses from stakeholders. The "underlying discourses" from our typology of change logics above—including, for example, messages gleaned from media reports about macro-economic conditions, industry trends, and company financial information—may lead stakeholders to anticipate certain changes. Additionally, their knowledge of and history with the organization and its leaders color their perceptions of the changes anticipated. Thus, stakeholders often begin to form views and attitudes about potential changes, and may discuss potential changes with peers, well before changes actually eventuate.

Furthermore, changes may be leaked or hinted at by managers. Here the "privately expressed" and "privately unexpressed" categories of change logics come into play. The important point is that formal announcements of changes and their publicly expressed logics often land in a context already saturated with discussion, opinions, and attitudes about those changes.

When a change initiative is finally made public, stakeholders often experience ambivalence about it (Piderit 2000), and thus engage in private and public sensemaking. The proposed change may engender a combination of emotions, (e.g., hope, excitement, fear), thoughts (e.g., about the need for, or potential problems with, the proposed change), and actions, and these may or may not align with each other (Piderit 2000). The ambivalence may occur because of the nature of the change and who is affected (Dent and Powley, 2002), because of beliefs about likely consequences, including injustices (Oreg et al. 2018; van Dijk and van Dick 2009), or perceived threats to stakeholders' identities (van Dijk and van Dick 2009).

Additionally, when a change is formally introduced, stakeholders do not necessarily choose to resist or support it immediately. Rather than seeing resistance as a sort of reflex response to one-way communication (sender to receiver) about the change, it may be more useful to conceptualize the process as a conversation (Ford et al. 2008) or a reciprocal communication system (Deline 2019). In Deline's conceptualization, there are three stages to the process, including the initial act (the change message), the response to the message (e.g., action or inaction) and the interpretation of the response (as resistance, compliance, etc.). Deline's third stage is important in recognizing that the labeling of stakeholders' response as resistance is itself a choice, not a given.

In our view, Deline's (2019) three-stage process is an important and useful contribution, but still understates the complexity of the change–resistance dynamic. Responses to change, as well as the labeling of those responses, evolve. A particular change may take place over many months or even years. For example, consider Piderit's (2000: 788) story of a manager's response to a major change initiative involving an enterprise-wide software system:

> His initial reaction to the restructuring included positive beliefs, because he felt the change was sorely needed, as well as positive emotions, reflected in expressions of enthusiasm. However, he reported increasingly negative intentions over time, and he planned to challenge his leadership to cancel the project if they would not provide the support that was needed.

The evolution of responses to change may be influenced by a number of factors. Two that have been studied are stakeholders' assessments of managers' ongoing handling of the change initiative, and stakeholders' comparisons of actual results to promised results. Regarding the former, Huy et al. (2014) found that as a change initiative progressed, employees continually tried to make sense of change agents' (managers') actions and that an important part of their sensemaking was assessing the competence and trustworthiness of the managers to implement change successfully. These researchers provided evidence that employees' assessments of managers' credibility directly affected the evolution of their inclination to support or resist. Regarding the comparison of actual and promised results, Andersén and Andersén (2014: 347) demonstrated how such comparisons as well as communication about the comparisons led to evolving attitudes toward the change, arguing that:

> Members of an organization will create meaning of the post-change situation by mainly anchoring the perceived post-change situation in the social representations of the current situation.... However, social representations are dynamic; new communication about the proposed change will occur and this will, of course, influence the different representations... and therefore the attitude to the proposed change.

Further complicating the dynamic nature of resistance and related responses is the visibility of resistance. Given the power dynamics present in the organizational context, overt resistance may not emerge or be visible even when stakeholders object or have deep reservations. On the other hand, in some organizations in which a high level of trust exists, stakeholders may articulate reservations and ask challenging questions very openly. Thus, it is easy to imagine one organization with very little resistance visible having less actual support for change than another organization in which employees raise objections quite vocally and extensively, depending on trust and organizational norms for allowing debate.

Additionally, some authors have pointed to ways that low-power stakeholders may express dissent in ways other than overt resistance. Lewis (2011) identifies a range of resistance forms, ranging from subtle to forceful, and suggests that subtle forms are more likely to be used in situations in which stakeholders fear reprisals from more direct confrontations. Some scholars have identified indirect forms of resistance that entail lesser risk, such as underground publications or posting on websites devoted to complaints about a company (Gossett and Kilker 2006). While such forms of resistance may seem unproductive in not directly addressing those driving the change, Lewis notes that they may garner support and eventually evolve into more forceful forms of resistance.

Of course, responses to change do not necessarily gravitate towards being more negative or forceful. In the example mentioned above of our university's introduction of a new student management system over a multi-year period, we have witnessed a complex evolution. Some university employees' responses evolved from initial enthusiasm at replacing an outdated system to concern as more was learned about the constraints that would be imposed by the new system, to anger, blaming, and workarounds as the system was implemented and experienced significant problems, and more recently to acceptance and support as bugs were worked out of the system and people learned to work within it.

Finally, in the context of resistance as a *process*, it is worth noting that it may be possible for change agents to actively influence how the process unfolds, minimizing the negative effects or even avoiding resistance to a change. For example, Stanley et al. (2005) suggest that managers consider explicitly tying outcomes valued by stakeholders to the stated objectives of the change, and identifying individuals within the organization who are trusted and supportive to act as ambassadors for the change. Others have found that participation can play a role in avoiding or minimizing resistance (e.g., Schweiger et al. 2018).

Our focus in this section has been on the ways that resistance and related response emerge and evolve. The clear message from the research cited is that resistance is not the inevitable response to change, and even when it does emerge, it may evolve from or evolve to other kinds of responses.

Outcomes: Consequences of Resistance

Finally, we consider *outcomes* of resistance, and factors that enable resistance behaviors to be, and to be seen as, producing constructive or destructive outcomes. In keeping with the contemporary approaches to resistance we have been highlighting, the consequences of resistance are not straightforwardly positive or negative. Empirical research has documented mostly negative consequences, although that is likely due to the much longer history of traditional research on resistance.

A number of studies demonstrate that, under some conditions at least, resistance results in detrimental outcomes in the change process. For example, one study found that salespeople who were inclined to resist change self-assessed as being less responsive to customers and less effective in their contributions overall (Jaramillo et al. 2012: 550). The authors explained their findings as follows:

> Resistance to change may likely impact the salesperson's ability to engage in performance enhancing behaviours like adopting new technologies, learning new selling techniques, embracing new customer relationship management initiatives, and

> engaging in adaptive selling behaviours. In addition, salespeople who resist change may not adequately respond to the ever-dynamic customer needs, which can ultimately compromise their ability to perform effectively.

Other studies also have found negative consequences of resistance in the change process but have added important qualifiers as to how and under what conditions such results are likely to manifest. For example, Schweiger et al. (2018) used a systems approach and identified various feedback loops in the change implementation process through which resistance and change outcomes are mutually influencing. One such feedback loop occurs if the situation precipitating the change is perceived as a crisis, in which case it can enhance resistance, which can in turn block change implementation. They quote (2018: 664) one of their participants as highlighting a "crisis means that some employees close up. They are not open anymore and close their minds to anything new." Their resistance then creates stress in the work group, which produces further resistance, and hampers successful change, creating a vicious cycle.

A second example (Jones and Van de Ven 2016) focuses on the effects of time on how resistance influences outcomes. In this study, the crucial finding was that the longer resistance persisted, the more negative the results. Over time, resistance to change was found to have increasingly negative relationships with employees' commitment to the organization and their perceptions of organizational effectiveness. They refer to this (2016: 484) as a "festering effect" of resistance and suggest this occurs because the change becomes experienced and tangible, not just imagined (2016: 487):

> As change progresses and resistant employees experience the realized effects of change, the impact of resistance is amplified. Their interpretation of the change shifts to become based on before-and-after understandings of the change. Their resistance remains, but what was anticipatory before is now (in their view) confirmed.

A third example focused on how underlying dimensions of resistance—affective, cognitive, and behavioral resistance—had differential negative effects. Specifically, affective resistance was associated with decreased job satisfaction, behavioral with intention to leave the organization, and cognitive with commitment to continue with the organization (Oreg 2006: 94):

> In other words, employees who reported being stressed, anxious, and angry because of the change, also reported being less satisfied with their jobs; those who reported having acted against the change also reported greater intention to leave the organization, and, similarly, those who reported having negative cognitive evaluations of the change when it was first introduced were also less likely to believe it is worth their while to remain in the organization.

Identifying positive outcomes of resistance in the organizational change literature has been primarily conceptual and anecdotal rather than the result of rigorous empirical research. However, some positive outcomes, while needing further study, seem apparent. First, behavioral resistance at the very least serves as a signal that stakeholders are paying attention and are engaged enough to raise objections. Second, as indicated previously, resistance can also inject energy into the change process and stimulate engagement by stakeholders in the change process (Ford et al. 2008). Third, resistance sometimes uncovers and hinders morally objectionable change plans and/or unethical methods (Moutousi and May 2018). That is, resistance can benefit the organization if it helps stop initiatives that are illegal or that would damage the organization's reputation. Fourth, resistance can force managers to question, defend, and change assumptions, potentially strengthening rationales and plans (Ford et al. 2008).

Studies have identified factors that may influence the likelihood of resistance having positive or negative effects as well as influencing the strength of those effects. For example, Schweiger et al. (2018) found that participative processes can decrease resistance and lessen its negative effects in certain circumstances. Specifically, they found (2018: 670) that participation can function to "(1) raise awareness that change is needed, (2) reduce employees' personal disadvantages, (3) create perceived empowerment and (4) accumulate trust in change agents." So, participation was found to be effective when stress levels were high and trust was low. However, they cautioned against the overuse of participation, because it slows progress, which can be demoralizing.

Similarly, Jones and Van de Ven (2016) found that perceived organizational fairness and supportive leadership were effective in reducing resistance and that fairness had stronger effects in the early stages of the change process and supportive leadership stronger effects later on—and recall that resistance in the later stages had stronger effects on commitment and perceived organizational effectiveness. Thus, supportive leadership, by decreasing resistance, could make those positive outcomes more likely. The authors further explained that supportive leadership served an important role in reducing threat which became particularly prominent as stakeholders began experiencing the actual effects of change later in the process.

On the whole, the research reviewed in this section suggests resistance certainly has negative effects on change-related outcomes in some circumstances. However, contemporary approaches to studying resistance encourage us to avoid seeing such outcomes as inevitable and to instead see that resistance has the potential to be constructive and in some cases lead to better results.

Conclusions and Implications

Our review of the dark side of change and resistance to change was intended to highlight perspectives that may not otherwise get sufficient attention in a handbook on organizational change research. Our purpose was not to suggest that all change initiatives are "dark" nor to valorize resistance, but to argue that explicating the potential dark side of change has conceptual and pragmatic value, as does considering resistance to change in a more nuanced way than has often been the case. A consideration of these perspectives promises to enable the potential for a richer understanding of both change and resistance. As Linstead et al. (2014: 175) argued:

> Most dark side research focuses on that which is non-obvious, hidden or unrealized—even, in some cases, by those involved. Ordinary and taken-for-granted behaviour that is not necessarily negative per se may at different times and within different consequential chains become pernicious as a result of changes in context, therefore rendering the dark side of organizational behaviour complex, ambiguous and emergent.

Pragmatically, an appreciation of these matters can help initiators and stakeholders to improve their management of change processes, as discussed below.

We conclude our chapter with several observations. First, our argument is an alternative to a traditional view of change as an unquestioned good, and resistance as unquestioned negative. There is support for this alternative perspective in recent literature. For example, Ford et al. (2008: 363) asserted that,

> By assuming that resistance is necessarily bad, change agents have missed its potential contributions of increasing the likelihood of successful implementation, helping build awareness and momentum for change, and eliminating unnecessary, impractical, or counterproductive elements in the design or conduct of the change process.

Second, our consideration of both the dark sides of change and resistance to change has placed a strong focus on these phenomena as complex and the product of sensemaking. As such, taking account of perspective and time are important. Change and responses to change are not givens, but fluid social constructions that vary by perspective and vary over time. As we have shown, and consistent with one of the major premises of this handbook, a change initiative may be seen quite differently by different stakeholders—including by initiators and others affected by the change—and their perspectives can change over time as processes of change and resistance (as well as other responses) play out. For example, one group of stakeholders may see a change as quite insidious early in the process and find themselves in opposition to another group who tout the change as positive and beneficial, only to have their positions reversed as the process evolves. And the group who initially saw the change as dark may resist vigorously early on and shift later towards much more supportive behavior.

Third, there are important implications for research and practice. In terms of theory and research, this chapter has raised a number of possibilities. We highlight two that we consider particularly timely. First, research should examine the interplay of the change logics and how these influence dark side perceptions. We made the case that the rationales or logics for change may have multiple layers and that a misalignment of those layers can signal hidden agendas and raise dark side concerns. Second, research should consider how and under what conditions positive consequences of resistance are realized. While a number of scholars have made logical arguments as to why resistance should produce benefits and what those benefits are, there is a dearth of research examining the process of resistance resulting in positive outcomes.

There are also implications for practice from our review. Using the *substance*, *processes*, and *outcomes* framework from this chapter provides a means for organizations to acknowledge and manage triggers of resistance in followers based on their perceptions of change. This framework can help to demonstrate important connections between the content and logic of a change initiative to overcome potential dark side judgments and resultant resistance behaviors.

First, recognition of the potential for change to have a dark side can assist managers to de-valorize change and approach change initiatives more soberly as phenomena that are likely in many cases not to be received with enthusiasm but, at least by some parties, with suspicion. Second, because dark side perceptions and responses to change are dynamic, managers should recognize that an opportunity exists both to lose and gain support over time, regardless of the initial reaction, and see garnering and maintaining support as long term and ongoing. Third, and closely related, several of the studies we reviewed demonstrated the importance of people skills in influencing perceptions and responses. Participation (Schweiger et al. 2018), supportive leadership and creating a sense of fairness (Jones and Van de Ven 2016), explaining risks (Lewis et al. 2013), and social accounting or framing (Tucker et al. 2012) were shown to have an important role to play in influencing stakeholders' perceptions and responses.

REFERENCES

Abrahamson, E., and Piazza, A. (2019), 'The Lifecycle of Management Ideas', in A. Sturdy, S. Heusinkveld, T. Reay, and D. Strang, eds., *Oxford Handbook of Management Ideas* (Oxford: Oxford University Press), 42–67.

Agocs, C. (1997), 'Institutionalized Resistance to Organizational Change: Denial, Inaction and Repression', *Journal of Business Ethics*, 16/9, 917–31.

Andersén, J. and Andersén, A. 2014. 'Deconstructing Resistance to Organizational Change: A Social Representation Theory Approach', *International Journal of Organizational Analysis*, 22/3, 342–55.

Asgarkhani, M., Cater-Steel, A., Toleman, M., and Ally, M. (2017), 'Failed IT projects: Is poor IT governance to blame?', in *Proceedings of the 28th Australasian Conference on Information Systems (ACIS 2017)*. Australian Association for Information Systems.

Bareil, C. (2013), 'Two Paradigms About Resistance to Change', *Organization Development Journal*, 31/3, 59–71.

Barker, J. R. (1993), 'Tightening the Iron Cage: Concertive Control in Self-Managing Teams', *Administrative Science Quarterly*, 38/3, 408–37.

Barrett, A. K., and Stephens, K. K. (2017), 'The Pivotal Role of Change Appropriation in the Implementation of Health Care Technology', *Management Communication Quarterly*. 31/2, 163–93.

Bernerth, J. B., Walker, H. J., and Harris, S. G. (2011), 'Change Fatigue: Development and Initial Validation of a New Measure', *Work and Stress: An International Journal of Work, Health and Organisations*, 25/4, 321–37.

Cooper, J. R. (1998), 'A Multidimensional Approach to the Adoption of Innovation', *Management Decision*, 36/8, 493–502.

Craine, K. (2007), 'Managing the Cycle of Change', *Information Management Journal*, 41/5, 44–9.

Davidson, J. O. (1994), 'The Sources and Limits of Resistance in a Privatized Utility', in J. M. Jermier, D. Knights, and W. R. Nord eds., *Resistance and Power in Organizations* (New York: Routledge), 69–101.

Dawson, P. (2003), *Reshaping Change: A Processual Perspective* (London: Routledge).

Deetz, S. A. (1992), *Democracy in an Age of Corporate Colonization: Developments in Communication and the Politics of Everyday Life* (Albany, NY: State University of New York Press).

Deline, M. B. (2019), 'Framing Resistance: Identifying Frames That Guide Resistance Interpretations at Work', *Management Communication Quarterly*, 33/1, 39–67.

Dent, E. B. and Goldberg, S. G. (1999), "Challenging 'Resistance to Change'", *The Journal of Applied Behavioral Science*, 35/1, 25–41.

Dent, E. and Powley, E. (2002), 'Employees Actually Embrace Change: The Chimera of Resistance', *Journal of Applied Management and Entrepreneurship*, 7/2, 40–56.

Drazin, R., Glynn, M. A., and Kazanjian, R. K. (2004), 'Dynamics of Structural Change', in M. S. Poole and A. H. Van de Ven (eds.), *Handbook of Organizational Change and Innovation* (Oxford: Oxford University Press), 161–89.

Felstead, A., Gallie, D., Green, F., and Henseke, G. (2019), 'The Determinants of Skills Use and Work Pressure: A Longitudinal Analysis'. *Economic and Industrial Democracy*, 40/3, 730–54.

Felstead, A., and Green, F. (2017), 'Working Longer and Harder? A Critical Assessment of Work Effort in Britain in Comparison to Europe', in D. Grimshaw, C. Fagan, G. Hebson, and I. Tavora, eds, *Making Work More Equal: A New Labour Market Segmentation Approach* (UK: Manchester University Press), 188–207.

Finkelstein, S. (1992), 'Power in Top Management Teams: Dimensions, Measurement, and Validation'. *Academy of Management Journal*, 35/3, 505–38.

Foucault, M. (1982), 'The Subject and Power', *Critical Inquiry*, 8/4, 777–95.

Ford, J. D., Ford, L. W., and D'Amelio, A. (2008), 'Resistance to Change: The Rest of the Story'. *Academy of Management Review*, 33/2, 362–77.

Gossett, L. (2009), 'Organizational Control Theory', in S. W. Littlejohn and K. A. Foss, eds., *Encyclopedia of Communication Theory* (Thousand Oaks, CA: Sage), 705–09.

Gossett, L. M., and Kilker, J. (2006), 'My Job Sucks: Examining Counter Institutional Web Sites as Locations for Organizational Member Voice, Dissent, and Resistance'. *Management Communication Quarterly*, 20/1, 63–90.

Green, F. (2004), 'Why Has Work Effort Become More Intense?' *Industrial Relations: A Journal of Economy and Society*, 43/4, 709–41.

Griffin, R. W., and O'Leary-Kelly, A. M. (2004), 'An Introduction to the Dark Side', in R.W. Griffin and A. M O'Leary-Kelly, eds., *The Dark Side of Organizational Behavior* (San Francisco: CA, John Wiley and Sons), 1–19.

Helms-Mills, J. (2003), *Making Sense of Organizational Change* (London, USA, and Canada: Routledge).

Higgins, M. C., Weiner, J., and Young, L. (2012), 'Implementation Teams: A New Lever for Organizational Change'. *Journal of Organizational Behavior*, 33/3: 366–88.

Hughes, M. (2011), 'Do 70 per cent of all Organizational Change Initiatives Really Fail?' *Journal of Change Management*, 11/4, 451–64.

Huy, Q. N., Corley, K. G., and Kraatz, M. S. (2014), 'From Support to Mutiny: Shifting Legitimacy Judgments and Emotional Reactions Impacting the Implementation of Radical Change'. *Academy of Management Journal*, 57/6, 1650–80.

Jacobs, G., van Witteloostuijn, A., and Christe-Zeyse, J. (2013), 'A Theoretical Framework of Organizational Change'. *Journal of Organizational Change Management*, 26/5, 772–92.

Jackson, B. (2001), *Management Gurus and Management Fashions: A Dramatistic Inquiry* (London: Routledge).

Jaramillo, F., Mulki, J. P., Vincent, O., and Pesquera, M. R. (2012), 'Salesperson Resistance to Change: An Empirical Investigation of Antecedents and Outcomes'. *International Journal of Bank Marketing*, 30/7, 548–66.

Jones, S. L., and Van de Ven, A. H. (2016), 'The Changing Nature of Change Resistance: An Examination of the Moderating Impact of Time'. *Journal of Applied Behavioral Science*, 52/4, 482–506.

Kelliher, C., and Anderson, D. (2010), 'Doing More with Less? Flexible Working Practices and the Intensification of Work'. *Human Relations*, 63/1, 83–106.

Korunka, C., Kubicek, B., and Paškvan, M. (2015), 'Changes in Work Intensification and Intensified Learning: Challenge or Hindrance Demands?' *Journal of Managerial Psychology*, 30/7, 786–800.

Krantz, J. (1999), 'Comment on "Challenging Resistance to Change"', *The Journal of Applied Behavioral Science*, 35/1, 42–4.

Lewis, L. K. (2011), *Organizational Change: Creating Change Through Strategic Communication* (Malden, MA: Wiley-Blackwell).

Lewis. L. (2021), 'Stakeholder Model of Change', in M. S. Poole and A. H. Van de Ven, eds., *The Oxford Handbook of Organizational Change and Innovation* (Oxford: Oxford University Press),

Lewis, L. K., Laster, N., and Kulkarni, V. (2013), 'Telling "Em How It Will Be": Previewing Pain of Risky Change in Initial Announcements', *Journal of Business Communication*, 50/3, 278–308.

Linstead, S., Maréchal, G., and Griffin, R. W. (2014), 'Theorizing and Researching the Dark Side of Organization', *Organization Studies*, 35/2, 165–88.

Magee, J. C., and Frasier, C. W. (2014), 'Status and Power: The Principal Inputs to Influence for Public Managers'. *Public Administration Review*, 74/3, 307–17.

Morgan, G., and Spicer, A. (2009), 'Critical Approaches to Organizational Change', in M. Alvesson, T. Bridgman, and H. Willmott, eds., *The Oxford Handbook of Critical Management Studies* (Oxford: Oxford University Press), 251–66.

Morris, J. A., Brotheridge, C. M., and Urbanski, J. C. (2005), 'Bringing Humility to Leadership: Antecedents and Consequences of Leader Humility', *Human Relations*, 58/10, 1323–50.

Moutousi, O., and May, D. (2018), 'How Change-Related Unethical Leadership Triggers Follower Resistance to Change: A Theoretical Account and Conceptual Model'. *Journal of Change Management*, 18/2, 142–61.

Norman, W., and MacDonald, C. (2004), 'Getting to the Bottom of "Triple Bottom Line"'. *Business Ethics Quarterly*, 14/2, 243–62.

Oreg, S. (2006), 'Personality, Context, and Resistance to Organizational Change'. *European Journal of Work and Organizational Psychology*, 15/1, 73–101.

Oreg, S., Bartunek, J. M., Lee, G., and Do, B. (2018), 'An Affect-Based Model of Recipients' Responses to Organizational Change Events', *Academy of Management Review*, 43/1, 65–86.

Piderit, S. K. (2000), 'Rethinking Resistance and Recognizing Ambivalence: A Multidimensional View of Attitudes Toward an Organizational Change'. *Academy of Management Review*, 25/4, 783–94.

Reichers, Arnon E., Wanous, J. P., and Austin, J. T. (1997), 'Understanding and Managing Cynicism About Organizational Change'. *Academy of Management Perspectives*, 11/1, 48–59.

Rigby, D., and Bilodeau, B. (2018,April 5) 'Management Tools and Trends', Bain and Company, https://www.bain.com/insights/management-tools-and-trends-2017/, accessed 30 September 2020.

Rosa, H. (2010), *Alienation and Acceleration. Towards a Critical Theory of Late-Modern Temporality* (Malmö/Aarhus: NSU Press).

Schein, E. H. (2017), Organizational Culture and Leadership (5th ed.) (Hoboken, New Jersey: Wiley).

Schweiger, S., Stouten, H., and Bleijenbergh, I. L. (2018), 'A System Dynamics Model of Resistance to Organizational Change: The Role of Participatory Strategies', *Systems Research and Behavioral Science Systems*, 35/6, 658–74.

Spicer, A., and Levay, C. (2012), 'Critical Theories of Organizational Change', in D. Boje, B. Burnes, and J. Hassard, eds., *The Routledge Companion to Organizational Change* (London and New York: Routledge), 276–90.

Stanley, D. J., Meyer, J. P., and Topolnytsky, L. (2005), "Employee Cynicism and Resistance to Organizational Change', *Journal of Business and Psychology*, 19/4: 429–59.

Thomas, R., and Hardy, C. (2011), 'Reframing Resistance to Organizational Change'. *Scandinavian Journal of Management*, 27/3, 322–31.

Thornton, P. H., and Ocasio, W. (2008), 'Institutional Logics', in C. Oliver, R. Suddaby, K. Sahlin, and R. Greenwood, eds., *The Sage Handbook of Organizational Institutionalism* (Thousand Oaks, CA: Sage), 99–128.

Thundiyil, T. G., Chiaburu, D. S., Oh, I. S., Banks, G. C., and Peng, A. C. (2015), 'Cynical About Change? A Preliminary Meta-Analysis and Future Research Agenda', *Journal of Applied Behavioral Science*, 51/4, 429–50.

Tompkins, P. K., and Cheney, G. (1985), 'Communication and Unobtrusive Control in Contemporary Organizations', in R. D. McPhee and P. K. Tompkins, eds., *Organizational Communication: Traditional Themes and New Directions* (Newbury Park, CA: Sage), 179–210.

Tucker, D. A., Yeow, P., and Viki, G. T. (2012), 'Communicating During Organizational Change Using Social Accounts: The Importance of Ideological Accounts'. *Management Communication Quarterly*, 27/2, 184–209.

Van de Ven, A. H., and Poole, M. S. (1995), 'Explaining Development and Change in Organizations'. *Academy of Management Review*, 20/3, 510–40.

van Dijk, R., and van Dick, R. (2009), 'Navigating Organizational Change: Change Leaders, Employee Resistance and Work-based Identities', *Journal of Change Management*, 9/2, 143–63.

Waddell, D., and Sohal, A. S. (1998), 'Resistance: A Constructive Tool for Change Management'. *Management Decision*, 36/8, 543–48.

Zorn, T. E. (2018), 'Management Fads and Fashions', in L. Lewis and C. Scott, eds., *The Encyclopedia of Organizational Communication* (Oxford, UK and Malden, MA: Wiley-Blackwell), 1476–83.

Zorn, T. E., Christensen, L. T., and Cheney, G. (1999), *Do We Really Want Constant Change?* (San Fancisco: Berrett-Koehler).

Zorn, T. E., Page, D., and Cheney, G. (2000), 'Nuts About Change: Multiple Perspectives on Change-Oriented Communication in a Public Sector Organization', *Management Communication* Quarterly, 13/4, 515–66.

Zorn, T. E., Roper, J., and Richardson, M. (2014), 'Positive Employment Practices or Reputational Capital? Tensions Inherent in Third-Party Legitimation Processes', *Management Communication Quarterly*, 28/3, 347–74.

CHAPTER 30

CHANGE THAT CONCLUDES

SAKU MANTERE AND RENE WIEDNER

Introduction

Endings are a crucial part of organizational change processes. For something new to emerge, something that has been needs to be concluded. Strategies, practices, routines, cultural symbols, identities, roles, structural configurations, governance policies, and many other aspects of organization come to an end at some point. Endings are a part of life, in organizations as anywhere else.

Classical teleological models of change accounted for this conclusive dimension in organizational change. Kurt Lewin (1947) and Edgar Schein (1996) talked of "unfreezing" the organization as the first step in the change process. When a social system is unfrozen, individuals acting within that system give up on routinized ways of acting and explore new ways. The old has to make way for something new. William Bridges (1986) argued that radical change endeavors, or "organizational transitions" start with letting go of old situations and old identities that go with them. Again, change was presented as ending things while beginning new ones.

Contemporary literature on organizational change seems to have lost at least some of its appreciation of conclusive aspects of change. In saying this, we do hope to avoid a significant misunderstanding, however. We are not referring to the conclusion *of* change, say a conclusion of an episode of radical change, followed by a period of relative stability, as suggested by the punctuated equilibrium view (Gersick 1991). Indeed, if our focus would be the ending *of* a change episode, we have no shortage of relevant contemporary work; from the perspective of Van De Ven and Poole's classic four-fold typology, teleological change ends in implementation, dialectical change in synthesis, life cycle in death or rebirth, and evolution in selection (see Chapter 1 in this volume).

Rather, we are referring to aspects of change which conclude *something else* than the change episode itself, such as a job, an organization, a unit, a practice, an institution. Such conclusions may happen at the beginning or middle of change episodes as much as their end stages. What we are focusing on are "subtractive" aspects of change (Albert 1992) which reduce something from an organization or other social entity. From this perspective, taking stock of contemporary literature, we seem to know much less overall on how to conclude things than how to start them. There also seems to be a predisposition to think of conclusion in negative terms; there is a clear bias towards additive change at the expense of subtractive change (Albert 1992; Corley and Gioia 2004; Wiedner and Mantere 2019). Communication of strategic change tends to favor sensegiving of new directions (Gioia and Chittipeddi 1991) whilst maintaining sense of continuity with organizational history (Chreim 2005; Sonenshein 2010), at the expense of discontinuing existing activities.

It seems that concluding things is as hard for change practitioners as it seems to be for their scholarly counterparts. Citing examples of projects that should have been concluded much earlier to avoid monumental costs to the firms that committed to them, Royer (2003) writes:

> No one comes to work saying, "I'm going to pursue a project that will waste my company millions of dollars." Quite the opposite. They come to work full of excitement about a project they believe in. And that, surprisingly, can be the root of all the trouble—a fervent belief in the inevitability of a project's ultimate success. Starting, naturally enough, with a project's champion, this faith can spread throughout the organization, leading everyone to believe collectively in the product's viability and to view any signs of impending doom merely as temporary setbacks.

Royer calls for the balancing of the influence of project champions with a new group of organizational actors: "exit champions", who weed out unsuccessful projects. Conclusions are indeed often necessary, or even inevitable. If companies fail to divest from non-productive businesses, flourishing business units might go down as well (Burgelman 1994). Being able to face the need to conclude a business rather than keep incurring sunk costs or fall prey to escalation of commitment is one part of mature strategic decision-making (Mellahi and Wilkinson 2004). Also, investing in future lines of business may not be possible without freeing resources from existing ones. This is particularly important in shifting strategic-level priorities, as decision-makers' attention is a scarce and valuable resource (Ocasio 1997).

If the art of concluding is a natural and often necessary part of change processes, it seems that regaining the interest of change classics would seem to be worthwhile as the alternative is to end up with one-sided theories of change, and misguided prescriptions to practitioners. In this chapter, we therefore seek to understand change that concludes. We structure our exploration of conclusive change with four simple sets of questions. We begin with: *Where and when does conclusive change happen*? Depending on the unit of analysis, conclusions can happen in various places. Looking at its various contexts and instantiations allows us to focus on *what* conclusive change *is*. How should it be conceptualized? What other kinds of change are there, and is conclusion necessary? The third question we will ask is: *Why* is conclusive change underappreciated? What drives the asymmetry in our attitudes between starting and concluding things in organizations? Integrating insight from the three previous questions, we conclude the paper by asking: *How* should conclusive change be approached by change agents? However different the unit of analysis, there may be general insights about how this type of change should be pursued, if only in the interest of minimizing human suffering.

Where and *When* do Conclusions Take Place?

Conclusions are ubiquitous. Like organizational change in general, we can think of organizational endings as ranging from small occurrences that are relatively common to organizational life to large-scale, dramatic events. Providing an overview of all of the different types of organizational conclusions that exist is impossible since everything dies. We have therefore decided to limit this overview to a small number of organizational phenomena that concern the discontinuation of entire organizations, as well as more and less central aspects thereof.

Structuring our overview this way may give the impression that the termination of an entire organization is in some way more significant than ending a supposedly marginal organizational routine. Yet we know that what matters is subjective and that a certain ending (regardless of the "size" or "centrality" of its subject and depending on a wide range of conditions), may be felt intensely by all, some, only a few, or none of its members or wider stakeholders. Rather than suggesting that certain types of endings are more fundamental than others, we compare and contrast them by considering the main types of loss that stakeholders may experience (see Table 30.1), while acknowledging that the same event can trigger different types of loss for different stakeholders.

Agents may not agree *when* a conclusion happens either. While a bankruptcy, for instance, implies conclusion of an organization, stakeholders may differ in their views on how, why, and exactly when the organization ended. A conclusion can be conceptualized as an experience that is subject to re-interpretation over time (see Hernes et al.'s phenomenological argument in Chapter 27 in this volume). What may appear to actors at a particular time as a decisive moment of conclusion, may later be regarded as largely irrelevant, or vice versa. The more time has elapsed and the longer the historical timeframe adopted, the more a decisive ending may appear as continuity. For instance, several commentators interpreted the announcement of large-scale restructuring of the National Health Service (NHS) in England in 2010 that involved abolishing over a hundred Primary Care Trusts at the time as the most significant change in the organization's seventy+ year history (Macdonald 2011)—marking the end of the NHS as many had

Table 30.1 Organizational Conclusions and Types of Loss

Type of ending	Potential feelings of loss experienced by organization members	Examples in literature
Termination of organization (e.g. bankruptcy)	Meaning; direction; social bonds; ability to exert influence; access to resources; stability; personal investment; recognition; status	(Sutton 1987)
Absorption of organization into another (e.g. M&A)	Organizational autonomy	(Ginter et al. 1992)
Closure of organizational unit; downsizing	See Termination of organization	(Fairhurst et al. 2002)
Organizational separation (e.g. divestiture)	Social bonds and direction	(Wiedner and Mantere 2019)
Departure of founder or other key figures (i.e. "leaders")	Meaning and direction	(Bell and Taylor 2016)
Ending imagined future (e.g. abandoning previously announced plans or vision)	Direction and stability	(Mantere et al. 2012)
Discontinuing labels (e.g. dropping or altering parts of name or brand)	Meaning and stability	(Sonenshein 2010)
Discontinuing organizational routines	See Termination of organization	(Kellogg 2011)
Ending projects (before and upon completion)	See Termination of organization	(Havila et al. 2013)

come to know it. Over time it has been interpreted increasingly as simply a continuation of the application of neoliberal principles that began at least twenty years earlier. Additionally, the more we "zoom in" to the final period of an entity's existence, the more we tend to struggle to identify the exact point of termination. Like a beginning, an ending constitutes a process.

Termination of Organization

The perhaps most extreme form of organizational conclusion is the termination of the organizational entity itself, which is referred to as "organizational death" by some academics and has attracted increased scholarly interest (Bell and Taylor 2011; Sheppard 1994; Sutton 1987). Given organizations' roles in people's everyday lives with respect to (1) providing income for employees to maintain their livelihood, (2) establishing and maintaining a sense of direction (via clear visions and career paths) and affiliation for individuals who may otherwise experience existential anxiety, and (3) providing opportunities for individuals to connect with others and develop communities, it is not surprising that the end of an organization (and even of its signifiers, such as name or logo) may trigger strong emotional reactions—even among former members (Do et al. 2019; Walsh et al. 2019).

Unlike human beings and other living organisms, legal entities do not have a natural life expectancy and thus, in theory, could continue to exist indefinitely (as long as they are somehow invoked).[1] They can be regarded as vehicles whose parts are replaceable to such an extent that none of its original elements—such as its members, processes, facilities, or products—need to survive. Some of the oldest, continually operating organizations in the world are Kongō Gumi (a Japanese construction company, allegedly founded in AD 578), The King's School in Canterbury, United Kingdom (founded in AD 597), and the University of Bologna in Italy (founded in AD 1088). These organizational lifespans contrast markedly with Stubbart and Knight's finding that "just surviving 5 to 10 years represents a large accomplishment for a new firm" (2006: 85).

Moreover, unlike human beings, organizational entities can merge with other entities or split to form new entities. This raises questions about what constitutes organizational death: Does a merger or divestiture signify an organizational ending—or continuation? What about if an organization has been declared bankrupt and a new entity acquires (most of) its resources. Does this represent an ending and new beginning or merely a hiatus? All of this suggests that determining what specifically constitutes the end of an organization is ultimately subjective and depends on how an organization and its boundaries are defined (Heracleous 2004; Hernes and Paulsen 2003; Santos and Eisenhardt 2005). In this respect, at least three quite different perspectives can be adopted, namely a legal, social arrangement, and practice-based view.

The legal perspective provides the most straightforward method of determining an organizational ending: The organization ceases to exist when it is no longer formally recognized as an entity. From a social arrangement perspective, such formal recognition is not necessary. Hence, an organization can continue to exist even when it is outlawed as long as people treat it as a going concern. A practice-based view, by contrast, sees organizations as patterns of enactments of interrelated practices, comprising bodily and mental activities, material elements, and meanings (Reckwitz 2002; Schatzki 2005). This last perspective calls into question the notion of an organization as a stable entity with stable boundaries altogether and draws attention to the minute, everyday dynamics that both reproduce and change social structures (Tsoukas and Chia 2002).[2] Hence, from this point of view, organizational death refers to an ending or change of a pattern and is ultimately dependent on where we draw the boundaries between one form and another (Wittgenstein 1958).

[1] This, however, does not mean that organizational lifespans are random, as population ecologists have shown (Freeman et al. 1983; Hannan and Freeman 1988).

[2] The notion of clearly identifiable boundaries is also increasingly questioned with respect to the human body: According to recent research, human cells make up less than 50% of the body's total cell count (Turnbaugh et al. 2007).

Notwithstanding these different perspectives, the term "organizational death" is generally used to designate "permanent closings" (Sutton 1987) that occur when an organization is declared bankrupt or wound down by its owners due to a lack of funding. In the case of public sector organizations and voluntary agencies, closure may follow an assessment that the organization is no longer relevant—either because it has achieved its goals (Brunsson and Sahlin-Andersson 2000) or is no longer compatible with the government's strategy (e.g., the abolition of certain agencies as part of NHS restructuring, as mentioned above).

According to Harris and Sutton (1986), organizational death can have a profound effect on members primarily because it breaks, or risks breaking, *social bonds*. Members may have become accustomed to interacting with one another on a regular basis and have formed emotional attachments that they find difficult to replace. Additionally, they highlight the affective and cognitive demands resulting from members' loss of established roles and transitions towards new roles (see also Sutton 1987). Since organizational affiliations and organizational roles define individuals to some extent, this requires discarding an old, and establishing a new, identity that provides meaning and direction.

The loss of employment that may come with the termination of the organization presents particular emotional challenges to individuals in cultures in which unemployment is regarded as an existential threat and/or shameful. For instance, in Japan, people who have lost their jobs may keep their unemployment secret from their closest family members and friends (Sutton et al. 2014). On a pragmatic level, the ending of an organization also signifies the closure of an arena (Mintzberg 1985) or field (Emirbayer and Johnson 2008) within which members could exert influence or access resources that may otherwise be difficult to obtain. Stakeholders including employees, shareholders, bondholders, suppliers, and clients may associate the end of an organization with the loss of their (financial and other types of) personal investments.

The term organizational death, however, is also occasionally used to describe M&A transactions (Ginter et al. 1992); in popular discourse, M&A's are sometimes referred to as "murders and executions". There are at least two reasons why a merger or acquisition can be associated with death. The first, as per the legal view of organizational death noted above, is that at least one of the original legal entities typically ceases to exist once an M&A transaction has been completed. Studies of organizational death rates that use large samples or populations (e.g., Daepp et al. 2015) tend to adopt this view. The second reason, which is linked to viewing organizations as social arrangements or bundles of practices, relates to organization members' perceptions of the consequences of an M&A transaction: Members of the acquired entity may interpret the transaction and its aftermath as signifying the end of the organization they used to know; for them the new organization is no longer recognizable as the old one.

Essentially, therefore, the types of loss that stakeholders may experience in the context of a merger or acquisition are the same as those already noted above. Along these lines, organizational death is also at times equated with organizational decline and used to describe events including downsizing, site closures, and large-scale restructuring efforts (Bell and Taylor 2011) that result in parts of an organization ceasing to exist. The termination of an entire organization, the closure of a factory, and the acquisition of a firm may trigger processes of mourning and the erection of temporary memorials (Bell 2012; Bell and Taylor 2016).

However, there is another type of loss that members of an acquired entity may experience: The loss of organizational autonomy. This is especially the case with start-ups or other small, entrepreneurial organizations that are acquired by large, established corporations and subsequently have to adhere to unfamiliar bureaucratic procedures (Datta and Grant 1990).

Separation: Concluding Relationships

Curiously, the splitting of organizations into two or more entities, either due to government-mandated break-ups, divestitures or spin-offs, is rarely explicitly associated with organizational death in the literature, despite dynamics being at play that are similar to those that may occur as part of downsizing, closures, and restructuring efforts. Splitting an organization into separate parts creates formal boundaries between members and entails the allocation of resources, such as equipment and patents, across these parts. For members of divesting and divested units, this division can trigger feelings of loss. An analogy that is commonly employed in this context is divorce (Wiedner and Ansari 2020). A divestiture is also sometimes compared to a child leaving the parents' home (Walter et al. 2014).

Case studies focusing on *divested* units reveal that their members may experience the divestment decision as "traumatic" and feel a sense of abandonment or rejection due to their contributions not being regarded as central or valuable to the divesting unit (Moschieri 2011). On the other hand, the thought of no longer being part of the old organization—and the increase in organizational autonomy this may occasion (Wiedner and Ansari 2020; Wiedner and Mantere 2019)—may also be experienced as liberating. Nevertheless, letting go of an old identity may be difficult (Corley and Gioia 2004; Ferriani et al. 2012).

For members of a *divesting* unit, a divestiture may also raise identity-related questions. Moreover, the increased autonomy gained by the divested unit can equate to a loss of control for the divesting unit, which may necessitate the adjustment of habits, such as no longer directing or guiding members of the newly separated unit (Wiedner and Mantere 2019).

As with mergers and acquisitions, organizational separation tends to involve implementation challenges, including emotional responses to a seemingly rational decision, that are frequently underestimated. Paradoxically, research suggests that organizational distancing—that is, the loosening of bonds between organizational units—may be most effectively supported via a period of approximation. This is because altering existing relations may require lengthy negotiations and the identification of linkages that were not necessarily apparent or obvious. Yet, increasing the level of communication following the decision to implement separation runs against the common conception or urge of achieving a "clean" or "clear" break (Wiedner and Ansari 2020; Wiedner and Mantere 2019).

Departure of Key Members

In addition to the above-mentioned phenomena, other types of organizational endings may strongly affect organization members or other stakeholders. Chief among these is the exit of the organization's founder(s) or other leadership figures that (formally or informally) represent or even personify the organization. The sudden absence of such (seemingly irreplaceable) figures may trigger an existential crisis among organization members, given that the perhaps most readily identifiable source of meaning or direction is gone.

A perhaps extreme case of mourning the departure of a founder of an organization is the response to the death of Steve Jobs. In this case, formal, organizational memorializing practices involved a virtual condolence book and an official memorial service, as well as unofficial practices in the form of unofficial websites and forums dedicated to mourning his death (Bell and Taylor 2016).

Critical management scholars suggest that the intensity of organization members' attachments to founders and other organizational leaders may be linked to charismatic authority, which creates dependencies on leaders and reduces dissent. Moreover, such attachments may be the results of more or less conscious efforts by organizations (rather than just the charismatic leaders themselves) to increase loyalty and "remould individuality" in ways that are "socially harmful" (Tourish and Pinnington 2002: 156–7). Hence, rather than occurring naturally, feelings of loss may be generated and exploited by organizations following the death of an individual to support powerful interests (Bell 2012).

The departure of a highly charismatic figure, or of one who has become associated with the organization's success, limits the ability for successors to gain acceptance since they may have to live up to unrealistic expectations (Bryman 1993). Ultimately, as Max Weber noted (1979), charismatic authority is a highly unstable source of organizational cohesion. Hence, the death of a leader can trigger the death of an organization.

Reversal: Concluding Imagined Futures

Given an organization's potential to provide meaning for its members, a loss of direction may not require the death or other form of exit of its leaders. It may also stem from the abandonment of a previously communicated and internalized strategy, large-scale change initiative, vision, or mission statement. Given the high failure rate of strategic change initiatives, such abandonment is a relatively common organizational phenomenon. Yet, very few studies of the aftermath of abandoning a previously communicated future exist.

Adopting a cognitive view of organization, successfully altering the strategic direction of an organization is dependent on changing organization members' interpretive schemas (Balogun and Johnson 2004; Bartunek 1984). This can be difficult in practice, as the extensive literature on resistance to change demonstrates (Val and Fuentes 2003). Given likely resistance, and members' assumed preferences for stability, abandoning change efforts would seem to be relatively unproblematic (Mantere et al. 2012).

Yet, as Mantere and colleagues (2012) have shown, such a view fails to consider the relevance of interpretive schema trajectories. Once a coherent narrative has been established it can be difficult to discard it, no matter how unpopular a particular, previously communicated change effort may have been. The cancellation of plans, targets, or other organizational objectives may trigger anxiety, cynicism, denial, and other responses from members who may feel that their efforts have been in vain, since what they have been working towards is no longer attainable. The organization's leadership team may also become associated with failure and incompetence. Naturally, this loss of a previously imagined future may also be met with relief by members who did not view it as desirable. An ending need not be interpreted as negative.

Discontinuation of Labels and Routines

Apart from removing a sense of certainty or direction, certain organizational endings may be primarily interpreted as removing potentially valued aspects of an organization's past—and therefore threaten the loss of a valued part of its identity. This loss may not require closing a site, divesting a unit, or involve the exit of the founder(s) or other leaders. It could also simply involve changing an organizations' name or other labels with which it has become associated. For example, when Daimler-Benz acquired Chrysler, the affix "Benz" was dropped as the legal entity was renamed DaimlerChrysler. When the company subsequently divested Chrysler, there were calls by several shareholders for the legal entity's name to be reverted to Daimler-Benz. As per a *New York Times* article, "[S]everal shareholders filed motions pleading for the Benz name, in one form or another," with one filing noting that "reinstating the name of one of the company's founding fathers would constitute a certain degree of compensation for the many years of frustration for the employees, particularly in the traditional Benz plants" (Landler 2007). The pleas were ultimately unsuccessful as the company was simply renamed Daimler AG.

Certain material objects, technologies, and routines may also be bound up with an organization's identity. They may therefore be kept even if they serve no direct economic purpose. For example, Piaggio refused to terminate the production of its flagship product, the Vespa scooter, even when it was no longer profitable (Ravasi and Canato 2010).

We have repeatedly referred to the potential importance of organizational identity in connection with organizational conclusions. Yet, we should also acknowledge that, for many organization members, organizational identification may be limited, especially in times and places in which life-long employment is not the norm; what may matter more to members in such situations is simply their ability to perform their everyday work (Amabile and Kramer 2007). A change may introduce uncomfortable breakdowns for organization members (Sandberg and Tsoukas 2011), such as when certain practices that they have become accustomed to are no longer possible or accepted (e.g., using fax or paper; or, for a medical practitioner, applying a certain treatment method). Even when replaced with an alternative, ending an organizational practice or a set of organizational practices may be associated with loss: Affected organization members may feel that their skills or contributions are no longer valued by, or relevant to, others; or they may feel that their interests are not being considered—that is that they are being disrespected (Grover 2014). This may give rise to seemingly irrational responses to endings. For instance, an academic who dislikes teaching a particular course—and would strongly prefer to teach another—may still attempt to resist its discontinuation if this decision is made without their consultation. In other words, feelings of loss are to some extent related to perceptions of consent: We may regret having given something up but generally only experience a sense of anger if we feel that something has been taken away from us against our will.

Project Closures

Finally, project endings are a particularly interesting case of organizational conclusion. This is because they are, by definition, time limited. Hence, in theory, their termination should not come as a surprise or be associated with loss. Yet, even planned project endings can trigger emotional responses if participants feel intimately connected to them due to their personal investments and the social bonds that may have emerged among team members. Terminating a project *before* its originally envisaged conclusion may be interpreted by those involved in its design and/or implementation as failure.

However, viewing projects as having clearly defined and expected endings is arguably simplistic. Projects routinely overrun, and this over-running and extending of originally communicated deadlines can itself become part of participants' expectations. Moreover, certain projects, such as highly ambitious organizational change initiatives, may perpetuate themselves because failure to achieve targets demands the instigation of further initiatives (Brunsson 2009; McKinley and Scherer 2000). By persuading themselves and others that complex organizational problems can be solved via relatively simple and clearly defined interventions, executives and management consultants ensure that projects that are destined to fail continue to be implemented (McGivern et al. 2018) and thus—contrary to their ostensive intentions—never end.

What is Change that Concludes

We have noted earlier that despite the seeming prevalence of conclusive change in managerial and organizational life, contemporary theorists and practitioners alike seem to shun it. Additive or cumulative change does have a nice ring to it these days. It is associated with experiences of progress, innovation, and growth, all of which tend to carry positive associations. Maintaining or continuing tends to be associated with stability, which tends to be evaluated positively in contrast to uncertainty and fragility (Chreim 2005; Sonenshein 2010). Against such ideals, we think of conclusions through such negative experiences as loss, decline, abandonment, or even death.

Yet, every change, however generative it may seem can be interpreted as "subtractive" as well as "additive". When an individual is promoted, old responsibilities are given up as new ones are endorsed. At the individual level, when experts are promoted to be managers, sustained focus on operational work begins to be regarded as "micromanagement" (Alvesson and Sveningsson 2003; Porter et al. 2004). At the organizational level, when strategic investments are made, resources are re-allocated, which almost inevitably means *de-funding* some activities to free resources for others (Barnett and Burgelman 1996), and shifting the focus of executive attention *from* old activities, as much as it means shifting it *to* new activities (Ocasio 1997). It would seem that depending on how things are framed, every change endeavor or episode, can be framed as a new beginning, continuation, or ending, or a more or less ambiguous combination of all of these.

Ontology of Concluding

Having seen the various contexts of conclusive change in the previous section, we will now turn to the task of defining what we mean by conclusive change. To provide a more solid definition, we turn to ontology, the branch of philosophy that examines existence and being.

What happens when something changes? In post-Platonic Western mainstream thought, change is conceived through *things*: the properties of things and relations between things; some draw a distinction between object- and process-based ontologies, where the Western mainstream thought is conceived as the first kind. In an object-based, post-Platonic ontology, if a change happens to object A, we tend to think of some property being deducted from A or added to A. Change may also mean a relation between two or several parties: if John and Wes fall in love, a new relation is brought to existence between the two of them. In his now classic paper "On what there is," philosopher Willard van Orman Quine (1948) defined "being" as "being the value of a bound variable." This implies that existence is found in sometimes complex entities, the complexity of which can be understood by virtue of which properties they carry; that is which variables are bound to them. To say that something "is" is to say some often complex object has a property, or that a relation exists between several such objects. In this view, to say

"the night is dark and full of terrors",

is to attach two properties: the one-place predicates

dark(x)

and

full of terrors(x)

to the complex object "night" so that

"*dark(night)* AND *full of terrors(night)*."

To say

"*John and Wes are married*,"

on the other hand, is to attribute a two-place, symmetrical and reciprocal relation

married(x,y)

with the individuals so that

"*married(John, Wes)*".

From this perspective, concluding something is one of four possible types of taking an action, that is, having an impact in the world by ceasing the existence of something (a complex entity, or some of its properties or relations with other entities). Separating two organizations, for instance, is an action of the form

"*same organization(x, y)* T NOT-*same organization*(x,y),"

that is, ending the existence of the relation "same organization(x,y)." The capital letter T denotes a transformation of one state of affairs into another through some agency. The other three forms of action are creating (bringing something that did not exist into existence), maintaining (keeping something in existence), and suppressing (keeping something in inexistence) (von Wright 1963).

The variety of phenomena that we saw in the previous section is explained by the range of changes that involve ending a significant property, a set of properties, or a relation. Conclusive change can end an entity, one or some of its aspects, or one or some of the relations it has with other entities.

Conceived in such terms, conclusive organizational change may mean anything from the conclusion of a temporary work contract to the adjourning of a team or a committee; from a strategic business exit (Burgelman 1994) to the bankruptcy or discontinuation of an entire organization. Conclusive change sometimes even takes place at the level of entire states or countries. While there are famous examples of states vanishing through military conquest or gradual decline, such as the Roman Empire, the decision by the Allied Forces to end the Prussian State at the conclusion of World War II is a clear example of conclusive change, which stands in symmetric comparison with the creation of the United Nations in the same year of 1945.

Process Ontology and Conclusive Change

From the Western, post-Platonic perspective, it is likely that all change endeavors in organizations will involve some elements of conclusion, as well as elements of all three other forms of action: suppressing undesired changes, maintaining continuity, starting new things, concluding old things.

The conception toward concluding would change dramatically, however, if we were to view it from the viewpoint of process ontology. Eschewing the platonic heritage where existence is regarded through objects as well as their properties and relations, process ontology conceives of reality as consisting of processes which are by nature dynamic (Tsoukas and Chia 2002). Concluding and starting lose much of their significance in this context. While change agents may announce many openings and maybe even a few closings, this happens in the contexts of an organization that is by nature shifting, in a state of flux (Hernes 2014). Agency that maintains stability becomes even more central to management and organizing than that which seeks change (Tsoukas and Chia 2002). We are also mentioning the process perspective as we find it contains many openings for understanding how conclusive change might be managed. We shall return to it in the Conclusion of this chapter, where we discuss how conclusions should be approached from a practical perspective.

Why Do We Tend To Ignore Or Avoid Concluding?

There is a puzzling asymmetry in how we think about beginnings and endings in theorizing organizational change. Beginning a new activity seems to be equated with "gaining" whereas concluding an activity seems to be equated with "losing." Considering that the experience of impermanence characterizes contemporary organizational experience (Weick 2009), and project-based work is a common experience even among workers under stable employment, this seems odd. One would think that ending a project would be no different than starting a new one. And, surely the conclusion of practices can be as much a source of hope as beginning new ones.

Why does the asymmetry exist between additive and subtractive change processes, or creative and conclusive change? There are several places to look for an answer. The first answer lies in psychology, human biases, and asymmetries in orienting towards beginnings and endings, risks, and opportunities. The second answer lies in organizational processes which seek to consolidate rather than conclude. The third lies at the macroscopic level, in institutionalized conceptions regarding the life of an autonomous individual, as well as conceptions of economic growth. The fourth and final answer lies in management fashion (Abrahamson 1996), which currently favors covert use of power and positive thinking.

Psychological Conditions

Several psychological mechanisms point to the asymmetry between starting and concluding change. Loss aversion (Tversky and Kahneman 1991) predicts that actors are likely to minimize potential loss over focusing on potential gains. In terms of organizational change, it is therefore not surprising that change agents would expect more resistance toward communication that is open about both subtractive as well as additive aspects of change, as opposed to communication that downplays the subtractive part.

Loss aversion raises a question about resistance to conclusive change. If we assume that organizational members are likely to be more resistant to conclusive changes rather than additive ones, then how do we conceive of the relationship between loss and conclusion? Does conclusive change necessarily involve loss, and consequently, resistance?

This relationship can be conceived in several ways. Perhaps the simplest is to focus on material interests. Critical literature on resistance to change (e.g., Ford et al. 2008) has noted that resistance to change cannot be regarded as a pathology to be overcome; change often acts againts the genuine interests of stakeholders and resistance is natural. Rather than as a matter of clearer or more convincing communication, or as a matter of more effective management, resistance should be conceived as negotiation where interests are re-aligned. Resistance can also point towards problems in the direction of change that have not been conceived by its architects, and can thus enhance the quality of both decisions and change outcomes.

The critical conception, as presented above at least, regards change recipients as rational promoters of their own interests. Once we relax the expectation of rationality, several further reasons for resistance toward conclusive change appear. Conclusions interact with emotional attachments, and significant losses tend to trigger avoidance behaviors (Smith 2006). Foundational losses such as organizational death may even trigger processes of grief and mourning (Bell and Taylor 2016).

Organizational Conditions

Organizations also tend to favor beginning new things rather than ending old ones; we hinted at this in Royer's (2003) call for "exit champions" in the Introduction. One reason for this is that overturning previous commitments may signal failure, which is hard to accept. There are two prominent explanations for organizational failure: previous success or previous failure (Mellahi and Wilkinson 2004). Successful organizations find it hard to give up on activities that they built their businesses on, despite the need for strategic change. Prominent examples range from Intel's struggles to exit the memory business (Burgelman 1994) to Nokia's failure to replace its mobile phones business (Vuori and Huy 2016). Miller (1991) has coined the term "Icarus paradox" to address situations where an organization starts to act as if it was afraid of change in fear of losing touch with its past successes. Flying too close to success can be a source of an organization's downfall. Conversely, admitting failure may lead to escalation of commitment to poor investments in fear of not accepting sunk costs (Staw 1981).

Both processes may also be amplified by visionary leadership which seeks to establish collective faith in new change endeavors (Kotter 1995). Visionary leadership builds collective faith on yet unproven lines of action, and once established, conflicting evidence will be harder to process (Royer 2003).

An even more foundational issue may lie in the very constitution of a business firm. Once a firm is established, it becomes a legal person, and the role of its governors is to promote its continued existence and flourishing (Bakan 2005). That is, even though most firms exist to deliver profits to shareholders, there seem to be few situations where the board decides to end the firm's existence, sell the firm's assets, pay severance packages to employees, and return the money to shareholders (Nielsen and Sarasvathy 2018). The governors of the firm are tasked to act in the interests of the firm rather than its shareholders, and while serving shareholders is certainly a crucial interest for a firm, its own survival may be even more fundamental.

Socio-Economic Conditions

A further driver for our dismissal of conclusive aspects of change may be found in the very project of capitalism, where stable employment acts as a significant governance mechanism. In many parts of the Western world, permanent work contracts are incentivized by legislators, and firms play a crucial role in providing a basis for stable life projects: providing life trajectories and self-respect, as well as a financial foundation for supporting families (Giddens 1991; Sennett 1999). As a result, the creation of X new jobs is rarely seen to be symmetrical to the conclusion of X jobs. The project of capitalism is also founded on the notion of continuous economic growth which drives growth expectations toward firms.

More recently, positive thinking and positive rhetoric have become defining characteristics of post-millennial management fashion (Cederström and Spicer 2014). Personal happiness, physical and mental wellness, and mindfulness are lauded as bases for meaningful work and good performance. While notions of individual purpose and leadership through cultivation of meaning can be traced back to such classics as Selznick (1949) and McGregor (1960), contemporary managers are encouraged to focus on the positive. Strategic change is communicated through ambiguity-by-design rather than clear messages of discontinuing (Gioia and Chittipeddi 1991). Employees are warned of performance problems by asking if they are *happy* at their work; with the implication that their performance could be an indication that they might be *happier* or more fulfilled elsewhere. Collinson (2012) has coined the term "Prozac leadership" to identify this trend.

Concluding Remarks: *How* Should We Approach Concluding?

We have discussed the various forms and contexts of conclusive change, traced its definition to a Western, object-based ontology where stability is the norm and change is the exception, and discussed the root causes why change theory and practice tends to disregard conclusive aspects of change. The final task ahead of us is to reflect on how these insights should inform the practice of conclusive change.

Avoiding or Managing Loss?

In managing conclusions, it would seem that the potential of *loss* is a significant consideration, that is, is the discontinuation of something that exists going to be experienced as a loss in the first place, and if yes, how this experience should be managed. One way to manage the risk of a conclusion being regarded as a loss is sensegiving (Gioia and Chittipeddi 1991). Change agents may seek to balance new directions with narratives that emphasize continuity with the organization's past (Sonenshein 2010), rooting new directions in a continuous historical development (Chreim 2005). Some managers may even deliberately brush over problematic or painful aspects of change; a practice called "sensehiding" (Monin et al. 2012). Seeking to downplay the loss interpretation of conclusion may border on dishonesty, and in some cases may not be possible due to the circumstances of change; in Mantere et al. (2012), the temporary CEO of the organization facing a canceled merger sought to reframe the cancellation as a fortunate escape from takeover—a strategy that backfired.

Another, much less explored strategy is to accept the loss aspects of change and manage the feelings involved in processing such loss. While there used to be an extensive discussion about tackling "resistance to change," following Lewin's classical idea of "unfreezing" (see Schein 1996), few practical accounts address the sense of loss involved in concluding. One approach is Schein's (1999) process consultation. Change is accomplished by helping the client to identify the problem that necessitates change, which helps consolidate the needs to overcome the forces of stasis that lead to resistance. While this in itself does not do away with the sense of loss, it should at least help make some sense of it.

The one model which explicitly addresses the sense of loss as a natural part of change is Bridges' (1986) framework for change as a process of transition. Bridges conceives of change as a three-phase transition, where a stage of letting go is followed by a transitional stage, concluded by an experience of a new beginning. The emotions experienced in the first stage include disenchantment, dislocation, and disidentification, sentiments that detach the subject from the old reality in anticipation of the transition. Bridges' framework suggests that a "neutral zone" follows the stage of letting go. This is experienced as disorienting and troubling by change recipients, echoing what Corley and

Gioia (2004) label as "a meaning void" that preceeds a strategic change. This period also sees nascent discovery that lays the groundwork of the final period of a new beginning.

Bridges suggests that the experiences of loss can be facilitated by various means. Interest-based losses can be addressed with negotiations, while loss of meaning requires what many organizational scholars have labeled sensemaking (Gioia and Chittipeddi 1991; Mantere et al. 2012). If loss of attachments is key, Bridges draws inspiration from the role of rites of passage as facilitators of transitions, and suggests collective rituals as facilitators of emotional labor. Finally, if the loss involves previously valued competences, then training is what is needed.

The two positions: one seeking to minimize experiences of loss during conclusions and the other seeking to acknowledge and manage such emotions seem to offer at least partially conflicting advice. Bridges' approach, rooted in psychodynamic theory (e.g. Bowlby 1998) accepts and embraces the emotional nature of organizational life, while more strategic approaches to change seem to be more suspicious of emotion. This is indeed a somewhat thorny issue, as one danger with a focus on emotion is to treat change agents as strategically rational and change recipients as emotional and resistant (Ford et al. 2008). This runs the risk of sending employees to grief counseling rather than acknowledging their rational concerns about conclusions (Bell and Taylor 2011). That said, Bridges does not promote such simplistic attitudes, and it would seem that an open approach to regulating emotions of loss in change management might be well worth reviving.

Liminality and Rites of Passage

There are institutional practices designed to facilitate transitions, but which have not been recognized by models of change. In traditional socieeties that conceived of an individual's life span as a series of fixed roles, life transitions were facilitated by collectively performed rites of passage. Rituals help facilitate life transitions and other events where social tensions are enlightened; transitioning from, say, childhood to adulthood involves loss as well as gain. Social tension arises from the individual's loss, but also from the risks accepted by the community in granting adulthood rights and responsibilities to an untested individual. Rites of passage often involve trials and other difficulties that initiates have to pass or at least endure (Bell 2009).

Another important aspect of life transitions in traditional societies is the notion of liminality, the "in-between-ness" that is experienced by individuals transitioning from one life stage to the next. In medieval craft guilds, graduating novices needed to become "journeymen," leaving their hometown to practice their craft elsewhere before they could become masters. In some tribal societies, youths are placed in a tent separated from the rest of the community to facilitate their preparation towards adulthood. Such periods of liminality provide the time necessary to prepare for transitions, processing the losses and gains of change (Bell 2009).

Periods of liminality are conducive of identity work, as individuals examine their self-narratives and explore new roles and new ways of being. Identity work itself is ongoing; as Weick (1995: 20) put it, the: "sensemaker is himself or herself an ongoing puzzle undergoing continual redefinition, coincident with presenting *some* self to others and trying to decide which self is appropriate." While liminality is in this sense an enduring aspect of identity (Daskalaki et al. 2016), explicit or even designed liminal periods do help individuals in experimenting with new social identities, as well as to reflect, question, and repair identity narratives towards personal renewal (Beech 2011; Mantere and Whittington 2020).

Contemporary organizations are certainly no strangers to the practice of ceremonies and rituals (Meyer and Rowan 1977). Rites of passage which acknowledge and dramatize the loss and rebirth involved in conclusions might well be worth exploring as parts of change management practice. Acknowledging personal and collective loss through the explicit performance of a ritual has the potential of managing the loss aspects of change. Designing liminal periods with loosely defined role expectations in career transition moments or reflective periods during those episodes in change processes where conclusions take place—Bridges suggests that these are often early parts of change processes—should help stakeholders process their losses and explore potential gains.

Back in Time: Shifting to a Process Ontology

Does change, conclusive or otherwise, need to be conceived in negative terms? Drawing on the metaphor of musical experience, where shifting dialectics of tension and resolution are not a source of discomfort but rather the basis of artistic experience, Mantere et al. (2007) explored the possibility of organizational members enjoying change. While all change cannot be a source of enjoyment, this perspective does raise the question of how general the expectation of loss should be in conclusive change. Looking into psychodynamic theory, for instance, a feeling of stability and non-change is endemic to a deep sense of hopelessness which is central to the experience of depression.

From this perspective, the type of object-based ontology that much change theory and practice endorses may be a root cause for the bitterness in conclusion experiences. A process-oriented ontology (Chapter 27 by Hernes et al. in this volume), on the other hand, has less use for the categories of starting and concluding. From the psychodynamic viewpoint, an experience of continuous change can be an experience of continuous growth and development which in many ways are antithetical to the experience of depression. Hernes et al. suggest that while individuals experience change in the moment as a continous experience, they make time actionable by structuring past and present into episodes and events. The appreciation of process ontology does not necessarily mean abandoning episode-based views of change.

Much of the practical relevance of the processual view when it comes to endings in particular lies in its impact in providing the subjective experience of *control* over one's circumstances (Giddens 1991). Our interest in conclusive change was sparked by two empirical projects. In a study of a cancelled merger in a Finnish governmental organization (Mantere et al. 2012), we saw an organization enter a crisis after the cancellation of a proposed merger. The staff had intitially resisted a merger, but had been convinced that it was a natural step forward for the organization and that the present organizational form was not sustainable for the long haul. An abrupt cancellation that was caused by a shift in legislation resulted in widespread cynicism and de-identification with the organization by staff members who had previously viewed their employer in overall positive terms. The second study (Wiedner and Mantere 2019) also had a negative outcome. A public organization within the framework of the UK National Health Service, was separated into two organizations in an effort to institute a purchaser–provider model, where the provider organization could be ultimately seen to start competing with other (public and private) service-providing organizations. The architects of the separation intended to "put clear water" between the two organizations to accomplish a clear boundary between them, which resulted in an escalation of disrespect and distress between the two parties, ultimately resulting in the failure of the entire separation.

Both cases have a common element, which also seems implied in many of the discussions above. This common element is a sense of control over a conclusion. The two parties of the NHS organization would have needed a period of processing the separation before they could reach autonomy as new organizational entities. A part of this was a matter of understanding how existing practices could be disentangled and new roles formulated, but another part was to accept the separation at an emotional level. In the Finnish case, the seeming paradox of staff who were basically content with their old organizational form becoming disillusioned with it after the abrupt cancellation can also be addressed by looking at the breach of a sense of control by the sudden cancellation.

A key consideration with managing a conclusion experience in a manner that allows for an element of control to stakeholders is *time* (see Hernes et al. in this volume). Change has rhythms (Albert and Bell 2002; Mintzberg and Huy 2003) which structure and syncronize action (Granqvist and Gustafsson 2015). Building on our discussion of liminality above, pacing change episodes to allow time for the processing of conclusions, and slowing down the pace of change during those episodes seems central. Another useful element is the accomplishment of collective rhythm, which makes change predictable to participants.

In this sense, time may become a resource that allows stakeholders to prepare and respond. Anticipating a (potential) cancellation or termination well ahead of time enables coming to terms with the ending, as well as directing efforts to other endeavors. Yet, the perception of having ample time to prepare for an ending can also inhibit preparatory efforts due to a lack of perceived urgency (Granqvist and Gustafsson 2015). Alternatively, being aware of an ending well in advance can also be debilitating. As we have noted above, we sometimes prefer not to imagine or accept that something we have become accustomed to will end. Confronting such an inevitable conclusion can enable better decision-making but it may also generate an overwhelming amount of anxiety. On the other hand, studies have shown that organizational performance may actually increase in the dying days of an organization or organizational unit as its remaining members either seek to signal their worth through hard work to other employers or develop a strong identity that increases motivation in the face of adversity (Hansson and Wigblad 2006).

Finally, with regard to timing, it is important to be aware that endings do not occur in a vacuum and that there are times when it may be relatively easy or difficult to manage a conclusion. On the one hand, the objects to be concluded may have a more or less natural lifespan or be associated with certain longevity expectations. Delaying attempts to enact a conclusion, such as terminating a project, so as to avoid relevant stakeholders interpreting them as premature, may limit resistance. But waiting too long may contribute to additional inertia.

On the other hand, organizational routines, projects, units, inter-organizational relationships, and organizational entities are often connected to many other objects. Given the many (potentially unanticipated) consequences, timing an ending—just like timing a beginning, such as a product launch—is an important skill. In much of the management and innovation literature, the importance of timing with respect to endings suggests that organizations are often too slow to abandon old routines or technologies, inhibiting their ability to adapt to changing circumstances. A classic example is the apparent reluctance by analog film and camera producers to abandon analog technology (Lucas and Goh 2009). Yet, there is an increasing realization that patience can also be a virtue and that keeping certain processes alive, rather than eliminating them, may generate value in the future—as the increased popularity of analog and craft-based objects and activities demonstrates (Ocejo 2017; Sax 2017). Hence, quickly and effectively managing a conclusion may eliminate potential gains arising from efforts to keep something alive.

Eternal Return

"You can't improvise on nothing man; you've gotta improvise on something," jazz legend Charles Mingus once said. We have reached the end of our paper about endings. We have looked at where conclusions take place, what they are, why we tend to avoid them, and finally, how they should be managed. We hope to have said something novel, but probably all our arguments can be traced back to what scholars before us have written. What we have done is to focus on a less explored topic and brought together existing resources to make sense of this domain.

As a final thought that may perhaps also be attributed to process philosophy is the idea of cyclicality in time, and the idea of eternal return. Organizations, careers, and practices revisit aspects of their past and are reborn into other organizations. New things are combinations of things that used to exist; creation is recombination as much as it is destruction. While all things will eventually end, they will also return.

References

Abrahamson, E. (1996), 'Management Fashion', *Academy of Management Review*, 21/1, 254–85.

Albert, S. (1992), 'The Algebra of Change', in B.M. Staw and L. L. Cummings, eds., *Research in Organizational Behavior* (Vol. 14) (Greenwich, Conn: JAI), 179–229.

Albert, S., and Bell, G. G. (2002), 'Timing and Music', *Academy of Management Review*, 27/4, 574–93.

Alvesson, M., and Sveningsson, S. (2003), 'The Great Disappearing Act: Difficulties in Doing "Leadership"', *The Leadership Quarterly*, 14/3, 359–81.

Amabile, T. M., and Kramer, S. J. (2007), 'Inner Work Life', *Harvard Business Review*, 85/5, 72–83.

Bakan, J. (2005), *The Corporation: The Pathological Pursuit of Profit and Power* (new edition) Robinson Publishing.

Balogun, J., and Johnson, G. (2004), 'Organizational Restructuring and Middle Manager Sensemaking', *The Academy of Management Journal*, 47/4, 523–49.

Barnett, W. P., and Burgelman, R. A. (1996), 'Evolutionary Perspectives on Strategy', *Strategic Management Journal*, 17(S1), 5–19.

Bartunek, J. M. (1984), 'Changing Interpretive Schemes and Organizational Restructuring: The Example of a Religious Order', *Administrative Science Quarterly*, 29/3, 355–72.

Beech, N. (2011), 'Liminality and the Practices of Identity Reconstruction', *Human Relations*, 64/2, 285–302.

Bell, C. (2009), *Ritual: Perspectives and Dimensions Revised Edition* (reissue edition) (New York: Oxford University Press).

Bell, E. (2012), 'Ways of Seeing Organisational Death: A Critical Semiotic Analysis of Organisational Memorialisation', *Visual Studies*, 27/1, 4–17.

Bell, E., and Taylor, S. (2011), 'Beyond Letting Go and Moving On: New Perspectives on Organizational Death, Loss and Grief', *Scandinavian Journal of Management*, 27/1, 1–10.

Bell, E., and Taylor, S. (2016), 'Vernacular Mourning and Corporate Memorialization in Framing the Death of Steve Jobs', *Organization*, 23/1, 114–32.

Bowlby, D. F. J. M. (1998), *Separation: Anxiety and Anger: Attachment and loss* (Vol. 2) Pimlico.

Bridges, W. (1986), 'Managing Organizational Transitions', *Organizational Dynamics*, 15/1, 24–33.

Brunsson, N. (2009), *Reform as Routine: Organizational Change and Stability in the Modern World* (Oxford: Oxford University Press).

Brunsson, N., and Sahlin-Andersson, K. (2000), Constructing Organizations: The Example of Public Sector Reform', *Organization Studies*, 21/4, 721–46.

Bryman, A. (1993), 'Charismatic Leadership in Business Organizations: Some Neglected Issues', *The Leadership Quarterly*, 4/3, 289–304.

Burgelman, R. A. (1994), 'Fading Memories: A Process Theory of Strategic Business Exit in Dynamic Environments', *Administrative Science Quarterly*, 39/1, 24–56.

Cederström, C., and Spicer, A. (2014), *The Wellness Syndrome* (1st edn) (Polity Press).

Chreim, S. (2005), 'The Continuity–Change Duality in Narrative Texts of Organizational Identity', *Journal of Management Studies*, 42/3, 567–93.

Collinson, D. (2012), 'Prozac Leadership and the Limits of Positive Thinking', *Leadership*, 8/2, 87–107.

Corley, K. G., and Gioia, D. A. (2004), 'Identity ambiguity and change in the wake of a corporate spin-off', *Administrative Science Quarterly*, 49/2, 173–208.

Daepp, M. I. G., Hamilton, M. J., West, G. B., and Bettencourt, L. M. A. (2015), The Mortality of Companies', *Journal of The Royal Society Interface*, 12/106, 20, 150, 120.

Daskalaki, M., Butler, C. L., and Petrovic, J. (2016), Somewhere in-between: Narratives of Place, Identity, and Translocal Work', *Journal of Management Inquiry*, 25/2, 184–98.

Datta, D. K., and Grant, J. H. (1990), 'Relationships Between Type of Acquisition, The Autonomy Given to the Acquired Firm, and Acquisition Success: An Empirical Analysis', *Journal of Management*, 16/1, 29–44.

Do, B., Lyle, M. C. B., and Walsh, I. J. (2019), 'Driving down Memory Lane: The Influence of Memories in a Community Following Organizational Demise', *Organization Studies*, 40/9, 1307–29.

Emirbayer, M., and Johnson, V. (2008), 'Bourdieu and Organizational Analysis', *Theory and Society*, 37/1, 1–44.

Fairhurst, G. T., Cooren, F., and Cahill, D. J. (2002), 'Discursiveness, Contradiction, and Unintended Consequences in Successive Downsizings', *Management Communication Quarterly*, 15/4, 501–40.

Ferriani, S., Garnsey, E., and Lorenzoni, G. (2012), 'Continuity and Change in a Spin-Off Venture: The Process of Reimprinting', *Industrial and Corporate Change*, 21/4, 1011–48.

Ford, J. D., Ford, L. W., and D'Amelio, A. (2008), 'Resistance to Change: The Rest of the Story', *Academy of Management Review*, 33/2, 362–77.

Freeman, J., Carroll, G. R., and Hannan, M. T. (1983), 'The Liability of Newness: Age Dependence in Organizational Death Rates', *American Sociological Review*, 48/5, 692–710,

Gersick, C. (1991), 'Revolutionary Change Theories—A Multilevel Exploration of the Punctuated Equilibrium Paradigm', *Academy of Management Review*, 16/1, 10–36.

Giddens, A. (1991), *Modernity and Self-identity: Self and Society in the Late Modern Age* (Polity Press).

Ginter, P. M., Swayne, L. E., Duncan, W. J., and Gordon Shelfer, A. (1992), 'When Merger Means Death: Organizational Euthanasia and Strategic Choice', *Organizational Dynamics*, 20/3, 21–33.

Gioia, D. A., and Chittipeddi, K. (1991), 'Sensemaking and Sensegiving in Strategic Change Initiation', *Strategic Management Journal*, 12/6, 433–48.

Gioia, D. A., Nag, R., and Corley, K. G. (2012), 'Visionary Ambiguity and Strategic Change: The Virtue of Vagueness in Launching Major Organizational Change', *Journal of Management Inquiry*, 21/4, 364–75.

Granqvist, N., and Gustafsson, R. (2015), 'Temporal Institutional Work', *Academy of Management Journal*, 59/3, 1009–35.

Grover, S. L. (2014), 'Unraveling Respect in Organization Studies', *Human Relations*, 67/1, 27–51.

Hannan, M. T., and Freeman, J. (1988), 'The Ecology of Organizational Mortality: American Labor Unions, 1836–985', *American Journal of Sociology*, 94/1, 25–52.

Hansson, M., and Wigblad, R. (2006), Pyrrhic Victories—Anticipating the Closedown Effect', *The International Journal of Human Resource Management*, 17/5, 938–58.

Harris, S. G., and Sutton, R. I. (1986), 'Functions of Parting Ceremonies in Dying Organizations', *The Academy of Management Journal*, 29/1, 5–30.

Havila, V., Medlin, C. J., and Salmi, A. (2013), 'Project-Ending Competence in Premature Project Closures', *International Journal of Project Management*, 31/1, 90–9.

Heracleous, L. (2004), 'Boundaries in the Study of Organization', *Human Relations*, 57/1, 95–103.

Hernes, T. (2014), *A Process Theory of Organization* (Oxford: Oxford University Press).

Hernes, T., Hussenot, A., and Pulk, A. (2021), 'Time and Temporality of Change Processes: Applying an Event-Based View to Integrate Episodic and Continuous Change', in M. S. Poole and A. H. Van de Ven, eds., *The Oxford Handbook of Organizational Change and Innovation* (Oxford: Oxford University Press).

Hernes, T., and Paulsen, N. (2003), 'Introduction: Boundaries and Organization', in N. Paulsen and T. Hernes, eds., *Managing Boundaries in Organizations: Multiple Perspectives* (Palgrave Macmillan), 1–13.

Kellogg, K. C. (2011), *Challenging Operations: Medical Reform And Resistance In Surgery* (Chicago: University of Chicago Press).

Kotter, J. P. (1995), 'Leading Change: Why Transformation Efforts Fail', *Harvard Business Review*, 73/2, 59–67.

Landler, M. (2007, October 5). 'From Now On, It's Just Plain Daimler', *The New York Times*.

Lewin, K. (1947), 'Frontiers in Group Dynamics: Concept, Method and Reality in Social Science; Social Equilibria and Social Change', *Human Relations*, 1/1, 5–41.

Lucas, H. C., and Goh, J. M. (2009), 'Disruptive Technology: How Kodak Missed the Digital Photography Revolution', *The Journal of Strategic Information Systems*, 18/1, 46–55.

Macdonald, V. (2011, January 19), 'NHS Reforms Signal Biggest Changes in Health Service History', Channel 4 News.

Mantere, S., Schildt, H., and Sillince, J. (2012), 'Reversal of Strategic Change', *Academy of Management Journal*, 55/1, 173–96.

Mantere, S., Sillince, J. A. A., and Hämäläinen, V. (2007), 'Music as a Metaphor for Organizational Change', *Journal of Organizational Change Management*, 20/3, 447–59.

Mantere, S. and Whittington, R. (2020), 'Becoming a Strategist: The Roles of Strategy Discourse and Ontological Security in Managerial Identity Work', *Strategic Organization*. 9/2, 136–62.

McGivern, G., Dopson, S., Ferlie, E., Fischer, M., Fitzgerald, L., Ledger, J., and Bennett, C. (2018), 'The Silent Politics of Temporal Work: A Case Study of a Management Consultancy Project to Redesign Public Health Care', *Organization Studies*, 39/8, 1007–30.

McGregor, D. (1960), *The Human Side of Enterprise* (New York: McGraw-Hill).

McKinley, W., and Scherer, A. G. (2000), 'Some Unanticipated Consequences of Organizational Restructuring', *The Academy of Management Review*, 25/4, 735–52.

Mellahi, K., and Wilkinson, A. (2004), 'Organizational Failure: A Critique of Recent Research and a Proposed Integrative Framework', *International Journal of Management Reviews*, 5–6/1, 21–41.

Meyer, J. W., and Rowan, B. (1977), 'Institutionalized Organizations: Formal Structure as Myth and Ceremony', *American Journal of Sociology*, 83/2, 340–63.

Miller, D. (1991), *The Icarus Paradox: How Exceptional Companies Bring About Their Own Downfall* (new edition) (New York: HarperBusiness).

Mintzberg, H. (1985), 'The Organization as Political Arena', *Journal of Management Studies*, 22/2, 133–54.

Mintzberg, H., and Huy, Q. N. (2003), 'The Rhythm of Change', *MIT Sloan Management Review*.

Monin, P., Noorderhaven, N., Vaara, E., and Kroon, D. (2012), 'Giving Sense to and Making Sense of Justice in Postmerger Integration', *Academy of Management Journal*, 56/1, 256–84.

Moschieri, C. (2011), 'The Implementation and Structuring of Divestitures: The Unit's Perspective', *Strategic Management Journal*, 32/4, 368–401.

Nielsen, K., and Sarasvathy, S. D. (2018), 'Exit Perspective on Entrepreneurship', in R. V. Turcan and N. M. Fraser, eds., *The Palgrave Handbook of Multidisciplinary Perspectives on Entrepreneurship* (Uitgever: Springer International Publishing), 223–45.

Ocasio, W. (1997), 'Towards an Attention-Based View of the Firm', *Strategic Management Journal*, 18, 187–206.

Ocejo, R. (2017), *Masters of Craft: Old Jobs in the New Urban Economy* (Princeton, NJ: Princeton University Press.

Porter, M. E., Lorsch, J. W., and Nohria, N. (2004, October 1), 'Seven Surprises for New CEOs' *Harvard Business Review*.

Quine, W. V. (1948) 'On What There Is', *The Review of Metaphysics*, 2/5, 21–38. JSTOR.

Ravasi, D., and Canato, A. (2010), 'We Are What We Do (and How We Do It): Organizational Technologies and the Construction of Organizational Identity', in P. Nelson, S. Graham , and G. Dorothy, eds., *Technology and Organization: Essays in Honour of Joan Woodward* (Vol. 29) (Bingley: Emerald Group Publishing Limited), 49–78.

Reckwitz, A. (2002), 'Toward a Theory of Social Practices A Development in Culturalist Theorizing', *European Journal of Social Theory*, 5/2, 243–63.

Royer, I. (2003, February 1), 'Why Bad Projects Are So Hard to Kill', *Harvard Business Review*, https://hbr.org/2003/02/why-bad-projects-are-so-hard-to-kill/, accessed 1 October 2020.

Sandberg, J., and Tsoukas, H. (2011), 'Grasping the Logic of Practice: Theorizing through Practical Rationality', *Academy of Management Review*, 36/2, 338–60.

Santos, F. M., and Eisenhardt, K. M. (2005), 'Organizational Boundaries and Theories of Organization', *Organization Science*, 16/5, 491–508.

Sax, D. (2017). *The Revenge of Analog: Real Things and Why They Matter* (reprint edition). PublicAffairs.

Schatzki, T. R. (2005), 'The Sites of Organizations', *Organization Studies*, 26/3, 465–84.

Schein, E. H. (1996), 'Kurt Lewin's Change Theory in the Field and in the Classroom: Notes toward a Model of Managed Learning', *Systems Practice*, 9/1, 27–47.

Schein, E. H. (1999), *Process Consultation Revisited: Building the Helping Relationship* (01 edition) (Reading, Mass: Addison Wesley).

Selznick, P. (1949), *TVA and the Grass Roots: A Study in the Sociology of Formal Organization* (Berkeley and Los Angeles: University of California Press).

Sennett, R. (1999). *The Corrosion of Character: The Personal Consequences of Work in the New Capitalism* (new edition) (W. W. Norton and Company).

Sheppard, J. P. (1994), 'Strategy and Bankruptcy: An Exploration into Organizational Death', *Journal of Management*, 20/4, 795–833.

Smith, W. (2006), 'Organizing Death: Remembrance and Re-collection', *Organization*, 13/2, 225–44.

Sonenshein, S. (2010), 'We're Changing—or Are We? Untangling the Role of Progressive, Regressive, and Stability Narratives During Strategic Change Implementation', *Academy of Management Journal*, 53/3, 477–512.

Staw, Barry M. (1981), 'The Escalation of Commitment To a Course of Action', *Academy of Management Review*, 6/4, 577–87.

Stubbart, C. I., and Knight, M. B. (2006), 'The Case of the Disappearing Firms: Empirical Evidence and Implications', *Journal of Organizational Behavior*, 27/1, 79–100.

Sutton, E., Pemberton, S., Fahmy, E., and Tamiya, Y. (2014), 'Stigma, Shame and the Experience of Poverty in Japan and the United Kingdom', *Social Policy and Society*, 13/1, 143–54.

Sutton, R. I. (1987), 'The Process of Organizational Death: Disbanding and Reconnecting', *Administrative Science Quarterly*, 32/4, 542–69.

Tourish, D., and Pinnington, A. (2002), 'Transformational Leadership, Corporate Cultism and the Spirituality Paradigm: An Unholy Trinity in the Workplace?' *Human Relations*, 55/2, 147–72.

Tsoukas, H., and Chia, R. (2002), 'On Organizational Becoming: Rethinking Organizational Change', *Organization Science*, 13/5, 567–82.

Turnbaugh, P. J., Ley, R. E., Hamady, M., Fraser-Liggett, C. M., Knight, R., and Gordon, J. I. (2007), 'The Human Microbiome Project', *Nature*, 449/7164, 804–10.

Tversky, A., and Kahneman, D. (1991), 'Loss Aversion in Riskless Choice: A Reference-Dependent Model', *The Quarterly Journal of Economics*, 106/4, 1039–61.

Val, M. P. del, and Fuentes, C. M. (2003), 'Resistance to Change: A Literature Review and Empirical Study', *Management Decision*, 41/2, 148–55.

Van de Ven,A. H., and Poole, M. S. (2021) 'Introduction: Central Issues in the Study of Organizational Change and Innovation', in M. S. Poole and A. H. Van de Ven, eds., *The Oxford Handbook of Organizational Change and Innovation* (Oxford: Oxford University Press).

von Wright, G. H. (1963), *Norm and Action: A Logical Enquiry*' (New York: Routledge and Kegan Paul).

Vuori, T. O., and Huy, Q. N. (2016), 'Distributed Attention and Shared Emotions in the Innovation Process: How Nokia Lost the Smartphone Battle', *Administrative Science Quarterly*, 61/1, 9–51.

Walsh, I. J., Pazzaglia, F., and Ergene, E. (2019), 'Loyal after the End: Understanding Organizational Identification in the Wake of Failure', *Human Relations*, 72/2, 163–87.

Walter, S. G., Heinrichs, S., and Walter, A. (2014), 'Parent Hostility and Spin-Out Performance', *Strategic Management Journal*, 35/13, 2031–42.

Weber, M., 1864–920. (1979), *Economy and Society: An Outline of Interpretive Sociology* (Berkeley: University of California Press).

Weick, K. 1995. *Sensemaking in Organizations*. London: Sage.

Weick, K. E. (2009), *The Impermanent Organization* (Chichester, UK: Wiley.
Wiedner, R., and Ansari, S. (2020), 'Collaborative Uncoupling: How to Break Up and Stay Together', in H. Berends and J. Sydow, eds., *Managing Inter-Organizational Collaborations* (Vol. 64) (Emerald Group Publishing Limited), 185–210.
Wiedner, R., and Mantere, S. (2019), 'Cutting the Cord: Mutual Respect, Organizational Autonomy, and Independence in Organizational Separation Processes', *Administrative Science Quarterly*, 64/3, 659–93.
Wittgenstein, L. (1958), *Philosophical Investigations* (2nd ed) (Oxford: Blackwell).

CHAPTER 31

THEORIES OF ORGANIZATIONAL CHANGE AS ASSEMBLAGES

MARSHALL SCOTT POOLE AND ANDREW H. VAN DE VEN

A famous image in Renaissance art shows a man peeping through the shell of the stars and planets to discern the glorious order behind their complex movements. What he sees is not a simple clockwork, but a dazzling manifold of spirits, and mechanisms that realize the will of these spirits. Sometimes the order beneath complexity—while more illuminating than the surface—is itself complex and difficult to understand. Our challenge is to sort out the images in this illumination, to discern the shadows and gradations that give it form.

Most observed processes of organization change far exceed the explanatory capabilities of any one theory. As the handbook chapters have shown, organization changes unfold in complex ways at multiple embedded levels over time on many interrelated issues, and involve multiple agents with diverse sensemakings, emotions, and actions. Explanations of change processes in organizations must often span more than one level of analysis, involve multiple actors or perspectives, and incorporate dynamic generative mechanisms. They must also take into account characteristics of organizational change such as its path dependence, the powerful influence that a single critical event often has on the direction and impacts of change, and the role of human agency in molding change according to plans or implicit models. Addressing all of these issues tends to make theories of organizational change and innovation very complex.

This presents the paradox of theory building. On the one hand, theories must be accurate enough to explain the complexity, yet simple enough to understand and use as a guide. Organizational theories have tended to favor simplification and parsimony, for simple ideas are often powerful and useful. However, an emphasis on simplicity tends to foster satisfaction with incomplete understandings that fail to capture important aspects of change. In addition, it has been difficult to find general principles that can be mastered and applied in organizations across the board. As Mauer et al. note in Chapter 19, prescriptive advice often must be so general as to leave change agents still without distinct guidance for practice. This challenges us to increase the complexity of our thinking. We attempt to address this paradox by proposing a few simple models that are useful for explaining general patterns, and then to unpack and reconnect these models as assemblages or modules for addressing different contexts and shifting conditions in organization change processes.

We do not propose to suggest that any one theory is *the best* theory of change or to derive a single broad integrative theory of change. Instead, we think it is more productive to consider a range of theories and models that can be applied to understanding change and innovation. As Popper (1962) argued, science is most likely to advance when a variety of theories and perspectives are in play. In some cases these will be competing alternatives, as Popper envisioned, while in others they will be compatible and even complementary.

Simple Theories of Complex Organizational Change and Innovation

The organizing framework for this handbook has been our typology of four simple process theories: teleology, life cycle, dialectics, and evolution (Van de Ven and Poole 1995). See Figure 31.1. Each of these theories relies on a different generative mechanism, or motor, that drives the change process. Complex change processes are generated by the interaction of more than one of these process theories. Indeed, very few applied theories of change, development, or innovation are built around a single ideal type theory as defined in Van de Ven and Poole (1995). Most involve hybrids of two or more theories operating together, at different levels, or during different time periods. In these cases, the simple theories are used as modules that are assembled together in different ways to address complex observed processes of organization change.

One reason for this is that organizational change and innovation are influenced by diverse units and actors, both inside and outside the organization. Their spatial dispersion means that different influences may be acting simultaneously on different parts of the organization, each imparting its own particular momentum to the change process. For example, in a study of the development of cochlear implants, Van de Ven and Garud (1993) found that a teleological process explained the course of development in the firm's R&D lab. In the regulatory affairs department, which focused on FDA approval of the product, a life cycle model corresponding to the steps in the approval process governed activity. These two different motors interacted as product development progressed. As the product progressed, yet another motor was operating in the larger field of the healthcare industry, an evolutionary process. The firm's pioneering product design was initially supported by the researchers, but evidence mounted which led most researchers and clinicians to switch allegiance to a competing firm's design, thus "selecting out" the product. Motors may also vary in strength as a process unfolds. As time passes, there is opportunity for different motors to come into play, especially given the spatial dispersion of influences. As the product studied by Van de Van and Garud matured, the life cycle motor governing regulatory approval became dominant, overshadowing the teleological process and entraining it to the stepwise approval process. The resulting observed process is multi-layered and complex, and to adequately capture it, a theory must incorporate more than one motor.

Organizational change and innovation processes are also complex due to the inherent incompleteness of any single motor. Each of the motors pictured in Figure 31.1 has one or more components that are determined exogenous to the model. For example, in the evolutionary model variations are assumed to arise randomly, but the process which gives rise to variation is left unspecified. In the dialectical model, the origin of thesis and antithesis is not accounted for, nor is the source of dissatisfaction in the teleological

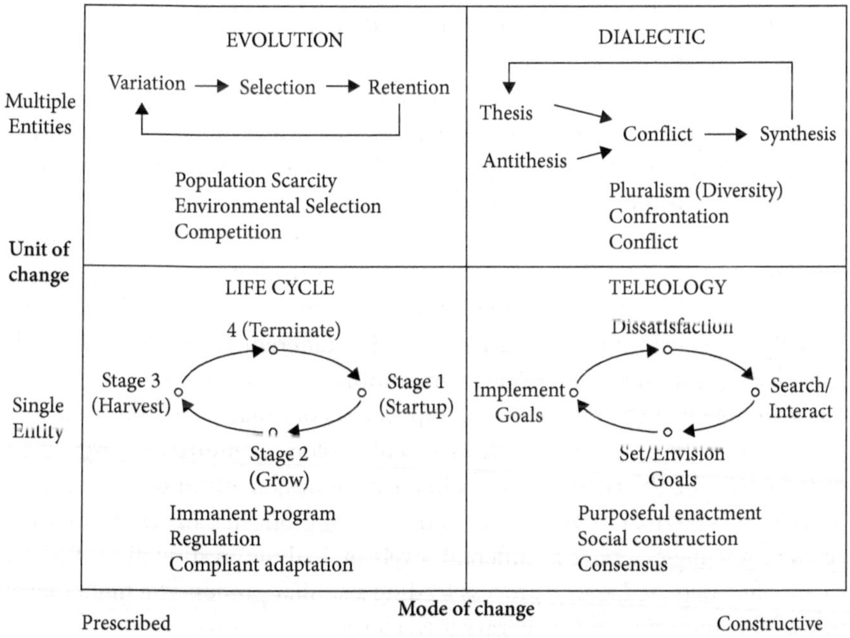

FIGURE 31.1 Process Theories of Organizational Development and Change

Note: Arrows on lines represent likely sequences among events, not causation between events.

Source: A.H. Van de Ven and M.S. Poole, "Explaining Development and Change in Organizations," *Academy of Management Review*, 20, 3, p. 520

model, and the processes that launch start-up and conclude termination in the life cycle model. The exogenous inputs to each model can be found in other models. For instance, the selection process in the evolutionary model can terminate the life cycle, and the implementation step in the teleological cycle can trigger the start-up step in the life cycle and the antithesis in the dialectic. The synthesis in the dialectic could be the source of variation in the evolutionary cycle. There are other possibilities whereby other models may complement the incompleteness of any single model of change.

Granting the likelihood that many theories of change and innovation will incorporate more than one motor, we will now consider the types of interactions among the motors. Throughout the subsequent discussion we will draw on and try to put into perspective the theories and ideas advanced in previous chapters.

Creating Complex Theories by Combining Simple Motors

A good composite theory of change or innovation specifies clearly and completely where the different motors fit—the spatial and temporal spheres within which they operate and the nature and degree of influence they have on each other. Three key aspects can be distinguished. First, we address different types of *inter-level relationships*. Organizations are multilevel phenomena, and theories of organizational change or innovation must consider how processes at different levels affect each other. The most common assumption is hierarchical relationships in which higher levels encapsulate and set the parameters for lower level processes. However, this is only one of three types of inter-level relationships that we will discuss. Second, we discuss the *form* relationships among motors may take, both across and within levels. While positive and negative linear relationships are the most common, recent work on complexity theory and nonlinear systems theory suggests that other more complex relationships may often hold. Finally, we consider the *time scales* at which different motors operate and how motors with different time scales relate to one another.

We should note that the motors in a composite theory may be either of the same or different types. A common approach in recent ecological models of organizational change is to describe the change process in terms of nested evolutionary motors (e.g., Van de Ven and Grazman 1999). Baum and Rao point out in Chapter 18 that in such models the same logic applies at different levels of analysis, and relationships among motors are often depicted as one process feeding a similar process at a higher level and one process shaping a similar process at a lower level.

However, things can be more complicated than this. We will now discuss several examples of theories that incorporate different types of motors, some at different levels of analysis and others operating on the same level. The issue in this case is how motors operating under different generative mechanisms mesh together.

Relationships among Motors at Different Levels

Most studies of organizational change have focused on a single level of analysis. However, most organizational units are situated in a multilevel system—individuals within departments within organizations within industries or communities within nation states or cultures. In some cases, the units are nested within a hierarchy such that they are interdependent, and so also is change in a unit at a given level dependent on changes in units at higher and lower levels. In other cases, different levels operate more independently, but still influence each other. While a multilevel model of change has been acknowledged as useful in *describing* organizational life, it has yet to be widely incorporated into *explanations* of organizational change. As a result, we know relatively little about how or why change processes in one level facilitate or constrain change at other levels of a hierarchy or series.

Meyer et al. (1993) provide an insightful account of how their research design, reflecting good contemporary theory, was unable to adequately measure or explain the hyper turbulent changes experienced by hospital organizations and the industry during the 1980s in the San Francisco Bay area. As Gaba and Meyer discuss in Chapter 16, "the most pressing need was to develop a broader framework for thinking about organizational change;... [one that examines] the *mode* of change [our four motors of change] and the *level* at which it occurs (organization or industry)" (Meyer et al. 1993: 71). In terms of social evolutionary theory, Baum and Singh in Chapter 18 and Maurer et al. in Chapter 19 also called for an expansion of the theory to include study of the processes of variation, selection, and retention *between* different levels of organizational entities.

If organizational change is a multilevel phenomenon, and motors are likely to operate on different levels of analysis, then what types of cross-level relationships might there be? We can distinguish *nested, entangled, and aggregated* motors.

Motors are *nested* when a lower-order motor is tightly linked with the higher-order motor, serving functions at the lower level that connect directly with the operation of the higher-level motor. For example, in Chapter 19 Mauer et al. discuss how a life cycle or teleological motor may describe the actions of individuals that participate in the VSR process in an evolutionary motor. In this case, the lower-level motor models the actors that go to make up the evolutionary process in a way that is compatible with the higher-level process. However, the functions performed by a nested motor need not be positive or supportive: they merely need to help drive the higher-level motor. Chapter 13 (Poole and Van de Ven) discuss Greiner's (1972) model of organizational development which posits a life cycle of creativity, direction, delegation, coordination, and collaboration. Each of these stages culminates in a different dialectical crisis (of leadership, autonomy, control, red tape, and "?"), which propels the organization into the next stage of growth. These crises are produced by struggles among individuals who are attempting to deal with organizational problems. The conflict process undermines the stage by precipitating a crisis that advances the process.

In the nested hierarchical structure of individuals within organizations within populations or industries, the organization itself represents but a single level of analysis, both encompassing and encompassed by other levels. Organizations are viewed as evolving systems nested in other co-evolving systems at higher (e.g., industry or population) and nesting lower (e.g., work groups or individual managers) levels of analysis, as described by Baum and Rao in Chapter 18. At the higher community level of analysis, Astley (1985) described how multiple populations of organizations also go through their own variation, selection, and retention processes as they co-evolve with lower-level organizational and management changes, as well as more macro technological and social developments, as illustrated in Schumpeterian cycles of creative destruction. The development of an explanatory role for hierarchical structure in evolutionary theory represents a vibrant vein of research in evolutionary biology (see, for example Arnold and Fristrup, 1982; Buss, 1987; Gould, 1982; Gould and Eldridge, 1977).

This multilevel view of evolution is important for understanding how selection and adaptation can occur at multiple levels. At any focal level, selection focuses on the evolutionary process of choosing or shifting between new branches (i.e., variations or speciations), while adaptation is the class of heritable characters that have a positive influence on the fitness of an entity within a constraining situation; that is, on extending the persistence of a branch that is chosen. So, selection assumes branching in a lineage, while adaptation assumes fitting or adjusting within a selected branch. Arnold and Fristrup (1982) go on to argue that branching and persistence are the essential components of fitness at all levels. Branching indicates variation or speciation rates, while persistence indicates the fitness (or extinction rates) of entities in selected branches.

While hierarchical relationships are attractive because of their order and elegance, other types of cross-level relationships also occur. Motors are *entangled* when lower and higher-order motors influence each other, but are not tightly linked into a single, coherent process. In this case, the motors operate independently to some degree. In contrast to nested motors, which have tight coupling, entangled motors are moderately or loosely coupled. As a result, the motors run their own courses and interact with each other but are not "in synch" to the extent nested motors are. For example, a teleological model of a planned change in an organization may be premised on development of a common mission shared by individuals (Bryson 1988). However, Chapter 3 (Bartunek et al.) discusses how these same individuals develop along their own life course and may experience the tension between inclusion and independence as the organization attempts to get them to hue to the common mission (Putnam and Stohl, 1996). These tensions may lead some individuals to choose to "opt out" of the organization by devoting their energy to other parts of their lives. In this case, individual-level processes may undermine organizational-level processes, or they may promote them, depending on how the individual processes intersect with the stages of the organization's life cycle. For example, in

Chapter 10 Prichard and Creed rely on narrative and psychoanalytic traditions to examine how unconscious drives, traumatic experiences, and socialized narratives of individuals may explain the formation of insurgent organizational change agents.

There is "slippage" in the relationships of entangled motors. The influence of a motor at one level on a motor at a different level is mediated by the process through which the motors engage each other. The nature of this process filters inter-level impacts and affects the strength and manner of influence. Depending on the process, inter-level influence may be strong or weak and may also change over time. As the examples illustrate, hierarchical relationships typically involve tight couplings whereby the interlock of motors is clear. In biological models, the genetic material offers a common boundary object on which the process can operate from several levels. In organizational versions of evolutionary theory, the analogue of genetic material has been difficult to identify, but Baum and Rao in Chapter 18 suggest that organizational form (defined in terms of dimensions such as mission, authority structure, technology, and market) is the basic stuff of organizational evolution. They posit that aspects of forms are borrowed, recombined, and created in the process of organizational evolution, resulting in a genealogy of organizational forms. Entangled motors do not have this common ground of operation. Instead, it is necessary to specify a process independent of the motors themselves that connects the entangled motors.

To continue the example of individual participation in organizational change efforts, the individual and organizational levels are connected by the process that governs the degree of investment individuals have in the higher-level entity. Individuals are members of many higher-order units—families, voluntary associations, friendship networks, and the focal organization—and because they have limited attention and energy to devote to these units, individuals must make choices about where they will invest their time and energy (Putnam and Stohl, 1996). Factors that affect this allocation process include the motivation the higher-level unit offers compared to other units, the individual's needs, and whether a transformational leader has emerged in the organization. The connecting process affects the nature and strength of inter-level influence. For example, a strong leader with a clear vision for change may galvanize individual energy around the change and draw it away from other units, resulting in a convergence of individuals around the change effort. This would show up as a strong inter-level influence. The nature and strength of influence may also change over time as the connecting process changes. If the leader is discredited, we would expect the strength of the connection to wane as individuals reallocate their energy to other agendas. This would show up as a decline in inter-level influence or perhaps even as a disconnect between levels.

It is more difficult to theorize entangled motors than hierarchies or the aggregated motors we will discuss next. Moreland and Levine's (1988) model of individual socialization into groups provides a good example. They offer a convincing picture of how individuals are shaped by groups and in turn influence the group. However, Moreland and Levine confine themselves to the case of single members and do not devote much attention to membership configurations or interactions among members. The complexity that this would add to the Moreland–Levine theory is daunting and it is often difficult to even conceive of how such connections could be modeled. However, that something is difficult does not mean it is impossible, and we hope that future theorists will turn their attention to questions such as this. Entangled motors are probably much more common than the existing literature would suggest. Their very difficulty may have discouraged researchers from conceptualizing them or encouraged them to force fit them into the hierarchical mold.

Aggregated motors, the third type, represent the case where a process on a higher level emerges from or is constituted by an aggregation of lower-level processes. In this case, a higher-level process is constituted by a collective of interdependent lower-level processes. Rheinhardt and Gioia in chapter 4 provide the example of aggregation with an "upside-down" process of sensemaking that is initiated by employees at the bottom of the organization. So also, Kim and Davis in chapter 9 discuss collective action models, in which rational action by a group of individuals eventuates in a change in a social structure or collectivity. Whereas nested motors are tightly coupled and entangled motors are moderately coupled, in aggregated motors the higher-level process is strongly dependent on the lower-level motors; however, rather than a linkage or coupling, the higher-level process literally *is* the combination of the lower-level motors. The different forms of combination determine different types of higher-order processes.

Theories of social action by Arrow (Arrow 1970) and Coleman (1973, 1986, 1990) offer one view of how aggregation could occur. Basically, their approach assumes individuals can act but organizations cannot, and attempts to specify models by which individual actions can combine to create collective outcomes at the organizational level. These system-level outcomes, may, in turn, impose constraints on individuals (Coleman, 1986: 1312). Coleman (1990) argues that a fully specified macro-micro system must consist of three types of propositions: (a) a proposition indicating how the higher level influences the lower level, which consists of an independent variable characterizing society and a dependent variable characterizing the individual; (b) a proposition indicating how one characteristic of the lower-level influences another characteristic on the same level, in which both independent and dependent variables characterize the individual; and (c) a proposition indicating how the lower level influences the higher level, which consists of an independent variable characterizing the individual and a dependent variable characterizing society. This third proposition, which marks the micro-macro transition, is not a simple effect of *a single* individual on society, but rather is a combined or aggregate effect of multiple individuals which is shaped by the nature of interdependence among them. The first proposition, which marks the macro-micro transition, also hinges on the nature of interdependence among individuals. Coleman conceives of these two components as "the rules of the game, rules which transmit consequences of an individual's action to other individuals and rules which derive macro-level outcomes from combinations of individuals' actions" (Coleman 1990: 19).

Coleman (1990) discusses a number of forms of interdependence among individual interests, which lead to different types of social organizations. He gives three examples of such organizations in his 1986 article:

> A pure market is a configuration in which there are "independent actors, each with differing private interests and goals and each with resources that can aid others' realization of interests. The actions that purposive actors will engage in when this configuration of interests and resources exists is social exchange, and when a number of these exchange processes are interdependent, we describe the whole set as a market institution.
>
> (Coleman 1986: 1324)

> A hierarchy is a set of relations "in which one actor's actions are carried out under the control of another and advance the other's interests." The associated institution is the formal organization or authority structure.
>
> (Coleman 1986: 1324–5)

> A federation (our term) is a set of independent actors linked by common interests. They are connected by a constitution embodying a set of norms regarding rights and obligations.
>
> (Coleman, 1986: 1326)

Each type of interdependence and associated organizational scheme has different formats for combining individual interests and actions into collective action and macro-structural outcomes.

While individuals are assumed to be the prime movers behind any organizational activity, Coleman's approach allows for several different kinds of macro-level actors (Coleman, 1990: 12–13). In some cases, the macro level is most appropriately conceived as the behavior of a system of actors whose actions are interdependent. In other cases, the system is sufficiently coherent that its behavior can be regarded as the behavior of a "supraindividual" actor, for example, an organization. And in still other cases,

> no unitary actor emerges at the macro level, but there are well-defined properties or concepts characterizing that level. The determination of price in an economic market is an example which illustrates this case well. The micro-level actors are the individual traders and the price of each good gives the exchange rate... for that good when there is equilibrium, that is, when no additional trades will take place beyond those already arranged. The relative prices of two goods as a concept characterizing the market as a whole... is an abstraction made possible by the fact that market competition compresses the various exchange rates for the same pair of goods among different trading partners toward a single rate, as each trader attempts to get the best exchange possible for the good or goods that the trader holds. (p. 13)

Aggregated motors enable researchers to directly address the issue of how macrolevel phenomena such as organizations or communities are constituted. Both nested and entangled motors presume the existence of the two levels without questioning how one or both come into being.

Forms of Relationships Among Motors

Regardless of what level relationships are at, we can distinguish several different forms that they may take. In our earlier paper (Van de Ven and Poole, 1995; for a summary see Chapter 1), we discussed how combinations of the motors create, in effect, hybrid change theories capable of capturing the complexity of change and innovation processes. The simplest type of combination is to determine which of the generating mechanisms underlying the four ideal types is in operation in the organizational change process. By specifying the presence (operation) or absence (non-operation) of the four motors in a given situation, we can define an array of sixteen logically possible explanations of organizational change and development. This array, shown in Table 31.1, is analogous to examining the simple main and interaction effects of each of the four motors on alternative applied theories in the management literature.

The first four alternatives represent the "main effects" of the generating mechanisms, "single-motor theories" that apply to cases when only one of the four generating mechanisms or change motors is in operation. The remaining twelve alternatives represent "interaction effects" of the interdependent operation of two or more of the four generative mechanisms. Alternatives 5 through 10 represent cases when only two of the four change motors are in operation. Alternatives 11 through 14 are "tri-motor theories", when three of the four change motors operate interdependently. Alternative 15 is the most complex situation, when all of the four generating mechanisms operate interdependently in a given situation. Examples of several of these motors are discussed in Chapters 1, 15, 16, 17, and 22 of this handbook., as well as Van de Ven and Poole (1995) and Poole et al. (2000).

There are sixteen logical combinations that represent *direct* relationships among the four motors, where one or more motors immediately influences another. For example, in Greiner's organizational development model, the maturation of a given stage of development fosters the emergence of crises. For sake of clarity, a direct relationship should be defined as unidirectional. Recursive relationships among motors are comprised of two direct relationships, one from motor A to motor B and a second from motor B to motor A. Continuing our example of Greiner's model, the crises fostered by the maturing stage advance the organization to its next stage of development. Hence there is a recursive influence of stages on crises and crises on stages.

In addition to these direct relationships, there may also be *indirect* relationships between motors when there is another process that mediates the relationship between them. In some cases, motors are linked not by the direct action of one on another, but because they operate in the same context or environment and therefore are subject to the same external influences or because they are linked by the action of a third process. Motors operating in the same context are coordinated by external forces and so may act in concert. The life cycles of organizations operating in a poor economy, for example, will be shaped by negative economic events and hence will exhibit similar patterns.

Table 31.1 Logically Possible Theories of Organizational Change and Development

	Interplays Among Generating Mechanisms			
	Imminent Program	Purposeful Enactment	Conflict & Synthesis	Competitive Selection
Single-Motor Theories				
1. Life Cycle	yes	no	No	no
2. Teleology	no	yes	No	no
3. Dialectics	no	no	yes	no
4. Evolution	no	no	No	yes
Dual Motor Theories				
5. Design Hierarchy theory (Clark 1985)	yes	yes	No	no
6. Group Conflict (Simmel 1908; Coser 1958)	no	yes	yes	no
7. Community & Population Ecologies (Astley 1985)	no	no	yes	yes
8. Adaptation-Selection models (Aldrich 1979)	yes	no	No	yes
9. Org. Growth & Crisis Stages (Greiner 1972)	yes	no	yes	no
10. Org. Punctuated Equilibrium (Tushman & Romanelli 1985)	no	yes	No	yes
Tri-Motor Theories				
11. Partisan Mutual Adjustment (Lindblom, 1965)	yes	yes	yes	no
12. ?	no	yes	yes	yes
13. Institutional Theory of Contradictions (Seo & Creed, 2002)	yes	no	yes	yes
14. Social Psychology of Organizing (Weick, 1979)	yes	yes	No	yes
Quad-Motor Theories				
15. Human Development Progressions (Riegel, 1976)	yes	yes	yes	yes
16. Garbage Can (Cohen March & Olsen, 1972)	no	no	no	no

Source: Van de Ven and Poole (1995, p. 528)

Motors linked by a third process may influence each other, but that influence is filtered, dampened, or sometimes even amplified by the intervening process.

The types of direct relationships are well known and include *reinforcing* (positive), *dampening* (negative), and *complex* (nonlinear). Direct relationships are fairly straightforward when considered individually, but they become less easy to fathom when three or more motors are linked in a system. In such a case, even if all have reinforcing relationships, the cumulative impact may be nonlinear. Oswick, Oswick, and Grant discuss in Chapter 12 several different approaches to modeling nonlinear relationships among motors. Multiple interlinked motors may also give rise to indirect relationships in which one motor mediates the effect of another. This type of relationship has been widely discussed in the literature on causal modeling as indirect effects (Bollen 1989).

Motors that operate across levels also add complexity, because the same motor may have different types of direct relationships on different levels, for example, a positive effect at one level and a negative effect at another. Organization and management strategy scholars have tended to draw attention to the harmony of functional alignment between organizational levels, but we cannot expect all units to have similar effects at all levels in the hierarchy. For example, a selfish or opportunistic top manager may select strategies and clone successors that extend the persistence of his/her leadership regime, at the expense of decreasing the fitness of the structural form of the encompassing organization. So also, overspecialization of organizational units, produced by exploiting the persistence of selected strategies' structures at the expense of exploring alternatives, increases short-term advantages of selected units at the aggregate organizational or industry disadvantage of limiting variations for adaptation and innovation.

In addition to mediated causal relationships, there are also two other notable types of *indirect* relationships among motors. *Entrainment* occurs when motors at the same or different levels operate independently but come into coordination due to an external pacing factor (see Chapter 3 by Bartunek et al.). In one common example, teleological motors of individual group members become entrained in terms of their pace of work and orientation to time by working on a common task with a characteristic pace. In this case, the task is the external pacing factor; other common pacing factors for individuals are diurnal cycles and pheromones, while for organizations, the calendar and government mandates are examples of pacing factors.

A *cyclical* relationship among motors occurs when two or more motors alternate in their impact on the change process. This alternation is choreographed by a factor or process that determines the relative weight given to the motors as a function of time. For example, in the sociological theory of morphogenesis (Buckley 1967), action and structure alternately dominate social processes in a cycle whereby active processes undermine current social structures and then commence to build up new ones. However, at a certain point the new structures become constraints on action and a period of structural inertia ensues until new actions can undermine structures and start the cycle anew. In this case, Mauer, Miner and Crossan point out in Chaper 19 that the cycle between the predominance of action and structure respectively is governed by an evolutionary process that determines the rate at which possible changes are introduced and accepted by the system (a VSR motor). This process determines the rate of the cycle and its regularity, as well as the particular direction in which the social system develops. An effective system would have relatively short cycles with fairly equal action and structure phases, which would enable it to respond effectively to changes in its external environment (Hernes, 1976). A less regular system might on the one hand exhibit longer phases of structural dominance, indicative of a system resistant to change, or on the other hand, longer phases of action dominance, indicative of disorganization and anomie. The pace and regularity of the evolutionary process is influenced by the balance between the openness of the social system to change and the degree of stability of relationships and institutions in the social system. Buckley notes, "[A sociocultural system with high adaptive potential, or integration as we might call it, requires some optimum level of both stability and flexibility" (1967: 206). He discusses several elements of complex adaptive systems that promote a good balance of stability and flexibility, including maintenance of an optimal level of tension for change, yet satisfaction of individual needs; a full communication network that provides adequate linkage of system components and feedback; a self-reflective selection system; and effective mechanisms for retention.

Terms commonly used in theories of change and innovation such as "influences," "causes," "generates," or "leads to" seem to be fairly specific. However, as this section indicates, much ambiguity remains as to the form of relationship to which they refer. The various forms discussed in this section, both direct and indirect, offer a "vocabulary" for theory building that focuses on the verbs in our theories in addition to the nouns—constructs—that are often the main concern. The models discussed by Dooley in Chapter 20 offer a still more precise means of specifying theories of change and development, when our thinking gets to that level of sophistication.

Temporal Relationships Among Motors

The interplay of motors depends also on issues of timing. Motors may operate with quite different temporal cadences, and the relationships among cadences shapes interactions among motors.

Poole et al.(2000) argued that the generality of a process explanation depended on its versatility, "the degree to which it can encompass a broad domain of developmental patterns without modification of its essential character" (p. 43). For a versatile model, the same change process applies to different cases, regardless of timing; for example, a group's development may take a few days or it may take years, yet the group may work through the same stages (Lacoursiere 1980). Hence, the most general process theories are developed without reference to actual timing. However, in composite theories timing must be considered, because it determines how motors interact. At least four temporal characteristics of change and innovation processes can be distinguished.

First, processes may vary in terms of their *temporal velocity*, how quickly the change process progresses. The same organizational life cycle, for example, may be completed in two months or two years. The first case clearly speeds the development process much more than the second. Processes may also vary in terms of *duration*, how long a process takes, controlling for velocity. Two life cycles with the same velocity of moving through their phases differ in duration if one is composed of three phases and the other of eight. Third, processes may vary in terms of their *acceleration*, whether and the degree to which their velocity changes. Some processes may accelerate or decelerate as they progress, while others maintain a constant pace. Finally, processes may differ in their *temporal orientation*, the degree to which past, present, and/or future influence the process. Usually temporal orientation is due to the focus of human agents in the change and innovation process, as they often highlight the past or future as they act. For example, organizations making strategy may be driven primarily by past defeats or victories or alternatively, by visions of future gains or threats. In each case the change process takes on a different coloration.

When motors with different temporal properties interact, the intersection of these properties should be taken into account in specifying relationships among them. However, these relationships are often complex, and we have not been able to work out reliable rules for inducing them a priori. For instance, it is often the case that higher-level processes have longer duration and slower velocity than lower-level processes. In a nested hierarchy, we would expect to see a greater number of changes to occur in lower-level units because changes at these lower levels are less complex, smaller in magnitude, and entail a shorter time scale to complete. Since time scales associated with these changes are far shorter for subunits than for higher-level units on average, the rate of adaptation and evolution at micro-levels tends to exceed that at macro-levels (Arnold and Fristrup 1982). However, there are also cases that run in the opposite direction. An individual's life cycle, for example, is usually longer and develops at a slower pace than a work group's life cycle, though the individual is nested within the group. Composite theories are best developed in response to the exigencies of specific cases rather than according to general rules.

Some Examples

To illustrate the application of the concepts developed in this review, we will consider five ambitious theories in this volume: (1) Baum and Rao's genealogical and ecological theory of organizational evolution in Chapter 18, (2) Mauer et al.'s extension of VSR processes to examine change within organizations in Chapter 19, (3) Ravasi and Schultz temporal examination of organization identity and culture change in Chapter 5, (4) Garud and Turunen's analysis of Usher's model of individual and collective partial cumulative synthesis in Chapter 22, and (5) Chapter 17 by Micelotta et al. on institutional change.

In Chapter 18, Baum and Rao examine organizational evolution as unfolding in genealogical lineages across an ecological hierarchy. Taking a Lamarckian stance they assume that in addition to random variation, organizations and their members learn and engage in planned entrepreneurial activity that generates variations in response to contextual demands. The variations are selected during interactions within the ecological hierarchy and retained within the genealogical hierarchy.

Cross-level influence runs downward in the ecological hierarchy with each level nested in the one above (job, workgroup, organization, population, community). Changes in the higher-level concepts which occur through various forms of competition and through community disruptions influence lower-level concepts directly. The closing of a factory, for instance, immediately eliminates its workgroups, but it does not necessarily change the population of like organizations materially. Since levels are nested, there are also indirect relationships between levels mediated by intervening levels. Influence may also jump a level in the hierarchy in the Baum and Rao model.

Temporal relationships in the genealogical hierarchy run both up and downward in the hierarchy. Upward influences in genealogical hierarchies come through the influence of retention on variation. Downward influence comes through the influence of variations at one level on those at another and through the influence of higher-level retention on lower-level variation. Just as with the ecological hierarchy, downward relationships are nested in that change in higher-level elements constrains lower-level elements. There are both direct and mediated downward relationships.

Baum and Rao's analysis is somewhat ambiguous on the nature of the upward relationships in the genealogical hierarchy. In some cases it may be aggregate, in that a change in enough units at the lower level will translate into a change on the higher level. Mauer et al. (Chapter 19) discuss these entangled relationships that unfold across levels and over time in VSR processes. Lower-level or bottom-up VSR processes may produce variations that happen to be successful. This "seed" is taken into the higher-level VSR process to be eliminated or to prosper, depending on the particular dynamics of the higher-level process. While the process at each level can be described as VSR, the specific means by which this occurs differs from level to level, thereby suggesting that the VSR motor is not wholly synchronized across levels. Hence, the different VSR processes are better regarded as entangled with respect to upward change.

In Chapter 5, Ravasi and Schultz extend the theory of organization culture and identity dynamics as originally developed by Hatch and Schultz (2002) by adding a temporal perspective on the process. They propose a teleological model of culture change that considers three different change pathways in which organizational identity may influence culture over time. The first pathway shows how newly forged claims may be used to consolidate an emergent trajectory, rooted in a relatively recent past, to ensure its continuity in the future. The second pathway shows how identity beliefs and understanding rooted in a distant past may shape how more recent events are interpreted, and induce members to adjust present behavior to realign past beliefs and future-oriented aspirations. The third pathway shows how visions of a distant future can be used to induce members to reconsider collective self-perceptions rooted in a distant past, thereby supporting changes in the present and near future. Ravasi and Schultz nicely illustrate how different temporal perspectives may explain different pathways of changing organizational identify and culture.

In Chapter 22, Garud and Turunen provide another example of linking micro individual and macro collective processes and temporal acts of insight in Usher's (1929; 1954) model of partial cumulative synthesis. Usher's historical studies of technological innovations provide detailed evidence that inventions entail an accretion of numerous events involving many people over extended periods of time. It was not a history of single inventors. Organizational change and innovation is a collective achievement. It is important to note that this achievement involves a stochastic (not deterministic) process. One person's insights and activities become engulfed and embedded in larger group and community initiatives. The steps one person takes may merge and influence the steps taken by others in the emergent stages of novelty through a stochastic process of partial cumulative syntheses.

Chapters 16 and 17 provide further examples of linking simple models in time and space to explain complex processes of organization change. Chapter 17 by Micelotta et al. introduce four pathways connecting institutional and organizational change: displacement, alignment, accretion, and accommodation. These four processes of institutional change are based on the scope (level) and temporal pace of change. In a similar way, Gaba and Meyer in Chapter 16 expand upon Meyer et al's (1990) framework of four different processes of change by distinguishing continuous versus episodic change and organizational vs. field-level changes. They use these distinctions in time and space to identify new social mechanisms that drive discontinuous change within organizations and organizational fields.

These examples illustrate how our framework can be employed to analyze and understand complex theories of change and innovation. This not only allows us to understand the theory better, but also suggests aspects that could be added to make the theory more complete.

As with all exercises in interpretation, alternative readings can be offered. For example, the long tradition of evolutionary theories of culture described in Chapter 7 suggests that the wheels of Hatch's theory might be interpreted as operating through VSR processes rather than dialectical tensions. Our view is that the dialectic better captures the interactions of the four processes, which are in constant tension, than the VSR cycle, which presumes atomic components in competition. A life cycle motor has obvious applications to the cycles in Ravasi and Schultz's model as well. Our view is that the dialectic offers an explanation of how and why cultures remain stable or change, whereas a stage theory would only describe movement through the cycles. To explain movement through the phases in a manner consistent with Hatch's discussion of her model requires a generative mechanism built on tension and systemic adjustment. A stagewise developmental process based on immanent programs in the culture is not as consistent with Hatch's description. These brief comments, however, are not sufficient to establish which combination of motors best represents Hatch's model. A lengthier discussion and debate would be required.

Translating theories into the well-specified terms of this framework enables us to think through how the relationships in a theory operate. It may also divulge gaps in the theory and may surface contradictions that have inadvertently been incorporated. Notwithstanding, there is little doubt that this framework itself is incomplete. Applying it to the analysis of other theories will assist in further development.

Summary

Developing specific explanations of change or innovation in terms of composite theories means working out the relationships among motors across levels and time scales. And it is not just at the level of theory that relationships should be specified. Empirical research, too, should be aimed at identifying relationships among models and at testing hypothesized relationships. In recent years considerable progress has been made in research on multilevel relationships (Klein and Koslowski, 2000). Temporal issues have also received increasing attention, though how to approach issues of timing and temporal relationships is less clear (see Chapter 1). Applying these insights and methods to change and innovation processes will raise a whole set of questions for future research to address and should lead to further advances.

Conclusion

We began this chapter with a hymn to complexity. We believe it is crucial that our theories rise to the challenge of organizational change and innovation processes. This means that we must meet complexity head on, acknowledging it and building commensurate theories. As Dooley in Chapter 20 and Albert and Ganco in chaper 21 discuss, complexity theory offers a way to do this by viewing phenomena as comprised of multiple interacting agents. The framework advanced in this chapter offers a similar view, but in this case the agents are simple theories of change that interact to produce complex patterns of change and innovation. Our theories are rather more complex than the agents of complexity theory, which typically are fairly simple programs that execute a few operations. The motors also interact with one another in a more complex fashion than the simple agents of complexity theory. However, just as unexpected results may emerge from agent-based models, so the interaction of multiple motors can produce complexities commonly found in change and innovation processes.

In conclusion we return to our scholar peeping through the shell of stars and planets to discern the glorious order behind their complex movements. His challenge is to appreciate this order, which at times seems confusing and perhaps even threatening. A natural human tendency is to project oneself onto this backdrop, to assume that our "clear and discrete ideas" offer adequate understanding, and that ultimately everything can be reduced to a few simple and powerful concepts and models. It is, however, becoming more and more evident that simple blinding insights are simply that—blinding. To appreciate the subtle complexities of change and innovation processes, we need to bring subtle tools to bear and avoid force-fitting our simple theories onto them. This means somehow achieving a degree of comfort with complicated theories. We offer this framework as one lens for discerning order in chaos.

But it would also be a mistake to complexify our thinking simply for the sake of complexity. There is a deceptive joy in finding connections and weaving webs of thought that ultimately tangle us and collapse from their own weight. Within the search for the sources of complexity there must also be an impulse toward the fundamental, toward simplicity. It is through the dialectic between simplicity and complexity that our understanding of change and innovation processes will ultimately advance.

References

Aldrich, H. (1979), 'Organization and Environments', (Englewood Cliffs, NJ: Prentice Hall).

Arnold, A. J., and Fristrup, K. (1982), 'The Theory of Evolution by Natural Selection: A Hierarchical Expansion', *Paleobiology, 8/2)* 113–29.

Arrow, K. (1970), *Social Choice and Individual Values* (2nd ed.) (New Haven: Yale University Press).

Astley, W. G. (1985), 'The Two Ecologies: Population and Community Perspectives on Organizational Evolution', *Administrative Science Quarterly*, 30, 224–41.

Bartunek, J., Putnam, L., and Myeong, G. S. (2021), 'Dualism and Dualities in the Ongoing Development of Organization Development', in M. S. Poole and A. H. Van de Ven, eds., *The Oxford Handbook of Organizational Change and Innovation* (2nd edn) (Oxford: Oxford University Press).

Baum, J. A. C., and Rao, H. (2021) 'Evolutionary Dynamics of Organizational Populations and Communities', in M. S. Poole and A. H. Van de Ven, eds., *The Oxford Handbook of Organizational Change and Innovation* (2nd edn) (Oxford: Oxford University Press).

Bollen, K. A. (1989), *Structural Equations with Latent Variables* (New York: Wiley).

Bryson, J. M. (1988), *Strategic Planning for Public and Nonprofit Organizations: A Guide to Strengthening and Sustaining Organizational Achievement* (San Francisco: Jossey-Bass).

Buckley, W. (1967), *Sociology and Modern Systems Theory* (Englewood Cliffs, NJ: Prentice-Hall).

Buss, L. W. (1987), *The Evolution of Individuality* (Princeton, NJ: Princeton University Press).

Clark, K. B. (1985), 'The Interaction of Design Hierarchies and Market Concepts in Technological Evolution', *Research Policy*, 14, 235–51.

Cohen, M. D., March, J. G., and Olsen, J. P. (1972), 'A Garbage can Model of Organizational Choice', *Administrative Science Quarterly*, 117, 1–25.

Coleman, J. S. (1973), *The Mathematics of Collective Action* (Chicago: Aldine).

Coleman, J. S. (1986), 'Social Theory, Social Research and a Theory of Action', *American Journal of Sociology*, 16, 1309–35.

Coleman, J. S. (1990), *Foundations of Social Theory* (Cambridge, MA: Harvard).

Coser, L. A. (1956), The Function of Social Conflict (New York: Free Press).

Dooley, K. (2021), 'Conceptualizing Organizational Change through the Lens of Complexity Science', in M. S. Poole and A. H. Van de Ven, eds., *The Oxford Handbook of Organizational Change and Innovation* (2nd edn) (Oxford: Oxford University Press).

Gaba, V. and Meyer, A. D. (2021), 'Discontinuous Change in Organizations and Fields', in M. S. Poole and A. H. Van de Ven, eds., *The Oxford Handbook of Organization Change and Innovation* (2nd edn) (Oxford: Oxford University Press).

Garud, R., and Turunen, M. (2021), 'Microfoundations of Innovation as Process: Usher's Cumulative Synthesis Model', in M. S. Poole and A. H. Van de Ven, eds., *The Oxford*

Handbook of Organizational Change and Innovation (2nd edn) (Oxford: Oxford University Press).

Gould, S. J. (1982), 'Darwinism and the Expansion of Evolutionary Theory', *Science*, 216, 380–7.

Gould, S. J., and Eldridge, N. (1977), 'Punctuated Equilibria: The Tempo and Model of Evolution Reconsidered', *Paleobiology*, 3, 115–51.

Greiner, L. (1972, July–August), 'Evolution and Revolution as Organizations Grow', *Harvard Business Review*, 165–74.

Hargrave, T. J. (2021), 'The Paradox Perspective and the Dialectics of Contradictions Research', in M. S. Poole and A. H. Van de Ven, eds., *The Oxford Handbook of Organizational Change and Innovation* (2nd edn) (Oxford: Oxford University Press).

Hatch, M. J. (1993), 'The Dynamics of Organizational Culture', *Academy of Management Review*, 18, 657–93.

Hatch, M. J. and Schultz, M. (2002), 'The Dynamics of Organizational Identity', *Human Relations*, 55(8), 989–1018.

Hernes, G. (1976), 'Structural Change in Social Processes', *American Journal of Sociology*, 82, 513–45.

Klein, K. J., and Koslowski, S. W. J. (2000), *Multilevel Theory, Research, and Methods in Organizations: Foundations, Extensions, and New Directions* (San Francisco: Jossey-Bass).

Lacoursiere, R. B. (1980), *The Life Cycle of Groups: Group Developmental Stage Theory* (New York: Human Sciences Press).

Lindblom, C. E. (1965), *The Intelligence of Democracy* (New York: Free Press).

Maurer, C., Miner, A. and Crossan, M. (2021), 'VSR Models of Change as Normative Practical Theory', in M. S. Poole and A. H. Van de Ven, eds., *The Oxford Handbook of Organizational Change and Innovation* (2nd edn) (Oxford: Oxford University Press).

Meyer, A.D.; Brooks, G.R.; Goes, J.B. (1990), 'Environmental Jolts and Industry Revolutions: Organizational Responses to Discontinuous Change', *Strategic Management Journal*, 11, 93–110.

Meyer, A. G., Goes, J. B., and Brooks, G. G. (1993), 'Organizational Reacting to Hyperturbulence', in G. P. Huber and W. Glick, eds., *Organizational Change and Redesign* (New York: Oxford University Press), 66–111.

Micelotta, E., Lounsbury, M., and Greenwood, R. (2021), 'Institutional Change', in M. S. Poole and A. H. Van de Ven, eds., *The Oxford Handbook of Organizational Change and Innovation* (2nd edn) (Oxford: Oxford University Press).

Moreland, R. L., and Levine, J. M. (1988), 'Group Dynamics over Time: Development and Socialization in Small Groups', in J. M. McGrath, ed., *The Social Psychology of Time* (Thousand Oaks, CA: Sage), 151–81.

Oswick, R., Oswick, C., and Grant D. (2021), 'Critical Approaches and Perspectives on Organizational Change', in M. S. Poole and A. H. Van de Ven, eds., *The Oxford Handbook of Organizational Change and Innovation* (2nd edn) (Oxford: Oxford University Press).

Poole, M. S., Van de Ven, A. H., Dooley, K., and Holmes, M. E. (2000), *Organizational Change and Innovation Processes: Theory and Methods for Research* (New York: Oxford University Press).

Poole, M. S., and Van de Ven, A.H. (2021), 'The Life Cycle Process Model', in M. S. Poole and A. H. Van de Ven, eds., *The Oxford Handbook of Organizational Change and Innovation* (2nd edn) (Oxford: Oxford University Press).

Popper, K. (1962), *Conjectures and Refutations* (New York: Harper).

Prichard, C., and Creed, D. (2021), 'Agency in Social Movements as Sources of Change', in M. S. Poole and A. H. Van de Ven, eds., *The Oxford Handbook of Organizational Change and Innovation* (2nd edn) (Oxford: Oxford University Press).

Putnam, L. L., and Stohl, C. (1996), 'Bona Fide Groups: An Alternative Perspective for Communication and Small Group Decision Making', in R. Y. Hirokawa and M. S. Poole, eds., *Communication and Group Decision Making* (2nd ed.) (Thousand Oaks, CA: Sage), 147–78.

Ravasi, D. and Schultz, M. (2021), 'Organizational Identity and Culture Change', in M. S. Poole and A. H. Van de Ven, eds., *The Oxford Handbook of Organizational Change and Innovation* (2nd edn) (Oxford: Oxford University Press).

Riegel, K. F. (1976), 'The Dialectics of Human Development', American Psychology, 31, 689–700.

Seo, M-G. and Creed, D. (2002), 'Institutional Contradictions, Praxis, and Institutional Change: A Dialectical Perspective', *The Academy of Management Review*, 27, 222–47.

Simmel, G. (1995), 'Der steit. [Chapter 4 in *Soziologie*]', in K. H. Wolff and R. Bendix (Trans.), *Georg Simmel: Conflict and the Web of Group Affiliations*. (New York: Free Press), 11–123. (Original work published 1908).

Tushman, M. L., and Romeanelli, E. (1985), 'Organization Evolution: A Metamorphosis Model of Convergence and Reorientation', in B. M. Staw and L. L. Cummings, eds., *Research in Organizational Behaviour* (Vol. 7) (Greenwich, CT: JAI Press), 171–222.

Usher, A. P. (1929), (1954). *A History of Mechanical Inventions* (Cambridge, MA: Harvard University Press).

Van de Ven, A. H., and Garud, R. (1993), 'Innovation and Industry Development: The Case of Cochelar Impacts', in R. Rosenbloom, ed., *Research on Technological Innovation, Management, and Policy* (Vol. 5) (Greenwich, CT: JAI Press), 1–46.

Van de Ven, A. H., and Grazman, D. N. (1999), 'Evolution in a Nested Hierarchy: A Genealogy of Twin Cities Health Care Organizations, 1853–1995', in J. A. C. Baum and B. McKelvey, eds., *Variations in Organizational Science: In Honor of Donald T. Campbell* (Thousand Oaks, CA: Sage), 185–12.

Van de Ven, A. H., and Poole, M. S. (1995), 'Explaining Development and Change in Organizations', *Academy of Management Review*, 20, 510–40.

Van de Ven, A. H., and Poole, M. S. (2021), 'Introduction: Central Issues in the Study of Organizational Change and Innovation', in M. S. Poole and A. H. Van de Ven, eds., *The Oxford Handbook of Organization Change and Innovation* (2nd edn) (Oxford: Oxford University Press).

Weick, K. E. (1979), The Social Psychology of Organizing (2nd ed.). Reading, MA: Addison Wesley.

PART VII

REFLECTIONS

CHAPTER 32

FROM RESISTANCE TO RESILIENCE

KATHLEEN M. SUTCLIFFE

INTRODUCTION

RESEARCH on change over the past fifty years has flourished across disciplines (Van de Ven and Poole 1995) and has continued to amass. It has even spawned new scientific specialties such as implementation science,[1] of which many organizational scholars may be unaware. But this wasn't always the case. The belief that actors could determinedly shape and reshape objects and situations hardly existed prior to the Enlightenment. For centuries it was common to think that the social world was fixed and immutable; that it couldn't be changed or improved by the actions of purposeful agents (Lawrence and Phillips 2019). But, as beliefs evolved, an abundance of technologies, frameworks, and "ideas and approaches to organizational change and development" arose (Lawrence and Phillips 2019: 3) in both the scholarly community and in the world of practice (Stouten et al. 2018). In response and over time organizational scholars have examined these various frameworks and accompanying ideas and assumptions, expanding and revising some, jettisoning others. Yet, decades of accumulating organizational scholarship have failed to budge two remarkably enduring ideas. The first is that change programs don't produce change (i.e., most change programs fail); the second is that change is often resisted. Fortunately Theodore Zorn's and Jennifer Scott's chapter—'Why Change? The Dark Side of Change and Change Resistance'—changes that. But will this perturbation endure? Given the strength of these long-held beliefs, it is going to take

[1] Implementation Science is the scientific study of the methods to promote the adoption and integration of evidence-based research findings into healthcare and public health at all levels of analysis (e.g., clinical, organizational, and/or institutional (i.e., policy)). Implementation science is inherently interdisciplinary. A journal *Implementation Science*, devoted to publishing translational research aimed at advancing the uptake of research into practice and policy was launched in 2006.

more than one chapter in a handbook of over thirty, to weaken scholarly wisdom about these aspects of change. More force is needed. Thus, this reflection.

My goals are to emphasize and reexamine vital aspects of Zorn and Scott's analysis, add additional nuances regarding change outcomes and resistance, and link it all with the concept of resilience. Although this essay addresses ideas specifically put forth by Zorn and Scott, the placement of their contribution in Part VI of this handbook—'Core Aspects in All Change Models'—is evidence that it holds implications for all chapters regardless of which model of change is espoused. It is hard to imagine change that does not occur without human beings, without their specific intended or unintended actions (or inactions). True, one can envision instances where some kind of change occurs through evolution or without direct human activity—for example, technology can break down through the wear and tear of constant exposure, or can become obsolete or be altered by the ravages of time. But it is hard to imagine many instances where human beings are not involved someway or somehow.

Change and its Darksides

Zorn and Scott clearly articulate their motivation at the outset: broaden perspectives about change, particularly perspectives that have long been taken for granted. As they note, much of the organizational change literature "has adopted and reproduced an ideology of change as an unquestioned good (p. 766)," and, resistance as an unquestioned bad. Yet as Shakespeare's Hamlet (Lowes 1914: 51) mid Act 2, Scene 2 implies in conversation with Rosencrantz and Guildenstern, nothing is really good or bad in itself—it's all what a person thinks about it. And that is precisely at the crux of Zorn and Scott's analysis, which they prime with a set of preliminary considerations. As they write, change and resistance to it are neither good nor bad. *It depends*. It depends on whose perspective about change is being privileged. It depends on what element of change is being judged. And, it depends on what point in time that judgment is being made. These three core considerations make salient the necessity of avoiding simplistic bifurcated views; dark versus bright, good versus bad, resistance versus acceptance. Three profound simple questions should be a wake-up call to all organizational scholars studying change. We all should be seeking more nuance to our theories. We all should be acknowledging issues of fluidity, ambiguity, and impermanence, if only because as has been repeated many times throughout these chapters, "change never starts because it never stops" (Weick and Quinn 1999: 381). Change is not an event; it is unequivocally a process—a series of acts, activities, or events that produce a result. We should study it as such.

Zorn and Scott's take on the dark side of change (i.e., the negative) revolves around two key points. The first is that dark side concerns derive from the change process itself. "Initiatives that are undertaken for ethically questionable reasons, using ethically questionable means, or having negative or harmful consequences" (p. 766) are likely to raise objections. Even when the substance of change is noncontroversial, stakeholders (i.e., those involved in or affected by change) are likely to report negative reactions to a change initiative when they perceive that the publicly expressed officially sanctioned rationale(s) for an initiative are incongruent with privately expressed or privately unexpressed rationale(s), when they perceive that a change process is being handled incompetently or unfairly, and/or when they perceive that the process is tainted by gross abuses of power or elements of manipulation. Incongruent rationales, incompetence, unfairness, manipulation, and power abuses diminish trust and increase distrust, which are at the core of dark-side suspicions and accusations.

The second key point central to Zorn and Scott's analysis is that stakeholders are likely to judge change initiatives in negative ways even if they have not observed the outcome, simply because they anticipate or assume that the outcome(s) will be bad. In fact, stakeholder skepticism and distrust have been linked to the popular persistent narrative that change programs don't produce change. For over four decades purported change program failure rates have been estimated at 50% to 70% (Hughes 2011), even though these estimates do not appear to be grounded in valid or reliable scholarly evidence (Burnes 2011; Hughes 2011).[2] Thus, as Zorn and Scott argue, "[I]t is not surprising that stakeholders are skeptical of change initiatives (p. 775)."

As critical as these two elements are to explaining why change processes have the potential to raise dark-side concerns they obscure an important assumption that is left unaddressed in the analysis; that is, the issue of intentionality. Do change agents intentionally engage in dark-side behaviors? Do they intentionally seek to harm individuals or organizations with their initiatives? In some cases, naturally this may occur. Yet, it is more plausible that things go wrong in change as a matter of course; that things that are known now weren't known then (i.e., at its inception). As sociologist Marianne Paget (1988) presented in her analysis of dark-side failures in medicine, mishaps and fiascoes only become apparent as events unfold. Acts are not mistakes, they become mistaken. As change is unfolding it is evolving in time and we often are unaware of having taken the wrong path. We go astray without knowing it. "[W]e take the wrong path as a cognition only after already having taken the wrong path in fact. Reflection returns to the act of becoming mistaken and embraces it with hindsight" (p. 45).

Acts of becoming are hard to capture in part because we often talk in terms of things rather than the movement of events in time (Paget 1988: 45). Moreover, we often talk about the world as it already happened rather than the world as it is happening. As Paget reminds us, things go wrong as a matter of course rather than intention. Change is not a solitary act or activity; it is a sequence of acts and activities although it is often described as a solitary event. Acts are embedded in other acts (or activities) and press into the

[2] Surprisingly, the idea that most change initiatives fail, which has been promoted in the scholarly literature and business press for over 40 years and often estimated at 50%-70% (see Burnes 2011), is unaddressed in the chapter. Although scholars in the past decade have challenged this ongoing narrative (see Hughes 2011), it is unclear why organizational scholars and practitioners continue to make this claim. Yet, it is perhaps even more important to understand why this has not received more attention by academics. Some have proposed that this is a self-serving unconscious collusion between academics, consultants, and managers (see Beer 2000; Hughes 2011).

unpredictable and unknown, which suggests that even with the best of intentions we don't always know how things will turn out in the end.

This line of thinking is exemplified more broadly in a study Gerry McNamara and I conducted of one Midwest financial institution's planned efforts to standardize their risk-rating decision process (i.e., the information loan officers used to assess risk and make loans) across its five branches (Sutcliffe and McNamara 2001). The change effort was fueled by a merger and structural reorganization that included a redesign of risk assessment and lending decision-making processes. The organization sought to increase the predictability and effectiveness of loan decisions by creating a best practice, and consistent process across all bank branches. The enactment of the change initiative was exemplary. The bank used a Delphi process to create the set of standard (i.e., prescribed) criteria that would be used to make decisions. And, before the new practices were rolled out, the bank trained all lending officers in using the prescribed set of risk-rating decision criteria to assess the risk of commercial borrowers.

As we hypothesized the planned change effort did influence decision-makers to alter their job-specific behavior. After the new process was implemented, loan officers were more likely to base their decisions on the prescribed criteria. And, the change in the criteria loan offers used contributed to greater stability in risk-rating decisions over time. But, in subsequent years reliance on prescribed criteria had unexpected and untoward consequences. Most importantly, loan officers who based their decisions on the new criteria were more likely to downgrade loan risk in the following periods, which is a central indicator of decision ineffectiveness. That is, decisions were ineffective because the profitability of a loan decreases as its risk increases (p. 496). Moreover, as time progressed, loan officers began to deviate from the standards, and adherence to the new practices eroded. It is certainly possible that decision-makers regressed to earlier learned behaviors, but a stronger and more plausible explanation is that over time decision-makers learned (either tacitly or explicitly) that the new criteria weren't leading to better decisions. Thus, loan officers over time continued to adapt their decision-making practices (e.g., decision criteria used) to make their practice more effective.

The point of all this is to say that we do not know how things are going to unfold ex ante and we do not know all the ways in which things can go astray or turn out contrary to what we expect. Volatility, uncertainty, complexity, and ambiguity exacerbate the unexpected (Weick and Sutcliffe 2015), and intervene in how things turn out. If change initiatives are not as intended, it isn't necessarily intentional.

Resistance as Resilience

Acknowledgment that the concept of change resistance is persistent, pervasive, and a "bankrupt model" (Dent and Goldberg 1999: 27), is not new. As Zorn and Scott point out scholars have challenged the concept of resistance for decades, yet the belief that change resistance is "as congenital as being frightened of the dark" (Craine 2007: 44) continues to be deeply ingrained in organizational life and scholarship. Disappointingly, research suggests that organizational scholarship on resistance has been normative rather than empirical, and if empirical has been grossly limited by a lack of diversity in research methods (Erwin and Garman 2010). Some critiques have revealed a lack of conceptual clarity. For example, Dent and Powley (2003: 40) show that definitions of the concept vary widely among scholars, and range from "willful opposition to valuable passion." This in itself suggests, as Zorn and Scott describe, that resistance is not simply an obstacle; rather it is a likely sensible reaction, part of a wider array of possible responses to change initiatives (Oreg et al. 2018). Thus, resistance isn't necessarily a threat or enemy of change initiatives—it also can be an important resource, a source of energy as well as front-line wisdom (Weick 2009: 19) that exposes elemental feedback. Moreover, resistance can be a means to enact resilience—a way to maintain organizational stability, equilibrium, or predictability under trying conditions (Weick 2009: 231). After all, resistance is not only a refusal to accept, comply, or prevent something by action or argument, it also is *the ability to not be affected by something*.

Whether a broader perspective on resistance (ranging from being an impediment to a resource) will take hold among scholars or practitioners remains to be seen. Still, the eventuality of conceptual transformation doesn't assuage curiosity (at least this scholar's curiosity) about the incredible staying power of the negative connotation. If we accept scholarly claims concerning the paucity of well-designed empirical studies on change resistance (Burnes 2011; Hughes 2011), and, findings suggesting that participants in change initiatives are looking for opportunities to unleash it rather than resist it (Kelman 2005) as well as findings suggesting that organizational members are more likely to make positive rather than negative responses about change (Dent and Powley 2003: 40), we might ask ourselves, why does the belief persist?

Cynical explanations accounting for its stickiness abound in the literature. For example, Dent and Powley (2003) argue that the belief persists among practitioners and organizational leaders so that they can purposely shift and deflect blame away from themselves to organizational members for bad ideas, poor execution, and unintended dynamics and results. A similar self-serving argument has been made for scholars: Organizational scientists continue to find resistance appealing because they do not want to lose the financial and emotional benefits they gain from scholarly activities (e.g., articles, books, executive education seminars, and consulting opportunities) aimed at solving this vexing problem (Dent and Powley 2003). Although these explanations make sense, there are other possibilities.

As this handbook and other research makes clear, there are many models of change. Still, change is often conceived of as an exceptional happening—a happening (or event) that separates the past and the future; an episode, or disruptive situation where meaning becomes precarious. Although the word "event" has multiple meanings, the most common definition is something that happens, a noteworthy occurrence or activity (Merriam Webster online edition (a)). Events (aka episodes, disruptions) can be contrasted with non-events (non-episodes, non-disruptions). A nonevent is defined as an expected event that fails to take place (Merriam Webster online edition (b)).

Nonevents in theory are smoothly running situations in which there is not much to pay attention to; situations in which there is not much need to make sense. Nonevent situations are often thought to be ones in which outcomes are constant and nothing is happening. If nothing is happening, there is no reason to study it, so we privilege studying events. In other words, situations that aren't running smoothly capture our attention and we label them as resistance. But the fact is that situations characterized by nonevents—situations where operations pass smoothly, where actions and activities progress unimpeded—are not associated with few "things" happening, but with many things happening (Weick 1987; Weick and Sutcliffe 2006; Weick 2009: 229-241). In these situations there are many smaller disturbances that occur as a natural consequence of unfolding ongoing activities, but there also are dynamic timely human adjustments and compensating adaptations. In other words, resistance to change in this context is an achievement; it is a form of resilience. As Karl Weick and I argued (Weick and Sutcliffe 2015: 98), "[R]esilience in the form of resistance should not be confused with constancy, which is explained by the simple law 'The *same* conditions lead to the same effect (italics in original).'" This may be subtle, but what produces these stable outcomes, this constancy, is continuous change, resilience not resistance. Scholarly attentiveness to more ordinary everyday change situations, rather than those that seem to be exceptions (i.e., that seemingly are going awry) may provide insight into the dynamics of resistance as resilience—the minute microdynamics of change and change resilience that may be more the norm than the exception.

Closing Comments

As I complete this essay the SARS-CoV-2 pandemic is proliferating across our planet. Organizational life and ways of working have changed on a dime. And although it is too early to understand all of its outcomes, ramifications, and implications, this calamity raises all sorts of interesting questions for scholars of organizational change. The pandemic has been particularly trying for nurses and other healthcare workers staffing hospitals, medical centers, nursing homes, and other healthcare facilities. Simone Hannah-Clark's observations in the 3 April 2020 *New York Times* are striking—not only relevant to several themes touched on here but also relevant to supporting the juxtaposition of change resistance and change resilience. As she writes:

> I am one of the many thousands of nurses who work in intensive care units in New York. We are not handmaidens or angels. We are professionals in our own right. We turn treatment plans into action. We question when things don't make sense or aren't going to work. We find solutions that work for our patients. Nurses assess and observe, question and console. We stand between the patient and the enemy. We are the front line.

People on the frontlines put plans into action, question when things don't make sense, and find solutions that work. I want to imagine that this view of the frontline would be similar for others working in other industries and other organizational contexts. Organizational members on the front lines are neither automatons nor rebels, although we continue to treat them as such. Rather, they are central actors whose mindful engagement with the context is critical; they apply their insight and contextually relevant knowledge to the jobs at hand. My work with a number of co-authors such as Michelle Barton (e.g., Barton and Sutcliffe 2009; Barton et al.2015), Tim Vogus (e.g., Vogus and Sutcliffe 2007), and Karl Weick (Weick and Sutcliffe 2015), has shown repeatedly that the cognitions, emotions, and interactions of those on the frontlines are crucial for picking up on weak signals of organizational vulnerability and using these and associated adaptive actions to turn vulnerability into organizational adaptability, resilience, and sustained performance. Our repeated findings suggest that predominant views of resistance as acts of problematic employee behavior (i.e., disobedience, defiance, opposition) or deviant responses of the less powerful to the more powerful belie the more probable explanation that resistance reflects more salutary efforts. The perspective advanced here suggests that resilience underlies resistance and is a natural part of organizational change. Unfortunately scholars studying these matters tend to overlook this possibility. This doesn't have to be the case.

References

Barton, M. A., and Sutcliffe, K. M. (2009), 'Overcoming Dysfunctional Momentum: Organizational Safety as a Social Achievement', *Human Relations*, 62/9, 1327–56.

Barton, M. A., Sutcliffe, K. M., Vogus, T. J., and DeWitt, T. (2015), 'Performing Under Uncertainty: Contextualized Engagement in Wildland Firefighting', *Journal of Contingencies and Crisis Management*, 23/2, 74–83.

Beer, M. (2000), 'Research That Will Break the Code of Change: The Role of Useful Normal Science and Usable Action Science, a Commentary on Van de Ven and Argyris', in M. Beer and N. Nohria, eds, *Breaking the Code of Change* (Boston, MA: Harvard Business School Press), 429–46.

Burnes, B. (2011), 'Introduction: Why Does Change Fail and What Can We Do About It?', *Journal of Change Management*, 11/4, 445–50.

Craine, K. (2007), 'Managing the Cycle of Change', *Information Management Journal*, 41/5, 44–9.

Dent, E. B., and Goldberg, S. G. (1999), 'Challenging 'Resistance to Change'', *The Journal of Applied Behavioral Science*, 35/1, 25–41.

Dent, E. B., and Powley, E. H. (2003), 'Employees Actually Embrace Change: The Chimera of Resistance'. *The Journal of Applied Management and Entrepreneurship*, 8/1, 40–56.

Erwin, D. G., and Garman, A. N. (2010), 'Resistance to Organizational Change: Linking Research and Practice'. *Leadership and Organizational Development Journal*, 31/1, 39–56.

Hannah-Clark, S. (2020), "An ICU Nurse's Coronavirus Diary'. *New York Times*, https://www.nytimes.com/2020/04/03/opinion/sunday/coronavirus-icu-nurse.html/, accessed 1 October 2020.

Hughes, M. (2011), 'Do 70 Per Cent of All Organizational Change Initiatives Really Fail?' *Journal of Change Management*, 11/4, 451–64.

Kelman, S. (2005), *Unleashing Change: A Study of Organizational Renewal in Government* (Washington DC: Brookings Institution).

Lawrence, T. B., and Phillips, N. (2019), *Constructing Organizational Life: How Social-Symbolic Work Shapes Selves, Organizations, and Institutions* (Oxford, UK: Oxford University Press).

Lowes, J. L. 1914. *Shakespeare's Hamlet* (New York: H. Holt).

Merriam Webster online edition (a), https://www.merriam-webster.com/dictionary/event/, accessed April 26, 2020.

Merriam Webster online edition (b), https://www.merriam-webster.com/dictionary/nonevent/, accessed April 26, 2020.

Oreg, S., Bartunek, J. M., Lee, G., and Do, B. (2018), 'An Affect-Based Model of Recipients' Responses to Organizational Change Events', *Academy of Management Review*, 43/1, 65–86.

Paget, M. (1988), *The Unity of Mistakes: A Phenomenological Interpretation of Medical Work* (Philadelphia, PA: Temple University Press).

Stouten, J., Rousseau, D. M., and de Cremer, D. (2018), 'Successful Organizational Change: Integrating the Management Practice and Scholarly Literatures', *Academy of Management Annals*, 12/2, 752–88.

Sutcliffe, K. M., and McNamara, G. (2001), 'Controlling Decision Making Practice in Organizations', *Organization Science*, 12/4, 484–501.

Van de Ven, A. J. and Poole, M. S. (1995), 'Explaining Development and Change in Organizations', *Academy of Management Review*, 20/3, 510–40.

Vogus, T. J., and Sutcliffe, K. M. (2007), 'The Impact of Safety Organizing, Trusted Leadership, and Care Pathways on Reported Medication Errors in Hospital Nursing Units', *Medical Care*, 41/10, 992–1002.

Weick, K.E. (1987), 'Organizational Culture as a Source of High Reliability', *California Management Review*, 29(2), 112–27.

Weick, K. E. (2009), *Making Sense of the Organization: The Impermanent Organization* (Vol II) (West Sussex, UK: Wiley).

Weick, K. E., and Quinn, R. E. (1999), 'Organizational Change and Development', *Annual Review of Psychology*, 50, 3344–61.

Weick, K. E., and Sutcliffe, K. M. (2006), 'Mindfulness and the Quality of Attention', *Organization Science*, 17/4, 514–25.

Weick, K. E., and Sutcliffe, K. M. (2015), *Managing the Unexpected: Sustained Performance in a Complex World* (San Francisco, CA: Wiley).

Zorn, T. E. and Scott, J. (2021), Must We Change? The Dark Side of Change and Change Resistance', in M. S. Poole and A. H. Van de Ven, eds., *The Oxford Handbook of Organizational Change and Innovation* (2nd edn) (Oxford: Oxford University Press).

CHAPTER 33

THE PERFORMATIVE "PICTURE"

Thinking about change as if change mattered

HARIDIMOS TSOUKAS

Tell me how you are searching, and I will tell you what you are searching for.

(Wittgenstein (1975: 67)

A picture held us captive. And we could not get outside it, fir it lay in our language and language seems to repeat it to us inexorably.

(Wittgenstein, 1953: 115)

How change comes about is an important question in organization studies and in the social sciences in general (Poole and Van de Ven, 2004; Tilly, 2008).[1] It is, of course, a critical question for practitioners too. How change is explained, understood or prescribed in scholarly accounts depends on how the phenomenon—change—is viewed: the intellectual "picture" (Wittgenstein 1953: 115) that underlies its conceptualization (Van de Ven and Poole 2021). "Pictures" (or images) of thought are important since they incorporate conscious and unconscious ways of thinking about a subject matter (Genoa 1995: 70–1). Change, in particular, has been a time-old philosophical problem, as, for example, Zeno's paradox testifies (Sainsbury 1988). Labels have been shifting over time, but, broadly, two perspectives are discernible: viewing change as a succession of states (the synoptic image) or viewing change as ongoing reweaving of agents' experience (the performative image).

[1] This chapter partly draws on the Distinguished Speaker's talk, Organizational Development and Change Division, Academy of Management, August 2013. My thanks to Andrew Van de Ven for his insightful editorial comments.

The synoptic (or entitative) image conceives of change as *happening to* organizations (or parts thereof) and, consequently, the latter are seen as moving along the time dimension (Langley and Tsoukas 2010; Langley et al. 2013). Change, typically, is seen as episodic ("infrequent, discontinuous and intentional," Weick and Quinn, 1999: 365), planned (i.e., intended by those high up the hierarchy and flowing to lower echelons, see Rheinhardt and Gioia 2021; Van de Ven and Poole 2021), and mandated from outside the entity in question. Exogenous stimuli abound, ranging from pandemics and new legislation to competitive pressures and technological development (Van de Ven and Poole 2021). Even when change is endogenous, the organization is typically seen to indirectly respond to changes in its environment (Rheinhardt and Gioia 2021). On this view, the organization is observed to be at state X1 at point in time T1 and then at state X2 at point in time T2. The difference between the two states is change (Poole 2004; Van de Ven and Poole 1995). Process, therefore, is seen as a succession of stages and is modeled on motion. A synoptic image views the organization as an entity leaving its traces along its action trajectory.

By contrast, the performative (or enactivist) image looks at change from within: *how* the organization responds to exogenous and endogenous stimuli. The organization is not viewed as a thing but as emerging from multiple interactions among agents distributed at different ranks, levels, and contexts (Weick 1979), and, therefore, change is continuous (Van de Ven and Poole 2021). Looked from within, the succession of states is not seen as preordained but as a contingent accomplishment. A particular state, even when it is the most likely, is not seen as inevitable but as a *possibility*; the question is to account for it by reconstructing the process that generated it. Similarly, studying change in real time (as, for example, in action research) aims to capture how the process of change ramifies, gathers momentum and/or is contested, and how some outcomes become more likely than others. If the synoptic image of change sees the latter as a journey whose most important features are its stops, for the performative image, change is the experience of the journey along the way. Put differently, the performative image views the organization as a bundle of contextually bounded interactions unfolding in time, with change endemic in it. Context and time are not variables to be factored in the explanation but constitutive of the unfolding process (Tilly, 2008: 134).

Both the synoptic and the performative images capture aspects of organizational behavior—a succession of patterns over time (the synoptic) and modification or patterns (or the creation of new ones) through enactment (the performative). Insofar as this is the case, they should be viewed "conjunctively" (Tsoukas 2019: 442), realizing the contributions and limitations of each. Weick (1979) has long argued that organizing is a process of generating recurrent behaviors through drawing on consensually validated cognitive categories. To put it differently, an activity becomes organized insofar as types of behavior in types of situations are systematically connected to types of agents. Insofar as *recurrence* is a distinguishing feature of organized activities, quasi-stable patterns emerge; recursive operations lead to a behavioral convergence on quasi-equilibrium points through agents' interaction (Tsoukas 2019: 440). However, viewed from the perspective of the agent, such stability is always a precarious accomplishment and, therefore, susceptible to change (Van de Ven and Poole 2021). Agents in organizations find themselves thrown into already existing quasi-stable patterns—that is, situations that have *already* been defined and structured -, which are potentially modified through further recursive interactions in open-ended contexts. "The creation of stabilities is an ongoing accomplishment—it is a process. Stability coexists with change: stability requires work for it to be accomplished and change requires stability from which to depart" (Tsoukas 2019: 441).

The synoptic image captures the succession of patterns (states), whereas the performative image favors "strong process" imagery (Langley and Tsoukas 2017: 4), whereby change is inferred not so much from the chronological succession of an entity's patterns as noticed or experienced from the reweaving of agents' beliefs and desires but as a result of their engagement in action. Agency is, therefore, primed. The closer we look into agency the more we see possibilities—what could have been otherwise (Giddens 1993: 81). The further away we are removed from agency, the more we synoptically see continuities punctuated by moments of disruption (Pettigrew 1985; Van de Ven and Poole 2021). Since organizational members are both observers of, and contributors to, patterns, they can alternate between the two, thus generating a more refined understanding of action: practitioners can view action from both within (i.e., experience its evolving, entangled, and differentiated character) and from outside (i.e., notice shifting patterns in retrospect, i.e., synoptically).

As contributors to patterns—that is, as agents—when practitioners describe their experience of organizational life, their language tends to be strongly processual. For example, drawing on his experience as dean of a US business school, for example, Vaill provides a vivid description of organizational life as continuously bubbling, evolving, and differentiated. He writes:

> [T]here was the problem of the intrusiveness of events: things did not occur one at a time; no competency could be practiced in pristine singularity. Instead, at any moment, I was flowing with the multiple, disjointed time streams of the various projects in which I was involved. Sometimes I had a little bit of influence over the pace and sequence of things in one of these steams, but as often I was "playing catch-up", "dodging someone else's bullets", "being overtaken by events", or "trying to get ahead" of a situation. The multiple time streams were, of course, not coordinated in space: they competed for my attention. (Vaill 1998: 29)

Notice that, from the perspective of the agent, change is ceaseless flow—neither a mere sequence of states, nor necessarily the outcome of intended action. To be part of an organization, especially to lead it, is to be part of, direct, and experience, ongoing flow. Change is not the exception but the norm—it is immanent (Orlikoswki 1996; Tsoukas and Chia 2002; Carlsen 2006; Gehman, et al. 2013; Lok and de Rond 2013).

If change is seen as immanent (i.e., constantly emerging, emic), how should it be further understood? How does it relate to episodic types of change, namely distinct change programs that aim at bringing about a new state of affairs in the organization (or part thereof)? What kind of language do we need to enable us, organizational researchers and practitioners alike, to account for, facilitate, and/or deliberately plan organizational change while acknowledging its immanence? Although the synoptic image enables us to see patterns (states) over chronological time, it lacks the vocabulary to provide insights concerning immanent change. For if change is viewed through the "logic of replacement" ("episodic change"—see Weick and Quinn 1999), as the synoptic image implies, we encounter the problem of motion: since change occurs between stages, it remains unaccounted. Even when, instead, "the logic of attraction" ("continuous change" as Weick and Quinn label it) is promisingly offered, vestiges of stage-based thinking remain ("freeze, rebalance, unfreeze", Weick and Quinn 1999: 379).

To view change through a performative lens does not merely let researchers capture continuous (ongoing) change. More fundamentally, it enables them to look for emergence even in the most episodic and planned types of change, as Rheinhardt and Gioia (2021) imply. Thus, even when change is episodic, as it often is in purposeful-cum-authoritative systems of recursive sociomaterial interaction that organizations are, it can also be illuminatingly viewed through a performative lens. Episodic change acquires *emergent* qualities as change projects are implemented in open-ended contexts. As Rheinhardt and Gioia (2021: 6) note, "[R]egardless of how well-planned or articulated proposed changes are, organizational members must make sense of the elements of the change(s), both in broad organizational terms and also in terms of personal implications," thus leading the ongoing re-interpretation and re-contextualization of a change program as it cascades down the organization (Balogun and Johnson, 2004).

And vice versa: even emergent change can have an ongoingly *episodic* character, as Garud and Turunen (2021) show in their discussion of 3M (see also Garud et al. 2011). The reason is that organizations represent—label, categorize, abstract—emergence in order to deal formally with it, thus turning it to events. What, therefore, is distinctive of the performative lens is that, through its emphasis on agency, it highlights what makes emergence possible—that is, relationality, experience, concrete time, and potentiality. Chapters by Hernes et al. (2021), Farjoun (2021), Garud and Turunen (2021), and Dooley (2021) in this volume bring out nicely these features of the performative lens.

Relationality implies that the qualities of an entity emerge from inter-connectedness and interactivity within a whole, a point highlighted by complexity science (Dooley 2021; see also Shotter 2013). It is not that no entities are assumed to exist but that what the subject-structure of language and our perceptual abilities lead us to treat as entities (a computer, an organization, a self, etc.) consist of bundles of ever-changing qualities (Mesle 2008: 46–9). The mental self, notes Hume (cited in Mesle 2008: 47), is "nothing but a bundle or collection of different perceptions, which succeed each other with an inconceivable rapidity, and are in perpetual flux and movement." Similarly, as Follett (cited in Weick 1995: 33) noted long time ago, "'I' can never influence 'you' because you have already influenced me; that is, in the very process of meeting, by the very process of meeting, we both become something different. It begins even before we meet, in the anticipation of meeting." Relationality, thus, in a strong sense, does not imply merely the inter-action of self-contained entities but their "intra-action" (Barad 2007: 139), namely that "things" are already entangled and mutually influenced within a broader whole (Shotter 2013:33).

Taking relationality seriously implies that events and experiences are seen as growing from other events and experiences, as Garud and Turunen (2021) aptly note. Past events are internally related to—they are constitutive of—a present one. While substances stand independent to one another and remain unchanged, events and experiences cannot be understood properly unless placed in the nexus of other events and experiences. Momentary human experience is meaningless if seen as isolated. On the contrary, it is meaningful to the extent it is seen as arising out of past experiences, just like listening to the final cord of a musical phrase and recognizing it as the completion of the phrase presupposes that earlier experiences of antecedent cords have become part of the present (Cobb 2007570). To use Whitehead's (1978: 19) term, the way we "prehend" a current experience incorporates elements of past experiences. Seeing the world as patterns of interrelated events and experiences enables us to see the endemic change the world undergoes: "every drop of experience is a novel weaving of the world of preceding experiences out of which that drop arises" (Mesle 2008: 43). Every event reconfigures an already established pattern.

A performative image enables a more complex understanding of temporality. Bergson draws a distinction between "abstract time" and "concrete time" (Bergson 1998: 21; see also Hernes 2014; Garud and Turunen 2021). Abstract time is, essentially, clock time, while concrete time is experienced time. Time as experienced by 3M's scientists involved in the invention of the Post-it® Note, as discussed by Garud and Turunen (2021), is concrete (or "kairotic") time, namely time that fitted their immediate awareness of their own particular experiences. As agents, practitioners are located in the present, which means they act according to the perceived priorities and needs of the time of action. However, for action at the present to be coherent, it always draws on the past while projecting to the future (Garud and Turunen 2021). Our perception of a melody would have been impossible had we not prehended not only what we hear at any moment but also what we heard just before. We prehend a current experience by incorporating elements of past experiences.

However, the whole past can never be fully present; it is felt as an "impulse" to act in a particular way (Bergson 1998:5). The whole past, far from being absent or indifferent, it exists in a virtual dimension. Although when agents act, attention is necessarily focused on the needs of the present, the whole past does not go away. Access to the virtual can happen, in concrete time, through "intuition", suggests Bergson. While analysis reduces an object to discrete elements already known, intuition involves "the sympathy by which one is transported into the interior of an object in order to coincide with what there is unique and constantly inexpressible in it" (Bergson 1992: 161). Intuition provides knowledge from within, which furnishes the agent with an immediate awareness of the seamless web of reality. This is an instance of intra-action: an agent does not merely *inter*-act with other independent agents but approaches the situation through having already formed certain dispositions and expectations. Once one's agency is foregrounded, reality is viewed more dynamically—potentiality is perceived. Skilled agents experience potentiality, in their effort to recover the virtuality of the past in ever-new contexts.

A common thread running through the chapters by Hernes et al (2021), Garud and Turunen (2021), Farjoun (2021), and Dooley (2021) is that they view organizational life in pluralistic, conjunctive, and non-deterministic terms. Thus, organizations are thought to include multiple temporalities, diverse contexts of action, multiple individual goals, and several contradictions and points of tension. In organizations, the explicit interacts with the implicit, the formal with the informal, the latent may guide the apparent, intended actions may give rise to unintended consequences, the organization co-evolves with its environment, and the present incorporates the past and the future. The outcome of the recursive interactions in organizations is open-ended. Since agency is critical, performatively oriented scholars highlight the possibilities that inhere in organizations and the immanence of change.

An explicitly integrative (or "conjunctive", Tsoukas 2019:442) approach that respects pluralism and allows for indeterminism is clear in all of the aforementioned chapters. Farjoun (2021) argues for a synthesis of dialectics and evolutionary theory through pragmatism. Hernes et al. (2021) aim at integrating episodic with continuous change. Garud and Turunen (2021) show the ordinariness of innovation (or novelty, more generally). Dooley (2021), drawing on versions of complexity science and systems thinking, highlights the connectivity of organizations to their environments, the existence of feedback loops (and the change they immanently engender) with latent assumptions (or goals) that impede genuine change, and how recurrent patterns of action include the possibility of change.

An important notion that is explicitly referred to (or implied in the case of Dooley) is that of "potentiality", a concept that is also found in Dewey (1998: 223), which strongly resonates with Gibson's (2015) "affordances"—the action possibilities the world affords agents (see also Ingolt 2011). Hernes et al. (2021) write: "As breaks in actors' experience, [events] constitute potentialities that actors may evoke from the past or project upon the future as they move through time." The potentiality is created as agents redefine events by relating them to other events over time. The authors illustrate this process through their study of how past and envisioned changes during an initially mundane meeting at a shipbuilding company led to the adoption of a new bow design. Similarly, following a project dealing with the development of a new HRM tool, Hussenot and Missonier (2016: 542) show that the "past is not over and the future is not merely expected," but both take part in the shaping of the present. Similar claims are made by Schultz and Hernes (2013) in their study of LEGO: articulating a new identity is a process through which past events are selectively evoked in light of anticipated futures.

Garud and Turunen (2021) go at length to point out the "potentialities" that inhere in organizations, especially in those, such as 3M, that have explicitly designed themselves to promote innovation. Acts of insight, they argue, occur at opportune moments (in *kairotic* time), which are known only by practitioners carrying out their tasks. Two related questions arise: (a) how the organizational stage is set for an act of insight to occur, and (b) how the organization avails itself of such individual insights to turn them to organizational innovations. Garud and Turunen's answer is, mainly, through narrative. Narratives of innovation preserve in the present, knowledge of the past and ideals informing the future. Thus, in 3M, as the authors point out, "[N]arratives of innovation celebrating the instincts of 3M's intrapreneurs [...] were in circulation" (Garud and Turunen 2021: xx).

Narrative knowledge is important for two reasons. First, narratives help, in Bruner's terms, "subjunctivize reality" (Bruner 1986: 35), that is they keep meaning open and "performable" by the agent. Secondly, narratively organized experiences provide agents with the tacitly held "subsidiary particulars" (Polanyi and Prosch 1975: 37–8), which bear on the focal activity *to* which agents are attending *from* them (Tsoukas 2011: 461). Stories make practitioners aware of historically accumulated knowledge and action-guiding ideals. When such awareness permeates the organization, it enters the collective unconscious: it becomes subsidiary and is merged into the focal awareness of agents. This accounts for Garud and Turunen's (2021) "diachronic temporal frame." A new idea is likely to be preserved in narrative memory that celebrates the ideal of novelty and is, thus, likely to be drawn upon when an agent encounters a challenge or "break in experience" (in Hernes et al's (2021) terms) or an "unsatisfactory pattern" (in Garud and Turunen's (2021) terms). Narratives preserve the virtuality of the organizational past, thus providing an "impulse" (Bergson 1998: 5) for action at a moment in the present.

In conclusion, by focusing on agency, the performative "picture" conceives of stability as an accomplishment. Even when stability is deliberately perturbed through episodic-cum-planned change, the latter always retains emergence—becomingness. As generators of recursive patterns of action, organizations create vortexes of stability. Change, however, is endemic since those vortexes constitute patterns that are always on the verge on being re-constituted through intra-action in ever-new contexts. From a performative perspective, when planned-cum-episodic change is initiated, what is worth exploring is how the rationale for change emerges, how it is articulated and connected with diverse narratives of change that may have been available, how diverse agents intra-act, and how possibilities emerge (for an apt illustration see Gehman et al. 2013).

Moreover, researchers may seek to further understand how: the past is brought forward to the present with what effects; conceptions of the future influence the present; predispositions to act orient change agents in particular ways; redirection of agents' attention is accomplished (or not); narratives of change gather momentum and/or get contested; multiple temporalities are played out; patterns of stability are maintained through change; or how new patterns may emerge through the disruption of dominant ones; and how power dynamics and politics shape the preceding processes. The performative "picture", being closer to agents' experience, is well suited to capturing the contingency, fluidity, and complexity of organizational life in the hyper-connected world of late modernity.

References

Balogun, K., and Johnson, G. (2004), 'Organizational Restructuring and Middle Manager Sensemaking', *Academy of Management Journal*, 47, 523–49.

Barad, K. (2007), *Meeting the Universe Halfway* (Durham, NC: Duke University Press).

Bergson, H. (1992), *The Creative Mind* (New York: Citadel Press).

Bergson H. (1998), *Creative Evolution*, authorized translation by A. Mitchell (Mineola, NY: Dover).

Bruner, J. (1986), *Actual Minds, Possible Worlds* (Cambridge, Mass.: Harvard University Press).

Carlsen, A. (2006), 'Organizational Becoming as Dialogic Imagination of Practice: The Case of the Indomitable Gauls', *Organization Science*, 17/1, 132–49.

Cobb, J. B. (2007), 'Person-in-Community: Whiteheadian Insights into Community and Institution', Organization Studies, 28/4, 567–88.

Dewey, J. (1998), 'Time and Individuality', in L. A. Hickman and T. M. Alexander, eds., *The Essential Dewey* (Vol.1) (Bloomington: Indiana University Press), 217–26.

Dooley, K. J. (2021), Conceptualizing Organizational Change through the Lens of Complexity Science', in M.S. Poole and A. Van de Ven, eds., *Oxford Handbook of Organizational Change and Innovation* (2nd edn) (Oxford: Oxford University Press).

Farjoun, M. (2021), 'The Becoming of Change in 3D: Dialectics, Darwin and Dewey', in M.S. Poole and A. Van de Ven, eds., *Oxford Handbook of Organizational Change and Innovation* (2nd edn) (Oxford: Oxford University Press).

Garud, R., Gehman, J. and Kumaraswamy, A. (2011), 'Complexity Arrangement for Sustaining Innovation: Lessons from 3M Corporation', *Organization Studies*, 32, 737–67.

Garud, R., and Turunen, M. (2021), 'Microfoundations of Innovation as Process: Usher's Cumulative Synthesis Model', in M. S. Poole and A. Van de Ven, eds. *Oxford Handbook of Organizational Change and Innovation* (2nd edn) (Oxford: Oxford University Press).

Gehman, J., Trevino, L. and Garud, R. (2013), 'Values Work: A Process Study of the Emergence and Performance of Organizational Values Practices', *Academy of Management Journal*, 56, 84–112.

Genoa, J. (1995), *Wittgenstein: A Way of Seeing* (New York: Routledge).

Gibson, J. J. (2015), *The Ecological Approach to Visual Perception* (Classic ed.) (New York: Psychology Press).

Giddens, A. (1993), *New Rules of Sociological Method* (Stanford: Stanford University Press).

Hernes, T. (2014), *A Process Theory of Organization* (Oxford: Oxford University Press).

Hernes, T., Hussenot, A. and Pulk, K. (2021), 'Time and temporality of change processes: Applying an event-based view to integrate episodic and continuous change', in M. S. Poole and A. Van de Ven, eds. *Oxford Handbook of Organizational Change and Innovation* (2nd edn) (Oxford: Oxford University Press).

Hussenot, A., and Missonier, S. (2016), 'Encompassing Stability and Novelty in Organization Studies: An Events-Based Approach', *Organization Studies*, 37, 523–46.

Ingold, T. (2011), *Being Alive* (London: Routledge).

Langley, A., Smallman, C., Tsoukas, H., and Van de Ven, A. (2013), 'Process Studies of Change in Organization and Management: Unveiling Temporality, Activity, and Flow', *Academy of Management Journal*, 56, 1–13.

Langley, A. and Tsoukas, H. (2010), 'Introducing "Perspectives on Process Organization Studies,"' in T. Hernes and S. Maitlis, eds., *Process, Sensemaking, & Organizing* (Oxford: Oxford University Press), 1–26.

Langley, A. and Tsoukas, H. (2017), 'Introduction', in A. Langley and H. Tsoukas, eds., *The SAGE Handbook of Process Organization Studies* (London: Sage), 1–25.

Lok, J. and de Rond, M. (2013), 'On the Plasticity of Institutions: Containing and Restoring Practice Breakdowns at the Cambridge University Boat Club', *Academy of Management Journal*, 56, 185–207.

Mesle, R. C. (2008), *Process-Relational Philosophy* (West Conshohocken, PS: Templeton Press).

Orlikowski, W. (1996), 'Improvising Organizational Transformation over Time: A Situated Change Perspective', *Information Systems Research*, 7, 63–92.

Pettigrew, A. (1985), *The Awakening Giant* (Oxford: Basil Blackwell).

Polanyi, M. and Prosch, H. (1975), *Meaning* (Chicago, Ill.: University of Chicago Press).

Poole, S. M. (2004), 'Central Issues in the Study of Change and Innovation', in M. S. Poole and C. Tilly (2008) *Explaining Social Processes* (Boulder, CO: Paradigm).

Poole, M. S. and Van de Ven, A. H. (eds.) (2004), *Handbook of Organizational Change and Innovation* (New York: Oxford University Press).

Rheinhardt, A. and Gioia, D. A. (2021), 'Upside-Down Organizational Change: Sensemaking, Sensegiving and the New Generation', in M. S. Poole and A. Van de Ven, eds., *Handbook of Organizational Change and Innovation* (2nd edn) (Oxford: Oxford University Press).

Sainsbury, R. M. (1988) *Paradoxes* (Cambridge: Cambridge University Press).

Schultz, M. and Hernes, T. (2013), 'A Temporal Perspective on Organizational Identity', *Organization Science*, 24, 1–21.

Shotter, J. (2013), 'Reflections on Sociomateriality and Dialogicality in Organization Studies: From "Inter-" to "Intra-Thinking"... in Performing Practices', in P. R. Carlile, D. Nicolini, A. Langley, and H. Tsoukas (eds.), *How Matter Matters* (Oxford: Oxford University Press), 32–55.

Tilly, C. (2008), *Explaining Social Processes* (Boulder, CO: Paradigm).

Tsoukas, H. (2011), 'How Should We Understand Tacit Knowledge? A Phenomenological View', In M. Easterby-Smith and M. Lyles, eds., *Handbook of Organizational Learning & Knowledge Management* (2nd edn) (Chichester, UK: Wiley), 453–76.

Tsoukas, H. (2019), 'Don't Simplify, Complexify: From Disjunctive to Conjunctive Theorizing in Organization and Management Studies, in H. Tsoukas, *Philosophical Organization Theory* (Oxford: Oxford University Press), 430–56 (originally published in the *Journal of Management Studies* (2017), 54/2, 132–53).

Tsoukas, H and Chia, R. (2002), 'On Organizational Becoming: Rethinking Organizational Change', *Organization Science*, 13, 567–82.

Van de Ven, A. H. and Poole, M. S. (1995), 'Explaining Development and Change in Organizations', *Academy of Management Review*, 20, 510–40.

Van de Ven, A. and Poole, S. M. (2021), 'Central Issues in the Study of Organizational Change and Innovation', in M. S. Poole and A. Van de Ven, eds., *Handbook of Organizational Change and Innovation* (2nd edn) (Oxford: Oxford University Press).

Vaill, P. (1998), 'The Unspeakable Texture of Process Wisdom', in D. L. Cooperrider and S. Srivastva, eds., *Organizational Wisdom and Executive Courage* (San Francisco: The New Lexington Press), 25–39.

Weick, K.E. (1995), *Sensemaking in Organizations* (Thousand Oaks, CA: Sage).

Weick, K. E. (1979), *The Social Psychology of Organizing* (second edn) (Reading, MA: Addison-Westley).

Weick, K. E., and Quinn, R. E. (1999), 'Organizational Change and Development', *Annual Review of Psychology*, 50, 361–86.

Wittgenstein. L. (1953), *Philosophical Investigations*, edited by G. E. Anscombe and R. Rhees, trans: G. E. Anscombe (Oxford: Blackwell).
Wittgenstein. L. (1975), *Philosophical Remarks*, edited by R, Rhees, trans: R. Hargreaves and R. White (Oxford: Basil Blackwell).
Whitehead, A. N. (1978), *Process and Reality* (New York: Free Press).

CHAPTER 34

DIALECTICAL CHANGE MODELS

An Escher-inspired reflection

MOSHE FARJOUN

M. C. ESCHER'S 'Drawing Hands' lithograph describes two hands, each drawing the other with a pencil.[1] Intriguing to many, this image holds significance for organization theorists. Czarniawska (2006) and Ansell (2011) have both used this artwork to highlight the notion of tangled hierarchies, or "strange loops" (Hofstadter 1979: 10): Czarniawska in relation to Weick's processual "organizing" theory, and Ansell in connection with complexity and pragmatist organization theory. For Orlikowski (2002), Escher's lithograph represents the mutual constitution of knowing and practice. This relation, which underlies the work of Giddens (1984), Maturana and Varela's (1998) notion of autopoiesis, and Lewontin's (1995) constructionist biology, is central to practice theory (Feldman and Orlikowski 2011). In all these examples, the authors viewed organizations in processual and relational terms and called attention to their ironic, paradoxical, recursive, and entangled features.

As I contemplated on how to structure my discussion of dialectical change models, Escher's 'Drawing Hands' presented itself as an attractive possibility. Dialectics ideas have inspired the above-mentioned organizational theories—from pragmatism and practice theory, to Weick's "organizing", to systems and complexity theory, to biology's niche construction theory (see Chapter 26 by author, this volume). Furthermore, the lithograph manifests several dialectical principles, such as essence and appearance, contradiction and irony, and the interplay between subject and object.[2]

[1] https://en.wikipedia.org/wiki/Drawing_Hands/, accessed 2 October 2020.

[2] The correspondence is only metaphorical. For instance, while a drawing converges into some end point where no more details are added, dialectics highlights how each element continuously develops over time.

Beyond its associations with dialectics, the lithograph provides a useful metaphor for organizing this essay's outline: the right hand in the drawing would include the different chapters in my review; the left hand, would then represent dialectics and its key principles. By analogy to 'Drawing Hands', my chapter would read dialectics into these various chapters; in turn, it would use this set of chapters to relay questions for dialectics scholars to reflect upon, perhaps redrawing dialectics contours in the process.

For convenience, I have grouped the dialectics-related chapters into three pairs: Chapter 7 by Hargrave and Chapter 8 by Runtian Jing, this volume, consider allied traditions; Chapter 9 by Davis and Kim and Chapter 10 by Prichard and Creed, this volume, highlight social movements, and Chapter 3 by Bartunek et al. and Chapter 12 by Oswick et al., this volume, focus on organizational interventions. The different pairs pose the following questions for organizational dialectics research: a) its standing vis-à-vis other models and literatures, b) how it can be applied to different phenomena, and c) how it relates to practice. Each of these subjects has elements of contention; therefore, while I share my evolving views on these subjects, I invite others to join the conversation.

Positioning Dialectics: Paradox, Yin-Yang and Other Allied Traditions

Within organization studies, the relationship between dialectics and paradox research has been a matter of some debate (e.g., Cunha and Putnam 2019). Hargrave, (Chapter 7 of this volume), presents a historical overview of the two traditions. He notes important differences between paradox and dialectics views, many of which concern their ontological underpinnings. Hargrave observes that paradox research tends to adopt an interventionist and problem-solving focus and is mostly associated with a managerial viewpoint; dialectics, by contrast, is more historical and explanatory, and can also be used as a tool by less prevalent groups to critique oppressive social arrangements. Moreover, while it too highlights agency, dialectics is more attuned to how it is constrained by factors such as social structure, unanticipated outcomes, and organizational politics.

Burrell and Morgan (1979) listed several generic responses for reconciling diverse views on organizations. Two of the solutions they discuss are a "dominance" approach, where one view strives to swallow the other, and a "synthesis", which builds on their complementarities. Observing that historically paradox research has attempted to assimilate dialectics—a position consistent with a "dominance" approach, Hargrave calls for a conceptual reversal where, while important, paradox features as only one "moment" in an ongoing dynamic dialectical process.

On reflection, while it trades the places of dialectics and paradox, this newly proposed view seems to also adopt a "dominance" solution. This position may well be justified, given the long and rich pedigree of dialectics and its standing as a broad social science perspective on social relations and processes. Hargrave, however, goes a step further by enfolding this position within a "synthesis" approach. His new vision combines the strengths of the dialectics and paradox perspectives to form a new "contradiction" lens. The proposed view would, for instance, negate the paradox perspective's assumption of the persistence of contradictions, and incorporate the dialectical assumption that contradictions can be transformed.

Runtian Jing, (Chapter 8, this volume), introduces an Eastern Yin-Yang Model of Change. Grounded in cultural philosophies such as Confucianism, Buddhism, and particularly Taoism, the Eastern model bears several similarities to dialectics. For instance, like dialectics, it stresses the unity and interplay of opposites, and highlights how one pole turns into another continuously over time (Yin-Yang). The two traditions also share a relational process worldview: they highlight "becoming" as opposed to "being", assume reality to be an "ever-changing flow", and stress interconnectedness. Another common feature of the two perspectives is their agreement with a critical realist ontology, which distinguishes observed change patterns from underlying, more hidden mechanisms and "deep" structures.[3] In Jing's view, the Yin-Yang model can be taken as a kind of dialectics. Nevertheless, as is the case with Hargrave's chapter, this model includes elements of paradox research as well.

As Jing claims, the Yin-Yang model adopts a historical rather than a social-psychological view of human behavior. This positioning resembles dialectics' stress on history, without fully admitting other of its aspects such as the interplay of agency and social structure. Cautioning against literal transfer of ideas from one culture to another, Jing notes additional differences. For instance, he contrasts the incremental change highlighted in the Yin-Yang model, with a radical, transformational change process accommodated in dialectics. In addition, the model offers several fresh ideas of its own. Taoism stresses timing and momentum as important ingredients in a successful change program (see also Chapter 9 by Kim and Davis, this volume, on this point).The Eastern model considers different ways in which momentum can evolve and several strategies for leveraging it. Lastly, the model highlights leaders' roles in managing paradoxes, leveraging momentum, and mitigating resistance by means of an "indirect" approach.

Hargrave and Jing raise an important question for dialectics scholarship to consider:

Q1: What scholarly traditions and models are most comparable to dialectics, and amenable to their possible synthesis?

Dialectics carries different meanings for different people (e.g., Schneider 1971; Langley and Sloan 2011) and therefore delineates a wide range of options for pairing dialectics with other models. For Van de Ven and Poole (1995), for example, dialectics is mostly associated with the Hegelian affirmation–negation–synthesis development

[3] Baxter and Montgomery (1996) note "remarkable communalities" between the views of Heraclitus, considered the father of dialectics, and Lau Tzu who lived around the same time. For Heraclitus' ideas, see also Chapter 26, by the author, this volume.

through conflict model. Within this representation, dialectics can be contrasted with other ideal-type models, along dimensions such as the key generating mechanisms, and the implied pace of change. Others, such as Hargrave, Chapter 7, this volume, take dialectical contradiction as their starting point. This view of dialectics leads him to contrast it with other models of organizational contradictions, such as paradox and dualities, along dimensions such as the sources of contradictions, or whether they persist or get resolved.

Scholars who view dialectics as a more general approach to social life consider it as a configuration of principles, such as social construction/production, totality, contradiction, and praxis. From this standpoint, there is no compelling reason to focus only on contradiction or change as bridges to other theories. For instance, dialectics' notion of praxis links it with other theories of social action, such as pragmatism and practice theory (Bernstein 2011).[4] Similarly, the dialectic notion of totality has clear commonalities with notions such as systems, complexity, ecology, and fields. A more general and abstract view of dialectics can provide a firmer foundation for comparison and synthesis, and along multiple dimensions—in other words, it provides a strong analogy. As a result, dialectics' configuration of principles can be matched with other broad traditions such as pragmatism, evolutionary theory and complexity (see also Chapter 26 by the author, this volume).

In sum, what other theory dialectics is best matched with depends on scholars' views on what dialectics entails. While historically dialectics has predominately been associated with organizational contradiction and change models, other pairings, narrow or broad, ought to be considered too.

Making Dialectics Relevant: Social Movements and Beyond

Social movement research is one area of inquiry in which dialectics theory—particularly its political strand—has historically been applied to organizational-related phenomena (e.g., Zald and Berger 1978; Davis et al. 2005; Hargrave and Van de Ven 2006; Rao and Dutta 2018). In Chapter 9 (Davis and Kim, this volume), highlight the role of social movements in organizational change and innovation. They observe that the confluence of technological changes and generational shifts in values have increased the scale, pervasiveness, and success of social activism within organizations. These changes have further erased the boundaries between social movements and organizations; for instance, movements can target organizations and industries, create conditions for new kinds of organizations to succeed, penetrate organizations, and draw on organizations as scaffoldings. These observations extend the authors' previous work (e.g., Davis 2016),

[4] While they differ in how they interpret praxis, all these theories are rooted in the Greek notion of pragma, which roughly means action.

and urge organizational change scholars to reconsider the reality of "organizations" (and their "environments") *before* they offer new conceptions of change.

Davis and Kim go further by sketching a political model of joint social movement/ organizational change. Their model identifies key targets for member–activist led changes, such as in products and services, practices, human resources, and communities. The chapter then offers general guidelines for how such change can be most effective. It highlights specifically, the opportunity structure and timing of change, how it is framed and mobilized within relational networks, and how change can be enabled by social, physical, and technological structures.

This chapter too resonates with several dialectical themes. For instance, it highlights change as stimulated by conflict and as coming "from within," originating from grassroots' initiatives. Further, it shares the sensitivity of dialectics to the arbitrariness of categories and boundaries, such as firms and industries; consistent with dialectics, the chapter implicitly adopts an ecological view that highlights overlap, interpenetration, and fuzzy boundaries instead. The proposed change model is inherently relational and processual, and fuses dichotomies such as subject and object, internal and external.

Davis and Kim's chapter also hints at a historical continuity between dialectics and social movement research. Like several influential theoretical statements on organizations, Benson's (1977) dialectical view of organizations, and Zald and Berger's (1978) paper on social movements, were published around the same time. Each of these two papers' authors clearly recognize their mutual interest in promoting a collective resource mobilization agenda. Indeed, themes such as mobilizing structures, framing processes, self-organizing, and influence tactics (or "dynamics of contention") have been a mainstay of both dialectical materialism and social movement research.

In Chapter 10, Prichard and Creed, this volume, highlight the role of social movements as the seedbeds of widescale organizational and institutional change in contemporary Western economies. They further stress the key role of individuals in mobilizing and molding collective reformative action. Given these two premises, the authors focus attention on the experiences, forces, and conditions leading these individuals to become change agents themselves.

To examine these factors, Prichard and Creed mainly draw on narrative and psychoanalytic traditions; their chapter, however, implicitly incorporates several dialectics motifs, such as the unconscious (or the hidden) and the manifest, self-emancipation, and radical reversals. Permeating their chapter is the theme of development through conflict. As the authors show, a conflict between an agent and its immediate family and social circle may be internalized early in the agent's life; elements of this conflict can subsequently be externalized and become incorporated in a rebellious social movement. Echoing another key dialectic theme, the authors uncover how social production and revolutions are conditioned by the existing social arrangements (e.g., Benson 1977). The dialectical notion of praxis is central to this process: as they mobilize others for a particular social cause, agents also shape and emancipate themselves.

This second pair of chapters poses another significant question for dialectics scholarship to consider:

Q2: How can dialectics be made most relevant to contemporary phenomena?

To address this question, it may be useful to distinguish between two common ways in which scholars interpret dialectics: literally vs. liberally. Scholars adopting a purist stance, interpret the ideas of key dialectics scholars *literally*. For instance, many consider Marx's writings as suggesting a clear hierarchical relation between superstructure (ideas) and material relations. Others, who take a more holistic and liberal view of Marx's work, interpret the relations between these two spheres as part of a totality, and as mutually implicated rather than linear or deterministic (e.g., Harvey 2018).

When carefully employed, this liberal alternative provides greater room for analogical transfer. For instance, Hegel used the master and slave parable to show how the idea of freedom bursts through the confines of a seemingly invulnerable institution of slavery. His story is dialectical: it unfolds out of the clash of opposing ideas and ideals which leads to new and more comprehensive ideas, including the idea of freedom. In theorizing about history, Marx drew on this dialectical account as an analogy: he changed the characters and modified the story, without changing the essential outlines of Hegel's tale. In Marx's view, the different, if not completely opposed interests and aims of different classes make class conflict inevitable, and true freedom can flourish only in a classless society (Ball 1991). As this example illustrates, selectively employed, liberal interpretations have been indispensable to dialectics' historical development.

A liberal approach to dialectics can extend its reach across diverse empirical phenomena. For instance, Prichard and Creed, (Chapter 10 this volume) draw inspiration from Rao and Dutta's (2018) model of identity movements as generators of new strategies. Similarly, Davis and Kim (Chapter 10, this volume), discuss "bureaucratic insurgence" as an indirect approach that enables agents to develop their offensive on the existing social order without being interrupted. Such a process parallels Burgelman's (1983) grassroots' model of how strategy and innovation develop in large organizations.

As the above examples show, to adopt a literal approach to dialectics scholarship is to also fix its ideas in time and space. A dialectical approach, by contrast, would view processes such as conceptual innovation, material restructuring, political revolutions, or social, cultural transformation, through which established orders are transformed, as potentially analogous, and often intertwined. For instance, the processes by which challengers develop their ideas and mobilize support largely apply to phenomena such as new strategy generation, institutional and organizational change, entrepreneurship, technological innovation, and social movements. Dialectics is not only useful for theorizing these phenomena, but it can help generate richer, more complete accounts. For instance, one can draw on a Hegelian model to explain how agents come up with new creative concepts and ideas and combine it with Marx's dialectical materialism to theorize how agents subsequently overcome resistance, and organize and mobilize support.

Dialectics in Whose Service? : Organizational Development (OD) and Other Interventions

Chapter 3 by Bartunek et al. and Chapter 12 by Oswick et al., this volume, which comprise the final pair, highlight how ideas about change affect organizational development (OD) interventions. In Chapter 3, Bartunek et al., this volume, provide a historical overview of organizational development models. Central to their narrative is a shift from "diagnostic" to "dialogical" interventionist approaches. The authors highlight how these two approaches to organizational change and development intertwine in practice, and how they both focus on the process rather than the content of change. The chapter also underscores how the practices of managing change in organizations are premised on several tensions and dualities, which can stimulate new intervention practices in turn.[5]

To frame their discussion, the authors draw on the conceptual distinction between "duality" and "dualism" or rigid opposition (e.g., Jackson 1999; Farjoun 2010). A mainstay of a relational process worldview, this distinction permeates dialectics and several other intellectual traditions (see Chapter 26, by author, this volume).[6] The notion of "dialogic" is linked to dialectics too: indeed, in ancient Greece, dialectics featured as an oppositional method of dialogue for progressively uncovering the truth (see Hargrave, Chapter 7, this volume).[7] In the dialectical notion of praxis, both diagnosis and critique

[5] Michel's (2014) ethnography examined how the notions of dualism and duality corresponded to episodic vs. continuous organizational changes in an empirical setting.

[6] Counter to prevailing conceptions (e.g., Feldman and Orlikowski 2011; Farjoun et al. 2015), Hegel and other dialectics scholars, do not reject outright the usefulness of classifications, categories, and binary distinctions. Rather, they consider them a vital part of the dialectic process and central to the emergence of contradictions. More accurately stated, the dialectics position emphasizes that, left alone, such distinctions and dualisms are incomplete and can become rigid, and in need of a dialectical logic that will account for change (Patterson 2018).

Overall, while the notion of duality is closely related to dialectics, the dialectical view is more processual, historical, and dynamic than the notion of duality implies: while it highlights how different elements coexist and interpenetrate, it also stresses how their relations change over time (for instance become more oppositional than complementary). Once we see the relations between the two terms as themselves evolving, we can then accommodate a range—from dualism, where the terms are separate, to a merger, where they become one. In this continuum, duality can be viewed as an intermediate, and at times transitory case.

[7] Bakhtin's dialogism conceives of change as a perpetual motion of centripetal–centrifugal forces. It thus rejects teleological change in favor of indeterminacy (Baxter and Montgomery 1996).

are needed for an effective reconstruction of the existing order (Benson 1977). Consequently, praxis combines elements of both the diagnostic and dialogic interventions highlighted in the chapter.

Oswick et al., (Chapter 12, this volume), discuss the evolution of organizational development intervention models too. While their account of a historical transition from diagnostic to dialogic approaches shares the view expressed by Bartunek et al. (in Chapter 3, this volume), it explicitly draws on dialectics. The dialectics influence is reflected in several ways: first, the chapter adopts a dialectics-inspired critical management approach (see Adler et al. 2007); second, it incorporates a critical realist ontology that questions the stress on discourse in dialogic interventions to highlight underlying structures and mechanisms instead; third, the chapter identifies a new wave of critical and more political approaches to intervention which is becoming increasingly pertinent and central to organizational development strategies.

As the authors highlight, critical theory is dialectical in nature insofar as it considers the unequal distribution of power and resources between stakeholder groups, such as management and employees (see also Lewis in Chapter 11, this volume). This inequality is sustained by political and ideological means: elites draw on knowledge and the distortion of communications to preserve their power and hegemony, whereas the marginalized are less knowledgeable or reflexive and are trained by the elite to accept the status quo as inevitable. The critical–informed change approaches that Oswick et al. advocate invert the dominant organizational development logic that views change as a top-down process, and foregrounds a more critically oriented bottom-up approach instead.

Oswick et al.'s critical, bottom-up approach highlights one way in which dialectics can be interventionist. Moreover, in stressing conflict and power imbalances, the critical intervention approach joins the social movement change models: both offer a less "romantic" counterpoint to dialogic approaches premised on cooperative problem-solving and communications practices.

In real organizational settings, where inequality and power imbalances are common, getting different parties to constructively exchange ideas may be effortful—a potential "moment" in ongoing power dynamics. Furthermore, the assumption of pluralism, which usually underpins traditional interventions, is often inconsistent with the reality of oppositional voices "encouraged" by power holders to exit the organization.

Implicit in this last pair of chapters is a third question for dialectics scholarship to ponder:

> *Q3: Qui bono? Can dialectics principles be more usefully applied to less privileged groups such as employees? Can dialectics be also applicable to management, or elites?*

Any intervention, from organizational development initiatives to strategy consulting, raises the question of who the key beneficiaries are. A key theme of dialectics, from its master and slave version in Hegel to the class conflict at the center of dialectical materialism, is that of power imbalance (Chapter 12 by Oswick et al., this volume). The humanistic interest of dialectics in self-emancipation and the development of individuals' creative potentials has predominantly been viewed as in the service of marginalized, less powerful parties such as certain groups of citizens, minorities, and employees (e.g., Adler 2009). At least for Marxists, the idea that dialectics principles are used to enhance the interests and ideology of managerial elites is likely to be alien.

An alternative view would suggest that whether they include specific theoretical insights or general philosophical principles, dialectics ideas are not limited to any particular social group. In this view, the theoretical insights and prescriptions of dialectics pertaining to influence tactics and to political means can serve *both* incumbents seeking to preserve their dominance or challengers working to upend the established order. Dialectics principles had been around long before they became central to contemporary theories of revolution and reconstruction. Moreover, several dialectics-inspired techniques and tools—system dynamics, red teams, and the like—have become part of managerial tool kits (also see Langley and Sloan 2011).

Yet, the idea that dialectics can be applied across a wider set of users and uses does not necessarily mean that this is the best way to draw on it. There is a real possibility that dialectics ideas will be subverted and abused—a charge that has been historically raised against other approaches, such as evolutionary theory. For instance, certain parties can use dialectics principles to exploit divisions for private gain or to stir up conflicts.[8] It is also important not to lose sight of the abundance of theories and models that are specifically designed to serve managerial elites and incumbents, or at least accept their hegemony. Here, dialectics can add its own unique insights, but in a space relatively crowded by other models. By contrast, when it comes to representing other, less vocal or powerless groups, followers and underdogs, dialectics is in a relative minority and its contribution is likely to be more distinctive as a result.

Conclusion

As the three pairs of chapters underscore, the dialectical lens on social life is unique and worth preserving. For social scientists and organizational scholars, dialectics has more than one use: it is a philosophy, a set of theories, a fund of empirical insights, and a potential guide for practice at the same time. A key question for dialectics scholars is how to best carry this tradition forward.

In this chapter, and benefiting from the contributions of other chapters, I explored this question across three different spheres: I discussed how dialectics can be paired with other key theories, either as a complement or as an alternative, how it can be applied to new emerging phenomena, and how it can be used as a tool for serving various groups of practitioners. In working in any of these spheres dialectics encounters tensions and frictions, which constitute some of the best means for dialectics to further grow and develop.

[8] I am indebted to William Jackson (personal communications) for highlighting this point.

References

Adler, P. S. (2009), 'Marx and Organization Studies Today', in P. S. Adler, ed., *The Oxford Handbook of Sociology and Organization Studies* (Oxford: Oxford University Press), 62–91.

Adler, P. S., Forbes, L. C., and Willmott, H. (2007), 'Critical Management Studies', *The Academy of Management Annals*, 1, 119–79.

Ansell, C. (2011), *Pragmatist Governance: Re-imagining Institutions and Democracy* (Oxford; New York: University Press).

Ball, T. (1991), 'History: Critique and Irony', in T. Carver, ed., *The Cambridge Companion to Marx* (Cambridge: Cambridge University Press).

Bartunek, J., Putnam, L. and Seo, M-G. (2021), 'Dualism and Dualities in the Ongoing Development of Organization Development', in M.S. Poole and A. Van de Ven, eds., *Oxford Handbook of Organizational Change and Innovation* (2nd edn) (Oxford: Oxford University Press).

Baxter, L. A. and Montgomery, B. M. (1996), *Relating: Dialogues and Dialectics* (New York: Guilford Press).

Benson, J. K. (1977), 'Organizations: A Dialectical View', *Administrative Science Quarterly*, 22/1, 1–21.

Bernstein, R. J. (2011), *Praxis and Action: Contemporary Philosophies of Human Activity* (Philadelphia: University of Pennsylvania Press).

Burgelman, R. A. (1983), 'A Process Model of Internal Corporate Venturing in the Diversified Major Firm', *Administrative Science Quarterly*, 28/2, 223–44.

Burrell, G., and G. Morgan (1979), *Sociological Paradigms and Organizational Analysis* (London: Heinemann).

Cunha, M. P., and L. L. Putnam (2019), 'Paradox Theory and the Paradox of Success', *Strategic Organization*, 17/1, 95–106.

Czarniawska, B. (2006), 'A Golden Braid: Allport, Goffman, Weick', *Organization Studies*, 27/11, 1661–74.

Davis, G. F. (2016), *The Vanishing American Corporation: Navigating the Hazards of a New Economy* (Vol. 16) (Oakland, CA: Berrett-Koehler Publishers.

Davis, G. F., and Kim, E. W. (2021), 'Social Movements and Organizational Change', in M.S. Poole and A. Van de Ven, eds., *Oxford Handbook of Organizational Change and Innovation* (2nd edn) (Oxford: Oxford University Press).

Davis, G. F., McAdam, D., Scott, W. R., and Zald, M. N. (eds.) (2005), *Social Movements and Organization Theory* (New York: Cambridge University Press).

Farjoun, M. (2010), 'Beyond Dualism: Stability and Change as a Duality'. *Academy of Management Review*, 35/2, 202–25.

Farjoun, M., Ansell, C. K., and Boin, A. (2015), 'Pragmatism in Organization Studies: Meeting the Challenges of a Dynamic and Complex World', *Organization Science*, 26/6, 1787–804.

Farjoun, M. (2021), 'The Becoming of Change in 3D: Dialectics, Darwin and Dewey', in M.S. Poole and A. Van de Ven, eds., *Oxford Handbook of Organizational Change and Innovation* (2nd edn) (Oxford: Oxford University Press).

Feldman, M. S., and Orlikowski, W. J. (2011), 'Theorizing Practice and Practicing Theory', *Organization Science*, 22/5, 1240–53.

Giddens, A. (1984), *The Constitution of Society: Outline of the Theory of Structure* (Berkeley, CA: University of California Press).

Hargrave, T. J., and Van de Ven, A. H. (2006), 'A Collective Action Model of Institutional Innovation', *Academy of Management Review*, 31/4, 864–88.
Hargrave, T. J. (2021), 'The Paradox Perspective and the Dialectics of Contradictions Research', in M.S. Poole and A. Van de Ven, eds., *Oxford Handbook of Organizational Change and Innovation* (2nd edn) (Oxford: Oxford University Press).
Harvey, D. (2018), *The Limits to Capital* (London: Verso Books).
Hofstadter, D. R. (1979), *Gödel, Escher, Bach* (Hassocks, Sussex: Harvester Press).
Jackson, W. A. (1999), 'Dualism, Duality, and the Complexity of Economic Institutions', *International Journal of Social Economics*, 26, 545–58.
Jing, R. (2021), 'Eastern *Yin-Yang* Model of Change', in M.S. Poole and A. Van de Ven, eds., *Oxford Handbook of Organizational Change and Innovation* (2nd edn) (Oxford: Oxford University Press).
Langley, A., and Sloan, P. (2011), 'Organizational Change and Dialectic Processes', in D. M. Boje, B. Burnes, and J. Hassard, eds., *The Routledge Companion to Organizational Change* (New York, NY: Routledge), 261–75.
Lewis, L. (2021), 'Stakeholder Model of Change', in M.S. Poole and A. Van de Ven, eds., *Oxford Handbook of Organizational Change and Innovation* (2nd edn) (Oxford: Oxford University Press).
Lewontin, R. (1995), 'Genes, Environment, and Organisms', in R. Silvers, ed., *Hidden Histories of Science* (New York, NY: New York Review of Books Publishers).
Maturana, H. R., and Varela, F. J. (1998), *The Tree of Knowledge: The Biological Roots of Human Understanding* (revised ed.) (Boston, MA: Shambhala Publications).
Michel, A. (2014), 'The Mutual Constitution of Persons and Organizations: An Ontological Perspective on Organizational Change', *Organization Science*, 25/4, 1082–110.
Orlikowski, W. J. (2002), 'Knowing in Practice: Enacting a Collective Capability in Distributed Organizing', *Organization Science*, 13/3, 249–73.
Oswick, R., Oswick, C., and Grant, D. (2021), 'Critical Approaches and Perspectives on Organizational Change', in M.S. Poole and A. Van de Ven, eds., *Oxford Handbook of Organizational Change and Innovation* (2nd edn) (Oxford: Oxford University Press).
Patterson, T. C. (2018), *Social Change Theories in Motion* (New York: Routledge).
Prichard, C., and Creed, D. (2021), 'Social Movements and Organizational Change', in M.S. Poole and A. Van de Ven, eds., *Oxford Handbook of Organizational Change and Innovation* (2nd edn) (Oxford: Oxford University Press).
Rao, H., and Dutta, S. (2018), 'Why Great Strategies Spring from Identity Movements', *Strategy Science*, 3/1, 313–22.
Schneider, L. (1971), 'Dialectic in Sociology', *American Sociological. Review*, 36/4, 667–78.
Van de Ven, A. H., and Poole, M. S. (1995), 'Explaining Development and Change in Organizations', *Academy of Management Review*, 20/3, 510–40.
Zald, M. N. and Berger, M. A. (1978), 'Social Movements in Organizations: Coup d'État, Insurgency, and Mass Movements', *American Journal of Sociology*, 83/4, 823–61.

CHAPTER 35

CONNECTING MORE DEEPLY WITH LIFE IN ORGANIZATIONS

STANLEY DEETZ

LET me begin with a bit of context. I read the chapters in the handbook and wrote my response in April 2020. Scientists are struggling to figure out a novel virus, to see how it is transmitted and works on the body, and finally to come up quickly with treatments and a vaccine. They are doing this without widespread testing, with incomplete and suspicious data sets. And the environment in which they work and give advice is highly politicized and filled with misinformation and opportunists.

Businesses of all sizes, in fact whole industries are struggling to survive. Governmental, corporate, and personal debt is mounting rapidly from already high levels. A roll of toilet paper is priced higher than a barrel of oil future. The infrastructure weaknesses in the US as well as many other societies is glaring. Globalization is showing its other side. And a massive social change process, a set of social experiments, is going on changing how many people live and work. Recall this if I seem impatient at times with academic writing. Criticism of the detachment will sometimes be unfair, for sure, since most of the chapters were written before this. And, of course, I have no idea of the state of affairs when this is read.

Much is to be learned about innovation and change in this context. In many ways it looks, albeit on a grand scale, much like nearly every organizational change process I have been a part of. I have intellectually enjoyed placing insights from each chapter into challenges faced daily. Clearly my voice, especially now, will be one of a practitioner at heart, if still a scholar in mind. I will spare you my current difficulties in working with a very difficult court-mandated assessment and change program.

The larger current situation is filled with social and business environmental changes that stress systems and demand new responses. It is filled with agreed upon and competing goals; it is political to the core with actors who will win and lose; it is filled with uncertainty and inadequate data; relationships between events are complex and emergent; routines are broken and fear leads to holding onto anything familiar. Resistance is as emergent—it is sometimes random, sometimes clumped and organic, sometimes heavily sponsored; it is beneficial to some systems, harmful to others; it sometimes leads to insight and growth, sometime protection and ignorance. Some things seem to work but whether by design or luck of co-occurrence of uncontrolled events giving affordance; some things fail but with emergence and long action chains should we see them as wrong, and might they yet be right in time. What and how often seem like the wrong questions, when *when* seems to matter a lot. Which moment of assessment matters? Whose criteria, whose values, whose benefits matter? Welcome to the world! This seems a large version of life in virtually every organization undergoing serious change.

Assessing Theories of Change and Innovation

Before I turn in more detail to my own values and assumptions, my own sense of the state of the field, and individual chapters, I want to briefly be explicit about assessing the contribution of theories. I suggest three assessment issues: 1. Validity: Is it cumulative and learning? 2. Utility: Can it explain outcomes or give direction to change processes? 3. Generativity: Does it provide a compelling way to think and talk about the world, challenging the taken-for-granted?

Validity: Is it cumulative and learning? Certainly the strong case of a good theory imitating the imagined physical science model is the capacity to gradually build block-by-block a body of timeless knowledge created by a theory's capacity to generate hypotheses that are falsifiable but not falsified. Such a theory could be generalized across a variety of organizations with the capacity to make correct predictions and control the process into the future with successful outcomes.

While potentially a useful metaphor to guide research, qualities of organizational life challenge the production of theories of this sort. Organizations change fundamentally over time, leaving theories to some extend time-bound. The sample-population relation is complex. Are we sampling events to generalize to an organization? Sampling organizations to a class of organizations? Generalization, even assessments, is of course hard. "Control" of the multitude of internal and external factors, market conditions, etc., is nearly impossible. Action chains are very long. People change based on what you say about them. Hawthorne effects challenge claims of right process. And systemic properties in organizations of emergence, indeterminacy, and complexity would challenge any type of traditional theory generalization. Hence, while I would expect to claim validity I am very cautious about generalizations. Few chapters in this volume venture to make big claims. But it does challenge Chapter 2's hope for organizational change that is evidence based (Burke 2021).

Utility: Can it explain outcomes or give direction to change processes? Most of the chapters in this volume I believe aim primarily at utility. The theories attempt to provide a conceptual frame that organizes a lot of disparate observations and events. While studies seeking validity might be expected to be demonstrative, studies reported here tend to be illustrative. The evidence is often an example, not a test, and case studies often serve this sufficiently. Coherence and confirmation rather than prediction and control tend to give the theories, or better, conceptual frameworks, longevity. Utility always has to answer to whom and for what. This is an issue I wish to explore in the chapters.

Generativity: Does it provide a compelling way to think and talk about the world providing insight into complex processes and challenging the taken-for-granted? In 1978 Kenneth Gergen proposed evaluating

> theoretical accounts in terms of their generative capacity, that is, the capacity to challenge the guiding assumptions of the culture, to raise fundamental questions regarding contemporary social life, to foster reconsideration of that which is 'taken for granted,' and thereby to furnish new alternatives for social action. It is the generative theory that can provoke debate, transform social reality, and ultimately serve to reorder social conduct." (Gergen 1978: 1346)

Many theories impacting organization studies such as Maslow's hierarchy of needs and much of Lewin' work offered new, interesting, and insightful ways of thinking and talking about organizations long before much data existed to support them. Many of these have made it into everyday organization members' ways of thinking and talking. Their value has come in this generativity: they are not just theories about but theories in use. Some have been misleading, but this assessment is more an assessment of qualities of impact and values than simply data. When a practitioner, I am often not applying theories to change processes, I am working with members to find a good way of talking about what is happening, in doing so raising to discussion native theories of people and processes through proposing alternative vocabularies. We work out an often hybrid language that I and they learn through and from. I refer to this as the co-generativity of theory (Deetz 2008). I think we need to be careful about elitism, of outsiders presuming superior understanding of insider's lives. Therefore I look at the chapters for genuine open contact with organization members, willing to invent a new way of talking and thinking with them. I see the relationship to problems as experienced by outside communities as important to all organizational research (Deetz 2000).

My Perspective

Of course my reflections here come from a perspective. I should be upfront about what that is. I have spent a fifty-year career employed by universities. As such I have been active as a scholar and researcher. But I have also been deeply involved in dozens of change projects in organizations, institutions, and communities. My work in critical management studies (CMS) is probably best known and most cited, but it is part of a larger project on the reformation of democracy (Deetz 1992). And, I do not fit neatly into the CMS camp as easily seen below in the contrast between my work and Chapter 12 (Oswick et al.) on critical studies. For me critique and understanding power-based one-dimensional (ir)rationality and ideology is only one step toward providing more open and productive organizational forms and practices.

Both my research and direct involvement in organizational change can be seen as directed by four goals: 1) understand deeply and with charity the lived experience of individuals in organizations allowing them to challenge my pre-understanding; 2) provide a unified way of understanding the complex processes of organizational life through focusing on organizational constructions and embedded power relations; 3) direct the evaluation of existing organizational forms and activities through looking at distorting reproductive activities focusing on unwitting consent, systematically distorted communication, and forms of discursive closure; and 4) provide guidance for the education of members and redesign of organizational structures and practices that allow earlier and deeper inclusion of diverse values in the decision chain, thereby increasing organizational agility and innovation and the ability to increase economic, social, and ecological goods.

From such a perspective I see organizations as conflict-filled, value-laden political sites making a variety of social and economic decisions for the external society as well as owners and employees. I have rarely seen any necessary contradiction between economic and social good, but it is often contrived as so from misrecognition, institutional structures and routines, and managerial self-interests. From a democratic value perspective, the question is whose and what values impact decisions and how to get social values earlier in the decision chain to enable more creativity for social and economic good. Most often organization members need a different perspective and many new skills to carry this off.

While the groups that employ me, and those with whom I work, may have much more narrow needs and objectives, I carry these basic commitments into change projects. I open this here not so much to advance my own values as to say I wish the chapters in this volume had been much more explicit about their value commitments and I cannot ask for that without being honest about my own. The change projects I have been involved with cut across industry and organizational types including manufacturing and high tech, large corporations and small businesses. Most recently I have focused on change in higher education with projects focusing on institutional change supportive of advancements in STEM education, as well as others, and even more so in industries with high employee and public safety impact, mostly in nuclear and fossil fuels. Most of my change work is proprietary and has not been published. Below I will talk a bit about the sheer difficulties of doing research while doing change.

Reactions to the Chapters

Each chapter in this volume was asked accomplish three very basic objectives: 1) Current state of research related to the theory; 2) Concrete description with some examples of the theory in practice, and 3) Research based principles of change (how does the theory suggest change may be promoted and how does it deal with resistance?).

The chapters are generally good at the first task. This should come as little surprise. Most of the authors are primarily academic researchers. But I think we should look at what they do a bit closer. Have they described programmatic lines of work that add detail and precision to the theory? Clearly in most cases the chapters demonstrate a lot of conceptual argument around core concepts and fairly detailed histories of conceptual development. This is understandable since a need exists to teach the theory, to show the variety of contributions different people have made to the conceptions, to present robust well-developed conceptions, and to answer potential objections.

The often lack of empirical studies is also understandable. Conducting research on a change process, especially following a specific theoretical frame is very difficult and the outcome often illustrates theoretical concepts rather than demonstrates the value or correctness of theoretical claims. Access into organizations is hard especially during change processes, owing to proprietary information, the need for privacy and confidentiality, and the fear of disruption. And many IRBs do not understand nor are favorable to studies of organizational change. Action and participation action research are especially hard since they involve emergent processes of data collection and even knowing in advance what data will be needed. And, organization members are a vulnerable population in several ways, as managers may give consent but members may not feel they have a choice. This is another reason, Chapter 2's call for evidence-based change processes is hard to see as accomplishable. Given all this, I would have liked the chapters to discuss more, given the difficulties of research, what they accept as support, and to explore more alternative forms of data.

I was generally disappointed by the often shallow ways the other two issues were addressed. [2) Concrete description with some examples of the theory in practice, and 3) Research based principles of change (how does the theory suggest change may be promoted and how does it deal with resistance?)]. The literatures drawn on by change practitioners have usually been quite different from those of academics, and writing to build theory is different from trying to change an organization, but I had hoped for more reaching across the silos. But even more than the different concerns and literatures, the chapters felt very abstracted from life in organizations. Most seemed very detached from real organizations and their complexity. They lacked texture and richness, a sense of being connected or situated in the lives of real people in real situations. In doing a change process, I am always taken by how complex things on the ground are, how varied interpretations are, how many work-arounds exist, and how personal life events matter. Even when talking about paradoxes and tensions in Chapter 3 (Bartunek et al. (2021)) for example, the discussion often seems very removed from life experiences. Real organizations are filled with stories of past change events, people often feel change fatigue, employees see individual motives and carry grudges, and so forth.

Some of the chapters present case studies of a change process. These get a little closer to life on the ground. But several of the case studies are familiar examples reported by others (e.g., 3M's Post-its®) and do not involve the authors nor show sensitivity to life in the organization. Perhaps this is not surprising, but I think academic work is often greatly enriched by more closeness to the phenomenon understudy.

I was surprised how little attention was given to or accounting for the strength of personal interests of managers. Certainly in Chapter 10, Prichard and Creed examine how agents and leaders of change become activists through some common conversion experience, which is produced by a pattern of unconscious drives, traumatic experiences, and redemptive self-narratives. But even here not so much attention is given to managers with clear self-aware career goals, political allies and enemies, and stock options. Most often managers seem to be treated as disinterested parties or just represent organization needs and goals. In actual change processes, I have found personal goals and needs of individual managers to be of central importance. Their careers and personal needs for control often are part of the initiation of a change process, direct choices in it, and guide the relationship to outside change agents. Personal interests tend to be the primary complications, root of barriers and resistance, and reason for resistance in others. In reading the chapters I found it very difficult to see how the theories would account for this.

I was also surprised how little attention was given to member identities and challenges to identities in change processes. This seems out of tune with wider social concerns with identities and identity politics and the fairly wide literatures in organization studies. As Brown (2015) demonstrated: "Identities, people's subjectively construed understandings of who they were, are and desire to become, are implicated in, and thus key to understanding and explaining, almost everything that happens in and around organizations" (p. 20; and Brown 2020). Chapter 5 (Ravasi and Schultz) did much to show the consequences of organizational identity on change, but even there member identities and the connection of member identities to the organizational identity received little attention. In some contexts this may be stronger than others. For example, implications for faculty identities as scientists and professors appeared as a significant barrier for implementation of reforms and institutional changes in STEM education (Reinholz et.al. 2016). But even beyond cases like this, especially in high tech industries, the impact on identities and identity work should not be missed.

Further few of the theories account for power dynamics in an organization (or between an organization and outside groups) before and during change processes. Sometime power is mentioned as important but seems to be used in a fairly simple sense of what is usually called first dimensional power. For example, Davis and Kim in Chapter 9 discuss mobilizing social movements in organizations and Sarasvarthy and Venkataraman in Chapter 6 describe the effectuation processes by entrepreneurs. Even in the critical organization studies chapter (Chapter 12, Oswick et al.), sophisticated theories of power are missing. But power has long been seen as a central aspect of organizational life, and the literature on power has been highly nuanced, providing much on types of power and how power enables and constrains organizational choices, especially in change (e.g., Bradshaw and Boonstra 2004).

Communication and especially the relation of communication and social construction in organizations is rarely addressed by the chapters. Where communication processes are addressed they seems reduced to the presentation of the change processes. But change in an organization works within complex interaction systems shaping interpretations and sensemaking as well as assessments and even financial reports. While Chapter 4 by Rheinhardt and Gioia examines bottom-up processes of sensemaking and communication of change with new technology and generations of employees, and social and relational constructionism appears in places, interaction processes are mostly oddly absent. Most today would see organizations as constituted in and by human interaction based in over fifty years of work regarding this (Deetz and Eger 2014). A narrow version of this today often goes by the name "communication constitution of organizations (CCO)." Change theories would be enriched by more attention to the complex processes by which meaning arises and changes in organizations.

Further little attention is given in the chapters here to collaborative processes within and between organizations, and most interaction appears to be seen as fairly linear. Practitioners most often see collaboration as central to contemporary organization and to change (see for example discussions in *Harvard Business Review* July/August 2011). Sometimes collaborations are seen as principally a means of increasing buy-in. But more often, collaboration is used to increase the quality of change by using local knowledge and cross-functional insight (Kwan 2019). Contractors and other organizations are often critical to goal accomplishment in change. Clearly organizations are rarely bounded entities. Chapter 11 (Lewis) focusing directly on stakeholder participation helps some in this regards but even there, collaborative processes themselves are not very well developed. I was especially disappointed with Chapter 12 (Oswick et al.). Critical studies are presented in a somewhat backward-looking critique of ideology and domination without looking to the collaborative organization it invites. Things like Habermas's concepts of systematically distorted communication and an ideal speech situation can be used for critique but also provide guidance creating organizations with more free and open communication and ways of enhancing a broader rationality.

Systems thinking and systems theories have always been somewhat difficult for organization scholars. They often find systems thinking at once highly useful in conceptualizing organizational processes and frustrating to publish quality research. But I think that good reasons exist for why the work of Argyris, Weick, Senge, and Luhmann keep appealing to those directing change projects. Interdependency, emergence, recursivity, autopoiesis, virtuous and vicious cycles, and relation to the environment remain helpful when one is in an organization. I have used a version of soft-systems methodology with many organizations. Even in the simplest form I am surprised how often members have reported that it was the first time they understood how much organization redundancy contributed to the maintenance of current forms and routines, how different the implications of change were for different parts of the organization, and the origin of resistance and unintended consequences. I listen to the organization at these times and wonder why we have not done more with the theory.

Finally, perhaps I should not be surprised (I know the time and other pressures) but still I am a bit taken-a-back by the silos that seem to still exist despite some active attempts to view change from multiple perspectives and use hybrid models. Integration appeared most often between theories that were fairly close in basic assumptions and reaching less across the larger conception divides within the change literature and larger organization studies literature. Theory silos are not new as are silos in any work, but innovation and change are complicated, frequently site dependent, and fluid. Being multilingual is critical for change agents and I think for theorists too. I'm not looking for a kind of cosmopolitan mash-up without serious concern with consistence and commitments, and certainly not cherry picking confirming parts of other work. Still so much of the work ignored competing conceptions or focused on making distinctions from *either/or* thinking when judicious *both/and* thinking might gain genuine ground.

I hope that my frequent expressed frustration does not take away from my appreciation of the volume. We all know that a tremendous amount of care, insightful, quality work is here. I only hope here to have posed some different conversations from a somewhat outside perspective. They are things I wonder about as I mess around with the very real lives of people in organizations and the real larger social, environmental, and economic impact of choices made in these organizations. I am concerned about the value commitments of organizational members and leaders but also about the value commitments of those developing theories of change and conducting research on it. Where do the *ought* enter into the descriptions of *is*?

References

Bartunek, J., Putnam. L. and Myeong-Gu, S. (2021), 'Dualism and Dualities in the Ongoing Development of Organization Development', in M.S. Poole and A. Van de Ven, eds., *Oxford Handbook of Organizational Change and Innovation* (2nd edn) (Oxford: Oxford University Press).

Bradshaw, P., and Boonstra, J. (2004), 'Power Dynamics in Organizational Change', in J. Boonstra, ed., *Dynamics of Organizational Change and Learning* (Hoboken, New Jersey: John Wiley & Sons), 279–300.

Brown, A. (2015), 'Identities and Identity Work in Organizations', *International Journal of Management Review*, 17, 20–40.

Brown, A. (ed.) (2020). *The Oxford Handbook of Identities in Organizations* (Oxford: Oxford University Press).

Burke, W. W. (2021),'Historical Currents in Scholarship of Organization Change', in M.S. Poole and A. Van de Ven, eds., *Oxford Handbook of Organizational Change and Innovation* (2nd edn) (Oxford: Oxford University Press).

Davis, G. F., and Kim, E. W. (2021), 'Social Movements and Organizational Change', in M.S. Poole and A. Van de Ven, eds., *Oxford Handbook of Organizational Change and Innovation* (2nd edn) (Oxford: Oxford University Press).

Deetz, S. (1992), *Democracy in an Age of Corporate Colonization: Developments in Communication and the Politics of Everyday Life* (Albany: State University of New York Press).

Deetz, S. (2000), 'Putting the Community into Organizational Science: Exploring the Construction of Knowledge Claims', *Organization Science*, 11, 732–38.

Deetz, S. (2008), 'Engagement as Co-Generative Theorizing', *Journal of Applied Communication Research*, 36, 288–96.

Deetz, S., and Eger, E. (2014), 'Developing a Metatheoretical Perspective for Organizational Communication Studies', in L. Putnam and D. Mumby, eds., *Handbook of Organizational Communication* (3rd edn) (Thousand Oaks, CA: Sage), 27–48.

Deetz, S., Tracy, S., and Simpson, J. (2000), *Leading Organizations through Transitions: Communication and Cultural Change* (Thousand Oaks, CA: Sage).

Gergen, K. (1978), 'Toward Generative Theory', *Journal of Personality and Social Psychology*, 36, 1344–60.

Harvard Business Review (July/August 2011), 'Special Issue: Collaboration', *Harvard Business Review* (Brighton, MA. Harvard Business Publishing).

Kwan, L. (March–April 2019), 'The Collaboration Blind Spot', *Harvard Business Review*. Brighton, MA. Harvard Business Publishing.

Lewis, L. (2021). 'Stakeholder Model of Change', in M.S. Poole and A. Van de Ven, eds., *Oxford Handbook of Organizational Change and Innovation* (2nd edn) (Oxford: Oxford University Press).

Oswick, R., Oswick, S., and Grant, D. (2021), 'Critical Approaches and Perspectives on Organizational Change', in M.S. Poole and A. Van de Ven, eds., *Oxford Handbook of Organizational Change and Innovation* (2nd edn) (Oxford: Oxford University Press).

Prichard, C., and Creed, D. (2021), 'Social Movements and Organizational Change', in M.S. Poole and A. Van de Ven, eds., *Oxford Handbook of Organizational Change and Innovation* (2nd edn) (Oxford: Oxford University Press).

Ravasi, D., and Schultz, M. (2021), 'Organizational Identity and Culture Change', in M.S. Poole and A. Van de Ven, eds., *Oxford Handbook of Organizational Change and Innovation* (2nd edn) (Oxford: Oxford University Press).

Rheinhardt, A., and Gioia, D. A. (2021), 'Upside-Down Organizational Change: Sensemaking, Sensegiving, and the New Generation', in M.S. Poole and A. Van de Ven, eds., *Oxford Handbook of Organizational Change and Innovation* (2nd edn) (Oxford: Oxford University Press).

Reinholz, D. L., Corbo, J. C., Dancy, M. H., Finkelstein, N., and Deetz, S. (2016), 'Towards a model of systematic change in university STEM education. In G. C. Weaver, W. D. Burgess, A. L. Childress, & L. Slakey (Eds.), *Transforming institutions: Undergraduate STEM education for the 21st century* (pp. 115–24). West Lafayette, IN: Purdue University Press.

Sarasvathy, S., and Venkataraman, S. (2021), 'An Effectual Entrepreneurial Model of Organizational Change: Acting on, Reacting to, and Interacting with Markets as Artifacts, in M.S. Poole and A. Van de Ven, eds., *Oxford Handbook of Organizational Change and Innovation* (2nd edn) (Oxford: Oxford University Press).

CHAPTER 36

ENTANGLED VIEWS OF EXOGENOUS AND ENDOGENOUS CHANGE

MARTHA S. FELDMAN

In keeping with identifying dialectics as one of four models of change (Van de Ven and Poole, 1995; Chapter 1, this volume), many of the chapters of this handbook identify various dualities as important to understanding organizational change. In Chapter 3, Bartunek et al. discuss the dualities of diagnostic/dialogic, life/death, and scholarship/practice as they relate to understanding the field of organizational development. They note that the either/or approach to these dualities has been more evident than the both-and approach. In Chapter 7, Hargrave discusses dialectics and paradoxes and proposes a contradictions perspective in which paradox is not a permanent state but a persistent moment in the unfolding of contradiction. In Chapter 8, Jing discusses the Yin-Yang model of change that presents an either-and alternative to the Western options of either-or and both-and. In Chapter 15, Pentland and Goh explore the duality of stability and change exemplified by patterning processes in organizational routines. In Chapter 26, Farjoun explores dialectics from a pragmatist perspective. In Chapter 27, Hernes et al. discuss the duality of episodic and continuous change, suggesting that the ontological differences may have been overstated, and showing how these two are entwined in practice.

Dichotomies (e.g., A and Not-A, black and white, subjective and objective, stability and change, individual and community) are powerful philosophical tools. As Farjoun (in Chapter 26) points out they are prevalent in Greek philosophy. As Jing (in Chapter 8) points out they are prevalent in Eastern philosophy. The tradition of practice theory (e.g., Giddens 1984; Bourdieu 1990) that I have worked in entails a philosophical movement from engaging dualisms that are separable to engaging dualities that are mutually constitutive (Feldman and Orlikowski 2011; Feldman and Worline 2016). For instance, the duality of stability and change is central to the field of routine dynamics that my work has helped to create (Feldman 2000; Feldman and Pentland 2003). Routine dynamics shows that organizational routines, which are sources of stability in organizational operations are also sources of change and that the ability to be simultaneously a source of stability and a source of change depends on the dynamics within routines or interdependent patterns of action. Scholars not working in the field of routine dynamics have also recognized the importance of the mutually constitutive nature of stability and change (e.g., Tsoukas and Chia 2002; Farjoun 2010). Viewing stability and change as part of each other rather than as separate states of being supports discussions of organizational change as continuous (Hernes et al, Chapter 27) and as an ongoing accomplishment.

Exploring the dynamics of stability and change in routines entails another duality related to where stability and change come from. The duality here is exogenous and endogenous. Exogenous is defined as "introduced from or produced outside the organism or system," while endogenous is defined as "caused by factors inside the organism or system."[1] The terms "external" and "internal" can often be used as synonyms. Identifying endogenous change was an important part of identifying organizational routines as a source of change, whether of the routine or of the organization. Identifying the possibility of endogenous change is particularly relevant if you otherwise think of a routine as an undifferentiated thing, such as a checklist, a rule, or a protocol. Undifferentiated things can only be stable since they don't have an inside that can generate change or stability. For undifferentiated things to change, there must be something or someone exogenous to them making the change. Endogenous change implies that what is inside matters and is worth exploring. For this reason, differentiating exogenous and endogenous change matters.

Differentiating, however, implies separation. Conceptual separating is an analytical process, that helps us understand how things work. Thus, identifying exogenous helps us see endogenous and vice versa. But differentiation and separation can also obscure the holistic nature of our focus—in this case change. For that reason, I have become curious about the various ways of thinking about how exogenous change and endogenous change are entangled.

Three Orientations to Exogenous and Endogenous Change

What better place to understand this entanglement than a cornucopia of perspectives on organizational change? Several chapters discuss issues of exogenous and endogenous change. Many of them use these terms, but not all. I have selected seven chapters that provide a range of perspectives on this issue. In each chapter exogenous and endogen-

[1] Merriam Webster, accessed online May 23, 2020.

ous (or external and internal) are focal concerns, though not necessarily the only focus. In the following I separate the range of orientations into three categories. There are chapters that take the difference between internal and external as an ontological fact and explore how separable entities interact with one another. There are chapters in which the difference between internal and external is an analytical process. These chapters are apparently agnostic about ontological differences. Finally, there are chapters that reject an ontological distinction between exogenous and endogenous and explore the entangled nature of exogenous and endogenous within a single ontology.

Ontologically and analytically separable but deeply entangled

Chapters 14, 17, and 19 each discuss the entanglement of external and internal as important and complex though relatively unproblematic ontologically and analytically separable. In these chapters external and internal may be different kinds of organizations as, for instance, in Chapter 14 that deals with the interactions of government organizations and corporations, or the connections between different levels of analysis as in Chapter 17 that deals with the relationship between change at the institutional level and change at the organizational level. In Chapter 19 the meanings of internal are more varied than in Chapters 14 and 17. In all three of these chapters, the exogenous affects the endogenous and vice versa in ways that are often complex and sometimes recursive.

Chapter 14

Hedging: Organizational Responses to the Formulation, Implementation, and Enforcement of Government Mandated Changes by Alfred Marcus and Joel Malen

This chapter discusses the interactions and dynamics of government as regulator and corporations/organizations as regulated. Government as regulator is multiple, creating uncertainty for corporations but also leeway for corporate responses. This multiplicity results in uncertainty that produces variance in corporate responses thereby adding to enforcement difficulties. Government and corporations are depicted as exogenous to one another (with different interests and motivations) but each is affected endogenously by the other's actions. Specifically, what the authors discuss is how endogenous change is affected by exogenous forces created through the actions of the opposing type of organization. The chapter focuses more on how corporations respond to regulation than on how governments respond to corporate responses to regulation. While positioning government and corporations as fundamentally exogenous to one another, the authors acknowledge the recursive nature of the relationship between the two.

Chapter 17
Institutional Change by Evelyn Micelotta, Michael Lounsbury, and Royston Greenwood

The focus in this chapter is on institutional change with an understanding that institutional change both affects and is affected by organizational change. While the authors point out that initial research in the field of institution theory primarily situated institutions as exogenous to organizations, many branches of institutional theory, including institutional logics, institutional entrepreneurship, practice-oriented studies, institutional maintenance studies, and studies that attend to time and temporality have theorized connections between institutions and organizations that break down the exogenous/endogenous distinction. From these perspectives, "the theoretical linkages between institutional and organizational change have become richer." Analysis of numerous articles across several branches of institution theory lead the authors to highlight four pathways of change in institutions and organizations based on differences in both the pace and the scope of change.

The case of Open Access the authors present "illuminates the connection between institutional change and organizational change in practice" by describing a movement that affected both the institutional level and the organizational level, though for the time being leaving most practices at both levels largely in place. The logic of research publishing continues to be a commercial logic and the subscription model continues to be the dominant means of distribution. Changes at the organizational level are scattered and heterogeneous, somewhat in line with the depiction of change in Chapter 14. But the introduction of temporality in the form of pace helps us to see the entanglement of actions and reactions at both institutional and organizational levels. As the story unfolds over time and, we presume, continues to unfold over time, the case illustrates how and why "once dominant assumptions about environmental fit and isomorphism dynamics between organizations and their broader contexts have been substantially loosened." While the ontological status of institutions and organizations as separate levels of analysis persists, the authors show that acknowledging the permeability of each is important for understanding how change happens.

Chapter 19
VSR Models of Change As Normative Practical Theory by Cara Mauer, Anne Miner, and Mary Crossan

The focus of this chapter is on internal VSR processes.[2] The authors theorize VSR as a process that may be agentic and that may be driven by action rather than action being a survival response. They describe internal processes as emanating from choices about technology, routines and strategies and individual actions. Internal takes on various meanings, including organizational as opposed to external to the organization, bottom-up

[2] My comments are based on the penultimate version of the chapter.

as opposed to top-down and individual as opposed to organizational or institutional. Internal VSR processes may not be ways for organizations to adapt internally to external conditions, but may also be part of the formation of the external context in a process the authors refer to as co-creation. Such outcomes can occur even over the resistance of internal leaders or managers.

As an example of co-creation, the authors discuss how academic women, who were blocked from changing their organizations through internal means, brought about change by first influencing policies of government organizations that regulate and provide resources to higher education and enforced rules relating to gender equity. This external pressure eventually produced internal change in the form of new routines and practices in universities.

This chapter is consistent with Chapter 17 on institutional change in showing that a theory that once was thought predominantly appropriate to explaining how organizations are affected by their external environments can be used to engage the entangled nature of the internal and external.

Analytically separable

Chapters 15 and 20 present a somewhat different view on the distinction between exogenous and endogenous. Here the focus is on endogenous dynamics of routines (Chapter 15) or of models (Chapter 20). Separating exogenous and endogenous is a matter of creating analytical boundaries that allow the focus on endogenous processes. Thus, this focus requires an ability to separate exogenous from endogenous analytically but does not require the authors to take a stand on ontology.

Chapter 15

Organizational Routines and Organizational Change by Brian T. Pentland and Kenneth T. Goh

This chapter discusses endogenous change in organizational routines as an alternative to change in response to exogenous forces. Organizational routines are conceptualized as networks of interdependent actions. The interdependence of the actions creates dynamics, which over time produces stability and change. The authors promote patterning as a way of understanding these endogenous dynamics. They suggest that patterns emerge through multiple iterations of a routine. Patterns are reinforced when over time people (or things) take the same actions and make the same connections between actions (e.g., action A is always followed by action B). Patterns change when people (or things) add or remove actions and when they make different connections between actions (e.g., action A may be followed (or preceded) by actions B, C, or D, assuming action A takes place). Patterning as conceptualized here is endogenous. The pattern emerges from taking action and what the authors refer to as hand-offs, which make connections between actions. An exogenous notion of patterning would, by contrast, entail matching actions and connections to an external referent such as a protocol or template.

The authors illustrate patterning by their research on videogame development. Endogeneity takes center stage. In comparing three versions of the "same" routine (a sprint), they show that the routines differ substantially (as indicated by the # of paths increasing from around 300 to around 43,000 and back again to the hundreds in the "same" routine) when actors make more connections between actions. Though the actions are the same, there are many more connections between these actions, creating many more paths. The authors note that time pressure is one of the differences between the sprints that have fewer paths and the sprint that has more paths. The focus of the analysis, however, is not on how the exogenous affects the endogenous but on the endogenous dynamics. Thus, the explanation is not a discussion of how or why time pressure (exogenous) affects hand-offs (endogenous), but on how hand-offs (endogenous) affect paths (endogenous). Thus, the endogenous explanation is that when people make more hand-offs, they produce exponentially more paths.

Chapter 20

Conceptualizing Organizational Change through the Lens of Complexity Science by Kevin J. Dooley

This chapter reviews complexity theory and four kinds of models used in relation to complexity theory: agent-based, computational, dynamical, and far-from-equilibrium. While the word "exogenous" is used a few times in the article to refer to events that are outside the activity of the model, the word "endogenous" does not appear in the text. Nonetheless the ability for some of these models to portray "dynamic interactions that occur across scales of an organizational system" make this chapter relevant to the issue at hand. The author discusses these dynamic interactions in relation to three of the four types of models: agent-based models, dynamical models, and far from equilibrium models.

Dooley states that in agent-based models agents learn from and evolve with an external environment. The boundary between inside and outside the system is a feature that modelers must specify, but where that boundary is placed is not necessarily self-evident from the phenomenon being modeled. In dynamical models the emphasis is on the interplay among elements in the system and the resultant aliveness of the system. While the author's general description of the model emphasizes internal elements, examples such as financial processes that respond to state and federal tax requirements or inventory levels that respond to seasonal variations suggest a relation between internal and external (though it is possible that what appears to be external in these examples is modeled as internal).

The far-from-equilibrium (FFE) models are the ones with the clearest reference to the interplay between external forces and internal processes. FFE models portray systems as self-organizing and self-organizing as requiring the existence of a boundary (or container) that defines inside and outside and constrains interaction between the two. While some descriptions of FFE models suggest that the relationship between internal and external is ontological and that transformation occurs through internal reactions to external triggers, the analytical nature of the distinction between inside and outside is evident from the suggestion that changing the boundaries (or containers), which is an analytical shift, can bring about organizational change.

Ontologically entangled

The third set of papers provides a view of exogenous and endogenous that is both deeply entangled and ontologically inseparable. The ontological inseparability means that any separation is provisional and fleeting. Separation is an act of analysis, whether by scholars or practitioners, and does not purport to be representative of reality. Ontological entanglement is supported by very different philosophical orientations. In Chapter 8, Jing presents a Taoist conceptualization; in Chapter 27, Hernes et al present an event-based conceptualization that draws on Western phenomenology. Both the event-based and the Taoist view have what some refer to as a strong process ontology (Langley et al, 2013) and show us the utility of reconsidering the idea that change happens at a particular time.

Chapter 8

Eastern Yin-Yang Model of Change by Runtian Jing

This chapter discusses exogenous and endogenous momentum and how actions that produce change can engage these momentums. Exogenous and endogenous, as all opposites in the yin-yang perspective, are interdependent. Using the familiar Yin-Yang symbol, the author explains that the opposite is always embedded within its contrary. There is, therefore, no absolute as the contrary is always already part of the focal quality (e.g., competition is always already part of cooperation; stability is always already part of change, etc., and, of course, vice versa). Jing provides a figure depicting how the growth of that contrary within transforms the focal quality. Failure transforms into success and success transforms into failure through the dynamics of their relation. And the cycle continues. Change is clearly continuous.

It is possible to engage the momentum of this cycle. While presumably this momentum can be internal (to an organization, to an individual), internal and external is just another intrinsically interdependent opposition. By the logic Jing describes, internal momentum transforms into external momentum and internal momentum transforms into external momentum. Jing notes that, in the Taoist view he describes, people are central to this transformation, and change becomes a matter of perceiving the fit between external and internal momentum and taking action in relation to this fit.

Jing provides the example of the Chengdu Bus Group (CBG). By making an internal change (slashing ticket prices), a move that was enabled by external conditions, CBG altered the competitive environment in which it operated, which allowed it to reorganize internal operations. While this interplay of internal and external is not unfamiliar from a Western perspective, the Yin-Yang perspective on momentum helped the CEO to recognize how the external momentum (competition among several bus companies) meshed with internal momentum (low morale and poor service) and to engage a process of continuous change needed to transform the way the company operated.

It is important to note that the strategy of the CBG is not something that can be transferred to other organizations or even other low-performing bus companies. While the general understanding of how the interplay between external and internal momentum can be transferred, action is taken in the specific context in which there are specific external and internal momentums. As Jing notes the perspective is metacognitive.

Chapter 27

Time and temporality of change processes. Applying an event-based view to integrate episodic and continuous change by Tor Hernes, Anthony Hussenot, and Kätlin Pulk

The authors integrate episodic and continuous change by viewing each through the lens of an event-based immanent temporal trajectory. This lens moves us within the experience of change. Viewed through this lens, episodes are breaks in continuous change. While it is possible that such breaks could be recognized at the time the event occurs, it is much more likely that the significance of the event only becomes evident through its connection with other events in the ongoing processes of continuous change. The authors note that their notion of breaks represents an endogenous view. Indeed, the event-based focus the authors present draws us into change as experienced from within the subjectivity of actors. As such, exogenous and endogenous here refer not to entities but to processes. From an event-based perspective, breaks are identified as they become part of the experience of change.

Their analysis of change in a shipbuilding company provides an example of this event-based perspective. A particular meeting has come to be identified as the moment that changed the company. During that meeting someone introduced a new design for a ship's bow. Over time the company began to make ships with that bow, which was both a distinctive and a successful innovation. Significantly, neither participants in the meeting nor observers (the researchers) experienced the meeting as a break/episode at the time of the meeting. It was only in the subsequent unfolding that the meeting became an episode and that the introduction of the new bow design could be identified as an episodic change. Thus, temporality is key to identifying what is exogenous and what is endogenous. Over time both participants and observers came to an exogenous view of the meeting, allowing them to pluck it out of the flow of continuous change and label it as a significant break. In the ongoing flow of continuous change, however, the meeting was endogenous—just part of the everyday activities of this organization.

The idea that events become significant only when they are retrospectively connected with other events is consistent with Garud and Turunen's depiction of the well-known story of the Post-it® note invention (Chapter 22) and descriptions of the equally well-known story of Rosa Parks' refusal to sit in the back of the bus (see Lovell 2003).

So What?

What have I learned from this exploration of the distinction between exogenous and endogenous? Most obviously, there are at least three ways of approaching the exogenous/endogenous distinction that acknowledges the relevance of and entangled nature of both parts of the duality. Each of the orientations to this distinction are productive, though in very different ways and for different explorations of change processes.

For instance, we can assume ontological differences and use the distinction to see how types of organizations and levels of analysis are related. In the chapters reviewed here, distinguishing types of organizations and levels of analysis, leads quickly to the ways in which they are entangled and to the importance of not only exogenous but also endogenous change. Studying processes and practices of organizational change have helped researchers see this entanglement. Indeed, one of the chapters in this category (Chapter 14) was already positioned within a literature that recognized entanglement as a result of studying practices of regulatory capture in which organizations or fields of organizations seek to control governmental regulatory agencies in order to create regulations that are beneficial to them. The other two chapters (Chapters 17 and 19) each make a point of saying that the research examining specific change processes and how those processes were enacted has moved their fields from an earlier understanding in which the focus was on how organizations responded to external pressures with little to no attention to the entangled nature of the relationship.

We don't, however, always have to take a stand on ontology. We make lots of choices about what we are going to look at. As shown in Chapters 15 and 20, we can choose to draw a boundary that identifies what is exogenous and what is endogenous. When we draw the boundary, though, we know we are drawing a boundary. Studying endogenous dynamics may entail analytically walling off the consistent din of things going on outside of the focal process. Drawing this analytical boundary does not necessarily reify an ontological distinction. Indeed, it is consistent with the practice theoretic idea that distinctions between mutually constituted constructs like exogenous and endogenous are mutually constituted in practice and are only separable analytically (Feldman and Worline 2016).

Finally, we should think twice about assuming that there is an ontological distinction between exogenous and endogenous. Questioning ontological assumptions is at the heart of practice theory and other theories of situated action that view social reality as ongoing accomplishments. Assuming the distinction between exogenous and endogenous is real can blind us to connections, particularly connections across time, and can reify categories that may, at best, be analytical. Not assuming ontological differences necessitates complex engagement with the flow of events and makes it difficult to produce explanations that are easily scalable. While the two chapters I reviewed here (Chapters 8 and 27) are most relevant to the exogenous/endogenous duality, many of the chapters in this handbook show in different ways the complexity of change and the importance of moving beyond explanations of change that focus on singular or spectacular events or heroic actions. They warn against assuming that change is something that happens once and for all or moves steadily in one direction. While scalable explanations may have the benefit of being easily transported, they may also obscure paths for understanding and making change in organizations and in society.

References

Bartunek, J. M., Putnam, L., and Seo, M-G. (2021), 'Dualisms and Dualities in the Ongoing Development of Organization Development', in M. S. Poole and A. H. Van de Ven, eds., *The Oxford Handbook of Organizational Change and Innovation* (2nd edn) (Oxford: Oxford University Press).

Bourdieu, P. (1990), *The Logic of Practice* (Stanford: Stanford University Press).

Dooley, K. J. (2021), Conceptualizing Organizational Change through the Lens of Complexity Science', in M. S. Poole and A. Van de Ven, eds., *Oxford Handbook of Organizational Change and Innovation* (2nd edn) (Oxford: Oxford University Press).

Farjoun, M. (2010), 'Beyond Dualism: Stability and Change as a Duality', *Academy of Management Review*, 35/2, 202–25.

Farjoun, M. (2021), 'The Becoming of Change in 3D: Dialectics, Darwin and Dewey', in M. S. Poole and A. Van de Ven, eds., *Oxford Handbook of Organizational Change and Innovation* (2nd edn) (Oxford: Oxford University Press).

Feldman, M. S. (2000), 'Organizational Routines as a Source of Continuous Change', *Organization Science*, 11/6, 611–29.

Feldman, M. S., and Orlikowski, W. J. (2011), 'Theorizing Practice and Practicing Theory', *Organization Science*, 22/5, 1240–53.

Feldman, M. S., and Pentland, B. T. (2003). Reconceptualizing organizational routines as a source of flexibility and change. *Administrative Science Quarterly*, 48/1: 94–118.

Feldman, M., and Worline, M. (2016), 'The Practicality of Practice Theory', *Academy of Management Learning and Education*, 15/2, 304–24.

Garud, R., and Turunen, M. (2021), 'Microfoundations of Innovation as Process: Usher's Cumulative Synthesis Model', in M. S. Poole and A. Van de Ven, eds. *Oxford Handbook of Organizational Change and Innovation* (2nd edn) (Oxford: Oxford University Press).

Giddens, A. (1984), *The Constitution of Society: Outline of the Theory of Structure* (Berkeley, CA: University of California Press).

Hargrave, T. J. (2021), 'The Paradox Perspective and the Dialectics of Contradictions Research', in M. S. Poole and A. H. Van de Ven, eds., *Oxford Handbook of Organizational Change and Innovation* (2nd edn) (Oxford: Oxford University Press).

Hernes, T., Hussenot, A., and Pulk, K. (2021), 'Time and Temporality of Change Processes. Applying an Event-Based View to Integrate Episodic and Continuous Change', in M. S. Poole and A. H. Van de Ven, eds., *Oxford Handbook of Organizational Change and Innovation* (2nd edn) (Oxford: Oxford University Press).

Jing, R. (2021), 'Eastern *Yin-Yang* Model of Change', in M. S. Poole and A. H. Van de Ven, eds., *Oxford Handbook of Organizational Change and Innovation* (2nd edn) (Oxford: Oxford University Press).

Lovell, T. (2003), 'Resisting with Authority: Historical Specificity, Agency and the Performative Self', *Theory, Culture & Society*, 20/1, 1–17.

Marcus, A and Malen, J. (2021), 'Hedging: Organizational Responses to the Formulation, Implementation, and Enforcement of Government Mandated Changes', in M. S. Poole and A. H. Van de Ven, eds., *Oxford Handbook of Organizational Change and Innovation* (2nd edn) (Oxford: Oxford University Press).

Micelotta, E. Lounsbury, M. and Greenwood, R. (2021), 'Institutional Change', in M. S. Poole and A. H. Van de Ven, eds., *Oxford Handbook of Organizational Change and Innovation* (2nd edn) (Oxford: Oxford University Press).

Maurer, C., Miner, A., and Crossan, M. (2021), 'VSR Models of Change as Normative Practical Theory', in M. S. Poole and A. H. Van de Ven, eds., *Oxford Handbook of Organizational Change and Innovation* (2nd edn) (Oxford: Oxford University Press).

Pentland, B. T. and Goh, K. T. (2021), 'Organizational Routines and Organizational Change', in M. S. Poole and A. H. Van de Ven, eds., *Oxford Handbook of Organizational Change and Innovation* (2nd edn) (Oxford: Oxford University Press).

Tsoukas, H., and Chia, R. (2002), 'On Organizational Becoming: Rethinking Organizational change. *Organization Science*, 13/5: 567–82.

Van de Ven, A. H., and Poole, M. S. (1995). Explaining development and change in Organizations, *Academy of Management Review*, 20, 510–40.

Van de Ven, A. and Poole, S. M. (2021), 'Central Issues in the Study of Organizational Change and Innovation', in M. S. Poole and A. H. Van de Ven, eds., *Handbook of Organizational Change and Innovation* (2nd edn) (Oxford: Oxford University Press).

Index of Authors

Note: Tables and figures are indicated by an italic "*t*" and "*f*", respectively, following the page number.

For the benefit of digital users, indexed terms that span two pages (e.g., 52–53) may, on occasion, appear on only one of those pages.

D

E

I

J

K

L

M

N

Q

R

S

T

X

Y

Z

INDEX

Note: Tables and figures are indicated by an italic "*t*" and "*f*" respectively, following the page number.

For the benefit of digital users, indexed terms that span two pages (e.g., 52–53) may, on occasion, appear on only one of those pages.

B

D

E

F

G

H

M

N

O

Q

R

S